Mathematics Standard Level

for the IB Diploma

Paul Fannon, Vesna Kadelburg,
Ben Woolley and Stephen Ward

CAMBRIDGE
UNIVERSITY PRESS

University Printing House, Cambridge CB2 8BS, United Kingdom

One Liberty Plaza, 20th Floor, New York, NY 10006, USA

477 Williamstown Road, Port Melbourne, VIC 3207, Australia

4843/24, 2nd Floor, Ansari Road, Daryaganj, Delhi – 110002, India

79 Anson Road, #06–04/06, Singapore 079906

Cambridge University Press is part of the University of Cambridge.

It furthers the University's mission by disseminating knowledge in the pursuit of education, learning and research at the highest international levels of excellence.

Information on this title: education.cambridge.org

First published 2012
20 19 18 17 16 15 14 13 12 11 10 9 8

Printed in India by Multivista Global Pvt Ltd

A catalogue record for this publication is available from the British Library

ISBN 978-1-107-61306-5 Paperback with CD-ROM for Windows® and Mac®

Cover image: David Robertson/Alamy

Contents

Geometry

(Topic 3: Circular functions & trigonometry & Topic 4: Vectors)

Calculus

(Topic 6: Calculus)

Statistics and probability

(Topic 5: Statistics & probability)

Introduction

Structure of the book

The book is split roughly into four blocks. Chapters 1 to 7 cover algebra and functions, chapters 8 to 11 cover geometry, chapters 12 to 15 cover calculus, and chapters 16 to 18 cover probability and statistics. Chapter 19 contains questions that mix together different parts of the course – a favourite trick in International Baccalaureate® (IB) examinations.

You do not have to work through the book in the order presented, but given how much the IB likes to mix up topics, you will find that some questions refer to material in previous chapters. In such cases, a 'rewind panel' will tell you that the material has been covered earlier, so that you can decide whether to remind yourself or move on.

In the book we have tried to include only material that will be examinable. There are many proofs and ideas that are useful and interesting but which are not included in the main text; these can be found on the CD-ROM should you wish to explore them.

Each chapter starts with a list of learning objectives which give you an idea about what the chapter contains. There is also an introductory problem that illustrates what you will be able to do after you have completed the chapter. Some introductory problems relate to 'real life' situations, while others are purely mathematical. You should not expect to be able to solve the problem at the start, but you may want to think about possible strategies and what sort of new facts and methods would help you. The solution to the introductory problem is provided at the end of the chapter, after the summary of the chapter contents.

Key point boxes

The most important ideas and formulae are emphasised in the Key point boxes. They also highlight which formulae are given in the Formula booklet.

Worked examples

Each worked example is split into two columns. On the right is what you should write down in your solution. Sometimes examples may go into more detail than you strictly need, but they are designed to give you an idea of what is required to score full method marks in examinations. Mathematics, however, is about much more than remembering methods and preparing for examinations. So, on the left of each worked example are notes that describe the thought processes and suggest which approach you could use to tackle the question. We hope that these will help you learn how to solve problems that differ from the worked examples. It is very deliberate that some of the exercise questions require you to do more than just repeat the methods in the worked examples – mathematics is about thinking!

Signposts

There are several kinds of boxes that appear throughout the book.

Theory of knowledge issues

Every lesson is really a 'theory of knowledge' lesson, but sometimes the connections may not be obvious. Although mathematics is frequently cited as an example of certainty and truth, things are often not so clear-cut. In these boxes we will try to highlight some of the weaknesses and ambiguities in mathematics, as well as showing how mathematics links to other areas of knowledge.

From another perspective

Mathematics is often described as a unified international language, but the International Baccalaureate encourages looking at things in various ways. As well as highlighting some differences between mathematicians from different parts of the world, these boxes also discuss other perspectives on the mathematics we are covering – historical, pragmatic and cultural.

Research explorer

As part of your course, you will be asked to write a report on an area of mathematics beyond the syllabus, related to a topic that changes from year to year. It is sometimes difficult to know which topics are suitable as a basis for such reports, so we have tried to show where a topic can act as a jumping-off point for further work. These can also give you ideas for the extended essay. There is a lot of great mathematics out there!

Exam hints

Although we encourage you to think of mathematics as more than just a subject to be studied in order to pass an examination, it is useful to be aware of some common errors so that you can try to avoid making them yourself. In these boxes we highlight common pitfalls; we also point out where graphical calculators can be used effectively to simplify a question or speed up your work, often referring to the relevant calculator skills sheet on the CD-ROM.

Fast forward / Rewind

Mathematics is all about making links. You might be interested in seeing how something you have just learned will be used elsewhere in the course, or you may need to go back and remind yourself of a previous topic. These boxes indicate connections with other sections of the book to help you find your way around.

How to use the questions

The colour coding

The questions are colour-coded to distinguish between different levels.

Black questions are drill questions. They are meant to help you practise the methods described in the book, but they are usually not structured like typical questions that appear in the examination. This does not mean they are easy – in fact, some of them are quite tough – but they are generally similar in style to the worked examples.

Each differently numbered drill question tests a different skill. Lettered subparts (a), (b), (c), … of a question are of increasing difficulty. Within each lettered part there may be multiple roman-numeral parts (i), (ii), (iii), …, which are all of similar difficulty. Unless you want to get lots of practice, we recommend that you do only one roman-numeral part and then check your answer. If you have made a mistake, you may want to think about what went wrong and then attempt another of the roman-numeral parts.

Green questions are examination-style questions which should be accessible to students on the way to achieving a grade 3 or 4.

Blue questions are harder examination-style questions. If you are aiming for a grade 5 or 6, you should be able to make significant progress through most of these.

Red questions are at the very top end of difficulty among examination-style questions. If you can do these, then you are likely to be on course for a grade 7.

Gold questions are those that are *not* typically set in the examination but which are designed to provoke thinking and discussion, in order to help you gain a better understanding of a particular concept.

At the end of each chapter you will see longer questions typical of the second section of the IB examination. The parts (a), (b), (c), … of these follow the same colour-coding scheme.

Of course, these are just **guidelines**. If you are aiming for a grade 6, do not be surprised if occasionally you find a green question you cannot do; people are rarely equally good at all areas of the syllabus. Similarly, even if you are able to do all the red questions, that does not guarantee you will get a grade 7 – after all, in the examination you will have to deal with time pressure and examination stress! It is also worth remembering that these questions are graded according to our experience of the final examination. When you first start the course, you may well find the questions harder than you would do by the end of the course, so try not to get discouraged.

Calculator versus non-calculator questions

In the final examination there will be one paper in which calculators are not allowed. Some questions require a calculator, but most could appear in either the calculator or the non-calculator paper.

Certain types of question are particularly common in the non-calculator paper, and you need to know how to deal with them. They are indicated by the non-calculator symbol.

On the other hand, some questions can be done in a clever way using a calculator, or cannot realistically be done without using a calculator. These are marked with a calculator symbol.

Note, however, that in the final examination you will not get any calculator/non-calculator indications, so you must make sure to learn which types of questions have an easy calculator method. The calculator skills sheets on the CD-ROM can help with this.

With questions that are not labelled with either the calculator or the non-calculator symbol, you could mix up practising with and without a calculator. Be careful not to become too reliant on your calculator – half of the core examination needs to be done without one!

On the CD-ROM

On the CD-ROM there are various materials that you might find useful.

Prior learning

The International Baccalaureate syllabus lists what candidates are expected to know before taking the examination. Not all the topics on the list are explicitly covered in the course, but knowledge of them may be needed to answer examination questions. Don't worry, you do not have to be familiar with all the 'prior learning' topics before starting the course: we have indicated in the rewind panels where a particular concept or skill is required, and on the CD-ROM you can find a self-assessment test for checking your knowledge, as well as some worksheets to help you learn any skills that you might be missing.

Coursebook support

Supporting worksheets include:

- calculator skills sheets that give instructions for making optimal use of some of the recommended graphical calculators
- fill-in proof sheets to allow you to re-create proofs that are not required in the examination
- self-discovery sheets to encourage you to investigate new results for yourself in the examination
- supplementary sheets exploring some applications, international and historical perspectives of the mathematics covered in the syllabus.

e-version

A flat pdf of the whole coursebook (for days when you don't want to carry the paperback!)

We hope that you will find Standard Level Mathematics for the IB diploma an interesting and enriching course. You may also find it quite challenging, but do not get intimidated – frequently, topics start to make sense only after lots of revision and practice. Persevere and you will succeed!

The author team.

1 Quadratic functions

In this chapter you will learn:

- about the shape and main features of graphs of quadratic functions
- about the uses of different forms of a quadratic function
- how to solve quadratic equations and simultaneous equations
- how to identify the number of solutions of a quadratic equation
- how to use quadratic functions to solve practical problems.

Introductory problem

A small dairy farmer wants to sell a new type of luxury cheese. After a fixed set-up cost of \$250, he can produce the cheese at a cost of \$9 per kilogram. He is able to produce up to 400 kg, but he plans to take advance orders and produce only what he can sell. His market research suggests that the amount he would be able to sell depends on the price in the following way: the amount decreases proportionally with the price; if he charged \$20 per kg he would not sell any, and if the cheese was free he would 'sell' the maximum 400 kg that he could produce. What price per kilogram should the farmer set in order to maximise his profit?

Problems like this, where we have to maximise or minimise a certain quantity, are known as optimisation problems. They are common in economics and business (e.g. minimising costs and maximising profits), biology (e.g. finding the maximum possible size of a population) and physics (e.g. electrons moving to the lowest energy state). The quadratic function is the simplest function with a maximum or minimum point, so it is often used to model such situations. Quadratic functions are also found in many natural phenomena, such as the motion of a projectile or the dependence of power on voltage in an electric circuit.

1A The quadratic form $y = ax^2 + bx + c$

A **quadratic function** has the general form $y = ax^2 + bx + c$ (where $a \neq 0$). In this chapter we will investigate graphs of quadratic functions and, in particular, how features of the graphs relate to the **coefficients** a, b and c.

A function is a rule that tells you what to do with any value you put in. We will study functions in general in chapter 4, but before then you will learn about some particular types of functions.

$x \in \mathbb{R}$ means that x can be any real number.

See Prior Learning section G on the CD-ROM for the meaning of such statements.

The word 'quadratic' indicates that the term with the highest power in the equation is x^2. It comes from the Latin *quadratus*, meaning 'square'.

Let us look at two examples of quadratic functions:

$$y_1 = 2x^2 - 2x - 4 \quad \text{and} \quad y_2 = -x^2 + 4x - 3 \quad (x \in \mathbb{R})$$

EXAM HINT

See Calculator Skills sheets 2 and 4 on the CD-ROM for how to sketch and analyse graphs on a graphic display calculator.

You can use your calculator to plot the two graphs:

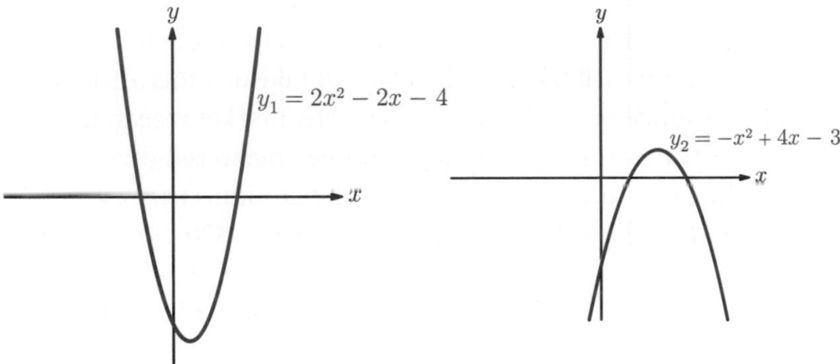

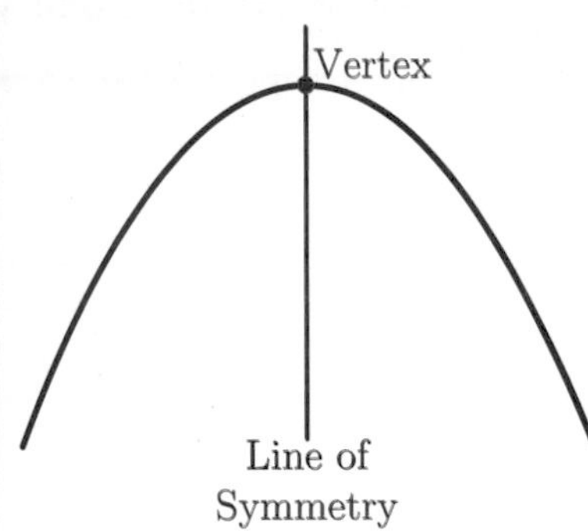

These two graphs have a similar shape, called a **parabola**. A parabola has a single turning point (called its vertex) and a vertical line of symmetry passing through the vertex. The most obvious difference between the two graphs above is that the first one has a minimum point whereas the second has a maximum point. This is due to the different signs of the x^2 term in y_1 and in y_2.

You can use your calculator to find the position of the vertex of a parabola. For the graphs above you should find that the coordinates of the vertices are (0.5, –4.5) and (2, 1); the lines of symmetry therefore have equations $x = 0.5$ and $x = 2$.

KEY POINT 1.1

For a quadratic function $f(x) = ax^2 + bx + c$:

If $a > 0$, $f(x)$ is a *positive* quadratic. The graph has a *minimum* point and goes *up* on both sides.

If $a < 0$, $f(x)$ is a *negative* quadratic. The graph has a *maximum* point and goes *down* on both sides.

The constant coefficient (denoted by c here) gives the position of the y-intercept of the graph, that is, where the curve crosses the y-axis.

Worked example 1.1

Match each equation to the corresponding graph, explaining your reasons.

(a) $y = 3x^2 - 4x - 1$

(b) $y = -2x^2 - 4x$

(c) $y = -x^2 - 4x + 2$

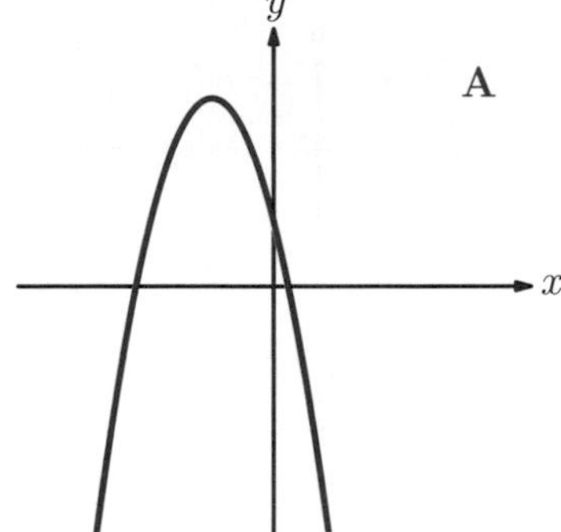

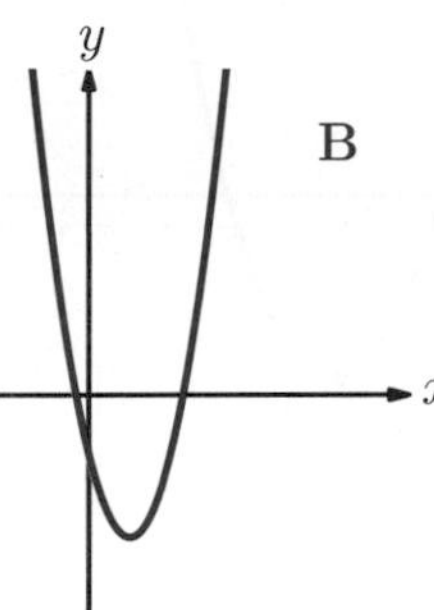

y C x

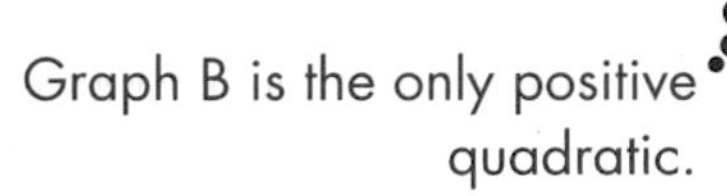

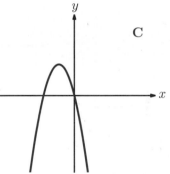

Graph B is the only positive quadratic.

Graph B shows a positive quadratic, so graph B corresponds to equation (a).

We can distinguish between the other two graphs by their y-intercepts.

Graph A has a positive y-intercept, so graph A corresponds to equation (c). Graph C corresponds to equation (b).

Although we are mainly concerned with investigating how the features of a graph are determined by the coefficients in the equation, it is often useful to be able to do the reverse. In other words, given a graph, can we find the coefficients? The following example illustrates how to tackle this type of problem.

Finding the equation of a given graph is important in *mathematical modelling,* where often a graph is generated from experimental data and we seek an equation to describe it.

Worked example 1.2

The graph shown below has the equation $y = ax^2 - 6x + c$.

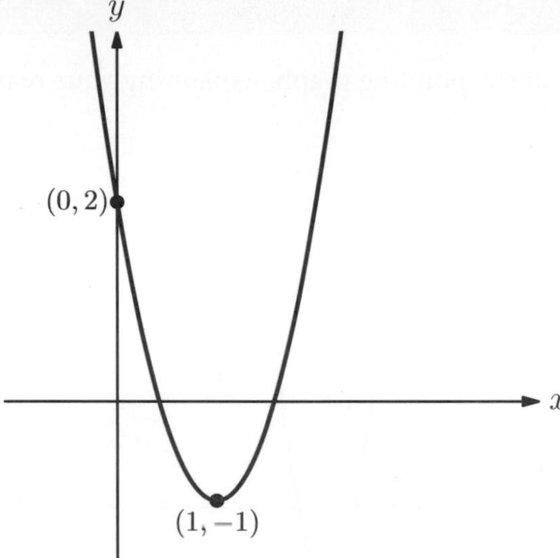

Find the values of c and a.

c is the y-intercept.

The y-intercept of the graph is (0, 2), so $c = 2$

The coordinates of the vertex need to satisfy the equation of the graph.

The vertex is at $x = 1$ and $y = -1$, so

$-1 = a(1)^2 - 6(1) + 2$

$-1 = a - 4$

$a = 3$

The shape of the graph and the position of the y-intercept are the only two features we can read directly from the quadratic equation. We may also be interested in other properties, such as

- the position of the line of symmetry
- the coordinates of the vertex
- the x-intercepts.

In the next two sections we will see how rewriting the equation of the graph in different forms allows us to identify these features. In some of the questions below you will need to find them using your calculator.

Exercise 1A

1. Match the equations to their corresponding graphs.

(i) A: $y = -x^2 - 3x + 6$ B: $y = 2x^2 - 3x + 3$ C: $y = x^2 - 3x + 6$

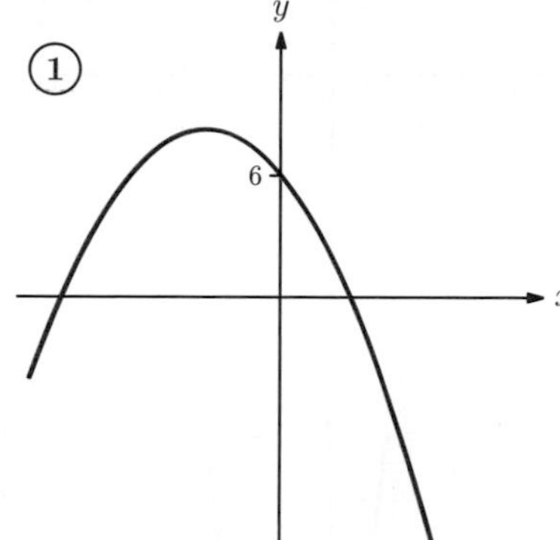

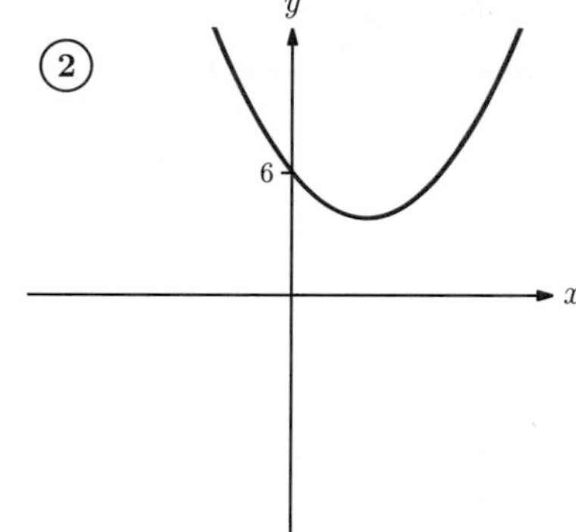

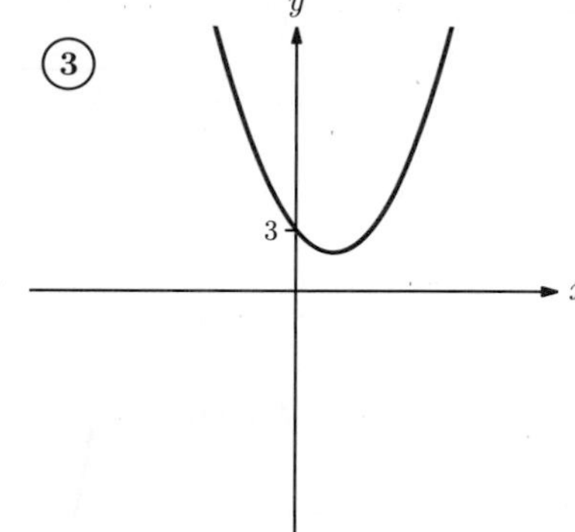

(ii) A: $y = -x^2 + 2x - 3$ B: $y = -x^2 + 2x + 3$ C: $y = x^2 + 2x + 3$

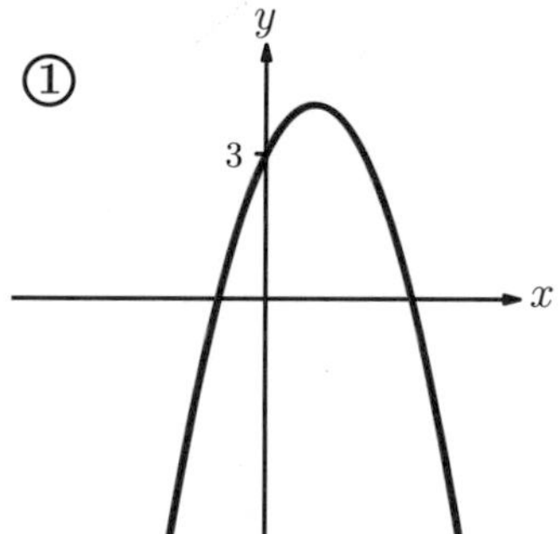

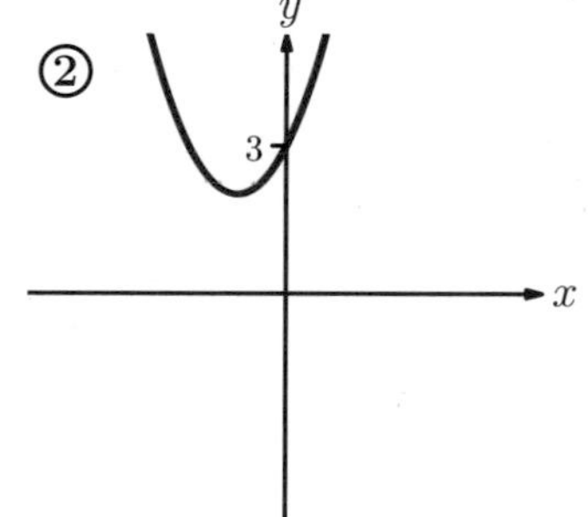

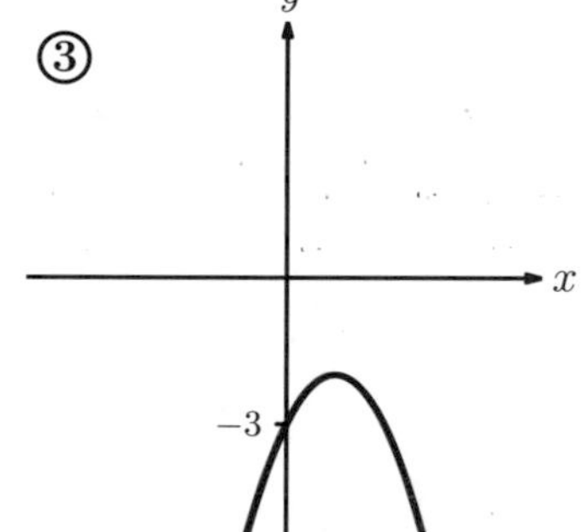

2. Write the following quadratic expressions in the form $ax^2 + bx + c$.

(a) (i) $2(x-1)(x+5)$ (ii) $5(x-1)(x-3)$

(b) (i) $-4(x+2)(4-x)$ (ii) $-(1-x)(2-x)$

(c) (i) $3(x-1)^2 + 3$ (ii) $4(x+2)^2 - 5$

(d) (i) $-4(x-1)^2 - 1$ (ii) $-2(x+2)^2 - 3$

See Prior Learning section K on the CD-ROM if you need to review the technique of expanding brackets.

3. Find the y-intercept of the graph of each equation.

(a) (i) $y = 2(x-1)(x+3)$ (ii) $y = 3(x+1)(x-1)$

(b) (i) $y = -3x(x-2)$ (ii) $y = -5x(x-1)$

(c) (i) $y = -(x-1)(x+2)$ (ii) $y = -3(x-1)(x+2)$

(d) (i) $y = 2(x-3)^2 + 1$ (ii) $y = 5(x-1)^2 - 3$

4. The diagrams show quadratic graphs and their equations. Find the value of c in each case.

(a) (i)

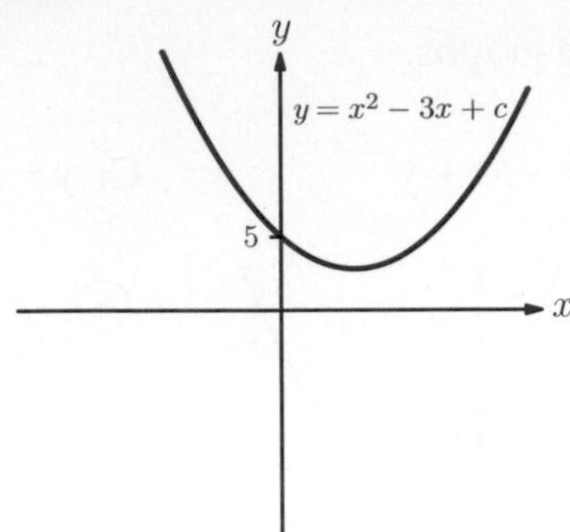

(ii)

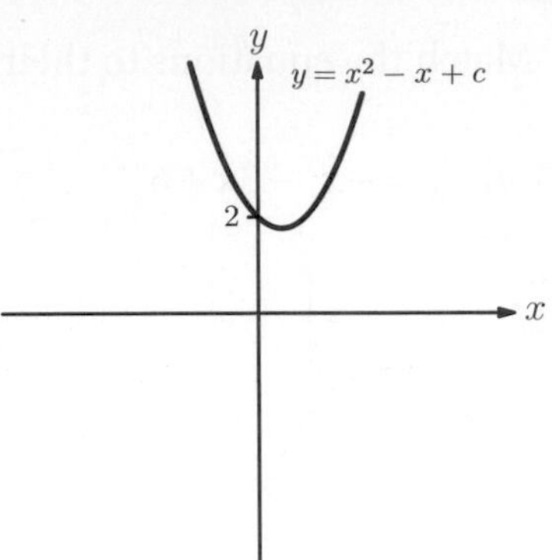

(b) (i)

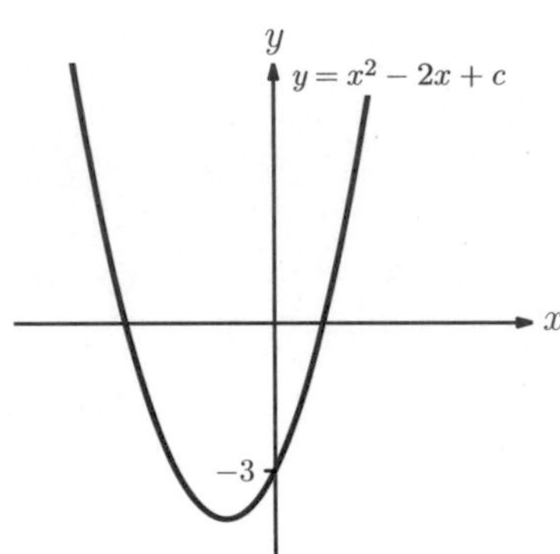

(ii)

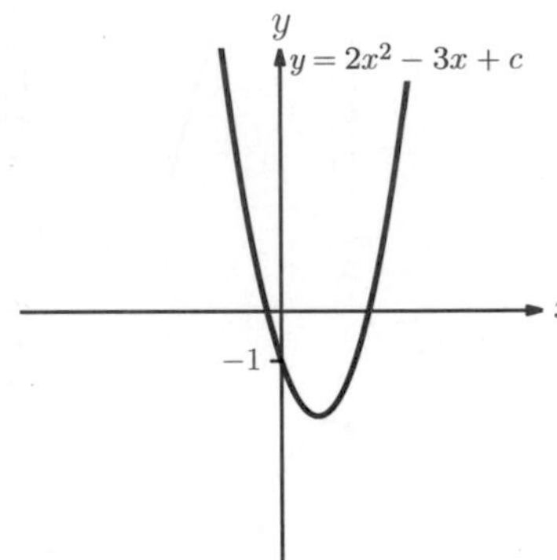

(c) (i)

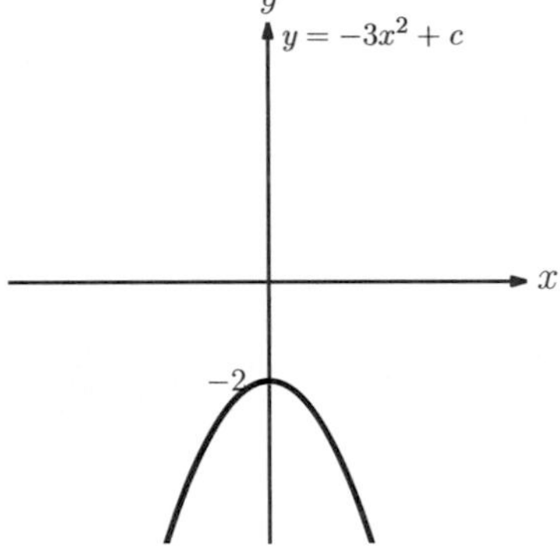

(ii)

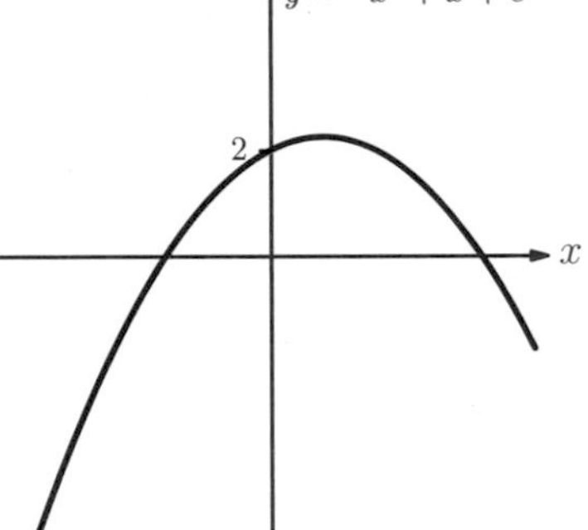

5. The diagrams show quadratic graphs and their equations. Find the value of a in each case.

(a) (i)

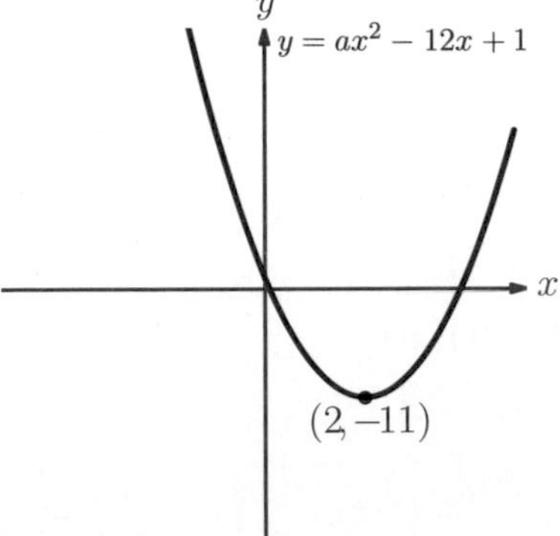

(ii)

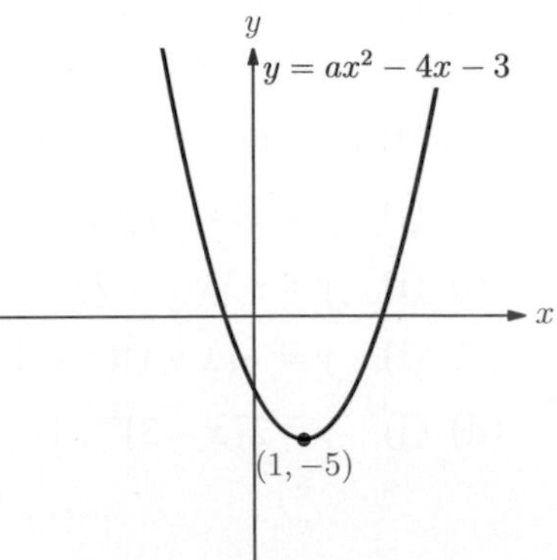

(b) (i)

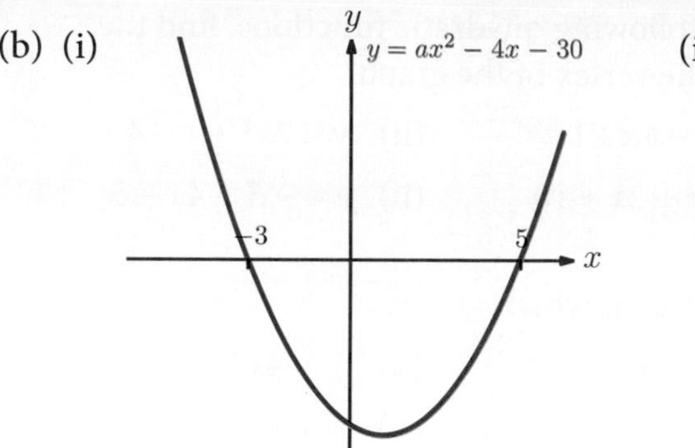

(ii)

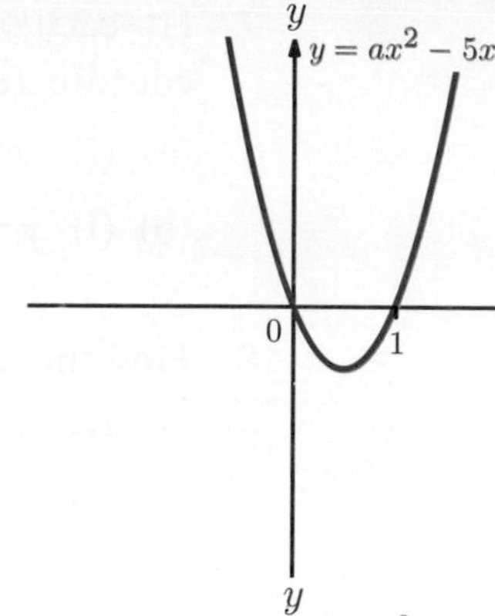

(c) (i)

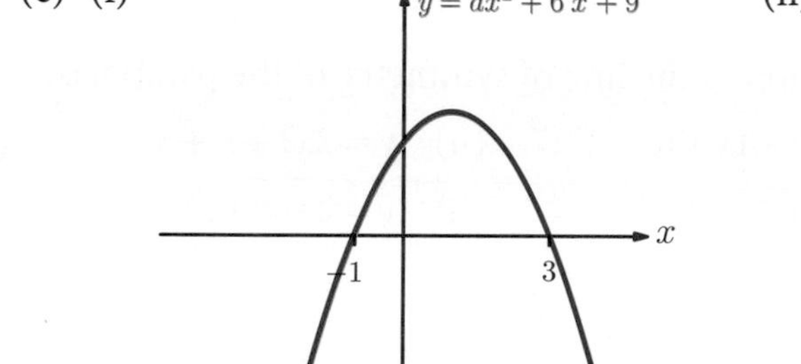

(ii)

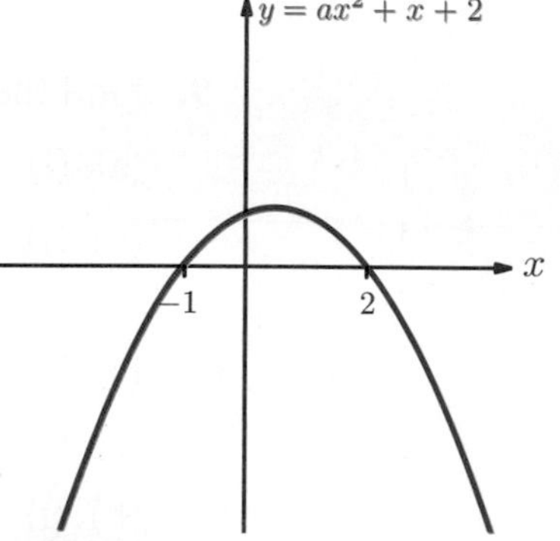

6. The diagrams show graphs of quadratic functions of the form $y = ax^2 + bx + c$. Write down the value of c and then find the values of a and b.

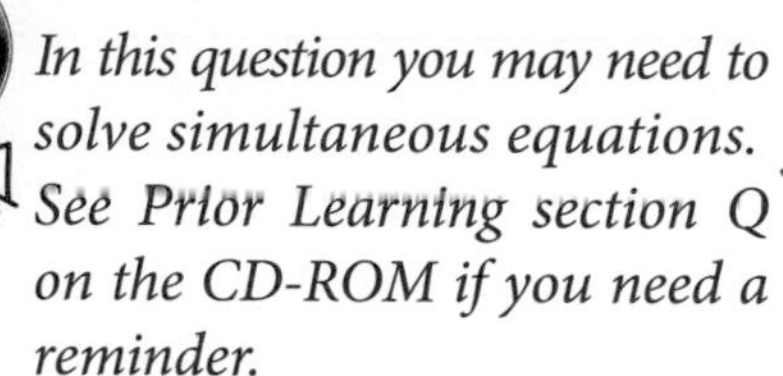

In this question you may need to solve simultaneous equations. See Prior Learning section Q on the CD-ROM if you need a reminder.

(a) (i)

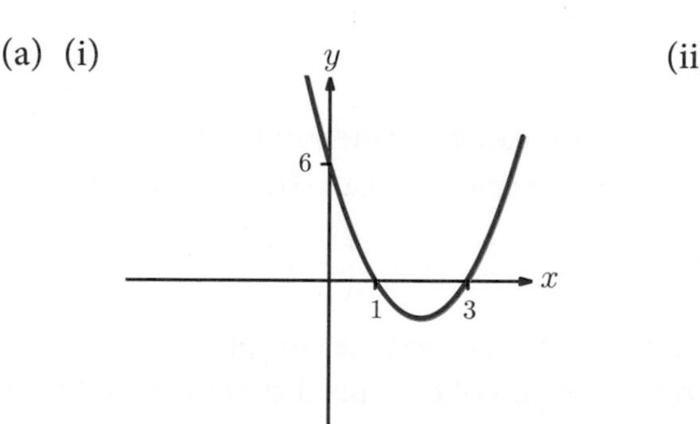

(ii)

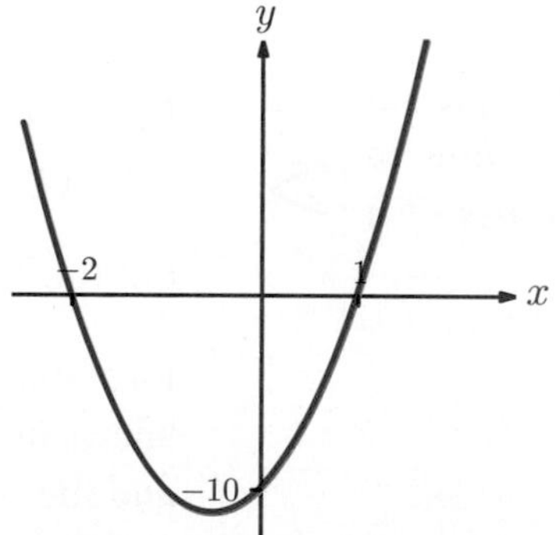

(b) (i)

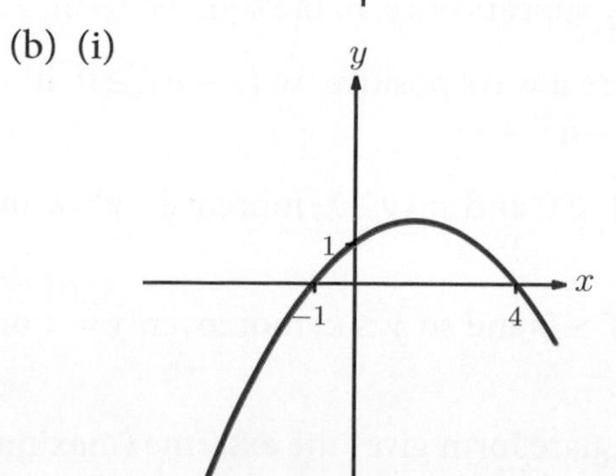

(ii)

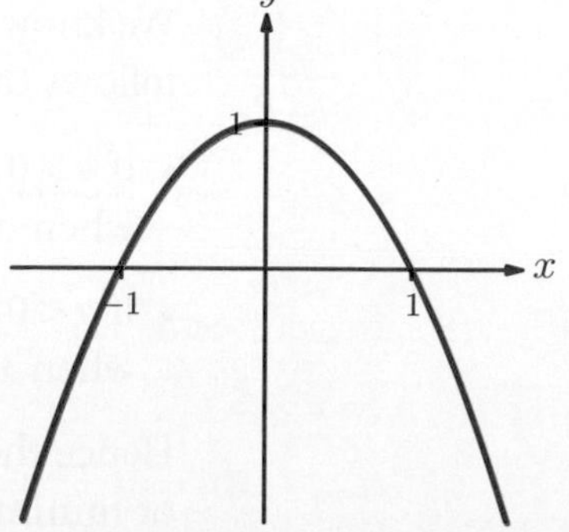

7. For each of the following quadratic functions, find the coordinates of the vertex of the graph.

(a) (i) $y = 3x^2 - 4x + 1$ (ii) $y = 2x^2 + x - 4$

(b) (i) $y = -5x^2 + 2x + 10$ (ii) $y = -x^2 + 4x - 5$

8. Find the x-values for which $y = 0$.

(a) (i) $y = 3x^2 - 4x - 3$ (ii) $y = 4x^2 + x - 3$

(b) (i) $y = 4x + 2 - x^2$ (ii) $y = x + 5 - 2x^2$

(c) (i) $y = -2x^2 + 12x - 18$ (ii) $y = 2x^2 - 6x + 4.5$

9. Find the equation of the line of symmetry of the parabolas.

(a) (i) $y = x^2 - 4x + 6$ (ii) $y = 2x^2 + x + 5$

(b) (i) $y = 4 + 3x - 2x^2$ (ii) $y = 2 - x + 3x^2$

10. Find the values of x for which

(a) (i) $3x^2 + 4x - 7 = 15$ (ii) $x^2 + x - 1 = 3$

(b) (i) $4x + 2 = 3x^2$ (ii) $3 - 5x = x^2 + 2$

1B The completed square form $y = a(x - h)^2 + k$

It is often useful to write a quadratic function in a different form.

Worked example 1.3 below shows how to find the values of h and k.

Every quadratic function can be written in the form $y = a(x-h)^2 + k$. For example, you can check by multiplying out the brackets that $2x^2 - 2x - 4 = 2\left(x - \frac{1}{2}\right)^2 - \frac{9}{2}$. This second form of a quadratic equation, called the **completed square form**, allows us to find the position of the line of symmetry of the graph and the coordinates of the vertex. It can also be used to solve equations because x only appears once, in the squared term.

We know that squares are always positive, so $(x-h)^2 \geq 0$. It follows that for $y = a(x-h)^2 + k$:

- if $a > 0$, then $a(x-h)^2 \geq 0$ and so $y \geq k$; moreover, $y = k$ only when $x = h$
- if $a < 0$, then $a(x-h)^2 \leq 0$ and so $y \leq k$; moreover, $y = k$ only when $x = h$.

Hence the completed square form gives the extreme (maximum or minimum) value of the quadratic function, namely k, as well as the value of x at which that extreme value occurs, h. The point at which the extreme value occurs is called a **turning point** or **vertex**.

KEY POINT 1.2

A quadratic function $y = a(x-h)^2 + k$ has turning point (h, k) and line of symmetry $x = h$.

For $a > 0$, $y \geq k$ for all x.

For $a < 0$, $y \leq k$ for all x.

The next example shows how the functions y_1 and y_2 from the previous section can be rearranged into completed square form.

Worked example 1.3

(a) Write $2x^2 - 2x - 4$ in the form $a(x-h)^2 + k$

(b) Hence write down the coordinates of the vertex and the equation of the line of symmetry of the graph $y_1 = 2x^2 - 2x - 4$.

Expand the brackets. Compare coefficients with the given expression.

(a) $a(x-h)^2 + k = ax^2 - 2ahx + ah^2 + k$

Comparing coefficients of x^2: $a = 2$

Comparing coefficients of x: $-2ah = -2$

But $a = 2$:

$\therefore -4h = -2$

$\Leftrightarrow h = \frac{1}{2}$

Comparing constants:

$ah^2 + k = -4$

But $a = 2, h = \frac{1}{2}$:

$\therefore \frac{1}{2} + k = -4$

$\Leftrightarrow k = -\frac{9}{2}$

Extract information from the turning point form (h, k).

(b) Line of symmetry is $x = \frac{1}{2}$ and the vertex is $\left(\frac{1}{2}, -\frac{9}{2}\right)$

We can also use the completed square form to solve equations. This is illustrated in the next example, which also shows you how to deal with negative coefficients.

Worked example 1.4

(a) Write $-x^2 + 4x - 3$ in the form $a(x - h)^2 + k$

(b) Hence solve the equation $y_2 = -8$

Expand the required form and compare coefficients

(a) $a(x-h)^2 + k = ax^2 - 2ahx + ah^2 + k$

Comparing the coefficients of x^2: $a = -1$

Comparing the coefficients of x:

$4 = -2ah$

$4 = 2h$

$\Leftrightarrow h = 2$

Comparing constants

$-3 = ah^2 + k$

$-3 = -4 + k$

$\Leftrightarrow \quad k = 1$

Therefore $-x^2 + 4x - 3 = -(x-2)^2 + 1$

Isolate the term containing x

(b) $y_2 = -(x-2)^2 + 1$

$-(x-2)^2 + 1 = -8$

$\Leftrightarrow -(x-2)^2 = -9$

$\Leftrightarrow (x-2)^2 = 9$

$\Leftrightarrow x - 2 = \pm 3$

$\therefore x = 5$ or $x = -1$

EXAM HINT

The line of symmetry (and the x-coordinate of the vertex) can also be found using the formula $x = -\dfrac{b}{2a}$, which is given in the Formula booklet. We will explain in section 1D where this formula comes from.

We can now label the lines of symmetry and the coordinates of the turning points on the graphs of y_1 and y_2.

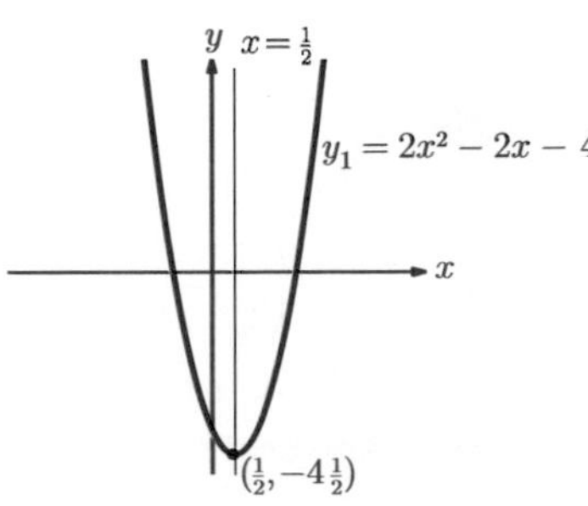

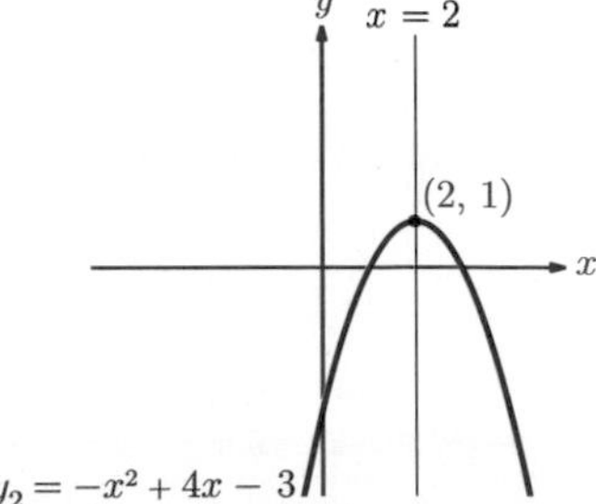

We can also reverse the process to find the equation of a given graph. If the coordinates of the maximum or minimum point are apparent from the graph, then it is easiest to write down the equation in completed square form.

Worked example 1.5

Find the quadratic relationship that fits this graph.

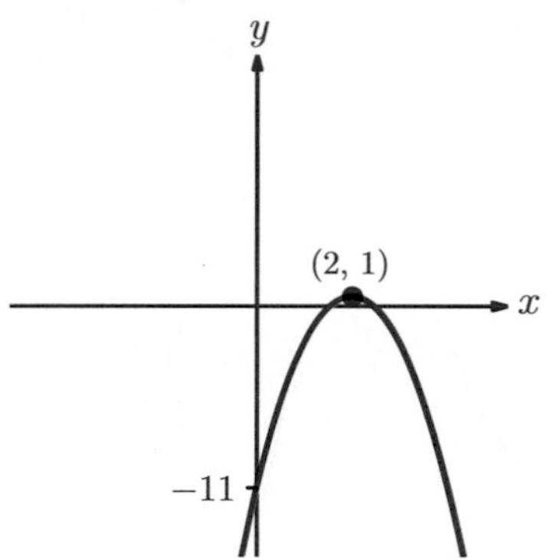

Since we are given information about the maximum point, we use the completed square form.

Maximum point is at (2, 1), so the function must be of the form $y = a(x-2)^2 + 1$

Use the remaining information to find a.

The y-intercept is at (0, −11). According to our function, when $x = 0$,

$$y = a(0-2)^2 + 1$$
$$= 4a + 1$$

Therefore

$$4a + 1 = -11$$
$$\Leftrightarrow \ a = -3$$

Answer the question.

So the relationship is $y = -3(x-2)^2 + 1$

Exercise 1B

1. Write down the coordinates of the vertex of each of the following quadratic functions.
   (a) (i) $y=(x-3)^2+4$ (ii) $y=(x-5)^2+1$
   (b) (i) $y=2(x-2)^2-1$ (ii) $y=3(x-1)^2-5$
   (c) (i) $y=(x+1)^2+3$ (ii) $y=(x+7)^2-3$
   (d) (i) $y=-5(x+2)^2-4$ (ii) $y=-(x+1)^2+5$

2. Write the following expressions in the form $a(x-h)^2+k$.

(a) (i) x^2-6x+4 (ii) $x^2-10x+21$

(b) (i) x^2+4x+1 (ii) x^2+6x-3

(c) (i) $2x^2-12x+5$ (ii) $3x^2+6x+10$

(d) (i) $-x^2+2x-5$ (ii) $-x^2-4x+1$

(e) (i) x^2+3x+1 (ii) $x^2-5x+10$

(f) (i) $2x^2+6x+15$ (ii) $2x^2-5x-1$

3. Find the equation of each graph in the form $y=a(x-h)^2+k$.

(a) (i)

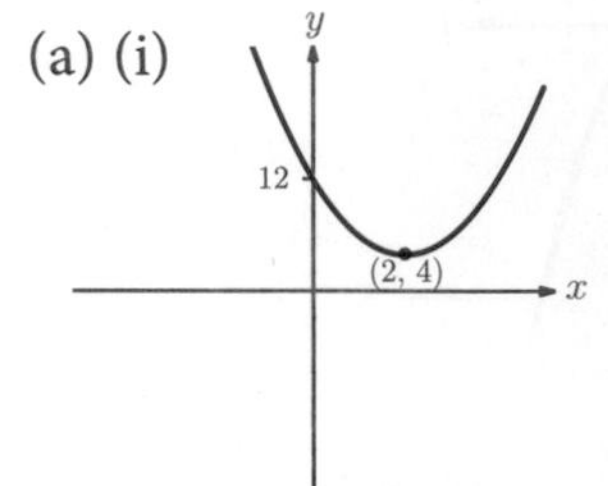

(ii)

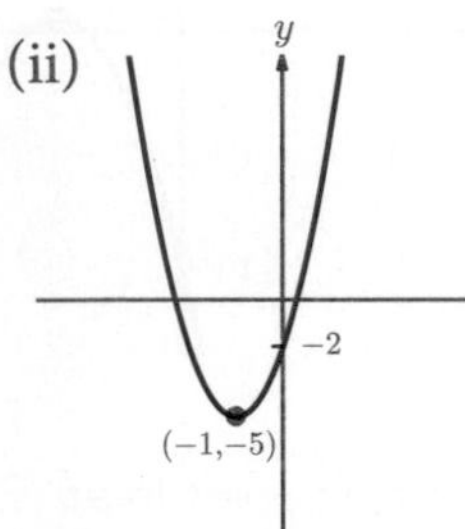

(b) (i)

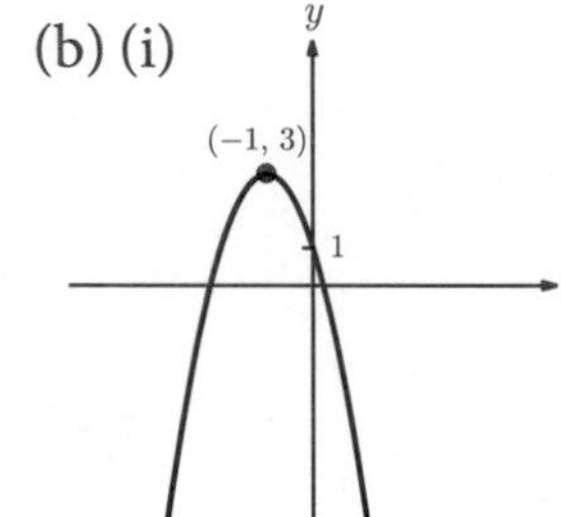

(ii)

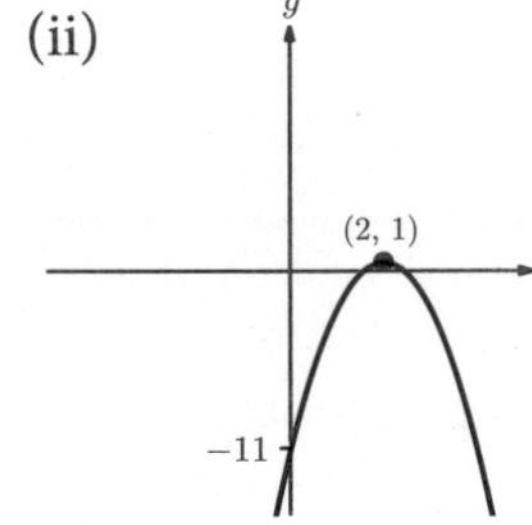

4. You are given that $y=x^2-6x+11$.

(a) Write y in the form $(x-h)+k$.

(b) Find the minimum value of y. *[3 marks]*

5. The curve $y=a(x+b)^2+c$ has a minimum point at (3, 6) and passes through the point (1, 14).

(a) Write down the values of b and c.

(b) Find the value of a. *[4 marks]*

6. (a) Write $2x^2+4x-1$ in the form $a(x-h)^2+k$.

(b) Hence write down the equation of the line of symmetry of the graph $y=2x^2+4x-1$.

(c) Find the exact solutions of the equation $2x^2+4x-1=0$.

[8 marks]

EXAM HINT

When you are asked to find *exact solutions*, leave your answer with roots and fractions rather than evaluating the decimal equivalent; this means that you should not use a calculator to find the answer (although you can still use it to check your answer).

1C The factorised form $y = a(x - p)(x - q)$

The **factorised form** is especially useful for determining another significant feature of a quadratic function, its **zeros**, defined as those values of x (if any) for which $y = 0$. Graphically, they are the values of x at which the curve crosses the x-axis. They are also called the **roots** of the equation $a(x-p)(x-q)=0$.

For each of the functions y_1 and y_2 that we studied earlier, there are two zeros, as you can see from their graphs. We may be able to find the values of these zeros by factorising the quadratic function.

See Prior Learning section N on the CD-ROM for how to factorise quadratics.

KEY POINT 1.3

A quadratic function $y = a(x - p)(x - q)$ has zeros at $x = p$ and $x = q$.

Check that the expression $a(x-p)(x-q)$ does equal zero when $x = p$ or when $x = q$.

Worked example 1.6

Using factorisation, find the zeros of functions y_1 and y_2.

Factorise the quadratic function, taking out the common factor 2 first.

$$y_1 = 2x^2 - 2x - 4$$
$$= 2(x^2 - x - 2)$$
$$= 2(x+1)(x-2)$$

Read off the values of p and q.

The zeros of y_1 are -1 and 2.

Factorise the quadratic function. It helps to take out the factor of -1 first.

$$y_2 = -x^2 + 4x - 3$$
$$= -(x^2 - 4x + 3)$$
$$= -(x-1)(x-3)$$

Read off the values of p and q.

The zeros of y_2 are 1 and 3.

EXAM HINT

The line of symmetry of the graph is half-way between the zeros. You can sometimes use this fact to help you factorise or to check your answer.

In some exam questions you may have to carry out these procedures in reverse. For example, you could be given information about the vertex or zeros of a quadratic function and asked to find the coefficients.

Worked example 1.7

A quadratic function has vertex at $(-1,-5)$, and one of its zeros is 4. Find the equation of the function in the form $y = ax^2 + bx + c$.

If we can find the other zero, then we can write down the factorised form of the function. Use the fact that the zeros are at an equal distance from the line of symmetry, on either side of it.

Line of symmetry is $x = -1$ and one zero is 4, so the other zero is -6.

Write down the factorised form; don't forget a.

$$y = a(x-4)(x+6)$$

We need to find a. To do this, we use the information about the vertex.

Vertex is at $x = -1$ and $y = -5$, so

$$-5 = a(-1-4)(-1+6)$$

$$\Leftrightarrow \quad -5 = -25a$$

$$\Leftrightarrow \quad a = \frac{1}{5}$$

Hence $y = \frac{1}{5}(x-4)(x+6)$

To put the equation in the required form, we need to multiply out the brackets.

$$y = \frac{1}{5}(x^2 + 2x - 24)$$

$$= \frac{1}{5}x^2 + \frac{2}{5}x - \frac{24}{5}$$

Exercise 1C

1. Write down the zeros of the following quadratic functions.

(a) (i) $(x+2)(x-3)$ (ii) $(x-5)(x+1)$

(b) (i) $x(x+3)$ (ii) $2x(x-2)$

(c) (i) $2(5-x)(2+x)$ (ii) $4(1-x)(1+x)$

(d) (i) $(2x-1)(3x+5)$ (ii) $(4x-3)(3x+1)$

2. By factorising, find the zeros of the following quadratic functions.

(a) (i) x^2+4x-5 (ii) x^2-6x+8

(b) (i) $2x^2+x-6$ (ii) $3x^2-x-10$

(c) (i) $6x^2-7x-3$ (ii) $8x^2-6x-5$

(d) (i) $12-x-x^2$ (ii) $10-3x-x^2$

3. For each graph, find its equation in the form $y=ax^2+bx+c$.

(a) (i)

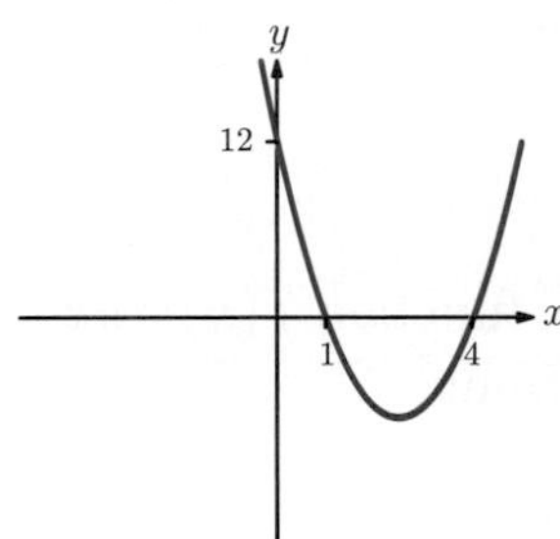

(ii)

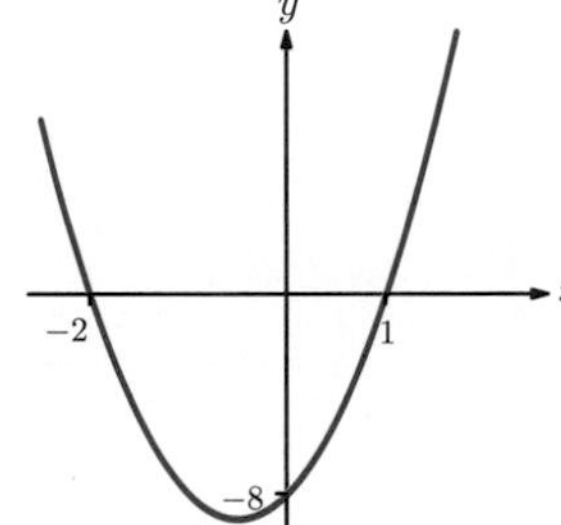

(b) (i)

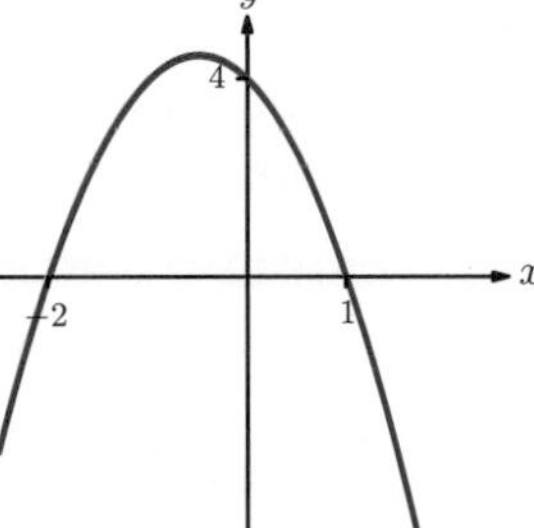

(ii)

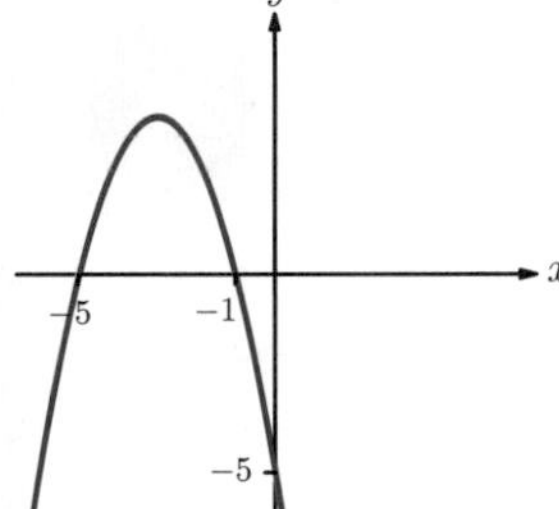

4. (a) Factorise $2x^2+5x-12$.

(b) Hence write down the coordinates of the points where the graph of $y=2x^2+5x-12$ crosses the x-axis. *[5 marks]*

5. This graph has equation $y=ax^2+bx+c$. Find the values of a, b and c. *[5 marks]*

1D The quadratic formula and the discriminant

It is not always possible to find the zeros of a quadratic function by factorising. For example, try factorising $y_1=x^2-3x-3$ and $y_2=x^2-3x+3$. It seems that neither of these equations can

EXAM HINT

Remember that finding zeros of a quadratic function is the same as solving a quadratic equation.

be factorised, but their graphs reveal that the first one has two zeros while the second has none.

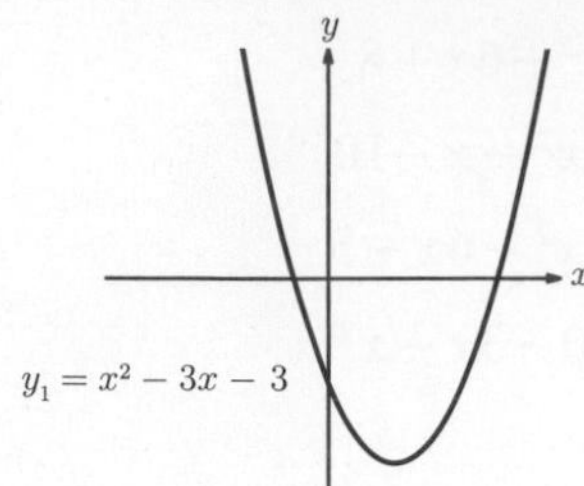

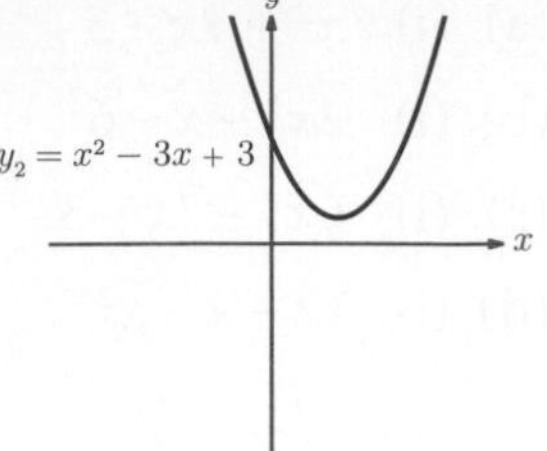

Instead of factorising, we can use the following formula to find zeros of a quadratic function.

KEY POINT 1.4

The zeros of the quadratic function $f(x) = ax^2 + bx + c$ are given by the quadratic formula

$$x = \frac{-b \pm \sqrt{b^2 - 4ac}}{2a}, a \neq 0$$

See Fill-in Proof sheet 1 'Proving the quadratic formula' on the CD-ROM for how to prove this formula.

EXAM HINT

Don't spend too long trying to factorise a quadratic – use the formula if you are asked to find exact solutions, and use a calculator (graph or equation solver) otherwise.

See Calculator Skills sheets 4 and 6 on the CD-ROM for how to do this.

Worked example 1.8

Use the quadratic formula to find the zeros of $x^2 - 5x - 3$.

As it is not obvious how to factorise the quadratic expression, we use the quadratic formula.

Here $a = 1,\ b = -5,\ c = -3$

$$x = \frac{5 \pm \sqrt{(-5)^2 - 4 \times 1 \times (-3)}}{2}$$

$$= \frac{5 \pm \sqrt{37}}{2}$$

The zeros are

$$\frac{5 + \sqrt{37}}{2} = 5.54 \text{ and } \frac{5 - \sqrt{37}}{2} = -0.541 \text{ (3 SF)}$$

Let us examine what happens if we try to apply the quadratic formula to find the zeros of $y_2 = x^2 - 3x + 3$:

$$x = \frac{3 \pm \sqrt{(-3)^2 - 4 \times 1 \times 3}}{2} = \frac{3 \pm \sqrt{-3}}{2}$$

As the square root of a negative number is not a real number, it follows that $x^2 - 3x + 3$ has no real zeros.

Worked example 1.8 is an example of a quadratic function with two zeros, just as the function y_1 on page 16. y_2 is an example of a quadratic function with no real zeros. It is also possible to have a quadratic function with one zero.

Looking more closely at the quadratic formula, we see that it can be separated into two parts:

$$x = \frac{-b}{2a} \pm \frac{\sqrt{b^2 - 4ac}}{2a}$$

You have already met the first term, $\frac{-b}{2a}$: $x = \frac{-b}{2a}$ is the line of symmetry of the parabola.

The second term in the formula involves a root expression: $\sqrt{b^2 - 4ac}$. The expression $b^2 - 4ac$ inside the square root is called the **discriminant** of the quadratic (often symbolised by the Greek letter Δ).

As noted above, the square root of a negative number is not a real number, so if the discriminant is negative, there can be no real zeros of the function.

If the discriminant is zero, the quadratic formula gives $x = -\frac{b}{2a} \pm 0$, so there is only one root, $x = -\frac{b}{2a}$. In this case, the graph is **tangent** to the x-axis (meaning that the graph touches the x-axis rather than crossing it) at a point that lies on the line of symmetry – the vertex, in fact.

The graphs at the top of page 18 demonstrate the three possible situations when finding the zeros of quadratic functions.

Note that $\frac{\sqrt{\Delta}}{2a}$ is the distance of the zeros from the line of symmetry $x = \frac{-b}{2a}$.

EXAM HINT

In exams you should either give exact answers (such as $\frac{5 + \sqrt{37}}{2}$) or round your answers to 3 significant figures, unless you are explicitly told otherwise.
See Prior Learning section B on the CD-ROM for the rules of rounding.

No real zeros

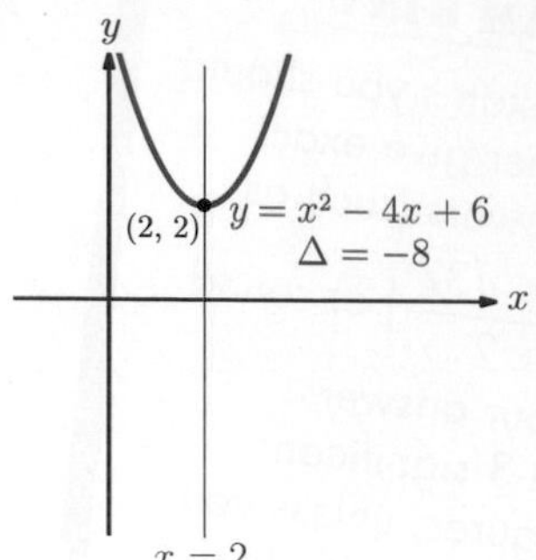

One real zero

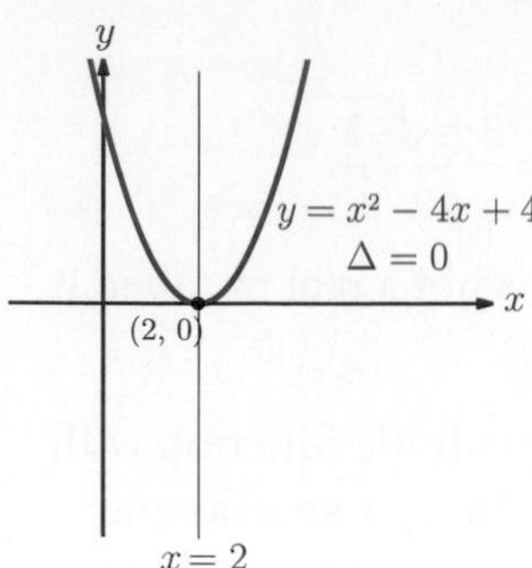

Two real zeros

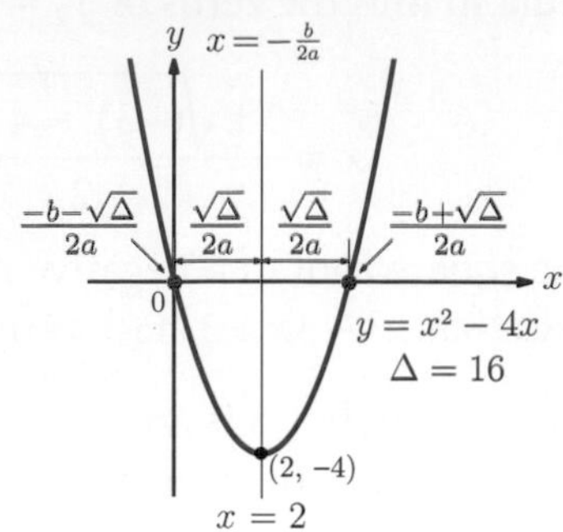

KEY POINT 1.5

For a quadratic function $y = ax^2 + bx + c$, the discriminant is $\Delta = b^2 - 4ac$.

- If $\Delta < 0$, the function has no real zeros.
- If $\Delta = 0$, the function has one (repeated) zero.
- If $\Delta > 0$, the function has two (distinct) real zeros.

The situation $\Delta = 0$ is often said to produce a 'repeated root' or 'equal roots' of $y = ax^2 + bx + c$, because in factorised form the function is $y = a(x - p)(x - p)$, which gives two equal root values p and q. An expression of the form $(x - p)(x - p)$ is also referred to as a 'perfect square'.

Worked example 1.9

Find the exact values of k for which the quadratic equation $kx^2 - (k+2)x + 3 = 0$ has a repeated root.

Repeated root means that $\Delta = b^2 - 4ac = 0$. So we identify a, b and c, and write down the equation $b^2 - 4ac = 0$.

$a = k, b = -(k+2), c = 3$

$(-k-2)^2 - 4(k)(3) = 0$

$\Leftrightarrow k^2 + 4k + 4 - 12k = 0$

This is a quadratic equation in k.

$\Rightarrow \quad k^2 - 8k + 4 = 0$

It doesn't look as if we can factorise, so use the quadratic formula.

$$k = \frac{8 \pm \sqrt{(-8)^2 - 4 \times 1 \times 4}}{2}$$

$$= \frac{8 \pm \sqrt{48}}{2}$$

$$= \frac{8 \pm 4\sqrt{3}}{2}$$

$$= 4 \pm 2\sqrt{3}$$

EXAM HINT

Questions of this type nearly always lead to a quadratic equation for k.

When $\Delta < 0$, the graph does not intersect the x-axis, so must lie entirely above or entirely below it. The two cases are distinguished by the value of a.

KEY POINT 1.6

For a quadratic function $y = ax^2 + bx + c$ with $\Delta < 0$:

- if $a > 0$, then $y > 0$ for all x
- if $a < 0$, then $y < 0$ for all x.

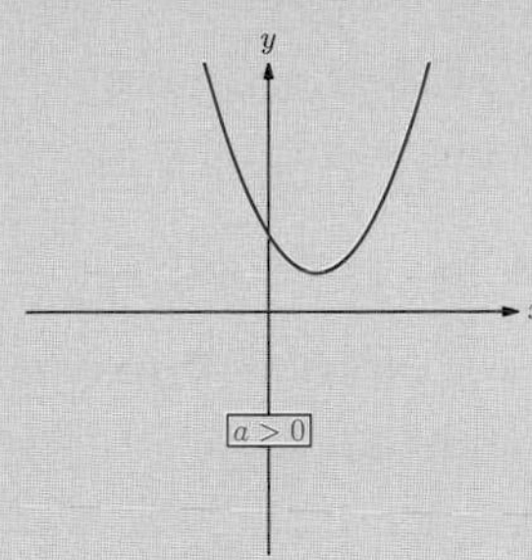

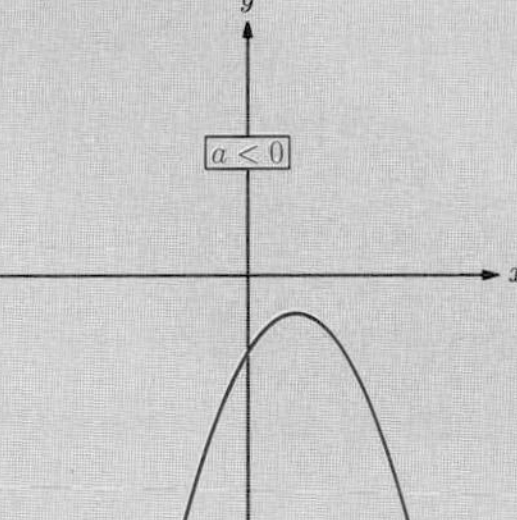

Worked example 1.10

Given the quadratic function $y = -3x^2 + kx - 12$, where $k > 0$, find the values of k such that $y < 0$ for all x.

y is a negative quadratic, so $y < 0$ means that the graph is entirely below the x-axis. This will happen when the quadratic has no real roots.

No real roots means $\Delta < 0$:

$$b^2 - 4ac < 0$$

$$k^2 - 4(-3)(-12) < 0$$

$$k^2 < 144$$

We are told that $k > 0$.

$$\therefore 0 < k < 12$$

Exercise 1D

1. Evaluate the discriminant of each quadratic expression.

(a) (i) $x^2 + 4x - 5$ (ii) $x^2 - 6x - 8$

(b) (i) $2x^2 + x + 6$ (ii) $3x^2 - x + 10$

(c) (i) $3x^2 - 6x + 3$ (ii) $9x^2 - 6x + 1$

(d) (i) $12 - x - x^2$ (ii) $-x^2 - 3x + 10$

2. State the number of zeros of each expression from Question 1.

3. Use the quadratic formula to find the exact solutions of the following equations.

(a) (i) $x^2 - 3x + 1 = 0$ (ii) $x^2 - x - 1 = 0$

(b) (i) $3x^2 + x - 2 = 0$ (ii) $2x^2 - 6x + 1 = 0$

(c) (i) $4 + x - 3x^2 = 0$ (ii) $1 - x - 2x^2 = 0$

(d) (i) $x^2 - 3 = 4x$ (ii) $3 - x = 2x^2$

4. Find the values of k for which

(a) (i) the equation $2x^2 - x + 3k = 0$ has two distinct real roots

(ii) the equation $3x^2 + 5x - k = 0$ has two distinct real roots

(b) (i) the equation $5x^2 - 2x + (2k - 1) = 0$ has equal roots

(ii) the equation $2x^2 + 3x - (3k + 1) = 0$ has equal roots

(c) (i) the equation $-x^2 + 3x + (k - 1) = 0$ has real roots

(ii) the equation $-2x^2 + 3x - (2k + 1) = 0$ has real roots

(d) (i) the equation $3kx^2 - 3x + 2 = 0$ has no solutions

(ii) the equation $-kx^2 + 5x + 3 = 0$ has no solutions

(e) (i) the quadratic expression $(k - 2)x^2 + 3x + 1$ has a repeated zero

(ii) the quadratic expression $-4x^2 + 5x + (2k - 5)$ has a repeated zero

(f) (i) the graph of $y = x^2 - 4x + (3k + 1)$ is tangent to the x-axis

(ii) the graph of $y = -2kx^2 + x - 4$ is tangent to the x-axis

(g) (i) the expression $-3x^2 + 5k$ has no real zeros

(ii) the expression $2kx^2 - 3$ has no real zeros

5. Find the exact solutions of the equation $3x^2 = 4x + 1$. *[3 marks]*

6. Show that the graph of $y = 4x^2 + x + \frac{1}{16}$ has its vertex on the x-axis. *[3 marks]*

7. Find the values of parameter m for which the quadratic equation $mx^2 - 4x + 2m = 0$ has equal roots. *[5 marks]*

8. Find the exact values of k such that the equation $-3x^2 + (2k + 1)x - 4k = 0$ is tangent to the x-axis. *[6 marks]*

9. Find the set of values of k for which the equation $x^2 - 6x + 2k = 0$ has no real solutions. *[5 marks]*

10. Find the range of values of the parameter c such that $2x^2 - 3x + (2c - 1) \geq 0$ for all x. *[5 marks]*

11. Find the possible values of m such that $mx^2 + 3x - 4 < 0$ for all x. *[5 marks]*

12. The positive difference between the zeros of the quadratic expression $x^2 + kx + 3$ is $\sqrt{69}$. Find the possible values of k. *[4 marks]*

1E Intersections of graphs and simultaneous equations

See Prior Learning section Q on the CD-ROM for revision of linear simultaneous equations.

Whenever we need to locate an intersection between two graphs, we are solving **simultaneous equations**. This means that we are trying to find values of x and y that satisfy both equations.

You can always find the intersections of two graphs by using a calculator. Remember, however, that a calculator only gives approximate solutions. If exact solutions are required, then we have to use an algebraic method. In many cases the best method is substitution, where we replace every occurrence of one variable in one of the equations by an expression for it derived from the other equation.

EXAM HINT

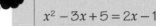

See Calculator Skills sheet 5 on the CD-ROM for how to find coordinates of intersection points.

Worked example 1.11

Find the coordinates of the points of intersection between the line $y = 2x - 1$ and the parabola $y = x^2 - 3x + 5$.

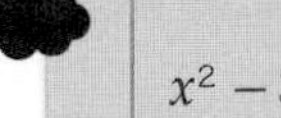

At intersection points the y-coordinates for the two curves are equal, so we can replace y in the first equation by the expression for y from the second equation.

$x^2 - 3x + 5 = 2x - 1$

continued . . .

This rearranges to a quadratic equation. Try to factorise it. In this case, factorisation gives the x-coordinates of the intersection points.

$$x^2 - 5x + 6 = 0$$
$$(x-2)(x-3) = 0$$
$$\Rightarrow \quad x = 2 \text{ or } 3$$

The corresponding y-coordinates can be found by substituting the x-values back into one of the original equations (both should give the same answer). Let us pick the first equation as it is simpler.

$y = 2x - 1$

$= 2 \Rightarrow y = 2\times2 - 1 = 3$

$= 3 \Rightarrow y = 2\times3 - 1 = 5$

The coordinates of the intersection points are (2, 3) and (3, 5).

Sometimes we only want to know how many intersection points there are, rather than to find their actual coordinates. The discriminant can be used to determine the number of intersections.

Worked example 1.12

Find the value of k for which the line with equation $y = x - k$ is tangent to the parabola $y = x^2$.

The line being tangent to the parabola means that the two graphs intersect at only one point. The number of intersections between the line and the parabola will depend on the value of k. This makes sense, as varying k moves the line up and down, so sometimes it will intersect the parabola and sometimes it won't.

Let us try to find the intersections. At intersection points the y-coordinates for the two curves are equal, so we can replace y in the second equation by the expression for y from the first equation.

Line equation: $y = x - k$

Substitute into the parabola equation $y = x^2$ to get

$$x - k = x^2$$

This is a quadratic equation; write it in the form of quadratic expression equal to zero.

$$x^2 - x + k = 0$$

For this to have only one solution, we need $\Delta = 0$.

One solution $\Rightarrow b^2 - 4ac = 0$

$$(-1)^2 - 4(1)(k) = 0$$
$$1 - 4k = 0$$
$$k = \frac{1}{4}$$

EXAM HINT

Questions about the *number* of intersections are often (though not always) solved using the discriminant.

Worked example 1.12 illustrates how a geometrical problem (intersections of two curves) can be solved by purely algebraic methods. There is a whole branch of mathematics studying such methods, called analytic geometry. It was developed in the 17th century by the French philosopher and mathematician René Descartes. Establishing a link between geometry and algebra was a major step in the development of modern mathematics.

The parabola belongs to a family of quadratic curves called 'conic sections', which also includes the circle, the ellipse and the hyperbola. There are many fascinating and beautiful results concerning conic sections, and a lot of these can be investigated using properties of the quadratic function.

Exercise 1E

1. Find the coordinates of intersection between the given parabola and the given straight line.

(a) (i) $y = x^2 + 2x - 3$ and $y = x - 1$

(ii) $y = x^2 - 4x + 3$ and $y = 2x - 6$

(b) (i) $y = -x^2 + 3x + 9$ and $2x - y = 3$

(ii) $y = x^2 - 2x + 8$ and $x - y = 6$

2. Solve the following simultaneous equations:

(a) (i) $x - 2y = 1,\ 3xy - y^2 = 8$

(ii) $x + 2y = 3,\ y^2 + 2xy + 9 = 0$

(b) (i) $xy = 3,\ x + y = 4$

(ii) $x + y + 8 = 0,\ xy = 15$

(c) (i) $x + y = 5,\ y = x^2 - 2x + 3$

(ii) $x - y = 4,\ y = x^2 + x - 5$

3. Find the coordinates of the points of intersection of the graph of $y = x^2 - 4$ and the line $y = 8 - x$. *[6 marks]*

4. Solve the simultaneous equations

$y = 2x^2 - 3x + 2$ and $3x + 2y = 5$ *[7 marks]*

5. A circle has equation $x^2 - 6x + y^2 - 2y - 8 = 0$.

(a) Show that the x-coordinates of the points of intersection of the circle with the line $y = x - 8$ satisfy the equation $x^2 - 12x + 36 = 0$.

(b) Hence show that the line is tangent to the circle. *[5 marks]*

6. Find the exact values of m for which the line $y = mx + 3$ and the curve with equation $y = 3x^2 - x + 5$ have only one point of intersection. *[6 marks]*

1F Using quadratic functions to solve problems

Quadratic functions are very common in applications of mathematics. Many natural phenomena can be modelled using quadratic functions. For example: the motion of a projectile follows a path which is approximately a parabola; the elastic energy of a particle attached to the end of a spring is proportional to the square of the extension; electric power in a circuit is a quadratic function of the voltage. Properties of quadratic functions are also widely used in optimisation problems, where a certain quantity has to be maximised or minimised. In this section we look at some typical examples.

Worked example 1.13

A rectangle has perimeter 100 cm. What is the largest its area can be?

The area of a rectangle is length × width. Introduce variables so we can write equations.	Let x = length, y = width. Then Area $= xy$
It is impossible to see from this equation alone what the maximum possible value of the area is. However, we can proceed by writing an equation relating x and y, using the known perimeter.	Perimeter $= 2x + 2y = 100$
This means that we can express the area in terms of only one of the variables.	$2y = 100 - 2x$ $\Rightarrow y = 50 - x$ $\therefore$ Area $= x(50 - x)$ $= 50x - x^2$

continued . . .

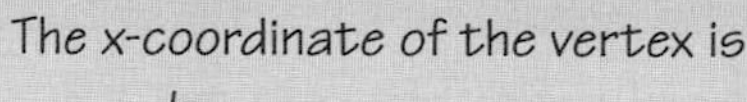

The area function is a negative quadratic, so we know how to find its maximum value (the y-coordinate of the vertex).

The x-coordinate of the vertex is

$$x = -\frac{b}{2a}$$

$$= -\frac{50}{2(-1)}$$

$$= 25$$

Negative quadratic, so the vertex is a maximum point with $f(25) = 50 \times 25 - 25^2 = 625$

Therefore the maximum area is 625 cm^2.

This is an example of *constrained optimisation*: we are trying to find a best possible solution while keeping some quantity fixed. It is intuitively clear that a short and wide or a tall and thin rectangle will have very small area, so we expect the largest area to occur somewhere in between.

A related problem is finding the minimum possible surface area for an object of fixed volume. Examples of this can be seen in nature: snakes have evolved to be long and thin in order to maximise their surface area – they are cold-blooded reptiles and need to gain as much heat as possible from the sun through their skin; polar bears, who live in the Arctic, avoid losing too much heat through their skin by adopting a rounder shape, which minimises the surface area for a given volume.

You may have noticed that in Worked example 1.13, the rectangle with the largest area is actually a square (with length = width = 25). It turns out that of all planar shapes with a fixed perimeter, the circle has the largest possible area. This so-called 'isoperimetric problem' has several intriguing proofs and many applications.

The next example presents an application to vertical motion under gravity. If we ignore air resistance, then the height above the ground of an object thrown vertically upwards will be a quadratic function of time.

Note that the path of the projectile can be represented by a similar parabola, as we shall see in Worked example 1.15.

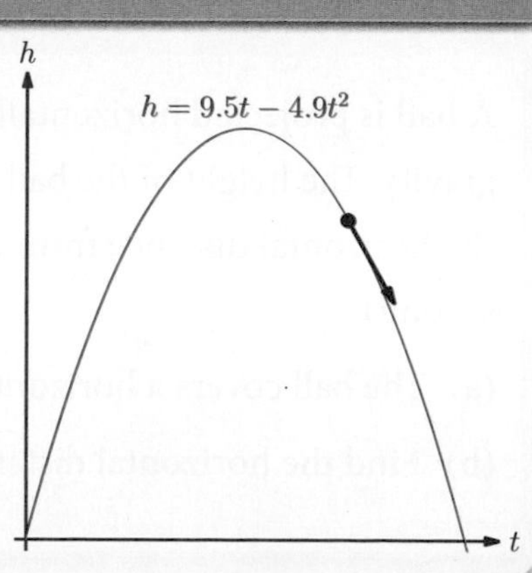

Worked example 1.14

A ball is thrown vertically upwards from ground level and moves freely under gravity. The height h of the ball above the ground can be modelled by the equation $h = 9.5t - 4.9t^2$, where t is the time, measured in seconds, after the ball is thrown.

(a) How long does the ball take to return to the ground?
(b) What height does the ball reach?

When the ball returns to the ground, $h = 0$, so we are looking for roots of the quadratic function. In this case, it is easy to factorise the quadratic.

(a) $9.5t - 4.9t^2 = 0$

$\Rightarrow t(9.5 - 4.9t) = 0$

$\Rightarrow t = 0$ or $t = \frac{9.5}{4.9} = 1.94$ (3 SF)

$t = 0$ is the time when the ball left the ground.

$\therefore$ the ball returns to the ground after 1.94 s.

We are now looking for the maximum point (vertex) of the quadratic function.

(b) Vertex is at

$t = -\frac{b}{2a}$

$= -\frac{9.5}{2 \times (-4.9)}$

$= 0.969$

$h = 9.5(0.969) - 4.9(0.969)^2$

$= 4.60$ (3 SF)

$\therefore$ the maximum height is 4.60 m.

A related problem is to describe the path of a projectile. In the absence of air resistance, this path is a parabola. The following example illustrates how we can use this fact. It also shows how to set out your working when you are using a calculator to analyse graphs.

Worked example 1.15

A ball is projected horizontally from a window 8 m above ground and then moves freely under gravity. The height of the ball above the ground, in metres, is given by $y = 8 - \frac{x^2}{2u}$, where x is the horizontal distance from the window and u is the initial speed of the ball (in metres per second).

(a) The ball covers a horizontal distance of 18 m before hitting the ground. Find the value of u.

(b) Find the horizontal distance that the ball covers while it is more than 4 m above ground.

→

continued . . .

The ball hits the ground when $y = 0$, so we know that $y = 0$ when $x = 18$.

(a) $y = 0$ when $x = 18$:

$$0 = 8 - \frac{18^2}{2u}$$

$$\Rightarrow \quad u = \frac{18^2}{16} = 20.25$$

We can draw the graph and find the values of x for which $y > 4$. To do this, we need the intersection of the graph with the horizontal line $y = 4$.

(b)

$$y = 8 - \frac{x^2}{40.5}$$

The graph is

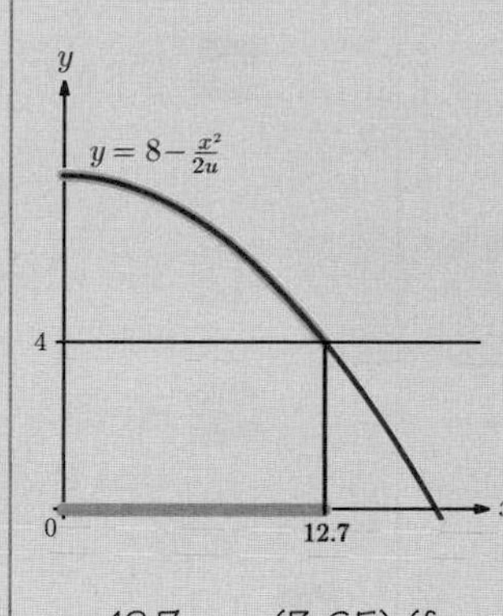

$x = 12.7\,m$ (3 SF) (from GDC)

Exercise 1F

1. The sum of two numbers is 8 and their product is 9.75. What are the two numbers? *[6 marks]*

2. A rectangle has perimeter equal to 12 cm. Let x cm be the length of one of the sides. Express the area of the rectangle in terms of x, and hence find the maximum possible area of the rectangle. *[6 marks]*

3. A farmer wishes to fence off a rectangular area adjacent to a wall. There is an existing piece of fence, 10 m in length, that is perpendicular to the wall, as shown in the diagram.

   The length of the new fencing is to be 200 m. Let x and y be the dimensions of the enclosure.

   (a) Write down an expression for the area of the enclosure in terms of x only.

   (b) Hence find the values of x and y that produce the maximum possible area. *[6 marks]*

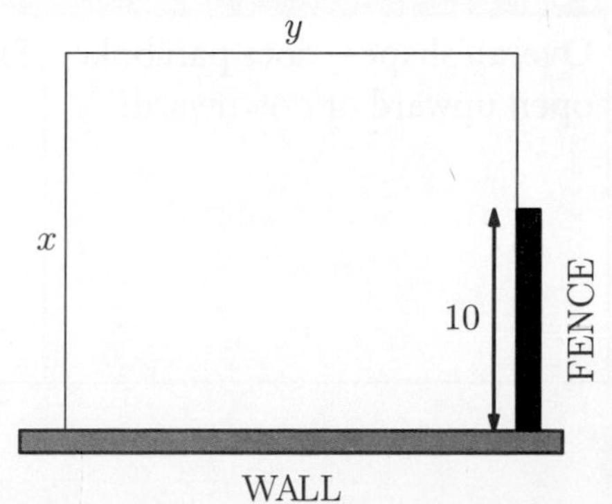

4. A ball is thrown upwards from ground level, and its height above the ground (in metres) is given by the equation $h = 8t - 4.9t^2$, where t is the time (in seconds) after the ball is thrown.

(a) When does the ball return to the ground?

(b) Find the maximum height of the ball. *[4 marks]*

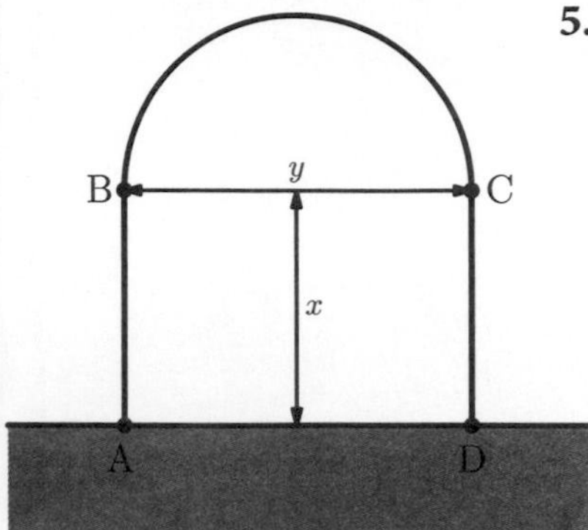

5. The enclosure ABCD consists of straight lines AB and CD together with a semi-circle BC. ABCD is a rectangle with sides x and y, as shown in the diagram. The perimeter of the enclosure is 60 m.

(a) Show that the area of the enclosure is given by

$$A = 30y - \frac{1}{8}\pi y^2.$$

(b) Show that the maximum possible area of the enclosure is when $x = 0$ (so that the enclosure is a semi-circle).

(c) Find the possible dimensions of the enclosure so that its area is 200 m^2. *[7 marks]*

6. A computer salesman finds that if he sells n computers, he can make a profit of $\$(200 - 4n)$ per computer. How many computers should he sell in order to maximise his profit? *[5 marks]*

Summary

Quadratic functions have the general form $f(x) = ax^2 + bx + c$, where a $\neq 0$.

The graphs of quadratic functions are **parabolas**, which have a single **turning point** or vertex. This point is either a minimum or a maximum point. The following table summarises their main features and how these are determined by the **coefficients** a,b and c.

Feature	What to look at	Conclusion
Overall shape – does parabola open upward or downward?	Sign of a	a > 0 minimum point

continued . . .

Feature	What to look at	Conclusion
		$a < 0$ maximum point
y-intercept	Value of c	y-intercept $(0, c)$
Vertex (or turning point)	Completed square form $y = a(x - h)^2 + k$	Vertex (h, k) for $a > 0$, $y \geq k$ for all x. for $a < 0$, $y \leq k$ for all x.
Line of symmetry	Completed square form or quadratic formula	$x = h$ or $x = -\dfrac{b}{2a}$
Zeros	Factorised form $y = a(x - p)(x - q)$ or quadratic formula $x = \dfrac{-b \pm \sqrt{b^2 - 4ac}}{2a}$	Roots p and q, x-intercepts $(p, 0)$ and $(q, 0)$
The number of real roots	Discriminant $\Delta = b^2 - 4ac$	$\Delta > 0 \Rightarrow$ two distinct real roots $\Delta = 0 \Rightarrow$ one root (repeated root, equal roots) $\Delta < 0 \Rightarrow$ no real roots

- It is also possible to determine some of the coefficients from the graph: the y-intercept, the ordinate of the vertex, the zeros and the shape of the graph (positive or negative a) can be read directly from the graph.
- We can solve quadratic equations by factorising, completing the square, applying the quadratic formula or using the graphing and equation solver programs on a calculator.
- We can also solve **simultaneous equations** using the points of intersection of two graphs, or using the method of substitution.
- Quadratic functions can be used to solve problems, especially optimisation problems, if we model the situation using a quadratic function.

Introductory problem revisited

A small dairy farmer wants to sell a new type of luxury cheese. After a fixed set-up cost of \$250, he can produce the cheese at a cost of \$9 per kilogram. He is able to produce up to 400 kg, but he plans to take advance orders and produce only what he can sell. His market research suggests that the amount he would be able to sell depends on the price in the following way: the amount decreases proportionally with the price; if he charged \$20 per kg he would not sell any, and if the cheese was free he would 'sell' the maximum 400 kg that he could produce. What price per kilogram should the farmer set in order to maximise his profit?

Let x (in dollars) be the selling price per kilogram of cheese, and let m be the amount produced (and sold). Then the production cost is $\$(250+9m)$ and the amount of money earned is $\$(mx)$, giving a profit of $P = mx-(250+9m)$ dollars.

The amount m depends on x. We are told that the relationship is 'proportional', i.e. linear; when $x = 20$, $m = 0$ (no one would buy the cheese if it cost \$20/kg), and when $x = 0$, $m = 400$ (the farmer would be able to 'sell' all 400 kg of cheese that he could produce if it were free). Hence m is a linear function of x (a straight line graph) that passes through the points (0, 400) and (20, 0). We can then find that its equation is $m = 400-20x$. So the total profit is

$$\begin{aligned} P &= mx-(250+9m) \\ &= (400-20x)x-\big(250+9(400-20x)\big) \\ &= -20x^2+580x-3850 \end{aligned}$$

This is a quadratic function of x. Since it is a negative quadratic, its vertex is a maximum point. The x-coordinate of the vertex is given by the equation for the line of symmetry, $x=-\frac{b}{2a}$. So the maximum profit is achieved when

$$x=-\frac{580}{2\times(-20)}=14.5$$

Thus, to maximise profit, the farmer should sell the cheese at \$14.50 per kilogram.
We can also graph the function to see how the profit depends on the selling price. Outside the range of x-values shown on the graph, the farmer would make a loss.

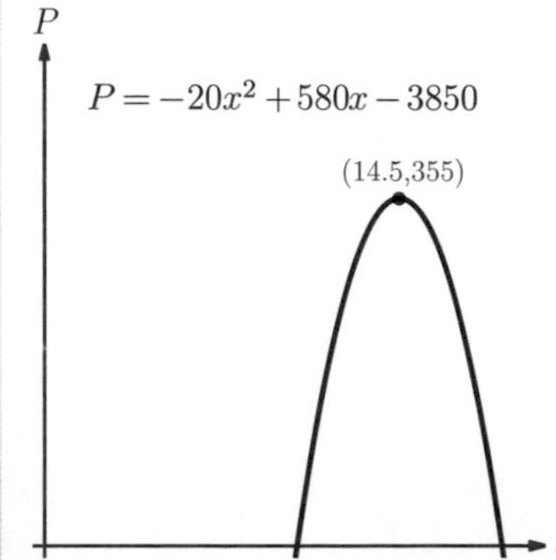

Mixed examination practice 1

Short questions

1. (a) Factorise $x^2+5x-14$.

(b) Solve $x^2+5x-14=0$. *[4 marks]*

2. The quadratic function $y=(x-a)^2+b$ has a turning point at (3, 7).

(a) State whether this turning point is a maximum or a minimum point.

(b) State the values of a and b. *[3 marks]*

3. The quadratic function $y=a(x-b)^2+c$ passes through the points (–2, 0) and (6, 0). Its maximum y-value is 48. Find the values of a, b and c. *[6 marks]*

4. A quadratic function passes through the points $(k,\ 0)$ and $(k+4,\ 0)$. Find in terms of k the x-coordinate of the turning point. *[2 marks]*

5. The diagram represents the graph of the function

$$f: x \mapsto (x-p)(x-q)$$

(a) Write down the values of p and q.

(b) The function has a minimum value at the point C. Find the x-coordinate of C. *[4 marks]*

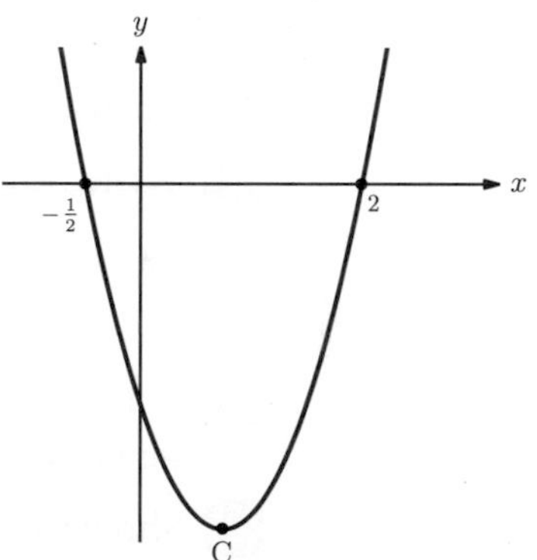

(© *IB Organization 1999*)

6. The diagram shows the graph of the function $y=ax^2+bx+c$.

Complete the table below to show whether each expression is positive, negative or zero.

Expression	Positive	Negative	zero
A			
C			
b^2-4ac			
B			

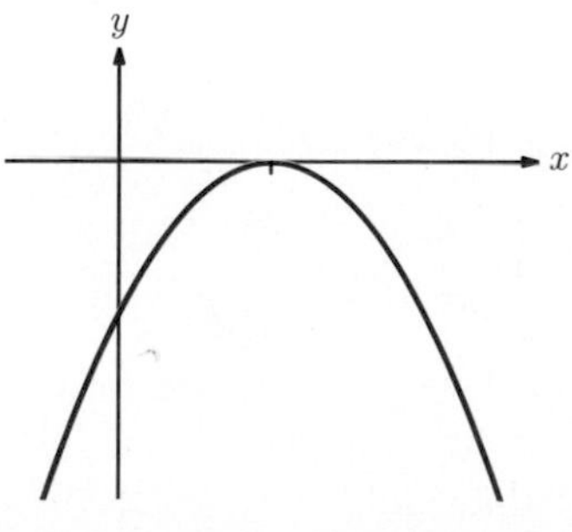

[4 marks]

(© *IB Organization 2000*)

 **7.** (a) Write $x^2 - 10x + 35$ in the form $(x-p)^2 + q$.

(b) Hence, or otherwise, find the maximum value of $\dfrac{1}{(x^2-10x+35)^3}$.

[5 marks]

8. Find the exact values of k for which the equation $2kx + (k+1)x + 1 = 0$ has equal roots. *[6 marks]*

9. Find the range of values of k for which the equation $2x^2 + 6x + k = 0$ has no real roots. *[6 marks]*

 **10.** Find the values of k for which the quadratic function $x^2 - (k+1)x + 3$ has only one zero. *[6 marks]*

11. Let α and β denote the roots of the quadratic equation $x^2 - kx + (k-1) = 0$.

(a) Express α and β in terms of k.

(b) Given that $\alpha^2 + \beta^2 = 17$, find the possible values of k. *[6 marks]*

Long questions

 **1.** The diagram shows a square with side x cm and a circle with radius y cm.

(a) Write down an expression for the perimeter

(i) of the square

(ii) of the circle

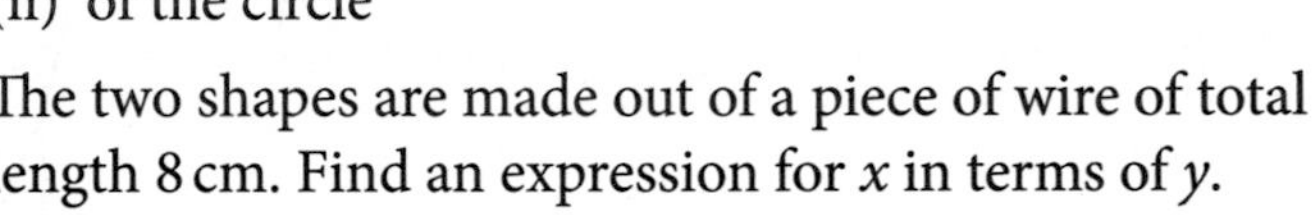

(b) The two shapes are made out of a piece of wire of total length 8 cm. Find an expression for x in terms of y.

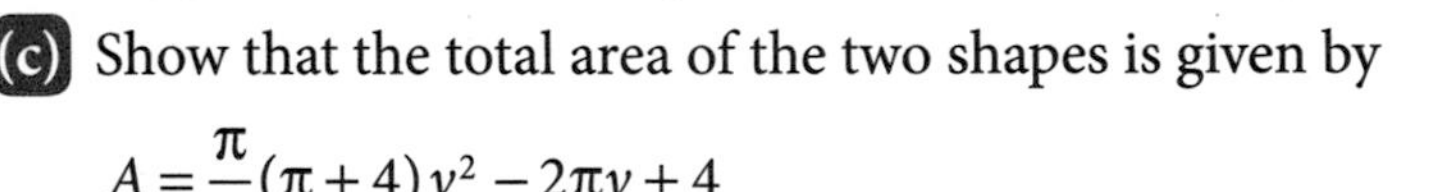

(c) Show that the total area of the two shapes is given by

$$A = \frac{\pi}{4}(\pi + 4)y^2 - 2\pi y + 4$$

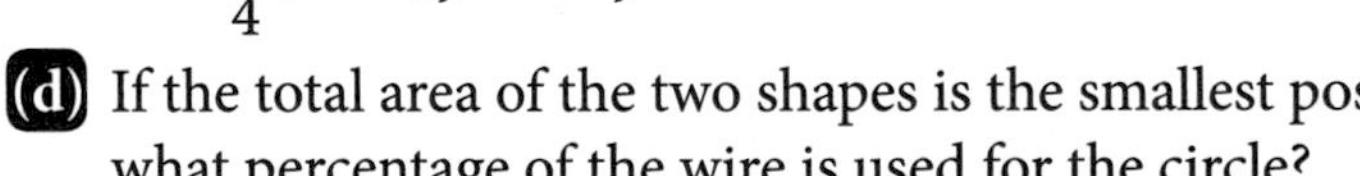

(d) If the total area of the two shapes is the smallest possible, what percentage of the wire is used for the circle?

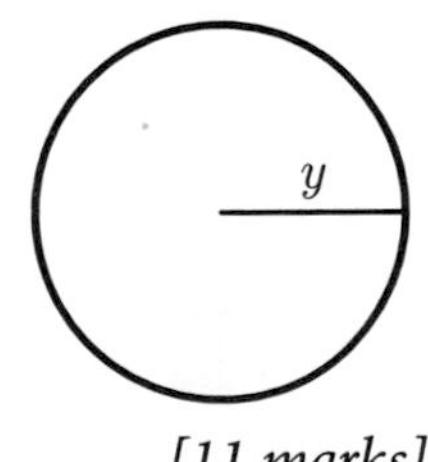

[11 marks]

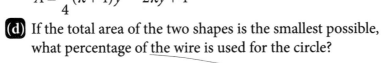

2. Two cars are travelling along two straight roads which are perpendicular to each other and meet at the point O, as shown in the diagram. The first car starts 50 km west of O and travels east at a constant speed of 20 km/h. The second car starts 30 km south of O at the same time and travels north at a constant speed of 15 km/h.

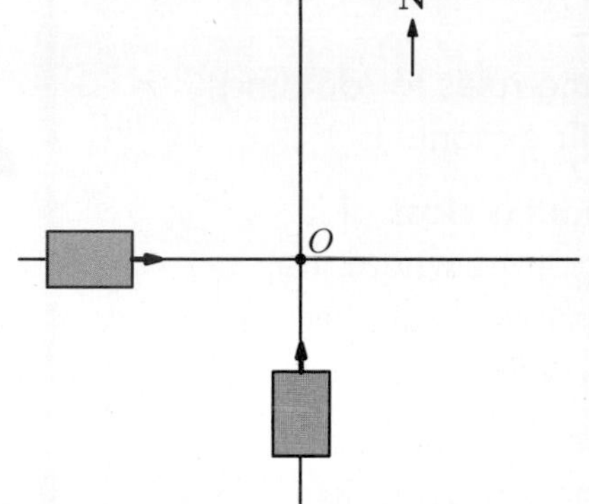

(a) Show that at time t, the distance d between the two cars satisfies $d^2 = 625t^2 - 2900t + 3400$.

(b) Hence find the closest distance between the two cars. *[9 marks]*

3. (a) The graph of $y = x^2 - 6x + k$ has its vertex on the x-axis. Find the value of k.

(b) A second parabola has its vertex at $(-2, 5)$ and passes through the vertex of the first graph. Find the equation of the second graph in the form $y = ax^2 + bx + c$.

(c) Find the coordinates of the other point of intersection between the two graphs. *[12 marks]*

2 Exponents and logarithms

In this chapter you will learn:

- some rules for dealing with exponents
- about a class of functions where the unknown is in the exponent
- about the number e and some of its properties
- about the inverse of an exponential function, called a logarithm
- the rules of logarithms
- about graphs of logarithms
- how to use logarithms to find solutions to simple exponential equations.

Introductory problem

A radioactive substance has a half-life of 72 years (this is the time it takes for half of the mass, and hence radioactivity, to decay). A 1 kg block of the substance is found to have a radioactivity of 25 million becquerels (Bq). How long, to the nearest 10 years, would it take for the radioactivity to fall to 10 000 Bq?

Many mathematical models (of biological, physical and financial phenomena, for instance) involve the concept of continuous growth or decay, where the rate of growth or decay of the population of interest depends on the size of that population. You may have encountered similar situations already – for example, for a bank account earning compound interest, the increase in the amount of money each year is given by the interest rate multiplied by the starting balance. Such situations are governed by exponential functions, which you will learn about in this chapter.

2A Laws of exponents

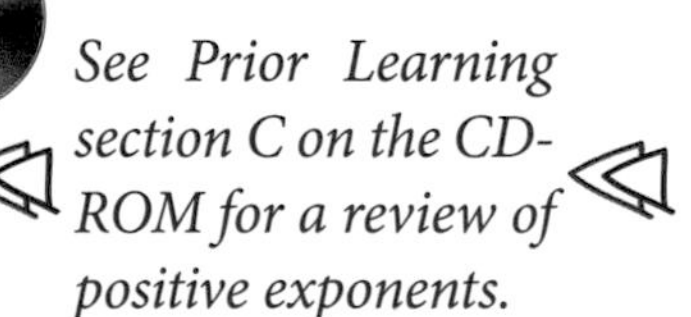

See Prior Learning section C on the CD-ROM for a review of positive exponents.

The exponent of a number tells you how many times the number is to be multiplied by itself. You will have met some of the rules for dealing with exponents before, and in this section we shall revisit and extend these rules.

An exponent is also called a 'power' or an 'index' (plural: indices). The operation of raising to a power is sometimes referred to as 'exponentiating'.

A number written in **exponent form** is one which explicitly looks like:

$$a^n \quad \text{where } n \text{ is referred to as the \textbf{exponent}; } a \text{ is referred to as the \textbf{base}}$$

The expression a^n is read as 'a to the exponent n' or, more simply, 'a to the n'.

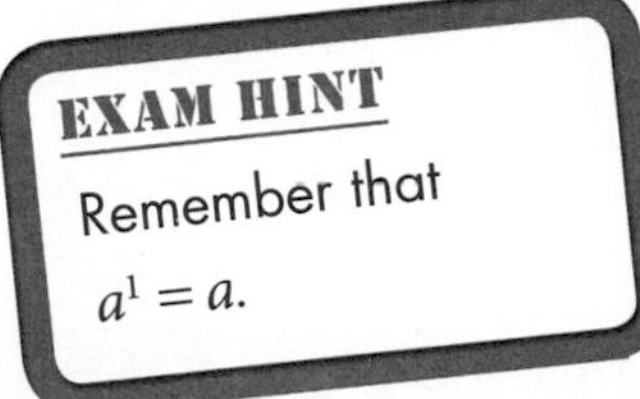
EXAM HINT
Remember that
$a^1 = a$.

Although we said earlier that an exponent shows how many times a number is multiplied by itself, if the exponent is a negative integer this interpretation would not apply. Nevertheless, we would like to give a meaning to negative integer exponents; to do this, we first need to look at the rules of exponents in more detail.

If the exponent is increased by one, the value of the expression is multiplied by the base. If the exponent is decreased by one, the value of the expression is divided by the base. It follows that the value of a^0 must be consistent with the value of a^1 divided by a, that is, $a^0 = a^{1-1} = a^1 \div a = 1$.

Mathematics is often considered a subject without ambiguity. However, if you ask what the value of 0^0 is, the answer is undetermined – it depends upon how you get there!

KEY POINT 2.1

$$a^0 = 1$$

If we continue dividing by the value of the base, we move into negative exponents:

$$a^{-1} = a^0 \div a = \frac{1}{a} \qquad \text{For example, } 3^{-1} = \frac{1}{3}$$

$$a^{-2} = a^{-1} \div a = \frac{1}{a^2} \qquad \text{For example, } 3^{-2} = \frac{1}{9}$$

Generalising this gives the following formula:

KEY POINT 2.2

$$a^{-n} = \frac{1}{a^n}$$

*$\frac{1}{x}$ is called the **reciprocal** of x. We will study this in more detail in section 4E.*

We now look at an example of what can happen when we apply operations to exponents.

Worked example 2.1

Simplify:

(a) $a^3 \times a^4$ (b) $a^3 \div a^4$ (c) $(a^4)^3$ (d) $a^4 + a^3$

The exponent counts the number of times you multiply the base to itself.

(a) $a^3 \times a^4 = (a \times a \times a \times a) \times (a \times a \times a) = a^7$

Divide top and bottom of the fraction by a three times.

(b) $a^3 \div a^4 = \dfrac{\not{a} \times \not{a} \times \not{a}}{\not{a} \times \not{a} \times \not{a} \times a} = \dfrac{1}{a} = a^{-1}$

Use the same idea as in part (a).

(c) $(a^4)^3 = a^4 \times a^4 \times a^4 = a^{12}$

All we can do here is factorise.

(d) $a^4 + a^3 = a^3(a+1)$

It is questionable whether in part (d) of the example we have actually simplified the expression. Sometimes the way mathematicians choose to 'simplify' expressions is governed by aesthetics, i.e. how the result looks, as well as how useful it might be.

Worked example 2.1 suggests some rules of exponents.

KEY POINT 2.3

$$a^m \times a^n = a^{m+n}$$

KEY POINT 2.4

$$a^m \div a^n = a^{m-n}$$

KEY POINT 2.5

$$(a^m)^n = a^{m \times n}$$

With these rules, we can interpret exponents that are fractions (rational numbers) as well.

Consider $a^{\frac{1}{2}}$. If the laws of exponents hold true for fractional exponents, then we must have

$$a^{\frac{1}{2}} \times a^{\frac{1}{2}} = a^{\frac{1}{2}+\frac{1}{2}} = a^1 = a$$

In other words, $\left(a^{\frac{1}{2}}\right)^2 = a$; so $a^{\frac{1}{2}}$ is a value which, when squared, gives a. This is, by definition, the square root of a.

By a similar argument, $a^{\frac{1}{3}}$ is a value such that $\left(a^{\frac{1}{3}}\right)^3 = a$, and so $a^{\frac{1}{3}}$ is the same as the cube root of a. We can continue on to larger powers and roots; for example, $32^{\frac{1}{5}} = \sqrt[5]{32} = 2$ since $2^5 = 32$.

EXAM HINT

These rules are *not* given in the Formula booklet, so make sure that you learn them and can use them in both directions. For example, if you see 2^6, know that you can rewrite it as either $(2^3)^2$ or $(2^2)^3$; and if you see $(2^3)^2$, recognise it as 2^6. Both ways will be important!

KEY POINT 2.6

$a^{\frac{1}{n}}$ means the nth root of a, that is, $\sqrt[n]{a}$.

We can combine Key points 2.5 and 2.6 to interpret $a^{\frac{m}{n}}$. We can express $a^{\frac{m}{n}}$ in two different ways, $a^{m \times \frac{1}{n}}$ or $a^{\frac{1}{n} \times m}$, and thus obtain the following rule.

KEY POINT 2.7

$$a^{\frac{m}{n}} = \sqrt[n]{a^m} = \left(\sqrt[n]{a}\right)^m$$

Worked example 2.2

Evaluate $64^{\frac{2}{3}}$.

Use $a^{\frac{m}{n}} = \left(\sqrt[n]{a}\right)^m$

$$64^{\frac{2}{3}} = \left(\sqrt[3]{64}\right)^2$$
$$= 4^2$$
$$= 16$$

You must take care when expressions with *different* bases are to be combined by multiplication or division, for example $2^3 \times 6^2$. The rule 'multiplication means add the exponents together' (Key point 2.3) is true only when *the bases are the same*. You cannot use the rule to simplify $2^3 \times 6^2$.

There is however, another rule that works when the bases are different but *the exponents are the same*. Consider the following example:

$$\begin{aligned} 3^2 \times 5^2 &= 3 \times 3 \times 5 \times 5 \\ &= 3 \times 5 \times 3 \times 5 \\ &= 15 \times 15 \\ &= 15^2 \end{aligned}$$

This suggests the following rule.

KEY POINT 2.8

$$a^n \times b^n = (ab)^n$$

Similarly, we can divide two expressions with the same exponent:

$$\frac{3^2}{5^2} = \frac{3 \times 3}{5 \times 5} = \frac{3}{5} \times \frac{3}{5} = \left(\frac{3}{5}\right)^2$$

KEY POINT 2.9

$$a^n \div b^n = \left(\frac{a}{b}\right)^n$$

Below is a summary of the rules of exponents covered so far.

If the base is the same and the exponents are different:	
Multiplication: keep the base the same, add the exponents	$a^m \times a^n = a^{m+n}$
Division: keep the base the same, subtract the exponents	$a^m \div a^n = a^{m-n}$
If the exponent is the same and the bases are different:	
Multiplication: keep the exponent the same, multiply the bases	$a^n \times b^n = (ab)^n$
Division: keep the exponent the same, divide the bases	$a^n \div b^n = \left(\frac{a}{b}\right)^n$
Any base to the exponent zero equals one	$a^0 = 1$
Any base to the exponent one is equal to the base itself	$a^1 = a$
Any base to a negative exponent is the same as the reciprocal of the same base to the equivalent positive exponent	$a^{-n} = \frac{1}{a^n}$
Any base to an exponent, all raised to another exponent, is the same as that base to the product of the exponents	$(a^m)^n = a^{m \times n}$
A base to a fractional exponent is a combination of an *n*th root and a power	$a^{\frac{m}{n}} = \left(\sqrt[n]{a}\right)^m = \sqrt[n]{a^m}$

You can use these rules to solve equations where the unknown is in the exponent.

Worked example 2.3

Solve the equation $4^{2x+1} = 8^{7-x}$.

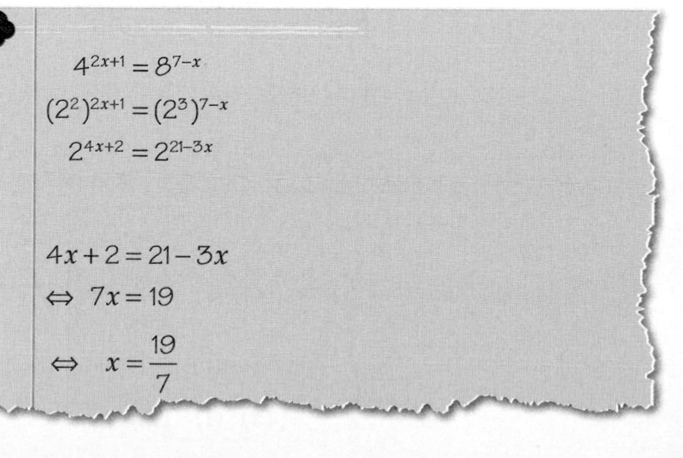

If both sides had the same base, we could compare the exponents. Notice that 4 and 8 are both powers of 2.

$$4^{2x+1} = 8^{7-x}$$
$$(2^2)^{2x+1} = (2^3)^{7-x}$$
$$2^{4x+2} = 2^{21-3x}$$

Now we can equate the exponents.

$$4x + 2 = 21 - 3x$$
$$\Leftrightarrow 7x = 19$$
$$\Leftrightarrow x = \frac{19}{7}$$

Exercise 2A

 **1.** Simplify the following, leaving your answer in exponent form.

(a) (i) $6^4 \times 6^3$ (ii) $5^3 \times 5^5$

(b) (i) $a^3 \times a^5$ (ii) $x^6 \times x^3$

(c) (i) $7^{11} \times 7^{-14}$ (ii) $5^7 \times 5^{-2}$

(d) (i) $x^4 \times x^{-2}$ (ii) $x^8 \times x^{-3}$

(e) (i) $g^{-3} \times g^{-9}$ (ii) $k^{-2} \times k^{-6}$

 **2.** Simplify the following, leaving your answer in exponent form.

(a) (i) $6^4 \div 6^3$ (ii) $5^3 \div 5^5$

(b) (i) $a^3 \div a^5$ (ii) $x^6 \div x^3$

(c) (i) $5^7 \div 5^{-2}$ (ii) $7^{11} \div 7^{-4}$

(d) (i) $x^4 \div x^{-2}$ (ii) $x^8 \div x^{-3}$

(e) (i) $2^{-5} \div 2^{-7}$ (ii) $3^{-6} \div 3^8$

(f) (i) $g^{-3} \div g^{-9}$ (ii) $k^{-2} \div k^6$

 **3.** Express the following in the specified form.

(a) (i) $(2^3)^4$ as 2^n (ii) $(3^2)^7$ as 3^n

(b) (i) $(5^{-1})^4$ as 5^n (ii) $(7^{-3})^2$ as 7^n

(c) (i) $(11^{-2})^{-1}$ as 11^n (ii) $(13^{-3})^{-5}$ as 13^n

(d) (i) $4 \times (2^5)^3$ as 2^n (ii) $3^{-5} \times (9^{-1})^{-4}$ as 3^n

(e) (i) $(4^2)^3 \times 3^{12}$ as 6^n (ii) $(6^3)^2 \div (2^2)^3$ as 3^n

4. Simplify each of the following, leaving your answer in exponent form with a prime number as the base.

(a) (i) 4^5 (ii) 9^7

(b) (i) 8^3 (ii) 16^5

(c) (i) $4^2 \times 8^3$ (ii) $9^5 \div 27^2$

(d) (i) $4^{-3} \times 8^5$ (ii) $3^7 \div 9^{-2}$

(e) (i) $\left(\frac{1}{4}\right)^3$ (ii) $\left(\frac{1}{9}\right)^3$

(f) (i) $\left(\frac{1}{8}\right)^2 \div \left(\frac{1}{4}\right)^4$ (ii) $9^7 \times \left(\frac{1}{3}\right)^4$

5. Write the following without brackets or negative exponents.

(a) (i) $(2x^2)^3$ (ii) $(3x^4)^2$

(b) (i) $2(x^2)^3$ (ii) $3(x^4)^2$

(c) (i) $\dfrac{(3a^3)^4}{9a^2}$ (ii) $\dfrac{(4x)^4}{8(2x)^4}$

(d) (i) $(2x)^{-1}$ (ii) $\left(\dfrac{3}{y}\right)^{-2}$

(e) (i) $2x^{-1}$ (ii) $\dfrac{3}{y^{-2}}$

(f) (i) $5 \div \left(\dfrac{3}{xy^2}\right)^2$ (ii) $\left(\dfrac{ab}{2}\right)^3 \div \left(\dfrac{a}{b}\right)^2$

(g) (i) $\left(\dfrac{2}{q}\right)^2 \div \left(\dfrac{p}{2}\right)^{-3}$ (ii) $\left(\dfrac{6}{x}\right)^4 \div \left(2\times\dfrac{3^2}{x}\right)^{-3}$

 **6.** Evaluate the following, leaving your answer in simplified rational form where appropriate.

(a) (i) 3×2^{-2} (ii) 7×3^{-4}

(b) (i) $(3\times2)^{-2}$ (ii) $(5\times2)^{-3}$

(c) (i) $10^3\times5^{-2}$ (ii) $12^2\times4^{-5}$

(d) (i) $6\div2^3$ (ii) $6^{-3}\div2^{-5}$

 **7.** Evaluate the following, leaving your answers as a fraction where appropriate.

(a) (i) $4^{\frac{1}{2}}$ (ii) $8^{\frac{1}{3}}$

(b) (i) $10000^{0.5}$ (ii) $81^{0.25}$

(c) (i) $\left(\dfrac{1}{25}\right)^{\frac{1}{2}}$ (ii) $\left(\dfrac{9}{16}\right)^{\frac{1}{2}}$

(d) (i) $8^{\frac{2}{3}}$ (ii) $25^{\frac{3}{2}}$

(e) (i) $100^{2.5}$ (ii) $81^{0.75}$

(f) (i) $\left(\dfrac{1}{16}\right)^{\frac{5}{4}}$ (ii) $\left(\dfrac{8}{27}\right)^{\frac{5}{3}}$

(g) (i) $8^{-\frac{1}{3}}$ (ii) $49^{-\frac{1}{2}}$

(h) (i) $\left(\dfrac{16}{9}\right)^{-\frac{1}{2}}$ (ii) $\left(\dfrac{9}{16}\right)^{-\frac{3}{2}}$

8. Simplify the following.

(a) (i) $(x^6)^{\frac{1}{2}}$ (ii) $(x^9)^{\frac{4}{3}}$

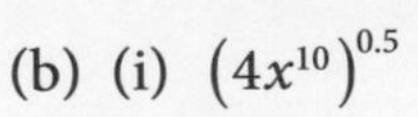

(b) (i) $(4x^{10})^{0.5}$ (ii) $(8x^{12})^{-\frac{1}{3}}$

(c) (i) $\left(\frac{27x^9}{64}\right)^{-\frac{1}{3}}$ (ii) $\left(\frac{x^4}{y^8}\right)^{-1.5}$

In section 2G you will see that there is another (often easier) way to solve equations like these, by using logarithms on a calculator.

9. Solve for x, giving your answer as a rational value.

(a) (i) $8^x = 32$ (ii) $25^x = \frac{1}{125}$

(b) (i) $\frac{1}{49^x} = 7$ (ii) $\frac{1}{16^x} = 8$

(c) (i) $2\times3^x = 162$ (ii) $3\div5^x = 0.12$

10. Suppose that a computer program is able to sort n input values in $k\times n^{1.5}$ microseconds. Observations show that it sorts a million values in half a second. Find the value of k. *[3 marks]*

11. A square-ended cuboid has volume xy^2, where x and y are its lengths. Such a cuboid for which $x = 2y$ has volume $128\,\text{cm}^3$. Find x. *[3 marks]*

12. The volume and surface area of a family of regular solid shapes are related by the formula $V = kA^{1.5}$, where V is given in cubic units and A in square units.

(a) For one such shape, $A = 81$ and $V = 243$. Find k.

(b) Hence determine the surface area of a shape with volume $\frac{64}{3}$ cm³. *[4 marks]*

13. Solve $2\times5^{x-1} = 250$ for x. *[5 marks]*

14. Solve $5+3^{x+2} = 14$ for x. *[5 marks]*

15. Solve $100^{x+5} = 10^{3x-1}$ for x. *[6 marks]*

16. Solve $16+2^x = 2^{x+1}$ for x. *[6 marks]*

17. Solve $6^{x+1} = 162\times2^x$ for x. *[6 marks]*

18. Solve $4^{1.5x} = 2\times16^{x-1}$ for x. *[6 marks]*

2B Exponential functions

In an exponential function, the unknown appears in the exponent. The general form of a simple exponential function is $f(x) = a^x$.

We will only consider situations where the base a is positive, because otherwise some exponents cannot easily be defined (for example, we cannot square root a negative number).

What is the meaning of $(-1)^{\frac{1}{2}}$? What about $\left((-1)^2\right)^{\frac{1}{4}}$? And $(-1)^{\frac{2}{4}}$? Not all mathematics is unambiguous!

Here is the graph of $y = 2^x$.

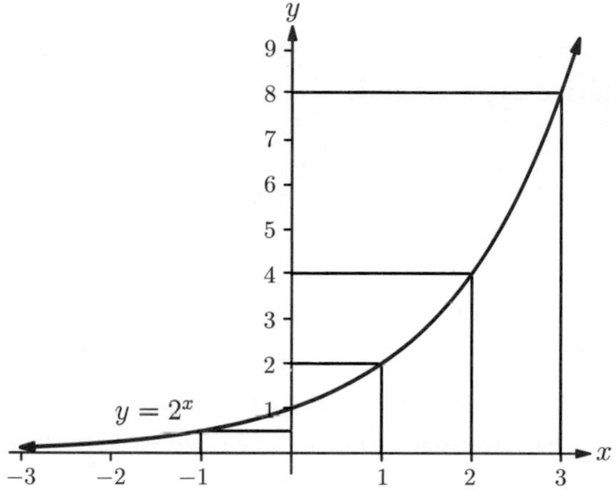

EXAM HINT
See Calculator Skills sheet 2 on the CD-ROM for how to plot graphs on your calculator.

For large positive values of x, the y-value gets very large ('approaches infinity'). For large negative values of x, the y-value approaches (but never reaches) zero. A line that a graph gets increasingly close to (but never touches) is called an **asymptote**. In this case we would say that the x-axis is an asymptote to the graph.

By looking at the graphs of exponential functions with different bases, we can begin to make some generalisations. Try plotting some exponential functions on your calculator; a few examples are shown below.

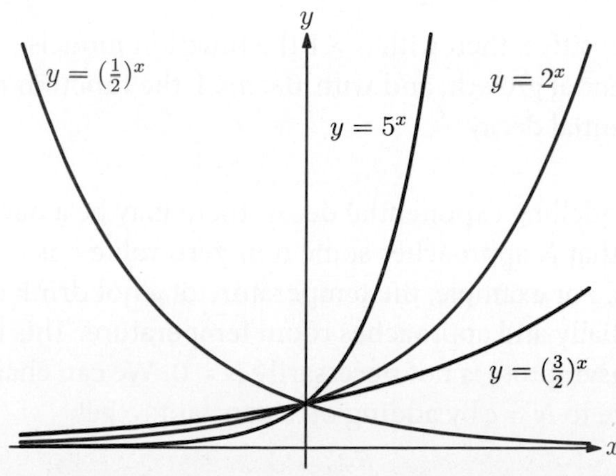

You may notice that the blue curve is a reflection of the black curve in the y-axis. You will see why this is the case in chapter 5.

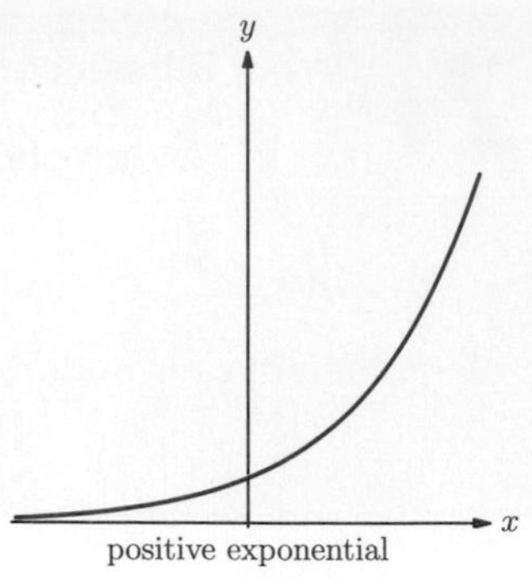

positive exponential

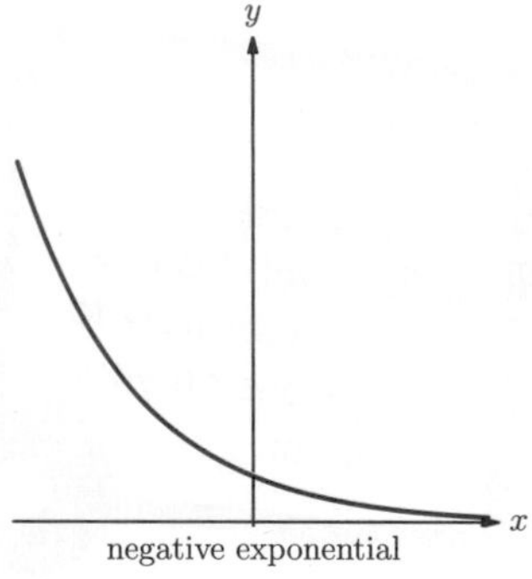

negative exponential

KEY POINT 2.10

For the graphs of $y = a^x$, where $a > 0$:

- The y-intercept is always (0, 1), because $a^0 = 1$.
- The graph of the function lies entirely above the x-axis, since $a^x > 0$ for all values of x.
- The x-axis is an asymptote.
- If $a > 1$, then as x increases, so does y. This is called a **positive exponential**.
- If $0 < a < 1$, then as x increases, y decreases. This is called a **negative exponential**.

EXAM HINT

Note that exponential decay can be written either as $y = a^x$ with $0 < a < 1$ or as $y = a^{-x}$ with $a > 1$. This is because, for example,

$$3^{-x} = (3^{-1})^x = \left(\frac{1}{3}\right)^x.$$

Many mathematical models are based on the following property of the exponential function $N = a^t$: as time (t) increases by a *fixed amount*, the quantity we are interested in (N) will rise by a *fixed factor*, called the **growth factor**. Exponential functions can therefore be used to represent many physical, financial and biological forms of **exponential growth** (positive exponential models) and **exponential decay** (negative exponential models).

To model more complex situations we may need to include more constants in our exponential function. A form that is commonly used is

$$N = Ba^{\left(\frac{t}{k}\right)}$$

We can interpret the constants in the following way:

- When $t = 0$ we have $N = B$, so B is the **initial value** of N.
- When $t = k$ we have $N = Ba$, so k is the time taken for N to increase by a factor of a.
- If $k = 1$, then a is the growth factor.
- If k is positive, then with $a > 1$ the function models exponential growth, and with $0 < a < 1$ the function models exponential decay.

In chapter 5 we will investigate how changing the constants in a function affects the shape and position of the graph.

When modelling exponential decay, there may be a **background level**, so that N approaches some non-zero value c as t increases. For example, the temperature of a hot drink decays exponentially and approaches room temperature. This means that the asymptote is not necessarily $N = 0$. We can change the asymptote to $N = c$ by adding on a constant to get

$$N = Ba^{\left(\frac{t}{k}\right)} + c$$

In this case, B represents how much N starts above the background level, so the initial value is $B+c$.

KEY POINT 2.11

For $N = Ba^{\left(\frac{t}{k}\right)} + c$:

- the background level is c (i.e. the asymptote is $N=c$)
- the initial value is $B+c$
- k is the time taken for the difference between N and the background level to increase by a factor of a
- if $a>1$ the function models exponential growth
- if $0<a<1$ the function models exponential decay.

EXAM HINT

Your calculator may not display asymptotes, as they are not really part of the graph; you can only guess approximately where they are by looking at large values of x. This is important to know how to find asymptotes directly from the equation.

EXAM HINT

Once you have plotted a graph on your calculator, you can use it to find x and y values, as well as check the value of the asymptote.

See Calculator Skills sheet 4 on the CD-ROM for how to analyse graphs.

Remember to round calculator answers to 3 significant figures, unless asked to do otherwise.

Worked example 2.4

The temperature T, in degrees Celsius, of a cooling liquid is modelled by the equation $T = 24 + 72 \times 0.6^{3t}$, where t is the time in minutes after the cooling begins.

(a) What was the initial temperature of the liquid?

(b) Find the temperature of the liquid after 2 minutes.

(c) How long does it take for the liquid to cool to 26°C?

(d) What temperature does the model predict the liquid will eventually reach?

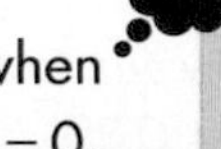

The word 'initial' means when $t=0$.

(a) When $t=0$,
$T = 24 + 72 = 96$°C

continued ...

When the answer is not exact, we should round it to 3 significant figures.

(b) When $t = 2$,

$T = 24 + 72 \times 0.6^6$

$= 27.4°C$ (3 SF)

We can answer this by looking at the graph on a calculator.

(c)

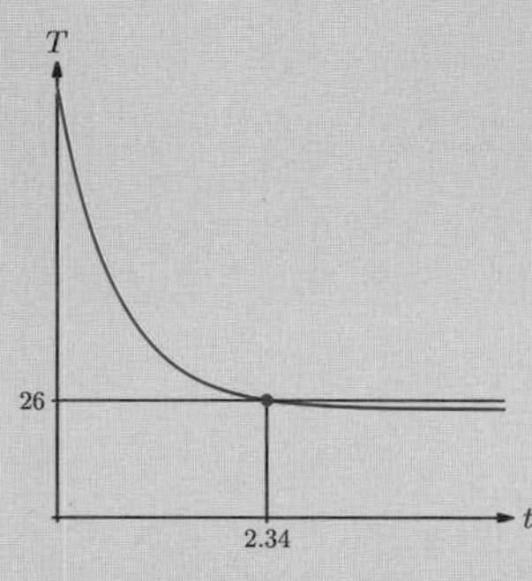

From GDC: $t = 2.34$ (3 SF)

It will take 2.34 minutes.

In the long term, the temperature approaches the asymptote.

(d) 24°C

In many applications, we first need to find the constants in the model using the information given.

Worked example 2.5

A population of bacteria in a culture medium doubles in size every 15 minutes. At 08:00 there are 1000 bacterial cells. Let N be the number of bacterial cells t hours after 08:00.

(a) Write down a model for N in terms of t.

(b) How many cells are there at

(i) 08:15?

(ii) 09:24?

There is a constant factor of increase, so we use an exponential growth model.

(a) $N = Ba^{\left(\frac{t}{k}\right)}$

Let N be the number of cells at time t hours after 08:00.

Every time t increases by 0.25 hours, N doubles.

Doubles every quarter hour $\Rightarrow$

$a = 2, k = 0.25$

$\therefore N = B \times 2^{4t}$

→

continued . . .

Initial value gives B.

(b) When $t = 0$, $N = 1000 = B$, so
$N = 1000 \times 2^{4t}$

Remember to convert minutes to hours.

(i) When $t = 0.25$, $N = 1000 \times 2 = 2000$ cells.
(ii) When $t = 1.4$, $N = 1000 \times 2^{5.6} = 48503$ cells.

When modelling exponential growth or decay, you may be given a percentage increase or decrease. This needs to be converted into a growth factor to be used in the exponential model.

We will meet similar questions again when we study geometric series in chapter 6.

Worked example 2.6

A car that cost $17 500 initially loses value at a rate of 18% each year.

(a) Write a model for the value (V) of the car after n years in the form $V = ka^n$.

(b) Hence or otherwise find the value of the car after 20 years.

Find the growth factor.

(a) The growth factor is $1 - \frac{18}{100} = 0.82$

Use initial value information.

When $n = 0$, $V = k = 17500$, hence
$V = 17500 \times 0.82^n$

Substitute for n.

(b) After 20 years, $V = 17500 \times 0.82^{20} = \$330.61$

EXAM HINT

'Hence or otherwise' means that you can use any method you like, but the word 'hence' suggests that the answers from previous parts of the question might be helpful.

Exercise 2B

1. Using your calculator, sketch the following functions on the same set of axes, for $-5 \le x \le 5$ and $0 \le y \le 10$. Show all the axis intercepts and state the equation of the horizontal asymptote.

   (a) (i) $y = 1.5^x$ (ii) $y = 3^x$

   (b) (i) $y = 2 \times 3^x$ (ii) $y = 6 \times 1.4^x$

   (c) (i) $y = \left(\frac{1}{2}\right)^x$ (ii) $y = \left(\frac{2}{3}\right)^x$

   (d) (i) $y = 5 + 2^x$ (ii) $y = 8 + 3^x$

   (e) (i) $y = 6 - 2^x$ (ii) $y = 1 - 5^x$

2. An algal population on the surface of a pond grows by 10% every day. The area it covers can be modelled by the equation $y = k \times 1.1^t$, where t is measured in days, starting from 09:00 on Tuesday, when the algae covered $10\,\text{m}^2$. What area will it cover by 09:00 on Friday? *[4 marks]*

3. A tree branch is observed to bend as the fruit growing on it increase in size. By estimating the mass of the developing fruit and plotting the data over time, a student finds that the height h in metres of the branch end above the ground is closely approximated by the function

$$h = 2 - 0.2 \times 1.6^{0.2m}$$

   where m is the estimated mass, in kilograms, of fruit on the branch.

   (a) Sketch the graph of h against m.

   (b) What height above ground is the branch without fruit?

   (c) The total mass of fruit on the branch at harvest was 7.5 kg. Find the height of the branch immediately prior to harvest.

   (d) The student wishes to estimate what mass of fruit would cause the branch end to touch the ground. Why might his model not be suitable to assess this? *[10 marks]*

4. (a) Sketch the graph of $y = 1 + 16^{1-x^2}$. Label clearly the horizontal asymptote and the maximum value.

   (b) Find all values of x for which $y = 3$. *[6 marks]*

5. A bowl of soup is served at a temperature of 55°C, in a room with air temperature 20°C. Every 5 minutes, the

temperature difference between the soup and the room air decreases by 30%. Assuming that the room air temperature remains constant, at what temperature will the soup be 7 minutes after serving? *[7 marks]*

6. The speed V (in metres per second) of a parachutist t seconds after jumping from an aeroplane is modelled by the equation

$$V = 40(1 - 3^{-0.1t})$$

(a) Find the parachutist's initial speed.

(b) What speed does the model predict that the parachutist will approach eventually? *[6 marks]*

7. The air temperature T (in degrees Celsius) around a light bulb is given by the equation

$$T = A + B \times 2^{-\frac{x}{k}}$$

where x is the distance in millimetres from the surface of the light bulb. The background temperature in the room is a constant 25°C, and the temperature on the surface of the light bulb is 125°C.

(a) Suppose that the air temperature 3 mm from the surface of the bulb is 75°C. Find the values of A, B and k.

(b) Determine the air temperature 2 cm from the surface of the bulb.

(c) Sketch a graph of air temperature against distance from the surface of the bulb. *[10 marks]*

2C The number e

In this section we introduce a special mathematical constant, e, which will be used extensively in the rest of this chapter and throughout the course.

Consider the following three situations, which might describe early population growth of a cell culture, for example.

There is a 100% increase every 100 seconds.

There is a 50% increase every 50 seconds.

There is a 25% increase every 25 seconds.

At first glance these may appear to be equivalent statements, but they are subtly different because of the compounding nature of percentage increases. If we begin with a population of size P, then after 100 seconds the population becomes, in the three cases,

$$P\times(1+1)=2P$$

$$P\times\left(1+\frac{1}{2}\right)^2=2.25P$$

$$P\times\left(1+\frac{1}{4}\right)^4=2.44P$$

Generalising, if we consider an increase of $\frac{100}{n}$ % which occurs n times in the course of 100 seconds, the population after 100 seconds would be given by $P\times\left(1+\frac{1}{n}\right)^n$.

From the above it may seem that as n increases, the overall increase in population over 100 seconds will keep getting larger. This is indeed the case, but not without limit. By taking larger and larger values of n, it can be seen that the population increase factor $\left(1+\frac{1}{n}\right)^n$ tends towards a value of approximately 2.71828182849. This number, much like π, arises so often in mathematics and is so useful in applications that it has been given its own letter, e.

KEY POINT 2.12

$$e=2.71828182849\ldots$$

The numbers π and e have many similar properties. Both are irrational, meaning that they cannot be written as a fraction of two whole numbers. They are also both transcendental, which means that they cannot be the solution to any polynomial equation (an equation involving only powers of x). The proofs of these facts are intricate but beautiful.

In chapter 12 you will see that e plays a major role in studying rates of change.

EXAM HINT

In questions involving the number e, you may be asked either to give an exact answer (for example, in the form of e^2) or to use your calculator, in which case you should round the answer to 3 significant figures unless told otherwise.

Although e has many important properties, it is after all just a number. Therefore, the standard rules of arithmetic and exponents still apply.

Exercise 2C

1. Find the values of the following to 3 significant figures.

(a) (i) $e+1$ (ii) $e-4$

(b) (i) $3e$ (ii) $\frac{e}{2}$

(c) (i) e^2 (ii) e^{-3}

(d) (i) $5e^{0.5}$ (ii) $\frac{3}{e^7}$

2. Evaluate $\sqrt[6]{(\pi^4+\pi^5)}$. What do you notice about the result?

3. Expand $\left(e^2+\frac{2}{e^2}\right)^2$. *[4 marks]*

2D Introduction to logarithms

See the Supplementary sheet 2 'Logarithmic scales and log-log graphs' on the CD-ROM if you are interested in discovering logarithms for yourself.

In this section we shall look at an operation which reverses the effect of exponentiating (raising to a power) and allows us to find an unknown power. If you are asked to solve

$$x^2 = 3 \text{ for } x \geq 0$$

then you can can either find a decimal approximation (for example by using a calculator or trial and improvement) or use the square root symbol to write

$$x = \sqrt{3}$$

This statement just says that 'x is the positive value which when squared gives 3'.

Similarly, to solve

$$10^x = 50$$

we could use trial and improvement to seek a decimal value:

$$10^1 = 10$$

$$10^2 = 100$$

So x must be between 1 and 2:

$$10^{1.5} = 31.6$$

$$10^{1.6} = 39.8$$

$$10^{1.7} = 50.1$$

So the answer is around 1.7.

Just as we can use the square root to answer the question 'what is the number which when squared gives this value?', there is also a function that can be used to answer the question 'what is the number which when put as the exponent of 10 gives this value?' This function is called a base-10 **logarithm**, written $\log_{10}$.

In the above example, we can write the solution as $x = \log_{10} 50$. More generally, the equation $y = 10^x$ can be re-expressed as $x = \log_{10} y$. In fact, the base need not be 10, but could be any positive value other than 1.

The symbol $\Leftrightarrow$ means that if the left-hand side is true then so is the right-hand side, and if the right-hand side is true then so is the left-hand side. When it appears between two statements, it means that the statements are equivalent and you can switch between them.

KEY POINT 2.13

$$b = a^x \Leftrightarrow x = \log_a b$$

It is worth noting that the two most common bases have abbreviations for their logarithms. Since we use a decimal system of counting, 10 is the default base for a logarithm, so $\log_{10} x$ is usually written simply as $\log x$ and is called the 'common logarithm'. Also, the number e that we met in section 2C is considered the 'natural' base, so the base-e logarithm is called the 'natural logarithm' and is denoted by $\ln x$.

EXAM HINT

Log x and ln x have a button on graphical calculators ('log' and 'ln') that you can use to evaluate. If the base is not 10 or e however, you will have to use the principles of Key point 2.15. Or, use the change-of-base rule in Key point 2.22.

KEY POINT 2.14

$\log_{10} x$ is often written as $\log x$

$\log_e x$ is often written as $\ln x$

Since taking a logarithm reverses the process of exponentiating, we have the following facts:

KEY POINT 2.15

$\log_a(a^x) = x$

$a^{\log_a x} = x$

These are referred to as the cancellation principles. This sort of 'cancellation', similar to stating that (for positive x) $\sqrt[n]{x^n} = x = \left(\sqrt[n]{x}\right)^n$, is often useful when simplifying logarithm expressions; but remember that you can only do such cancellations when the base of the logarithm and the base of the exponential match and are immediately adjacent in the expression.

The cancellation principles can be combined with the rules of exponents to derive an interesting relationship between the base-e exponential function and any other exponential function. From the second cancellation principle it follows that $e^{\ln a} = a$. By raising both sides to the power x and using the rule of exponents $(b^y)^x = b^{yx}$ (Key point 2.5), we obtain the following useful formula.

A related change-of-base rule for logarithms is given in Key point 2.22.

When we study rates of change in chapter 12, we will need to use base e for exponential functions.

KEY POINT 2.16

$$e^{x\ln a} = a^x$$

This says that we can always change the base of an exponential function to e.

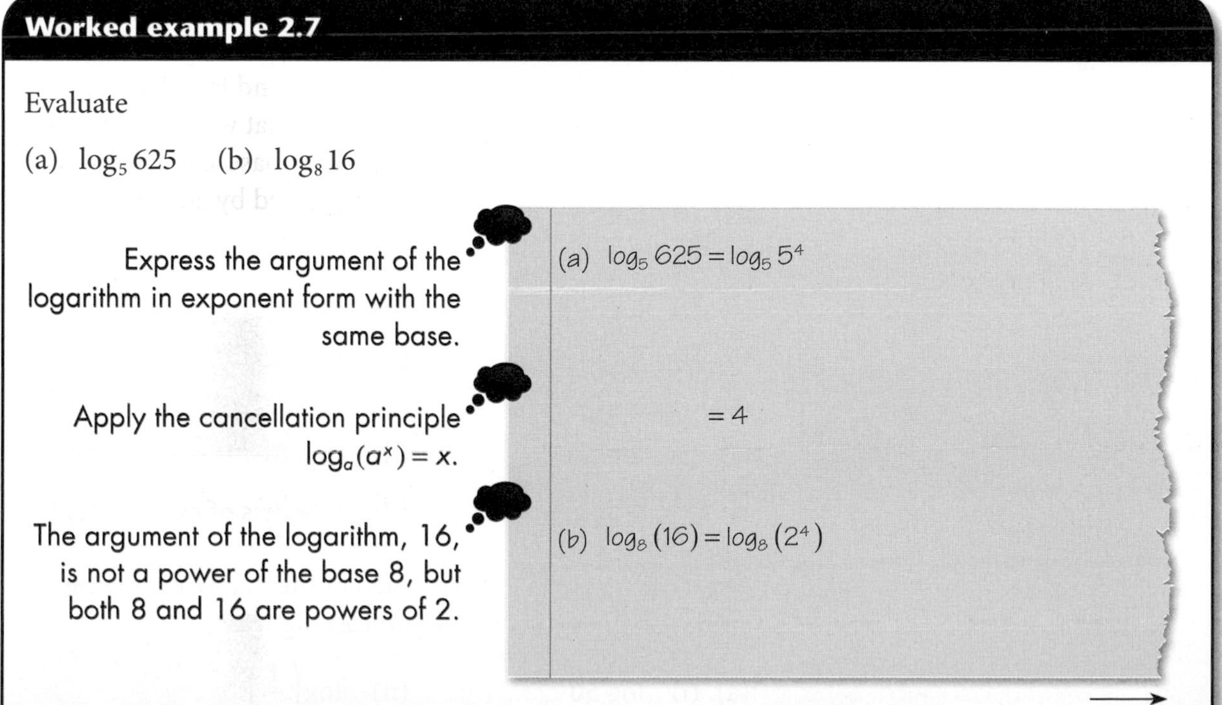

Worked example 2.7

Evaluate

(a) $\log_5 625$ (b) $\log_8 16$

Express the argument of the logarithm in exponent form with the same base.	(a) $\log_5 625 = \log_5 5^4$
Apply the cancellation principle $\log_a(a^x) = x$.	$= 4$
The argument of the logarithm, 16, is not a power of the base 8, but both 8 and 16 are powers of 2.	(b) $\log_8(16) = \log_8(2^4)$

continued . . .

Using a rule of exponents, convert 2^4 to an exponent of $8 = 2^3$.	$= \log_8\left(2^{3\times\frac{4}{3}}\right)$
	$= \log_8\left(8^{\frac{4}{3}}\right)$
Apply the cancellation principle $\log_a(a^x) = x$.	$= \frac{4}{3}$

Whenever you raise a positive number to a power, whether positive or negative, the result is always positive. Therefore a question such as 'to what power do you raise 10 to get −3?' has no answer.

KEY POINT 2.17

You cannot take the logarithm of a negative number or zero.

Exercise 2D

1. Evaluate the following:

(a) (i) $\log_3 27$ (ii) $\log_4 16$

(b) (i) $\log_5 5$ (ii) $\log_3 3$

(c) (i) $\log_{12} 1$ (ii) $\log_{15} 1$

(d) (i) $\log_3 \frac{1}{3}$ (ii) $\log_4 \frac{1}{64}$

(e) (i) $\log_4 2$ (ii) $\log_{27} 3$

(f) (i) $\log_8 \sqrt{8}$ (ii) $\log_2 \sqrt{2}$

(g) (i) $\log_8 4$ (ii) $\log_{81} 27$

(h) (i) $\log_{25} 125$ (ii) $\log_{16} 32$

(i) (i) $\log_4 2\sqrt{2}$ (ii) $\log_9 81\sqrt{3}$

(j) (i) $\log_{25} 0.2$ (ii) $\log_4 0.5$

2. Use a calculator to evaluate each of the following, giving your answer correct to 3 significant figures.

(a) (i) $\log 50$ (ii) $\log\left(\frac{1}{4}\right)$

(b) (i) $\ln 0.1$ (ii) $\ln 10$

3. Simplify the following expressions:

(a) (i) $7\log x - 2\log x$ (ii) $2\log x + 3\log x$

(b) (i) $(\log x - 1)(\log y + 3)$ (ii) $(\log x + 2)^2$

(c) (i) $\dfrac{\log a + \log b}{\log a \log b}$ (ii) $\dfrac{(\log a)^2 - 1}{\log a - 1}$

See Prior Learning section O on the CD-ROM if you need to brush up on simplifying fractions.

4. Make x the subject of the following:

(a) (i) $\log_3 x = y$ (ii) $\log_4 x = 2y$

(b) (i) $\log_a x = 1 + y$ (ii) $\log_a x = y^2$

(c) (i) $\log_x 3y = 3$ (ii) $\log_x y = 2$

EXAM HINT

Remember that 'log x' is just another value so can be treated the same way as any variable.

5. Find the value of x in each of the following:

(a) (i) $\log_2 x = 32$ (ii) $\log_2 x = 4$

(b) (i) $\log_5 25 = 5x$ (ii) $\log_{49} 7 = 2x$

(c) (i) $\log_x 36 = 2$ (ii) $\log_x 10 = \dfrac{1}{2}$

6. Solve the equation $\log_{10}(9x+1) = 3$. *[4 marks]*

7. Solve the equation $\log_8 \sqrt{1-x} = \dfrac{1}{3}$. *[4 marks]*

8. Find the exact solution to the equation $\ln(3x-1) = 2$. *[5 marks]*

9. Find all values of x which satisfy $(\log_3 x)^2 = 4$. *[5 marks]*

10. Solve the equation $3(1 + \log x) = 6 + \log x$. *[5 marks]*

11. Solve the equation $\log_x 4 = 9$. *[4 marks]*

12. Solve the simultaneous equations

$$\log_3 x + \log_5 y = 6$$

$$\log_3 x - \log_5 y = 2$$

[6 marks]

13. The Richter scale is a way of measuring the strength of earthquakes. An increase of one unit on the Richter scale corresponds to an increase by a factor of 10 in the strength of the earthquake. What would be the Richter level of an earthquake which is twice as strong as a level 5.2 earthquake? *[5 marks]*

2E Laws of logarithms

Just as there are rules to follow when performing arithmetic with exponents, so there are corresponding rules which apply to logarithms.

See Fill-in proof 2 'Proving log rules' on the CD-ROM for how these rules for logarithms can be derived from the laws of exponents.

KEY POINT 2.18

The logarithm of a *product* is the *sum* of the logarithms.

$$\log_a xy = \log_a x + \log_a y$$

For example, you can check that $\log_2 32 = \log_2 8 + \log_2 4$.

KEY POINT 2.19

The logarithm of a *quotient* is the *difference* of the logarithms.

$$\log_a \frac{x}{y} = \log_a x - \log_a y$$

For example, $\log 6 = \log 42 - \log 7$.

KEY POINT 2.20

The logarithm of an *exponent* is the *multiple* of the logarithm.

$$\log_a x^r = r \log_a x$$

For example, $\log_5 8 = \log_5 (2^3) = 3\log_5 2$.

A special case of this is the logarithm of a reciprocal:

$$\log x^{-1} = -\log x$$

We know that $a^0 = 1$ irrespective of a. We can express this in terms of logarithms:

KEY POINT 2.21

The logarithm of 1 is always 0, irrespective of the base.

$$\log_a 1 = 0$$

We can use the laws of logarithms to manipulate expressions and solve equations involving logarithms, as the next two examples illustrate.

EXAM HINT

It is just as important to know what you *cannot* do with logarithms. One very common mistake is to rewrite $\log(x+y)$ as $\log x + \log y$ or as $\log x \times \log y$.

Worked example 2.8

If $x = \log_{10} a$ and $y = \log_{10} b$, express $\log_{10} \frac{100a^2}{b}$ in terms of x, y and integers.

Use laws of logs to isolate $\log_{10} a$ and $\log_{10} b$ in the given expression. First, use the law about the logarithm of a fraction.

$$\log_{10} \frac{100a^2}{b} = \log_{10}(100a^2) - \log_{10} b$$

Then use the law about the log of a product.

$$= \log_{10} 100 + \log_{10} a^2 - \log_{10} b$$

For the second term use the law about the log of an exponent.

$$= \log_{10} 100 + 2\log_{10} a - \log_{10} b$$

Finally, simplify (by evaluating) $\log_{10} 100$.

$$= 2 + 2\log_{10} a - \log_{10} b$$
$$= 2 + 2x - y$$

Worked example 2.9

Solve the equation $\log_2 x + \log_2(x+4) = 5$.

Rewrite the left-hand side as a single logarithm.

$\log_2 x + \log_2(x+4) = 5$

$\Leftrightarrow \quad \log_2(x(x+4)) = 5$

Undo the logarithm by exponentiating both sides; the base must be the same as the base of the logarithm, 2.

$2^{\log_2(x(x+4))} = 2^5$

Apply the cancellation principle to the left-hand side.

$x(x+4) = 32$

$x^2 + 4x = 32$

This is a quadratic equation, which can be factorised.

$x^2 + 4x - 32 = 0$

$(x+8)(x-4) = 0$

$x = -8 \text{ or } x = 4$

Check the validity of the solutions by putting them into the original equation.

When $x = -8$:

$\text{LHS} = \log_2(-8) + \log_2(-4)$, and since we cannot take logarithms of negative numbers, this solution does not work.

When $x = 4$:

$\text{LHS} = \log_2 4 + \log_2 8$

$= 2 + 3 = 5 = \text{RHS}$

So $x = 4$ is the only solution of the given equation.

EXAM HINT

Checking your answers is an important part of solving mathematical problems, and involves more than looking for arithmetic errors. As this example shows, false solutions may arise through correct algebraic manipulations.

Although we have discussed logarithms with a general base a, your calculator may only have buttons for the common logarithm and the natural logarithm ($\log x$ and $\ln x$). To use a calculator to evaluate a logarithm with base other than 10 or e (for example, $\log_5 20$), we use the following **change-of-base rule** for logarithms.

KEY POINT 2.22

Change-of-base rule for logarithms:

$$\log_a x = \frac{\log_b x}{\log_b a}$$

So, we can calculate $\log_5 20$ using the logarithm with base 10 as follows:

$$\log_5 20 = \frac{\log 20}{\log 5} = 1.86 \text{ (3 SF)}$$

The change-of-base rule is useful for more than just evaluating logarithms.

Worked example 2.10

Solve the equation $\log_3 x + \log_9 x = 2$.

We want to have logarithms involving just one base, so use the change-of-base rule to turn the log with base 9 into a log with base 3.

$$\log_9 x = \frac{\log_3 x}{\log_3 9} = \frac{\log_3 x}{2}$$

Therefore the equation is

$$\log_3 x + \frac{\log_3 x}{2} = 2$$

Collect the logs together.

$$\Leftrightarrow \frac{3}{2}\log_3 x = 2$$

$$\Leftrightarrow \log_3 x = \frac{4}{3}$$

Exponentiate both sides with base 3.

Hence

$$x = 3^{\frac{4}{3}} = 4.33 \text{ (3SF)}$$

Exercise 2E

 **1.** Given that $b>0$, simplify each of the following.

(a) (i) $\log_b b^4$ (ii) $\log_b \sqrt{b}$

(b) (i) $\log_{\sqrt{b}} b^3$ (ii) $\log_b b^2 - \log_{b^2} b$

 **2.** If $x=\log a$, $y=\log b$ and $z=\log c$, express the following in terms of x, y and z.

(a) (i) $\log(bc)$ (ii) $\log\left(\frac{c}{a}\right)$

(b) (i) $\log a^3$ (ii) $\log b^5$

(c) (i) $\log cb^7$ (ii) $\log a^2 b$

(d) (i) $\log\left(\frac{ab^2}{c}\right)$ (ii) $\log\left(\frac{a^2}{bc^3}\right)$

(e) (i) $\log\left(\frac{100}{bc^5}\right)$ (ii) $\log(5b)+\log(2c^2)$

 **3.** Solve the following equations for x.

(a) (i) $\log_3\left(\frac{2+x}{2-x}\right)=3$ (ii) $\log_2(7x+4)=5$

(b) (i) $\log_3 x - \log_3(x-6)=1$ (ii) $\log_8 x - 2\log_8\left(\frac{1}{x}\right)=1$

(c) (i) $\log_2 x + 1 = \log_4 x$ (ii) $\log_8 x + \log_2 x = 4$

(d) (i) $\log_4 x + \log_8 x = 2$ (ii) $\log_{16} x - \log_{32} x = 0.5$

(e) (i) $\log_3(x-7)+\log_3(x+1)=2$

(ii) $2\log(x-2)-\log(x)=0$

(f) (i) $\log(x^2+1)=1+2\log(x)$

(ii) $\log(3x+6)=\log(3)+1$

4. Find the exact solution to the equation $2\ln x + \ln 9 = 3$, giving your answer in the form Ae^B where A and B are rational numbers. *[5 marks]*

 **5.** If $a=\ln 2$ and $b=\ln 5$, write the following in terms of a and b.

(a) $\ln 50$

(b) $\ln 0.16$ *[6 marks]*

6. Solve $\log_2 x = \log_x 2$. *[5 marks]*

7. If $x = \log a$, $y = \log b$ and $z = \log c$, express the following in terms of x, y and z.

(a) $\log a^3 - 2\log ab^2$

(b) $\log(4b) + 2\log(5ac)$ *[8 marks]*

8. Evaluate $\log\frac{1}{2} + \log\frac{2}{3} + \log\frac{3}{4} + \log\frac{4}{3} + \cdots + \log\frac{8}{9} + \log\frac{9}{10}$.

[4 marks]

9. If $x = \log a$, $y = \log b$ and $z = \log c$, express the following in terms of x, y and z.

(a) $\log_a a^2 b$

(b) $\log_{ab} ac^2$ *[6 marks]*

10. If $x = \log a$, $y = \log b$ and $z = \log c$, express the following in terms of x, y and z.

(a) $\log_b\left(\frac{a}{bc}\right)$

(b) $\log_{a^b}(b^a)$ *[7 marks]*

2F Graphs of logarithms

Let us now look at the graph of the logarithm function and the various properties of logarithms that we can deduce from it. Here are the graphs of $y = \log x$, $y = \log_2 x$ and $y = \ln x$.

In chapter 5 you will see how this type of change in the function causes a vertical stretch of the graph.

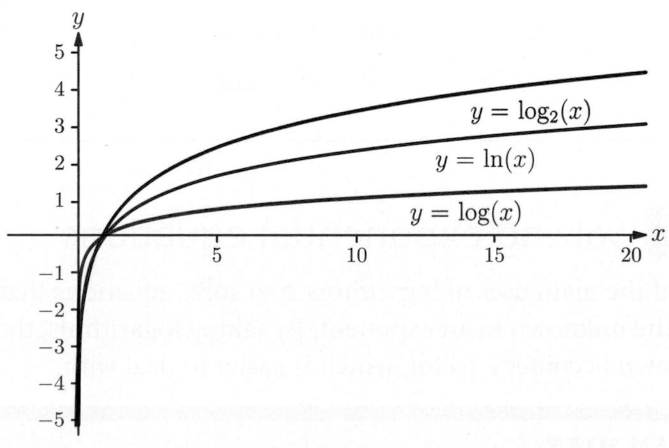

Given the change-of-base rule from section E (Key point 2.22), it is not surprising that these curves all have a similar shape: since $\log_2 x = \frac{\log x}{\log 2}$ and $\ln x = \frac{\log x}{\log e}$, each of the logarithm functions is a multiple of the common logarithm function.

> **EXAM HINT**
> Vertical asymptotes are even harder to detect accurately from a calculator display than horizontal ones. This is why it is essential that you know where the asymptote is for a logarithmic graph.

From the graphs above, we can observe the following important properties of the logarithm function.

KEY POINT 2.23

If $y = \log_a x$ (for any positive value of a), then

- the graph of y against x crosses the x-axis at (1, 0), because $\log_a 1 = 0$
- $\log x$ is negative for $0 < x < 1$ and positive for $x > 1$
- the graph lies entirely to the right of the y-axis, since the logarithm of a negative value of x is not a real number
- the graph increases (slopes upward from left to right) throughout, and as x tends to infinity so does y
- the y-axis is an asymptote to the curve.

Note that a logarithm graph is the reflection of an exponential graph. You will see why this is in chapter 5.

It is unlikely you will find exam questions testing just this topic, but you may have to sketch a graph involving a logarithm as part of another question.

Exercise 2F

1. Sketch the following graphs, labelling clearly the vertical asymptote and all axis intercepts.

(a) (i) $y = \log(x^2)$ (ii) $y = \log(x^3)$

(b) (i) $y = \log 4x$ (ii) $y = \log 2x$

(c) (i) $y = \log(x-2)$ (ii) $y = \log(x+1)$

2G Solving exponential equations

One of the main uses of logarithms is to solve equations that have the unknown in an exponent. By taking logarithms, the unknown becomes a factor, which is easier to deal with.

> **EXAM HINT**
> When taking logarithms of both sides of an equation, you can use any base. We usually choose log or ln so that we can easily find or check the answer with a calculator.

Worked example 2.11

Find the exact solution of the equation $3^{x-2} = 5$.

Take logs of both sides.

$\log(3^{x-2}) = \log 5$

The log of an exponent is the multiple of the log (Key point 2.20).

$\Leftrightarrow (x-2)\log 3 = \log 5$

$\Leftrightarrow x-2 = \dfrac{\log 5}{\log 3}$

$\Leftrightarrow x = \dfrac{\log 5}{\log 3} + 2$

Note that we can use the rules of logarithms to make the answer more compact:

$$\frac{\log 5}{\log 3} + 2 = \frac{\log 5 + 2\log 3}{\log 3} = \frac{\log(5\times 3^2)}{\log 3} = \frac{\log 45}{\log 3}$$

You need to be able to carry out this sort of simplification, but you do not *have* to do it unless the question explicitly asks you to – for instance, if the above example specified that you should write the answer in the form $\dfrac{\log a}{\log b}$ where a and b are integers.

If you are allowed to use a calculator, you can plot both sides of the equation and find the solution by looking for intersections of the graphs.

EXAM HINT

See Calculator skills sheet 5 on the CD-ROM for how to use graphs to solve equations.

Worked example 2.12

The number of bacteria in a culture medium is given by $N = 1000 \times 2^{4t}$, where t is the number of hours since 08:00. At what time will the population first reach one million?

We need to solve the equation $1000 \times 2^{4t} = 1000000$. First, sketch the graph of $N = 1000 \times 2^{4t}$ with t on the x-axis and N on the y-axis.

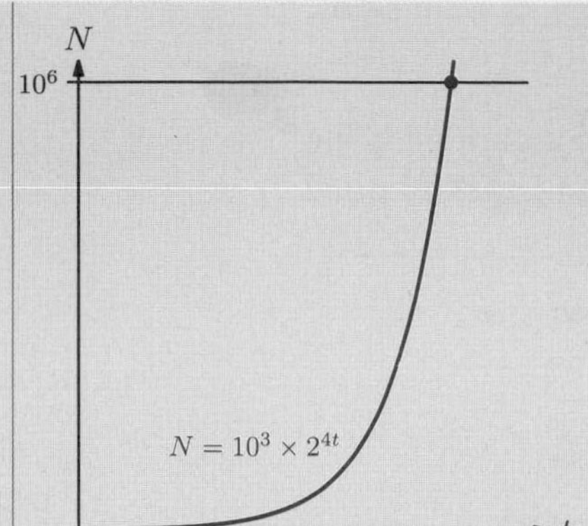

The solution is the intersection of the curve with the line $y = 1000000$.

From GDC: $t = 2.49$ (hours after 08:00)

Convert this t-value into hours and minutes.

$0.49 \times 60 = 29$ minutes

So the population will reach 1 million at 10:29.

The next example shows how to solve a more complicated exponential equation, where the unknown appears in the exponent on both sides. The method of taking logarithms of both sides works here as well, but a little more algebraic manipulation is needed.

There is another type of exponential equation that sometimes comes up: a disguised quadratic equation, for example $2^{2x} - 5 \times 2^{x} + 6 = 0$. Such equations are explored in section 3B.

Worked example 2.13

Solve the equation $10^x = 5 \times 2^{3x}$, giving your answer in terms of natural logarithms.

Take the natural logarithm of both sides.

$\ln(10^x) = \ln(5 \times 2^{3x})$

On the RHS, the log of a product is the sum of logs.

$\Leftrightarrow \ln(10^x) = \ln 5 + \ln(2^{3x})$

continued . . .

The log of an exponent is the multiple of the log.

$\Leftrightarrow x\ln 10 = \ln 5 + 3x\ln 2$

Collect all terms containing x.

$\Leftrightarrow x\ln 10 - 3x\ln 2 = \ln 5$

We want only one term with x, so take x out as a factor.

$\Leftrightarrow x(\ln 10 - 3\ln 2) = \ln 5$

$$\Leftrightarrow x = \frac{\ln 5}{\ln 10 - 3\ln 2}$$

Exercise 2G

1. Solve for x, giving your answer correct to 3 significant figures.

(a) (i) $3\times 4^x = 90$ (ii) $1000\times 1.02^x = 10000$

(b) (i) $6\times 7^{3x+1} = 1.2$ (ii) $5\times 2^{2x-5} = 94$

(c) (i) $3^{2x} = 4^{x-1}$ (ii) $5^x = 6^{1-x}$

(d) (i) $3\times 2^{3x} = 7\times 3^{3x-2}$ (ii) $4\times 8^{x-1} = 3\times 5^{2x+1}$

EXAM HINT

In question 1 above, where you are allowed to use a calculator, you need to judge whether it will be faster to plot graphs or to rearrange the equation and then evaluate the logarithms with your calculator, for example:

$$2^{x-1} = 5$$

$$\Rightarrow (x-1)\log 2 = \log 5$$

$$\Rightarrow x - 1 = \frac{\log 5}{\log 2}$$

$$\Rightarrow x = 1 + \frac{\log 5}{\log 2} = 3.32 \text{ (3SF)}$$

2. Solve the following equations, giving your answers in terms of natural logarithms.

(a) (i) $3^{2x} = 5$ (ii) $10^{3x} = 7$

(b) (i) $2^{x+1} = 5^x$ (ii) $5^{x-2} = 3^x$

(c) (i) $2^{3x} = 3e^x$ (ii) $e^{2x} = 5\times 2^x$

3. In a yeast culture, cell numbers are given by $N = 100e^{1.03t}$, where t is measured in hours after the cells are introduced to the culture.

(a) What is the initial number of cells?

(b) How many cells will be present after 6 hours?

(c) How long will it take for the population to reach one thousand cells? *[4 marks]*

4. A rumour spreads exponentially through a school, so that the number of people who know it can be modelled by the equation $N = Ae^{kt}$, where t is the time, in minutes, after 9 a.m. When school begins (at 9 a.m.), 18 people know the rumour. By 10 a.m. 42 people know it.

(a) Write down the value of A.

(b) Show that $k = 0.0141$, correct to three significant figures.

(c) How many people know the rumour at 10:30 a.m.?

(d) There are 1200 people in the school. According to the exponential model, at what time will everyone know the rumour? *[6 marks]*

5. The mass M of a piece of plutonium at time t seconds is given by

$$M = ke^{-0.01t}$$

(a) Write down the initial mass of the plutonium.

(b) Sketch the graph of M against t.

(c) How long will it take for the plutonium to reach 25% of its original mass? Give your answer in minutes. *[5 marks]*

6. Find the solution to the equation $15^{2x} = 3 \times 5^{x+1}$ in the form $\frac{\log a}{\log b}$ where a and b are positive integers. *[6 marks]*

7. Solve the equation, $\frac{1}{7^x} = 3 \times 49^{5-x}$, giving your answer in the form $a + \log_7 b$ where $a, b \in \mathbb{Z}$. *[6 marks]*

8. Solve the equation $5 \times 4^{x-1} = \frac{1}{3^{2x}}$, giving your answer in the form $x = \frac{\ln p}{\ln q}$ where p and q are rational numbers. *[6 marks]*

9. (a) Show that the equation $3^x = 3 - x$ has only one solution.

(b) Find the solution, giving your answer to 3 significant figures. *[6 marks]*

Summary

- In this chapter, we revisited the rules for exponents and explored the meaning of fractional and negative exponents. (These rules are not in the Formula booklet.)

$a^m \times a^n = a^{m+n}$ $\qquad (a^m)^n = a^{m \times n}$

$a^m \div a^n = a^{m-n}$ $\qquad a^{\frac{m}{n}} = \left(\sqrt[n]{a}\right)^m = \sqrt[n]{a^m}$

$a^n \times b^n = (ab)^n$ $\qquad a^0 = 1 \quad (a \neq 0)$

$a^n \div b^n = \left(\frac{a}{b}\right)^n$ $\qquad a^{-n} = \frac{1}{a^n} \quad (a \neq 0)$

- Exponential functions can be used to model growth or decay of some simple real-life systems, taking as a general form the function: $N = Ba^{\left(\frac{t}{k}\right)} + c$
- $\log_a b$ represents the answer to the question 'to what exponent do I have to raise a to get b?'

$$b = a^x \Leftrightarrow x = \log_a b$$

- Logarithms undo the effect of exponentiating, and vice versa:

$$\log_a(a^x) = x = a^{\log_a x}$$

- The following properties of the logarithm function can be deduced from its graph, if $y = \log x$ then:
  - the graph of y against x crosses the x-axis at (1,0)
  - $\log x$ is negative for $0 < x < 1$ and positive for $x > 1$
  - the graph lies to the right of the y-axis; the y-axis is an asymptote to the curve
  - the logarithm graph increases throughout; as x tends to infinity so does y.
- Logarithms obey a number of rules, most of which are given in the Formula booklet:

$$\log_a xy = \log_a x + \log_a y$$

$$\log_a\left(\frac{x}{y}\right) = \log_a x - \log_a y$$

$$\log_a\left(\frac{1}{x}\right) = -\log_a x \text{ (not in Formula booklet)}$$

$$\log_a x^p = p\log_a x$$

$$\log_a 1 = 0 \text{ (not in Formula booklet)}$$

- e is the mathematical constant (Euler's number): e = 2.71828182849...
- Logarithms with base 10 (common logarithms, $\log_{10} x$), are often written simply as $\log x$. Logarithms with base e (natural logarithms) are usually written as $\ln x$.

- A change-of-base formula for logarithms, and a related rule for exponents, are given in the formula book:

$$\log_b a = \frac{\log_c a}{\log_c b}$$

$$a^x = e^{x \ln a}$$

- Many exponential equations can be solved by taking logarithms of both sides.

Introductory problem revisited

A radioactive substance has a half-life of 72 years (this is the time it takes for half of the mass, and hence radioactivity, to decay). A 1 kg block of the substance is found to have a radioactivity of 25 million becquerels (Bq). How long, to the nearest 10 years, would it take for the radioactivity to fall to 10 000 Bq?

Write down the exponential equation.

Let R be the radioactivity after t years. Then

$$R = Ba^{\frac{t}{k}}$$

Initial condition gives B.

When $t = 0$, $R = 25 \times 10^6 = B$

Every time t increases by 72, R falls by 50%.

$a = 0.5$, $k = 72$

$\therefore R = (25 \times 10^6) \times 0.5^{\frac{t}{72}}$

We want to find the value of t for which $R = 10000$.

$R = 10^4$

$\Leftrightarrow 25 \times 10^6 \times 0.5^{\frac{t}{72}} = 10^4$

$\Leftrightarrow 0.5^{\frac{t}{72}} = 0.0004$

The unknown is in the exponent, so use logarithms.

$\log\left(0.5^{\frac{t}{72}}\right) = \log(0.0004)$

$\frac{t}{72}\log(0.5) = \log(0.0004)$

Now rearrange to find t.

$t = \frac{72 \log(0.0004)}{\log(0.5)} = 812.7$

It takes around 810 years for the radioactivity to fall to 10 000 Bq.

Mixed examination practice 2

Short questions

1. Solve $\log_5\left(\sqrt{x^2+49}\right)=2$. *[4 marks]*

2. If $a=\log x$, $b=\log y$ and $c=\log z$ (where all logs are with base 10), express the following in terms of a, b and c.

   (a) $\log\frac{x^2\sqrt{y}}{z}$ (b) $\log\sqrt{0.1x}$ (c) $\log_{100}\left(\frac{y}{z}\right)$ *[6 marks]*

3. Given that $B=4+12e^{\frac{t}{3}}$, find the value of t for which $B=25$. *[3 marks]*

4. Find the exact solution of the equation $4\times 3^{2x}=5^x$, giving your answer in terms of natural logarithms. *[6 marks]*

5. Solve the simultaneous equations

$$\ln x+\ln y^2=8$$

$$\ln x^2+\ln y=6$$

[6 marks]

6. If $y=\ln x-\ln(x+2)+\ln(4-x^2)$, express x in terms of y. *[6 marks]*

7. Find the exact value of x which satisfies the equation

$$2\times 3^{x-2}=36^{x-1}$$

giving your answer in the simplified form $\frac{\ln p}{\ln q}$ where $p,q\in\mathbb{Z}$. *[5 marks]*

8. Given that $\log_a b^2=c$ and $\log_b a=c-1$ for some value c, where $0<a<b$, express a in terms of b. *[6 marks]*

9. Find the exact solutions of the equation $\ln x=4\log_x e$. *[5 marks]*

Long questions

1. The speed V in metres per second of a parachutist t seconds after jumping is modelled by the expression

$$V=42(1-e^{-0.2t})$$

(a) Sketch a graph of V against t.

(b) What is the initial speed?

(c) What is the maximum speed that the parachutist could approach?

The parachutist opens the parachute when his speed reaches 22 m s^{-1}.

(d) How long is he falling before opening the parachute? *[9 marks]*

2. Scientists think that the global population of tigers is falling exponentially. Estimates suggest that in 1970 there were 37 000 tigers but by 1980 the number had dropped to 22 000.

(a) The number T of tigers n years after 1970 can be modelled by $T = ka^n$.

(i) Write down the value of k.

(ii) Show that $a = 0.949$ to three significant figures.

(b) What does the model predict that the population will be in 2020?

(c) When the population reaches 1000, the tiger population will be described as 'near extinction'. In which year will this happen?

In the year 2000 a worldwide ban on the sale of tiger products was implemented, and it is believed that by 2010 the population of tigers had recovered to 10 000.

(d) If the recovery has been exponential, find a model of the form $T = ka^m$ connecting the number of tigers (T) with the number of years after 2000 (m).

(e) If each year since 2000 the rate of growth has been the same, find the percentage increase in the tiger population each year. *[12 marks]*

3. A sum of \$2000 is paid into a bank account which pays 3.5% annual interest. Assume that no money is taken out of the account.

(a) What is the amount of money in the account after

(i) 1 year?

(ii) 5 years?

(b) How long, to the nearest year, does it take for the amount of money in the account to double?

(c) Sketch a graph showing how the amount of money in the account varies with time over the first 20 years.

(d) Another bank account pays only 2% annual interest, but the initial investment is \$3000. After how many years, to the nearest year, will the amount of money in the two accounts be the same?

(e) How much should be invested in the second account so that after 20 years the amount of money in the two accounts is the same? *[14 marks]*

3 Algebraic structures

In this chapter you will learn:

- some standard algebraic strategies for solving equations
- how to sketch graphs, and some limitations of graphical calculators
- how to use a graphical calculator to solve equations
- how to work with identities.

Introductory problem

Solve the equation $\frac{1}{x^2} = \ln x$.

Equations are the building blocks of mathematics. There are many different types: some have no solutions; some have many solutions; some have solutions which cannot be expressed in terms of any function you have met.

Graphs are an alternative way of expressing a relationship between two variables. If you understand the connection between graphs and equations, and can switch readily between the two representations, you will have a wider variety of tools for solving mathematical problems. The International Baccalaureate® places great emphasis on using graphical calculators to analyse graphs.

Identities are used to rewrite an expression in a different form, which can be very useful when solving equations. In much of mathematics we do not distinguish between equations and identities, although they are fundamentally different. In this chapter we shall explore some of these differences and look at the different techniques we can apply to equations and identities.

Very few examination questions are set on this topic alone, but the techniques of this chapter are involved in virtually every examination question.

3A Solving equations by factorising

We start by looking at some common algebraic methods for solving equations. You have already seen how factorising can be used to help sketch the graphs of quadratic functions; in this chapter we will apply the same principles in a wider context.

If two numbers multiply together to give 5, what can you say about those two numbers? They could be 1 and 5, 10 and $\frac{1}{2}$, π and $\frac{5}{\pi}$, …. In fact, there are an infinite number of possibilities. So, just knowing that two numbers multiply together to give 5 is not of much help in determining what the numbers actually are.

This is true for real numbers, but if the numbers you are looking for are integers, then knowing that they multiply together to give a non-zero constant is extremely useful. For example, can you solve $xy = 14$ if x and y are known to be integers? This type of equation is called a *Diophantine equation*.

However, if you know that two (or more) numbers multiply together to give zero, then you can deduce that at least one of those numbers must be zero. Therefore, if we can factorise the expression we would have a powerful tool for solving equations that take the form of an expression equal to zero.

KEY POINT 3.1

For factorising to be useful in solving an equation, one side of the equation must be zero.

Worked example 3.1

Solve the equation $e^x(\ln(x)-1)(2x-1)=0$.

If a product is equal to zero, then one of the factors must be zero.

Either $e^x = 0$ (1)

or $\ln(x)-1=0$ (2)

or $2x-1=0$ (3)

From (1): $e^x = 0$ has no solution

From (2): $\ln(x)=1$

$\Leftrightarrow x = e$

From (3): $2x=1$

$\Leftrightarrow x=\frac{1}{2}$

$\therefore x = e$ or $\frac{1}{2}$

If, instead of factorising an expression, you divide it by another expression, it is possible that you will lose solutions. For example, consider the equation $x^3 = x$. If you divide both sides by x, you get $x^2 = 1$ and hence $x = \pm 1$. But, by substituting $x = 0$ into the original equation, you can see that it is also a solution, which was missed by the method of dividing through by x. The correct way to solve this equation is:

$$
\begin{aligned}
& x^3 = x \\
\Leftrightarrow\quad & x^3 - x = 0 \\
\Leftrightarrow\quad & x(x^2 - 1) = 0 \\
\Leftrightarrow\quad & x(x-1)(x+1) = 0 \\
\Leftrightarrow\quad & x = 0 \text{ or } x = 1 \text{ or } x = -1
\end{aligned}
$$

EXAM HINT

Whenever you are tempted to divide both sides by an expression involving x, rearrange the equation so that one side is zero and then factorise the other side.

Exercise 3A

1. Solve the following equations.
   (a) (i) $3(x-3)^3 = 0$ (ii) $-4(x+1)^5 = 0$
   (b) (i) $7(2x-1)(5x+3)^2 = 0$ (ii) $5(3-x)^2(2x+6)^2 = 0$
   (c) (i) $(\log_3 x - 3)(3^x - 3) = 0$ (ii) $(\sqrt{x} - 4)(9\sqrt{x} - 1) = 0$
   (d) (i) $x(x^2 - 3) = 7(x^2 - 3)$
   (ii) $5x(x^2 - 5x + 4) = 6(x^2 - 5x + 4)$

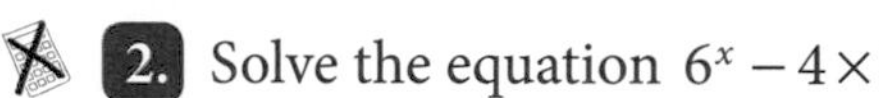

2. Solve the equation $6^x - 4 \times 3^x = 0$. *[5 marks]*

3. Find the exact solution to the equation $2 \times 5^x - 7 \times 10^x = 0$. *[6 marks]*

4. Solve $(3x-1)^{x^2-4} = 1$. *[4 marks]*

3B Solving equations by substitution

There are certain types of equation which you should know how to solve. In this section we shall focus particularly on quadratic equations, since we have a formula for solving them. We will see how some complicated-looking equations can be turned into quadratic equations by means of a substitution.

Worked example 3.2

Solve the equation $x^4 - 4 = 3x^2$.

A substitution $y = x^2$ turns this into a quadratic equation, since $x^4 = y^2$.

Let $y = x^2$. Then the equation becomes

$$y^2 - 4 = 3y$$

This is a standard quadratic equation, which can be factorised.

$$y^2 - 3y - 4 = 0$$
$$\Leftrightarrow (y+1)(y-4) = 0$$
$$\Leftrightarrow y = -1 \text{ or } y = 4$$

Use the substitution to find the corresponding values of x.

$x^2 = -1$ (not possible, reject)

or

$x^2 = 4$

$x = 2$ or $x = -2$

EXAM HINT

Note that you should explicitly state that you have rejected the possibility $x^2 = -1$. Do not just cross it out.

It may not always be obvious what substitution to use. It is quite common to be given an exponential equation which needs a substitution; in such cases, look out for an a^{2x} or $(a^2)^x$ term, both of which can be rewritten as $(a^x)^2$.

Worked example 3.3

Solve the equation $2(4^x + 2) = 9 \times 2^x$.

Note that $4^x = (2^2)^x = 2^{2x} = (2^x)^2$, so a substitution $y = 2^x$ turns this into a quadratic equation.

Let $y = 2^x$. Then the equation becomes

$$2(y^2 + 2) = 9y$$

continued . . .

This is a standard quadratic equation, which can be factorised.

$$2y^2 - 9y + 4 = 0$$
$$\Leftrightarrow (2y-1)(y-4) = 0$$
$$\Leftrightarrow y = \frac{1}{2} \text{ or } y = 4$$

Use the substitution to find the values of x.

Therefore $2^x = \frac{1}{2} \Rightarrow x = -1$

$2^x = 4$

$\Rightarrow x = 2$

Exercise 3B

1. Solve the following equations, giving your answers in exact form.

   (a) (i) $a^4 - 10a^2 + 21 = 0$ (ii) $x^4 - 7x^2 + 12 = 0$

   (b) (i) $2x^6 + 7x^3 = 15$ (ii) $a^6 + 7a^3 = 8$

   (c) (i) $x^2 - 4 = \frac{2}{x^2}$ (ii) $x^2 + \frac{36}{x^2} = 12$

   (d) (i) $x - 6\sqrt{x} + 8 = 0$ (ii) $x - 10\sqrt{x} + 24 = 0$

2. Solve the following equations.

   (a) $e^{2x} + 16e^x = 80$

   (b) $25^x - 15 \times 5^x + 50 = 0$

   (c) $\log_4 x = (\log_4 x^2)^2$

3. Solve the following equations.

   (a) $e^{2x} - 9e^x + 20 = 0$

   (b) $4^x - 7 \times 2^x + 12 = 0$

   (c) $(\log_3 x)^2 - 3\log_3 x + 2 = 0$ *[15 marks]*

4. Solve the equation $9(1 + 9^{x-1}) = 10 \times 3^x$. *[5 marks]*

5. If $a^x = \frac{-5}{a^x} + 6$ where $a > 0$ is a constant, solve for x, leaving your answer in terms of a. *[5 marks]*

6. Solve the equation $\log_2 x = 6 - 5\log_x 2$. *[6 marks]*

3C Features of graphs

In this course you will meet many different types of equations and will learn various techniques for solving them. You already encountered quadratic, exponential and logarithmic equations in chapters 1 and 2, and they are very common in applications, but you may also need to solve equations which do not belong to one of these standard types. Approximate solutions to such equations can be found by using graphs.

Graphs are simply another way of representing a relationship between two variables. For example, we can write $y = x^2$ or draw

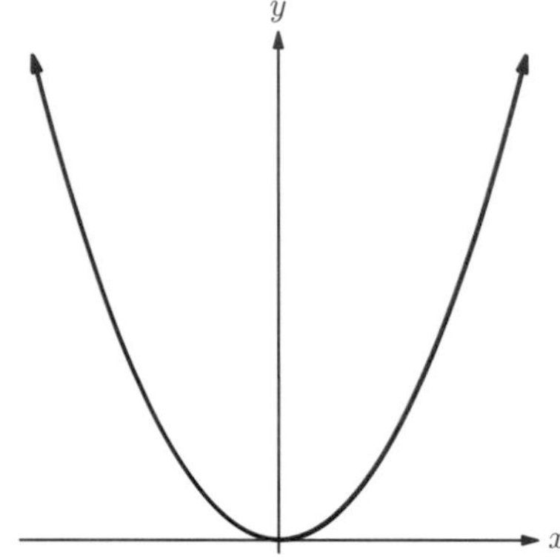

Graphical calculators can be very helpful in sketching or drawing graphs. In this section we will examine important features you should look for when plotting graphs with your graphical calculator; we will also discuss some limitations of this method.

The main features you should indicate on your sketch are:

- the y-intercept – this is where $x = 0$
- the x-intercepts (zeros) – these are where $y = 0$
- maximum and minimum points.

If the graph you are sketching is completely unfamiliar, it can be difficult to choose a good viewing window. If the window is too small, you may miss important parts of the graph; if it is too large, you may not be able to distinguish between features that are close together. This is why it is useful to have a general idea of the overall shape of the graph before trying to plot it. It is important to learn about the graphs of different types of functions, even if you have a graphical calculator available.

EXAM HINT

If you are asked to *sketch* a graph, you only need to show the overall shape and indicate the important features. Occasionally you may be asked to *draw* a graph, in which case the graph should be accurate and to scale, and you should use a ruler for straight lines.

EXAM HINT

See Calculator Skills sheets 2 and 4 on the CD-ROM for a guide to sketching graphs and finding the main features.

Worked example 3.4

Sketch the graph of $y = \dfrac{x^3 - 16x}{x^2 + 1}$.

Can we quickly deduce any of the important features?
When $x = 0$, $y = 0$, so the graph goes through (0, 0).
We also know that the zeros (x-intercepts) occur when the numerator is zero, and we can find those points by factorising.

Zeros occur where

$$x^3 - 16x = 0$$
$$x(x^2 - 16) = 0$$
$$x(x-4)(x+4) = 0$$
$$x = 0, 4, -4$$

We don't know much about the shape of the graph, so use a GDC to plot it.
The viewing window should include −4 and 4.
There appear to be one maximum and one minimum point; if needed, we can find their coordinates with the GDC too.

From GDC:

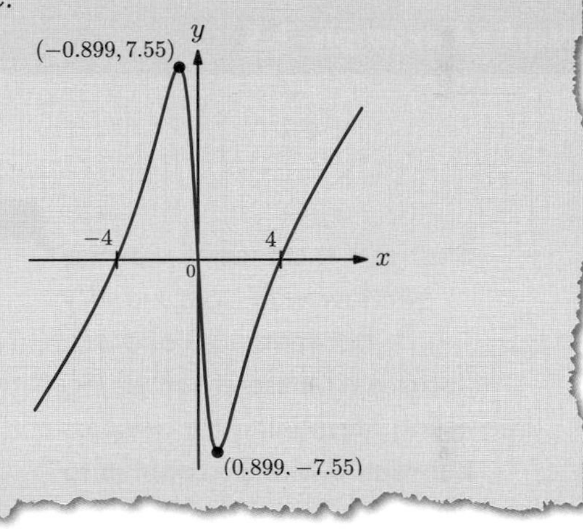

Some graphs may have asymptotes.

KEY POINT 3.2

> An **asymptote** is a straight line which the graph approaches as either x or y gets very large.

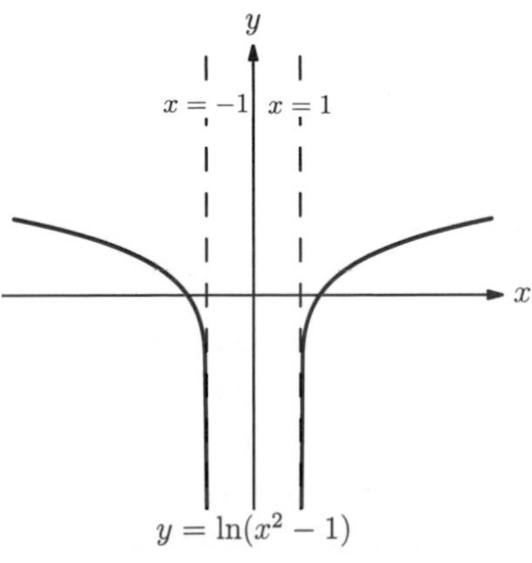

Asymptotes are usually shown on graphs as dotted lines.

Vertical asymptotes occur where a function ceases to be defined. They are vertical lines of the form $x = a$. For example, $y = \dfrac{1}{x-3}$ has an asymptote $x = 3$ (because we cannot divide by zero), and $y = \ln(x^2 - 1)$ has asymptotes $x = -1$ and $x = 1$ (because we cannot take a logarithm of zero).

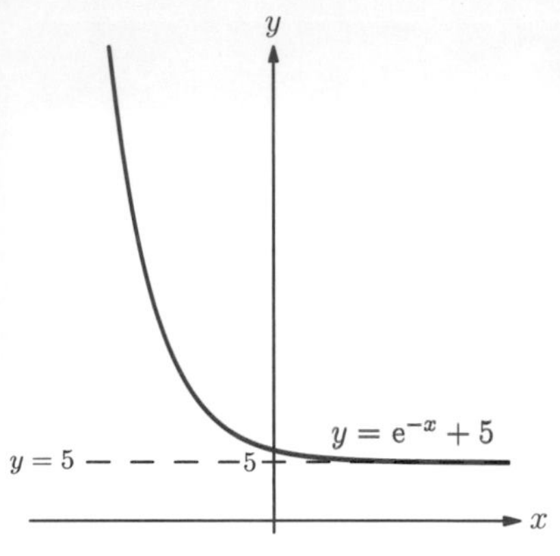

Horizontal asymptotes indicate long-term behaviour of the function; they are lines that the graph approaches for large values of x (positive or negative). They are horizontal lines of the form $y = a$. For example, $y = e^{-x} + 5$ has an asymptote $y = 5$.

Since asymptotes are not actually part of the graph, they will not show up on your calculator sketch. But you can find approximately where they are by moving the cursor along the graph towards large values of x or y and estimating what y or x value the graph seems to be approaching. To find the exact location of an asymptote, you need to use knowledge of the function in question – for example, the fact that you cannot divide by zero or that e^{-x} approaches zero as x gets large. You will only be asked to identify the exact position of asymptotes for familiar functions.

Worked example 3.5

Sketch the graph of $y = xe^{-x} + 2$.

Start with a standard viewing window with both x and y between −10 and 10. It looks as if there is something interesting happening for x-values between 0 and 3; zoom in to confirm that there is a maximum point at $x = 1$. There also seems to be a horizontal asymptote. We know that e^{-x} approaches 0, so it is likely that the asymptote is $y = 2$.

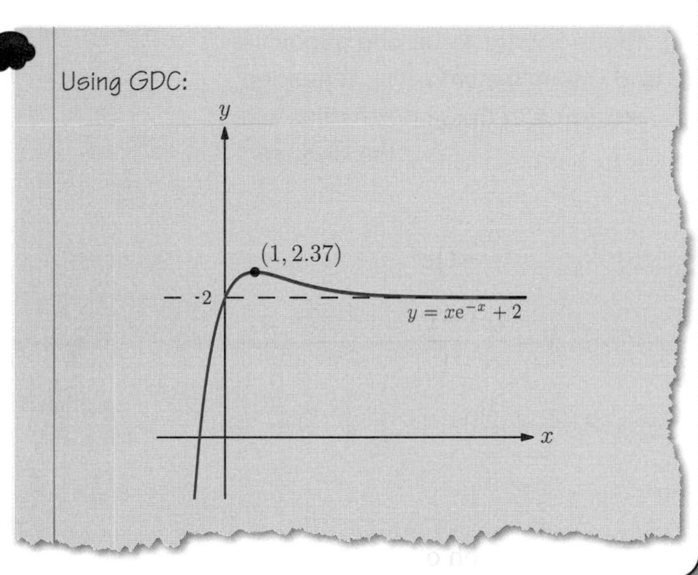

Note that in the above example, although the line $y = 2$ is an asymptote, the graph actually crosses it when $x = 0$. This is fine, as the asymptote is only relevant for large values of x.

See Prior learning section I on the CD-ROM for an introduction to the modulus function $|x|$. Make sure you know where to find it on your calculator.

Vertical asymptotes can sometimes be unclear. In the next example, the graph approaches the vertical asymptote from both sides, so your calculator may attempt to 'connect the points' into a 'V' shape. You must be able to identify for yourself that there is a vertical asymptote between the two arms of the 'V' and draw it correctly.

Worked example 3.6

Sketch the graph of $y = \ln|x-2|$.

It looks as if the two branches of the graph join at a point with x-coordinate equal to 2. However, we know that ln 0 is not defined, so there should instead be an asymptote at $x = 2$.

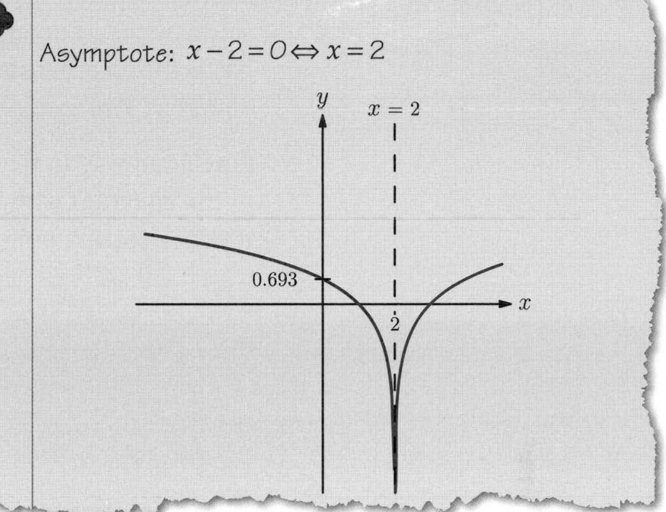

Exercise 3C

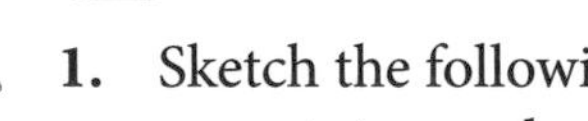

1. Sketch the following graphs, indicating the axis intercepts, asymptotes, and maximum and minimum points.

   (a) (i) $y = x^4 - x^3 + 1$ (ii) $x^4 - x^2$

   (b) (i) $y = (x-1)e^x$ (ii) $y = (e^x - 1)^2$

   (c) (i) $y = \frac{\frac{1}{2}e^x - 1}{x-1}$ (ii) $y = \ln\left(\frac{x+2}{x-1}\right)^2$

   (d) (i) $\left|\frac{x^2-1}{x+2}\right|$ (ii) $y = \frac{|x^2-4|}{x+1}$

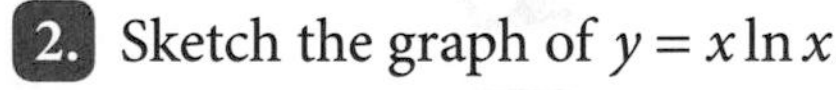

2. Sketch the graph of $y = x\ln x$. *[4 marks]*

3. Sketch the graph of $y = \frac{e^x}{\ln x}$. *[6 marks]*

4. Sketch the graph of $y = \frac{x^2(x^2-9)}{e^x}$ for $-5 \le x \le 6$. Mark the coordinates of all zeros and maximum and minimum points. *[6 marks]*

EXAM HINT

In question 4 you need to explore different viewing windows to locate all the maximum and minimum points.

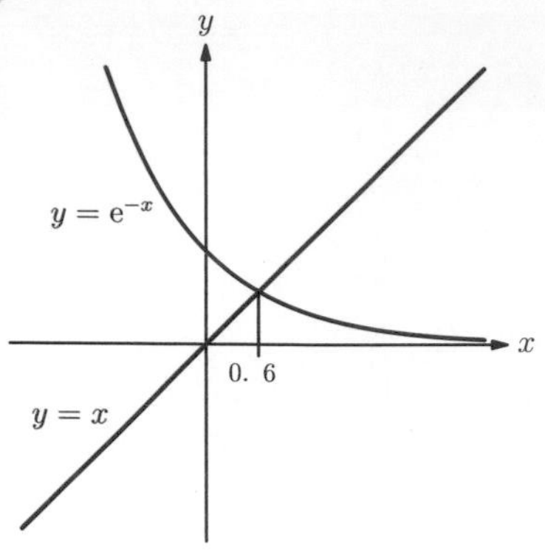

3D Using a graphical calculator to solve equations

Some equations cannot be solved analytically, that is, you cannot rearrange them to get $x =$ a certain number using the standard set of operations and functions mathematicians allow. Nevertheless, there may still be values of x which satisfy the equation. An example of such an equation is $x = e^{-x}$.

One good way to find these solutions is by plotting both sides of the equation with a graphical calculator. The x-coordinate of the intersection point gives the solution to the equation – in this case 0.567 to three significant figures.

The solution to $x = e^{-x}$ can actually be written in terms of the 'Lambert W Function'. In fact, it is $W(1)$. However, does knowing this actually give us any more information about the solution to the above equation?

Worked example 3.7

Solve the equation $x^2 = 3\ln x + 2$.

There is no obvious substitution or factorisation, so plot both sides of the equation on the calculator and make a sketch.

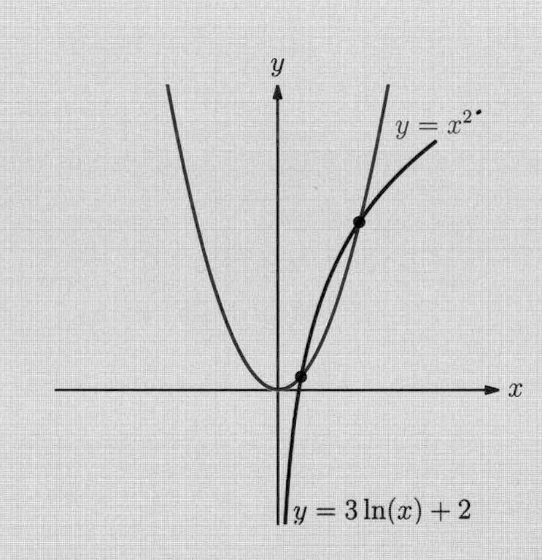

Use the calculator to find the intersection points.

$x = 2.03$ or $x = 0.573$ (3SF)

(from GDC)

EXAM HINT

When using your calculator to solve an equation, you must show a sketch of the graph and round the answer to an appropriate degree of accuracy (usually 3 SF).

Solving equations graphically has some problems: you may not know how many solutions to look for, or how to set the viewing window so you can see them all; if two solutions are very close together, you may miss one of them. This is where you need to rely on your knowledge of the graphs of different types of functions to make sure that the calculator is showing all the important features.

Many graphical calculators have functions for solving special types of equations. In particular, you may be able to solve polynomial equations (those involving only positive integer powers of x) without having to graph them. Your calculator may also have some sort of equation solver tool, although this has drawbacks similar to those associated with graphical methods.

See Calculator skills sheet 5 and 6 on the CD-ROM for more details.

If the question does not ask for an exact answer, you can take it as an indication that a graphical solution might be appropriate. If you cannot see another quick way to solve the equation, try using your calculator.

Worked example 3.8

Solve the equation $x^3 = 5x^2 - 2$.

As we don't yet know any algebraic methods for solving cubic equations, let's try using the polynomial equation solver on the calculator. First, the equation needs to be rearranged.

$$x^3 - 5x^2 + 2 = 0$$

$$x = -0.598, 0.680, 4.92 \text{ (3SF)}$$

(using GDC)

EXAM HINT

You can use the graphical method in the non-calculator paper, too. Questions in the non-calculator paper usually just ask you to find the number of solutions, rather than to actually solve the equation.

Worked example 3.9

Find the number of solutions of the equation $e^x = 4 - x^2$.

Sketch graphs of both sides of the equation; these are graphs you should know how to sketch without a calculator.

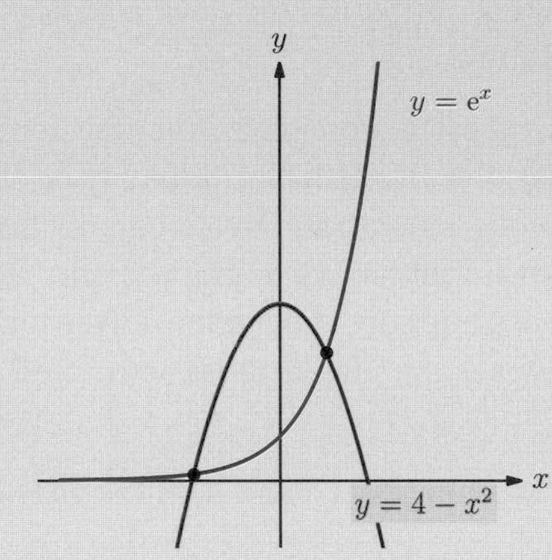

The solutions correspond to the intersections of the two curves.

There are 2 solutions.

Exercise 3D

1. Solve the following equations, giving your answers to 3 significant figures.

   (a) (i) $x^3 = 3x - 1$ (ii) $x^3 + 4x^2 = 2x - 1$

   (b) (i) $e^x = x + 1$ (ii) $e^{2x} = x^2 - 3$

   (c) (i) $e^x = \ln x$ (ii) $e^x \ln x = x^3 - x$

2. Solve the equation $x \ln x = 3 - x^2$. *[4 marks]*

3. The equation $\ln x = kx$, where $k > 0$, has one solution. How many solutions do the following equations have?

   (a) $\ln x^2 = kx$

   (b) $\ln\left(\frac{1}{x}\right) = kx$

   (c) $\ln\sqrt{x} = kx$ *[6 marks]*

4. Find a value of k such that the equation $\sin x = kx$ has 7 solutions, where x is measured in degrees. *[6 marks]*

3E Working with identities

KEY POINT 3.3

An **identity** is an equation which is true for all values of x, for example $x \times x \equiv x^2$.

The identity sign $\equiv$ is used to emphasise that the left-hand side and right-hand side are equal for all values of x, but frequently an equals sign is written instead.

Identities are very useful for manipulating algebraic expressions. Operations such as multiplying out brackets are actually applications of identities; for example, when expanding the expression $(x-2)(x+1)$ to give $x^2 - x - 2$, we are actually using the identity $(x+a)(x+b) \equiv x^2 + (a+b)x + ab$, which holds for all a, b and x (in particular for $a = -2$, $b = 1$ and unknown x).

When solving equations, we can use any known identities or derive a new one where needed. To derive or 'show' an identity, we essentially rewrite a given expression. We must start from one side, and use known rules and identities to transform the expression step by step until we reach the other side of the identity.

You may be unsure about which rules and identities you are allowed to use. Anything listed as a 'Key point' in this book is acceptable, as are basic algebraic manipulations such as multiplying out brackets and simplifying fractions.

Identities are very important in trigonometry; see chapter 9.

EXAM HINT

You can choose which side of the identity to start from. It is usually a good idea to start from the more complicated expression and work towards the simpler one.

Worked example 3.10

Show that $e^{(2\ln x + \ln 3)} = 3x^2$.

Start from the more complicated expression on the left-hand side.	$\text{LHS} = e^{(2\ln x + \ln 3)}$
First, take the multiple inside the log: $p\ln a = \ln(a^p)$.	$= e^{\ln x^2 + \ln 3}$
Then $\ln a + \ln b = \ln(ab)$.	$= e^{\ln(3x^2)}$
Finally, apply the cancellation principle.	$= 3x^2$ $= \text{RHS}$

Exercise 3E

1. Show that the following equations are identities.

   (a) (i) $(x-y)^2+4xy=(x+y)^2$

   (ii) $x^3+y^3=(x+y)(x^2-xy+y^2)$

   (b) (i) $\log(xyz)=\log x+\log y+\log z$

   (ii) $\log_a b=\dfrac{1}{\log_b a}$

   (c) (i) $\dfrac{a^2-b^2}{a-b}=a+b$ (ii) $\dfrac{x-y}{y-x}=-1$

   (d) (i) $\sqrt[a]{x^b}=\left(\sqrt[a]{x}\right)^b$ (ii) $2^a+2^a=2^{a+1}$

Summary

- Important methods for solving **equations** include factorising and substitution.
- When sketching graphs on your calculator, you may need to use your knowledge of the shapes of common graphs to make sure you do not miss any important features, such as zeros and asymptotes.
- You can use a graphical calculator to solve equations involving unfamiliar functions by finding intersections of two graphs, one for each side of the equation.
- **Identities** are equations that are true for all values of x. We derive identities by transforming one side into the other, using known identities.

Introductory problem revisited

Solve the equation $\dfrac{1}{x^2}=\ln x$.

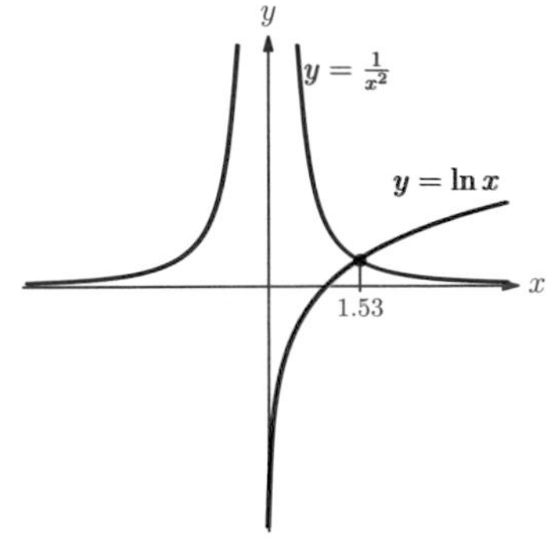

If you try to rearrange this equation to isolate x, you will find that it is impossible. It is better to plot the graphs of $y=\dfrac{1}{x^2}$ and $y=\ln x$:

There is one intersection point, and we find its x-coordinate using the calculator. The solution is $x=1.53$ (3 SF).

Mixed examination practice 3

Questions on this topic usually come as parts of longer questions. This exercise is intended to give you a feel for the level of difficulty you may encounter in the examination.

1. (a) Sketch the graphs of $y = 2^x$ and $y = 1 - x^2$ on the same axes.

(b) Hence write down the number of solutions of the equation $2^x = 1 - x^2$.

[6 marks]

2. Find the largest possible value of $y = x^2 e^{-x}$ for $x \in [0,5]$. *[4 marks]*

3. Find the exact solution of the equation $e^x \ln x = 3e^x$. *[5 marks]*

4. Find the equations of the vertical asymptotes of $y = \dfrac{1}{(ax+b)(x-c)}$. *[3 marks]*

5. (a) Sketch the graph of $\dfrac{1}{e^x - 2}$.

(b) State the exact equation of the vertical asymptote. *[6 marks]*

6. By using an appropriate substitution, find the exact solutions to the equation $x^4 + 36 = 13x^2$. *[6 marks]*

7. Solve the equation $x \ln x + 4 \ln x = 0$. *[5 marks]*

4 The theory of functions

In this chapter you will learn:

- about the concept of function
- the notation used to represent functions
- about what happens when one function acts after another function
- how to reverse the effect of a function
- about the reciprocal function, simple rational functions and their graphs.

Introductory problem
Think of any number. Add on 3. Double your answer. Take away 6. Divide by the number you first thought of. Is your answer always prime? Why?

Doubling, adding five, finding the largest prime factor, … these are all actions that can be applied to numbers, producing a result. This idea of performing operations on numbers to get another value out comes up a lot in mathematics, and its formal study leads to the concept of functions.

4A Function notation

A function is a rule where for each value you put in there is exactly one value that comes out. In this section we will see how to describe functions using mathematical expressions.

Suppose we have the rule 'add 3 to the input', and we call this rule 'f'. In function notation, this is written as:

$$f: x \mapsto x+3$$

We read this as 'the function f transforms x into $x+3$'. An alternative way of writing this is:

$$f(x) = x+3$$

Although conventionally the letters f and x are often used, they are not intrinsically special. We could replace f with any other name and x with any input value we like; whatever we call this function and its input, the function will always do the same thing to the input (e.g. add 3). The input is sometimes called the **argument** of the function and the output is called the image of the input.

Is the notation $f(x)$ just a label for a rule, or does it help to open up new techniques and new knowledge? It may surprise you to learn that the latter is actually the case. Particularly in many applications of calculus, we do not need to know exactly what the rule is, but simply that it depends on 'x', which may stand for time, or height, or some other quantity of interest in the application.

Worked example 4.1

Given a function defined by $g(x) = x^2 + x$, find and simplify the following:

(a) $g(2)$ (b) $g(y)$ (c) $g(x+1)$ (d) $g(3x)$ (e) $4g(x-1)-3$

Replace x with 2.

(a) $g(2) = 2^2 + 2 = 6$

Replace x with y.

(b) $g(y) = y^2 + y$

Replace x with $(x+1)$. Don't forget brackets!

(c) $g(x+1) = (x+1)^2 + (x+1)$
$= x^2 + 2x + 1 + x + 1$
$= x^2 + 3x + 2$

Replace x with $(3x)$. Don't forget brackets!

(d) $g(3x) = (3x)^2 + (3x)$
$= 9x^2 + 3x$

Replace x with $(x-1)$ and then multiply by 4 and subtract 3.

(e) $4g(x-1)-3 = 4((x-1)^2 + (x-1)) - 3$
$= 4(x^2 - 2x + 1 + x - 1) - 3$
$= 4(x^2 - x) - 3$
$= 4x^2 - 4x - 3$

Exercise 4A

1. If $h(x) = 3x^2 - x$, find and simplify the following.
   (a) (i) $h(3)$ (ii) $h(7)$
   (b) (i) $h(-2)$ (ii) $h(-1)$
   (c) (i) $h(z)$ (ii) $h(a)$
   (d) (i) $h(x+1)$ (ii) $h(x-2)$
   (e) (i) $\frac{1}{2}(h(x) - h(-x))$ (ii) $3h(x) + 4h(2x)$
   (f) (i) $h\left(\frac{1}{x}\right)$ (ii) $h(\sqrt{x})$

2. If $g: x \mapsto 1 + \log_{10} x$, find and simplify the following.
   (a) (i) $g(100)$ (ii) $g(1\,000\,000)$
   (b) (i) $g(0.1)$ (ii) $g(1)$
   (c) (i) $g(y)$ (ii) $g(z)$
   (d) (i) $g(10x)$ (ii) $g(100y)$
   (e) (i) $g(x) + g(x^2)$ (ii) $\frac{1}{2}\left(g(x) + g\left(\frac{1}{x}\right)\right)$

Calculations with logarithms were covered in chapter 2.

3. If $u(x)=3x+1$ and $v(x)=-\sqrt{x}$, find and simplify the following.

(a) (i) $u(2)+v(9)$ (ii) $u(1)v(4)$

(b) (i) $u(x)+v(y)$ (ii) $u(2x+1)-v(4x)$

(c) (i) $2u(4x)+3v(4x)$ (ii) $v(x^2+1)+xu(2x)$

4B Domain and range

A function is a rule that tells you what to do with the input, but, to be completely defined, it also needs to specify what type of input values are allowed.

KEY POINT 4.1

> The set of allowed input values is called the **domain** of the function. Conventionally, we write it after the rule using set notation or inequalities.

Worked example 4.2

Sketch the graph of $f(x)=x+1$ over the domain

(a) $x\in\mathbb{R}, x>1$ (b) $x\in\mathbb{Z}$

> **EXAM HINT**
> If you are instructed to sketch the graph of $f(x)$, this means the graph of $y=f(x)$.

First, sketch the graph for $x\in\mathbb{R}$ (all real numbers).

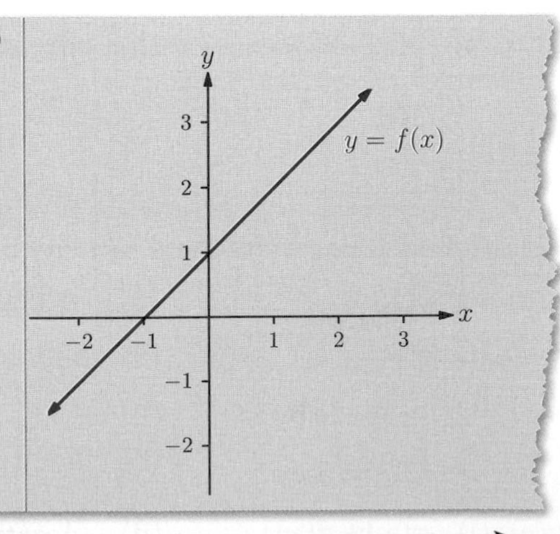

continued ...

Discard the part of the graph which is outside the given domain. Since '$x > 1$' does not include the endpoint 1, we label the point (1, 2) with an open circle.

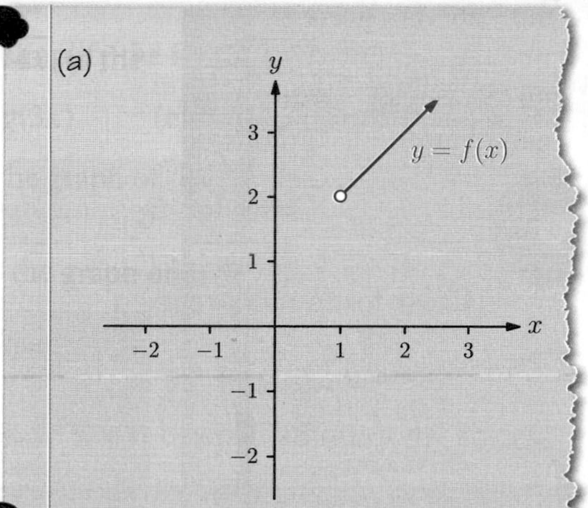

If the domain is $x \in \mathbb{Z}$, the graph exists only at whole numbers, which we label with closed circles.

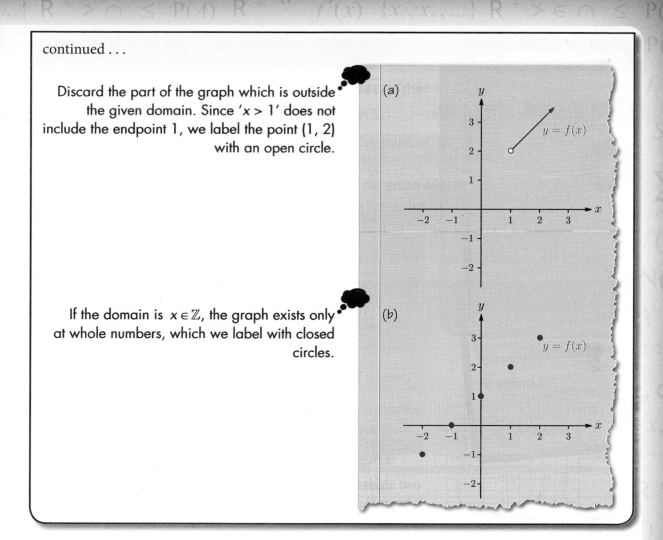

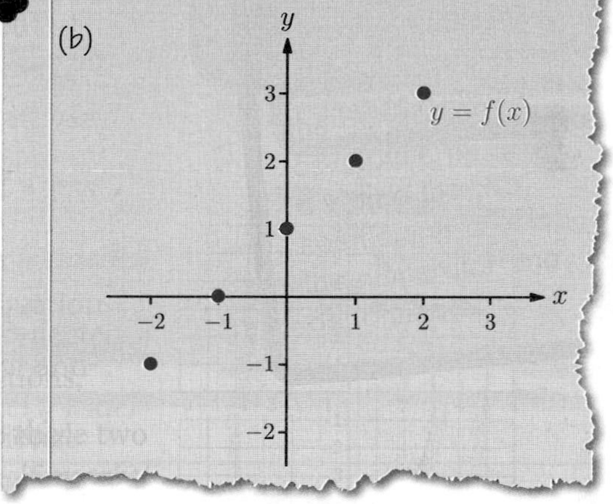

If the domain is not explicitly stated, you can assume that it consists of all real numbers. You may wonder why we would ever need to consider any other domain. One reason might be that we are modelling a physical situation where the variables can only take particular values; for example, if x represented the age of humans, it would not make sense for x to be negative or much greater than 120.

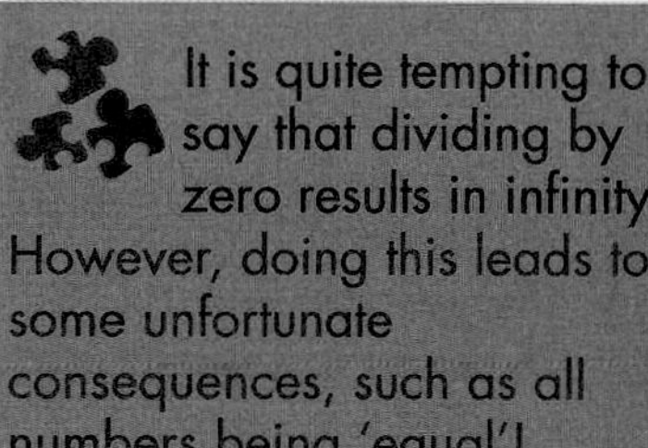

It is quite tempting to say that dividing by zero results in infinity. However, doing this leads to some unfortunate consequences, such as all numbers being 'equal'!

Another reason is that the function may involve a mathematical operation that cannot handle certain types of numbers. For example, if we want to find the largest prime factor of a number, we should only be looking at positive integers. When working with real numbers, the three most common reasons to restrict the domain are:

- you cannot divide by zero
- you cannot take the square root of a negative number
- you cannot take the logarithm of a negative number or zero.

Worked example 4.3

What is the largest possible domain of $h: x \mapsto \frac{1}{x-2} + \sqrt{x+3}$?

Check for division by zero.	There will be division by zero when $x-2=0$.
Check for square rooting of a negative number.	There will be square rooting of a negative number when $x+3<0$.
Decide what can be allowed in the function.	$x \geq -3$ and $x \neq 2$

We can also use interval notation to write domains; in the previous example we could write the answer as $x \in [-3, 2[\cup]2, \infty[$.

Once we have specified what can go into a function, it is interesting to see what values can come out of the function.

EXAM HINT

Remember that you can restrict the viewing window to the x-values in the domain.

KEY POINT 4.2

The set of all possible *outputs* of a function (y-values on the graph) is called the **range** of the function. The easiest way of finding the range is to sketch the graph (possibly using your GDC). Be aware that the range depends on the domain.

Worked example 4.4

Find the range of $f(x) = x^2 + 3$ if the domain is

(a) $x \in \mathbb{R}$ (b) $x > 2$

Sketch the graph of $y = x^2 + 3$ for $x \in \mathbb{R}$.

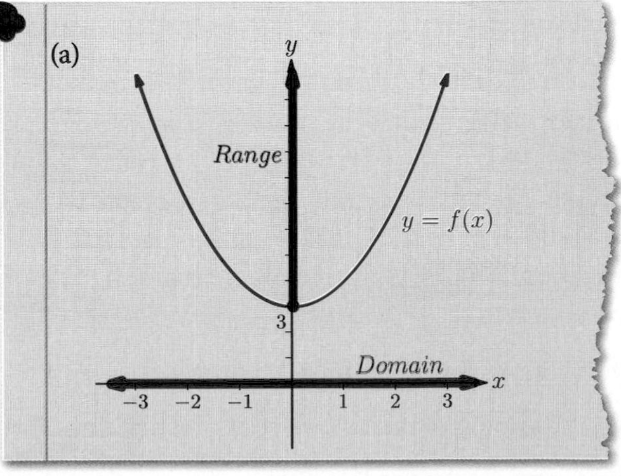

→

continued . . .

From the graph, observe which y-values can occur.

Range: $y \geq 3$

Sketch the graph of $y = x^2 + 3$ for $x > 2$.

(b)

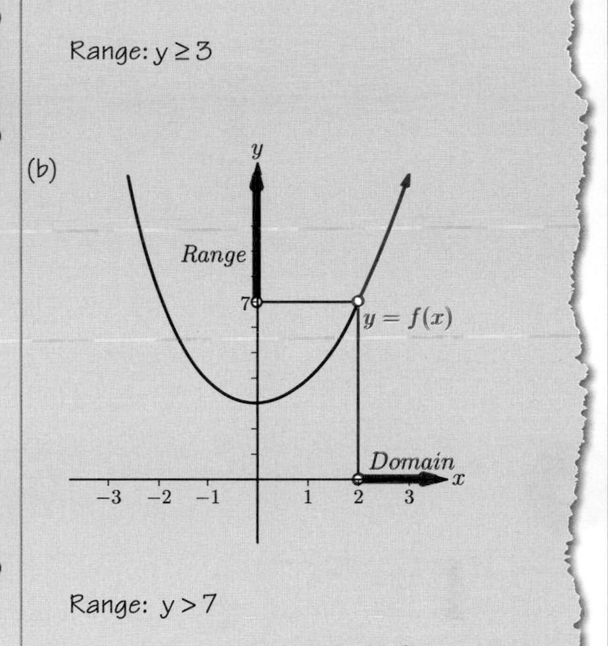

From the graph, observe which y-values can occur.

Range: $y > 7$

Exercise 4B

1. State the largest possible domain and range of the following functions:

   (a) $f(x) = 2^x$.

   (b) $f(x) = a^x$, $a > 0$.

   State the largest possible range and domain of the following functions:

   (c) $f(x) = \log_{10} x$.

   (d) $f(x) = \log_b x, b > 0$.

Exponential and logarithm functions were covered in chapter 2.

What are the largest possible domain and range of $f(x) = (-2)^x$? This function illustrates why it is important to be careful in deciding how to define a continuous function – an important concept in higher mathematics.

2. Find the largest possible domain of the following functions.

   (a) (i) $f(x) = \dfrac{1}{x+2}$ (ii) $f(x) = \dfrac{5}{x-7}$

   (b) (i) $f(x) = \dfrac{3}{(x-2)(x+4)}$ (ii) $g(x) = \dfrac{x}{x^2-9}$

   (c) (i) $r(y) = \sqrt{y^3 - 1}$ (ii) $h(x) = \sqrt{x+3}$

   (d) (i) $f(a) = \dfrac{1}{\sqrt{a-1}}$ (ii) $f(x) = \dfrac{5x}{\sqrt{2-5x}}$

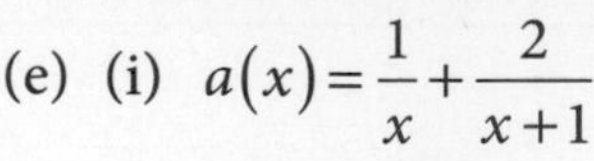

(e) (i) $a(x)=\dfrac{1}{x}+\dfrac{2}{x+1}$ (ii) $f(x)=\sqrt{x+1}+\dfrac{1}{x+2}$

(f) (i) $f(x)=\sqrt{x^2-5}$ (ii) $f(x)=4\sqrt{x^2+2x-3}$

(g) (i) $f(x)=\sqrt{x}+\dfrac{1}{x+7}-x^3+5$

(ii) $f(x)=e^x+\sqrt{2x+3}-\dfrac{1}{x^2+4}-2$

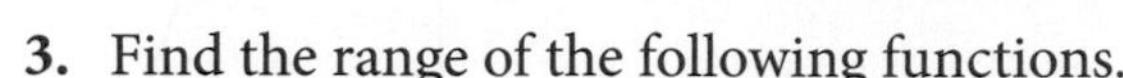

3. Find the range of the following functions.

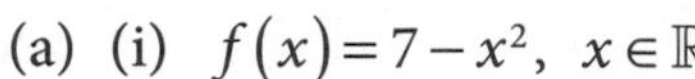

(a) (i) $f(x)=7-x^2,\ x\in\mathbb{R}$ (ii) $f(x)=x^2+3,\ x\in\mathbb{R}$

(b) (i) $g(x)=x^2+3,\ x\geq 3$ (ii) $h(x)=x+1,\ x>3,\ x\in\mathbb{Z}$

(c) (i) $f(x)=|x-1|$ (ii) $f(x)=|2x+3|$

(d) (i) $d(x)=\dfrac{1}{x},\ x\geq -1,\ x\neq 0$ (ii) $q(x)=3\sqrt{x},\ x>0$

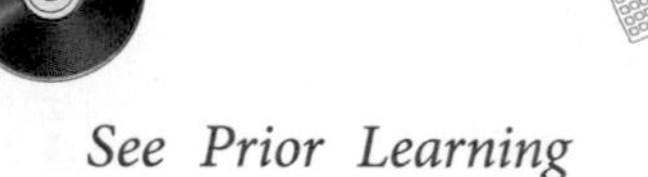

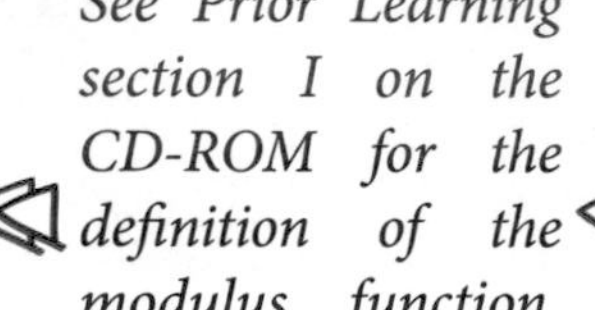

See Prior Learning section I on the CD-ROM for the definition of the modulus function, $|x|$.

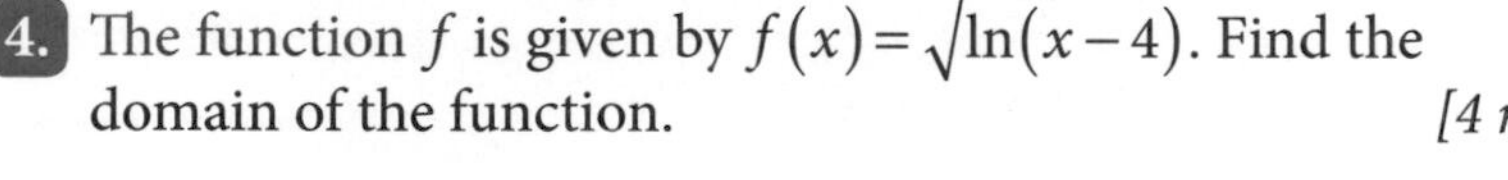

4. The function f is given by $f(x)=\sqrt{\ln(x-4)}$. Find the domain of the function. *[4 marks]*

5. Find the largest possible domain of the function

$$f(x)=\frac{4^{\sqrt{x-1}}}{x+2}-\frac{1}{x^2-5x+6}+x^2+1$$ *[5 marks]*

6. Find the largest possible domain of the function $g(x)=\ln(x^2+3x+2)$. *[5 marks]*

7. Find the largest set of values of x such that the function f given by $f(x)=\sqrt{\dfrac{8x-4}{x-12}}$ takes real values. *[5 marks]*

8. Define $f(x)=\sqrt{x-a}+\ln(b-x)$.

(a) State the domain of the function if

(i) $a<b$ (ii) $a>b$

(b) Evaluate $f(a)$. *[6 marks]*

4C Composite functions

We can apply one function to a number and then apply another function to that result. The overall rule linking the original input value with the final output value is called a **composite function**.

KEY POINT 4.3

If we first apply the function g to x and then apply the function f to the result, we write this composite function as

$$f(g(x)) \quad or \quad fg(x) \quad or \quad f \circ g(x)$$

EXAM HINT

None of these three expressions for a composite function is 'better' than the others. Use whichever one suits you, but be aware that in the exam you must be able to interpret any of them. Remember the correct order: the function nearest to x acts first!

As we shall see later, it is useful to refer to $g(x)$ as the **inner function** and $f(x)$ as the **outer function**.

For the composite function $fg(x)$ to exist, the range of $g(x)$ must lie entirely within the domain of $f(x)$, otherwise we would be trying to put values into $f(x)$ which cannot be calculated.

Worked example 4.5

If $f(x) = x^2$ and $g(x) = x - 3$, find

(a) $f \circ g(1)$ (b) $f \circ g(x)$ (c) $gf(x)$

We need to evaluate $g(1)$ and then apply f to the result.

(a) $g(1) = 1 - 3 = -2$

$f(-2) = (-2)^2 = 4$

$\therefore f(g(1)) = 4$

EXAM HINT

Notice that to work this out we did not need to find the general expression for $f \circ g(x)$

Replace the x in $f(x)$ with the expression for $g(x)$.

(b) $f(g(x)) = f(x-3) = (x-3)^2$

$= x^2 - 6x + 9$

Replace the x in $g(x)$ with the expression for $f(x)$.

(c) $g(f(x)) = g(x^2)$

$= x^2 - 3$

Notice that $f(g(x))$ and $g(f(x))$ are not the same function.

It is more difficult to recover one of the original functions from a composite function. The best way to do this is by using a substitution.

Worked example 4.6

If $f(x+1)=4x^2+x$, find $f(x)$.

Substitute y = inner function.

Let

$y=x+1$

Rearrange to make x the subject.

$x=y-1$

Replace all the x's by $y-1$.

$$f(y)=4(y-1)^2+(y-1)$$
$$=4y^2-8y+4+y-1$$
$$=4y^2-7y+3$$

We were asked to write the answer in terms of x.

$f(x)=4x^2-7x+3$

Exercise 4C

1. If $f(x)=x^2+1$ and $g(x)=3x+2$, find:

(a) (i) $g(f(0))$ (ii) $fg(1)$

(b) (i) $gg(x)$ (ii) $f\circ g(x)$

(c) (i) $gg(\sqrt{a}+1)$ (ii) $f\bullet f(y-1)$

(d) (i) $ggf(y)$ (ii) $gfg(z)$

2. Find $f(x)$ given the following conditions:

(a) (i) $f(2a)=4a^2$ (ii) $f\left(\frac{b}{3}\right)=\frac{b^3}{27}$

(b) (i) $f(x+1)=3x-2$ (ii) $f(x-2)=x^2+x$

(c) (i) $f(1-y)=5-y$ (ii) $f(y^3)=y^2$

(d) (i) $f(e^k)=\ln k$ (ii) $f(3n+2)=\ln(n+1)$

3. If $f(x)=x^2+1$ and $g(x)=3x+2$, solve $fg(x)=gf(x)$. *[4 marks]*

4. If $f(x)=3x+1$ and $g(x)=\dfrac{x}{x^2+25}$, solve $gf(x)=0$. *[5 marks]*

5. Functions g and h are defined by $g(x)=\sqrt{x}$ and $h(x)=\dfrac{2x-3}{x+1}$.

(a) Find the range of h.

(b) Solve the equation $h(x)=0$.

(c) Find the domain and range of $g \circ h$. *[6 marks]*

6. The function f is defined by $f: x \to x^3$. Find an expression for $g(x)$ in terms of x in each of the following cases:

(a) $(f \circ g)(x)=2x+3$

(b) $(g \circ f)(x)=2x+3$ *[6 marks]*

7. Functions f and g are defined by $f(x)=\sqrt{x^2-2x}$ and $g(x)=3x+4$. The composite function $f \circ g$ is *undefined* for $x \in \,]a,b[$.

(a) Find the value of a and the value of b.

(b) Find the range of $f \circ g$. *[7 marks]*

8. Define $f(x)=x-1$, $x>3$ and $g(x)=x^2$, $x \in \mathbb{R}$.

(a) Explain why $g \circ f$ exists but $f \circ g$ does not.

(b) Find the largest possible domain for g so that $f \circ g$ is defined. *[6 marks]*

9. Let f and g be two functions. Given that $(f \circ g)(x)=\dfrac{x+2}{3}$ and $g(x)=2x+5$, find $f(x-1)$. *[6 marks]*

4D Inverse functions

Functions transform an input into an output, but sometimes we need to reverse this process – that is, to find out what input produced a particular output. When it is possible to reverse the actions of a function f, we can define its **inverse function**, usually written as f^{-1}.

For example, if $f(x)=3x$, then $f^{-1}(12)$ is a number which when put into f produces the output 12; in other words, we

EXAM HINT

Make sure you do not get confused by this notation. With numbers, the superscript '−1' denotes the reciprocal, e.g. $3^{-1} = \frac{1}{3}$ and $x^{-1} = \frac{1}{x}$. With functions, f^{-1} denotes the inverse function of f.

are looking for a number x such that $f(x) = 12$. In this case, $f^{-1}(12) = 4$.

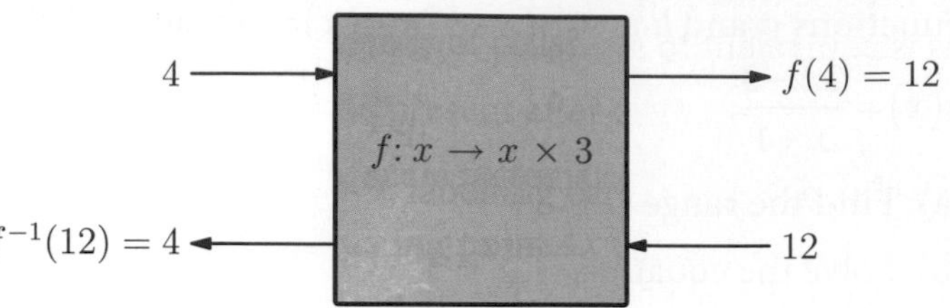

To find a formula for the inverse function, you must rearrange the formula of the original function to find the input (x) in terms of the output (y).

KEY POINT 4.4

To find the inverse function $f^{-1}(x)$ given an expression for $f(x)$:

1. Start off with $y = f(x)$.
2. Rearrange to get x (the input) in terms of y (the output).
3. This gives us $f^{-1}(y)$, but often we are asked to find $f^{-1}(x)$; we do this by replacing every occurrence of y in the expression with x.

Worked example 4.7

Find the inverse function of $f(x) = \frac{1+x}{3-x}$.

Write $y = f(x)$.

$$y = \frac{1+x}{3-x}$$

Make x the subject of the formula. Then the right-hand side expression is $f^{-1}(y)$.

$$y(3-x) = 1+x$$
$$\Leftrightarrow 3y - yx = 1+x$$
$$\Leftrightarrow 3y - 1 = x + xy$$
$$\Leftrightarrow 3y - 1 = x(1+y)$$
$$\Leftrightarrow x = \frac{3y-1}{1+y}$$
$$\therefore f^{-1}(y) = \frac{3y-1}{1+y}$$

Replace y with x to get $f^{-1}(x)$.

$$f^{-1}(x) = \frac{3x-1}{1+x}$$

Now we have learned how to find inverse functions, there are some important facts we need to know about them:

- The inverse function switches inputs and outputs; graphically this is equivalent to switching the x- and y-axes.

KEY POINT 4.5

The graph of $y = f^{-1}(x)$ is the reflection of the graph of $y = f(x)$ in the line $y = x$.

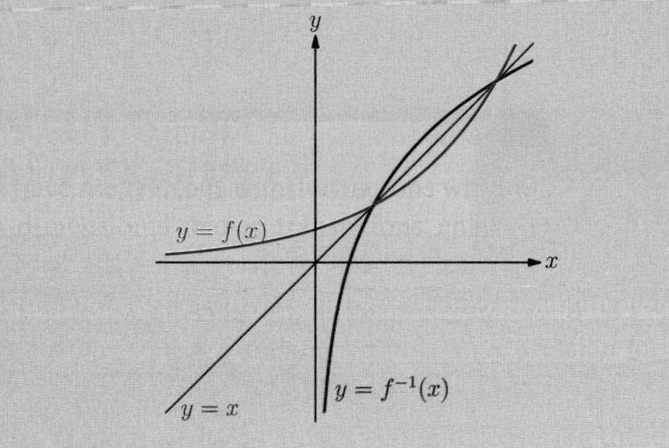

- If you apply a function and then undo it, you get back to where you started.

KEY POINT 4.6

$$f^{-1}(f(x)) = f(f^{-1}(x)) = x$$

The function $g(x) = x$, for which the output is always the same as the input, is called the **identity function**. Thus $f^{-1} \circ f$ and $f \circ f^{-1}$ are both equal to the identity function.

EXAM HINT

See Calculator Skills sheet 7 on the CD-ROM for how to sketch the graph of an inverse function on your calculator.

EXAM HINT

If you have found an algebraic expression for $f^{-1}(x)$, you can check whether it is correct by plotting both $f(x)$ and $f^{-1}(x)$ on the same axes and looking for symmetry.

Worked example 4.8

The graph of $y = h(x)$ is shown. Sketch the graphs of $y = h^{-1}(x)$ and $y = h \circ h^{-1}(x)$.

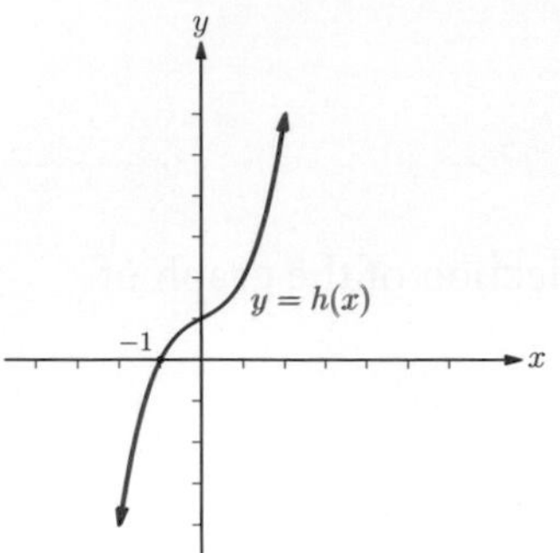

The graph of $y = h^{-1}(x)$ is obtained by reflecting the graph of $y = h(x)$ in the line $y = x$.

$h \circ h^{-1}$ is the identity function, so $y = h \circ h^{-1}(x)$ simplifies to $y = x$.

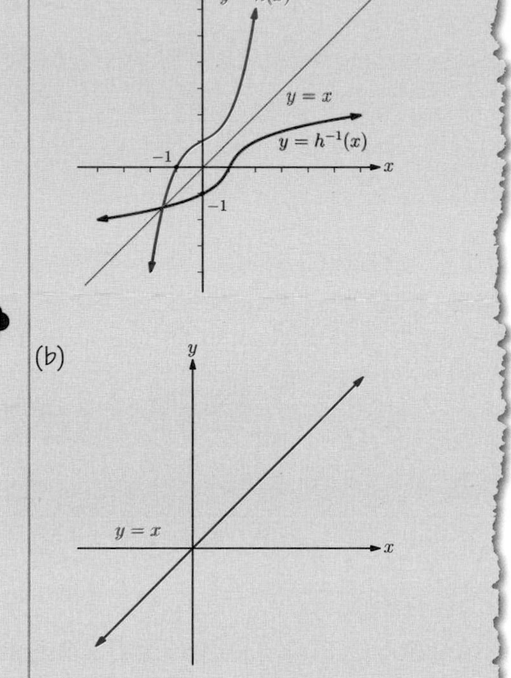

- Reflection in the line $y = x$ swaps the domain and the range of a function (because it swaps the x- and y-coordinates).

KEY POINT 4.7

> The domain of $f^{-1}(x)$ is the same as the range of $f(x)$.
>
> The range of $f^{-1}(x)$ is the same as the domain of $f(x)$.

Exercise 4D

1. Find $f^{-1}(x)$ if

(a) (i) $f(x)=3x+1$ (ii) $f(x)=7x-3$

(b) (i) $f(x)=\dfrac{2x}{3x-2},\ x\neq\dfrac{2}{3}$ (ii) $f(x)=\dfrac{x}{2x+1},\ x\neq-\dfrac{1}{2}$

(c) (i) $f(x)=\dfrac{x-a}{x-b},\ x\neq b$ (ii) $f(x)=\dfrac{ax-1}{bx-1},\ x\neq\dfrac{1}{b}$

(d) (i) $f(a)=1-a$ (ii) $f(y)=3y+2$

(e) (i) $f(x)=\sqrt{3x-2},\ x\geq\dfrac{2}{3}$ (ii) $f(x)=\sqrt{2-5x},\ x\leq\dfrac{2}{5}$

(f) (i) $f(x)=\ln(1-5x),\ x<0.2$ (ii) $f(x)=\ln(2x+2),\ x>-1$

(g) (i) $f(x)=7\mathrm{e}^{\frac{x}{2}}$ (ii) $f(x)=9\mathrm{e}^{10x}$

(h) (i) $f(x)=x^2-10x+6,\ x<5$ (ii) $f(x)=x^2+6x-1,\ x>0$

2. Sketch the inverse functions of the following functions.

(a)

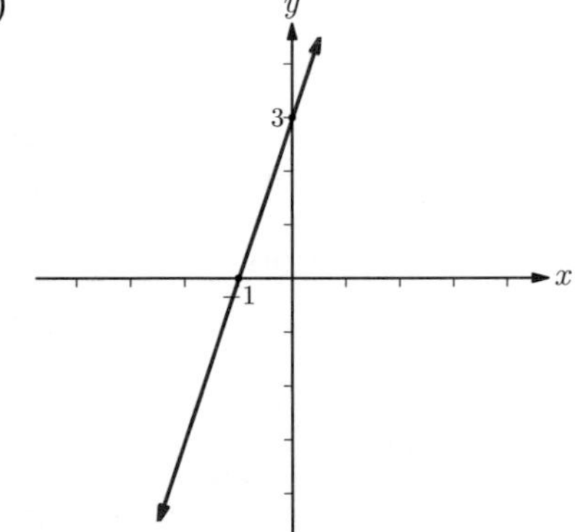

(b)

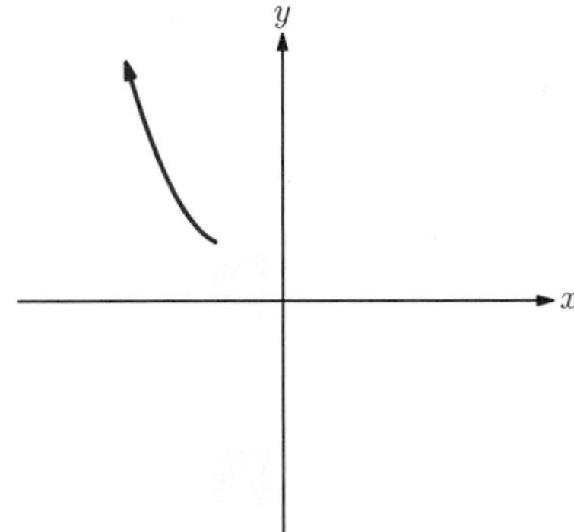

(c)

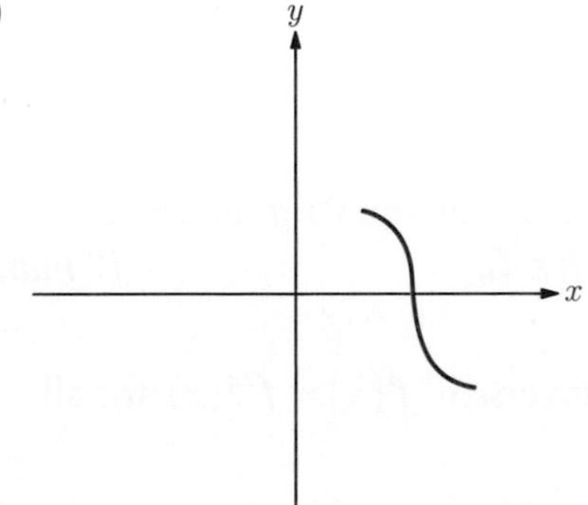

(d)

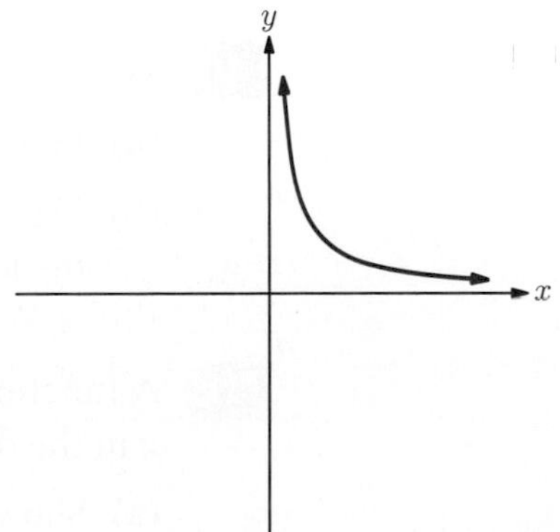

3. The following table gives selected values of the function $f(x)$.

x	-1	0	1	2	3	4
$f(x)$	-4	-1	3	0	7	2

(a) Evaluate $ff(2)$.

(b) Evaluate $f^{-1}(3)$. *[4 marks]*

4. The function f is defined by $f: x \mapsto \sqrt{3-2x},\ x \leq \frac{3}{2}$.

Evaluate $f^{-1}(7)$. *[4 marks]*

5. Given that $f(x) = 3e^{2x}$, find the inverse function $f^{-1}(x)$. *[4 marks]*

6. Given functions $f: x \mapsto 2x+3$ and $g: x \to x^3$, find the function $(f \circ g)^{-1}$. *[5 marks]*

7. The functions f and g are defined by $f: x \mapsto e^{2x}$ and $g: x \mapsto x+1$.

(a) Calculate $f^{-1}(3) \times g^{-1}(3)$.

(b) Show that $(f \circ g)^{-1}(3) = \ln\sqrt{3} - 1$. *[6 marks]*

8. Let $f(x) = \sqrt{x}$ and $g(x) = 2x$. Solve the equation $(f^{-1} \circ g)(x) = 0.25$. *[5 marks]*

9. The function f is defined for $x \leq 0$ by $f(x) = \dfrac{x^2-4}{x^2+9}$.

Find an expression for $f^{-1}(x)$. *[5 marks]*

10. Let $f(x) = \ln(x-1) + \ln 3$ for $x > 1$.

(a) Find $f^{-1}(x)$.

(b) Let $g(x) = e^x$. Find $(g \circ f)(x)$, giving your answer in the form $ax+b$ where $a, b \in \mathbb{Z}$. *[7 marks]*

11. A function is said to be *self-inverse* if $f(x) = f^{-1}(x)$ for all x in the domain.

(a) Show that $f(x) = \dfrac{1}{x}$ is a self-inverse function.

(b) Find the value of the constant k so that $g(x) = \dfrac{3x-5}{x+k}$ is a self-inverse function. *[8 marks]*

4E Rational functions

There are many situations where one quantity decreases as another increases.

For example, the amount of your phone credit decreases as the number of text messages you send increases; moreover, as the number of messages increases by a fixed number, the credit decreases by a fixed amount – this is called linear decay.

Another example is radioactive decay, where the amount of a radioactive substance halves in a fixed time period, called the half-life; in this case, as time increases by a fixed number, the amount of substance decreases by a fixed factor – this is called exponential decay.

Exponential functions were covered in chapter 2. See Prior Learning section Q on the CD-ROM for a review of linear functions.

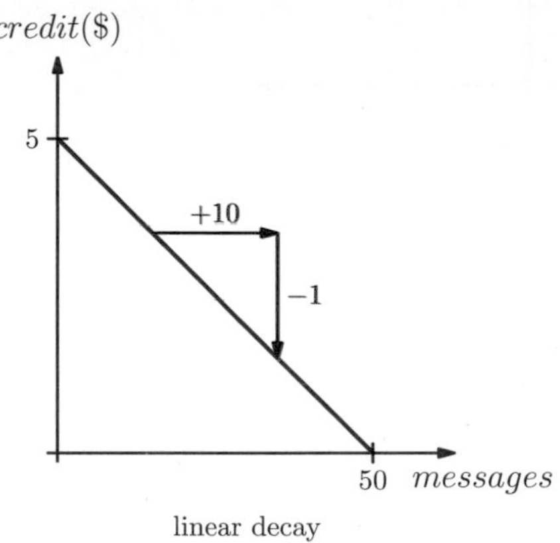

linear decay

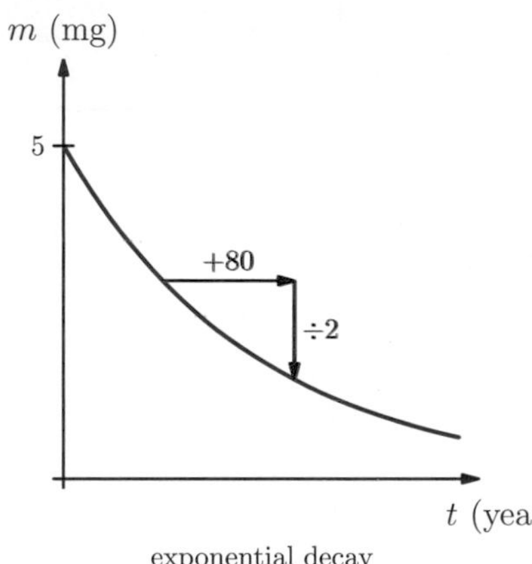

exponential decay

In this section we look at a third type of decay, called inverse proportion, where as one quantity increases by a fixed factor, another decreases by the same factor. For example, if you double your speed, the amount of time it takes to travel a given distance will halve. If the total distance travelled is 12 km, then the equation for travel time (in hours) in terms of speed (in km/h) is $t = \frac{12}{v}$. This is an example of a **reciprocal function**, which has the general form $f(x) = \frac{k}{x}$.

EXAM HINT

The reciprocal of a non-zero real number x is $\frac{1}{x}$.

For example, the reciprocal of -2 is $-\frac{1}{2}$ and the reciprocal of $\frac{2}{3}$ is $\frac{3}{2}$.

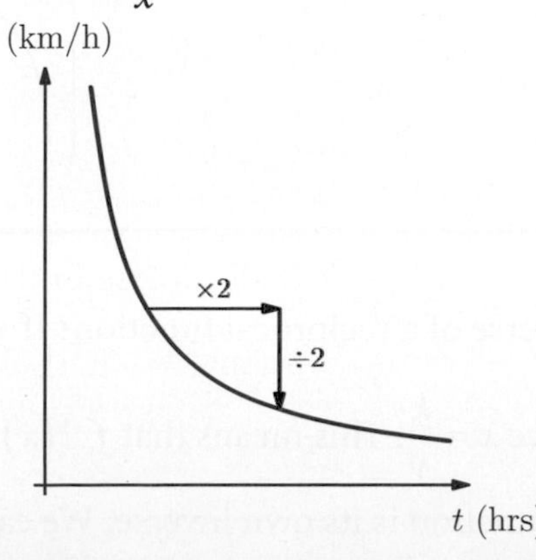

Graphs of reciprocal functions all have the same shape, called a **hyperbola**. A hyperbola is made up of two curves, with the axes as asymptotes. The function is not defined for $x = 0$ (the y-axis is a vertical asymptote), and as x gets very large (positive or negative) y approaches zero (the x-axis is a horizontal asymptote). This means that neither x nor y can equal zero. The two parts of the hyperbola can be either in the first and third **quadrants** or in the second and fourth quadrants, depending on the sign of k.

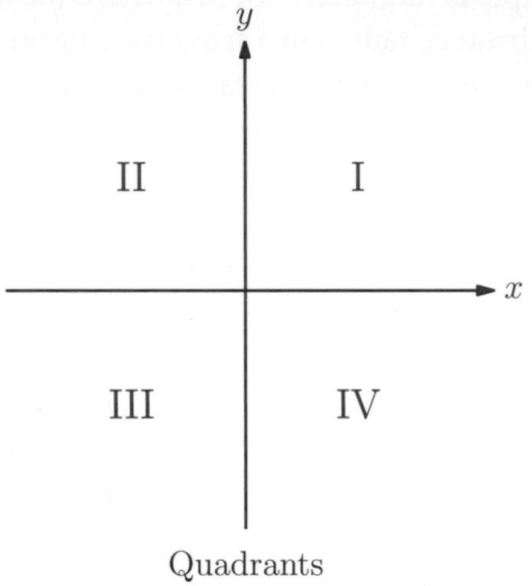

Quadrants

KEY POINT 4.8

A reciprocal function has the form $f(x) = \frac{k}{x}$.

The domain of f is $x \neq 0$ and the range is $y \neq 0$.

The graph of $f(x)$ is a hyperbola.

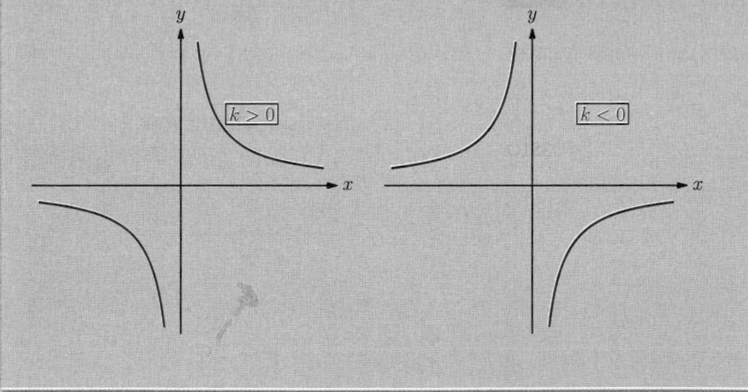

What is the inverse of a reciprocal function? If $y = \frac{k}{x}$, then $xy = k$ and hence $x = \frac{k}{y}$. This means that $f^{-1}(x) = \frac{k}{x} = f(x)$, so the reciprocal function is its own inverse. We can also see this from the graph: a hyperbola is symmetrical about the line $y = x$, so its reflection in the line is the same as itself.

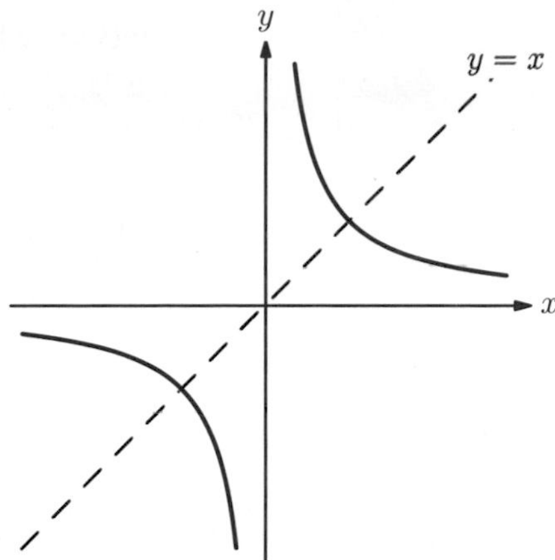

KEY POINT 4.9

The reciprocal function $f(x) = \frac{k}{x}$ is a **self-inverse function**; that is, $f^{-1}(x) = f(x)$.

Related to reciprocal functions, **rational functions** are a ratio of two polynomials: $f(x) = \frac{p(x)}{q(x)}$ can be used to model a wider variety of situations where one quantity decreases as another increases. The following example illustrates one such situation.

Worked example 4.9

A rectangular piece of card has dimensions 30 cm by 20 cm. Strips of width x cm and y cm are cut off the ends, as shown in the diagram, so that the remaining card has area 450 cm^2.

(a) Find an expression for y in terms of x in the form $y = \frac{ax - b}{cx - d}$.

(b) Sketch the graph of y against x.

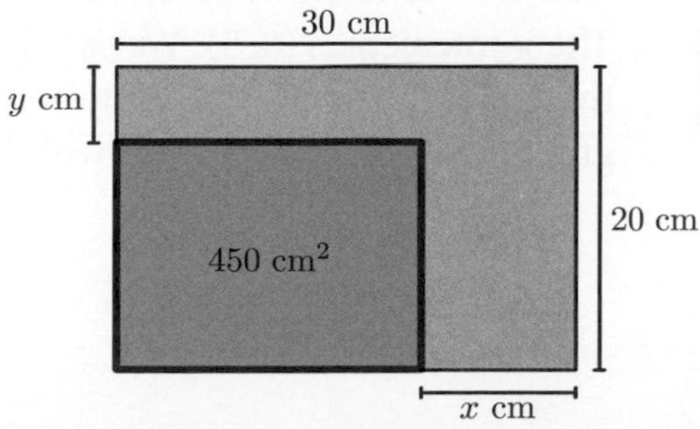

continued . . .

Write the equation for the remaining area in terms of x and y.

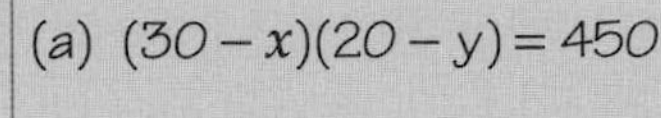

(a) $(30-x)(20-y)=450$

we want to make y the subject, so divide by $(30-x)$ (rather than expanding the brackets).

$$20-y=\frac{450}{30-x}$$

$$y=20-\frac{450}{30-x}$$

$$=\frac{20(30-x)-450}{30-x}$$

$$=\frac{150-20x}{30-x}$$

To get the expression in the required form, multiply top and bottom by -1.

$$\therefore y=\frac{20x-150}{x-30}$$

We can use a GDC to sketch the graph. Only positive values of x and y are relevant in this situation.

(b)

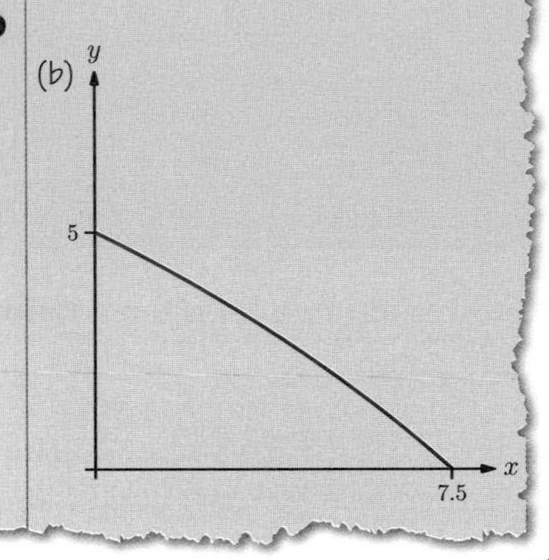

Is zero the same as 'nothing'? What happens if you say that the result of dividing by zero is infinity? What would $\frac{0}{0}$ be then?

In the above example only positive values of x and y were relevant, but let us look at the graph of $f(x)=\frac{20x-150}{x-30}$ over the whole of $\mathbb{R}$. The function is not defined at $x=30$ (as we would be dividing by zero), so there is a vertical asymptote there. The y-intercept is (0, 5). We can find the x-intercept by setting the top of the fraction equal to zero, which gives (7.5, 0). The graph looks like a hyperbola with horizontal asymptote $y=20$.

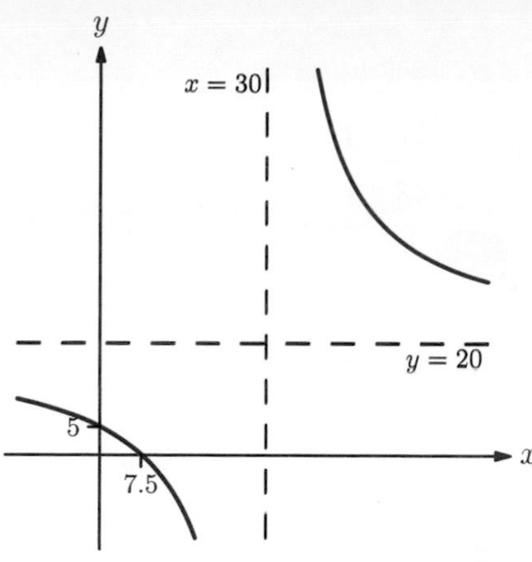

The position of the horizontal asymptote can be discovered by looking at the first equation we found for y in Worked example 4.9, which can also be written as $y = 20 + \frac{450}{x-30}$. As x gets very large (either positive or negative), $x - 30$ gets very large, so $\frac{450}{x-30}$ gets very small. Therefore the value of y gets closer and closer to 20. Another way to find the asymptote is to think about what happens as x gets very large in the equation $y = \frac{20x-150}{x-30}$: the terms containing x in the numerator and denominator become much larger than 150 and 30, so these two constant terms can be ignored, leaving $y \approx \frac{20x}{x} = 20$.

The example $f(x) = \frac{20x-150}{x-30}$ illustrates all the important properties of rational functions of the form $f(x) = \frac{ax+b}{cx+d}$.

EXAM HINT

In the examination you can just find the horizontal asymptote by dividing the two coefficients of x in the numerator and denominator.

KEY POINT 4.10

The graph of a rational function of the form $f(x) = \frac{ax+b}{cx+d}$ is a hyperbola which has

- vertical asymptote $x = -\frac{d}{c}$ (where $cx + d = 0$)
- horizontal asymptote $y = \frac{a}{c}$
- x-intercept at $x = -\frac{b}{a}$ (where $ax + b = 0$)
- y-intercept at $y = \frac{b}{d}$ (where $x = 0$)

EXAM HINT

Make sure you include all asymptotes and intercepts when sketching graphs of rational functions. The intercepts should help you determine which quadrants the graph lies in.

Knowing the position of the asymptotes tells you the domain and range of the function.

Worked example 4.10

 Find the domain and range of the function $f(x)=\dfrac{3x-4}{2x+1}$.

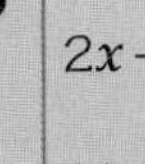

The only value excluded from the domain is where the denominator is zero.

$2x+1=0$

$\Leftrightarrow x=-\dfrac{1}{2}$

The domain is $x\in\mathbb{R},\ x\neq-\dfrac{1}{2}$

Sketching the graph can show us the range. Find the horizontal asymptote by dividing the coefficients of x.

Horizontal asymptote:

$y=\dfrac{3}{2}$

Find the intercepts to decide which quadrants the graph lies in.

Intercepts:

$x=0\Rightarrow y=-4$

$y=0\Rightarrow 3x-4=0\Rightarrow x=\dfrac{4}{3}$

Sketch the graph.

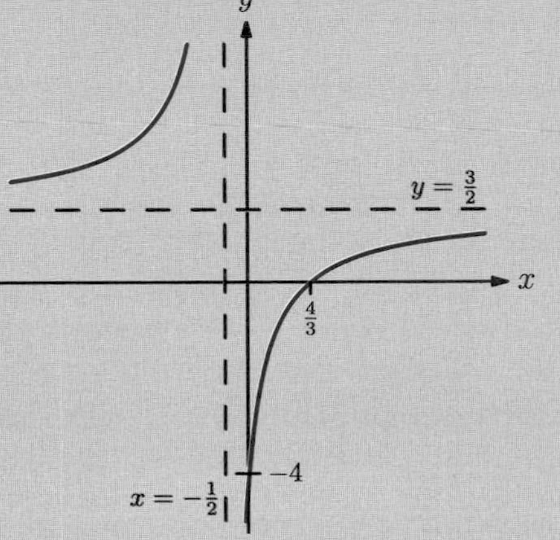

The range is $y\in\mathbb{R}, y\neq\dfrac{3}{2}$

Exercise 4E

 **1.** Find the coordinates of the axes intercepts of the following rational functions.

(a) (i) $f(x)=\dfrac{3x+1}{x+3}$ (ii) $f(x)=\dfrac{2x+5}{x+1}$

(b) (i) $f(x)=\dfrac{2x-3}{2x+7}$ (ii) $f(x)=\dfrac{3x-5}{x+2}$

2. Find the equations of the asymptotes of the following graphs.

(a) (i) $y=\frac{4x+3}{x-1}$ (ii) $y=\frac{2x+1}{x-7}$

(b) (i) $y=\frac{3x+2}{2x-1}$ (ii) $y=\frac{4x+1}{3x-5}$

(c) (i) $y=\frac{3-x}{2x+5}$ (ii) $y=\frac{2x+1}{2-3x}$

(d) (i) $y=\frac{3}{x-2}$ (ii) $y=\frac{2}{2x+1}$

3. Sketch the graphs of the following rational functions, labelling all the axes intercepts and asymptotes.

(a) (i) $y=\frac{2x+1}{x-2}$ (ii) $y=\frac{3x+1}{x-3}$

(b) (i) $y=\frac{x-3}{4-x}$ (ii) $y=\frac{5-x}{x-2}$

(c) (i) $y=\frac{2}{x+3}$ (ii) $y=\frac{1}{x-2}$

(d) (i) $y=-\frac{3}{x}$ (ii) $y=-\frac{2}{x}$

4. Find the domain, range and inverse function of the following rational functions.

(a) (i) $f(x)=\frac{3}{x}$ (ii) $f(x)=\frac{7}{x}$

(b) (i) $f(x)=\frac{2}{x-3}$ (ii) $f(x)=\frac{5}{x+1}$

(c) (i) $f(x)=\frac{2x+1}{3x-1}$ (ii) $f(x)=\frac{4x-5}{2x+1}$

(d) (i) $f(x)=\frac{5-2x}{x+2}$ (ii) $f(x)=\frac{3x-1}{4x-3}$

5. Find the equations of the asymptotes of the graph of $y=\frac{3x-1}{4-5x}$. *[3 marks]*

6. Let $f(x)=\frac{1}{x+3}$.

(a) Find the domain and range of $f(x)$.

(b) Find $f^{-1}(x)$. *[5 marks]*

7. (a) Sketch the graph of $y = -\frac{3}{x}$.

(b) Let $f(x) = -\frac{3}{x}$, $x \neq 0$. Write down an equation for $f^{-1}(x)$. *[4 marks]*

8. Sketch the graph of $y = \frac{3x-1}{x-5}$. *[5 marks]*

9. A function is defined by $f: x \mapsto \frac{ax+3}{2x-8}$, $x \neq 4$, where $a \in \mathbb{R}$.

(a) Find, in terms of a, the range of f.

(b) Find the inverse function $f^{-1}(x)$.

(c) Find the value of a such that f is a self-inverse function. *[5 marks]*

Summary

- In this chapter we introduced the concept of a **function**: a rule where for each value you put in there is exactly one value that comes out.
- To fully define a function, as well as stating the rule, we also need to specify the **domain** – the set of allowed inputs. Once we know the domain we can also find the **range** – the set of outputs that can be produced.
- A function can act upon the output of another function. The result is called a **composite function** and we write $f(g(x))$ or $fg(x)$ or $f \circ g(x)$ for $g(x)$ followed by $f(x)$.
- Reversing the effect of a function $f(x)$ is done by applying an **inverse function**, $f^{-1}(x)$. The general method of finding an inverse function is:
  1. Start with $y = f(x)$.
  2. Rearrange to get x in terms of y.
  3. Replace each occurrence of y with an x.
- Inverse functions have the following important properties:
  - the graph of an inverse function is the reflection in the line $y = x$ of the graph of the original function
  - the domain of the inverse function is the range of the original function, and the range of the inverse function is the domain of the original function
  - the inverse function and the original function cancel each other out to give the **identity function**: $f(f^{-1}(x)) = f^{-1}(f(x)) = x$

- For **rational functions** of the form $f(x)=\frac{ax+b}{cx+d}$, the graph is a **hyperbola** with the following properties:
  - vertical asymptote $x=-\frac{d}{c}$
  - horizontal asymptote $y=\frac{a}{c}$
  - x-intercept at $x=-\frac{b}{a}$
  - y-intercept at $y=\frac{b}{d}$
- A special case of a rational function is a **reciprocal function**, $f(x)=\frac{k}{x}$. This is an example of a **self-inverse** function.

Introductory problem revisited

Think of any number. Add on 3. Double your answer. Take away 6. Divide by the number you first thought of. Is your answer always prime? Why?

We can write the actions on the number as a function:

$$f(x)=\frac{2(x+3)-6}{x}$$

In most cases this expression simplifies to give 2, which is a prime number. However, we now know that a function is more than just a rule; it also needs a domain. The domain for this function must exclude zero, so the function produces a prime number for any input other than zero.

Mixed examination practice 4

Short questions

1. If $f(x)=x^2+1$, find $f(2x-1)$. *[3 marks]*

2. If $f(x)=x+2$ and $g(x)=x^2$, solve the equation $fg(x)=gf(x)$. *[5 marks]*

3. If $f(x)=e^{2x}$, evaluate $f^{-1}(3)$. *[3 marks]*

4. (a) Write down the equations of all asymptotes of the graph of $y=\dfrac{4x-3}{5-x}$.

(b) Find the inverse function of $f(x)=\dfrac{4x-3}{5-x}$. *[6 marks]*

5. Find the inverse of the following functions.

(a) $f(x)=\log_3(x+3),\ x>-3$

(b) $f(x)=3e^{x^3-1}$ *[4 marks]*

6. The diagram shows three graphs.

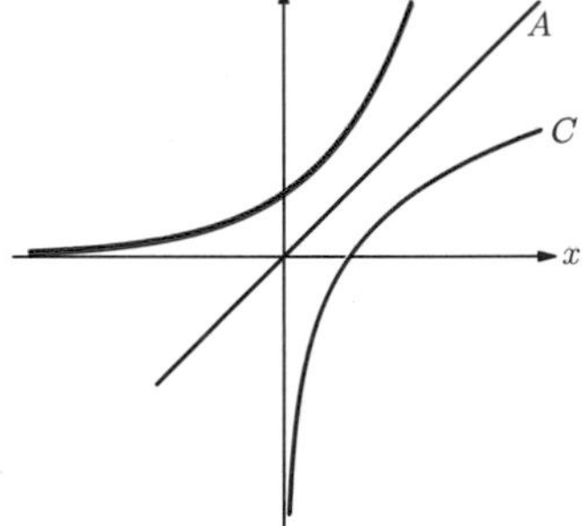

A is part of the graph of $y=x$
B is part of the graph of $y=2^x$
C is the reflection of graph *B* in line *A*

Write down:

(a) the equation of *C* in the form $y=f(x)$

(b) the coordinates of the point where *C* cuts the *x*-axis. *[5 marks]*

7. The function *f* is given by $f(x)=x^2-6x+10$ for $x\geq 3$.

(a) Write $f(x)$ in the form $(x-p)^2+q$.

(b) Find the inverse function $f^{-1}(x)$.

(c) State the domain of $f^{-1}(x)$. *[6 marks]*

8. The function $f(x)$ is defined by $f(x)=\dfrac{3-x}{x+1}, x\neq -1$.

(a) Find the range of f.

(b) Sketch the graph of $y=f(x)$.

(c) Find the inverse function of f in the form $f^{-1}(x)=\dfrac{ax+b}{cx+d}$, and state its domain and range. *[11 marks]*

9. Let $h(x)=x^2-6x+2$ for $x>3$.

(a) Write $h(x)$ in the form $(x-p)^2+q$.

(b) Hence or otherwise, find the range of $h(x)$.

(c) Find the inverse function $h^{-1}(x)$. *[7 marks]*

10. The functions $f(x)$ and $g(x)$ are given by $f(x)=\sqrt{x-2}$ and $g(x)=x^2+x$. The function $(f\circ g)(x)$ is defined for $x\in\mathbb{R}$ except on the interval $]a,b[$.

(a) Calculate the value of a and of b.

(b) Find the range of $f\circ g$. *[7 marks]*

(© IB Organization 2002)

Long questions

1. Let $f(x)=x^2+1,\ x\geq 3$ and $g(x)=5-x$.

(a) Evaluate $f(3)$.

(b) Find and simplify an expression for $gf(x)$.

(c) State the geometric relationship between the graphs of $y=f(x)$ and $y=f^{-1}(x)$.

(d) (i) Find an expression for $f^{-1}(x)$.

(ii) Find the range of $f^{-1}(x)$.

(iii) Find the domain of $f^{-1}(x)$.

(e) Solve the equation $f(x)=g(3x)$. *[10 marks]*

2. Define $f(x)=2x+1$ and $g(x)=\dfrac{x+3}{x-1},\ x\neq 1$.

(a) Find and simplify

(i) $f(7)$ (ii) the range of $f(x)$ (iii) $f(z)$

(iv) $fg(x)$ (v) $ff(x)$

(b) Explain why $gf(x)$ does not exist.

(c) (i) Find an expression for $g^{-1}(x)$.

(ii) State the geometric relationship between the graphs of $y=g(x)$ and $y=g^{-1}(x)$.

(iii) State the domain of $g^{-1}(x)$.

(iv) State the range of $g^{-1}(x)$. *[9 marks]*

3. The functions f and g are defined over the domain of all real numbers by

$$f(x) = x^2 + 4x + 9$$
$$g(x) = e^x$$

(a) Write $f(x)$ in the form $f(x) = (x+p)^2 + q$.

(b) Hence sketch the graph of $y = x^2 + 4x + 9$, labelling carefully all axis intercepts and the coordinates of the turning point.

(c) State the range of $f(x)$ and of $g(x)$.

(d) Hence or otherwise, find the range of $h(x) = e^{2x} + 4e^x + 9$. *[10 marks]*

4. You are given that $(2x+3)(4-y) = 12$ for $x, y \in \mathbb{R}$.

(a) Write y in terms of x, giving your answer in the form $y = \frac{ax+b}{cx+d}$.

(b) Sketch the graph of y against x.

Let $g(x) = 2x + k$ and $h(x) = \frac{8x}{2x+3}$.

(c) Find $h(g(x))$.

(d) Write down the equations of the asymptotes of the graph of $y = h(g(x))$.

(e) Show that when $k = -\frac{19}{2}$, $h(g(x))$ is a self-inverse function. *[17 marks]*

5 Transformations of graphs

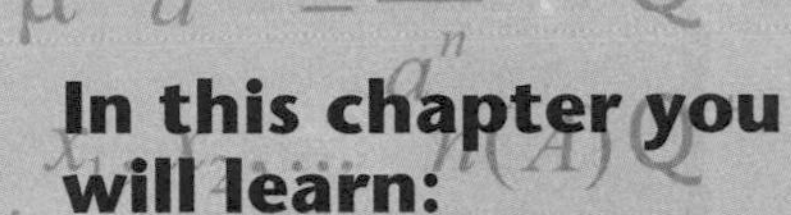

In this chapter you will learn:

- how certain changes to functions affect their graphs
- how to sketch complicated functions by considering them as transformations of simpler functions.

Introductory problem

Sketch the graph of $y = \log(x^2 - 6x + 9)$ without using a calculator.

You have met various transformations which can be applied to two-dimensional shapes: translations, enlargements, reflections and rotations. In this chapter you will learn how translations, stretches and reflections of a graph relate to changing parts of its equation.

Self-Discovery Worksheet 2 'Changing functions and their graphs' on the CD-ROM guides you in discovering these rules for yourself.

5A Translations

Compare these graphs of two functions which differ only by a constant:

$$y = x^2 - x + 1$$
$$y = x^2 - x - 2$$

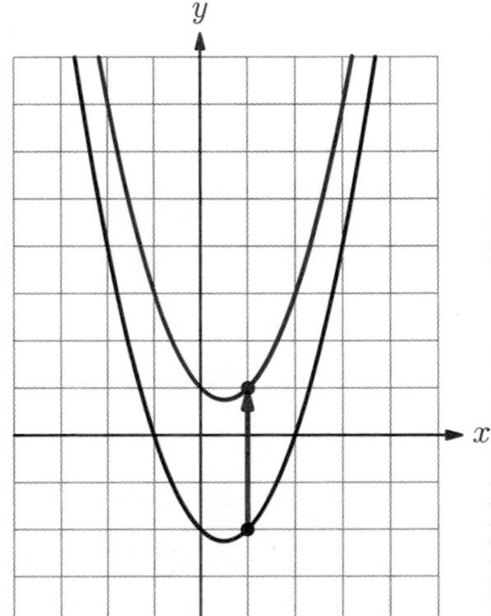

When the x-coordinates on the two graphs are the same (where $x = x$) the y-coordinates differ by 3 ($y = y + 3$). We can interpret this as meaning that at the same x-coordinate, the blue graph is three units above the red graph – it has been translated vertically.

KEY POINT 5.1

The graph of $y = f(x) + c$ is the graph of $y = f(x)$ moved up by c units. If c is negative, the graph is moved down.

Vector notation is explained in more detail in chapter 11.

It is common to use vector notation to describe translations.

A translation by c units up is described by $\begin{pmatrix} 0 \\ c \end{pmatrix}$.

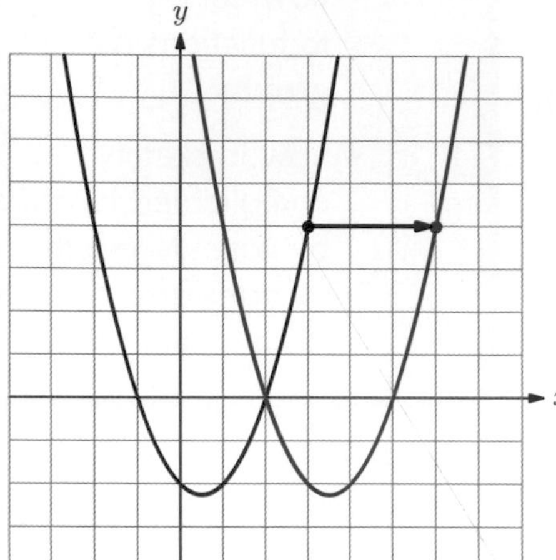

In this next case, the blue graph is obtained from the red graph upon replacing x by $x - 3$ in the function.

$$y = x^2 - x - 2$$

$$y = (x-3)^2 - (x-3) - 2$$

Here, when $x = x$ there is nothing obvious we can say about the relationship between y and y. However, note that a way of getting $y = y$ is to have $x = x - 3$ or, equivalently, $x = x + 3$. We can interpret this as meaning that the two graphs are at the same height when the blue graph is three units to the right of the red graph – it has been translated horizontally.

KEY POINT 5.2

> The graph $y = f(x+d)$ is the same as the graph of $y = f(x)$ moved *left* by d units. If d is negative, the graph is moved *right*.

In vector notation, a translation to the left by d units is written $\begin{pmatrix} -d \\ 0 \end{pmatrix}$.

Worked example 5.1

The graph of $y = x^2 + 2x$ is translated 5 units to the left. Find the equation of the resulting graph in the form $y = ax^2 + bx + c$.

Relate the transformation to function notation.	If $f(x) = x^2 + 2x$, then the new graph is $y = f(x+5)$.
Replace all occurrences of x by $(x + 5)$ in the expression for $f(x)$.	$y = (x+5)^2 + 2(x+5)$ $= x^2 + 12x + 35$

Exercise 5A

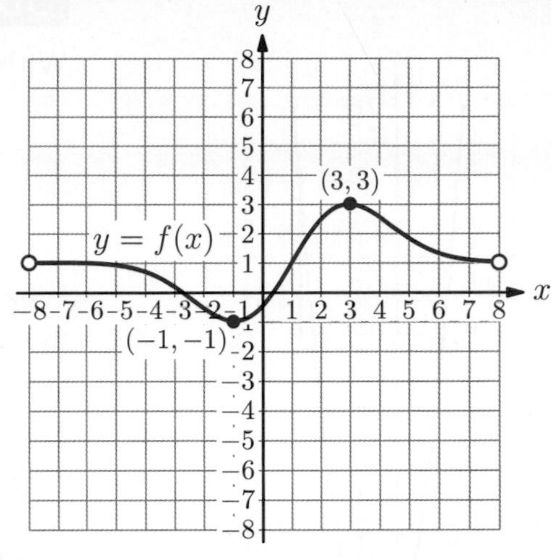

1. Given the graph of $y = f(x)$, sketch the graph of the following functions, indicating the positions of the minimum and maximum points.

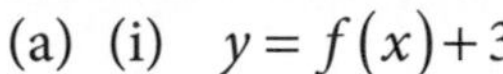

(a) (i) $y = f(x) + 3$ (ii) $y = f(x) + 5$

(b) (i) $y = f(x) - 7$ (ii) $y = f(x) - 0.5$

(c) (i) $y = f(x+2)$ (ii) $y = f(x+4)$

(d) (i) $y = f(x-1.5)$ (ii) $y = f(x-2)$

2. Find the equation of the graph after the given transformation is applied.

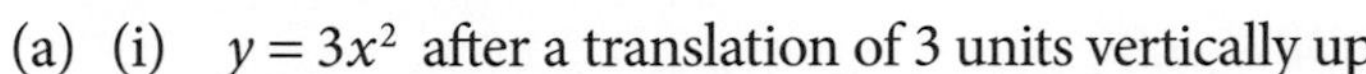

(a) (i) $y = 3x^2$ after a translation of 3 units vertically up

(ii) $y = 9x^3$ after a translation of 7 units vertically down

(b) (i) $y = 7x^3 - 3x + 6$ after a translation of 2 units down

(ii) $y = 8x^2 - 7x + 1$ after a translation of 5 units up

(c) (i) $y = 4x^2$ after a translation of 5 units to the right

(ii) $y = 7x^2$ after a translation of 3 units to the left

(d) (i) $y = 3x^3 - 5x^2 + 4$ after a translation of 4 units to the left

(ii) $y = x^3 + 6x + 2$ after a translation of 3 units to the right

3. Find the required translations.

(a) (i) Transforming the graph of $y = x^2 + 3x + 7$ to the graph of $y = x^2 + 3x + 2$

(ii) Transforming the graph of $y = x^3 - 5x$ to the graph of $y = x^3 - 5x - 4$

(b) (i) Transforming the graph of $y = x^2 + 2x + 7$ to the graph of $y = (x+1)^2 + 2(x+1) + 7$

(ii) Transforming the graph of $y = x^2 + 5x - 2$ to the graph of $y = (x+5)^2 + 5(x+5) - 2$

(c) (i) Transforming the graph of $y = e^x + x^2$ to the graph of $y = e^{x-4} + (x-4)^2$

(ii) Transforming the graph of $y = \log(3x) - \sqrt{4x}$ to the graph of $y = \log(3(x-5)) - \sqrt{4(x-5)}$

(d) (i) Transforming the graph of $y = \ln(4x)$ to the graph of $y = \ln(4x + 12)$

(ii) Transforming the graph of $y = \sqrt{2x+1}$ to the graph of $y = \sqrt{2x-3}$

5B Stretches

With these two graphs, one function is 3 times the other.

$$y = x^2 - x - 2$$

$$y = 3(x^2 - x - 2)$$

When the x-coordinates on the two graphs are the same ($x = x$), the y-coordinates of the blue graph are three times larger ($y = 3y$). We can interpret this as meaning that at the same x-coordinate, the blue graph is three times further from the x-axis than the red graph – it has been stretched *vertically*.

KEY POINT 5.3

> The graph of $y = pf(x)$, with $p > 0$, is the same as the graph of $y = f(x)$ *stretched* vertically relative to the x-axis (away from) with scale factor p. If $0 < p < 1$, then $y = f(x)$ is *compressed* vertically relative to the x-axis (towards). If $p < 0$, you have a negative scale factor $(-p)$ and it might be easier to think of the transformation as a stretch by scale factor p followed by a reflection in the x-axis.

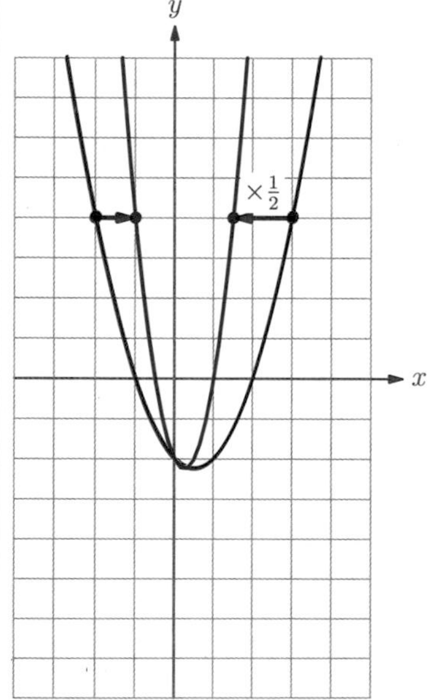

These graphs illustrate what happens when you replace x in the function by $2x$.

$$y = x^2 - x - 2$$

$$y = (2x)^2 - (2x) - 2$$

When $x = x$, there is nothing obvious we can say about the relationship between y and y. But note that a way of getting $y = y$ is to have $x = 2x$ or, equivalently, $x = \frac{x}{2}$. We can interpret this as meaning that the two graphs are at the same height when the distance from the y-axis of the blue graph is half the distance of the red graph – it has been stretched *horizontally*.

KEY POINT 5.4

The graph of $y = f(qx)$ is the same as the graph of $y = f(x)$ stretched horizontally relative to the y-axis by scale factor $\frac{1}{q}$. This can be considered a compression relative to the y-axis (towards) when $q > 0$. When $0 < q < 1$, it is considered a stretch relative to the y-axis (away from) and when $q < 0$ you have a negative scale factor $(-\frac{1}{q})$ and it is easier to think of the transformation as a stretch/compression by scale factor $\frac{1}{q}$ followed by a reflection in the y-axis.

Although we have used the terms 'stretched' and 'compressed', both transformations are generally referred to as 'stretches'.

Worked example 5.2

Describe a transformation which transforms the graph of $y = \ln x - 1$ to the graph of $y = \ln x^4 - 4$.

Try to relate the two equations using function notation.

Let $f(x) = \ln x - 1$.
Then

None of the transformations we know involves raising x to a power, so first think of a different way to write $\ln x^4$.

$$\ln x^4 - 4 = 4\ln x - 4$$
$$= 4(\ln x - 1)$$
$$= 4f(x)$$

Relate the function notation to the transformation.

It is a vertical stretch with scale factor 4.

Exercise 5B

1. Given the graph of $y = f(x)$, sketch the graph of the following functions, indicating the positions of the minimum and maximum points.

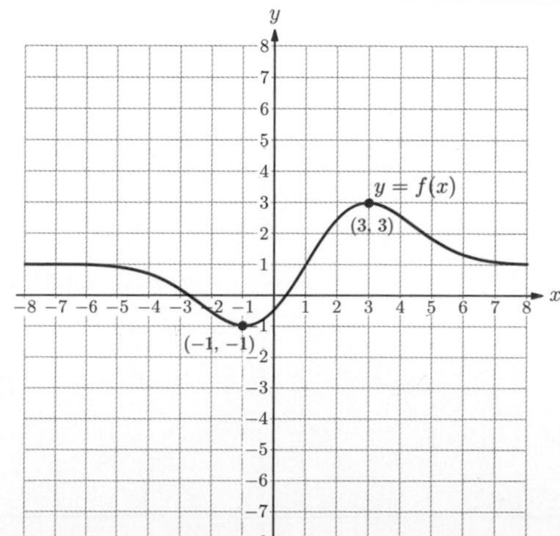

(a) (i) $y = 3f(x)$ (ii) $y = 5f(x)$

(b) (i) $y = \frac{f(x)}{4}$ (ii) $y = \frac{f(x)}{2}$

(c) (i) $y = f(2x)$ (ii) $y = f(6x)$

(d) (i) $y = f\left(\frac{2x}{3}\right)$ (ii) $y = f\left(\frac{5x}{6}\right)$

2. Find the equation of the graph after the given transformation is applied.

(a) (i) $y = 3x^2$ after a vertical stretch 7 relative to the x-axis

(ii) $y = 9x^3$ after a vertical stretch 2 relative to the x-axis

(b) (i) $y = 7x^3 - 3x + 6$ after a vertical stretch factor $\frac{1}{3}$ relative to the x-axis

(ii) $y = 8x^2 - 7x + 1$ after a vertical stretch factor $\frac{4}{5}$ relative to the x-axis

(c) (i) $y = 4x^2$ after a horizontal stretch factor 2 relative to the y-axis

(ii) $y = 7x^2$ after a horizontal stretch factor 5 relative to the y-axis

(d) (i) $y = 3x^3 - 5x^2 + 4$ after a horizontal stretch factor $\frac{1}{2}$ relative to the y-axis

(ii) $y = x^3 + 6x + 2$ after a horizontal stretch factor $\frac{2}{3}$ relative to the y-axis

3. Describe the following stretches.

(a) (i) Transforming the graph of $y = x^2 + 3x + 7$ to the graph of $y = 4x^2 + 12x + 28$

(ii) Transforming the graph of $y = x^3 - 5x$ to the graph of $y = 6x^3 - 30x$

(b) (i) Transforming the graph of $y = x^2 + 2x + 7$ to the graph of $y = (3x)^2 + 2(3x) + 7$

(ii) Transforming the graph of $y = x^2 + 5x - 2$ to the graph of $y = (4x)^2 + 5(4x) - 2$

(c) (i) Transforming the graph of $y = e^x + x^2$ to the graph of $y = e^{\frac{x}{2}} + \left(\frac{x}{2}\right)^2$

(ii) Transforming the graph of $y = \log(3x) - \sqrt{4x}$ to the graph of $y = \log\left(\frac{3x}{5}\right) - \sqrt{\frac{4x}{5}}$

(d) (i) Transforming the graph of $y = \ln(4x)$ to the graph of $y = \ln(12x)$

(ii) Transforming the graph of $y = \sqrt{2x+1}$ to the graph of $y = \sqrt{x+1}$

5C Reflections

Compare these two graphs and their equations:

$$y = x^2 - x - 2$$

$$y = -(x^2 - x - 2)$$

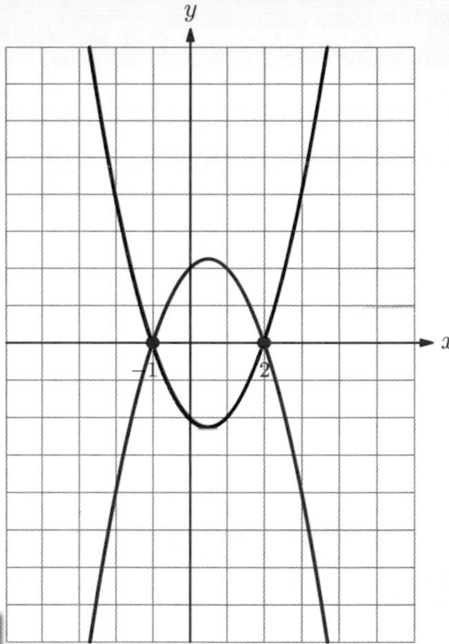

When the x-coordinates on the two graphs are the same ($x = x$), the y-coordinates are negatives of each other ($y = -y$). We can interpret this as meaning that at the same x-coordinate, the blue graph is the same vertical distance from the x-axis as the red graph but on the opposite side of the axis – it has been reflected vertically.

KEY POINT 5.5

> The graph of $y = -f(x)$ is the same as the graph of $y = f(x)$ reflected in the x-axis.

Next, see what happens when we replace x by $-x$ in the equations:

$$y = x^2 - x - 2$$

$$y = (-x)^2 - (-x) - 2$$

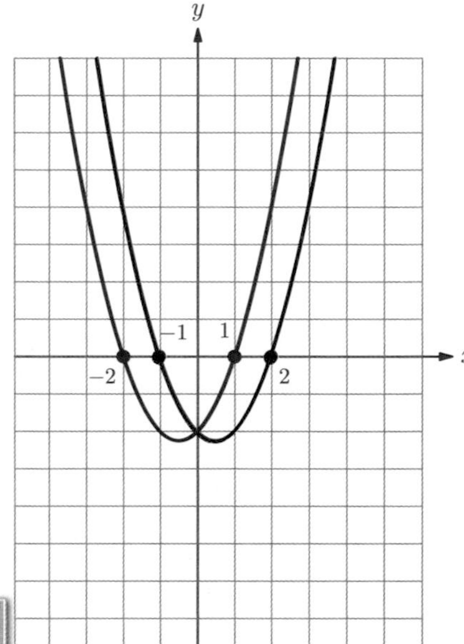

When $x = x$, there is nothing obvious we can say about the relationship between y and y. But note that for $x = -x$ we have $y = y$. This means that the heights of the two graphs are the same when the blue graph is at the same position relative to the y-axis as the red graph, but on the opposite side of the y-axis – it has been reflected horizontally.

KEY POINT 5.6

> The graph of $y = f(-x)$ is the same as the graph of $y = f(x)$ reflected in the y-axis.

Worked example 5.3

The graph of $y = f(x)$ has a single maximum point with coordinates $(4,-3)$. Find the coordinates of the maximum point on the graph of $y = f(-x)$.

Relate the function notation to an appropriate transformation.

The transformation taking $y = f(x)$ to $y = f(-x)$ is reflection in the y-axis.

Reflection in the y-axis leaves y-coordinates unchanged but switches the sign of x-coordinates.

The maximum point is $(-4,-3)$.

Exercise 5C

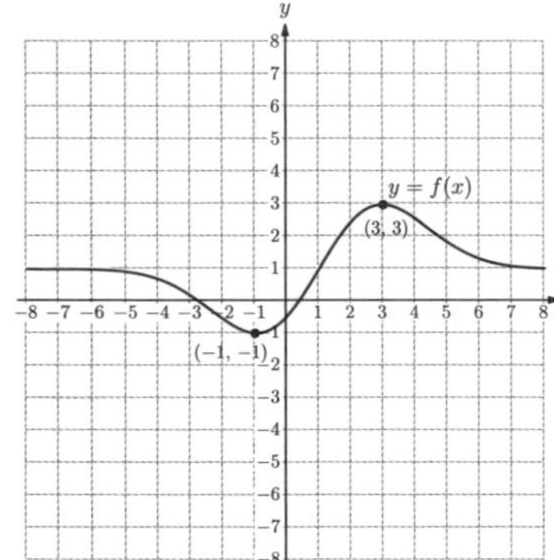

1. Given the graph of $y = f(x)$, sketch the graph of the following functions, indicating the positions of the minimum and maximum points.
   (a) $y = -f(x)$
   (b) $y = f(-x)$

2. Find the equation of the graph after the given transformation is applied.
   (a) (i) $y = 3x^2$ after reflection in the x-axis
   (ii) $y = 9x^3$ after reflection in the x-axis
   (b) (i) $y = 7x^3 - 3x + 6$ after reflection in the x-axis
   (ii) $y = 8x^2 - 7x + 1$ after reflection in the x-axis
   (c) (i) $y = 4x^2$ after reflection in the y-axis
   (ii) $y = 7x^3$ after reflection in the y-axis
   (d) (i) $y = 3x^3 - 5x^2 + 4$ after reflection in the y-axis
   (ii) $y = x^3 + 6x + 2$ after reflection in the y-axis

3. Describe the following transformations
   (a) (i) Transforming the graph of $y = x^2 + 3x + 7$ to the graph of $y = -x^2 - 3x - 7$
   (ii) Transforming the graph of $y = x^3 - 5x$ to the graph of $y = 5x - x^3$
   (b) (i) Transforming the graph of $y = x^2 + 2x + 7$ to the graph of $y = x^2 - 2x + 7$
   (ii) Transforming the graph of $y = x^2 - 5x - 2$ to the graph of $y = x^2 + 5x - 2$

(c) (i) Transforming the graph of $y = e^x + x^2$ to the graph of $y = e^{-x} + x^2$

(ii) Transforming the graph of $y = \log(3x) - \sqrt{4x}$ to the graph of $y = \sqrt{4x} - \log(3x)$

(d) (i) Transforming the graph of $y = \ln(4x)$ to the graph of $y = \ln(-4x)$

(ii) Transforming the graph of $y = \sqrt{2x - 1}$ to the graph of $y = \sqrt{-1 - 2x}$

5D Consecutive transformations

In this section we look at what happens when we apply two transformations in succession.

If the point (1, 3) is translated two units up and then reflected in the x-axis, there have been two vertical transformations, and the new point is (1, –5).

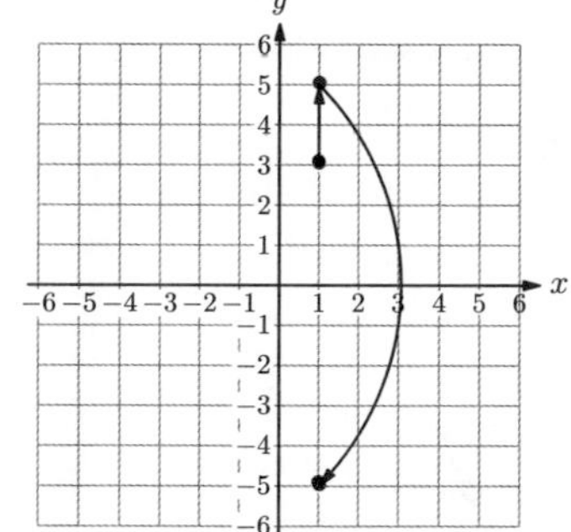

If (1, 3) is first reflected in the x-axis and then translated two units up, there have been two vertical transformations, and the new point is (1, –1).

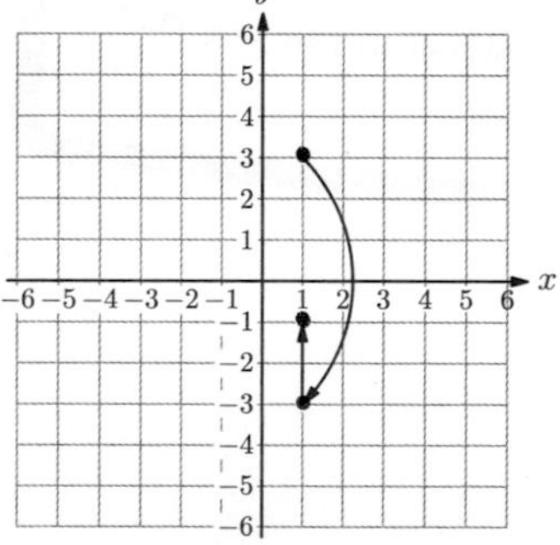

However, if the two transformations were a translation by two units up and a reflection in the y-axis, there has been one vertical transformation and one horizontal transformation, and the new point will be (–1, 5) regardless of the order in which the transformations were applied.

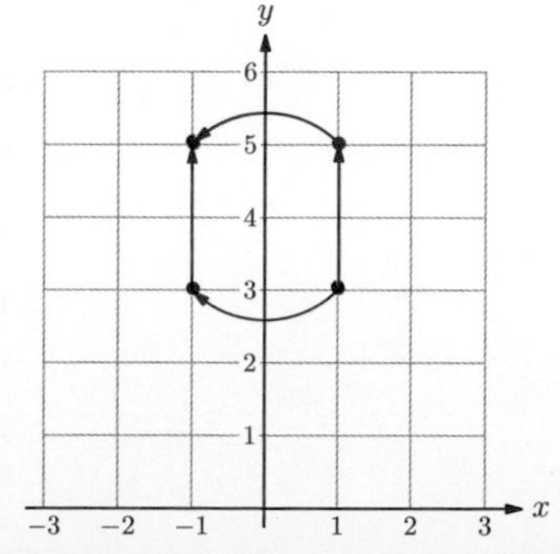

In advanced mathematics, algebra involves much more than using letters to represent numbers. Unknowns can be transformations and many other things besides numbers. As you can see in this section, the rules for transformations are different from the rules for numbers, but there are certain similarities too. The study of this more general form of algebra is called group theory, and it has many applications, ranging from particle physics to painting polyhedra.

EXAM HINT

You may find it helpful to remember that when resolving vertical transformations we follow the normal order of operations, while horizontal transformations are resolved in the opposite order.

KEY POINT 5.7

> When two vertical transformations or two horizontal transformations are combined, the order in which they are applied affects the outcome.
>
> When one vertical and one horizontal transformation are combined, the outcome does not depend on the order.

There is a very important rule to remember when resolving horizontal or vertical transformations:

- vertical transformations follow the 'normal' order of operations as applied to arithmetic
- horizontal transformations are resolved in the opposite order to the 'normal' order of operations.

This is demonstrated below:

First, let us consider how we could combine two vertical transformations to transform the graph of $y = f(x)$ into the graph of

$$y = pf(x) + c$$

We can achieve this by first multiplying $f(x)$ by p and then adding on c, so this process is composed of a stretch (and/or reflection if $p < 0$) followed by a translation.

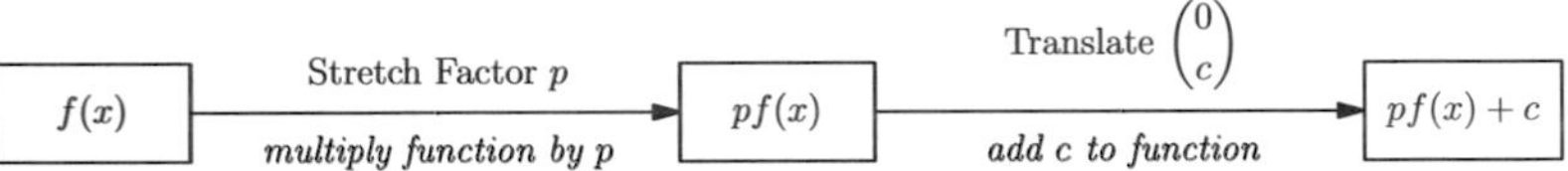

This follows the order of operations as you would expect.

Next, think about how we could combine two horizontal transformations to transform the graph of $y = f(x)$ into the graph of

$$y = f(qx + d)$$

We can achieve this by first replacing x with $x + d$ and then replacing all occurrences of x by qx, so this process consists of a translation followed by a stretch (and/or reflection if $q < 0$).

$f(x)$ → Translate $\binom{-d}{0}$ (Replace x with $x + d$) → $f(x+d)$ → Stretch Factor q (Replace x with qx) → $f(qx+d)$

Following the normal order of operations, you would expect to resolve 'qx' before '$+d$' but you resolve the transformation in the opposite order.

The first question in Exercise 5D asks you what happens if you apply these transformations in the reverse order.

Worked example 5.4

Given the graph of $y = f(x)$, sketch the corresponding graph of $y = 3 - 2f(2x+1)$.

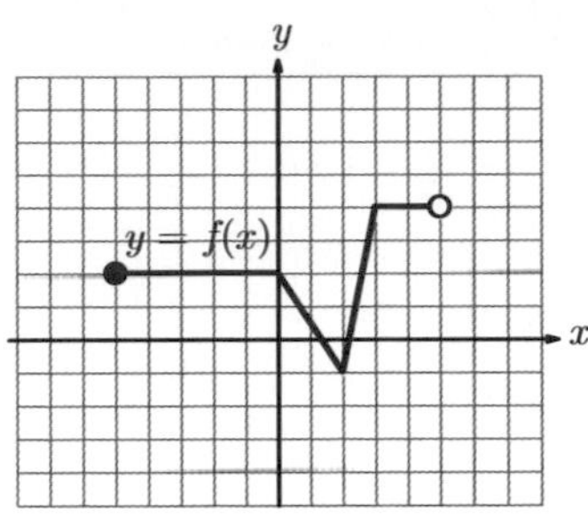

Break down the changes to the function into components.

$(2x + 1)$ is two horizontal transformations (changes x); $3 - 2f(2x + 1)$ is two vertical transformations (changes y)

Changing x: add 1, then multiply x by 2

Changing y: multiply by -2, then add 3

Relate each component to a transformation of the graph.

Replace x with $x+1$; change $y = f(x)$ to $y = f(x+1)$.

Horizontal translation by $\begin{pmatrix} -1 \\ 0 \end{pmatrix}$

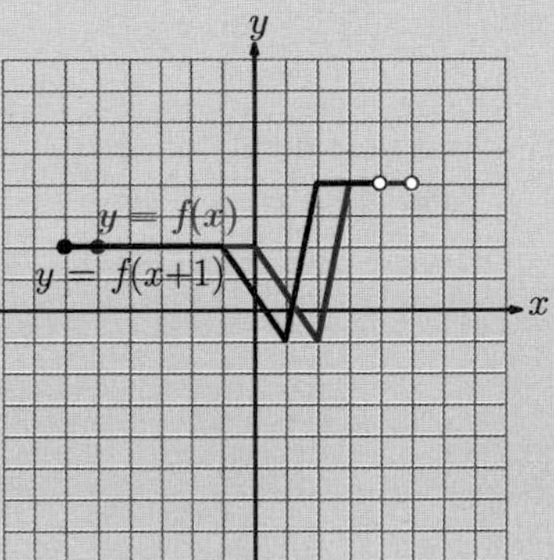

Replace x with $2x$; change $y = f(x+1)$ to $y = f(2x+1)$.

Horizontal stretch with scale factor $\frac{1}{2}$

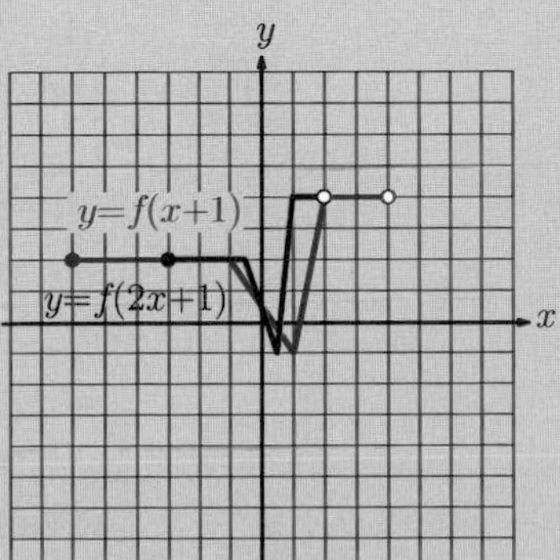

continued . . .

Multiply RHS by −2;
change $y = f(2x+1)$ to $y = -2f(2x+1)$.

Reflection in the x-axis and vertical stretch with scale factor 2

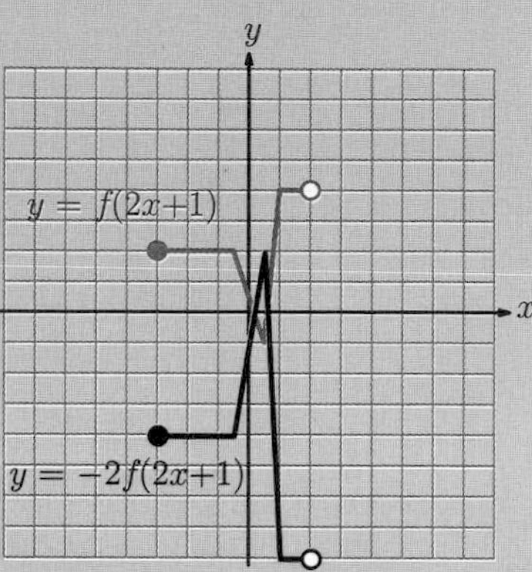

Add 3 to RHS;
change $y = -2f(2x+1)$ to $y = 3 - 2f(2x+1)$.

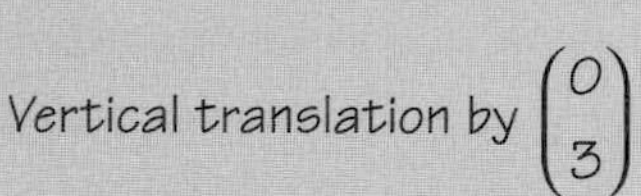

Vertical translation by $\begin{pmatrix}0\\3\end{pmatrix}$

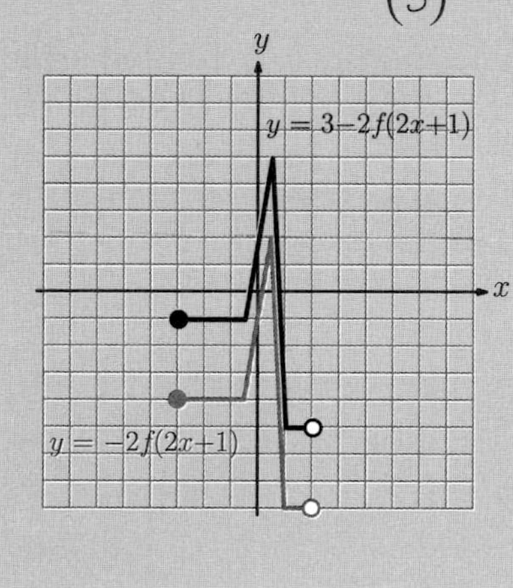

Exercise 5D

1. (a) The graph of $y = f(x)$ is transformed by applying first a vertical translation by c units up and then a vertical stretch with factor p relative to the x-axis. What is the equation of the resulting graph?

(b) The graph of $y = f(x)$ is transformed by applying first a horizontal stretch with factor q relative to the y-axis, then a horizontal translation by d units to the left. What is the equation of the resulting graph?

2. The graphs of $y = f(x)$ and $y = g(x)$ are given.
Sketch the graphs of the following.

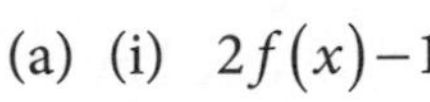

(a) (i) $2f(x)-1$ (ii) $\frac{1}{2}g(x)+3$

(b) (i) $4-f(x)$ (ii) $2-2g(x)$

(c) (i) $3(f(x)-2)$ (ii) $\frac{1-g(x)}{2}$

(d) (i) $f\left(\frac{x}{2}-1\right)$ (ii) $g(2x+3)$

(e) (i) $f\left(\frac{4-x}{5}\right)$ (ii) $g\left(\frac{x-3}{2}\right)$

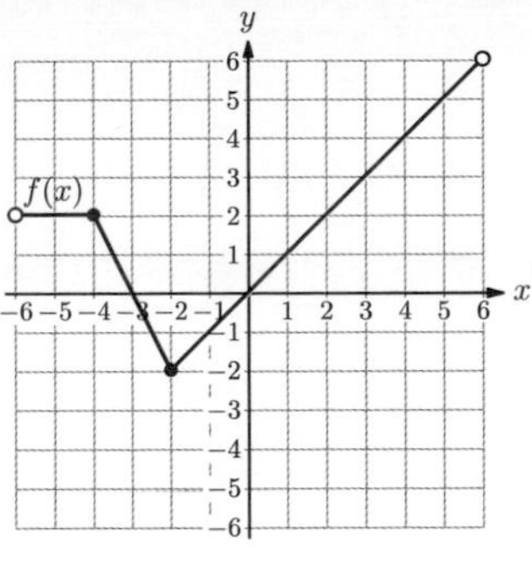

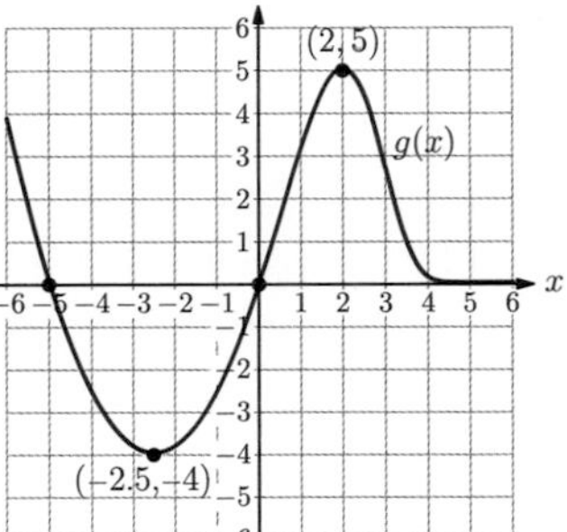

3. If $f(x) = x^2$, express each of the following functions as $af(x)+b$ and hence describe the transformation(s) mapping $f(x)$ to the given function.

(a) (i) $k(x) = 2x^2 - 6$ (ii) $k(x) = 5x^2 + 4$

(b) (i) $h(x) = 5 - 3x^2$ (ii) $h(x) = 4 - 8x^2$

4. If $f(x) = 2x^2 - 4$, write down the function $g(x)$ which gives the graph of $f(x)$ after:

(a) (i) translation $\begin{pmatrix} 0 \\ 2 \end{pmatrix}$, followed by a vertical stretch of scale factor 3

(ii) translation $\begin{pmatrix} 0 \\ 6 \end{pmatrix}$, followed by a vertical stretch of scale factor $\frac{1}{2}$

(b) (i) vertical stretch of scale factor $\frac{1}{2}$, followed by a translation $\begin{pmatrix} 0 \\ 6 \end{pmatrix}$

(ii) vertical stretch of scale factor $\frac{7}{2}$, followed by a translation $\begin{pmatrix} 0 \\ 10 \end{pmatrix}$

(c) (i) reflection through the horizontal axis

(ii) reflection through the horizontal axis followed by a translation $\begin{pmatrix} 0 \\ 2 \end{pmatrix}$

(d) (i) reflection through the horizontal axis and vertical stretch of scale factor $\frac{1}{2}$, followed by a translation $\begin{pmatrix} 0 \\ 3 \end{pmatrix}$

(ii) reflection through the horizontal axis followed by a translation $\begin{pmatrix} 0 \\ -6 \end{pmatrix}$ followed by a vertical stretch, scale factor $\frac{3}{2}$

5. If $f(x)=x^2$, express each of the following functions as $f(ax+b)$ and hence describe the transformation(s) mapping $f(x)$ to the given function.

(a) (i) $g(x)=x^2+2x+1$ (ii) $g(x)=x^2-6x+9$

(b) (i) $h(x)=4x^2$ (ii) $h(x)=\frac{x^2}{9}$

(c) (i) $k(x)=4x^2+8x+4$ (ii) $k(x)=9x^2-6x+1$

6. If $f(x)=2x^2-4$, write down the function $g(x)$ which gives the graph of $f(x)$ after:

(a) (i) translation $\begin{pmatrix} 1 \\ 0 \end{pmatrix}$ followed by a horizontal stretch of scale factor $\frac{1}{4}$

(ii) translation $\begin{pmatrix} -2 \\ 0 \end{pmatrix}$, followed by a horizontal stretch of scale factor $\frac{1}{2}$

(b) (i) horizontal stretch of scale factor $\frac{1}{2}$, followed by a translation $\begin{pmatrix} -4 \\ 0 \end{pmatrix}$

(ii) horizontal stretch of scale factor $\frac{2}{3}$, followed by a translation $\begin{pmatrix} 1 \\ 0 \end{pmatrix}$

(c) (i) translation $\begin{pmatrix} -3 \\ 0 \end{pmatrix}$ followed by a reflection through the vertical axis

(ii) reflection through the vertical axis followed by a translation $\begin{pmatrix} -3 \\ 0 \end{pmatrix}$

7. For each of the following functions $f(x)$ and $g(x)$, express $g(x)$ in the form a: $f(x+b)+c$ for some values a, b and c, and hence describe a sequence of horizontal and vertical transformations which map $f(x)$ to $g(x)$.

(a) (i) $f(x)=x^2,\ g(x)=2x^2+4x$

(ii) $f(x)=x^2,\ g(x)=3x^2-24x+8$

(b) (i) $f(x)=x^2+3,\ g(x)=x^2-6x+8$

(ii) $f(x)=x^2-2,\ g(x)=2+8x-4x^2$

8. If $f(x)=2^x+x$, give in simplest terms the formula for $h(x)$, which is obtained from transforming $f(x)$ by the following sequence of transformations:

- vertical stretch, scale factor 8 relative to $y=0$
- translation by $\begin{pmatrix}1\\4\end{pmatrix}$
- horizontal stretch, scale factor $\frac{1}{2}$ relative to $x=0$ *[6 marks]*

9. Sketch the following graphs. In each case, indicate clearly the positions of the vertical asymptote and the x-intercept.

(a) $y=\ln x$

(b) $y=3\ln(x+2)$

(c) $y=\ln(2x-1)$ *[6 marks]*

10. (a) The graph of the function $f(x)=ax+b$ is transformed by the following sequence:

- translation by $\begin{pmatrix}1\\2\end{pmatrix}$
- reflection in $y=0$
- horizontal stretch, scale factor $\frac{1}{3}$ relative to $x=0$

The resultant function is $g(x)=4-15x$. Find a and b.

(b) The graph of the function $f(x) = ax^2 + bx + c$ is transformed by the following sequence:

- reflection in $x = 0$
- translation by $\begin{pmatrix} -1 \\ 3 \end{pmatrix}$
- horizontal stretch, scale factor 2 relative to $y = 0$

The resultant function is $g(x) = 4x^2 + ax - 6$. Find a, b and c. *[10 marks]*

Summary

- Here are the most important transformations that you need to know:

Transformation of $y = f(x)$	Transformation of the graph
$y = f(x) + c$	Translation $\begin{pmatrix} 0 \\ c \end{pmatrix}$
$y = f(x + d)$	Translation $\begin{pmatrix} -d \\ 0 \end{pmatrix}$
$y = pf(x)$	Vertical stretch, scale factor p: when $p > 0$ stretches away from the x-axis; when $0 < p < 1$ stretches towards x-axis; when $p < 0$ stretch by factor p then reflect in x-axis.
$y = f(qx)$	Horizontal stretch, scale factor $\frac{1}{q}$: when $q > 0$ stretches towards the y-axis; when $0 < q < 1$ stretches away from the y-axis; when $q < 0$ stretch by $-\frac{1}{q}$ then reflect in the y-axis.
$y = -f(x)$	Reflection in the x-axis.
$y = f(-x)$	Reflection in the y-axis.

- When combining two or more transformations,
  - when two horizontal transformations, or two vertical transformations, are combined, the order in which they are applied will change the outcome
  - when one horizontal and one vertical transformation are combined, the outcome will be the same regardless of the order in which the transformations were applied.

Introductory problem revisited

Sketch the graph of $y = \log(x^2 - 6x + 9)$ without using a calculator.

First, simplify the equation algebraically:

$$\begin{aligned} y &= \log(x^2 - 6x + 9) \\ &= \log(x-3)^2 \\ &= 2\log(x-3) \end{aligned}$$

We can relate this to a graph we know:

$$y = f(x) = \log x$$

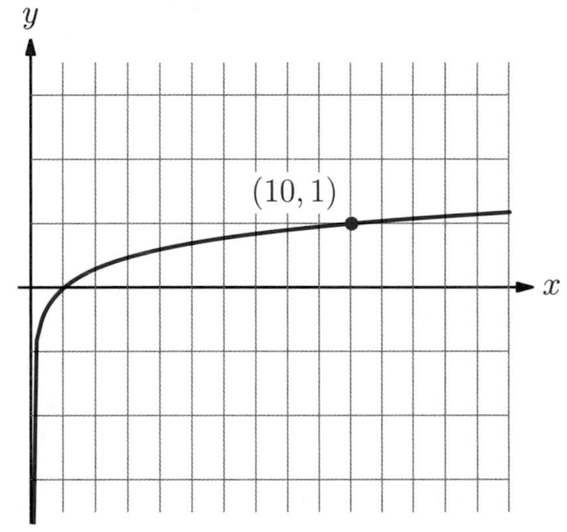

The required graph is $y = 2f(x-3)$, which is obtained from the graph of $y = f(x)$ by applying a vertical stretch with scale factor 2 and a translation $\begin{pmatrix} 3 \\ 0 \end{pmatrix}$.

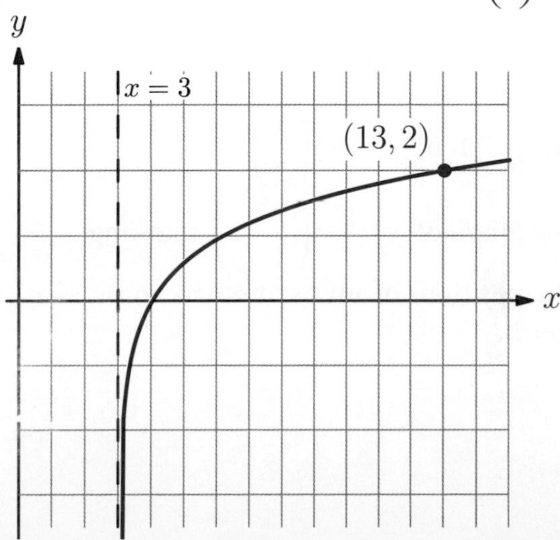

Mixed examination practice 5

Short questions

1. The graph of $y = f(x)$ is shown.

Sketch on separate diagrams the graphs of

(a) $y = 3f(x-2)$

(b) $f\left(\frac{x}{3}\right) - 2$

Indicate clearly the positions of any x-intercepts and asymptotes. *[6 marks]*

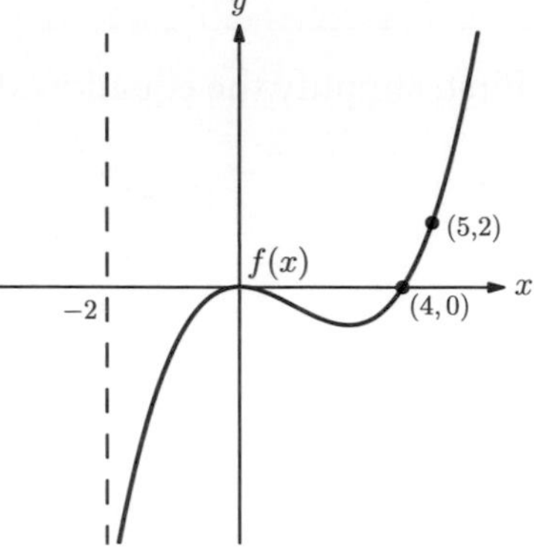

2. The graph of $y = x^3 - 1$ is transformed by applying a translation with vector $\begin{pmatrix} 2 \\ 0 \end{pmatrix}$ followed by a vertical stretch with scale factor 2. Find the equation of the resulting graph in the form $y = ax^3 + bx^2 + cx + d$. *[4 marks]*

3. The graph of $y = f(x)$ is shown.

(a) Sketch the graph of $y = f(x-1) + 2$.

(b) State the coordinates of the minimum points on $y = f(x-1) + 2$. *[5 marks]*

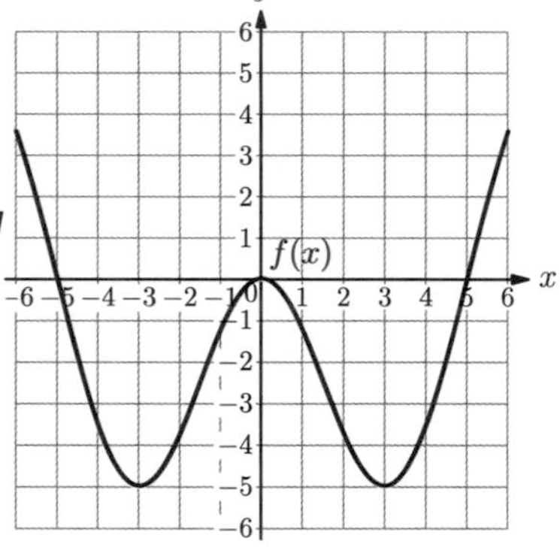

4. Find two transformations whose composition transforms the graph of $y = (x-1)^2$ to the graph of $y = 3(x+2)^2$. *[4 marks]*

5. (a) Describe two transformations whose composition transforms the graph of $y = f(x)$ to the graph of $y = 3f\left(\frac{x}{2}\right)$.

(b) Sketch the graph of $y = 3\ln\left(\frac{x}{2}\right)$.

(c) Sketch the graph of $y = 3\ln\left(\frac{x}{2} + 1\right)$, marking clearly the positions of any asymptotes and x-intercepts. *[7 marks]*

6. The diagram on the right shows a part of the graph of $y = f(x)$.

Sketch the graph of $y = f(3x - 2)$. *[4 marks]*

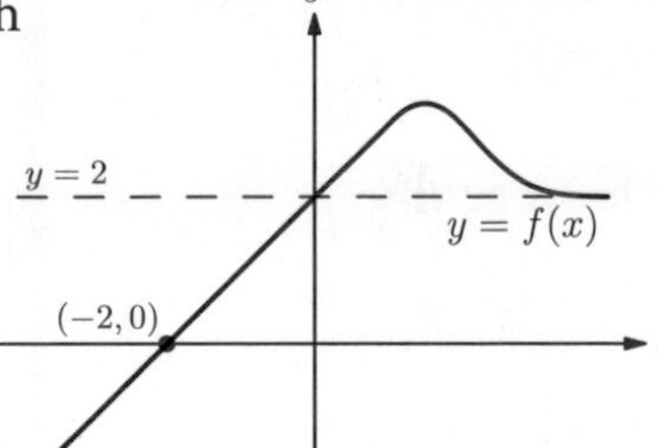

Long questions

1. **(a)** Describe two transformations which transform the graph of $y = x^2$ to the graph of $y = 3x^2 - 12x + 12$.

(b) Describe two transformations which transform the graph of $y = x^2 + 6x - 1$ to the graph of $y = x^2$.

(c) Hence describe a sequence of transformations which transform the graph of $y = x^2 + 6x - 1$ to the graph of $y = 3x^2 - 12x + 12$. *[10 marks]*

2. **(a)** Describe a transformation which transforms the graph of $y = f(x)$ to the graph of $y = f(x + 2)$.

(b) Sketch on the same diagram the graphs of

(i) $y = \ln(x + 2)$ (ii) $y = \ln(x^2 + 4x + 4)$

Mark clearly any asymptotes and x-intercepts on your sketches.

(c) The graph of the function $y = g(x)$ has been translated and then reflected in the x-axis to produce the graph of $y = h(x)$.

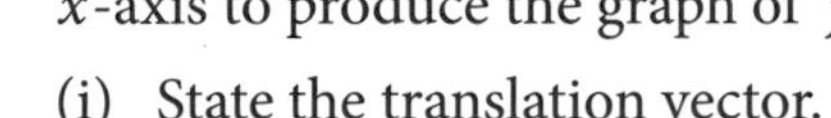

(i) State the translation vector.

(ii) If $g(x) = x^3 - 2x + 5$, find constants a, b, c, d such that $h(x) = ax^3 + bx^2 + cx + d$. *[12 marks]*

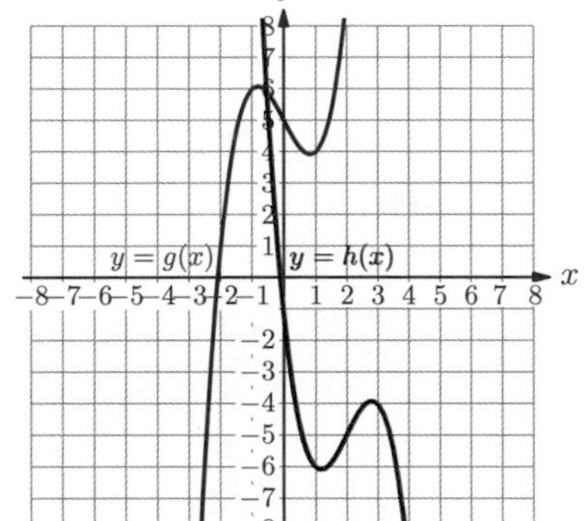

3. Let $f(x) = \dfrac{3x - 5}{x - 2}$.

(a) Write down the equation of the horizontal asymptote of the graph of $y = f(x)$.

(b) Find the value of constants p and q such that $f(x) = p + \dfrac{q}{x - 2}$.

(c) Hence describe a single transformation which transforms the graph of $y = \dfrac{1}{x}$ to the graph of $y = f(x)$.

(d) Find an expression for $f^{-1}(x)$ and state its domain.

(e) Describe the transformation which transforms the graph of $y = f(x)$ to the graph of $y = f^{-1}(x)$. *[11 marks]*

6 Sequences and series

In this chapter you will learn:

- how to describe sequences mathematically
- a way to describe sums of sequences
- about sequences with a constant difference between terms
- about finite sums of sequences with a constant difference between terms
- about sequences with a constant ratio between terms
- about finite sums of sequences with a constant ratio between terms
- about infinite sums of sequences with a constant ratio between terms
- how to apply sequences to real-life problems.

Introductory problem

A mortgage of $100 000 has a fixed rate of 5% compound interest. It needs to be paid off in 25 years by fixed annual instalments. Interest is debited at the end of each year, just before the payment is made. How much should be paid each year?

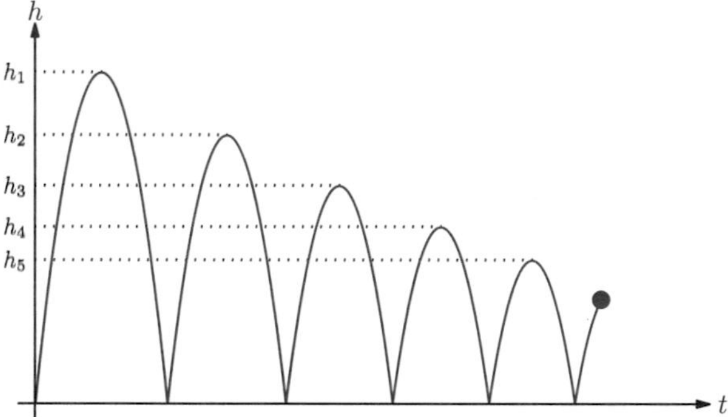

If you drop a ball, it will bounce a little lower each time it hits the ground. The heights that the ball reaches after each bounce form a sequence. Although the study of sequences may seem to be just about abstract number patterns, it actually has a remarkable number of applications in the real world – from calculating mortgages to estimating harvests on farms.

6A General sequences

A **sequence** is a list of numbers in a specified order. Examples include:

1, 3, 5, 7, 9, 11, ...

1, 4, 9, 16, 25, ...

100, 50, 25, 12.5, ...

The numbers in a sequence are called **terms**; so in the first sequence above, the first term is 1, the second term is 3, and so on. To study sequences, it is useful to have some special notation to describe them.

EXAM HINT

While u_n is a conventional symbol for a sequence, there is nothing special about the letters used. We could also call a sequence t_x or a_h. The important thing to remember is that the subscript (n) tells us where the term is in the sequence, and the letter together with the subscript (u_n) represents the value of that term.

KEY POINT 6.1

u_n denotes the value of the nth term of a sequence.

In the first sequence above, we would write $u_1 = 1$, $u_2 = 3$, $u_5 = 9$, etc.

We are mainly interested in sequences with well-defined mathematical rules. There are two types of rules for defining a sequence: recursive rules and deductive rules.

A **recursive rule** links new terms to previous terms in the sequence. For example, if each term is three times the previous term, we would write $u_{n+1} = 3u_n$.

Worked example 6.1

A sequence is defined by $u_{n+1} = u_n + u_{n-1}$ with $u_1 = 1$ and $u_2 = 1$. What is the fifth term of this sequence?

The sequence is defined by a recursive rule, so we have to work our way up to u_5. We are given u_1 and u_2. To find u_3 set $n = 2$ in the inductive formula.

$$u_3 = u_2 + u_1$$
$$= 1 + 1$$
$$= 2$$

To find u_4 set $n = 3$.

$$u_4 = u_3 + u_2$$
$$= 2 + 1$$
$$= 3$$

To find u_5 set $n = 4$.

$$u_5 = u_4 + u_3$$
$$= 3 + 2$$
$$= 5$$

You may recognise the sequence in Worked example 6.1 as the famous 'Fibonacci sequence', based on a model Leonardo Fibonacci proposed for rabbit populations. This sequence has arisen in many applications, from the arrangement of seeds in pine cones to a proof of the infinity of prime numbers. There is also a beautiful link to a special number called the 'golden ratio', $\frac{1+\sqrt{5}}{2}$.

A **deductive rule** links the value of the term to where it is in the sequence. For example, if each term is the square of its position in the sequence, we would write $u_n = n^2$.

EXAM HINT

There are several alternative names for deductive and recursive rules. A recursive rule may also be referred to as a 'term-to-term rule', 'recurrence relation' or 'inductive rule'. A deductive rule may also be called a 'position-to-term rule', '*n*th term rule' or simply 'formula'.

Worked example 6.2

A sequence is defined by $u_n = 2n-1$.

(a) Find the fourth term of this sequence.

(b) Find and simplify an expression for $u_{n+1} - u_n$.

With a deductive rule, we can jump straight to the fourth term by setting $n = 4$ in the formula.

(a) $u_4 = 2\times 4-1$
$= 7$

To get u_{n+1}, put $n + 1$ in place of n in the formula.

(b) $u_{n+1} = 2(n+1)-1$

$u_{n+1} - u_n = (2(n+1)-1)-(2n-1)$
$= 2n+2-1-2n+1$
$= 2$

(You might be intersted to know that the answer to part (b) is the difference between each term in the sequence.)

Exercise 6A

1. Write out the first five terms of the following inductively defined sequences.

(a) (i) $u_{n+1} = u_n + 5,\ u_1 = 3.1$ (ii) $u_{n+1} = u_n - 3.8,\ u_1 = 10$

(b) (i) $u_{n+1} = 3u_n + 1,\ u_1 = 0$ (ii) $u_{n+1} = 9u_n - 10,\ u_1 = 1$

(c) (i) $u_{n+2} = u_{n+1} \times u_n,\ u_1 = 2, u_2 = 3$

(ii) $u_{n+2} = u_{n+1} \div u_n,\ u_1 = 2, u_2 = 1$

(d) (i) $u_{n+2} = u_n + 5,\ u_1 = 3, u_2 = 4$

(ii) $u_{n+2} = 2u_n + 1,\ u_1 = -3, u_2 = 3$

(e) (i) $u_{n+1} = u_n + 4,\ u_4 = 12$ (ii) $u_{n+1} = u_n - 2,\ u_6 = 3$

2. Write out the first five terms of the following deductively defined sequences.

(a) (i) $u_n = 3n + 2$ (ii) $u_n = 1.5n - 6$

(b) (i) $u_n = n^3 - 1$ (ii) $u_n = 5n^2$

(c) (i) $u_n = 3^n$ (ii) $u_n = 8 \times (0.5)^n$

(d) (i) $u_n = n^n$ (ii) $u_n = \sin(90n°)$

3. Give a possible inductive definition for each of the following sequences.

(a) (i) $7, 10, 13, 16, \ldots$ (ii) $1, 0.2, -0.6, -1.4, \ldots$

(b) (i) $3, 6, 12, 24, \ldots$ (ii) $12, 18, 27, 40.5, \ldots$

(c) (i) $1, 3, 6, 10, \ldots$ (ii) $1, 2, 6, 24, \ldots$

4. Give a deductive definition for each of the following sequences.

(a) (i) $2, 4, 6, 8, \ldots$ (ii) $1, 3, 5, 7, \ldots$

(b) (i) $2, 4, 8, 16, \ldots$ (ii) $5, 25, 125, 625, \ldots$

(c) (i) $1, 4, 9, 16, \ldots$ (ii) $1, 8, 27, 64, \ldots$

(d) (i) $\frac{1}{2}, \frac{2}{3}, \frac{3}{4}, \frac{4}{5}, \ldots$ (ii) $\frac{1}{2}, \frac{3}{4}, \frac{5}{8}, \frac{7}{16}, \ldots$

In science we may state an observed pattern as a law if there is no contradictory evidence, but this is not the case in mathematics. For instance, given the first four terms of a sequence, we cannot be sure that the sequence will continue on for ever with the same pattern. Nevertheless, a principle in philosophy called 'Occam's Razor' suggests that the simplest answer is often the right one.

5. The sequence u_n is defined by $u_n = n2^n$.

(a) Write down u_1.

(b) Find and simplify an expression for $\frac{u_{n+1}}{u_n}$. *[4 marks]*

6. A sequence $\{u_n\}$ is defined by $u_0 = 1$, $u_1 = 2$, $u_{n+1} = 3u_n - 2u_{n-1}$ where $n \in \mathbb{Z}$.

(a) Find u_2, u_3 and u_4.

(b) (i) Using the results in part (a), suggest an expression for u_n in terms of n.

(ii) Verify that your answer to part (b)(i) satisfies the equation $u_{n+1} = 2(3u_n - 2u_{n-1})$. *[6 marks]*

6B General series and sigma notation

If 10% interest is paid on money in a bank account each year, the amounts paid form a sequence. While it is good to know how much interest is paid each year, you may be even more interested in knowing how much interest will be paid in total over a certain number of years. This is an example of a situation where we may want to add up the terms of a sequence. The sum of a sequence up to a certain point is called a **series**. We often use the symbol S_n to denote the sum of the first n terms of a sequence.

Worked example 6.3

The sum of consecutive odd numbers, starting from 1, forms a series. Let S_n denote the sum of the first n terms. List the first five terms of the sequence S_n and suggest a rule for it.

Start by examining the first few terms.

$S_1 = 1$
$S_2 = 1+3 = 4$
$S_3 = 1+3+5 = 9$
$S_4 = 1+3+5+7 = 16$
$S_5 = 1+3+5+7+9 = 25$

Do we recognise these numbers?

It seems that $S_n = n^2$

You will learn how to prove this result in section 6D.

EXAM HINT

Do not be intimidated by this complicated-looking notation. If you struggle with an expression given in sigma notation, try writing out the first few terms of the series.

To work with series mathematically, it is often too tedious to specify adding up a defined sequence from a given start point to a certain end point, or to write $u_1 + u_2 + u_3 + u_4 + \cdots + u_n$. The same thing can be expressed in a shorter (although not necessarily simpler) way by using **sigma notation**:

KEY POINT 6.2

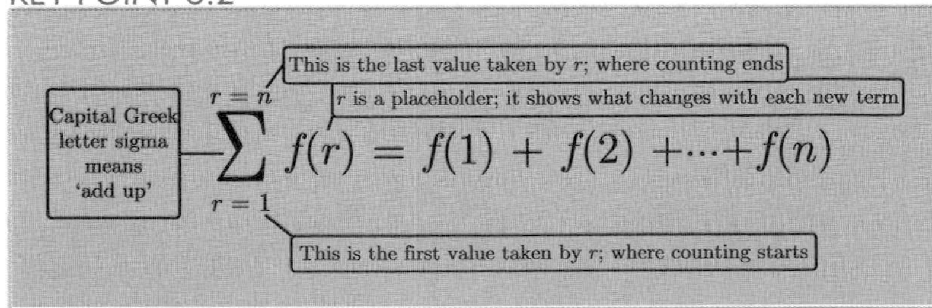
This is the last value taken by r; where counting ends
r is a placeholder; it shows what changes with each new term
Capital Greek letter sigma means 'add up'
$\sum_{r=1}^{r=n} f(r) = f(1) + f(2) + \cdots + f(n)$
This is the first value taken by r; where counting starts

Note that although in Key point 6.2 the counting started at $r = 1$, this does not necessarily have to be the case: you can replace 1

by any other starting value. However, r always increases by 1 until it reaches the end value. If there is only one variable in the expression being summed, it is acceptable to omit the '$r=$' above and below the sigma.

Worked example 6.4

Given that $T_n = \sum_{2}^{n} r^2$, find the value of T_4.

Put the starting value, $r = 2$ into the expression being summed, r^2. — $T_4 = 2^2 + \ldots$

We've not reached the end value 4, so put in $r = 3$. — $T_4 = 2^2 + 3^2 + \ldots$

We've still not reached the end value, so put in $r = 4$. — $T_4 = 2^2 + 3^2 + 4^2$

Now we have reached the end value and can proceed to evaluate the sum. — $T_4 = 4 + 9 + 16$
$= 29$

In the example, both the letters n and r are unknowns, but they are not the same type of unknown. If we replace r by any other letter (except n), the sum will keep the same value. For example, $T_4 = \sum_{k=2}^{k=4} k^2 = 29$; $\sum_{r=2}^{r=n} r^2$ and $\sum_{k=2}^{k=n} k^2$ have exactly the same meaning.
Thus, r is called a 'dummy variable'. However, if we replace n with anything else, the value of the expression may change; for example, $T_3 = 13$, $T_4 = 29$.

Worked example 6.5

Write the series $\frac{1}{2} + \frac{1}{3} + \frac{1}{4} + \frac{1}{5} + \frac{1}{6}$ in sigma notation.

We must describe each term of the series using a dummy variable r. — General term: $\frac{1}{r}$

What is the first value of r? — Starts from $r = 2$

What is the final value of r? — Ends at $r = 6$

Express in sigma notation. — Series is $\sum_{2}^{6} \frac{1}{r}$

Exercise 6B

1. Evaluate the following expressions.

   (a) (i) $\sum_{2}^{4} 3r$ (ii) $\sum_{5}^{7}(2r+1)$

   (b) (i) $\sum_{3}^{6}(2^r-1)$ (ii) $\sum_{-1}^{4}1.5^r$

   (c) (i) $\sum_{a=1}^{a=4} b(a+1)$ (ii) $\sum_{q=-3}^{q=2} pq^2$

2. Write the following expressions in sigma notation. Be aware that in each case there is more than one correct answer.

   (a) (i) $2+3+4+\cdots+43$ (ii) $6+8+10+\ldots+60$

   (b) (i) $\frac{1}{4}+\frac{1}{8}+\frac{1}{16}+\cdots+\frac{1}{128}$ (ii) $2+\frac{2}{3}+\frac{2}{9}+\cdots+\frac{2}{243}$

   (c) (i) $14a+21a+28a+\cdots+70a$ (ii) $0+1+2^b+3^b+\cdots+19^b$

6C Arithmetic sequences

We now focus on a particular type of sequence – one where there is a constant difference between consecutive terms. Such sequences are called **arithmetic sequences** or **arithmetic progressions**. The constant difference between consecutive terms is called the *common difference*, usually denoted by d, so arithmetic sequences obey the recursive rule

$$u_{n+1} = u_n + d$$

This formula is not enough to fully define the sequence. There are many different sequences with common difference 2, for example 1,3,5,7,9,11,... and 106,108,110,112,.... To fully define the sequence we also need to specify the first term, u_1. So the second sequence above is defined by $u_1 = 106, d = 2$.

Worked example 6.6

What is the fourth term of an arithmetic sequence with $u_1 = 300, d = -5$?

Use the recursive rule to find the first four terms.

$u_1 = 300$
$u_2 = u_1 - 5 = 295$
$u_3 = u_2 - 5 = 290$
$u_4 = u_3 - 5 = 285$

In the above example it did not take long to find the first four terms, but what if you had been asked to find the hundredth term? To do this efficiently, we need to move from the inductive definition of an arithmetic sequence to a deductive rule. Think about how arithmetic sequences are built up:

$$u_2 = u_1 + d$$
$$u_3 = u_2 + d = u_1 + d + d$$
$$u_4 = u_3 + d = u_1 + d + d + d$$

and so on. To get to the nth term, we start at the first term and add on the common difference $n-1$ times. This suggests the following formula.

KEY POINT 6.3

$$u_n = u_1 + (n-1)d$$

Worked example 6.7

The fifth term of an arithmetic sequence is 7 and the eighth term is 16. What is the 100th term?

We need to find a deductive rule for u_n, which we can do once we know u_1 and d. So let's write down the information given and relate it to u_1 and d. Write an expression for the 5th term in terms of u_1 and d.

$u_5 = u_1 + 4d$

We are told that $u_5 = 7$

$7 = u_1 + 4d$ (1)

Repeat for the 8th term.

$16 = u_1 + 7d$ (2)

Solve this pair of equations simultaneously.

(2) − (1) gives
$9 = 3d$
$\therefore d = 3$
and hence
$u_1 = -5$

Write down the general term and use it to answer the question.

$u_n = -5 + (n-1) \times 3$
$u_{100} = -5 + 99 \times 3$
$= 292$

EXAM HINT

Many exam questions on this topic involve writing the given information in the form of simultaneous equations and then solving them.

Worked example 6.8

An arithmetic progression has first term 5 and common difference 7. What is the term number corresponding to the value 355?

The question is asking us to find n when $u_n = 355$. Write this as an equation.

$$355 = u_1 + (n-1)d$$
$$= 5 + 7(n-1)$$

Solve this equation.

$$\Leftrightarrow 350 = 7(n-1)$$
$$\Leftrightarrow 50 = n-1$$
$$\Leftrightarrow n = 51$$

So 355 is the 51st term.

EXAM HINT

'Arithmetic progression' is just another way of saying 'arithmetic sequence'. Make sure you are familiar with these different expressions for the same thing.

Exercise 6C

1. Find the general formula for the arithmetic sequence that satisfies the following conditions.

(a) (i) First term 9, common difference 3

(ii) First term 57, common difference 0.2

(b) (i) First term 12, common difference −1

(ii) First term 18, common difference $-\frac{1}{2}$

(c) (i) First term 1, second term 4

(ii) First term 9, second term 19

(d) (i) First term 4, second term 0

(ii) First term 27, second term 20

(e) (i) Third term 5, eighth term 60

(ii) Fifth term 8, eighth term 38

2. How many terms are there in each of the following sequences?

(a) (i) 1,3,5,…,65 (ii) 18,13,8,…,−122

(b) (i) First term 8, common difference 9, last term 899

(ii) First term 0, ninth term 16, last term 450

3. An arithmetic sequence has 5 and 13 as its first term and second term, respectively.

(a) Write down, in terms of n, an expression for the nth term a_n.

(b) Find the number of terms of the sequence which are less than 400. *[8 marks]*

4. The 10th term of an arithmetic sequence is 61 and the 13th term is 79. Find the value of the 20th term. *[4 marks]*

5. The 8th term of an arithmetic sequence is 74 and the 15th term is 137. Which term has the value 227? *[4 marks]*

6. The heights above ground of the rungs in a ladder form an arithmetic sequence. The third rung is 70 cm above the ground and the tenth rung is 210 cm above the ground. If the top rung is 350 cm above the ground, how many rungs does the ladder have? *[5 marks]*

7. The first four terms of an arithmetic sequence are 2, $a - b$, $2a + b + 7$ and $a - 3b$, where a and b are constants. Find a and b. *[5 marks]*

8. A book starts at page 1 and is numbered on every page.

(a) Show that the first eleven pages contain thirteen digits.

(b) If the total number of digits used is 1260, how many pages are in the book? *[8 marks]*

6D Arithmetic series

When you add up the terms of an arithmetic sequence, you get an arithmetic series. There is a formula for the arithmetic series of n terms. See the Fill-in proof 3 'Arithmetic series and the story of Gauss' on the CD-ROM if you are interested in how it is derived, though you are not required to know this derivation for the International Baccalaureate.

There are two different forms of the formula.

KEY POINT 6.4

If you know the first and last terms:

$$S_n = \frac{n}{2}(u_1 + u_n)$$

If you know the first term and the common difference:

$$S_n = \frac{n}{2}(2u_1 + (n-1)d)$$

Worked example 6.9

Find the sum of the first 30 terms of an arithmetic progression with first term 8 and common difference 0.5.

We have all of the information needed to use the second sum formula.

$$S_{30} = \frac{30}{2}(2\times 8 + (30-1)\times 0.5)$$
$$= 457.5$$

Sometimes you have to interpret the question carefully to realise that it is about an arithmetic sequence.

Worked example 6.10

Find the sum of all the multiples of 3 between 100 and 1000.

Write out a few terms to see what is happening.

Sum $= 102 + 105 + 108 + \cdots + 999$

This is an arithmetic series with $u_1 = 102$ and $d = 3$.

Since we know the first and last terms, we can use the first formula; but in order to do so, we also need to know how many terms are in the sequence. We find the number of terms by solving $u_n = 999$.

$$\Leftrightarrow \quad 999 = 102 + 3(n-1)$$
$$\Leftrightarrow \quad 897 = 3(n-1)$$
$$\Leftrightarrow \quad n = 300$$

Use the first sum formula.

$$S_{300} = \frac{300}{2}(102 + 999)$$
$$= 165150$$

You need to be able to work backwards too – for example, to find out how many terms are in a series given its sum and some other information. Remember that the number of terms can only be a positive integer.

Worked example 6.11

An arithmetic sequence has first term 5 and common difference 10. If the sum of all the terms is 720, how many terms are in the sequence?

We know u_1, d and S_n, so in the second sum formula n is the only unknown.

$$720 = \frac{n}{2}(2\times 5 + (n-1)\times 10)$$
$$= \frac{n}{2}(10 + 10n - 10)$$
$$= 5n^2$$

Solve this equation to find n.

$$n^2 = 144$$

Therefore

$$n = \pm 12$$

But n must be a positive integer, so $n = 12$.

Exercise 6D

1. Find the sum of the following arithmetic sequences.
   (a) (i) 12,33,54,... (17 terms)
   (ii) −100,−85,−70,... (23 terms)
   (b) (i) 3,15,...,459 (ii) 2,11,...,650
   (c) (i) 28,23,...,−52 (ii) 100,97,...,40
   (d) (i) 15,15.5,...,29.5 (ii) $\frac{1}{12},\frac{1}{6},\ldots,1.5$

2. An arithmetic sequence has first term 4 and common difference 8. Find the number of terms required to get a sum of:
   (a) (i) 676 (ii) 4096 (iii) 11236
   (b) x^2, $x > 0$

3. The second term of an arithmetic sequence is 7. The sum of the first four terms of the sequence is 12. Find the first term, a, and the common difference, d, of the sequence. *[5 marks]*

4. Consider the arithmetic series 2 + 5 + 8 + ...
   (a) Find an expression for S_n, the sum of the first n terms.
   (b) Find the value of n for which $S_n = 1365$. *[5 marks]*

5. The sum of the first n terms of a series is given by $S_n = 2n^2 - n$, where $n \in \mathbb{Z}^+$.

(a) Find the first three terms of the series.

(b) Find an expression for the nth term of the series, giving your answer in terms of n. *[7 marks]*

6. Find the sum of the positive terms of the arithmetic sequence 85, 78, 71, ... *[6 marks]*

7. The second term of an arithmetic sequence is 6, and the sum of the first four terms of the sequence is 8. Find the first term, a, and the common difference, d, of the sequence. *[6 marks]*

8. Consider the arithmetic series $-6+1+8+15+\cdots$

Find the least number of terms so that the sum of the series is greater than 10 000. *[6 marks]*

9. The sum of the first n terms of an arithmetic sequence is $S_{\text{n}} = 3n^2 - 2n$. Find the nth term, u_n. *[6 marks]*

10. A circular disc is cut into twelve sectors whose angles are in an arithmetic sequence. The angle of the largest sector is twice the angle of the smallest sector. Find the size of the angle of the smallest sector. *[6 marks]*

11. The ratio of the fifth term to the twelfth term of a sequence in an arithmetic progression is $\frac{6}{13}$. If each term of this sequence is positive, and the product of the first term and the third term is 32, find the sum of the first 100 terms of the sequence. *[7 marks]*

12. What is the sum of all three-digit numbers which are multiples of 14 but not 21? *[8 marks]*

6E Geometric sequences

A **geometric sequence** has a constant ratio between terms. To get from one term (u_n) to the next (u_{n+1}), you always multiply by the same number, which is called the *common ratio* and usually denoted by r. So geometric sequences obey the recursive rule

$$u_{n+1} = r\,u_n$$

Here are some examples of geometric sequences:

$$1,2,4,8,16,\ldots \quad (r = 2)$$

$$100,50,25,12.5,6.25,\ldots \quad (r = \frac{1}{2})$$

$$1,-3,9,-27,81,\ldots \quad (r = -3)$$

As with arithmetic sequences, to fully define a geometric sequence we also need to know the first term, u_1.

To obtain the deductive rule, observe that in order to get to the nth term starting from the first term, you need to multiply by the common ratio $n-1$ times. For example, $u_2 = ru_1$, $u_3 = ru_2 = r^2u_1$, and so on.

KEY POINT 6.5

$$u_n = u_1\,r^{n-1}$$

Worked example 6.12

The 7th term of a geometric sequence is 13. The 9th term is 52. What values could the common ratio take?

Write an expression for the 7th term in terms of u_1 and r.	$u_7 = u_1r^6$
But we know $u_7 = 13$.	$13 = u_1r^6$ (1)
Repeat the same process for the 9th term.	$52 = u_1r^8$ (2)
Divide the two equations to eliminate u_1 and hence solve for r.	$(2) \div (1)$ gives $4 = r^2$ $r = \pm 2$

EXAM HINT

Notice that the question asked for *values* rather than a value. This is a big hint that there is more than one answer.

When questions on geometric sequences ask which term satisfies a particular condition, you can either generate the sequence with your calculator and inspect the values, or use logarithms to solve an equation.

Worked example 6.13

A geometric sequence has first term 2 and common ratio −3. Which term has the value −4374?

Write down the formula for the *n*th term.

$u_n = 2\times(-3)^{n-1}$

Use a table on your GDC to list the terms of the sequence and search for −4374. (See calculator skills sheet 10 on the CD-ROM.)

From GDC: $u_8 = -4374$

It is the 8th term.

It may be that the value of *n* you seek is large, in which case it could be impractical to search through a table on your calculator. Instead, try to set up an equation and solve it using logarithms.

Worked example 6.14

A geometric sequence has first term 5000 and common ratio 0.2.

Which term is equal to 3.36×10^{-15}, correct to three significant figures?

Express the condition as an equation.

$$5000\times(0.2)^{n-1} = 3.36\times10^{-15}$$

The unknown is in the exponent, so solve using logarithms.

$$(0.2)^{n-1} = \frac{3.36\times10^{-15}}{5000} = 6.72\times10^{-19}$$

$$\log\left((0.2)^{n-1}\right) = \log\left(6.72\times10^{-19}\right)$$

$$(n-1)\log0.2 = -18.17...$$

$$n-1 = \frac{-18.17...}{\log0.2} = 25.9991...$$

$$\therefore n = 27$$

See section 2G if you need a reminder of how to solve exponential equations using logarithms.

Exercise 6E

1. Find an expression for the nth term of the following geometric sequences.

(a) (i) $6, 12, 24, \ldots$ (ii) $12, 18, 27, \ldots$

(b) (i) $20, 5, 1.25, \ldots$ (ii) $1, \frac{1}{2}, \frac{1}{4}, \ldots$

(c) (i) $1, -2, 4, \ldots$ (ii) $5, -5, 5, \ldots$

(d) (i) $a, ax, ax^2, \ldots$ (ii) $3, 6x, 12x^2, \ldots$

2. Find the number of terms in each of the following geometric sequences.

(a) (i) $6, 12, 24, \ldots, 24576$ (ii) $20, 50, \ldots, 4882.8125$

(b) (i) $1, -3, \ldots, -19683$ (ii) $2, -4, 8, \ldots, -1024$

(c) (i) $\frac{1}{2}, \frac{1}{4}, \ldots, \frac{1}{1024}$ (ii) $3, 2, \frac{4}{3}, \ldots, \frac{128}{729}$

3. How many terms are needed in the following geometric sequences to get within 10^{-9} of zero?

(a) (i) $5, 1, \frac{1}{5}, \ldots$ (ii) $0.6, 0.3, 0.15, \ldots$

(b) (i) $4, -2, 1, \ldots$ (ii) $-125, 25, -5, \ldots$

4. The second term of a geometric sequence is 6 and the fifth term is 162. Find the tenth term. *[5 marks]*

5. The third term of a geometric sequence is 112 and the sixth term is 7168. Which term takes the value 1 835 008? *[5 marks]*

6. Which is the first term of the sequence $\frac{2}{5}, \frac{4}{25}, \ldots, \frac{2^n}{5^n}$ that is less than 10^{-6}? *[6 marks]*

7. The difference between the fourth and the third term of a geometric sequence is $\frac{75}{8}$ times the first term. Find the common ratio given that $r > 0$. *[6 marks]*

8. The third term of a geometric progression is 12 and the fifth term is 48. Find the two possible values of the eighth term. *[6 marks]*

9. The first three terms of a geometric sequence are $a, a+14, 9a$. Find the value of a. *[6 marks]*

10. The three terms a, 1, b are in arithmetic progression. The three terms 1, a, b are in geometric progression. Find the values of a and b given that $a \neq b$. *[7 marks]*

11. The sum of the first n terms of an arithmetic sequence $\{u_n\}$ is given by $S_n = 4n^2 - 2n$. Three terms of this sequence, u_2, u_m and u_{32}, are consecutive terms in a geometric sequence. Find m. *[7 marks]*

6F Geometric series

When you add up the terms of a geometric sequence, you get a geometric series. As with arithmetic series, there is a formula for the sum of n terms in a geometric sequence. See the Fill-in proof 4 'Self-similarity and geometric series' on the CD-ROM if you are interested in learning where this formula comes from.

KEY POINT 6.6

$$S_n = \frac{u_1(1-r^n)}{1-r} \quad (r \neq 1)$$

or equivalently

$$S_n = \frac{u_1(r^n-1)}{r-1} \quad (r \neq 1)$$

EXAM HINT

Generally we use the first of these formulas when the common ratio is less than one, the second when the common ratio is greater than one. This way we can avoid working with negative numbers as much as possible.

Worked example 6.15

Find the exact value of the sum of the first 6 terms of the geometric sequence with first term 8 and common ratio $\frac{1}{2}$.

Since $r < 1$, we use the first sum formula.

$$S_6 = \frac{8\left(1-\left(\frac{1}{2}\right)^6\right)}{1-\frac{1}{2}}$$

$$= \frac{8\left(1-\frac{1}{64}\right)}{\frac{1}{2}}$$

$$= 16\left(\frac{63}{64}\right)$$

$$= \frac{63}{4}$$

We may be given information about the sum and have to deduce other information.

Worked example 6.16

How many terms are needed for the sum of the geometric series $3+6+12+24+\ldots$ to exceed 100 000?

We need to find n, but first we need the values of u_1 and r.

$$u_1 = 3$$
$$r = 2$$

As $r > 1$, use the second sum formula and express the condition as an inequality.

$$S_n = \frac{3(2^n-1)}{2-1} > 100\,000$$

We can use a calculator to generate values for S_n.

From GDC:

$S_{15} = 98\,301$

$S_{16} = 196\,605$

So 16 terms are needed.

Exercise 6F

1. Find the sums of the following geometric series. (Some of these may have more than one possible answer.)
   (a) (i) $7, 35, 175, \ldots$ (10 terms)
   (ii) $1152, 576, 288, \ldots$ (12 terms)

(b) (i) 16, 24, 36, …, 182.25

(ii) 1, 1.1, 1.21, …, 1.771561

(c) (i) First term 8, common ratio −3, last term 52 488

(ii) First term −6, common ratio −3, last term 13 122

(d) (i) Third term 24, fifth term 6, 12 terms

(ii) Ninth term 50, thirteenth term 0.08, last term 0.0032

2. Find the value of the common ratio if

(a) (i) the first term is 11, sum of the first 12 terms is 2 922 920

(ii) the first term is 1, sum of the first 6 terms is 1.24992

(b) (i) the first term is 12, sum of the first 6 terms is −79 980

(ii) the first term is 10, sum of the first 4 terms is 1

3. The nth term, u_n, of a geometric sequence is given by $u_n = 3\times 5^{n+2}$.

(a) Find the common ratio r.

(b) Hence or otherwise find S_n, the sum of the first n terms of this sequence. *[5 marks]*

4. The sum of the first three terms of a geometric sequence is $23\frac{3}{4}$, and the sum of the first four terms is $40\frac{5}{8}$. Find the first term and the common ratio. *[6 marks]*

5. The first term of a geometric series is 6, and the sum of the first 15 terms is 29. Find the common ratio. *[5 marks]*

6. The sum of the first four terms of a geometric series is 520. The sum of the first five terms is 844. The sum of the first six terms is 1330.

(a) Find the common ratio of the geometric progression.

(b) Find the sum of the first two terms. *[6 marks]*

6G Infinite geometric series

If we keep adding together terms of an arithmetic sequence, the sum will grow (or decrease) without limit, and is said to be **divergent**. This can occur with some geometric series, too, but it could also happen that the sum gets closer and closer to and 'settles down' to a finite number; in this case we say that the geometric series is **convergent**.

The graph shows the values of S_n for a geometric series with first term $u_1 = 4$ and common ratio $r = 0.2$. As n increases, the value of S_n seems to be getting closer and closer to 5; thus we say that the series converges to 5.

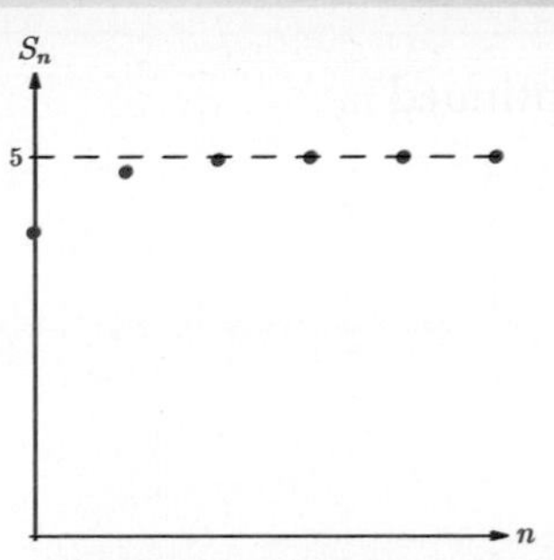

Not all geometric series converge. To determine which ones do, we need to look at the formula for a geometric series:

$$S_n = \frac{u_1(1-r^n)}{1-r}$$

We want to know what happens to S_n as n gets large, so we focus on the r^n term. With most numbers, when you raise the number to a larger power the result gets bigger; for example, $1.2^{20} = 38.3$ and $1.2^{30} = 237$. The exception is when r is a number between -1 and 1. In this case, r^n gets smaller as n increases – in fact, it approaches zero; for example, $0.2^2 = 0.04, 0.2^3 = 0.008$ and $0.2^{20} = 1.05\times10^{-14}$. This means that for $-1 < r < 1$, as n increases the value of S_n will get closer and closer to $\frac{u_1}{1-r}$.

When $r = 1$, the geometric series certainly diverges. But when $r = -1$, it is not clear whether the series converges or diverges: the sum could have value 0, u_1 or $\frac{u_1}{2}$ depending on how the terms in the series are grouped. This is an example of a situation where mathematics is open to debate.

KEY POINT 6.7

As n increases, the sum of a geometric series converges to

$$S_\infty = \frac{u_1}{1-r} \text{ if } |r|<1.$$

This is called the **sum to infinity of the series.**

EXAM HINT

The condition that $|r|<1$ is just as important as the formula itself.

$|r|$ is the modulus, or absolute value, of r. The modulus leaves positive values unchanged but reverses the sign of negative values. So, $|8| = 8$ and $|-8| = 8$.

Worked example 6.17

The sum to infinity of a geometric sequence is 5. The second term is $-\frac{6}{5}$. Find the common ratio.

Write the given information as equations in u_1 and r.

$$S_\infty = \frac{u_1}{1-r} = 5 \quad (1)$$

$$u_2 = u_1 r = -\frac{6}{5} \quad (2)$$

continued . . .

Solve the equations simultaneously.

From (2):

$$u_1 = -\frac{6}{5r}$$

Substituting into (1):

$$-\frac{6}{5r(1-r)} = 5$$

$$-6 = 25(r - r^2)$$

$$25r^2 - 25r - 6 = 0$$

$$(5r - 6)(5r + 1) = 0$$

Therefore $r = \frac{6}{5}$ or $r = -\frac{1}{5}$

Watch out! Check whether the series actually converges for the r-values found.

But since the sum to infinity exists, we must have $|r| < 1$, so $r = -\frac{1}{5}$

Some questions may focus on the condition for the sequence to converge rather than the value that it converges to.

Worked example 6.18

The geometric series $(2-x)+(2-x)^2+(2-x)^3+\cdots$ converges. What values can x take?

Identify r.

$$r = (2 - x)$$

Use the fact that the series converges.

Since the series converges,

$$|2 - x| < 1$$

Convert the modulus expression into a double inequality.

$$-1 < 2 - x < 1$$

$$\Leftrightarrow -3 < -x < -1$$

Therefore

$$1 < x < 3$$

Exercise 6G

1. Find the value of each of the following infinite geometric series, or state that the series is divergent.

(a) (i) $9+3+1+\frac{1}{3}+\dots$ (ii) $56+8+1\frac{1}{7}+\dots$

(b) (i) $0.3+0.03+0.003+\dots$

(ii) $0.78+0.0078+0.000078+\dots$

(c) (i) $0.01+0.02+0.04+\dots$ (ii) $\frac{19}{10000}+\frac{19}{1000}+\frac{19}{100}+\dots$

(d) (i) $10-2+0.4+\dots$ (ii) $6-4+\frac{8}{3}+\dots$

(e) (i) $10-40+160+\dots$ (ii) $4.2-3.36+2.688+\dots$

2. Find the values of x which allow the following geometric series to converge.

(a) (i) $9+9x+9x^2+\dots$ (ii) $-2-2x-2x^2+\dots$

(b) (i) $1+3x+9x^2+\dots$ (ii) $1+10x+100x^2+\dots$

(c) (i) $-2-10x-50x^2+\dots$ (ii) $8+24x+72x^2+\dots$

(d) (i) $40+10x+2.5x^2+\dots$ (ii) $144+12x+x^2+\dots$

(e) (i) $243-81x+27x^2+\dots$ (ii) $1-\frac{5}{4}x+\frac{25}{16}x^2+\dots$

(f) (i) $3-\frac{6}{x}+\frac{12}{x^2}+\dots$ (ii) $18-\frac{9}{x}+\frac{1}{x^2}+\dots$

(g) (i) $5+5(3-2x)+5(3-2x)^2+\dots$

(ii) $7+\frac{7(2-x)}{2}+\frac{7(2-x)^2}{4}+\dots$

(h) (i) $1+\left(3-\frac{2}{x}\right)+\left(3-\frac{2}{x}\right)^2+\dots$ (ii) $1+\frac{1+x}{x}+\frac{(1+x)^2}{x^2}+\dots$

(i) (i) $7+7x^2+7x^4+\dots$ (ii) $12-48x^3+192x^6+\dots$

3. Find the sum to infinity of the geometric sequence $-18, 12, -8, \dots$. *[4 marks]*

4. The first and fourth terms of a geometric sequence are 18 and $-\frac{2}{3}$ respectively.

(a) Find the sum of the first n terms of the sequence.

(b) Find the sum to infinity of the sequence. *[5 marks]*

5. $f(x) = 1 + 2x + 4x^2 + 8x^3 + \ldots$ is an infinitely long expression. Evaluate

(a) $f\left(\frac{1}{3}\right)$

(b) $f\left(\frac{2}{3}\right)$ *[6 marks]*

6. A geometric sequence has all positive terms. The sum of the first two terms is 15 and the sum to infinity is 27. Find the value of

(a) the common ratio

(b) the first term. *[5 marks]*

7. The sum to infinity of a geometric series is 32. The sum of the first four terms is 30 and all the terms are positive. Find the difference between the sum to infinity and the sum of the first eight terms. *[5 marks]*

8. Consider the infinite geometric series

$$1 + \left(\frac{2x}{3}\right) + \left(\frac{2x}{3}\right)^2 + \ldots$$

(a) For what values of x does the series converge?

(b) Find the sum of the series if $x = 1.2$. *[6 marks]*

9. The sum of an infinite geometric sequence is 13.5, and the sum of the first three terms is 13. Find the first term. *[6 marks]*

10. An infinite geometric series is given by $\sum_{k=1}^{\infty} 2(4-3x)^k$.

(a) Find the values of x for which the series has a finite sum.

(b) When $x = 1.2$, find the minimum number of terms needed to give a sum which is greater than 1.328. *[7 marks]*

11. The common ratio of the terms in a geometric series is 2^x.

(a) State the set of values of x for which the sum to infinity of the series exists.

(b) If the first term of the series is 35, find the value of x for which the sum to infinity is 40. *[6 marks]*

6H Mixed questions on sequences and series

Be very careful when dealing with questions on sequences and series. It is vital that you first:

- identify whether the question is about a geometric or an arithmetic sequence
- determine whether you are being asked for a term in the sequence or a sum of terms in the sequence
- translate the information given into equations that you can work with.

One frequently examined topic is **compound interest**. The questions are usually about savings or loans, where the interest added is a percentage of the current amount. As long as no other money is added or removed, the balance of the savings account or loan will follow a geometric sequence. A compound interest rate of $p\%$ is equivalent to a common ratio of $r = 1 + \frac{p}{100}$.

Worked example 6.19

A savings account pays 2.4% annual interest, added at the end of each year. If $200 is paid into the account at the start of the first year, how much will there be in the account at the start of the 7th year?

Each year the balance of the account is increased by the same percentage, so this gives a geometric sequence.

Geometric sequence with

$$r = 1 + \frac{2.4}{100} = 1.024$$

$$u_1 = 200$$

If the start of the first year is u_1, the start of the 7th year is u_7.

$$u_7 = u_1 r^6$$

$$= 230.58$$

There will be $230.58.

EXAM HINT

Think carefully about whether the amount you are calculating is for the beginning or the end of a year.

Exercise 6H

1. Philippa invests £1000 at 3% compound interest for 6 years.
   (a) How much interest does she get paid in the 6th year?
   (b) How much does she get back after 6 years? *[6 marks]*

2. Lars starts a job on an annual salary of \$32 000 and is promised an annual increase of \$1500.
   (a) How much will his salary be in the 20th year?
   (b) After how many complete years will he have earned a total of \$1 million? *[6 marks]*

3. A sum of \$5000 is invested at a compound interest rate of 6.3% per annum.
   (a) Write down an expression for the value of the investment after n full years.
   (b) What will be the value of the investment at the end of five years?
   (c) The value of the investment will exceed \$10 000 after n full years.
      (i) Write an inequality to represent this information.
      (ii) Calculate the minimum value of n. *[8 marks]*

4. Suppose that each row of seats in a theatre has 200 more seats than the previous row. There are 50 seats in the front row and the designer wants the theatre's capacity to be at least 8000.
   (a) How many rows are required?
   (b) Assuming the rows are equally spread, what percentage of people are seated in the front half of the theatre? *[7 marks]*

5. A sum of \$100 is invested.
   (a) If the interest is compounded annually at a rate of 5% per year, find the total value V of the investment after 20 years.
   (b) If the interest is compounded monthly at a rate of $\frac{5}{12}$% per month, find the minimum number of months for the value of the investment to exceed V. *[6 marks]*

6. A marathon is a 26-mile race. In a training regime for a marathon, a runner runs 1 mile on his first day of training and increases his distance by $\frac{1}{4}$ of a mile each day.

(a) After how many days has he run a total of 26 miles?

(b) On which day does he first run over 26 miles? *[6 marks]*

7. A football is dropped vertically from 2 m above the ground. A model suggests that each time it bounces up to a height of 80% of its previous height.

(a) How high does it bounce on the 4th bounce?

(b) How far has it travelled when it hits the ground for the 9th time?

(c) Give one reason why this model is unlikely to work after 20 bounces. *[7 marks]*

8. Samantha puts \$1000 into a bank account at the beginning of each year, starting in 2010, which corresponds to year 1. At the end of each year, 4% interest is added to the account.

(a) Show that at the beginning of 2012 there is $\$1000+\$1000\times1.04+\$1000\times(1.04)^2$ in the account.

(b) Find an expression for the amount in the account at the beginning of year *n*.

(c) When Samantha has a total of at least \$50 000 in her account at the beginning of a year she will start looking for a house to buy. In which year will this happen? *[7 marks]*

Summary

- Sequences can be described by either **recursive** (term to term) or **deductive** (*n*th term) rules.
- A **series** is a sum of terms in a sequence; it can be described concisely using **sigma notation**:

$$\sum_{r=1}^{r=n} f(r) = f(1) + f(2) + \ldots + f(n)$$

- One very important type of sequence is an **arithmetic sequence**, which has a constant difference, *d*, between consecutive terms. The relevant formulas are given in the information booklet:
  - if you know the first term u_1, the *n*th term in the sequence is: $u_n = u_1 + (n-1)d$
  - if you know the first and last terms, the sum to the *n*th term in the series is: $S_n = \frac{n}{2}(u_1 + u_n)$

- if you know the first term and the common difference, the sum to the nth term in the series is: $S_n = \frac{n}{2}(2u_1 + (n-1)d)$

- Another frequently encountered type of sequence is a **geometric sequence**, which has a constant ratio, r, between consecutive terms. The following formulas are also given in the information booklet:
  - if you know the first term u_1, the nth term in the sequence is: $u_n = u_1\, r^{n-1}$
  - the sum of the first n terms in the series is: $S_n = \frac{u_1(1-r^n)}{1-r}$ or $\frac{u_1(r^n-1)}{r-1} (r \neq 1)$

- As the number of terms being added increases, a series can be **convergent** (the sum gets closer and closer to a single finite value) or **divergent** (the sum increases or decreases without bound).
  - if $|r|<1$, the **sum to infinity** of a geometric series is given by

$$S_\infty = \frac{u_1}{1-r}$$

Introductory problem revisited

A mortgage of \$100 000 has a fixed rate of 5% compound interest. It needs to be paid off in 25 years by fixed annual instalments. Interest is debited at the end of each year, just before the payment is made. How much should be paid each year?

Imagine two separate accounts: one in which the debt is accumulating interest, and another in which you deposit your payments, where they acquire interest at the same rate. The first payment you make will have interest paid on it 24 times, the second payment will have 23 interest payments, and so on.

After 25 years, the amount in the debt account will be $100\,000 \times 1.05^{25}$.

If the annual payment is \$$x$, the amount in the credit account will be:

$$x \times 1.05^{24} + x \times 1.05^{23} + x \times 1.05^{22} + \ldots + x \times 1.05^{1} + x$$

This is a finite geometric series with 25 terms, where the first term is x and the common ratio is 1.05. Therefore, using the second sum formula in Key point 6.6, it can be simplified to

$$\frac{x(1.05^{25}-1)}{1.05-1}$$

If the debt is to be paid off, the amount in the credit account must equal the amount in the debt account; that is,

$$100\,000 \times 1.05^{25} = \frac{x(1.05^{25}-1)}{1.05-1}$$

Solving this gives $x = 7095.25$, so the annual instalment should be \$7095.25.

Mixed examination practice 6

Short questions

1. The fourth term of an arithmetic sequence is 9.6 and the ninth term is 15.6. Find the sum of the first nine terms. *[5 marks]*

2. Which is the first term of the sequence $\frac{1}{3}, \frac{1}{9}, \ldots, \frac{1}{3^n}$ that is less than 10^{-6}? *[5 marks]*

3. The fifth term of an arithmetic sequence is three times larger than the second term. Find the ratio $\frac{\text{common difference}}{\text{first term}}$. *[6 marks]*

4. Evaluate $\sum_{n=0}^{n=\infty} \frac{(2^n + 4^n)}{6^n}$ *[6 marks]*

5. Find the sum of all the integers between 300 and 600 which are divisible by 7. *[7 marks]*

6. A geometric sequence and an arithmetic sequence both have 1 as their first term. The third term of the arithmetic sequence is the same as the second term of the geometric sequence. The fourth term of the arithmetic sequence is the same as the third term of the geometric sequence. Find the possible values of the common difference of the arithmetic sequence. *[7 marks]*

7. Find an expression for the sum of the first 23 terms of the series

$$\ln\frac{a^3}{\sqrt{b}} + \ln\frac{a^3}{b} + \ln\frac{a^3}{b\sqrt{b}} + \ln\frac{a^3}{b^2} + \cdots$$

giving your answer in the form $\ln\left(\frac{a^m}{b^n}\right)$ where $m, n \in \mathbb{Z}$. *[7 marks]*

Long questions

1. Kenny is offered a choice of two investment plans, each requiring an initial investment of $10 000.

Plan A offers a fixed return of $800 per year.

Plan B offers a return of 5% each year, reinvested in the plan.

(a) Find an expression for the amount in plan A after n years.

(b) Find an expression for the amount in plan B after n years.

(c) Over what period of time is plan A better than plan B? *[10 marks]*

2. Ben builds a pyramid out of toy bricks. The top row contains one brick, the second row contains three bricks, and each row beneath that contains two more bricks than the row above.

(a) How many bricks does the nth row (from the top) contain?

(b) If a total of 36 bricks are used, how many rows are there?

(c) In Ben's largest ever pyramid, he noticed that the total number of bricks was four more than four times the number of bricks in the bottom row. What is the total number of bricks in this pyramid? *[10 marks]*

3. A student writes '1' on the first line of a page, then the next two integers '2,3' on the second line of the page, then the next three integers '4,5,6' on the third line. She continues this pattern.

(a) How many integers are there on the nth line?

(b) What is the last integer on the nth line?

(c) What is the first integer on the nth line?

(d) Show that the sum of all the integers on the nth line is $\frac{n}{2}(n^2+1)$.

(e) The sum of all the integers on the last line of the page is 16 400. How many lines are on the page? *[10 marks]*

4. Selma has taken out a mortgage for £150 000. At the end of each year, 6% interest is added, and then Selma pays £10 000.

(a) Explain why at the end of the third year the amount still owed is

$$150\,000\times(1.06)^3-10\,000\times(1.06)^2-10\,000\times1.06-10\,000$$

(b) Find an expression for how much is owed at the end of the nth year.

(c) After how many years will the mortgage be paid off? *[10 marks]*

7 Binomial expansion

In this chapter you will learn:

- how to expand an expression of the form $(a+b)^n$ for a positive integer n
- how to find individual terms in the expansion of $(a+b)^n$ for a positive integer n.

Introductory problem

Without using a calculator, find the value of $(1.002)^{10}$ correct to 8 decimal places.

A **binomial** expression is an expression that contains two terms, for example $a+b$.

Expanding a power of a binomial expression could be performed laboriously by expanding brackets; for example, $(a+b)^7$ could be found by multiplying out, at length,

$$(a+b)(a+b)(a+b)(a+b)(a+b)(a+b)(a+b)$$

This is time-consuming and mistakes could easily be made, but fortunately there is a much quicker approach.

7A Introduction to the binomial theorem

To see how we might rapidly expand an expression of the form $(a+b)^n$ for an integer power n, let us first look at some expansions of $(a+b)^n$ done using the slow method of multiplying out brackets repeatedly. The table shows the results for $n=1,2,3$ and 4; in the rightmost column, the coefficients and powers in the expansions are coloured to highlight the pattern.

$(a+b)^0$	$=1$	$=1a^0b^0$
$(a+b)^1$	$=a+b$	$=1a^1b^0+1a^0b^1$
$(a+b)^2$	$=a^2+2ab+b^2$	$=1a^2b^0+2a^1b^1+1a^0b^2$
$(a+b)^3$	$=a^3+3a^2b+3ab^2+b^3$	$=1a^3b^0+3a^2b^1+3a^1b^2+1a^0b^3$
$(a+b)^4$	$=a^4+4a^3b+6a^2b^2+4ab^3+b^4$	$=1a^4b^0+4a^3b^1+6a^2b^2+4a^1b^3+1a^0b^4$

The red numbers form a famous mathematical structure called *Pascal's triangle*. There are many amazing patterns in Pascal's triangle – for example, by highlighting all the even numbers you can generate an ever-repeating pattern called a *fractal*.

EXAM HINT
See Calculator Skills sheet 3 on the CD-ROM for how to find $\binom{n}{r}$ using your calculator.

We can see several patterns in each expansion:

- The powers of a and b (coloured green) in each term always add up to n.
- Every power of a from 0 up to n is present in one of the terms, with the corresponding complementary power of b.
- The pattern of coefficients (coloured red) is symmetrical.

The red numbers are called **binomial coefficients**. The expansion of $(a+b)^n$ has $n+1$ binomial coefficients, and the one associated with the terms $a^{n-r}b^r$ and $a^r b^{n-r}$ is denoted by $\binom{n}{r}$.

KEY POINT 7.1

Binomial theorem

The coefficient of the term containing $a^{n-r}b^r$ in the expansion of $(a+b)^n$ is $\binom{n}{r}$.

Worked example 7.1

Find the coefficient of x^5y^3 in the expansion of $(x+y)^8$.

Write down the required term in the form $\binom{n}{r}(a)^{n-r}(b)^r$. Here $a=x$, $b=y$, $r=3$, $n=8$.	The required term is $\binom{8}{3}(x)^5(y)^3$
Calculate the coefficient and apply the powers to the bracketed terms.	$\binom{8}{3}=56$ $(x)^5=x^5$ $(y)^3=y^3$ The term is $56x^5y^3$ The coefficient is 56

Sometimes one of a and b is just a number, but we treat the expansion in exactly the same way as if both were variables.

Worked example 7.2

Find the y^3 term in $(2+y)^5$.

Write down the required term in the form $\binom{n}{r}(a)^{n-r}(b)^r$.

Here $a=2,\ b=y,\ r=3,\ n=5.$

The relevant term is $\binom{5}{3}(2)^2(y)^3$

Calculate the coefficient and apply the powers to the bracketed terms.

$\binom{5}{3}=10$

$(2)^2=4$

$(y)^3=y^3$

The term is $40y^3$

EXAM HINT

A question may ask for the whole term or just the coefficient. Make sure that your answer gives what was requested!

Exercise 7A

1. (i) Find the x^5y^7 term in the expansion of $(x+y)^{12}$.
   (ii) Find the a^7b^9 term in the expansion of $(a+b)^{16}$.
   (iii) Find the c^3d^2 term in the expansion of $(c+d)^5$.
   (iv) Find the a^2b^7 term in the expansion of $(a+b)^9$.
   (v) Find the x^2y^4 term in the expansion of $(x+y)^6$.

2. (a) Find the coefficient of x^3 in $(3+x)^4$.
   (b) Find the coefficient of y^2 in $(y+5)^6$.
   (c) Find the coefficient of z in $(5+z)^5$.
3. Find the coefficient of x^5y^3 in the expansion of $(x+y)^6$.

7B Binomial coefficients

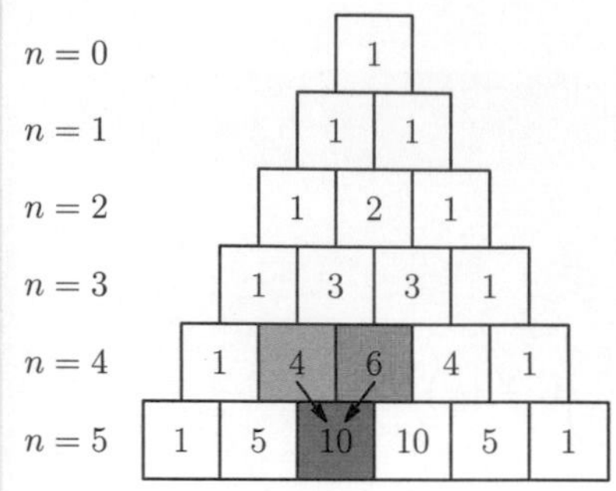

The easiest way to find binomial coefficients is by using a calculator, but in some situations you may need to find them without a calculator. One method of doing this is to use Pascal's triangle – the pattern of red numbers in the table of binomial expansions from the previous section arranged in the shape of a pyramid.

The slanted sides are made up of 1s. Each of the other values is obtained by adding the two values above it. The binomial coefficients of $(a + b)^n$ are found in the $(n + 1)$th row from the top.

Although it is not difficult to generate Pascal's triangle, finding binomial coefficients in this way is impractical when n is large. In such cases, there is a formula that can be used. Before introducing this formula we need to define a new function, the factorial function $n!$ (pronounced 'n factorial').

KEY POINT 7.2

> For a positive integer n,
>
> $n! = 1 \times 2 \times 3 \times \cdots \times (n-1) \times n$

$0!$ is defined to be 1.

> One reason that $0! = 1$ was agreed on as a convention is because it is useful to have this in other formulas involving factorials. Is this a valid mathematical reason for assigning a certain value to an undefined expression?

Using the factorial function, it is possible to write down a simple formula for the binomial coefficients. You do not need to know the proof of this formula.

KEY POINT 7.3

> Binomial coefficient: $\binom{n}{r} = \dfrac{n!}{r!(n-r)!}$

Worked example 7.3

Evaluate $\binom{6}{4}$.

Using the formula with $n = 6$, $r = 4$ and $n - r = 2$.

$$\binom{6}{4} = \frac{6!}{4! \times 2!}$$
$$= \frac{1 \times 2 \times 3 \times 4 \times 5 \times 6}{(1 \times 2 \times 3 \times 4) \times (1 \times 2)}$$
$$= \frac{5 \times 6}{2}$$
$$= 15$$

Using the formula, we can find expressions for binomial coefficients with general n and small values of r.

KEY POINT 7.4

$$\binom{n}{0} = 1 \quad \binom{n}{1} = n \quad \binom{n}{2} = \frac{n(n-1)}{2}$$

These expressions are useful when part of an expansion has been given.

Worked example 7.4

The expansion of $(1+x)^n$ up to the third term is given by $1+6x+ax^2$. Find the value of n and of a.

Write out the first three terms of the expansion of the left-hand side in terms of n.

$$(1+x)^n = 1 + \binom{n}{1}x + \binom{n}{2}x^2 + \cdots$$
$$= 1 + nx + \frac{n(n-1)}{2}x^2 + \cdots$$

Compare this with the given expression $1+6x+ax^2$.

Comparing coefficients of x gives

$n = 6$

Comparing coefficients of x^2 gives

$$\frac{n(n-1)}{2} = a$$

$$\therefore \quad a = \frac{6 \times 5}{2} = 15$$

Exercise 7B

1. If we say that the first row of Pascal's triangle is 1,1, find:
   (a) the second row
   (b) the third row
   (c) the fifth row

2. Find the following binomial coefficients.
   (a) (i) $\binom{7}{3}$ (ii) $\binom{9}{2}$
   (b) (i) $\binom{9}{0}$ (ii) $\binom{6}{0}$
   (c) (i) $\binom{8}{7}$ (ii) $\binom{10}{8}$

3. (i) Find the coefficient of xy^3 in the expansion of $(x+y)^4$.
   (ii) Find the coefficient of x^3y^4 in the expansion of $(x+y)^7$.
   (iii) Find the coefficient of ab^6 in the expansion of $(a+b)^7$.
   (iv) Find the coefficient of a^5b^3 in the expansion of $(a+b)^8$.

4. Find the coefficient of x^4 in $(3+2x)^5$. *[4 marks]*

5. Suppose that $(2+x)^n = 32+ax+\cdots$
   (a) Find the value of n.
   (b) Find the value of a. *[5 marks]*

6. Suppose that $(1+2x)^n = 1+20x+ax^2+\cdots$
   (a) Find the value of n.
   (b) Find the value of a. *[5 marks]*

7C Applying the binomial theorem

In section 7A you learned the general pattern for expanding powers of a binomial expression $(a+b)$. Many expansions can be done using this method, if we substitute more complicated expressions for a and b.

Worked example 7.5

Find the term in x^6y^4 in the expansion of $(x+3y^2)^8$.

Write down the required term in the form $\binom{n}{r}(a)^{n-r}(b)^r$, with $a=x,\ b=3y^2,\ r=2,\ n=8$.

The relevant term is $\binom{8}{2}(x)^6(3y^2)^2$

Calculate the coefficient and apply the powers to the bracketed terms.

$\binom{8}{2}=28$

$(x)^6=x^6$

$(3y^2)^2=9y^4$

The required term is $28\times x^6\times 9y^4=252x^6y^4$

EXAM HINT

A common mistake is to assume that the powers of each variable in the term you're asked to find correspond to the value of r in the expansion; but as you can see in this example, y is raised to the power 4 while r is 2.
Take care also to apply the power not only to the variable but also to its coefficient. In this example, $(3y^2)^2=9y^4$, not $3y^4$.

Although examination questions typically ask you to calculate just one term, you should also be able to find the entire expansion. To do this, repeat the calculation for each of the values that r can take (from 0 up to n) and then add together all these terms. This leads to the following formula given in the Formula booklet.

KEY POINT 7.5

Binomial theorem

$$(a+b)^n=a^n+\binom{n}{1}a^{n-1}b+\cdots+\binom{n}{r}a^{n-r}b^r+\cdots+b^n$$

Worked example 7.6

Use the binomial theorem to expand and simplify $(2x-3y)^5$.

Write down each term in the form $\binom{n}{r}(a)^{n-r}(b)^r$, with

$a=2x,\ b=-3y,\ n=5.$

Coefficients are 1,5,10,10,5,1

The expansion is

$1(2x)^5 + 5(2x)^4(-3y)^1 + 10(2x)^3(-3y)^2 + 10(2x)^2(-3y)^3 + 5(2x)^1(-3y)^4 + 1(-3y)^5$

Apply the powers to the bracketed terms and multiply through.

$= 32x^5 - 240x^4y + 720x^3y^2 - 1080x^2y^3 + 810xy^4 - 243y^5$

A question may ask for a term in a binomial expansion where '*a*' and '*b*' in the binomial expression both contain the same variable. You can use the rules of exponents to determine which term of the expansion is needed.

Worked example 7.7

Find the coefficient of x^5 in the expansion of $\left(2x^2 - \frac{1}{x}\right)^7$.

Start with the form of a general term and simplify using the rules of exponents.

Each term will be of the form

$\binom{7}{r}(2x^2)^{7-r}(-x^{-1})^r$

$=\binom{7}{r}(2)^{7-r}x^{14-2r}(-1)^r x^{-r}$

$=\binom{7}{r}(2)^{7-r}(-1)^r x^{14-3r}$

→

continued . . .

The power of x in the required term is 5, so equate that to the power of x in the general term.

Need $14-3r=5$

$3r=9$

$r=3$

Write down the required term in the form $\binom{n}{r}(a)^{n-r}(b)^r$, with $a=2x^2,\ b=-x^{-1},\ n=7,\ r=3$.

The relevant term is $\binom{7}{3}(2x^2)^4(-x^{-1})^3$

Calculate the coefficient and apply the powers to the bracketed terms.

$\binom{7}{3}=35$

$(2x^2)^4=16x^8$

$(-x^{-1})^3=-x^{-3}$

Combine the elements to calculate the coefficient.

The term is $35\times16x^8\times(-x^{-3})=-560x^5$

The coefficient is -560

EXAM HINT

If 'a' or 'b' has a negative sign, it must stay with each of the terms $a^{n-r}b^r$ in the expansion and needs to be acted upon by the corresponding power. Lots of people forget the negative signs!

You may need to work with the product of a binomial expression and a power of another binomial expression.

Worked example 7.8

Use the binomial theorem to expand and simplify $(5-3x)(2-x)^4$.

To expand $(2-x)^4$, write down each term in the form $\binom{n}{r}(a)^{n-r}(b)^r$.

Here $a=2$, $b=-x$, $n=4$
Coefficients are 1,4,6,4,1

The expansion is

$$(5-3x)[1(2)^4+4(2)^3(-x)+6(2)^2(-x)^2+4(2)^1(-x)^3+1(-x)^4]$$

5 multiplies the square bracket and $-3x$ multiplies the square bracket.

$$=5[16-32x+24x^2-8x^3+x^4]$$
$$-3x[16-32x+24x^2-8x^3+x^4]$$
$$=80-208x+216x^2-112x^3+29x^4-3x^5$$

When x is a small number (modulus less than 1), high powers of x will be very small, even after multiplying by a binomial coefficient. Thus, if we take a binomial expansion involving values of x very close to zero and throw away terms containing higher powers of x, this should have little impact on the overall value of the expansion. Truncated binomial expansions, which retain only a few terms containing low powers of x, are useful for calculating approximate values of powers of numbers.

KEY POINT 7.6

If the value of x is close to zero, large powers of x will be extremely small.

Worked example 7.9

Find the first 3 terms of the expansion of $(2-x)^5$ in ascending powers of x. By setting $x=0.01$, use your answer to find an approximate value of 1.99^5.

Write down each term of the expansion in the form $\binom{n}{r}(a)^{n-r}(b)^r$, with $a=2$, $b=-x$, $n=5$.

The first 3 terms are

$$1(2)^5+5(2)^4(-x)^1+10(2)^3(-x)^2$$

Apply the powers to the bracketed terms and multiply through.

$$=32-80x+80x^2$$

Calculate the powers of the given value of x and hence the value of each term in the expansion.

$x^0=1 \Rightarrow 32x^0=32$

$x=0.01 \Rightarrow -80x=-0.8$

$x^2=0.0001 \Rightarrow 80x^2=0.008$

Add up the values of the terms.

Hence, approximately,

$$1.99^5=32-0.8+0.008=31.208$$

Exercise 7C

1. (a) Find the coefficient of xy^3 in

(i) $(2x+3y)^4$ (ii) $(5x+y)^4$

(b) Find the term in x^3y^4 in

(i) $(x-2y)^7$ (ii) $(y-2x)^7$

(c) Find the coefficient of a^2b^3 in

(i) $\left(2a-\frac{1}{2}b\right)^5$ (ii) $(17a+3b)^5$

2. (a) (i) Fully expand and simplify $(2-x)^5$.

(ii) Fully expand and simplify $(3+x)^6$.

(b) (i) Find the first three terms in the expansion of $(3x+y)^5$ in descending powers of x.

(ii) Find the first three terms in the expansion of $(2c-d)^4$ in ascending powers of d.

(c) Fully expand and simplify $(2x^2-3x)^3$.

3. (a) Find the first 3 terms in the expansion of $(3-5x)^4$.

(b) By choosing a suitable value of x, use your answer from part (a) to find an approximation for 2.995^4.

[7 marks]

4. Find the first 4 terms in the expansion of $(y+3y^2)^6$ in ascending powers of y. *[6 marks]*

5. Which term in the expansion of $(x-2y)^5$ has coefficient

(a) 40 ?

(b) −80 ? *[6 marks]*

6. Find the coefficient of x^3 in $(1-5x)^9$. *[4 marks]*

7. Find the x^2 term in $(3-2x)^7$. *[4 marks]*

8. Find the coefficient of x^2y^6 in $(3x+2y^2)^5$. *[5 marks]*

9. Find the coefficient of x^2 in the expansion of $\left(x+\frac{1}{x}\right)^8$.

10. (a) Find the first 3 terms in the expansion of $(2+3x)^7$.

(b) Hence find an approximation to

(i) 2.3^7 (ii) 2.03^7

(c) Which of your answers in part (b) provides a more accurate approximation? Justify your answer. *[6 marks]*

11. (a) Expand $\left(\text{e}+\frac{2}{\text{e}}\right)^5$.

(b) Simplify $\left(\text{e}+\frac{2}{\text{e}}\right)^5+\left(\text{e}-\frac{2}{\text{e}}\right)^5$. *[7 marks]*

12. The expansion of $(x+ay)^n$ contains the term $60x^4y^2$.

(a) Write down the value of n.

(b) Find the value of a. *[4 marks]*

13. Complete and simplify the expansion of $\left(2z^2+\frac{3}{z}\right)^4$, which begins with $16z^8+96z^5$. *[4 marks]*

14. (a) Write the expression $(1+x)^n(1-x)^n$ in the form $(f(x))^n$.

(b) Find the first three non-zero terms in the expansion of $(1-x)^{10}(1+x)^{10}$ in ascending powers of x. *[6 marks]*

15. The expansion of $\left(3x^2y+\frac{5x}{y}\right)^n$ begins with $27x^6y^3+135x^5y$.

(a) Write down the value of n

(b) Complete and simplify the expansion *[5 marks]*

16. Find the coefficient of x^2 in the expansion of $\left(2x+\frac{1}{\sqrt{x}}\right)^5$.

[4 marks]

17. Find the constant coefficient in the expansion of $(x-2x^{-2})^9$.

[4 marks]

EXAM HINT

The 'constant coefficient' is the term in x^0. It may also be described as 'the term independent of x'.

18. Find the term in x^5 in $\left(x^2-\frac{3}{x}\right)^7$. *[6 marks]*

19. Find the term that is independent of x in the expansion of $\left(2x-\frac{5}{x^2}\right)^{12}$. *[6 marks]*

20. Find the coefficient of x^5 in the expansion of $(1+3x)(1+x)^7$.

21. If $(1+ax)^n = 1+10x+40x^2+\cdots$, find the values of a and of n.

Summary

- A binomial expression is one that contains two terms, e.g. $a+b$.
- The binomial coefficient, $\binom{n}{r}$, is the coefficient of the term containing $a^{n-r}b^r$ in the expansion of $(a+b)^n$.
- The expansion of $(a+b)^n$ can be accomplished directly by using the **binomial theorem**:

$$(a+b)^n = a^n + \binom{n}{1}a^{n-1}b+\cdots+\binom{n}{r}a^{n-r}b^r+\cdots+b^n$$

- The coefficient of individual terms in a **binomial expansion** can be found by looking at the powers of the algebraic components and using the formula for the rth term

$$\binom{n}{r}(a)^{n-r}(b)^r$$

with appropriate choices of n, r, a and b.
- Approximations to powers of numbers can be made by taking the first few terms of a binomial expansion $(a + bx)^n$ and substituting an appropriate small value for x, so that terms containing higher powers of x will be negligible.

Introductory problem revisited

Without using a calculator, find the value of $(1.002)^{10}$ correct to 8 decimal places.

The first step is to recognise that $(1.002)^{10}$ can be obtained by evaluating the binomial expansion $(1 + 2x)^{10}$ with $x = 0.001$.

To ensure accuracy to 8 decimal places, we need to include terms up to $x^3 = 10^{-9}$ at least; we can safely disregard terms in x^4 and greater powers, since these will be too small to affect the first 8 decimal places of the result.

Write down each term in the form $\binom{n}{r}(a)^{n-r}(b)^r$ with $a=1, b=2x, n=10$.

The first 4 terms are
$1(1)^{10} + 10(1)^9(2x)^1 + 45(1)^8(2x)^2 + 120(1)^7(2x)^3$

Apply the powers to the bracketed terms and multiply through.

The first 4 terms are
$1 + 20x + 180x^2 + 960x^3$

Calculate the powers of the appropriate value of x and thus the value of each term.

$x^0 = 1$ $\quad$ $1 = 1$
$x^1 = 0.001$ $\quad$ $20x^1 = 0.02$
$x^2 = 0.000\,001$ $\quad$ $180x^2 = 0.000\,18$
$x^3 = 0.000\,000\,001$ $\quad$ $960x^3 = 0.000\,000\,96$

Total the values of the terms.

Hence $1.002^{10} \simeq 1.02018096$

From calculator, $1.002^{10} = 1.020\,180\,963\,368\,08\ldots$
So approximation error is $3.30 \times 10^{-9} = 0.000\,000\,33\%$

Mixed examination practice 7

Short questions

1. Find the coefficient of x^5 in the expansion of $(2-x)^{12}$. *[5 marks]*

2. Fully expand and simplify $(2x^{-1}+5y)^3$. *[4 marks]*

3. Let $a=2-\sqrt{2}$. Using binomial expansion or otherwise, express a^5 in the form $m+n\sqrt{2}$. *[5 marks]*

4. Find the constant coefficient in the expansion of $(x^3-2x^{-1})^4$. *[4 marks]*

5. Fully expand and simplify $\left(x^2-\frac{2}{x}\right)^4$. *[6 marks]*

6. Find the coefficient of c^4d^{11} in the expansion of $(2c+5d)(c+d)^{14}$. *[6 marks]*

7. Find the coefficient of x^6 in the expansion of $(1-x^2)(1+x)^5$. *[5 marks]*

Long questions

1. (a) Sketch the graph of $y=(x+2)^3$.

(b) Find the binomial expansion of $(x+2)^3$.

(c) Find the exact value of 2.001^3.

(d) Solve the equation $x^3+6x^2+12x+16=0$. *[12 marks]*

2. The expansion of $(2x+ay)^n$ contains the term $20x^3y^2$.

(a) Write down the value of n.

(b) Find the value of a.

(c) Find the first four terms in ascending powers of y.

(d) Hence or otherwise, find 20.05^n correct to the nearest hundred. You do not need to justify the accuracy of your approximation. *[11 marks]*

8 Circular measure and trigonometric functions

In this chapter you will learn:

- about different units for measuring angles, and how measuring angles is related to distance travelled around a circle
- the definitions of the sine, cosine and tangent functions, their basic properties and their graphs
- how to calculate certain special values of trigonometric functions
- how to apply your knowledge of transformations of graphs to sketch more complicated trigonometric functions
- how to use trigonometric functions to model periodic phenomena.

Introductory problem

A clock has an hour hand of length 10 cm, and the centre of the clock is 4 m above the floor. Find an expression for the height, h metres, of the tip of the hour hand above the floor at a time t hours after midnight.

Measuring angles is related to measuring lengths around the perimeter of a circle. This observation leads to a new unit for measuring angles, the **radian**, which will turn out to be more useful than the degree as a unit of angle measurement in advanced mathematics.

Periodic motion is motion that repeats after a fixed time interval. Motion in a circle is just one example of this; other examples include oscillation of a particle attached to the end of a spring or vibration of a guitar string. There are also periodic phenomena where a pattern is repeated in space rather than in time – for example, the shape of a water wave. All of these can be modelled using **trigonometric functions**.

8A Measuring angles

An angle measures the amount of rotation between two straight lines. You are already familiar with measuring angles in degrees, where a full turn measures 360°. There are two directions (or senses) of rotation: clockwise and anti-clockwise (counter-clockwise). In mathematics, the convention is to take anti-clockwise as the positive direction. In the first diagram below, the line OA rotates 60° anti-clockwise into position OB. Therefore $A\hat{O}B = 60°$.

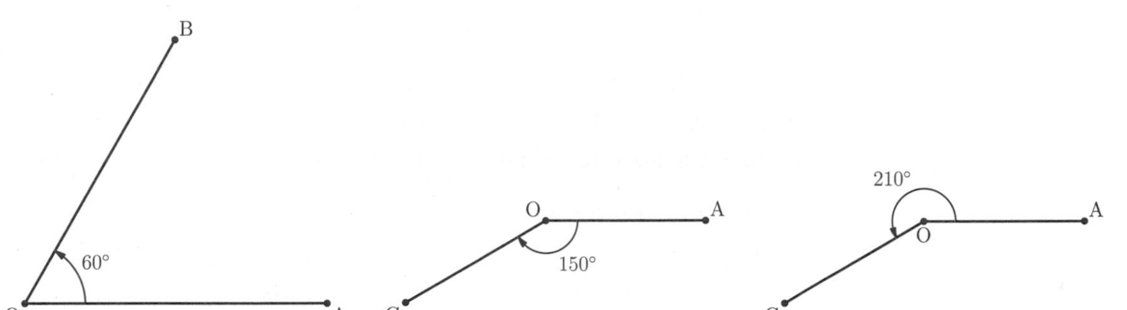

In the second diagram, the line OA rotates 150° clockwise into position OC. Clockwise rotations are represented by negative angle measures; therefore $A\hat{O}C = -150°$. Note that we can also move OA to position OC by rotating 210° anti-clockwise, as shown in the third diagram, so it is equally correct to say that $A\hat{O}C = 210°$. In this book, as well as in exam questions, it will always be made clear which of the two angles is required.

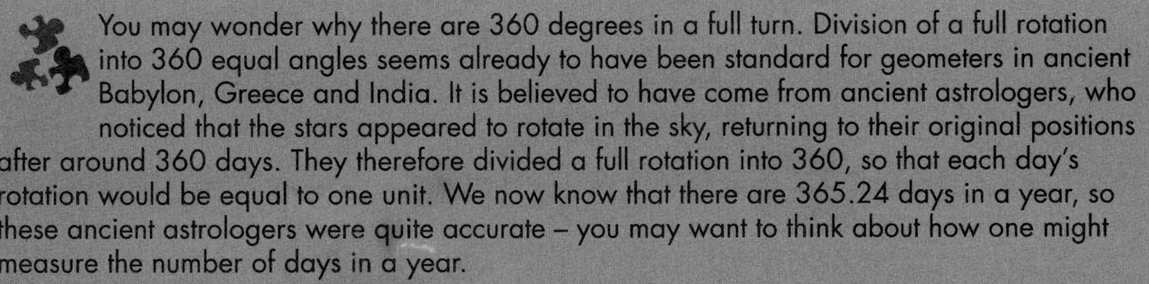
You may wonder why there are 360 degrees in a full turn. Division of a full rotation into 360 equal angles seems already to have been standard for geometers in ancient Babylon, Greece and India. It is believed to have come from ancient astrologers, who noticed that the stars appeared to rotate in the sky, returning to their original positions after around 360 days. They therefore divided a full rotation into 360, so that each day's rotation would be equal to one unit. We now know that there are 365.24 days in a year, so these ancient astrologers were quite accurate – you may want to think about how one might measure the number of days in a year.

Defining a full turn to be 360° is somewhat arbitrary, and there are other ways of measuring sizes of angles. In advanced mathematics, the most useful unit of angle measurement is the **radian**. This measure relates the size of the angle to the distance moved by a point around a circle.

The unit circle will be used when defining trigonometric functions in Section 8B.

Consider a circle with centre O and radius 1; this is called the **unit circle**. Let A and B be two points on its circumference. As the line OA rotates into position OB, point A moves a distance equal to the length of the arc AB. The measure of the angle $A\hat{O}B$ in radians is defined to be this arc length.

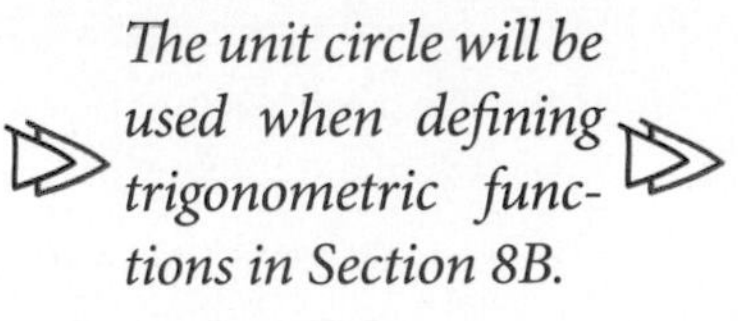
Recall that an arc is the path joining two points on a curve.

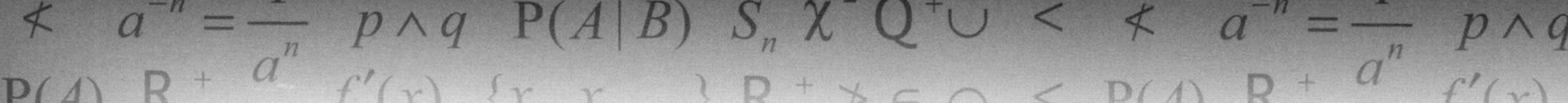

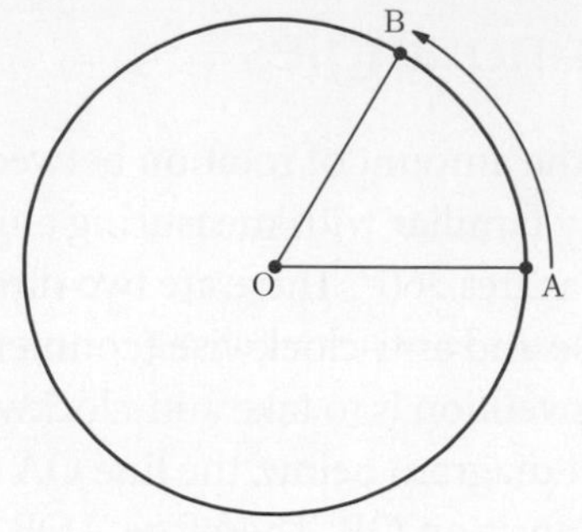

If point A makes a full rotation around the circle, it will cover a distance equal to the length of the circumference of the circle. As the radius of the circle is 1, the length of the circumference is 2π. Hence a full turn measures 2π radians. From this we can deduce the sizes in radians of other angles; for example, a right angle is one quarter of a full turn, so it measures $2\pi \div 4 = \frac{\pi}{2}$ radians. Although the sizes of common angles measured in radians are often expressed as fractions of π, we can also use decimal approximations. Thus a right angle measures approximately 1.57 radians. The fact that a full turn measures 2π radians can be used to convert any angle measurement from degrees to radians, and vice versa.

Worked example 8.1

(a) Convert 75° to radians.

(b) Convert 2.5 radians to degrees.

What fraction of a full turn is 75°?

(a) $\frac{75}{360} = \frac{5}{24}$

Calculate the same fraction of 2π.

$\frac{5}{24} \times 2\pi = \frac{5\pi}{12}$

$\therefore 75° = \frac{5\pi}{12}$ radians

This is the *exact* answer. Using a calculator, we can find the decimal equivalent to 3 significant figures.

75° = 1.31 radians (3 SF)

What fraction of a full turn is 2.5 radians?

(b) $\frac{2.5}{2\pi} (\approx 0.3979)$

Calculate the same fraction of 360°.

$\frac{2.5}{2\pi} \times 360 = 143.239\ldots$

2.5 radians = 143° (3 SF)

KEY POINT 8.1

$$\text{full turn} = 360° = 2\pi \text{ radians}$$

$$\text{half turn} = 180° = \pi \text{ radians}$$

To convert from degrees to radians, divide by 180 and multiply by π:

$$\text{radians} = \frac{\pi \times \text{degrees}}{180}$$

To convert from radians to degrees, divide by π and multiply by 180:

$$\text{degrees} = \frac{180 \times \text{radians}}{\pi}$$

There are various other measures of angle. For example, a unit that originated in France when the metric system was introduced is the gradian, which is one-hundredth of a right angle. In most countries today, use of the gradian continues only within a few specialised fields, such as architectural surveying and artillery. Since there are so many different ways of defining angle units, does this mean that the facts you have learnt – such as there being 180 degrees in a triangle – are purely consequences of particular definitions and have no link to truth?

Our definition of radian measure used the unit circle. However, we can consider a point moving around a circle of any radius.

Think about what happens as the line OA rotates into position OB.

The distance covered by point A will be the arc length, l.

Since the entire circumference is $2\pi r$, the fraction of the circle travelled is $\frac{l}{2\pi r}$.

Let θ be the measure of $A\hat{O}B$ in radians; this corresponds to a fraction $\frac{\theta}{2\pi}$ of a full rotation.

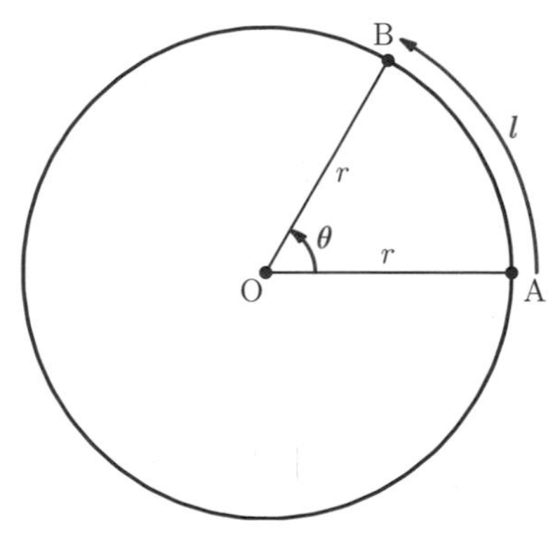

Now we have two expressions for the proportion of the circle covered as we move from OA to OB: one from considering the length of the arc, and the other from considering the size of the angle. Both give the fraction of the circle covered by the sector AOB, so they must be equal:

$$\frac{\theta}{2\pi} = \frac{l}{2\pi r} \Rightarrow \theta = \frac{l}{r}$$

KEY POINT 8.2

The radian measure of an angle in a circle is given by

$$\theta = \frac{l}{r}$$

That is, the measure of the angle is the ratio of the length of the arc to the radius of the circle.

In particular, an angle of 1 radian corresponds to an arc whose length is equal to the radius of the circle.

EXAM HINT

Some people write angles in radians as, for instance, $\theta = 1.31\text{rad}$ or $\theta = 1.31^c$, but the International Baccalaureate does not use this notation.

In the unit circle (where $r = 1$), the size of an angle is numerically equal to the length of the arc; however, these two quantities have different units. If we think of the size of an angle as a ratio of two lengths (as in Key point 8.2), then it should have no units. This is why the radian is said to be a *dimensionless unit* and, when writing the size of an angle in radians, we need only give the angle as a number, for example $\theta = 1.31$.

All this may sound complicated, and you may wonder why we cannot just use degrees to measure angles. You will see in the next two sections that the formulas for calculating lengths and areas of parts of circles are much simpler when radians are used, and the advantages of using radians will become even clearer when you study calculus.

Radians will be used whenever we differentiate or integrate trigonometric functions (from chapter 12 onwards).

If we think of angles as measuring the amount of rotation around the unit circle, then we can represent an angle of any size by its corresponding point on the unit circle. As mentioned earlier, the convention in mathematics is to measure positive angles by anti-clockwise rotations. Another convention is that we consider the unit circle as having its centre at the origin of the coordinate system, and start measuring from the point on the circle which lies on the positive x-axis. In the first diagram below, the starting point is labelled A, and the point P corresponds to the angle 60°. In other words, to get from the starting point to point P, we need to rotate 60°, or one-sixth of a full turn, anti-clockwise around the circle.

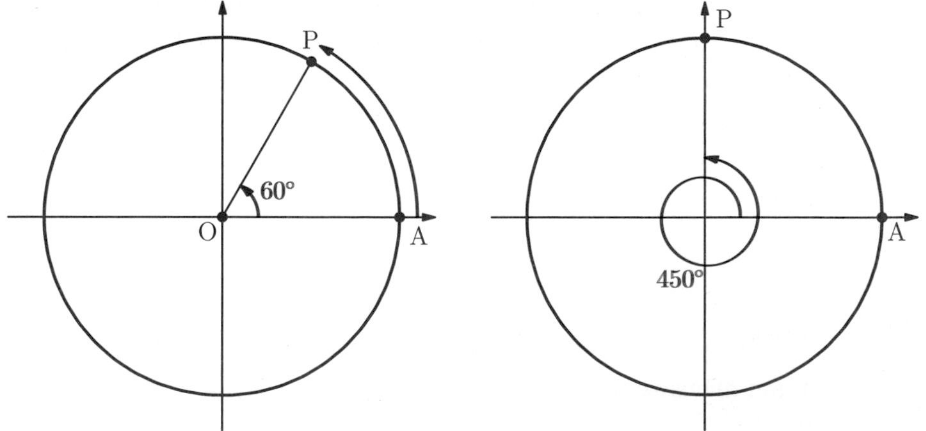

We can also represent negative angles (by clockwise rotations) and angles larger than 360° (by rotating through more than one full turn). The second diagram above shows point P representing the angle of 450°, or one and a quarter turns.

There is a three-dimensional analogue of an angle, called a solid angle. The size of a solid angle has units of *steradians*, which measure the fraction of the surface area of a sphere covered. Many aspects of two-dimensional trigonometry can be transferred to these solid angles.

Worked example 8.2

(a) Mark on the unit circle the points corresponding to the following angles, measured in degrees:

A: 135°   B: 270°   C: −120°   D: 765°

(b) Mark on the unit circle the points corresponding to the following angles, measured in radians:

A: π B: $-\frac{\pi}{2}$ C: $\frac{5\pi}{2}$ D: $\frac{13\pi}{3}$

$135 = 90 + 45$, so point A represents quarter plus another eighth of a full turn.

$270 = 3 \times 90$, so point B represents rotation through three right angles.

$120 = 360 \div 3$, so point C represents a third of a full turn, but clockwise (because of the minus sign).

$765 = 2 \times 360 + 45$, so point D represents two full turns plus one half of a right angle.

π radians is one half of a full turn so point A represents half a turn.

$\frac{\pi}{2} = \frac{1}{4} \times 2\pi$, so point B represents one quarter of a full turn in the clockwise direction.

$\frac{5\pi}{2} = 2\pi + \frac{\pi}{2}$, so point C represents a full turn followed by another quarter of a turn.

$\frac{13\pi}{3} = 4\pi + \frac{\pi}{3}$, so point D represents two full turns followed by another $\frac{1}{6}$ of a turn.

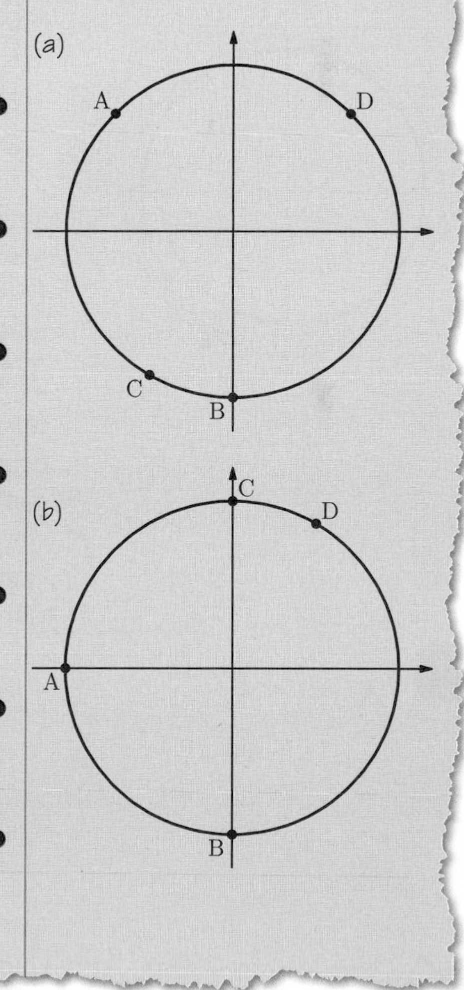

Looking at the number line in this way should suggest why radians are a more natural measure of angle than degrees. While radians are rarely used outside the mathematical community, within mathematics they are the unit of choice.

The idea of representing angles by points on the unit circle can be applied to numbers too: instead of representing numbers by points on a number line, we can represent them by points on the unit circle. To do this, imagine wrapping the number line around the unit circle: start by placing zero on the positive x-axis (point S in the diagram) and then, going anti-clockwise, lay positive numbers on the circle. As the circumference of the circle has length 2π, the numbers $2\pi, 4\pi$ and so on will also be represented by point S. The numbers π, 3π, 5π and so on are represented by point P. The number 3, which is a little less than π, is represented by point A.

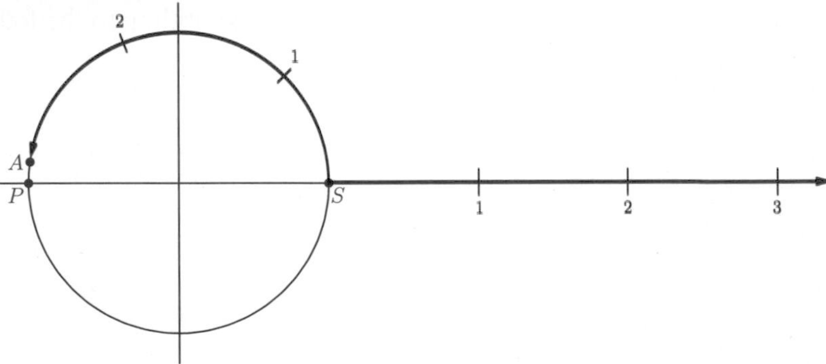

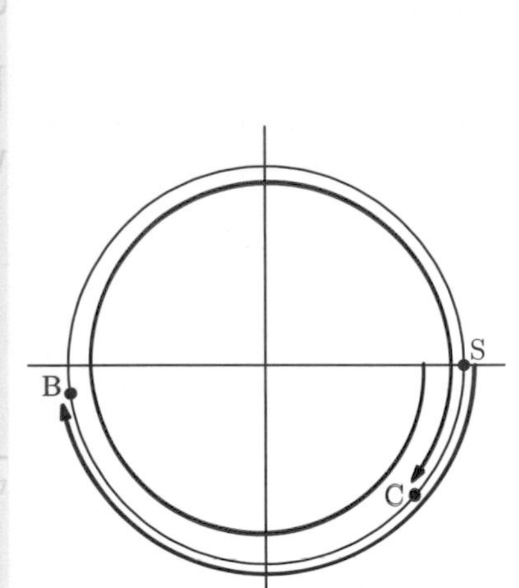

Similarly, we can represent negative numbers by wrapping the negative part of the number line clockwise around the circle. For example, the number −3 is represented by point B and the number −7 by point C (7 is a bit bigger than 2π, which means wrapping once and a bit around the circle).

It is useful to describe where points are on the unit circle by using quadrants. A **quadrant** is one quarter of the circle, and conventionally quadrants are labelled going anti-clockwise, starting from the top right one. So in part (a) of Worked example 8.2, point A is in the second quadrant, point B in the third quadrant and point D in the first quadrant.

Exercise 8A

1. Draw a unit circle for each part and mark the points corresponding to the given angles:
   (a) (i) 60° (ii) 150°
   (b) (i) −120° (ii) −90°
   (c) (i) 495° (ii) 390°

2. Draw a unit circle for each part and mark the points corresponding to the following angles:

(a) (i) $\frac{\pi}{4}$ (ii) $\frac{\pi}{3}$

(b) (i) $\frac{4\pi}{3}$ (ii) $\frac{3\pi}{4}$

(c) (i) $-\frac{\pi}{3}$ (ii) $-\frac{\pi}{6}$

(d) (i) -2π (ii) -4π

3. Express the following angles in radians, giving your answers in terms of π:

(a) (i) 135° (ii) 45°

(b) (i) 90° (ii) 270°

(c) (i) 120° (ii) 150°

(d) (i) 50° (ii) 80°

4. Express the following angles in radians, correct to 3 decimal places:

(a) (i) 320° (ii) 20°

(b) (i) 270° (ii) 90°

(c) (i) 65° (ii) 145°

(d) (i) 100° (ii) 83°

5. Express the following angles in degrees:

(a) (i) $\frac{\pi}{3}$ (ii) $\frac{\pi}{4}$

(b) (i) $\frac{5\pi}{6}$ (ii) $\frac{2\pi}{3}$

(c) (i) $\frac{3\pi}{2}$ (ii) $\frac{5\pi}{3}$

(d) (i) 1.22 (ii) 4.63

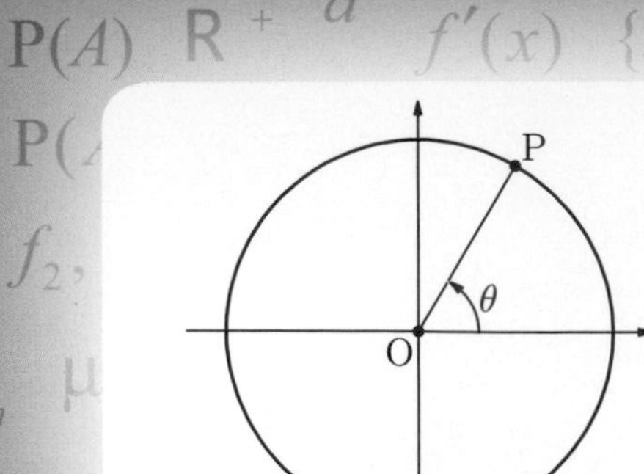

6. The diagram shows point P on the unit circle corresponding to angle θ (measured in degrees). Copy the diagram and mark the points corresponding to the following angles.
   (a) (i) $180° - \theta$ (ii) $180° + \theta$
   (b) (i) $\theta + 180°$ (ii) $\theta + 90°$
   (c) (i) $90° - \theta$ (ii) $270° - \theta$
   (d) (i) $\theta - 360°$ (ii) $\theta + 360°$

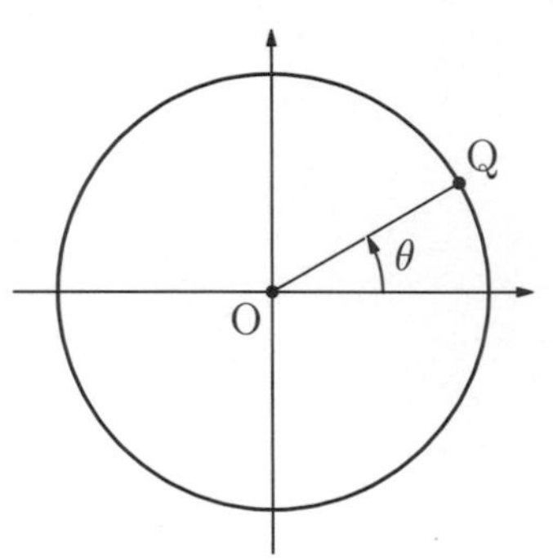

7. The diagram shows point Q on the unit circle corresponding to the real number θ.
   Copy the diagram and mark the points corresponding to the following real numbers.
   (a) (i) $2\pi - \theta$ (ii) $\pi - \theta$
   (b) (i) $\theta + \pi$ (ii) $-\pi - \theta$
   (c) (i) $\frac{\pi}{2} + \theta$ (ii) $\frac{\pi}{2} - \theta$
   (d) (i) $\theta - 2\pi$ (ii) $\theta + 2\pi$

8B Definitions and graphs of the sine and cosine functions

We now define trigonometric functions.

For a real number α, mark the point A on the unit circle that represents the number α (or, equivalently, the angle α radians).

The sine and cosine of α are defined in terms of the distance from point A to the x- and y-axes. (Remember that, by convention, the unit circle has its centre at the origin of the coordinate axes.)

KEY POINT 8.3

The **sine** of the number α, written sin α, is the distance of the point A above the horizontal axis (its *y*-coordinate).

The **cosine** of the number α, written cos α, is the distance of the point A to the right of the vertical axis (its *x*-coordinate).

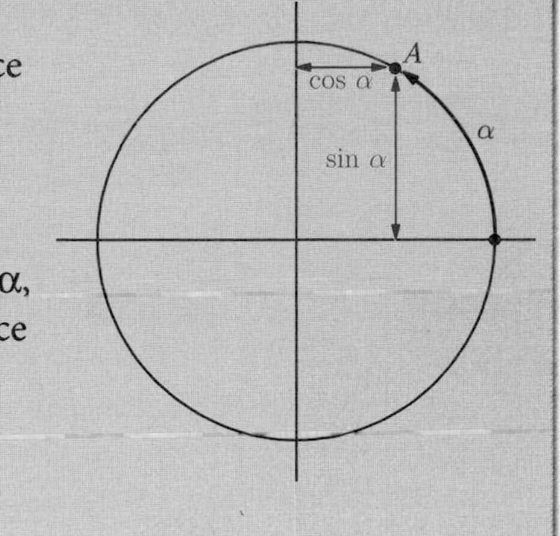

You have previously seen sine and cosine defined using right-angled triangles. See Prior Learning section U on the CD-ROM for a reminder.

The definition in Key point 8.3 is consistent with the definition by right-angled triangles, but it further allows us to define sine and cosine for angles beyond 90°. This raises the question of how to decide which of several alternative definitions to use – should we go with the one that came first historically, the one that is more understandable, or the one that is more general?

Worked example 8.3

By marking the corresponding point on the unit circle, estimate the value of $\cos 2.4$.

$\frac{\pi}{2} \approx 1.6$ and $\pi \approx 3.1$, so the point is around the middle of the second quadrant.

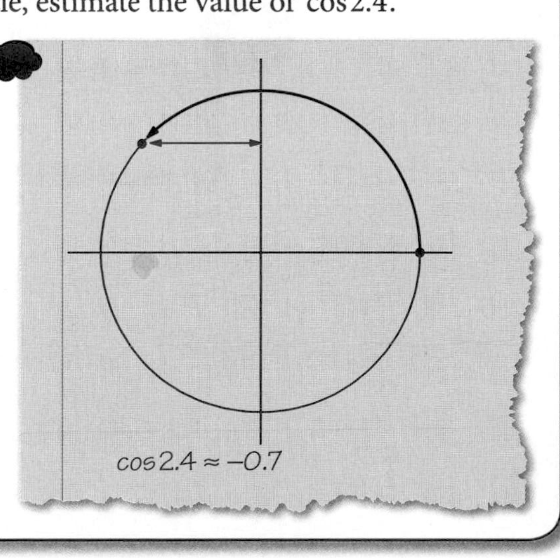

$\cos 2.4 \approx -0.7$

Notice that in the above example cos 2.4 was a negative number. This is because the point corresponding to 2.4 lies to the left of the vertical axis, so we take the distance to be negative.

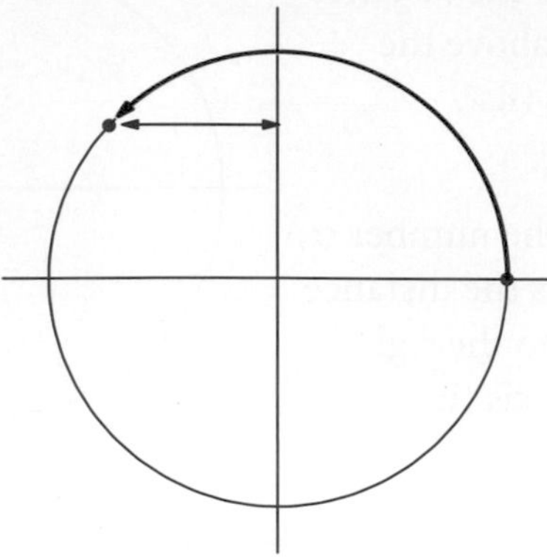

You can find sine and cosine values, such as the ones in the previous example, using your calculator.

Most GDC calculators have buttons for the sine, cosine (and tan) functions. If you were to work out the answer to the question in Worked example 8.3 using your GDC, you would simply press [cos] [2][.][4][EXE] and you would get the answer −0.737... (provided your calculator was in radian mode). As the question used an angle measured in radians, you would need to make sure your calculator was set to radians. If your calculator was in degree mode, your calculator would interpret cos 2.4 as the cosine of 2.4° rather than 2.4 radians and you would get an answer of 0.999..., which is incorrect.

See Calculator skills sheet 1 for how to determine if your calculator is in radians or degree mode, and how to change between them.

Key point 8.1 describes how to change from radians to degrees and vice versa.

Note however, that if your calculator had been in degree mode and you had keyed in the cosine of the equivalent angle in degrees, i.e. 137.5° (which is approximately 2.4 radians), then you would have got the correct answer of −0.737.... This demonstrates that it does not matter whether you find the sine or cosine of an angle in degrees or radians (the answer will be the same) provided that your calculator is in the correct mode according to the form of the angle you enter into your calculator.

We can use the unit circle to get information about functions of angles related to one we already know about.

Remember that $\sin\alpha$ is the distance of the point of interest (e.g. A) on the circumference above the horizontal axis (its y-coordinate) and $\cos\alpha$ is the distance of A to the right of the vertical axis (its x-coordinate).

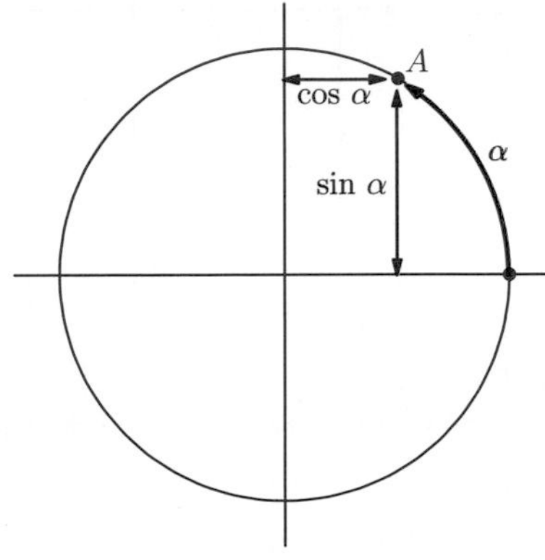

Worked example 8.4

Given that $\sin\theta = 0.6$, find the values of

(a) $\sin(\pi - \theta)$ (b) $\sin(\theta + \pi)$

Mark the points corresponding to θ and $\pi - \theta$ on the circle.

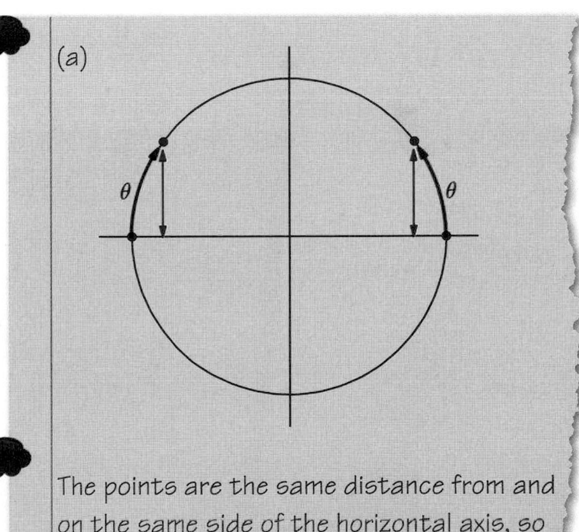

Since sine of a number is defined to be the y-coordinate of the corresponding point on the unit circle, compare the positions of the points relative to the horizontal axis.

The points are the same distance from and on the same side of the horizontal axis, so

$\sin(\pi - \theta) = 0.6$

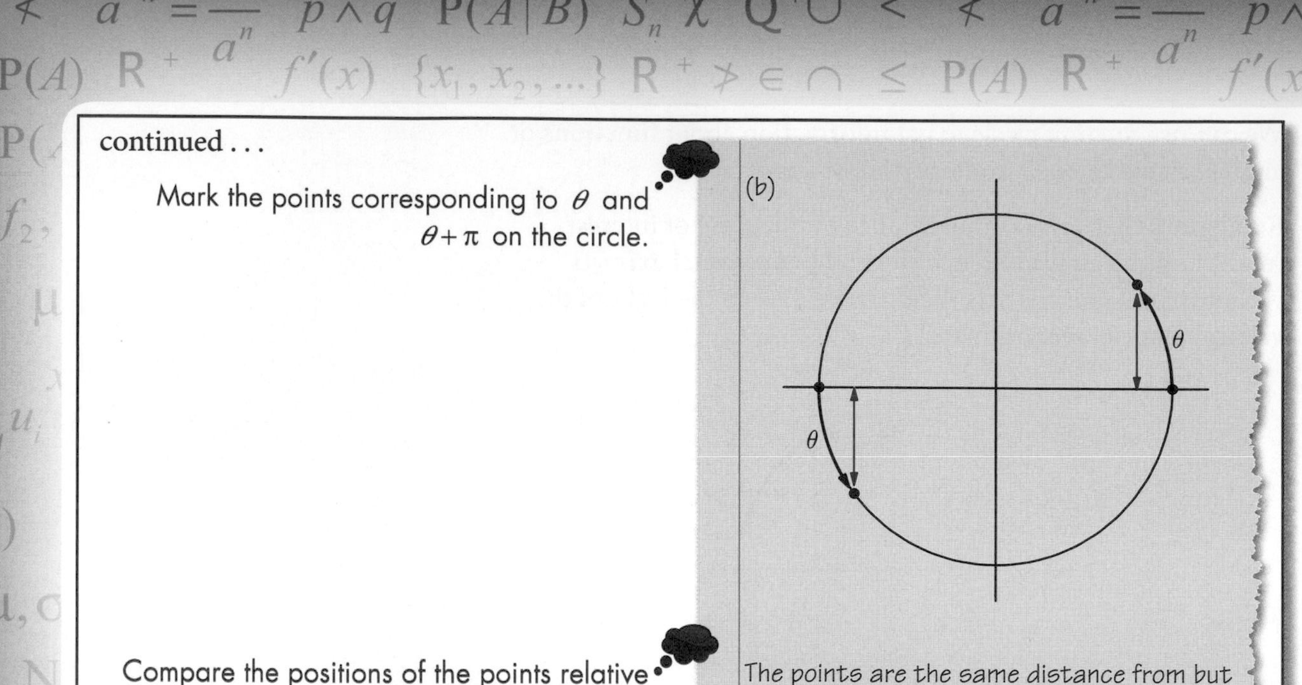
continued . . .
Mark the points corresponding to θ and θ+π on the circle.
(b)
θ
θ
Compare the positions of the points relative to the horizontal axis.
The points are the same distance from but on opposite sides of the horizontal axis, so
sin(θ+π) = −0.6

The above example illustrates some of the properties of the sine function. Similar properties hold for the cosine function. The symmetry results summarised below are useful to remember. They can all be derived using circle diagrams.

EXAM HINT

These results are not given in the Formula booklet, so make sure that you are able to work them out from a quick sketch of a circle by considering the symmetries involved.

KEY POINT 8.4

For any real number x:

$\sin x = \sin(\pi - x) = \sin(x + 2\pi)$

$\sin(\pi + x) = \sin(-x) = -\sin x$

$\cos x = \cos(-x) = \cos(x + 2\pi)$

$\cos(\pi - x) = \cos(\pi + x) = -\cos x$

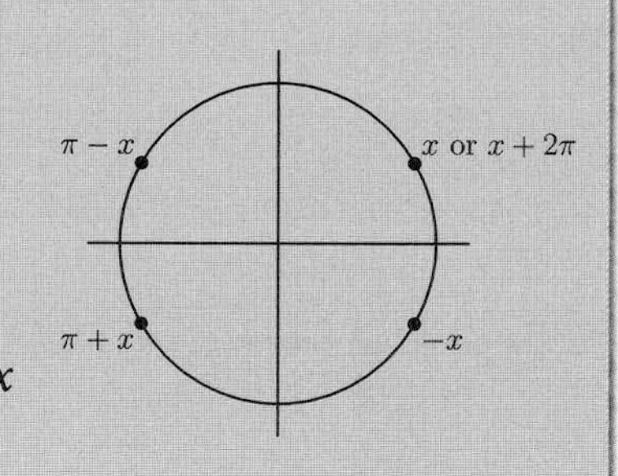
π − x
x or x + 2π
π + x
−x

Worked example 8.5

Given that $\sin x = 0.4$, find the value of:

(a) $\cos\left(\frac{\pi}{2} - x\right)$ (b) $\cos\left(x + \frac{\pi}{2}\right)$

Mark on the unit circle the points corresponding to x, $\frac{\pi}{2} - x$ and $x + \frac{\pi}{2}$. The point P represents the number x, and we know that $PX = \sin x = 0.4$.

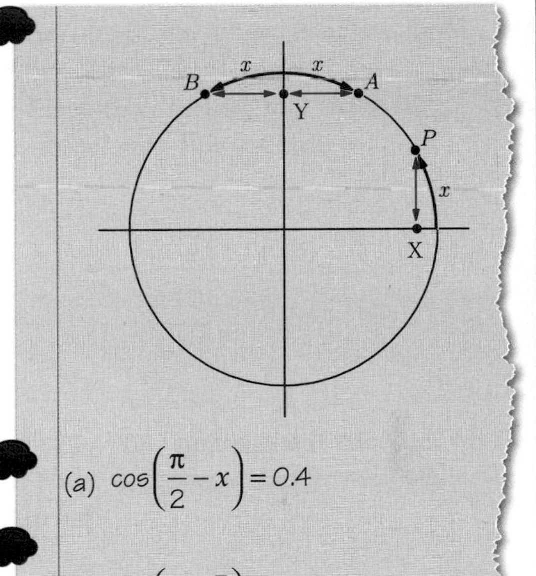

$\frac{\pi}{2} - x$ is represented by point A, and AY = PX.

(a) $\cos\left(\frac{\pi}{2} - x\right) = 0.4$

$x + \frac{\pi}{2}$ is represented by point B, and BY = PX, but B is to the left of the vertical axis.

(b) $\cos\left(x + \frac{\pi}{2}\right) = -0.4$

The above example illustrates a relationship between sine and cosine functions. It will be useful to remember the following results, or be able to derive them from a circle diagram.

KEY POINT 8.5

For any real number x:

$$\cos\left(\frac{\pi}{2} - x\right) = \sin x$$

$$\cos\left(\frac{\pi}{2} + x\right) = -\sin x$$

$$\sin\left(\frac{\pi}{2} - x\right) = \cos x$$

$$\sin\left(\frac{\pi}{2} + x\right) = \cos x$$

In chapter 9 you will see another connection between the sine and cosine functions, which arises from Pythagoras' Theorem.

In Key points 8.4 and 8.5, the variable x was an angle measured in radians. Analogous results can be derived when the variable represents an angle measured in degrees.

Worked example 8.6

Given that θ is an angle measured in degrees such that $\cos\theta = 0.8$, find the value of

(a) $\cos(180° + \theta)$ (b) $\sin(90° - \theta)$

Mark on the circle the points corresponding to angles θ, $180° + \theta$ and $90° - \theta$. We know that the point representing θ is at distance 0.8 from the vertical axis.

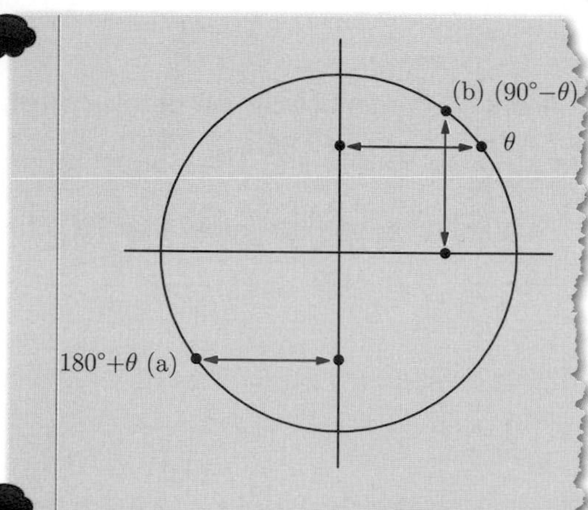

For the point representing $180° + \theta$, its distance from the vertical axis is also 0.8, but it lies to the left of the axis.

(a) $\cos(180° + \theta) = -0.8$

The point representing $90° - \theta$ is the reflection of the point representing θ in the diagonal line $y = x$, so the distance from the *horizontal* axis is 0.8.

(b) $\sin(90° - \theta) = 0.8$

So far we have focused on the sine and cosine of angles, but in reality the domain of the sine and cosine functions is all real numbers.

Having defined the sine function for all real numbers, we can draw its graph. To do this, let's go back to thinking about the real number line wrapped around the unit circle. Each real number corresponds to a point on the circle, and the value of the sine function is the distance of the point from the horizontal axis.

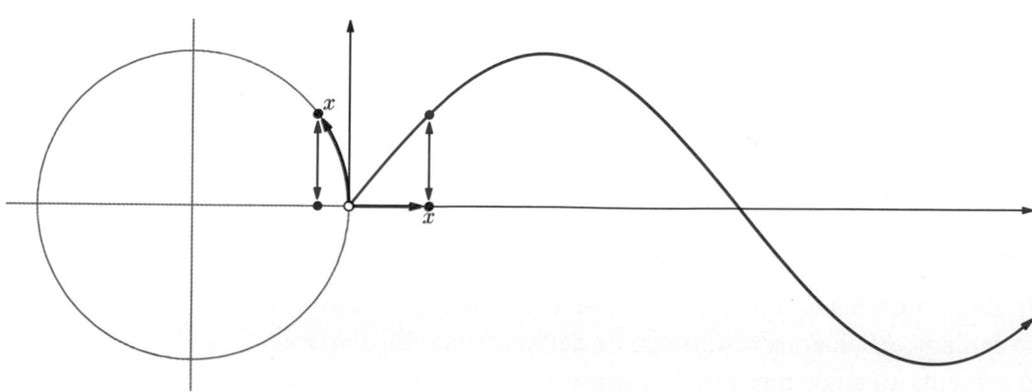

All of the properties of the sine function discussed above can be seen in its graph. For example, increasing x by 2π corresponds to making a full turn around the circle and returning to the same point; therefore, $\sin(x+2\pi)=\sin x$. We say that the sine function is **periodic** with **period** 2π. Looking at the graph below, by considering points A and B we can see that $\sin(-x)=-\sin x$. We can also see that the minimum possible value of $\sin x$ is -1 and the maximum value is 1. Thus we say that the sine function has **amplitude** 1.

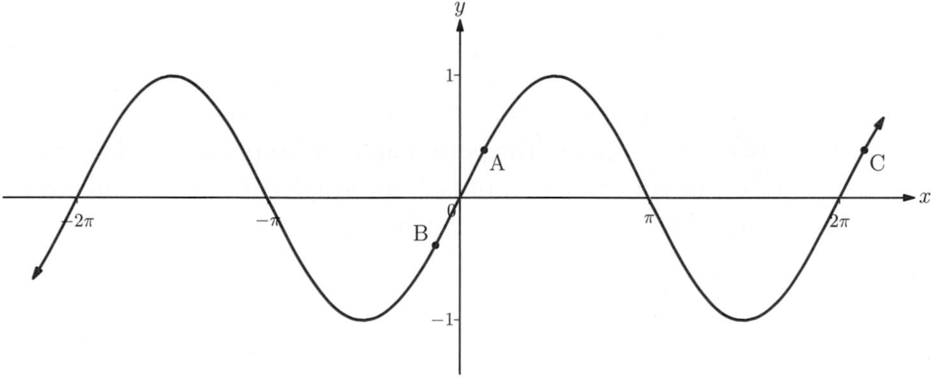

KEY POINT 8.6

A function is **periodic** if its pattern repeats regularly. The interval between the start of two consecutive repeating blocks is called the **period**.

The **amplitude** of a periodic function is half the distance between the maximum and minimum values.

To draw the graph of the cosine function, we look at the distance from the vertical axis of the point on the unit circle representing the real number x.

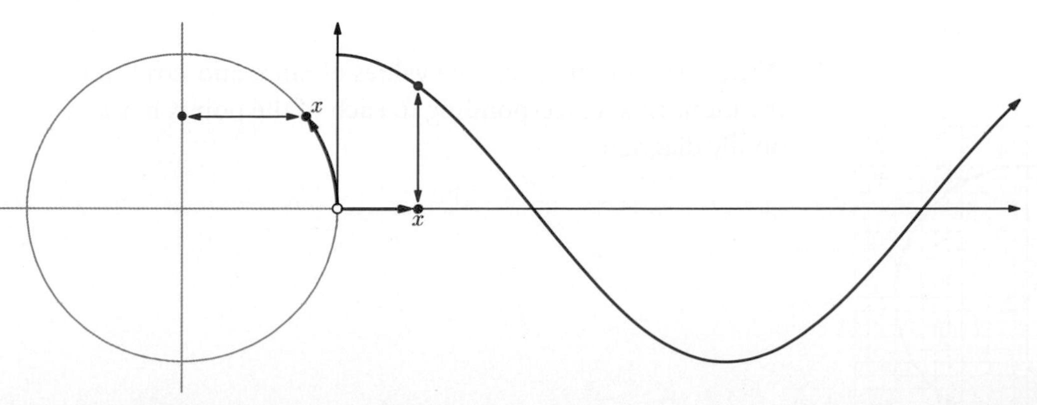

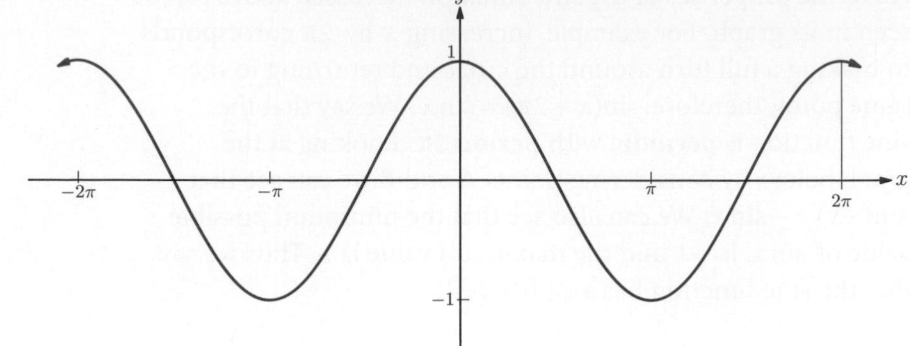

Again, we can see on this graph many of the properties discussed previously; for example, $\cos(-x) = \cos x$ and $\cos(\pi - x) = -\cos x$. The period and the amplitude are the same as for the sine function. In fact, the graphs of the sine and cosine functions are related to each other in a simple way: the graph of $y = \cos x$ is obtained from the graph of $y = \sin x$ by translating it $\frac{\pi}{2}$ units to the left. This corresponds to one of the properties listed in Key point 8.5: $\cos x = \sin\left(x + \frac{\pi}{2}\right)$.

We discussed the transformations of graphs in chapter 5.

KEY POINT 8.7

The sine and cosine functions are periodic with period 2π.

The sine and cosine functions have amplitude 1.

Trigonometric functions can be used to define *polar coordinates*. This alternative to the Cartesian coordinate system makes it easier to write equations of certain graphs. Equations in polar coordinates produce some beautiful curves, such as the cardioid and the polar rose.

Exercise 8B

1. Write down the approximate values of $\sin x$ and $\cos x$ for the number x corresponding to each of the points marked on the diagram.

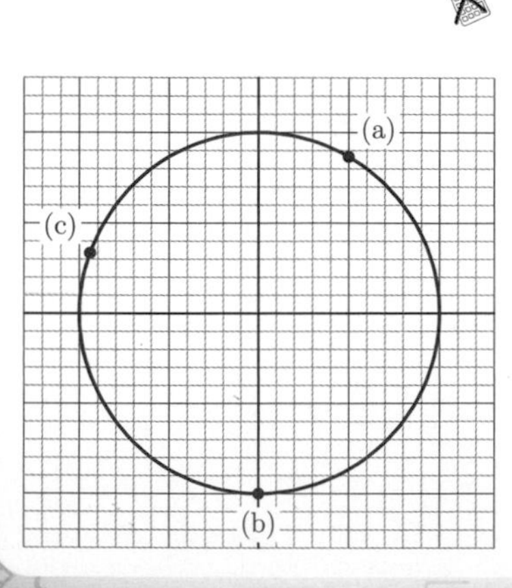

2. Use the unit circle to find the following values:

(a) (i) $\sin\frac{\pi}{2}$ (ii) $\sin 2\pi$

(b) (i) $\cos 0$ (ii) $\cos(-\pi)$

(c) (i) $\sin\left(-\frac{\pi}{2}\right)$ (ii) $\cos\frac{5\pi}{2}$

3. Use the unit circle to find the following values:

(a) (i) $\cos 90°$ (ii) $\cos 180°$

(b) (i) $\sin 270°$ (ii) $\sin 90°$

(c) (i) $\sin 720°$ (ii) $\cos 450°$

4. Given that $\cos\frac{\pi}{5} = 0.809$, find the value of:

(a) $\cos\frac{4\pi}{5}$ (b) $\cos\frac{21\pi}{5}$

(c) $\cos\frac{9\pi}{5}$ (d) $\cos\frac{6\pi}{5}$

5. Given that $\sin\frac{2\pi}{3} = 0.866$, find the value of:

(a) $\sin\left(\frac{-2\pi}{3}\right)$ (b) $\sin\frac{4\pi}{3}$

(c) $\sin\frac{10\pi}{3}$ (d) $\sin\frac{\pi}{3}$

6. Given that $\cos 40° = 0.766$, find the value of:

(a) $\cos 400°$ (b) $\cos 320°$

(c) $\cos(-220°)$ (d) $\cos 140°$

7. Given that $\sin 130° = 0.766$, find the value of:

(a) $\sin 490°$ (b) $\sin 50°$

(c) $\sin(-130°)$ (d) $\sin 230°$

8. Sketch the graph of $y = \sin x$ for:

(a) (i) $0° \le x \le 180°$ (ii) $90° \le x \le 360°$

(b) (i) $-\frac{\pi}{2} \le x \le \frac{\pi}{2}$ (ii) $-\pi \le x \le 2\pi$

9. Sketch the graph of $y = \cos x$ for:

(a) (i) $-180° \le x \le 180°$ (ii) $0 \le x \le 270°$

(b) (i) $\frac{\pi}{2} \le x \le \frac{3\pi}{2}$ (ii) $-\pi \le x \le 2\pi$

10. (a) On the unit circle, mark the points representing $\frac{\pi}{6}, \frac{\pi}{3}$ and $\frac{2\pi}{3}$.

(b) Given that $\sin\frac{\pi}{6} = 0.5$, find the value of:

(i) $\cos\frac{\pi}{3}$ (ii) $\cos\frac{2\pi}{3}$

11. Use your calculator to evaluate the following, giving your answers to 3 significant figures:

(a) (i) $\cos 1.25$ (ii) $\sin 0.68$

(b) (i) $\cos(-0.72)$ (ii) $\sin(-2.35)$

12. Use your calculator to evaluate the following, giving your answers to 3 significant figures:

(a) (i) $\sin 42°$ (ii) $\cos 168°$

(b) (i) $\sin(-50°)$ (ii) $\cos(-227°)$

13. Simplify $\cos(\pi + x) + \cos(\pi - x)$. *[3 marks]*

14. Simplify the following expression:

$$\sin x + \sin\left(x + \frac{\pi}{2}\right) + \sin(x + \pi) + \sin\left(x + \frac{3\pi}{2}\right) + \sin(x + 2\pi)$$

[5 marks]

8C Definition and graph of the tangent function

We now introduce another trigonometric function: the **tangent** function. It is defined as the ratio between the sine and the cosine functions.

KEY POINT 8.8

$$\tan x = \frac{\sin x}{\cos x}$$

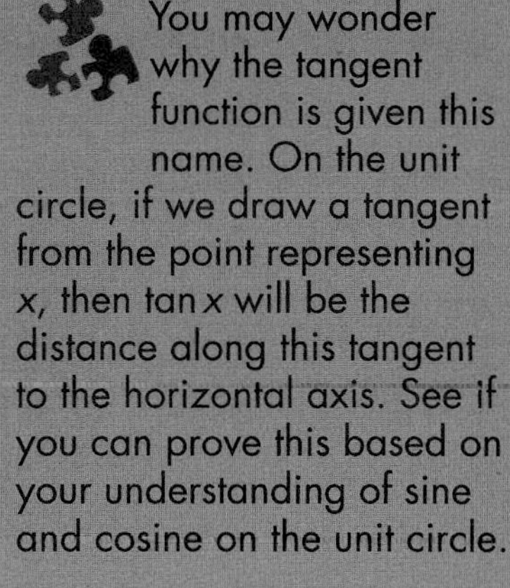

You may wonder why the tangent function is given this name. On the unit circle, if we draw a tangent from the point representing x, then $\tan x$ will be the distance along this tangent to the horizontal axis. See if you can prove this based on your understanding of sine and cosine on the unit circle.

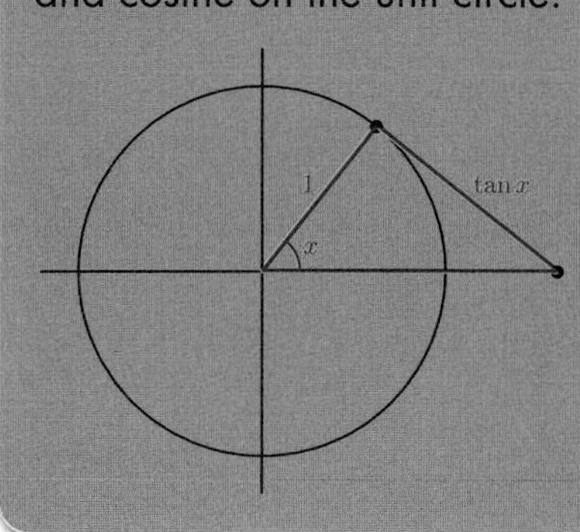

You may notice that there is a problem with this definition: we cannot divide by $\cos x$ when it is zero. Thus the tangent function is undefined at values of x where $\cos x = 0$; that is,

$\tan x$ is undefined for $x = \frac{\pi}{2}, \frac{3\pi}{2}, \frac{5\pi}{2}, \ldots$.

By considering the signs of $\sin x$ and $\cos x$ in different quadrants, we can see that $\tan x$ is positive in the first and third quadrants, and negative in the second and fourth quadrants. It is equal to zero when $\sin x = 0$, that is, at $x = 0, \pi, 2\pi, \ldots$

Since $\sin(x+\pi) = -\sin x$ and $\cos(x+\pi) = -\cos x$ (see Key point 8.4), we have

$$\tan(x+\pi) = \frac{\sin(x+\pi)}{\cos(x+\pi)} = \frac{-\sin x}{-\cos x} = \frac{\sin x}{\cos x} = \tan x$$

So the tangent function is periodic with period π:

$$\tan x = \tan(x+\pi) = \tan(x+2\pi) = \ldots$$

Using the information we have collected above, we can sketch the graph of the tangent function. The graph will have vertical asymptotes at $x = \frac{\pi}{2}, \frac{3\pi}{2}, \frac{5\pi}{2}, \ldots$

Vertical asymptotes were discussed in chapters 2 and 4.

KEY POINT 8.9

The graph of the tangent function is:

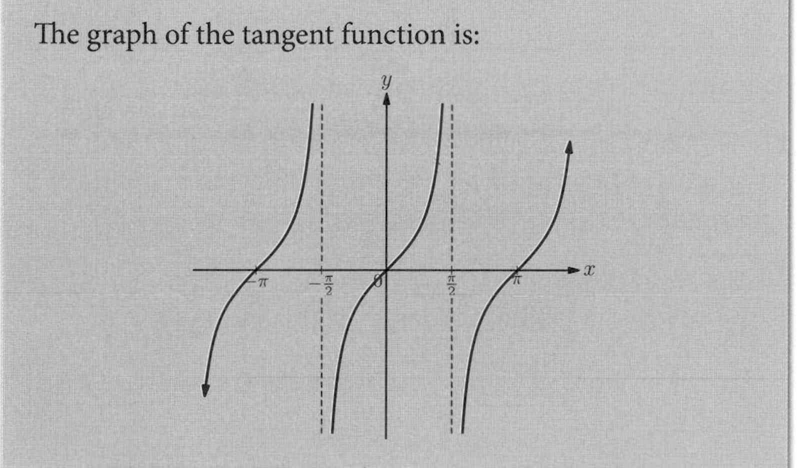

Remember that points on the unit circle can also represent angles measured in degrees. Sometimes you may be asked to work in degrees.

EXAM HINT

You should always use radians unless explicitly told to use degrees.

Worked example 8.7

Sketch the graph of $y = \tan x$ for $-90° < x < 270°$.

The given domain $-90° < x < 270°$ covers the fourth quadrant, first quadrant, second quadrant, and then third quadrant. Find the values of x for which $\tan x$ is not defined.

$\tan x$ is undefined when $\cos x = 0$, i.e. at

$x = -90°, 90°, 270°$

When is the function positive/negative? When is it zero?

$\tan x$ is:
negative in the fourth quadrant,
positive in the first quadrant,
negative in the second quadrant,
positive in the third quadrant.
$\tan x = 0$ at $x = 0°$ and $180°$

Start by marking the asymptotes and zeros.

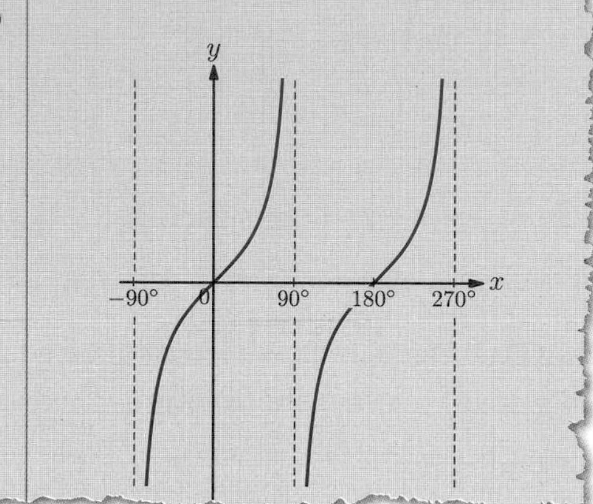

Exercise 8C

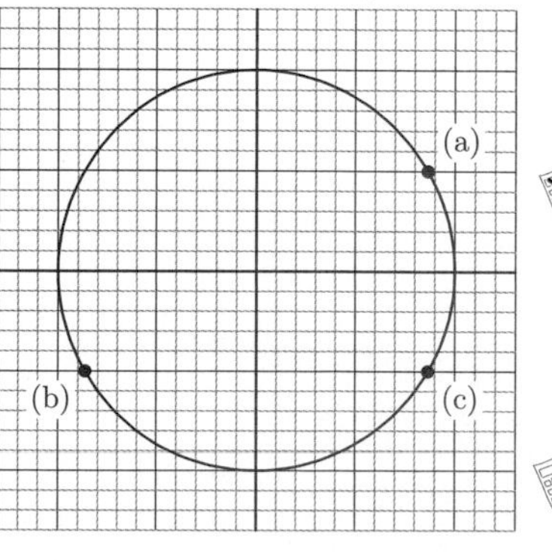

1. By estimating the values of $\sin\theta$ and $\cos\theta$, find the approximate value of $\tan\theta$ for the points shown on the diagram.

2. Sketch the graph of $y = \tan x$ for:
   (a) (i) $0° \le x \le 360°$ (ii) $-90° \le x \le 270°$
   (b) (i) $\frac{\pi}{2} \le x \le \frac{5\pi}{2}$ (ii) $-\pi \le x \le \pi$

3. Use your calculator to evaluate the following, giving your answers to 2 decimal places:
   (a) (i) $\tan 1.2$ (ii) $\tan 4.7$
   (b) (i) $\tan(-0.65)$ (ii) $\tan(-7.3)$

4. Use your calculator to evaluate the following, giving your answers to 3 significant figures:

(a) (i) $\tan 32°$ (ii) $\tan 168°$

(b) (i) $\tan(-540°)$ (ii) $\tan(-128°)$

5. Use the properties of sine and cosine to express the following in terms of $\tan x$:

(a) $\tan(\pi - x)$ (b) $\tan\left(x + \frac{\pi}{2}\right)$

(c) $\tan(x + \pi)$ (d) $\tan(x + 3\pi)$

6. Use the properties of sine and cosine to express the following in terms of $\tan \theta°$:

(a) $\tan(-\theta°)$ (b) $\tan(360° - \theta°)$

(c) $\tan(90° - \theta°)$ (d) $\tan(180° + \theta°)$

7. Sketch the graph of:

(i) $y = 2\sin x - \tan x$ for $-\frac{\pi}{2} \le x \le 2\pi$

(ii) $y = 3\cos x + \tan x$ for $-\pi \le x \le \pi$

8. Find the zeros of the following functions:

(i) $y = 2\tan x° + \sin x°$ for $0 \le x \le 360$

(ii) $y = 3\cos x° - \tan x°$ for $-180 \le x \le 360$

9. Find the coordinates of the maximum and minimum points on the following graphs:

(i) $y = 3\sin x - \tan x$ for $0 \le x \le 2\pi$

(ii) $y = \cos x - 2\sin x$ for $-\pi \le x \le \pi$

10. Find approximate solutions of the following equations, giving your answers correct to 3 significant figures:

(i) $\cos x - \tan x = 3,\ x \in]0, 2\pi[$

(ii) $\sin x + \cos x = 1,\ x \in [0, 2\pi]$

8D Exact values of trigonometric functions

Although generally values of trigonometric functions are difficult to find without a calculator, there are a few special numbers for which exact values can easily be found. The method relies on the properties of two special right-angled triangles.

Worked example 8.8

Find the exact values of $\sin\frac{\pi}{4}$, $\cos\frac{\pi}{4}$ and $\tan\frac{\pi}{4}$.

Mark the point corresponding to $\frac{\pi}{4}$ on the unit circle (point A in the diagram).

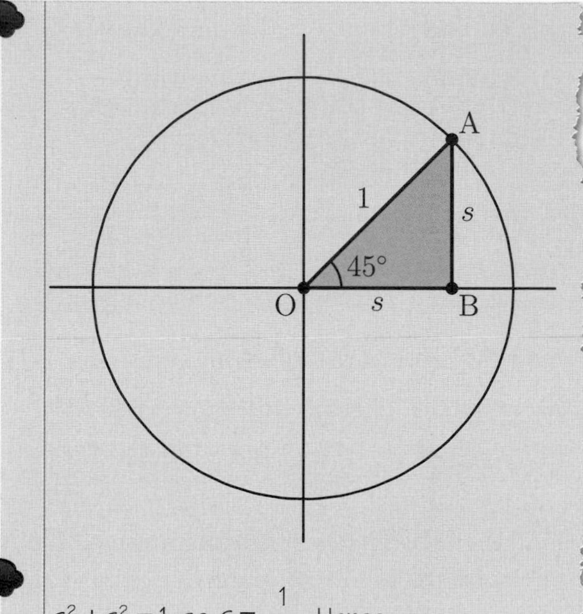

Look at the triangle OAB. It has a right angle at B, and the angle at O is equal to 45° (because $\frac{\pi}{4}$ is one-eighth of a full turn).

$s^2 + s^2 = 1$, so $s = \frac{1}{\sqrt{2}}$. Hence

$$\sin\frac{\pi}{4} = \cos\frac{\pi}{4} = \frac{1}{\sqrt{2}}$$

We can now use the definition of tan x.

$$\tan\frac{\pi}{4} = \frac{\sin\frac{\pi}{4}}{\cos\frac{\pi}{4}} = 1$$

The other special right-angled triangle is made by cutting an equilateral triangle in half.

Worked example 8.9

Find the exact values of the three trigonometric functions of $\frac{2\pi}{3}$.

Mark the point corresponding to $\frac{2\pi}{3}$ on the unit circle. $\frac{2\pi}{3}$ is one-third of a full turn (120°), so angle $A\hat{O}B$ is 60°.

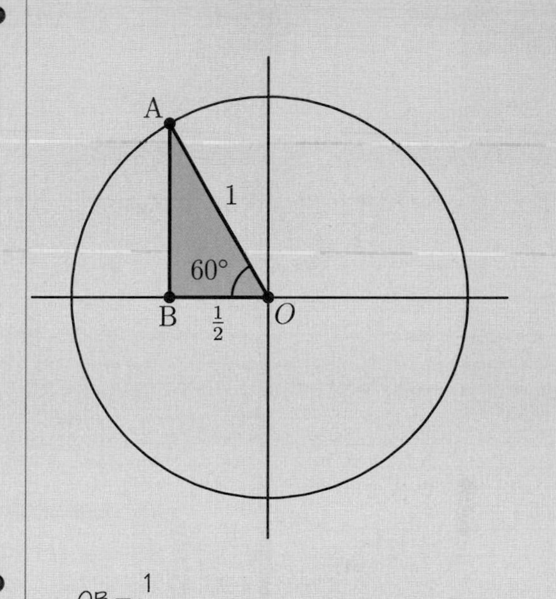

Triangle AOB is half of an equilateral triangle with side length 1. OB is equal to half the side of the equilateral triangle.

$OB = \frac{1}{2}$

Point A is to the left of the vertical axis, so $\cos\frac{2\pi}{3} < 0$

$\therefore \cos\frac{2\pi}{3} = -\frac{1}{2}$

To find AB, use Pythagoras' Theorem.

$AB^2 = 1^2 - \left(\frac{1}{2}\right)^2 = \frac{3}{4}$

$\therefore \sin\frac{2\pi}{3} = \frac{\sqrt{3}}{2}$

Use the definition of tan *x*.

$\tan\frac{2\pi}{3} = \frac{\frac{\sqrt{3}}{2}}{-\frac{1}{2}} = -\sqrt{3}$

The sine, cosine and tangent values of other special numbers are summarised below. You should understand how they are derived, as shown in Worked examples 8.8 and 8.9.

KEY POINT 8.10

Radians	0	$\frac{\pi}{6}$	$\frac{\pi}{4}$	$\frac{\pi}{3}$	$\frac{\pi}{2}$	$\frac{2\pi}{3}$	$\frac{3\pi}{4}$	$\frac{5\pi}{6}$	π
Degrees	0	30	45	60	90	120	135	150	180
sin *x*	0	$\frac{1}{2}$	$\frac{\sqrt{2}}{2}$	$\frac{\sqrt{3}}{2}$	1	$\frac{\sqrt{3}}{2}$	$\frac{\sqrt{2}}{2}$	$\frac{1}{2}$	0
cos *x*	1	$\frac{\sqrt{3}}{2}$	$\frac{\sqrt{2}}{2}$	$\frac{1}{2}$	0	$-\frac{1}{2}$	$-\frac{\sqrt{2}}{2}$	$-\frac{\sqrt{3}}{2}$	-1
tan *x*	0	$\frac{1}{\sqrt{3}}$	1	$\sqrt{3}$	not defined	$-\sqrt{3}$	-1	$-\frac{1}{\sqrt{3}}$	0

EXAM HINT

The angles $\frac{\pi}{6}, \frac{\pi}{4}$ and $\frac{\pi}{3}$ come up so frequently in exam questions that it is useful to memorise the results for them, rather than having to repeatedly derive the values from triangles. The table might be easier to remember if you notice the pattern in the values of sin and cos: $0, \frac{1}{2}, \frac{\sqrt{2}}{2}, \frac{\sqrt{3}}{2}, 1\left(=\frac{\sqrt{4}}{2}\right)$.

Exercise 8D

1. By marking the corresponding points on the unit circle, find the exact values of

   (a) $\cos\frac{3\pi}{4}$ (b) $\cos\frac{\pi}{2}$

   (c) $\sin\frac{5\pi}{4}$ (d) $\tan\frac{3\pi}{4}$

2. Find the exact values of

   (a) $\sin\frac{\pi}{6}$ (b) $\sin\frac{7\pi}{6}$

   (c) $\cos\left(\frac{4\pi}{3}\right)$ (d) $\tan\left(-\frac{\pi}{3}\right)$

3. Find the exact values of

(a) $\cos 45°$ (b) $\sin 135°$

(c) $\cos 225°$ (d) $\tan 225°$

4. Find the exact values of

(a) $\sin 210°$ (b) $\cos 210°$

(c) $\tan 210°$ (d) $\tan 330°$

5. Evaluate the following, simplifying as far as possible.

(a) $1-\sin^2\left(\frac{\pi}{6}\right)$

(b) $\sin\left(\frac{\pi}{4}\right)+\sin\left(\frac{\pi}{3}\right)$

(c) $\cos\frac{\pi}{3}-\cos\frac{\pi}{6}$

6. Show that

(a) $\sin 60°\cos 30°+\cos 60°\sin 30°=\sin 90°$

(b) $(\sin 45°)^2+(\cos 45°)^2=1$

(c) $\cos^2\left(\frac{\pi}{6}\right)-\sin^2\left(\frac{\pi}{6}\right)=\cos\left(\frac{\pi}{3}\right)$

(d) $\left(1+\tan\frac{\pi}{3}\right)^2=4+2\sqrt{3}$

8E Transformations of trigonometric graphs

Transformations of functions and graphs were introduced in chapter 5.

In this section we shall apply the ideas from chapter 5 to the trigonometric graphs we have met. This will enable us to model many real-life situations which show periodic behaviour (see section 8F), and will also be useful in solving equations involving trigonometric functions.

First, consider how we might obtain the graph of $y=\sin 2x$ by using its relationship with $y=\sin x$. The equation $y=\sin 2x$ is of the form $y=f(2x)$ where $f(x)=\sin x$, so we need to apply a horizontal stretch with scale factor $\frac{1}{2}$ to the graph of $y=\sin x$.

We can see that the amplitude of $\sin 2x$ is still 1, but its period is halved to π.

EXAM HINT

$\sin 2x$ is not the same as $2\sin x$. Importantly, $\frac{\sin 2x}{2}$ cannot be simplified to $\sin x$! Plot the functions on your GDC and compare the results.

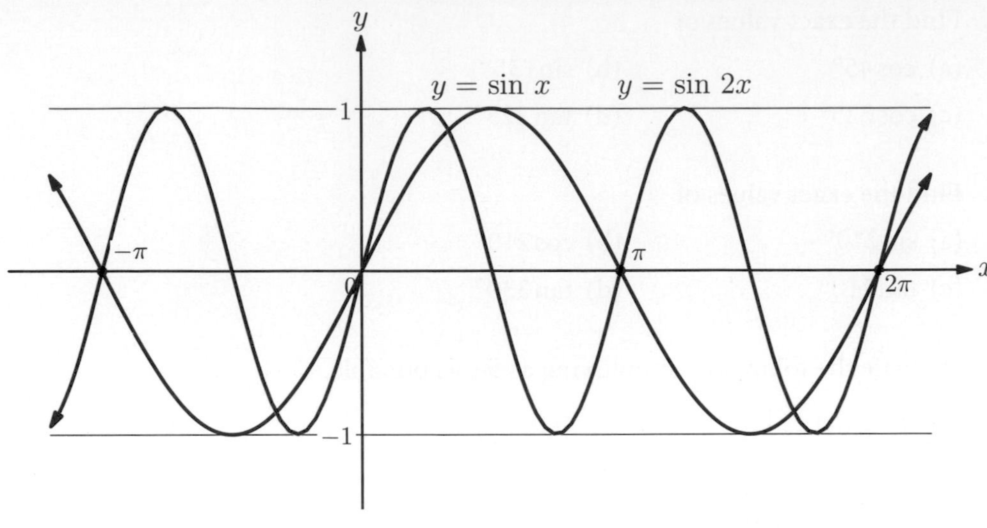

Now let us sketch the graph of $y = 2\sin x$. This is of the form $y = 2f(x)$ where $f(x) = \sin x$, so we need to apply a vertical stretch with scale factor 2 to the graph of $y = \sin x$. The resulting function has amplitude 2, while the period is unchanged.

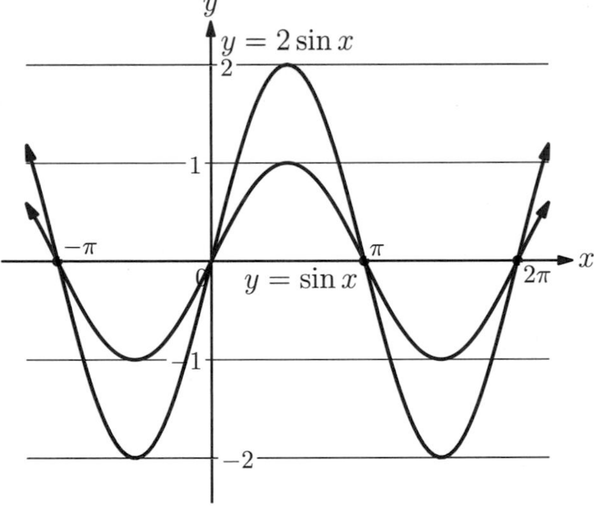

We can combine these two types of transformation (horizontal and vertical stretches) to change both the amplitude and the period of the sine function. The same transformations can also be applied to the graph of the cosine function.

KEY POINT 8.11

The functions $y = a\sin bx$ and $y = a\cos bx$ have amplitude a and period $\frac{2\pi}{b}$.

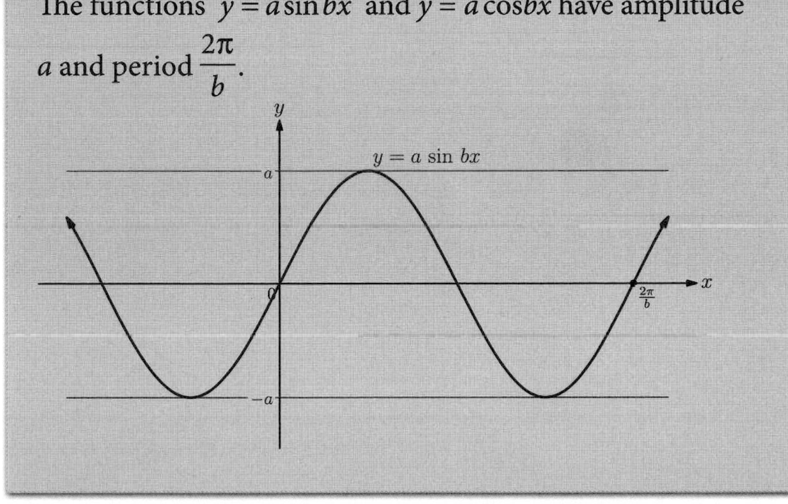

Worked example 8.10

(a) Sketch the graph of $y = 4\cos\left(\frac{x}{3}\right)$ for $0 \le x \le 6\pi$.

(b) Write down the amplitude and the period of the function.

Start with the graph of $y = \cos x$ and think about what transformations to apply to it.

(a) Vertical stretch with scale factor 4
Horizontal stretch with scale factor 3

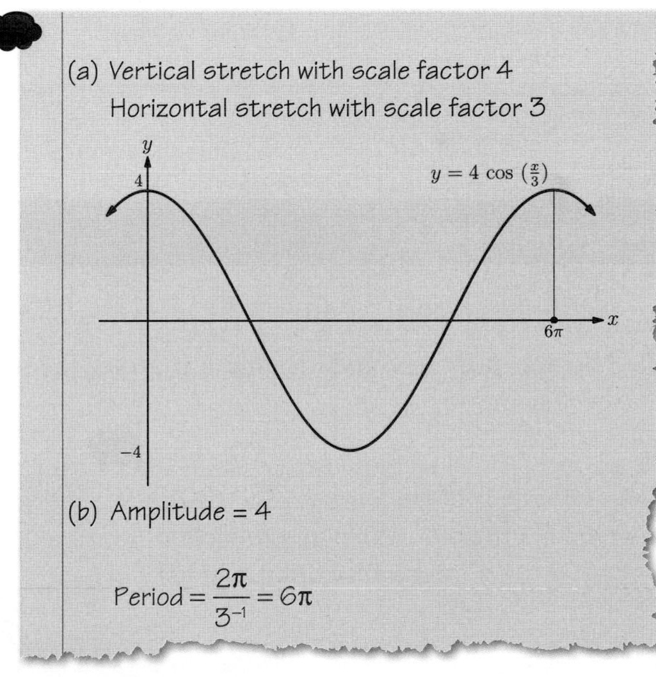

(b) Amplitude = 4

$$\text{Period} = \frac{2\pi}{3^{-1}} = 6\pi$$

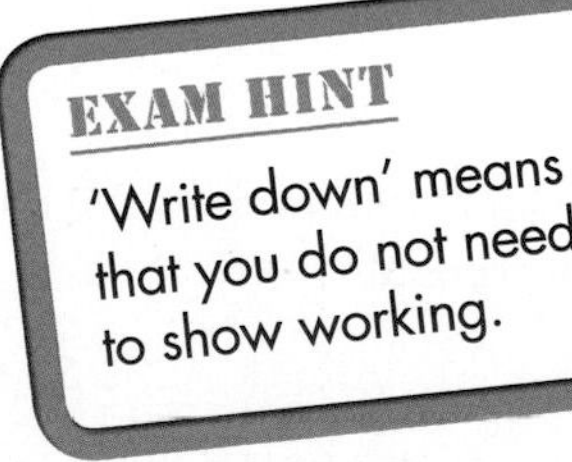

EXAM HINT
'Write down' means that you do not need to show working.

Besides vertical and horizontal stretches, we can also apply translations to graphs of trigonometric functions. They will leave the period and the amplitude unchanged, but will change the positions of maximum and minimum points and the axis intercepts.

Worked example 8.11

(a) Sketch the graph of $y = \sin x + 2$ for $x \in [0, 2\pi]$.

(b) Find the maximum and the minimum values of the function.

The equation is of the form $y = f(x) + 2$ where $f(x) = \sin x$. What transformation does this correspond to?

(a) Apply vertical translation by 2 units upward to $y = \sin x$

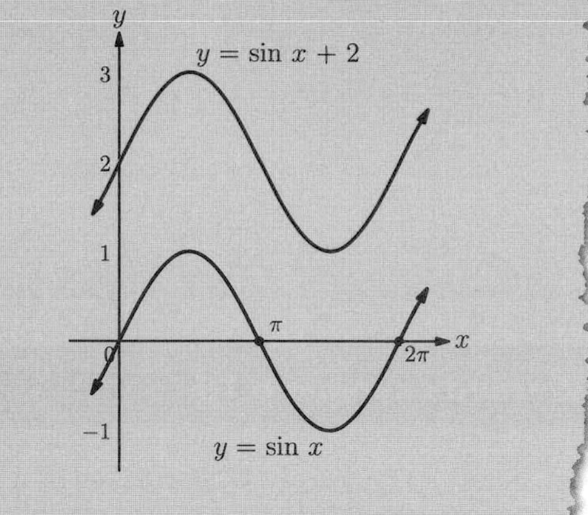

We know that the minimum and maximum values of $\sin x$ are 1 and −1, so add 2 to those values.

(b) Minimum value: $-1 + 2 = 1$

Maximum value: $1 + 2 = 3$

In the next example we consider a horizontal translation.

Worked example 8.12

(a) Sketch the graph of $y = \cos(x + 30°)$ for $0° \le x \le 360°$.

(b) State the minimum and maximum values of the function, and the values of x at which they occur.

The equation is of the form $y = f(x + 30)$ where $f(x) = \cos x$. What transformation does this correspond to?

(a) Apply horizontal translation by 30 units leftward to $y = \cos x$.

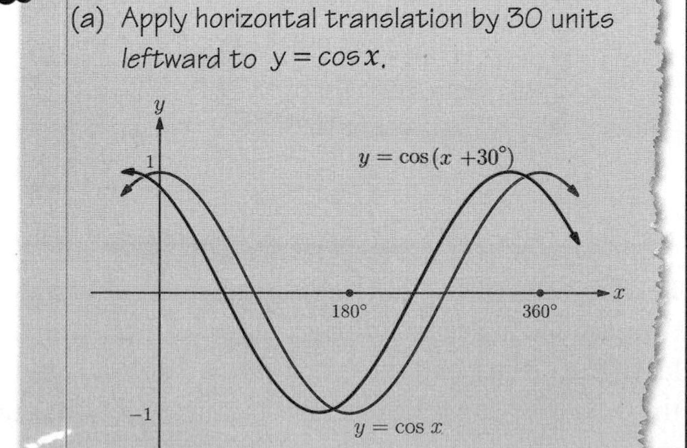

continued . . .

The minimum value of $\cos x$ is -1, and in the interval $[0°, 360°]$ it occurs at $x = 180°$. Since the graph is translated 30 units to the left, we subtract 30.

(b) Minimum value is -1

It occurs at $x = 180° - 30° = 150°$

The maximum value of $\cos x$ is 1, and in the interval $[0°, 360°]$ it occurs at $x = 0°, 360°$. Pick the value which is in the required interval *after* translation to the left.

Maximum value is 1

It occurs at $x = 360° - 30° = 330°$

The result of applying the two types of translations and two types of stretches to the sine and cosine functions can be summarised as follows.

KEY POINT 8.12

The functions $y = a\sin b(x+c)+d$ and $y = a\cos b(x+c)+d$ have

- amplitude a
- period $\frac{2\pi}{b}$
- minimum value $d-a$ and maximum value $d+a$

Note that the value of d is always half-way between the minimum and maximum values; in other words, $d = \frac{min+max}{2}$.

The amplitude is half the difference between the minimum and maximum values: $a = \frac{max-min}{2}$.

The value of c in the above equation determines the horizontal translation of the graph; therefore it affects the position of the maximum and minimum points. The following example shows how to work out these positions.

Worked example 8.13

Find the exact values of x for which the function $y = \sin 3(x+1)$ attains its maximum value.

When does the sine function attain its maximum value?

$\sin x$ has a maximum when $x = \frac{\pi}{2}, \frac{5\pi}{2}, \frac{9\pi}{2}$ etc.

The given function is of the form $f(3(x+1))$; this means that x has been replaced by $3(x+1)$.

$3(x+1) = \frac{\pi}{2}, \frac{5\pi}{2}, \frac{9\pi}{2}, \ldots$

Now solve for x.

$x = \frac{\pi}{6} - 1, \frac{5\pi}{6} - 1$, etc.

We can use our knowledge of transformations of graphs to find an equation of a function given its graph.

Worked example 8.14

The graph shown has equation $y = a\sin(bx) + d$. Find the values of a, b and d.

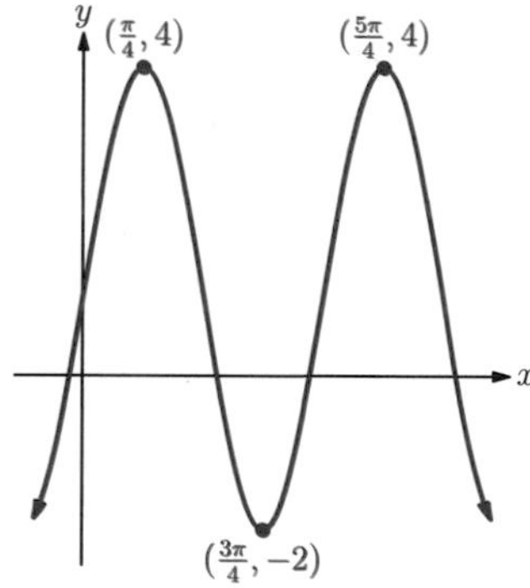

a is the amplitude, which is half the difference between the minimum and maximum values.

$a = \frac{4-(-2)}{2} = 3$

b is related to the period via the formula $period = \frac{2\pi}{b}$. The period is also the distance between two consecutive maximum points, which we can find from the graph.

$period = \frac{5\pi}{4} - \frac{\pi}{4} = \pi$

$\therefore \pi = \frac{2\pi}{b}$

Hence $b = 2$

d represents the vertical translation of the graph. It is the value half-way between the minimum and the maximum values.

$d = \frac{4+(-2)}{2} = 1$

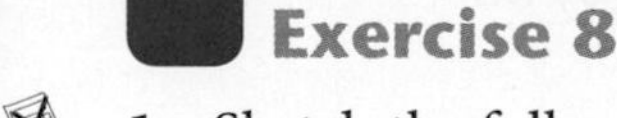

Exercise 8E

1. Sketch the following graphs, indicating any axis intercepts.
   (a) (i) $y = \sin 2x$ for $-180° \le x \le 180°$
   (ii) $y = \cos 3x$ for $0° \le x \le 360°$
   (b) (i) $y = \tan\left(x - \frac{\pi}{2}\right)$ for $0 \le x \le \pi$
   (ii) $y = \tan\left(x + \frac{\pi}{3}\right)$ for $0 \le x \le \pi$
   (c) (i) $y = 3\cos x - 2$ for $0° \le x \le 720°$
   (ii) $y = 2\sin x + 1$ for $-360° \le x \le 360°$

2. Sketch the following graphs, giving the coordinates of maximum and minimum points.
   (a) (i) $y = \cos\left(x - \frac{\pi}{3}\right)$ for $0 \le x \le 2\pi$
   (ii) $y = \sin\left(x + \frac{\pi}{2}\right)$ for $0 \le x \le 2\pi$
   (b) (i) $y = 2\sin(x + 45°)$ for $-180° \le x \le 180°$
   (ii) $y = 3\cos(x - 60°)$ for $-180° \le x \le 180°$
   (c) (i) $y = -3\sin 2x$ for $-\pi \le x \le \pi$
   (ii) $y = 3 - 2\cos x$ for $0° \le x \le 360°$

3. Find the amplitude and period of the following functions.
   (a) $f(x) = 3\sin 4x$, where x is in degrees
   (b) $f(x) = \tan 3x$, where x is in radians
   (c) $f(x) = \cos 3x$, where x is in degrees
   (d) $f(x) = 2\sin \pi x$, where x is in radians

4. The graph shown has equation $y = p\sin(qx)$ for $0 \le x \le 2\pi$. Find the values of p and q.

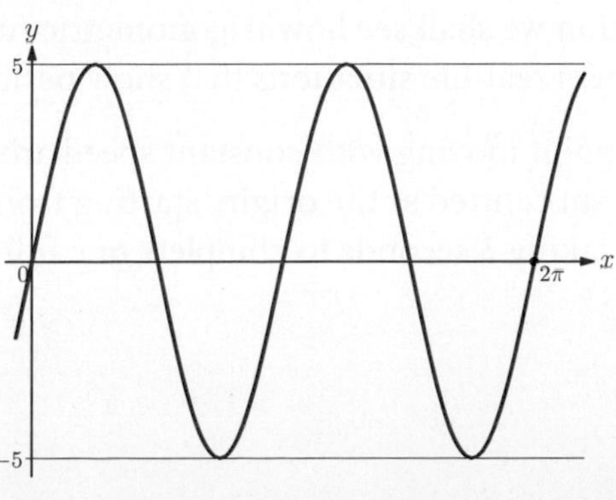

[3 marks]

5. The graph shown has equation $y = a\cos(x - b)$ for $0° \le x \le 720°$. Find the values of a and b.

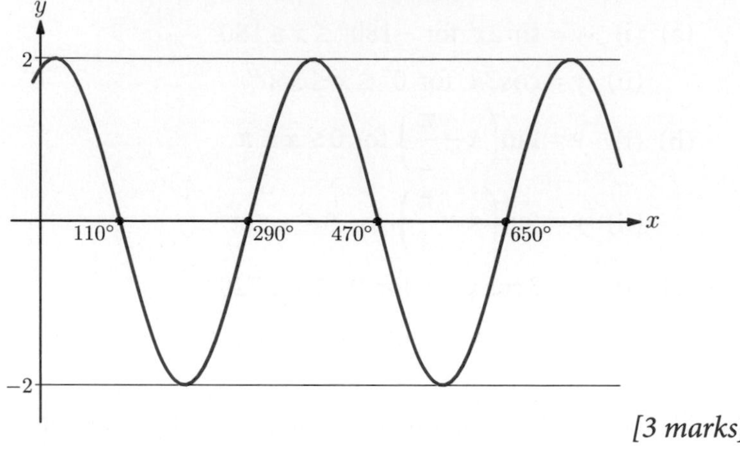

[3 marks]

6. (a) On the same set of axes sketch the graphs of $y = 1 + \sin 2x$ and $y = 2\cos x$ for $0 \le x \le 2\pi$.

(b) Hence state the number of solutions of the equation $1 + \sin 2x = 2\cos x$ for $0 \le x \le 2\pi$.

(c) Write down the number of solutions of the equation $1 + \sin 2x = 2\cos x$ for $-2\pi \le x \le 6\pi$. [6 marks]

7. (a) Sketch the graph of $y = 2\cos(x + 60°)$ for $x \in [0°, 360°]$.

(b) Find the coordinates of the maximum and minimum points on the graph.

(c) Write down the coordinates of the maximum and minimum points on the graph of $y = 2\cos(x + 60°) - 1$ for $x \in [0°, 360°]$. [6 marks]

8F Modelling using trigonometric functions

In this section we shall see how trigonometric functions can be used to model real-life situations that show periodic behaviour.

Imagine a point moving with constant speed around a circle of radius 2 cm centred at the origin, starting from the positive x-axis and taking 3 seconds to complete one full rotation.

Let h be the height of the point above the x-axis. How does h vary with time t (measured in seconds)?

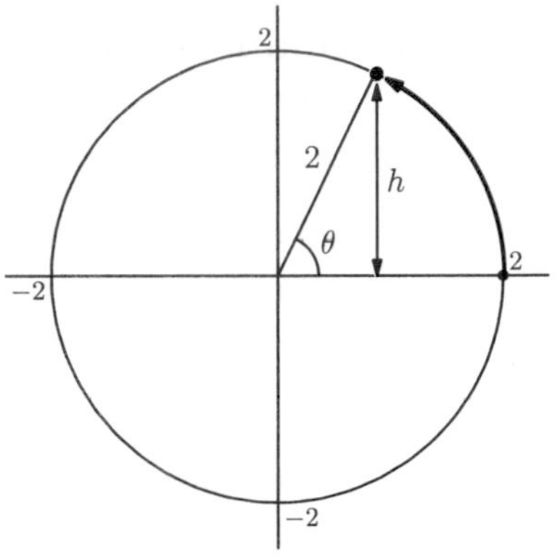

We know that if the point is moving around the unit circle, the height above the x-axis would be $\sin\theta$, where θ is the angle between the radius and the x-axis. As the circle now has radius 2, the height is $2\sin\theta$.

So, to find how h varies with time, we need to find how θ depends on time. As the point starts on the positive x-axis, $\theta = 0$ when $t = 0$. After one complete rotation, we have $\theta = 2\pi$ and $t = 3$. Because the point is moving with constant speed, we can use ratios to state that $\frac{\theta}{2\pi} = \frac{t}{3}$, so $\theta = \frac{2\pi}{3}t$.

Therefore the equation for the height in terms of time is $h = 2\sin\left(\frac{2\pi}{3}t\right)$. The diagram below shows the graph of this function.

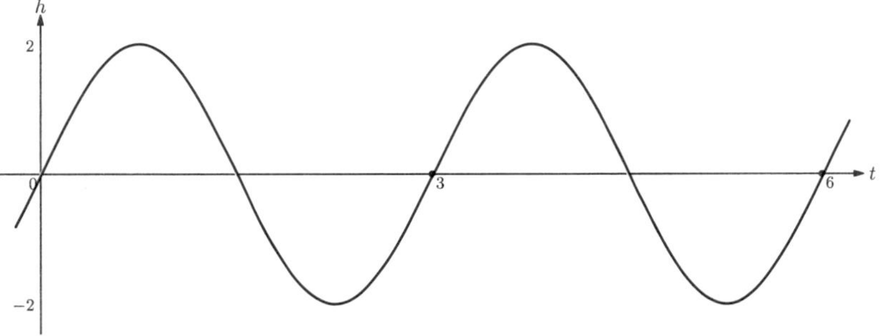

This is an example of **modelling** using trigonometric functions. We can use sine and cosine functions to model periodic motion, such as motion around a circle, oscillation of a particle attached to the end of a spring, water waves, or heights of tides. In practice, we would collect experimental data to sketch a graph and then use our knowledge of trigonometric functions to find its equation. We can then use the equation to do further calculations.

Summary

- The unit circle is a circle with centre 0 and radius 1.
- Radian measure for angles is defined in terms of distance travelled around the unit circle, so that a full turn = 2π radians.
- To convert from degrees to radians, divide by 180 and multiply by π.
  To convert from radians to degrees, divide by π and multiply by 180.
- Using the unit circle and the real number α, the **sine** and **cosine** of this number is defined in terms of distance to the axes:

  $\sin\alpha$ is the distance of a point from the horizontal axis

  $\cos\alpha$ is the distance of the point from the vertical axis
- Useful properties of the sine and cosine function are summarised in Key point 8.4.
- The relationship between the sine and cosine function is summarised in Key point 8.5.
- The **tangent** function is another trigonometric function. It is defined as the ratio between the sine and cosine functions: $\tan x = \dfrac{\sin x}{\cos x}$
- The sine and cosine functions can be defined for all real numbers:

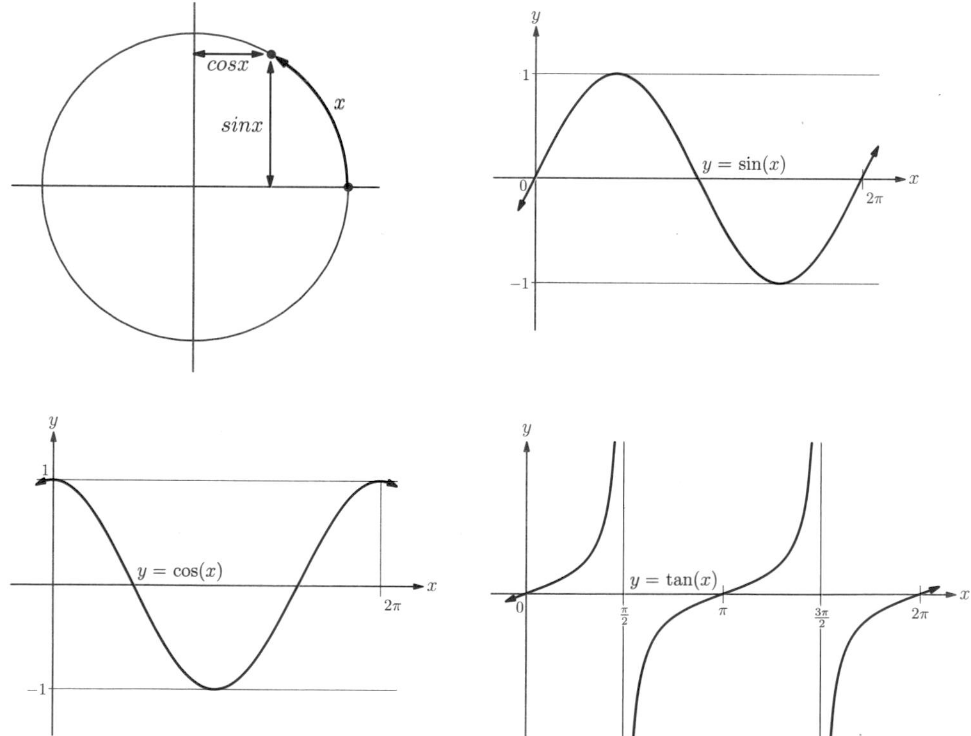

- For some real numbers trigonometric functions have exact values, which are useful to remember (see Key point 8.10).

- The sine and cosine functions are periodic with period 2π and amplitude 1.
- The tangent function is periodic with period π.

$$\tan(x) = \tan(x \pm \pi) = \tan(x \pm 2\pi) = \ldots$$

- We can apply translations and stretches to the sine and cosine functions. The resulting functions $y = a\sin b(x+c)+d$ and $y = a\cos b(x+c)+d$ are very useful in modelling periodic phenomena; they have:
  - amplitude a
  - period $\frac{2\pi}{b}$
  - minimum value $d-a$ and maximum value $d+a$ (the value d is half-way between the minimum and maximum values).

Introductory problem revisited

> A clock has an hour hand of length 10 cm, and the centre of the clock is 4 m above the floor. Find an expression for the height, *h* metres, of the tip of the hour hand above the floor at a time *t* hours after midnight.

We can model the height using a cosine function (because when $t = 0$, the graph should be at the maximum height). The period is 12 hours, the amplitude is 0.1 m (the length of the hand), and the half-way height is 4 m (the position of the centre of the clock). Therefore the function is

$$h = 4 + 0.1\cos\left(\frac{\pi}{6}t\right)$$

Mixed examination practice 8

Short questions

1. The height of a wave, in metres, at a distance x metres from a buoy is modelled by the function $f(x)=1.4\sin(3x-0.1)-0.6$.

(a) State the amplitude of the wave.

(b) Find the distance between consecutive peaks of the wave. *[4 marks]*

2. A runner is jogging around a level circular track. His distance north of the centre of the track in metres is given by $60\cos 0.08t$, where t is measured in seconds.

(a) How long does is take the runner to complete one lap?

(b) What is the length of the track?

(c) At what speed is the runner jogging? *[7 marks]*

3. Let $f(x)=3\sin 2\left(x-\frac{\pi}{3}\right)$.

(a) State the period of the function.

(b) Find the coordinates of the zeros of $f(x)$ for $x\in[0,2\pi]$.

(c) Hence sketch the graph of $y=f(x)$ for $x\in[0, 2\pi]$, showing the coordinates of the maximum and minimum points. *[7 marks]*

4. The diagram shows the graph of the function $f(x)=a\sin(bx)$. Find the values of a and b.

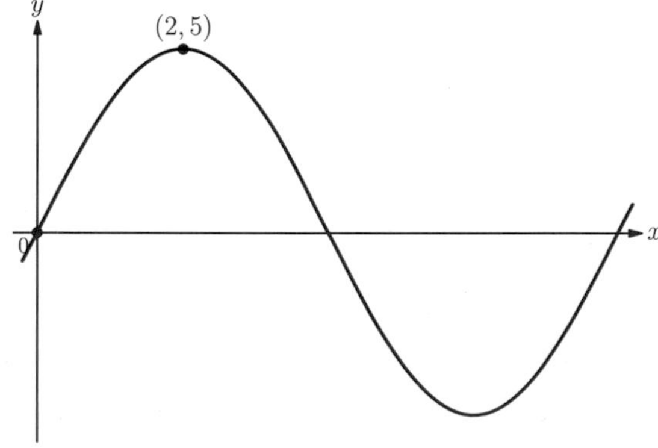

[4 marks]

Long questions

1. The graph shows the function $f(x)=\sin(x-k)+c$.

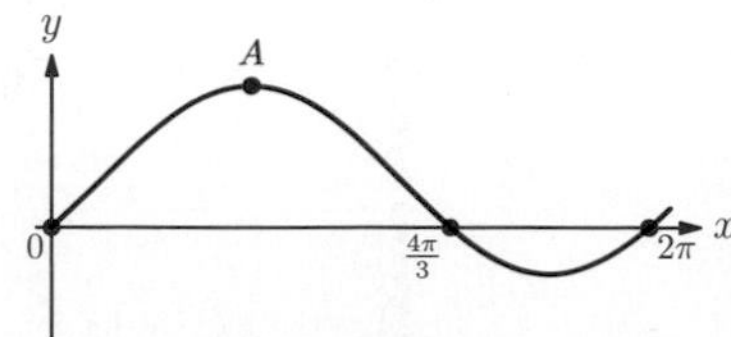

(a) (i) Write down the coordinates of A.

(ii) Hence find the values of k and c.

(b) Find all the zeros of the function in the interval $[-4\pi, 0]$.

(c) Consider the equation $f(x) = k$ with $-0.5 < k < 0$.

(i) Write down the number of solutions of this equation in the interval $[0, 9\pi]$.

(ii) Given that the smallest positive solution is α, write the next two solutions in terms of α. *[11 marks]*

2. **(a)** (i) Sketch the graph of $y = \tan x$ for $0 \le x \le 2\pi$.

(ii) On the same graph, sketch the line $y = \pi - x$.

(b) Consider the equation $x + \tan x = \pi$. Denote by x_0 the solution of this equation in the interval $]0, \frac{\pi}{2}[$.

(i) Find, in terms of x_0 and π, the remaining solutions of the equation in the interval $[0, 2\pi]$.

(ii) How many solutions does the equation $x + \tan x = \pi$ have for $x \in \mathbb{R}$?

(c) Given that $\cos A = c$ and $\sin A = s$:

(i) Write down the values of $\cos\left(\frac{\pi}{2} - A\right)$ and $\sin\left(\frac{\pi}{2} - A\right)$.

(ii) Hence show that $\tan\left(\frac{\pi}{2} - A\right) = \frac{1}{\tan A}$.

(iii) Given that $\tan A + \tan\left(\frac{\pi}{2} - A\right) = \frac{4}{\sqrt{3}}$, find the possible values of $\tan A$.

(iv) Hence find the values of $x \in]0, \frac{\pi}{2}[$ for which

$$\tan A + \tan\left(\frac{\pi}{2} - A\right) = \frac{4}{\sqrt{3}}.$$

[16 marks]

3. **(a)** Write down the minimum value of $\cos x$ and the smallest positive value of x (in radians) for which the minimum occurs.

(b) (i) Describe two transformations which transform the graph of $y = \cos x$ to the graph of $y = 2\cos\left(x + \frac{\pi}{6}\right)$.

(ii) Hence state the minimum value of $2\cos\left(x + \frac{\pi}{6}\right)$ and find the value of $x \in [0, 2\pi]$ for which the minimum occurs.

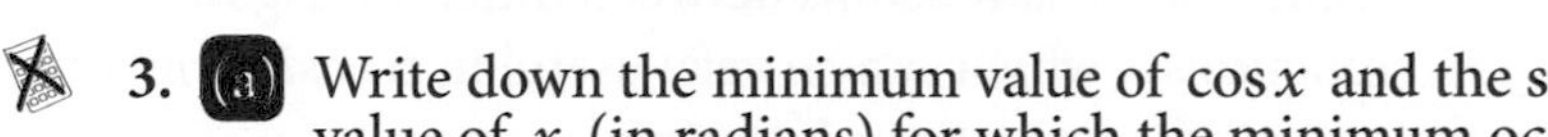

(c) The function f is defined for $x \in [0, 2\pi]$ by $f(x) = \dfrac{5}{2\cos\left(x + \frac{\pi}{6}\right) + 3}$.

(i) State, with a reason, whether f has any vertical asymptotes.

(ii) Find the range of f. *[13 marks]*

9 Trigonometric equations and identities

In this chapter you will learn:

- how to solve equations involving trigonometric functions
- about relationships between different trigonometric functions, called identities
- how to use identities to solve more complicated trigonometric equations
- about relationships between trigonometric functions of an angle and trigonometric functions of twice that angle.

Introductory problem

The original Ferris Wheel was constructed in 1893 in Chicago. It was just over 80 m tall and could complete one full revolution in 9 minutes. During each revolution, how much time did the passengers spend more than 50 m above the ground?

Often, when using trigonometric functions to model real-life situations we need to solve equations where the unknown is in the argument of a trigonometric function; for example, $5\sin(2x+1)=3$ or $\cos 2x - \sin^2 x = -2$. Because trigonometric functions are periodic, such equations may have more than one solution. In this chapter you will see how to find all solutions in a given interval. You will also learn some trigonometric identities – relationships between different trigonometric functions – which can be very useful in transforming more complicated equations into simpler ones.

9A Introducing trigonometric equations

Inverse functions and their graphs were covered in section 4D.

To solve trigonometric equations it is important that we can 'undo' trigonometric functions. If you were told that the sine of a value is $\frac{1}{2}$, you would know from section 8D that the original value could be $\frac{\pi}{6}$, but if you were told that the sine of a value is 0.8 the original value would not be so easy to find. The answer is given by the inverse function of sine, written as $\arcsin x$ or $\sin^{-1} x$.

The inverse function of cosine is denoted by $\arccos x$ or $\cos^{-1} x$, and the inverse tangent function is $\arctan x$ or $\tan^{-1} x$.

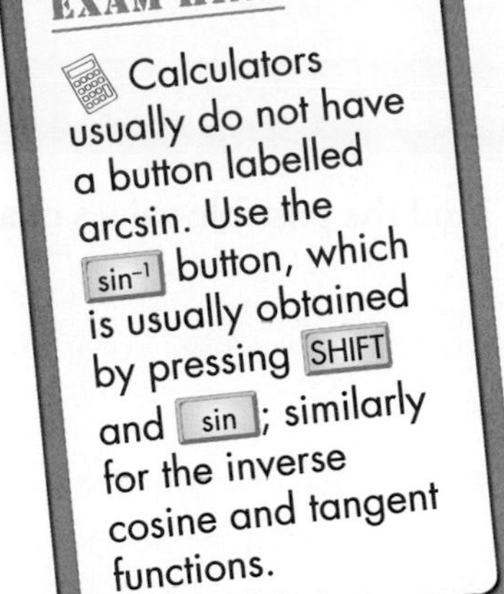

Suppose we want to find the values of x which satisfy $\sin x = 0.6$. Applying the inverse sine function, we get $x = \sin^{-1} 0.6$; then, using a calculator we find $\sin^{-1} 0.6 = 0.644$ (3 SF). The $\sin^{-1}$ function gives us only one solution. However, from the graph of $y = \sin x$ we can see that there are many x-values that satisfy the equation (these correspond to the intersections of the curve $y = \sin x$ and the line $y = 0.6$).

The solutions come in pairs – one in the green sections of the graph and one in the blue sections. The $\sin^{-1}$ function will always give us only one solution: the one in the green section closest to zero (x_1). To find the solution x_2 in the blue section we use the fact that the graph has a line of symmetry at $x = \frac{\pi}{2}$, so x_2 is as far below π as x_1 is above zero; in our example, this means that $x_2 = \pi - 0.644 = 2.50$. Once we have this pair of solutions, we can use the fact that the sine graph repeats with period 2π to find the other solutions: $x_3 = x_1 + 2\pi = 6.93$, $x_4 = x_2 + 2\pi = 8.78$, and so on.

EXAM HINT

If you have found a value using an inverse trigonometric function and need to do further calculations with it, save the value in your calculator's memory and always use the stored value or the ANS button in subsequent calculations – not the rounded answer. See Calculator Skills sheet 1 on the CD-ROM for how to do this.

KEY POINT 9.1

To find the possible values of x which satisfy $\sin x = a$:

- Use the calculator to find $x_1 = \sin^{-1} a$.
- A second solution is given by $x_2 = \pi - x_1$ (or $180° - x_1$ if working in degrees).
- Other solutions are found by adding (or subtracting) multiples of 2π (or 360°) to x_1 or x_2.

In the International Baccalaureate you will only be asked to find solutions in a given interval.

Worked example 9.1

Find the possible values of angle $\theta \in [0°, 360°]$ for which $\sin\theta = -0.3$.

Put the calculator in degree mode.

$\sin^{-1}(-0.3) = -17.5°$

Look at the graph to see how many solutions there are in the required interval.

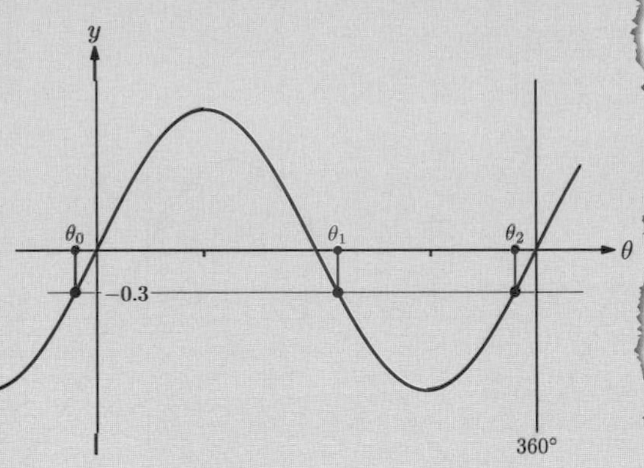

There are two solutions.

The second solution is given by $180° - \theta$.

$180° - (-17.5°) = 197.5°$

The solution $-17.5°$ is not in the required interval, so add 360°.

$\theta_1 = 197.5°$
$\theta_2 = -17.5° + 360° = 342.5°$

EXAM HINT

Always make sure that your calculator is in the appropriate mode, degree or radian, as indicated in the question. See Calculator Skills sheet 1 on the CD-ROM for how to set the mode.

We can solve the equation $\cos x = k$ in a similar way.

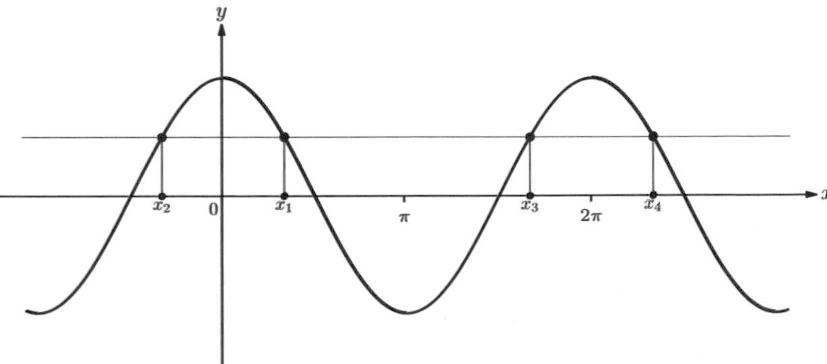

The function $\cos^{-1} k$ gives the solution x_1 in the green region closest to zero. We use the symmetry of the cosine graph to find x_2: it is simply the negative of x_1. Once we have this pair of solutions, we can use the fact that the cosine graph repeats with period 2π to find the other solutions.

KEY POINT 9.2

To find the possible values of x which satisfy $\cos x = a$:

- Use the calculator to find $x_1 = \cos^{-1} a$.
- A second solution is given by $x_2 = -x_1$.
- Other solutions are found by adding (or subtracting) multiples of 2π (or $360°$) to x_1 or x_2.

EXAM HINT

It is useful to remember that the first two positive solutions will be $\cos^{-1} a$ and $2\pi - \cos^{-1} a$.

Worked example 9.2

Find the values of x between $-\pi$ and 2π for which $\cos x = \frac{\sqrt{2}}{2}$.

Sketch the graph.

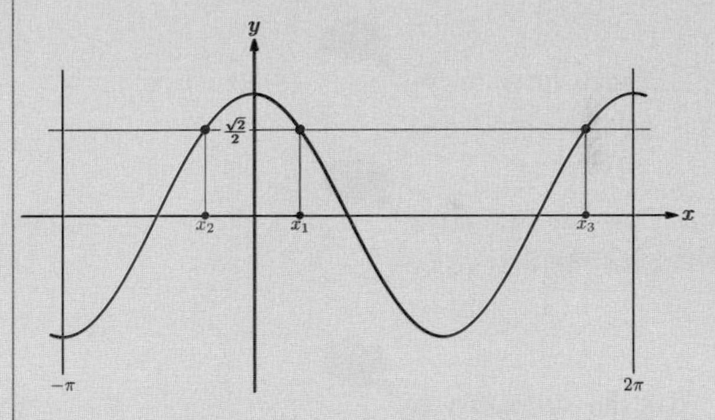

Note how many solutions there are.

There are 3 solutions

$\cos^{-1}\frac{\sqrt{2}}{2}$ is a value that we should know.

$x_1 = \cos^{-1}\left(\frac{\sqrt{2}}{2}\right) = \frac{\pi}{4}$

Use the symmetry of the graph to find the other solutions.

$x_2 = -\frac{\pi}{4}$

$x_3 = 2\pi - \frac{\pi}{4} = \frac{7\pi}{4}$

It can be difficult to know how many times to add or subtract 2π to make sure that we have found all the solutions in a given interval. Sketching a graph can help, as we can then see how many solutions we are looking for and approximately where they are. A good rule of thumb is that, apart from maximum and minimum values, there are two solutions within each period for sin and cos.

Worked example 9.3

Find all the values of x between 0 and 4π for which $\cos x = 0.8$.

Sketch the graph.

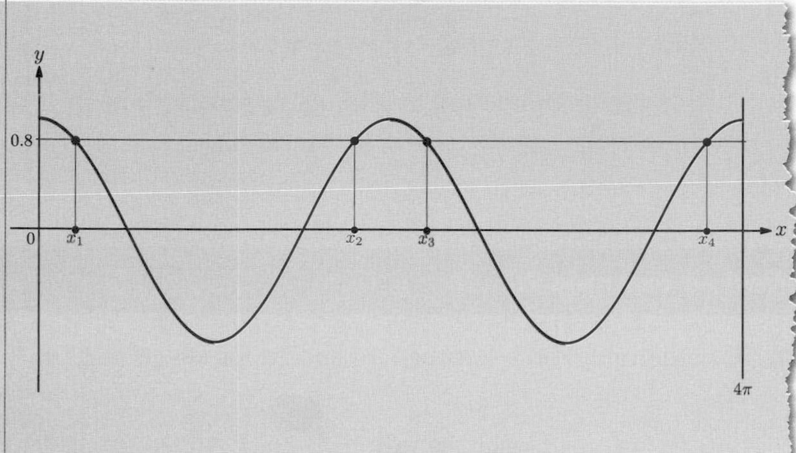

Note how many solutions there are.

4 solutions

$\cos^{-1}$ on the calculator will give the first value of x.

$x_1 = \cos^{-1} 0.8 = 0.644$ (3 SF)

Use the symmetry of the graph to find the other values.

$x_2 = 2\pi - 0.644 = 5.64$ (3SF)
$x_3 = x_1 + 2\pi = 6.93$ (3SF)
$x_4 = x_2 + 2\pi = 11.9$ (3SF)

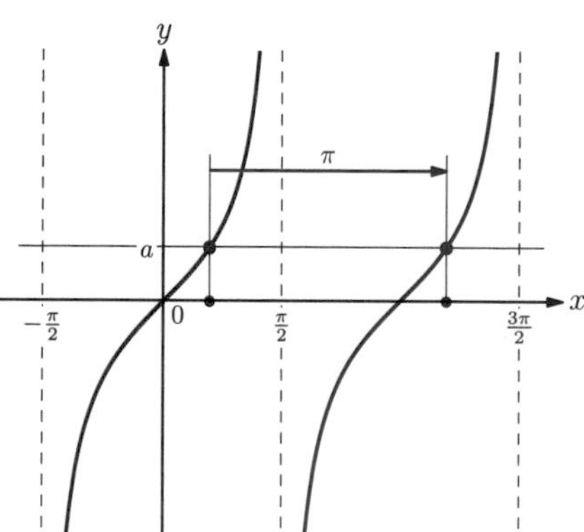

The procedure for solving equations of the type $\tan x = a$ is slightly different because the tangent function has period π rather than 2π. It is best understood by looking at the graph of the tangent function.

KEY POINT 9.3

To find the possible values of x which satisfy $\tan x = a$:

- Use the calculator to find $x_1 = \tan^{-1} a$.
- Other solutions are found by adding (or subtracting) multiples of π (or 180°).

Worked example 9.4

Find all real values of $x \in [-\pi, 3\pi]$ such that $\tan x = 2.5$.

Sketch the graph.

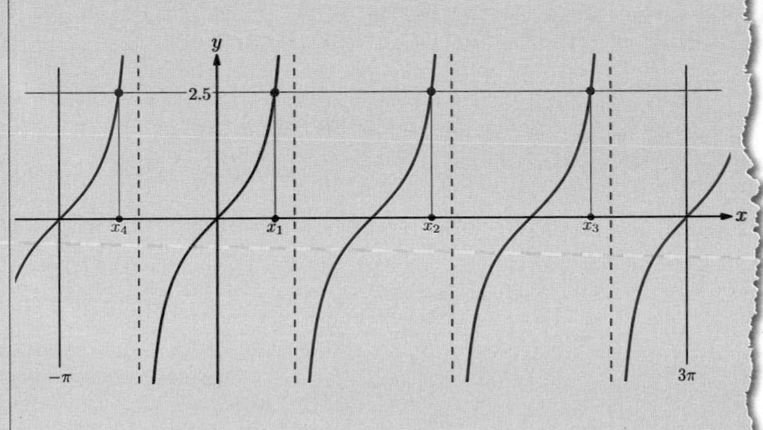

Note the number of solutions.

There are four solutions.

Use a calculator to find $\tan^{-1}$.

$x_1 = \tan^{-1} 2.5 = 1.19$

The other solutions are found by adding or subtracting π.

$x_2 = x_1 + \pi = 4.33$
$x_3 = x_2 + \pi = 7.47$
$x_4 = x_1 - \pi = -1.95$

Exercise 9A

1. Use your calculator to evaluate the following in radians, correct to three significant figures.
   (a) (i) $\cos^{-1} 0.6$ (ii) $\sin^{-1}(0.2)$
   (b) (i) $\tan^{-1}(-3)$ (ii) $\sin^{-1}(-0.8)$

 2. Evaluate the following in radians without using a calculator.
   (a) (i) $\sin^{-1}\left(\frac{1}{2}\right)$ (ii) $\cos^{-1}\left(\frac{\sqrt{3}}{2}\right)$
   (b) (i) $\tan^{-1}(-\sqrt{3})$ (ii) $\cos^{-1}\left(-\frac{1}{\sqrt{2}}\right)$
   (c) (i) $\sin^{-1}(-1)$ (ii) $\tan^{-1}(1)$

3. Evaluate the following, giving your answer in degrees correct to one decimal place.

(a) (i) $\sin^{-1} 0.7$ (ii) $\sin^{-1} 0.3$

(b) (i) $\cos^{-1}(-0.62)$ (ii) $\cos^{-1}(-0.75)$

(c) (i) $\tan^{-1} 6.4$ (ii) $\tan^{-1}(-7.1)$

4. Find the value of

(a) (i) $\sin(\sin^{-1} 0.6)$ (ii) $\cos(\cos^{-1}(-0.3))$

(b) (i) $\tan(\tan^{-1}(-2))$ (ii) $\sin(\sin^{-1}(-1))$

5. Find the exact values of x between 0° and 360° which satisfy the following equations.

(a) (i) $\sin x = \frac{1}{2}$ (ii) $\sin x = \frac{\sqrt{2}}{2}$

(b) (i) $\cos x = \frac{1}{2}$ (ii) $\cos x = \frac{\sqrt{3}}{2}$

(c) (i) $\sin x = -\frac{\sqrt{3}}{2}$ (ii) $\sin x = -\frac{1}{2}$

(d) (i) $\tan x = 1$ (ii) $\tan x = \sqrt{3}$

6. Find the exact values of x between 0 and 2π which satisfy the following equations.

(a) (i) $\cos x = \frac{\sqrt{3}}{2}$ (ii) $\cos x = \frac{\sqrt{2}}{2}$

(b) (i) $\cos x = -\frac{1}{2}$ (ii) $\cos x = -\frac{\sqrt{3}}{2}$

(c) (i) $\sin x = \frac{\sqrt{2}}{2}$ (ii) $\sin x = \frac{\sqrt{3}}{2}$

(d) (i) $\tan x = \frac{1}{\sqrt{3}}$ (ii) $\tan x = -1$

7. Solve these equations in the given interval, giving your answers to one decimal place.

(a) (i) $\sin x = 0.45$ for $x \in [0°, 360°]$

(ii) $\sin x = 0.7$ for $x \in [0°, 360°]$

(b) (i) $\cos x = -0.75$ for $-180° \le x \le 180°$

(ii) $\cos x = -0.2$ for $-180° \le x \le 180°$

(c) (i) $\tan\theta = \frac{1}{3}$ for $0° \le \theta \le 720°$

(ii) $\tan\theta = \frac{4}{3}$ for $0° \le \theta \le 720°$

(d) (i) $\sin t = -\frac{2}{3}$ for $t \in [-180°, 360°]$

(ii) $\sin t = -\frac{1}{4}$ for $t \in [-180°, 360°]$

8. Solve these equations in the given interval, giving your answers to three significant figures.

(a) (i) $\cos t = \frac{4}{5}$ for $t \in [0, 4\pi]$

(ii) $\cos t = \frac{2}{3}$ for $t \in [0, 4\pi]$

(b) (i) $\sin\theta = -0.8$ for $\theta \in [-2\pi, 2\pi]$

(i) $\sin\theta = -0.35$ for $\theta \in [-2\pi, 2\pi]$

(c) (i) $\tan\theta = -\frac{2}{3}$ for $-\pi \le \theta \le \pi$

(ii) $\tan\theta = -3$ for $-\pi \le \theta \le \pi$

(d) (i) $\cos\theta = 1$ for $\theta \in [0, 4\pi]$

(ii) $\cos\theta = 0$ for $\theta \in [0, 4\pi]$

9. Solve the following equations in the given interval, giving exact answers.

(a) (i) $\sin x = \frac{1}{2}$ for $-360° \le x \le 360°$

(ii) $\sin x = \frac{\sqrt{2}}{2}$ for $-360° \le x \le 360°$

(b) (i) $\cos x = -1$ for $-180° \le x \le 180°$

(ii) $\sin x = -1$ for $-180° \le x \le 180°$

(c) (i) $\tan x = \sqrt{3}$ for $-360° < x < 0°$

(ii) $\tan x = 1$ for $-360° < x < 0°$

(d) (i) $\cos x = -\frac{\sqrt{2}}{2}$ for $-360° \le x \le 360°$

(ii) $\cos x = -\frac{\sqrt{3}}{2}$ for $-360° \le x \le 360°$

10. Find the exact solutions of the following equations.

(a) (i) $\cos\theta = \frac{1}{2}$ for $-2\pi < \theta < 2\pi$

(ii) $\cos\theta = \frac{\sqrt{3}}{2}$ for $-2\pi < \theta < 2\pi$

(b) (i) $\sin\theta = -\frac{\sqrt{3}}{2}$ for $-\pi < \theta < 3\pi$

(ii) $\sin\theta = -\frac{\sqrt{2}}{2}$ for $-\pi < \theta < 3\pi$

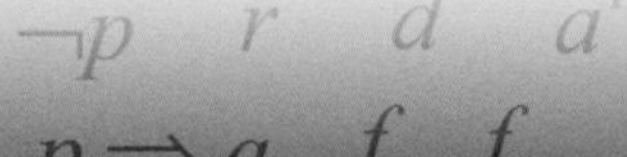

(c) (i) $\tan\theta = -\frac{1}{\sqrt{3}}$ for $-\pi < \theta < \pi$

(ii) $\tan\theta = -1$ for $-\pi < \theta < \pi$

(d) (i) $\cos\theta = 0$ for $0 < \theta < 3\pi$

(ii) $\sin\theta = 0$ for $0 < \theta < 3\pi$

(e) $\sin\theta = \frac{1}{\sqrt{2}}$ for $-2\pi < \theta < 0$

11. Solve the following equations:

(a) (i) $2\sin\theta + 1 = 1.2$ for $0° < \theta < 360°$

(ii) $4\sin x + 3 = 2$ for $-90° < x < 270°$

(b) (i) $3\cos x - 1 = \frac{1}{3}$ for $0 < x < 2\pi$

(ii) $5\cos x + 2 = 4.7$ for $0 < x < 2\pi$

(c) (i) $3\tan t - 1 = 4$ for $-\pi < t < \pi$

(ii) $5\tan t - 3 = 8$ for $0 < t < 2\pi$

12. Find the exact values of $x \in (-\pi, \pi)$ for which $2\sin x + 1 = 0$. *[5 marks]*

13 Show by a counterexample that $\tan^{-1} x \neq \frac{\sin^{-1} x}{\cos^{-1} x}$.

9B Harder trigonometric equations

In this section we shall look at two kinds of trigonometric equations that are more difficult to deal with: equations that need to be rearranged first and equations in which the argument of the trigonometric function is more complicated.

See chapter 3 for a reminder on disguised quadratics and solving equations by factorising.

The previous section showed how to solve equations of the form 'trigonometric function = constant'. It is not always obvious how to write an equation in this form. There are three tactics which are often used:

- look for disguised quadratics
- take everything over to one side and factorise
- use trigonometric identities.

Section 9D covers how to use identities to solve trigonometric equations.

Worked example 9.5

Solve the equation $\cos^2\theta = \frac{4}{9}$ for $\theta \in [0°, 360°]$.

Give answers correct to one decimal place.

EXAM HINT

$\cos^2\theta$ means $(\cos\theta)^2$.

First, find the possible values of $\cos\theta$. Remember $\pm$ signs when taking the square root.

$\cos^2\theta = \frac{4}{9} \Rightarrow \cos\theta = \pm\frac{2}{3}$

Sketch the graph to see how many solutions there are in the required interval.

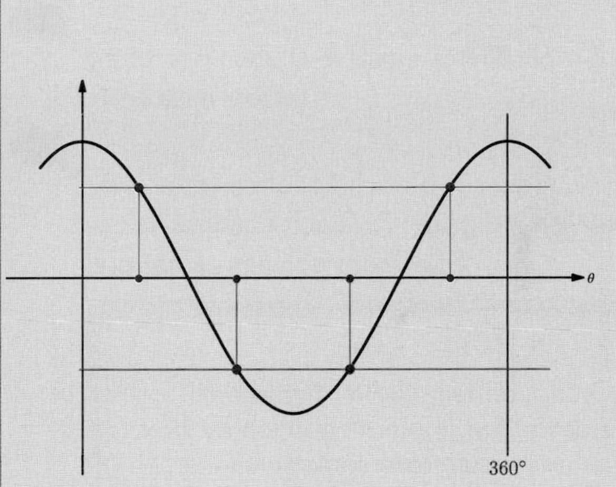

2 solutions for each of $\pm\frac{2}{3}$.

Solve each equation separately.

When $\cos\theta = \frac{2}{3}$:

$\cos^{-1}\left(\frac{2}{3}\right) = 48.2°$

$\theta = 48.2°$ or $360° - 48.2° = 311.8°$

When $\cos\theta = -\frac{2}{3}$:

$\cos^{-1}\left(-\frac{2}{3}\right) = 131.8°$

$\theta = 131.8°$ or $360° - 131.8° = 228.2°$

List all the solutions.

$\theta_1 = 48.2°$
$\theta_2 = 131.8°$
$\theta_3 = 228.2°$
$\theta_4 = 311.8°$

In the next example we need to use factorising.

Worked example 9.6

Solve the equation $3\sin x\cos x = 2\sin x$ for $-\pi \le x \le \pi$.

The equation is not in the form 'trig function = constant', so we cannot take the inverse directly. However, both sides have a factor of sin x, so we can rearrange the equation so that the RHS is zero and then factorise the LHS.

$3\sin x\cos x - 2\sin x = 0$

$\Leftrightarrow \sin x(3\cos x - 2) = 0$

If a product is equal to 0, then one of the factors must be 0.

$\sin x = 0$ or $\cos x = \frac{2}{3}$

Now solve each equation separately. Sketch the graph for each equation to see how many solutions there are.

When $\sin x = 0$:

$\sin^{-1} 0 = 0$

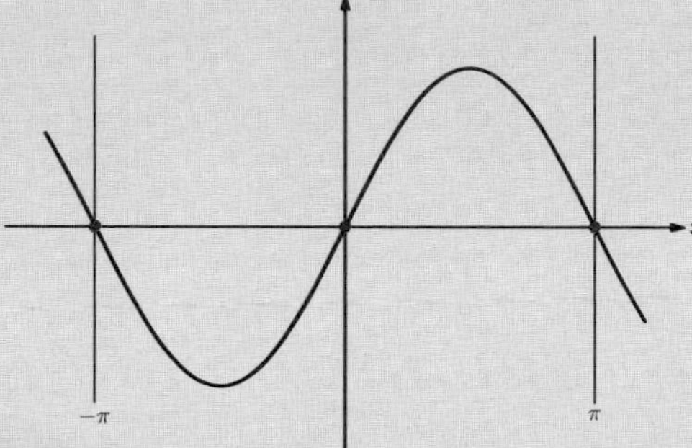

$x = 0$ or $\pi - 0 = \pi$ or $0 - \pi = -\pi$

When $\cos x = \frac{2}{3}$:

$\cos^{-1}\left(\frac{2}{3}\right) = 0.841$

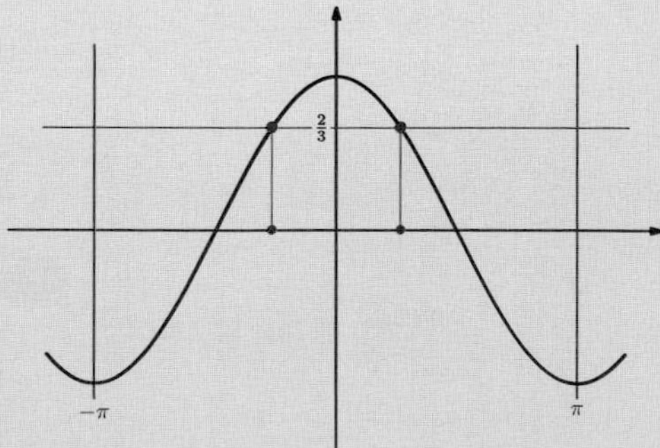

$2\pi - 0.841 = 5.44$ is not in the interval, but $5.44 - 2\pi = -0.841$ is in the interval.

We have found five solutions.

$x = -\pi, -0.841, 0, 0.841, \pi$

EXAM HINT

Do not be tempted to divide both sides of the original equation by sinx as you would lose some solutions (the ones coming from $\sin x = 0$).

Check these solutions by looking at graphs on your calculator. If you plot the graphs of $y=3\sin x\cos x$ and $y=2\sin x$ on the same set of axes over the given interval, you will see that they intersect at five points.

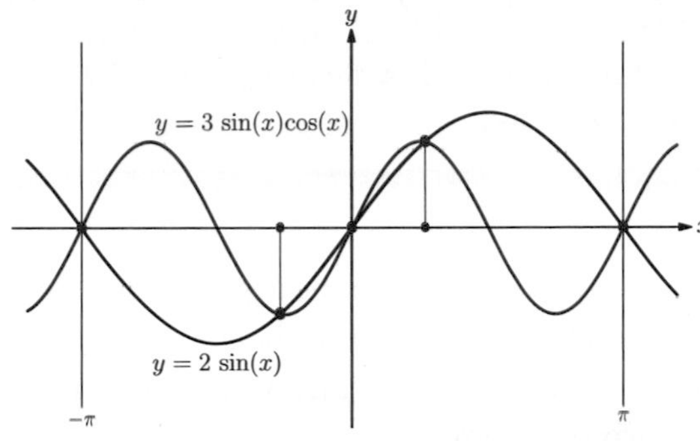

Another common type of trigonometric equation is a disguised quadratic.

Worked example 9.7

(a) Given that $3\sin^2 x-5\sin x+1=0$, find the possible values of $\sin x$.
(b) Hence solve the equation $3\sin^2 x-5\sin x+1=0$ for $0<x<2\pi$.

Recognise that this is a quadratic equation in sinx. Since we cannot factorise it, use the quadratic formula.

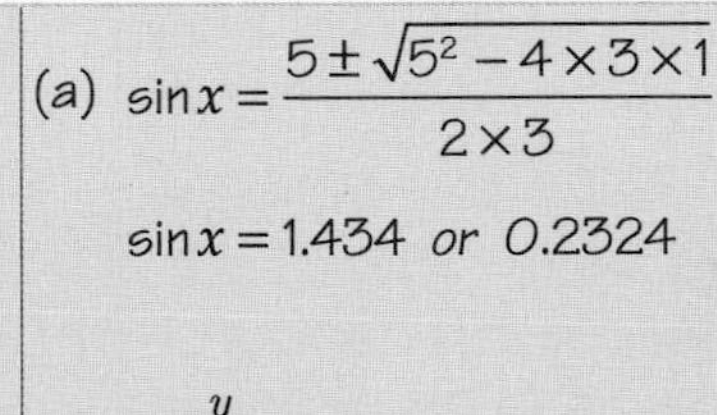

(a) $\sin x=\dfrac{5\pm\sqrt{5^2-4\times3\times1}}{2\times3}$

$\sin x=1.434$ or 0.2324

Sketch the graph of sinx to see how many solutions there are to $\sin x=1.434$ and $\sin x=0.2324$.

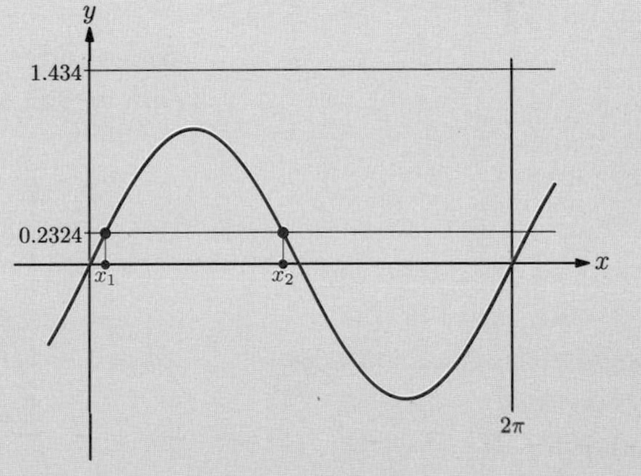

There are two solutions in total.

sinx is always between −1 and 1, so only $\sin x=0.2324$ has solutions.

$\sin x=1.434>1$ is impossible.
Hence $\sin x=0.2324$

Solve this equation as before.

(b) $\sin^{-1}(0.2324)=0.235$
$x=0.235$ or $\pi-0.235=2.91$

> **EXAM HINT**
>
> Questions like the one in Worked example 9.7 force you to use algebraic methods to solve the equation, but you should still use a graph on your calculator to check your solution. If the question did not include part (a), then you could solve the equation directly using your GDC, without any algebraic working.

Next, we look at equations where the argument of the trigonometric function is more complicated than just x. For the equation $\sin x = 0.6$ with $0 \le x \le 2\pi$, we can see from the graph that there are two solutions.

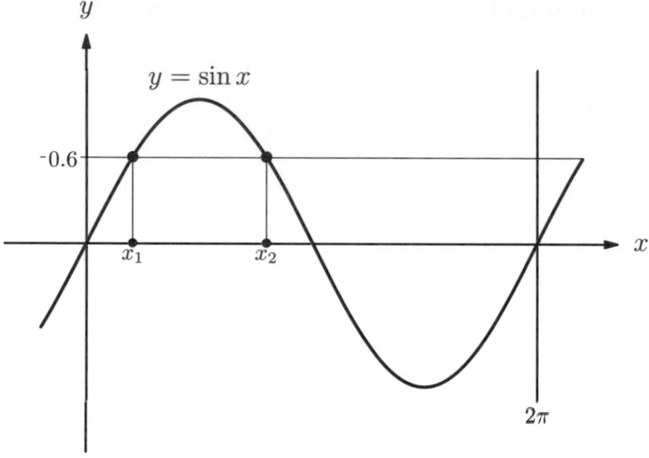

Now consider the equation $\sin 2x = 0.6$ for $0 \le x \le 2\pi$. From the graph we can see that there are four solutions.

Notice this is the graph of sinx squashed by a factor of 2. See section 5B.

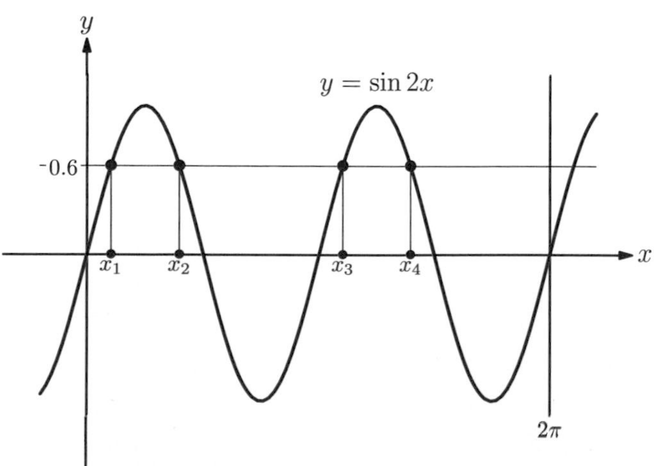

We need to extend the methods from section 9A to deal with equations like this. A substitution is a useful step in converting such an equation to the form 'trigonometric function = constant'.

Worked example 9.8

Find the zeros of the function $3\sin(2x)+1$ for $x \in [0, 2\pi]$.

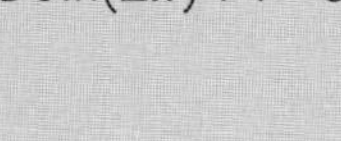

Write down the equation to be solved.

$3\sin(2x)+1=0$

Rearrange it into the form $\sin(A)=k$.

$\Leftrightarrow \sin(2x) = -\frac{1}{3}$

Make a substitution for the argument.

Let $A = 2x$

Rewrite the interval in terms of A.

$x \in [0, 2\pi] \Leftrightarrow A \in [0, 4\pi]$

Solve the equation for A.

$\sin A = -\frac{1}{3}$

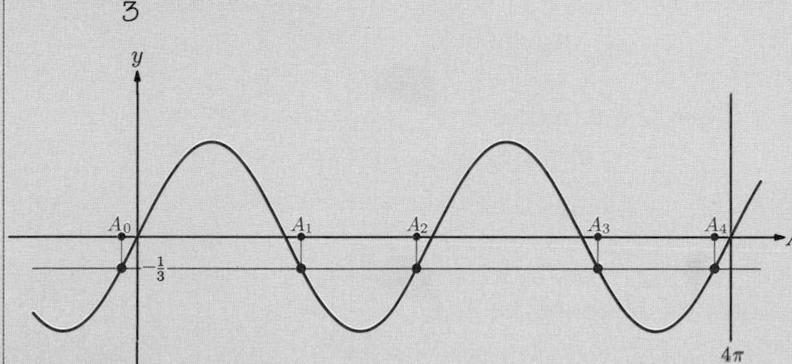

There are four solutions.

$A_0 = \sin^{-1}\left(-\frac{1}{3}\right) = -0.3398$ is outside of the interval.

$A_1 = \pi - A_0 = 3.481$
$A_2 = A_0 + 2\pi = 5.943$
$A_3 = A_1 + 2\pi = 9.764$
$A_4 = A_2 + 2\pi = 12.23$

Transform the solutions back into x.

$x = \frac{A}{2}$
$= 1.74, 2.97, 4.88, 6.11$ (3 SF)

This procedure can be summarised in the following four-step process.

KEY POINT 9.4

To solve trigonometric equations:

1. Make a substitution for the argument of the trigonometric function (such as $A = 2x$).
2. Change the interval for x into an interval for A.
3. Solve the equation for A in the usual way.
4. Transform the solutions back into the original variable.

The following example illustrates this method in a more complicated situation.

Worked example 9.9

Solve the equation $3\cos(2x+1) = 2$ for $x \in [-\pi, \pi]$.

Write the equation in the form $\cos(A) = k$.

$\cos(2x+1) = \frac{2}{3}$

Make a substitution for the argument.

Let $A = 2x+1$

Rewrite the interval in terms of A.

$-\pi \leq x \leq \pi$

$\Leftrightarrow -2\pi \leq 2x \leq 2\pi$

$\Leftrightarrow -2\pi + 1 \leq 2x + 1 \leq 2\pi + 1$

So $A \in [-2\pi + 1, 2\pi + 1]$

Solve the equation for A.

$\cos A = \frac{2}{3}$

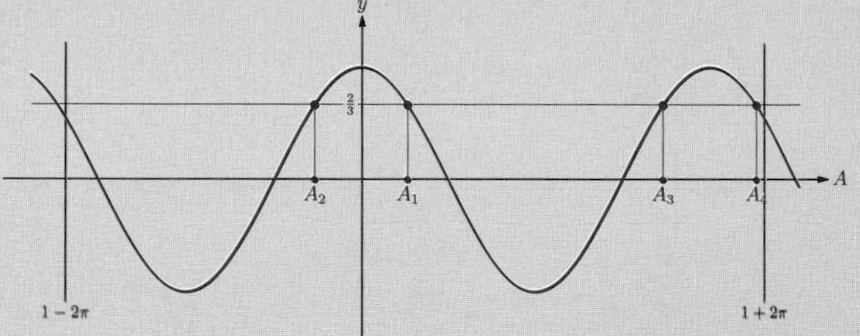

There are four solutions:

$A_1 = \cos^{-1}\left(\frac{2}{3}\right) = 0.841$

$A_2 = -A_1 = -0.841$

$A_3 = A_2 + 2\pi = 5.44$

$A_4 = A_1 + 2\pi = 7.12$

Transform the solutions back into x.

$x = \frac{A-1}{2} = -0.0795, 2.22, 6.2035, -0.921$

In the next example we revisit the tangent function, working in degrees and finding exact solutions.

Worked example 9.10

Solve the equation $3\tan\left(\frac{1}{2}\theta° - 30°\right) = \sqrt{3}$ for $0 \le \theta \le 720$.

Rearrange the equation into the form $\tan(A) = k$.

$\tan\left(\frac{1}{2}\theta° - 30°\right) = \frac{\sqrt{3}}{3} = \frac{1}{\sqrt{3}}$

Make a substitution for the argument.

$A = \frac{1}{2}\theta° - 30°$

Rewrite the interval in terms of A.

$0 \le \theta \le 720$

$\Leftrightarrow 0 \le \frac{1}{2}\theta \le 360$

$\Leftrightarrow -30 \le \frac{1}{2}\theta - 30 \le 330$

$\Leftrightarrow -30° \le A \le 330°$

Solve the equation for A. $\frac{1}{\sqrt{3}}$ is one of the exact values from Section 8D.

$\tan A = \frac{1}{\sqrt{3}}$

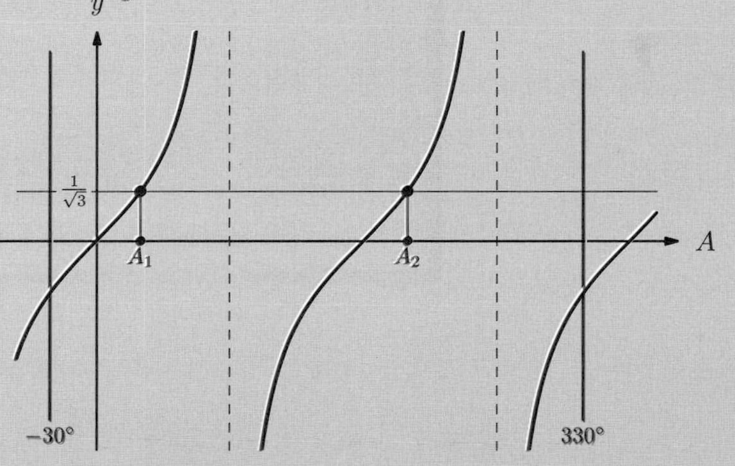

There are two solutions:

$A_1 = \tan^{-1}\left(\frac{1}{\sqrt{3}}\right) = 30°$

$A_2 = A_1 + 180° = 210°$

Transform the solutions back into θ.

$\theta° = 2(A + 30°)$

$\theta = 120°$ or $480°$

Exercise 9B

1. Solve the following equations, giving your answers to 3 significant figures.

   (a) (i) $\tan^2 x = 2$ for $-\pi \le x \le \pi$

   (ii) $\sin^2 x = 0.6$ for $-\pi \le x \le \pi$

   (b) (i) $9\cos^2\theta = 4$ for $0° < \theta < 360°$

   (ii) $3\tan^2\theta = 5$ for $0° < \theta < 360°$

2. Without using graphs on your calculator, find all solutions of each equation in the given interval. Use graphs on your calculator to check your answers.

   (a) (i) $3\sin x - 2\sin x\cos x = 0$ for $0° \le x \le 360°$

   (ii) $4\cos x - \sin x\cos x = 0$ for $0° \le x \le 360°$

   (b) (i) $4\sin^2\theta = 3\sin\theta$ for $\theta \in [-\pi, \pi]$

   (ii) $3\cos^2\theta = -\cos\theta$ for $\theta \in [-\pi, \pi]$

   (c) (i) $\tan^2 t - 5\tan t + 5 = 0$ for $t \in]0, 2\pi[$

   (ii) $2\tan^2 t + \tan t - 1 = 0$ for $t \in]0, 2\pi[$

   (d) (i) $\sin\theta\tan\theta + \frac{1}{2}\tan\theta = 0$ for $\theta \in [0, 2\pi]$

   (ii) $2\cos\theta\tan\theta - 3\cos\theta = 0$ for $\theta \in [0, 2\pi]$

   (e) (i) $2\cos^2 x + 3\cos x = 2$ for $0° < x < 180°$

   (ii) $\cos^2 x - 2\cos x = 3$ for $0° < x < 180°$

3. Solve the following equations in the given interval, giving your answers to 3 significant figures.

   (a) (i) $\cos 2x = \frac{1}{3}$ for $0° \le x \le 360°$

   (ii) $\cos 3x = \frac{2}{5}$ for $0° \le x \le 360°$

   (b) (i) $\sin(3x - 1) = -0.2$ for $0 \le x \le \pi$

   (ii) $\sin(2x + 1) = \frac{2}{3}$ for $0 \le x \le 2\pi$

   (c) (i) $\tan(x - 45°) = 2$ for $-180° \le x \le 180°$

   (ii) $\tan(x + 60°) = -3$ for $-180° \le x \le 180°$

4. Find the exact solutions in the given interval.

   (a) (i) $\sin 2x = \frac{1}{2}$ for $0 \le x \le 2\pi$

   (ii) $\sin 3x = -\frac{1}{2}$ for $0 \le x \le 2\pi$

(b) (i) $\cos 2x = -\frac{\sqrt{2}}{2}$ for $0° \le x \le 360°$

(ii) $\cos 3x = \frac{1}{2}$ for $-180° \le x \le 180°$

(c) (i) $\tan 4x = \sqrt{3}$ for $0 \le x \le \pi$

(ii) $\tan 2x = \frac{1}{\sqrt{3}}$ for $0 \le x \le \pi$

5. Find the exact solutions of the following in the given interval.

(a) (i) $\cos(x + 60°) = \frac{\sqrt{3}}{2}$ for $0° \le x \le 360°$

(ii) $\cos\left(x - \frac{\pi}{3}\right) = \frac{1}{2}$ for $-\pi \le x \le \pi$

(b) (i) $\sin\left(x - \frac{\pi}{3}\right) = -\frac{1}{2}$ for $-\pi \le x \le \pi$

(ii) $\sin(x - 120°) = -\frac{\sqrt{2}}{2}$ for $0° \le x \le 360°$

(c) (i) $\tan\left(x + \frac{\pi}{2}\right) = 1$ for $0 < x < 2\pi$

(ii) $\tan\left(x - \frac{\pi}{4}\right) = -1$ for $0 < x < 2\pi$

6. Solve the equation $3\cos x = \tan x$ for $0 \le x \le 2\pi$. *[8 marks]*

7. (a) Given that $2\sin^2 x - 3\sin x = 2$, find the *exact* value of $\sin x$.

(b) Hence solve the equation $2\sin^2 x - 3\sin x = 2$ for $0 < x < 360°$. *[6 marks]*

8. Solve the equation $\sin x \tan x = \sin^2 x$ for $-\pi \le x \le \pi$. *[8 marks]*

9. Find the exact solutions of the equation $\sin(x^2) = \frac{1}{2}$ for $-\pi < x < \pi$. *[5 marks]*

9C Trigonometric identities

We have already seen one example of a trigonometric identity: $\frac{\sin x}{\cos x} = \tan x$. The two sides are equal for all values of x (except when $\cos x = 0$ and $\tan x$ is undefined). There are many other identities involving trigonometric functions, and we will meet some of them in this section.

EXAM HINT

The identity symbol $\equiv$ means that the equality holds for all values of the variable(s). Many people write $\frac{\sin x}{\cos x} \equiv \tan x$ to emphasise that the statement is an identity (true for all values of x) rather than an equation (true only for some values of x, which need to be found). However, the IB syllabus and most exam questions use the equals sign in identities, so we will do the same in this book, except where there is a possibility of confusion.

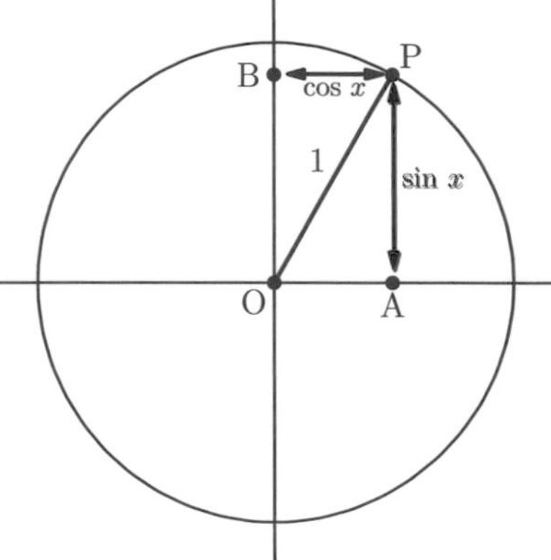

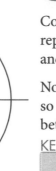

Consider again the unit circle diagram, with point P representing number x. According to the definitions of the sine and cosine functions, $\text{AP} = \sin x$ and $\text{BP} = \text{OA} = \cos x$.

Note that the triangle is right-angled, with hypotenuse 1, so using Pythagoras' Theorem we get the following relation between sine and cosine.

KEY POINT 9.5

Pythagorean identity:

$\sin^2 x + \cos^2 x = 1$

Worked example 9.11

Given that $\sin x = \frac{1}{3}$, find the possible values of $\cos x$ and $\tan x$.

Think of an identity relating sin and cos. Put in the known value.

$$\sin^2 x + \cos^2 x = 1$$

$$\left(\frac{1}{3}\right)^2 + \cos^2 x = 1$$

Find the value of the other function. Remember ± signs when taking the square root.

$$\cos^2 x = 1 - \frac{1}{9} = \frac{8}{9}$$

$$\therefore \cos x = \pm\sqrt{\frac{8}{9}} = \pm\frac{2\sqrt{2}}{3}$$

We know how to find tan given sin and cos.

$$\tan x = \frac{\sin x}{\cos x}$$

$$\therefore \tan x = \frac{\frac{1}{3}}{\pm\frac{2\sqrt{2}}{3}} = \pm\frac{\sqrt{2}}{4}$$

We have already seen examples where the values of $\sin x$ and $\cos x$ were used to find the value of $\tan x$. Using the Pythagorean identity, we only need to know the value of one of the functions to find the values of the other two.

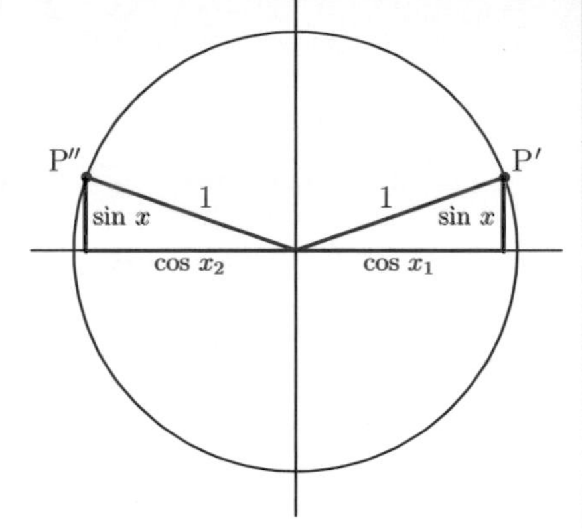

Notice that for a given value of $\sin x$, there are two possible values of $\cos x$. The circle diagram makes this clear: points P′ and P″ are the same distance, namely $\sin x$, above the horizontal axis, but have different values of $\cos x$ (equal in size but opposite in sign).

Notice also that we do not need to know what x is to find the possible values of $\cos x$ given $\sin x$ (and vice versa). However by restricting x to a particular quadrant we can select one of the two possible values.

Worked example 9.12

If $\tan x = 2$ and $\frac{\pi}{2} < x < \pi$, find the value of $\cos x$.

We need a relationship between $\cos x$ and $\tan x$. The only two identities we know so far are $\sin^2 x + \cos^2 x = 1$ and $\frac{\sin x}{\cos x} = \tan x$. We can substitute $\sin x$ from the second identity into the first.

$\frac{\sin x}{\cos x} = \tan x$

$\Rightarrow \sin x = \tan x \cos x$

So the Pythagorean identity becomes

$\tan^2 x \cos^2 x + \cos^2 x = 1$

Now put in the given value of $\tan x$.

$2^2 \cos^2 x + \cos^2 x = 1$

$\Leftrightarrow 5\cos^2 x = 1$

$\Leftrightarrow \cos x = \pm\frac{\sqrt{5}}{5}$

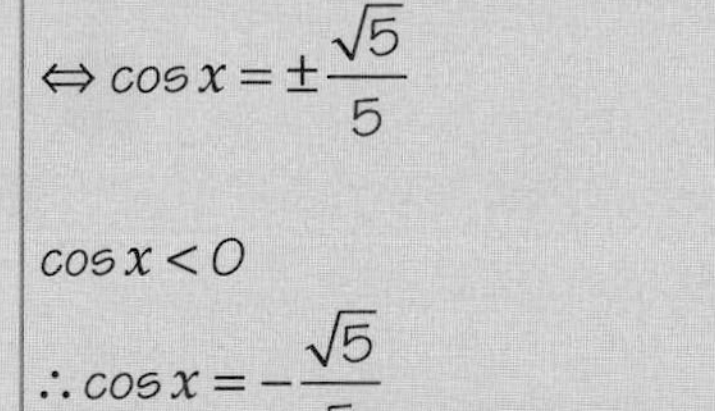

We are told that x is in the second quadrant, so $\cos x$ is negative.

$\cos x < 0$

$\therefore \cos x = -\frac{\sqrt{5}}{5}$

Exercise 9C

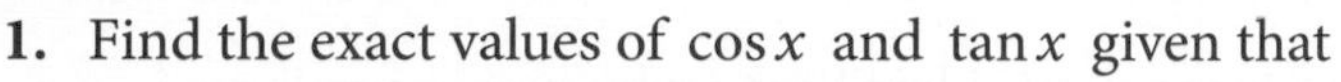

1. Find the exact values of $\cos x$ and $\tan x$ given that

(i) $\sin x = \frac{1}{3}$ and $0° < x < 90°$ (ii) $\sin x = \frac{4}{5}$ and $0° < x < 90°$

2. Find the exact values of $\sin\theta$ and $\tan\theta$ given that

   (i) $\cos\theta = -\frac{1}{3}$ and $180° < \theta < 270°$

   (ii) $\cos\theta = -\frac{3}{4}$ and $180° < \theta < 270°$

3. (a) Find the exact value of $\cos x$ if

   (i) $\sin x = \frac{1}{5}$ and $\frac{\pi}{2} < x < \pi$

   (ii) $\sin x = -\frac{1}{2}$ and $\frac{3\pi}{2} < x < 2\pi$

   (b) Find the exact value of $\tan x$ if

   (i) $\cos x = \frac{3}{5}$ and $-\frac{\pi}{2} < x < 0$

   (ii) $\cos x = -1$ and $\frac{\pi}{2} < x < \frac{3\pi}{2}$

4. (i) Find the possible values of $\cos x$ if $\tan x = \frac{2}{3}$.

   (ii) Find the possible values of $\sin x$ if $\tan x = -\frac{1}{2}$.

5. Find the exact value of:

   (a) $3\sin^2 x + 3\cos^2 x$ (b) $\sin^2 5x + \cos^2 5x$

   (c) $-2\cos^2 2x - 2\sin^2 2x$ (d) $2\tan^2 2x - \frac{2}{\cos^2 2x}$

   (e) $\frac{1}{\sin^2 x} - \frac{1}{\tan^2 x}$ (f) $\frac{3}{2\sin^2 4x} - \frac{3}{2\tan^2 4x}$

6. (i) Express $3\sin^2 x + 4\cos^2 x$ in terms of $\sin x$ only.

   (ii) Express $\cos^2 x - \sin^2 x$ in terms of $\cos x$ only.

7. (a) Express $3 - 2\tan^2 x$ in terms of $\cos x$ only.

   (b) Express $\frac{1+\tan^2 x}{\cos^2 x}$ in terms of $\sin x$ only, simplifying your answer as fully as possible. *[7 marks]*

8. If $t = \tan x$, express the following in terms of t:

   (a) $\cos^2 x$ (b) $\sin^2 x$ (c) $\cos^2 x - \sin^2 x$ (d) $\frac{2}{\sin^2 x} + 1$ *[8 marks]*

9D Using identities to solve equations

We can use trigonometric identities to solve more complicated equations. Usually we start by replacing $\tan x$ by $\frac{\sin x}{\cos x}$ or by using the Pythagorean identity. The latter can only be used if the equation contains squares and typically results in a quadratic equation.

Worked example 9.13

Solve the equation $4\sin x = \tan x$ in the interval $0 \le x \le 2\pi$.

The applicable identity here is the one for tan.

$$4\sin x = \frac{\sin x}{\cos x}$$

To eliminate fractions, multiply both sides by $\cos x$.

$$\Leftrightarrow 4\sin x\cos x = \sin x$$

Both sides contain $\sin x$, so rearrange the equation to make one side zero and factorise.

$$\Leftrightarrow 4\sin x\cos x - \sin x = 0$$
$$\Leftrightarrow \sin x(4\cos x - 1) = 0$$

One of the factors must be equal to zero.

$$\sin x = 0 \text{ or } \cos x = \frac{1}{4}$$

Now solve each equation separately.

When $\sin x = 0$:
$x = 0, \pi, 2\pi$

When $\cos x = \frac{1}{4}$:

$x = \cos^{-1}\left(\frac{1}{4}\right) = 1.32(3SF)$

or $x = 2\pi - 1.32 = 4.97(3SF)$

List all the solutions.

$\therefore x = 0, 1.32, \pi, 4.97, 2\pi$

The next example shows how using the Pythagorean identity can lead to a quadratic equation. You could solve the resulting equation using a graph on your calculator, but the question may require you to use an algebraic method, for instance by asking you to find possible values of $\cos\theta$ first.

Worked example 9.14

Find all values of θ in the interval $[-180°, 180°]$ which satisfy the equation $2\sin^2\theta + 3\cos\theta = 1$.

The equation contains both sin and cos terms. The sin term is squared, so replace $\sin^2\theta$ by $1-\cos^2\theta$.

$$2(1-\cos^2\theta) + 3\cos\theta = 1$$
$$\Leftrightarrow 2 - 2\cos^2\theta + 3\cos\theta = 1$$

This is a quadratic equation in $\cos\theta$. Write it in the standard form and then solve it.

$$\Leftrightarrow 2\cos^2\theta - 3\cos\theta - 1 = 0$$
$\cos\theta = 1.78$ or -0.281

continued . . .

cos values must be between −1 and 1.

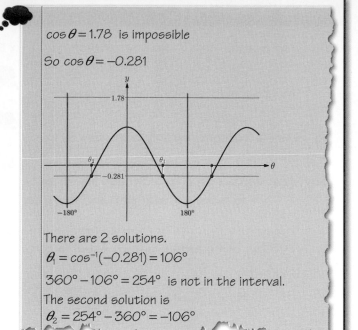

$\cos\theta = 1.78$ is impossible

So $\cos\theta = -0.281$

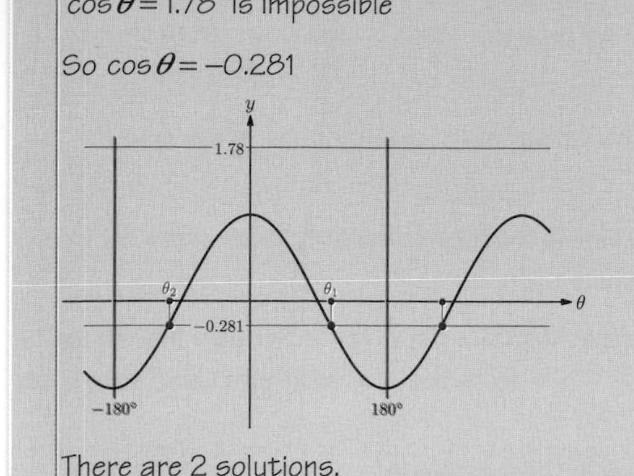

There are 2 solutions.

$\theta_1 = \cos^{-1}(-0.281) = 106°$

$360° - 106° = 254°$ is not in the interval.

The second solution is

$\theta_2 = 254° - 360° = -106°$

Exercise 9D

1. By using the identity $\tan x = \dfrac{\sin x}{\cos x}$, solve the following equations.

   (a) (i) $3\sin x = 2\cos x$ for $0° \le x \le 180°$

   (ii) $3\sin x = 5\cos x$ for $0° \le x \le 180°$

   (b) (i) $\cos x = 3\sin x$ for $0 \le x \le \dfrac{\pi}{2}$

   (ii) $3\cos x = -\sin x$ for $0 \le x \le \pi$

   (c) (i) $3\sin x + 5\cos x = 0$ for $0 \le x \le \pi$

   (ii) $4\cos x + 3\sin x = 0$ for $0 \le x \le 2\pi$

   (d) (i) $7\cos x - 3\sin x = 0$ for $-180° \le x \le 180°$

   (ii) $\sin x - 5\cos x = 0$ for $-180° \le x \le 180°$

2. Solve the following equations in the given interval, giving exact answers.

   (a) (i) $\sin 3\theta = \cos 3\theta$ for $0 < \theta < \dfrac{\pi}{2}$

   (ii) $\sin 2t = \sqrt{3}\cos 2t$ for $t \in [0, \pi]$

   (b) (i) $\sin 2x + \sqrt{3}\cos 2x = 0$ for $0 \le x \le 2\pi$

   (ii) $\sin 3a + \cos 3a = 0$ for $a \in \left[0, \dfrac{\pi}{2}\right]$

3. Use trigonometric identities to solve these equations. (Do not use graphs or the equation solver function on your calculator.)

(a) $\sin x + \dfrac{\sin^2 x}{\cos x} = 0$ for $0° \le x \le 360°$

(b) $3\sin^2 x = 2\sin x \cos x$ for $x \in [-\pi, \pi]$

(c) $\dfrac{\cos\theta}{\sin\theta} - 2 = 0$ for $\theta \in [-90°, 90°]$

(d) $3\cos^2\theta + 4\sin\theta\cos\theta = 0$ for $0 \le \theta \le 2\pi$

4. Use the identity $\sin^2 x + \cos^2 x = 1$ to solve the following equations in the interval $[0°, 360°]$.

(a) (i) $7\sin^2 x + 3\cos^2 x = 5$ (ii) $\sin^2 x + 4\cos^2 x = 2$

(b) (i) $3\sin^2 x - \cos^2 x = 1$ (ii) $\cos^2 x - \sin^2 x = 1$

5. Use an algebraic method to solve the equation $5\sin^2\theta = 4\cos^2\theta$ for $-180° \le \theta \le 180°$. *[4 marks]*

6. Solve the equation $2\cos^2 t - \sin t - 1 = 0$ for $0 \le t \le 2\pi$. *[4 marks]*

7. Solve the equation $4\cos^2 x - 5\sin x - 5 = 0$ for $x \in [-\pi, \pi]$. *[4 marks]*

8. Given that $\cos^2 t + 5\cos t = 2\sin^2 t$, find the *exact* value of $\cos t$. *[4 marks]*

9. (a) Given that $6\sin^2 x + \cos x = 4$, find the exact values of $\cos x$.

(b) Hence solve the equation $6\sin^2 x + \cos x = 4$ for $0° \le x \le 360°$. *[6 marks]*

10. (a) Show that the equation $2\sin^2 x - 3\sin x\cos x + \cos^2 x = 0$ can be written in the form $2\tan^2 x - 3\tan x + 1 = 0$.

(b) Hence solve the equation $2\sin^2 x - 3\sin x\cos x + \cos^2 x = 0$, giving all solutions in the interval $-\pi < x < \pi$. *[6 marks]*

9E Double angle identities

This section looks at the relationships between trigonometric functions of a certain argument and trigonometric functions with double that argument.

Working in radians, use your calculator to find

$\sin 1.2$ and $\sin 2.4$

$\cos 1.2$ and $\cos 2.4$

Are there any rules that relate $\sin 2x$ and $\cos 2x$ to $\sin x$ and $\cos x$? At first glance it may appear that there is no connection between the values of trigonometric functions of an angle and those of twice that angle. To try to discover any relationships that might exist, a sensible starting point would be the familiar right-angled triangle containing the angle x. We are interested in the angle $2x$, which can be formed by adjoining an identical right-angled triangle as shown below.

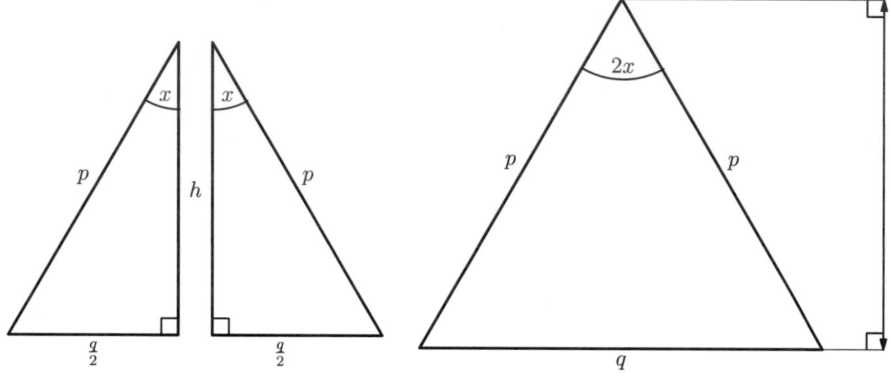

If you have not seen this formula before, you will meet it in chapter 10.

First consider the whole isosceles triangle. Using the formula $\text{Area} = \frac{1}{2}ab\sin C$, we find:

$$\text{Area} = \frac{1}{2}p^2\sin(2x)$$

We can also calculate the area from the base and the height of the triangle ($\text{Area} = \frac{1}{2}bh$). To find the height h and the length of the base b, look at one of the right-angled triangles with angle x. We have

$$\frac{h}{p} = \cos x \quad \Rightarrow \quad h = p\cos x$$

$$\frac{\frac{q}{2}}{p} = \sin x \quad \Rightarrow \quad q = 2p\sin x$$

So another expression for the area of the triangle is:

$$\begin{aligned}\text{Area} &= \frac{1}{2}(2p\sin x)(p\cos x)\\ &= p^2\sin x\cos x\end{aligned}$$

Comparing the two expressions for the area, we get

$$\frac{1}{2}p^2\sin(2x) = p^2\sin x\cos x$$

and rearranging this equation gives the **double angle identity** for sine.

EXAM HINT

You will often see sin, cos and tan of a multiple of x written without brackets: sin 2x, cos 5x, etc.

KEY POINT 9.6

$$\sin(2x) = 2\sin x\cos x$$

Although x was assumed to be an acute angle in our derivation of this formula, the identity actually holds for all values of x.

Working from the same triangle, it is possible to find a double angle identity for cosine:

$$\cos(2x) = \cos^2 x - \sin^2 x$$

Substituting $\sin^2 x = 1 - \cos^2 x$ or $\cos^2 x = 1 - \sin^2 x$ in this formula gives us two further ways of expressing the double angle identity for cosine.

KEY POINT 9.7

$$\cos(2x) = \begin{cases} 2\cos^2 x - 1 \\ 1 - 2\sin^2 x \\ \cos^2 x - \sin^2 x \end{cases}$$

One application of double angle identities is finding the exact values of half-angles.

Worked example 9.15

Using the exact value of $\cos 30°$, show that $\sin 15° = \sqrt{\frac{2-\sqrt{3}}{4}}$.

We know that $\cos 30° = \frac{\sqrt{3}}{2}$, and we need to relate this to $\sin 15°$.
Since $30 = 2 \times 15$, the obvious choice is the cosine double angle identity that involves sine: $\cos(2x) = 1 - \sin^2 x$.

Using $\cos(2x) = 1 - \sin^2 x$:

$$\cos(2 \times 15°) = 1 - 2\sin^2 15°$$

$$\cos 30° = 1 - 2\sin^2 15°$$

Using $\cos 30° = \frac{\sqrt{3}}{2}$:

$$\frac{\sqrt{3}}{2} = 1 - 2\sin^2 15°$$

$$\Leftrightarrow \sqrt{3} = 2 - 4\sin^2 15°$$

$$\Leftrightarrow 4\sin^2 15° = 2 - \sqrt{3}$$

$$\Leftrightarrow \sin^2 15° = \frac{2-\sqrt{3}}{4}$$

We have to choose between the positive and negative square root. Since 15° is in the first quadrant, $\sin 15° > 0$ and so we take the positive square root.

$$\therefore \sin 15° = \sqrt{\frac{2-\sqrt{3}}{4}} \quad (\text{as } \sin 15° > 0)$$

In chapter 15 we will see how double angle identities can be used to integrate some trigonometric functions.

Double angle identities are also very useful in proving more complex trigonometric identities and solving equations. Although they are called double angle identities, these formulas can be applied to any multiple of an angle.

Worked example 9.16

Find an expression for $\cos 4x$ in terms of

(a) $\cos 2x$ (b) $\cos x$

Notice that $4x = 2 \times (2x)$, so one of the cosine double angle identities seems suitable. Since we want an expression involving only cos, the most appropriate formula is $\cos(2x) = 2\cos^2 x - 1$, with $x = 2x$.

(a) Using $\cos(2x) = 2\cos^2 x - 1$:

$$\cos(2(2x)) = 2\cos^2(2x) - 1$$

$$\cos(4x) = 2\cos^2(2x) - 1$$

continued . . .

Can we use the answer from the part (i)? Yes – we just need to replace $\cos(2x)$ in the previous result with an expression involving only $\cos x$. Replace $\cos(2x)$ in the answer to part (a) with an expression involving only $\cos x$.

(b) From part (i),

$$\cos(4x) = 2\cos^2(2x) - 1$$
$$= 2(2\cos^2 x - 1)^2 - 1$$
$$(\text{as } \cos(2x) = 2\cos^2 x - 1)$$

EXAM HINT

In the exam, any equivalent form of the answer would be acceptable; therefore, unless explicitly asked to do so, you need not go any further than this, for example by expanding the brackets.

Recognising the form of double angle formulas can be helpful in solving trigonometric equations.

Worked example 9.17

Solve the equation $6\sin x\cos x = 1$ for $-\pi < x < \pi$.

To solve this equation we need to rewrite it in the form 'trigonometric function = constant'. Here the $\sin x \cos x$ on the LHS should remind us of the $\sin(2x)$ identity.

$$6\sin x\cos x = 1$$
$$\Leftrightarrow 2\sin x\cos x = \frac{1}{3}$$
$$\Leftrightarrow \sin(2x) = \frac{1}{3} \quad (\text{as } 2\sin x\cos x = \sin(2x))$$

Now we can follow the standard procedure. First, make a substitution for the argument. Sketching the graph, we see that there are 4 solutions in the given domain.

Let $A = 2x$

$-\pi < x < \pi \Leftrightarrow -2\pi < A < 2\pi$

$$\sin^{-1}\left(\frac{1}{3}\right) = 0.3398$$

so the 4 solutions are

$A = 0.3398, 2.802, -5.943, -3.481$

and hence

$x = 0.170, 1.40, -2.97, -1.74$ (3 SF)

If an equation contains both $\cos 2\theta$ and $\cos\theta$, we need to use identities to turn it into a quadratic equation involving only $\cos\theta$.

Worked example 9.18

Solve the equation $\cos 2x = \cos x$ for $0° \le x \le 360°$.

We need to write the equation in terms of only one trig function. (Watch out: cos2x and cosx are not the same function!) Use the identity for cos(2x) that involves just cosx.	$\cos(2x) = \cos x$ $\Leftrightarrow 2\cos^2 x - 1 = \cos x$ (as $\cos(2x) = 2\cos^2 x - 1$)
Recognise this as a quadratic equation in cosx. Try to factorise.	$2\cos^2 x - \cos x - 1 = 0$ $(2\cos x + 1)(\cos x - 1) = 0$ $\cos x = -\frac{1}{2}$ or $\cos x = 1$
Solve each equation separately.	When $\cos x = -\frac{1}{2}$: $x = 120°$ or $360° - 120° = 240°$ When $\cos x = 1$: $x = 0°$ or $360°$
List all the solutions.	$x = 0°, 120°, 240°, 360°$

We can use the double angle identities for sine and cosine to derive a double angle identity for the tangent function, $\tan 2x = \frac{2\tan x}{1 - \tan^2 x}$.

Worked example 9.19

Express $\tan 2x$ in terms of $\tan x$.

First, write $\tan 2x$ in terms of $\sin 2x$ and $\cos 2x$.	$\tan 2x = \frac{\sin 2x}{\cos 2x}$ $= \frac{2\sin x\cos x}{\cos^2 x - \sin^2 x}$ (as $\cos(2x) = \cos^2 x - \sin^2 x$)
Then, express in terms of $\sin x$ and $\cos x$ by using the sin and cos double angle identities. We have to decide which of the $\cos 2x$ identities to use. If we use $\cos(2x) = \cos^2 x - \sin^2 x$, we can divide through by $\cos^2 x$ to leave $1 - \tan^2 x$ in the denominator.	Dividing top and bottom by $\cos^2 x$: $\tan 2x = \frac{2\left(\frac{\sin x}{\cos x}\right)}{1 - \frac{\sin^2 x}{\cos^2 x}}$ So $\tan(2x) = \frac{2\tan x}{1 - \tan^2 x}$

It may not be obvious which version of the cos(2x) identity to use. The good news is that, in this example and most other cases, even if you choose the 'wrong' version to begin with you will still be able to complete the calculation – it may just take a little longer.

Exercise 9E

1. (a) (i) Given that $\cos\theta = -\frac{1}{4}$, find the exact value of $\cos 2\theta$.

   (ii) Given that $\sin A = -\frac{2}{3}$, find the exact value of $\cos 2A$.

   (b) (i) Given that $\sin x = \frac{1}{3}$ and $0 < x < \frac{\pi}{2}$, find the exact value of $\cos x$.

   (ii) Given that $\sin x = \frac{3}{5}$ and $0 < x < \frac{\pi}{2}$, find the exact value of $\cos x$.

   (c) (i) Given that $\sin x = \frac{1}{3}$ and $0 < x < \frac{\pi}{2}$, find the exact value of $\sin 2x$.

   (ii) Given that $\sin x = \frac{3}{5}$ and $0 < x < \frac{\pi}{2}$, find the exact value of $\sin 2x$.

2. Find the exact value of

   (a) $\sin^2 22.5°$ (b) $\cos^2 75°$

   (c) $\cos^2\left(\frac{\pi}{12}\right)$

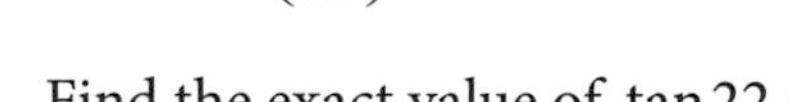

3. Find the exact value of $\tan 22.5°$.

4. Simplify the following by using double angle identities.

   (a) $2\cos^2(3A) - 1$ (b) $4\sin 5x \cos 5x$

   (c) $3 - 6\sin^2\left(\frac{b}{2}\right)$ (d) $5\sin\left(\frac{x}{3}\right)\cos\left(\frac{x}{3}\right)$

5. Use an algebraic method to solve each of the following equations.

   (a) $\sin 2x = 3\sin x$ for $x \in [0, 2\pi]$

   (b) $\cos 2x - \sin^2 x = -2$ for $0° \le x \le 180°$

   (c) $5\sin 2x = 3\cos x$ for $-\pi < x < \pi$

   (d) $\tan 2x - \tan x = 0$ for $0° \le x \le 360°$

6. Find all the values of $\theta \in [-\pi, \pi]$ which satisfy the equation $\cos^2\theta + \cos 2\theta = 0$. *[5 marks]*

7. Show that $\dfrac{1-\cos 2\theta}{1+\cos 2\theta} = \tan^2\theta$. *[4 marks]*

8. Express $\cos 4\theta$ in terms of

(a) $\cos\theta$ (b) $\sin\theta$ *[7 marks]*

9. (a) Show that

(i) $\cos^2\left(\dfrac{1}{2}x\right) = \dfrac{1}{2}(1+\cos x)$

(ii) $\sin^2\left(\dfrac{1}{2}x\right) = \dfrac{1}{2}(1-\cos x)$

(b) Express $\tan^2\left(\dfrac{1}{2}x\right)$ in terms of $\cos x$. *[7 marks]*

10. Given that $a\sin 4x = b\sin 2x$ and $0 < x < \dfrac{\pi}{2}$, express $\sin^2 x$ in terms of a and b. *[6 marks]*

Summary

- To solve trigonometric equations, follow this procedure:
  - First, rearrange the equation into the form $\sin A = k$, $\cos A = k$ or $\tan A = k$.
  - Make a substitution for the argument of the trigonometric function, e.g. $A = 2x + 1$ then sketch a graph over the required interval to see how many solutions there are (it is not necessary to substitute A for x in simple trigonometric equations).
  - Find solutions in the interval $[0, 2\pi]$:

$$\sin A = k \Rightarrow A_1 = \sin^{-1} k,\ A_2 = \pi - A_1$$
$$\cos A = k \Rightarrow A_1 = \cos^{-1} k,\ A_2 = 2\pi - A_1 \text{ (i.e. the reflection of } A_1\text{)}$$
$$\tan A = k \Rightarrow A_1 = \tan^{-1} k,\ A_2 = \pi + A_1$$

  - Find other solutions in the required interval by adding or subtracting multiples of 2π for sine and cosine and multiples of π for tangent.
- Use the values of A to find the value of x, i.e. transform the solutions back into the original variable.
- Trigonometric functions are related through identities, e.g.
  - $\tan x = \dfrac{\sin x}{\cos x}$
  - Pythagorean identity: $\sin^2 x + \cos^2 x = 1$
  - double angle identities: $\sin 2\theta = 2\sin\theta\cos\theta$;

$$\cos(2\theta) = \begin{cases} 2\cos^2\theta - 1 \\ 1 - 2\sin^2\theta \\ \cos^2\theta - \sin^2\theta \end{cases}$$

Introductory problem revisited

The original Ferris Wheel was constructed in 1893 in Chicago. It was just over 80 m tall and could complete one full revolution in 9 minutes. During each revolution, how much time did the passengers spend more than 5 m above the ground?

A car on the Ferris Wheel moves in a circle. Its height above the ground can therefore be modelled by a suitably transformed sine or cosine function. The car starts on the ground, climbs to a maximum height of 80 m and then returns to the ground; this takes 9 minutes. We can sketch a graph showing the height of the car above the ground as a function of time:

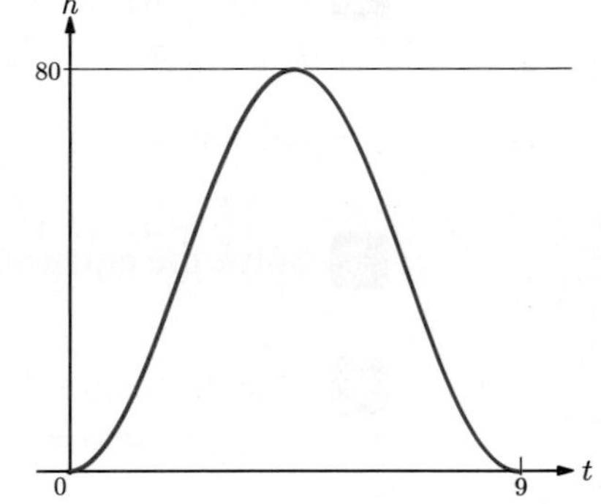

The period of the function is 9 and the amplitude is 40, so the function should involve $40\sin\left(\frac{2\pi}{9}t\right)$ or $40\cos\left(\frac{2\pi}{9}t\right)$. Either the sine or the cosine function can be used as the model; let us choose the cosine function, so that no horizontal translation is needed. The centre of the circle is at height 40, which means the graph is translated up by 40 units. Thus, an appropriate equation for height in terms of time is

$$h = 40 - 40\cos\left(\frac{2\pi}{9}t\right)$$

The minus sign in front of the cosine term ensures that when $t = 0$ we have $h = 0$.

To find the amount of time that the car spends more than 50 m above the ground, we need to find the times at which the height is exactly 50 m. This involves solving the equation

$$40 - 40\cos\left(\frac{2\pi}{9}t\right) = 50$$

Using the methods in this chapter, we get

$$\cos\left(\frac{2\pi}{9}t\right) = -0.25$$

$$\cos^{-1}(-0.25) = 1.82$$

$$\therefore \frac{2\pi}{9}t = 1.82 \text{ or } 2\pi - 1.82 = 4.46$$

$$\Rightarrow t_1 = 2.61,\ t_2 = 6.39$$

Therefore the time spent more than 50 m above ground is $6.39 - 2.61 \approx 3.78$ minutes.

Mixed examination practice 9

Short questions

1. Solve the equation $\tan x° = -0.62$ for $x \in]-90°, 270°[$. *[4 marks]*

2. Given that $0 < \theta < \frac{\pi}{2}$ and $\sin\theta = \frac{2}{3}$, find the exact value of
   (a) $\cos\theta$
   (b) $\cos 2\theta$ *[6 marks]*

3. Solve the equation $5\sin^2\theta = 4\cos^2\theta$ for $-\pi \le \theta \le \pi$. *[5 marks]*

4. Sketch the graph of $y = \sin(2x) + 2\sin(6x)$ and hence find the exact period of the function. *[4 marks]*

5. Prove the identity $\frac{2}{\cos^2 x} - \tan^2 x = 2 + \tan^2 x$. *[5 marks]*

6. Solve the equation $\cos\theta - 2\sin^2\theta + 2 = 0$ for $\theta \in [0, 2\pi]$. *[6 marks]*

7. Use an algebraic method to solve the equation $6\sin^2 x + \cos x = 4$ for $0° \le x \le 360°$. *[6 marks]*

8. Solve the equation $\sin 2\theta = \cos\theta$ for $0 \le \theta \le 2\pi$. *[7 marks]*

Long questions

1. The shape of a small bridge can be modelled by the equation $y = 1.8\sin\left(\frac{x}{3}\right)$, where y is the height of the bridge above the water and x is the distance from one river bank, both measured in metres. The bridge is just long enough to span the river.
   (a) Find the width of the river.
   (b) A barge has height 1.2 metres above the water level. Find the maximum possible width of the barge so that it can pass under the bridge.
   (c) Another barge has width 3.5 m. What is the maximum possible height of the barge so that it can pass under the bridge? *[10 marks]*

2. **(a)** Sketch the graph of the function $C(x) = \cos x + \frac{1}{2}\cos 2x$ for $-2\pi \le x \le 2\pi$.

(b) Prove that the function $C(x)$ is periodic and state its period.

(c) For what values of x, with $-2\pi \le x \le 2\pi$, is $C(x)$ a maximum?

(d) Let $x = x_0$ be the smallest positive value of x for which $C(x) = 0$. Find an approximate value of x_0 which is correct to two significant figures.

(e) (i) Prove that $C(x) = C(-x)$ for all x.

(ii) Let $x = x_1$ be that value of x with $\pi < x < 2\pi$ for which $C(x) = 0$. Find the value of x_1 in terms of x_0. *[16 marks]*

(© IB Organization 2004)

3. **(a)** Find the value of k for which the equation $4x^2 - kx + 1 = 0$ has a repeated root.

(b) Show that the equation $4\sin^2\theta = 5 - k\cos\theta$ can be written as $4\cos^2\theta - k\cos\theta + 1 = 0$.

(c) Let $f_k(\theta) = 4\cos^2\theta - k\cos\theta + 1$.

(i) State the number of values of $\cos\theta$ which satisfy the equation $f_4(\theta) = 0$.

(ii) Find all the values of $\theta \in [-2\pi, 2\pi]$ which satisfy the equation $f_4(\theta) = 0$.

(iii) Find the value of k for which $x = 1$ is a solution of the equation $4x^2 - kx + 1 = 0$.

(iv) For this value of k, find the number of solutions in $[-2\pi, 2\pi]$ of the equation $f_k(\theta) = 0$. *[14 marks]*

10 Geometry of triangles and circles

In this chapter you will learn:

- some important trigonometric relations in right-angled triangles
- how to use the sine rule to find sides and angles of a triangle
- how to use the cosine rule to find sides and angles of a triangle
- an alternative formula for the area of a triangle
- techniques for solving geometry problems in two and three dimensions
- how to calculate the length of an arc of a circle
- how to calculate the area of a sector of a circle
- to use trigonometry to solve problems involving circles and triangles.

Introductory problem

Two people are trying to measure the width of a river. There is no bridge across the river, but they have instruments for measuring lengths and angles. When they stand 50 m apart on the same side of the river, at points A and B, the person at A measures that the angle between line (AB) and the line from A to the tower on the other side of the river is 25.6°. The person at B finds the corresponding angle to be 28.3°, as shown in the diagram. Use this information to calculate the width of the river.

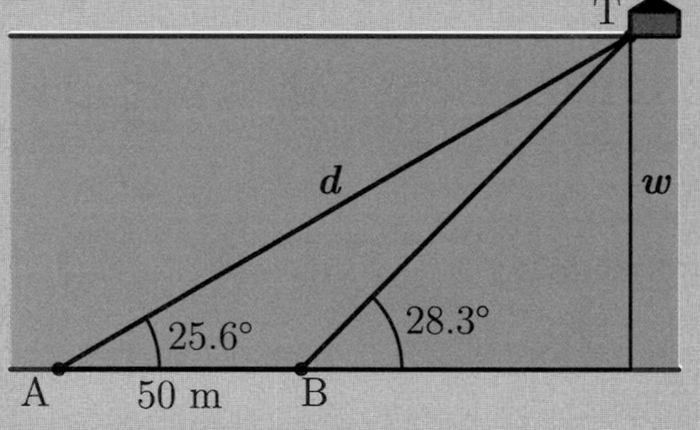

The first steps in developing trigonometry were taken by Babylonian astronomers as early as the second millennium BCE. It is thought that the Egyptians used trigonometric calculations when building their pyramids. Trigonometry was further developed by the Greeks and Indians. Some of the most significant contributions were made by Islamic mathematicians in the second half of the first millennium BCE.

The problem above involves finding lengths and angles in triangles. Such problems can be solved using trigonometric functions. In fact, the word *trigonometry* means 'measuring triangles', and historically trigonometry was used to solve similar problems in land measurement, building and astronomy. In this chapter we will use what we have already learned about trigonometric functions and develop some new results to enable us to calculate lengths and angles in triangles.

10A Right-angled triangles

In previous courses, you may have been introduced to the sine, cosine and tangent functions in the context of a right-angled triangle. We will now briefly discuss how this view relates to the definitions given in chapter 8.

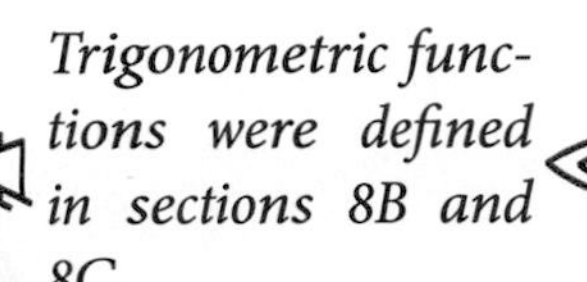

Trigonometric functions were defined in sections 8B and 8C.

Recall how sine and cosine were defined using the unit circle. Let $0° < \theta < 90°$, and let P be the point on the unit circle such that $\text{S}\hat{\text{O}}\text{P} = \theta$. Then $\text{PQ} = \sin\theta$ and $\text{OQ} = \cos\theta$.

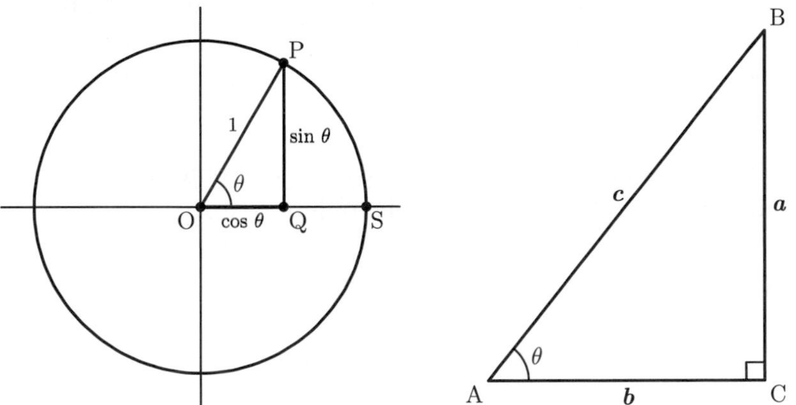

Now consider a right-angled triangle ABC with right angle at C and $\text{B}\hat{\text{A}}\text{C} = \theta$.

The triangles OPQ and ABC have the same angles, so they are similar triangles. Therefore

See Prior Learning section T on the CD-ROM for a reminder about similar triangles.

$$\frac{a}{\sin\theta} = \frac{b}{\cos\theta} = \frac{c}{1}$$

By rearranging these equations we find that the ratios of sides in a right-angled triangle are trigonometric functions of the angle θ.

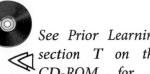

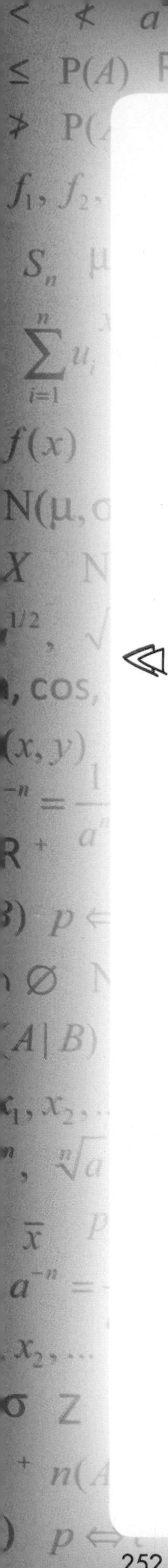

KEY POINT 10.1

In a right-angled triangle:

$$\frac{a}{c} = \sin\theta$$

$$\frac{b}{c} = \cos\theta$$

$$\frac{a}{b} = \frac{\sin\theta}{\cos\theta} = \tan\theta$$

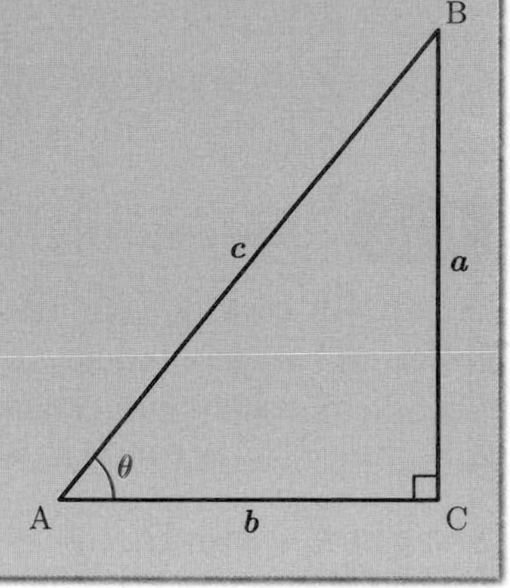

See Prior Learning section U on the CD-ROM for practice questions on right-angled triangles.

These equations apply only to acute angles. In the rest of this chapter we shall deal with triangles in general, including those containing obtuse angles, in which case we would need to use the definitions of trigonometric functions based on the unit circle.

Two terms that come up frequently in trigonometry are the **angle of elevation** and the **angle of depression**.

KEY POINT 10.2

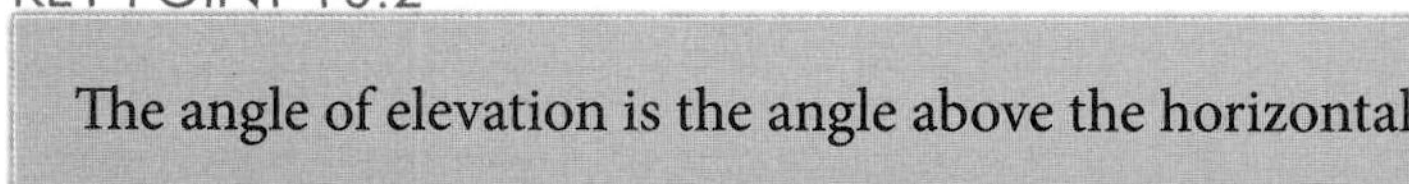

The angle of elevation is the angle above the horizontal.

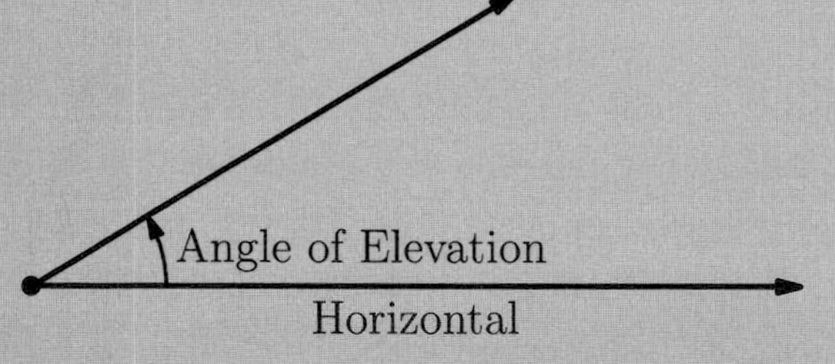

The angle of depression is the angle below the horizontal.

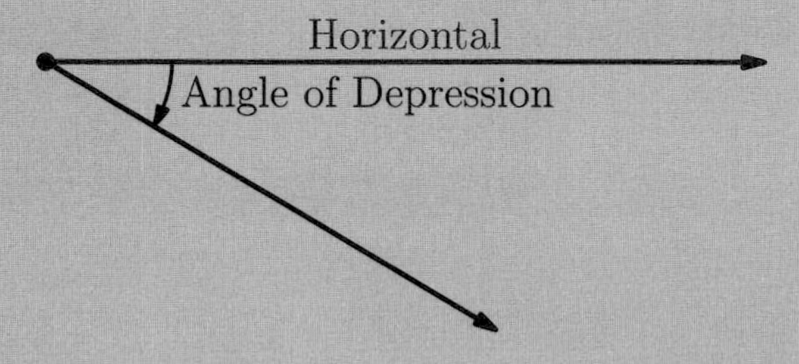

Worked example 10.1

Daniel and Theo are trying to work out the height of a bird's nest in their garden. From Theo's bedroom window, which is 4 m above the ground, the angle of depression of the nest is 10°. From Daniel's position at the end of the flat garden, 8 m away from the house, the angle of elevation is 30°. Find the height of the nest above the ground.

EXAM HINT

If a diagram is not given, it is always a good idea to sketch one, labelling any points that you refer to in your working.

Sketch a diagram. The letters B, D and T represent the positions of the bird's nest, Daniel and Theo, respectively. The letters A and C refer to points directly above and below the nest.

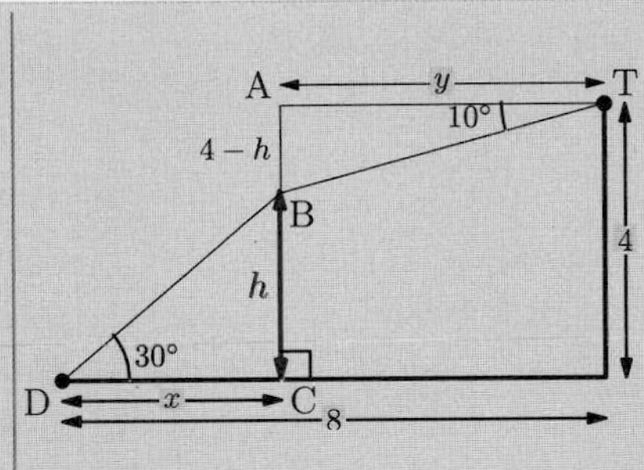

Apply trigonometry to the right-angled triangles to find the horizontal distances x and y in terms of the height h.

From triangle TAB,

$$\tan 10° = \frac{4-h}{y}$$

$$\Rightarrow y = \frac{4-h}{\tan 10°}$$

From triangle BCD,

$$\tan 30° = \frac{h}{x}$$

$$\Rightarrow x = \frac{h}{\tan 30°}$$

Now use the length of the garden, which is the total horizontal distance.

$$x + y = 8$$

Substitute the trigonometric expressions for x and y.

$$\therefore \frac{4-h}{\tan 10°} + \frac{h}{\tan 30°} = 8$$

→

continued . . .

Rearrange the equation to find h. If you find it cumbersome to write out tan 10° and tan 30° repeatedly, you can define a short name for each.

Let $a = \tan 10°$ and $b = \tan 30°$.

Then $\frac{4-h}{a} + \frac{h}{b} = 8$

$\Rightarrow (4-h)b + ha = 8ab$

$\Rightarrow \quad h(a-b) = 8ab - 4b$

$\Rightarrow \quad h = \frac{8ab - 4b}{a-b}$

Finally, evaluate a and b and hence find h.

$a = 0.176,\ b = 0.577$

$\therefore h = 3.73\text{m}$ (3 SF)

EXAM HINT

While it is acceptable to put in the values for tan 10° and tan 30° before rearranging the equation, this can easily lead to arithmetic errors. It is safer to rearrange first and calculate values at the end. Remember that you can save values to each of the lettered memory sites in your calculator, so you could assign tan 10° to memory A and tan 30° to memory B, for example; this would make it much faster to evaluate the final expression for h.

10B The sine rule

Can we use trigonometry to calculate sides and angles of triangles that do not have a right angle? The answer is yes, and one way to do this is by using a set of identities called the **sine rule**. In the diagram on the left at the top of the next page, the triangle has AB = 7, $\hat{BAC} = 55°$ and $\hat{ACB} = 80°$. Can we find the length BC?

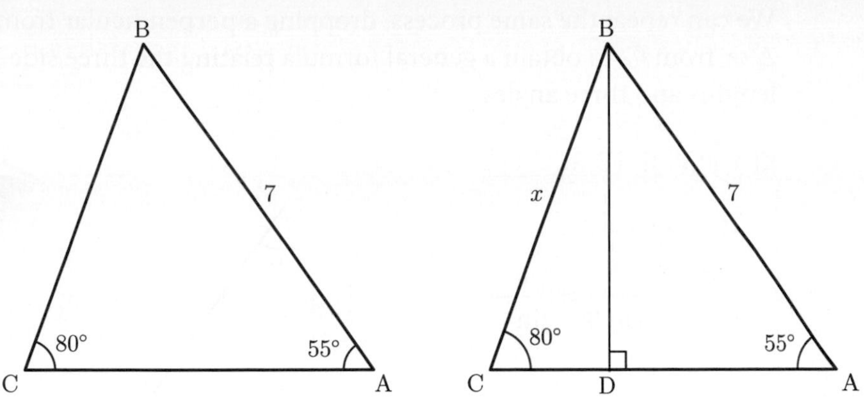

There are no right angles in the diagram, but we can create some by drawing the line [BD] perpendicular to [AC], as shown in the second diagram.

We now have two right-angled triangles: ABD and BCD.

In triangle ABD, $\frac{BD}{7} = \sin 55°$, so $BD = 7\sin 55°$.

In triangle BCD, $\frac{BD}{x} = \sin 80°$, so $BD = x\sin 80°$.

Comparing the two expressions for BD, we get

$$x \sin 80° = 7 \sin 55° \qquad (*)$$

and rearranging gives

$$x = \frac{7\sin 55°}{\sin 80°} = 5.82$$

In fact, we did not even need to write down expressions for BD but can go straight to equation (*). This equation can also be written as

$$\frac{x}{\sin 55°} = \frac{7}{\sin 80°}$$

which is an example of the sine rule. Note that the length of each side is divided by the sine of the angle *opposite* that side.

EXAM HINT

Remember the International Baccalaureate® notation for lines and line segments: (AB) stands for the straight line through A and B that extends indefinitely in both directions, [AB] denotes the line segment between A and B, and AB is the length of [AB].

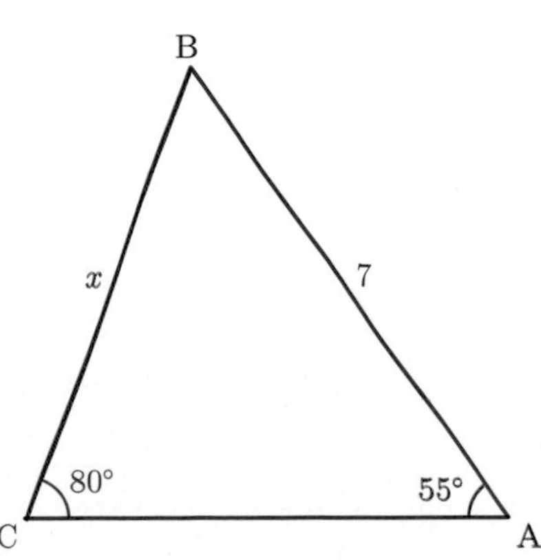

We can repeat the same process, dropping a perpendicular from A or from C, to obtain a general formula relating the three side lengths and three angles.

KEY POINT 10.3

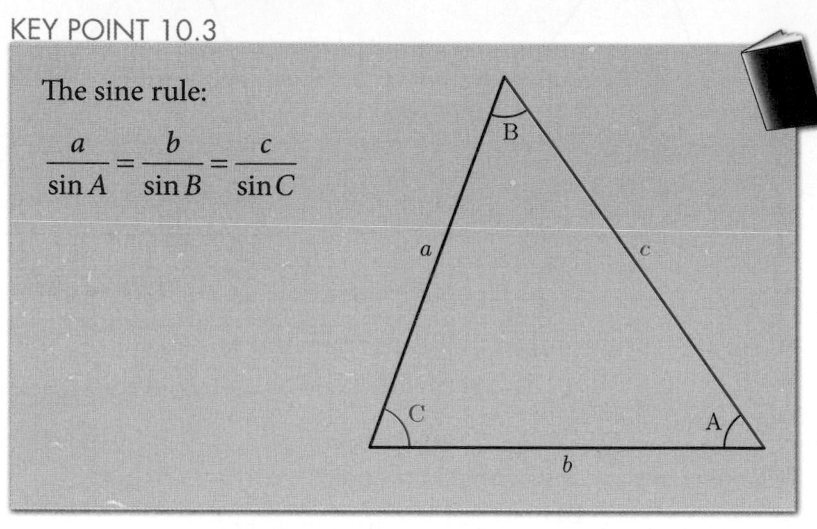

The sine rule:

$$\frac{a}{\sin A} = \frac{b}{\sin B} = \frac{c}{\sin C}$$

Normally, you would use only two of the three ratios in the sine rule. To decide which ones to use, look at what information is given in the question. In any case, you always need to know one angle and its opposite side to be able to apply the sine rule.

Worked example 10.2

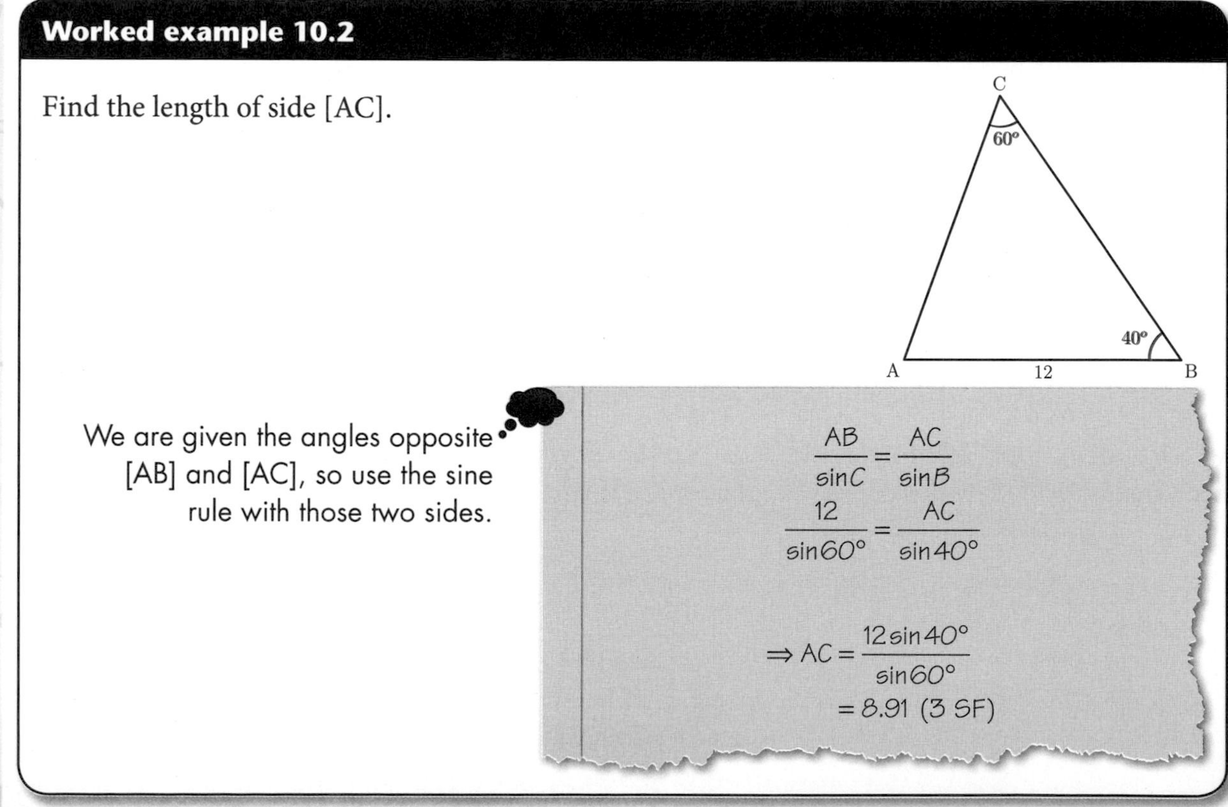

Find the length of side [AC].

We are given the angles opposite [AB] and [AC], so use the sine rule with those two sides.

$$\frac{AB}{\sin C} = \frac{AC}{\sin B}$$

$$\frac{12}{\sin 60°} = \frac{AC}{\sin 40°}$$

$$\Rightarrow AC = \frac{12 \sin 40°}{\sin 60°}$$

$$= 8.91 \text{ (3 SF)}$$

We can use the sine rule to find angles as well as side lengths.

Worked example 10.3

Find the size of the angle marked θ.

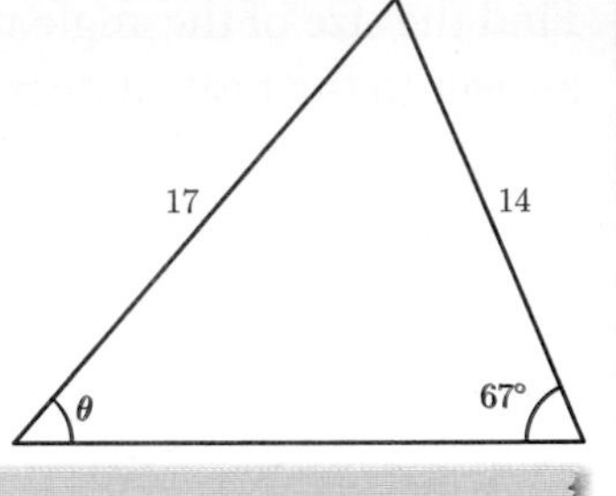
17
14
θ
67°

We can use the sine rule because we know an angle together with its opposite side, are given one of the other sides, and want to find the angle opposite that side.

$$\frac{17}{\sin 67^\circ} = \frac{14}{\sin \theta}$$

$$\Rightarrow \sin \theta = \frac{14 \sin 67^\circ}{17} = 0.758$$

$$\therefore \quad \theta = \sin^{-1} 0.758 = 49.3^\circ$$

In the above example, once we have found θ we can deduce the size of the third angle even though we do not know the length of the side opposite it: the third angle must be $180^\circ - 67^\circ - \theta = 63.7^\circ$. So, provided that we know one side length and the angle opposite it, we can use either of the remaining side lengths to calculate both remaining angles.

You should remember from chapter 9 that there is more than one value of θ with $\sin\theta = 0.758$; besides 49.3°, another solution of the equation is $180^\circ - 49.3^\circ = 130.7^\circ$. Does this mean that Worked example 10.3 actually has more than one possible answer?

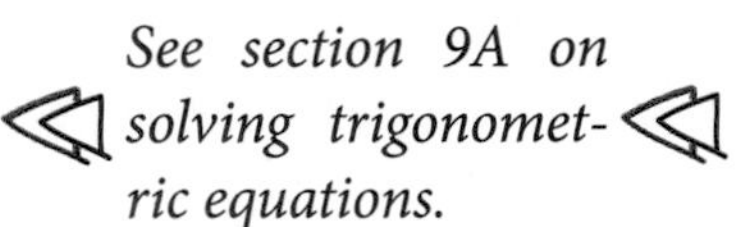
See section 9A on solving trigonometric equations.

Note, however, that because the given angle is 67°, the solution 130.7° for θ is impossible: the three angles of the triangle must add up to 180°, but $67 + 130.7 = 190.7$ is already greater than 180. All other solutions of $\sin\theta = 0.758$ are outside the interval $]0^\circ, 180^\circ[$, so cannot be angles of a triangle. Therefore, in Worked example 10.3, there is only one possible value for the angle θ.

The next example shows that this is not always the case.

Worked example 10.4

Find the size of the angle marked θ, giving your answer to the nearest degree.

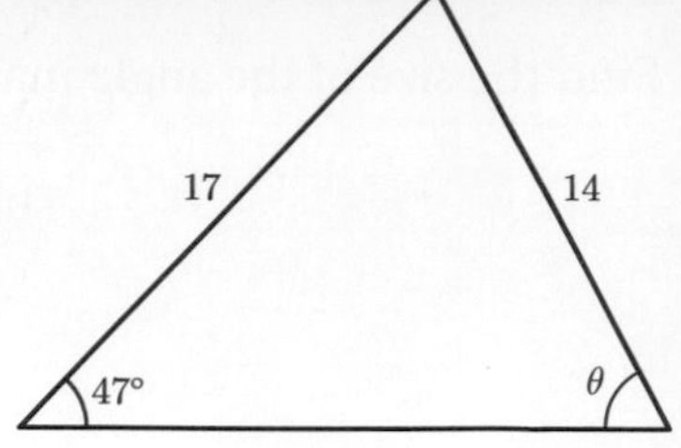

Use the sine rule with the two given sides.	$\dfrac{17}{\sin\theta} = \dfrac{14}{\sin 47°}$ $\Rightarrow \sin\theta = \dfrac{17\sin 47°}{14} = 0.888$
Find the two possible values of θ in $]0°, 180°[$.	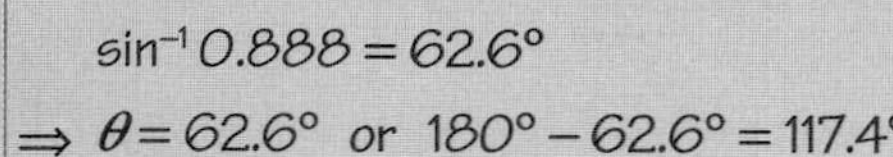 $\sin^{-1} 0.888 = 62.6°$ $\Rightarrow \theta = 62.6°$ or $180° - 62.6° = 117.4°$
Check whether each solution is possible: do the two known angles add up to less than 180°?	$62.6 + 47 = 109.6 < 180$ $117.4 + 47 = 164.4 < 180$
Both solutions are possible.	$\therefore \theta = 63°$ or $117°$

EXAM HINT

In the examination, a question will often alert you to look for two possible answers, or instruct you which one to choose, for example by specifying that θ is obtuse. However, if the question gives no clue, you should always check whether the second solution is possible by finding the sum of the known angles.

The diagram below shows the two possible triangles for Worked example 10.4. In both triangles, the side of length 14 is opposite the angle 47°, with another side having length 17, which could be opposite an angle of either 63° or 117°. If these two triangles are placed adjacent to each other, they would form an isosceles triangle with base angles 47° and equal sides of length 17.

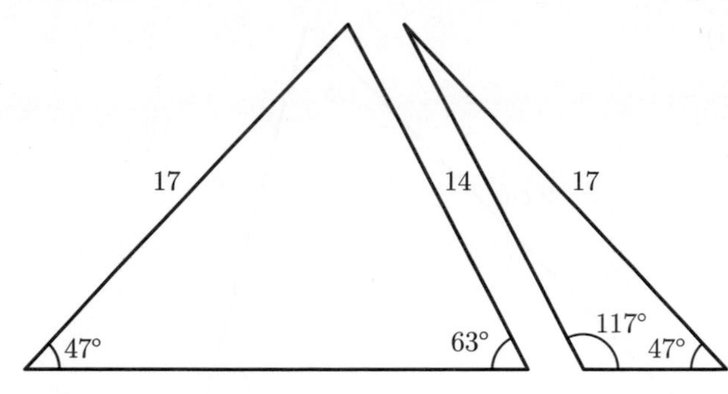

Exercise 10B

1. Find the lengths of the sides marked with letters.

(a) (i)

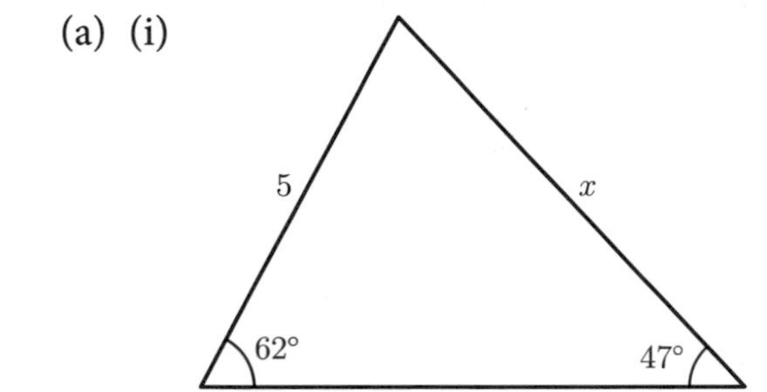

(ii)

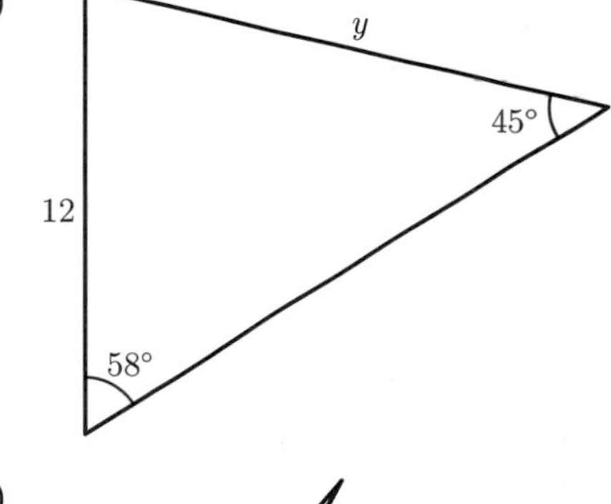

(b) (i)

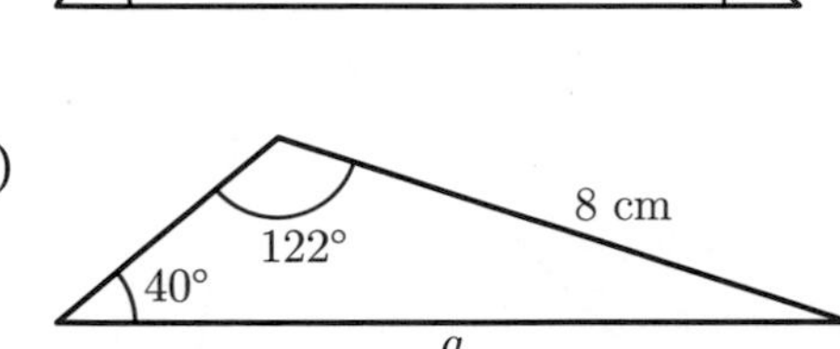

(ii)

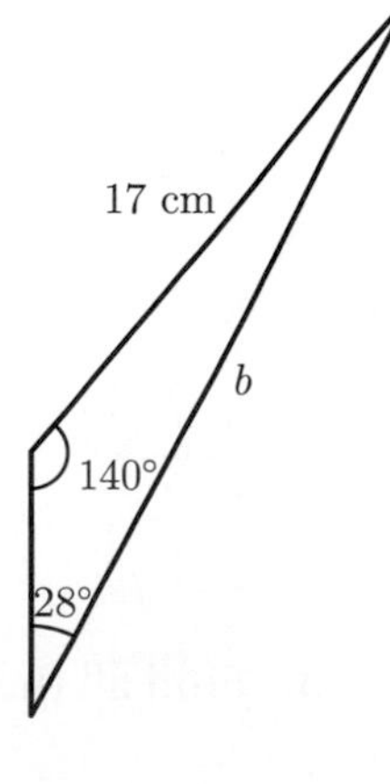

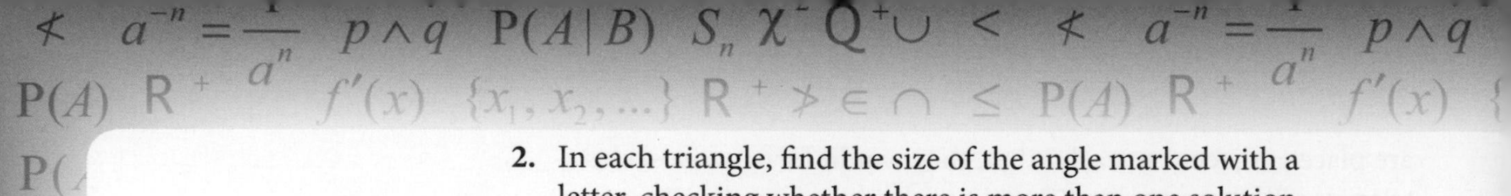

2. In each triangle, find the size of the angle marked with a letter, checking whether there is more than one solution.

(a) (i)

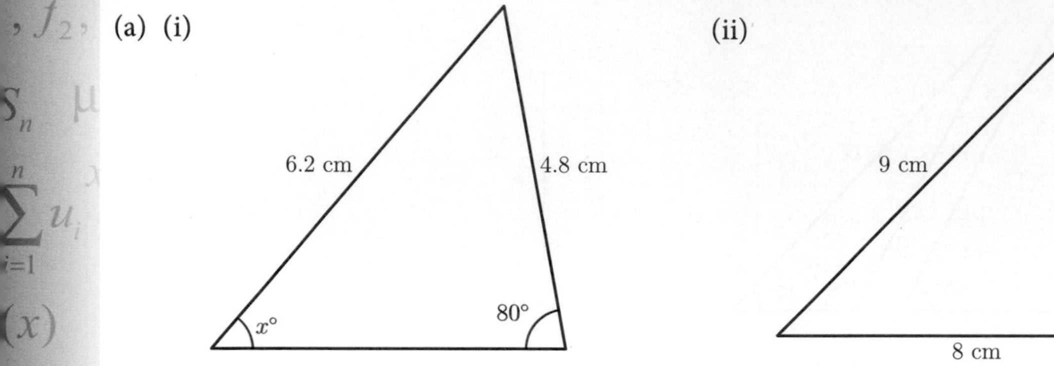

(ii)

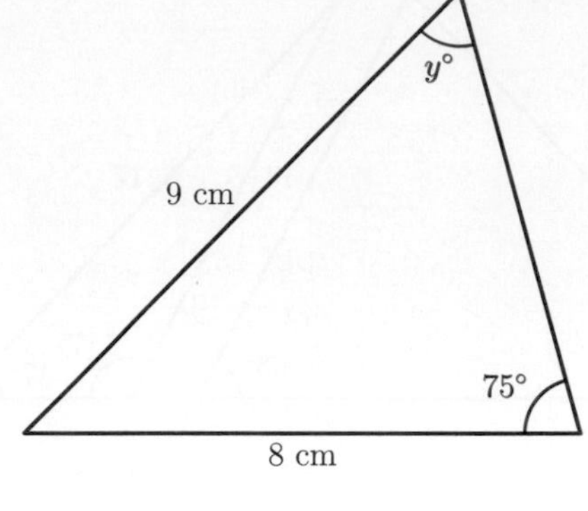

(b) (i)

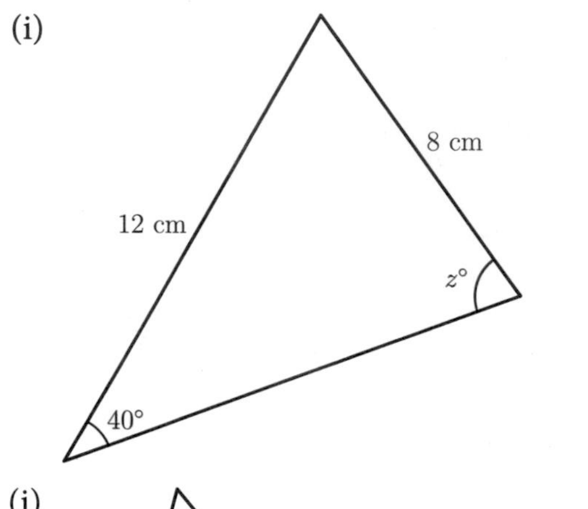

(ii)

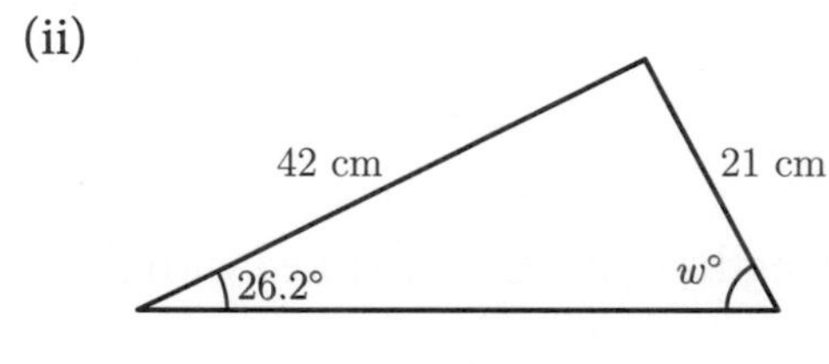

(c) (i)

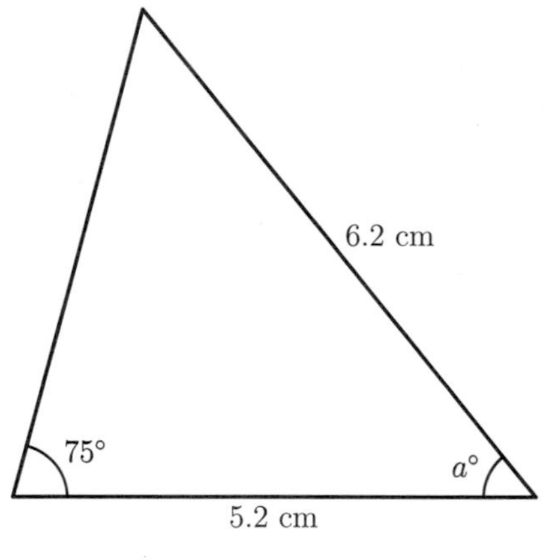

(ii)

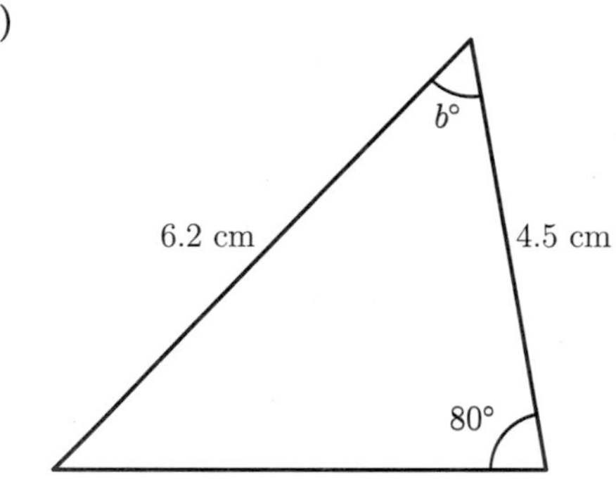

3. Find all the unknown sides and angles in triangle ABC.

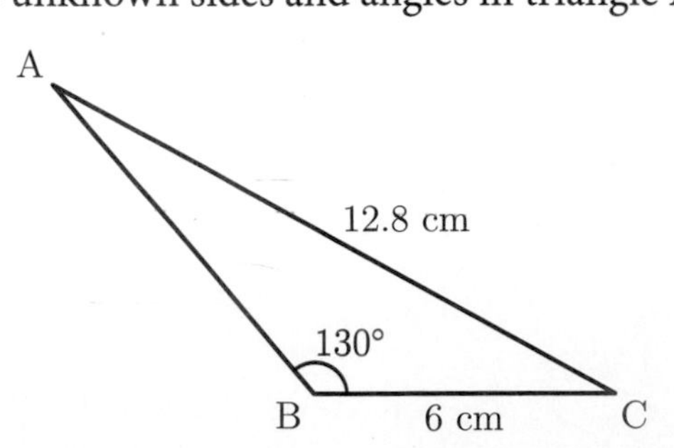

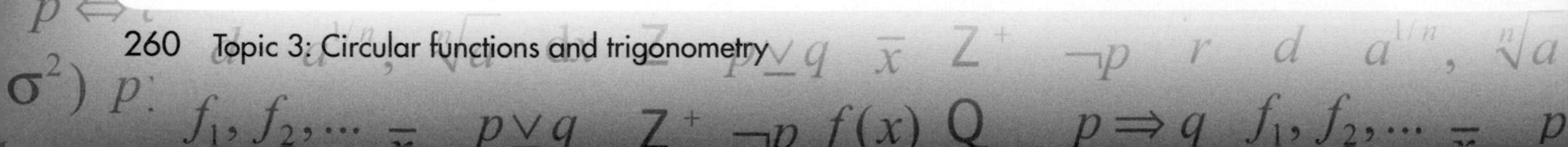

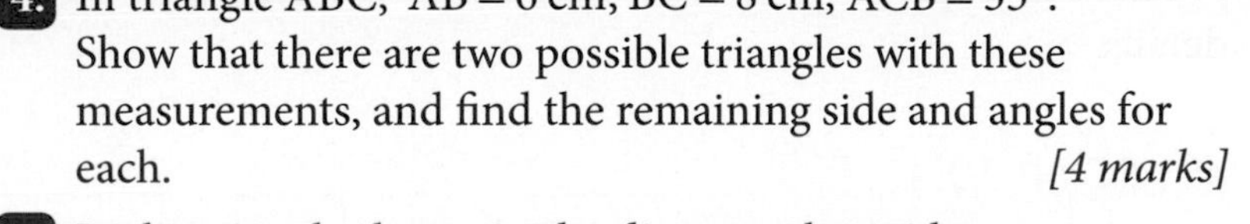

4. In triangle ABC, AB = 6 cm, BC = 8 cm, $A\hat{C}B = 35°$. Show that there are two possible triangles with these measurements, and find the remaining side and angles for each. *[4 marks]*

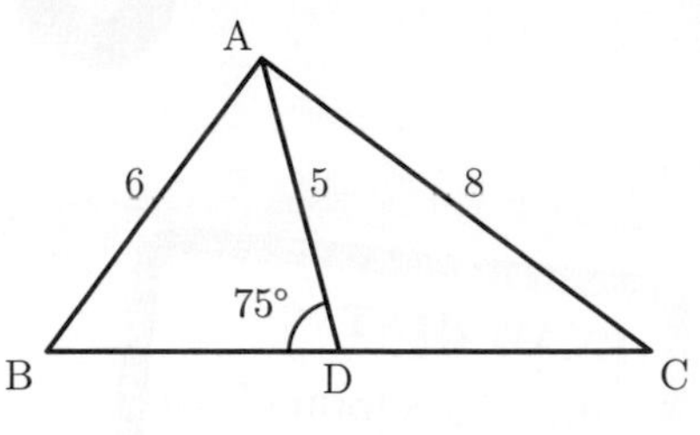

5. In the triangle shown in the diagram alongside, AB = 6, AC = 8, AD = 5 and $A\hat{D}B = 75°$. Find the length of the side [BC]. *[5 marks]*

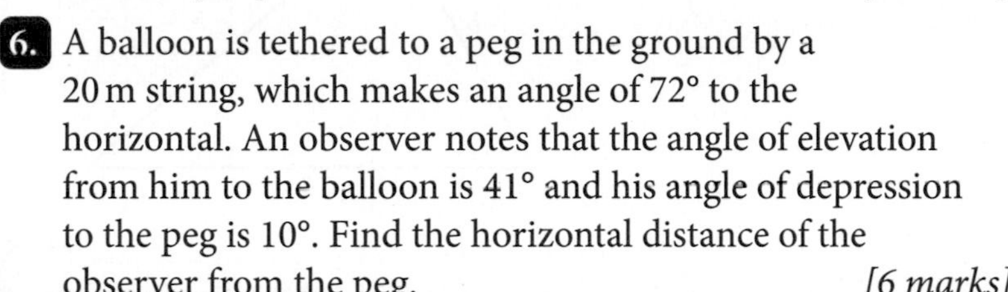

6. A balloon is tethered to a peg in the ground by a 20 m string, which makes an angle of 72° to the horizontal. An observer notes that the angle of elevation from him to the balloon is 41° and his angle of depression to the peg is 10°. Find the horizontal distance of the observer from the peg. *[6 marks]*

7. Show that it is impossible to draw a triangle ABC with AB = 12 cm, AC = 8 cm and $A\hat{B}C = 47°$. *[5 marks]*

10C The cosine rule

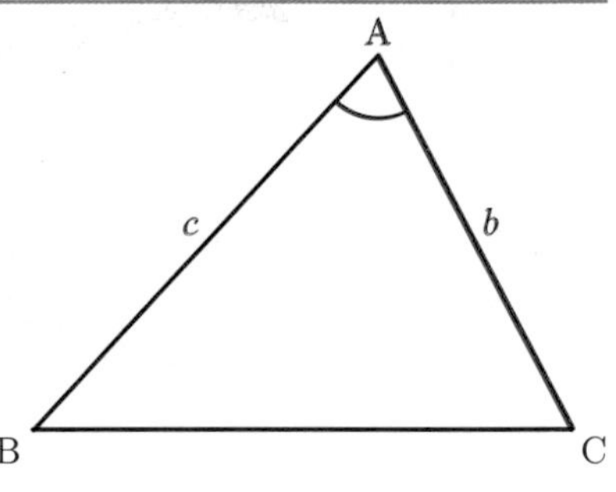

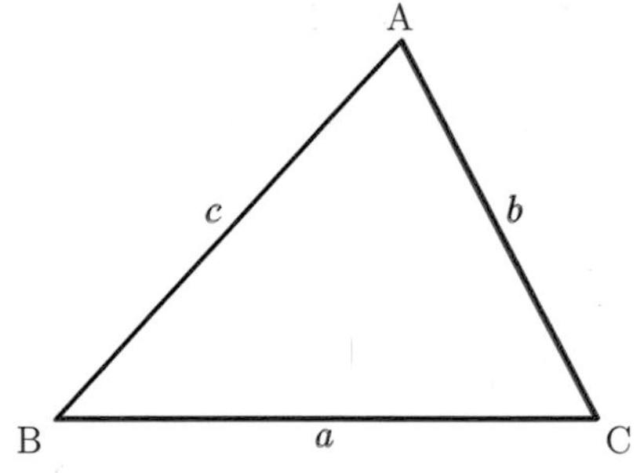

The sine rule allows us to calculate angles and side lengths of a triangle provided that we know one side and its opposite angle, together with one other angle or side length. If we know two sides and the angle between them (the upper diagram alongside), or if we know all three side lengths but no angles (the lower diagram alongside), then we cannot use the sine rule. However, in these cases we can still find the remaining angles and side lengths of the triangle – we just need to apply a different rule, called the cosine rule.

Can we find the length of side [AB] in the triangle below?

The sine rule for this triangle says $\frac{AB}{\sin 70°} = \frac{8}{\sin B} = \frac{12}{\sin A}$, but since we do not know either of the angles A or B, it is impossible to find the length AB from this formula. However, just like for the sine rule, by creating two right-angled triangles in the original triangle we can derive a different formula for AB.

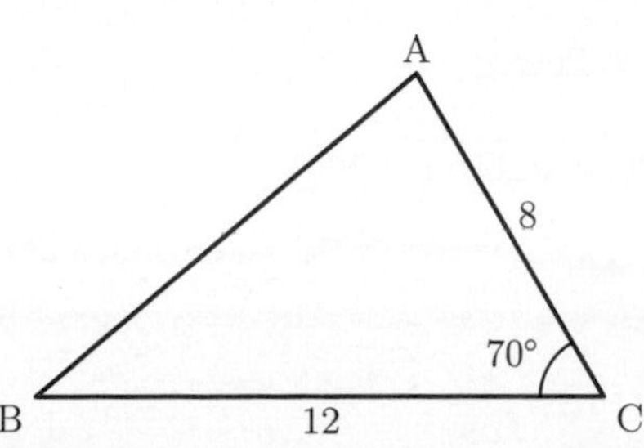

See the Fill-in proof sheet 7 'Cosine rule' on the CD-ROM for details.

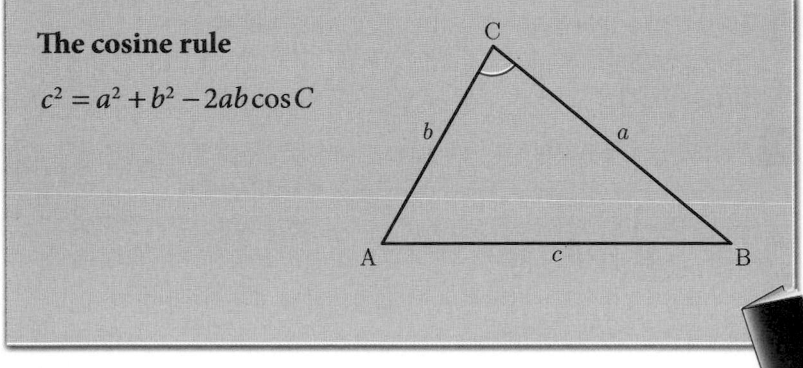

EXAM HINT

This is the form of the cosine rule given in the Formula booklet, but you can change the names of the variables to whatever you like as long as the angle on the right-hand side (the argument of cosine) corresponds to (i.e. is opposite to) the length on the left-hand side of the equation.

Note that the capital letter C stands for the angle at vertex C, that is, angle $\text{A}\hat{\text{C}}\text{B}$, which lies opposite the side marked c. (Similarly, B would stand for $\text{A}\hat{\text{B}}\text{C}$ opposite b, and A for $\text{B}\hat{\text{A}}\text{C}$ opposite a.)

The cosine rule can be used to find the third side of a triangle when we know the other two sides and the angle between them.

Worked example 10.5

Find the length of the side [PQ].

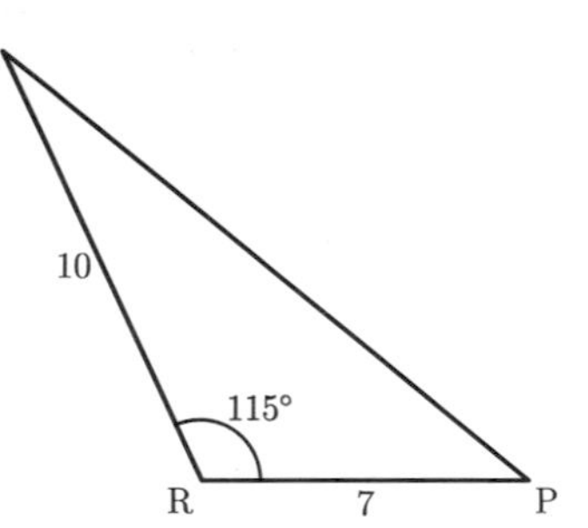

As we are given two sides and the angle between them, we can use the cosine rule.

$PQ^2 = 7^2 + 10^2 - 2 \times 7 \times 10 \times \cos 115°$

$PQ^2 = 208.2$

$\therefore\ PQ = \sqrt{208.2} = 14.4$

We can also use the cosine rule to find an angle if we know all three sides of a triangle. To do this, we need to rearrange the formula.

KEY POINT 10.5

$$\cos C = \frac{a^2 + b^2 - c^2}{2ab}$$

Worked example 10.6

Find the size of the angle $\hat{ACB}$ correct to the nearest degree.

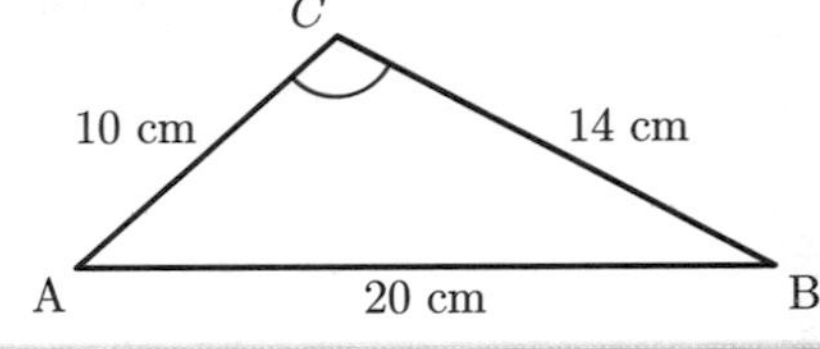

Apply the rearranged cosine rule.

$$\cos C = \frac{14^2 + 10^2 - 20^2}{2 \times 14 \times 10}$$
$$= -\frac{104}{280}$$
$$= -0.371$$

Use inverse cosine to find the angle.

$$\therefore C = \cos^{-1}(-0.371) = 112°$$

Notice that in both Worked examples 10.5 and 10.6, the angle was obtuse and thus its cosine turned out negative. Note also that, unlike with the sine rule, when using the cosine rule to find an angle there is no second solution: recall that the second solution of $\cos x = k$ is $360° - \cos^{-1} k$, and this will always be greater than 180°, so it cannot be an angle in a triangle.

It is possible to use the cosine rule even when the given angle is not opposite the required side, as illustrated in the next example. This example also reminds you that there are some exact values of trigonometric functions you need to remember.

Exact values of trigonometric functions were covered in section 8D.

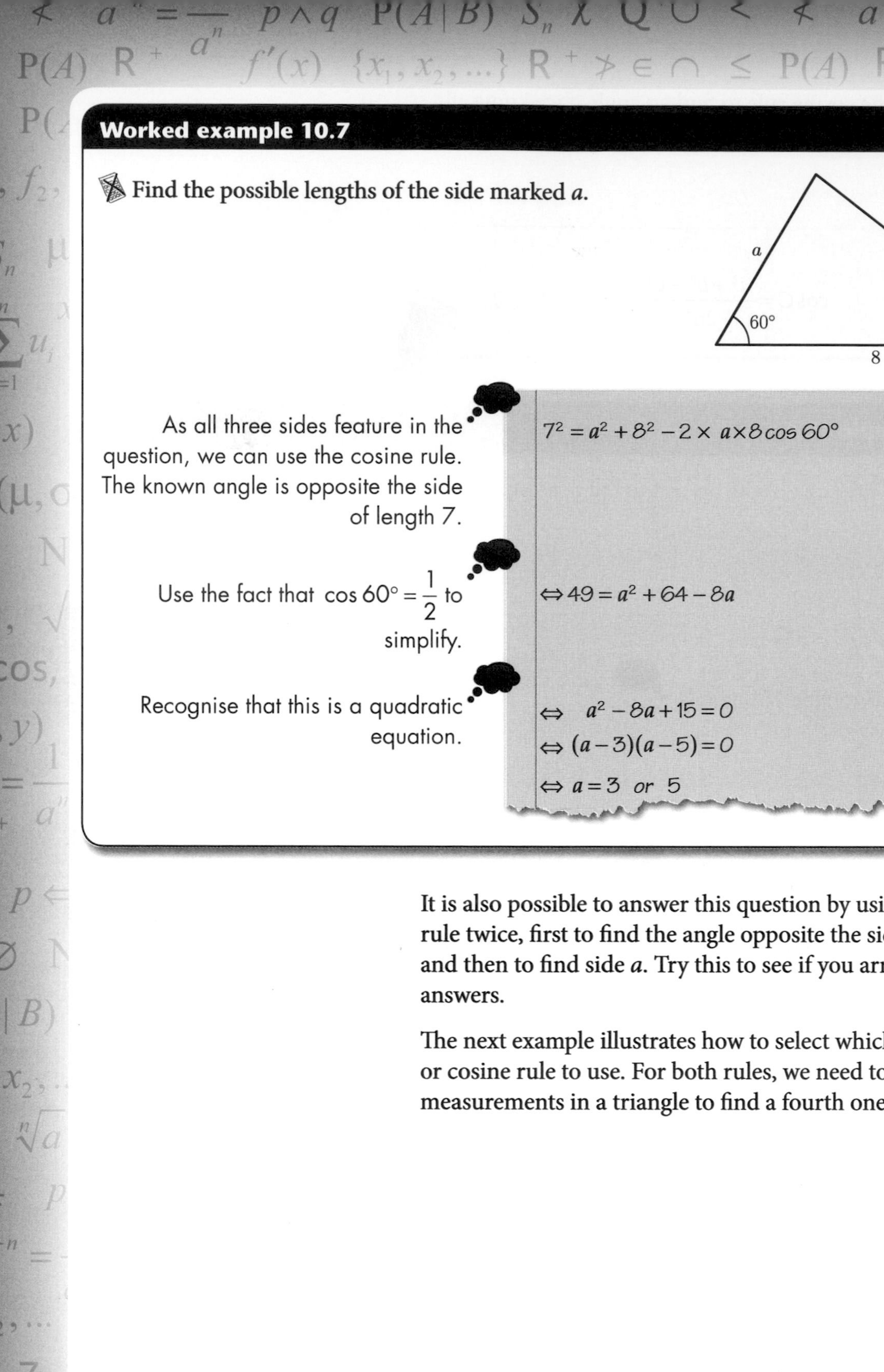

Worked example 10.7

Find the possible lengths of the side marked a.

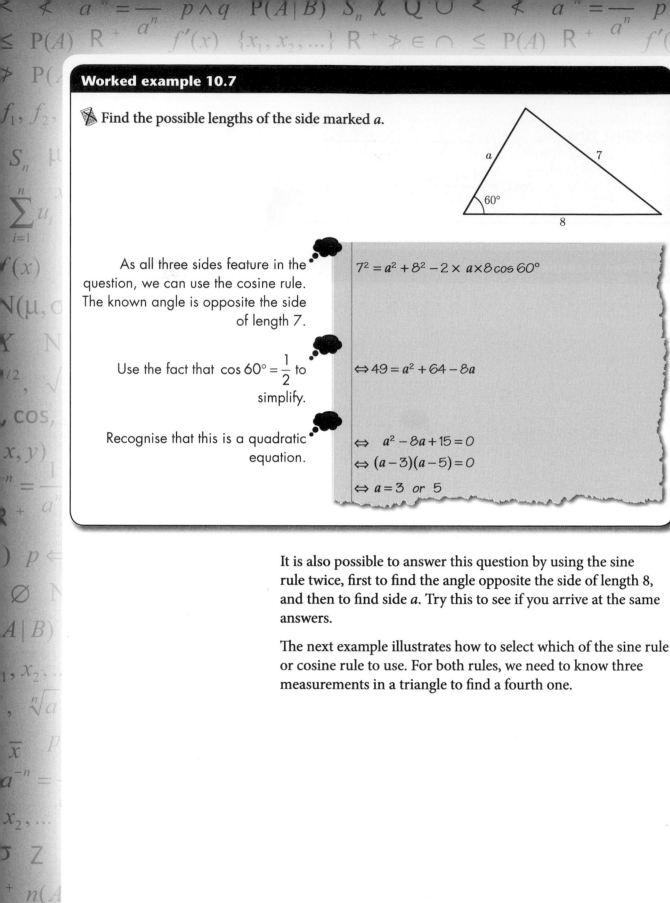

As all three sides feature in the question, we can use the cosine rule. The known angle is opposite the side of length 7.

$$7^2 = a^2 + 8^2 - 2 \times a \times 8 \cos 60°$$

Use the fact that $\cos 60° = \frac{1}{2}$ to simplify.

$$\Leftrightarrow 49 = a^2 + 64 - 8a$$

Recognise that this is a quadratic equation.

$$\Leftrightarrow \quad a^2 - 8a + 15 = 0$$

$$\Leftrightarrow (a-3)(a-5) = 0$$

$$\Leftrightarrow a = 3 \text{ or } 5$$

It is also possible to answer this question by using the sine rule twice, first to find the angle opposite the side of length 8, and then to find side a. Try this to see if you arrive at the same answers.

The next example illustrates how to select which of the sine rule or cosine rule to use. For both rules, we need to know three measurements in a triangle to find a fourth one.

Worked example 10.8

In the triangle shown in the diagram, AB = 6.5 cm, AD = 7 cm, CD = 5.8 cm, $\hat{ABC} = 52°$ and AC = x cm. Find the value of x correct to one decimal place.

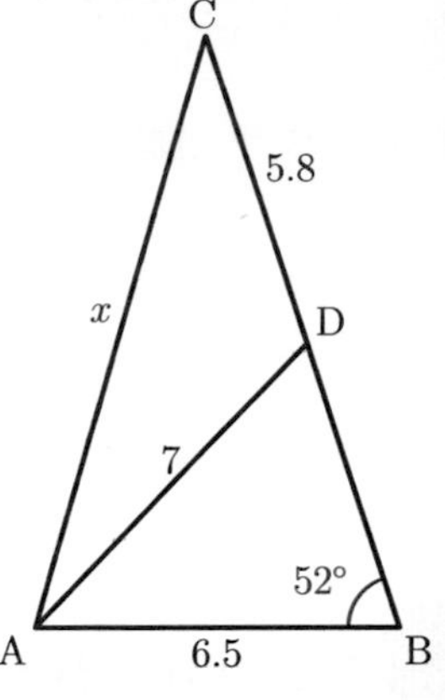

The only triangle in which we know three measurements is ABD. We know two side lengths and an angle opposite one of these sides, so we can use the sine rule to find $\hat{ADB}$.

Sine rule in triangle ABD:

let $\hat{ADB} = \theta$; then

$$\frac{6.5}{\sin\theta} = \frac{7}{\sin 52°}$$

$$\Rightarrow \sin\theta = \frac{6.5\sin 52°}{7} = 0.7317$$

$\sin^{-1} 0.7317 = 47.0°$

Are there two possible solutions?

$180 - 47 = 133$ but $133 + 52 > 180$, so there is only one solution, $\theta = 47°$

In triangle ADC, we know two sides and want to find the third. If we knew $\hat{ADC}$, we could use the cosine rule, but this angle can be found easily.

$\hat{ADC} = 180° - 47° = 133°$

Now we can now apply the cosine rule.

Cosine rule in triangle ADC:

$x^2 = 7^2 + 5.8^2 - 2 \times 7 \times 5.8 \cos 133°$

$x^2 = 137.99$

$x = \sqrt{137.99} = 11.7$ cm

EXAM HINT

In a question like this where the solution has several steps, it is important not to round intermediate calculation results. Use the memory or ANS button on your calculator and round answers only at the end. You do not, however, have to write down all the digits on your calculator display in the intermediate steps of working.

Exercise 10C

1. Find the lengths of the sides marked with letters.

(a) (i)

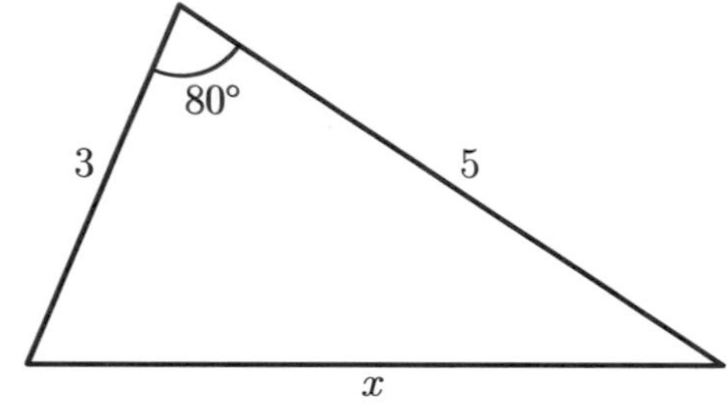

(ii)

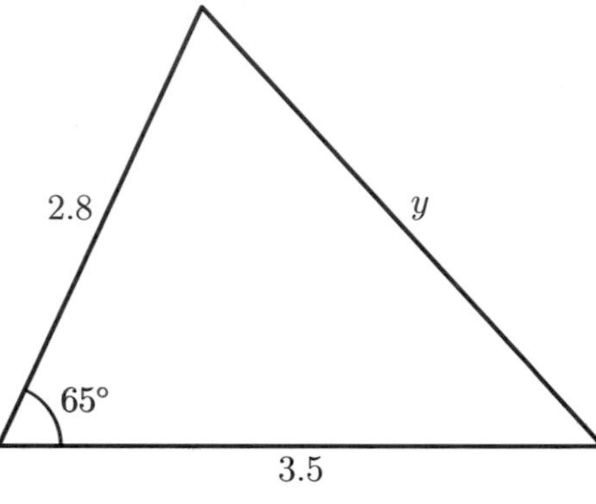

(b) (i)

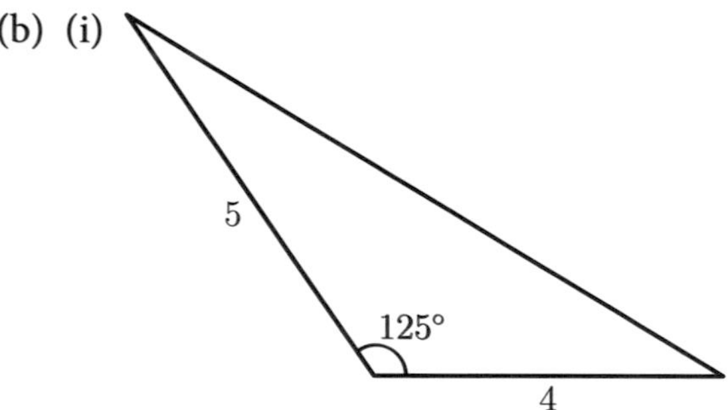

(ii)

2. Find the angles marked with letters.

(a) (i)

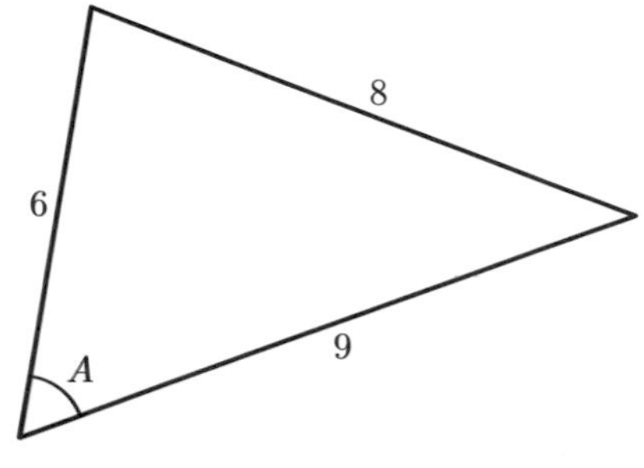

(ii)

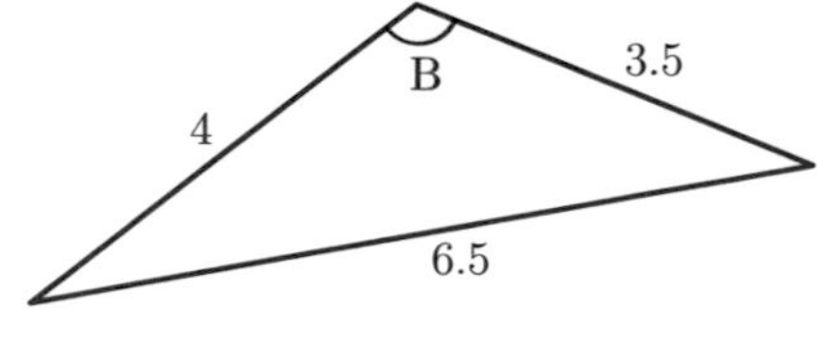

(b) (i)

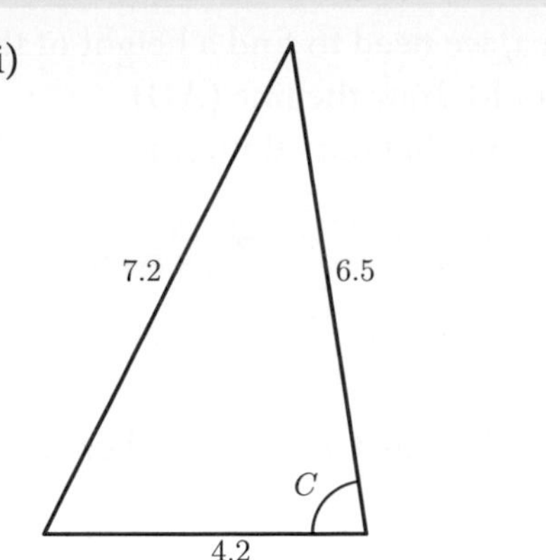

(ii)

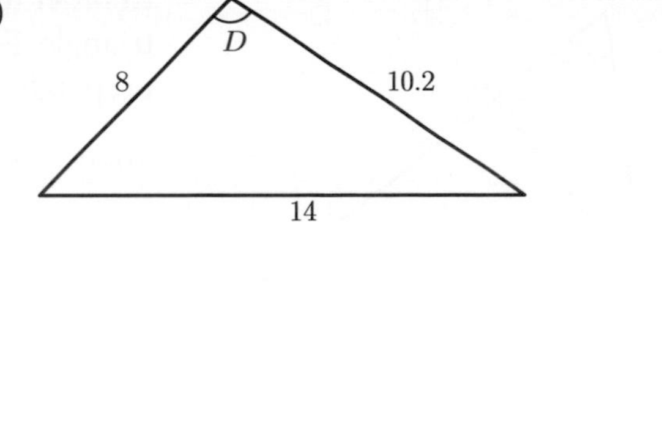

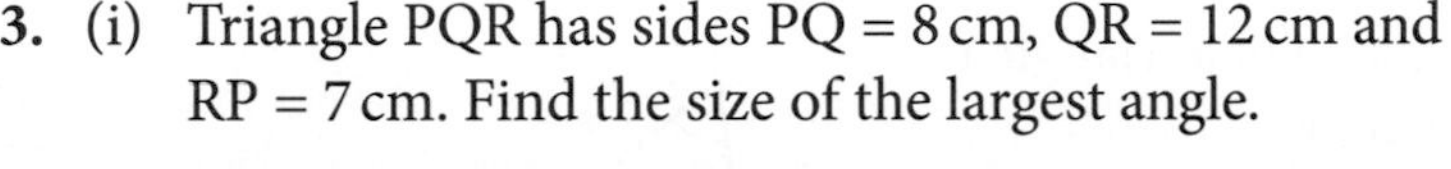

3. (i) Triangle PQR has sides PQ = 8 cm, QR = 12 cm and RP = 7 cm. Find the size of the largest angle.

   (ii) Triangle ABC has sides AB = 4.5 cm, BC = 6.2 cm and CA = 3.7 cm. Find the size of the smallest angle.

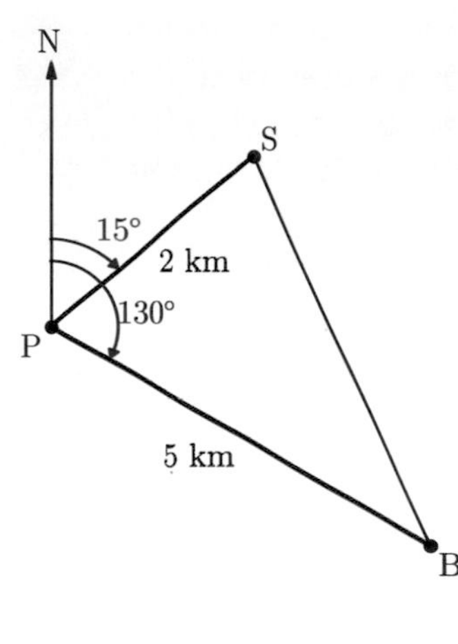

4. Ship S is 2 km from port P on a bearing of 15°, and boat B is 5 km from the port on a bearing of 130°, as shown in the diagram. Find the distance between the ship and the boat. *[6 marks]*

5. Find the value of x in the diagram.

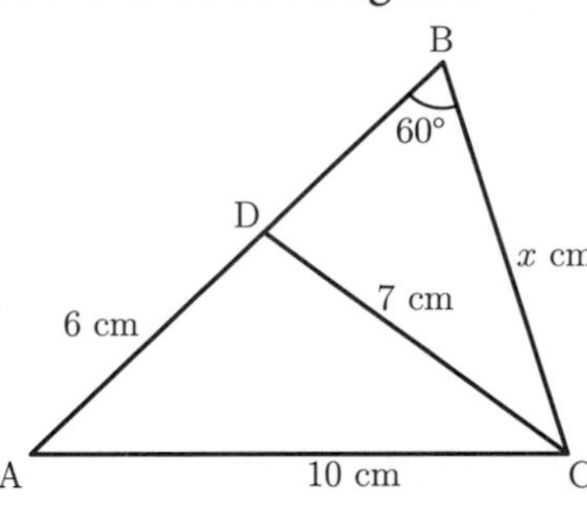

[6 marks]

6. In triangle ABC, $\text{AB} = (x-3)\text{cm}$, $\text{BC} = (x+3)\text{cm}$, $\text{AC} = 8\text{ cm}$ and $\text{B}\hat{\text{A}}\text{C} = 60°$. Find the value of x. *[6 marks]*

7. In triangle KLM, KL = 4, LM = 7 and $\text{L}\hat{\text{K}}\text{M} = 45°$. Find the exact length KM. *[6 marks]*

10D Area of a triangle

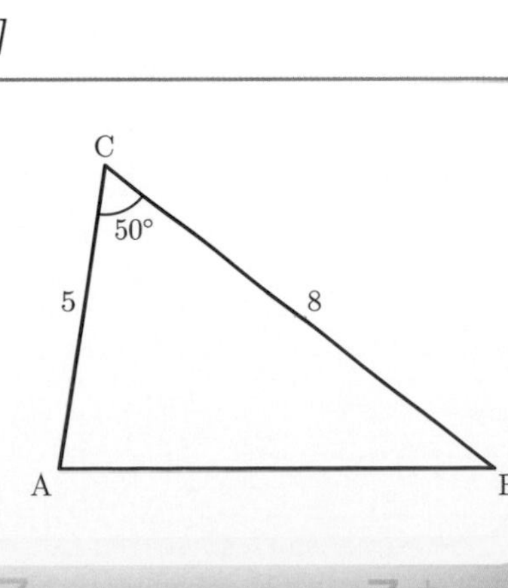

We have seen how to calculate side lengths and angles of a triangle; another quantity that we might be interested in finding is the area of the triangle. The formula $\frac{1}{2}\text{base} \times \text{perpendicular height}$ should be familiar, and we can use this to find the area of the triangle shown in the diagram.

In order to calculate the area, we need to find a height of the triangle. For instance, we could draw the line (AD) perpendicular to (BC), as in the diagram alongside.

Then $AD = 5\sin 50°$, so the area of the triangle is

$$\frac{1}{2}BC \times AD = \frac{1}{2} \times 8 \times 5\sin 50° = 15.3 \text{ cm}^2$$

We can use the same method for any triangle, and hence obtain a general formula for the area.

There is also a formula for the area of a triangle involving its three sides; it is called *Heron's formula*.

KEY POINT 10.6

The area of a triangle is given by

$$\text{Area} = \frac{1}{2}ab\sin C$$

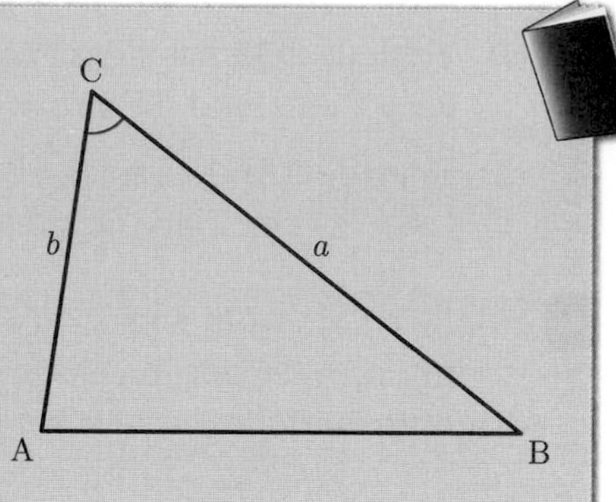

As well as calculating the area given two sides and the angle between them, we could also be asked to find the angle (or one of the side lengths) given the area.

Worked example 10.9

The area of the triangle in the diagram is 52 cm^2.
Find the two possible values of $A\hat{B}C$, correct to one decimal place.

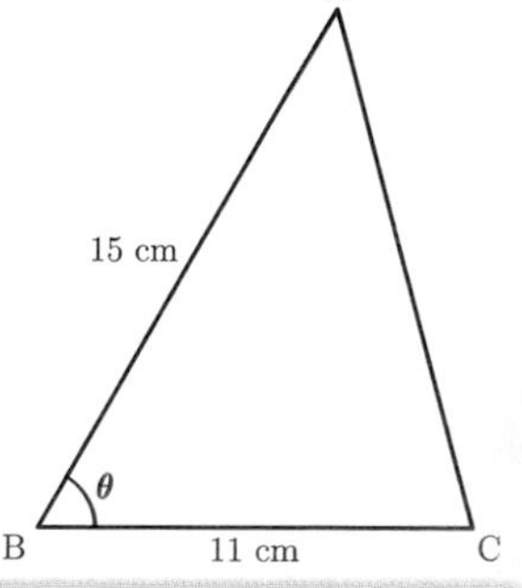

We can directly use the formula from Key point 10.6.

$$\frac{1}{2} \times 11 \times 15 \sin\theta = 52$$

$$\Rightarrow \quad \sin\theta = \frac{2 \times 52}{11 \times 15} = 0.6303$$

$$\sin^{-1} 0.6303 = 39.07°$$

$$\therefore \ \theta = 39.1° \ \text{or} \ 180° - 39.1° = 141° \ (3SF)$$

In the next example, we use the sine rule to calculate the information needed, and then apply the formula for the area of the triangle.

Worked example 10.10

Triangle PQR is shown in the diagram.

(a) Calculate the exact value of x.

(b) Find the area of the triangle.

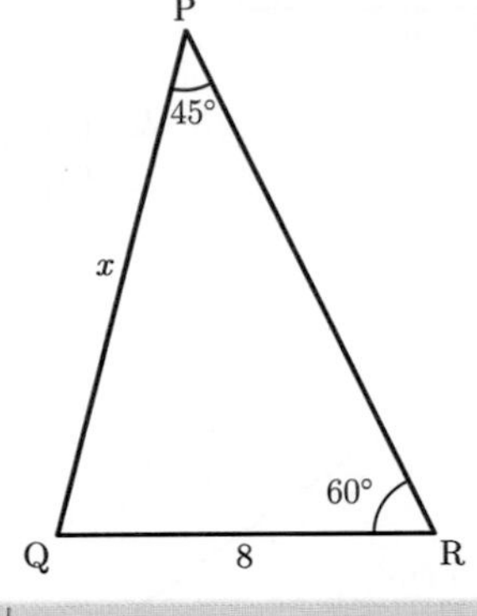

Since we know two angles and a side that is opposite one of the angles, we can use the sine rule.

(a) $\frac{8}{\sin 45°} = \frac{x}{\sin 60°}$

We are asked to find the *exact* value of x, so use the exact values for $\sin 45°$ and $\sin 60°$.

$\Rightarrow \frac{8}{\frac{\sqrt{2}}{2}} = \frac{x}{\frac{\sqrt{3}}{2}}$

$\Rightarrow \frac{16}{\sqrt{2}} = \frac{2x}{\sqrt{3}}$

$\Rightarrow \quad x = \frac{16\sqrt{3}}{2\sqrt{2}} = 4\sqrt{6}$

To use the formula for the area of the triangle, we need $P\hat{Q}R$.

(b) $P\hat{Q}R = 180° - 60° - 45° = 75°$

$\text{Area} = \frac{1}{2}(8 \times 4\sqrt{6})\sin 75°$

$= 37.9 \text{ (3SF)}$

Exercise 10D

1. Calculate the areas of these triangles.

(a) (i)

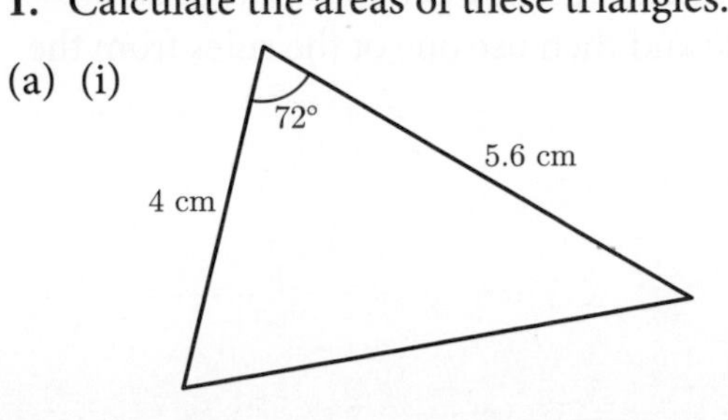

(ii)

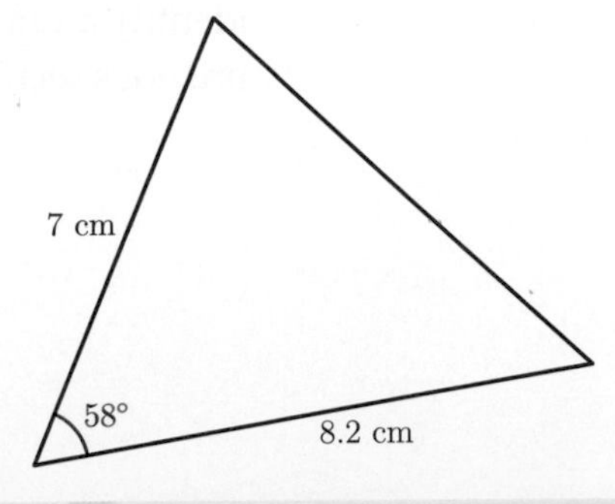

(b) (i) 9 cm, 130°, 8 cm

(ii) 6.2 cm, 97°, 8.5 cm

2. Each triangle has the area shown. Find two possible values for each marked angle.

(i) 12 cm, 16 cm, $x°$, 95 cm^2

(ii) 8.2 cm, 6.7 cm, $y°$, 24 cm^2

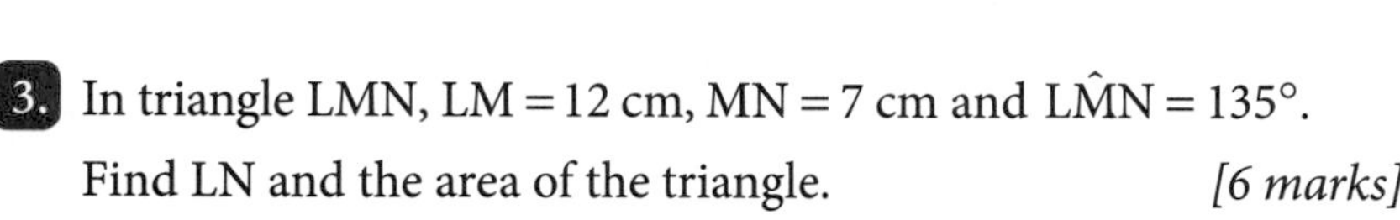

3. In triangle LMN, LM = 12 cm, MN = 7 cm and $L\hat{M}N = 135°$.
Find LN and the area of the triangle. *[6 marks]*

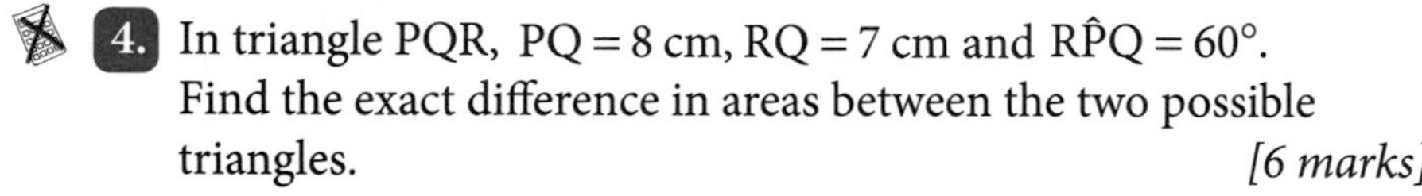

4. In triangle PQR, PQ = 8 cm, RQ = 7 cm and $R\hat{P}Q = 60°$.
Find the exact difference in areas between the two possible triangles. *[6 marks]*

10E Trigonometry in three dimensions

In many applications we need to work with three-dimensional objects. The examples in this section show you how trigonometry can be applied in three dimensions. The general strategy is to identify a suitable triangle and then use one of the rules from the previous sections.

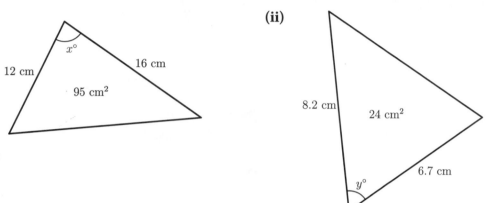

Worked example 10.11

A cuboid has sides of length 8 cm, 12 cm and 15 cm. The diagram shows diagonals of three of the faces.

(a) Find the lengths AB, BC and CA.
(b) Find the size of the angle $A\hat{C}B$.
(c) Calculate the area of the triangle ABC.
(d) Find the length AD.

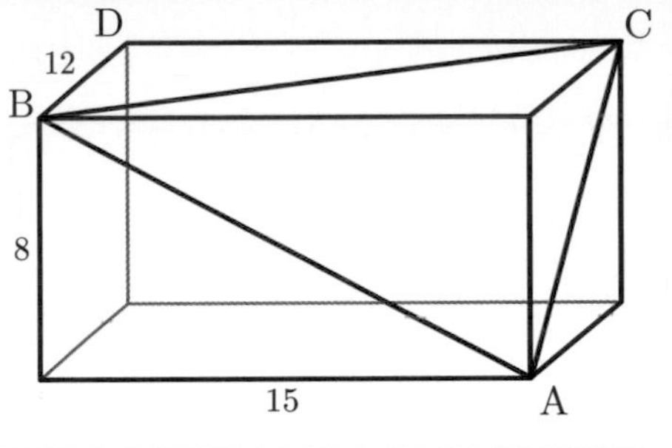

[AB] is the diagonal of the front face, so it is the hypotenuse of a right-angled triangle with sides 8 and 15.

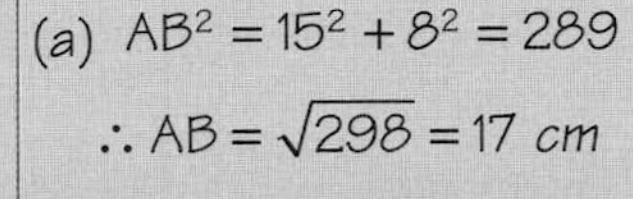

(a) $AB^2 = 15^2 + 8^2 = 289$

$\therefore AB = \sqrt{298} = 17 \text{ cm}$

Find BC and CA in a similar way.

$BC = \sqrt{12^2 + 15^2} = 19.2 \text{ cm}$

$CA = \sqrt{12^2 + 8^2} = 14.4 \text{ cm}$

Now look at triangle ABC. Draw the triangle by itself if it helps.

(b)

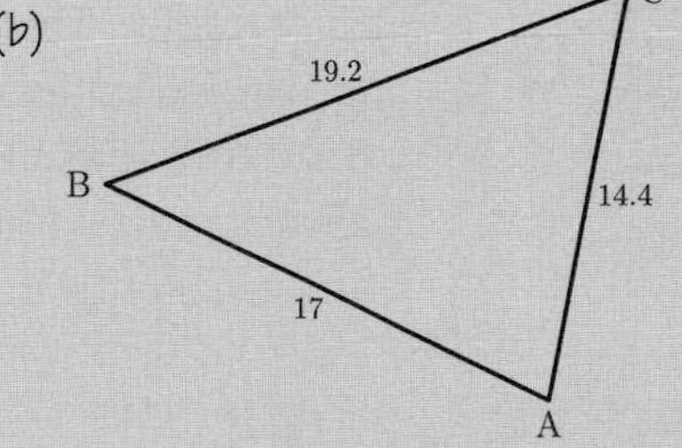

We know all three sides and want to find an angle, so we use the cosine rule.

$$\cos C = \frac{14.4^2 + 19.2^2 - 17^2}{2 \times 14.4 \times 19.2} = 0.519$$

$\therefore C = \cos^{-1} 0.519 = 58.7°$

Use the formula for the area, with the angle we found in (b).

(c) $\text{Area} = \frac{1}{2}(14.4 \times 19.2)\sin 58.7°$

$= 118 \text{ cm}^2$

ABD is a right-angled triangle.

(d)

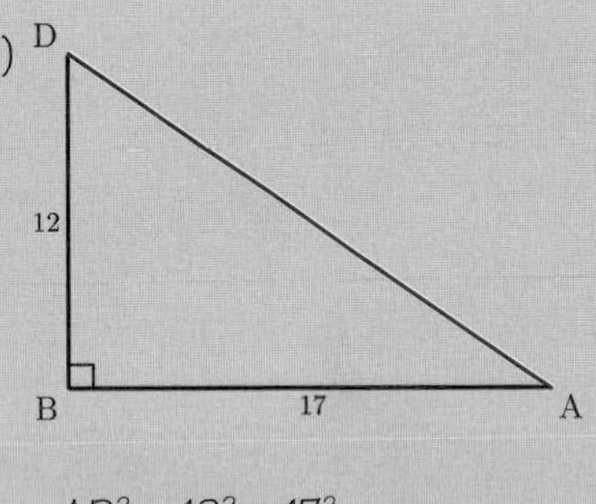

$AD^2 = 12^2 + 17^2$

$\therefore AD = \sqrt{433} = 20.8 \text{ cm}$

Part (d) of the previous example illustrates a very useful fact about the diagonal of a cuboid.

KEY POINT 10.7

The diagonal of a cuboid with dimensions p, q and r has length $\sqrt{p^2+q^2+r^2}$

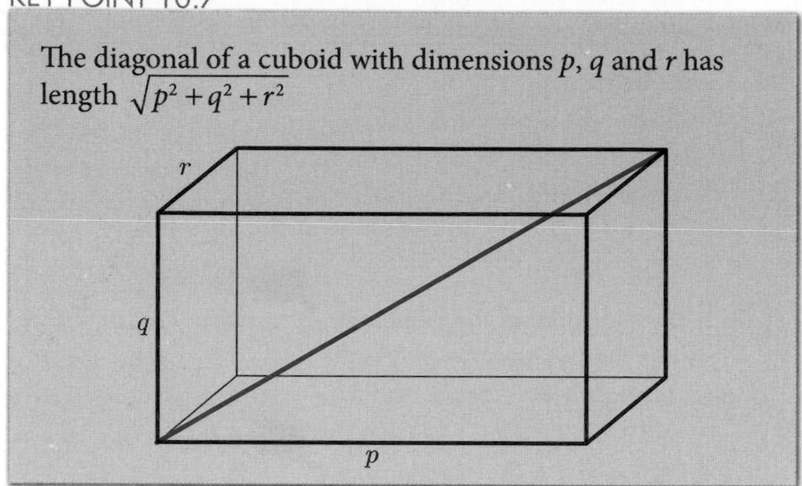

In chapter 11 you will meet vectors, which can also be used to solve three-dimensional problems.

The key to solving many three-dimensional problems is spotting right angles. This is not always easy to do from diagrams that are drawn in perspective, but there are some common configurations to look for; for example, a vertical edge will always meet a horizontal edge at 90°, and the symmetry line of an isosceles triangle is perpendicular to its base.

Worked example 10.12

The base of a pyramid is a square of side length 4 cm. The other four faces are isosceles triangles with sides of length 7 cm. The height of one of the side faces is labelled h.

(a) Find the exact value of h.

(b) Find the exact height of the pyramid.

(c) Calculate the volume of the pyramid, correct to 3 significant figures.

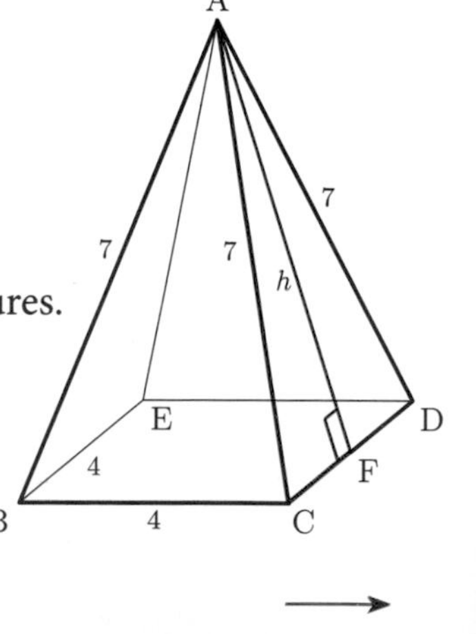

continued . . .

Triangle AFC is right-angled. Draw it separately and label the sides.

(a)

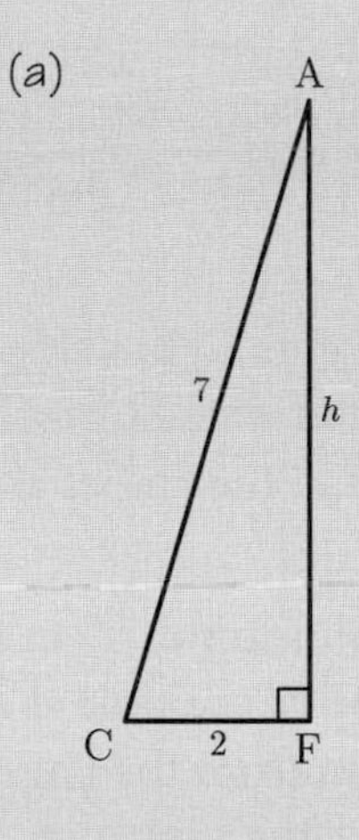

Use Pythagoras' Theorem to find h.

$h^2 = 7^2 - 2^2$

$\therefore h = \sqrt{45}$ cm

Add the height of the pyramid to the diagram. It is the length of a vertical line [AM] which is perpendicular to the base. The point M is the centre of the base, so MF = 2 cm, and $A\widehat{M}F$ is a right angle. Draw the triangle AMF.

(b)

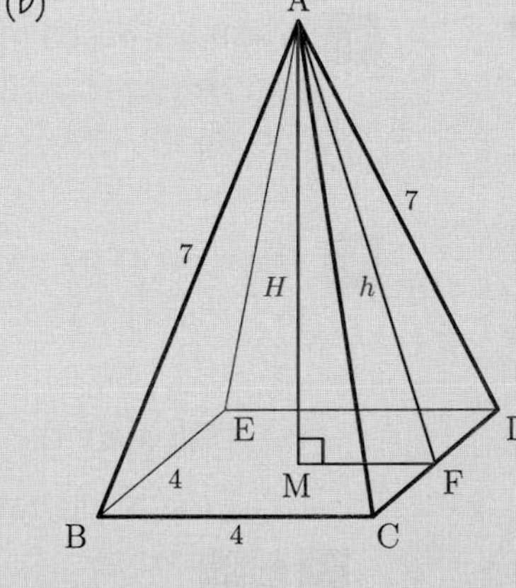

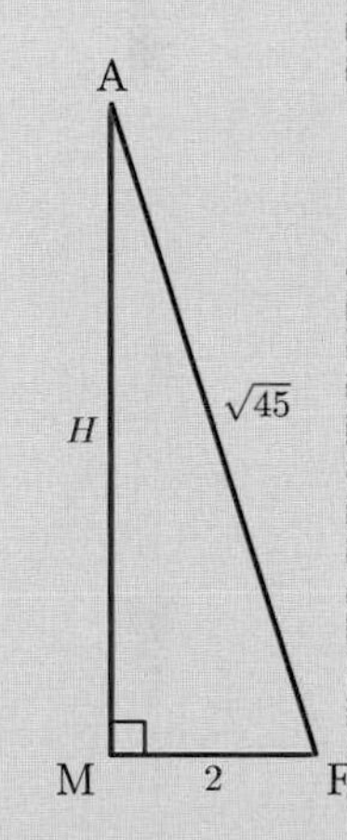

Use Pythagoras' Theorem to find H.

$H^2 = \left(\sqrt{45}\right)^2 - 2^2$

$\therefore H = \sqrt{41}$ cm

The formula for the volume of a pyramid (from the Formula booklet) is

$\frac{1}{3} \times$ area of base $\times$ vertical height.

(c) $V = \frac{1}{3} \times 4^2 \times \sqrt{41})$

$= 34.1$ cm^3 (3SF)

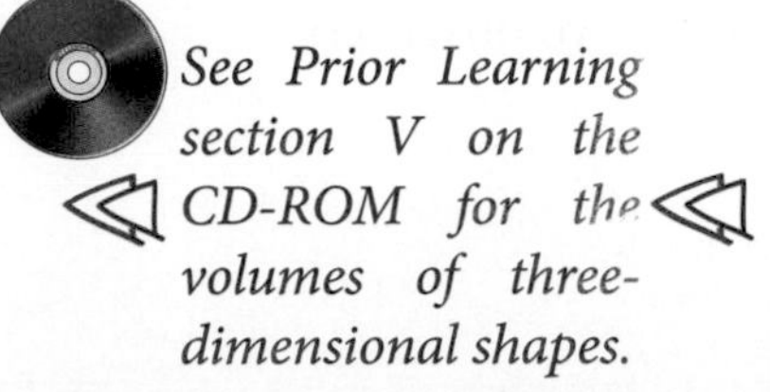

See Prior Learning section V on the CD-ROM for the volumes of three-dimensional shapes.

Exercise 10E

1. Find the length of the diagonal of the cuboid with the following dimensions.

   (i) 3 cm × 5 cm × 10 cm (ii) 4 cm × 4 cm × 8 cm

2. A cuboid has sides of length 12.5 cm, 10 cm and 7.3 cm. It is intersected by a plane passing through vertices A, B and C. Find the angles and the area of triangle ABC. *[8 marks]*

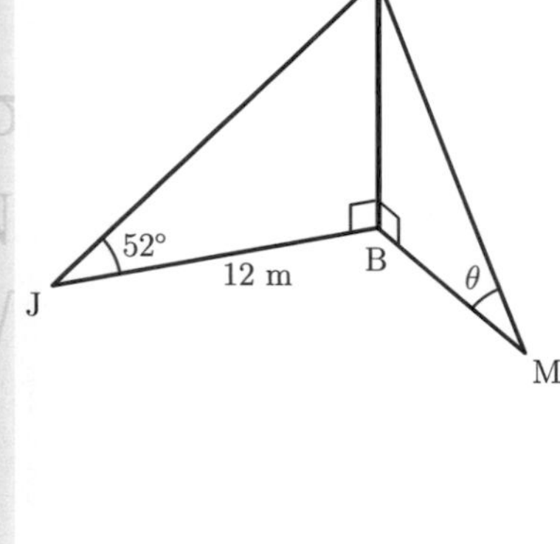

3. John stands 12 m from the base of a flagpole and sees the top of the pole at an angle of elevation of 52°. Marit stands 8 m from the flagpole. At what angle of elevation does she see the top? *[6 marks]*

4. A square-based pyramid has a base of side length $a = 8$ cm and height $H = 12$ cm. Find the length l of the sloping side. *[6 marks]*

5. The base of pyramid TABCD is a square. The height of the pyramid is TM = 12 cm, and the length of a sloping side is TC = 17 cm.

   (a) Calculate the length MC.

   (b) Find the length of the side of the base. *[6 marks]*

6. The diagram shows a vertical tree PQ and two observers, A and B, standing on horizontal ground. The following quantities are known:

$$AQ = 25\text{ m}, Q\hat{A}P = 37°, Q\hat{B}P = 42°, A\hat{Q}B = 75°$$

   (a) Find the height of the tree, h.

   (b) Find the distance between the two observers. *[8 marks]*

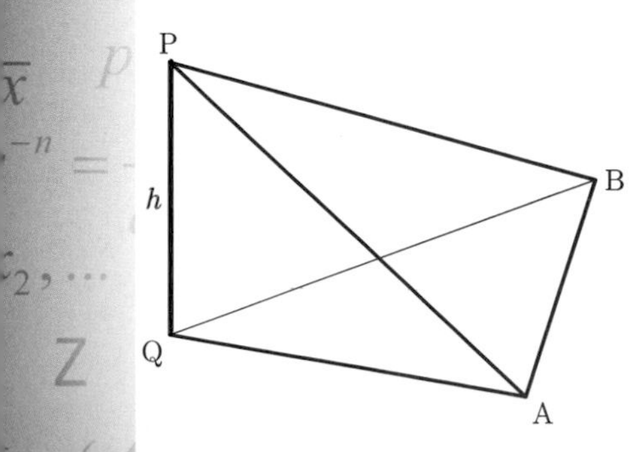

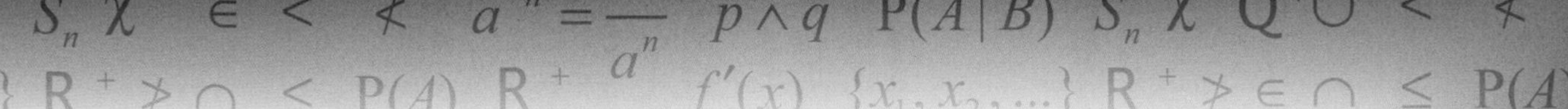

7. Annabel and Bertha are trying to measure the height, h, of a vertical tree RT. They stand on horizontal ground, distance d apart, so that $\hat{ARB}$ is a right angle. From where Annabel is standing, the angle of elevation of the top of the tree is α and from where Bertha is standing, the angle of elevation of the top of the tree is β.

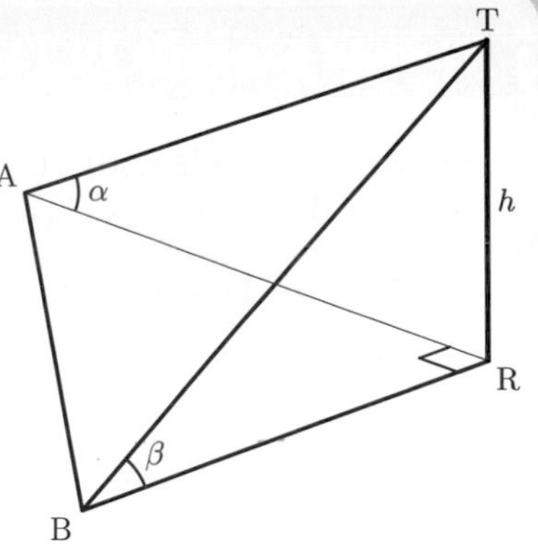

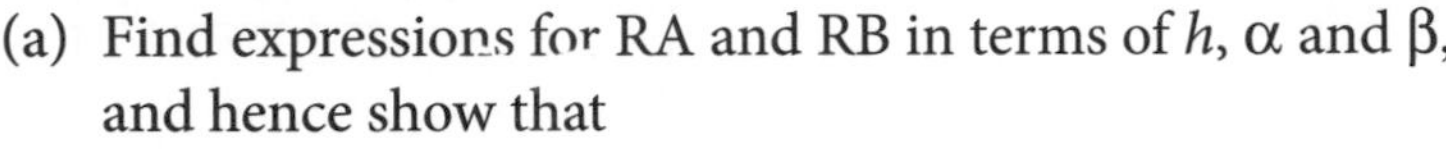

(a) Find expressions for RA and RB in terms of h, α and β, and hence show that

$$h^2\left(\frac{1}{\tan^2\alpha}+\frac{1}{\tan^2\beta}\right)=d^2$$

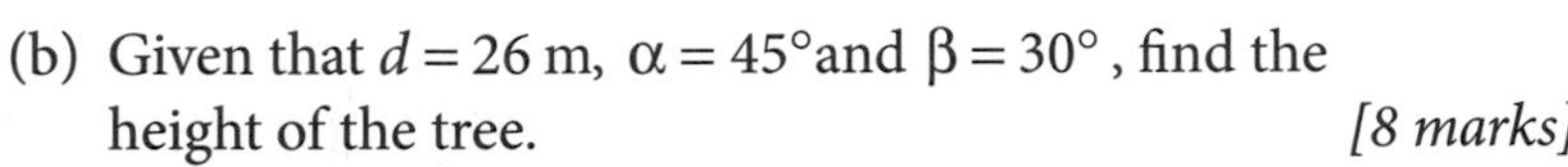

(b) Given that $d = 26$ m, $\alpha = 45°$ and $\beta = 30°$, find the height of the tree. *[8 marks]*

10F Length of an arc

The diagram shows a circle with centre O and radius r, and points A and B on its circumference. The part of the circumference between points A and B is called an **arc** of the circle. As you can see, there are in fact two arcs: the shorter one is called the *minor arc*, and the longer one the *major arc*. We say that the minor arc AB **subtends** angle θ at the centre of the circle; that is, the angle $\hat{AOB}$ beneath the arc is θ.

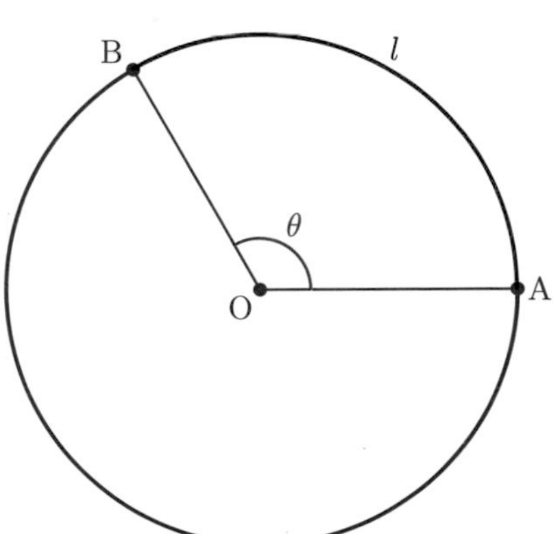

You learned in chapter 8 that the measure of angle θ in radians is equal to the ratio of the length of the arc AB to the radius of the circle; in other words, $\theta = \frac{l}{r}$. This gives us a very simple formula for the length of an arc of a circle, if we know the angle it subtends at the centre.

KEY POINT 10.8

The length of an arc of a circle is

$$l = r\theta$$

where r is the radius of the circle and θ is the angle subtended at the centre, measured in radians.

Worked example 10.13

Arc AB of a circle with radius 5 cm subtends an angle of 0.6 at the centre, as shown in the diagram.

(a) Find the length of the minor arc AB.

(b) Find the length of the major arc AB.

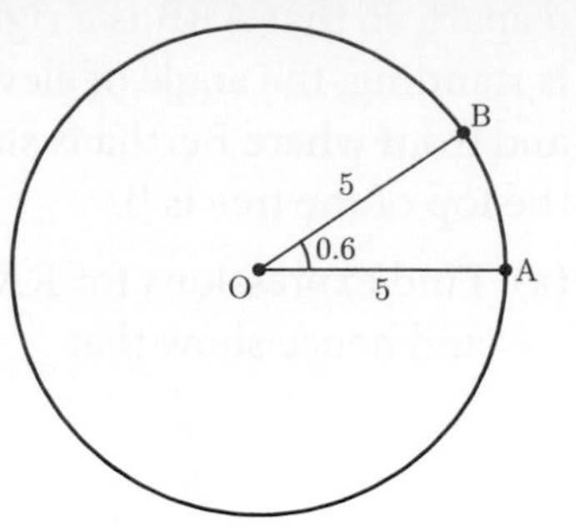

Use the formula for the length of an arc.

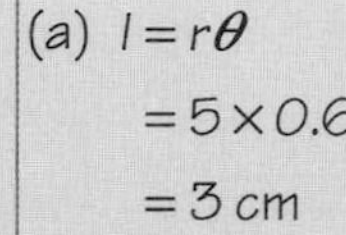

(a) $l = r\theta$
$= 5 \times 0.6$
$= 3$ cm

The angle subtended by the major arc is equal to a full turn (2π radians) minus the smaller angle.

(b) $\theta_1 = 2\pi - 0.6$
$= 5.683$
$l = r\theta_1$
$= 5 \times 5.683$
$= 28.4$ cm (3 SF)

We could have done part (b) differently, by finding the length of the whole circumference and then taking away the minor arc: the circumference is $2\pi r = 2\pi \times 5 = 31.42$, so the length of the major arc is $31.42 - 3 = 28.4$ cm (3 SF).

If the angle is given in degrees, we must convert to radians before using the formula for arc length.

Worked example 10.14

Two points A and B lie on the circumference of a circle of radius r cm. The arc AB has length 10.9 cm and subtends an angle of 52° at the centre of the circle.

(a) Find the value of r.

(b) Calculate the perimeter of the shaded region.

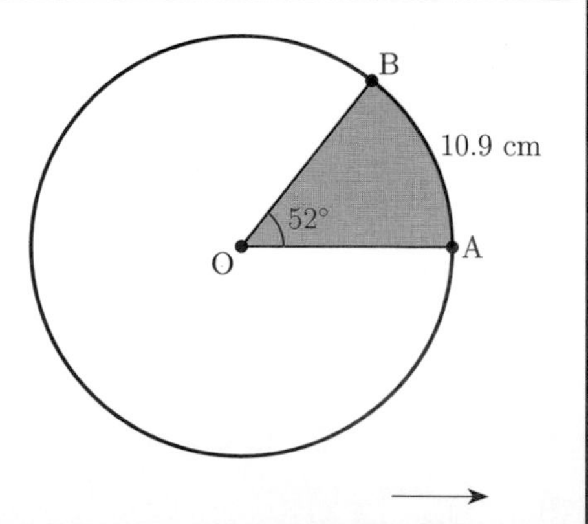

→

continued . . .

We know the arc length and the angle, so we can find the radius.

(a) $l = r\theta \Rightarrow r = \frac{l}{\theta}$

Remember that in order to use the arc length formula, the angle must be in radians.

$\theta = 52 \times \frac{\pi}{180} = 0.908$

$\therefore r = \frac{10.9}{0.908} = 12.0 \text{ cm}$

The perimeter is made up of two radii and the arc length.

(b) $p = 2r + l$

$= 2 \times 12.0 + 10.9$

$= 34.9 \text{ cm}$

Exercise 10F

1. Calculate the length of the minor arc subtending an angle of θ radians at the centre of the circle of radius r cm.

   (i) $\theta = 1.2, \ r = 6.5$ (ii) $\theta = 0.4, \ r = 4.5$

2. Points A and B lie on the circumference of a circle with centre O and radius r cm. Angle $A\hat{O}B$ is θ radians. Calculate the length of the major arc AB.

   (i) $r = 15, \ \theta = 0.8$ (ii) $r = 1.4, \ \theta = 1.4$

3. Calculate the length of the minor arc AB in the diagram below.

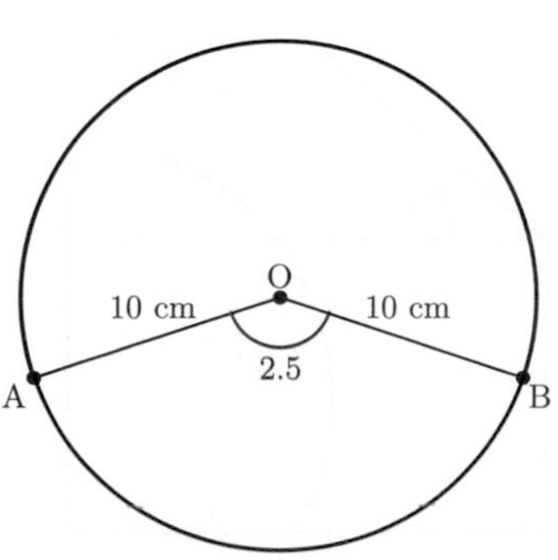

[4 marks]

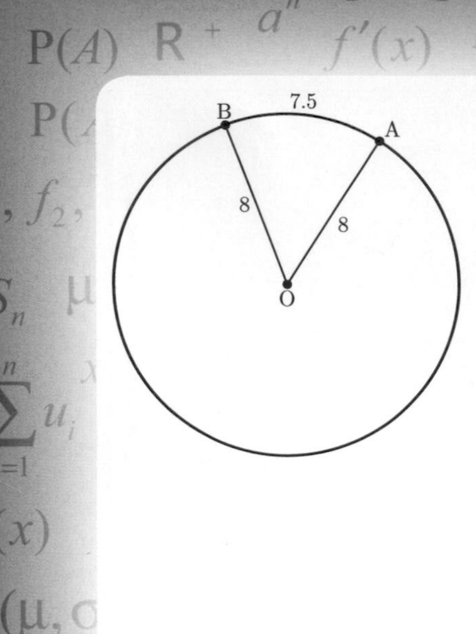

4. In the diagram alongside, the radius of the circle is 8 cm and the length of the minor arc AB is 7.5 cm. Calculate the size of the angle $A\hat{O}B$

(a) in radians

(b) in degrees. *[5 marks]*

5. Points M and N lie on the circumference of a circle with centre C and radius 4 cm. The length of the *major* arc MN is 15 cm. Calculate the size of the *smaller* angle $M\hat{C}N$. *[4 marks]*

6. Points P and Q lie on the circumference of a circle with centre O. The length of the minor arc PQ is 12 cm and $P\hat{O}Q = 1.6$. Find the radius of the circle. *[4 marks]*

7. In the diagram below, the length of the major arc XY is 28 cm. Find the radius of the circle.

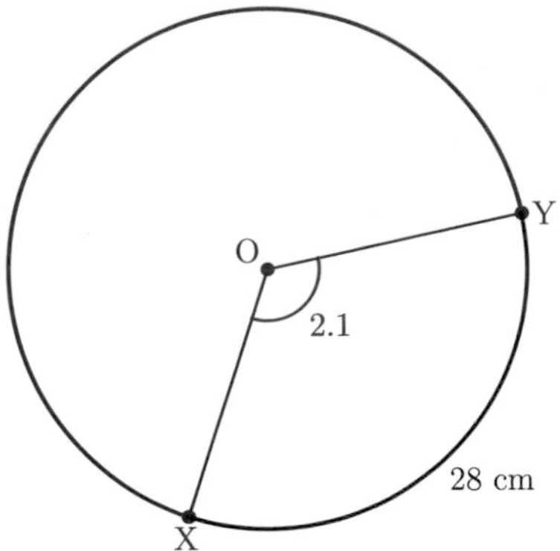

[4 marks]

8. The diagram alongside shows an equilateral triangle ABC with side length $a = 5$ cm. A figure (outlined in red) is made up of arcs of three circles whose centres are at the vertices of the triangle. Calculate the perimeter of the figure. *[5 marks]*

9. Calculate the perimeter of the figure shown in the diagram below.

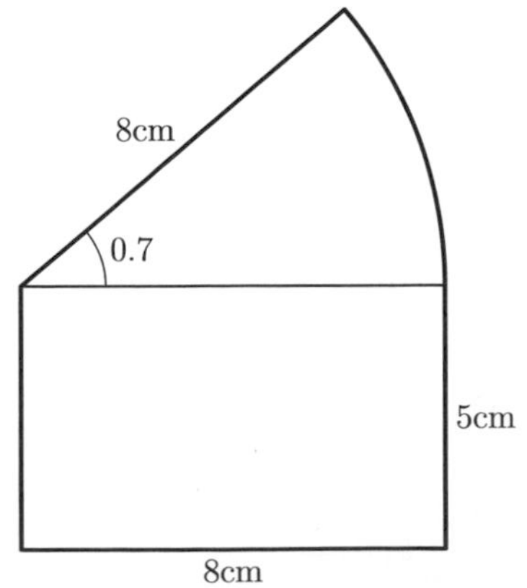

[6 marks]

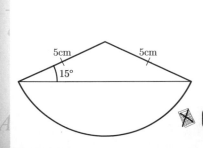

10. Find the exact perimeter of the figure shown in the diagram alongside. *[6 marks]*

11. A sector of a circle has perimeter $p = 12$ cm and angle $\theta = 0.4$ at the centre. Find the radius of the circle. *[5 marks]*

12. A cone is made by rolling a piece of paper shown in the diagram below.

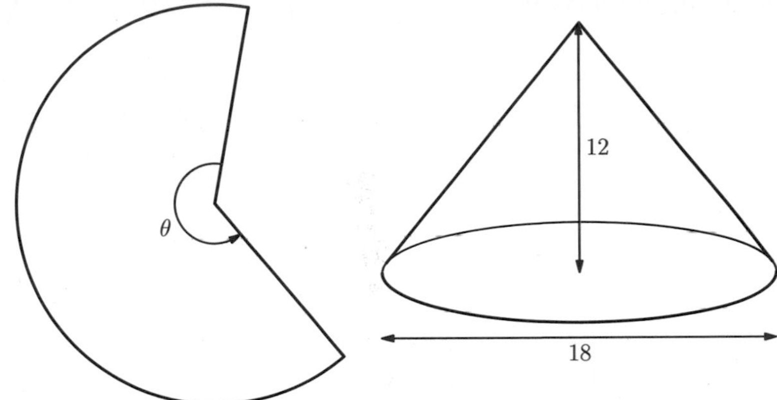

If the cone is to have height 12 cm and base diameter 18 cm, find the size of the angle marked θ. *[6 marks]*

10G Area of a sector

A **sector** is a part of a circle bounded by two radii and an arc. As with arcs, we can distinguish between a *minor sector* and a *major sector.*

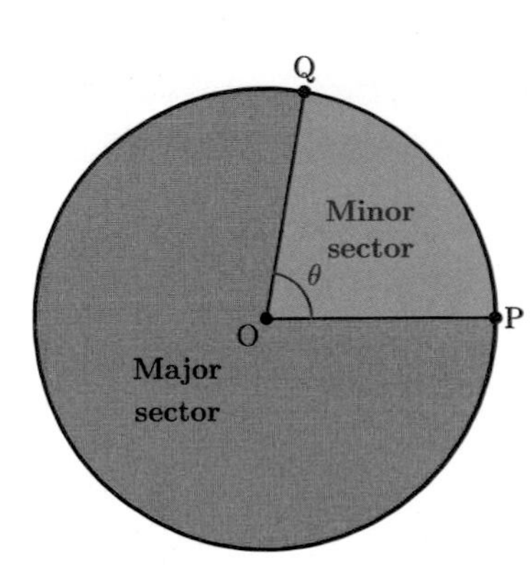

Consider the blue-shaded region. What fraction of the circle does this account for?

Thinking in terms of angles, the fraction should be $\frac{\theta}{2\pi}$.

If we compare areas, then since we know that the total circle area is πr^2, the fraction can also be expressed as $\frac{A}{\pi r^2}$ where A represents the area of the sector.

Both expressions define the same fraction, so they must be equal:

$$\frac{A}{\pi r^2} = \frac{\theta}{2\pi}$$

Rearranging this equation gives a formula for the area of the sector.

KEY POINT 10.9

> The area of a sector of a circle is
>
> $$A = \frac{1}{2} r^2 \theta$$
>
> where r is the radius of the circle and θ is the angle subtended at the centre, measured in radians.

Worked example 10.15

The diagram shows a circle with centre O and radius 6 cm, and two points A and B on its circumference such that $A\hat{O}B = 1.2$. Find the area of the minor sector AOB.

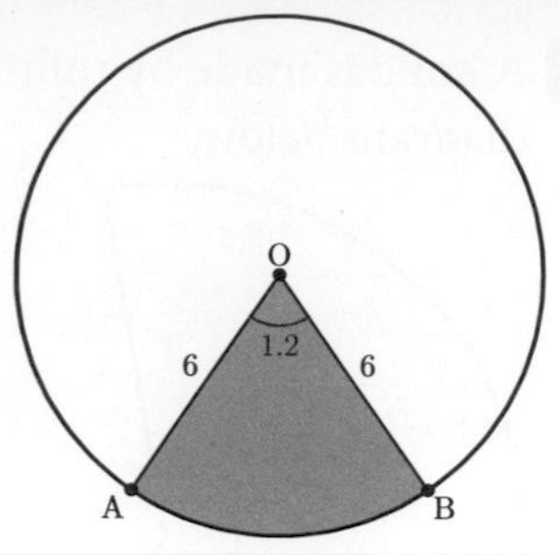

Use the formula for the area of a sector.

$$A = \frac{1}{2}r^2\theta$$
$$= \frac{1}{2} \times 6^2 \times 1.2$$
$$= 21.6 \text{ cm}^2$$

We may have to use the formulas for arc length and area in reverse.

Worked example 10.16

A sector of a circle has perimeter $p = 12$ cm and angle $\theta = 50°$ at the centre. Find the area of the sector.

To find the area we can use $A = \frac{1}{2}r^2\theta$, but first we need to find r.

We are given the perimeter, which is the sum of the arc length and two radii. We can use this equation to find r.

$$p = r\theta + 2r$$

Remember that the angle needs to be in radians.

and,

$$\theta = 50 \times \frac{\pi}{180} = 0.873$$

Substitute the values into the formula for perimeter to find r.

So,

$$12 = 0.873r + 2r = 2.873r$$
$$\Leftrightarrow r = \frac{12}{2.873} = 4.177$$

Substitute θ and r into the formula for sector area.

$$\therefore \quad A = \frac{1}{2}(4.177)^2(0.873)$$
$$= 7.62 \text{ cm}^2 \text{ (3SF)}$$

Exercise 10G

1. Points M and N lie on the circumference of a circle with centre O and radius r cm, and $\hat{MON} = \alpha$. Calculate the area of the minor sector MON if

   (i) $r = 5, \alpha = 1.3$ (ii) $r = 0.4, \alpha = 0.9$

2. Points A and B lie on the circumference of a circle with centre C and radius r cm. The size of the angle $\hat{ACB}$ is θ radians. Calculate the area of the major sector ACB if

   (i) $r = 13, \theta = 0.8$ (ii) $r = 1.4, \theta = 1.4$

3. A circle has centre O and radius 10 cm. Points A and B lie on the circumference so that the area of the minor sector AOB is 40 cm². Calculate the size of the acute angle $\hat{AOB}$. *[5 marks]*

4. Points P and Q lie on the circumference of a circle with radius 21 cm. The area of the *major* sector POQ is 744 cm². Find the size of the *smaller* angle $\hat{POQ}$ in *degrees*. *[5 marks]*

5. A sector of a circle with angle 1.2 radians has area 54 cm². Find the radius of the circle. *[4 marks]*

6. A sector of a circle with angle 162° has area 180 cm². Find the radius of the circle. *[4 marks]*

7. Find the area of the shaded region in the diagram below.

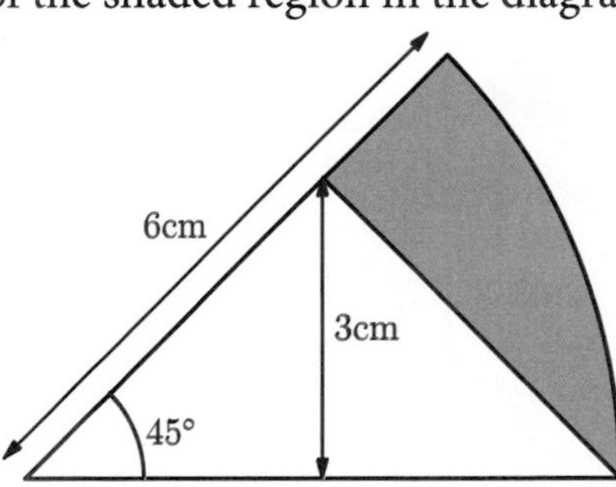

[6 marks]

8. The perimeter of the sector MON shown in the diagram alongside is 28 cm. Find its area. *[5 marks]*

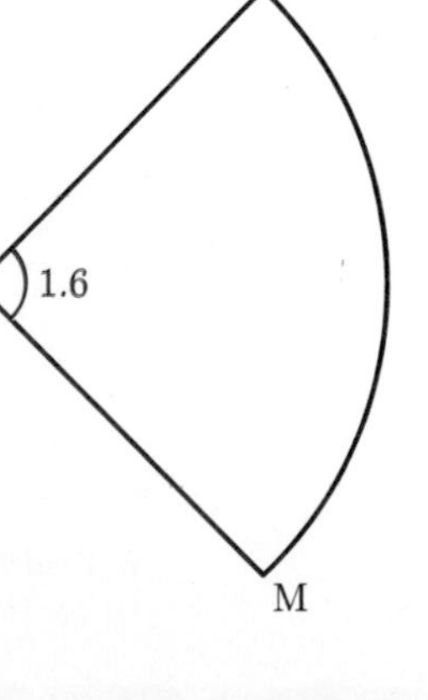

9. A sector of a circle has perimeter 7 cm and area 3 cm². Find the possible values of the radius of the circle. *[6 marks]*

10. Points P and Q lie on the circumference of a circle with centre O and radius 5 cm. The difference between the areas of the major sector POQ and the minor sector POQ is 15 cm². Find the size of the angle $\hat{POQ}$. *[5 marks]*

10H Triangles and circles

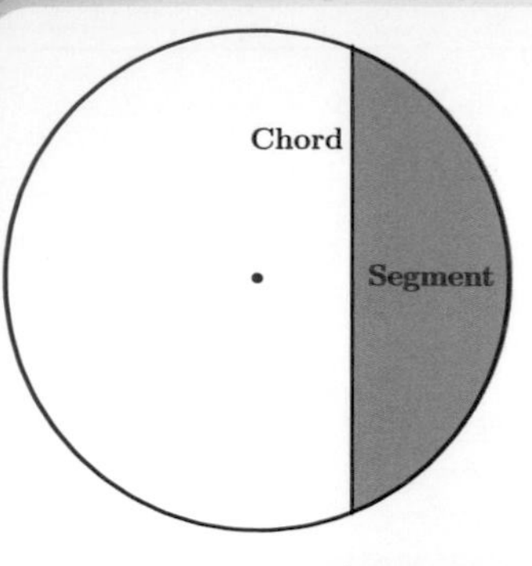

Besides arcs and sectors, there are two other important parts of circles that you need to know about: **chords** and **segments**.

Worked example 10.17

The diagram shows a sector of a circle with radius 7 cm; the angle at the centre is 0.8 radians. Find

(a) the perimeter of the shaded region
(b) the area of the shaded region.

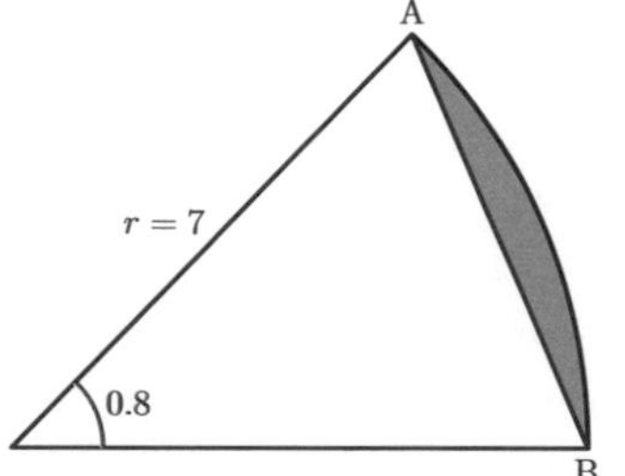

The perimeter is made up of the arc AB and the chord [AB].

(a) $p = \text{arc} + \text{chord}$

The formula for the arc length is $l = r\theta$.

$l = 7 \times 0.8$
$= 5.6$ cm

The chord [AB] is the third side of the isosceles triangle ABC. We can split ABC into two identical right-angled triangles with base $\frac{AB}{2}$ and hypotenuse 7; therefore $\frac{AB}{2} = 7\sin\frac{0.8}{2}$. (Alternatively, you can use the cosine rule on triangle ABC to find AB.)

$AB = 2 \times 7 \times \sin 0.4$
$= 5.45$ cm

Now we can calculate the perimeter.

$\therefore p = 5.6 + 5.45$
$= 11.1$ cm

If we calculate the area of the sector and then subtract the area of triangle ABC, we are left with the area of the segment.

(b) $A = \text{sector} - \text{triangle}$

continued . . .

The formula for the area of a sector is $\frac{1}{2}r^2\theta$.

The formula for the area of a triangle is $\frac{1}{2}ab\sin C$.

We can now find the area of the segment.

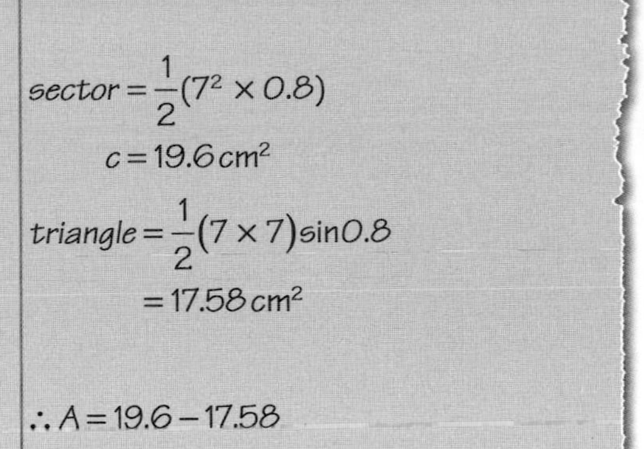

$sector = \frac{1}{2}(7^2 \times 0.8)$
$c = 19.6\text{ cm}^2$
$triangle = \frac{1}{2}(7 \times 7)\sin 0.8$
$= 17.58\text{ cm}^2$
$\therefore A = 19.6 - 17.58$
$= 2.02\text{ cm}^2$

Following the method used in Worked example 10.17, we can derive general formulas for the length of a chord and the area of a segment.

KEY POINT 10.10

The length of a chord of a circle is given by

$$AB = 2r\sin\left(\frac{\theta}{2}\right)$$

and the area of the shaded segment is

$$\frac{1}{2}r^2(\theta - \sin\theta)$$

where the angle θ is measured in radians and is the angle subtended at the centre.

EXAM HINT

These formulae are not given in the Formula booklet, so you need to know how to derive them.

The next example shows how we can solve more complex geometry problems by splitting up the figure into basic shapes such as triangles and sectors.

Worked example 10.18

The diagram shows two identical circles of radius 12 such that the centre of one circle is on the circumference of the other.

(a) Find the exact size of angle $P\hat{C}_1Q$ in radians.

(b) Calculate the exact area of the shaded region.

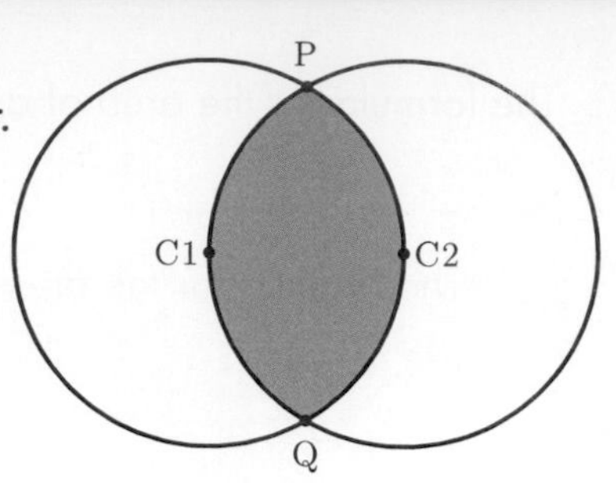

The only thing we know is the radius of the circles, so draw in all the lengths which are equal to the radius.

(a)

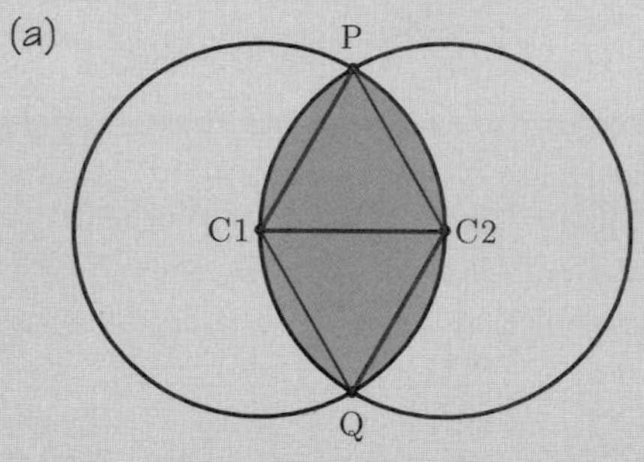

The lengths C_1P, C_2P *and* C_1C_2 are all equal to the radius of the circle, so triangle PC_1C_2 is equilateral; similarly for triangle QC_1C_2.

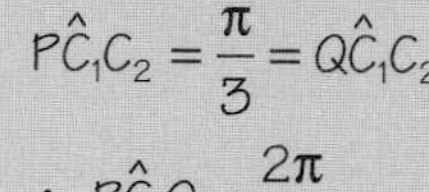

$$P\hat{C}_1C_2 = \frac{\pi}{3} = Q\hat{C}_1C_2$$

$$\therefore\ P\hat{C}_1Q = \frac{2\pi}{3}$$

The shaded area is made up of two equal segments, one for each circle, each with angle $\frac{2\pi}{3}$ at the centre.

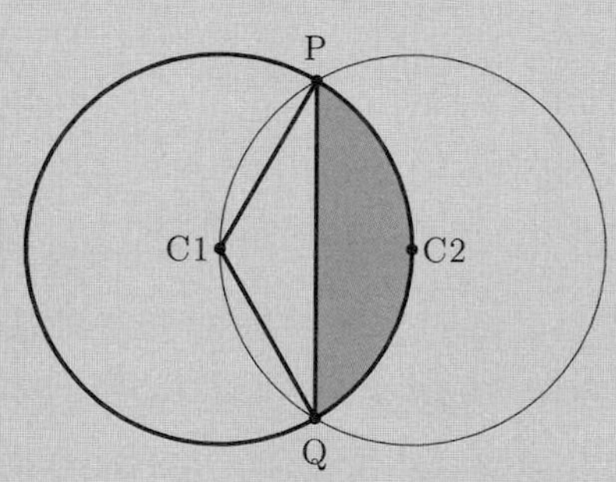

We can find the area of one segment by using the formula. Since we are asked for the exact area, we should use the exact value of $\sin\left(\frac{2\pi}{3}\right)$.

(b) Area of one segment

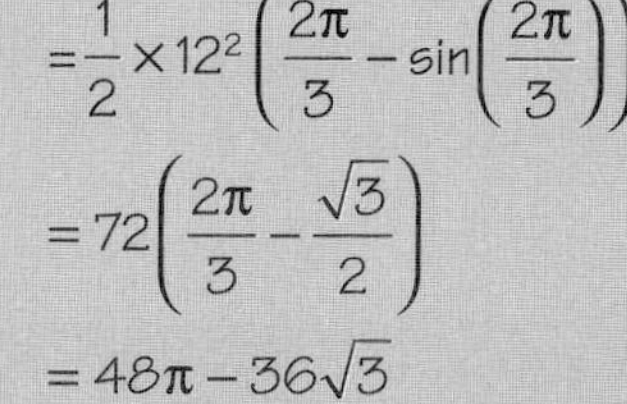

$$= \frac{1}{2} \times 12^2 \left(\frac{2\pi}{3} - \sin\left(\frac{2\pi}{3}\right)\right)$$

$$= 72\left(\frac{2\pi}{3} - \frac{\sqrt{3}}{2}\right)$$

$$= 48\pi - 36\sqrt{3}$$

Remember that the shaded area consists of two segments.

$\therefore$ *shaded area* $= 96\pi - 72\sqrt{3}$

Exercise 10H

1. Find the length of the chord AB in each diagram.

(a) (i)

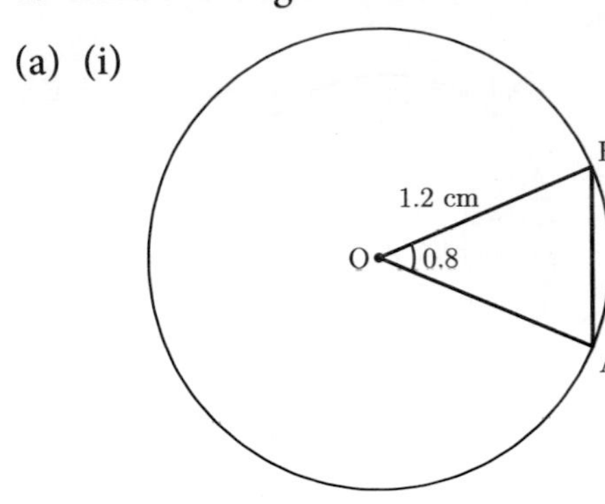

(ii)

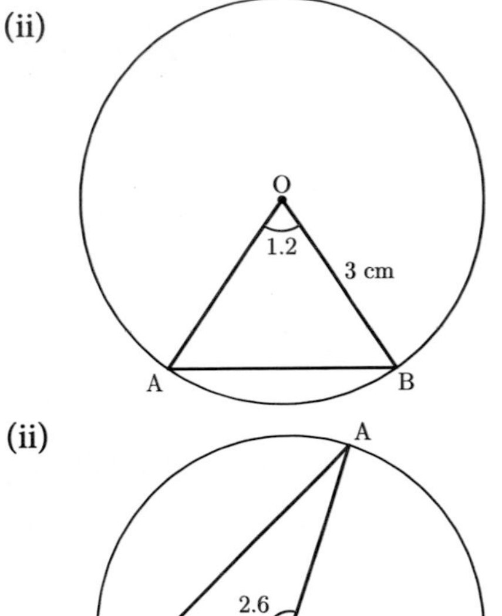

(b) (i)

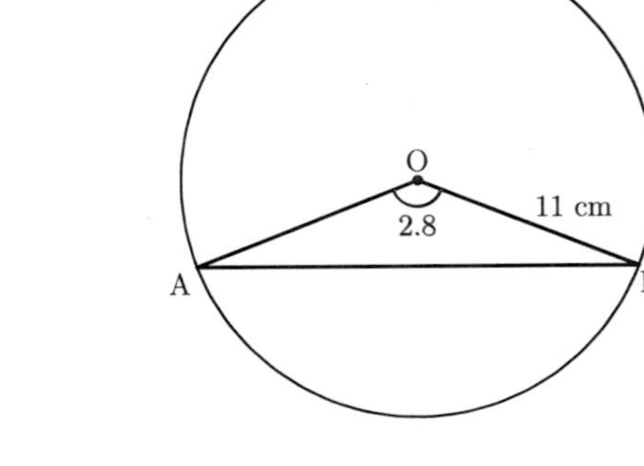

(ii)

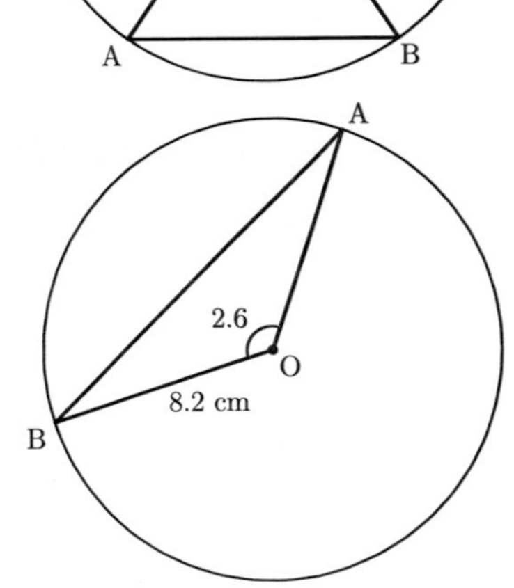

2. Find the perimeters of the minor segments from Question 1.

3. Find the areas of the minor segments from Question 1.

4. A circle has centre O and radius 5 cm. Chord PQ subtends angle θ at the centre of the circle.

(a) Write down an expression for the area of the minor segment.

(b) Given that the area of the minor segment is 15 cm², find the value of θ. *[6 marks]*

5. Two circles, with centres A and B, intersect at points P and Q. The radii of the circles are 6 cm and 4 cm, and $P\hat{A}Q = 45°$.

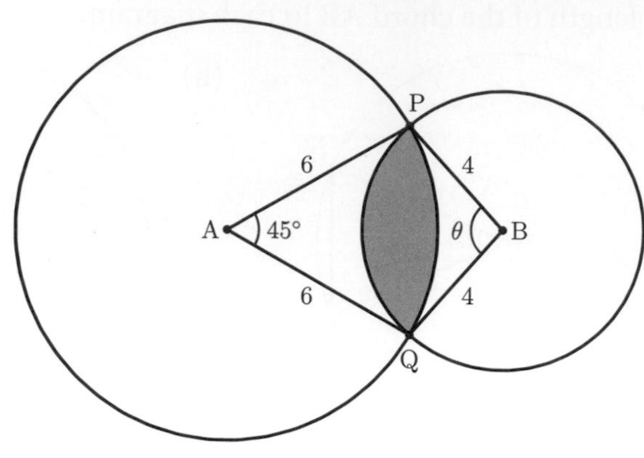

(a) Show that $PQ = 6\sqrt{2-\sqrt{2}}$.

(b) Find the size of $P\hat{B}Q$.

(c) Find the area of the shaded region. *[9 marks]*

Summary

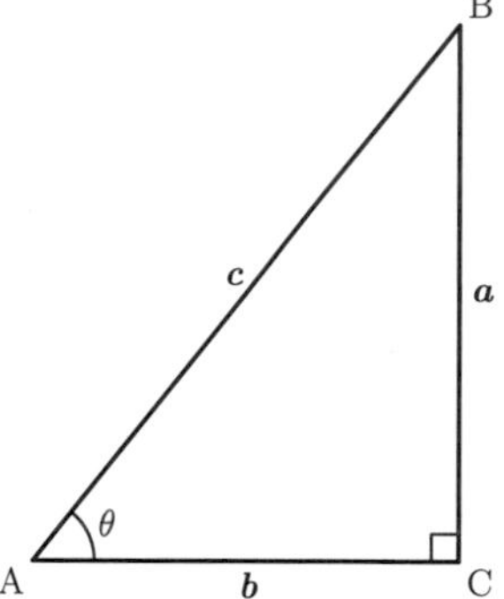

- In a right-angled triangle: $\frac{a}{c} = \sin\theta$; $\frac{b}{c} = \cos\theta$; $\frac{a}{b} = \frac{\sin\theta}{\cos\theta} = \tan\theta$
- The angle of elevation is the angle above the horizontal.
- The angle of depression is the angle below the horizontal.
- To find a side length of a triangle when two angles and a side are given, or to find an angle when two sides and a non-included angle are given, we can use the **sine rule**:

$$\frac{a}{\sin A} = \frac{b}{\sin B} = \frac{c}{\sin C}$$

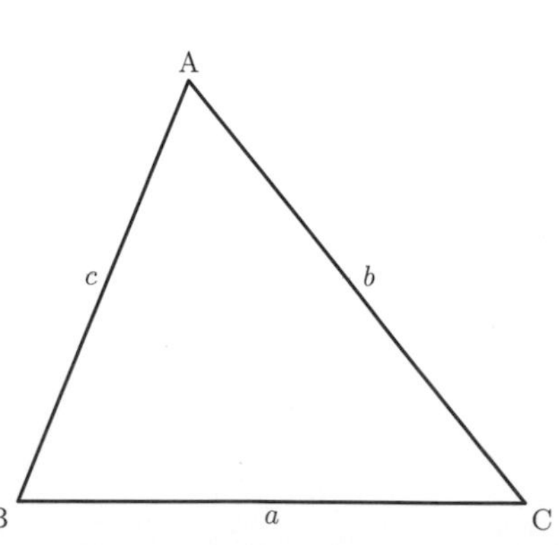

- To find a side length of a triangle when two sides and the angle between them are given, or to find an angle when all three sides are given, we can use the **cosine rule**:

$$c^2 = a^2 + b^2 - 2ab\cos C$$

Or:

$$\cos C = \frac{a^2 + b^2 - c^2}{2ab}$$

- The diagonal of a cuboid, $p \times q \times r$, has length $\sqrt{p^2 + q^2 + r^2}$.

- An alternative formula for the area of a triangle is:

$$\text{Area} = \frac{1}{2}ab\sin C$$

- To solve geometry problems in three dimensions, try to find a suitable triangle and use one of the above formulas or Pythagoras' Theorem. Look out especially for right angles.
- In a circle of radius r, for an angle θ in radians subtended at the centre:
  - arc length $l = r\theta$
  - area of sector $A = \frac{1}{2}r^2\theta$
- Know how to derive the formulae for the length of a chord AB and the area of a segment subtending an angle θ radians at the centre:

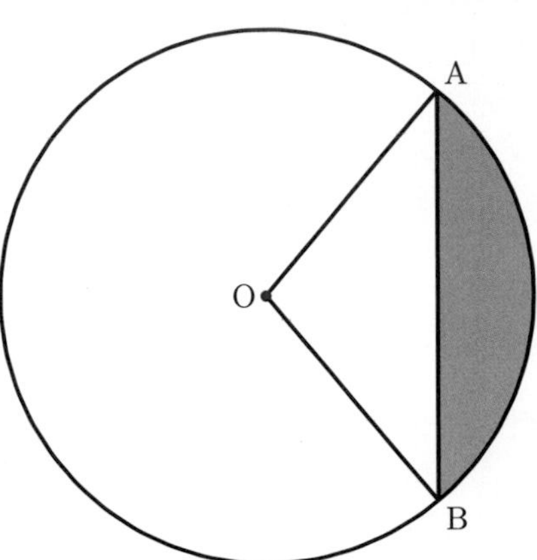

$$\text{AB} = 2r\sin\left(\frac{\theta}{2}\right)$$

$$\text{Area} = \frac{1}{2}r^2(\theta - \sin\theta)$$

Introductory problem revisited

Two people are trying to measure the width of a river. There is no bridge across the river, but they have instruments for measuring lengths and angles. When they stand 50 m apart on the same side of the river, at points A and B, the person at A measures that the angle between line (AB) and the line from A to the tower on the other side of the river is 25.6°. The person at B finds the corresponding angle to be 28.3°, as shown in the diagram. Use this information to calculate the width of the river.

Draw a diagram of the triangles in the problem. We want to find w. There are two right-angled triangles, ACT and BCT, but we do not know the lengths of any of their sides. However, in triangle ABT we know two angles and one side, so we can calculate the remaining sides. In particular, once we find the length of BT, we will be able to find w from triangle BCT.

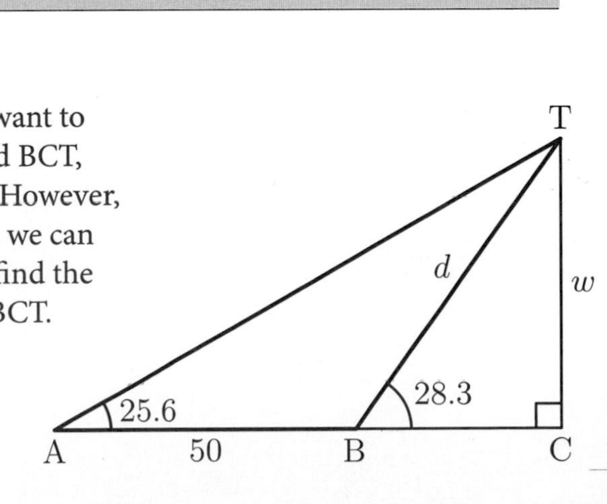

In order to use the sine rule in triangle ABT, we need to know the size of the angle opposite [AB], namely $A\hat{T}B$. Since $A\hat{B}T = 180° - 28.3° = 151.7°$, we find that $A\hat{T}B = 180° - 25.6° - 151.7° = 2.7°$.

Now we apply the sine rule:

$$\frac{d}{\sin 25.6°} = \frac{50}{\sin 2.7°}$$

$$\Rightarrow \quad d = \frac{50 \sin 25.6°}{\sin 2.7°}$$

$$= 458.6$$

Finally, use the right-angled triangle BCT to find the width of the river:

$$w = d \sin 28.3°$$

$$= 217 \text{ m} (3 \text{ SF})$$

Mixed examination practice 10

Short questions

1. In the diagram, OABC is a rectangle with sides 7 cm and 2 cm. PQ is a straight line. AP and CQ are circular arcs, and $A\hat{O}P = \frac{\pi}{6}$.

(a) Write down the size of $C\hat{O}Q$.

(b) Find the area of the whole shape.

(c) Find the perimeter of the whole shape.

[9 marks]

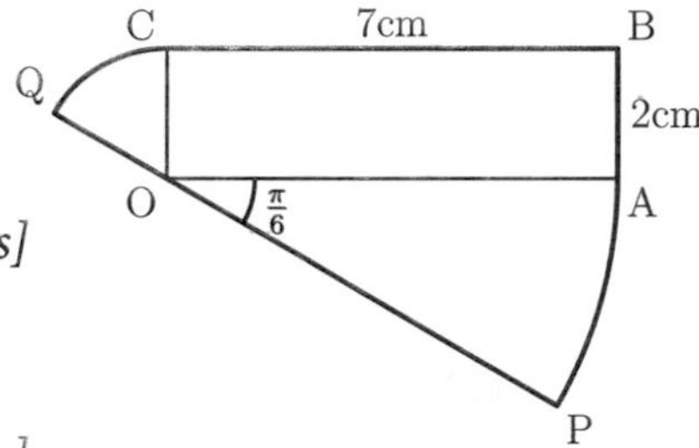

2. A sector has perimeter 36 cm and radius 10 cm. Find its area. *[6 marks]*

3. In triangle ABC, AB = 6.2 cm, CA = 8.7 cm and $A\hat{C}B = 37.5°$. Find the two possible values of $A\hat{B}C$. *[6 marks]*

4. A vertical tree of height 12 m stands on horizontal ground. The bottom of the tree is at the point B. Observer A, standing on the ground, sees the top of the tree at an angle of elevation of 56°.

(a) Find the distance of A from the bottom of the tree.

Another observer, M, stands the same distance away from the tree, with $A\hat{B}M = 48°$.

(b) Find the distance AM. *[6 marks]*

5. The diagram shows a circle with centre O and radius $r = 7$ cm. The chord PQ subtends angle $\theta = 1.4$ radians at the centre of the circle.

(a) Find the area of the shaded region.

(b) Find the perimeter of the shaded region.

[6 marks]

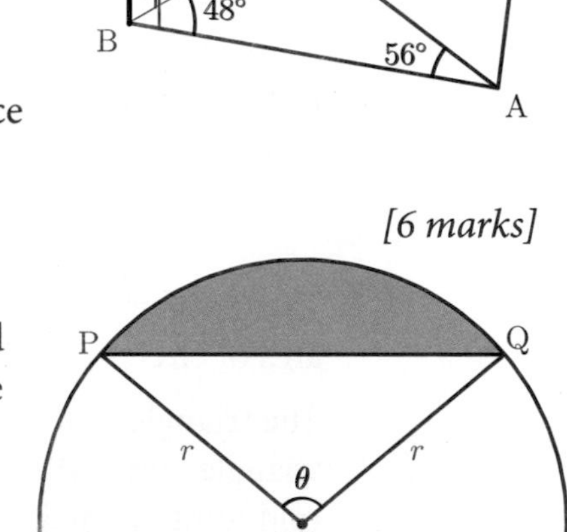

6. The diagram shows two circular sectors with angle θ at the centre. The radius of the larger sector is 10 cm, the radius of the smaller sector is x cm shorter.

(a) Show that the area of the shaded region is given by $\frac{x(20-x)\theta}{2}$.

(b) If $\theta = 1.2$, find the value of x such that the area of the shaded region is equal to 54.6 cm². *[8 marks]*

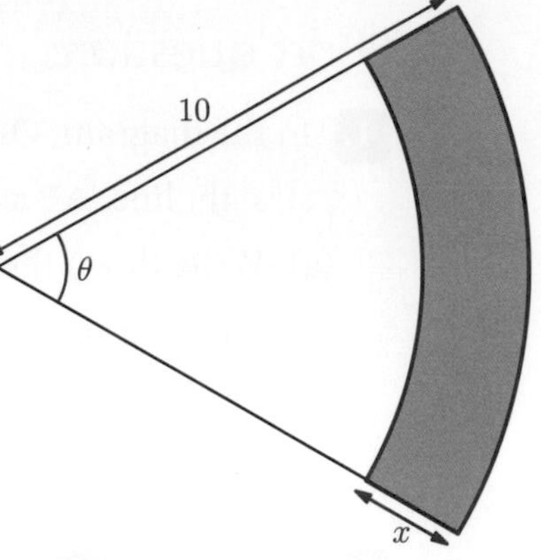

7. In the diagram, O is the centre of the circle and (AT) is the tangent to the circle at T.

See Prior Learning sections U and W on the CD-ROM for a review of properties of circles and basic trigonometry.

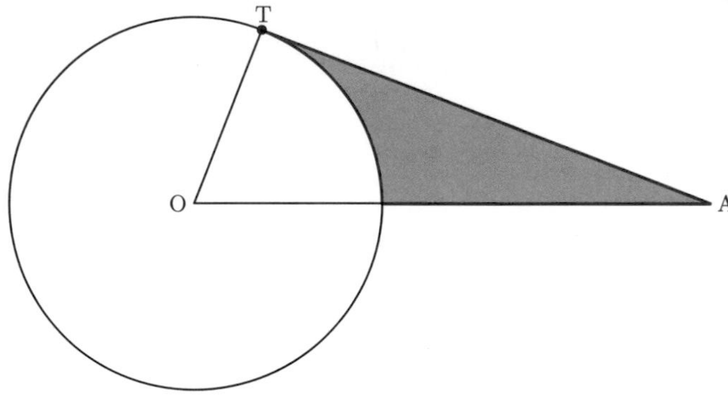

If OA = 12 cm and the circle has a radius of 6 cm, find the area of the shaded region. *[4 marks]*

(© IB Organization 2001)

8. The diagram shows a triangle and two arcs of circles.

The triangle ABC is a right-angled isosceles triangle, with AB = AC = 2. The point P is the midpoint of [BC].

The arc BDC is part of a circle with centre A.

The arc BEC is part of a circle with centre P.

(a) Calculate the area of the segment BDCP.

(b) Calculate the area of the shaded region BECD.

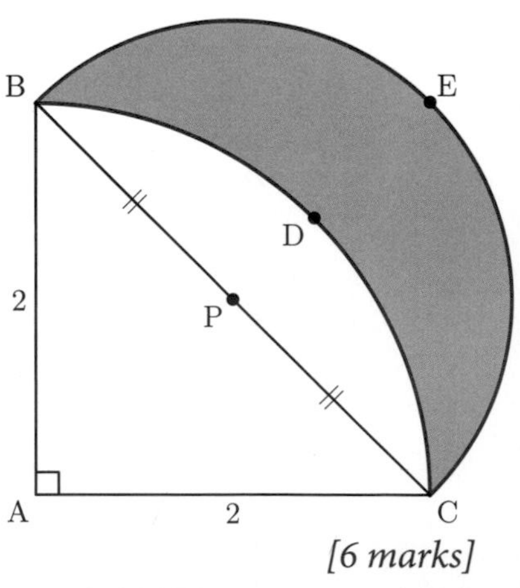

[6 marks]

(© IB Organization 2003)

9. A right-angled triangle has sides 12 cm and 9 cm. At each vertex, a sector of radius 2 cm is cut out, as shown in the diagram. The angle of sector 1 is θ radians.

(a) Write down an expression for the area of sector 2 in terms of θ.

(b) Find the remaining area after the triangle has had the corners removed. *[6 marks]*

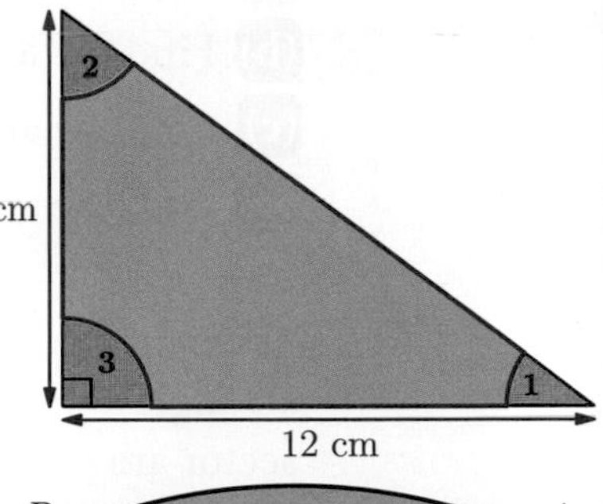

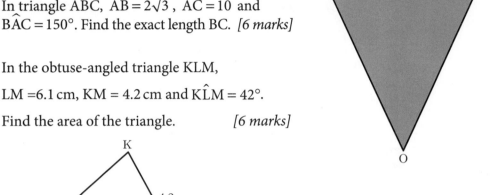

10. The perimeter of the sector shown in the diagram is 34 cm and its area is 52 cm². Find the radius of the sector. *[6 marks]*

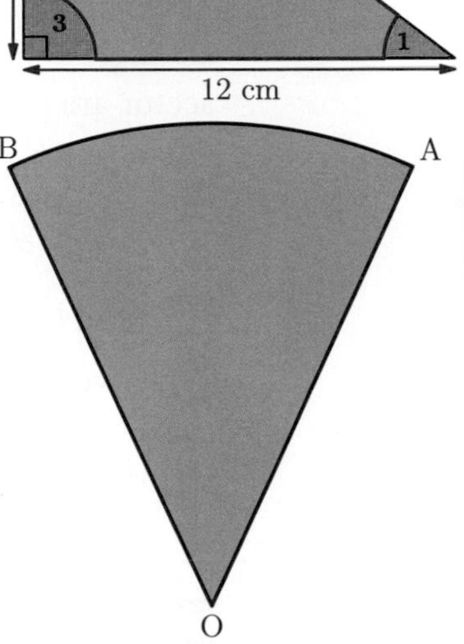

11. In triangle ABC, $AB = 2\sqrt{3}$, $AC = 10$ and $B\hat{A}C = 150°$. Find the exact length BC. *[6 marks]*

12. In the obtuse-angled triangle KLM,

LM = 6.1 cm, KM = 4.2 cm and $K\hat{L}M = 42°$.

Find the area of the triangle. *[6 marks]*

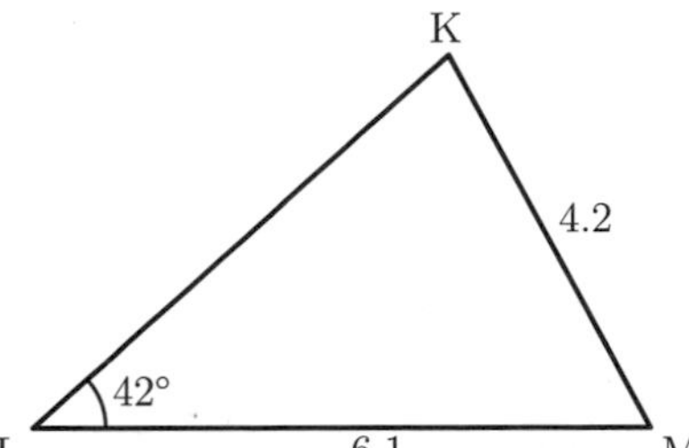

13. In triangle ABC, AB = 10 cm, BC = 8 cm and CA = 7 cm.

(a) Find the exact value of $\cos A\hat{B}C$.

(b) Find the exact value of $\sin A\hat{B}C$.

(c) Find the exact value of the area of the triangle. *[8 marks]*

Long questions

1. In triangle ABC, AB = 5, AC = x, and $B\hat{A}C = \theta$; M is the midpoint of the side [AC].

(a) Use the cosine rule to find an expression for MB^2 in terms of x and θ.

(b) Given that BC = MB, show that $\cos\theta = \frac{3x}{20}$.

(c) If $x = 5$, find the value of the angle θ such that MB = BC. *[9 marks]*

2. Two circles have equal radius r and intersect at points S and T. The centres of the circles are A and B, and $A\hat{S}B = 90°$.

   (a) Explain why $S\hat{A}T$ is also 90°.

   (b) Find the length AB in terms of r.

   (c) Find the area of the sector AST.

   (d) Find the area of overlap of the two circles. *[10 marks]*

3. The diagram shows a circle with centre O and radius r. Chord AB subtends an angle at the centre of size θ radians. The minor segment and the major sector are shaded.

   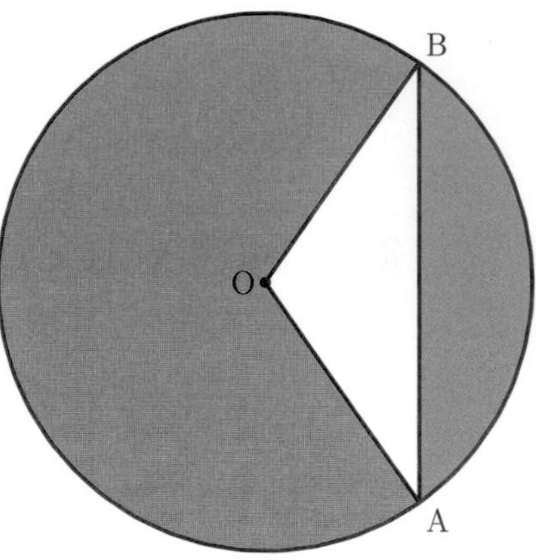

   (a) Show that the area of the minor *segment* is $\frac{1}{2}r^2(\theta - \sin\theta)$.

   (b) Find the area of the major *sector*.

   (c) Given that the ratio of the area of the blue region to the area of the pink region is 1:2, show that

   $$\sin\theta = \frac{3}{2}\theta - \pi$$

   (d) Find the value of θ. *[10 marks]*

4. The area of the triangle shown is 2.21 cm². The length of the shortest side is x cm and the other two sides are $3x$ cm and $(x+3)$ cm.

   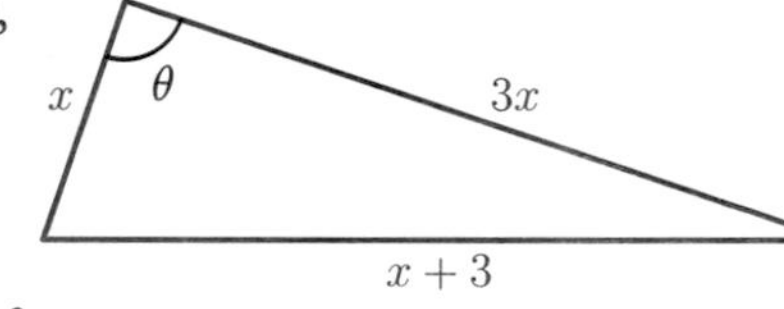

   (a) Using the formula for the area of a triangle, write down an expression for $\sin\theta$ in terms of x.

   (b) Using the cosine rule, write down and simplify an expression for $\cos\theta$ in terms of x.

   (c) Using your answers to parts (a) and (b), show that,

   $$\left(\frac{3x^2 - 2x - 3}{2x^2}\right)^2 = 1 - \left(\frac{4.42}{3x^2}\right)^2$$

   (d) Hence find

   (i) the possible values of x

   (ii) the corresponding values of θ, in *radians*, using your answer to part (b) above. *[10 marks]*

(© IB Organization 2000)

 5. In triangle ABC, AB = 5, BC = 10, CA = x and $A\hat{C}B = \theta$.

(a) Show that $x^2 - 20x\cos\theta + 75 = 0$.

(b) Find the range of values of $\cos\theta$ for which the above equation has real solutions for x.

(c) Hence find the set of values of θ for which it is possible to construct triangle ABC with the given measurements. *[8 marks]*

6. In the diagram, the points O(0,0) and A(8,6) are fixed. The angle $O\hat{P}A$ varies as the point $P(x,10)$ moves along the horizontal line $y = 10$.

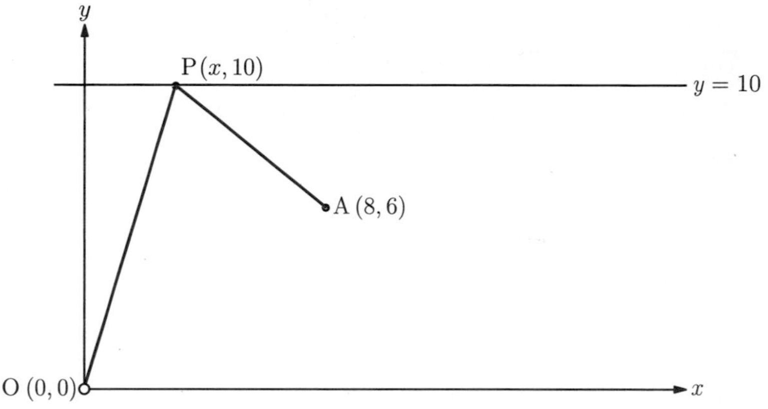

(a) (i) Show that $AP = \sqrt{x^2 - 16x + 80}$.

(ii) Write down a similar expression for OP in terms of x.

(b) Hence show that

$$\cos O\hat{P}A = \frac{x^2 - 8x + 40}{\sqrt{(x^2 - 16x + 80)(x^2 + 100)}}$$

(c) Find, in degrees, the angle $O\hat{P}A$ when $x = 8$.

(d) Find the positive value of x such that $O\hat{P}A = 60°$.

Let the function f be defined by

$$f(x) = \cos O\hat{P}A = \frac{x^2 - 8x + 40}{\sqrt{(x^2 - 16x + 80)(x^2 + 100)}},\ 0 \le x \le 15$$

(e) Consider the equation $f(x) = 1$.

(i) Explain, in terms of the position of the points O, A and P, why this equation has a solution.

(ii) Find the *exact* solution to the equation. *[17 marks]*

(© IB Organization 2001)

7. **(a)** Let $y = -16x^2 + 160x - 256$. Given that y has a maximum value, find

   (i) the value of x that gives the maximum value of y

   (ii) this maximum value of y.

The triangle XYZ has XZ = 6, YZ = x and XY = z, as shown in the diagram. The perimeter of triangle XYZ is 16.

(b) (i) Express z in terms of x.

   (ii) Using the cosine rule, express z^2 in terms of x and cos Z.

   (iii) Hence show that $\cos Z = \dfrac{5x-16}{3x}$.

Let the area of triangle XYZ be A.

(c) Show that $A^2 = 9x^2 \sin^2 Z$.

(d) Hence show that $A^2 = -16x^2 + 160x - 256$.

(e) (i) Hence write down the maximum area for triangle XYZ.

   (ii) What type of triangle is the triangle with maximum area? *[15 marks]*

8. Two circular cogs are connected by a chain as shown in Diagram 1. The radii of the cogs are 3 cm and 8 cm, and the distance between their centres is 25 cm.

Diagram 2 shows the quadrilateral O_1ABO_2. Line O_2P is drawn parallel to AB.

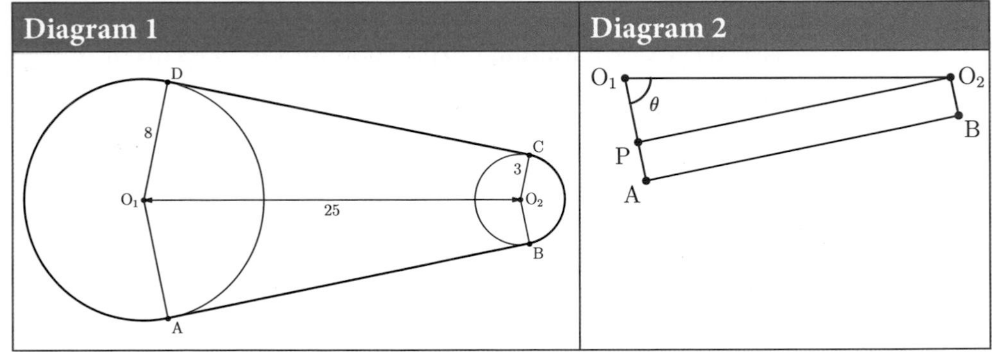

(a) Write down the size of $O_1\hat{A}B$ in radians, giving a reason for your answer.

(b) Explain why $PO_2 = AB$.

(c) Hence find the length AB.

(d) Find the size of the angle marked θ, giving your answer in radians correct to 4 SF.

(e) Calculate the length of the chain (shown in red in Diagram 1). *[11 marks]*

11 Vectors

In this chapter you will learn:

- to use vectors to represent displacements and positions in two and three dimensions
- to perform algebraic operations with vectors, and understand their geometric interpretation
- how to calculate the distance between two points
- how to use vectors to calculate the angle between two lines
- a new operation on vectors, called the scalar product
- how to describe a straight line using vectors
- to find intersections and angles between lines using vector methods.

Introductory problem

What is the angle between the diagonals of a cube?

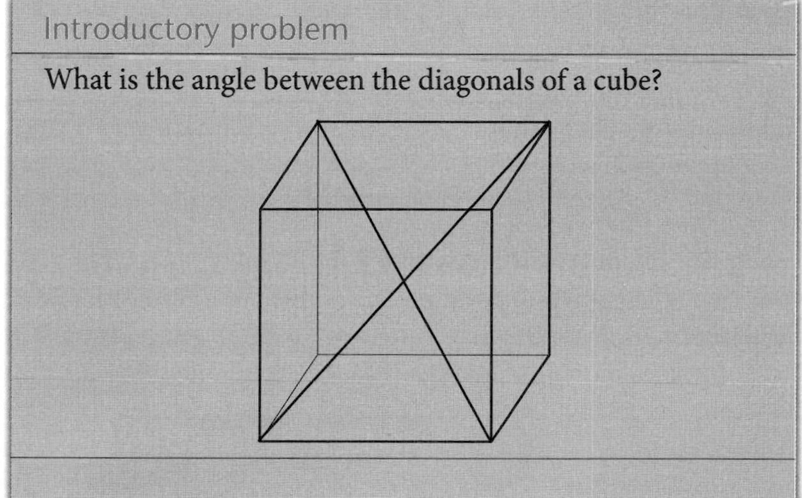

Solving problems in three dimensions can be difficult, as it is not always straightforward to visualise the geometry. Vectors provide a useful tool for translating geometrical properties into equations, which can often be analysed more easily. In this chapter we will develop techniques to calculate angles and distances in two and three dimensions; we will also look at how vectors can be used to describe lines in three dimensions and to find their intersections.

Vectors are an example of abstraction in mathematics – a single concept that can be applied to many different situations. Forces, velocities and displacements appear to have little in common, yet they can all be described and manipulated using the rules of vectors. In the words of the French mathematician and physicist Henri Poincaré (1854–1912), 'Mathematics is the art of giving the same name to different things.'

11A Positions and displacements

You may know from studying physics that **vectors** are used to represent quantities which have both magnitude (size) and direction, such as force or velocity. **Scalar** quantities, in contrast, are fully described by a single number. In pure mathematics, vectors are also used to represent displacements from one point to another, and thus to describe geometrical figures.

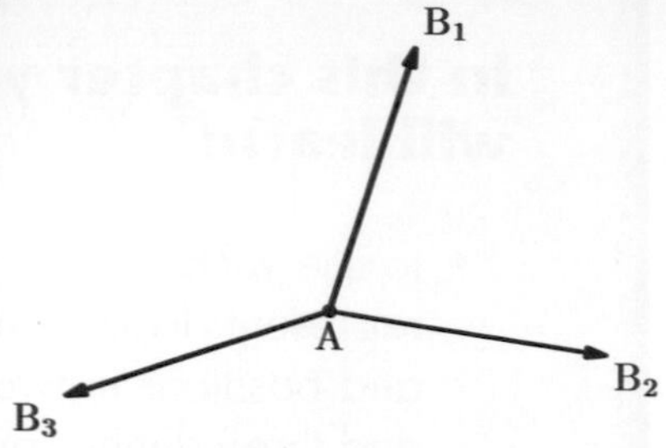

Consider a fixed point A and another point B that is 10 cm away from it. This information alone does not tell you where B is; for example, it could be any of the three positions shown in the diagram.

The position of B relative to A can be represented by the **displacement vector** $\overrightarrow{AB}$. The vector contains both distance and direction information. We can think of $\overrightarrow{AB}$ as describing a way of getting from A to B.

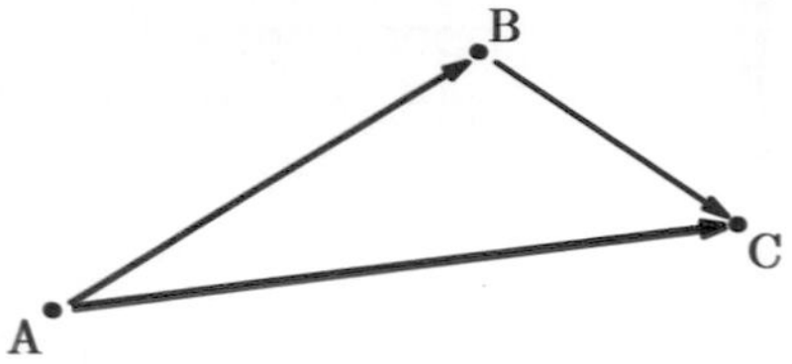

If we now add a third point, C, then there are two ways of getting from A to C: either directly, or via B. To express the second possibility using vectors, we write $\overrightarrow{AC} = \overrightarrow{AB} + \overrightarrow{BC}$; the addition sign means that moving from A to B is followed by moving from B to C.

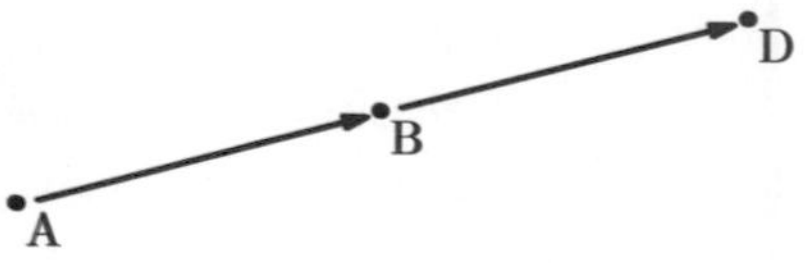

Remember that while a vector represents a way of getting from one point to another, it does not tell us anything about the position of the starting point or end point; nor does it provide any information about what route was taken. If getting from B to D involves moving the same distance and in the same direction as getting from A to B, then the displacement vectors are the same: $\overrightarrow{BD} = \overrightarrow{AB}$.

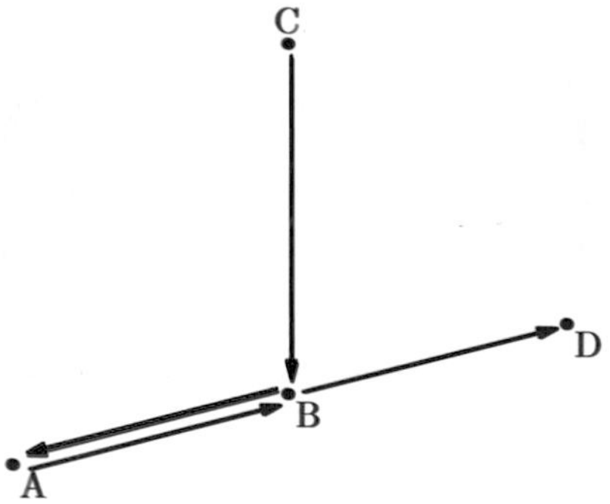

To return from the end point to the starting point, we have to reverse direction; this is represented by a minus sign, so $\overrightarrow{BA} = -\overrightarrow{AB}$. We can also use a subtraction sign between two vectors; for example, $\overrightarrow{CB} - \overrightarrow{AB} = \overrightarrow{CB} + \overrightarrow{BA}$.

To get from A to D we need to move in the same direction, but twice as far, as in getting from A to B. We express this as $\overrightarrow{AD} = 2\overrightarrow{AB}$ or, equivalently, $\overrightarrow{AB} = \frac{1}{2}\overrightarrow{AD}$.

To refer to vectors conveniently, we often give them letters as names, just as we do with variables in algebra. To emphasise that something is a vector rather than a scalar (number), we use either bold type or an arrow on top. When writing by hand, we use underlining instead of bold type. For example, we can denote vector $\overrightarrow{AB}$ by $\boldsymbol{a}$ (you may also see $\vec{a}$ used in some texts). Then in the diagrams above, $\overrightarrow{BD} = \boldsymbol{a}$, $\overrightarrow{BA} = -\boldsymbol{a}$ and $\overrightarrow{AD} = 2\boldsymbol{a}$.

EXAM HINT

Fractions of a vector are usually written as multiples, e.g. $\frac{1}{2}\overrightarrow{AD}$ rather than $\frac{\overrightarrow{AD}}{2}$.

Worked example 11.1

The diagram shows a parallelogram ABCD. Let $\overrightarrow{AB} = \boldsymbol{a}$ and $\overrightarrow{AD} = \boldsymbol{b}$. M is the midpoint of [CD], and N is the point on (BC) such that CN = BC.

Express the vectors $\overrightarrow{CM}$, $\overrightarrow{BN}$ and $\overrightarrow{MN}$ in terms of $\boldsymbol{a}$ and $\boldsymbol{b}$.

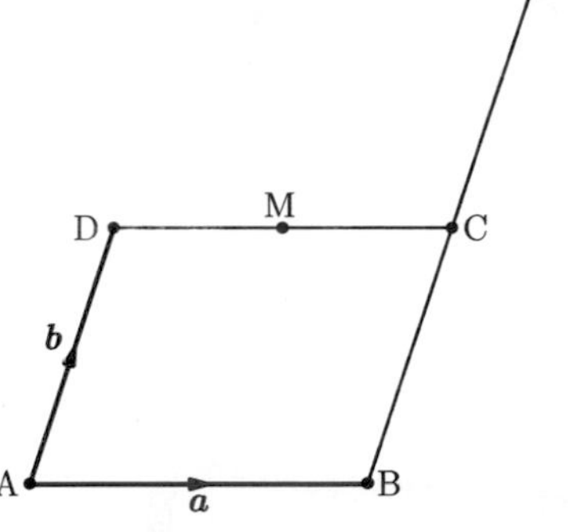

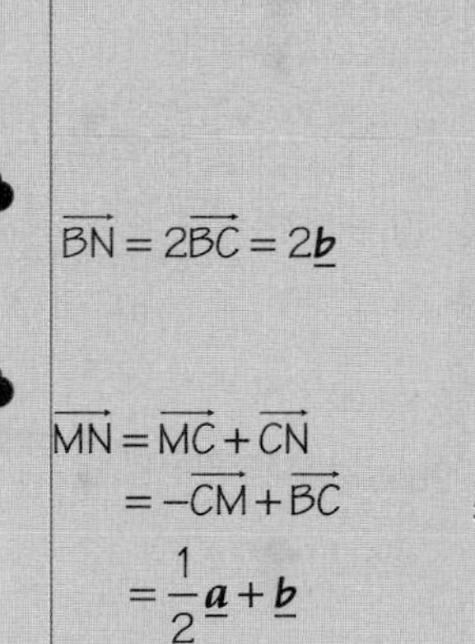

Think of $\overrightarrow{CM}$ as describing a way of getting from C to M by moving only along the directions of $\boldsymbol{a}$ and $\boldsymbol{b}$. Going from C to M is the same as going half way from B to A, and we know $\overrightarrow{BA} = -\overrightarrow{AB}$.

$\overrightarrow{CM} = \frac{1}{2}\overrightarrow{BA} = -\frac{1}{2}\underline{a}$

Going from B to N involves moving twice the distance in the same direction as from B to C, and $\overrightarrow{BC} = \overrightarrow{AD}$.

$\overrightarrow{BN} = 2\overrightarrow{BC} = 2\underline{b}$

To get from M to N, we can go from M to C and then from C to N. $\overrightarrow{MC} = -\overrightarrow{CM}$ and $\overrightarrow{CN} = \overrightarrow{BC}$.

$$\begin{aligned}\overrightarrow{MN} &= \overrightarrow{MC} + \overrightarrow{CN}\\ &= -\overrightarrow{CM} + \overrightarrow{BC}\\ &= \frac{1}{2}\underline{a} + \underline{b}\end{aligned}$$

To make it easier to do further calculations with vectors, we need a way of describing them using numbers, not just diagrams. You are already familiar with coordinates, which are used to represent positions of points. A similar idea can be used to represent vectors.

Let us start by looking at displacements in the plane. Select two directions perpendicular to each other, and let $\boldsymbol{i}$ and $\boldsymbol{j}$ denote vectors of length 1 in those two directions. Then any vector in the plane can be expressed in terms of $\boldsymbol{i}$ and $\boldsymbol{j}$, as shown in the diagram. The vectors $\boldsymbol{i}$ and $\boldsymbol{j}$ are called **base vectors**.

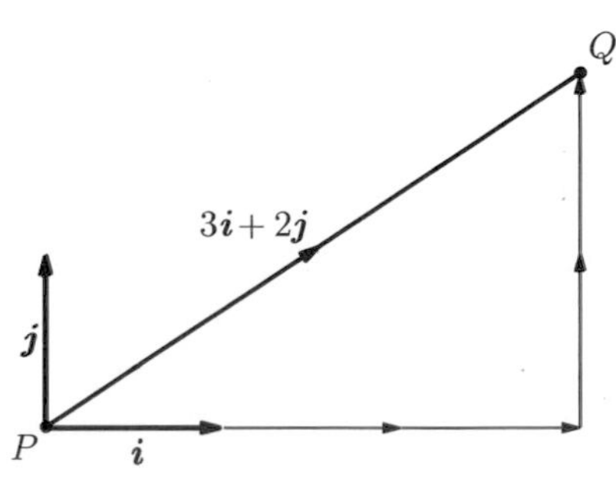

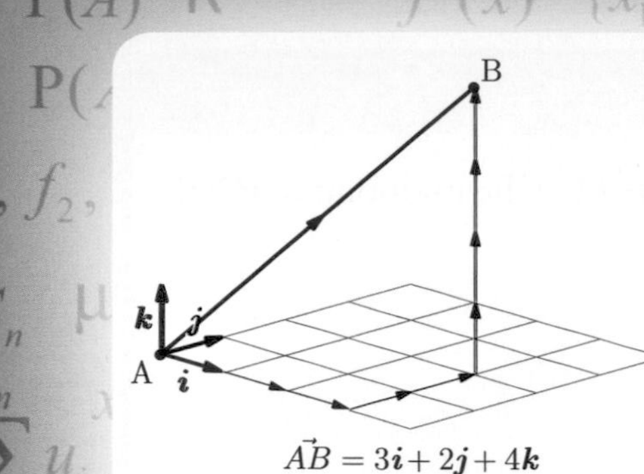

$\vec{AB} = 3i + 2j + 4k$

To represent displacements in three-dimensional space, we need three base vectors, all perpendicular to each other. They are conventionally called $\boldsymbol{i}$, $\boldsymbol{j}$ and $\boldsymbol{k}$, where $\boldsymbol{i}$ represents one unit in the x direction, $\boldsymbol{j}$ represents one unit in the y direction and $\boldsymbol{k}$ represents one unit in the z direction. In the diagram alongside, $\overrightarrow{AB} = 3\boldsymbol{i} + 2\boldsymbol{j} + 4\boldsymbol{k}$.

Alternatively, displacements can be written as **column vectors**. In this notation, the displacements in the diagrams above would be expressed as $\overrightarrow{PQ} = \begin{pmatrix} 3 \\ 2 \end{pmatrix}$ and $\overrightarrow{AB} = \begin{pmatrix} 3 \\ 2 \\ 4 \end{pmatrix}$.

EXAM HINT

You need to be familiar with both base vector and column vector notation, as both will be used in exam questions. When writing answers, you can use whichever notation you prefer.

The numbers in each column are called the **components** of the vector.

Using components makes it easy to add displacements. In the diagram below, to get from A to B we need to move 3 units in the $\boldsymbol{i}$ direction, and to get from B to P we need to move 5 units in the $\boldsymbol{i}$ direction; thus, getting from A to P requires moving a total of 8 units in the $\boldsymbol{i}$ direction. Similarly, in the $\boldsymbol{j}$ direction we move −2 units from A to B and 4 units from B to P, making the total movement in the $\boldsymbol{j}$ direction from A to P equal to +2 units. As the total displacement from A to P is $\overrightarrow{AP} = \overrightarrow{AB} + \overrightarrow{BP}$, we can write $(3\boldsymbol{i} - 2\boldsymbol{j}) + (5\boldsymbol{i} + 4\boldsymbol{j}) = 8\boldsymbol{i} + 2\boldsymbol{j}$ or, in column vector notation,

$$\begin{pmatrix} 3 \\ -2 \end{pmatrix} + \begin{pmatrix} 5 \\ 4 \end{pmatrix} = \begin{pmatrix} 8 \\ 2 \end{pmatrix}.$$

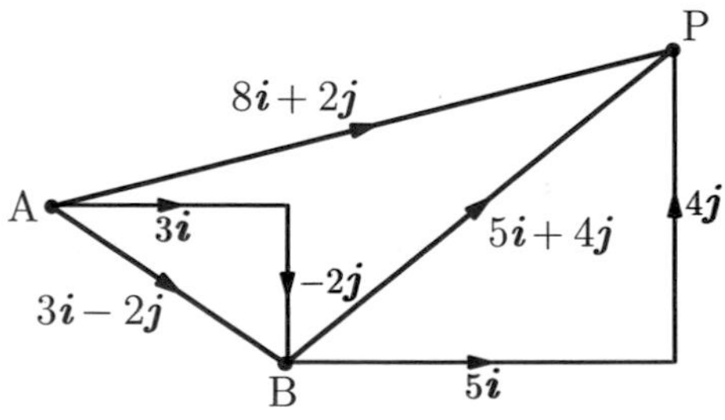

Reversing the direction of a vector is also simple in component notation: to get from B to A we need to move −3 units in the $\boldsymbol{i}$ direction and 2 units in the $\boldsymbol{j}$ direction; thus $\overrightarrow{BA} = -\overrightarrow{AB} = \begin{pmatrix} -3 \\ 2 \end{pmatrix}$.

Analogous rules for adding and subtracting vectors – that is, doing so component by component – apply in three dimensions as well.

Worked example 11.2

The diagram shows points M, N, P and Q such that $\overrightarrow{MN} = 3\boldsymbol{i} - 2\boldsymbol{j} + 6\boldsymbol{k}$, $\overrightarrow{NP} = \boldsymbol{i} + \boldsymbol{j} - 3\boldsymbol{k}$ and $\overrightarrow{MQ} = -2\boldsymbol{j} + 5\boldsymbol{k}$.

Write the following vectors in component form:

(a) $\overrightarrow{MP}$

(b) $\overrightarrow{PM}$

(c) $\overrightarrow{PQ}$

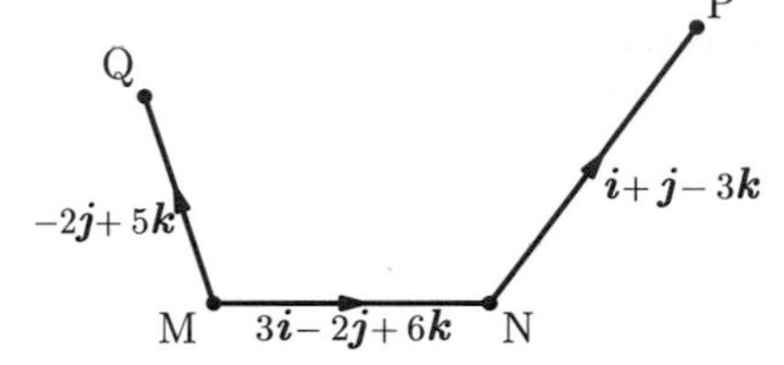

We can get from M to P via N.

(a) $\overrightarrow{MP} = \overrightarrow{MN} + \overrightarrow{NP}$
$= (3\underline{i} - 2\underline{j} + 6\underline{k}) + (\underline{i} + \underline{j} - 3\underline{k})$
$= 4\underline{i} - \underline{j} + 3\underline{k}$

We have already found $\overrightarrow{MP}$.

(b) $\overrightarrow{PM} = -\overrightarrow{MP} = -4\underline{i} + \underline{j} - 3\underline{k}$

We can get from P to Q via M, using the answers from the previous parts.

(c) $\overrightarrow{PQ} = \overrightarrow{PM} + \overrightarrow{MQ}$
$= (-4\underline{i} + \underline{j} - 3\underline{k}) + (-2\underline{j} + 5\underline{k})$
$= -4\underline{i} - \underline{j} + 2\underline{k}$

EXAM HINT

As you can see from this example, vector diagrams do not have to be accurate or to scale to be useful: a two-dimensional sketch of a 3D situation is often enough to show you what is going on.

We have been speaking of vectors as representing displacements, but they can also be used to represent positions of points. To do this, we fix one particular point, called the *origin*; then the position of any point can be thought of as its displacement from the origin. For example, the position of point P in the diagram can be described by its **position vector** $\overrightarrow{OP}$.

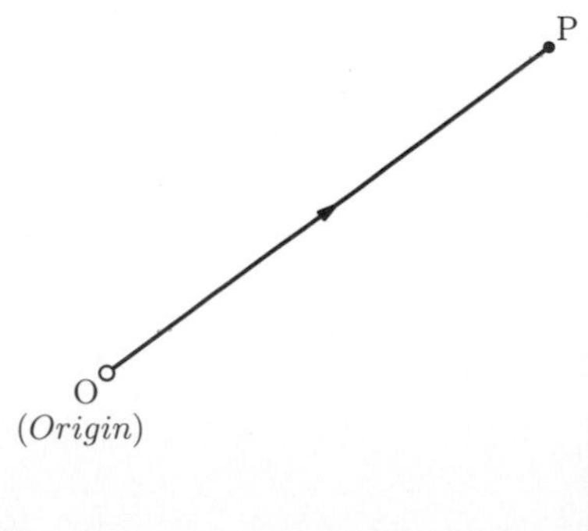

If we know the position vectors of two points A and B, we can find the displacement $\overrightarrow{AB}$ as shown in the diagram in Key point 11.1 on the next page.

Taking the route from A to O and then on to B, we get $\overrightarrow{AB} = \overrightarrow{AO} + \overrightarrow{OB}$. But since $\overrightarrow{AO} = -\overrightarrow{OA}$, we find that $\overrightarrow{AB} = -\overrightarrow{OA} + \overrightarrow{OB} = \overrightarrow{OB} - \overrightarrow{OA}$.

EXAM HINT

The position vector of point A is usually denoted by $\boldsymbol{a}$.

If points A and B have position vectors $\boldsymbol{a}$ and $\boldsymbol{b}$, then $\overrightarrow{AB} = \boldsymbol{b} - \boldsymbol{a}$.

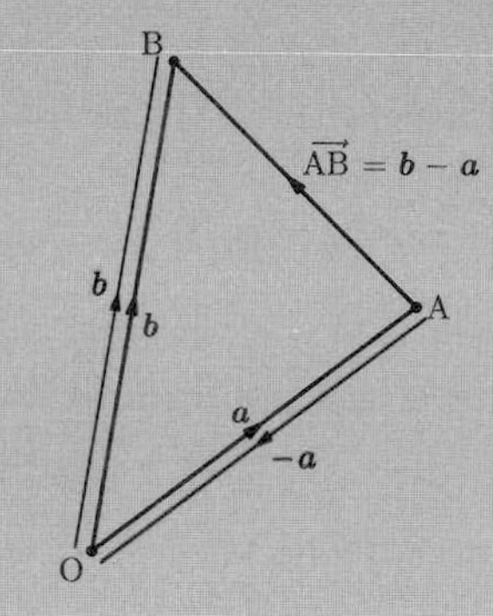

Position vectors are closely related to coordinates. As the base vectors $\boldsymbol{i}, \boldsymbol{j}$ and $\boldsymbol{k}$ are chosen to have directions along the coordinate axes, the components of the position vector will simply be the coordinates of the point.

Worked example 11.3

Points A and B have coordinates (3,−1,2) and (5,0,3), respectively. Write as column vectors

(a) the position vectors of A and B

(b) the displacement vector $\overrightarrow{AB}$.

The components of the position vectors are the coordinates of the point.

(a) $\underline{a} = \begin{pmatrix} 3 \\ -1 \\ 2 \end{pmatrix} \quad \underline{b} = \begin{pmatrix} 5 \\ 0 \\ 3 \end{pmatrix}$

(b) $\overrightarrow{AB} = \underline{b} - \underline{a}$

$= \begin{pmatrix} 5 \\ 0 \\ 3 \end{pmatrix} - \begin{pmatrix} 3 \\ -1 \\ 2 \end{pmatrix}$

$= \begin{pmatrix} 2 \\ 1 \\ 1 \end{pmatrix}$

Worked example 11.4

Points A, B, C and D have position vectors $\boldsymbol{a} = \begin{pmatrix} 3 \\ -1 \\ 1 \end{pmatrix}$, $\boldsymbol{b} = \begin{pmatrix} 5 \\ 0 \\ 3 \end{pmatrix}$, $\boldsymbol{c} = \begin{pmatrix} 7 \\ 8 \\ -3 \end{pmatrix}$, $\boldsymbol{d} = \begin{pmatrix} 4 \\ 3 \\ -2 \end{pmatrix}$.

Point E is the midpoint of [BC].

(a) Find the position vector of E.

(b) Show that ABED is a parallelogram.

Make a sketch to try to see what is going on.

For part (a), we only need to look at points B, C and E. As we are given the position vectors, it will help to show the origin on the diagram.

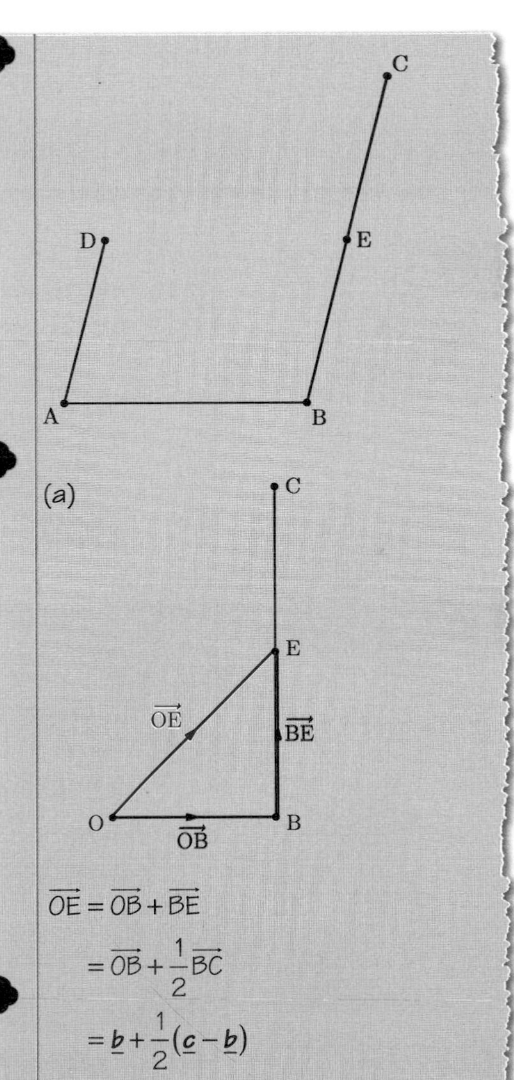

Use relationship $\overrightarrow{AB} = \boldsymbol{b} - \boldsymbol{a}$

$$\overrightarrow{OE} = \overrightarrow{OB} + \overrightarrow{BE}$$

$$= \overrightarrow{OB} + \frac{1}{2}\overrightarrow{BC}$$

$$= \underline{b} + \frac{1}{2}(\underline{c} - \underline{b})$$

$$= \frac{1}{2}\underline{b} + \frac{1}{2}\underline{c}$$

$$= \begin{pmatrix} 2.5 \\ 0 \\ 1.5 \end{pmatrix} + \begin{pmatrix} 3.5 \\ 4 \\ -1.5 \end{pmatrix} = \begin{pmatrix} 6 \\ 4 \\ 0 \end{pmatrix}$$

continued . . .

In a parallelogram, opposite sides are parallel and of the same length, which means that the vectors corresponding to those sides are equal. So we need to show that $\overrightarrow{AD} = \overrightarrow{BE}$.

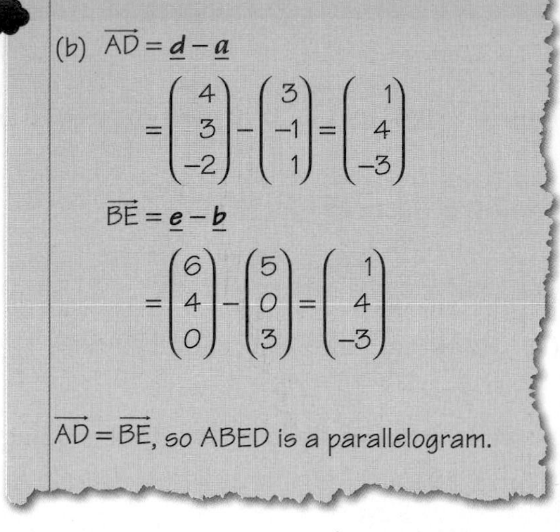
(b) $\overrightarrow{AD} = \underline{d} - \underline{a}$
$= \begin{pmatrix} 4 \\ 3 \\ -2 \end{pmatrix} - \begin{pmatrix} 3 \\ -1 \\ 1 \end{pmatrix} = \begin{pmatrix} 1 \\ 4 \\ -3 \end{pmatrix}$
$\overrightarrow{BE} = \underline{e} - \underline{b}$
$= \begin{pmatrix} 6 \\ 4 \\ 0 \end{pmatrix} - \begin{pmatrix} 5 \\ 0 \\ 3 \end{pmatrix} = \begin{pmatrix} 1 \\ 4 \\ -3 \end{pmatrix}$
$\overrightarrow{AD} = \overrightarrow{BE}$, so ABED is a parallelogram.

In part (a) of the above example we derived a general formula for the position vector of the midpoint of a line segment.

KEY POINT 11.2

The position vector of the midpoint of [AB] is $\frac{1}{2}(\boldsymbol{a} + \boldsymbol{b})$.

Exercise 11A

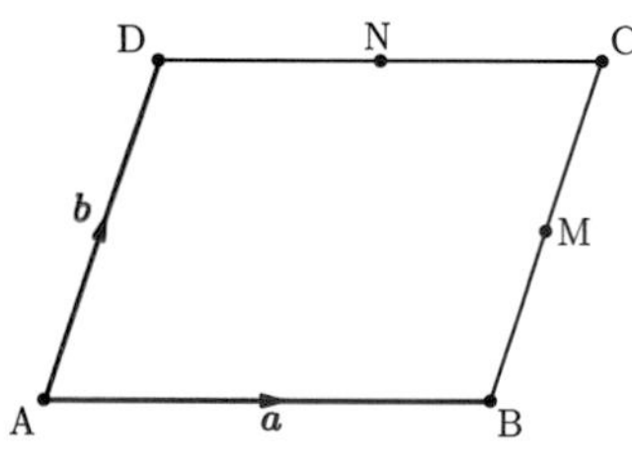
D
N
C
b
M
A
a
B

1. The diagram shows a parallelogram ABCD with $\overrightarrow{AB} = \boldsymbol{a}$ and $\overrightarrow{AD} = \boldsymbol{b}$. M is the midpoint of [BC] and N is the midpoint of [CD]. Express the following vectors in terms of $\boldsymbol{a}$ and $\boldsymbol{b}$.

   (a) (i) $\overrightarrow{BC}$ (ii) $\overrightarrow{AC}$

   (b) (i) $\overrightarrow{CD}$ (ii) $\overrightarrow{ND}$

   (c) (i) $\overrightarrow{AM}$ (ii) $\overrightarrow{MN}$

2. In the parallelogram ABCD, $\overrightarrow{AB} = \boldsymbol{a}$ and $\overrightarrow{AD} = \boldsymbol{b}$. M is the midpoint of [BC], Q is the point on (AB) such that $BQ = \frac{1}{2}AB$, and P is the point on (BC) such that $BC : CP = 3 : 1$, as shown in the diagram.

Express the following vectors in terms of $\boldsymbol{a}$ and $\boldsymbol{b}$.

(a) (i) $\overrightarrow{AP}$ (ii) $\overrightarrow{AM}$

(b) (i) $\overrightarrow{QD}$ (ii) $\overrightarrow{MQ}$

(c) (i) $\overrightarrow{DQ}$ (ii) $\overrightarrow{PQ}$

3. Write the following vectors in three-dimensional column vector notation.

(a) (i) $4\boldsymbol{i}$ (ii) $-5\boldsymbol{j}$

(b) (i) $3\boldsymbol{i}+\boldsymbol{k}$ (ii) $2\boldsymbol{j}-\boldsymbol{k}$

4. Three points O, A and B are given. Let $\overrightarrow{OA}=\boldsymbol{a}$ and $\overrightarrow{OB}=\boldsymbol{b}$.

(a) Express $\overrightarrow{AB}$ in terms of $\boldsymbol{a}$ and $\boldsymbol{b}$.

(b) C is the midpoint of [AB]. Express $\overrightarrow{OC}$ in terms of $\boldsymbol{a}$ and $\boldsymbol{b}$.

(c) Point D lies on the line (AB), on the same side of B as A, so that AD = [3AB]. Express $\overrightarrow{OD}$ in terms of $\boldsymbol{a}$ and $\boldsymbol{b}$. *[5 marks]*

5. Points A and B lie in a plane and have coordinates (3, 0) and (4,2) respectively. C is the midpoint of [AB].

(a) Express $\overrightarrow{AB}$ and $\overrightarrow{AC}$ as column vectors.

(b) Point D is such that $\overrightarrow{AD}=\begin{pmatrix}7\\-2\end{pmatrix}$. Find the coordinates of D. *[5 marks]*

6. Points A and B have position vectors $\overrightarrow{OA}=\begin{pmatrix}3\\1\\-2\end{pmatrix}$ and $\overrightarrow{OB}=\begin{pmatrix}4\\-2\\5\end{pmatrix}$.

(a) Write $\overrightarrow{AB}$ as a column vector.

(b) Find the position vector of the midpoint of [AB]. *[5 marks]*

7. Point A has position vector $\boldsymbol{a}=2\boldsymbol{i}-3\boldsymbol{j}$, and point D is such that $\overrightarrow{AD}=\boldsymbol{i}-\boldsymbol{j}$. Find the position vector of point D. *[4 marks]*

8. Points A and B have position vectors $\boldsymbol{a}=\begin{pmatrix}2\\2\\1\end{pmatrix}$ and $\boldsymbol{b}=\begin{pmatrix}1\\-1\\3\end{pmatrix}$.

Point C lies on [AB] so that AC : BC = 2 : 3. Find the position vector of C. *[5 marks]*

9. Points P and Q have position vectors $\boldsymbol{p} = 2\boldsymbol{i} - \boldsymbol{j} - 3\boldsymbol{k}$ and $\boldsymbol{q} = \boldsymbol{i} + 4\boldsymbol{j} - \boldsymbol{k}$.

(a) Find the position vector of the midpoint M of [PQ].

(b) Point R lies on the line (PQ) such that QR = QM. Find the coordinates of R if R and M are distinct points. *[6 marks]*

10. Points A, B and C have position vectors $\boldsymbol{a} = \begin{pmatrix} 2 \\ -1 \\ 4 \end{pmatrix}$, $\boldsymbol{b} = \begin{pmatrix} 5 \\ 1 \\ 2 \end{pmatrix}$ and $\boldsymbol{c} = \begin{pmatrix} 3 \\ 1 \\ 4 \end{pmatrix}$. Find the position vector of point D such that ABCD is a parallelogram. *[5 marks]*

EXAM HINT

The ability to switch between diagrams and equations is essential for solving harder vector problems.

EXAM HINT

Remember that vectors only show the *relative* positions of two points; they don't have a fixed starting point. This means we are free to 'move' the second vector so that its starting point coincides with the end point of the first.

11B Vector algebra

In the previous section we used vectors to describe positions and displacements of points in space; we also mentioned that vectors can represent quantities other than displacements, for example velocities or forces. Whatever the vectors represent, they always follow the same algebraic rules. In this section we will summarise those rules, which can be expressed using either diagrams or equations.

Vector addition can be done on a diagram by joining the starting point of the second vector to the end point of the first; the sum of the two vectors is the vector which starts at the starting point of the first vector and ends at the end point of the second vector. In component form, we add vectors by adding their corresponding components. When the vectors describe displacements, addition represents one displacement followed by another.

$$\begin{pmatrix} 3 \\ 1 \\ -2 \end{pmatrix} + \begin{pmatrix} 2 \\ 2 \\ 6 \end{pmatrix} = \begin{pmatrix} 5 \\ 3 \\ 4 \end{pmatrix}$$

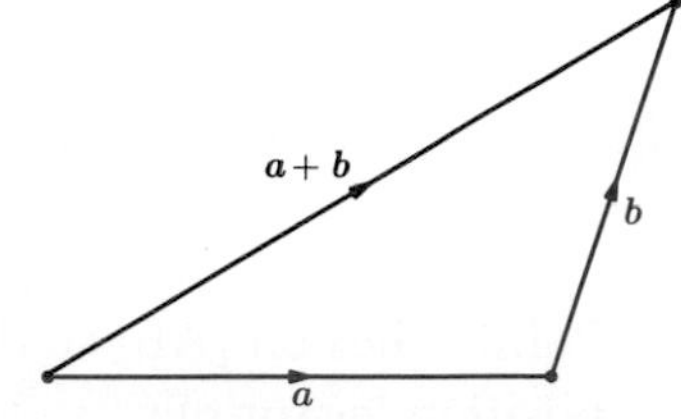

Another way of visualising the sum of two vectors is as the diagonal of the parallelogram formed by the two vectors being added.

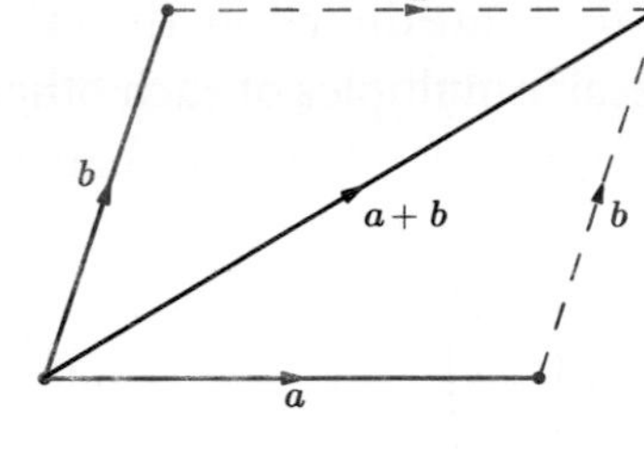

As we saw in section 11A, reversing the direction of a vector is represented by taking its negative; in component form, this means switching the signs of all the components. *Subtracting* a vector is the same as adding its negative. It is carried out in component form by subtracting corresponding components. When the vectors describe displacements, subtracting a vector represents moving along the vector from the end point back to the starting point.

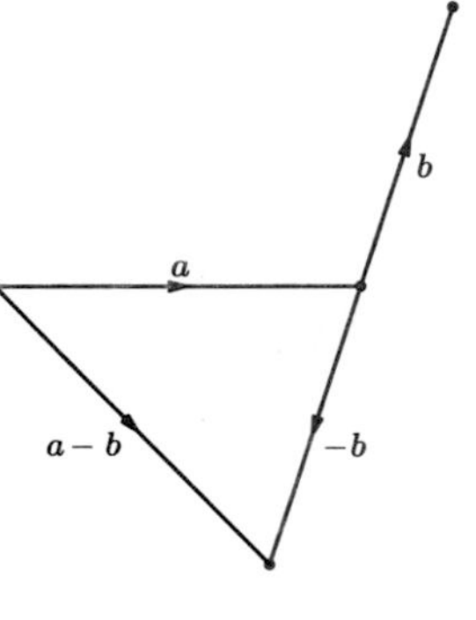

$$\begin{pmatrix} 5 \\ 1 \\ -2 \end{pmatrix} - \begin{pmatrix} 3 \\ 3 \\ -3 \end{pmatrix} = \begin{pmatrix} 5 \\ 1 \\ -2 \end{pmatrix} + \begin{pmatrix} -3 \\ -3 \\ 3 \end{pmatrix} = \begin{pmatrix} 2 \\ -2 \\ 1 \end{pmatrix}$$

The difference of two vectors can be represented by the other diagonal of the parallelogram formed by the two vectors.

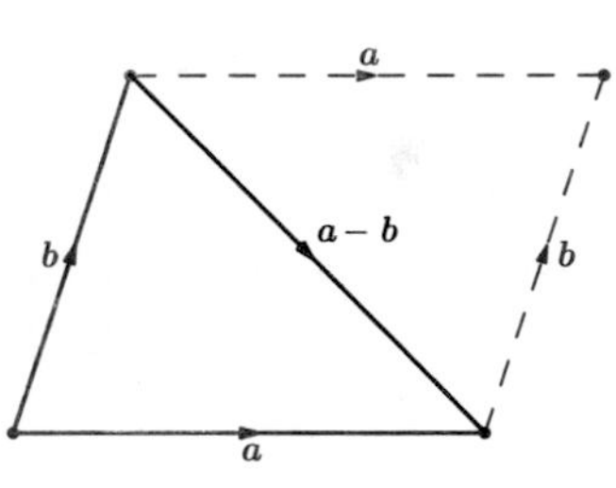

Scalar multiplication changes the magnitude (length) of the vector, leaving the direction the same. In component form, each component is multiplied by the scalar. For a displacement vector ***a***, k***a*** represents a displacement in the same direction but with distance multiplied by k.

$$2\begin{pmatrix} 3 \\ -5 \\ 0 \end{pmatrix} = \begin{pmatrix} 6 \\ -10 \\ 0 \end{pmatrix}$$

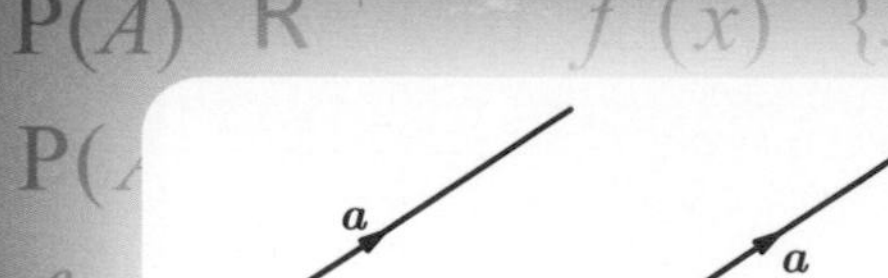

Two vectors are *equal* if they have the same magnitude and direction. All their components are equal. They represent the same displacements but may have different start and end points.

If two vectors are in the same direction, then they are **parallel**. Parallel vectors are scalar multiples of each other, since multiplying a vector by a scalar does not change its direction.

$\begin{pmatrix} 2 \\ -3 \\ 1 \end{pmatrix}$ is parallel to $\begin{pmatrix} 6 \\ -9 \\ 3 \end{pmatrix}$

because $\begin{pmatrix} 6 \\ -9 \\ 3 \end{pmatrix} = 3\begin{pmatrix} 2 \\ -3 \\ 1 \end{pmatrix}$

KEY POINT 11.3

If vectors $\boldsymbol{a}$ and $\boldsymbol{b}$ are parallel, we can write $\boldsymbol{b} = t\boldsymbol{a}$ for some scalar t.

The following example illustrates the vector operations we have just described.

Worked example 11.5

Given the vectors $\boldsymbol{a} = \begin{pmatrix} 1 \\ 2 \\ 7 \end{pmatrix}$, $\boldsymbol{b} = \begin{pmatrix} -3 \\ 4 \\ 2 \end{pmatrix}$ and $\boldsymbol{c} = \begin{pmatrix} -2 \\ p \\ q \end{pmatrix}$

(a) Find $2\boldsymbol{a} - 3\boldsymbol{b}$.

(b) Find the values of p and q such that $\boldsymbol{c}$ is parallel to $\boldsymbol{a}$.

(c) Find the value of the scalar k such that $\boldsymbol{a} + k\boldsymbol{b}$ is parallel to vector $\begin{pmatrix} 0 \\ 10 \\ 23 \end{pmatrix}$.

(a) $2\underline{a} - 3\underline{b} = 2\begin{pmatrix} 1 \\ 2 \\ 7 \end{pmatrix} - 3\begin{pmatrix} -3 \\ 4 \\ 2 \end{pmatrix}$

$= \begin{pmatrix} 2 \\ 4 \\ 14 \end{pmatrix} - \begin{pmatrix} -9 \\ 12 \\ 6 \end{pmatrix} = \begin{pmatrix} 11 \\ -8 \\ 8 \end{pmatrix}$

continued . . .

If two vectors are parallel we can write $\mathbf{v}_2 = t\mathbf{v}_1$.

(b) Write $\underline{c} = t\underline{a}$ for some scalar t. Then

$$\begin{pmatrix}-2\\p\\q\end{pmatrix} = t\begin{pmatrix}1\\2\\7\end{pmatrix} = \begin{pmatrix}t\\2t\\7t\end{pmatrix}$$

Two vectors being equal means that all their components are equal.

$$\Leftrightarrow \begin{cases}-2 = t\\ p = 2t\\ q = 7t\end{cases}$$

$\therefore p = -4, q = -14$

We can write vector $\boldsymbol{a} + k\boldsymbol{b}$ in terms of k and then solve $\boldsymbol{a} + k\boldsymbol{b} = t\begin{pmatrix}0\\10\\23\end{pmatrix}$.

(c) $\underline{a} + k\underline{b} = \begin{pmatrix}1\\2\\7\end{pmatrix} + \begin{pmatrix}-3k\\4k\\2k\end{pmatrix} = \begin{pmatrix}1-3k\\2+4k\\7+2k\end{pmatrix}$

Parallel to $\begin{pmatrix}0\\10\\23\end{pmatrix}$

$$\Rightarrow \begin{pmatrix}1-3k\\2+4k\\7+2k\end{pmatrix} = t\begin{pmatrix}0\\10\\23\end{pmatrix}$$

$$\Leftrightarrow \begin{cases}1-3k = 0\\ 2+4k = 10t\\ 7+2k = 23t\end{cases}$$

We can find k from just the first equation; however, we still need to check that all three equations can be satisfied by this value of k.

$1-3k = 0 \Rightarrow k = \frac{1}{3}$

From 2nd equation,

$2+4\left(\frac{1}{3}\right) = 10t \Rightarrow t = \frac{1}{3}$

Put values into 3rd equation:

$\text{LHS} = 7+2\left(\frac{1}{3}\right) = \frac{23}{3}$

$\text{RHS} = 23\left(\frac{1}{3}\right)$ $\therefore$ satisfied

$\therefore k = \frac{1}{3}$

Exercise 11B

1. Let $\boldsymbol{a} = \begin{pmatrix} 7 \\ 1 \\ 12 \end{pmatrix}$, $\boldsymbol{b} = \begin{pmatrix} 5 \\ -2 \\ 3 \end{pmatrix}$ and $\boldsymbol{c} = \begin{pmatrix} 1 \\ 1 \\ 2 \end{pmatrix}$. Find the following vectors.

   (a) (i) $3\boldsymbol{a}$ (ii) $4\boldsymbol{b}$

   (b) (i) $\boldsymbol{a} - \boldsymbol{b}$ (ii) $\boldsymbol{b} + \boldsymbol{c}$

   (c) (i) $2\boldsymbol{b} + \boldsymbol{c}$ (ii) $\boldsymbol{a} - 2\boldsymbol{b}$

   (d) (i) $\boldsymbol{a} + \boldsymbol{b} - 2\boldsymbol{c}$ (ii) $3\boldsymbol{a} - \boldsymbol{b} + \boldsymbol{c}$

2. Let $\boldsymbol{a} = \boldsymbol{i} + 2\boldsymbol{j}$, $\boldsymbol{b} = \boldsymbol{i} - \boldsymbol{k}$ and $\boldsymbol{c} = 2\boldsymbol{i} - \boldsymbol{j} + 3\boldsymbol{k}$. Find the following vectors:

   (a) (i) $-5\boldsymbol{b}$ (ii) $4\boldsymbol{a}$

   (b) (i) $\boldsymbol{c} - \boldsymbol{a}$ (ii) $\boldsymbol{a} - \boldsymbol{b}$

   (c) (i) $\boldsymbol{a} - \boldsymbol{b} + 2\boldsymbol{c}$ (ii) $4\boldsymbol{c} - 3\boldsymbol{b}$

3. Given that $\boldsymbol{a} = 4\boldsymbol{i} - 2\boldsymbol{j} + \boldsymbol{k}$, find the vector $\boldsymbol{b}$ such that

   (a) $\boldsymbol{a} + \boldsymbol{b}$ is the zero vector

   (b) $2\boldsymbol{a} + 3\boldsymbol{b}$ is the zero vector

   (c) $\boldsymbol{a} - \boldsymbol{b} = \boldsymbol{j}$

   (d) $\boldsymbol{a} + 2\boldsymbol{b} = 3\boldsymbol{i}$

4. Given that $\boldsymbol{a} = \begin{pmatrix} -1 \\ 1 \\ 2 \end{pmatrix}$ and $\boldsymbol{b} = \begin{pmatrix} 5 \\ 3 \\ 3 \end{pmatrix}$, find the vector $\boldsymbol{x}$ such that

   $3\boldsymbol{a} + 4\boldsymbol{x} = \boldsymbol{b}$. *[4 marks]*

5. Given that $\boldsymbol{a} = 3\boldsymbol{i} - 2\boldsymbol{j} + 5\boldsymbol{k}$, $\boldsymbol{b} = \boldsymbol{i} - \boldsymbol{j} + 2\boldsymbol{k}$ and $\boldsymbol{c} = \boldsymbol{i} + \boldsymbol{k}$, find the value of the scalar t such that $\boldsymbol{a} + t\boldsymbol{b} = \boldsymbol{c}$. *[4 marks]*

6. Given that $\boldsymbol{a} = \begin{pmatrix} 2 \\ 0 \\ 2 \end{pmatrix}$ and $\boldsymbol{b} = \begin{pmatrix} 3 \\ 1 \\ 3 \end{pmatrix}$, find the value of the scalar p

   such that $\boldsymbol{a} + p\boldsymbol{b}$ is parallel to the vector $\begin{pmatrix} 3 \\ 2 \\ 3 \end{pmatrix}$. *[5 marks]*

7. Given that $\boldsymbol{x} = 2\boldsymbol{i} + 3\boldsymbol{j} + \boldsymbol{k}$ and $\boldsymbol{y} = 4\boldsymbol{i} + \boldsymbol{j} + 2\boldsymbol{k}$, find the value of the scalar λ such that $\lambda\boldsymbol{x} + \boldsymbol{y}$ is parallel to vector $\boldsymbol{j}$. *[5 marks]*

8. Given that $\boldsymbol{a} = \boldsymbol{i} - \boldsymbol{j} + 3\boldsymbol{k}$ and $\boldsymbol{b} = 2q\boldsymbol{i} + \boldsymbol{j} + q\boldsymbol{k}$, find the values of scalars p and q such that $p\boldsymbol{a} + \boldsymbol{b}$ is parallel to the vector $\boldsymbol{i} + \boldsymbol{j} + 2\boldsymbol{k}$. *[6 marks]*

11C Distances

Geometry problems often involve finding distances between points. In this section we will see how to do this using vectors.

Consider two points A and B such that the displacement between them is $\overrightarrow{AB} = \begin{pmatrix} 3 \\ 1 \\ 4 \end{pmatrix}$. The distance AB can be found by using Pythagoras' Theorem in three dimensions:

$AB = \sqrt{3^2 + 1^2 + 4^2} = \sqrt{26}$.

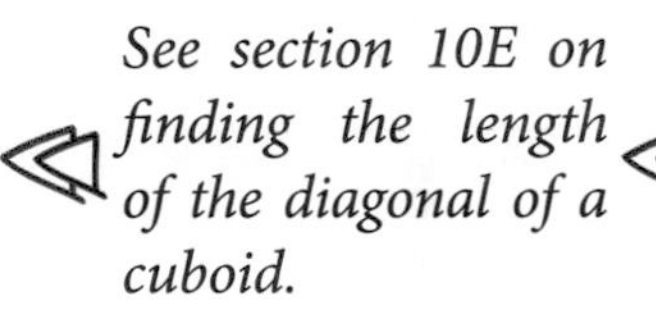

See section 10E on finding the length of the diagonal of a cuboid.

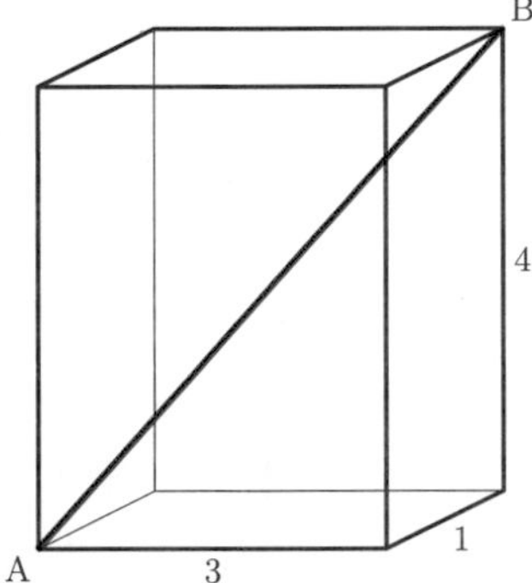

This quantity is called the **magnitude** of $\overrightarrow{AB}$, and is denoted by $\left|\overrightarrow{AB}\right|$.

If we know the position vectors of A and B, then to find the distance between A and B we need to find the displacement vector $\overrightarrow{AB}$ and then calculate its magnitude.

Worked example 11.6

Points A and B have position vectors $\boldsymbol{a} = \begin{pmatrix} 2 \\ -1 \\ 5 \end{pmatrix}$ and $\boldsymbol{b} = \begin{pmatrix} 5 \\ 2 \\ 3 \end{pmatrix}$. Find the exact distance AB.

The distance is the magnitude of the displacement vector, so we need to find $\overrightarrow{AB}$ first.

$\overrightarrow{AB} = \underline{b} - \underline{a}$

$= \begin{pmatrix} 5 \\ 2 \\ 3 \end{pmatrix} - \begin{pmatrix} 2 \\ -1 \\ 5 \end{pmatrix} = \begin{pmatrix} 3 \\ 3 \\ -2 \end{pmatrix}$

Now use the formula for the magnitude.

$\left|\overrightarrow{AB}\right| = \sqrt{3^2 + 3^2 + (-2)^2} = \sqrt{22}$

EXAM HINT

Don't forget that squaring a negative number gives a positive value.

KEY POINT 11.4

The magnitude of a vector $\boldsymbol{a} = \begin{pmatrix} a_1 \\ a_2 \\ a_3 \end{pmatrix}$ is $|\boldsymbol{a}| = \sqrt{a_1^2 + a_2^2 + a_3^2}$.

A useful point that is not in the Formula booklet is: the distance between points with position vectors $\boldsymbol{a}$ and $\boldsymbol{b}$ is $|\boldsymbol{b} - \boldsymbol{a}|$.

We saw in section 11B that multiplying a vector by a scalar (other than 0 or 1) produces a vector in the same direction but of different magnitude. In more advanced applications of vectors it will be useful to produce vectors of length 1, called **unit vectors**. The base vectors $\boldsymbol{i}$, $\boldsymbol{j}$ and $\boldsymbol{k}$ are examples of unit vectors. For any vector $\boldsymbol{v}$, the unit vector in the direction of $\boldsymbol{v}$ is often written as $\hat{\boldsymbol{v}}$.

Worked example 11.7

(a) Find the unit vector in the same direction as $\boldsymbol{a} = \begin{pmatrix} 2 \\ -2 \\ 1 \end{pmatrix}$.

(b) Find a vector of magnitude 5 that is parallel to $\boldsymbol{a}$.

To produce a vector in the same direction as $\boldsymbol{a}$ but with a different magnitude, we need to multiply $\boldsymbol{a}$ by a scalar. We need to find the value of this scalar.

(a) Call the required unit vector $\hat{\underline{a}}$.

Then $\hat{\underline{a}} = k\underline{a}$ and $|\hat{\underline{a}}| = 1$.

$|k\underline{a}| = k|\underline{a}| = 1$

$\Rightarrow k = \frac{1}{|\underline{a}|}$

$|\underline{a}| = \sqrt{2^2 + 2^2 + 1^2} = 3$

$\therefore k = \frac{1}{3}$

Now find the vector $\hat{\boldsymbol{a}}$.

The unit vector is

$\hat{\underline{a}} = \frac{1}{3}\begin{pmatrix} 2 \\ -2 \\ 1 \end{pmatrix} = \begin{pmatrix} \frac{2}{3} \\ -\frac{2}{3} \\ \frac{1}{3} \end{pmatrix}$

To get a vector of magnitude 5, we multiply the unit vector by 5.

(b) Let $\underline{b}$ be parallel to $\underline{a}$ and $|\underline{b}| = 5$.

Then $\underline{b} = 5\hat{\underline{a}} = \begin{pmatrix} \frac{10}{3} \\ -\frac{10}{3} \\ \frac{5}{3} \end{pmatrix}$

EXAM HINT

In fact, part (b) has two possible answers, as **b** could be in the opposite direction to the one we found. To get the second answer, multiply the unit vector by –5 instead of 5.

Worked example 11.7 showed the general method for finding the unit vector in a given direction.

KEY POINT 11.5

The unit vector in the same direction as $\boldsymbol{a}$ is $\hat{\boldsymbol{a}} = \frac{1}{|\boldsymbol{a}|}\boldsymbol{a}$.

Exercise 11C

1. Find the magnitude of the following vectors in two dimensions:

   $\boldsymbol{a} = \begin{pmatrix} 4 \\ 2 \end{pmatrix}$ $\boldsymbol{b} = \begin{pmatrix} -1 \\ 5 \end{pmatrix}$ $\boldsymbol{c} = 2\boldsymbol{i} - 4\boldsymbol{j}$ $\boldsymbol{d} = -\boldsymbol{i} + \boldsymbol{j}$

2. Find the magnitude of the following vectors in three dimensions:

   $\boldsymbol{a} = \begin{pmatrix} 4 \\ 1 \\ 2 \end{pmatrix}$ $\boldsymbol{b} = \begin{pmatrix} 1 \\ -1 \\ 0 \end{pmatrix}$ $\boldsymbol{c} = 2\boldsymbol{i} - 4\boldsymbol{j} + \boldsymbol{k}$ $\boldsymbol{d} = \boldsymbol{j} - \boldsymbol{k}$

3. Find the distance between the following pairs of points in the plane.

   (a) (i) A(1,2) and B(3,7) (ii) C(2,1) and D(1,2)

   (b) (i) P(–1,–5) and Q(–4,2) (ii) M(1,0) and N(0,–2)

4. Find the distance between the following pairs of points in three dimensions.

   (a) (i) A(1,0,2) and B(2,3,5) (ii) C(2,1,7) and D(1,2,1)

   (b) (i) P(3,–1,–5) and Q(–1,–4,2) (ii) M(0,0,2) and N(0,–3,0)

5. Find the distance between the points with the given position vectors:

(a) $\boldsymbol{a} = 2\boldsymbol{i} + 4\boldsymbol{j} - 2\boldsymbol{k}$ and $\boldsymbol{b} = \boldsymbol{i} - 2\boldsymbol{j} - 6\boldsymbol{k}$

(b) $\boldsymbol{a} = \begin{pmatrix} 3 \\ 7 \\ -2 \end{pmatrix}$ and $\boldsymbol{b} = \begin{pmatrix} 1 \\ -2 \\ -5 \end{pmatrix}$

(c) $\boldsymbol{a} = \begin{pmatrix} 2 \\ 0 \\ -2 \end{pmatrix}$ and $\boldsymbol{b} = \begin{pmatrix} 0 \\ 0 \\ 5 \end{pmatrix}$

(d) $\boldsymbol{a} = \boldsymbol{i} + \boldsymbol{j}$ and $\boldsymbol{b} = \boldsymbol{j} - \boldsymbol{k}$

6. (a) (i) Find a unit vector parallel to $\begin{pmatrix} 2 \\ 2 \\ 1 \end{pmatrix}$.

(ii) Find a unit vector parallel to $6\boldsymbol{i} + 6\boldsymbol{j} - 3\boldsymbol{k}$.

(b) (i) Find a unit vector in the same direction as $\boldsymbol{i} + \boldsymbol{j} + \boldsymbol{k}$.

(ii) Find a unit vector in the same direction as $\begin{pmatrix} 4 \\ -1 \\ 2\sqrt{2} \end{pmatrix}$.

7. Find the possible values of the constant c such that the vector $\begin{pmatrix} 2c \\ c \\ -c \end{pmatrix}$ has magnitude 12. *[4 marks]*

8. Points A and B have position vectors $\boldsymbol{a} = \begin{pmatrix} 4 \\ 1 \\ 2 \end{pmatrix}$ and $\boldsymbol{b} = \begin{pmatrix} 2 \\ -1 \\ 3 \end{pmatrix}$. C is the midpoint of [AB]. Find the exact distance AC. *[4 marks]*

9. Let $\boldsymbol{a} = \begin{pmatrix} -2 \\ 0 \\ -1 \end{pmatrix}$ and $\boldsymbol{b} = \begin{pmatrix} 2 \\ -1 \\ 2 \end{pmatrix}$. Find the possible values of λ such that $|\boldsymbol{a} + \lambda\boldsymbol{b}| = 5\sqrt{2}$. *[6 marks]*

10. (a) Find a vector of magnitude 6 that is parallel to $\begin{pmatrix} 4 \\ -1 \\ 1 \end{pmatrix}$.

(b) Find a vector of magnitude 3 in the same direction as $2\boldsymbol{i} - \boldsymbol{j} + \boldsymbol{k}$. *[6 marks]*

11. Points A and B are such that $\overrightarrow{OA} = \begin{pmatrix} -1 \\ -6 \\ 13 \end{pmatrix}$ and $\overrightarrow{OB} = \begin{pmatrix} 1 \\ -2 \\ 4 \end{pmatrix} + t\begin{pmatrix} 2 \\ 1 \\ -5 \end{pmatrix}$ where O is the origin. Find the possible values of t such that $AB = 3$. *[5 marks]*

12. Points P and Q have position vectors $\boldsymbol{p} = \boldsymbol{i} + \boldsymbol{j} + 3\boldsymbol{k}$ and $\boldsymbol{q} = (2+t)\boldsymbol{i} + (1-t)\boldsymbol{j} + (1+t)\boldsymbol{k}$. Find the value of t for which the distance PQ is as small as possible and find this minimum distance. *[6 marks]*

11D Angles

In solving geometry problems, we often need to find angles between lines. The diagram shows two lines with angle θ between them; $\boldsymbol{a}$ and $\boldsymbol{b}$ are vectors in the directions of the two lines, arranged so that both arrows point away from the intersection point. It turns out that $\cos\theta$ can be expressed in terms of the components of $\boldsymbol{a}$ and $\boldsymbol{b}$.

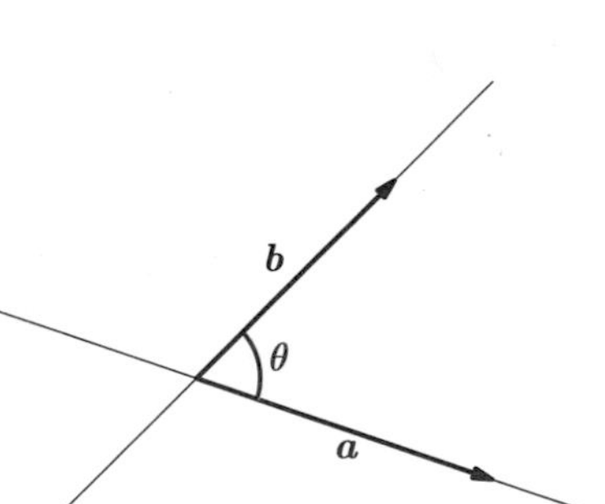

KEY POINT 11.6

If θ is the angle between vectors $\boldsymbol{a} = \begin{pmatrix} a_1 \\ a_2 \\ a_3 \end{pmatrix}$ and $\boldsymbol{b} = \begin{pmatrix} b_1 \\ b_2 \\ b_3 \end{pmatrix}$, then

$$\cos\theta = \frac{a_1b_1 + a_2b_2 + a_3b_3}{|\boldsymbol{a}||\boldsymbol{b}|}.$$

See the Fill-in proof 8 'Deriving scalar product' on the CD-ROM for how to derive this result using the cosine rule.

The expression in the numerator of the fraction in the formula has some very important uses, so it has been given a special name.

KEY POINT 11.7

The quantity $a_1b_1 + a_2b_2 + a_3b_3$ is called the **scalar product** (or *dot product*) of ***a*** and ***b*** and is denoted by $\boldsymbol{a} \cdot \boldsymbol{b}$.

Worked example 11.8

Given points A(3,−5,2), B(4,1,1) and C(−1,1,2), find the size of the acute angle $\text{B}\hat{\text{A}}\text{C}$ in degrees.

It is always a good idea to draw a diagram.

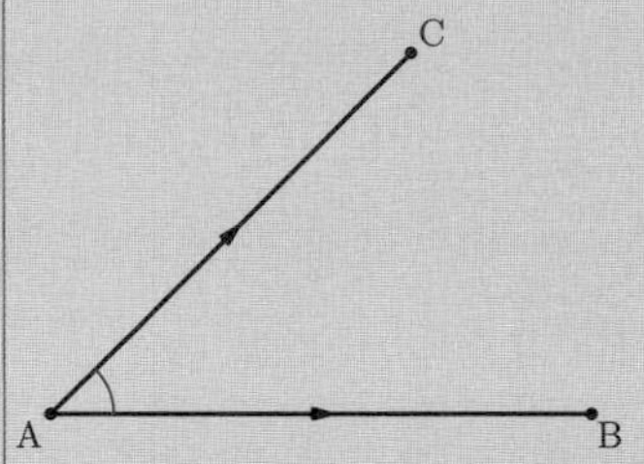

We can see that the required angle is between vectors $\overrightarrow{AB}$ and $\overrightarrow{AC}$. Use the formula with $\boldsymbol{a} = \overrightarrow{AB}$ and $\boldsymbol{b} = \overrightarrow{AC}$.

Let $\theta = \text{B}\hat{\text{A}}\text{C}$. Then

$$\cos\theta = \frac{\overrightarrow{AB} \cdot \overrightarrow{AC}}{|\overrightarrow{AB}||\overrightarrow{AC}|}$$

First, we need to find the components of vectors $\overrightarrow{AB}$ and $\overrightarrow{AC}$.

$$\overrightarrow{AB} = \begin{pmatrix} 4 \\ 1 \\ 1 \end{pmatrix} - \begin{pmatrix} 3 \\ -5 \\ 2 \end{pmatrix} = \begin{pmatrix} 1 \\ 6 \\ -1 \end{pmatrix}$$

$$\overrightarrow{AC} = \begin{pmatrix} -1 \\ 1 \\ 2 \end{pmatrix} - \begin{pmatrix} 3 \\ -5 \\ 2 \end{pmatrix} = \begin{pmatrix} -4 \\ 6 \\ 0 \end{pmatrix}$$

$$\therefore \cos\theta = \frac{1\times(-4) + 6\times 6 + (-1)\times 0}{\sqrt{1^2+6^2+1^2}\sqrt{4^2+6^2+0^2}}$$

$$= \frac{32}{\sqrt{38}\sqrt{52}}$$

$$= 0.7199$$

$$\theta = \cos^{-1}(0.7199)$$

$$= 44.0°$$

The formula in Key point 11.6 makes it very straightforward to check whether two vectors are perpendicular. If $\theta = 90°$, then $\cos\theta = 0$, and so the numerator of the fraction in the formula must be zero. We do not even need to calculate the magnitudes of the two vectors.

KEY POINT 11.8

Two vectors $\boldsymbol{a}$ and $\boldsymbol{b}$ are perpendicular if $\boldsymbol{a}\cdot\boldsymbol{b} = 0$.

Worked example 11.9

Given that $\boldsymbol{p} = \begin{pmatrix} 4 \\ -1 \\ 2 \end{pmatrix}$ and $\boldsymbol{q} = \begin{pmatrix} 2 \\ 1 \\ 1 \end{pmatrix}$, find the value of the scalar t such that $\boldsymbol{p} + t\boldsymbol{q}$ is perpendicular to $\begin{pmatrix} 3 \\ 5 \\ 1 \end{pmatrix}$.

Two vectors are perpendicular if their scalar product equals 0.

$$(\underline{p} + t\underline{q}) \cdot \begin{pmatrix} 3 \\ 5 \\ 1 \end{pmatrix} = 0$$

Write the components of $\boldsymbol{p} + t\boldsymbol{q}$ in terms of t and then form an equation.

$$\underline{p} + t\underline{q} = \begin{pmatrix} 4+2t \\ -1+t \\ 2+t \end{pmatrix}$$

So

$$\begin{pmatrix} 4+2t \\ -1+t \\ 2+t \end{pmatrix} \cdot \begin{pmatrix} 3 \\ 5 \\ 1 \end{pmatrix} = 0$$

Form and solve the equation.

$$\Leftrightarrow 3(4+2t) + 5(-1+t) + 1(2+t) = 0$$

$$\Leftrightarrow 9 + 12t = 0$$

$$\Leftrightarrow t = -\frac{3}{4}$$

Exercise 11D

1. Calculate the angle between each pair of vectors, giving your answers in radians.

   (a) (i) $\begin{pmatrix}5\\1\\2\end{pmatrix}$ and $\begin{pmatrix}1\\-2\\3\end{pmatrix}$ (ii) $\begin{pmatrix}3\\0\\2\end{pmatrix}$ and $\begin{pmatrix}0\\-1\\1\end{pmatrix}$

   (b) (i) $2\boldsymbol{i}+2\boldsymbol{j}-\boldsymbol{k}$ and $\boldsymbol{i}-\boldsymbol{j}+3\boldsymbol{k}$

   (ii) $3\boldsymbol{i}+\boldsymbol{j}$ and $\boldsymbol{i}-2\boldsymbol{k}$

   (c) (i) $\begin{pmatrix}3\\2\end{pmatrix}$ and $\begin{pmatrix}-1\\4\end{pmatrix}$ (ii) $\boldsymbol{i}-\boldsymbol{j}$ and $2\boldsymbol{i}+3\boldsymbol{j}$

2. The angle between vectors $\boldsymbol{a}$ and $\boldsymbol{b}$ is θ. Find the exact value of $\cos\theta$ in the following cases.

   (a) (i) $\boldsymbol{a}=2\boldsymbol{i}+3\boldsymbol{j}-\boldsymbol{k}$ and $\boldsymbol{b}=\boldsymbol{i}-2\boldsymbol{j}+\boldsymbol{k}$

   (ii) $\boldsymbol{a}=\boldsymbol{i}-3\boldsymbol{j}+3\boldsymbol{k}$ and $\boldsymbol{b}=\boldsymbol{i}+5\boldsymbol{j}-2\boldsymbol{k}$

   (b) (i) $\boldsymbol{a}=\begin{pmatrix}2\\2\\3\end{pmatrix}$ and $\boldsymbol{b}=\begin{pmatrix}1\\1\\-2\end{pmatrix}$ (ii) $\boldsymbol{a}=\begin{pmatrix}5\\1\\-3\end{pmatrix}$ and $\boldsymbol{b}=\begin{pmatrix}2\\-1\\2\end{pmatrix}$

   (c) (i) $\boldsymbol{a}=-2\boldsymbol{k}$ and $\boldsymbol{b}=4\boldsymbol{i}$ (ii) $\boldsymbol{a}=5\boldsymbol{i}$ and $\boldsymbol{b}=3\boldsymbol{j}$

3. (i) The vertices of a triangle have position vectors $\boldsymbol{a}=\begin{pmatrix}1\\1\\3\end{pmatrix}$, $\boldsymbol{b}=\begin{pmatrix}2\\-1\\1\end{pmatrix}$ and $\boldsymbol{c}=\begin{pmatrix}5\\1\\2\end{pmatrix}$. Find, in degrees, the angles of the triangle.

   (ii) Find, in degrees, the angles of the triangle with vertices (2, 1, 2),(4, –1, 5) and (7, 1, –2).

4. Determine whether each pair of vectors is perpendicular.

(a) (i) $\begin{pmatrix}2\\1\\-3\end{pmatrix}$ and $\begin{pmatrix}1\\-2\\2\end{pmatrix}$ (ii) $\begin{pmatrix}3\\-1\\2\end{pmatrix}$ and $\begin{pmatrix}2\\6\\0\end{pmatrix}$

(b) (i) $5\boldsymbol{i}-2\boldsymbol{j}+\boldsymbol{k}$ and $3\boldsymbol{i}+4\boldsymbol{j}-7\boldsymbol{k}$

(ii) $\boldsymbol{i}-3\boldsymbol{k}$ and $2\boldsymbol{i}+\boldsymbol{j}+\boldsymbol{k}$

5. Points A and B have position vectors $\overrightarrow{OA}=\begin{pmatrix}2\\2\\3\end{pmatrix}$ and $\overrightarrow{OB}=\begin{pmatrix}-1\\7\\2\end{pmatrix}$. Find the angle between $\overrightarrow{AB}$ and $\overrightarrow{OA}$. *[5 marks]*

6. Four points have coordinates A(2, −1, 3), B(1, 1, 2), C(6, −1, 2) and D(7, −3, 3). Find the angle between $\overrightarrow{AC}$ and $\overrightarrow{BD}$. *[5 marks]*

7. Four points have coordinates A(2, 4, 1), B(k, 4, 2k), C($k+4$, $2k+4$, $2k+2$) and D(6, $2k+4$, 3).

(a) Show that ABCD is a parallelogram for all values of k.

(b) When $k=1$, find the angles of the parallelogram.

(c) Find the value of k for which ABCD is a rectangle. *[8 marks]*

8. Vertices of a triangle have position vectors $\boldsymbol{a}=\boldsymbol{i}-2\boldsymbol{j}+2\boldsymbol{k}$, $\boldsymbol{b}=3\boldsymbol{i}-\boldsymbol{j}+7\boldsymbol{k}$ and $\boldsymbol{c}=5\boldsymbol{i}$.

(a) Show that the triangle is right-angled.

(b) Calculate the other two angles of the triangle.

(c) Find the area of the triangle. *[8 marks]*

11E Properties of the scalar product

In section 11D we defined the scalar product of vectors

$$\boldsymbol{a} = \begin{pmatrix} a_1 \\ a_2 \\ a_3 \end{pmatrix} \text{ and } \boldsymbol{b} = \begin{pmatrix} b_1 \\ b_2 \\ b_3 \end{pmatrix} \text{ as}$$

$$\boldsymbol{a} \cdot \boldsymbol{b} = a_1 b_1 + a_2 b_2 + a_3 b_3$$

and we saw that if θ is the angle between the directions of $\boldsymbol{a}$ and $\boldsymbol{b}$, then

$$\boldsymbol{a} \cdot \boldsymbol{b} = |\boldsymbol{a}||\boldsymbol{b}|\cos\theta$$

In this section we will look at various properties of the scalar product in more detail – in particular, the algebraic rules it follows. The scalar product has many properties similar to the multiplication of numbers; these can be proved by using the components of the vectors.

KEY POINT 11.9

Algebraic properties of the scalar product:

$$\boldsymbol{a} \cdot \boldsymbol{b} = \boldsymbol{b} \cdot \boldsymbol{a}$$

$$(-\boldsymbol{a}) \cdot \boldsymbol{b} = -(\boldsymbol{a} \cdot \boldsymbol{b})$$

$$(k\boldsymbol{a}) \cdot \boldsymbol{b} = k(\boldsymbol{a} \cdot \boldsymbol{b})$$

$$\boldsymbol{a} \cdot (\boldsymbol{b} + \boldsymbol{c}) = (\boldsymbol{a} \cdot \boldsymbol{b}) + (\boldsymbol{a} \cdot \boldsymbol{c})$$

All the operations with vectors work the same way in two and three dimensions. If there were a fourth dimension, so that the position of each point is described using four numbers, we could use analogous rules to calculate 'distances' and 'angles'. Does this mean that we can acquire knowledge about a four-dimensional world which we can't see, or even imagine?

There are also some properties of multiplication of numbers which do not hold for the scalar product. For example, it is not possible to calculate the scalar product of three vectors: the expression $(\boldsymbol{a} \cdot \boldsymbol{b}) \cdot \boldsymbol{c}$ has no meaning, as $\boldsymbol{a} \cdot \boldsymbol{b}$ is a scalar, and the scalar product involves multiplying two vectors.

Another important property of the scalar product concerns parallel vectors.

KEY POINT 11.10

If $\boldsymbol{a}$ and $\boldsymbol{b}$ are parallel vectors, then $\boldsymbol{a} \cdot \boldsymbol{b} = |\boldsymbol{a}||\boldsymbol{b}|$.

In particular, $\boldsymbol{a} \cdot \boldsymbol{a} = |\boldsymbol{a}|^2$.

The next two examples show how you can use the rules discussed in this section.

Worked example 11.10

Given that $\boldsymbol{a}$ and $\boldsymbol{b}$ are perpendicular vectors such that $|\boldsymbol{a}|=5$ and $|\boldsymbol{b}|=3$, evaluate $(2\boldsymbol{a}-\boldsymbol{b})\cdot(\boldsymbol{a}+4\boldsymbol{b})$.

According to Key point 11.9, we can multiply out the brackets just as we would with numbers.

$(2\underline{a}-\underline{b})\cdot(\underline{a}+4\underline{b})=2\underline{a}\cdot\underline{a}+8\underline{a}\cdot\underline{b}-\underline{b}\cdot\underline{a}-4\underline{b}\cdot\underline{b}$

As $\boldsymbol{a}$ and $\boldsymbol{b}$ are perpendicular, $\boldsymbol{a}\cdot\boldsymbol{b}=\boldsymbol{b}\cdot\boldsymbol{a}=0$.

$=2\underline{a}\cdot\underline{a}-4\underline{b}\cdot\underline{b}$

Now use the fact that $\boldsymbol{a}\cdot\boldsymbol{a}=|\boldsymbol{a}|^2$ and similarly for $\boldsymbol{b}$, and then substitute the given magnitudes.

$=2|\underline{a}|^2-4|\underline{b}|^2$

$=2\times5^2-4\times3^2$

$=14$

Worked example 11.11

Points A, B and C have position vectors $\boldsymbol{a}=k\begin{pmatrix}3\\-1\\1\end{pmatrix}$, $\boldsymbol{b}=\begin{pmatrix}3\\4\\-2\end{pmatrix}$ and $\boldsymbol{c}=\begin{pmatrix}1\\1\\5\end{pmatrix}$.

(a) Find $\overrightarrow{BC}$.

(b) Find $\overrightarrow{AB}$ in terms of k.

(c) Find the value of k for which (AB) is perpendicular to (BC).

Use $\overrightarrow{BC}=\boldsymbol{c}-\boldsymbol{b}$.

(a) $\overrightarrow{BC}=\underline{c}-\underline{b}$

$$=\begin{pmatrix}1\\1\\5\end{pmatrix}-\begin{pmatrix}3\\4\\-2\end{pmatrix}=\begin{pmatrix}-2\\-3\\7\end{pmatrix}$$

Use $\overrightarrow{AB}=\boldsymbol{b}-\boldsymbol{a}$.

(b) $\overrightarrow{AB}=\underline{b}-\underline{a}$

$$=\begin{pmatrix}3\\4\\-2\end{pmatrix}-\begin{pmatrix}3k\\-k\\k\end{pmatrix}=\begin{pmatrix}3-3k\\4+k\\-2-k\end{pmatrix}$$

→

continued . . .

For (AB) and (BC) to be perpendicular, we must have $\overrightarrow{AB}\cdot\overrightarrow{BC}=0$.

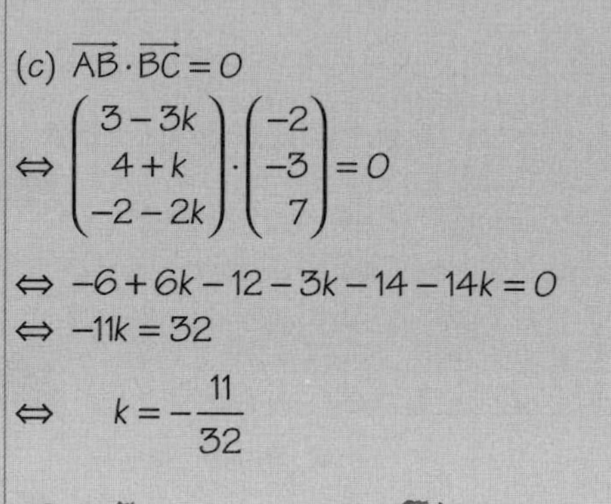

(c) $\overrightarrow{AB}\cdot\overrightarrow{BC}=0$

$\Leftrightarrow \begin{pmatrix}3-3k\\4+k\\-2-2k\end{pmatrix}\cdot\begin{pmatrix}-2\\-3\\7\end{pmatrix}=0$

$\Leftrightarrow -6+6k-12-3k-14-14k=0$

$\Leftrightarrow -11k=32$

$\Leftrightarrow \quad k=-\frac{11}{32}$

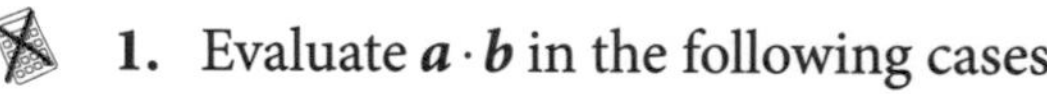

Exercise 11E

1. Evaluate $\boldsymbol{a}\cdot\boldsymbol{b}$ in the following cases.

(a) (i) $\boldsymbol{a}=\begin{pmatrix}2\\1\\2\end{pmatrix}$ and $\boldsymbol{b}=\begin{pmatrix}5\\2\\2\end{pmatrix}$ (ii) $\boldsymbol{a}=\begin{pmatrix}3\\-1\\2\end{pmatrix}$ and $\boldsymbol{b}=\begin{pmatrix}-12\\4\\-8\end{pmatrix}$

(b) (i) $\boldsymbol{a}=\begin{pmatrix}2\\-1\\2\end{pmatrix}$ and $\boldsymbol{b}=\begin{pmatrix}5\\-2\\2\end{pmatrix}$ (ii) $\boldsymbol{a}=\begin{pmatrix}3\\0\\2\end{pmatrix}$ and $\boldsymbol{b}=\begin{pmatrix}0\\0\\-8\end{pmatrix}$

(c) (i) $\boldsymbol{a}=4\boldsymbol{i}+2\boldsymbol{j}+\boldsymbol{k}$ and $\boldsymbol{b}=\boldsymbol{i}+\boldsymbol{j}+3\boldsymbol{k}$

(ii) $\boldsymbol{a}=4\boldsymbol{i}-2\boldsymbol{j}+\boldsymbol{k}$ and $\boldsymbol{b}=\boldsymbol{i}-\boldsymbol{j}+3\boldsymbol{k}$

(d) (i) $\boldsymbol{a}=-3\boldsymbol{j}+\boldsymbol{k}$ and $\boldsymbol{b}=2\boldsymbol{i}-4\boldsymbol{k}$ (ii) $\boldsymbol{a}=-3\boldsymbol{j}$ and $\boldsymbol{b}=4\boldsymbol{k}$

2. Given that θ is the angle between vectors $\boldsymbol{p}$ and $\boldsymbol{q}$, find the exact value of $\cos\theta$.

(a) (i) $\boldsymbol{p}=\begin{pmatrix}1\\1\\2\end{pmatrix}$ and $\boldsymbol{q}=\begin{pmatrix}2\\1\\2\end{pmatrix}$ (ii) $\boldsymbol{p}=\begin{pmatrix}3\\0\\2\end{pmatrix}$ and $\boldsymbol{q}=\begin{pmatrix}1\\1\\1\end{pmatrix}$

(b) (i) $\boldsymbol{p}=\begin{pmatrix}-1\\1\\2\end{pmatrix}$ and $\boldsymbol{q}=\begin{pmatrix}1\\1\\2\end{pmatrix}$ (ii) $\boldsymbol{p}=\begin{pmatrix}-1\\1\\0\end{pmatrix}$ and $\boldsymbol{q}=\begin{pmatrix}0\\1\\2\end{pmatrix}$

3. (i) Given that $|\boldsymbol{a}| = 3, |\boldsymbol{b}| = 5$ and $\boldsymbol{a} \cdot \boldsymbol{b} = 10$, find, in degrees, the angle between $\boldsymbol{a}$ and $\boldsymbol{b}$.

(ii) Given that $|\boldsymbol{c}| = 9, |\boldsymbol{d}| = 12$ and $\boldsymbol{c} \cdot \boldsymbol{d} = -15$, find, in degrees, the angle between $\boldsymbol{c}$ and $\boldsymbol{d}$.

4. (a) Given that $|\boldsymbol{a}| = 6, |\boldsymbol{b}| = 4$ and the angle between $\boldsymbol{a}$ and $\boldsymbol{b}$ is 37°, calculate $\boldsymbol{a} \cdot \boldsymbol{b}$.

(b) Given that $|\boldsymbol{a}| = 8, \boldsymbol{a} \cdot \boldsymbol{b} = 12$ and the angle between $\boldsymbol{a}$ and $\boldsymbol{b}$ is 60°, find the exact value of $|\boldsymbol{b}|$.

5. Given that $\boldsymbol{a} = 2\boldsymbol{i} + \boldsymbol{j} - 2\boldsymbol{k}, \boldsymbol{b} = \boldsymbol{i} + 3\boldsymbol{j} - \boldsymbol{k}, \boldsymbol{c} = 5\boldsymbol{i} - 3\boldsymbol{k}$ and $\boldsymbol{d} = -2\boldsymbol{j} + \boldsymbol{k}$ verify that

(a) $\boldsymbol{b} \cdot \boldsymbol{d} = \boldsymbol{d} \cdot \boldsymbol{b}$

(b) $\boldsymbol{a} \cdot (\boldsymbol{b} + \boldsymbol{c}) = \boldsymbol{a} \cdot \boldsymbol{b} + \boldsymbol{a} \cdot \boldsymbol{c}$

(c) $(\boldsymbol{c} - \boldsymbol{d}) \cdot \boldsymbol{c} = |\boldsymbol{c}|^2 - \boldsymbol{c} \cdot \boldsymbol{d}$

(d) $(\boldsymbol{a} + \boldsymbol{b}) \cdot (\boldsymbol{a} + \boldsymbol{b}) = |\boldsymbol{a}|^2 + |\boldsymbol{b}|^2 + 2\boldsymbol{a} \cdot \boldsymbol{b}$

6. Find the values of t for which the following pairs of vectors are perpendicular.

(a) (i) $\begin{pmatrix} 2t \\ 1 \\ -3t \end{pmatrix}$ and $\begin{pmatrix} 1 \\ -2 \\ 2 \end{pmatrix}$ (ii) $\begin{pmatrix} t+1 \\ 2t-1 \\ 2t \end{pmatrix}$ and $\begin{pmatrix} 2 \\ 6 \\ 0 \end{pmatrix}$

(b) (i) $5t\boldsymbol{i} - (2+t)\boldsymbol{j} + \boldsymbol{k}$ and $3\boldsymbol{i} + 4\boldsymbol{j} - t\boldsymbol{k}$

(ii) $t\boldsymbol{i} - 3\boldsymbol{k}$ and $2t\boldsymbol{i} + \boldsymbol{j} + t\boldsymbol{k}$

7. Given that $\boldsymbol{a} = \begin{pmatrix} 2 \\ -2 \\ 1 \end{pmatrix}, \boldsymbol{b} = \begin{pmatrix} 1 \\ 1 \\ 2 \end{pmatrix}, \boldsymbol{c} = \begin{pmatrix} 3 \\ -5 \\ 1 \end{pmatrix}$ and $\boldsymbol{d} = \begin{pmatrix} 3 \\ -3 \\ 2 \end{pmatrix}$, calculate

(a) $\boldsymbol{a} \cdot (\boldsymbol{b} + \boldsymbol{c})$

(b) $(\boldsymbol{b} - \boldsymbol{a}) \cdot (\boldsymbol{d} - \boldsymbol{c})$

(c) $(\boldsymbol{b} + \boldsymbol{d}) \cdot (2\boldsymbol{a})$ *[7 marks]*

8. (a) If $\boldsymbol{a}$ is a unit vector perpendicular to $\boldsymbol{b}$, find the value of $\boldsymbol{a} \cdot (2\boldsymbol{a} - 3\boldsymbol{b})$.

(b) If $\boldsymbol{p}$ is a unit vector making a 45° angle with vector $\boldsymbol{q}$, and $\boldsymbol{p} \cdot \boldsymbol{q} = 3\sqrt{2}$, find $|\boldsymbol{q}|$. *[6 marks]*

9. (a) $\boldsymbol{a}$ is a vector of magnitude 3 and $\boldsymbol{b}$ makes an angle of 60° with $\boldsymbol{a}$. Given that $\boldsymbol{a}\cdot(\boldsymbol{a}-\boldsymbol{b})=\frac{1}{3}$, find the value of $|\boldsymbol{b}|$.

(b) Given that $\boldsymbol{a}$ and $\boldsymbol{b}$ are two vectors of equal magnitude such that $(3\boldsymbol{a}+\boldsymbol{b})$ is perpendicular to $(\boldsymbol{a}-3\boldsymbol{b})$, show that $\boldsymbol{a}$ and $\boldsymbol{b}$ are perpendicular. *[6 marks]*

10. Points A, B and C have position vectors $\boldsymbol{a}=\boldsymbol{i}-19\boldsymbol{j}+5\boldsymbol{k}$, $\boldsymbol{b}=2\lambda\boldsymbol{i}+(\lambda+2)\boldsymbol{j}+2\boldsymbol{k}$ and $\boldsymbol{c}=-6\boldsymbol{i}-15\boldsymbol{j}+7\boldsymbol{k}$.

(a) Find the value of λ for which (BC) is perpendicular to (AC).

For the value of λ found above, find

(b) the angles of the triangle ABC

(c) the area of the triangle ABC. *[8 marks]*

11. ABCD is a parallelogram with [AB] parallel to [DC]. Let $\overrightarrow{AB}=\boldsymbol{a}$ and $\overrightarrow{AD}=\boldsymbol{b}$.

(a) Express $\overrightarrow{AC}$ and $\overrightarrow{BD}$ in terms of $\boldsymbol{a}$ and $\boldsymbol{b}$.

(b) Simplify $(\boldsymbol{a}+\boldsymbol{b})\cdot(\boldsymbol{b}-\boldsymbol{a})$.

(c) Hence show that if ABCD is a rhombus, then its diagonals are perpendicular. *[8 marks]*

12. Points A and B have position vectors $\begin{pmatrix}2\\1\\4\end{pmatrix}$ and $\begin{pmatrix}2\lambda\\\lambda\\4\lambda\end{pmatrix}$.

(a) Show that B lies on the line (OA) for all values of λ.

Point C has position vector $\begin{pmatrix}12\\2\\4\end{pmatrix}$.

(b) Find the value of λ for which $\hat{CBA}$ is a right angle.

(c) For the value of λ found above, calculate the exact distance from C to the line (OA). *[8 marks]*

11F Vector equation of a line

Before we can solve problems involving lines in space, we need a way of deciding whether a given point lies on a certain straight line.

Consider two points A(−1, 1, 4) and B(1, 4, 2); they determine a unique straight line (by 'straight line' we mean a line that extends indefinitely in both directions). If we are given a third point C, how can we check whether it lies on the same line? We can use vectors to answer this question. For example, if C has coordinates (5, 10, –2), then

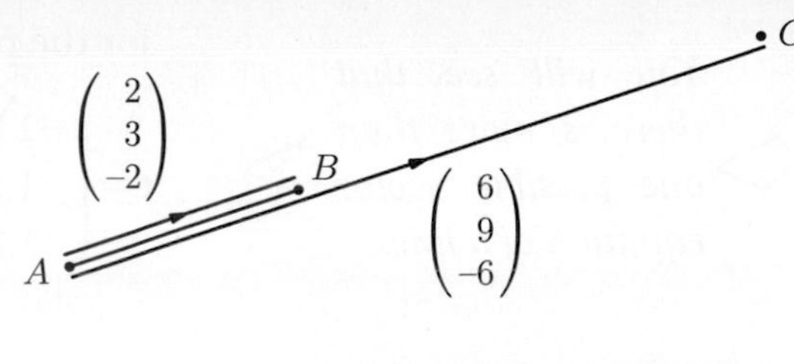

$$\overrightarrow{AC} = \begin{pmatrix} 6 \\ 9 \\ -6 \end{pmatrix} = 3\begin{pmatrix} 2 \\ 3 \\ -2 \end{pmatrix} = 3\overrightarrow{AB}$$

This means that (AC) is parallel to (AB). But since they both contain the point A, (AC) and (AB) must then be the same straight line; in other words, C lies on the line (AB).

EXAM HINT

Remember the International Baccalaureate ® notation for lines and line segments: (AB) stands for the (infinite) straight line through A and B, [AB] for the line segment between A and B, and AB for the length of [AB].

The next question is: how can we characterise all the points on the line (AB)? Following the above reasoning, we realise that a point R lies on (AB) if (AR) and (AB) are parallel; this can be expressed using vectors by saying that $\overrightarrow{AR} = \lambda\overrightarrow{AB}$ for some value of the scalar λ, so $\overrightarrow{AR} = \begin{pmatrix} 2\lambda \\ 3\lambda \\ -2\lambda \end{pmatrix}$ in our example. On the other hand, we also know that $\overrightarrow{AR} = \boldsymbol{r} - \boldsymbol{a}$, where $\boldsymbol{r}$ and $\boldsymbol{a}$ are the position vectors of R and A.

Recall that a scalar is a number without direction.

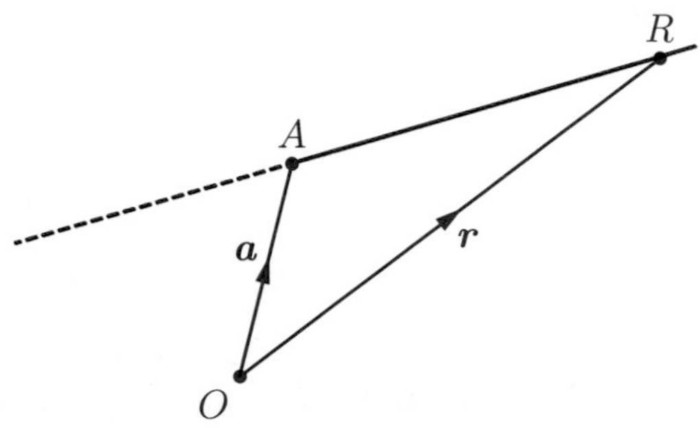

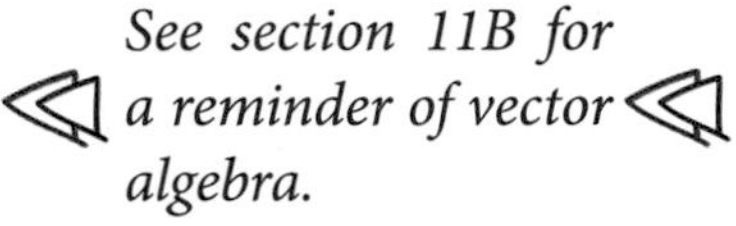
See section 11B for a reminder of vector algebra.

Hence $\boldsymbol{r} = \boldsymbol{a} + \overrightarrow{AR} = \begin{pmatrix} -1 \\ 1 \\ 4 \end{pmatrix} + \begin{pmatrix} 2\lambda \\ 3\lambda \\ -2\lambda \end{pmatrix}$ is the position vector of a general point R on the line (AB). In other words, R has coordinates $(-1+2\lambda, 1+3\lambda, 4-2\lambda)$ for some value of λ.

Different values of λ correspond to different points on the line; for example, $\lambda = 0$ corresponds to point A, $\lambda = 1$ to point B and $\lambda = 3$ to point C. The line is parallel to the vector $\begin{pmatrix} 2 \\ 3 \\ -2 \end{pmatrix}$, so this vector determines the direction of the line. The expression

You will see that there is more than one possible vector equation of a line.

for the position vector of R is usually written in the form

$r = \begin{pmatrix} -1 \\ 1 \\ 4 \end{pmatrix} + \lambda \begin{pmatrix} 2 \\ 3 \\ -2 \end{pmatrix}$ to make it easy to identify the direction vector.

KEY POINT 11.11

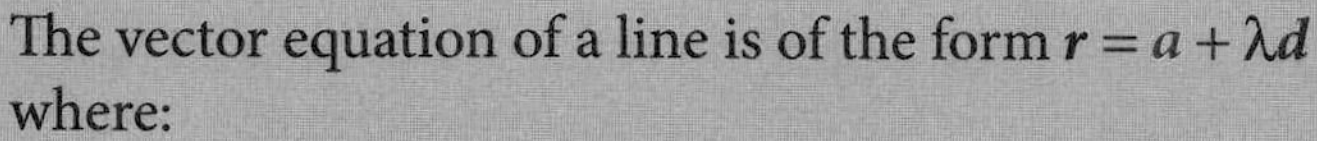

The vector equation of a line is of the form $\boldsymbol{r} = \boldsymbol{a} + \lambda\boldsymbol{d}$ where:

$\boldsymbol{r}$ is the position vector of a general point on the line

$\boldsymbol{d}$ is the direction vector of the line

$\boldsymbol{a}$ is the position vector of one point on the line

Different values of the parameter λ give the positions of different points on the line.

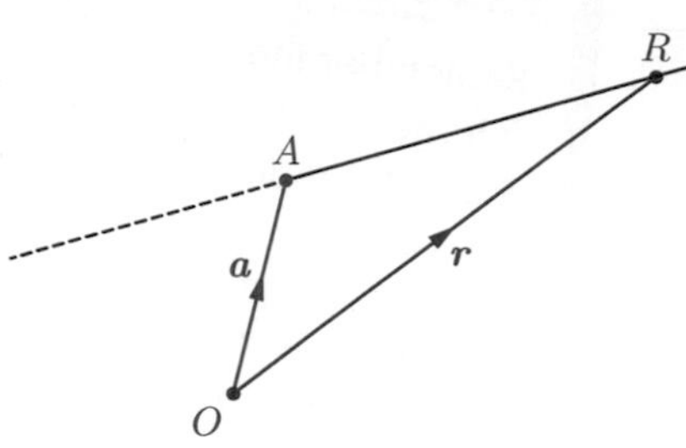

Worked example 11.12

Write down a vector equation of the line passing through the point (−1, 1, 2) in the direction of the vector $\begin{pmatrix} 2 \\ 2 \\ 1 \end{pmatrix}$.

The equation of the line is $\boldsymbol{r} = \boldsymbol{a} + \lambda\boldsymbol{d}$, where $\boldsymbol{a}$ is the position vector of a point on the line and $\boldsymbol{d}$ is the direction vector.

$$r = \begin{pmatrix} -1 \\ 1 \\ 2 \end{pmatrix} + \lambda \begin{pmatrix} 2 \\ 2 \\ 1 \end{pmatrix}$$

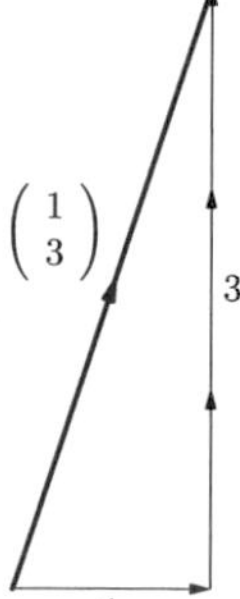

In two dimensions, a straight line is determined by its gradient and one point. The gradient is a number that tells us the direction of the line. For example, for a line with gradient 3, an increase of 1 unit in x produces an increase of 3 units in y; thus the line is in the direction of the vector $\begin{pmatrix} 1 \\ 3 \end{pmatrix}$.

In three dimensions, a straight line is still determined by its direction and one point, but it is no longer possible to use a single number to represent the direction vector. The line in Worked example 11.12 had direction vector $\begin{pmatrix} 2 \\ 2 \\ 1 \end{pmatrix}$, which means that an increase of 2 units in x will produce an increase of 2 units in y *and* an increase of 1 unit in z; we cannot describe these different increase amounts by just one number.

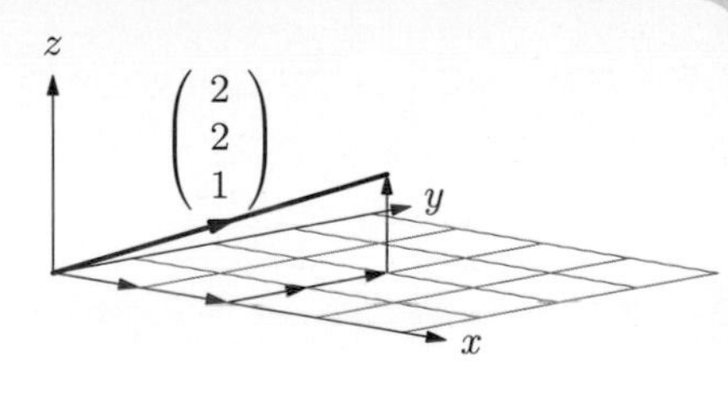

As you know, two points determine a straight line. The next example shows how to find a vector equation when two points on the line are given.

Worked example 11.13

Find a vector equation of the line through the points A(−1, 1, 2) and B(3, 5, 4).

To find an equation of the line, we need to know one point and the direction vector.

$\underline{r} = \underline{a} + \lambda \underline{d}$

The line passes through A(−1, 1, 2).

$\underline{a} = \begin{pmatrix} -1 \\ 1 \\ 2 \end{pmatrix}$

Draw a diagram. The line is in the direction of $\overrightarrow{AB} = \boldsymbol{b} - \boldsymbol{a}$.

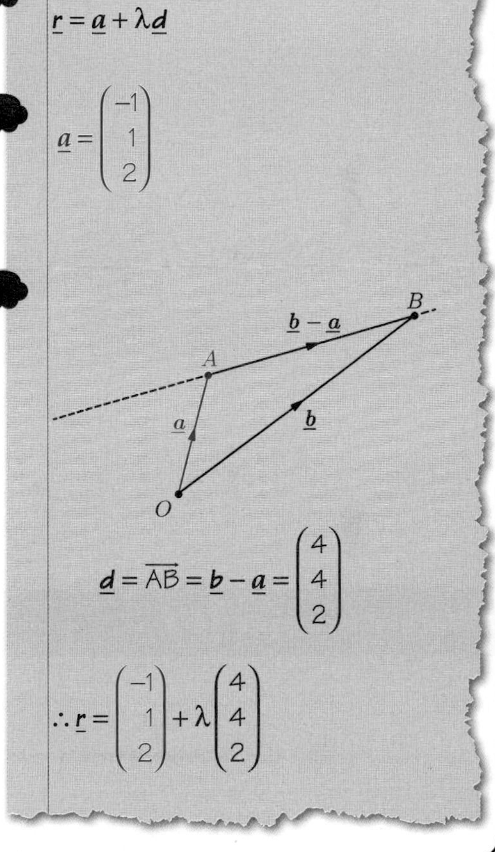

$\underline{d} = \overrightarrow{AB} = \underline{b} - \underline{a} = \begin{pmatrix} 4 \\ 4 \\ 2 \end{pmatrix}$

$\therefore \underline{r} = \begin{pmatrix} -1 \\ 1 \\ 2 \end{pmatrix} + \lambda \begin{pmatrix} 4 \\ 4 \\ 2 \end{pmatrix}$

What if, for '$\boldsymbol{a}$' in the formula, we had used the position vector of point B instead? Then we would have got the equation

$\boldsymbol{r} = \begin{pmatrix} 3 \\ 5 \\ 4 \end{pmatrix} + \lambda \begin{pmatrix} 4 \\ 4 \\ 2 \end{pmatrix}$. This equation represents the same line as the one given as the answer to Worked example 11.13, but the values of λ corresponding to particular points will be different.

For example, with the equation $\boldsymbol{r} = \begin{pmatrix} -1 \\ 1 \\ 2 \end{pmatrix} + \lambda \begin{pmatrix} 4 \\ 4 \\ 2 \end{pmatrix}$, point A has $\lambda = 0$ and point B has $\lambda = 1$, while with the equation $\boldsymbol{r} = \begin{pmatrix} 3 \\ 5 \\ 4 \end{pmatrix} + \lambda \begin{pmatrix} 4 \\ 4 \\ 2 \end{pmatrix}$ point A has $\lambda = -1$ and point B has $\lambda = 0$.

The direction vector is not unique either: as we are only interested in its direction and not its magnitude, any (non-zero) scalar multiple of the direction vector will also be a direction vector. Hence $\begin{pmatrix} 2 \\ 2 \\ 1 \end{pmatrix}$ or $\begin{pmatrix} -6 \\ -6 \\ -3 \end{pmatrix}$ could also be used as direction vectors for the line in Worked example 11.13, and yet another form of the equation of the same line would be $\boldsymbol{r} = \begin{pmatrix} -1 \\ 1 \\ 2 \end{pmatrix} + \lambda \begin{pmatrix} -6 \\ -6 \\ -3 \end{pmatrix}$. With this equation, point A has $\lambda = 0$ and point B has $\lambda = -\frac{2}{3}$. To simplify calculations, we usually choose the direction vector to be the one whose components are smallest possible integer values, although sometimes it will be convenient to use the corresponding unit vector.

Worked example 11.4

(a) Show that the equations $\boldsymbol{r} = \begin{pmatrix} -1 \\ 1 \\ 2 \end{pmatrix} + \lambda \begin{pmatrix} 2 \\ 2 \\ 1 \end{pmatrix}$ and $\boldsymbol{r} = \begin{pmatrix} 5 \\ 7 \\ 5 \end{pmatrix} + \mu \begin{pmatrix} 6 \\ 6 \\ 3 \end{pmatrix}$ represent the same straight line.

(b) Show that the equation $\boldsymbol{r} = \begin{pmatrix} -5 \\ -3 \\ 1 \end{pmatrix} + t \begin{pmatrix} -4 \\ -4 \\ -2 \end{pmatrix}$ represents a different straight line.

EXAM HINT

When a problem involves more than one line, different letters should be used for the parameters in their vector equations. The most commonly used letters are λ (lambda), μ (mu), *t* and *s*.

→

continued . . .

We need to show that the two lines have parallel direction vectors (so that the lines are parallel) and one common point (then they will be the same line). Two vectors are parallel if one is a scalar multiple of the other (Key point 11.3).

(a) Direction vectors are parallel, because

$$\begin{pmatrix}6\\6\\3\end{pmatrix}=3\begin{pmatrix}2\\2\\1\end{pmatrix}$$

We know that the second line contains the point (5, 7, 5). Now check that (5, 7, 5) also lies on the first line: this will be the case if we can find a value of λ which, when substituted in the equation of the first line, will give the position vector of (5, 7, 5).

Show that (5, 7, 5) lies on the first line:

Find the value of λ which gives the first coordinate.

$$-1+2\lambda=5$$
$$\Rightarrow\lambda=3$$

Check whether this value of λ also gives the other two coordinates.

$$\begin{cases}1+3\times2=7\\2+3\times1=5\end{cases}$$

so (5, 7, 5) lies on the first line. Hence the two lines are the same.

Check whether the direction vectors are parallel.

(b) $$\begin{pmatrix}-4\\-4\\-2\end{pmatrix}=-2\begin{pmatrix}2\\2\\1\end{pmatrix}$$

So this line is parallel to the other two.

Check whether (–5, –3, 1) lies on the first line. Find the value of λ which gives the first coordinate.

$$-1+2\lambda=-5$$
$$\Rightarrow\lambda=-2$$

Check whether this value of λ also gives the other two coordinates.

$$\begin{cases}1+(-2)\times2=-3\\2+(-2)\times1=0\neq1\end{cases}$$

so (–5, –3, 1) does not lie on the line. Hence the line is not the same as the first line.

In the above example we used the coordinates of the point to find the corresponding value of λ. Sometimes, however, we know only that a point lies on a given line, but not its precise coordinates. The next example shows how we can work with a general point on the line (with an unknown value of λ).

Worked example 11.15

Point B(3, 5, 4) lies on the line with equation $\boldsymbol{r}=\begin{pmatrix}-1\\1\\2\end{pmatrix}+\lambda\begin{pmatrix}2\\2\\1\end{pmatrix}$. Find the possible positions of a point Q on the line such that BQ = 15.

We know that Q lies on the line, so it has position vector $\begin{pmatrix}-1\\1\\2\end{pmatrix}+\lambda\begin{pmatrix}2\\2\\1\end{pmatrix}$ for some value of λ. We will find the possible values of λ and hence the possible position vectors of Q.

$$\boldsymbol{q}=\begin{pmatrix}-1\\1\\2\end{pmatrix}+\lambda\begin{pmatrix}2\\2\\1\end{pmatrix}=\begin{pmatrix}-1+2\lambda\\1+2\lambda\\2+\lambda\end{pmatrix}$$

Express vector $\overrightarrow{BQ}$ in terms of λ and then set its magnitude equal to 15.

$$\overrightarrow{BQ}=\boldsymbol{q}-\boldsymbol{b}$$

$$=\begin{pmatrix}-1+2\lambda\\1+2\lambda\\2+\lambda\end{pmatrix}-\begin{pmatrix}3\\5\\4\end{pmatrix}=\begin{pmatrix}2\lambda-4\\2\lambda-4\\\lambda-2\end{pmatrix}$$

It is easier to work without square roots, so let us square the magnitude equation $\left|\overrightarrow{BQ}\right|=15$.

$$\left|\overrightarrow{BQ}\right|^2=15^2$$

$$\Leftrightarrow(2\lambda-4)^2+(2\lambda-4)^2+(\lambda-2)^2=15^2$$

$$\Leftrightarrow 9\lambda^2-36\lambda-189=0$$

$$\Leftrightarrow \lambda=-3 \text{ or } 7$$

Now we can find the position vector of Q.

$$\therefore \boldsymbol{q}=\begin{pmatrix}-7\\-5\\-1\end{pmatrix} \text{ or } \begin{pmatrix}13\\15\\9\end{pmatrix}$$

Exercise 11F

1. Find a vector equation of the line in the given direction through the given point.

   (a) (i) Direction $\begin{pmatrix}1\\4\end{pmatrix}$, point (4,–1)

   (ii) Direction $\begin{pmatrix}2\\-3\end{pmatrix}$, point (4,1)

   (b) (i) Point (1,0,5), direction $\begin{pmatrix}1\\3\\-3\end{pmatrix}$

   (ii) Point (–1,1,5), direction $\begin{pmatrix}3\\-2\\2\end{pmatrix}$

   (c) (i) Point (4,0), direction $2\boldsymbol{i}+3\boldsymbol{j}$

   (ii) Point (0,2), direction $\boldsymbol{i}-3\boldsymbol{j}$

   (d) (i) Direction $\boldsymbol{i}-3\boldsymbol{k}$, point (0,2,3)

   (ii) Direction $2\boldsymbol{i}+3\boldsymbol{j}-\boldsymbol{k}$, point (4,–3,0)

2. Find a vector equation of the line through the two given points (there is more than one right answer for each part).

   (a) (i) (4,1) and (1,2) (ii) (2,7) and (4,–2)

   (b) (i) (–5,–2,3) and (4,–2,3) (ii) (1,1,3) and (10,–5,0)

3. Decide whether or not the given point lies on the given line.

   (a) (i) Line $\boldsymbol{r}=\begin{pmatrix}2\\1\\5\end{pmatrix}+t\begin{pmatrix}-1\\2\\2\end{pmatrix}$, point (0,5,9)

   (ii) Line $\boldsymbol{r}=\begin{pmatrix}-1\\0\\3\end{pmatrix}+t\begin{pmatrix}4\\1\\5\end{pmatrix}$, point (–1,0,3)

   (b) (i) Line $\boldsymbol{r}=\begin{pmatrix}-1\\5\\1\end{pmatrix}+t\begin{pmatrix}0\\0\\7\end{pmatrix}$, point (–1,3,8)

   (ii) Line $\boldsymbol{r}=\begin{pmatrix}4\\0\\3\end{pmatrix}+t\begin{pmatrix}4\\0\\3\end{pmatrix}$, point (0,0,0)

4. (a) Show that the points A(4,–1,–8) and B(2,1,–4) lie on the line l with equation $\mathbf{r} = \begin{pmatrix} 2 \\ 1 \\ -4 \end{pmatrix} + t\begin{pmatrix} -1 \\ 1 \\ 2 \end{pmatrix}$.

(b) Find the coordinates of the point C on the line l such that AB = BC. *[6 marks]*

5. (a) Find a vector equation of the line l through points P(7,1,2) and Q(3,–1,5).

(b) Point R lies on l and PR = 2 PQ. Find the possible coordinates of R. *[6 marks]*

6. (a) Write down a vector equation of the line l through the point A(2,1,4) parallel to the vector $2\mathbf{i} - 3\mathbf{j} + 6\mathbf{k}$.

(b) Calculate the magnitude of the vector $2\mathbf{i} - 3\mathbf{j} + 6\mathbf{k}$.

(c) Find possible coordinates of the point P on l such that AP = 35. *[8 marks]*

11G Solving problems involving lines

In this section we will use vector equations of lines to solve problems about angles and intersections.

Worked example 11.16

Find the acute angle between the lines with equations $\mathbf{r} = \begin{pmatrix} 4 \\ 1 \\ -2 \end{pmatrix} + t\begin{pmatrix} 1 \\ -1 \\ 3 \end{pmatrix}$ and $\mathbf{r} = \begin{pmatrix} 4 \\ 1 \\ -2 \end{pmatrix} + \lambda\begin{pmatrix} -1 \\ 4 \\ 1 \end{pmatrix}$.

We know a formula for the angle between two vectors (Key point 11.6). The question is which vectors to choose as our '**a**' and '**b**'.

$$\cos\theta = \frac{\mathbf{a}\cdot\mathbf{b}}{|\mathbf{a}||\mathbf{b}|}$$

Drawing a diagram is a good way of identifying which two vectors make the required angle. This indicates that we should take **a** and **b** to be the direction vectors of the two lines.

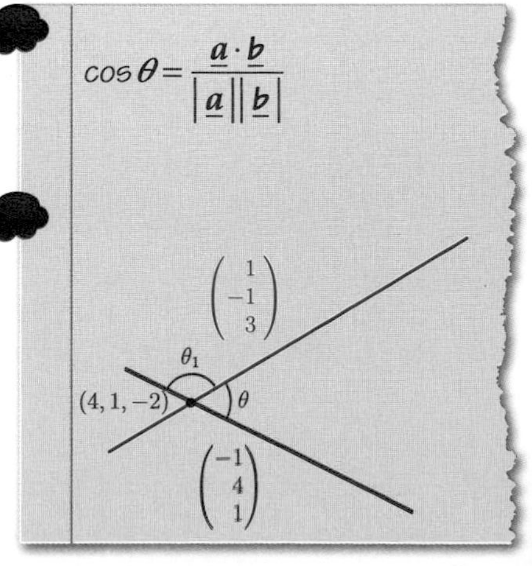

continued . . .

The two vectors are in the directions of the two lines, so we take $\boldsymbol{a}$ and $\boldsymbol{b}$ to be the direction vectors of the two lines.

$\underline{a} = \begin{pmatrix} 1 \\ -1 \\ 3 \end{pmatrix} \quad \underline{b} = \begin{pmatrix} -1 \\ 4 \\ 1 \end{pmatrix}$

Now use the formula to calculate the angle.

$$\cos\theta = \frac{-1-4+3}{\sqrt{1+1+9}\sqrt{1+16+1}} = \frac{-2}{\sqrt{11}\sqrt{18}}$$

$\therefore \theta = 98.2°$

Note, however, that the angle we found is obtuse – it is the angle marked θ_1 in the diagram. The question asked for the acute angle.

acute angle $= 180° - 98.2°$
$= 81.8°$

The example above illustrates the general approach to finding an angle between two lines.

KEY POINT 11.12

The angle between two lines is the angle between their direction vectors.

Since we only need to look at direction vectors to determine the angle between two lines, it is easy to identify parallel and perpendicular lines.

Parallel and perpendicular vectors were covered in sections 11B and 11E.

KEY POINT 11.13

Two lines with direction vectors $\boldsymbol{d}_1$ and $\boldsymbol{d}_2$ are

- parallel if $\boldsymbol{d}_1 = k\boldsymbol{d}_2$
- perpendicular if $\boldsymbol{d}_1 \cdot \boldsymbol{d}_2 = 0$.

Worked example 11.17

Decide whether the following pairs of lines are parallel, perpendicular, or neither:

(a) $\boldsymbol{r} = \begin{pmatrix} 2 \\ -1 \\ 5 \end{pmatrix} + \lambda \begin{pmatrix} 4 \\ -1 \\ 2 \end{pmatrix}$ and $\boldsymbol{r} = \begin{pmatrix} -2 \\ 0 \\ 3 \end{pmatrix} + \mu \begin{pmatrix} 1 \\ -2 \\ -3 \end{pmatrix}$

(b) $\boldsymbol{r} = \begin{pmatrix} 0 \\ 0 \\ 1 \end{pmatrix} + \lambda \begin{pmatrix} 2 \\ 1 \\ 1 \end{pmatrix}$ and $\boldsymbol{r} = \begin{pmatrix} 2 \\ 1 \\ 2 \end{pmatrix} + t \begin{pmatrix} 1 \\ 0 \\ -3 \end{pmatrix}$

(c) $\boldsymbol{r} = \begin{pmatrix} 2 \\ -1 \\ 5 \end{pmatrix} + t \begin{pmatrix} 4 \\ -6 \\ 2 \end{pmatrix}$ and $\boldsymbol{r} = \begin{pmatrix} -2 \\ 0 \\ 3 \end{pmatrix} + s \begin{pmatrix} -10 \\ 15 \\ -5 \end{pmatrix}$

Is $\boldsymbol{d}_1$ a multiple of $\boldsymbol{d}_2$?

(a)

If $\begin{pmatrix} 4 \\ -1 \\ 2 \end{pmatrix} = k \begin{pmatrix} 1 \\ -2 \\ -3 \end{pmatrix}$

then

$$\begin{cases} 4 = k \times 1 \Rightarrow k = 4 \\ -1 = k \times (-2) \Rightarrow k = \dfrac{1}{2} \end{cases}$$

$4 \neq \dfrac{1}{2}$

$\therefore$ the lines are not parallel.

Is $\boldsymbol{d}_1 \cdot \boldsymbol{d}_2 = 0$?

$$\begin{pmatrix} 4 \\ -1 \\ 2 \end{pmatrix} \cdot \begin{pmatrix} 1 \\ -2 \\ -3 \end{pmatrix} = 4 + 2 - 6 = 0$$

$\therefore$ they are perpendicular.

Is $\boldsymbol{d}_1$ a multiple of $\boldsymbol{d}_2$?

(b)

If $\begin{pmatrix} 2 \\ 1 \\ 1 \end{pmatrix} = k \begin{pmatrix} 1 \\ 0 \\ -3 \end{pmatrix}$

then

$$\begin{cases} 2 = k \times 1 \Rightarrow k = 2 \\ 1 = k \times 0 \text{ impossible} \end{cases}$$

$\therefore$ the lines are not parallel.

→

continued . . .

Is $\boldsymbol{d}_1 \cdot \boldsymbol{d}_2 = 0$?

$$\begin{pmatrix}2\\1\\2\end{pmatrix} \cdot \begin{pmatrix}1\\0\\3\end{pmatrix} = 2+0+6 = 8 \neq 0$$

∴ they are not perpendicular.

The lines are neither parallel nor perpendicular.

Is $\boldsymbol{d}_1$ a multiple of $\boldsymbol{d}_2$?

(c)

If $\begin{pmatrix}4\\-6\\2\end{pmatrix} = k\begin{pmatrix}-10\\15\\-5\end{pmatrix}$

then

$$\begin{cases} 4 = k \times (-10) \Rightarrow k = -\frac{2}{5} \\ -6 = k \times 15 \Rightarrow k = -\frac{2}{5} \\ 2 = k \times (-5) \Rightarrow k = -\frac{2}{5} \end{cases}$$

∴ the lines have parallel directions.

But they could be the same line, so we need to check this.

If the point $\begin{pmatrix}-2\\0\\3\end{pmatrix}$ on the second line also lies on the first line then

$$\begin{cases} 2 + 4t = -2 \Rightarrow t = -1 \\ -1 - 6t = 0 \Rightarrow t = -\frac{1}{6} \end{cases}$$

∴ they are not the same line.

The lines are parallel.

We will now see how to find the point of intersection of two lines. Suppose two lines l_1 and l_2 have vector equations $\boldsymbol{r}_1 = \boldsymbol{a}_1 + \lambda \boldsymbol{d}_1$ and $\boldsymbol{r}_2 = \boldsymbol{a}_2 + \mu \boldsymbol{d}_2$. If they intersect, then there is a point which lies on both lines. As the position vector of a general point on a line is given by $\boldsymbol{r}$, finding the intersection of l_1 and l_2 means finding values of λ and μ which make $\boldsymbol{r}_1 = \boldsymbol{r}_2$.

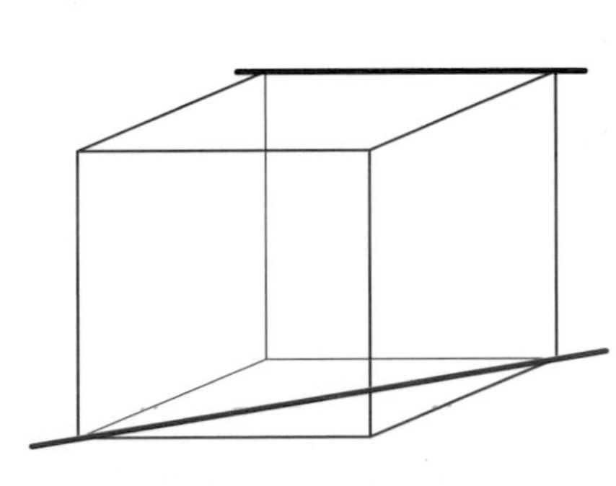

In a plane, two different straight lines either intersect or are parallel. However, in three dimensions it is possible to have lines which are not parallel but do not intersect either, like the red and blue lines in the diagram.

Such non-parallel, non-intersecting lines are called **skew lines**.

As we shall see, if l_1 and l_2 are skew lines, we will not be able to find values of λ and μ such that $\boldsymbol{r}_1 = \boldsymbol{r}_2$.

Worked example 11.18

Find the coordinates of the point of intersection of the following pairs of lines.

(a) $\boldsymbol{r}_1 = \begin{pmatrix} 0 \\ -4 \\ 1 \end{pmatrix} + \lambda \begin{pmatrix} 1 \\ 2 \\ 1 \end{pmatrix}$ and $\boldsymbol{r}_2 = \begin{pmatrix} 1 \\ 3 \\ 5 \end{pmatrix} + \mu \begin{pmatrix} 4 \\ -2 \\ -2 \end{pmatrix}$

(b) $\boldsymbol{r}_1 = \begin{pmatrix} -4 \\ 1 \\ 3 \end{pmatrix} + t \begin{pmatrix} 1 \\ 1 \\ 4 \end{pmatrix}$ and $\boldsymbol{r}_2 = \begin{pmatrix} 2 \\ 1 \\ 1 \end{pmatrix} + \lambda \begin{pmatrix} 2 \\ -3 \\ 2 \end{pmatrix}$

Try to make $\boldsymbol{r}_1 = \boldsymbol{r}_2$.

(a)

$$\begin{pmatrix} 0 \\ -4 \\ 1 \end{pmatrix} + \lambda \begin{pmatrix} 1 \\ 2 \\ 1 \end{pmatrix} = \begin{pmatrix} 1 \\ 3 \\ 5 \end{pmatrix} + \mu \begin{pmatrix} 4 \\ -2 \\ -2 \end{pmatrix}$$

$$\Leftrightarrow \begin{pmatrix} 0+\lambda \\ -4+2\lambda \\ 1+\lambda \end{pmatrix} = \begin{pmatrix} 1+4\mu \\ 3-2\mu \\ 5-2\mu \end{pmatrix}$$

For two vectors to be equal, all their components must be equal.

$$\Leftrightarrow \begin{cases} 0+\lambda = 1+4\mu \\ -4+2\lambda = 3-2\mu \\ 1+\lambda = 5-2\mu \end{cases}$$

$$\Leftrightarrow \begin{cases} \lambda - 4\mu = 1 & (1) \\ 2\lambda + 2\mu = 7 & (2) \\ \lambda + 2\mu = 4 & (3) \end{cases}$$

We know how to solve two simultaneous equations in two variables. Pick any two of the three equations. Let us use the first and third (because subtracting them eliminates λ).

$(3) - (1) \Leftrightarrow 6\mu = 3$

$\therefore \mu = \frac{1}{2}, \lambda = 3$

The values of λ and μ that we have found must also satisfy the remaining (i.e. second) equation. Check whether this is the case.

$(2): 2\times 3 + 2\times\frac{1}{2} = 7$

$\therefore$ the lines intersect

→

continued . . .

The position of the intersection point is given by $\boldsymbol{r}_1$ with the value of λ we found (or $\boldsymbol{r}_2$ with the value of μ we found – they should be the same).

$$\underline{r}_1 = \begin{pmatrix} 0 \\ -4 \\ 1 \end{pmatrix} + 3\begin{pmatrix} 1 \\ 2 \\ 1 \end{pmatrix} = \begin{pmatrix} 3 \\ 2 \\ 4 \end{pmatrix}$$

The lines intersect at the point (3, 2, 4).

Repeat the same procedure for the second pair of lines.

(b)

$$\begin{pmatrix} -4 \\ 3 \\ 3 \end{pmatrix} + t\begin{pmatrix} 1 \\ 1 \\ 4 \end{pmatrix} = \begin{pmatrix} 2 \\ 1 \\ 1 \end{pmatrix} + \lambda\begin{pmatrix} 2 \\ -3 \\ 2 \end{pmatrix}$$

$$\Leftrightarrow \begin{cases} t - 2\lambda = 6 & (1) \\ t + 3\lambda = -2 & (2) \\ 4t - 2\lambda = -2 & (3) \end{cases}$$

Solve for t and λ from the first two equations.

$$(2)-(1) \Rightarrow \lambda = -\frac{8}{5}, t = \frac{14}{5}$$

The values found should also satisfy the third equation.

$$(3): 4\times\frac{14}{5} - 2\times\left(-\frac{8}{5}\right) = \frac{72}{5} \neq -2$$

This tells us that it is impossible to find t and λ that make $\boldsymbol{r}_1 = \boldsymbol{r}_2$.

$\therefore$ the two lines do not intersect.

In vector problems you often need to find a point on a given line which satisfies certain conditions. We have already seen (in Worked example 11.15) how to use the position vector $\boldsymbol{r}$ of a general point on the line together with the given condition to write an equation for the parameter λ. In the next example we use more complicated conditions.

EXAM HINT

You may be able to use your calculator to solve simultaneous equations. See Calculator Skills sheet 6 on the CD-ROM for guidance on how to do this.

Worked example 11.19

Line l has equation $\boldsymbol{r} = \begin{pmatrix} 3 \\ -1 \\ 0 \end{pmatrix} + \lambda \begin{pmatrix} 1 \\ -1 \\ 1 \end{pmatrix}$, and point A has coordinates $(3, 9, -2)$.

(a) Find the coordinates of point B on l such that (AB) is perpendicular to l.

(b) Hence find the shortest distance from A to l.

(c) Find the coordinates of the reflection of the point A in l.

Draw a diagram. The line (AB) should be perpendicular to the direction vector of l.

(a)

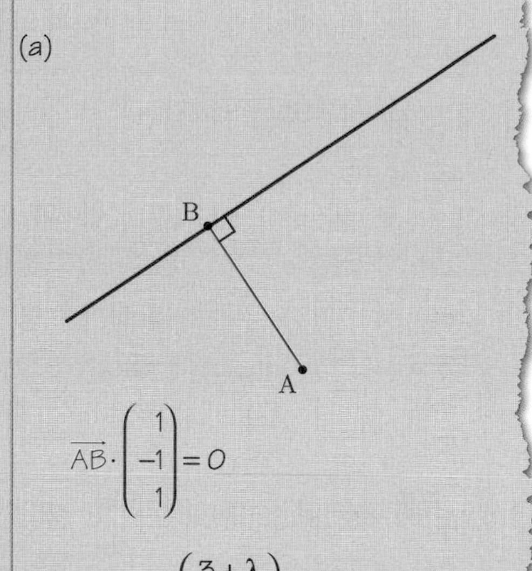

$\overrightarrow{AB} \cdot \begin{pmatrix} 1 \\ -1 \\ 1 \end{pmatrix} = 0$

We know that B lies on l, so its position vector is given by $\boldsymbol{r}$.

$\overrightarrow{OB} = \underline{r} = \begin{pmatrix} 3+\lambda \\ -1-\lambda \\ \lambda \end{pmatrix}$

$\overrightarrow{AB} = \boldsymbol{b} - \boldsymbol{a}$.

$\therefore \overrightarrow{AB} = \begin{pmatrix} 3+\lambda \\ -1-\lambda \\ \lambda \end{pmatrix} - \begin{pmatrix} 3 \\ 9 \\ -2 \end{pmatrix} = \begin{pmatrix} \lambda \\ -10-\lambda \\ \lambda+2 \end{pmatrix}$

We can now find the value of λ for which the two lines are perpendicular.

$\begin{pmatrix} \lambda \\ -10-\lambda \\ \lambda+2 \end{pmatrix} \cdot \begin{pmatrix} 1 \\ -1 \\ 1 \end{pmatrix} = 0$

$\Leftrightarrow (\lambda) + (10+\lambda) + (\lambda+2) = 0$

$\Leftrightarrow \lambda = -4$

Substitute the value we found for λ in the equation of the line to get the position vector of B.

$\therefore \underline{r} = \begin{pmatrix} -1 \\ 3 \\ -4 \end{pmatrix}$

B has coordinates $(-1, 3, -4)$

→

continued . . .

The shortest distance from a point to a line is the perpendicular distance, that is, the distance AB.

The reflection A_1 lies on the line (AB), with $BA_1 = AB$. As A_1 and A are on opposite sides of the line l, we have $\overrightarrow{BA_1} = \overrightarrow{AB}$ (draw a diagram to make this clear).

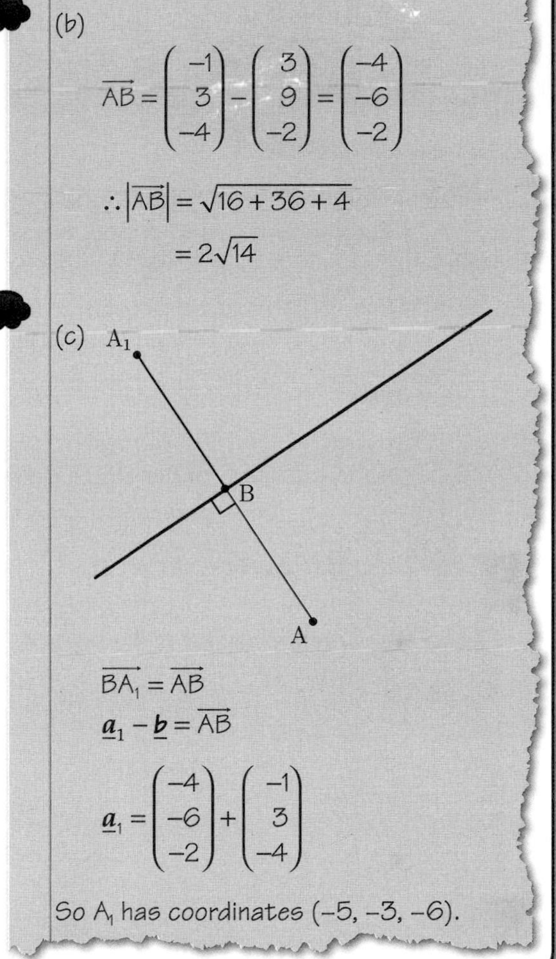

(b)
$\overrightarrow{AB} = \begin{pmatrix} -1 \\ 3 \\ -4 \end{pmatrix} - \begin{pmatrix} 3 \\ 9 \\ -2 \end{pmatrix} = \begin{pmatrix} -4 \\ -6 \\ -2 \end{pmatrix}$
$\therefore |\overrightarrow{AB}| = \sqrt{16+36+4}$
$= 2\sqrt{14}$
(c) A1
B
A
$\overrightarrow{BA_1} = \overrightarrow{AB}$
$\underline{a}_1 - \underline{b} = \overrightarrow{AB}$
$\underline{a}_1 = \begin{pmatrix} -4 \\ -6 \\ -2 \end{pmatrix} + \begin{pmatrix} -1 \\ 3 \\ -4 \end{pmatrix}$
So A_1 has coordinates (−5, −3, −6).

Part (c) of the above example illustrates the power of vectors: as vectors contain both distance and direction information, just one equation ($\overrightarrow{BA_1} = \overrightarrow{AB}$) was needed to express both the fact that A_1 is on the line (AB) and that $BA_1 = AB$.

One of the common applications of vectors is in mechanics. You may encounter questions in which the velocity of a moving object is given as a vector, and you have to use the information to find positions. In such a situation, remember that the position $\boldsymbol{r}$ of the object can be expressed as a vector equation where the parameter represents time (and hence is usually denoted by t) and the direction vector is the velocity vector:

$$\boldsymbol{r} = \boldsymbol{a} + t\boldsymbol{v}$$

In this equation, $\boldsymbol{a}$ is the position vector of the object at time $t = 0$.

Worked example 11.20

A ship leaves a port at (0, 1) and moves in a straight line so that after 5 hours it has reached point (20, 5). A lighthouse is situated at point (8, 2). At what time is the ship closest to the lighthouse, and what is the distance between them at that time?

Sketch a diagram. Mark the start position A, the lighthouse L, and the point B at which the boat is closest to the lighthouse. The line (BL) should be perpendicular to (AB).

(20, 5)
B
L (8, 2)
A (0, 1)

Write down the equation of the ship's path in terms of time t.

The start point has position vector $\boldsymbol{a} = \begin{pmatrix} 0 \\ 1 \end{pmatrix}$, and the direction vector is the velocity.

In 5 hours, the ship has moved from (0, 1) to (20, 5), so its velocity is $v = \frac{1}{5}\begin{pmatrix} 20 \\ 4 \end{pmatrix} = \begin{pmatrix} 4 \\ 0.8 \end{pmatrix}$

At time t hours, the ship has position

$$\boldsymbol{r} = \begin{pmatrix} 0 \\ 1 \end{pmatrix} + t\begin{pmatrix} 4 \\ 0.8 \end{pmatrix} = \begin{pmatrix} 4t \\ 1+0.8t \end{pmatrix}$$

The lighthouse has position vector

$$\boldsymbol{l} = \begin{pmatrix} 8 \\ 2 \end{pmatrix}$$

When the ship is at B, $\boldsymbol{r} - \boldsymbol{l}$ is perpendicular to the path of the ship.

$$\boldsymbol{r} - \boldsymbol{l} = \begin{pmatrix} 4t-8 \\ 0.8t-1 \end{pmatrix}$$

When the ship is at B,

$$(\boldsymbol{r} - \boldsymbol{l}) \cdot \begin{pmatrix} 4 \\ 0.8 \end{pmatrix} = 0$$

Now we can solve for the value of t at which the ship is at B.

$$\begin{pmatrix} 4t-8 \\ 0.8t-1 \end{pmatrix} \cdot \begin{pmatrix} 4 \\ 0.8 \end{pmatrix} = 0$$

$\Leftrightarrow 16t - 32 + 0.64t - 0.8 = 0$

$\Leftrightarrow 16.64t = 32.8$

$\Leftrightarrow t = 1.971$

The ship is closest to the lighthouse 1.97 hours (1 hour and 58 minutes) after leaving port.

→

continued . . .

Substitute this value for t in the equation of the line to find the position vector of B.

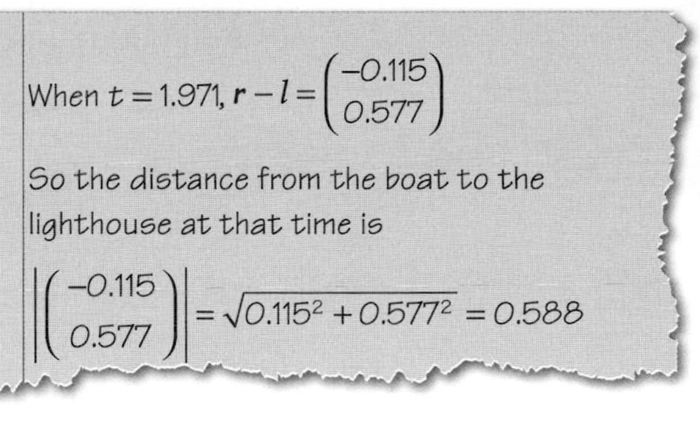

When $t = 1.971$, $r - l = \begin{pmatrix} -0.115 \\ 0.577 \end{pmatrix}$
So the distance from the boat to the lighthouse at that time is
$\left| \begin{pmatrix} -0.115 \\ 0.577 \end{pmatrix} \right| = \sqrt{0.115^2 + 0.577^2} = 0.588$

Exercise 11G

1. Find the acute angle between the following pairs of lines, giving your answer in degrees.

   (a) (i) $\boldsymbol{r} = \begin{pmatrix} 5 \\ -1 \\ 2 \end{pmatrix} + \lambda \begin{pmatrix} 2 \\ 2 \\ 3 \end{pmatrix}$ and $\boldsymbol{r} = \begin{pmatrix} 1 \\ 1 \\ 0 \end{pmatrix} + \mu \begin{pmatrix} 4 \\ -1 \\ 3 \end{pmatrix}$

   (ii) $\boldsymbol{r} = \begin{pmatrix} 4 \\ 0 \\ 2 \end{pmatrix} + \lambda \begin{pmatrix} 2 \\ -1 \\ 1 \end{pmatrix}$ and $\boldsymbol{r} = \begin{pmatrix} 1 \\ 0 \\ 2 \end{pmatrix} + \mu \begin{pmatrix} -5 \\ 1 \\ 3 \end{pmatrix}$

   (b) (i) $\boldsymbol{r} = (2\boldsymbol{i} + \boldsymbol{k}) - t\,\boldsymbol{i}$ and $\boldsymbol{r} = (\boldsymbol{i} + 3\boldsymbol{j} + 3\boldsymbol{k}) + 5\,(4\boldsymbol{i} + 2\boldsymbol{k})$

   (ii) $\boldsymbol{r} = (6\boldsymbol{i} + 6\boldsymbol{j} + 2\boldsymbol{k}) + t\,(-\boldsymbol{i} + 3\boldsymbol{k})$ and $\boldsymbol{r} = \boldsymbol{i} + 5\,(4\boldsymbol{i} - \boldsymbol{j} + 2\boldsymbol{k})$

2. For each pair of lines state whether they are parallel, perpendicular, the same line, or none of the above.

   (a) $\boldsymbol{r} = \boldsymbol{k} + \lambda(2\boldsymbol{i} - \boldsymbol{j} + 3\boldsymbol{k})$ and $\boldsymbol{r} = \boldsymbol{k} + \mu\,(2\boldsymbol{i} + \boldsymbol{j} - \boldsymbol{k})$

   (b) $\boldsymbol{r} = (4\boldsymbol{i} + \boldsymbol{j} + 2\boldsymbol{k}) + 5\,(-\boldsymbol{i} + 2\boldsymbol{j} + 2\boldsymbol{k})$ and $\boldsymbol{r} = (2\boldsymbol{i} + \boldsymbol{j} + \boldsymbol{k})$ $+ \boldsymbol{t}\,(2\boldsymbol{i} - 4\boldsymbol{i} + 4\boldsymbol{k})$

(c) $r = \begin{pmatrix} 1 \\ 5 \\ 2 \end{pmatrix} + \lambda \begin{pmatrix} 3 \\ 3 \\ 1 \end{pmatrix}$ and $r = \begin{pmatrix} 0 \\ 0 \\ 1 \end{pmatrix} + t \begin{pmatrix} 3 \\ 3 \\ 1 \end{pmatrix}$

(d) $r = \begin{pmatrix} 2 \\ 2 \\ 1 \end{pmatrix} + t \begin{pmatrix} 1 \\ -1 \\ 3 \end{pmatrix}$ and $r = \begin{pmatrix} 5 \\ -1 \\ 10 \end{pmatrix} + s \begin{pmatrix} 1 \\ -1 \\ 3 \end{pmatrix}$

3. Determine whether the following pairs of lines intersect; if they do, find the coordinates of the intersection point.

(a) (i) $r = \begin{pmatrix} 6 \\ 1 \\ 2 \end{pmatrix} + \lambda \begin{pmatrix} -1 \\ 2 \\ 1 \end{pmatrix}$ and $r = \begin{pmatrix} 2 \\ 1 \\ -14 \end{pmatrix} + \mu \begin{pmatrix} 2 \\ -2 \\ 3 \end{pmatrix}$

(ii) $r = \begin{pmatrix} 4 \\ -1 \\ 2 \end{pmatrix} + \lambda \begin{pmatrix} 1 \\ 2 \\ -4 \end{pmatrix}$ and $r = \begin{pmatrix} 6 \\ -2 \\ 0 \end{pmatrix} + \mu \begin{pmatrix} 3 \\ -4 \\ 0 \end{pmatrix}$

(b) (i) $r = (i - 2j + 3k) + t(-i + j + 2k)$ and $r = (-4i - 4j - 11k) + 5(5i + j + 2k)$

(ii) $r = (4i + 2k) + t(2i + k)$ and $r = (-i + 2j + 3k) + 5(i - 2i - 2j)$

4. Line l has equation $r = \begin{pmatrix} 4 \\ 2 \\ -1 \end{pmatrix} + \lambda \begin{pmatrix} 2 \\ -1 \\ 2 \end{pmatrix}$, and point P has coordinates (7,2,3). Point C lies on l and [PC] is perpendicular to l. Find the coordinates of C. *[6 marks]*

5. Find the shortest distance from the point (–1,1,2) to the line with equation $r = (i + 2k) + t(-3i + j + k)$ *[6 marks]*

6. Two lines are given by $l_1 : \boldsymbol{r} = \begin{pmatrix} -5 \\ 1 \\ 10 \end{pmatrix} + \lambda \begin{pmatrix} -3 \\ 0 \\ 4 \end{pmatrix}$ and

$l_2 : \boldsymbol{r} = \begin{pmatrix} 3 \\ 0 \\ -9 \end{pmatrix} + \mu \begin{pmatrix} 1 \\ 1 \\ 7 \end{pmatrix}$.

(a) l_1 and l_2 intersect at P. Find the coordinates of P.

(b) Show that the point Q(5, 2, 5) lies on l_2.

(c) Find the coordinates of the point M on l_1 such that [QM] is perpendicular to l_1.

(d) Find the area of the triangle PQM. *[10 marks]*

7. Find the distance of the line with equation $\boldsymbol{r} = \begin{pmatrix} 1 \\ -2 \\ 2 \end{pmatrix} + \lambda \begin{pmatrix} 2 \\ 2 \\ 1 \end{pmatrix}$ from the origin. *[7 marks]*

8. Two lines $l_1 : \boldsymbol{r} = \begin{pmatrix} 0 \\ -1 \\ 2 \end{pmatrix} + \lambda \begin{pmatrix} 1 \\ 5 \\ 3 \end{pmatrix}$ and $l_2 : \boldsymbol{r} = \begin{pmatrix} 2 \\ 2 \\ 1 \end{pmatrix} + t \begin{pmatrix} -1 \\ 1 \\ 3 \end{pmatrix}$ intersect at point P.

(a) Find the coordinates of P.

(b) Find, in degrees, the acute angle between the two lines.

Point Q has coordinates (−1,5,10).

(c) Show that Q lies on l_2.

(d) Find the distance PQ

(e) Hence find the shortest distance from Q to the line l_1. *[12 marks]*

9. Consider the line $\boldsymbol{r} = (5\boldsymbol{i} + \boldsymbol{j} + 2\boldsymbol{k}) + \lambda\,(2\boldsymbol{i} - 3\boldsymbol{j} + 3\boldsymbol{k})$ and the point P(21, 5, 10).

(a) Find the coordinates of point M on l such that [PM] is perpendicular to l.

(b) Show that the point Q(15,−14,17) lies on l.

(c) Find the coordinates of point R on l such that PR = PQ. *[10 marks]*

10. Two lines have equations $l_1 : \boldsymbol{r} = \begin{pmatrix} 2 \\ -1 \\ 0 \end{pmatrix} + \lambda \begin{pmatrix} 1 \\ -2 \\ 2 \end{pmatrix}$ and

$l_2 : \boldsymbol{r} = \begin{pmatrix} 2 \\ -1 \\ 0 \end{pmatrix} + \mu \begin{pmatrix} 1 \\ 1 \\ 2 \end{pmatrix}$ and intersect at point P.

(a) Show that Q(5, 2, 6) lies on l_2.

(b) R is a point on l_1 such that PR = PQ. Find the possible coordinates of R. *[8 marks]*

Summary

- A vector represents the displacement of one point from another.
- The displacement of a point from the origin is the point's **position vector**. The displacement between points with position vectors $\boldsymbol{a}$ and $\boldsymbol{b}$ is $\boldsymbol{b} - \boldsymbol{a}$; the midpoint between them has position vector $\frac{1}{2}(\boldsymbol{a} + \boldsymbol{b})$.
- Vectors can be expressed in terms of **base vectors** $\boldsymbol{i}$, $\boldsymbol{j}$ and $\boldsymbol{k}$ or as column vectors using **components**.
- The vector algebra operations of addition, subtraction and scalar multiplication can be carried out component by component, but it is also important to understand the geometric interpretation of these operations. When solving problems using vectors, drawing diagrams helps us see what calculations we need to do. Three-dimensional situations can be represented by two-dimensional diagrams, which do not have to be accurate to be useful.
- The **magnitude** of a vector can be calculated from the components of the vector:

$$|\boldsymbol{a}| = \sqrt{a_1^2 + a_2^2 + a_3^2}$$

- The distance between points with position vectors $\boldsymbol{a}$ and $\boldsymbol{b}$ is given by $|\boldsymbol{b} - \boldsymbol{a}|$.
- The unit vector in the direction of $\boldsymbol{a}$ is $|\hat{\boldsymbol{a}}| = \frac{1}{|\boldsymbol{a}|}\boldsymbol{a}$.
- The angle θ between the directions of vectors $\boldsymbol{a}$ and $\boldsymbol{b}$ is given by $\cos\theta = \frac{\boldsymbol{a} \cdot \boldsymbol{b}}{|\boldsymbol{a}||\boldsymbol{b}|}$ where $\boldsymbol{a} \cdot \boldsymbol{b}$ is the **scalar product**, defined in terms of the components as

$$\boldsymbol{a} \cdot \boldsymbol{b} = a_1 b_1 + a_2 b_2 + a_3 b_3$$

- For perpendicular vectors, $\boldsymbol{a} \cdot \boldsymbol{b} = 0$.
- For parallel vectors, $\boldsymbol{a} \cdot \boldsymbol{b} = |\boldsymbol{a}||\boldsymbol{b}|$ and $\boldsymbol{a} = t\boldsymbol{b}$ for some non-zero scalar t.
- A **vector equation** of a line gives the position vectors of points on the line. It is of the form

$$\boldsymbol{r} = \boldsymbol{a} + \lambda \boldsymbol{d}$$

where $\boldsymbol{d}$ is a vector in the direction of the line, $\boldsymbol{a}$ is the position vector of one point on the line, and λ is a parameter whose values correspond to different points on the line.

- The angle between two lines is the angle between their direction vectors.
- Two lines with direction vectors $\boldsymbol{d}_1$ and $\boldsymbol{d}_2$ are
  - parallel if $\mathbf{d}_1 = k\mathbf{d}_2$
  - perpendicular if $\boldsymbol{d}_1 \cdot \boldsymbol{d}_2 = 0$
- To find the intersection of two lines with three-dimensional vector equations $\boldsymbol{r}_1 = \boldsymbol{a}_1 + \lambda \boldsymbol{d}_1$ and $\boldsymbol{r}_2 = \boldsymbol{a}_2 + \mu \boldsymbol{d}_2$, set the position vectors equal to each other: $\boldsymbol{a}_1 + \lambda \boldsymbol{d}_1 = \boldsymbol{a}_2 + \mu \boldsymbol{d}_2$. This gives three equations (one for each component); solve two of the them to find λ and μ. If these values also satisfy the remaining equation, they give the point of intersection of the two lines; if not, the lines are **skew**.

Introductory problem revisited

What is the angle between the diagonals of a cube?

This problem can be solved by applying the cosine rule to one of the triangles made by the diagonals and one side. However, using vectors gives a slightly faster solution, as we do not have to find the lengths of the sides of the triangle.

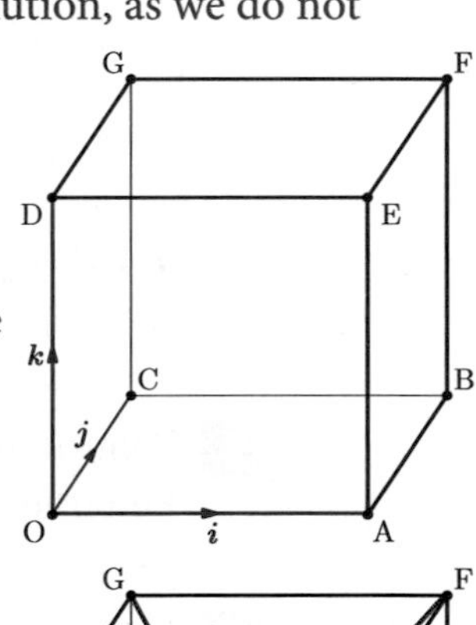

The angle between two lines can be found from the direction vectors of the lines and the formula involving the scalar product. We do not know the actual positions of the vertices of the cube, or even the length of its sides. But the angle between the diagonals does not depend on the size of the cube, so we can, for simplicity, look at the cube with side length 1 that has one vertex at the origin and sides parallel to the base vectors.

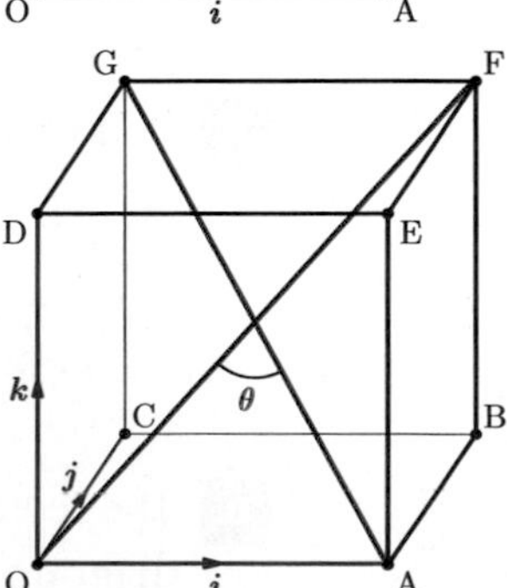

We want to find the angle between the diagonals OF and AG, so we need the coordinates of those four vertices; they are O(0, 0, 0), A(1, 0, 0), F(1, 1, 1) and G(0, 1, 1). The required angle θ is between the lines OF and AG. The corresponding vectors are

$$\overrightarrow{OF} = \begin{pmatrix} 1 \\ 1 \\ 1 \end{pmatrix} \text{ and } \overrightarrow{AG} = \begin{pmatrix} -1 \\ 1 \\ 1 \end{pmatrix}$$

Now we can use the formula:

$$\begin{aligned} \cos\theta &= \frac{\overrightarrow{OF} \cdot \overrightarrow{AG}}{|\overrightarrow{OF}||\overrightarrow{AG}|} \\ &= \frac{-1+1+1}{\sqrt{3}\sqrt{3}} = \frac{1}{3} \\ \therefore \theta &= 70.5° \end{aligned}$$

Mixed examination practice 11

Short questions

1. Find a vector equation of the line passing through points (3,−1,1) and (6,0,1). *[4 marks]*

2. The diagram shows a rectangle ABCD. M is the midpoint of [BC].

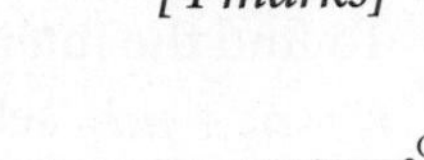

(a) Express $\overrightarrow{MD}$ in terms of $\overrightarrow{AB}$ and $\overrightarrow{AD}$.

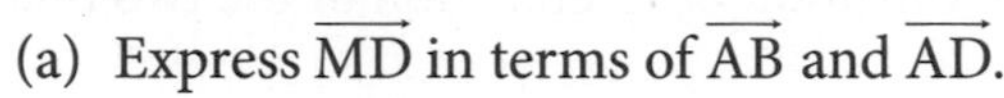

(b) Given that AB = 6 and AD = 4, show that $\overrightarrow{MD} \cdot \overrightarrow{MC} = 4$. *[5 marks]*

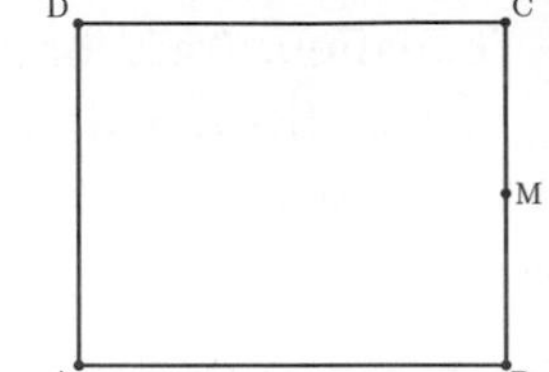

3. Points A(−1,1,2) and B(3,5,4) lie on the line with equation

$$\boldsymbol{r} = \begin{pmatrix} -1 \\ 1 \\ 2 \end{pmatrix} + \lambda \begin{pmatrix} 2 \\ 2 \\ 1 \end{pmatrix}.$$ Find the coordinates

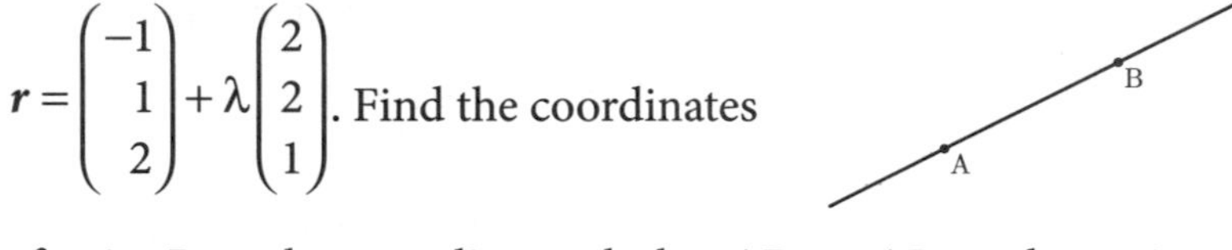

of point P on the same line such that AP = 3 AB, as shown in the diagram. *[5 marks]*

4. Point A(−3,0,4) lies on the line with equation $\boldsymbol{r} = -3\boldsymbol{i} + 4\boldsymbol{k} + \lambda(2\boldsymbol{i} + 2\boldsymbol{j} - \boldsymbol{k})$. Find the coordinates of one point on the line which is 10 units from A. *[6 marks]*

5. Points A(4,1,12) and B(8,−11,20) lie on the line l.

(a) Find an equation for line l, giving your answer in vector form.

(b) The point P is on l such that $\overrightarrow{OP}$ is perpendicular to l. Find the coordinates of P. *[6 marks]*

6. The rectangular box shown in the diagram has dimensions 6cm × 5cm × 3cm. Find, correct to the nearest one-tenth of a degree, the size of the angle $A\hat{H}C$. *[6 marks]*

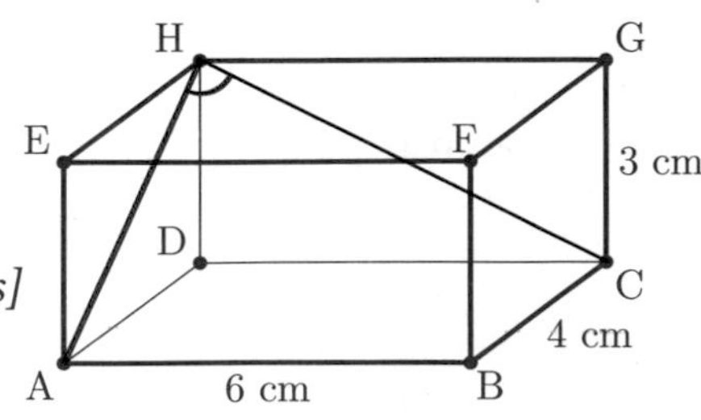

7. Let α be the angle between vectors $\boldsymbol{a}$ and $\boldsymbol{b}$, where $\boldsymbol{a} = (\cos\theta)\boldsymbol{i} + (\sin\theta)\boldsymbol{j}$ and $\boldsymbol{b} = (\sin\theta)\boldsymbol{i} + (\cos\theta)\boldsymbol{j}$, with $0 < \theta < \pi/4$. Express α in terms of θ.

[6 marks]

(© *IB Organization 2000*)

8. Given two non-zero vectors $\boldsymbol{a}$ and $\boldsymbol{b}$ such that $|\boldsymbol{a}+\boldsymbol{b}| = |\boldsymbol{a}-\boldsymbol{b}|$, find the value of $\boldsymbol{a}\cdot\boldsymbol{b}$.

[6 marks]

(© *IB Organization 2002*)

9. (a) Show that $(\boldsymbol{b}-\boldsymbol{a})\cdot(\boldsymbol{b}-\boldsymbol{a}) = |\boldsymbol{a}|^2 + |\boldsymbol{b}|^2 - 2\boldsymbol{a}\cdot\boldsymbol{b}$.

(b) In triangle MNP, $\text{M}\hat{\text{P}}\text{N} = \theta$. Let $\overrightarrow{\text{PM}} = \boldsymbol{a}$ and $\overrightarrow{\text{PN}} = \boldsymbol{b}$. Use the result from part (a) to derive the cosine rule: $\text{MN}^2 = \text{PM}^2 + \text{PN}^2 - 2\text{PM}\times\text{PN}\cos\theta$.

[6 marks]

Long questions

1. Points A, B and D have coordinates (1,1,7), (−1,6,3) and (3,1,k), respectively. (AD) is perpendicular to (AB).

(a) Write down, in terms of k, the vector $\overrightarrow{\text{AD}}$.

(b) Show that $k = 6$.

Point C is such that $\overrightarrow{\text{BC}} = 2\overrightarrow{\text{AD}}$.

(c) Find the coordinates of C.

(d) Find the exact value of $\cos(\text{A}\hat{\text{D}}\text{C})$.

[10 marks]

2. Points A and B have coordinates (4,1,2) and (0,5,1). Line l_1 passes through A and has equation $\boldsymbol{r}_1 = \begin{pmatrix}4\\1\\2\end{pmatrix} + \lambda\begin{pmatrix}2\\-1\\3\end{pmatrix}$. Line l_2 passes through B and has equation $\boldsymbol{r}_2 = \begin{pmatrix}0\\5\\1\end{pmatrix} + t\begin{pmatrix}4\\-4\\1\end{pmatrix}$.

(a) Show that the line l_2 also passes through A.

(b) Calculate the distance AB.

(c) Find the angle between l_1 and l_2 in degrees.

(d) Hence find the shortest distance from A to l_1.

[10 marks]

3. A triangle has vertices A(1,1,2), B(4,4,2) and C(2,1,6). Point D lies on the side [AB] and AD : DB = 1 : k.

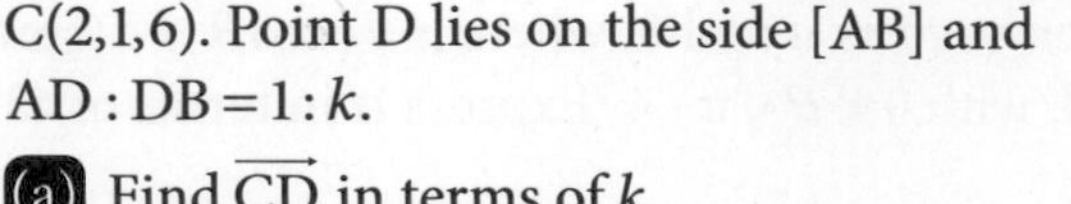

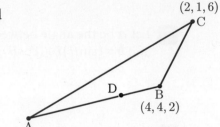

(a) Find $\overrightarrow{CD}$ in terms of k.

(b) Find the value of k such that [CD] is perpendicular to [AB].

(c) For the above value of k, find the coordinates of D.

(d) Hence find the length of the perpendicular line from vertex C which passes through [AB]. *[10 marks]*

4. Point P lies on the parabola $y = x^2$ and has x-coordinate a ($a > 0$).

(a) Write down, in terms of a, the coordinates of P.

Point S has coordinates (0, 4).

(b) Write down the vectors $\overrightarrow{PO}$ and $\overrightarrow{PS}$.

(c) Use the scalar product to find the value of a for which [OP] is perpendicular to [PS].

(d) For the value of a found above, calculate the exact area of the triangle OPS.

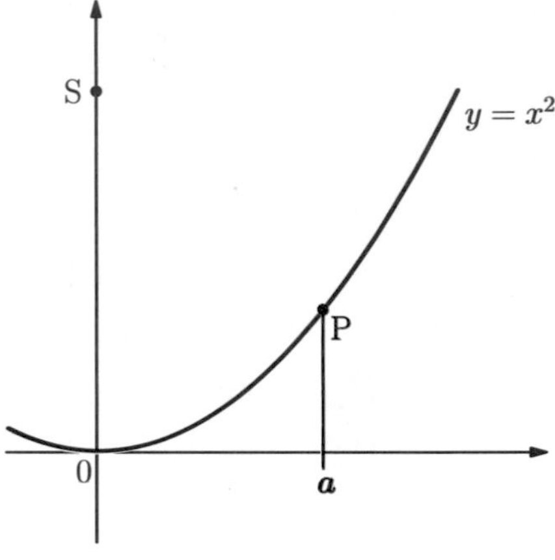

[10 marks]

5. *In this question, the base vectors* **i** *and* **j** *point due east and due north, respectively.*

A port is located at the origin. One ship starts from the port and moves with velocity $v_1 = (3\boldsymbol{i} + 4\boldsymbol{j})$ km/h.

(a) Write down the ship's position vector at time t hours after leaving port.

A second ship starts at the same time from 18 km north of the port and moves with velocity $v_2 = (3\boldsymbol{i} - 5\boldsymbol{j})$ km/h.

(b) Write down the position vector of the second ship at time t hours.

(c) Show that after half an hour, the distance between the two ships is 13.5 km.

(d) Show that the ships meet, and find the time at which this happens.

(e) How long after the ships meet are they 18 km apart? *[12 marks]*

6. At time $t = 0$ two aircraft have position vectors $5\boldsymbol{j}$ and $7\boldsymbol{k}$. The first moves with velocity $3\boldsymbol{i} - 4\boldsymbol{j} + \boldsymbol{k}$ and the second with velocity $5\boldsymbol{i} + 2\boldsymbol{j} - \boldsymbol{k}$.

(a) Write down the position vector of the first aircraft at time t.

(b) Show that at time t, the distance d between the two aircraft is given by $d^2 = 44t^2 - 88t + 74$.

(c) Show that the two aircraft will not collide.

(d) Find the minimum distance between the two aircraft. *[12 marks]*

7. (a) Show that the lines $l_1 : \boldsymbol{r} = \begin{pmatrix} -3 \\ 3 \\ 18 \end{pmatrix} + \lambda \begin{pmatrix} 2 \\ -1 \\ -8 \end{pmatrix}$ and $l_2 : \boldsymbol{r} = \begin{pmatrix} 5 \\ 0 \\ 2 \end{pmatrix} + \mu \begin{pmatrix} 1 \\ 1 \\ -1 \end{pmatrix}$ do not intersect.

(b) Points P and Q lie on l_1 and l_2, respectively. (PQ) is perpendicular to both lines.

(i) Write down $\overrightarrow{PQ}$ in terms of λ and μ.

(ii) Show that $9\mu - 69\lambda + 147 = 0$.

(iii) Find a second equation for λ and μ.

(iv) Find the coordinates of P and the coordinates of Q.

(v) Hence find the shortest distance between l_1 and l_2. *[14 marks]*

8. (a) Find the vector equation of the line L through point $A(-2,4,2)$ parallel to the vector $\boldsymbol{l} = \begin{pmatrix} 1 \\ 1 \\ 0 \end{pmatrix}$.

(b) Point B has coordinates (2,3,3). Find the cosine of the angle between (AB) and the line L.

(c) Calculate the distance AB.

(d) Point C lies on L and [BC] is perpendicular to L. Find the exact distance AC. *[10 marks]*

12 Basic differentiation and its applications

In this chapter you will learn:

- how to find the gradients of curves from first principles – a process called differentiation
- to differentiate x^n
- to differentiate $\sin x$, $\cos x$ and $\tan x$
- to differentiate e^x and $\ln x$
- how to find the equations of tangents and normals to curves at given points
- how to find maximum and minimum points on curves, as well as points of inflexion.

Introductory problem

The cost of petrol consumed by a car is £$\left(12+\frac{v^2}{100}\right)$ per hour, where the speed $v\ (>0)$ is measured in miles per hour. If Daniel wants to travel 50 miles as cheaply as possible, what speed should he go at?

In real life things change: planets move, babies grow and prices rise. Calculus is the study of change, and one of its most important tools is differentiation, that is, finding the rate at which the y-coordinate of a curve is changing when the x-coordinate changes. For a straight-line graph, this rate of change was given by the gradient of the line. In this chapter we apply the same idea to curves, where the gradient is different at different points.

We already met tangents in chapters 3 and 9.

12A Sketching derivatives

Our first task is to establish exactly what is meant by the gradient of a function. We are clear on what is meant by the gradient of a straight line, so we will use this idea to make a more general definition. A **tangent** to a curve is a straight line which touches the curve without crossing it. We define the **gradient** of a function at a point P to be the gradient of the tangent to the function's graph at that point.

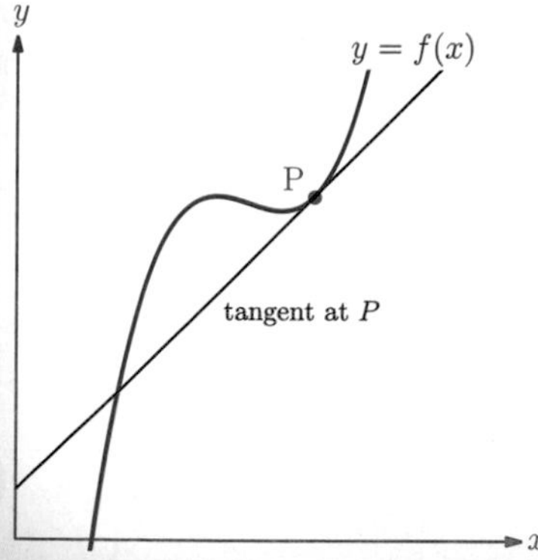

Note that when we say the tangent at P does not cross the curve, we mean this in a 'local' sense – that is, the tangent does not cross the curve close to the point P; it can intersect a different part of the curve (as shown in the diagram).

The **derivative** of a function $f(x)$ is a function which gives the gradient of $y = f(x)$ at any point x in the domain. It is often useful to be able to roughly sketch the derivative of a given function.

Worked example 12.1

Sketch the derivative of this function.

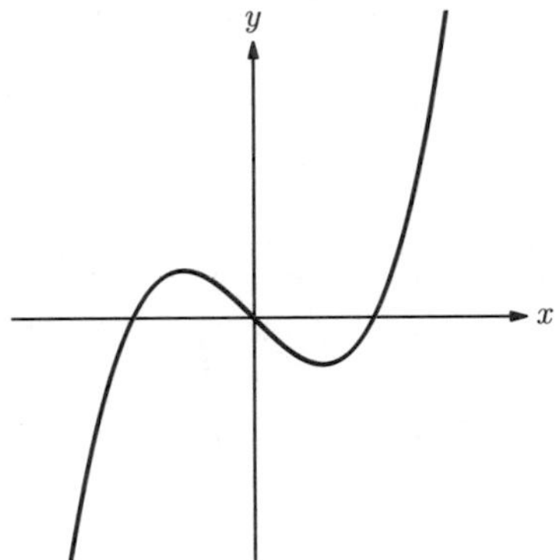

y
x

Imagine a point moving along the curve from left to right; we will track the tangent to the curve at the moving point and form the graph of its gradient.

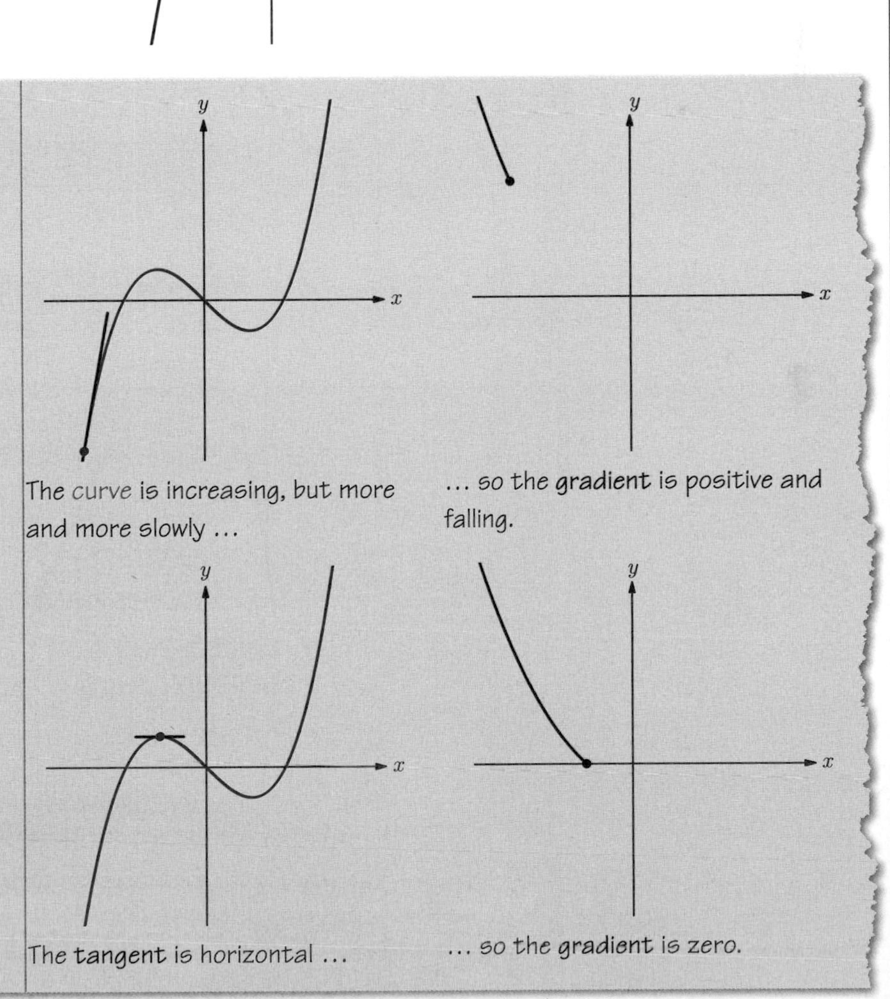

y
x
The curve is increasing, but more and more slowly ...
... so the gradient is positive and falling.
The tangent is horizontal ...
... so the gradient is zero.

continued . . .

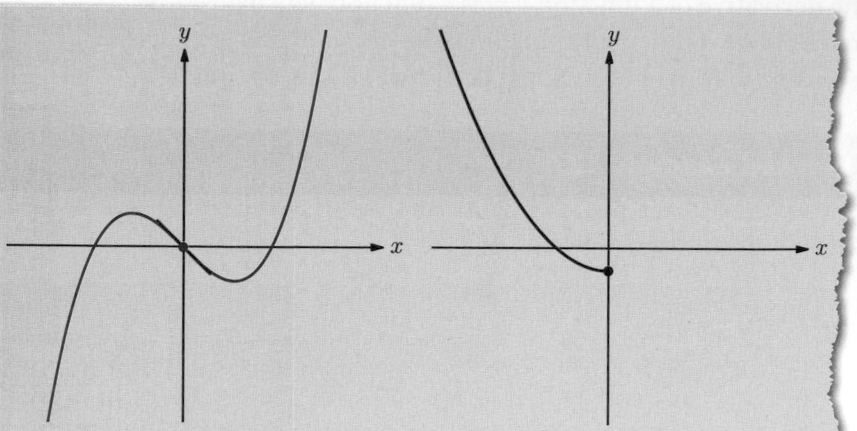

The curve is now decreasing ...

... so the gradient is negative.

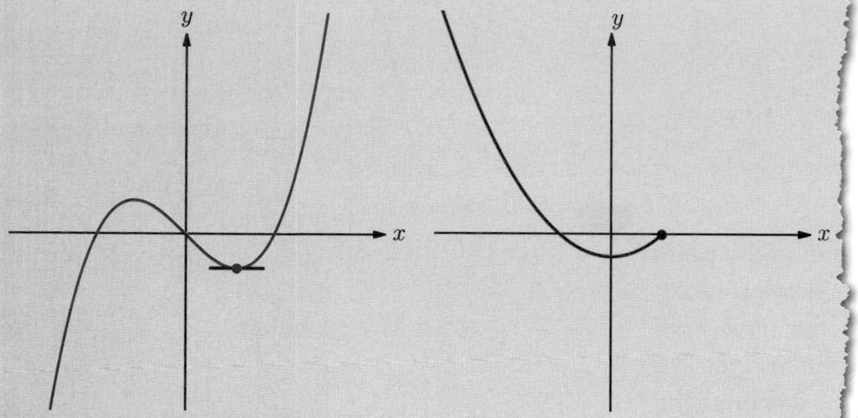

The tangent becomes horizontal again ...

... so the gradient is zero.

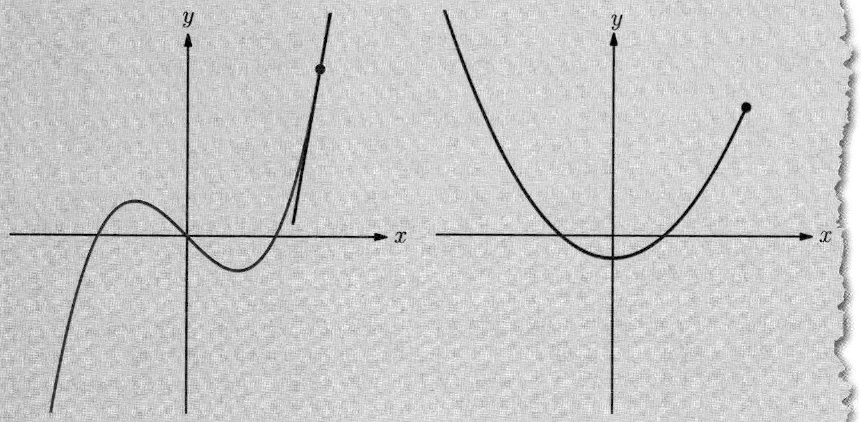

The curve increases again, and does so faster and faster ...

... so the gradient is positive and getting larger.

We can also apply the same reasoning backwards.

Worked example 12.2

The graph shows the derivative of a function. Sketch a possible graph of the original function.

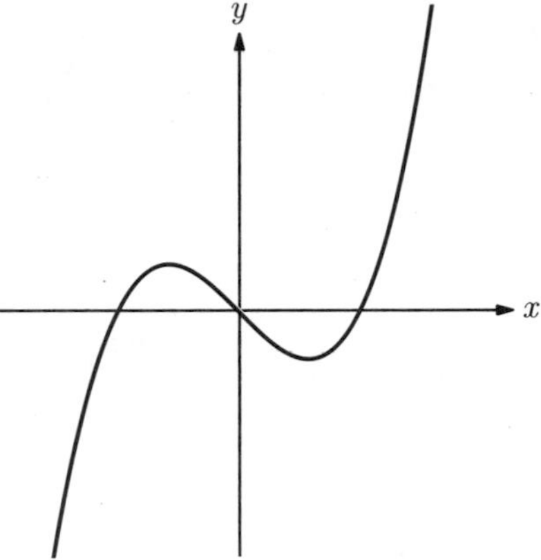

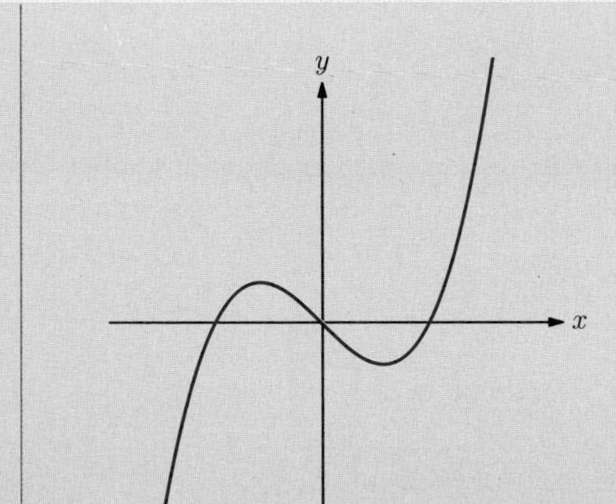

The gradient is negative ...

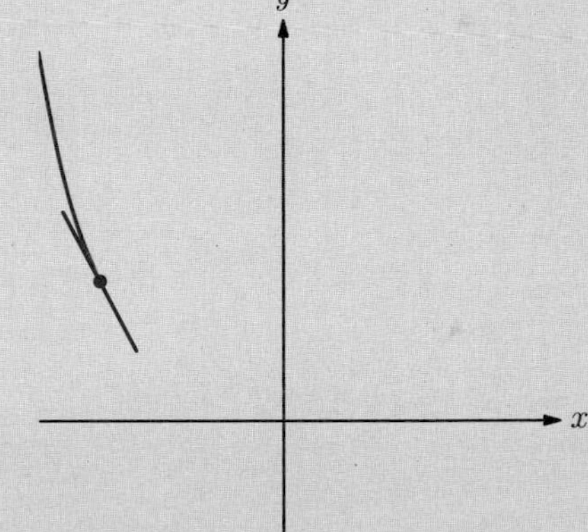

... so the curve is decreasing.

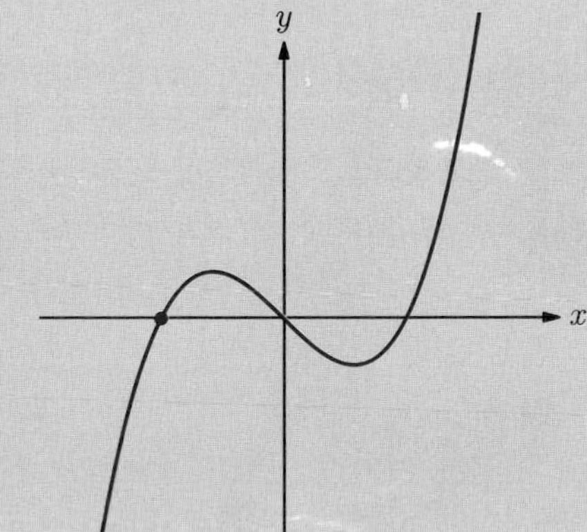

The gradient is zero ...

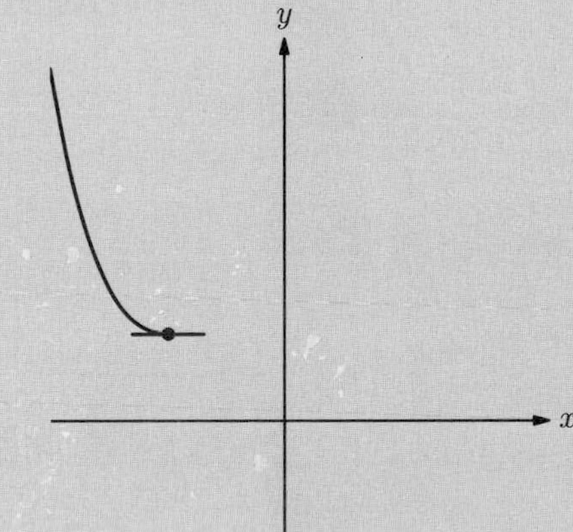

... so the tangent is horizontal.

→

continued . . .

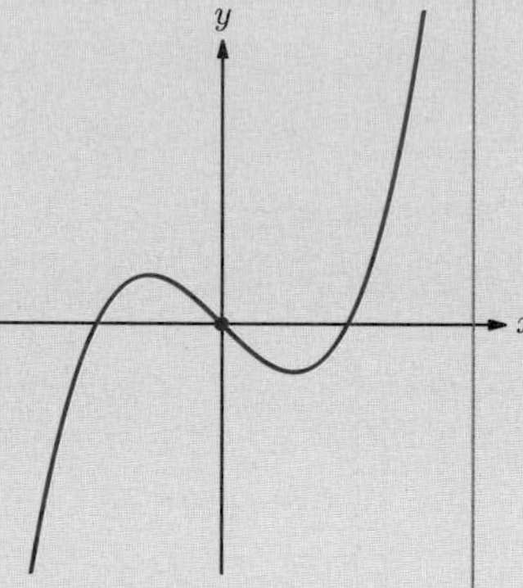

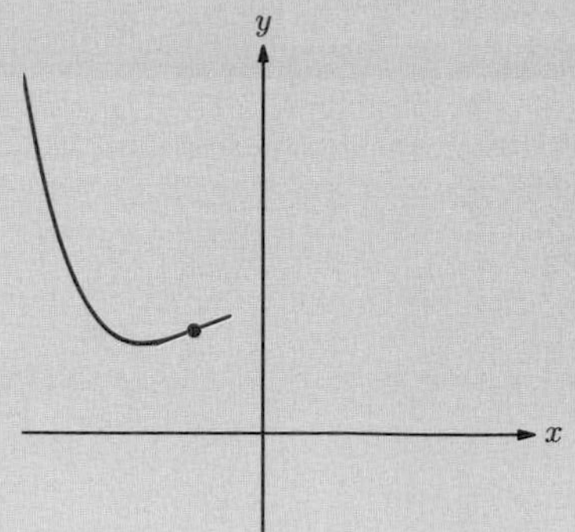

The gradient is positive ... ... so the curve is increasing.

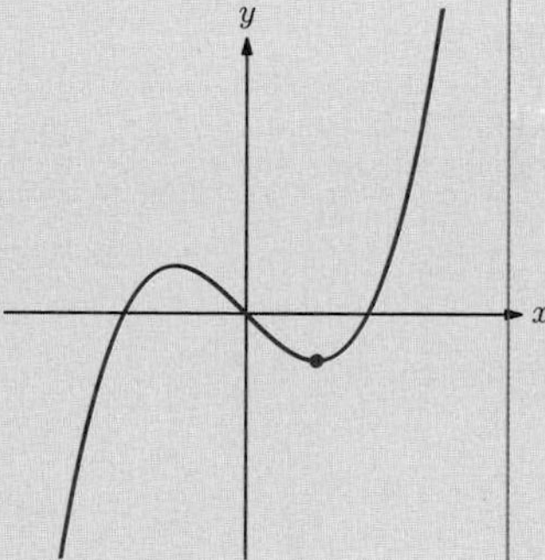

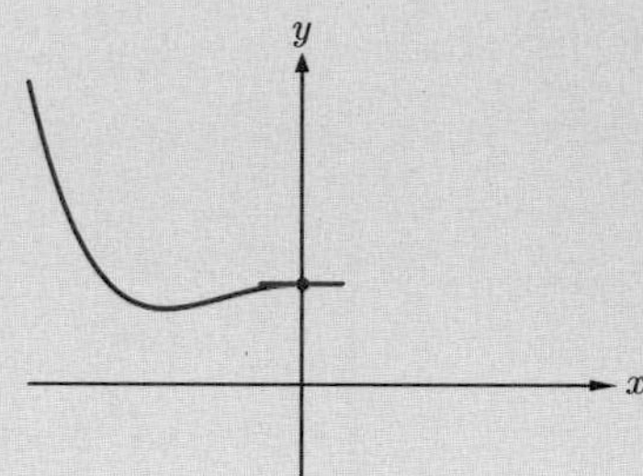

The gradient is zero ... ... so the tangent is horizontal.

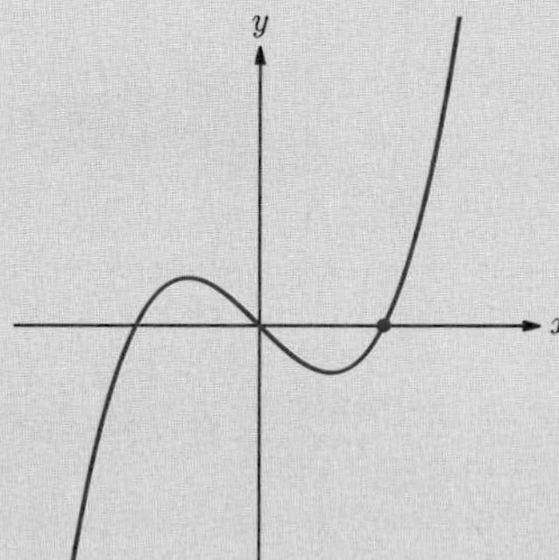

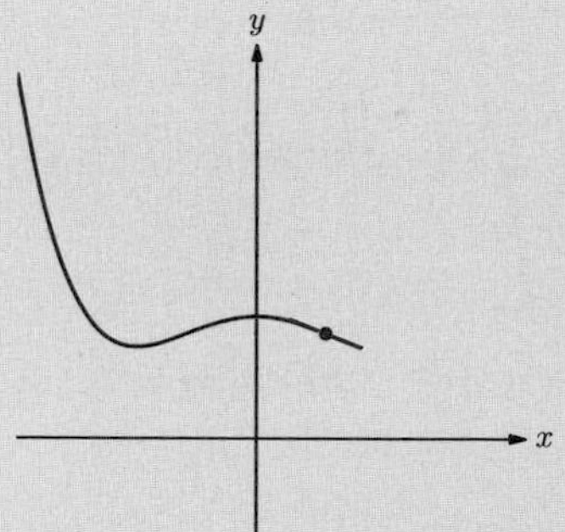

The gradient is negative ... ... so the curve is decreasing.

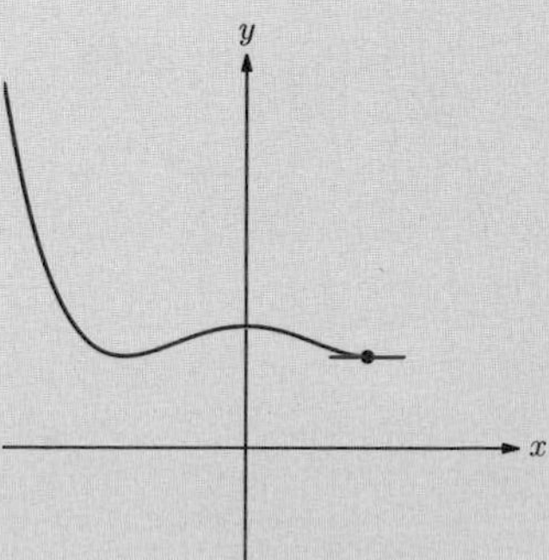

The gradient is zero ... ... so the tangent is horizontal.

continued . . .

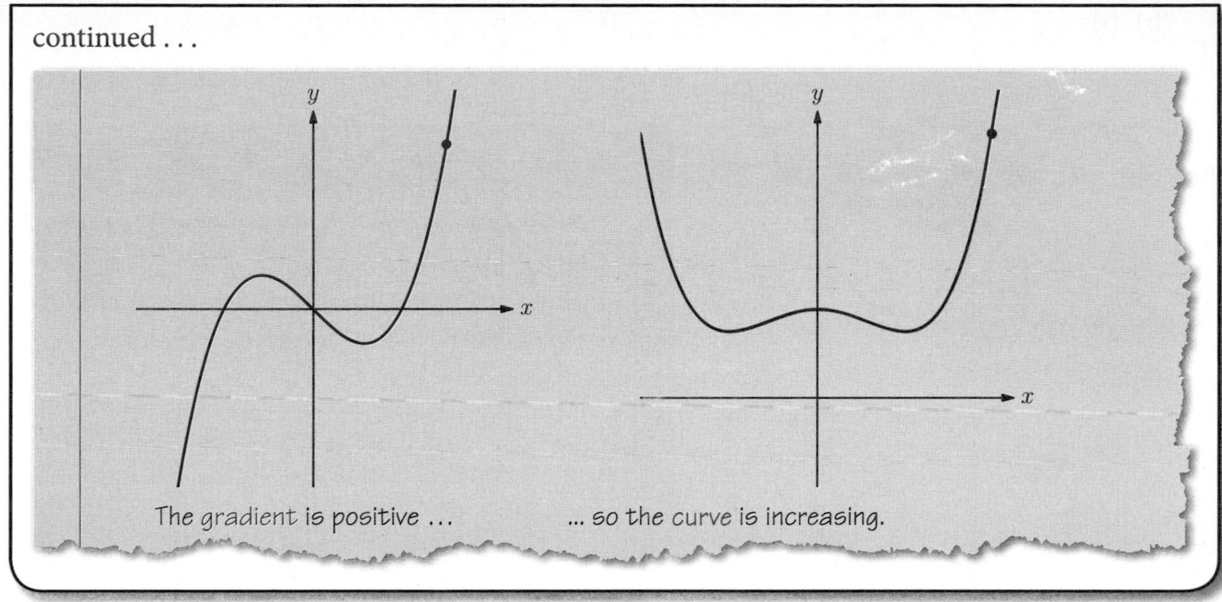

Note that in Worked example 12.2 there was more than one possible graph we could have drawn, depending on where we started the sketch. In chapter 13 you will see more about this ambiguity when you learn how to 'undo' differentiation.

The relationship between a graph and its derivative can be summarised as follows.

KEY POINT 12.1

When the curve is increasing the gradient is positive.

When the curve is decreasing the gradient is negative.

When the tangent is horizontal the gradient is zero. A point on the curve where this occurs is called a **stationary point** or **turning point**.

Exercise 12A

1. Sketch the derivatives of the following, showing intercepts with the x-axis.

(a) (i)

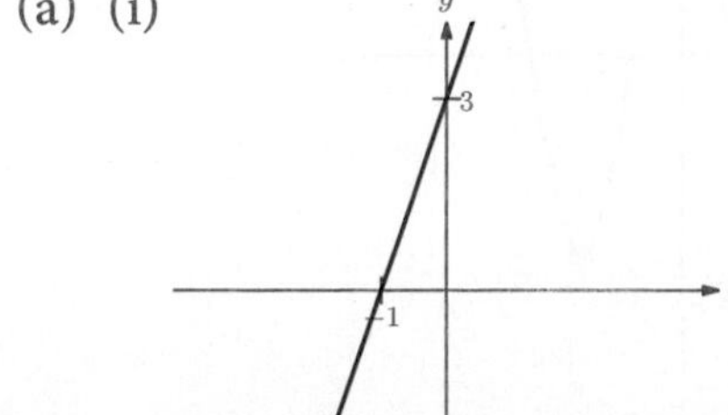

(ii)

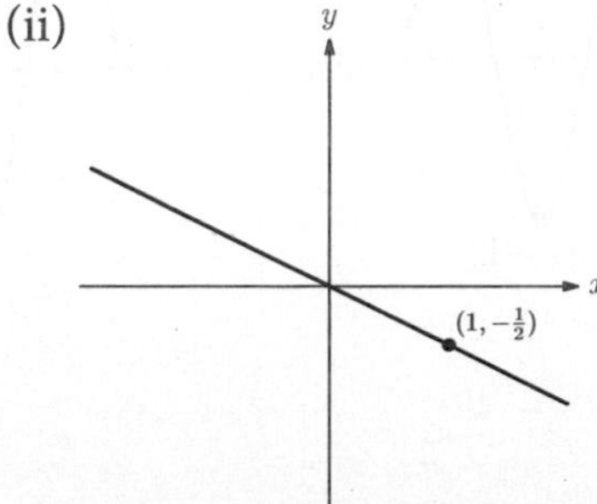

(b) (i)

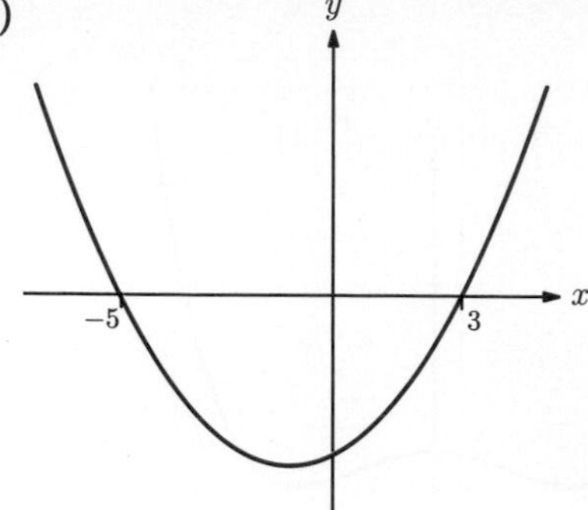

(ii)

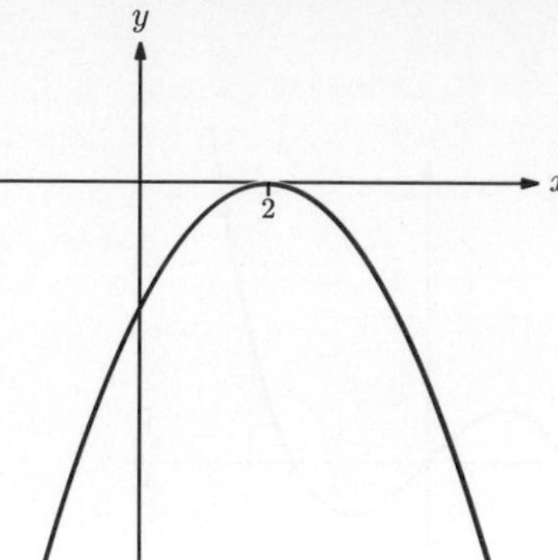

(c) (i)

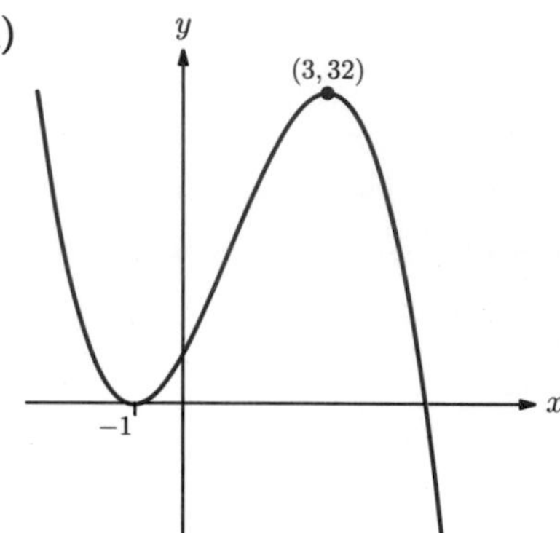

(ii)

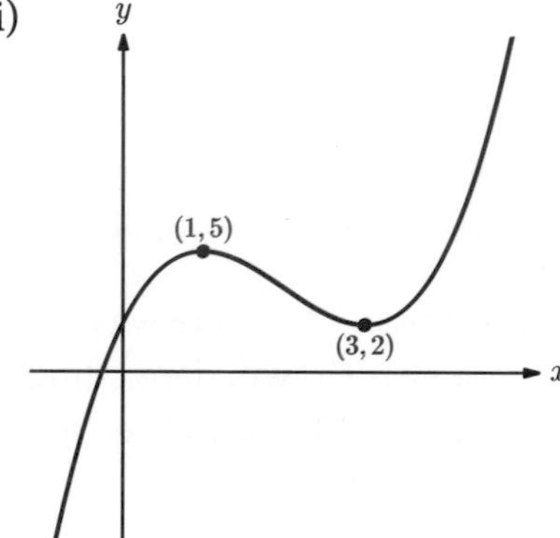

(d) (i)

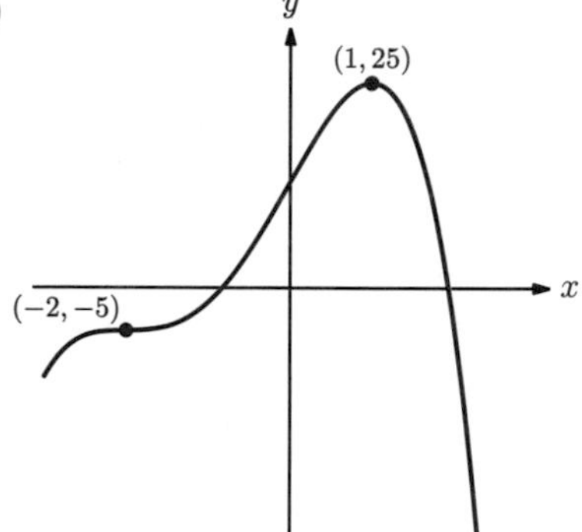

(ii)

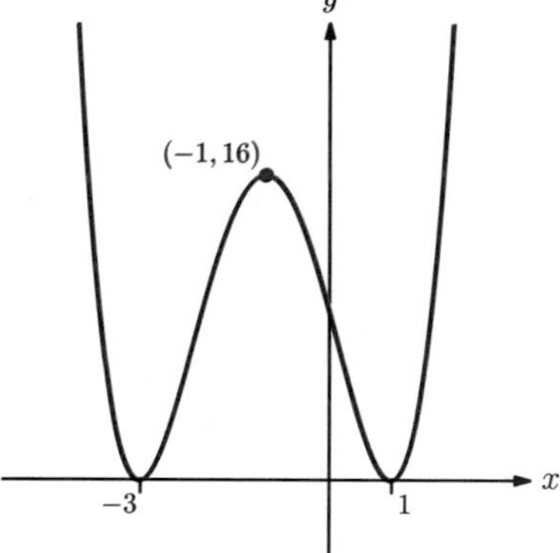

(e) (i)

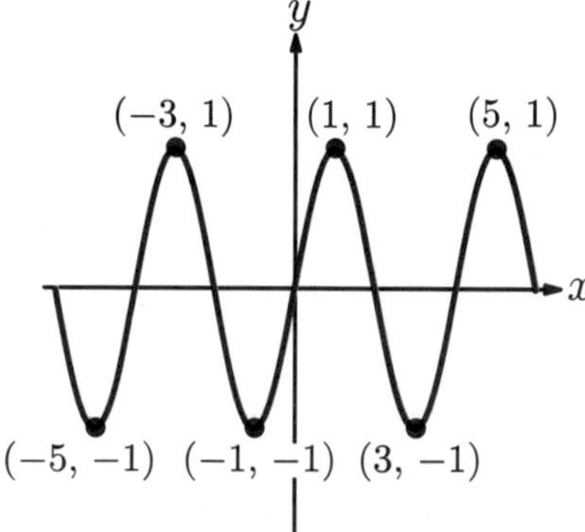

(ii)

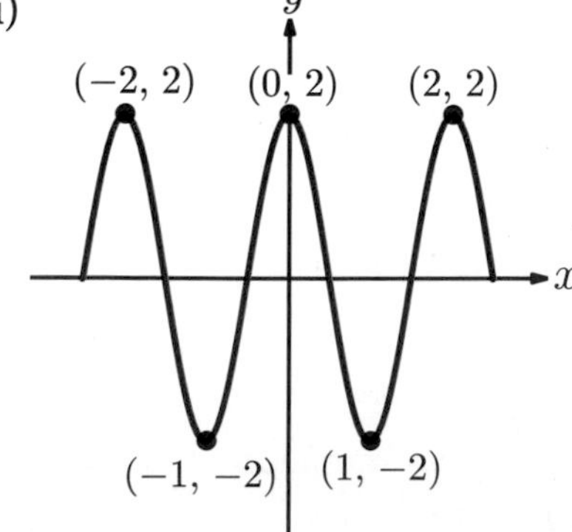

(f) (i)

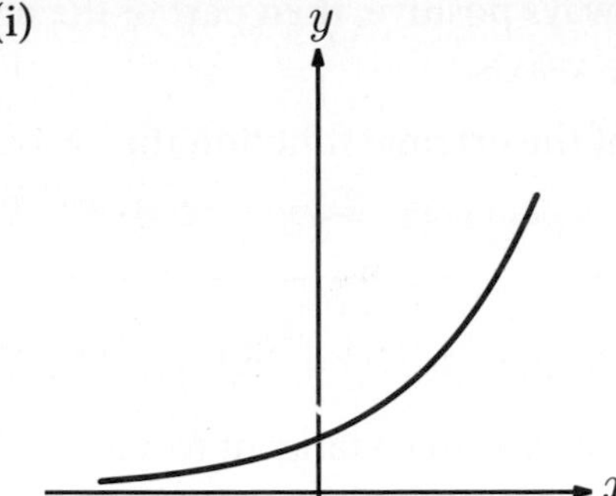

(ii)

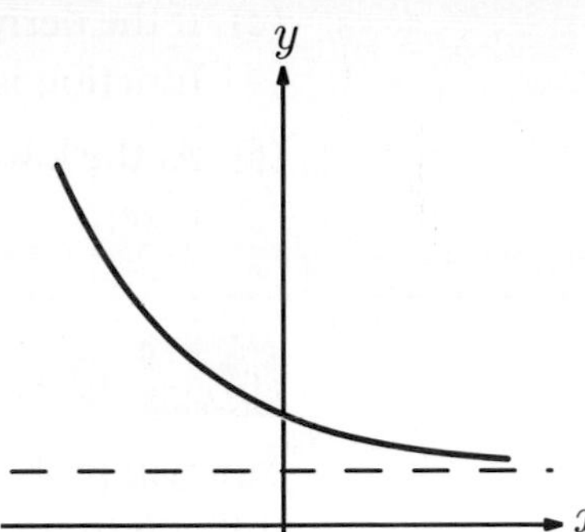

2. Each of the following graphs represents a function's derivative. Sketch a possible graph for the original function, indicating any stationary points.

(a)

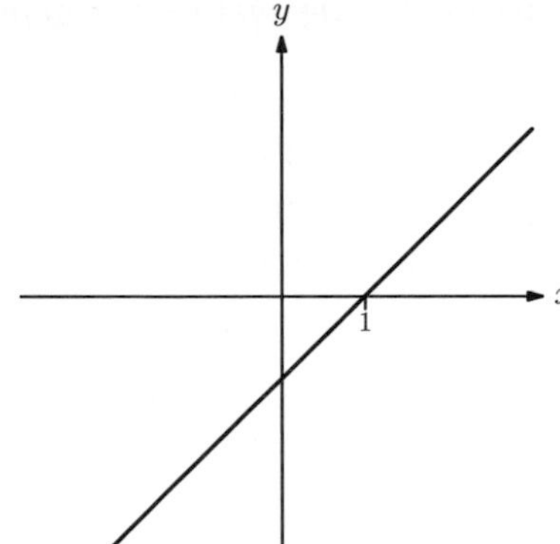

(b)

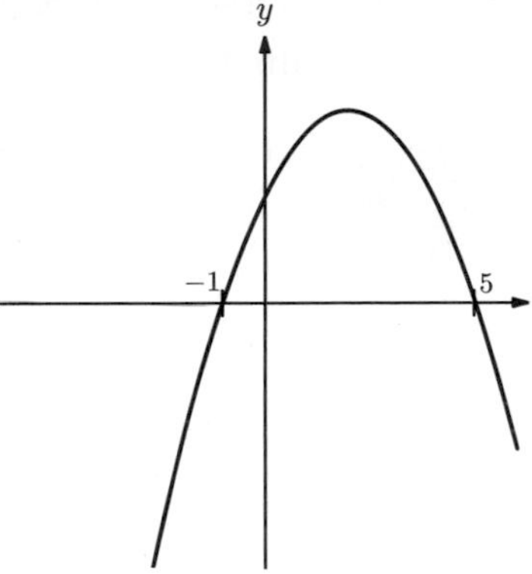

(c)

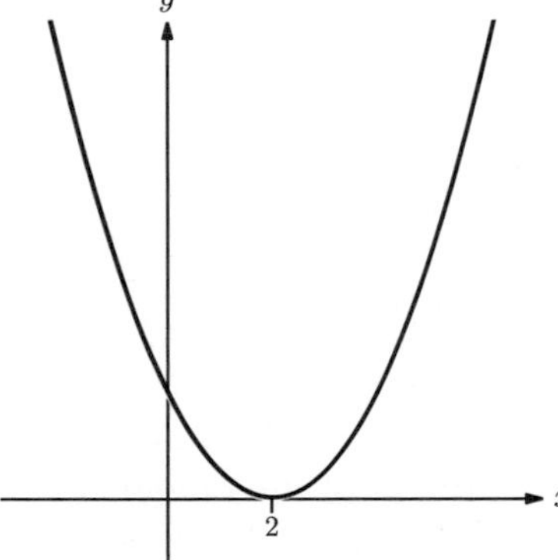

(d)

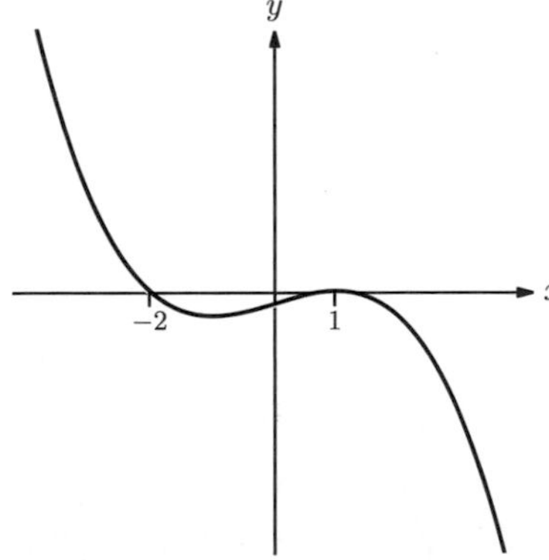

3. Decide whether each of the following statements is always true, sometimes true or always false.

(a) At a point where the derivative is positive the original function is positive.

(b) When the original function is negative the derivative is also negative.

(c) The derivative crossing the x-axis corresponds to a stationary point on the function's graph.

(d) When the derivative is zero the graph is at a local maximum or minimum point.

(e) If the derivative is always positive, then part of the original function is above the x-axis.

(f) At the lowest value of the original function the derivative is zero.

12B Differentiation from first principles

You will probably find that drawing a tangent to a graph is quite difficult to do accurately, and that the line you draw typically crosses the curve at two points. The line segment between these two intersection points is called a **chord**. If the two points are close together, the gradient of the chord will be very close to the gradient of the tangent. We can use this geometric insight to develop a method for calculating the derivative of a given function.

Self-Discovery Worksheet 3 'Investigating derivatives of polynomials' on the CD-ROM leads you through several concrete examples of using this method. Here we summarise the general procedure.

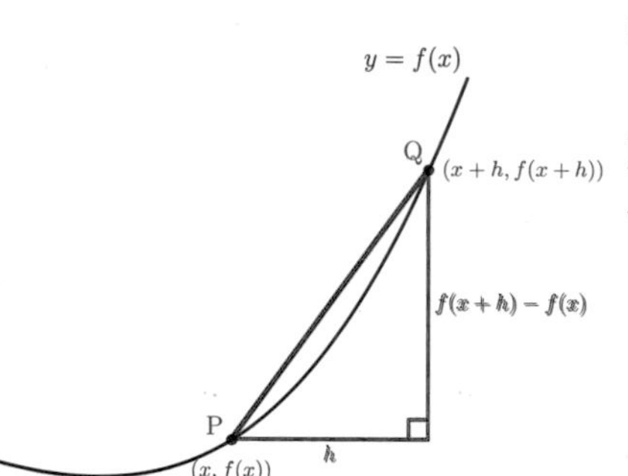

Consider a point $\mathrm{P}(x, f(x))$ on the graph of the function $y = f(x)$, and move a horizontal distance h away from x to the point $\mathrm{Q}(x+h, f(x+h))$.

We can find an expression for the gradient of the chord [PQ]:

$$\begin{aligned} m_{PQ} &= \frac{y_2 - y_1}{x_2 - x_1} \\ &= \frac{f(x+h) - f(x)}{(x+h) - x} \\ &= \frac{f(x+h) - f(x)}{h} \end{aligned}$$

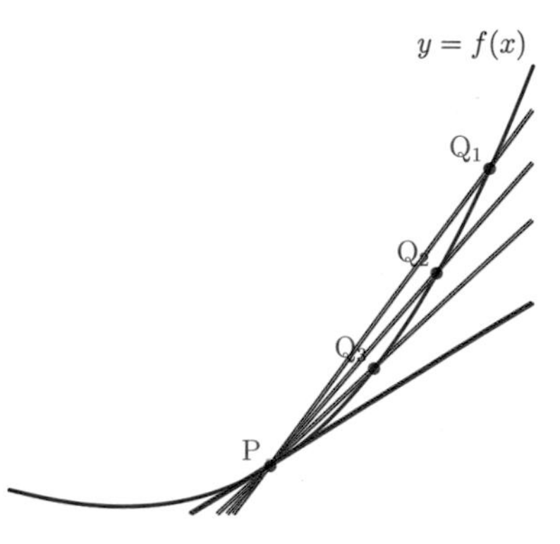

As the point Q gets closer and closer to P, the gradient of the chord [PQ] approximates the gradient of the tangent at P more and more closely.

To denote the distance h between P and Q approaching zero, we use $\lim_{h\to 0}$, which reads as 'the limit as h tends to zero'. This idea of a limit is very much like that encountered in chapters 2 and 3 with asymptotes on graphs, where the graph approaches the asymptote (the limit) as x tends to ∞.

The process of finding $\lim_{h\to 0}$ of the gradient of the chord [PQ] is called **differentiation from first principles**, and we have the following definition.

KEY POINT 12.2

Differentiation from first principles

$$f'(x) = \lim_{h\to 0} \frac{f(x+h) - f(x)}{h}$$

EXAM HINT

Differentiation from first principles means finding the derivative using the definition in Key point 12.2, rather than any of the rules we will meet in later sections.

The expression $f'(x)$ is referred to as the **derivative** of $f(x)$. It is also written as just f', or as y' or $\frac{dy}{dx}$ where $y = f(x)$. The process of finding the derivative is called **differentiation**.

We can use this definition to find the derivative of simple polynomial functions.

Worked example 12.3

For the function $y = x^2$, find $\frac{dy}{dx}$ from first principles.

Use the formula; here $f(x) = x^2$.

$$\frac{dy}{dx} = \lim_{h\to 0} \frac{(x+h)^2 - x^2}{h}$$

We do not want to have the denominator go to zero, so first try to simplify the numerator and hope that the h in the denominator will cancel out.

$$= \lim_{h\to 0} \frac{x^2 + 2xh + h^2 - x^2}{h}$$

$$= \lim_{h\to 0} \frac{2xh + h^2}{h}$$

Now, as hoped, we can divide top and bottom by h.

$$= \lim_{h\to 0} 2x + h$$

Finally, since we don't have to worry about zero in the denominator, we are free to let $h \to 0$.

$$= 2x$$

Let us see how we can use the formula derived in the above example. On the curve $y = x^2$, at the point where $x = 3$ the y-coordinate is 9. Now we also know from the formula $\frac{dy}{dx} = 2x$ that the gradient at that point is 6. We could, of course, use this formula for $\frac{dy}{dx}$ to find the gradient at any point on the curve $y = x^2$.

Exercise 12B

1. Find the derivatives of the following functions from first principles.

   (a) (i) $f(x) = x^3$ (ii) $f(x) = x^4$

   (b) (i) $f(x) = -4x$ (ii) $f(x) = 3x^2$

   (c) (i) $f(x) = x^2 - 6x$ (ii) $f(x) = x^2 - 3x + 4$

2. Prove from first principles that the derivative of $x^2 + 1$ is $2x$.

[4 marks]

3. Prove from first principles that the derivative of 8 is zero.

[4 marks]

4. If k is a constant, prove from first principles that the derivative of $kf(x)$ is $kf'(x)$. *[4 marks]*

12C Rules of differentiation

From Exercise 12B and the results of Self-Discovery Worksheet 3 'Investigating derivatives of polynomials' on the CD-ROM, it seems that we have the following formula for the derivative of a power function.

KEY POINT 12.3

If $y = x^n$, then $\frac{dy}{dx} = nx^{n-1}$.

The Fill-in Proof 9 'Differentiating polynomials' on the CD-ROM guides you through deriving this result for positive integer values of *n*; however, the formula actually holds for all rational powers.

A special case is when $n = 0$: the function is $y = x^0 = 1$, and the formula gives $\frac{dy}{dx} = 0x^{-1} = 0$. The geometric interpretation is that the graph $y = 1$ is a horizontal line and thus has zero gradient everywhere. In fact, the derivative of any constant is zero (see Exercise 12B question 3).

See chapter 2 if you need to review the rules of exponents.

Often you may have to simplify a function using rules of algebra, in particular the laws of exponents, before you can differentiate it.

Worked example 12.4

Find the derivatives of the following functions:

(a) $f(x)=x^2\sqrt{x}$

(b) $g(x)=\frac{1}{\sqrt[3]{x}}$

First, rewrite the function in the form x^n using the laws of exponents.

(a) $f(x)=x^2\sqrt{x}$

$=x^2x^{\frac{1}{2}}$

$=x^{2+\frac{1}{2}}$

$=x^{\frac{5}{2}}$

Then use the differentiation formula.

$f'(x)=\frac{5}{2}x^{\frac{5}{2}-1}$

$=\frac{5}{2}x^{\frac{3}{2}}$

Rewrite the function in the form x^n using the laws of exponents.

(b) $g(x)=\frac{1}{\sqrt[3]{x}}$

$=x^{-\frac{1}{3}}$

Then use the differentiation formula.

$g'(x)=-\frac{1}{3}x^{-\frac{1}{3}-1}$

$=-\frac{1}{3}x^{-\frac{4}{3}}$

The results of Exercise 12B questions 1(c) and 4 suggest some properties of differentiation.

KEY POINT 12.4

- If we differentiate $kf(x)$, where k is a constant, we get $kf'(x)$.
- To differentiate a sum, we can differentiate its terms one at a time and then add up the results.

EXAM HINT

Note: you cannot differentiate a product by differentiating each of the factors and multiplying the results together – we will see in chapter 14 that there is a more complicated rule for dealing with products.

See Fill-in Proof 9 'Differentiating polynomials' on the CD-ROM for the derivation of these rules.

The following example illustrates these properties.

Worked example 12.5

Find the derivatives of the following functions.

(a) $f(x)=5x^3$

(b) $g(x)=x^4-\frac{3}{2}x^2+5x-4$

(c) $h(x)=\frac{2(2x-7)}{\sqrt{x}}$

Differentiate x^3 and then multiply by 5.

(a) $f'(x)=5\times 3x^2$
$=15x^2$

Differentiate each term separately and add up the results.

(b) $g'(x)=4x^3-\frac{3}{2}\times 2x+5+0$
$=4x^3-3x+5$

We need to write this as a sum of terms of the form x^n.

(c) $h(x)=\frac{2(2x-7)}{\sqrt{x}}$

Use the laws of exponents.

$=\frac{4x-14}{x^{\frac{1}{2}}}$

$=4x^{1-\frac{1}{2}}-14x^{-\frac{1}{2}}$

$=4x^{\frac{1}{2}}-14x^{-\frac{1}{2}}$

Now differentiate term by term.

$h'(x)=4\times\frac{1}{2}x^{\frac{1}{2}-1}-14\left(-\frac{1}{2}\right)x^{-\frac{1}{2}-1}$

$=2x^{-\frac{1}{2}}+7x^{-\frac{3}{2}}$

Exercise 12C

1. Differentiate the following.

(a) (i) $y=x^4$ (ii) $y=x$

(b) (i) $y=3x^7$ (ii) $y=-4x^5$

(c) (i) $y=10$ (ii) $y=-3$

(d) (i) $y=4x^3-5x^2+2x-8$ (ii) $y=2x^4+3x^3-x$

(e) (i) $y=\frac{1}{3}x^6$ (ii) $y=-\frac{3}{4}x^2$

(f) (i) $y=7x-\frac{1}{2}x^3$ (ii) $y=2-5x^4+\frac{1}{5}x^5$

(g) (i) $y=x^{\frac{3}{2}}$ (ii) $y=x^{\frac{2}{3}}$

(h) (i) $y=6x^{\frac{4}{3}}$ (ii) $y=\frac{3}{5}x^{\frac{5}{6}}$

(i) (i) $y=3x^4-x^2+15x^{\frac{2}{5}}-2$ (ii) $y=x^3-\frac{3}{5}x^{\frac{5}{3}}+\frac{4}{3}x^{\frac{1}{2}}$

(j) (i) $y=x^{-1}$ (ii) $y=-x^{-3}$

(k) (i) $y=x^{-\frac{1}{2}}$ (ii) $y=-8x^{-\frac{3}{4}}$

(l) (i) $y=5x-\frac{8}{15}x^{-\frac{5}{2}}$ (ii) $y=-\frac{7}{3}x^{-\frac{3}{7}}+\frac{4}{3}x^{-6}$

2. Find $\frac{dy}{dx}$ for each of the following.

(a) (i) $y=\sqrt[3]{x}$ (ii) $y=\sqrt[5]{x^4}$

(b) (i) $y=\frac{3}{x^2}$ (ii) $y=-\frac{2}{5x^{10}}$

(c) (i) $y=\frac{1}{\sqrt{x}}$ (ii) $y=\frac{8}{3\sqrt[4]{x^3}}$

(d) (i) $y=x^2(3x-4)$ (ii) $y=\sqrt{x}(x^3-2x+8)$

(e) (i) $y=(x+2)(\sqrt[3]{x}-1)$ (ii) $y=\left(x+\frac{2}{x}\right)^2$

(f) (i) $y=\frac{3x^5-2x}{x^2}$ (ii) $y=\frac{9x^2+3}{2\sqrt[3]{x}}$

3. Find $\frac{dy}{dx}$ if

(a) (i) $x+y=8$ (ii) $3x-2y=7$

(b) (i) $y+x+x^2=0$ (ii) $y-x^4=2x$

12D Interpreting derivatives and second derivatives

The derivative $\frac{dy}{dx}$ has two related interpretations:

- It is the gradient of the graph of y against x.
- It measures how fast y changes when x is changed, that is, the **rate of change** of y with respect to x.

EXAM HINT

We can also write this using function notation: if $f(x) = x^2$, then $f'(x) = 2x$; so $f'(3) = 6$ and $f'(-1) = -2$.

Remember that $\frac{dy}{dx}$ is itself a function whose value depends on x.

For example, if $y = x^2$, then $\frac{dy}{dx} = 2x$; so $\frac{dy}{dx}$ is equal to 6 when $x = 3$, and it is equal to -2 when $x = -1$. This corresponds to the fact that the gradient of the graph of $y = x^2$ changes with x, or that the rate of change of y varies with x.

To calculate the gradient (or the rate of change) at any particular point, we simply substitute the value of x into the expression for the derivative.

Worked example 12.6

Find the gradient of the graph of $y = 4x^3$ at the point where $x = 2$.

The gradient is given by the derivative, so find $\frac{dy}{dx}$.

$\frac{dy}{dx} = 12x^2$

Substitute the given value for x.

When $x = 2$,

$\frac{dy}{dx} = 12 \times 2^2 = 48$

So the gradient is 48

EXAM HINT

Most calculators are not able to find the general expression for the derivative of a function, but can find the gradient of a curve at a specific point. See Calculator Skills sheet 8 on the CD-ROM for instructions on how to do this.

If we know the gradient of a graph at a particular point, we can find the value of x at that point. This involves solving an equation involving $\frac{dy}{dx}$.

Worked example 12.7

Find the values of x for which the graph of $y = x^3 - 7x + 1$ has gradient 5.

The gradient is given by the derivative.

$$\frac{dy}{dx} = 3x^2 - 7$$

We know the value of $\frac{dy}{dx}$, so we can write down an equation for x and solve it.

$$3x^2 - 7 = 5$$
$$\Leftrightarrow 3x^2 = 12$$
$$\Leftrightarrow x^2 = 4$$
$$\Leftrightarrow x = 2 \text{ or } -2$$

The sign of the gradient tells us whether the function is increasing or decreasing.

KEY POINT 12.5

If $\frac{dy}{dx}$ is positive, the function is increasing: as x gets larger, so does y.

If $\frac{dy}{dx}$ is negative, the function is decreasing: as x gets larger, y gets smaller.

In section 12H we will discuss what happens when $\frac{dy}{dx} = 0$.

Worked example 12.8

Find the range of values of x for which the function $f(x) = 2x^2 - 6x$ is decreasing.

A decreasing function has negative gradient.

$$f'(x) < 0$$
$$\Leftrightarrow 4x - 6 < 0$$
$$\Leftrightarrow x < 1.5$$

You may wonder why it is important to emphasise that we are differentiating with respect to x (or Q or 'monkeys'). In this course we only consider functions of one variable, but it is possible to generalise calculus to deal with functions that depend on several variables. Multivariable calculus has many applications, particularly in physics and engineering.

There is nothing special about the variables y and x. We can just as well say that $\frac{dB}{dQ}$ is the gradient of the graph of B against Q or that $\frac{d(\text{bananas})}{d(\text{monkeys})}$ measures how fast the 'bananas' variable changes when you change the variable 'monkeys'.

To emphasise which variables we are using, we call $\frac{dy}{dx}$ the *derivative of y with respect to x.*

Worked example 12.9

Given that $a = \sqrt{S}$, find the rate of change of a when $S = 9$.

The rate of change is given by the derivative.

$$a = S^{\frac{1}{2}}$$

$$\frac{da}{dS} = \frac{1}{2}S^{-\frac{1}{2}}$$

$$= \frac{1}{2\sqrt{S}}$$

Substitute the given value for S.

When $S = 9$,

$$\frac{da}{dS} = \frac{1}{2\sqrt{9}}$$

$$= \frac{1}{6}$$

$\frac{d}{dx}$ is an example of what is called an *operator* – something that acts on functions to turn them into other functions. In this case, the operation that $\frac{d}{dx}$ performs on a function is differentiation with respect to x. For example, we can think of differentiating $y = 3x^2$ as applying the $\frac{d}{dx}$ operator to both sides of the equation:

$$\frac{d}{dx}(y) = \frac{d}{dx}(3x^2)$$

$$\Rightarrow \frac{dy}{dx} = 6x$$

So $\frac{dy}{dx}$ just means the operator $\frac{d}{dx}$ applied to y.

Since, as discussed earlier, the derivative $\frac{dy}{dx}$ is itself a function of x, we can also apply the $\frac{d}{dx}$ operator to it. The result is called the **second derivative**.

KEY POINT 12.6

> The second derivative $\frac{d}{dx}\left(\frac{dy}{dx}\right)$ is denoted by $\frac{d^2y}{dx^2}$ or $f''(x)$ and measures the rate of change of the gradient.

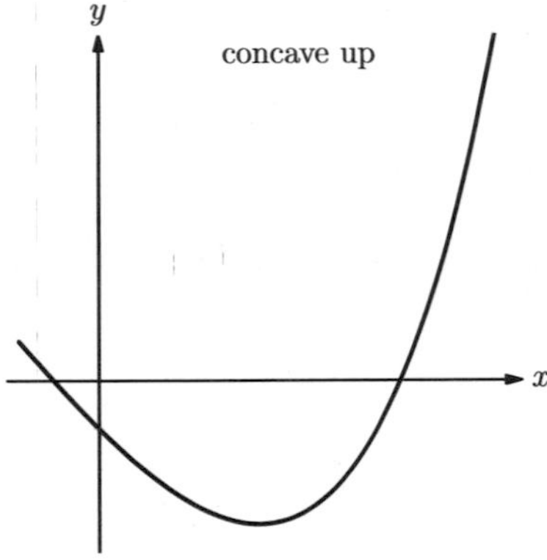

The sign of the second derivative tells us whether the gradient is increasing or decreasing.

If the gradient is increasing, the curve is said to be 'concave-up'. If the gradient is decreasing, the curve is described as 'concave-down'.

KEY POINT 12.7

> If $\frac{d^2y}{dx^2} > 0$, the curve is concave-up.
>
> If $\frac{d^2y}{dx^2} < 0$, the curve is concave-down.

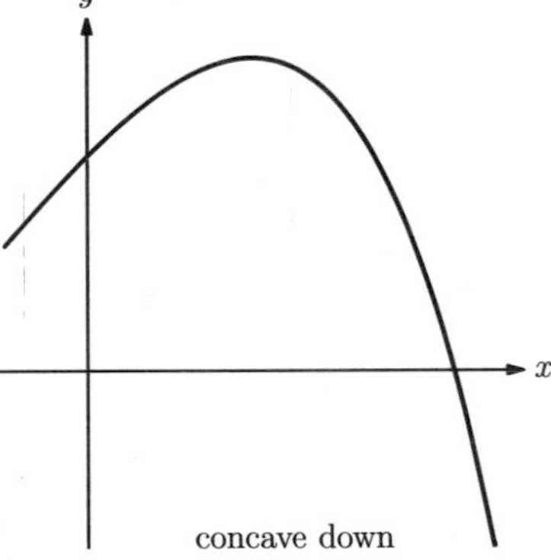

We can differentiate the second derivative to get the third derivative, denoted by $\frac{d^3y}{dx^3}$ or $f'''(x)$, and then differentiate again to find the fourth derivative, written $\frac{d^4y}{dx^4}$ or $f^{(4)}(x)$, and so on.

Worked example 12.10

Let $f(x) = 5x^3 - 4x$.

(a) Find $f''(x)$.

(b) Find the rate of change of the gradient of the graph of $y = f(x)$ at the point where $x = -1$.

Differentiate $f(x)$ and then differentiate the result.	(a) $f'(x) = 15x^2 - 4$ $f''(x) = 30x$
The rate of change of the gradient means the second derivative.	(b) $f''(-1) = -30$

Exercise 12D

1. Write the following rates of change as derivatives.
   (a) The rate of change of z as t changes.
   (b) The rate of change of Q with respect to p.
   (c) How fast R changes when m is changed.
   (d) How quickly the volume of a balloon (V) changes over time (t).
   (e) The rate of increase of the cost of apples (y) as the average weight of an apple (x) increases.
   (f) The rate of change of the rate of change of z as y changes.
   (g) The second derivative of H with respect to m.

2. (a) (i) If $f = 5x^{\frac{1}{3}}$, what is the derivative of f with respect to x?
   (ii) If $p = 3q^5$, what is the derivative of p with respect to q?
   (b) (i) Differentiate $d = 3t + 7t^{-1}$ with respect to t.
   (ii) Differentiate $r = c + \frac{1}{c}$ with respect to c.
   (c) (i) Find the second derivative of $y = 9x^2 + x^3$ with respect to x.
   (ii) Find the second derivative of $z = \frac{3}{t}$ with respect to t.

3. (a) (i) If $y = 5x^2$, find $\frac{dy}{dx}$ when $x = 3$.
   (ii) If $y = x^3 + \frac{1}{x}$, find $\frac{dy}{dx}$ when $x = 1.5$.
   (b) (i) If $A = 7b + 3$, find $\frac{dA}{db}$ when $b = -1$.
   (ii) If $\phi = \theta^2 + \theta^{-3}$, find $\frac{d\phi}{d\theta}$ when $\theta = 0.1$.
   (c) (i) Find the gradient of the graph of $A = x^3$ when $x = 2$.
   (ii) Find the gradient of the tangent to the graph of $z = 2a + a^2$ when $a = -6$.
   (d) (i) How quickly does $f = 4T^2$ change as T changes when $T = 3$?
   (ii) How quickly does $g = y^4$ change as y changes when $y = 2$?
   (e) (i) What is the rate of increase of W with respect to p when p is -3 if $W = -p^2$?
   (ii) What is the rate of change of L with respect to c when $c = 6$ if $L = 7\sqrt{c} - 8$?

You may consider it paradoxical to talk about the rate of change of y as x changes when we are fixing x at a certain value; think of it as the rate at which y is changing at the instant when x is passing through this particular point.

4. (a) (i) If $y = ax^2 + (1-a)x$ where a is a constant, find $\frac{dy}{dx}$.

(ii) If $y = x^3 + b^2$ where b is a constant, find $\frac{dy}{dx}$.

(b) (i) If $Q = \sqrt{ab} + \sqrt{b}$ where b is a constant, find $\frac{dQ}{da}$.

(ii) If $D = 3(av)^2$ where a is a constant, find $\frac{dD}{dv}$.

5. (a) (i) If $y = x^3 - 5x$, find $\frac{d^2y}{dx^2}$ when $x = 9$.

(ii) If $y = 8 + 2x^4$, find $\frac{d^2y}{dx^2}$ when $x = 4$.

(b) (i) If $S = 3A^2 + \frac{1}{A}$, find $\frac{d^2S}{dA^2}$ when $A = 1$.

(ii) If $J = v - \sqrt{v}$, find $\frac{d^2J}{dv^2}$ when $v = 9$.

(c) (i) Find the second derivative of B with respect to n if $B = 8n$ and $n = 2$.

(ii) Find the second derivative of g with respect to r if $g = r^7$ and $r = 1$.

6. (a) (i) Given that $y = 3x^3$ and $\frac{dy}{dx} = 36$, find x.

(ii) Given that $y = x^4 + 2x$ and $\frac{dy}{dx} = 6$, find x.

(b) (i) If $y = 2x + \frac{8}{x}$ and $\frac{dy}{dx} = -30$, find y.

(ii) If $y = \sqrt{x} + 3$ and $\frac{dy}{dx} = \frac{1}{6}$, find y.

7. (a) (i) Find the interval in which $x^2 - x$ is an increasing function.

(ii) Find the interval in which $x^2 + 2x - 5$ is a decreasing function.

(b) (i) Find the interval in which $y = x^3 - 3x^2$ is concave-up.

(ii) Find the interval in which $y = x^3 + 5x$ is concave-down.

8. Show that $y = x^3 + kx + c$ is always increasing if $k > 0$.

[4 marks]

9. Find all points on the graph of $y = x^3 - 2x^2 + 1$ where the gradient equals the y-coordinate. *[5 marks]*

10. In what interval is the gradient of the graph of $y = 7x - x^2 - x^3$ decreasing? *[5 marks]*

11. Find an alternative expression for $\frac{\mathrm{d}^n}{\mathrm{d}x^n}(x^n)$.

12E Differentiating trigonometric functions

Using the techniques from section 12A we can sketch the derivative of the graph of $y = \sin x$. The result is a graph that looks just like $y = \cos x$. See Fill-in Proof 11 'Differentiating trigonometric functions' on the CD-ROM to find out why this is the case.

The derivatives of $y = \cos x$ and $y = \tan x$ can be established in a similar manner, giving the following results.

EXAM HINT

Whenever you are doing calculus you *must* work in radians.

KEY POINT 12.8

$$\frac{\mathrm{d}}{\mathrm{d}x}(\sin x) = \cos x$$

$$\frac{\mathrm{d}}{\mathrm{d}x}(\cos x) = -\sin x$$

$$\frac{\mathrm{d}}{\mathrm{d}x}(\tan x) = \frac{1}{\cos^2 x}$$

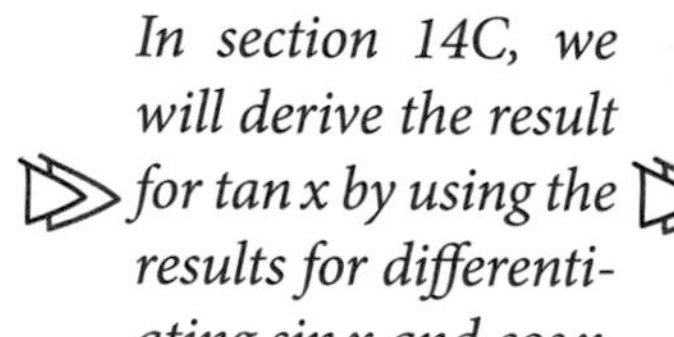

In section 14C, we will derive the result for $\tan x$ by using the results for differentiating $\sin x$ and $\cos x$.

It is important to remember that these formulas are valid only if x is measured in radians. This is because they are based on the assumption that the value of $\sin x$ is very close to x when x is small; you can use your calculator to confirm that this is true for x in radians but not for x in degrees.

See Fill-in Proof 10 'Small angle approximations' on the CD-ROM for a derivation of the $\sin x \approx x$ approximation, which is also shown on the graph on the next page.

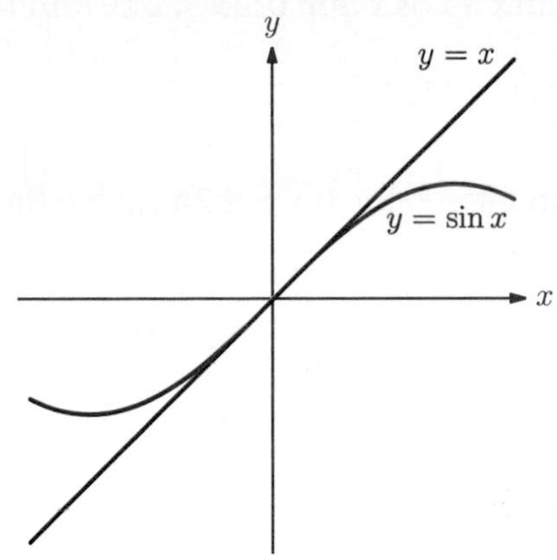

It is possible to do calculus using degrees, or any other unit for measuring angles, but using radians gives the simplest rules, which is why they are the unit of choice for mathematicians.

All the rules of differentiation from section 12C apply to trigonometric functions as well.

Worked example 12.11

Differentiate $y = 3\tan x - 2\cos x$.

Differentiate term by term, using the formulas in Key point 12.8.

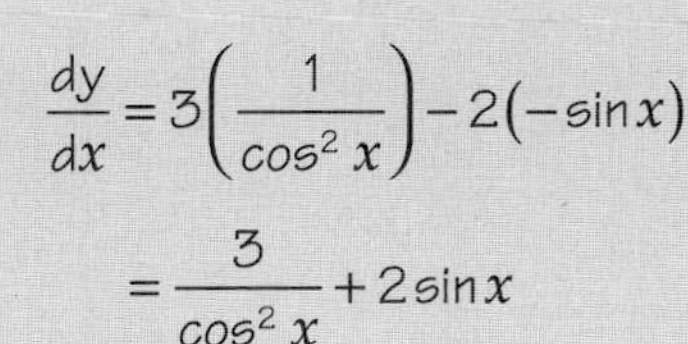

$$\frac{dy}{dx} = 3\left(\frac{1}{\cos^2 x}\right) - 2(-\sin x)$$

$$= \frac{3}{\cos^2 x} + 2\sin x$$

Exercise 12E

1. Differentiate the following.

   (a) (i) $y = 3\sin x$ (ii) $y = 2\cos x$

   (b) (i) $y = 2x - 5\cos x$ (ii) $y = \tan x + 5$

   (c) (i) $y = \dfrac{\sin x + 2\cos x}{5}$ (ii) $y = \dfrac{1}{2}\tan x - \dfrac{1}{3}\sin x$

2. Find the gradient of $f(x) = \sin x + x^2$ at the point $x = \dfrac{\pi}{2}$. *[5 marks]*

3. Find the gradient of $g(x) = \dfrac{1}{4}\tan x - 3\cos x - x^3$ at the point $x = \dfrac{\pi}{6}$. *[5 marks]*

4. Given $h(x) = \sin x + \cos x$ for $0 \le x < 2\pi$, find the values of x for which $h'(x) = 0$. *[6 marks]*

5. Given $y = \frac{1}{4}\tan x + \frac{1}{x^2}$ for $0 < x \le 2\pi$, solve the equation $\frac{dy}{dx} = 1 - \frac{2}{x^3}$. *[6 marks]*

12F Differentiating exponential and natural logarithm functions

Use your calculator to sketch the graphs of $y = 2^x$ and $y = 3^x$ and their derivatives. The derivative graphs look like exponential functions too.

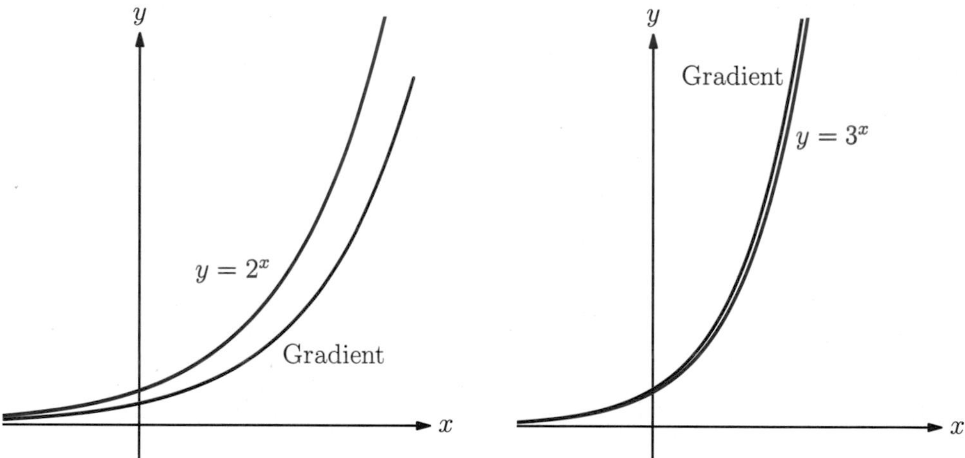

Notice that the graph of the derivative of $y = 2^x$ lies below the graph of $y = 2^x$ itself, whereas the graph of the derivative of $y = 3^x$ lies slightly above the graph of $y = 3^x$ itself. It seems that there should be a number a somewhere between 2 and 3 for which the graph of the derivative of $y = a^x$ would be exactly the same as the graph of $y = a^x$ itself. It turns out that this number 'a' is e = 2.71828… which we met in section 2C.

KEY POINT 12.9

$$\frac{d}{dx}(e^x) = e^x$$

The derivative of the natural logarithm (the logarithm with base e) $y = \ln x$ is somewhat surprising, being of a completely different form from the original function.

KEY POINT 12.10

$$\frac{d}{dx}(\ln x) = \frac{1}{x}$$

See Fill-in Proof 12 'Differentiating logarithmic functions graphically' on the CD-ROM for a derivation of this result.

Worked example 12.12

Differentiate $y = 2e^x + 3\ln x + 4x$.

Differentiate term by term, using the formulas in Key points 12.9 and 12.10.

$$\frac{dy}{dx} = 2e^x + \frac{3}{x} + 4$$

Exercise 12F

1. Differentiate the following.

(a) (i) $y = 3e^x$ (ii) $y = \frac{2e^x}{5}$

(b) (i) $y = -2\ln x$ (ii) $y = \frac{1}{3}\ln x$

(c) (i) $y = \frac{\ln x}{5} - 3x + 4e^x$ (ii) $y = 4 - \frac{e^x}{2} + 3\ln x$

2. Find the value of the gradient of the graph of $f(x) = \frac{1}{2}e^x - 7\ln x$ at the point $x = \ln 4$. *[2 marks]*

3. Find the exact value of the gradient of the graph of $f(x) = e^x - \frac{\ln x}{2}$ when $x = \ln 3$. *[2 marks]*

4. Find the value of x where the gradient of $f(x) = 5 - 2e^x$ is -6.

[4 marks]

5. Find the interval in which $e^x - 2x$ is an increasing function.

[5 marks]

6. Find the value of x at which the gradient of $g(x) = x^2 - 12\ln x$ is 2.

[4 marks]

There is an easier way to do some of the parts in this question, using a method from chapter 14. For now, you will have to rely on your algebra skills!

7. Differentiate the following.

(a) (i) $y = \ln x^3$ (ii) $y = \ln 5x$

(b) (i) $y = e^{x+3}$ (ii) $y = e^{x-3}$

(c) (i) $y = e^{2\ln x}$ (ii) $y = e^{3\ln x+2}$

12G Tangents and normals

See Prior Learning section R on the CD-ROM for how to find the equation of a straight line from its gradient and a point on the line.

The tangent to a curve at a given point is a straight line which touches the curve at that point and (by definition) has the same gradient as the curve at that point. Therefore, if we need to find the equation of the tangent, we first have to know the gradient of the curve at that point, which can be obtained by differentiating the curve function. Once we have both the gradient of the tangent and the coordinates of the point where it touches the curve, we can apply the standard procedure for finding the equation of a straight line.

The **normal** to a curve at a given point is a straight line which crosses the curve at that point and is perpendicular to the tangent at that point. Normals have many uses, such as in finding the centres of curvature of shapes and in working out how light is reflected from curved mirrors. In the International Baccalaureate® you are only likely to be expected to find their equations. To do this, use the fact that if two (non-horizontal, non-vertical) lines are perpendicular, their gradients m_1 and m_2 are related by $m_1 m_2 = -1$.

Worked example 12.13

(a) Find the equation of the tangent to the function $f(x) = \cos x + e^x$ at the point $x = 0$.

(b) Find the equation of the normal to the function $g(x) = x^3 - 5x^2 - x^{\frac{3}{2}} + 22$ at $(4, -2)$.

In each case give your answer in the form $ax + by + c = 0$, where a, b and c are integers.

We need the gradient at $x = 0$, which is $f'(0)$.

(a)

$$f'(x) = -\sin x + e^x$$

$$\therefore f'(0) = -\sin 0 + e^0 = 1$$

We also need coordinates of the point at which the tangent touches the graph. This is where $x = 0$. The corresponding y-coordinate is $f(0)$.

When $x = 0$,

$$\begin{aligned} y &= f(0) \\ &= \cos 0 + e^0 \\ &= 1 + 1 \\ &= 2 \end{aligned}$$

Put the information into the general equation of a line.

$$\begin{aligned} y - y_1 &= m(x - x_1) \\ y - 2 &= 1(x - 0) \\ \Leftrightarrow \quad y &= x + 2 \\ \Leftrightarrow x - y + 2 &= 0 \end{aligned}$$

The normal is perpendicular to the tangent, so find the gradient of the tangent at $x = 4$ first.

(b)

$$f'(x) = 3x^2 - 10x - \frac{3}{2}x^{\frac{1}{2}}$$

$$\begin{aligned} \therefore f'(4) &= 3(4)^2 - 10(4) - \frac{3}{2}(4)^{\frac{1}{2}} \\ &= 48 - 40 - 3 \\ &= 5 \end{aligned}$$

For perpendicular lines, $m_1 m_2 = -1$.

Therefore gradient of normal is

$$m = \frac{-1}{5}$$

Both x- and y-coordinates of the point are given, so we can put all the information into the general equation of a line.

$$\begin{aligned} y - y_1 &= m(x - x_1) \\ y - (-2) &= \frac{-1}{5}(x - 4) \\ \Leftrightarrow \quad 5y + 10 &= -x + 4 \\ \Leftrightarrow x + 5y + 6 &= 0 \end{aligned}$$

EXAM HINT

Your calculator may be able to find the equation of the tangent at a given point.

We summarise the procedure for finding equations of tangents and normals as follows.

KEY POINT 12.11

At the point on the curve $y = f(x)$ with $x = a$:

- the gradient of the tangent is $f'(a)$
- the gradient of the normal is $\frac{-1}{f'(a)}$
- the coordinates of the point are $x_1 = a, y_1 = f(a)$

To find the equation of the tangent or the normal, use $y - y_1 = m(x - x_1)$ with the appropriate gradient.

Sometimes you may be given limited information about the tangent and have to use this to find out other information.

Worked example 12.14

The tangent at point P on the curve $y = x^2 + 1$ passes through the origin. Find the possible coordinates of P.

We can find the equation of the tangent at P, but we need to use unknowns for the coordinates of P.	Let P have coordinates (p, q).
As P lies on the curve, (p, q) must satisfy $y = x^2 + 1$.	Then $q = p^2 + 1$
The gradient of the tangent is given by $\frac{dy}{dx}$ with $x = p$.	$\frac{dy}{dx} = 2x$ When $x = p$, $\frac{dy}{dx} = 2p$ $\therefore m = 2p$
Write down the equation of the tangent.	Equation of the tangent: $y - q = 2p(x - p)$ $y - (p^2 + 1) = 2p(x - p)$
The tangent passes through the origin, so set $x = 0$ and $y = 0$ in the equation.	Passes through (0,0): $0 - (p^2 + 1) = 2p(0 - p)$ $\Leftrightarrow -p^2 - 1 = -2p^2$ $\Leftrightarrow p^2 = 1$ Hence $p = 1$ or -1

→

continued . . .

Now find the corresponding y-coordinate q.

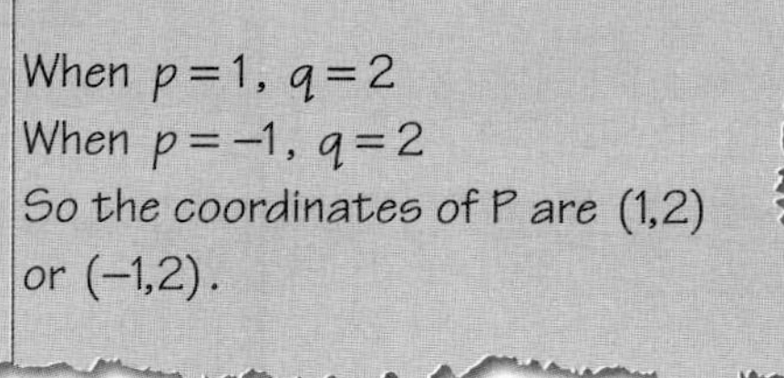

When $p=1$, $q=2$
When $p=-1$, $q=2$
So the coordinates of P are (1,2) or (−1,2).

Exercise 12G

1. Find the equations of the tangent and the normal to each of the following curves at the given point. Write your equations in the form $ax+by+c=0$.

   (a) $y=\dfrac{x^2+4}{\sqrt{x}}$ at $x=4$

   (b) $y=3\tan x-2\sqrt{2}\sin x$ at $x=\dfrac{\pi}{4}$

2. Find the equation of the normal to the curve $y=3-\dfrac{1}{5}e^x$ at $x=2\ln 5$. *[7 marks]*

3. Find the coordinates of the point at which the tangent to the curve $y=x^3-3x^2$ at $x=2$ meets the curve again. *[6 marks]*

4. Find the x-coordinates of the points on the curve $y=x^3-3x^2$ where the tangent is parallel to the normal to the curve at $(1,-2)$. *[6 marks]*

5. Find the equation of the tangent to the curve $y=e^x+x$ which is parallel to $y=3x$. *[4 marks]*

6. Find the coordinates of the point on the curve $y=(x-1)^2$ for which the normal passes through the origin. *[5 marks]*

7. A tangent is drawn on the graph $y=\dfrac{k}{x}$ at the point where $x=a$ $(a>0)$. The tangent intersects the y-axis at P and the x-axis at Q. If O is the origin, show that the area of the triangle OPQ is independent of a. *[8 marks]*

8. Show that any tangent to the curve $y=x^3-x$ at the point with x-coordinate a meets the curve again at a point with x-coordinate $-2a$. *[6 marks]*

12H Stationary points

In real life people might be interested in maximising profits or minimising the drag on a car. We can use calculus to describe such goals mathematically as points on a graph.

Note that at both the maximum point and the minimum point on the graph, the gradient is zero.

KEY POINT 12.12

> To find local maximum and local minimum points, solve the equation $\frac{\mathrm{d}y}{\mathrm{d}x} = 0$.

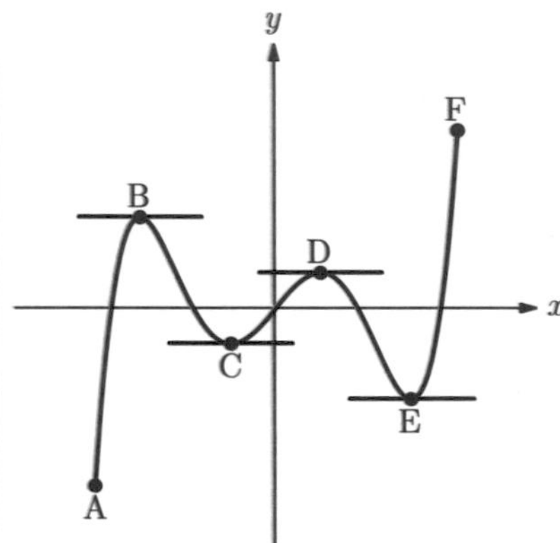

We use the phrases **local maximum** and **local minimum** because it is possible that the overall largest or smallest value of the function occurs at an endpoint of the graph, or that there are multiple peaks or troughs on the graph. The word 'local' means that each peak or trough just represents the largest or smallest y-value in that particular 'neighbourhood' on the graph.

Points at which the graph has a gradient of zero are called **stationary points**.

Worked example 12.15

Find the coordinates of the stationary points of $y = 2x^3 - 15x^2 + 24x + 8$.

Stationary points have $\frac{dy}{dx} = 0$, so we need to differentiate and then set the derivative equal to zero.

$$\frac{dy}{dx} = 6x^2 - 30x + 24$$

For stationary points $\frac{dy}{dx} = 0$:

$$6x^2 - 30x + 24 = 0$$
$$\Leftrightarrow x^2 - 5x + 4 = 0$$
$$\Leftrightarrow (x-4)(x-1) = 0$$
$$\Leftrightarrow x = 1 \text{ or } x = 4$$

Remember to find the y-coordinate for each point.

When $x = 1$:

$$y = 2(1)^3 - 15(1)^2 + 24(1) + 8 = 19$$

When $x = 4$:

$$y = 2(4)^3 - 15(4)^2 + 24(4) + 8 = -8$$

Therefore, stationary points are (1, 19) and (4, −8)

The calculation in Worked example 12.15 does not tell us whether the stationary points we found are maximum or minimum points. One way of testing for the nature of a stationary point is to check the gradient on either side of the point by substituting nearby x-values into the expression for $\frac{dy}{dx}$. For a minimum point, the gradient goes from negative to positive as x moves from left to right through the stationary point; for a maximum point, the gradient changes from positive to negative.

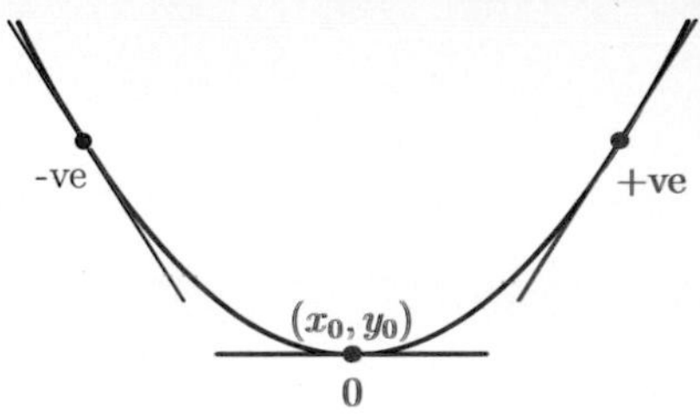

We can also interpret these conditions in terms of the rate of change of the gradient – that is, the second derivative $\frac{d^2y}{dx^2}$. At a minimum point, the gradient is increasing (changing from negative to positive) and hence $\frac{d^2y}{dx^2}$ is positive; at a maximum point, the gradient is decreasing (changing from positive to negative) and so $\frac{d^2y}{dx^2}$ is negative. This leads to the following test.

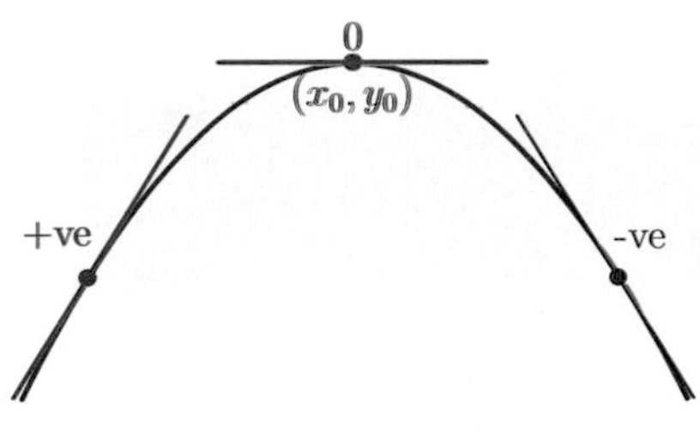

KEY POINT 12.13

Given a stationary point (x_0, y_0) of a function $y = f(x)$:

- if $\frac{d^2y}{dx^2} < 0$ at x_0, then (x_0, y_0) is a *maximum*
- if $\frac{d^2y}{dx^2} > 0$ at x_0, then (x_0, y_0) is a *minimum*
- if $\frac{d^2y}{dx^2} = 0$ at x_0, then no conclusion can be drawn, so check the sign of the gradient $\frac{dy}{dx}$ on either side of (x_0, y_0)

EXAM HINT

You can find maximum and minimum points on your calculator, as described on Calculator Skills sheet 4. However, questions of this type often appear on the non-calculator paper.

All local maximum and local minimum points have $\frac{dy}{dx} = 0$, but the converse is not true: a point with $\frac{dy}{dx} = 0$ does not have to be a maximum or a minimum point. There are two other possibilities:

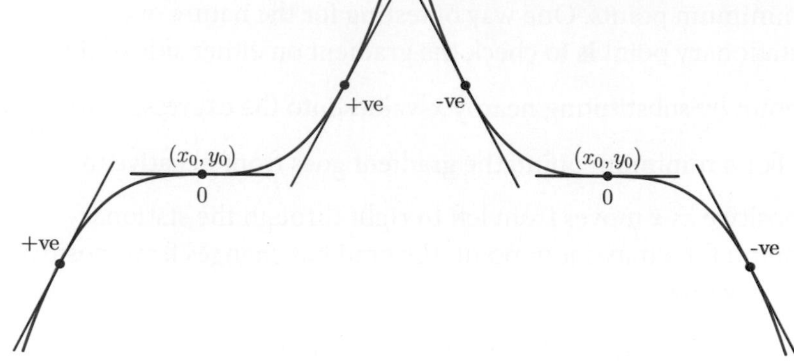

The stationary points labelled (x_0, y_0) on the above graphs are called **points of inflexion**. Note that at these points, the line with zero gradient actually passes through the curve. The gradient of the curve is either positive on both sides of a point of inflexion (which is then called a positive point of inflexion, like the one on the left-hand graph), or negative on both sides (in which case we have a negative point of inflexion, like the one on the right-hand graph).

In UK English, 'inflexion' might be spelt 'inflection'.

If a question asks you to 'find and classify' the stationary points on a curve, it means you have to find the coordinates of all points which have $\frac{dy}{dx} = 0$ and decide whether each one is a maximum point, minimum point or point of inflexion. This may also be referred to as the 'nature' of the stationary points.

Worked example 12.16

Find and classify the stationary points of $y = 3 + 4x^3 - x^4$.

Stationary points have $\frac{dy}{dx} = 0$.

$$\frac{dy}{dx} = 12x^2 - 4x^3$$

For stationary points $\frac{dy}{dx} = 0$:

$$12x^2 - 4x^3 = 0$$

$$\Leftrightarrow 4x^2(3 - x) = 0$$

$$\Leftrightarrow x = 0 \text{ or } x = 3$$

continued . . .

Find the y-coordinates.

When $x = 0$:

$$y = 3 + 4(0)^3 - (0)^4 = 3$$

When $x = 3$:

$$y = 3 + 4(3)^3 - (3)^4 = 30$$

Therefore, stationary points are $(0,3)$ and $(3,30)$

Use the second derivative to determine the nature of each stationary point.

$$\frac{d^2y}{dx^2} = 24x - 12x^2$$

At $x = 0$:

$$\frac{d^2y}{dx^2} = 24(0) - 12(0)^2 = 0$$

As $\frac{d^2y}{dx^2} = 0$, we need to check the gradient on either side of the stationary point.

Inconclusive, so examine $\frac{dy}{dx}$ on either side of $x = 0$:

At $x = -1$:

$$\frac{dy}{dx} = 12(-1)^2 - 4(-1)^3$$
$$= 12 + 4$$
$$= 16 > 0$$

At $x = 1$:

$$\frac{dy}{dx} = 12(1)^2 - 4(1)^3$$
$$= 12 - 4$$
$$= 8 > 0$$

$\therefore$ $(0, 3)$ is a positive point of inflexion.

At $x = 3$:

$$\frac{d^2y}{dx^2} = 24(3) - 12(3)^2$$
$$= 72 - 108$$
$$= -36 < 0$$

$\therefore$ $(3, 30)$ is a local maximum.

When $\frac{d^2y}{dx^2} = 0$, be careful not to jump to the conclusion that the stationary point is a point of inflexion – this is not necessarily the case, as the next example shows.

Worked example 12.17

Find the coordinates and nature of the stationary points of $f(x)=x^4$.

Stationary points have $f'(x)=0$.

$f'(x)=4x^3$

For stationary points $f'(x)=0$:

$$4x^3=0$$
$$\Leftrightarrow x=0$$

Find the y-coordinate.

$$f(0)=0$$

Therefore, stationary point is $(0, 0)$

Look at $f''(x)$ to determine the nature of the stationary point..

$$f''(x)=12x^2$$
$$f''(0)=0$$

As $f''(0)=0$, we need to check the gradient on either side of $x=0$.

Therefore, examine $f'(x)$:

$$f'(-1)=4(-1)^3$$
$$=-4<0$$
$$f'(1)=4(1)^3$$
$$=4>0$$

$\therefore$ $(0, 0)$ is a local minimum.

You can use stationary points to determine the range of a function.

Worked example 12.18

The graph shows $f(x)=e^x-2x$. Find the range of $f(x)$.

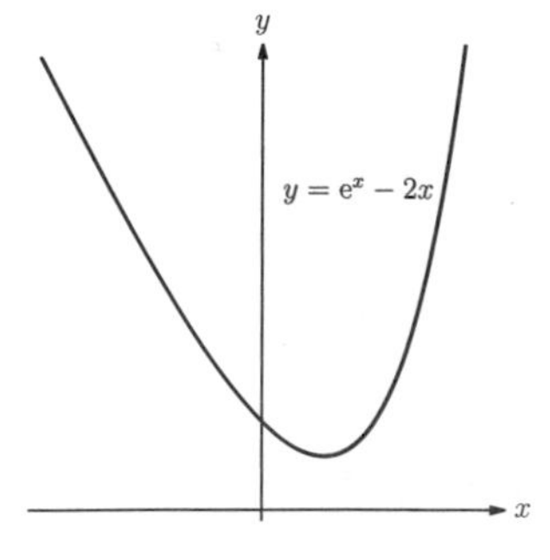

→

continued . . .

From the graph it is clear that $f(x)$ can take any value above the minimum point. So we need to find the minimum point.

$f'(x) = e^x - 2$

At the minimum point $f'(x) = 0$:

$e^x - 2 = 0$

$\Leftrightarrow e^x = 2$

$\Leftrightarrow x = \ln 2$

When $x = \ln 2$,

$f(x) = e^{\ln 2} - 2\ln 2$

$= 2 - 2\ln 2$

This is the minimum value of $f(x)$, so the range of $f(x)$ is

$f(x) \geq 2 - 2\ln 2$

See section 4B for a reminder of range and domain.

Exercise 12H

1. Find and classify the stationary points on the following curves.

(a) (i) $y = x^3 - 5x^2$ (ii) $y = x^4 - 8x^2$

(b) (i) $y = \sin x + \frac{x}{2}$, $-\pi \leq x \leq \pi$

(ii) $y = 2\cos x + 1$, $0 \leq x < 2\pi$

(c) (i) $y = \ln x - \sqrt{x}$ (ii) $y = 2e^x - 5x$

2. Find and classify the stationary points on the curve $y = x^3 + 3x^2 - 24x + 12$. *[6 marks]*

3. Find the coordinates of the stationary point on the curve $y = x - \sqrt{x}$ and determine its nature. *[6 marks]*

4. Find and classify the stationary points on the curve $y = \sin x + 4\cos x$ in the interval $0 < x < 2\pi$. *[6 marks]*

5. Show that the function $f(x) = \ln x + \frac{1}{x^k}$ has a stationary point with y-coordinate $\frac{\ln(k)+1}{k}$. *[6 marks]*

6. Find the range of the function $f: x \mapsto 3x^4 - 16x^3 + 18x^2 + 6$. *[5 marks]*

7. Find the range of the function $f: x \mapsto e^x - 4x + 2$. [5 marks]

8. Find in terms of k the stationary points on the curve $y = kx^3 + 6x^2$ and determine their nature. [6 marks]

12I General points of inflexion

In the previous section we met stationary points of inflexion, but the idea of a point of inflexion is more general than this.

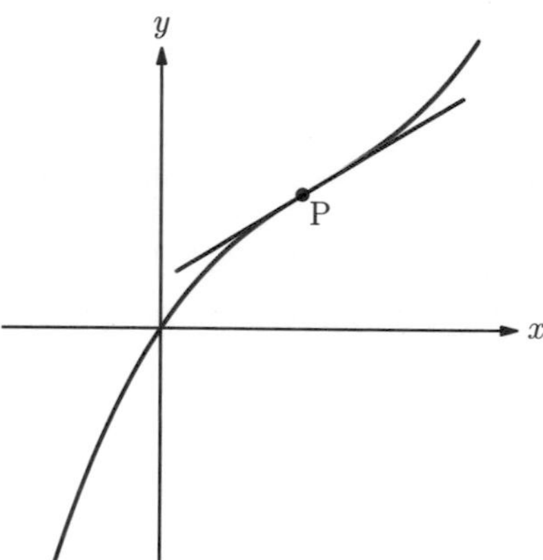

One definition of a point of inflexion is as a point where the tangent to the curve crosses the curve at that point. This does not require the point to be a stationary point. Geometrically, the portion of the graph around a point of inflexion can be interpreted as an 'S-bend' – a curve whose gradient goes from decreasing to increasing (as shown in the diagram) or vice versa; this is equivalent to the curve switching from concave-down to concave-up or vice versa. At the point of inflexion itself, the gradient is neither decreasing nor increasing.

EXAM HINT

Although the red line actually crosses the graph at P, it is still referred to as the tangent, because it has the same gradient as the curve at P.

KEY POINT 12.14

At a point of inflexion, $\frac{d^2y}{dx^2} = 0$.

Although a point of inflexion must have zero second derivative, the converse is not true: just because a point has $\frac{d^2y}{dx^2} = 0$, it is not necessarily a point of inflexion. You can see this from the function $f(x) = x^4$ of Worked example 12.17: at $x = 0$ we have $f''(x) = 0$, but $f''(x) = 12x^2$ is positive on *both* sides of $x = 0$, which means that the gradient is increasing on both sides; so $x = 0$ is not a point of inflexion.

Worked example 12.19

Find the coordinates of the point of inflexion on the curve $y = x^3 - 3x^2 + 5x - 1$.

Find $\frac{d^2y}{dx^2}$.

$$\frac{dy}{dx} = 3x^2 - 6x + 5$$

$$\frac{d^2y}{dx^2} = 6x - 6$$

At a point of inflexion $\frac{d^2y}{dx^2} = 0$:

$$6x - 6 = 0$$

$$\Leftrightarrow x = 1$$

Remember to calculate the other coordinate!

When $x = 1$, $y = 1 - 3 + 5 - 1 = 2$

So point of inflexion is at (1, 2)

EXAM HINT

If a question states that a curve has a point of inflexion and you find only one solution to the equation $\frac{d^2y}{dx^2} = 0$, you can then assume that you have found the point of inflexion, with no need to check the sign of $\frac{d^2y}{dx^2}$ on either side.

Exercise 12I

1. Find the coordinates of the point of inflexion on the curve $y = e^x - x^2$. *[5 marks]*

2. The curve $y = x^4 - 6x^2 + 7x + 2$ has two points of inflexion. Find their coordinates. *[5 marks]*

3. Show that all points of inflexion on the curve $y = \sin x$ lie on the x-axis. *[6 marks]*

4. Find the coordinates of the points of inflexion on the curve $y = 2\cos x + x$ for $0 \le x \le 2\pi$. Justify carefully that these points are points of inflexion. *[5 marks]*

5. The point of inflexion on the curve $y = x^3 - ax^2 - bx + c$ is a stationary point of inflexion. Show that $b = -\frac{a^2}{3}$. *[6 marks]*

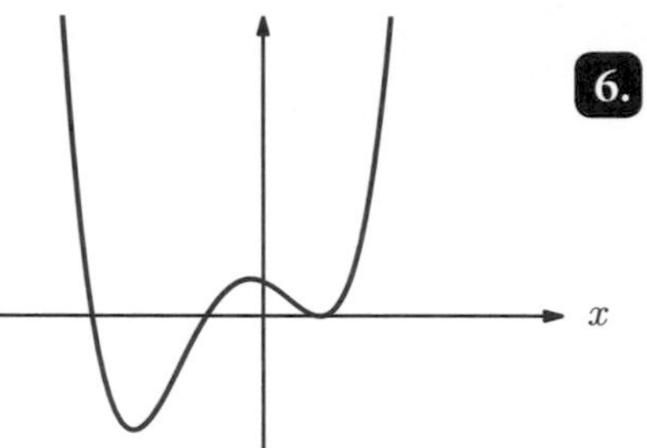

6. The graph shows $y = f'(x)$.

On a copy of the graph:

(a) mark points corresponding to a local minimum of $f(x)$ with an A

(b) mark points corresponding to a local maximum of $f(x)$ with a B

(c) mark points corresponding to a point of inflexion of $f(x)$ with a C. *[6 marks]*

12J Optimisation

We now have enough tools to start using differentiation to maximise or minimise quantities.

KEY POINT 12.15

> To maximise or minimise quantity A by changing quantity B, we follow a four-stage procedure:
>
> 1. Find the relationship between A and B.
> 2. Solve the equation $\frac{dA}{dB} = 0$ to find stationary points.
> 3. Determine whether each stationary point is a local maximum, local minimum or point of inflexion by checking $\frac{d^2A}{dB^2}$ and, if necessary, the sign of $\frac{dA}{dB}$ on either side of the point.
> 4. Check whether each end point of the domain is actually a global maximum or global minimum point, and check that there are no vertical asymptotes.

The first stage of this process is often the most difficult, and there are many situations in which we have to make this link in a geometric context. Fortunately, in many questions this relationship is given to you.

Worked example 12.20

The height h in metres of a swing above the ground at time t seconds is given by $h = 2 - 1.5\sin t$ for $0 < t < 3$. Find the minimum and maximum heights of the swing.

Find stationary points.

$\frac{dh}{dt} = -1.5\cos t = 0$ at a stationary point

$\Rightarrow \cos t = 0$

$0 < t < 3 \ \therefore t = \frac{\pi}{2}$ (only one solution)

Classify stationary points.

$\frac{d^2h}{dt^2} = 1.5\sin t$

When $t = \frac{\pi}{2}$:

$\frac{d^2h}{dt^2} = 1.5 > 0$,

so $t = \frac{\pi}{2}$ is a local minimum.

The minimum height is

$h = 2 - 1.5\sin\frac{\pi}{2} = 0.5$ metres.

There are no vertical asymptotes. Check end points.

When $t = 0, h = 2$

When $t = 3, h = 1.79$

So maximum height is 2 metres.

Exercise 12J

1. What are the minimum and maximum values of e^x for $0 \le x \le 1$? *[4 marks]*

2. A rectangle has width x metres and length $30 - x$ metres.
   (a) Find the maximum area of the rectangle.
   (b) Show that as x changes the perimeter stays constant, and find the value of this perimeter. *[5 marks]*

3. Find the maximum and minimum values of the function $y = x^3 - 9x$ for $-2 \leq x \leq 5$. *[4 marks]*

4. What are the maximum and minimum values of $f(x) = e^x - 3x$ for $0 \leq x \leq 2$? *[5 marks]*

5. What are the minimum and maximum values of $y = \sin x + 2x$ for $0 \leq x \leq 2\pi$? *[5 marks]*

6. Find the minimum value of the sum of a positive real number and its reciprocal. *[5 marks]*

7. A paper aeroplane of weight $w > 1$ will travel at a constant speed of $1 - \frac{1}{\sqrt{w}}$ metres per second for $\frac{5}{w}$ seconds. What weight will achieve the maximum distance travelled? *[6 marks]*

8. The time t in minutes taken to melt 100 g of butter depends upon the percentage p of the butter that consists of saturated fats, as described by the following function:

$$t = \frac{p^2}{10000} + \frac{p}{100} + 2$$

Find the maximum and minimum times to melt 100 g of butter. *[6 marks]*

9. The volume V of water in a tidal lake, in millions of litres, is modelled by $V = 60\cos t + 100$, where t is the time in days after the tidal lake mechanism is switched on.

(a) What is the smallest volume of the lake?

(b) A hydroelectric plant produces an amount of electricity proportional to the rate of flow of lake water. During the first 6 days, when is the plant producing the maximum amount of electricity? *[6 marks]*

10. A fast-food merchant finds that there is a relationship between the amount of salt, s, that he puts on his fries and his weekly sales of fries, F:

$$F(s) = 4s + 1 - s^2, \quad 0 \leq s \leq 4.2$$

(a) Find the amount of salt he should put on his fries to maximise sales.

(b) The total cost C associated with selling the fries is given by

$$C(s) = 0.3 + 0.2F(s) + 0.1s$$

Find the amount of salt the merchant should put on his fries to minimise costs.

(c) The profit made on the fries is given by the difference between the sales and the costs. How much salt should the merchant add to maximise profit? *[8 marks]*

11. A car tank is being filled with petrol such that the volume V of petrol in the tank, in litres, after time t minutes is given by

$$V = 300(t^2 - t^3) + 4, \quad 0 < t < 0.5$$

(a) How much petrol was initially in the tank?

(b) After 30 seconds the tank was full. What is the capacity of the tank?

(c) At what time is petrol flowing into the tank at the greatest rate? *[8 marks]*

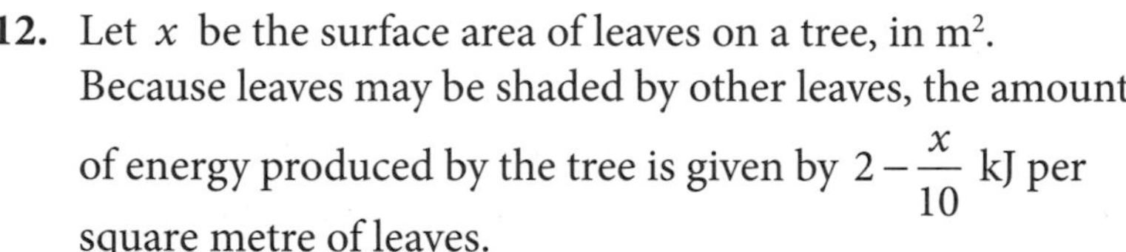

12. Let x be the surface area of leaves on a tree, in m^2. Because leaves may be shaded by other leaves, the amount of energy produced by the tree is given by $2 - \frac{x}{10}$ kJ per square metre of leaves.

(a) Find an expression for the total energy produced by the tree.

(b) What area of leaves provides the maximum energy for the tree?

(c) Leaves also require energy for maintenance. The total energy requirement is given by $0.01x^3$. The *net* energy produced is the difference between the total energy produced by the leaves and the energy required by the leaves. For what range of x do the leaves produce more energy than they require?

(d) Show that the maximum net energy is produced when the tree has leaves with a surface area of $\frac{10(\sqrt{7}-1)}{3}$.

[12 marks]

Summary

- The gradient of a function at a point is the gradient of the **tangent** to the function's graph at that point.
- The gradient of a function $f(x)$ at point x is called the **derivative** and is given by

$$f'(x) = \lim_{h \to 0} \frac{f(x+h) - f(x)}{h}$$

  The process of finding the derivative of a function is called **differentiation**.

  The derivative is also written as $\frac{\mathrm{d}}{\mathrm{d}x} f(x)$, where $\frac{\mathrm{d}}{\mathrm{d}x}$ means 'differentiate with respect to x'.
- The derivative of a sum is obtained by differentiating the terms one by one and then adding up the results. If k is a constant, the derivative of $kf(x)$ is $kf'(x)$.
- The derivatives of some common functions are:

$$\frac{\mathrm{d}}{\mathrm{d}x}(x^n) = nx^{n-1}$$

$$\frac{\mathrm{d}}{\mathrm{d}x}(\sin x) = \cos x$$

$$\frac{\mathrm{d}}{\mathrm{d}x}(\cos x) = -\sin x$$

$$\frac{\mathrm{d}}{\mathrm{d}x}(\tan x) = \frac{1}{\cos^2 x}$$

$$\frac{\mathrm{d}}{\mathrm{d}x}(\mathrm{e}^x) = \mathrm{e}^x$$

$$\frac{\mathrm{d}}{\mathrm{d}x}(\ln x) = \frac{1}{x}$$

- At the point on the curve $y = f(x)$ with $x = a$:
  - the gradient of the tangent is $f'(a)$
  - the gradient of the **normal** is $-\frac{1}{f'(a)}$
  - the coordinates of the point are $x_1 = a$, $y_1 = f(a)$

  The equation of the tangent or normal is $y - y_1 = m(x - x_1)$ with the appropriate gradient.
- **Stationary points** of a function are points where the gradient is zero: $\frac{\mathrm{d}y}{\mathrm{d}x} = 0$

  There are four types of stationary point:
  - local maximum
  - local minimum
  - positive point of inflexion
  - negative point of inflexion

- To determine the type of a stationary point, we can use the **second derivative**. At a stationary point (x_0, y_0):

  - if $\frac{d^2y}{dx^2} < 0$ at x_0, then (x_0, y_0) is a maximum
  - if $\frac{d^2y}{dx^2} > 0$ at x_0, then (x_0, y_0) is a minimum
  - if $\frac{d^2y}{dx^2} = 0$ at x_0, then no conclusion can be drawn, so check the sign of the gradient $\frac{dy}{dx}$ on either side of (x_0, y_0)

- A **point of inflexion** is a point where the curve switches from being concave-up to being concave-down or vice versa. At a point of inflexion, $\frac{d^2y}{dx^2} = 0$.
- To solve optimisation problems – that is, to maximise or minimise a function – we find and classify the stationary points, and also check the function values at the end points of the domain; the global maximum or minimum of a function may occur at an end point.

Introductory problem revisited

The cost of petrol consumed by a car is £$\left(12 + \frac{v^2}{100}\right)$ per hour, where the speed $v\ (>0)$ is measured in miles per hour. If Daniel wants to travel 50 miles as cheaply as possible, what speed should he go at?

We know the cost per hour and want the total cost, so we need to find the total time. The time taken is $\frac{50}{v}$ hours, hence the total cost is $C = \frac{50}{v}\left(12 + \frac{v^2}{100}\right) = \frac{600}{v} + \frac{v}{2}$.

We wish to minimise C. To do this, we first look for stationary points by setting $\frac{dC}{dv} = 0$:

$$\frac{dC}{dv} = -\frac{600}{v^2} + \frac{1}{2}$$

$$\therefore -\frac{600}{v^2} + \frac{1}{2} = 0$$

$$\Leftrightarrow -1200 + v^2 = 0$$

$$\Leftrightarrow v = \sqrt{1200} = 34.6 \text{ (3SF)}$$

We take the positive square root since $v > 0$.

To check whether we have found a minimum point, calculate $\frac{d^2C}{dv^2} = 1200v^{-3}$. This is positive for any positive v, so the stationary point is a local minimum.

Next, to see if it is in fact the global minimum, we must consider the end points of the domain. Although v is never actually zero, as it gets close to zero the $\frac{600}{v}$ term becomes very large (the function has a vertical asymptote at $v = 0$). At the other end, when v gets very large, the $\frac{v}{2}$ term gets very large. Therefore the global minimum cannot be found at either end, and so the minimum cost is achieved at speed 34.6 miles per hour.

Mixed examination practice 12

Short questions

1. Find the equation of the tangent to the curve $y = e^x + 2\sin x$ at the point where $x = \frac{\pi}{2}$. *[5 marks]*

2. Find the equation of the normal to the curve $y = (x-2)^3$ at the point where $x = 2$. *[5 marks]*

3. $f(x)$ is a quadratic function taking the form $x^2 + bx + c$. If $f(1) = 2$ and $f'(2) = 12$, find the values of b and c. *[5 marks]*

4. Find the coordinates of the point on the curve $y = \sqrt{x} + 3x$ where the gradient is 5. *[4 marks]*

5. Find the coordinates of the point of inflexion on the graph of $y = \frac{x^3}{6} - x^2 + x$. *[5 marks]*

6. Find and classify the stationary points on the curve $y = \tan x - \frac{4x}{3}$. *[6 marks]*

7. The graph shows $y = f'(x)$.

On a copy of this graph:

(a) mark points corresponding to a local minimum of $f(x)$ with an A

(b) mark points corresponding to a local maximum of $f(x)$ with a B

(c) mark points corresponding to a point of inflexion of $f(x)$ with a C. *[6 marks]*

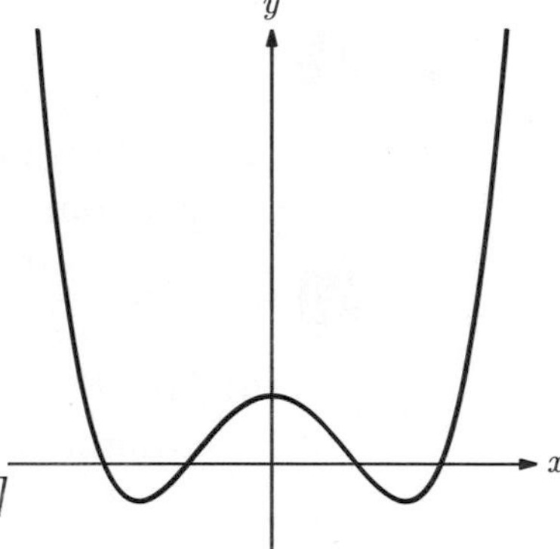

8. On the curve $y = x^3$, a tangent is drawn from the point (a, a^3) and a normal is drawn from the point $(-a, -a^3)$. The tangent and the normal meet on the y-axis. Find the value of a. *[6 marks]*

Long questions

1. The line $y = 24(x-1)$ is tangent to the curve $y = ax^3 + bx^2 + 4$ at $x = 2$.

(a) Use the fact that the tangent meets the curve to show that $2a + b = 5$.

(b) Use the fact that the tangent has the same gradient as the curve to find another relationship between a and b.

(c) Hence find the values of a and b.

(d) The line meets the curve again. Find the coordinates of the other point of intersection. *[12 marks]*

2. The curve shown is part of the graph of

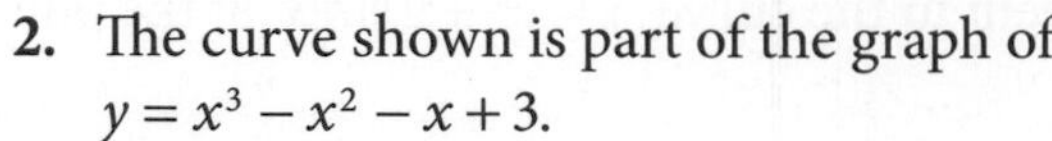

$y = x^3 - x^2 - x + 3$.

The point A is a local maximum and the point B is a point of inflexion.

(a) (i) Find the coordinates of A.

(ii) Find the coordinates of B.

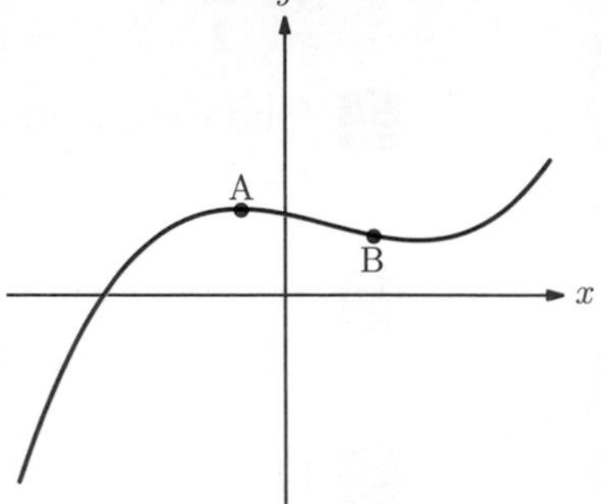

(b) (i) Find the equation of the line containing both A and B.

(ii) Find the equation of a tangent to the curve which is parallel to this line. *[10 marks]*

3. The population P of bacteria in thousands at a time t in hours is modelled by

$$P = 10 + e^t - 3t,\ t \geq 0$$

(a) (i) Find the initial population of bacteria.

(ii) At what time does the number of bacteria reach 14 million?

(b) (i) Find $\frac{dP}{dt}$.

(ii) Find the time at which the bacteria are growing at a rate of 6 million per hour.

(c) (i) Find $\frac{d^2P}{dt^2}$ and explain the physical significance of this quantity.

(ii) Find the minimum number of bacteria, justifying that it is a minimum. *[12 marks]*

13 Basic integration and its applications

In this chapter you will learn:

- how to reverse differentiation, a process called integration
- how to find the equation of a curve given its derivative and a point on the curve
- to integrate $\sin x$ and $\cos x$
- to integrate e^x and $\frac{1}{x}$
- how to find the area between a curve and the x-axis
- how to find the area enclosed between two curves.

Introductory problem

The amount of charge stored in a capacitor is given by the area under the graph of current (I) against time (t). For alternating current the relationship between I and t is $I = \sin t$; for direct current the relationship is $I = k$, where k is a constant. For what value of k is the amount of charge stored in the capacitor from $t = 0$ to $t = \pi$ the same whether alternating or direct current is used?

As in many areas of mathematics, as soon as we learn a new process we must then learn how to undo it. It turns out that undoing the process of differentiation opens up a way to solve a seemingly unconnected problem: how to calculate the area under a curve.

13A Reversing differentiation

We saw in chapter 12 how differentiation gives us the gradient of a curve or the rate of change of one quantity with another. What if we already know the function describing a curve's gradient, or the expression for a rate of change, and want to find the original function? This is the same as asking how we can 'undo' the differentiation that has already taken place; the process of reversing differentiation is known as **integration**.

Let us look at two particular cases to get a feel for this process. Each time we will be given $\frac{dy}{dx}$ and need to answer the question, 'what function was differentiated to give this?'

Suppose that $\frac{dy}{dx} = 2x$.

Since $\frac{dy}{dx} = 2x$, the original function y must contain x^2, as we know that differentiation decreases the power by 1. In fact, differentiating x^2 gives exactly $2x$, so we can say that

if $\frac{dy}{dx} = 2x$, then $y = x^2$.

Now suppose that $\frac{dy}{dx} = x^{\frac{1}{2}}$.

Using the same reasoning as above, since $\frac{dy}{dx} = x^{\frac{1}{2}}$, we deduce that the original function y must contain $x^{\frac{3}{2}}$. But if we differentiate $x^{\frac{3}{2}}$ we will get $y = \frac{3}{2}x^{\frac{1}{2}}$, so there is an extra factor of $\frac{3}{2}$ which we do not want. However, if we multiply $x^{\frac{3}{2}}$ by $\frac{2}{3}$, then when we differentiate, the coefficient will cancel to leave 1.

Therefore we can say that if $\frac{dy}{dx} = x^{\frac{1}{2}}$, then $y = \frac{2}{3}x^{\frac{3}{2}}$.

The integration symbol comes from the old English way of writing the letter 'S'. Originally it stood for the word 'sum' (or rather, ∫um). As you will see later, the integral does indeed represent a sum of infinitesimally small quantities.

Writing out 'if $\frac{dy}{dx} = x^{\frac{1}{2}}$ then $y = \frac{2}{3}x^{\frac{3}{2}}$' is rather laborious, so we use a shorthand notation for integration:

$$\int x^{\frac{1}{2}}\,dx = \frac{2}{3}x^{\frac{3}{2}}$$

The dx states that integration is taking place with respect to the variable x, in exactly the same way that $\frac{d}{dx}$ tells us that the differentiation is taking place with respect to x. We could equally well write, for example,

$$\int t^{\frac{1}{2}}\,dt = \frac{2}{3}t^{\frac{3}{2}}$$

Exercise 13A

1. Find a possible expression for y in terms of x for each of the following.

   (a) (i) $\frac{dy}{dx} = 3x^2$ (ii) $\frac{dy}{dx} = 5x^4$

   (b) (i) $\frac{dy}{dx} = -\frac{1}{x^2}$ (ii) $\frac{dy}{dx} = -\frac{4}{x^5}$

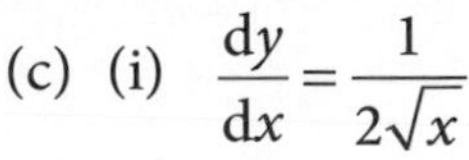

(c) (i) $\frac{dy}{dx} = \frac{1}{2\sqrt{x}}$ (ii) $\frac{dy}{dx} = \frac{1}{3\sqrt[3]{x^2}}$

(d) (i) $\frac{dy}{dx} = 10x^4$ (ii) $\frac{dy}{dx} = 12x^2$

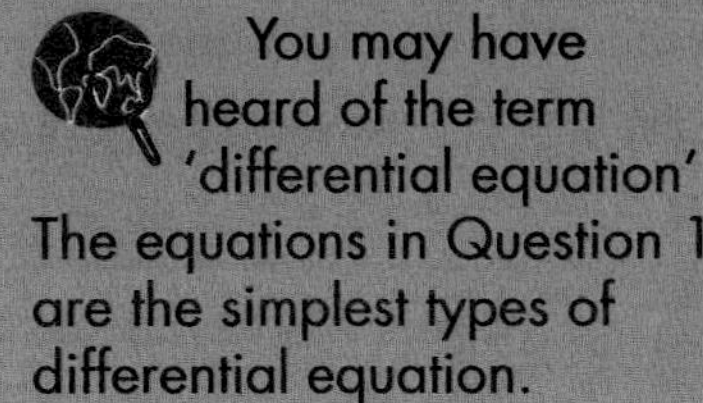

You may have heard of the term 'differential equation'. The equations in Question 1 are the simplest types of differential equation.

13B Constant of integration

We have seen how to integrate some functions of the form x^n by reversing the effects of differentiation. However, the process as carried out above was not quite complete.

Let us consider again the example $\frac{dy}{dx} = 2x$, where we stated that

$$\int 2x \, dx = x^2$$

because the derivative of x^2 is $2x$. But besides x^2, there are other functions which when differentiated give $2x$, for example $x^2 + 1$ or $x^2 - \frac{3}{5}$. This is because when we differentiate the additional constant ($+1$ or $-\frac{3}{5}$) we just get zero. So we could write

$$\int 2x \, dx = x^2 + 1$$

or

$$\int 2x \, dx = x^2 - \frac{3}{5}$$

and both of these answers would be just as valid as $\int 2x dx = x^2$. In fact, we could have added any constant to x^2; without further information we cannot know what constant term the original function had before it was differentiated.

Therefore, the complete answers to the integrals considered in section 13A should be

$$\int 2x \, dx = x^2 + c$$

$$\int x^{\frac{1}{2}} \, dx = \frac{2}{3}x^{\frac{3}{2}} + c$$

where c represents an unknown **constant of integration**. We will see later that, given further information, we can find the value of this constant.

We will see how to determine the constant of integration in section 13F.

Exercise 13B

1. Give three possible functions which when differentiated with respect to x give the following.

(a) $3x^3$ (b) 0

2. Find the following integrals.

(a) (i) $\int 7x^4 \, \mathrm{d}x$ (ii) $\int \frac{1}{3}x^2 \, \mathrm{d}x$

(b) (i) $\int \frac{1}{2t^2} \, \mathrm{d}t$ (ii) $\int \frac{8}{y^3} \, \mathrm{d}y$

13C Rules of integration

First, let us think about how to reverse the general rule of differentiating a power function.

We know that if $y = x^n$, then $\frac{\mathrm{d}y}{\mathrm{d}x} = nx^{n-1}$, or in words:

To differentiate x^n, **multiply** by the **old** power and then **decrease** the power by 1.

The reverse of this process is:

To integrate x^n, **increase** the power by 1 and then **divide** by the **new** power.

Using integral notation, the general rule for integrating x^n is expressed as follows.

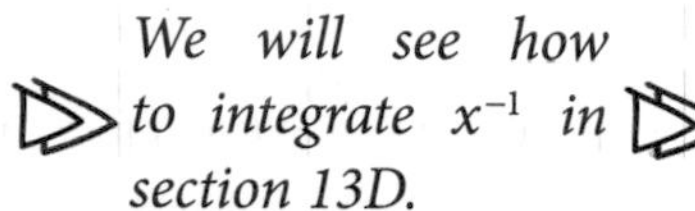
We will see how to integrate x^{-1} in section 13D.

KEY POINT 13.1

$$\int x^n \, \mathrm{d}x = \frac{1}{n+1}x^{n+1} + c$$

This holds for any rational power $n \neq -1$.

EXAM HINT

The +c is an essential part of the answer; you must write it every time.

Note the condition $n \neq -1$ which ensures that we are not dividing by zero.

It is worth remembering the formula for integrating a constant: $\int k \, \mathrm{d}x = kx + c$, which is a special case of the above rule with $n = 0$: $\int k \, \mathrm{d}x = \int kx^0 \, \mathrm{d}x = \frac{k}{1}x^1 + c$.

EXAM HINT

This rule holds only if k is a constant – a number or expression that does not change with the integration variable.

When we differentiate a function multiplied by a constant k, we get k times the derivative of the function (Key point 12.4). Reversing this gives the following rule for integration:

KEY POINT 13.2

$$\int kf(x) \, \mathrm{d}x = k\int f(x) \, \mathrm{d}x$$

As we can differentiate term by term (Key point 12.4), we can also split up integrals of sums and do them term by term.

KEY POINT 13.3

For the sum of integrals:

$$\int f(x)+g(x)\,dx = \int f(x)\,dx + \int g(x)\,dx$$

EXAM HINT

Be warned – you cannot integrate products or quotients by integrating each part separately.

By combining Key point 13.3 and Key point 13.2 with $k = -1$, we can also show that the integral of a difference is the difference of the integrals of the separate terms.

These ideas are demonstrated in the following examples.

Worked example 13.1

Find (a) $\int 6x^{-3}\,dx$ (b) $\int \left(3x^4 - 8x^{-\frac{4}{3}} + 2\right) dx$

Add one to the power and divide by the new power.

(a) $\int 6x^{-3}\,dx = \dfrac{6}{-3+1}x^{-3+1} + c$

$= \dfrac{6}{-2}x^{-2} + c$

$= -3x^{-2} + c$

Go through term by term, adding one to the power of x and dividing by the new power. Remember the special rule for integrating a constant.

(b) $\int 3x^4 - 8x^{-\frac{4}{3}} + 2\,dx$

$= \dfrac{3}{4+1}x^{4+1} - \dfrac{8}{-\frac{4}{3}+1}x^{-\frac{4}{3}+1} + 2x + c$

$= \dfrac{3}{5}x^5 - \dfrac{8}{-\frac{1}{3}}x^{-\frac{1}{3}} + 2x + c$

$= \dfrac{3}{5}x^5 + 24x^{-\frac{1}{3}} + 2x + c$

Just as for differentiation, it may be necessary to manipulate terms into the form kx^n before integrating.

Worked example 13.2

Find (a) $\int 5x^2\sqrt[3]{x}\,dx$ (b) $\int \dfrac{(x-3)^2}{\sqrt{x}}\,dx$

Write the cube root as a power and use the laws of exponents to combine the two powers.

(a) $\int 5x^2\sqrt[3]{x}\,dx = \int 5x^2x^{\frac{1}{3}}\,dx$

$= \int 5x^{\frac{7}{3}}\,dx$

→

continued . . .

Dividing by $\frac{10}{3}\left(\text{which is from } \frac{7}{3}+1\right)$ is the same as multiplying by $\frac{3}{10}$.

$$=5\times\frac{3}{10}x^{\frac{10}{3}}+c$$

$$=\frac{3}{2}x^{\frac{10}{3}}+c$$

Expand the brackets first, then use rules of exponents to write as a sum of powers.

(b) $$\int\frac{(x-3)^2}{\sqrt{x}}dx=\int\frac{x^2-6x+9}{x^{\frac{1}{2}}}dx$$

$$=\int\frac{x^2}{x^{\frac{1}{2}}}-\frac{6x}{x^{\frac{1}{2}}}+\frac{9}{x^{\frac{1}{2}}}dx$$

$$=\int x^{\frac{3}{2}}-6x^{\frac{1}{2}}+9x^{-\frac{1}{2}}\,dx$$

Dividing by a fraction is the same as multiplying by its reciprocal.

$$=\frac{2}{5}x^{\frac{5}{2}}-6\times\frac{2}{3}x^{\frac{3}{2}}+9\times2x^{\frac{1}{2}}+c$$

$$=\frac{2}{5}x^{\frac{5}{2}}-4x^{\frac{3}{2}}+18x^{\frac{1}{2}}+c$$

Exercise 13C

1. Find the following integrals

(a) (i) $\int 9x^8\,dx$ (ii) $\int 12x^{11}\,dx$

(b) (i) $\int x\,dx$ (ii) $\int x^3\,dx$

(c) (i) $\int 9\,dx$ (ii) $\int \frac{1}{2}\,dx$

(d) (i) $\int 3x^5\,dx$ (ii) $\int 9x^4\,dx$

(e) (i) $\int 3\sqrt{x}\,dx$ (ii) $\int 3\sqrt[3]{x}\,dx$

(f) (i) $\int \frac{5}{x^2}\,dx$ (ii) $\int \frac{2}{x^3}\,dx$

EXAM HINT

Do not neglect the dx or equivalent in the integral; it tells you what letter represents the variable – see Questions 2 and 3, for example. We will make more use of it later. You can think of the function you are integrating as being multiplied by 'dx', so sometimes you will see integrals written as, for instance, $\int\frac{2\,dx}{x^3}$.

2. Find the following integrals

(a) (i) $\int 3\,dt$ (ii) $\int 7\,dz$

(b) (i) $\int q^5 \, dq$ (ii) $\int r^{10} \, dr$

(c) (i) $\int 12g^{\frac{3}{5}} \, dg$ (ii) $\int 5y^{\frac{7}{2}} \, dy$

(d) (i) $\int 4\frac{dh}{h^2}$ (ii) $\int \frac{dp}{p^4}$

3. Find the following integrals.

(a) (i) $\int x^2 - x^3 + 2 \, dx$ (ii) $\int x^4 - 2x + 5 \, dx$

(b) (i) $\int \frac{1}{3t^3} + \frac{1}{4t^4} \, dt$ (ii) $\int 5 \times \frac{1}{v^2} - 4 \times \frac{1}{v^5} \, dv$

(c) (i) $\int x\sqrt{x} \, dx$ (ii) $\int \frac{3\sqrt{x}}{\sqrt[3]{x}} \, dx$

(d) (i) $\int (x+1)^3 \, dx$ (ii) $\int x(x+2)^2 \, dx$

4. Find $\int \frac{1+x}{\sqrt{x}} \, dx$. *[4 marks]*

13D Integrating x^{-1} and e^x

We can now integrate x^n for any rational power n with one exception: in the formula $\int x^n \, dx = \frac{1}{n+1} x^{n+1} + c$ we had to exclude $n = -1$. How, then, do we cope with this case?

In section 12F we learned that $\frac{d}{dx}(\ln x) = \frac{1}{x}$ (Key point 12.10).

Reversing this gives the integration rule for x^{-1}.

KEY POINT 13.4

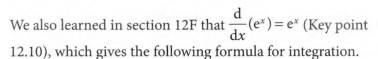

For $x > 0$,

$$\int x^{-1} \, dx = \ln x + c$$

We also learned in section 12F that $\frac{d}{dx}(e^x) = e^x$ (Key point 12.10), which gives the following formula for integration.

KEY POINT 13.5

$$\int e^x \, dx = e^x + c$$

Worked example 13.3

Find the integral $\int \frac{1+x}{x} \, dx$.

Divide each term of the numerator by the denominator x to split it into two terms.

$$\int \frac{1+x}{3x} dx = \int \frac{1}{3x} + \frac{1}{3} dx$$

$\frac{1}{3x}$ is the same as $\frac{1}{3} \times \frac{1}{x}$.

$$= \int \frac{1}{3} \times \frac{1}{x} + \frac{1}{3} dx$$

Use Key point 13.4 to integrate the first term.

$$= \frac{1}{3} \ln x + \frac{x}{3} + c$$

Exercise 13D

1. Find the following integrals.

   (a) (i) $\int \frac{2}{x} \, dx$ (ii) $\int \frac{3}{x} \, dx$

   (b) (i) $\int \frac{1}{2x} \, dx$ (ii) $\int \frac{1}{3x} \, dx$

   (c) (i) $\int \frac{x^2-1}{x} \, dx$ (ii) $\int \frac{x^3+5}{x} \, dx$

   (d) (i) $\int \frac{3x+2}{x^2} \, dx$ (ii) $\int \frac{x-\sqrt{x}}{x^2} \, dx$

2. Find the following integrals.

   (a) (i) $\int 5e^x \, dx$ (ii) $\int 9e^x \, dx$

   (b) (i) $\int \frac{2e^x}{5} \, dx$ (ii) $\int \frac{7e^x}{11} \, dx$

   (c) (i) $\int \frac{(e^x+3x)}{2} \, dx$ (ii) $\int \frac{(e^x+x^3)}{5} \, dx$

13E Integrating trigonometric functions

We will expand the set of functions that we can integrate by continuing to refer back to chapter 12. In section 12E we saw that $\frac{d}{dx}(\sin x) = \cos x$ (Key point 12.8), which means that

$\int \cos x \, dx = \sin x + c$. Similarly, since $\frac{d}{dx}(\cos x) = -\sin x$, we also have $\int \sin x \, dx = -\cos x + c$.

KEY POINT 13.6

$$\int \sin x \, dx = -\cos x + c$$
$$\int \cos x \, dx = \sin x + c$$

Exercise 13E

1. Evaluate the following integrals.

   (a) (i) $\int \sin x - \cos x \, dx$ (ii) $\int 3\cos x + 4\sin x \, dx$

   (b) (i) $\int \frac{x + \sin x}{7} \, dx$ (ii) $\int \frac{\sqrt{x} + \cos x}{6} \, dx$

   (c) (i) $\int 1 - (\cos x + \sin x) dx$

   (ii) $\int \cos x - 2(\cos x - \sin x) dx$

2. Find $\int \pi(\cos x - 1) dx$. *[3 marks]*

3. Find $\int \frac{\cos 2x}{\cos x - \sin x} dx$. *[5 marks]*

13F Finding the equation of a curve

We have seen how, given $\frac{dy}{dx}$, we can integrate it to find the equation of the original curve, except for the unknown constant of integration. Geometrically, this means that the gradient determines the shape of the curve, but not exactly where it is. However, if we also know the coordinates of a point on the curve (essentially 'fixing' the curve at a certain position), then we can determine the constant and hence specify the original function precisely.

Consider again the example $\frac{dy}{dx} = 2x$ discussed in sections 13A and 13B. We found that the original curve must have equation $y = x^2 + c$ for some value of the constant c. Each different value of c gives a different curve, but all these graphs have the same shape (a parabola symmetric about the y-axis) and are related to one another by vertical translations; they form a *family* of

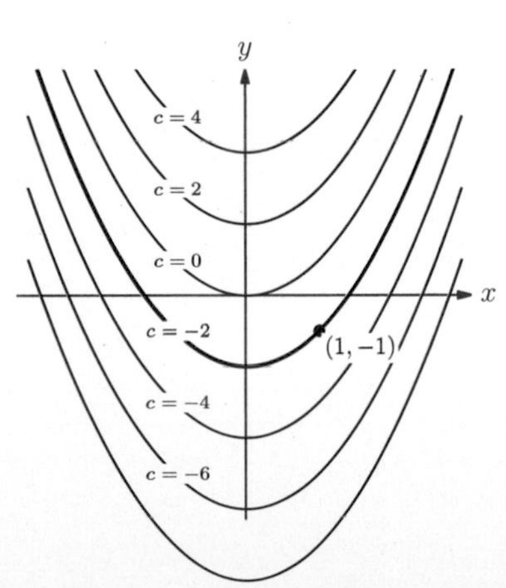

curves. Now, if we are also told that the curve passes through the point (1, −1), then we can substitute these x and y values into the equation, find c, and thus specify which curve of the family our function corresponds to.

Worked example 13.4

The gradient of a curve is given by $\frac{dy}{dx} = 3x^2 - 8x + 5$, and the curve passes through the point $(1, -4)$. Find the equation of the curve.

To find y from $\frac{dy}{dx}$ we need to integrate. Don't forget + c.

$$y = \int 3x^2 - 8x + 5 \, dx$$
$$= x^3 - 4x^2 + 5x + c$$

The coordinates of the given point must satisfy this equation, so we can find c.

When $x = 1$, $y = -4$, so

$$-4 = (1)^3 - 4(1)^2 + 5(1) + c$$
$$\Rightarrow -4 = 1 - 4 + 5 + c$$
$$\Rightarrow c = -6$$
$$\therefore y = x^3 - 4x^2 + 5x - 6$$

The above example illustrates the general procedure for finding the equation of a curve from its gradient and a point on the curve.

KEY POINT 13.7

To find the equation for y given the gradient $\frac{dy}{dx}$ and one point (p, q) on the curve:

- Integrate $\frac{dy}{dx}$ to get an equation for y in terms of x, remembering $+c$.
- Find the value of c by substituting $x = p$ and $y = q$ into the equation.
- Rewrite the equation, putting in the value of c that was found.

Exercise 13F

1. Find the equation of the original curve if:

   (a) (i) $\frac{dy}{dx} = x$ and the curve passes through $(-2,7)$

   (ii) $\frac{dy}{dx} = 6x^2$ and the curve passes through (0, 5)

   (b) (i) $\frac{dy}{dx} = \frac{1}{\sqrt{x}}$ and the curve passes through (4, 8)

   (ii) $\frac{dy}{dx} = \frac{1}{x^2}$ and the curve passes through (1,3)

   (c) (i) $\frac{dy}{dx} = 2e^x + 2$ and the curve passes through (1, 1)

   (ii) $\frac{dy}{dx} = e^x$ and the curve passes through $(\ln 5, 0)$

   (d) (i) $\frac{dy}{dx} = \frac{x+1}{x}$ and the curve passes through (e, e)

   (ii) $\frac{dy}{dx} = \frac{1}{2x}$ and the curve passes through $(e^2, 5)$

   (e) (i) $\frac{dy}{dx} = \cos x + \sin x$ and the curve passes through $(\pi, 1)$

   (ii) $\frac{dy}{dx} = -3\sin x$ and the curve passes through (0, 4)

2. The derivative of the function $f(x)$ is $\frac{1}{2x}$.

   (a) Find an expression for all possible functions $f(x)$.

   (b) If the curve $y = f(x)$ passes through the point (2, 7), find the equation of the curve. *[5 marks]*

3. The gradient of a curve is found to be $\frac{dy}{dx} = x^2 - 4$.

   (a) Find the x-coordinate of the maximum point, justifying that it is a maximum.

   (b) Given that the curve passes through the point (0, 2), show that the y-coordinate of the maximum point is $7\frac{1}{3}$. *[5 marks]*

4. A curve is defined only for positive values of x, and the gradient of the normal to the curve at any point is equal to the x-coordinate at that point. If the curve passes through the point $(e^2, 3)$, find the equation of the curve in the form $y = \ln g(x)$ where $g(x)$ is a rational function. *[6 marks]*

13G Definite integration

Until now we have been carrying out a process called **indefinite integration**: indefinite in the sense that we have an unknown constant each time, for example $\int x^2 \, dx = \frac{1}{3}x^3 + c$.

There is also a process known as **definite integration**, which yields a numerical answer. To calculate a definite integral, we evaluate the indefinite integral at two points and take the difference of the results:

$$\begin{aligned}\int_2^3 x^2 \, dx &= \left[\frac{1}{3}x^3 + c\right]_2^3 \\ &= \left(\frac{1}{3}3^3 + c\right) - \left(\frac{1}{3}2^3 + c\right) \\ &= 6\frac{1}{3}\end{aligned}$$

Note that the constant of integration, c, cancels out in the subtraction, so we can omit it altogether from the definite integral calculation and just write

$$\begin{aligned}\int_2^3 x^2 \, dx &= \left[\frac{1}{3}x^3\right]_2^3 \\ &= \left(\frac{1}{3}3^3\right) - \left(\frac{1}{3}2^3\right) \\ &= 6\frac{1}{3}.\end{aligned}$$

The numbers 2 and 3 here are known as the **limits of integration**; 2 is the lower limit and 3 is the upper limit.

EXAM HINT

Make sure you know how to evaluate definite integrals on your calculator. See Calculator Skills sheet 9 on the CD-ROM for guidance on how to do this.
Besides saving you time, your calculator can help you evaluate integrals that you don't know how to do algebraically. And even when you are asked to find the exact value of the integral, it is still a good idea to use your calculator to check the answer.

We could calculate the definite integral of x^2 with any numbers a and b as the lower and upper limits; the answer will, of course, depend on a and b:

$$\begin{aligned}\int_a^b x^2 \, dx &= \left[\frac{1}{3}x^3\right]_a^b \\ &= \frac{1}{3}b^3 - \frac{1}{3}a^3\end{aligned}$$

The integration variable x does *not* come into the answer – it has taken on the values of the limits and is referred to as a 'dummy variable'.

The square bracket notation indicates that integration has taken place but the limits have not yet been applied. 'Applying the limits' just means to evaluate the integrated expression at the upper limit and subtract the integrated expression evaluated at the lower limit.

Worked example 13.5

Find the exact value of $\int_1^e \frac{1}{x} + 4 \, dx$.

Integrate and write in square brackets.

$$\int_1^e \frac{1}{x} + 4\, dx = [\ln x + 4x]_1^e$$

Evaluate the integrated expression at the upper and lower limits and subtract the lower from the upper.

$$= (\ln(e) + 4(e)) - (\ln(1) + 4(1))$$
$$= (1 + 4e) - (0 + 4)$$
$$= 4e - 3$$

Exercise 13G

1. Evaluate the following definite integrals, giving exact answers.

(a) (i) $\int_2^6 x^3 \, dx$ (ii) $\int_1^4 x^2 + x \, dx$

(b) (i) $\int_0^{\pi/2} \cos x \, dx$ (ii) $\int_\pi^{2\pi} \sin x \, dx$

(c) (i) $\int_0^1 e^x \, dx$ (ii) $\int_{-1}^1 3e^x \, dx$

2. Evaluate the following definite integrals.

(a) (i) $\int_{0.3}^{1.4} \sqrt{x}\,dx$ (ii) $\int_{9}^{9.1} \frac{3}{\sqrt{x}}\,dx$

(b) (i) $\int_{0}^{1} e^{x^2}\,dx$ (ii) $\int_{1}^{e} \ln x\,dx$

3. Find the exact value of the integral $\int_0^{\pi} e^x + \sin x + 1\,dx$. *[5 marks]*

4. Show that the value of the integral $\int_k^{2k} \frac{1}{x}\,dx$ is independent of k. *[4 marks]*

5. If $\int_3^9 f(x)\,dx = 7$, evaluate $\int_3^9 2f(x)+1\,dx$. *[4 marks]*

6. Solve the equation $\int_1^a \sqrt{t}\,dt = 42$. *[5 marks]*

13H Geometrical significance of definite integration

Now we have a method that gives a numerical value for an integral, the natural question to ask is: what does this number mean? The answer is that the definite integral represents the area under a curve; more precisely, $\int_a^b f(x)\,dx$ is the area enclosed between the curve $y = f(x)$, the x-axis, and the lines $x = a$ and $x = b$.

KEY POINT 13.8

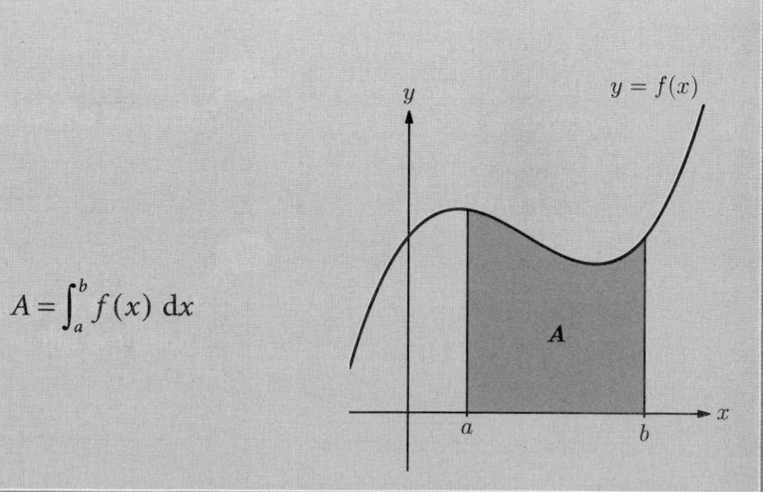

See Fill-in proof 14 'The fundamental theorem of calculus' on the CD-ROM for a justification of this result. Strictly speaking, it holds only if the graph lies above the x-axis, but we shall see later how we can also find areas associated with graphs that go below the x-axis.

In the 17th century the integral was defined as the area under a curve. The region under the curve $y=f(x)$ was broken down into thin rectangles, each with height $f(x)$ and width being a small distance in the x direction, written Δx. The total area can be approximated by the sum of the areas of all these rectangles.

The height of the first rectangle is $f(a)$ and its width is Δx, so its area is $\Delta x f(a)$.

The height of the second rectangle is $f(a+\Delta x)$, so its area is $\Delta x f(a+\Delta x)$.

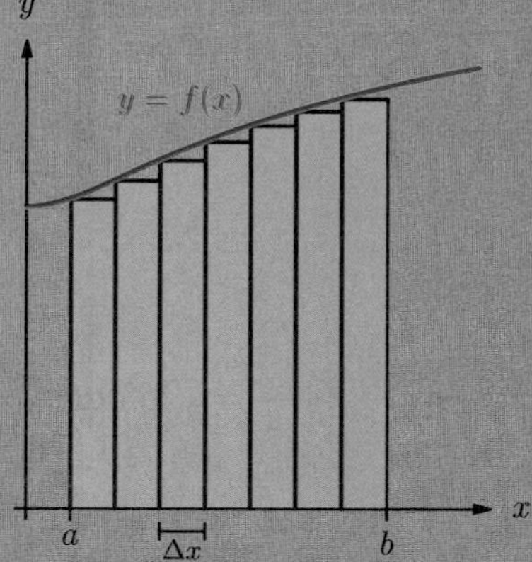

This pattern continues until the final rectangle with left edge at $b-\Delta x$, which has area $\Delta x f(b-\Delta x)$.

Thus, the area under the curve is approximately

$$\left[f(a)+f(a+\Delta x)+f(a+2\Delta x)+\cdots+f(b-\Delta x)\right]\Delta x$$

which can be written more briefly, in sigma notation (see chapter 6), as

$$\sum_{x=a}^{x=b-\Delta x} f(x)\Delta x$$

This approximation to the area gets better as the rectangles become thinner and more numerous. If we take the limit as the width of the rectangles becomes very small ($\Delta x \to 0$), while their number tends to infinity, we should be able to obtain the exact area under the curve.

Isaac Newton, one of the pioneers of calculus, was a big fan of writing in English rather than Greek. 'Sigma' became the English letter 'S' and 'delta' became the English letter 'd', so when the limit $\Delta x \to 0$ is taken, the expression for the sum of rectangle areas becomes

$$\int_a^b f(x)\,dx$$

This illustrates another very important interpretation of integration – as the infinite sum of infinitesimally small parts.

The ancient Greeks had already developed ideas of limiting processes similar to those used in calculus, but it took nearly 2000 years for the ideas to be formalised. This was done almost simultaneously by Isaac Newton and Gottfried Leibniz in the 17th century. Was this a coincidence, or is it often the case that a long period of slow progress is needed to reach a stage of readiness for major breakthroughs? Supplementary sheet 13 looks at some other people who made contributions to the development of calculus.

Worked example 13.6

Find the exact area enclosed between the x-axis, the curve $y = \sin x$ and the lines $x = 0$ and $x = \frac{\pi}{3}$.

Sketch the graph and identify the area required.

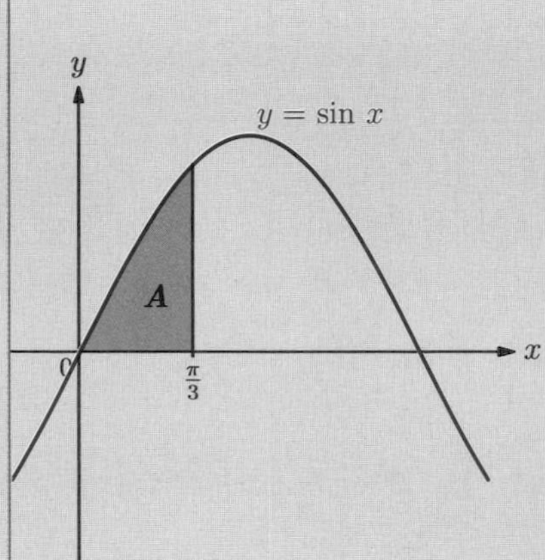

Integrate and write in square brackets.

$$A = \int_0^{\pi/3} \sin x \, dx = [-\cos x]_0^{\pi/3}$$

Evaluate the integrated expression at the upper and lower limits and subtract the lower from the upper.

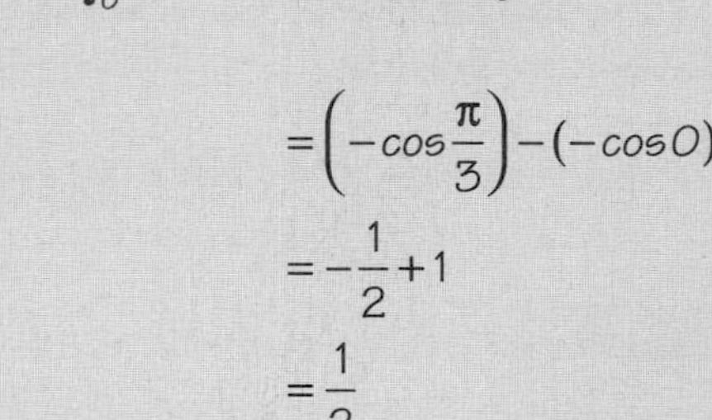

$$= \left(-\cos\frac{\pi}{3}\right) - (-\cos 0)$$

$$= -\frac{1}{2} + 1$$

$$= \frac{1}{2}$$

EXAM HINT

If you sketch the graph on a calculator, you can get it to shade and evaluate the required area, as explained on Calculator Skills sheet 9 on the CD-ROM. If it is not already given in the question, you should show the sketch as part of your working.

When the curve is entirely below the x-axis the integral will give us a negative value. In this case, the modulus of the definite integral is the area bounded by the curve and the x-axis.

Worked example 13.7

Find the area A in the diagram.

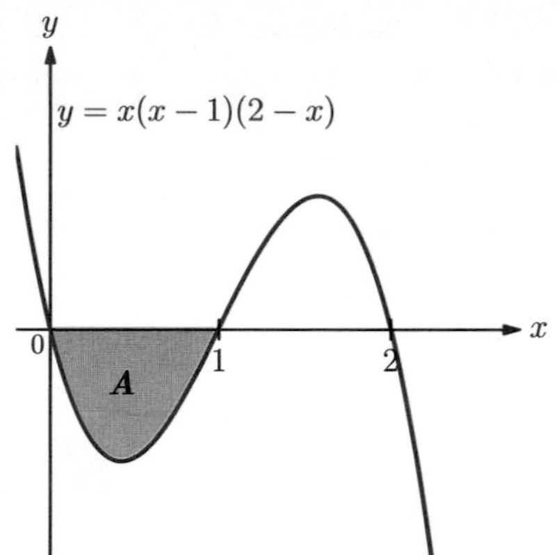

Write down the integral we need, then use the calculator to evaluate it.

$\int_0^1 x(x-1)(2-x)dx = -0.25$ (by GDC)

The area must be positive.

$\therefore A = 0.25$

Unfortunately, the relationship between integrals and areas is not so simple when there are parts of the curve above and below the x-axis. Those parts above the axis contribute positively to the area, but portions below the axis contribute negatively to the area. Therefore, to calculate the total area enclosed between the curve and the x-axis, we must separate out the sections above the axis and those below the axis.

Worked example 13.8

(a) Find $\int_1^4 x^2 - 4x + 3\,dx$.

(b) Find the area enclosed between the x-axis, the curve $y = x^2 - 4x + 3$ and the lines $x = 1$ and $x = 4$.

continued . . .

Integrate and evaluate at the upper and lower limits.

(a) $\int_1^4 x^2 - 4x + 3\, dx$

$= \left[\frac{1}{3}x^3 - 2x^2 + 3x\right]_1^4$

$= \left(\frac{1}{3}(4)^3 - 2(4)^2 + 3(4)\right) - \left(\frac{1}{3}(1)^3 - 2(1)^2 + 3(1)\right)$

$= \frac{4}{3} - \frac{4}{3} = 0$

The value found above cannot be the area asked for in part (b). Sketch the curve to see exactly what area we are being asked to find.

(b)

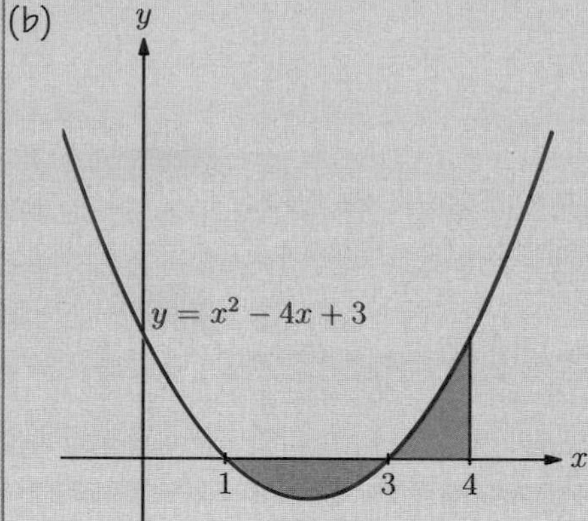

The required area is made up of two parts, one below the axis and one above, so evaluate each of them separately.

$\int_1^3 x^2 - 4x + 3\, dx = \left[\frac{1}{3}x^3 - 2x^2 + 3x\right]_1^3$

$= (0) - \left(\frac{4}{3}\right)$

$= -\frac{4}{3}$

$\therefore$ area below the axis is $\frac{4}{3}$

$\int_3^4 x^2 - 4x + 3\, dx = \left[\frac{1}{3}x^3 - 2x^2 + 3x\right]_3^4$

$= \left(\frac{4}{3}\right) - (0)$

$= \frac{4}{3}$

$\therefore$ area above the axis is $\frac{4}{3}$

Total area $= \frac{4}{3} + \frac{4}{3} = \frac{8}{3}$

The integral being zero in part (a) of the example means that the area above the x-axis is exactly cancelled by the area below the axis.

As you can see from the example above, when you are asked to find an area it is essential to sketch the graph and identify exactly where each part of the area is. The area bounded by $y = f(x)$, the x-axis and the lines $x = a$ and $x = b$ is given by $\int_a^b f(x)\,dx$ only when $f(x)$ is entirely positive between a and b. If the curve crosses the x-axis somewhere between a and b, then we have to split up the integral and find each piece of area separately.

See Prior Learning Section I if you are unfamiliar with the modulus function and Calculator Skills Sheet 3 for how to find it on your calculator.

If you are evaluating the area on your calculator, you can use the modulus function to ensure that all parts of the area are counted as positive:

$$\text{Area} = \int_a^b |f(x)|\,dx$$

Exercise 13H

1. Find the shaded areas.

(a) (i)

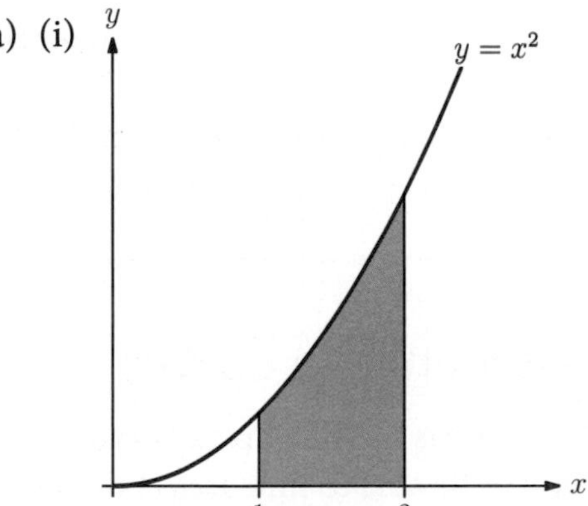

(ii)

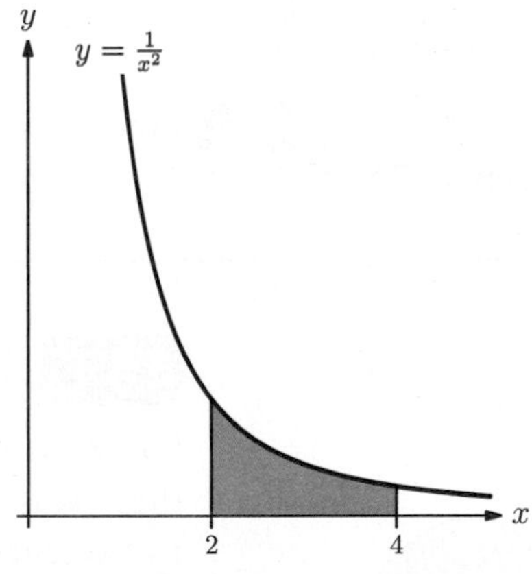

(b) (i)

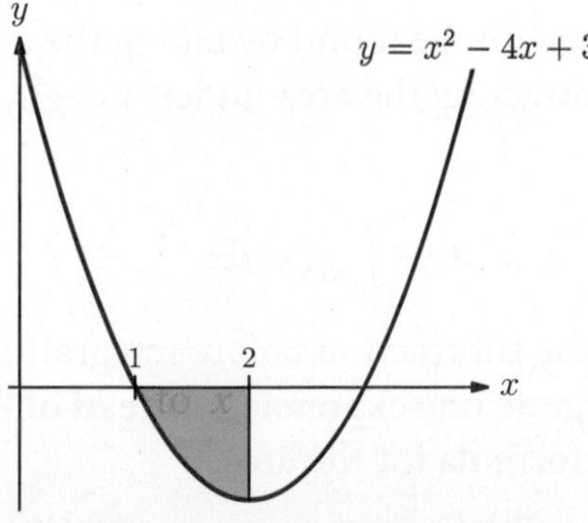

(ii)

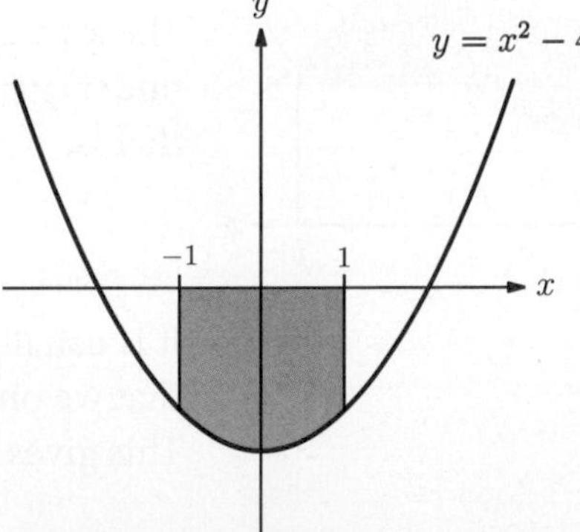

(c) (i)

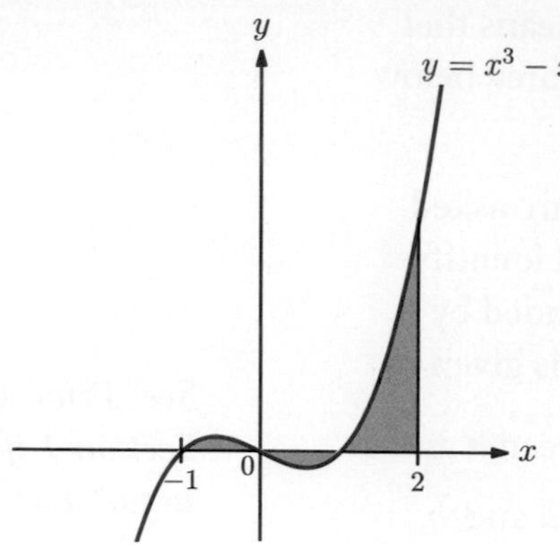

(ii)

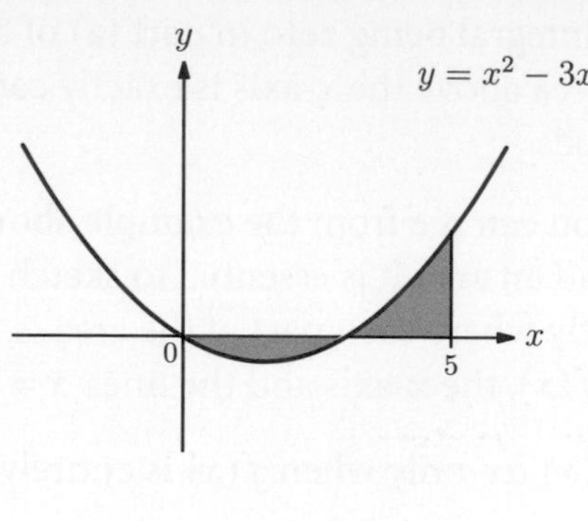

2. The area enclosed by the x-axis, the curve $y = \sqrt{x}$ and the line $x = k$ is 18. Find the value of k. *[6 marks]*

EXAM HINT

'Find the area enclosed' means to first identify a closed region bounded by the curves mentioned, and then find its area. A sketch is a very useful tool.

3. (a) Find $\int_0^3 x^2 - 1\,\mathrm{d}x$.

(b) Find the area between the curve $y = x^2 - 1$ and the x-axis between $x = 0$ and $x = 3$. *[5 marks]*

4. Between $x = 0$ and $x = 3$, the area of the graph $y = x^2 - kx$ below the x-axis equals the area above the x-axis. Find the value of k. *[6 marks]*

5. Find the area enclosed by the curve $y = 7x - x^2 - 10$ and the x-axis. *[7 marks]*

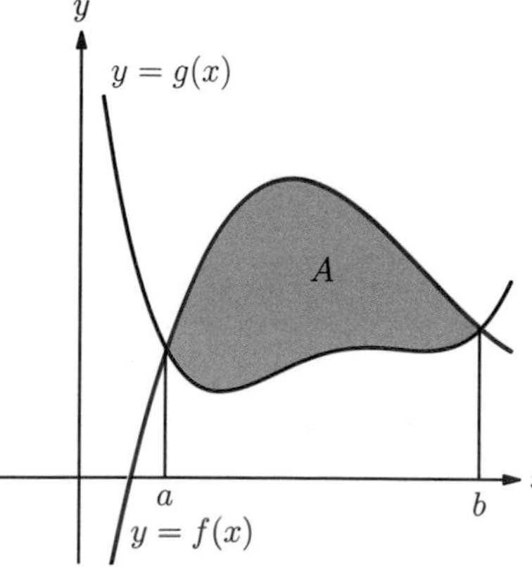

13I The area between two curves

So far we have considered only areas bounded by a curve and the x-axis, but it is also useful to be able to find areas bounded by two curves.

The area A in the diagram can be found by taking the area under $y = f(x)$ and subtracting the area under $y = g(x)$, that is,

$$A = \int_a^b f(x)\,\mathrm{d}x - \int_a^b g(x)\,\mathrm{d}x$$

It is usually easier to do the subtraction before integrating, so that we only have to integrate one expression instead of two. This gives an alternative formula for the area.

KEY POINT 13.9

The area bounded above by the curve $y = f(x)$ and below by the curve $y = g(x)$ is

$$A = \int_a^b |f(x) - g(x)| \mathrm{d}x$$

where a and b are the x-coordinates of the intersection points of the two curves.

Worked example 13.9

Find the area A enclosed between $y = 2x + 1$ and $y = x^2 - 3x + 5$.

First find the x-coordinates of intersection.

For intersection:

$x^2 - 3x + 5 = 2x + 1$

$\Leftrightarrow x^2 - 5x + 4 = 0$

$\Leftrightarrow (x-1)(x-4) = 0$

$\Leftrightarrow x = 1, 4$

Make a rough sketch to see the relative positions of the two curves.

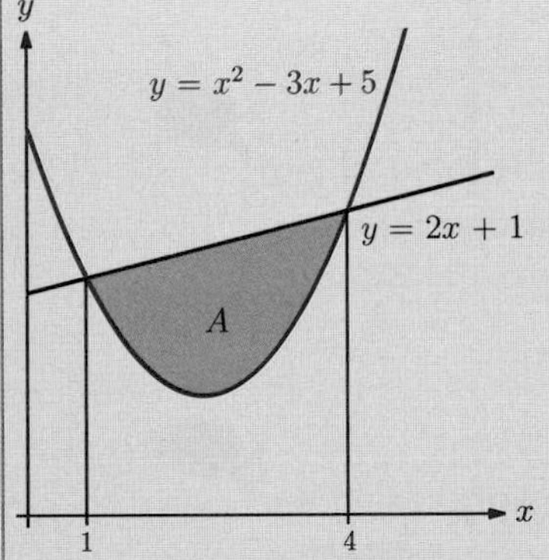

Subtract the lower curve from the higher before integrating.

$A = \int_1^4 (2x+1) - (x^2 - 3x + 5)\, dx$

$= \int_1^4 -x^2 + 5x - 4\, dx$

$= \left[-\frac{x^3}{3} + \frac{5x^2}{2} - 4x \right]_1^4$

$= \frac{8}{3}\left(-\frac{11}{6} \right) = \frac{9}{2}$

Subtracting the two equations before integrating is particularly convenient when one of the curves is partially below the x-axis: as long as $f(x)$ is above $g(x)$, the expression we are integrating, $f(x)-g(x)$, will always be positive, so we do not have to worry about the signs of $f(x)$ and $g(x)$ themselves.

Worked example 13.10

Find the area bounded by the curves $y = e^x - 5$ and $y = 3 - x^2$.

Sketch the graph to see the relative positions of the two curves.

Using GDC:

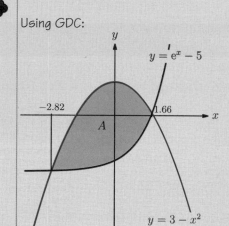

Find the intersection points – use the calculator.

Intersections: $x = -2.818$ and 1.658

Write down the integral that represents the area.

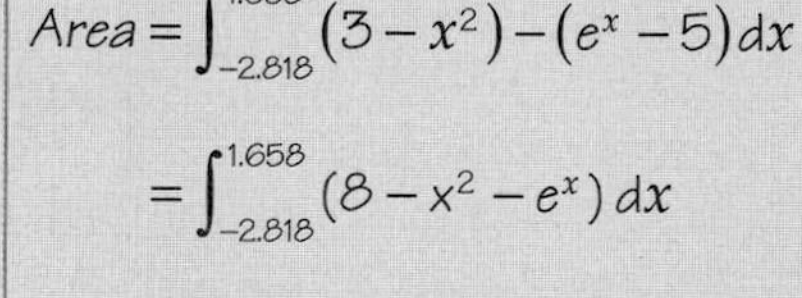

$$\text{Area} = \int_{-2.818}^{1.658} (3 - x^2) - (e^x - 5)\,dx$$

$$= \int_{-2.818}^{1.658} (8 - x^2 - e^x)\,dx$$

Evaluate the integral using the calculator.

$= 21.6$ (3 SF) using GDC

Exercise 13I

1. Find the shaded areas.

(a) (i)

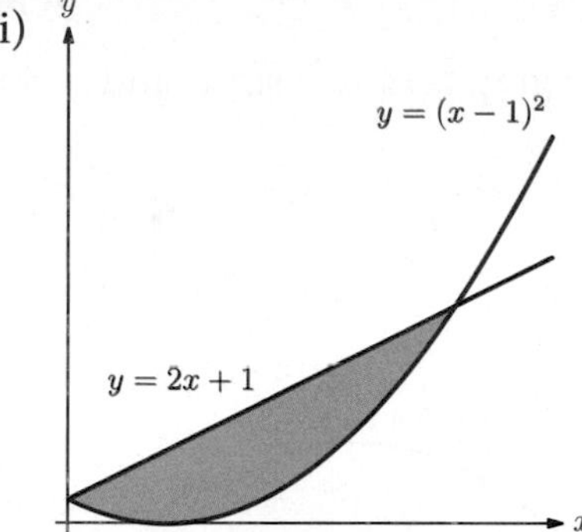

(ii)

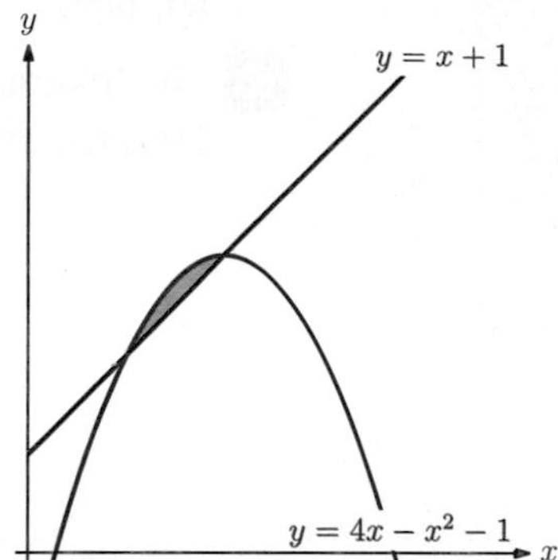

(b) (i)

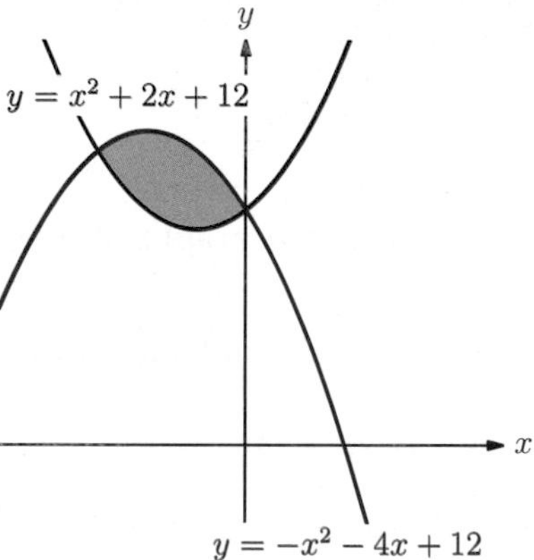

(ii)

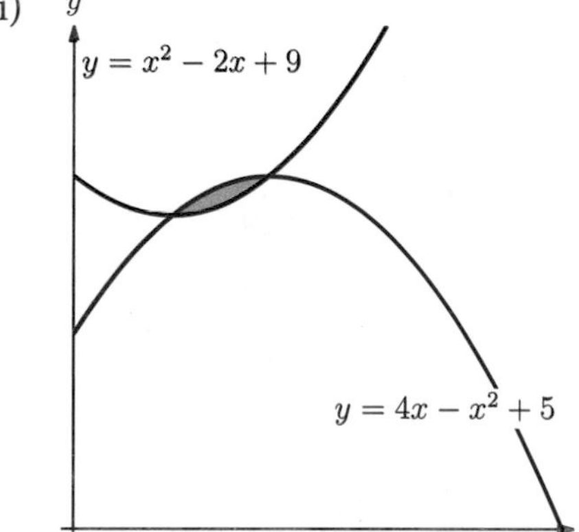

(c) (i)

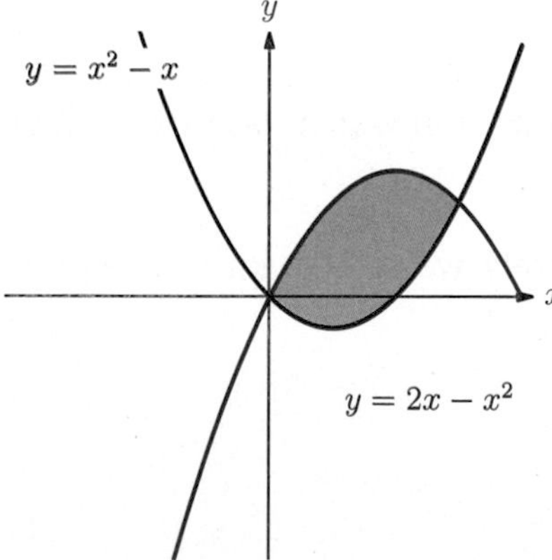

(ii)

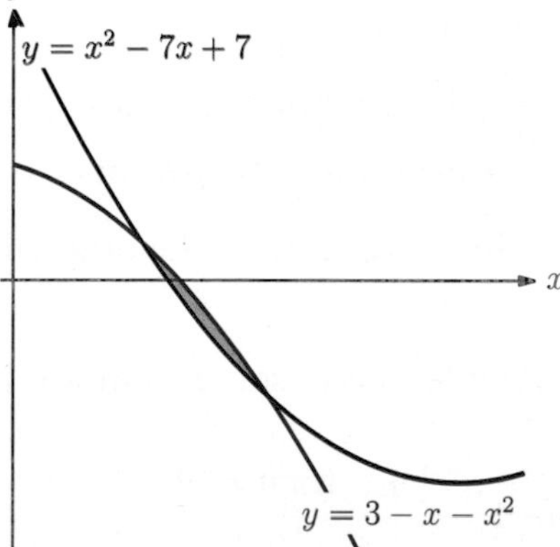

2. Find the area enclosed between the graphs of $y = x^2 + x - 2$ and $y = x + 2$. *[6 marks]*

3. Find the area enclosed by the curves $y = e^x$ and $y = x^2$, the y-axis and the line $x = 2$. *[6 marks]*

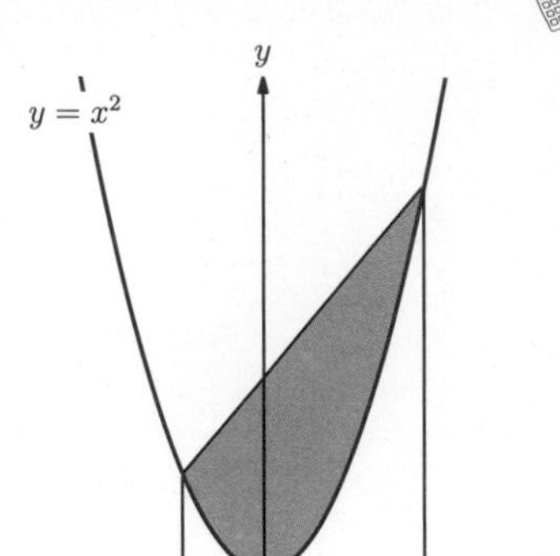

4. Find the area between the curves $y = \frac{1}{x}$ and $y = \sin x$ in the region $0 < x < \pi$. *[6 marks]*

5. Show that the area of the shaded region in the diagram on the left is $\frac{9}{2}$. *[6 marks]*

6. The diagram below shows the graphs of $y = \sin x$ and $y = \cos x$. Find the shaded area.

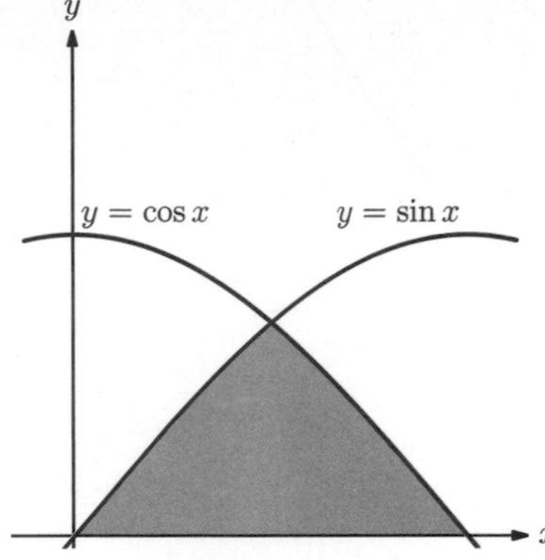

[6 marks]

7. Find the total area enclosed between the graphs of $y = x(x-4)^2$ and $y = x^2 - 7x + 15$. *[6 marks]*

8. The area enclosed between the curve $y = x^2$ and the line $y = mx$ is $10\frac{2}{3}$. Find the value of m if $m > 0$. *[7 marks]*

Summary

- **Integration** is the reverse process of differentiation.
- If we know $\frac{dy}{dx}$, the **indefinite integral** gives the original function which has this gradient, with an unknown **constant of integration** c.
- To find c and hence determine the original function precisely, we need to know one point (p, q) on the curve.
- The indefinite integrals of some common functions are:

$$\int x^n \, dx = \frac{1}{n+1} x^{n+1} + c \quad \text{for } n \neq -1$$

$$\int x^{-1} \, dx = \ln|x| + c \quad \text{for } x > 0$$

$$\int e^x \, dx = e^x + c$$

$$\int \sin x \, dx = -\cos x + c$$

$$\int \cos x \, dx = \sin x + c$$

- The **definite integral** $\int_a^b f(x)\,dx$ is found by evaluating the integrated expression at the upper limit b and then subtracting the integrated expression evaluated at the lower limit a.
- The area between the curve $y = f(x)$, the x-axis and the lines $x = a$ and $x = b$ is given by

  $$A = \int_a^b f(x)\,dx$$

  provided that the curve lies entirely above the x-axis between $x = a$ and $x = b$.

  If the curve goes below the x-axis, then the integral of the part below the axis will be *negative*. On a calculator we can use the modulus function to ensure we are always integrating a positive function.
- The area bounded above by the curve $y = f(x)$ and below by the curve $y = g(x)$ is

  $$A = \int_a^b |f(x) - g(x)|\,dx$$

  where a and b are the x-coordinates of the intersection points of the two curves.

Introductory problem revisited

The amount of charge stored in a capacitor is given by the area under the graph of current (I) against time (t). For alternating current the relationship between I and t is $I = \sin t$; for direct current the relationship is $I = k$, where k is a constant. For what value of k is the amount of charge stored in the capacitor from $t = 0$ to $t = \pi$ the same whether alternating or direct current is used?

For alternating current, the area under the curve of I against t is $\int_0^\pi \sin t\,dt = [-\cos t]_0^\pi = 2$.

For direct current, the area is $\int_0^\pi k\,dt = [kt]_0^\pi = k\pi$.

These two quantities are equal if $k = \dfrac{2}{\pi}$.

In this example, $k = \frac{1}{\pi}\int_0^\pi \sin t\,dt$ can be interpreted as the average value of the current I over the time interval $0 \le t \le \pi$. In fact, integration is a sophisticated way of finding the average value of a quantity.

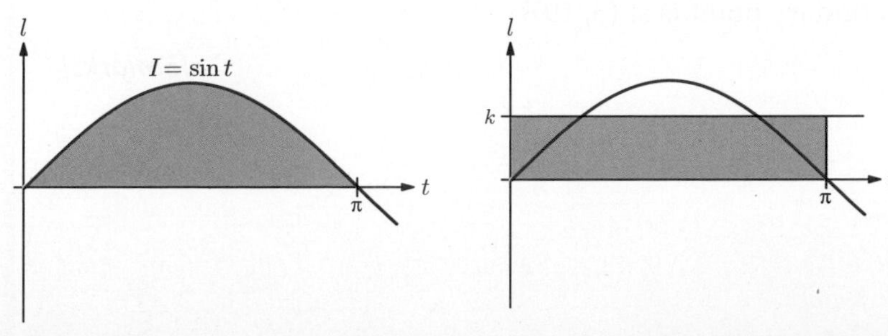

Mixed examination practice 13

Short questions

1. If $f'(x) = \sin x$ and $f\left(\frac{\pi}{3}\right) = 0$, find $f(x)$. *[4 marks]*

2. Find the area enclosed between the graph of $y = k^2 - x^2$ and the x-axis, giving your answer in terms of k. *[6 marks]*

3. Find the indefinite integral $\int \frac{1 + x^2\sqrt{x}}{x} \mathrm{d}x$. *[5 marks]*

4. (a) Solve the equation

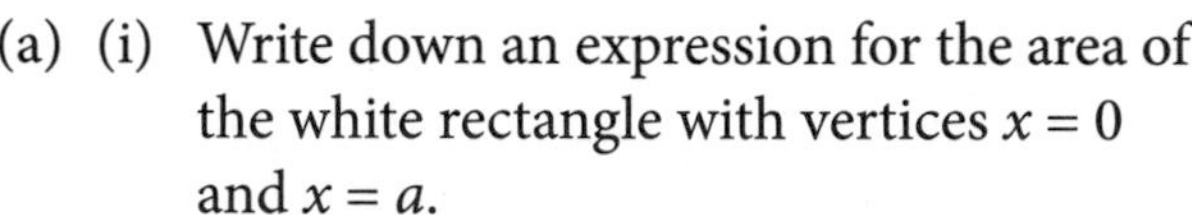

$$\int_0^a x^3 - x \, \mathrm{d}x = 0, a > 0$$

(b) For this value of a, find the total area enclosed between the x-axis and the curve $y = x^3 - x$ for $0 \le x \le a$. *[6 marks]*

5. The diagram shows the graph of $y = x^n$ for $n > 1$.

(a) (i) Write down an expression for the area of the white rectangle with vertices $x = 0$ and $x = a$.

(ii) If B is the area of the blue shaded region, find an expression for B in terms of a, b and n.

(b) If the red area is three times larger than the blue area, find the value of n. *[6 marks]*

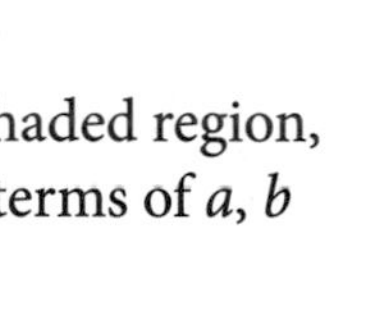

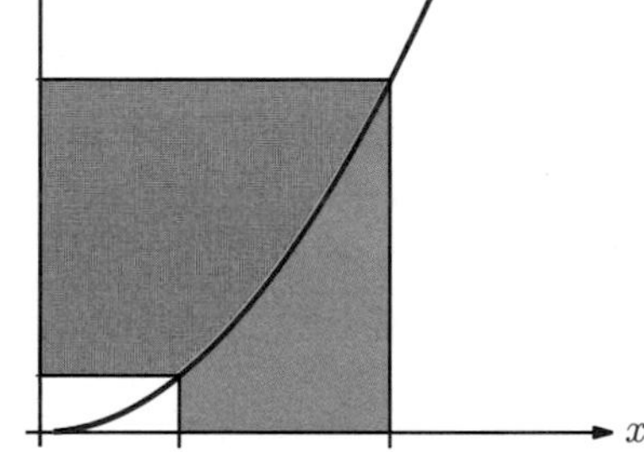

6. Find the area enclosed between the graphs of $y = \sin x$ and $y = 1 - \sin x$ for $0 < x < \pi$. *[3 marks]*

7. The function $f(x)$ has a stationary point at (3, 19), and $f''(x) = 6x + 6$.

(a) What kind of stationary point is at (3, 19)?

(b) Find $f(x)$. *[5 marks]*

Long questions

1. The derivative of $f(x)$ is $f'(x) = e^x + c$. The line $y = 3x + 2$ is tangent to the graph $y = f(x)$ at $x = 1$.
   (a) Find the value of c.
   (b) Find the value of $f(1)$.
   (c) Find an expression for $f(x)$.
   (d) Find the area under the graph $y = f(x)$ between $x = 0$ and $x = 1$.
   [11 marks]

2. (a) Show that $5a^2 + 4ax - x^2 = (5a - x)(x + a)$.
   (b) Find the coordinates of the points of intersection of the graphs $y = 5a^2 + 4ax - x^2$ and $y = x^2 - a^2$.
   (c) Find the area enclosed between these two graphs.
   (d) Show that the fraction of this area above the x-axis is independent of a, and state the value that this fraction takes. *[10 marks]*

14 Further differentiation

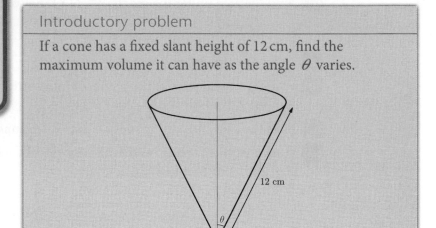

In this chapter you will learn:

- how to differentiate composite functions
- how to differentiate products of functions
- how to differentiate quotients of functions
- how to maximise or minimise functions with constraints.

Introductory problem

If a cone has a fixed slant height of 12 cm, find the maximum volume it can have as the angle θ varies.

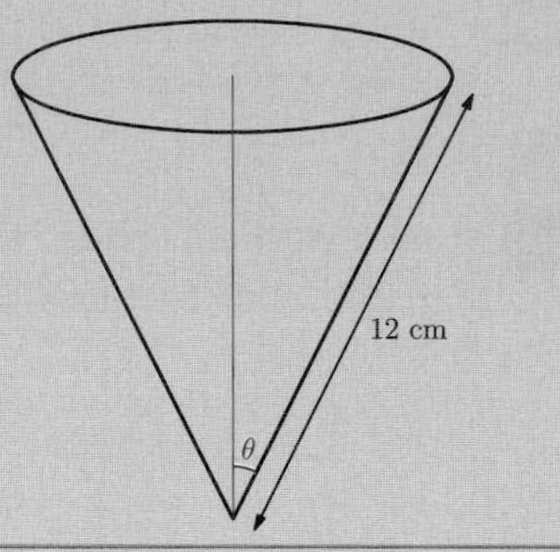

In this chapter we will build on the techniques developed in chapter 12 and learn new tools for differentiating a wider range of functions. Much of the work here will also be used in chapter 15, where we expand our integration techniques.

14A Differentiating composite functions using the chain rule

We can already differentiate functions such as $y=(3x^2+5x)^2$ by expanding the brackets and differentiating term by term:

$$y=(3x^2)^2+2(3x^2)(5x)+(5x)^2$$
$$=9x^4+30x^3+25x^2$$

$$\therefore \frac{\mathrm{d}y}{\mathrm{d}x}=36x^3+90x^2+50x$$
$$=2x(18x^2+45x+25)$$

But what if the function is more complicated – for instance, having a higher power or more terms in the brackets? While the same method would work, it is clearly not efficient to expand, say, $y=(3x^2+5x+2)^7$ and then differentiate each term. And what about functions such as $y = \sin 3x$ or $y = e^{x^2}$? Although we know how to differentiate $y = \sin x$ and $y = e^x$, we do not yet know any rules that tell us what to do when the argument of the function is changed to $3x$ or x^2.

The functions $y = (3x^2 + 5x + 2)^7$, $y = \sin 3x$ and $y = e^{x^2}$ may seem quite different but do have something in common – they are all *composite functions*.

We met composite functions in section 4C.

$y = (3x^2 + 5x + 2)^7$ is $y = u^7$ where $u(x) = 3x^2 + 5x + 2$

$y = \sin 3x$ is $y = \sin u$ where $u(x) = 3x$

$y = e^{x^2}$ is $y = e^u$ where $u(x) = x^2$

There is a general rule for differentiating any composite function.

KEY POINT 14.1

The **chain rule**:

If $y = f(u)$ where $u = g(x)$, then

$$\frac{dy}{dx} = \frac{dy}{du} \times \frac{du}{dx}$$

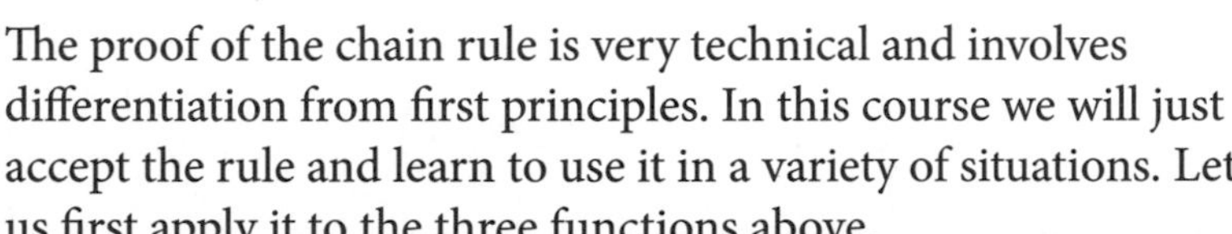

The proof of the chain rule is very technical and involves differentiation from first principles. In this course we will just accept the rule and learn to use it in a variety of situations. Let us first apply it to the three functions above.

Worked example 14.1

Differentiate the following functions.

(a) $y = (3x^2 + 5x + 2)^7$ (b) $y = \sin 3x$ (c) $y = e^{x^2}$

As these are all composite functions, we can use the chain rule on each of them.

(a) $y = u^7$ where $u = 3x^2 + 5x + 2$

$$\frac{dy}{dx} = \frac{dy}{du} \times \frac{du}{dx} = 7u^6 \times (6x + 5)$$

Write the answer in terms of x.

$$= 7(3x^2 + 5x + 2)^6(6x + 5)$$

continued . . .

(b) $y = \sin u$ where $u = 3x$

$$\frac{dy}{dx} = \frac{dy}{du} \times \frac{du}{dx}$$

$$= (\cos u) \times 3$$

Write the answer in terms of x and rearrange into the conventional form.

$$= 3\cos 3x$$

(c) $y = e^u$ where $u = x^2$

$$\frac{dy}{dx} = \frac{dy}{du} \times \frac{du}{dx}$$

$$= e^u \times 2x$$

Write the answer in terms of x and rearrange into the conventional form.

$$= 2xe^{x^2}$$

Part (b) of Worked example 14.1 illustrates a special case of the chain rule, where the 'inside' function is of the form $ax + b$.

KEY POINT 14.2

$$\frac{d}{dx} f(ax+b) = af'(ax+b)$$

For example,

$$\frac{d}{dx}(4x+1)^7 = 4 \times 7(4x+1)^6 \text{ and } \frac{d}{dx}(e^{3-2x}) = -2e^{3-2x}.$$

It is useful to remember this shortcut and it is not necessary to write down the 'inner function' u each time. The chain rule calculation can then be done more concisely, as demonstrated in the next example. The basic idea is to imagine brackets around the inner function, differentiate the outer function as if the bracketed expression were a single argument, and then multiply by the derivative of the bracketed expression.

Worked example 14.2

Differentiate the following composite functions.

(a) $y = e^{x^2-3x}$

(b) $y = \dfrac{3}{\sqrt{x^3 - 5}}$

$e^{()}$ differentiates to $e^{()}$. $x^2 - 3x$ differentiates to $2x - 3$.

(a) $y = e^{(x^2-3x)}$

$\dfrac{dy}{dx} = (2x-3)e^{(x^2-3x)}$

First, rewrite the square root as a power.

(b) $y = 3(x^3 - 5)^{-\frac{1}{2}}$

$3(\ )^{-\frac{1}{2}}$ differentiates to $-\frac{3}{2}(\ )^{-\frac{3}{2}}$. $x^3 - 5$ differentiates to $3x^2$.

$\dfrac{dy}{dx} = -\dfrac{3}{2}(x^3-5)^{-\frac{3}{2}}(3x^2)$

$= -\dfrac{9}{2}x^2(x^3-5)^{-\frac{3}{2}}$

EXAM HINT

It takes practice to be able to apply the chain rule without writing down *u* explicitly. Don't worry if you find this method confusing; although it is often quicker, you will never be forced to use it.

Sometimes it is necessary to apply the chain rule more than once.

Worked Example 14.3

Differentiate $y = \cos^3(\ln 2x)$.

Remember that $\cos^3 A$ means $(\cos A)^3$. You can think of this as a composite of three functions.

$y = (\cos(\ln 2x))^3$

$(\ )^3$ differentiates to $3(\ )^2$

$\cos(\ )$ differentiates to $-\sin(\ )$

$\ln 2x$ differentiates to $2 \times \dfrac{1}{2x} = \dfrac{1}{x}$ (by Key point 14.2).

$\dfrac{dy}{dx} = 3(\cos(\ln 2x))^2 \times (-\sin(\ln 2x)) \times \dfrac{1}{x}$

$= -\dfrac{3}{x}\cos^2(\ln 2x)\sin(\ln 2x)$

Exercise 14A

1. Use the chain rule to differentiate the following expressions with respect to x.

(a) (i) $(3x+4)^5$ (ii) $(5x+4)^7$

(b) (i) $\sqrt{3x-2}$ (ii) $\sqrt{x+1}$

(c) (i) $\frac{1}{3-x}$ (ii) $\frac{1}{(2x+3)^2}$

(d) (i) e^{10x+1} (ii) e^{4-3x}

(e) (i) $\sin 4x$ (ii) $\cos(3x+\pi)$

(f) (i) $\ln(5-x)$ (ii) $\ln(3-2x)$

2. Use the chain rule to differentiate the following expressions with respect to x.

(a) (i) $(x^2-3x+1)^7$ (ii) $(x^3+1)^5$

(b) (i) e^{x^2-2x} (ii) e^{4-x^3}

(c) (i) $(2e^x+1)^{-3}$ (ii) $(2-5e^x)^{-4}$

(d) (i) $\sin(3x^2+1)$ (ii) $\cos(x^2+2x)$

(e) (i) $\cos^3 x$ (ii) $\sin^4 x$

(f) (i) $\ln(2x-5x^3)$ (ii) $\ln(4x^2-1)$

(g) (i) $(4\ln x-1)^4$ (ii) $(\ln x+3)^{-5}$

3. Differentiate the following using the short cut from Key point 14.2.

(a) (i) $(2x+3)^5$ (ii) $(4x-1)^8$

(b) (i) $(5-x)^{-4}$ (ii) $(1-x)^{-7}$

(c) (i) $\cos(1-4x)$ (ii) $\cos(2-x)$

(d) (i) $\ln(5x+2)$ (ii) $\ln(x-4)$

4. Differentiate the following using the chain rule twice.

(a) (i) $\frac{1}{\cos^2 3x}$ (ii) $\tan^2 2x$

(b) (i) $e^{\sin^2 3x}$ (ii) $e^{(\ln 2x)^2}$

(c) (i) $(1-2\sin^2 2x)^2$ (ii) $(4\cos 3x+1)^2$

(d) (i) $\ln(1-3\cos 2x)$ (ii) $\ln(2-\cos 5x)$

5. Find the equation of the tangent to $y=(3x+5)^2$ at the point where $x=2$. *[7 marks]*

6. Find the equation of the normal to the curve $y=\frac{1}{\sqrt{4x^2+1}}$ at the point where $x=\sqrt{2}$. *[7 marks]*

7. Find the exact coordinates of stationary points on the curve $y=e^{\sin x}$ for $x\in[0,2\pi]$. *[5 marks]*

8. For what values of x does the function $f(x)=\ln(x^2-35)$ have a gradient of 1? *[5 marks]*

9. A non-uniform chain hangs from two posts. Its height h above the ground is described by the equation

$$h=e^x+\frac{1}{e^{2x}},\ -1\le x\le 2$$

The left post is positioned at $x=-1$, and the right post is at $x=2$.

(a) State, with reasons, which post is taller.

(b) Show that the minimum height occurs at $x=\frac{1}{3}\ln 2$.

(c) Find the exact value of the minimum height of the chain. *[8 marks]*

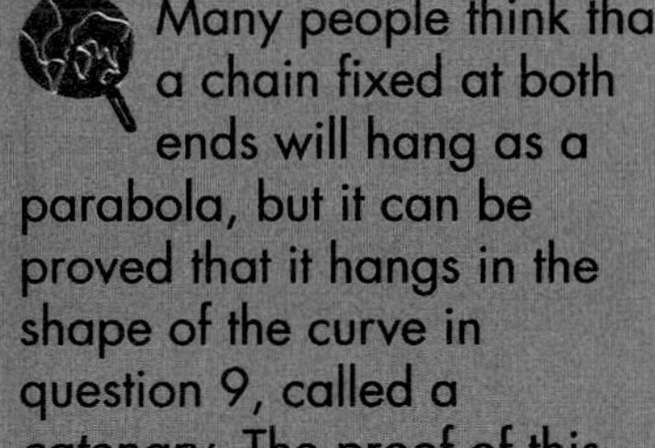

Many people think that a chain fixed at both ends will hang as a parabola, but it can be proved that it hangs in the shape of the curve in question 9, called a *catenary*. The proof of this requires techniques from a mathematical area called *differential geometry*.

14B Differentiating products using the product rule

We now move on to products of two functions. We can already differentiate some products, such as $y=x^4(3x^2-5)$, by expanding and then differentiating term by term. However, as for composite functions, this method is rather impractical when the function is more complicated, for example $y=x^4(3x^2-5)^9$; moreover, expanding does not help with functions such as $y=x^2\cos x$ or $y=x\ln x$.

Just as there is a rule for differentiating composite functions, there is a rule for differentiating products.

KEY POINT 14.3

The product rule

If $y = u(x)v(x)$, then

$$\frac{dy}{dx} = v\frac{du}{dx} + u\frac{dv}{dx}$$

See Fill-in proof sheet 15 on the CD-ROM if you are interested in how this rule is derived.

Worked example 14.4

Differentiate $y = x^4(3x^2 - 5)$ using the product rule.

It doesn't make any difference which function you call u and which you call v.

Let $u = x^4$ and $v = 3x^2 - 5$. Then

$$\frac{du}{dx} = 4x^3$$

and

$$\frac{dv}{dx} = 6x$$

Apply the product rule.

$$\begin{aligned}\frac{dy}{dx} &= v\frac{du}{dx} + u\frac{dv}{dx}\\ &= (3x^2 - 5)4x^3 + x^4 \times 6x\\ &= 12x^5 - 20x^3 + 6x^5\\ &= 18x^5 - 20x^3\end{aligned}$$

EXAM HINT

After applying the product rule, you do not need to simplify the resulting expression unless the question explicitly tells you to do so.

When differentiating a more complicated product, be aware that the chain rule may be needed as well as the product rule.

Worked example 14.5

Differentiate $y = x^4(3x^2-5)^5$ and factorise your answer.

This is a product of two functions x^4 and $(3x^2-5)^5$. It does not matter which we take as u and which as v.

Let $u = x^4$ and $v = (3x^2-5)^5$.
Then

$$\frac{du}{dx} = 4x^3$$

v(x) is a composite function, so use the chain rule to find its derivative.

and

$$\frac{dv}{dx} = 5(3x^2-5)^4(6x)$$
$$= 30x(3x^2-5)^4$$

Now apply the product rule.

$$\frac{dy}{dx} = v\frac{du}{dx} + u\frac{dv}{dx}$$
$$= (3x^2-5)^5 4x^3 + x^4 30x(3x^2-5)^4$$

We are asked to factorise the answer, so instead of expanding the brackets, look for common factors.

$$= 2x^3(3x^2-5)^4[2(3x^2-5)+15x^2]$$
$$= 2x^3(3x^2-5)^4(6x^2-10+15x^2)$$
$$= 2x^3(3x^2-5)^4(21x^2-10)$$

Exercise 14B

1. Differentiate the following using the product rule.
   (a) (i) $y = x(1+x)^3$ (ii) $y = 4x^2(x+3)^4$
   (b) (i) $x^2 \sin x$ (ii) $5x \tan x$
   (c) (i) $e^x \ln x$ (ii) $e^x \sin x$

2. Differentiate the following using the product rule.
   (a) (i) $y = x^2 \cos x$ (ii) $y = x^{-1} \sin x$
   (b) (i) $y = x^{-2} \ln x$ (ii) $y = x^3 \ln x$
   (c) (i) $y = x^3\sqrt{2x+1}$ (ii) $y = x^{-1}\sqrt{4x}$
   (d) (i) $e^{2x} \tan x$ (ii) $e^{x+1} \sin 3x$

3. Find $f'(x)$ and fully factorise your answer.
   (a) (i) $f(x) = (x+1)^4(x-2)^5$ (ii) $f(x) = (x-3)^7(x+5)^4$
   (b) (i) $f(x) = (2x-1)^4(1-3x)^3$ (ii) $f(x) = (1-x)^5(4x+1)^2$

4. Differentiate $y=(3x^2-x+2)e^{2x}$, giving your answer in the form $P(x)e^{2x}$. *[4 marks]*

5. Find the equation of the tangent to $y=xe^x$ where $x=1$. *[7 marks]*

6. Given that $f(x)=x^2e^{3x}$, find $f''(x)$ in the form $(ax^2+bx+c)e^{3x}$. *[4 marks]*

7. Find the x-coordinates of the stationary points on the curve $y=(2x+1)^5 e^{-2x}$. *[5 marks]*

8. Find the coordinates of the stationary point on the graph of $y=x\sqrt{x+1}$. *[3 marks]*

9. Find the exact values of the x-coordinates of the stationary points on the curve $y=(3x+1)^5(3-x)^3$. *[6 marks]*

10. Consider the graph of $y=x\sin 2x$ for $x\in[0,2\pi]$.

(a) Show that the x-coordinates of the points of inflexion satisfy $\cos 2x = x\sin 2x$.

(b) Hence find the coordinates of the points of inflexion. *[6 marks]*

11. Find the derivative of $\sin(xe^x)$ with respect to x. *[5 marks]*

12. (a) If $f(x)=x\ln x$, find $f'(x)$.

(b) Hence find $\int \ln x\,dx$. *[5 marks]*

13. Find the exact coordinates of the minimum point on the curve $y=e^{-x}\cos x$, for $0\le x\le\pi$. *[6 marks]*

14. Given that $f(x)=x^2\sqrt{1+x}$, show that $f'(x)=\dfrac{x(a+bx)}{2\sqrt{1+x}}$ where a and b are constants to be found. *[6 marks]*

15. (a) Write $y=x^x$ in the form $y=e^{f(x)}$.

(b) Hence or otherwise, find $\dfrac{dy}{dx}$.

(c) Find the exact coordinates of the stationary points on the curve $y=x^x$. *[8 marks]*

14C Differentiating quotients using the quotient rule

By combining the product rule and the chain rule, we can differentiate quotients such as

$$y=\frac{x^2-4x+12}{(x-3)^2}$$

This function can be expressed as

$$y=(x^2-4x+12)(x-3)^{-2}$$

Then, taking $u=(x^2-4x+12)$ and $v=(x-3)^{-2}$, with $\frac{du}{dx}=2x-4$ and $\frac{dv}{dx}=(-2)(x-3)^{-3}$, we get

$$\frac{dy}{dx}=(x-3)^{-2}(2x-4)+(x^2-4x+12)(-2)(x-3)^{-3}$$

After tidying up the negative powers and fractions, this simplifies to $\frac{dy}{dx}=\frac{-2x-12}{(x-3)^3}$.

If we apply the same process to a general function of the form $\frac{u(x)}{v(x)}$, we can derive a new rule for differentiating quotients.

See Fill-in proof 16 on the CD-ROM for details.

In this course you are only expected to know how to use the result.

KEY POINT 14.4

The quotient rule

If $y=\frac{u(x)}{v(x)}$, then

$$\frac{dy}{dx}=\frac{v\frac{du}{dx}-u\frac{dv}{dx}}{v^2}$$

Worked example 14.6

Differentiate $y=\frac{x^2-4x+12}{(x-3)^2}$ using the quotient rule and simplify your answer as far as possible.

The function is a quotient. Make sure to get u and v the right way round.

$y=\frac{u}{v}$ where $u=x^2-4x+12$, $v=(x-3)^2$

$$\frac{dy}{dx}=\frac{v\frac{du}{dx}-u\frac{dv}{dx}}{v^2}$$

Use chain rule to differentiate v.

$$=\frac{(x-3)^2(2x-4)-(x^2-4x+12)\times 2(x-3)}{\left[(x-3)^2\right]^2}$$

Notice that we can cancel a factor of $(x-3)$ from top and bottom.

$$=\frac{(x-3)(2x-4)-(x^2-4x+12)\times 2}{(x-3)^3}$$

$$=\frac{2x^2-10x+12-2x^2+8x-24}{(x-3)^3}$$

$$=\frac{-2x-12}{(x-3)^3}$$

$$=\frac{-2(x+6)}{(x-3)^3}$$

In section 12E we stated that the derivative of $\tan x$ is $\frac{1}{\cos^2 x}$.

We can now use the quotient rule, together with the derivatives of $\sin x$ and $\cos x$, to prove this result.

Worked example 14.7

Prove that $\frac{d}{dx}(\tan x)=\frac{1}{\cos^2 x}$.

Express $\tan x$ in terms of $\sin x$ and $\cos x$, whose derivatives we know.

$\tan x=\frac{\sin x}{\cos x}$

Let $u=\sin x$, $v=\cos x$

→

continued . . .

Use the quotient rule.

$$\frac{dy}{dx}=\frac{v\frac{du}{dx}-u\frac{dv}{dx}}{v^2}$$

$$=\frac{\cos x\cos x-\sin x(-\sin x)}{(\cos x)^2}$$

$$=\frac{\cos^2 x+\sin^2 x}{\cos^2 x}$$

Use the identity $\sin^2 x+\cos^2 x=1$ to simplify.

$$=\frac{1}{\cos^2 x}$$

The quotient rule, like the product rule, often leads to a long expression. Sometimes product and quotient rule questions are used to test your skill with fractions and exponents, as in the following example.

Worked example 14.8

Differentiate $\frac{x}{\sqrt{x+1}}$ and give your answer in the form $\frac{x+c}{k\sqrt{(x+1)^p}}$ where $c,k,p\in\mathbb{N}$.

The function is a quotient. Identify u and v.

$$y=\frac{x}{\sqrt{x+1}}$$

Let $u=x$, $v=\sqrt{x+1}=(x+1)^{\frac{1}{2}}$

Use the quotient rule

$$\frac{dy}{dx}=\frac{v\frac{du}{dx}-u\frac{dv}{dx}}{v^2}$$

$$=\frac{(x+1)^{\frac{1}{2}}\times 1-x\times\frac{1}{2}(x+1)^{-\frac{1}{2}}}{\left((x+1)^{\frac{1}{2}}\right)^2}$$

As we want a square root in the answer, turn the fractional powers back into roots.

$$=\frac{\sqrt{x+1}-\frac{x}{2\sqrt{x+1}}}{x+1}$$

→

continued . . .

Remove 'fractions within fractions' by multiplying top and bottom by $2\sqrt{x+1}$.

$$=\frac{2(x+1)-x}{2(x+1)\sqrt{x+1}}$$

Notice that $x\sqrt{x}=x^{\frac{3}{2}}=\sqrt{x^3}$.

$$=\frac{x+2}{2\sqrt{(x+1)^3}}$$

Exercise 14C

1. Differentiate the following using the quotient rule.

(a) (i) $y=\frac{x-1}{x+1}$ (ii) $y=\frac{x+2}{x-3}$

(b) (i) $y=\frac{\sqrt{2x+1}}{x}$ (ii) $y=\frac{x^2}{\sqrt{x-1}}$

(c) (i) $y=\frac{1-2x}{x^2+2}$ (ii) $y=\frac{4-x^2}{1+x}$

(d) (i) $y=\frac{\ln 3x}{x}$ (ii) $y=\frac{\ln 2x}{x^2}$

2. Find the coordinates of the stationary points on the graph of $y=\frac{x^2}{2x-1}$. *[5 marks]*

3. Find the equation of the normal to the curve $y=\frac{\sin x}{x}$ at the point where $x=\frac{\pi}{2}$, giving your answer in the form $y=mx+c$ where m and c are exact. *[7 marks]*

4. The graph of $y=\frac{x-a}{x+2}$ has gradient 1 at the point $(a,0)$, where $a\neq -2$. Find the value of a. *[5 marks]*

5. Find the exact coordinates of the stationary point on the curve $y=\frac{\ln x}{x}$ and determine its nature. *[6 marks]*

6. Find the range of values of x for which the function $f(x)=\frac{x^2}{1-x}$ is increasing. *[6 marks]*

7. Given that $y=\dfrac{x^2}{\sqrt{x+1}}$, show that $\dfrac{dy}{dx}=\dfrac{x(ax+b)}{2(x+1)^p}$, stating clearly the value of the constants a,b and p. *[6 marks]*

8. Show that if the curve $y=f(x)$ has a maximum stationary point at $x=a$, then the curve $y=\dfrac{1}{f(x)}$ has a minimum stationary point at $x=a$, provided $f(a)\neq 0$. *[7 marks]*

14D Optimisation with constraints

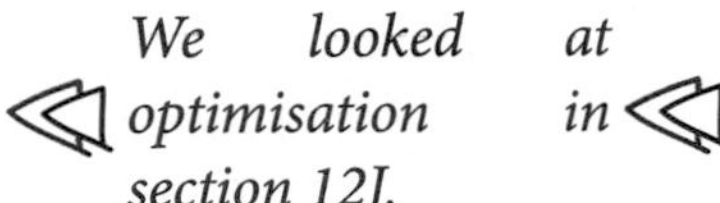
We looked at optimisation in section 12J.

In this section we shall look at how to maximise or minimise functions which at first sight appear to depend on two different variables. However, the two variables will be related by a constraint, which allows us to eliminate one of them; we can then follow the usual procedure for finding maxima or minima.

Worked example 14.9

Find the maximum value of $xy-y$ given that $x+3y=7$.

Give the function a name.

We wish to maximise $F=xy-y$

Use the constraint to write one variable in terms of the other, and hence express F as a function of one variable only.

$$x+3y=7$$
$$\Rightarrow x=7-3y$$
$$\therefore F=(7-3y)y-y$$
$$=6y-3y^2$$

Find stationary points.

$$\frac{dF}{dy}=6-6y$$

At a stationary point $\dfrac{dF}{dy}=0$:

$$6-6y=0$$
$$\Leftrightarrow \quad y=1$$

and so $x=7-3y=4$

The value of F at this point is

$$F=4\times1-1=3$$

Classify the stationary point.

$$\frac{d^2F}{dx^2}=-6<0$$

So $F=3$ is a local maximum.

→

continued . . .

Check end points and asymptotes.

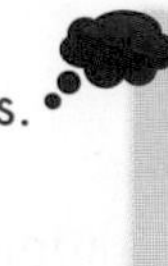

There are no asymptotes, and as $|y|$ gets large $F = 6y - 3y^2$ becomes large and negative.
So 3 is the global maximum value.

Sometimes the constraint is not explicitly given, and needs to be deduced from the context. Two common types of constraints are:

- A shape has a fixed perimeter, area or volume – this gives an equation relating different variables (height, length, radius, etc.).
- A point lies on a given curve – this gives a relationship between x and y.

Worked example 14.10

Find the point on the curve $y = x^3$ that is closest to the point (2, 0).

Give a name to the quantity we need to optimise.

Let L be the distance from (2, 0) to the point $P(x, y)$.

Then $L = \sqrt{(x-2)^2 + y^2}$

Write the function in terms of one variable only.

If P lies on the curve, then $y = x^3$, so

$$L = \sqrt{(x-2)^2 + x^6}$$

Find stationary points. This function looks complicated and the question does not require exact answers, so we can use the GDC.

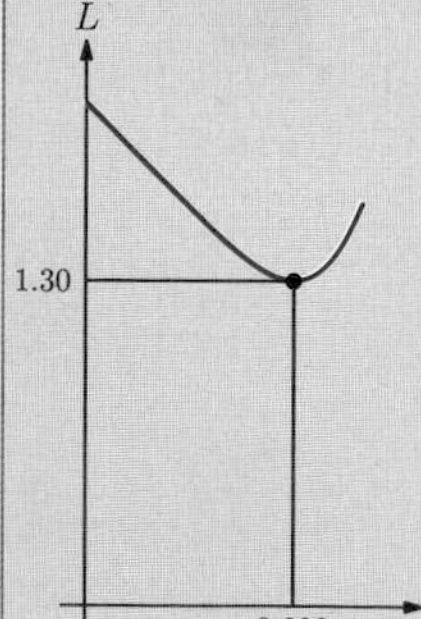

From GDC, the minimum occurs at $x = 0.829$ (3 SF).
The corresponding y-value is $y = 0.569$ (3 SF).
So the coordinates are (0.829, 0.569).

Exercise 14D

1. (a) (i) Find the maximum possible value of xy given that $x+2y=4$.

 (ii) Find the maximum possible value of xy given that $3x+y=7$.

 (b) (i) Find the minimum possible value of $a+b$ given that $ab=3$ and $a,b>0$.

 (ii) Find the minimum possible value of $2a+b$ given that $ab=4$ and $a,b>0$.

 (c) (i) Find the maximum possible value of $4r^2h$ if $2r^2+rh=3$ and $r,h>0$.

 (ii) Find the maximum possible value of rh^2 if $4r^2+3h^2=12$ and $r,h>0$.

2. A square sheet of card with 12 cm sides has four squares of side x cm cut from the corners. The sides are then folded to make a small open box.

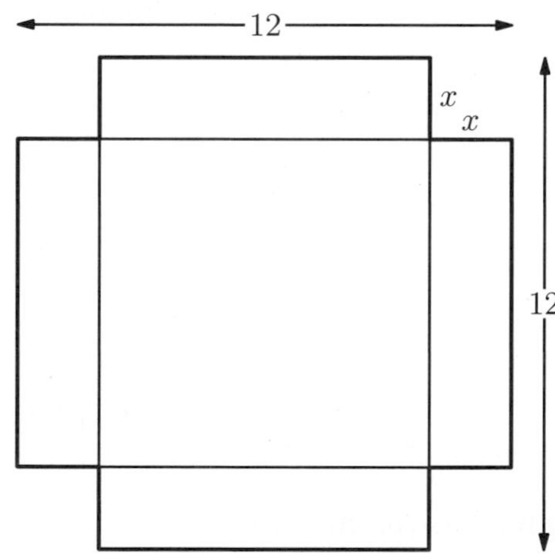

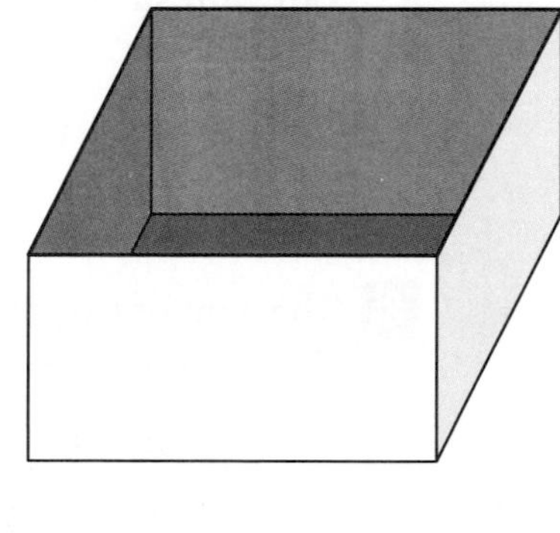

 (a) Find an expression for the volume of the box in terms of x.

 (b) Find the value of x for which the volume is maximum possible, and prove that it is a maximum. *[6 marks]*

3. An open box in the shape of a square-based prism has volume 32 cm^2. Find the minimum possible surface area of the box. *[6 marks]*

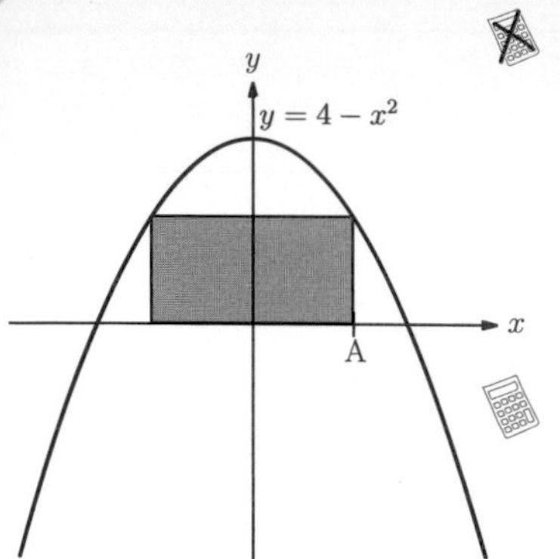

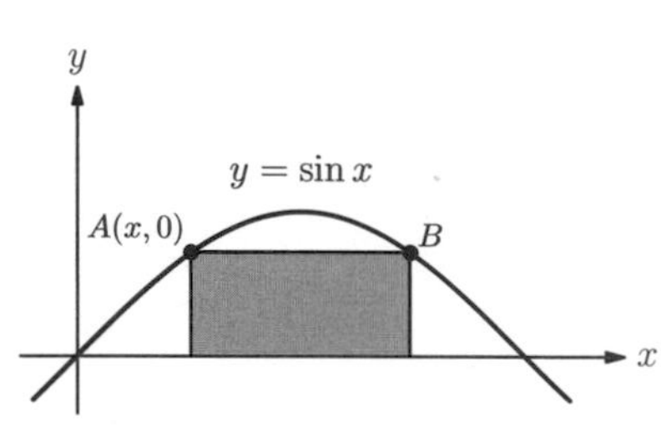

4. A rectangle is drawn inside the region bounded by the curve $y = 4 - x^2$ and the x-axis, so that two of its vertices lie on the x-axis and the other two lie on the curve.

Find the x-coordinate of vertex A so that the area of the rectangle is the maximum possible. *[6 marks]*

5. A rectangle is drawn inside the region bounded by the curve $y = \sin x$ and the x-axis, as shown in the diagram. The vertex A has coordinates $(x, 0)$.

(a) (i) Write down the coordinates of point B.

(ii) Find an expression for the area of the rectangle in terms of x.

(b) Show that the rectangle has maximum area when $2\tan x = \pi - 2x$.

(c) Find the maximum possible area of the rectangle. *[8 marks]*

6. What is the largest possible capacity of a closed cylindrical can with surface area $450\,\text{cm}^2$? *[6 marks]*

7. What is the largest possible capacity of a closed square-based can with surface area $450\,\text{cm}^2$? *[6 marks]*

8. The sum of two numbers x and y is 6, and $x, y \geq 0$. Find the two numbers if the sum of their squares is

(a) the minimum possible

(b) the maximum possible. *[7 marks]*

9. A cone of radius r and height h has volume 81π.

(a) Show that the curved surface area of the cone is given by $S = \frac{\pi}{r}\sqrt{r^6 + 243^2}$.

(b) Find the radius and height of the cone that make the curved surface area of the cone as small as possible. *[7 marks]*

 **10.** A 20 cm piece of wire is bent to form an isosceles triangle with base b.

(a) Show that the area of the triangle is given by $A = \frac{b}{2}\sqrt{100 - 10b}$.

(b) Show that the area of the triangle is the largest possible when the triangle is equilateral. *[6 marks]*

 **11.** The sum of the squares of two positive numbers is a. Prove that their product is the maximum possible when the two numbers are equal. *[6 marks]*

 **12.** Find the coordinates of the point on the curve $y = x^2$, $x \geq 0$, that is closest to the point (0, 4). *[7 marks]*

Summary

- The **chain rule** is used to differentiate composite functions.
  If $y = f(u)$ where $u = g(x)$, then
  $$\frac{dy}{dx} = \frac{dy}{du} \times \frac{du}{dx}$$

- The **product rule** is used to differentiate two functions multiplied together.
  If $y = u(x)v(x)$, then
  $$\frac{dy}{dx} = v\frac{du}{dx} + u\frac{dv}{dx}$$

- The **quotient rule** is used to differentiate one function divided by another.
  If $y = \frac{u(x)}{v(x)}$, then
  $$\frac{dy}{dx} = \frac{v\frac{du}{dx} - u\frac{dv}{dx}}{v^2}$$

- When solving optimisation problems that involve a function which depends on two variables, the variables will be related by a constraint. It is possible to use the constraint to express the quantity we wish to minimise or maximise in terms of one variable only (by eliminating the other variable); then we can differentiate this function and find its stationary points.

- Two common types of constraint are:
  - a shape with a fixed perimeter, area or volume (this gives an equation relating different variables)
  - a point that lies on a given curve (this gives a relationship between x and y).

Introductory problem revisited

If a cone has a fixed slant height of 12 cm, find the maximum volume it can have as the angle θ varies.

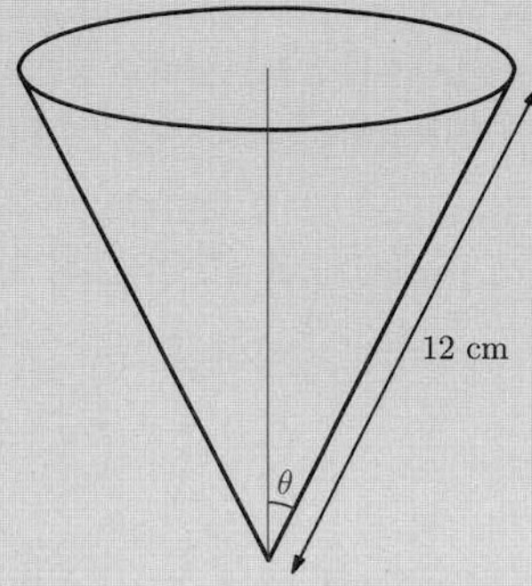

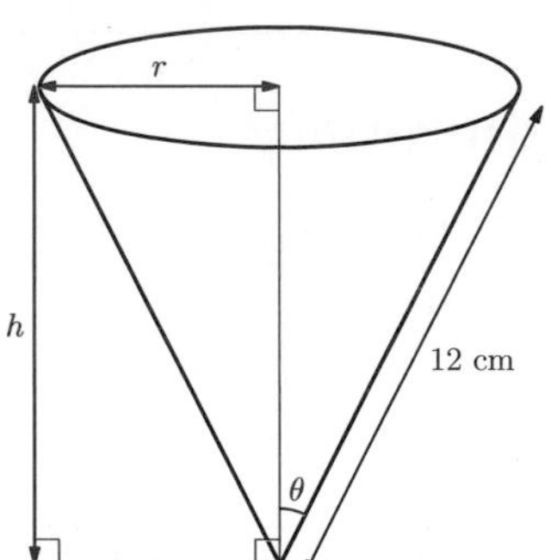

The first thing we need to do is write an expression for the volume V of the cone. Then we will aim to differentiate with respect to θ and solve $\frac{dV}{d\theta}=0$ to find the value of θ at which the maximum occurs.

The formula for the volume of a cone is

$$V=\frac{1}{3}\pi r^2 h$$

Using the right-angled triangle shown in the diagram, we have

$$r=12\sin\theta$$

$$h=12\cos\theta$$

Substituting these into the formula for V gives

$$\begin{aligned}V&=\frac{1}{3}\pi(12\sin\theta)^2(12\cos\theta)\\&=\frac{12^3}{3}\pi\sin^2\theta\cos\theta\end{aligned}$$

Now that V is expressed in terms of θ only, we can differentiate:

$$\begin{aligned}\frac{dV}{d\theta}&=\frac{12^3}{3}\pi\left[(2\sin\theta\cos\theta)\cos\theta+\sin^2\theta(-\sin\theta)\right]\\&=\frac{12^3}{3}\pi\left[2\sin\theta\cos^2\theta-\sin^3\theta\right]\end{aligned}$$

For stationary points, $\frac{dV}{d\theta}=0$:

$$\frac{12^3}{3}\pi\left[2\sin\theta\cos^2\theta-\sin^3\theta\right]=0$$

$$\Leftrightarrow 2\sin\theta\cos^2\theta-\sin^3\theta=0$$

$$\Leftrightarrow \sin\theta(2\cos^2\theta-\sin^2\theta)=0$$

$$\Leftrightarrow \sin\theta=0 \quad\text{or}\quad 2\cos^2\theta-\sin^2\theta=0$$

$\sin\theta = 0$ has no valid solutions, as $0° < \theta < 90°$ for the cone.

The other equation, $2\cos^2\theta - \sin^2\theta = 0$, is satisfied when

$$\sin^2\theta = 2\cos^2\theta$$
$$\Leftrightarrow \tan^2\theta = 2$$
$$\therefore \tan\theta = \sqrt{2}$$

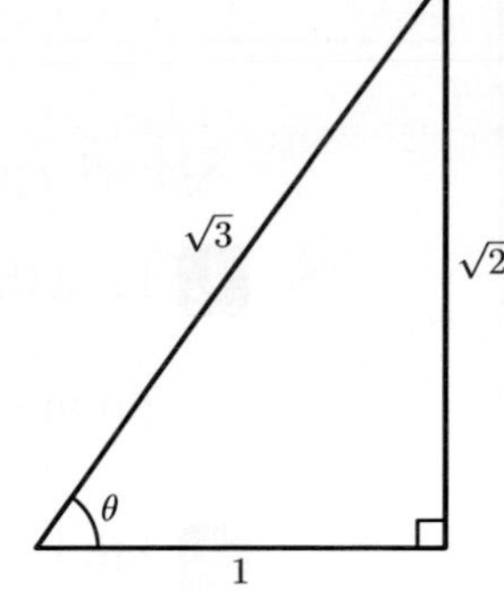

($\tan\theta = -\sqrt{2}$ has no solutions in $0° < \theta < 90°$).

Therefore the maximum volume is attained when $\tan\theta = \sqrt{2}$, which implies that $\sin\theta = \frac{\sqrt{2}}{\sqrt{3}}$ and $\cos\theta = \frac{1}{\sqrt{3}}$ (see the right-angled triangle diagram).

Finally, substitute these values of $\sin\theta$ and $\cos\theta$ into the expression $V = \frac{12^3}{3}\pi\sin^2\theta\cos\theta$ to find the maximum volume:

$$\begin{aligned} V_{\text{max}} &= \frac{12^3}{3}\pi\left(\frac{\sqrt{2}}{\sqrt{3}}\right)^2\left(\frac{1}{\sqrt{3}}\right) \\ &= \frac{12^3 \times 2\sqrt{3}\pi}{3^3} \\ &= 128\sqrt{3}\pi \end{aligned}$$

Mixed examination practice 14

Short questions

1. Find the exact value of the gradient of the curve with equation $y=\frac{1}{4-x^2}$ at the point where $x=\frac{1}{2}$. *[5 marks]*

2. Find $\frac{dy}{dx}$ if

(a) $y=e^{5x}$

(b) $y=\sqrt{3x+2}$

(c) $y=e^{5x}\sqrt{3x+2}$ *[8 marks]*

3. The graph of $y=xe^{-kx}$ has a stationary point at $x=\frac{2}{5}$. Find the value of k. *[4 marks]*

4. The diagram shows a rectangular area ABCD bounded on three sides by 60 m of fencing, and on the fourth by a wall AB.

Find the width of the rectangle (that is, the length AD) that gives its maximum area. *[5 marks]*

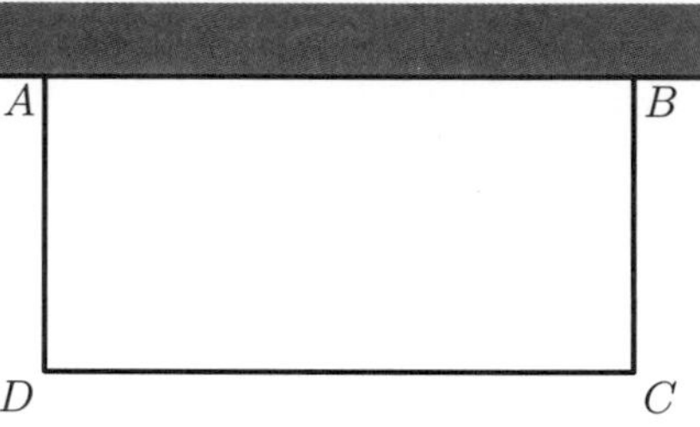

(© IB Organization 2005)

5. A curve has equation

$$f(x)=\frac{a}{b+e^{-cx}} \text{ where } a\neq 0 \text{ and } b,c>0$$

(a) Show that

$$f''(x)=\frac{ac^2e^{-cx}\left(e^{-cx}-b\right)}{\left(b+e^{-cx}\right)^3}$$

(b) Find the coordinates of the point on the curve where $f''(x)=0$. *[11 marks]*

(© IB Organization 2003)

Long questions

1. The function f is defined as $f(x) = e^x \sin x$, where x is in radians. Part of the curve of f is shown in the diagram. There is a point of inflexion at A and a local maximum point at B. The graph of f intersects the x-axis at the point C.

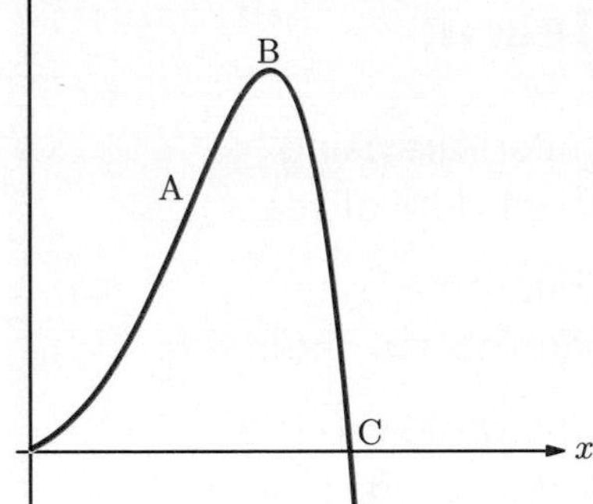

   (a) Write down the x-coordinate of the point C. *[1 mark]*

   (b) (i) Find $f'(x)$.

   (ii) Write down the value of $f'(x)$ at the point B.

   (c) Show that $f''(x) = 2e^x \cos x$.

   (d) (i) Write down the value of $f''(x)$ at A, the point of inflexion.

   (ii) Hence, calculate the coordinates of A. *[11 marks]*

(*© IB Organization 2007*)

2. A curve has equation $y = \dfrac{x^2}{1-2x}$.

   (a) Write down the equation of the vertical asymptote of the curve.

   (b) Use differentiation to find the coordinates of stationary points on the curve.

   (c) Determine the nature of the stationary points.

   (d) Sketch the graph of $y = \dfrac{x^2}{1-2x}$. *[17 marks]*

3. The function f is defined by $f(x) = \dfrac{x^2}{2^x}$ for $x > 0$.

   (a) (i) Show that $2^x = e^{x\ln 2}$.

   (ii) Hence show that $\dfrac{d}{dx}(2^x) = 2^x \ln 2$.

   (b) (i) Show that $f'(x) = \dfrac{2x - x^2 \ln 2}{2^x}$.

   (ii) Obtain an expression for $f''(x)$, simplifying your answer as far as possible.

   (c) (i) Find the *exact* value of x satisfying the equation $f'(x) = 0$.

   (ii) Show that this value gives a maximum value for $f(x)$. *[14 marks]*

15 Further integration

In this chapter you will learn:

- to integrate using known derivatives
- to integrate by reversing the chain rule
- to integrate using a change of variable (substitution)
- to apply integration to problems involving motion (kinematics)
- how to find volumes of rotationally symmetrical shapes.

Introductory problem

Prove that the area of a circle with radius r is πr^2.

Having extended the range of functions we can differentiate, we now do the same for integration. Sometimes we will be able to use results from previous chapters directly, but in other cases we have to develop new techniques. In this chapter we look at the most commonly used integration method – substitution or reversing the chain rule – and show how integration can be used to solve some problems that arise in applications.

15A Reversing standard derivatives

In chapter 13 we reversed a number of standard derivatives that had been established in chapter 12, thus obtaining the following list of basic integrals:

$$\int x^n \, dx = \frac{1}{n+1} x^{n+1} + c, \qquad n \neq -1$$

$$\int e^x \, dx = e^x + c$$

$$\int \frac{1}{x} \, dx = \ln x + c, \qquad x > 0$$

$$\int \sin x \, dx = -\cos x + c$$

$$\int \cos x \, dx = \sin x + c$$

The chain rule for differentiation (section 14A) allows us to go further and deal with integrals such as $\int 2\cos(2x)\,dx$. Here the idea is to integrate cos to sin and then think about what the chain rule would give us if we differentiated back. In this case, $\frac{d}{dx}(\sin 2x) = 2\cos 2x$, and the factor 2 (the derivative of $2x$) that came from applying the chain rule happens to match precisely the factor in the original integral, so we have the correct answer straight away:

$$\int 2\cos(2x)\,\mathrm{d}x = \sin 2x + c$$

However, in a similar situation, we may find that the factor coming from the chain rule does not match the factor in the integral. If these factors are constants, we can compensate for the discrepancy by cancelling out the constant factor generated by the chain rule. For example, to find $\int \sin(3x)\,\mathrm{d}x$ we proceed as before, integrating sin to −cos; but this time, when we differentiate back, the chain rule gives us an unwanted factor of 3: $\frac{\mathrm{d}}{\mathrm{d}x}(-\cos 3x) = 3\sin 3x$.
Therefore, we simply divide by 3 to cancel it out:

$$\int \sin(3x)\,\mathrm{d}x = -\frac{1}{3}\cos 3x + c$$

This method can be used with any of the standard derivatives and integrals in the list above.

Worked example 15.1

Find the following integrals.

(a) $\int (2x-3)^4\,\mathrm{d}x$ (b) $\int (1-4x)^{-\frac{2}{3}}\,\mathrm{d}x$

Integrate $(\ )^4$ to $\frac{1}{5}(\ )^5$ and then consider the effect of the chain rule.

We know that $\frac{\mathrm{d}}{\mathrm{d}x}\left(\frac{1}{5}(2x-3)^5\right) = 2(2x-3)^4$, so multiply by $\frac{1}{2}$ to remove the unwanted factor of 2.

(a)

$$\int (2x-3)^4\,dx = \frac{1}{2}\times\frac{1}{5}(2x-3)^5 + c$$
$$= \frac{1}{10}(2x-3)^5 + c$$

Integrate $(\ )^{-\frac{2}{3}}$ to $3(\ )^{\frac{1}{3}}$ and then consider the effect of the chain rule.

We know that $\frac{\mathrm{d}}{\mathrm{d}x}\left(3(1-4x)^{\frac{1}{3}}\right) = (-4)(1-4x)^{-\frac{2}{3}}$ so multiply by $-\frac{1}{4}$ to remove the unwanted −4.

(b)

$$\int (1-4x)^{-\frac{2}{3}}\,dx = \left(-\frac{1}{4}\right)3(1-4x)^{\frac{1}{3}} + c$$
$$= -\frac{3}{4}(1-4x)^{\frac{1}{3}} + c$$

You may notice a pattern here: we always divide by the coefficient of x. This is indeed a general rule, which comes from reversing the special case of the chain rule given in Key point 14.2.

EXAM HINT

This rule only applies when the 'inside' function is of the form $ax+b$, where a and b are constants.

KEY POINT 15.1

If a and b are constants, then

$$\int f(ax+b)\,\mathrm{d}x = \frac{1}{a}F(ax+b)+c$$

where $F(x)$ is the integral of $f(x)$

With this shortcut in hand, we no longer need to consciously consider the effect of the chain rule every time.

Worked example 15.2

Find the following:

(a) $\int \frac{1}{2}\mathrm{e}^{4x}\,\mathrm{d}x$ (b) $\int \frac{2}{6x+5}\,\mathrm{d}x$

Integrate $\mathrm{e}^{(\,)}$ to $\mathrm{e}^{(\,)}$ and divide by the coefficient of x.

(a)
$$\int \frac{1}{2}e^{4x}dx = \frac{1}{2}\times\frac{1}{4}e^{4x}+c$$
$$= \frac{1}{8}e^{4x}+c$$

Integrate $\frac{1}{(\,)}$ to $\ln(\,)$ and divide by the coefficient of x.

(b)
$$\int \frac{2}{6x+5}dx = 2\times\frac{1}{6}\ln(6x+5)+c$$
$$= \frac{1}{3}\ln(6x+5)+c$$

You may need to use algebra to rewrite the expression in the form of a standard derivative which can then be reversed.

Worked example 15.3

Find the integral

$$\int \frac{x+4}{12-5x-2x^2}\,\mathrm{d}x$$

If there are polynomials in the expression, it is generally a good idea to check whether they factorise.

$$\int \frac{x+4}{12-5x-2x^2}dx = \int \frac{x+4}{(3-2x)(x+4)}dx$$

Now the function resembles one of the standard derivatives.

$$= \int \frac{1}{3-2x}dx$$

So we can use the rule in Key point 15.1.

$$= -\frac{1}{2}\ln(3-2x)+c$$

Exercise 15A

1. Find the following integrals.

(a) (i) $\int 5(x+3)^4 \, dx$ (ii) $\int (x-2)^5 \, dx$

(b) (i) $\int (4x-5)^7 \, dx$ (ii) $\int \left(\frac{1}{8}x+1\right)^3 dx$

(c) (i) $\int (4-x)^8 \, dx$ (ii) $\int 4\left(3-\frac{1}{2}x\right)^6 dx$

(d) (i) $\int \sqrt{2x-1} \, dx$ (ii) $\int 7(2-5x)^{\frac{3}{4}} \, dx$

(e) (i) $\int \frac{6}{(4-3x)^2} \, dx$ (ii) $\int \frac{1}{\sqrt[4]{2+\frac{x}{3}}} \, dx$

2. Find the following integrals.

(a) (i) $\int 3e^{3x} \, dx$ (ii) $\int e^{2x+5} \, dx$

(b) (i) $\int e^{\frac{1}{2}x} \, dx$ (ii) $\int 4e^{\frac{2x-1}{3}} \, dx$

(c) (i) $\int -6e^{-3x} \, dx$ (ii) $\int \frac{1}{e^{4x}} \, dx$

(d) (i) $\int e^{-\frac{2}{3}x} \, dx$ (ii) $\int \frac{-2}{e^{x/4}} \, dx$

3. Find the following integrals.

(a) (i) $\int \frac{1}{x+4} \, dx$ (ii) $\int \frac{5}{5x-2} \, dx$

(b) (i) $\int \frac{2}{3x+4} \, dx$ (ii) $\int \frac{-8}{2x-5} \, dx$

(c) (i) $\int \frac{1}{7-2x} \, dx$ (ii) $\int \frac{-3}{1-4x} \, dx$

4. Integrate the following.

(a) $\int \sin(2-3x) \, dx$ (b) $\int 2\cos 4x \, dx$

5. By first simplifying, find the following integrals.

(a) $\int \frac{(4x^2-9)^2}{(2x+3)^2} \, dx$

(b) $\int e^{2x}e^{4x} \, dx$

(c) $\int \frac{x+3}{6-13x-5x^2} \, dx$

6. Two students integrate $\int \frac{1}{3x}\,\mathrm{d}x$ in different ways.

Marina writes

$$\int \frac{1}{3x}\,\mathrm{d}x = \frac{1}{3}\int \frac{1}{x}\,\mathrm{d}x = \frac{1}{3}\ln x + c$$

while Jack uses the rule from Key point 15. 1 and divides by the coefficient of x:

$$\int \frac{1}{3x}\,\mathrm{d}x = \frac{1}{3}\ln(3x) + c$$

Who has the right answer?

7. Given that $0 < a < 1$ and that the area enclosed between the graph of $y = \frac{1}{1-x}$, the x-axis, and the lines $x = a^2$ and $x = a$ is 0.4, find the value of a correct to 3 significant figures. *[5 marks]*

15B Integration by substitution

The shortcut for reversing the chain rule (Key point 15.1) works only when the derivative of the 'inside' function is a constant. This is because a constant factor can 'move through the integral sign' (see Key point 13.2 from section 13C); for example,

$$\begin{aligned}\int \cos 2x\,\mathrm{d}x &= \int \frac{1}{2}\times 2\cos 2x\,\mathrm{d}x\\ &= \frac{1}{2}\int 2\cos 2x\,\mathrm{d}x\\ &= \frac{1}{2}\sin 2x + c\end{aligned}$$

However, any expression containing the integration variable *cannot* be moved across the integral sign: $\int x\sin x\,\mathrm{d}x$ is not the same as $x\int \sin x\,\mathrm{d}x$. So we need different ways to integrate a product of two functions. Some products of a special form can be integrated by extending the principle of reversing the chain rule, which leads to the method of **integration by substitution**.

When we use the chain rule to differentiate a composite function, we differentiate the outer function and multiply by the derivative of the inner function; for example,

$$\frac{\mathrm{d}}{\mathrm{d}x}\left(\sin\left(x^2+2\right)\right) = \cos(x^2+2)\times 2x$$

We can think of this as using a substitution $u = x^2 + 2$, and then $\frac{dy}{dx} = \frac{dy}{du} \times \frac{du}{dx}$.

Now look at $\int x\cos(x^2 + 2)\,dx$. Since $\cos(x^2 + 2)$ is a composite function, we can write it as $\cos u$ where $u = x^2 + 2$. Thus our integral becomes $\int x\cos u\,dx$. We know how to integrate $\cos u$ with respect to u, so we would like our integration variable to be u; in other words, we want du instead of dx. These two are not the same (so we cannot simply replace dx by du), but they are related because $u = x^2 + 2 \Rightarrow \frac{du}{dx} = 2x$. We can then 'rearrange' the derivative equation to get $dx = \frac{1}{2x}du$.

Substituting all this into our integral gives

$$\begin{aligned}\int x\cos(x^2+2)\,dx &= \int x\cos u\left(\frac{1}{2x}\right)\,du\\ &= \int \frac{1}{2}\cos u\,du\\ &= \frac{1}{2}\sin u + c\\ &= \frac{1}{2}\sin(x^2+2) + c\end{aligned}$$

Note that after obtaining the integral with respect to u we should rewrite it in terms of the original variable x.

A word of warning here: $\frac{du}{dx}$ is not really a fraction (as we saw in section 12D; it means the differentiation operator $\frac{d}{dx}$ applied to u), so it is not clear that 'rearranging' the equation $\frac{du}{dx} = f'(x)$ is valid. Nevertheless, it can be shown that as a consequence of the chain rule, dx *can be replaced by* $\frac{1}{f'(x)}du$.

We summarise the method of integration by substitution as follows.

KEY POINT 15.2

Integration by substitution

1. Select a substitution u = inner function (if not already given one).
2. Differentiate the substitution and rearrange to write dx in terms of du.
3. In the integral, replace dx by the expression from step 2, and replace any obvious occurrences of u.
4. Simplify as far as possible.
5. If any terms with x remain, write them in terms of u.
6. Find the new integral with respect to u.
7. Write the answer in terms of x.

Worked example 15.4

Find $\int x e^{x^2} dx$ using the substitution $u = x^2$.

We are given the substitution, so differentiate it and then write dx in terms of du.

$$\frac{du}{dx} = 2x$$

$$\therefore \; dx = \frac{1}{2x} du$$

In the integral, replace dx by the above expression, and replace any obvious occurrences of u.

$$\int x e^{x^2} dx = \int x e^u \frac{1}{2x} du$$

$$= \frac{1}{2} \int e^u du$$

Find the new integral in terms of u.

$$= \frac{1}{2} e^u + c$$

Write the answer in terms of x.

$$= \frac{1}{2} e^{x^2} + c$$

We can use integration by substitution with definite integrals as well. It is usually best to wait until the integration has been completed and written in terms of the original variable before you apply the limits (but see the solution to the introductory problem at the end of the chapter for an alternative approach). You can remind yourself of this by writing '$x =$' in the limits.

Worked example 15.5

Use the substitution $u = x^2 + 1$ to evaluate the integral $\int_0^1 \frac{x}{\sqrt{x^2+1}}\,dx$.

Differentiate the given substitution and write dx in terms of du.

$$\frac{du}{dx} = 2x$$

$$\therefore\ dx = \frac{1}{2x}\,du$$

Replace dx by the above expression, and replace any obvious occurrences of u.

$$\int_{x=0}^{x=1} \frac{x}{\sqrt{x^2+1}}\,dx = \int_{x=0}^{x=1} \frac{x}{\sqrt{u}}\frac{1}{2x}\,du$$

$$= \frac{1}{2}\int_{x=0}^{x=1} \frac{1}{\sqrt{u}}\,du$$

Find the new integral in terms of u.

$$= \frac{1}{2}\int_{x=0}^{x=1} u^{-\frac{1}{2}}\,du$$

$$= \left[\frac{1}{2}\times 2u^{\frac{1}{2}}\right]_{x=0}^{x=1}$$

$$= \left[\sqrt{u}\right]_{x=0}^{x=1}$$

Write the answer in terms of x. Then apply the limits.

$$= \left[\sqrt{x^2+1}\right]_{x=0}^{x=1}$$

$$= \sqrt{1^2+1} - \sqrt{0^2+1}$$

$$= \sqrt{2} - 1$$

You will nearly always be told what substitution to use. If you are not given a substitution, look for a composite function and take u = inner function.

Worked example 15.6

Find the following integrals.

(a) $\int \sin^5 x \cos x\,dx$ (b) $\int x^2 e^{x^3+4}\,dx$

Remember that $\sin^5 x$ means $(\sin x)^5$, which is a composite function with inner function $\sin x$.

(a) Let $u = \sin x$.

Then $\frac{du}{dx} = \cos x$ and so $dx = \frac{1}{\cos x}\,du$

→

continued . . .

Make the substitution.

$$\int(\sin x)^5 \cos x\,dx = \int u^5 \cos x \frac{1}{\cos x}\,du$$
$$= \int u^5\,du$$
$$= \frac{1}{6}u^6 + c$$

Write the answer in terms of x.

$$= \frac{1}{6}\sin^6 x + c$$

e^{x^3+4} is a composite function with inner function $x^3 + 4$.

(b) Let $u = x^3 + 4$.

Then $\frac{du}{dx} = 3x^2$ and hence $dx = \frac{1}{3x^2}\,du$

Make the substitution.

$$\int x^2 e^{x^3+4}\,dx = \int x^2 e^u \frac{1}{3x^2}\,du$$
$$= \int \frac{1}{3}e^u\,du$$
$$= \frac{1}{3}e^u + c$$

Write the answer in terms of x.

$$= \frac{1}{3}e^{x^3+4} + c$$

It is quite common to have to integrate a quotient where the numerator is a multiple of the derivative of the denominator. In this situation, use the substitution u = denominator.

Worked example 15.7

Find $\int \frac{x-3}{x^2-6x+7}\,dx$.

The derivative of the denominator is $2x - 6$, which is 2 times the numerator, so substitute u = denominator.

Let $u = x^2 - 6x + 7$. Then

$$\frac{du}{dx} = 2x - 6$$
$$\therefore\ dx = \frac{1}{2x-6}du = \frac{1}{2(x-3)}du$$

→

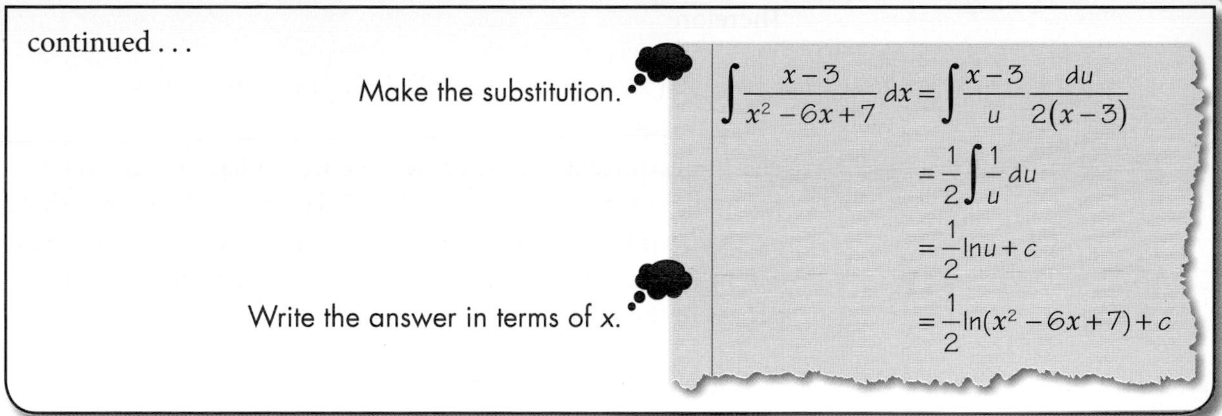

continued . . .
Make the substitution.
$\int \frac{x-3}{x^2-6x+7}\,dx = \int \frac{x-3}{u}\,\frac{du}{2(x-3)}$
$= \frac{1}{2}\int \frac{1}{u}\,du$
$= \frac{1}{2}\ln u + c$
Write the answer in terms of x.
$= \frac{1}{2}\ln(x^2-6x+7)+c$

Whenever you have a quotient to integrate, always look out for this situation. In fact, if an integral is of the form $\int \frac{f'(x)}{f(x)}\,\mathrm{d}x$, you can immediately write down the result as $\ln(f(x)) + c$.

You may have noticed in all of the above examples that, after making the substitution, the part of the integrand which was still in terms of x cancelled with a similar term coming from $\frac{du}{dx}$. For instance, in Worked example 15.6 part (b),

$$\int x^2 e^{x^3+4}\,\mathrm{d}x = \int x^2 e^u \frac{1}{3x^2}\,\mathrm{d}u = \int \frac{1}{3}e^u\,\mathrm{d}u.$$

When integrating a product of functions, this cancellation will always happen if one part of the product is a composite function and the other part is a constant multiple of the derivative of the inner function. The explanation comes from the chain rule.

For example, consider the integral

$$\int (2x+3)(x^2+3x-5)^4\,\mathrm{d}x$$

To find this integral, think about what we would need to differentiate to get $(2x+3)(x^2+3x-5)^4$. Notice that $(x^2+3x-5)^4$ is a composite function and that $2x+3$ is the derivative of the inner function x^2+3x-5, so we know that we would get $2x+3$ 'for free' when differentiating some power of x^2+3x-5 using the chain rule. To end up with $(x^2+3x-5)^4$, we would have to be differentiating $\frac{1}{5}(x^2+3x-5)^5$. Check that

$$\frac{\mathrm{d}}{\mathrm{d}x}\left(\frac{1}{5}(x^2+3x-5)^5\right) = (2x+3)(x^2+3x-5)^4$$

Therefore

$$\int (2x+3)(x^2+3x-5)^4\, dx = \frac{1}{5}(x^2+3x-5)^5 + c$$

This is of course the same answer we would have obtained by using the substitution $u = x^2+3x-5$. However, if you spot that a particular integral can be found by reversing the chain rule, you can just write down the answer without working through the details of the substitution.

Exercise 15B

1. Find the following integrals using the given substitutions.

(a) (i) $\int x\sqrt{x^2+2}\, dx$; $u = x^2+2$

(ii) $\int (x+3)\sqrt{x^2+6x+4}\, dx$; $u = x^2+6x+4$

(b) (i) $\int \frac{x^2}{x^3+1}\, dx$; $u = x^3+1$

(ii) $\int \frac{3x}{x^2+5}\, dx$; $u = x^2+5$

(c) (i) $\int \sin x \cos^2 x\, dx$; $u = \cos x$

(ii) $\int \frac{1}{x}\ln x\, dx$; $u = \ln x$

2. Find the following integrals using appropriate substitutions.

(a) (i) $\int x(x^2+3)^3\, dx$ (ii) $\int 3x(x^2-1)^5\, dx$

(b) (i) $\int (2x-5)(3x^2-15x+4)^4\, dx$

(ii) $\int (x^2+2x)(x^3+3x^2-5)^3\, dx$

(c) (i) $\int \frac{2x}{x^2+3}\, dx$ (ii) $\int \frac{6x^2-12}{x^3-6x+1}\, dx$

(d) (i) $\int 4\cos^5 3x \sin 3x\, dx$ (ii) $\int \cos 2x \sin^3 2x\, dx$

(e) (i) $\int 3x\mathrm{e}^{3x^2-1}\, dx$ (ii) $\int 3x\mathrm{e}^{x^2}\, dx$

(f) (i) $\int \frac{\mathrm{e}^{2x+3}}{\mathrm{e}^{2x+3}+4}\, dx$ (ii) $\int \frac{\cos x}{3+4\sin x}\, dx$

3. Use the substitution $u = \sin x$ to find the value

of $\int_0^{\pi/2} \cos x\, \mathrm{e}^{\sin x}\, dx$. *[7 marks]*

4. Use the substitution $u = x^3 + 5$ to find the indefinite integral $\int x^2\sqrt{x^3+5}\,\mathrm{d}x$. [5 marks]

 **5.** Use the substitution $u = \mathrm{e}^x$ to evaluate $\int_0^1 \frac{\mathrm{e}^x}{\sqrt{\mathrm{e}^x+1}}\,\mathrm{d}x$.

6. Find the exact value of $\int_0^2 (2x+1)\mathrm{e}^{x^2+x-1}\,\mathrm{d}x$. [6 marks]

7. Evaluate $\int_2^5 \frac{2x}{x^2-1}\,\mathrm{d}x$, giving your answer in the form $\ln k$. [4 marks]

8. (a) Write $\tan x$ in terms of $\sin x$ and $\cos x$.

(b) Hence or otherwise, find $\int \tan x\,\mathrm{d}x$. [7 marks]

 **9.** Evaluate $\int_1^3 \frac{(2x-3)\sqrt{x^2-3x+3}}{x^2-3x+3}\,\mathrm{d}x$. [5 marks]

10. Three students integrate $\cos x \sin x$ in three different ways.

Amara uses the chain rule in reverse with $u = \sin x$:

$$\frac{\mathrm{d}u}{\mathrm{d}x} = \cos x, \text{ so } \int \cos x \sin x\,\mathrm{d}x = \int u\,\mathrm{d}u = \frac{1}{2}\sin^2 x + c.$$

Ben uses the chain rule in reverse with $u = \cos x$:

$$\frac{\mathrm{d}u}{\mathrm{d}x} = -\sin x, \text{ so } \int \cos x \sin x\,\mathrm{d}x = \int -u\,\mathrm{d}u = -\frac{1}{2}\cos^2 x + c.$$

Carlos uses a double-angle formula:

$$\int \cos x \sin x\,\mathrm{d}x = \int \frac{1}{2}\sin 2x\,\mathrm{d}x = -\frac{1}{4}\cos 2x + c.$$

Who is right?

15C Kinematics

Kinematics is the study of movement – in particular position, velocity and acceleration. We first need to define some terms carefully.

- *Time* is normally given the symbol t. We can define $t = 0$ to be any convenient time.
- In a standard 400-metre race athletes run a single lap, so despite running 400 m they return to where they started. The distance is how much ground someone has covered,

> In the International Baccalaureate® you will only have to deal with movement in one dimension. In reality, however, motion often occurs in two or three dimensions. To deal with this requires a combination of vectors and calculus called (unsurprisingly) vector calculus.

400 m in this case; the **displacement** is how far away they are from a particular position (called the origin), so the athletes' displacement upon finishing the race is 0 m. Displacement is usually represented by the symbol s.

- The rate of change of displacement with respect to time is called **velocity**, usually denoted by v.

KEY POINT 15.3

> **Velocity** is $v = \frac{ds}{dt}$.
> **Speed** is the magnitude of velocity, $|v|$.

The rate of change of velocity with respect to time is called **acceleration** and is typically given the symbol a.

KEY POINT 15.4

> **Acceleration** is $a = \frac{dv}{dt}$.

We differentiate to go from displacement to velocity to acceleration. Therefore, reversing the process – going from acceleration to velocity to displacement – is done by integration.

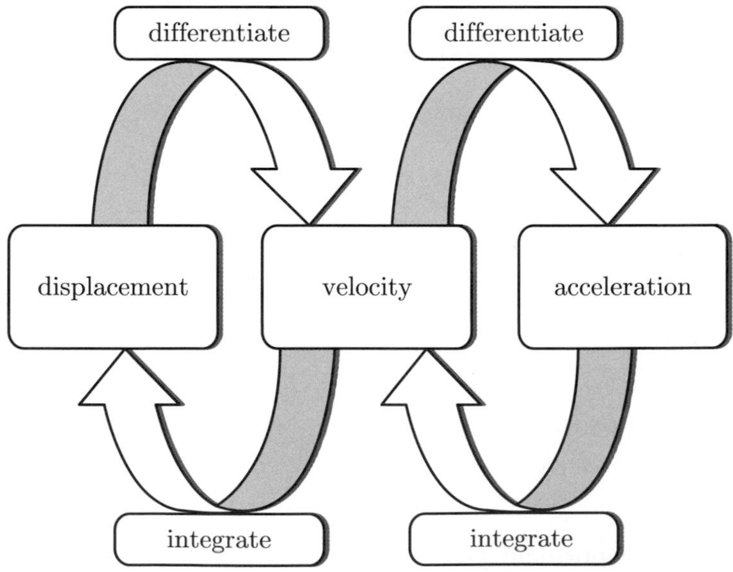

There is an important difference between finding the distance and finding the displacement from time $t = a$ to time $t = b$.

KEY POINT 15.5

Displacement between times $t = a$ and $t = b$ is the integral $\int_a^b v\, dt$.

Distance travelled between times $t = a$ and $t = b$ is the area $\int_a^b |v|\, dt$, that is, the total area enclosed between the graph of v against t, the t-axis, and the lines $t = a$ and $t = b$.

See section 13H if you need to refresh your memory on the relationship and differences between areas and integrals.

Worked example 15.8

The velocity (ms^{-1}) of a car at time t after passing a flag is modelled by $v = 17 - 4t$ for $0 \le t < 5$.

(a) What is the initial speed of the car?

(b) Find the acceleration of the car.

(c) What is the maximum displacement of the car from the flag?

(d) Find the distance that the car travels.

'Initial' means at $t = 0$.

(a) When $t = 0$, $v = 17$, so speed is 17 ms^{-1}.

To find acceleration, differentiate the velocity.

(b) $a = \frac{dv}{dt} = -4$ ms^{-1}

Maximum displacement occurs at a stationary point of s, i.e. when $\frac{ds}{dt} = 0$, which is the same as $v = 0$

(c) $v = 0 \Rightarrow t = 4.25$

At this time the displacement is

$$s = \int_0^{4.25} v\, dt$$

$$= \int_0^{4.25} 17 - 4t\, dt$$

$$= 36.125\text{ m (from GDC)}$$

Distance is the actual area enclosed between the graph of v against t, the t-axis, and the lines $t = a$ and $t = b$.

(d)

The area above the t-axis is 36.125 from part (c).

The area below the axis is $\int_{4.25}^{5} |v|\, dt = 1.125$ (from GDC)

So total distance is 37.25 m

Exercise 15C

1. Find expressions for the velocity and acceleration in terms of time if the displacement is given by the following.

   (a) (i) $s = 4e^{-2t}$ (ii) $s = 5 - 2e^{3t}$

   (b) (i) $s = 5\sin\left(\frac{t}{2}\right)$ (ii) $s = 2 - 3\cos(2t)$

2. A particle is at the origin ($s = 0$) at $t = 0$ and moves with the given velocity. Find the displacement in terms of t.

   (a) (i) $v = 3t^2 - 1$ (ii) $v = \frac{1}{2}(1 - t^3)$

   (b) (i) $v = 2e^{-t}$ (ii) $v = 1 + e^{2t}$

   (c) (i) $v = \frac{3}{t+2}$ (ii) $v = 3 - \frac{1}{t+1}$

3. For the given velocity function, find the distance travelled between the specified times.

   (a) (i) $v = 2e^{-t}$ between $t = 0$ and $t = 2$

   (ii) $v = 4(\ln t)^3$ between $t = 2$ and $t = 3$

   (b) (i) $v = 1 - 5\cos t$ between $t = 0.2$ and $t = 0.9$

   (ii) $v = 2\cos(3t)$ between $t = 1$ and $t = 1.5$

   (c) (i) $v = t^2 - 2$ between $t = 0$ and $t = 2.3$

   (ii) $v = 5\sin(2t)$ between $t = 0.5$ and $t = 2.5$

4. Use integration to derive the following constant acceleration formulas: for an object moving with constant acceleration a from an initial velocity u, these give the velocity v at time t and the displacement s from the starting position.

   (i) $v = u + at$

   (ii) $s = ut + \frac{1}{2}at^2$

5. The velocity of an object, in metres per second, is given by $v = 5\cos\left(\frac{t}{3}\right)$.

   (a) Find the displacement of the object from the starting point when $t = 6$.

   (b) Find the total distance travelled by the object in the first 6 seconds. *[6 marks]*

6. A ball is projected vertically upwards so that its velocity in metres per second at time t seconds is given by $v = 12 - 9.8t$.

(a) Find the displacement of the ball relative to its starting position after 2 seconds.

(b) Find the distance travelled by the ball in the first 2 seconds of motion. *[5 marks]*

7. An object moves in a straight line so that its velocity at time t is given by $v = \dfrac{t}{t^2 + 1}$.

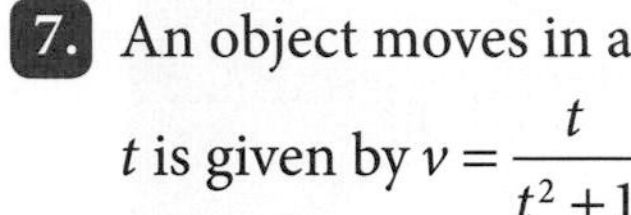

(a) Find an expression for the acceleration of the object at time t.

(b) Given that the object is initially at the origin, find its displacement from the origin when $t = 5$. *[6 marks]*

8. The displacement of an object varies with time as
$s = -\dfrac{1}{3}t^3 + \dfrac{3}{2}t^2 + 4t$ for $0 \le t \le 5$.
Find the maximum velocity of the object. *[5 marks]*

9. A car leaving a parking space has velocity (in metres per second) given by the equation $v = \dfrac{1}{2}t^2 - 2t$, where t is the time in seconds. The car is assumed to move along a straight line at all times.

(a) Show that the car is stationary when $t = 0$ and when $t = 4$.

(b) Describe the car's motion during the first eight seconds.

(c) Find the distance travelled in the first four seconds.

(d) Find the distance travelled in the first eight seconds.

(e) Find the displacement after eight seconds.

(f) At what time is the acceleration $5\,\text{m/s}^2$?

(g) Find the maximum speed in the first eight seconds. *[20 marks]*

15D Volumes of revolution

In chapter 13 you saw that the area between a curve and the x-axis from $x = a$ to $x = b$ is given by $\int_a^b y \, dx$ as long as $y > 0$. In this section we shall find a similar formula to calculate the volume of a shape that can be formed by rotating a curve around the x-axis.

Imagine a curve $y = f(x)$ being rotated fully around the x-axis; the resulting shape is called a **volume of revolution**.

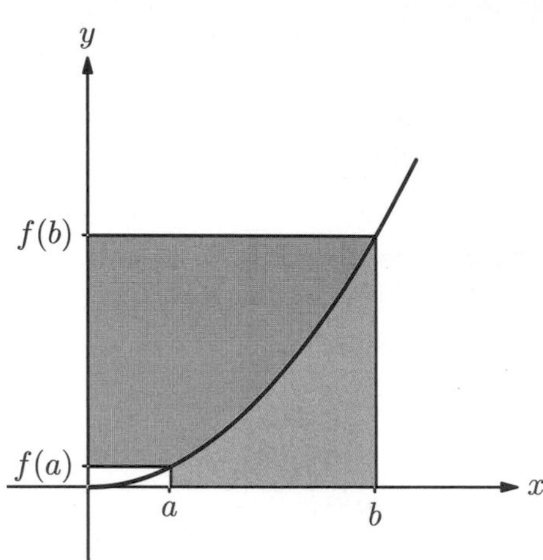

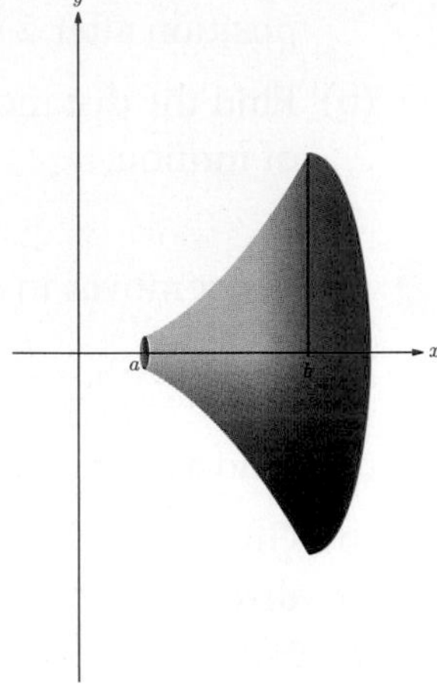

KEY POINT 15.6

The volume of revolution formed by rotating a portion of a curve between $x = a$ and $x = b$ around the x-axis is given by $V = \int_{x=a}^{x=b} \pi y^2 \, dx$

for clarity

See Fill-in proof sheet 17 'Volumes of revolution' on the CD-ROM for the derivation of this formula.

Worked example 15.9

The graph of $y = \sqrt{\sin 2x}$, $0 \le x \le \frac{\pi}{2}$, is rotated 360° around the x-axis. Find, in terms of π, the volume of the solid generated.

Use the formula for the volume of revolution.

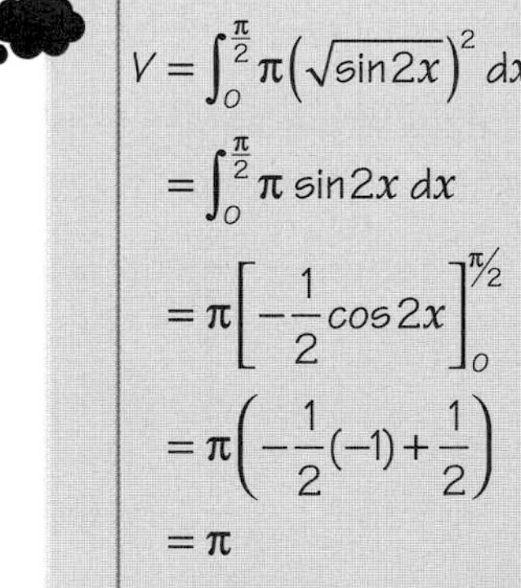

$$V = \int_0^{\frac{\pi}{2}} \pi\left(\sqrt{\sin 2x}\right)^2 dx$$

$$= \int_0^{\frac{\pi}{2}} \pi \sin 2x \, dx$$

$$= \pi\left[-\frac{1}{2}\cos 2x\right]_0^{\pi/2}$$

$$= \pi\left(-\frac{1}{2}(-1) + \frac{1}{2}\right)$$

$$= \pi$$

We can extend this idea to find a volume of revolution formed by rotating a region between two curves. The argument is similar to the one we used for calculating the area enclosed between two curves in section 13I.

The volume formed when the region R is rotated around the x-axis is given by the volume of revolution obtained from rotating $y = g(x)$ minus the volume of revolution obtained from rotating $y = f(x)$.

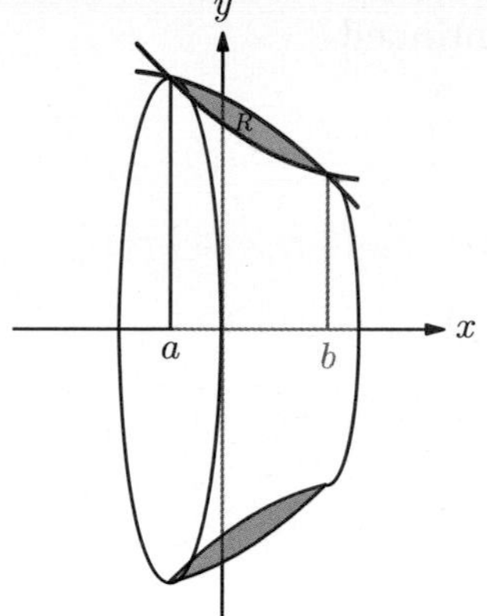

KEY POINT 15.7

The volume of revolution formed by rotating the region bounded above by the curve $y = f(x)$ and below by the curve $y = g(x)$ (i.e. where $g(x)$ is above $f(x)$) around the x-axis is

$$\int_a^b \pi\left[g(x)^2 - f(x)^2\right]\mathrm{d}x$$

where a and b are the x-coordinates of the points of intersection between the curves.

EXAM HINT

Be careful to square each term *within* the bracket. Do not fall into the trap of squaring the whole bracket, saying that the volume is $\int_a^b \pi\left[g(x) - f(x)\right]^2 \mathrm{d}x$.

Worked example 15.10

The region bounded by the curves $y = x^2 + 6$ and $y = 8x - x^2$ is rotated 360° about the x-axis.

(a) Show that the volume of revolution is given by $4\pi\int_1^3 13x^2 - 4x^3 - 9\,\mathrm{d}x$.

(b) Evaluate this volume, correct to 3 significant figures.

The limits of integration are the intersection points.

(a)

Intersections:

$x^2 + 6 = 8x - x^2$

$\Leftrightarrow 2x^2 - 8x + 6 = 0$

$\Leftrightarrow 2(x-1)(x-2) = 0$

$\Leftrightarrow x = 1 \text{ or } 3$

Use $V = \pi\int_b^a [g(x)]^2 - [f(x)]^2\,\mathrm{d}x$. Draw a sketch to see which curve is above.

continued . . .

$$V = \pi\int_1^3 (8x - x^2)^2 - (x^2 + 6)^2 dx$$

$$= \pi\int_1^3 (64x^2 - 16x^3 + x^4) - (x^4 + 12x^3 + 36)\, dx$$

$$= \pi\int_1^3 52x^2 - 16x^3 - 36\, dx$$

$$= 4\pi\int_1^3 13x^2 - 4x^3 - 9\, dx$$

We can evaluate the integral using the GDC.

(b)
Using GDC,
$V = 184$ (3 SF)

EXAM HINT

Notice that, due to the possibility of cancelling or combining terms, subtracting the squares of the two functions first and then integrating (i.e. doing $\int [g(x)]^2 - [f(x)]^2 dx$) is often easier than integrating $f(x)^2$ and $g(x)^2$ separately and then subtracting (i.e. doing $\int [g(x)]^2 dx - \int [f(x)]^2 dx$).

There are also formulas for finding the surface area of a solid formed by rotating a region around an axis. Some particularly interesting examples arise if we allow one end of the region to extend infinitely far; for example, rotating the region to the right of $x = 1$ between the curve $y = \frac{1}{x}$ and the x-axis gives a solid called Gabriel's horn or Torricelli's trumpet.

Surface areas and volumes generated by such unbounded regions can still be calculated, by using so-called improper integrals, and it turns out that it is possible to have a solid with finite volume but infinite surface area!

Exercise 15D

1. Find the volume of revolution formed when the curve $y = f(x)$, with $a \le x \le b$, is rotated through 2π radians about the x-axis.

(a) (i) $f(x) = x^2 + 6; a = -1, b = 3$

(ii) $f(x) = 2x^3 + 1; a = 0, b = 1$

(b) (i) $f(x) = e^{2x} + 1; a = 0, b = 1$

(ii) $f(x) = e^{-x} + 2; a = 0, b = 2$

(c) (i) $f(x) = \sqrt{\sin x}; a = 0, b = \pi$

(ii) $f(x) = \sqrt{\cos x}; a = 0, b = \frac{\pi}{2}$

2. The part of the curve $y = g(x)$ with $a \le x \le b$ is rotated 360° around the x-axis. Find the volume of revolution generated, correct to 3 significant figures.

(a) (i) $g(x) = 4x^2 + 1; a = 0, b = 2$

(ii) $g(x) = \dfrac{x^2 - 1}{3}; a = 1, b = 4$

(b) (i) $g(x) = \ln x + 1; a = 1, b = 3$

(ii) $g(x) = \ln(2x - 1); a = 1, b = 5$

(c) (i) $g(x) = \cos x; a = 0, b = \dfrac{\pi}{2}$

(ii) $g(x) = \tan x; a = 0, b = \dfrac{\pi}{4}$

3. The part of the graph of $y = \ln x$ between $x = 1$ and $x = 2\text{e}$ is rotated 360° around the x-axis. Find the volume generated. *[4 marks]*

4. The part of the curve $y^2 = \sin x$ between $x = 0$ and $x = \dfrac{\pi}{2}$ is rotated 2π radians around the x-axis. Find the exact volume of the solid generated. *[4 marks]*

5. The part of the curve $y = \sqrt{\dfrac{3}{x}}$ between $x = 1$ and $x = a$ is rotated 2π radians around the x-axis. The volume of the resulting solid is $\pi \ln\left(\dfrac{64}{27}\right)$. Find the exact value of a. *[7 marks]*

6. (a) Find the coordinates of the points of intersection of the curves $y = x^2 + 3$ and $y = 4x + 3$.

(b) Find the volume of revolution generated when the region between the curves $y = x^2 + 3$ and $y = 4x + 3$ is rotated 360° around the x-axis. *[7 marks]*

Summary

- Look for **standard derivatives** before attempting any more complicated methods. A list of standard derivatives and integrals is given in the Formula booklet. You may need to divide by the coefficient of x to get the correct constant factor.
- If the expression to be integrated is a product that contains both a function and (a constant multiple of) its derivative, then you should be able to reverse the chain rule or use a substitution to convert the expression into a standard derivative:
  - a general rule, which comes from reversing the special case of the chain rule in Key point 14.2, is: if a and b are constants, then
    $\int f(ax + b)\text{d}x = \dfrac{1}{a}F(ax + b) + c$ where $F(x)$ is the integral of $f(x)$.

- the above shortcut only works when the 'inside' function is a constant. When integrating the product of two functions, you can sometimes use integration by substitution, following the steps in Key point 15.2. This method can also be used with definite integrals: complete the integration first and then apply the limits.

- In **kinematics**,
  - distance is the amount of ground covered; displacement is how far away something is from the origin; velocity is the rate of change of displacement with respect to time ($v = \frac{ds}{dt}$); speed is the magnitude of velocity, $|v|$; and acceleration is the rate of change of velocity with respect to time ($a = \frac{dv}{dt}$).
  - differentiate to go from **displacement** to **velocity** to **acceleration**
  - integrate to go from acceleration to velocity to displacement.

  Do not confuse displacement with distance travelled:
  - displacement between times $t = a$ and $t = b$ is the integral $\int_a^b v \, dt$
  - distance travelled between times $t = a$ and $t = b$ is the area $\int_a^b |v| \, dt$.

- The **volume of revolution** formed by rotating a portion of curve between $x = a$ and $x = b$ around the x-axis is $\int_{x=a}^{x=b} \pi y^2 \, dx$.

- The volume of revolution formed by rotating the region bounded above by curve $y = f(x)$ and below by curve $y = g(x)$ (i.e, $g(x)$ is above $f(x)$) around the x-axis is

$$\int_a^b \pi\left[g(x)^2 - f(x)^2\right] dx$$

where a and b are the x-coordinates of the points of intersection between the curves.

Introductory problem revisited

Prove that the area of a circle with radius r is πr^2.

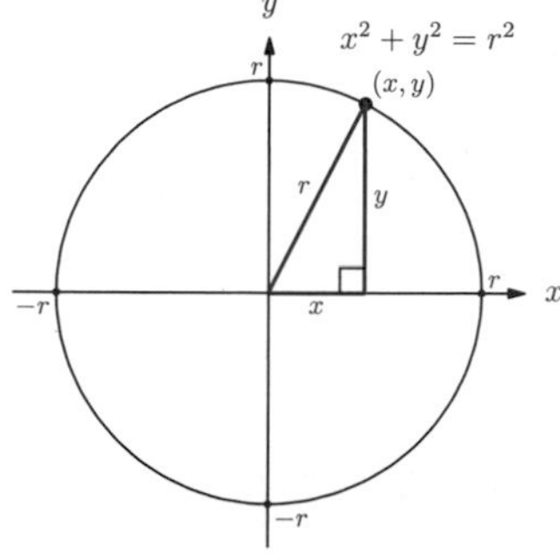

To do this using integration, we need to find an equation for the circle. Suppose that the circle is centred at the origin of the coordinate axes. By Pythagoras' theorem, any point on the circle must satisfy $x^2 + y^2 = r^2$.

We can rearrange this equation to get $y = \pm\sqrt{r^2 - x^2}$. The positive root represents the top half of the circle and the negative root the bottom half. To find the area of the circle, we can find the area enclosed between the graph of $y = \sqrt{r^2 - x^2}$ and the x-axis, and then double the answer.

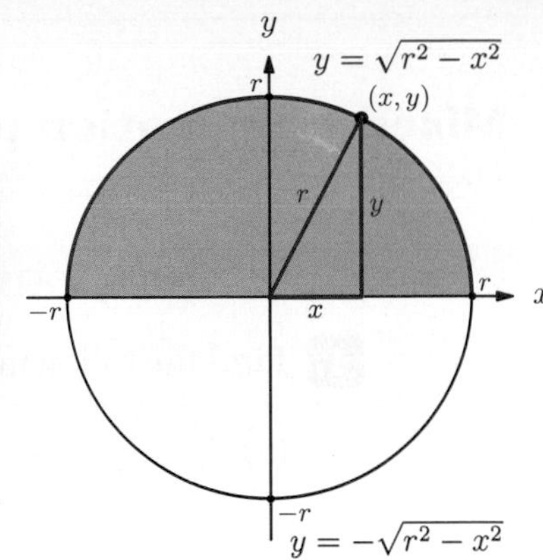

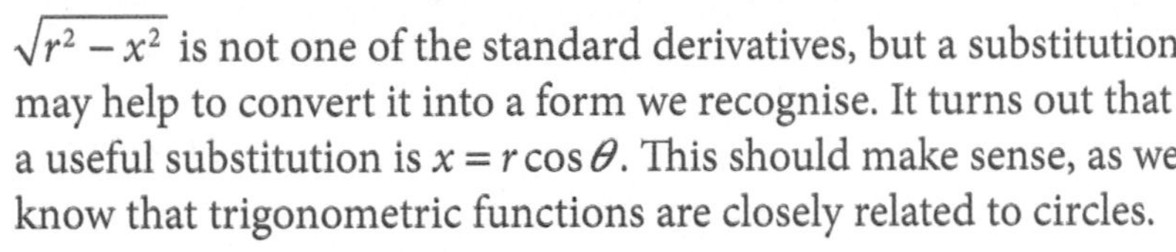

EXAM HINT

If you have to integrate a function like this in the exam, i.e. one that is not standard you will be given the substitution to use or a hint.

$\sqrt{r^2 - x^2}$ is not one of the standard derivatives, but a substitution may help to convert it into a form we recognise. It turns out that a useful substitution is $x = r\cos\theta$. This should make sense, as we know that trigonometric functions are closely related to circles.

Now we can carry out the integration.

Write down the integral to be evaluated.

The area of the top half of the circle is

$$\frac{A}{2} = \int_{-r}^{r} \sqrt{r^2 - x^2}\, dx$$

State the method to be used.

Substitute $x = r\cos\theta$

Differentiate the substitution and rearrange.

$$\frac{dx}{d\theta} = -r\sin\theta$$

$$\therefore dx = -r\sin\theta\, d\theta$$

Express the function in terms of θ.

$$r^2 - x^2 = r^2 - (r\cos\theta)^2$$

$$= r^2(1 - \cos^2\theta) = r^2\sin^2\theta$$

Notice that $\sin\theta$ is positive on the top half of the circle.

$$\Rightarrow \sqrt{r^2 - x^2} = r\sin\theta$$

It will be easier for later calculations to transform the integration limits for x to limits in θ (so we will not need to change back to the x variable after doing the integration).

Limits:

when $x = -r$, $\cos\theta = -1$, so $\theta = \pi$

when $x = r$, $\cos\theta = 1$, so $\theta = 0$

Write the integral in terms of θ.

$$\frac{A}{2} = \int_{\pi}^{0} (r\sin\theta)(-r\sin\theta)\, d\theta$$

$$= -r^2 \int_{\pi}^{0} \sin^2\theta\, d\theta$$

Use a double angle identity to convert $\sin^2\theta$ to $\frac{1 - \cos 2\theta}{2}$, which is the sum of two standard derivatives.

$$= -r^2 \int_{\pi}^{0} \frac{1}{2} - \frac{1}{2}\cos 2\theta\, d\theta$$

$$= -r^2 \left[\frac{\theta}{2} - \frac{\sin 2\theta}{4}\right]_{\pi}^{0}$$

$$= -r^2 \left\{(0 - 0) - \left(\frac{\pi}{2} - \frac{\sin 2\pi}{4}\right)\right\}$$

$$= \frac{\pi r^2}{2}$$

Hence the area of the whole circle is $2 \times \frac{\pi r^2}{2} = \pi r^2$ as required.

Mixed examination practice 15

Short questions

1. Find the following integrals.

(a) $\int \frac{1}{1-3x}\, dx$

(b) $\int \frac{1}{(2x+3)^2}\, dx$ *[4 marks]*

2. Using the substitution $u = e^x + 1$ or otherwise, find the integral

$$\int \frac{e^x}{e^x + 1}\, dx$$ *[6 marks]*

3. Given that $\int_0^m \frac{dx}{3x+1} = 1$, calculate the value of m to 3 significant figures. *[6 marks]*

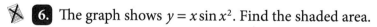

4. (a) Find the derivative of $x \ln x$.

(b) Hence find $\int \ln x \, dx$. *[5 marks]*

5. Find the volume formed when the graph of $\frac{1}{x}$ between $x = 1$ and $x = 2$ is rotated by 360° around the x-axis.

6. The graph shows $y = x \sin x^2$. Find the shaded area.

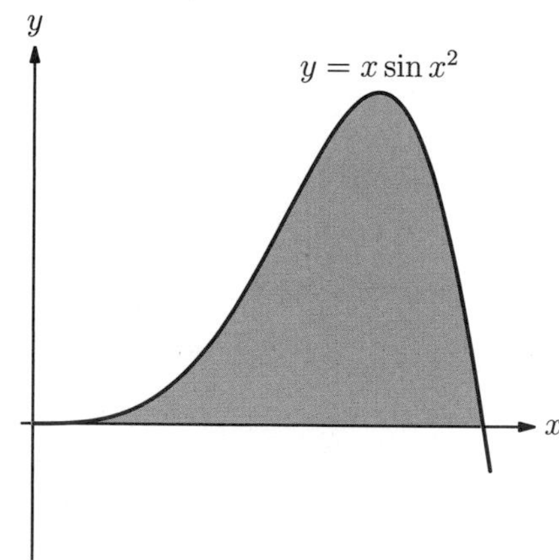

[7 marks]

7. The graph of $y = e^x$ between $x = 0$ and $x = a$ is rotated by 360° around the x-axis. The volume of the shape created is $\frac{3\pi}{2}$. Find the exact value of a. *[7 marks]*

8. (a) Show that $\frac{1}{x-2}+\frac{5}{(x-2)^2}=\frac{x+3}{(x-2)^2}$.

(b) Hence, find $\int \frac{x+3}{(x-2)^2}\,dx$. *[4 marks]*

9. Find $\int \frac{1}{x\ln x}\,dx$. *[6 marks]*

Long questions

1. Let $I=\int \frac{\sin x}{\sin x+\cos x}\,dx$ and $J=\int \frac{\cos x}{\sin x+\cos x}\,dx$.

(a) Find $I+J$.

(b) By using the substitution $u=\sin x+\cos x$, find $J-I$.

(c) Hence find $\int \frac{\sin x}{\sin x+\cos x}\,dx$. *[12 marks]*

2. (a) Show that $\cos^2\theta=\frac{1}{2}(1+\cos 2\theta)$.

(b) Hence find $\int \cos^2 x\,dx$.

(c) Find the exact value of $\int_0^{\pi}\cos^2(3x)\,dx$. *[12 marks]*

3. Amy does a bungee jump from a platform 50 m above a river. Let h be her height above the river, in metres, at a time t seconds after jumping. Her velocity is given by $v=2t^2-10t$.

(a) What is the initial acceleration that Amy experiences?

(b) At what time is Amy's velocity zero?

(c) How close to the river does Amy get?

(d) What distance does Amy travel in the first seven seconds?

(e) How long does it take for Amy to return to the platform? *[12 marks]*

16 Summarising data

In this chapter you will learn:

- different ways to measure the centre of data
- different ways to measure the spread of data
- how to work with data that has been summarised
- some useful ways of representing data
- the effects of constant changes to data
- how to describe the strength of a relationship between two variables
- to find the equation of the line of best fit for two variables.

Introductory problem

The magnetic dipole of an electron is measured three times in a very sensitive experiment. The values obtained are 2.000 0015, 2.000 0012 and 2.000 0009. Does this data support the theory that the magnetic dipole is 2?

Huge amounts of data are collected in scientific experiments and social surveys. This data in its raw state can be very difficult to interpret, so we often summarise the important features using statistics – individual numbers or diagrams that display some aspect of the data, such as where its centre lies or how spread out it is.

16A Measures of the centre of data

In everyday language the word *average* is often used without specifying whether it refers to the mean, median or mode. This can lead to some confusing newspaper headlines. In mathematics it is important to be precise.

What are the pros and cons of representing a complex set of data by a single number?

See Prior Learning section Y on the CD-ROM for how to find the mean, median and mode.

One of the things we very often want to know about a set of data is a single number that could represent the whole set. This value is called an *average*. There are several different types of average. For the International Baccalaureate® you need to know about three kinds: the mean, the median and the mode.

The **mean** is the value you get when you add up all the numbers in a set and divide by the number of items in the set. It is what is usually meant when people refer to an 'average'. If the numbers in the set are $x_1, x_2, \ldots$, then the mean is usually denoted by $\bar{x}$; sometimes it is also given the symbol μ.

Technically, this is the *arithmetic* mean. There are several other types of 'mean' – the geometric mean, the harmonic mean and the quadratic mean, to name a few. Each has many uses, and perhaps most interestingly, if all the numbers in the data set are positive, these means always come out in the same order: harmonic ≤ geometric ≤ arithmetic ≤ quadratic.

The **median** is the number you get when you put all the data in order and find the middle value. If there is not just one middle value, you take the mean of the two middle values.

The **mode** is the value that occurs most frequently in the data set. There can be no mode or more than one mode for a given set of data.

Why are there so many different averages? They all have advantages and disadvantages, and depending on the situation, one type may be more suitable than the others for representing the data.

Type of average	Advantage	Disadvantage
Mean	Takes into account all of the data values	Can be skewed by outliers
Median	Is not skewed by outliers	Does not take into account all of the data
Mode	Can be used for non-numeric data	Can take more than one value

Worked example 16.1

Wages in a factory are £3000, £5000, £10 000 and £150 000. Find the mean, median and mode. Why does the mean give an unrepresentative average?

The mean is the sum of all the data values divided by the number of data items.

$$\text{mean} = \frac{£3000 + £5000 + £10000 + £150\,000}{4}$$
$$= £42000$$

With 4 items, the median is the average of the second and third in the ordered list.

$$\text{median} = \frac{£5000 + £10000}{2}$$
$$= £7500$$

→

continued . . .

The mode is the most frequent value. 

There is no mode because all 4 values occur equally often.

The mean is unrepresentative because it is skewed by the extra-large value of £150 000 (an outlier).

EXAM HINT

You can use a calculator to find the mean and median of a set of data. See Calculator skills sheets 10 and 11 on the CD-ROM for how to do this. However, when the data set is small, you may find it faster to carry out the calculation by hand as above.

Exercise 16A

1. Find the mean, median and mode for the following sets of data.

   (a) (i) 19.0, 23.4, 36.2, 18.7, 15.7

   (ii) 0.4, −1.3, 7.9, 8.4, −9.4

   (b) (i) 28, 31, 54, 28, 17, 30

   (ii) 60, 18, 42, 113, 95, 23

2. Find the mean, median and mode for the following sets of data.

   (a) 15, 15, 34, 15, 34, 4

   (b) 3, −8, 6, −8, 14, 22

3. A newspaper headline says 'Half of children have below average intelligence'. Is such a statement always true?

4. For each of the following statements, decide whether it is always true, sometimes true or never true.

   (a) The median is smaller than the mean.

   (b) The median takes the value of one of the data items.

(c) The mean is a whole number.

(d) If all of the data items are whole numbers then so is the mean.

(e) If all of the data items are whole numbers then so is the mode.

(f) The mode is larger than the median.

(g) The mean is less than or equal to the maximum data value.

(h) There are the same number of data items with value below the median as above the median.

5. A sample of 14 measurements has a mean of 20.4, and another sample of 20 measurements has a mean of 16.8. Find the mean of all 34 measurements. *[5 marks]*

6. Jenny must sit four papers for an exam. The mean of the first three papers Jenny has sat is 72%.

(a) If she wants to get an overall mean of at least 75%, what is the lowest mark she can get in her fourth paper?

(b) What is the highest possible mean she can get over all four papers? *[6 marks]*

7. Five data items are as follows: $x, y, 1, 3, 10$

The mean is 5.4, and the median is 5. Find the values of x and y. *[5 marks]*

8. The table summarises the marks gained in a test by a group of students.

Mark	1	2	3	4	5
Number of students	5	10	p	6	2

The median mark is 3 and the mode is 2. Find the **two** possible values of p. *[6 marks]*

(*© IB Organization 2004*)

9. Amy and Bob are playing a computer game. Amy's average score on both level one and level two is higher than Bob's. Show that it is possible for Bob to still have a higher overall average across levels one and two.

The word *range* is used in several different contexts in mathematics, both technical and informal, and can have very different meanings. When talking about the range of a function, we mean the *set of values* which the function can output; the range of a data set, however, is a *single number* that represents the length of the interval in which the data values lie.

16B Measures of spread

Once we have a representative value for the centre of a data set, we may also be interested in how far away from this centre the other data values lie. This 'distance from the average' is called the spread (or dispersion) of the data, and, just as with the average, there are several different ways to measure the spread.

The simplest measure of spread is the **range**, which is the difference between the largest and smallest data values. The main disadvantage of the range is that it is extremely sensitive to outliers.

An improved measure that avoids the undue influence of outliers is the **interquartile range**, usually abbreviated IQR. Instead of taking the difference between the extreme values of the data, we arrange the data values in order and look at the difference between the data item one-quarter of the way up, called the **lower quartile** (abbreviated LQ or Q_1), and the data item three-quarters of the way up, called the **upper quartile** (UQ or Q_3). To find the quartiles Q_1 and Q_3 we split the ordered data into two halves, discarding the central item if there are an odd number of values, and then find the median of each half. In the same notation, the median of the whole data set can be called Q_2, the minimum value Q_0, and the maximum value Q_4.

KEY POINT 16.1

$$IQR = Q_3 - Q_1$$

As with the median, one disadvantage of the IQR is that it does not take into account all of the data. A commonly used measure that does use all the data values is the **standard deviation**, usually given the symbol σ. This measures the average distance of data items from the mean.

EXAM HINT

In the International Baccalaureate Standard Level Mathematics course, you will only be expected to find standard deviations using your calculator. See Calculator skills sheets 10 and 11 on the CD-ROM for instructions on how to do this.

EXAM HINT

Look carefully at whether a question is asking for standard deviation or variance.

The square of the standard deviation is called the **variance**. It is not a direct measure of spread, but in more advanced statistics it is a very convenient quantity to work with algebraically.

Worked example 16.2

Find the range, interquartile range and standard deviation of the following set of numbers:

1, 12, 9, 9, 15, 7, 5

Range = 15 − 1 = 14

Order the data and then split into halves. The number of values is odd, so omit the middle value.

Data in order:
1, 5, 7, [9], 9, 12, 15

LQ = 5, UQ = 12, so IQR = 12 − 5 = 7

Use GDC to find the standard deviation.

$\sigma = 4.23$ (3 SF)

As a rough guide, about two-thirds of the data will be less than one standard deviation away from the mean. In a large data set, nearly all of the values will be within two standard deviations from the mean, and any value more than three standard deviations from the mean would be very unusual.

Exercise 16B

1. For each set of data calculate the standard deviation and interquartile range.
   (a) (i) 19.0, 23.4, 36.2, 18.7, 15.7
       (ii) 0.4, −1.3, 7.9, 8.4, −9.4
   (b) (i) 28, 31, 54, 28, 17, 30
       (ii) 60, 18, 42, 113, 95, 23

2. Six people live in a house. They record their ages in whole years. The oldest is 32 and the youngest is 20. State whether each of the following statements is true, false or impossible to be sure. For cases where it is impossible to be sure, give an example for which the statement is true.
   (a) The range is greater than the mean.
   (b) The median is 26.
   (c) The mean is greater than 10.
   (d) The mean is greater than the mode
   (e) The median is not a whole number.

3. Find the interquartile range of the following set of data:
3, 4, 5, 5, 6, 8, 11, 13 *[3 marks]*

4. The ordered set of data 5, 5, 7, 8, 9, x, 13 has interquartile range equal to 7.
   (a) Find the value of x.
   (b) Find the standard deviation of the data set. *[5 marks]*

5. Three numbers a, b, c are such that $a < b < c$. The median is 12, the range is 12 and the mean is 14. Find the value of c. *[4 marks]*

16C Frequency tables and grouped data

It is very common to summarise large amounts of data in a frequency table. This is a list of all the values that the data items take, along with how often each value occurs. Given a frequency table, we could always expand it into a list of all the data values and then calculate the statistics discussed in sections 16A and 16B, but usually it is enough to just imagine writing out the whole list.

For example, suppose we are given the following data:

x	Frequency
1	2
2	5
3	3

We could write this out as a list:

$$\underbrace{1,1}_{\text{2 ones}},\ \overbrace{2,2,2,2,2}^{\text{5 twos}},\underbrace{3,3,3}_{\text{3 threes}}$$

From this list we could calculate statistics such as the mean and standard deviation as before. With large data sets, however, it would be impractical to write out the full list. Instead, to find the mean we use the fact that we would add up each data value as often as it occurs. This leads to the following formula.

KEY POINT 16.2

From a frequency table, $\bar{x} = \frac{\sum_{i=1}^{n} f_i x_i}{\sum_{i=1}^{n} f_i}$

where f_i is the frequency of the ith data value and $\sum_{i=1}^{n} f_i$, the sum of all the frequencies, is the total number of data items.

See section 6B for a reminder about $\sum$ notation.

Worked example 16.3

The numbers of passengers observed in cars passing a school are as follows:

Passengers	Frequency
0	32
1	16
2	2
3 or more	0

Find the median and mean number of passengers in each car.

There are 32 + 16 + 2 = 50 data items, so the median is the average of the 25th and 26th items. Both of these lie in the group corresponding to 0 passengers.

median = average of 25th and 26th numbers

so median = 0

For the mean, use the formula in Key point 16.2.

$$\bar{x} = \frac{(32\times 0)+(16\times 1)+(2\times 2)}{32+16+2}$$

$$= \frac{20}{50}$$

$$= 0.4$$

EXAM HINT

The mean does not have to be one of the data values, so do not round to the nearest whole number.

Data is often grouped because, even though some detail is lost, it is easier to get an overview of the data set. Would having the original data values necessarily be better?

So far we have been given the exact data values, but when dealing with **grouped data**, we no longer have this information. The simplest way of estimating the mean and standard deviation of grouped data is to assume that all the original data values in each group are located at the centre of the group, called the **mid-interval value**. To find the mid-interval value of a group, we take the mean of the largest and smallest possible values in the group, called the **upper and lower interval boundaries**. You can use your calculator to find the mean and standard deviation of grouped data by entering the mid-interval values for each group.

To find the median and interquartile range for grouped data you need to use cumulative frequency, which is covered in section 16D.

Worked example 16.4

Find the mean and standard deviation of the mass of eggs produced at a chicken farm. Explain why these answers are only estimates.

Mass of eggs (grams)	Frequency
[100,120[	26
[120,140[	52
[140,160[	84
[160,180[	60
[180,200[	12

Rewrite the table, replacing each group by the mid-interval value.

Midpoint	f_i
110	26
130	52
150	84
170	60
190	12

EXAM HINT

Any values that you have found which are not given in the question must be written down.

continued . . .

Use GDC to calculate the mean and standard deviation.

$\bar{x} = 148.3g$ (3 SF)
$\sigma = 21.2g$ (3 SF)

These answers are only estimates because we have assumed that all the data in each group is at the centre, rather than using the actual data values.

EXAM HINT

Whenever you find a mean or a standard deviation, it is always worth checking that the numbers make sense in the given context. For this data, an average of about 150g seems reasonable.

Exercise 16C

1. Calculate the mean, standard deviation and median for the given data sets.

(a)

x	Frequency
10	7
12	19
14	2
16	0
18	2

(b)

x	Frequency
0.1	16
0.2	15
0.3	12
0.4	9
0.5	8

2 A group is described as '17–20'. State the upper and lower boundaries of this group if the data is measuring:

(a) age in completed years

(b) number of pencils

(c) length of a worm to the nearest centimetre

(d) hourly earnings, rounded *up* to whole dollars.

3. Find the mean and standard deviation of each of the following sets of data.

(a) (i) x is the time taken to complete a puzzle in seconds.

x	Frequency
[0,15[	19
[15,30[	15
[30,45[	7
[45,60[	5
[60,90[	4

(ii) x is the weight of plants in grams.

x	Frequency
[50,100[	17
[100,200[	23
[200,300[	42
[300,500[	21
[500,1000[	5

(b) (i) x is the length of fossils found at a geological dig, rounded to the nearest centimetre.

x	Frequency
0 to 4	71
5 to 10	43
11 to 15	22
16 to 30	6

(ii) x is the power consumption of light bulbs, rounded to the nearest watt.

x	Frequency
90 to 95	17
96 to 100	23
101 to 105	42
106 to 110	21
111 to 120	5

(c) (i) x is the age of children in a hospital ward, in completed years.

x	Frequency
0 to 2	12
3 to 5	15
6 to 10	7
11 to 16	6
17 to 18	3

(ii) x is the amount of tip customers paid in a restaurant, rounded *down* to the nearest dollar.

x	Frequency
0 to 5	17
6 to 10	29
11 to 20	44
21 to 30	16
31 to 50	8

4. In a sample of 50 boxes of eggs, the number of broken eggs per box is shown in the table.

Number of broken eggs per box	0	1	2	3	4	5	6
Number of boxes	17	8	7	7	6	5	0

(a) Calculate the median number of broken eggs per box.

(b) Calculate the mean number of broken eggs per box.

[4 marks]

5. The mean of the data in the table is 12.6 and the range is 15. Find the values of p and q.

x	Frequency
5	6
10	p
15	$2p$
q	2

[4 marks]

6. The mean of the data in the table is 30.4 and the range is 20. Find the values of p and q.

x	Frequency
20	12
40	p
60	q

[3 marks]

16D Cumulative frequency

In the previous section we saw how to estimate the mean and standard deviation of grouped data. Now we move on to finding the median and quartiles. This is easiest if we represent the data in a new way, using a **cumulative frequency** table or diagram. Cumulative frequency is a count of the total number of data items *up to a certain value.*

Worked example 16.5

Convert the 'masses of eggs' table from Worked example 16.4 into a cumulative frequency table.

Here is the original table of grouped data.

Mass of eggs (grams)	Frequency
[100,120[	26
[120,140[	52
[140,160[	84
[160,180[	60
[180,200[	12

→

continued . . .

The first column of the cumulative frequency table consists of the upper boundaries of the data groups. The second column counts how many items there are up to that point.

Mass of eggs (grams)	Cumulative frequency
120	26
140	78
160	162
180	222
200	234

Once we have organised the data in cumulative frequency form, we can draw a cumulative frequency diagram. This is a graph with data values along the x-axis and cumulative frequencies along the y-axis. For the example above, we know that 26 eggs are under 120 g, 78 eggs are under 140 g, and so on. Therefore we plot the points (120, 26), (140, 78), etc. In other words, for grouped data, we plot the cumulative frequency against the upper bound of each group.

There is always an additional data point to be plotted, of the lowest lower bound and zero cumulative frequency.

Also, notice that besides the values in the cumulative frequency table of Worked example 16.5, there is another point we can plot: from the original data table we know that there are no eggs lighter than 100 g, so (100, 0) is the leftmost point in the diagram.

Worked example 16.6

Plot a cumulative frequency curve for the 'mass of eggs' data from Worked examples 16.4 and 16.5.

Plot the five points from the cumulative frequency table of Worked example 16.5, plus the additional point (100, 0), and join them up with an increasing curve.

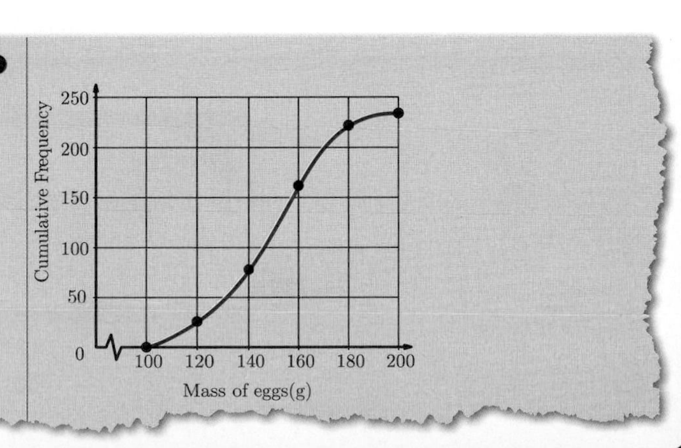

We can use the cumulative frequency graph to estimate the median and the quartiles. The median is the data value corresponding to the middle data item, so draw a horizontal line from the y-axis at *half* the total frequency (maximum y-value) until it meets the cumulative frequency curve, and then draw a vertical line down to the x-axis to obtain the median value.

To find the quartiles Q_1 and Q_3, the process is similar, except that the horizontal lines should be drawn at one-quarter and three-quarters of the total frequency.

Worked example 16.7

Find the median and interquartile range of the eggs data from Worked examples 16.4–16.6.

The total frequency is 234, so draw lines across from the y-axis at $0.5\times 234=117$ for the median, $0.25\times 234=58.5$ for the lower quartile, and $0.75\times 234=175.5$ for the upper quartile. Where these horizontal lines meet the cumulative frequency curve, draw vertical lines downward to the x-axis to find the values of the median and quartiles.

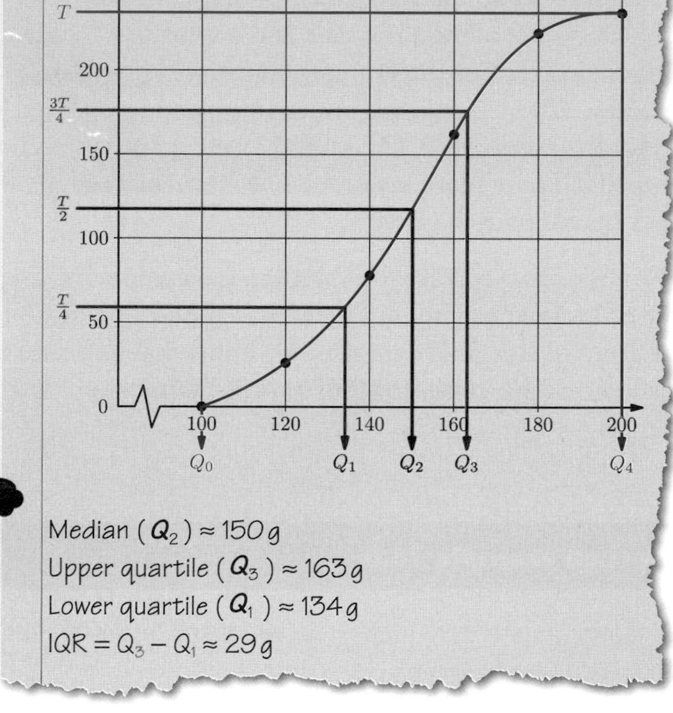

Read off the values on the x-axis for Q_1, Q_2 and Q_3.

Median (Q_2) ≈ 150 g
Upper quartile (Q_3) ≈ 163 g
Lower quartile (Q_1) ≈ 134 g
$\text{IQR} = Q_3 - Q_1 \approx 29$ g

EXAM HINT

Drawing in appropriate vertical and horizontal lines on cumulative frequency graphs can get you method marks in the exam even if the cumulative frequency graph itself is wrong.

The median and quartiles are specific examples of *percentiles*, which tell you the data value at a given percentage of the way through the data when the items are arranged in ascending order. The median is the 50th percentile and the lower quartile is the 25th percentile.

Worked example 16.8

(a) Find the 90th percentile of the mass of eggs from Worked examples 16.4–16.7.

(b) The top 10% of eggs are classed as 'extra large'. What range of masses corresponds to extra large?

The total frequency is 234, so draw a line across from the y-axis at $0.9 \times 234 \approx 211$. Where this horizontal line meets the cumulative frequency curve, draw a vertical line downward to the x-axis to find the 90th percentile.

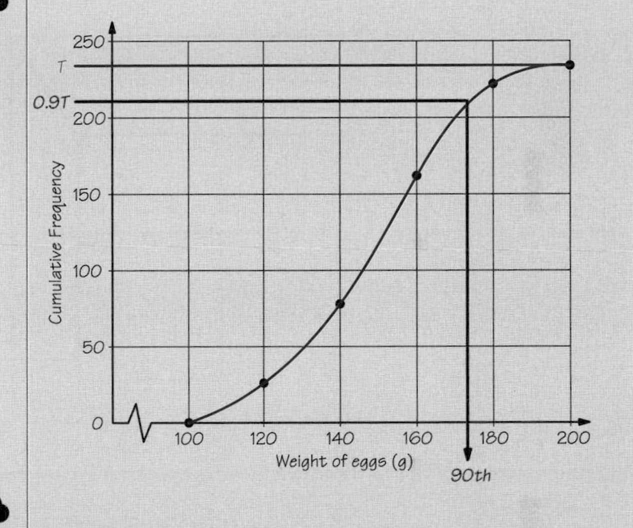

Read off the value on the x-axis.

(a) From the diagram the 90th percentile is approximately 173 g.

Top 10% means 90th percentile and above.

(b) Eggs with weights in the range [173, 200[are classified as extra large.

A useful way of visually representing the information in a cumulative frequency diagram is a **box and whisker plot**, which shows the median and lower and upper quartiles in a 'box', and the smallest and largest data values at the ends of 'whiskers'. The IQR is the length of the central box.

To obtain a box and whisker plot from a cumulative frequency graph, draw the same lines you would for finding the median and quartiles, but extend the vertical lines beyond the x-axis.

Worked example 16.9

Draw a box and whisker plot for the eggs data from Worked examples 16.4–16.8.

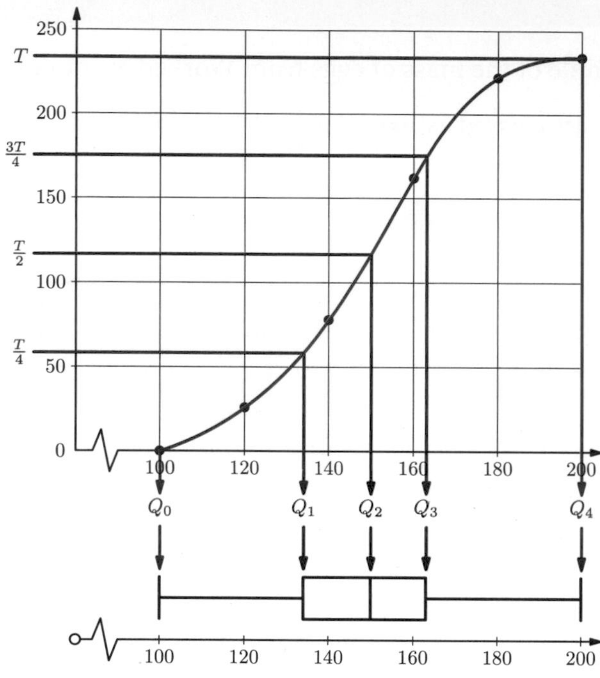

Since quartiles and the interquartile range are less influenced by extreme data values, they can be used to define such 'outliers'.

KEY POINT 16.3

An **outlier** is any data value that is more than 1.5 × IQR above the upper quartile or more than 1.5 × IQR below the lower quartile.

An outlier is usually marked with a cross on a box and whisker plot; the whiskers are ended at the most extreme data values that are not outliers.

So, for a data set with least value 12, lower quartile 24, median 40, upper quartile 50 and highest two values 87 and 102, the box and whisker, graph would be represented as shown below.

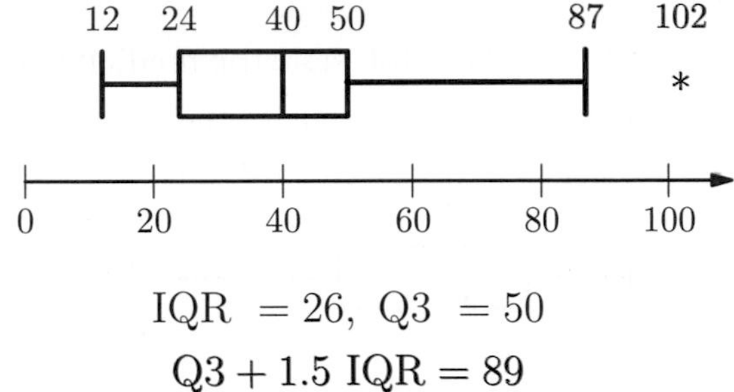

$$\text{IQR} = 26, \ \text{Q3} = 50$$

$$\text{Q3} + 1.5\ \text{IQR} = 89$$

End whisker at 87, label outlier 102 with $*$

Exercise 16D

1. Draw cumulative frequency diagrams for each of the data

   sets in Exercise 16C question 3. Hence estimate the median and the interquartile range.

2. For each of the data sets in question 1 (Exercise 16C question 3) draw a box and whisker plot.

3. 80 students were asked to solve a simple word puzzle, and the times they took, in seconds, were recorded. The results are shown in a cumulative frequency graph.
   (a) Estimate the median.
   (b) Estimate the interquartile range.
   (c) If the middle 50% of students took between c and d seconds to solve the puzzle, write down the values of c and d.

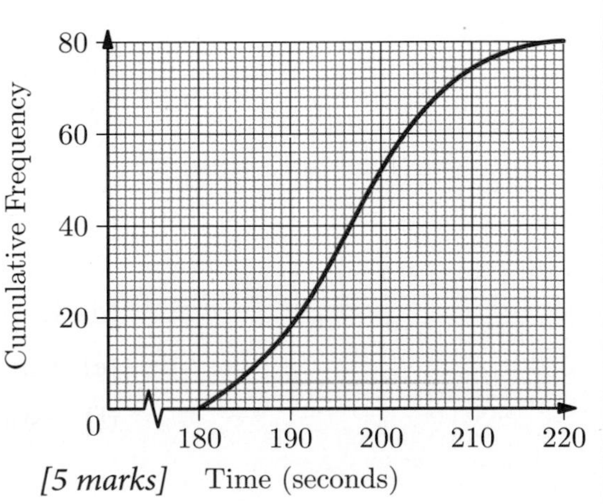

[5 marks]

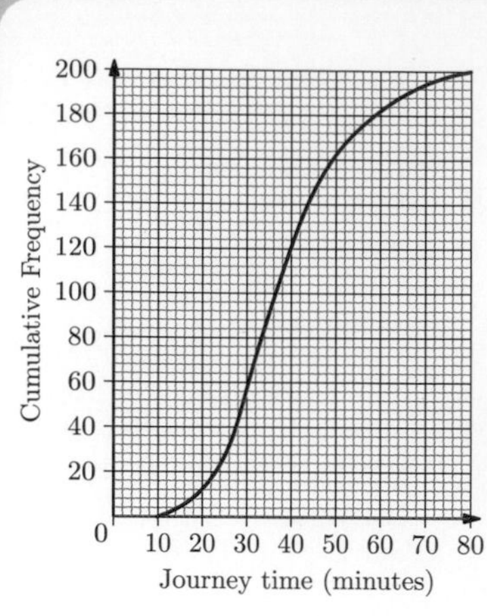

4. The cumulative frequency curve shows the amount of time 200 students spend travelling to school.

(a) Estimate the percentage of students who spend between 30 and 50 minutes travelling to school.

(b) If 80% of the students spend more than x minutes travelling to school, estimate the value of x. *[6 marks]*

5. From the box and whisker plot, state the median and interquartile range.

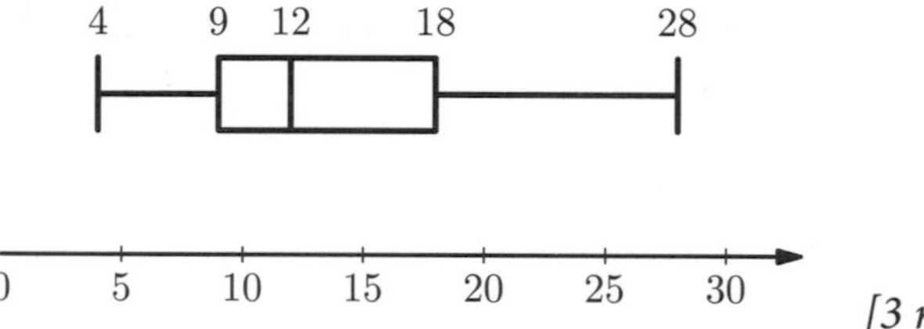

[3 marks]

6. The table summarises the number of pages in 200 books in a library.

No. pages	100–199	200–299	300–399	400–499	500–599	600–699	700–799
Frequency	12	36	42	53	33	20	4

(a) Estimate the mean number of pages.

(b) Fill in the following cumulative frequency table.

No. pages	199	299	399	499	599	699	799
Cumulative frequency	12	48					200

(c) On graph paper plot a cumulative frequency graph representing the data.

(d) Estimate the median of the data.

(e) Estimate the interquartile range of the data.

(f) Estimate the percentage of books with more than 450 pages. *[14 marks]*

16E Histograms

Another way of displaying data is to draw a histogram, which shows clearly how the data is distributed. At first sight a histogram may look just like a bar chart – in both types of diagram, the size of each bar represents the frequency. However, a bar chart is used for categorical or discrete data, and the width of the bars does not matter. A histogram, on the other hand, is used for continuous data (where data items may take any real value in a certain range); the axis along the bottom of the histogram represents a continuous interval of real numbers, and each bar is positioned over the entirety of the group to which it corresponds.

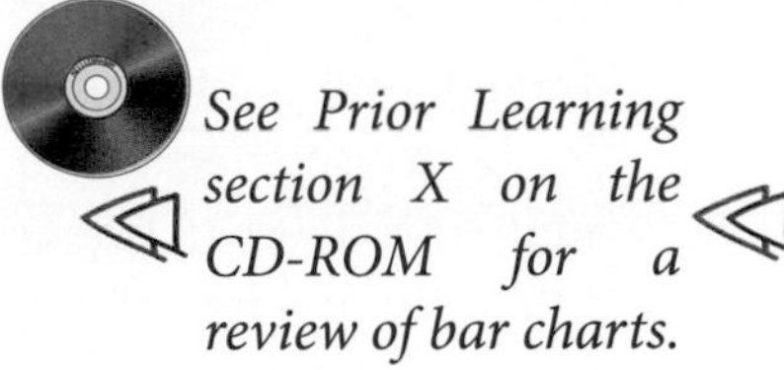

See Prior Learning section X on the CD-ROM for a review of bar charts.

Why are diagrams more useful than raw data? Statistical diagrams can be hugely informative, but they can also be very misleading. See if you can find some examples of misleading statistical diagrams. Are there any common features which lead you to a particular interpretation of the data?

Histograms can be drawn for grouped data where the groups are of unequal size. In this case, the area rather than the height of each bar represents the frequency associated with that group. You will not be expected to deal with this situation in the International Baccalaureate® course.

Worked example 16.10

Draw a histogram to represent the following data.

Length of arm (to the nearest cm)	Frequency
40–49	12
50–59	18
60–69	6
70–79	0
80–89	1

→

continued . . .

The left and right ends of each bar are positioned at the lower and upper interval boundaries. Since the measurements have been rounded to the nearest cm, the group '40–49' actually represents all data values in the interval [39.5, 49.5 [,so 39.5 and 49.5 determine the boundaries of the first bar. Similarly, the second bar has its boundaries at 49.5 and 59.5, and so on. The height of each bar is the frequency of the group.

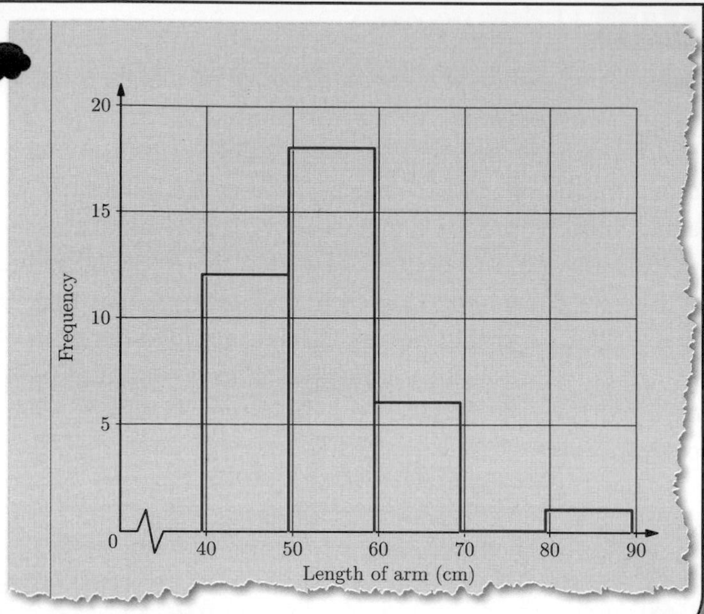

Exercise 16E

1. Draw histograms to represent the following data sets.

   (a) (i) x is the time taken to complete a puzzle, in seconds.

x	Frequency
[0, 15[	19
[15, 30[	15
[30, 45[	7
[45, 60[	5
[60, 75[	3
[75, 90[	1

   (ii) x is the birth weight of full-term babies in a delivery ward over the course of a week, in kilograms.

x	Frequency
[2.0, 2.5[	5
[2.5, 3.0[	49
[3.0, 3.5[	84
[3.5, 4.0[	63
[4.0, 4.5[	31
[4.5, 5.0[	9

(b) (i) x is the blood glucose level in a sample of 50 cats, to the nearest mmol l^{-1}.

x	Frequency
1 to 5	7
6 to 10	24
11 to 15	13
16 to 20	5
21 to 25	1

(ii) x is the power consumption of light bulbs, to the nearest watt.

x	Frequency
91 to 95	17
96 to 100	23
101 to 105	42
106 to 110	21
111 to 115	5

(c) (i) x is the age of teachers in a school.

x	Frequency
21 to 25	7
26 to 30	16
31 to 35	23
36 to 40	18
41 to 45	3
46 to 50	8

(ii) x is the total bill in a cafe, rounded up to the nearest dollar.

x	Frequency
1 to 10	16
11 to 20	21
21 to 30	43
31 to 40	26
41 to 50	8
51 to 60	2

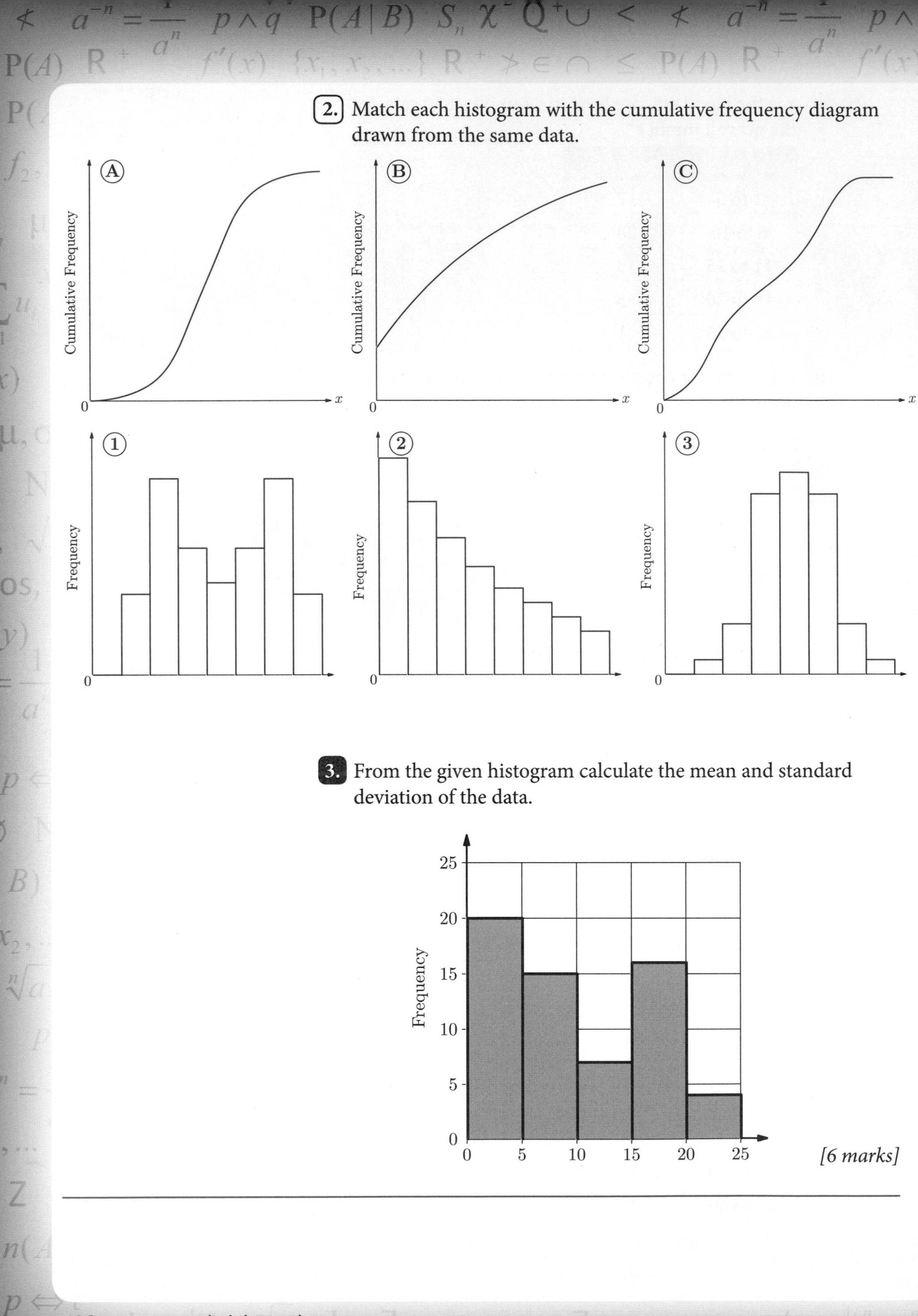

2. Match each histogram with the cumulative frequency diagram drawn from the same data.

3. From the given histogram calculate the mean and standard deviation of the data.

[6 marks]

16F Constant changes to data

Suppose you need to calculate the mean of the following data:

135408, 135409, 135405

You do not actually have to add up these values; you can just look at the last digit, since this is the only thing that differs between the items. The mean of 8, 9 and 4 is 7, so the mean of the data is 135407.

Effectively, what we have done is subtract 135400 from each of the data items, calculate the mean of the much smaller numbers and then add the 135400 back. This is a common trick for simplifying statistical calculations. It relies on the following fact.

KEY POINT 16.4

> If you increase (or decrease) every data item by the value x, all measures of the centre of the data will also increase (or decrease) by x.

Adding on the same quantity to every data item does not change how spread out the data is.

KEY POINT 16.5

> If you increase (or decrease) every data item by the value x, all measures of the spread of the data will remain unchanged.

What about the effects of multiplying or dividing all of the data by the same value?

KEY POINT 16.6

> If you multiply (or divide) every data item by the value x, all measures of the centre of the data will also be multiplied (or divided) by x.

KEY POINT 16.7

> If you multiply (or divide) every data item by the value x, all direct measures of the spread of the data will also be multiplied (or divided) by x.

Since standard deviation is multiplied by x, it follows that the variance will be multiplied by x^2.

Worked example 16.11

A taxi driver records the distance travelled per journey, d, in kilometres. The cost of each journey, c, is given by \$4 plus \$3 per km travelled. On one particular day the average distance travelled was 2.9 km, with a standard deviation of 1.1 km. Find the mean and standard deviation of the cost per journey on that day.

Express c in terms of d.

$c = 3d + 4$

The mean is transformed in the same way as each individual value in the data set.

$\bar{c} = 3\bar{d} + 4$
$= 3 \times 2.9 + 4$
$= 12.7$

The standard deviation is only affected by the multiplication.

$\sigma_c = 3\sigma_d$
$= 3 \times 1.1$
$= 3.3$

Exercise 16F

1. In each of the following situations find $\bar{y}$ and σ_y.
   - (a) (i) $y = x - 25$, $\bar{x} = 28$, $\sigma_x = 14$
     - (ii) $y = x + 5$, $\bar{x} = 12$, $\sigma_x = 3$
   - (b) (i) $y = 2x$, $\bar{x} = 9.3$, $\sigma_x = 2.4$
     - (ii) $y = \frac{x}{7}$, $\bar{x} = 49$, $\sigma_x = 14$
   - (c) (i) $y = 5x - 2$, $\bar{x} = 0$, $\sigma_x = 1$
     - (ii) $y = 3x + 7$, $\bar{x} = 9$, $\sigma_x = 10$
   - (d) (i) $y = 3(x - 2) + 1$, $\bar{x} = 4$, $\sigma_x = 4$
     - (ii) $y = 4(x + 1)$, $\bar{x} = 10$, $\sigma_x = 3$

2. In each of the following situations find the median and interquartile range of b.
   - (a) (i) a has median 2.3 and IQR 2.4; $b = a + 4$
     - (ii) a has median 7.1 and IQR 2; $b = a - 3$
   - (b) (i) a has median 9 and IQR 3; $b = 2.5a$
     - (ii) a has median 8 and IQR 6; $b = 1.2a$
   - (c) (i) a has median 22 and IQR 7; $b = 2.4a + 1.8$
     - (ii) a has median 10 and IQR 8; $b = 9a - 4$

3. Consider the data set $\{x-2, x, x+1, x+5\}$.

(a) Find the mean of this data set in terms of x.

Each number in the above data set is now decreased by 6.

(b) Find the mean of the new data set in terms of x. *[4 marks]*

4. In some countries the fuel efficiency of a car is measured in miles per gallon (mpg); in other countries it is measured in kilometres per litre (kpl). 1 mile per gallon is equivalent to 0.354 kilometres per litre. A certain make of car has a median efficiency of 32 mpg with variance 60 mpg^2. Find the median and variance of the efficiency in kilometres per litre. *[4 marks]*

5. A website gives the following instructions for converting temperatures in Celsius to temperatures in Fahrenheit:

Take the temperature in Celsius and multiply by 1.8.

Add 32.

The result is in degrees Fahrenheit.

(a) The mean temperature in a fridge is 4°C. Find the mean temperature in Fahrenheit.

(b) The interquartile range of the temperatures in the fridge is 2°F. Find the interquartile range of the temperature in Celsius. *[5 marks]*

6. The variable x has median 20 and interquartile range 10. The variable y is related to x by $y = ax - b$. Find the relationship between a and b so that the median of y equals the interquartile range of y. *[5 marks]*

7. Key point 16.7 assumes that x is positive. Investigate what happens when x is negative. Find a rule that works for all values of x.

16G Correlation

So far we have been focusing on one variable at a time, such as the mass of eggs or the time taken to complete a puzzle. Now we will look at two variables, represented by two data sets, and investigate whether there is a relationship between them. The two sets of data are collected such that from each individual source (a person, for example) we record two values, one for each variable (for example, age and mass). Data that comes in pairs in this fashion is said to be **bivariate**.

Two variables may be *independent*: knowing the value of one gives us no information about the other – for example, the IQ and house number of a randomly chosen person. Alternatively, there may be a fixed relationship between the variables: once we know the value of one, we can determine exactly the value of the other – for example, the length of a side of a cube and the volume of the cube. Usually, however, the situation is somewhere in between: if we know the value of one variable, we can make a better guess at the value of the other variable, but we cannot be absolutely certain – for example, the total mark achieved by a student in paper 1 of an examination and their mark in paper 2. Where the relationship between two variables lies on this spectrum from completely independent to totally deterministic is called the **correlation** of the two variables.

In this course we shall focus on *linear* correlation – the extent to which two variables X and Y are related by a relationship of the form $Y = mX + c$. If the gradient m of the linear relationship is positive, we say that the correlation is positive; if the gradient is negative, we describe the correlation as negative.

The relationship between two variables is best illustrated using a scatter diagram.

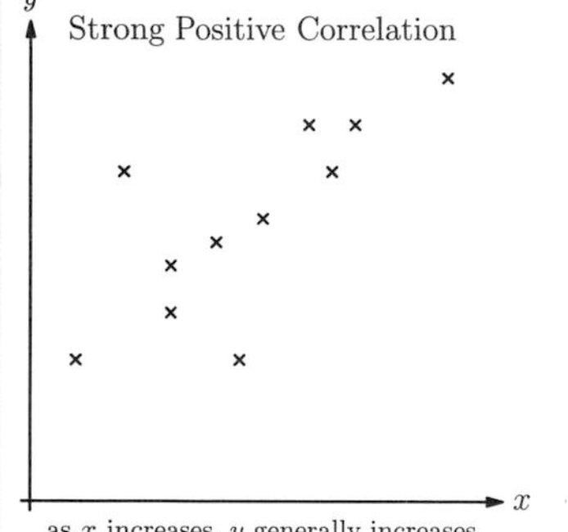

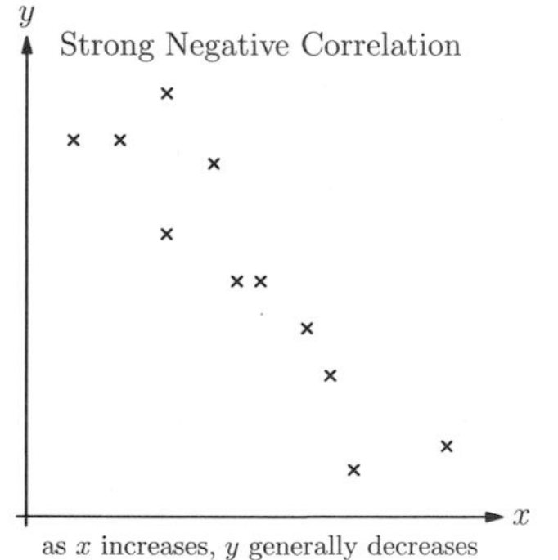

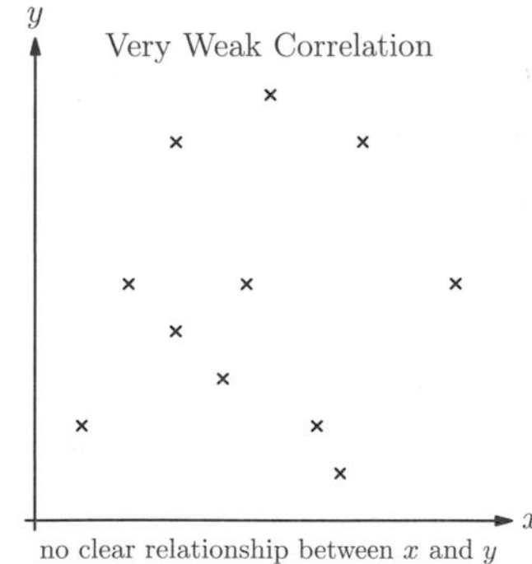

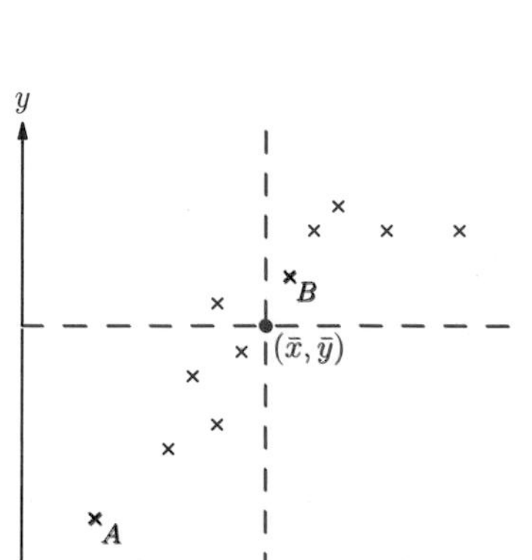

Rather than simply describing the relationship in words, we can try to find a numerical value to represent the linear correlation. The idea is to split a scatter diagram into quadrants around the mean point.

If there is a positive linear relationship, we would expect most of the data points to lie in quadrant 1 and quadrant 3. Points lying in those regions should increase our measure of correlation, while points lying in quadrants 2 and 4 should decrease the measure. We do not, however, want all points to be treated equally: point A seems to provide stronger evidence of a positive linear relationship than point B, so we would like it to count more.

KEY POINT 16.8

The **product–moment correlation coefficient**, usually denoted by r, is a measure of the strength of the relationship between two variables.

EXAMINERS' HINT

In the International Baccalaureate Standard Level Mathematics course, you will only be expected to find this coefficient using your calculator. See Calculator Skills sheet 14 on the CD-ROM for instructions.

r can take values between -1 and 1 inclusive. You need to know how to interpret the value of r that you find:

Value of r	Interpretation
$r \approx 1$	Strong positive linear correlation
$r \approx 0$	No linear correlation
$r \approx -1$	Strong negative linear correlation

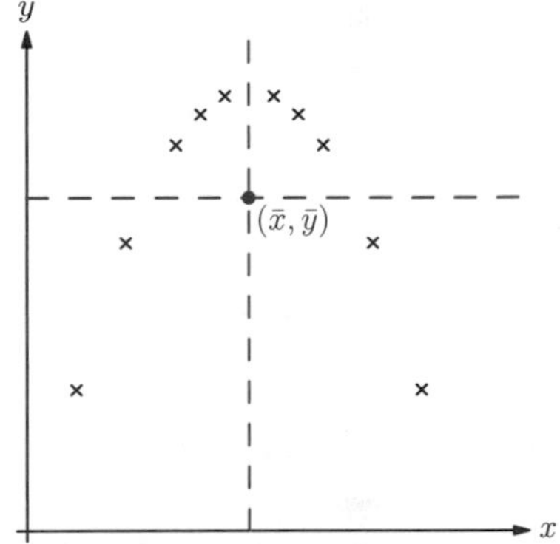

Just because $r = 0$ does not mean that there is no relationship between the two variables – only that there is no *linear* relationship. The graph alongside shows bivariate data with a correlation coefficient of zero, but clearly there is a relationship between the two variables.

While the product–moment correlation coefficient can provide a measure of correlation between two variables, it is important to realise that even when r is close to ± 1, a change in one variable does not necessarily cause a change in the other. The correlation might simply be due to coincidence or the influence of a third, hidden variable. For example, there may be a strong correlation between ice-cream sales and instances of drowning at a certain beach, but this does not imply that eating more ice cream leads to increased chances of drowning; rather, the hidden variable of temperature could cause both variables to rise.

There are actually many different measures of correlation. The r in Key point 16.8 is referred to as Pearson's product–moment correlation coefficient, or PPMCC.

Worked example 16.12

The following data were collected:

Score in a maths test (M)	Number of hours spent revising (R)
42	1.0
50	1.25
67	2.0
71	2.3
92	3.0

(a) Calculate the product–moment correlation coefficient.

(b) Interpret the value you found in part (a).

(a) From GDC, $r = 0.996$

The value is close to +1.

(b) This suggests a strong positive linear correlation between M and R.

Exercise 16G

1. Find the correlation coefficient for each of the following bivariate data sets.

   (a) (i) $(2,-5),(0,3),(8,12),(5,19),(4,10),(10,24)$

   (ii) $(1,0),(1,3),(2,6),(2,2),(4,4),(5,9)$

   (b) (i) $(3,15),(17,9),(22,10),(33,7)$

   (ii) $(22,50),(54,19),(100,0),(93,12)$

   (c) (i) $(-2,3),(0,0),(2,1),(3,5),(4,2)$

   (ii) $(5,1),(9,3),(7,-2),(8,8)$

   (d) (i) $(1,3),(2,5),(3,7),(5,11)$

   (ii) $(9,1),(4,6),(5,5),(11,-1)$

2. Match the scatter diagrams with the following values of r:

A : $r = 0.98$ B : $r = -0.34$ C : $r = -0.93$ D : $r = 0.58$

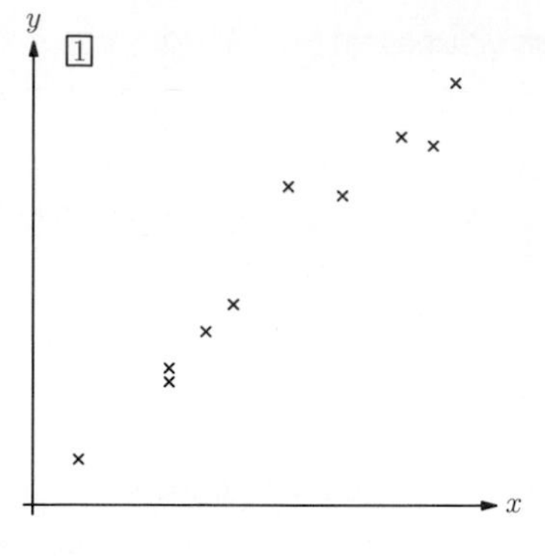
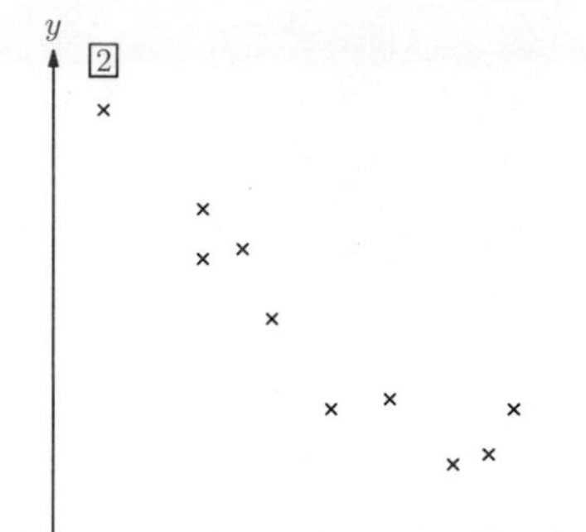
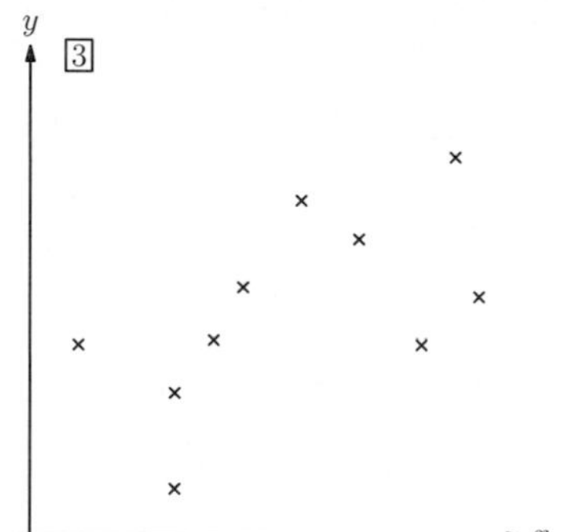
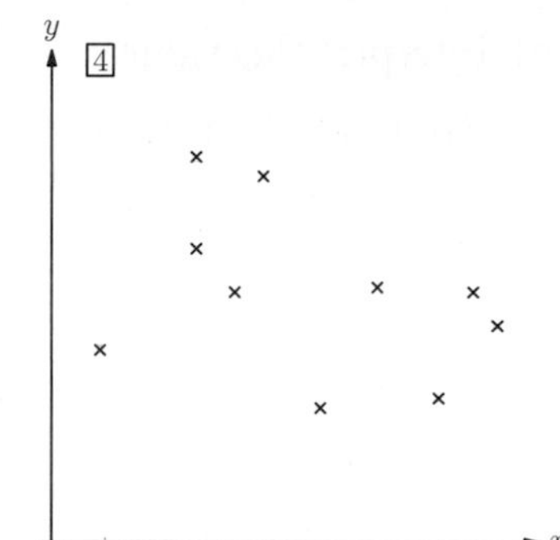

3. The following table gives data on life expectancy and average CPU speed of PCs over the past 20 years:

Year	Processor speed (Hz)	Life expectancy (months)
1990	6.6×10^7	74
1995	1.2×10^8	75
2000	1.0×10^9	77
2005	1.8×10^9	79
2010	2.4×10^9	80

(a) Calculate the correlation coefficient between processor speed and life expectancy.

(b) Interpret the value you found in (a).

(c) Does this result imply that CPU speed affects life expectancy? *[5 marks]*

4. A road safety group has tested the braking distance of cars of different ages.

Age in years	Braking distance in metres
3	31.3
6	38.6
7	40.1
7	35.1
9	48.4

(a) Find the correlation coefficient between a car's age and braking distance.

(b) Interpret this value.

(c) Farah says that this provides evidence that older cars tend to have longer stopping distances. State with a reason whether you agree with her. *[6 marks]*

5. The time spent in education and the income of six different 45-year-olds is recorded:

Years in education	Income ($)
12	64 000
14	31 000
14	36 000
18	54 000
18	62 000
20	48 000

(a) Find the correlation coefficient between these two variables.

(b) Gavin says that this provides evidence that spending more time in education means you will be paid more. State with two reasons whether you agree with him. *[5 marks]*

6. The following table shows the time taken for a chemical reaction to complete at different temperatures. The temperatures were recorded in both degrees Celsius and degrees Fahrenheit.

Temperature in °C (C)	Temperature in °F (f)	Time in seconds (t)
10	50	43
15	59	39
20	68	34
25	77	29
30	86	22
35	95	18
40	104	15

(a) Find the correlation coefficient between c and t.

(b) Find the correlation coefficient between f and t.

(c) Comment on your results in parts (a) and (b).

16H Linear regression

Suppose we have established that there is a linear relationship between two variables. We would then want to find the equation that best describes this relationship. To do this we use a method called *least-squares regression.*

If we assume that two variables X and Y are related by $Y = mX + c$, then for each x-value (i.e. data value for the X variable), we can measure the distance of the corresponding y-value from the line $Y = mX + c$.

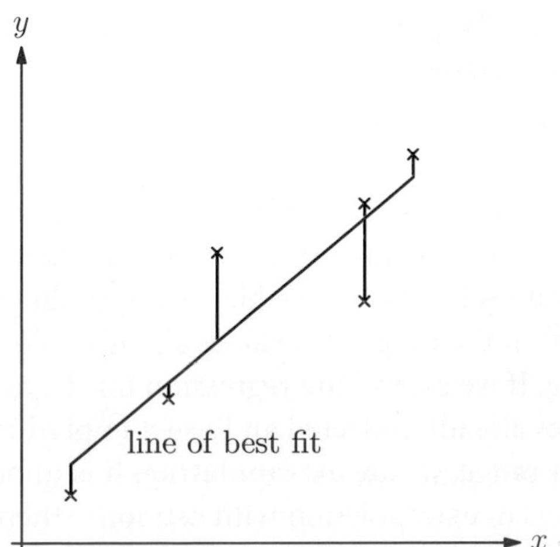

We could add up these distances and then try to minimise the total distance by varying the gradient and intercept of the line, but it turns out to be better to minimise the sum of the *squares* of these distances.

EXAM HINT

You may be asked whether a linear model is appropriate for a given set of bivariate data. In exam questions it will always be clear whether the correlation coefficient is strong enough to justify using a linear model (that is, r will be obviously close to or far away from ± 1).

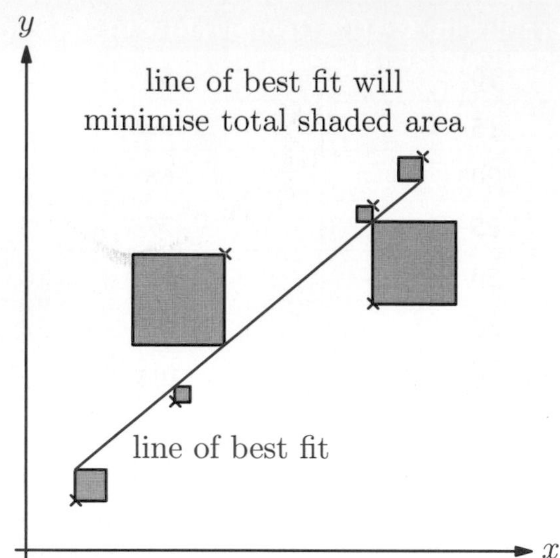

EXAM HINT
See Calculator skills sheet 14 on the CD-ROM for instructions.

To do this minimisation requires some fairly advanced calculus. Fortunately, as with the correlation coefficient r, you can use your calculator to obtain the equation of this **line of best fit**, also referred to as a **regression line**.

The line of best fit always passes through the mean point – the point with coordinates $(\overline{x}, \overline{y})$.

KEY POINT 16.9

> The variable to be plotted on the x-axis is called the **independent variable**; it is the variable that can be controlled by the experimenter.
>
> The variable to be plotted on the y-axis is known as the **dependent variable**.

Once you have found the line of best fit, you can use it to estimate values that are not among the data already collected. If we estimate values for the Y variable corresponding to values of X that are within the range of x-values already collected, we are **interpolating**. If we extend the regression line beyond the range of the x-values already collected and use it to predict a value of Y outside this range, we are **extrapolating**. It is important to treat the results of extrapolation with caution – there is no guarantee that the pattern will continue beyond the observed values.

Worked example 16.13

The following data were collected:

Score in a maths test (M)	Number of hours spent revising (R)
42	1.0
50	1.25
67	2.0
71	2.3
92	3.0

(a) Which is the independent and which is the dependent variable? Justify your answer.

(b) Find the equation of the regression line.

(a) Time spent revising is the independent variable, as it can be controlled. The score in the test is the dependent variable; we assume it can be affected by the time spent revising.

(b) From GDC: $M = 24.0R + 18.5$

Exercise 16H

1. Find the line of best fit for each of the following sets of bivariate data.

   (a) (i) $(2,-5),(0,3),(8,12),(5,19),(4,10),(10,24)$

   (ii) $(1,0),(1,3),(2,6),(2,2),(4,4),(5,9)$

   (b) (i) $(3,15),(17,9),(22,10),(33,7)$

   (ii) $(22,50),(54,19),(100,0),(93,12)$

   (c) (i) $(-2,3),(0,0),(2,1),(3,5),(4,2)$

   (ii) $(5,1),(9,3),(7,-2),(8,8)$

   (d) (i) $(1,3),(2,5),(3,7),(5,11)$

   (ii) $(9,1),(4,6),(5,5),(11,-1)$

2. In a restaurant, the regression line relating the number of calories, d, in a dessert and the quantity sold, n, is given by $n = 0.14d - 20$. The mean number of desserts sold is 36 and the median number of desserts sold is 32.

(a) Find the mean number of calories in a dessert, or state that it cannot be found.

(b) Find the median number of calories in a dessert, or state that it cannot be found. *[3 marks]*

3. The table shows the average speed v of cars passing positions d at 10 m intervals after a junction.

d (m)	v (km/hr)
10	12.3
20	17.6
30	21.4
40	23.4
50	25.7
60	26.3

(a) Find the correlation coefficient.

(b) State, with a reason, which is the independent variable.

(c) Using an appropriate regression line, find the value of v when $d = 45$.

(d) Explain why you cannot use your regression line to accurately estimate v when $d = 80$. *[9 marks]*

4. The following data gives the height h of a cake baked at different temperatures T.

T (°F)	h (cm)
300	16.4
320	17.3
340	18.1
360	16.2
380	15.1
400	14.8

(a) Find the correlation coefficient.

(b) State which variable is the independent variable.

(c) Find the regression line for this data.

(d) State two reasons why it would be inappropriate to use the regression line found in part (c) to estimate the temperature required to get a cake of height 20 cm. *[7 marks]*

5. State whether the following statements are true or false for bivariate data.

(a) If $r = 0$, there is no relationship between the two variables.

(b) If $Y = kX$, then $r = 1$.

(c) If $r < 0$, then the gradient of the line of best fit is negative.

(d) As r increases, so does the gradient of the line of best fit.

6. Data from an experiment is given in the following table:

x	y
−5	25
7	52
−6	35
−8	62
−4	13
−9	89
0	−3
−6	38

(a) Find the correlation coefficient for

(i) y and x

(ii) y and x^2

(b) Use least-squares regression to find a model for the data of the form $y = kx^2 + c$.

[7 marks]

Summary

- Measures of the *centre* of a data set include the **mean**, **median** and **mode**. The *spread* of the data values around the centre can be measured with the **range**, **interquartile range** ($\text{IQR} = Q_3 - Q_1$) or **standard deviation** (σ). The square of the standard deviation is called the **variance**. These values can all be worked out using your calculator for large data sets, or by hand for small data sets.
- To calculate the mean from a frequency table, see Key point 16.2.
- To estimate the mean and standard deviation of grouped data, we assume that every data item of a group is at the **mid-interval value** of the group, which is the mean of the upper and lower interval boundaries. The mid-interval value of each group is multiplied by the frequency in that group, and the mean and standard deviation can be worked out as normal using your calculator.
- **Histograms,** which are used for continuous data, provide a useful visual summary of data, giving an immediate impression of centre and spread.
- **Cumulative frequency** is a count of the total number of data items up to a certain value.
- Cumulative frequency diagrams involve plotting the cumulative frequency against the upper bound of each group as well as the leftmost point that represents a frequency of zero. These graphs are useful for finding the median, interquartile range and various percentiles, especially for grouped data. They also facilitate the construction of **box and whisker plots**, which are another good way of summarising data visually.

- If you increase (or decrease) every item in a data set by a value x, all measures of the centre of the data will also increase (or decrease) by x, while all measures of the spread of the data will remain unchanged.
- If you multiply (or divide) every item in a data set by a positive value x, all measures of the centre and all measures of the spread of the data will also be multiplied (or divided) by x.
- **Bivariate data** represents the paired measurements of two variables. The relationship, or correlation, between such variables can be visualised on a scatter diagram.
- The linear correlation is the extent to which two variables, X and Y, are related by a relationship of the form $Y = mX + c$. If m is positive, the correlation is also positive; if m is negative, so is the correlation. A numerical value to represent the linear correlation is the product-moment correlation coefficient.
- The **product-moment correlation coefficient** is a value between -1 and 1 which measures the strength of the linear relationship between two variables. 1 indicates a strong positive correlation.
- We can use least-squares regression to find the line equation of the **line of best fit** (or **regression line**) for the two variables. The line of best fit always passes through the mean point: $(\bar{x}, \bar{y})$
  - the x-variable is the **independent variable**; it is controlled
  - the y-variable is the **dependent variable**; its value depends on x.
- The line of best fit can be used to estimate data that is not among the collected data set:
  - **interpolating** is estimating Y from values of X within the range of the collected x-values
  - **extrapolating** is the process of extending the regression line beyond the range of collected x-values and using this to estimate the y-values; this is not very reliable because there is no guarantee that the pattern will continue beyond the observed values.

Introductory problem revisited

The magnetic dipole of an electron is measured three times in a very sensitive experiment. The values obtained are 2.000 0015, 2.000 0012 and 2.000 0009. Does this data support the theory that the magnetic dipole is 2?

From these three measurements, the mean magnetic dipole is 2.000 0012, which seems pretty close to 2. However, the standard deviation of the data is 0.000 000 245, so the mean is approximately 5 sample standard deviations away from 2. Therefore, within the natural variation observed, we cannot say with confidence that the magnetic dipole is 2.

The difference between 2.000 0012 and 2 may seem trivial, but it was what inspired Richard Feynman to create a new theory of physics called Quantum Electrodynamics, which did indeed predict this tiny difference from 2! This is an example of theory driving experiment, which in turn creates new theory – the interplay between theoretical mathematics and reality.

Mixed examination practice 16

Short questions

1. For the set of data

115, 108, 135, 122, 127, 140, 139, 111, 124

find:

(a) the interquartile range

(b) the mean

(c) the variance. *[7 marks]*

2. Four populations A, B, C and D are the same size and have the same range. Frequency histograms for the four populations are given below.

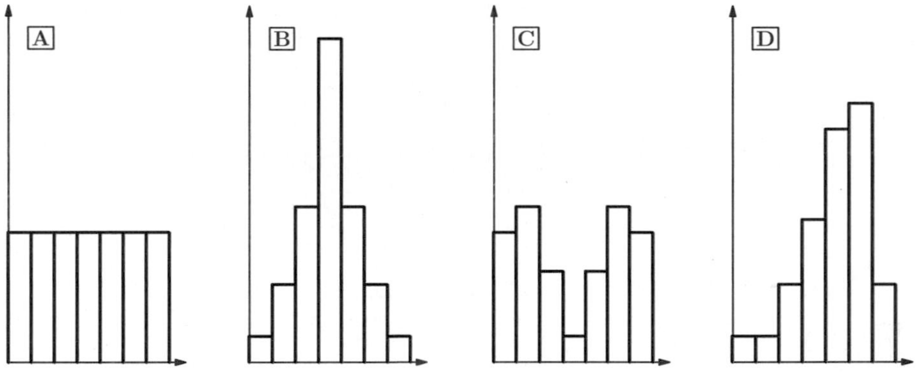

(a) Each of the three box and whisker plots shown corresponds to one of the four populations. Write the letter of the correct population for each of α, β and γ.

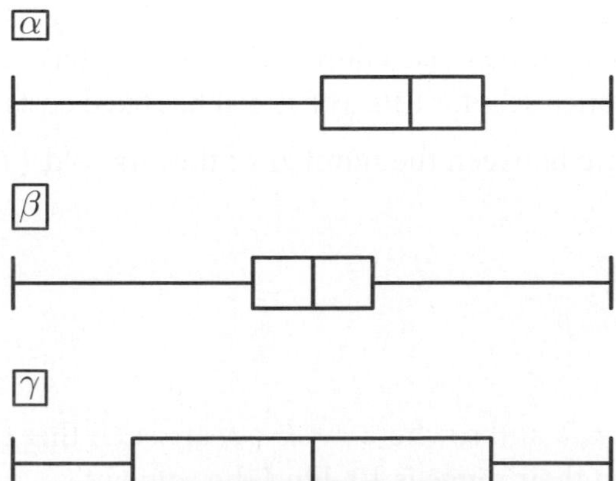

(b) Each of the three cumulative frequency diagrams below corresponds to one of the four populations. Write the letter of the correct population for each of (i), (ii) and (iii).

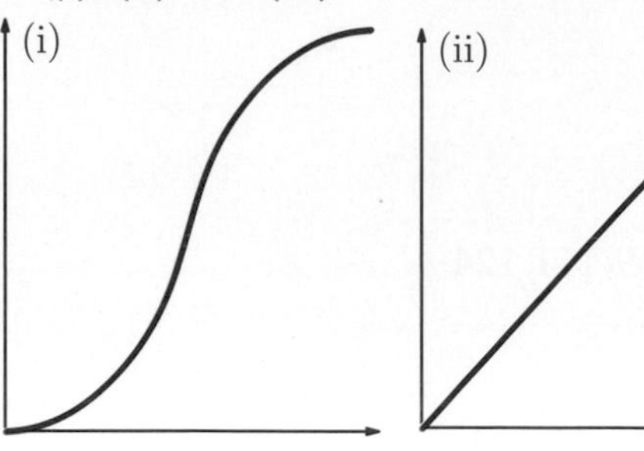

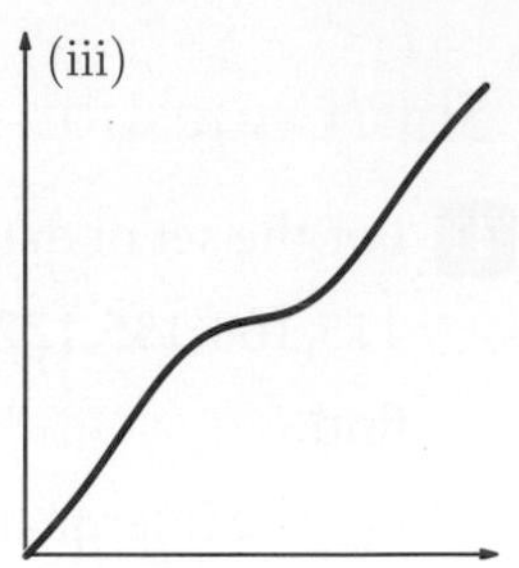

[6 marks]

(© IB Organization 2006)

3. A test marked out of 100 is taken by 800 students. The cumulative frequency graph for the marks is shown.

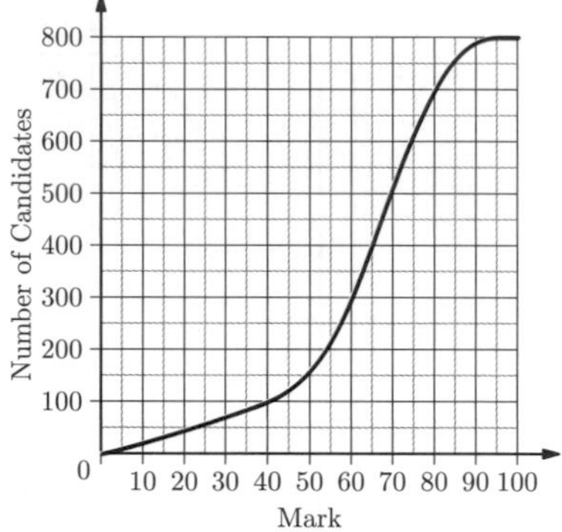

(a) Write down the number of students who scored 40 marks or less on the test.

(b) The middle 50% of test results lie between marks a and b, where $a<b$. Find a and b. *[6 marks]*

(© IB Organization 2005)

4. The number of bunches of flowers that a florist sells each day has a mean of 83 and a variance of 60. Each bunch sells for £10. The florist has fixed costs of £100 per day.

(a) Find the relationship between the number of flowers sold (f) and the profit made (p).

(b) Find the mean of p.

(c) Find the variance of p. *[6 marks]*

5. Three positive integers a, b and c, where $a < b < c$, are such that their median is 15, their mean is 13 and their range is 10. Find the value of c. *[6 marks]*

Long questions

1. The following is the cumulative frequency diagram for the heights of 30 plants given in centimetres.

   (a) Use the diagram to estimate the median height.

   (b) Complete the following frequency table.

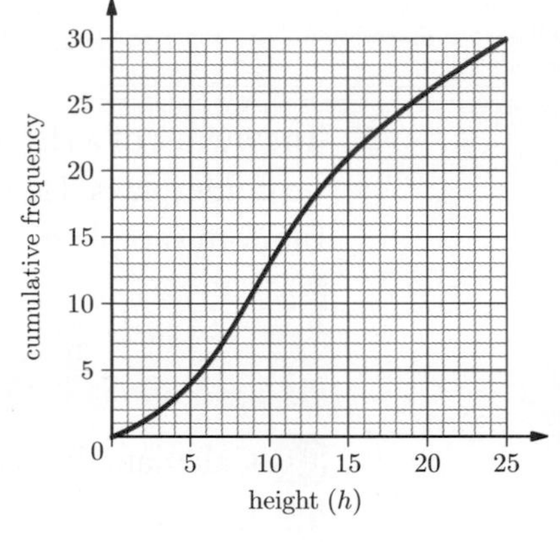

Height (h)	Frequency
$0 < h \leq 5$	4
$5 < h \leq 10$	9
$10 < h \leq 15$	
$15 < h \leq 20$	
$20 < h \leq 25$	

   (c) Hence estimate the mean height. *[8 marks]*

(*© IB Organization 2006*)

2. One thousand candidates sit an examination. The distribution of marks is shown in the following grouped frequency table.

Marks	1–10	11–20	21–30	31–40	41–50	51–60	61–70	71–80	81–90	91–100
Number of candidates	15	50	100	170	260	220	90	45	30	20

   (a) Copy and complete the following table, which presents the above data as a cumulative frequency distribution.

Mark	≤10	≤20	≤30	≤40	≤50	≤60	≤70	≤80	≤90	≤100
Number of candidates	15	65					905			

   (b) Draw a cumulative frequency graph of the distribution, using a scale of 1 cm for 100 candidates on the vertical axis and 1 cm for 10 marks on the horizontal axis.

   (c) Use your graph to answer parts (i)–(iii) below.

      (i) Find an estimate for the median score.

(ii) Candidates who scored less than 35 were required to retake the examination. How many candidates had to retake?

(iii) The highest-scoring 15% of candidates were awarded a distinction. Find the mark above which a distinction was awarded.

[16 marks]

(© IB Organization 1999)

3. The owner of a shop selling hats and gloves thinks that his sales are higher on colder days. He records the temperature and the value of goods sold on a random sample of 8 days:

Temperature (°C)	13	5	10	–2	10	7	–5	5
Sales (£)	345	450	370	812	683	380	662	412

(a) Calculate the correlation coefficient for the two sets of data.

(b) Suggest one other factor that might cause the sales to vary from day to day.

(c) Explain why temperature could be considered the independent variable.

(d) Find the equation of the regression line.

(e) Use this line to estimate the sales when the temperature is 0°C.

(f) Explain why it would not be appropriate to use the regression line to estimate sales when the temperature is –20°C. *[9 marks]*

4. A shopkeeper records the amount of ice cream sold on a summer's day along with the temperature at noon. He does this for several days, and gets the following results:

Temperature (°C)	Ice creams sold
26	41
29	51
30	72
24	23
23	29
19	12

(a) Find the correlation coefficient.

(b) By finding the equation of the appropriate regression line, estimate the number of ice creams that would be sold if the temperature were 25°C.

(c) Give two reasons why it would not be appropriate to use the regression line from part (b) to estimate the temperature on a day when no ice creams are sold. *[8 marks]*

17 Probability

In this chapter you will learn:

- how probability can be estimated from data
- how probability can be predicted theoretically
- how to work out probabilities when you are interested in more than one outcome
- how to work out the probability of a sequence of events occurring
- how to work out probabilities of simple functions of independent random events
- how being given additional information changes our estimate of a probability.

Introductory problem

A woman gives birth to non-identical twins. One of them is a girl. What is the probability that the other one is a girl?

In real life we often deal with uncertain events, but not all events are equally uncertain. It is not certain that the next Steven Spielberg film will be a big hit, nor is it certain that it will snow in India next summer. However, intuitively, these two events are not equally likely. We can put events on a scale with impossible at one end and certain at the other. To indicate where an event lies on this scale, we assign it a number between 0 and 1; this number is called the **probability** of the event.

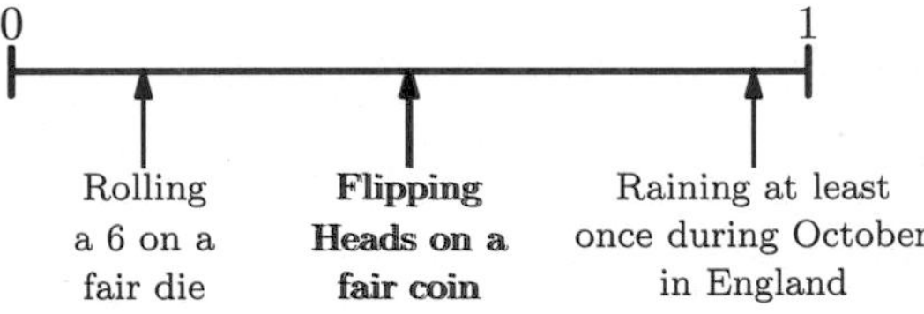

For the concept of probability to be useful, it must be more than just a reflection of past experience. We also have to be able to predict probabilities of events in the future, and use these predictions to make decisions. This is the focus of this chapter.

Probability is one of the most recent additions to the field of mathematics. It was formalised by the French mathematician Pierre de Fermat (1601–1655) in response to a request from his patron, the Chevalier de Méré, a notorious gambler who wanted help at the gambling table.

17A Empirical probability

In this section we shall look at how we can use data to estimate the probability of an event occurring. A probability that is estimated from observations is called *empirical* or *experimental probability*.

Out of 291 240 births in Australia in 2009, there were 4444 multiple births (twins, triplets, etc.). The fraction of multiple births is $\frac{4444}{291240}$ or about 0.015; this is an estimate of the probability of a pregnancy being a multiple birth in Australia.

KEY POINT 17.1

The probability of an event A occurring is denoted by $P(A)$.

From observation, we can estimate $P(A)$ as:

$$P(A) = \frac{\text{number of times } A \text{ occurs}}{\text{number of times } A \text{ could have occurred}}$$

Notice that, according to this definition, $P(A)$ must be between 0 and 1 inclusive.

We can turn this idea around or, in other words, use a rearranged form of the equation: if we are given a probability and the number of times the event could have occurred, we can estimate how many times we think that the event might occur.

Worked example 17.1

A six-sided die is rolled 200 times and a '6' comes up 40 times.

(a) Use this data to estimate the probability of rolling a '6'.

(b) Suppose the die is rolled a further 35 times. Assuming that the probability remains the same, estimate the number of '6's that would occur.

Use the formula in Key point 17.1.

(a) $P(6) = \frac{40}{200} = \frac{1}{5}$

Rearrange the formula.

(b) Expected number of '6's that occur

$= \text{number of attempts} \times P(6)$

$= 35 \times \frac{1}{5}$

$= 7$

Suppose that in part (b) of the above example, the first seven outcomes were all '6'. Would we then expect to get no more '6's in the next 28 rolls? This idea, though tempting, is incorrect: the outcome of the first 7 rolls does not affect the remaining rolls. This misconception illustrates how a conflict between language and logic can sometimes lead to incorrect conclusions; it is so famous that it has been given a special name – the Gambler's Fallacy.

Exercise 17A

1. In this question, give your answers correct to three significant figures.

   (a) (i) 600 boxes of cereal are opened and 400 contain plastic toys. Estimate the probability that a randomly opened box contains a plastic toy.

   (ii) 2000 people are surveyed and 300 say that they will vote for the Green party in an upcoming election. Estimate the probability that a randomly chosen voter will vote for the Green party.

   (b) (i) In a board game some cards are drawn: 4 of the cards give positive effects and 3 of them give negative effects. Estimate the probability that a randomly chosen card gives a positive effect.

   (ii) While practising basketball free throws, Brian scores 12 and misses 18. Estimate the probability that Brian scores in his next attempt.

   (c) (i) From a large bag of marbles several are drawn: 3 are red, 6 are blue and 5 are green. Estimate the probability that the next randomly drawn marble is blue.

   (ii) Yuna picked 20 DVDs randomly from her collection: 12 were comedy, 6 were action and the remainder were documentaries. Estimate the probability that another randomly chosen DVD from her collection is a documentary.

2. (a) The probability of getting a heart when a card is drawn from a normal pack of cards is $\frac{1}{4}$. If 20 cards are chosen with replacement (i.e. put back into the pack each time), how many hearts would you expect to draw?

   (b) A cancer drug shows a positive effect within one year in 15% of cases. If 500 cancer patients are put on a trial of the drug, how many would you expect to show a positive effect in one year?

3. In one clinical trial a drug was found to have a positive effect in 18 out of 20 cases. A larger study was then conducted, in which the drug showed a positive effect in 68 cases, a negative effect in 10 cases and no effect in 30 cases. Based on all the available evidence, estimate the probability that in a randomly chosen patient the drug will have a positive effect. *[3 marks]*

4. Two independent studies examined the number of light bulbs that last over 100 hours. In the first study, 40% of light bulbs passed the test. In the second study, 60% of light bulbs passed the test. Is it true that if the studies are combined, it will be shown that 50% of light bulbs pass the test? Justify your answer.

17B Theoretical probability

We can always estimate the probability of an event empirically by performing an experiment repeatedly, but in some situations it is possible to predict the probability *before* doing any experiments. To do this we need to be able to make a list of all possible outcomes, called the **sample space**.

For example, when you toss a coin, there are two possible outcomes: heads and tails. Since the two are equally likely, the probability of each must be one half. This leads to the theoretical definition of probability.

There are two possible outcomes if you enter a lottery: either you win or you don't win. But this does not mean that the probability of winning is one half, because there is no reason to believe that the outcomes are *equally likely*. Many mistakes in probability come from making such an erroneous assumption.

KEY POINT 17.2

$$\mathrm{P}(A) = \frac{\text{number of times } A \text{ occurs in the sample space}}{\text{number of items in the sample space}}$$

In the formula booklet:

$$\mathrm{P}(A) = \frac{n(A)}{n(U)}$$

This definition again ensures that $0 \le \mathrm{P}(A) \le 1$. It also gives the following interpretation to $\mathrm{P}(A)$: if $\mathrm{P}(A) = 0$, the event A is impossible; if $\mathrm{P}(A) = 1$, the event A is certain; as $\mathrm{P}(A)$ rises, the likelihood of A occurring increases.

You might consider it obvious that the definitions of empirical and theoretical probability are equivalent. However, this is quite tricky to prove. If you would like to see how it is done, do some research on the 'law of large numbers'.

Worked example 17.2

(a) For a family with two children, list the sample space for the sexes of the children, assuming no twins.

(b) Hence find the theoretical probability that the two children are a boy and a girl.

A systematic way to list the possibilities is to make a table.

EXAM HINT

Although the 'boy first, girl second' and 'girl first, boy second' cases can be described as a 'boy and a girl', we must remember to count them separately in the sample space.

(a)

First child	Second Child
Boy	Boy
Boy	Girl
Girl	Boy
Girl	Girl

There are four outcomes, two of which consist of a boy and a girl.

(b) $P(\text{a boy and a girl}) = \frac{2}{4} = \frac{1}{2}$

When the sample space is more complicated, it is important to list the possible outcomes in a systematic way, so that you do not miss any. For example, consider a board game in which players face a penalty whenever the sum of two rolled dice is 7. It does not matter how the 7 is achieved – it may be from a 1 and a 6, or a 3 and a 4, among other possibilities. In this situation it helps to make a probability grid diagram, in which you list each possibility of the first die on one axis, each possibility of the second die on the other axis, and the result of interest (the sum of numbers on the dice) in each cell of the grid.

EXAM HINT

Expressions such as 'fair die' and 'fair coin' mean that all possible outcomes of rolling the die (singular for dice) or tossing the coin are equally likely.

Worked example 17.3

What is the probability of getting a sum of 7 when two fair dice are rolled?

Draw a probability grid diagram showing all possible totals when two dice are rolled.

EXAM HINT

Notice that a '3' on die A and a '1' on die B has to be counted as a separate outcome from a '1' on die A and a '3' on die B. However, a '3' on die A and a '3' on die B is only one outcome. This often causes confusion.

		Die A					
		1	2	3	4	5	6
Die B	1	2	3	4	5	6	7
	2	3	4	5	6	7	8
	3	4	5	6	7	8	9
	4	5	6	7	8	9	10
	5	6	7	8	9	10	11
	6	7	8	9	10	11	12

→

continued . . .

Count how many items are in the sample space.

36 items in the sample space, each of equal probability.

Count how many sums of 7 there are.

6 sums of 7, therefore the probability of getting a sum of 7 is

$$\frac{6}{36}=\frac{1}{6}$$

Saying that an event either happens or does not happen is called the 'law of the excluded middle', and it is a basic axiom of standard logic. However, there is an alternative logical system called 'fuzzy logic', where an event could be in a state of 'maybe happening'. Fuzzy logic is used in a philosophical physics problem called 'Schrödinger's cat', and also has many real-world applications.

An event either happens or does not happen. Everything other than the event happening is called the **complement** of the event. For example, the complement of rolling a 6 on a die is rolling a 1, 2, 3, 4 or 5. The complement of event A is denoted by A'.

An event and its complement are said to be *mutually exclusive*, which means that they cannot both happen. We also know that one of the two must happen, so they have a total probability of 1. From this we can deduce a formula linking the probability of an event and the probability of its complement.

KEY POINT 17.3

$$\mathrm{P}(A)+\mathrm{P}(A')=1$$

This looks like a simple and trivial formula, but it can be really useful in simplifying probability calculations, because there are many situations in which the probability of the complement of an event is much easier to find than the probability of the event itself. The next example illustrates one such case.

Worked example 17.4

Two fair dice are rolled. What is the probability that the sum of the scores is greater than 2?

The sum of the scores must be at least 2, and we can get a total of 2 in just one way, so it is easier to find this probability first, which is the probability of the complement of the required event.

Let A be the event 'the sum of the scores is greater than 2'.
Then A' is the event 'the sum of the scores is 2'.
The total number of possible outcomes is 36.

continued . . .

Out of those, only (1, 1) has sum 2.

$\therefore P(A') = \frac{1}{36}$

Use $P(A)+P(A')=1$.

$P(A) = 1 - P(A') = \frac{35}{36}$

Often we are interested in more complicated events, such as 'today is Tuesday *and* it is raining' or 'getting an A in Extended Essay *or* TOK'. When describing such combined events we need to be very clear about the meaning of the words used. The word 'and' indicates that the desired outcome is *both* of the component events happening.

In everyday language the word 'or' is used ambiguously. If you say 'Peter is a doctor or a lawyer', you generally do not mean that he could be both. However, in a game, if you say 'I win if I get a black number or an even number', you would expect to win if you got a black even number. In probability we use the word 'or' in the second sense: 'A or B' means A or B *or both* happening.

In the next two sections we will see how the probability of a combined event is related to the probabilities of the individual events.

Worked example 17.5

When a die is rolled, find the probability that the outcome is

(a) odd *and* a prime number

(b) odd *or* a prime number.

List the sample space.

Possible outcomes: 1, 2, 3, 4, 5, 6

List the outcomes that satisfy *both* of the given conditions.

(a) Odd and prime: 3, 5

Probability $= \frac{2}{6} = \frac{1}{3}$

List the outcomes that satisfy *one or both* of the conditions.

(b) Odd or prime: 1, 2, 3, 5

Probability $= \frac{4}{6} = \frac{2}{3}$

Exercise 17B

1. List the sample space for each of the following:
   (a) a fair six-sided die
   (b) rearrangements of the word RED
   (c) the sexes of three children in a family
   (d) a six-sided die with three sides labelled 1 and the remaining sides labelled 2, 3 and 4.

2. In a standard pack of 52 playing cards there are four different suits (red hearts, red diamonds, black clubs and black spades). Each suit consists of number cards from 2 to 10 and four 'picture cards': jack, queen, king and ace. Find the probability that a randomly chosen card is
   (a) (i) red (ii) a spade
   (b) (i) a jack (ii) a picture card
   (c) (i) a black number card (ii) a club picture card
   (d) (i) not a heart (ii) not a picture card
   (e) (i) a club or a picture card (ii) a red card or a number card
   (f) (i) a red number card strictly between 3 and 9
   (ii) a picture card that is not a jack

3. A bag contains marbles of three different colours: six are red, four are blue and five are yellow. One marble is taken from the bag. Calculate the probability that it is
   (a) (i) red (ii) yellow
   (b) (i) not blue (ii) not red
   (c) (i) blue or yellow (ii) red or blue
   (d) (i) green (ii) not green
   (e) (i) neither red nor yellow (ii) neither yellow nor blue
   (f) (i) red or green (ii) neither blue nor green
   (g) (i) red and green (ii) red and blue

4. By means of an example, show that $\mathrm{P}(A)+\mathrm{P}(B)=1$ does not mean that B is the complement of A.

5. Two fair six-sided dice numbered 1 to 6 are rolled. By drawing probability grid diagrams, find the probability that
   (a) the sum is 8
   (b) the product is greater than or equal to 8
   (c) the product is 24 or 12
   (d) the maximum value is 4
   (e) the larger value is more than twice the other value
   (f) the value on the first die divided by the value on the second die is a whole number.

6. A fair four-sided die (numbered 1 to 4) and a fair eight-sided die (numbered 1 to 8) are rolled. Find the probability that
   (a) the sum is 8
   (b) the product is greater than or equal to 8
   (c) the product is 24 or 12
   (d) the maximum value is 4
   (e) the larger value is more than twice the other value
   (f) the value on the eight-sided die divided by the value on the four-sided die is a whole number.

7. Two fair six-sided dice are thrown, and the score is the highest common factor of the two outcomes. If this were done 180 times, how many times would you expect the score to be 1? *[5 marks]*

8. Three fair six-sided dice are thrown, and the score is the sum of the three results. What is the probability that the score is less than 6? *[5 marks]*

17C Combined events and Venn diagrams

In this section we shall generalise the sample space method to efficiently calculate probabilities of combined events.

Which is more likely when you roll a die once:

- getting a prime number *and* an odd number
- getting a prime number *or* an odd number?

The first possibility is more restrictive – we have to satisfy both conditions. For the second, we can satisfy either condition, so it must be more likely.

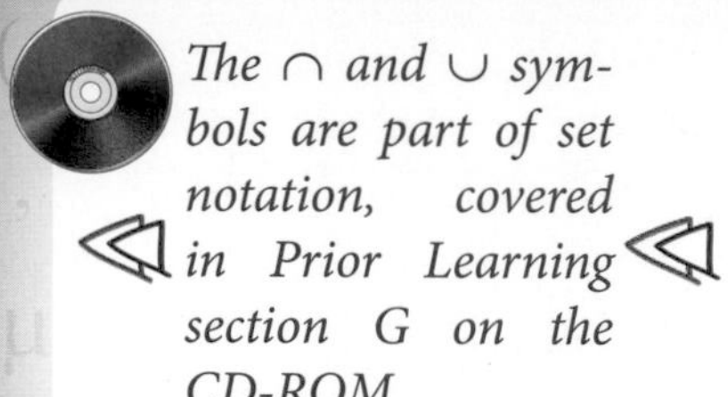

The $\cap$ and $\cup$ symbols are part of set notation, covered in Prior Learning section G on the CD-ROM.

The 'and' and 'or' are two of the most common ways of combining events, known respectively as 'intersection' and 'union' in mathematical language. These are given the following symbols:

$A \cap B$ is the **intersection** of A and B, meaning that *both* A *and* B happen.

$A \cup B$ is the **union** of A and B, meaning that *either* A happens, *or* B happens, *or both* happen.

If you have neither apples nor pears, then you have no apples *and* no pears. In set notation this can be written as $(A \cup B)' = A' \cap B'$. This is one of De Morgan's laws – a description of the algebraic rules obeyed by sets and hence events in probability.

Why do mathematicians use complicated words such as 'union' and 'intersection'? One reason is that everyday language can be ambiguous. If I say that I play football or hockey, some people will take this to mean that I do not play both. Mathematicians hate ambiguity.

See Prior Learning section J on the CD-ROM for explanation of Venn diagrams.

We can use **Venn diagrams** to illustrate the concepts of union and intersection:

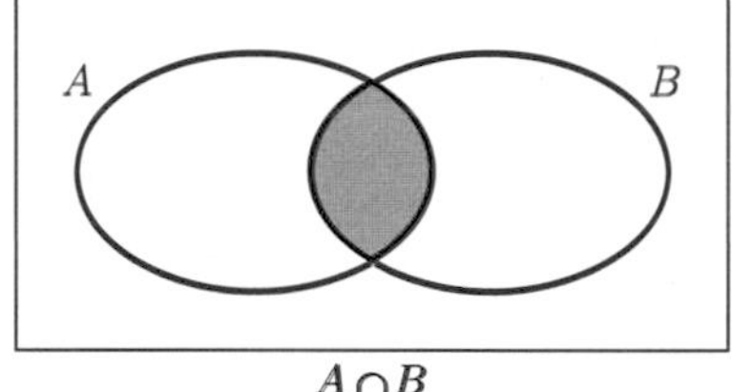

$A \cap B$

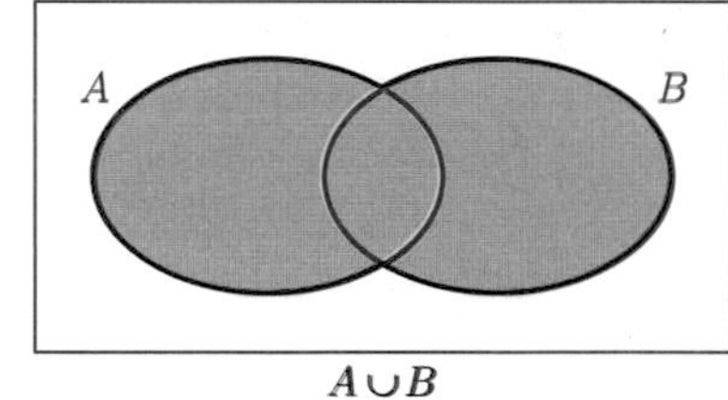

$A \cup B$

Venn diagrams can help us calculate the probability of the union of two events. The diagrams below show that the union of two sets which have some overlap can be viewed as the sum of the two separate sets minus the region of overlap.

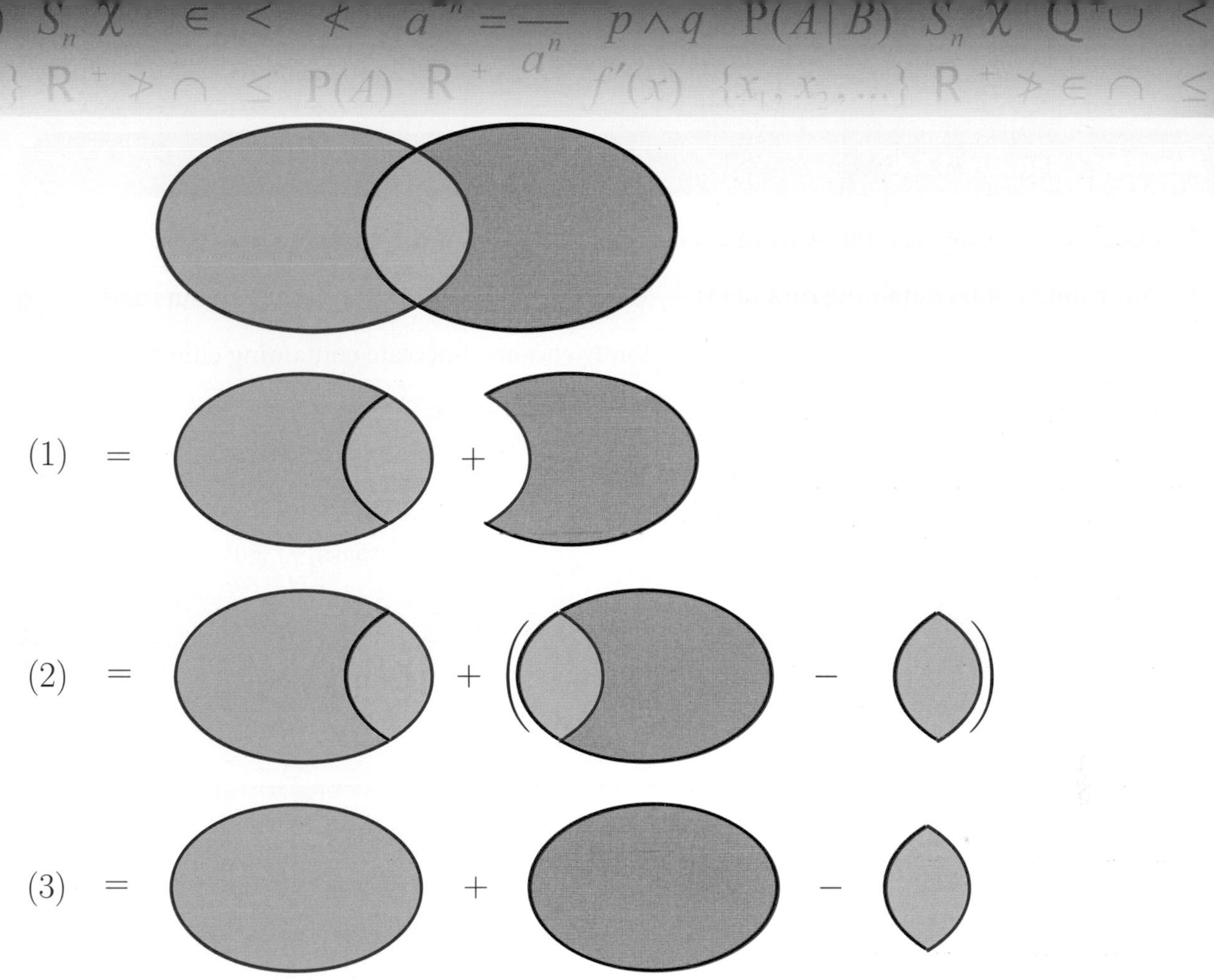

This gives a very important formula.

KEY POINT 17.4

$$P(A \cup B) = P(A) + P(B) - P(A \cap B)$$

In section 17B we already met one example of mutually exclusive events: A and its complement A′.

Essentially, this formula is saying that if you want to count the number of ways of getting A or B, count the number of ways of getting A and add to that the number of ways of getting B; however, the number of ways of getting *A and B* would have been counted twice, so we compensate by subtracting it.

If there is no possibility of A and B occurring at the same time, then $P(A \cap B) = 0$. These events are said to be *mutually exclusive*, and in this case the formula reduces to $P(A \cup B) = P(A) + P(B)$.

EXAM HINT

Be careful that you do not use this formula for mutually exclusive events *unless* you are sure that the events cannot both occur at the same time.

Worked example 17.6

A chocolate is selected randomly from a box. The probability of it containing nuts is $\frac{1}{4}$. The probability of it containing caramel is $\frac{1}{3}$. The probability of it containing both nuts and caramel is $\frac{1}{6}$. What is the probability of a randomly chosen chocolate containing either nuts or caramel or both?

The event we are interested in is 'nuts ∪ caramel', so we can use the formula from Key point 17.4.

P(nuts ∪ caramel)
$= \text{P(nuts)} + \text{P(caramel)} - \text{P(nuts} \cap \text{caramel)}$
$= \frac{1}{4} + \frac{1}{3} - \frac{1}{6}$
$= \frac{5}{12}$

Exercise 17C

1. (a) (i) $\text{P}(A)=0.4$, $\text{P}(B)=0.3$ and $\text{P}(A\cap B)=0.2$. Find $\text{P}(A\cup B)$.

   (ii) $\text{P}(A)=\frac{3}{10}$, $\text{P}(B)=\frac{4}{5}$ and $\text{P}(A\cap B)=\frac{1}{10}$. Find $\text{P}(A\cup B)$.

   (b) (i) $\text{P}(A)=\frac{2}{3}$, $\text{P}(B)=\frac{1}{8}$ and $\text{P}(A\cup B)=\frac{5}{8}$. Find $\text{P}(A\cap B)$.

   (ii) $\text{P}(A)=0.2$, $\text{P}(B)=0.1$ and $\text{P}(A\cup B)=0.25$. Find $\text{P}(A\cap B)$.

   (c) (i) $\text{P}(A\cap B)=20\%$, $\text{P}(A\cup B)=0.4$ and $\text{P}(A)=\frac{1}{3}$. Find $\text{P}(B)$.

   (ii) $\text{P}(A\cup B)=1$, $\text{P}(A\cap B)=0$ and $\text{P}(B)=0.8$. Find $\text{P}(A)$.

   (d) (i) Find $\text{P}(A\cup B)$ if $\text{P}(A)=0.4$, $\text{P}(B)=0.3$ and A and B are mutually exclusive.

   (ii) Find $\text{P}(A\cup B)$ if $\text{P}(A)=0.1$, $\text{P}(B)=0.01$ and A and B are mutually exclusive.

2. (a) (i) When a fruit pie is selected at random, $\text{P(it contains pears)} = \frac{1}{5}$ and $\text{P(it contains apples)} = \frac{1}{4}$. 10% of the pies contain both apples and pears. What is the probability that a randomly selected pie contains apples or pears?

(ii) In a library, 80% of books are classed as fiction and 70% are classed as 20th century. Half of the books are 20th-century fiction. What proportion of the books are fiction or from the 20th century?

(b) (i) 25% of students in a school play football or tennis. The probability of a randomly chosen student playing football is $\frac{3}{5}$, and the probability that they play tennis is $\frac{5}{8}$. What percentage of students play both football and tennis?

(ii) Two in five people at a school study Spanish, and one in three study French. Half of the school study French or Spanish. What fraction study both French and Spanish?

(c) (i) 90% of students in a school have a Facebook account, and three out of five have a Twitter account. One-twentieth of students have neither a Facebook account nor a Twitter account. What percentage of students are on both Facebook and Twitter?

(ii) 25% of teams in a football league have French players and a third have Italian players. 60% have neither French nor Italian players. What percentage have both French and Italian players?

3. Simplify the following expressions where possible.

(a) $\text{P}(x > 2 \cap x > 4)$

(b) $\text{P}(y \leq 3 \cup y < 2)$

(c) $\text{P}(a < 3 \cap a > 4)$

(d) $\text{P}(a < 5 \cup a \geq 0)$

(e) $\text{P(apple} \cup \text{fruit)}$

(f) $\text{P(apple} \cap \text{fruit)}$

(g) $\text{P(multiple of 4} \cap \text{multiple of 2)}$

(h) $\text{P(square} \cup \text{rectangle)}$

(i) $\text{P(blue} \cap \text{(blue} \cup \text{red))}$

(j) $\text{P(blue} \cap \text{(blue} \cap \text{red))}$

4. In a survey, 60% of people are in favour of a new primary school and 85% are in favour of a new library. Half of all those surveyed would like both a new primary school and a new library. What percentage supported neither a new library nor a new primary school? *[5 marks]*

5. If $P(A) = 0.2$, $P(A \cap B) = 0.1$ and $P(A \cup B) = 0.7$ find $P(B')$. *[5 marks]*

6. Events A and B satisfy $P((A \cup B)') = 0.2$ and $P(A) = P(B) = 0.5$. Find $P(A \cap B')$. *[5 marks]*

7. An integer is chosen at random from the first one thousand positive integers. Find the probability that the integer chosen is

(a) a multiple of 6

(b) a multiple of *both* 6 and 8. *[5 marks]*

17D Tree diagrams and finding intersections

Venn diagrams have given us a useful formula connecting the intersection and union of two events. However, they are not of much help in calculating the probability of an intersection or union by itself. Another method – tree diagrams – is more useful for doing this.

When several events happen, either in succession or simultaneously, a tree diagram displays all the possible combinations of outcomes. It starts out with branches representing all the possible outcomes for one of the events; then from each branch we draw further branches that represent all possible outcomes for the next event. Along each branch we write the probability of taking that branch. Tree diagrams have an advantage over the sample space method as they can accommodate outcomes that are not equally likely.

The following is an example of a tree diagram, showing meal combinations at a school.

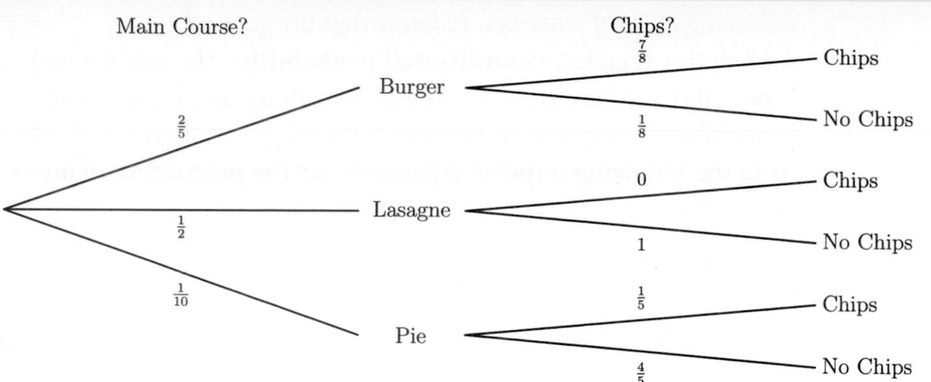

We can think of there being a filtering process at each branching point. Consider 100 days of school food. On $\frac{2}{5}$ of these days (i.e. 40 days) there will be burgers. On $\frac{7}{8}$ of these burger days there will also be chips. So overall there will be 35 days out of the 100 that have both burgers and chips, equivalent to a probability of $\frac{7}{20}$.

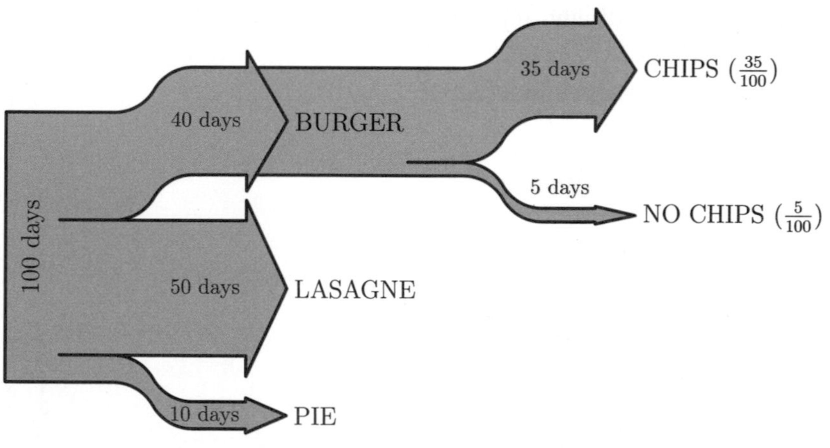

To find the probability of getting to each branch tip at the far right of the diagram, we calculate a fraction of a fraction; in other words, we multiply the probabilities on the branches we travelled along to reach that branch tip. What do these two probabilities represent in our burger and chips example? Clearly the $\frac{2}{5}$ represents the probability of getting burgers, and it might be tempting to say that the $\frac{7}{8}$ is the probability of getting chips – but this is not true. If we complete the filtering diagram above, we will see that chips are served on 37 out of 100 days, and this is certainly not $\frac{7}{8}$. Rather, the $\frac{7}{8}$ represents the probability of having chips *if you already know* that burgers are being served; this is called a **conditional probability**. The conditional probability in this case is written P(chips|burgers), read as 'the probability of chips given burgers'. Tree diagrams therefore lead us to the following important formula for the probability of an intersection of two events.

KEY POINT 17.5

$$P(A \cap B) = P(A)P(B|A)$$

Worked example 17.7

If I revise, there is an 80% chance I will pass the test; but if I do not revise, there is only a 30% chance of passing. I revise for ¾ of tests. What proportion of tests can I expect to pass?

EXAM HINT

This question uses the words 'chance' and 'proportion'. These are just other ways of referring to probability. Try not to get put off by unusually worded questions.

Decide which of the given probabilities is not conditional. Start the tree diagram with this event. Since the probability of passing the test is conditional on revision, the revision branches should come first.

Add the conditional event: passing or not passing the test.

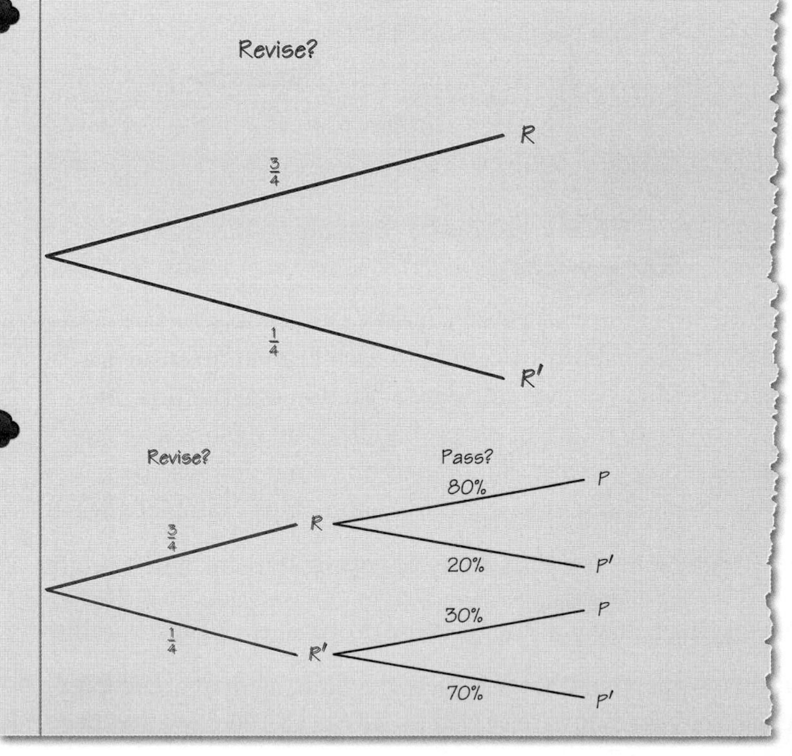

continued . . .

Identify which branch sequences result in passing the test.

Multiply the probabilities along each branch sequence to find the probability at the end.

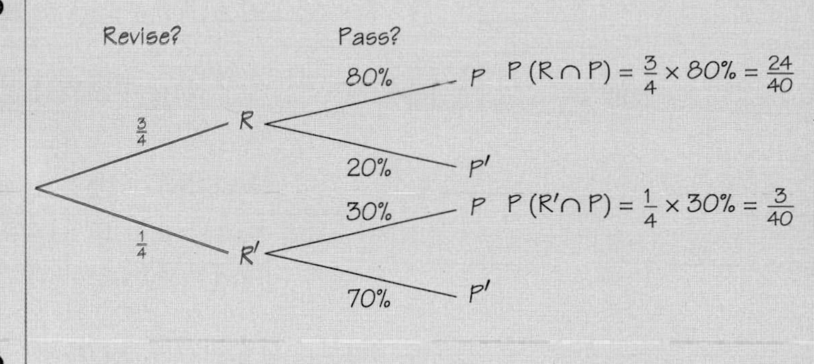

Add up the end probabilities associated with passing the test.

$$P(\text{passing}) = P(\text{revising} \cap \text{passing}) + P(\text{not revising} \cap \text{passing})$$

$$= \frac{24}{40} + \frac{3}{40}$$

$$= \frac{27}{40}$$

EXAM HINT

Frequently, when a question says to find the probability of 'at least ...' or 'at most ...', looking at the complement is a good idea.

As we saw in section 17B, sometimes the probability we are asked for may be quite difficult to find directly, but the probability of its complement is much easier to work out.

Worked example 17.8

Find the probability of getting at least one head when you toss four fair coins.

We could draw a tree diagram, find the probabilities of getting 1, 2, 3 or 4 heads, and add them up. But it is easier to look at the complement – getting 0 heads (all tails).

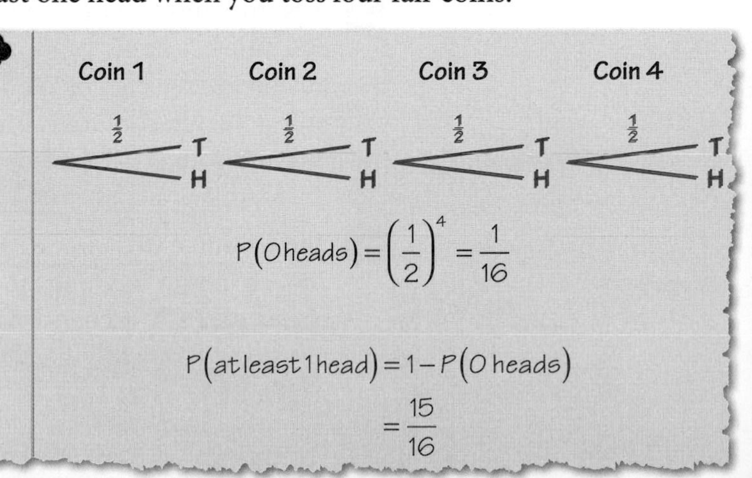

$$P(0\,\text{heads}) = \left(\frac{1}{2}\right)^4 = \frac{1}{16}$$

$$P(\text{at least 1 head}) = 1 - P(0\,\text{heads})$$

$$= \frac{15}{16}$$

Exercise 17D

1. (a) (i) $P(A) = 0.4$ and $P(B|A) = 0.3$. Find $P(A \cap B)$.

   (ii) $P(X) = \frac{3}{5}$ and $P(Y|X) = 0$. Find $P(X \cap Y)$.

   (b) (i) $P(A) = 0.3$, $P(B) = 0.2$ and $P(B|A) = 0.8$. Find $P(A \cap B)$.

   (ii) $P(A) = 0.4$, $P(B) = 0.8$ and $P(A|B) = 0.3$. Find $P(A \cap B)$.

   (c) (i) $P(A) = \frac{2}{5}$, $P(B) = \frac{1}{3}$ and $P(A|B) = \frac{1}{4}$. Find $P(A \cup B)$.

   (ii) $P(A) = \frac{3}{4}$, $P(B) = \frac{1}{4}$ and $P(B|A) = \frac{1}{3}$. Find $P(A \cup B)$.

2. A class contains 6 boys and 8 girls. If two students are picked at random, what is the probability that they are both boys? *[4 marks]*

3. A bag contains 4 red balls, 3 blue balls and 2 green balls. A ball is chosen at random from the bag and is not replaced; then a second ball is chosen. Find the probability of choosing one green ball and one blue ball in any order. *[5 marks]*

4. Given that $P(X) = \frac{1}{3}$, $P(Y|X) = \frac{2}{9}$ and $P(Y|X') = \frac{1}{3}$, find

   (a) $P(Y')$

   (b) $P(X' \cup Y')$ *[6 marks]*

5. A factory has two machines for making widgets. The older machine has larger capacity, so it makes 60% of the widgets, but 6% are rejected by quality control. The newer machine has only a 3% rejection rate. Find the probability that a randomly selected widget is rejected. *[5 marks]*

6. The school tennis league consists of 12 players. Daniel has a 30% chance of winning any game against a higher-ranked player, and a 70% chance of winning any game against a

lower-ranked player. If Daniel is currently in third place, find the probability that he wins his next game against a random opponent. *[5 marks]*

7. There are 36 disks in a bag. Some of them are black and the rest are white. Two are simultaneously selected at random. Given that the probability of selecting two disks of the same colour is equal to the probability of selecting two disks of different colour, how many black disks are there in the bag? *[6 marks]*

17E Independent events

We can now evaluate the probabilities of the intersection and union of two events A and B if we know $\mathrm{P}(A)$, $\mathrm{P}(B)$ and $\mathrm{P}(A|B)$ or $\mathrm{P}(B|A)$, but finding the conditional probabilities can be quite difficult. There is one important exception: if the two events do not affect each other. Such events are called **independent events**. In this case, knowing that B has occurred has no impact on the probability of A occurring; in probability notation, $\mathrm{P}(A|B) = \mathrm{P}(A)$. Since $\mathrm{P}(A \cap B) = \mathrm{P}(A|B)\mathrm{P}(B)$, we get the following relationship that applies to independent events.

KEY POINT 17.6

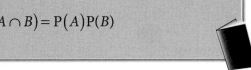

For independent events,

$$\mathrm{P}(A \cap B) = \mathrm{P}(A)\mathrm{P}(B)$$

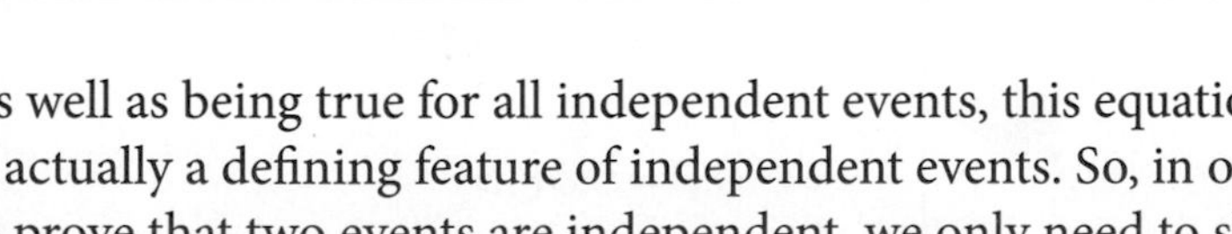

As well as being true for all independent events, this equation is actually a defining feature of independent events. So, in order to prove that two events are independent, we only need to show that they satisfy the equation in Key point 17.6.

All strawberries are red, but not all red things are strawberries. It can be difficult to distinguish between a property and a defining feature. A circle has a constant width, but is every plane shape with constant width necessarily a circle?

Worked example 17.9

$P(A)=0.5$, $P(B)=0.2$ and $P(A\cup B)=0.6$. Are the events A and B independent?

Use the given information to find $P(A\cap B)$.

$$P(A\cup B)=P(A)+P(B)-P(A\cap B)$$
$$0.6=0.5+0.2-P(A\cap B)$$
$$\therefore P(A\cap B)=0.1$$

Evaluate $P(A)P(B)$.

$$P(A)P(B)=0.5\times 0.2=0.1$$

Compare the two.

$$P(A\cap B)=P(A)P(B)$$

So A and B are independent.

If we know that two events are independent, we can use this fact to help calculate other probabilities.

Worked example 17.10

A and B are independent events with $P(A\cup B)=0.8$ and $P(A)=0.2$. Find $P(B)$.

Write $P(A\cap B)$ in terms of other probabilities.

$$P(A\cup B)=P(A)+P(B)-P(A\cap B)$$
$$0.8=0.2+P(B)-P(A\cap B)$$

Use independence.

$$=0.2+P(B)-0.2\times P(B)$$
$$=0.2+0.8P(B)$$

Solve the equation for $P(B)$.

$$\Rightarrow 0.6=0.8P(B)$$
$$\therefore P(B)=\frac{3}{4}\text{(or 0.75)}$$

Exercise 17E

1. In this question, assume that events A and B are independent.
   (a) (i) $P(A)=0.3$ and $P(B)=0.7$. Find $P(A\cap B)$.
   (ii) $P(A)=\frac{1}{5}$ and $P(B)=\frac{1}{3}$. Find $P(A\cap B)$.

(b) (i) $P(A)=\frac{4}{5}$ and $P(A\cap B)=\frac{3}{7}$. Find $P(B)$.

(ii) $P(A\cap B)=0.5$ and $P(B)=0.9$. Find $P(A)$.

(c) (i) $P(A)=40\%$ and $P(B)=16\%$. Find $P(A\cup B)$.

(ii) $P(A)=0.2$ and $P(B)=\frac{1}{4}$. Find $P(A\cup B)$.

(d) (i) $P(A\cup B)=0.6$ and $P(A)=0.4$. Find $P(B)$.

(ii) $P(A\cup B)=0.5$ and $P(A)=0.1$. Find $P(B)$.

2. Determine which of the following pairs of events are independent.

(a) (i) $P(A)=0.6$, $P(B)=0.5$ and $P(A\cap B)=0.3$.

(ii) $P(A)=0.8$, $P(B)=0.1$ and $P(A\cap B)=0.05$.

(b) (i) $P(A)=\frac{1}{5}$, $P(B)=\frac{1}{4}$ and $P(A\cup B)=\frac{2}{5}$.

(ii) $P(A)=56\%$, $P(B)=32\%$ and $P(A\cup B)=72\%$.

3. The independent events A and B are such that $P(A)=0.6$ and $P(A\cup B)=0.72$. Find

(a) $P(B)$

(b) the probability that either A occurs or B occurs, *but not both.* *[5 marks]*

4. A school has two photocopiers, one for teachers and one for students. The probability of the teachers' photocopier working is 92%. The probability of the students' photocopier working is 68%. The two outcomes do not affect each other. What is the probability that

(a) both photocopiers are working

(b) neither photocopier is working

(c) at least one photocopier is working? *[7 marks]*

5. As part of a promotion a toy is put in each packet of crisps sold. There are eight different toys available. Each toy is equally likely to be found in any packet of crisps.

David buys four packets of crisps.

(a) Find the probability that the four toys in these packets are all different.

(b) Of the eight toys in the packets, his favourites are the yo-yo and the gyroscope. What is the probability that he finds at least one of his favourite toys in the four packets? *[7 marks]*

6. Given that events A and B are independent with $P(A \cap B) = 0.3$ and $P(A \cap B') = 0.6$, find $P(A \cup B)$. *[5 marks]*

17F Conditional probability

Estimate the probability that a randomly chosen person is a dollar millionaire. Would your estimate change if you were told that they live in a mansion?

When we get additional information, probabilities change. In the above example, P(millionaire) is very different from P(millionaire|lives in mansion). The second is a **conditional probability**, which we already used in section 17D when working with tree diagrams.

To find conditional probabilities, one useful method is restricting the sample space: we write out a list of all equally likely possibilities before we know any extra information (the full sample space); then we cross out any possibilities ruled out by the extra information given.

Worked example 17.11

Given that the number rolled on a die is prime, show that the probability that it is odd is $\frac{2}{3}$.

Write out the full sample space for a single roll of a die.	On one roll we could get 1, 2, 3, 4, 5 or 6.
We are told that the number is prime.	If the number is prime it can only be 2, 3 or 5.
Decide how many of the remaining numbers are odd.	Two of these are odd, so the probability is $\frac{2}{3}$.

In section 17D (Key point 17.5) we saw that $P(A \cap B) = P(A)P(B|A)$. Rearranging this equation gives a very important formula for conditional probability.

KEY POINT 17.7

$$P(B|A)=\frac{P(A\cap B)}{P(A)}$$

EXAM HINT

This rearranged form is not given in the Formula booklet.

We can visualise this formula in a Venn diagram.

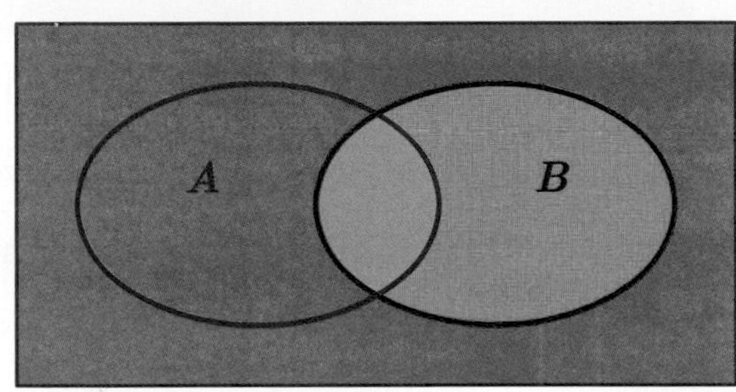

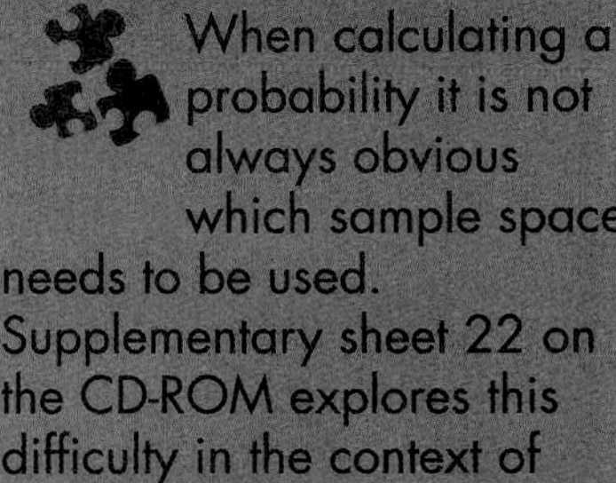

When calculating a probability it is not always obvious which sample space needs to be used. Supplementary sheet 22 on the CD-ROM explores this difficulty in the context of estimating the risk of a transport accident.

If we know that event B has occurred, we can focus on B and ignore the rest of the Venn diagram. The portion of the region B in which A occurs is $A\cap B$. We will look at such Venn diagrams in more detail in section 17G.

Worked example 17.12

The probability that a randomly chosen resident of a certain city is a millionaire is $\frac{1}{10000}$.

The probability that a randomly chosen resident lives in a mansion is $\frac{1}{30000}$. Only 1 in 40 000 residents are millionaires who live in mansions. What is the probability of a randomly chosen individual being a millionaire given that they live in a mansion?

Write the required probability in 'given' notation and apply the formula.

$$P(\text{millionaire}|\text{mansion})=\frac{P(\text{millionaire}\cap\text{mansion})}{P(\text{mansion})}$$

$$=\frac{\frac{1}{40000}}{\frac{1}{30000}}$$

$$=\frac{3}{4}$$

It can be difficult to tell whether a question is asking for conditional probability or combined probability. For example, if the question says that a boy has green eyes and asks what is the probability that he also has brown hair, it is tempting to think this is P(green eyes $\cap$ brown hair). However, the fact that the boy has green eyes has been given, so we should actually find P(brown hair|green eyes).

Sometimes we are given one conditional probability and need to find another.

Worked example 17.13

If it is raining in the morning, there is a 90% chance that I will bring my umbrella. If it is not raining in the morning, there is only a $\frac{1}{5}$ chance of me taking my umbrella. On any given morning the probability of rain is 0.1. If you see me with an umbrella, what is the probability that it was raining that morning?

First draw a tree diagram.

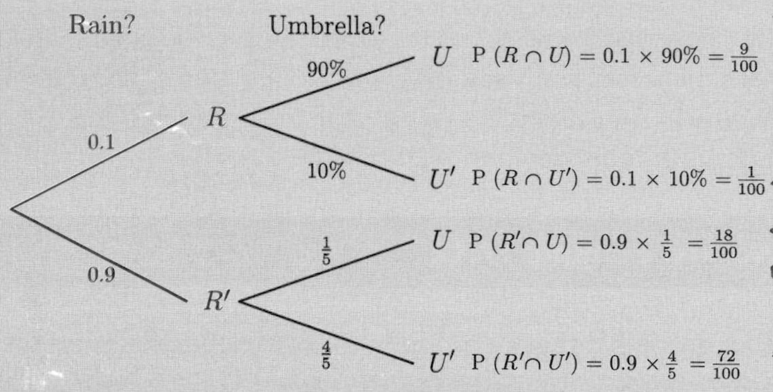

Rain? Umbrella?

R (0.1): U (90%) $P(R \cap U) = 0.1 \times 90\% = \frac{9}{100}$; U′ (10%) $P(R \cap U') = 0.1 \times 10\% = \frac{1}{100}$

R′ (0.9): U ($\frac{1}{5}$) $P(R' \cap U) = 0.9 \times \frac{1}{5} = \frac{18}{100}$; U′ ($\frac{4}{5}$) $P(R' \cap U') = 0.9 \times \frac{4}{5} = \frac{72}{100}$

Write the required quantity in probability notation. We realise that it is a conditional probability, so use the formula.

$$P(\text{rain} \mid \text{umbrella}) = \frac{P(\text{rain} \cap \text{umbrella})}{P(\text{umbrella})}$$

Use the tree diagram to find the relevant probabilities.

$$P(\text{rain} \cap \text{umbrella}) = \frac{9}{100}$$

$$P(\text{umbrella}) = \frac{9}{100} + \frac{18}{100} = \frac{27}{100}$$

Put these numbers into the formula.

$$\therefore P(\text{rain} \mid \text{umbrella}) = \frac{P(\text{rain} \cap \text{umbrella})}{P(\text{umbrella})} = \frac{\frac{9}{100}}{\frac{27}{100}} = \frac{1}{3}$$

Exercise 17F

1. For each of the questions below, write the probability required in mathematical notation; you are not required to calculate the probability. For example, the probability that I revise and pass the test would be written P(revise $\cap$ pass).
   (a) Find the probability that the outcome of rolling a die is a prime and odd number.
   (b) Find the probability that a person is from either Senegal or Taiwan.
   (c) A student is studying the IB. Find the probability that he is also studying French.
   (d) If a playing card is a red card, find the probability that it is a heart.
   (e) What proportion of German people live in Munich?
   (f) What is the probability that someone is wearing neither black nor white socks?
   (g) What is the probability that a vegetable is a potato if it is not a cabbage?
   (h) What is the probability that a ball drawn from a bag is red, given that the ball is either red or blue?

2. (a) (i) If $P(X)=0.3$ and $P(X\cap Y)=\frac{1}{5}$, find $P(Y\,|\,X)$.
   (ii) If $P(Y)=0.8$ and $P(X\cap Y)=\frac{3}{7}$, find $P(X\,|\,Y)$.
   (b) (i) If $P(X)=0.4$, $P(Y)=0.7$ and $P(X\cap Y)=\frac{1}{4}$, find $P(X\,|\,Y)$.
   (ii) If $P(X)=0.6$, $P(Y)=0.9$ and $P(X\cap Y)=\frac{1}{2}$, find $P(Y\,|\,X)$.

3. The events A and B are such that $P(A)=0.6$, $P(B)=0.2$ and $P(A\cup B)=0.7$.
   (a) (i) Find $P(A\cap B)$.
   (ii) Hence show that A and B are not independent.
   (b) Find $P(B\,|\,A)$. *[7 marks]*

4. Let A and B be events such that $\mathrm{P}(A)=\frac{2}{3}$, $\mathrm{P}(B|A)=\frac{1}{2}$ and $\mathrm{P}(A\cup B)=\frac{4}{5}$.

(a) Find $\mathrm{P}(A\cap B)$.

(b) Find $\mathrm{P}(B)$.

(c) Show that A and B are not independent. *[7 marks]*

5. Box A contains 6 red balls and 4 green balls. Box B contains 5 red balls and 3 green balls. A standard fair cubical die is thrown. If a '6' is obtained, a ball is selected from box A; otherwise a ball is selected from box B.

(a) Calculate the probability that the ball selected was red.

(b) Given that the ball selected was red, calculate the probability that it came from box B. *[7 marks]*

6. Robert travels to work by train every weekday from Monday to Friday. The probability that he catches the 7.30 a.m. train on Monday is $\frac{2}{3}$. The probability that he catches the 7.30 a.m. train on any other weekday is 90%. A weekday is chosen at random.

(a) Find the probability that Robert catches the 7.30 a.m. train on that day.

(b) Given that he catches the 7.30 a.m. train on that day, find the probability that the chosen day is Monday. *[7 marks]*

7. Bag 1 contains 6 red cubes and 10 blue cubes. Bag 2 contains 7 red cubes and 3 blue cubes.

Two cubes are drawn at random, the first from bag 1 and the second from bag 2.

(a) Find the probability that the cubes are of the same colour.

(b) Given that the cubes selected are of different colours, find the probability that the red cube was selected from bag 1. *[8 marks]*

8. On any day in April, there is a $\frac{2}{3}$ chance of rain in the morning. If it is raining, there is a $\frac{4}{5}$ chance I will remember my umbrella, but if it is not raining, there is only a $\frac{2}{5}$ chance of my remembering to bring an umbrella.

(a) On a random day in April, what is the probability I have my umbrella with me?

(b) Given that I have an umbrella on a day in April, what is the probability that it was raining? *[6 marks]*

9. The probability that a man leaves his umbrella in any shop he visits is $\frac{1}{5}$. After visiting two shops in succession, he finds he has left his umbrella in one of them. What is the probability that he left his umbrella in the second shop? *[4 marks]*

10. $P(A)=\frac{2}{3}, P(A|B)=\frac{1}{5}$ and $P(A\cup B)=\frac{4}{5}$. Find $P(B)$. *[6 marks]*

17G Further Venn diagrams

A Venn diagram is a very helpful way of representing information about events or groups which overlap one another.

When labelling the various events or groups in the diagram, the convention is that the number we put into each region is the probability or size unique to that region. It is therefore a good idea to label the intersection of all the regions first, assigning it a variable if necessary, and then work outwards. Do not try to label the total for all the regions joined together.

Worked example 17.14

In a class of 32, 19 have a bicycle, 21 have a mobile phone and 16 have a laptop computer; 11 have both a bike and a phone, 12 have both a phone and a laptop, and 6 have both a bike and a laptop. Two have none of these objects. How many people have a bike, a phone and a laptop?

Draw a Venn diagram, showing three overlapping groups.
Label the size of the central region (where all three groups overlap) as x. We know that 2 people are outside all three groups.

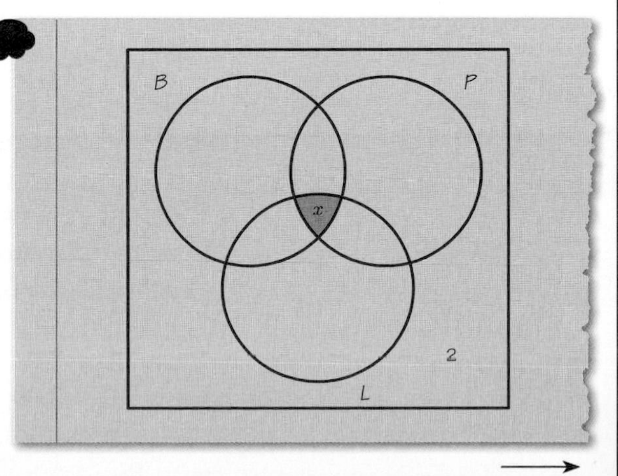

continued . . .

Work outwards from the centre, and look at the three regions where only two of the groups overlap. For example, the number who have a bicycle and a phone but not a laptop is $11-x$.

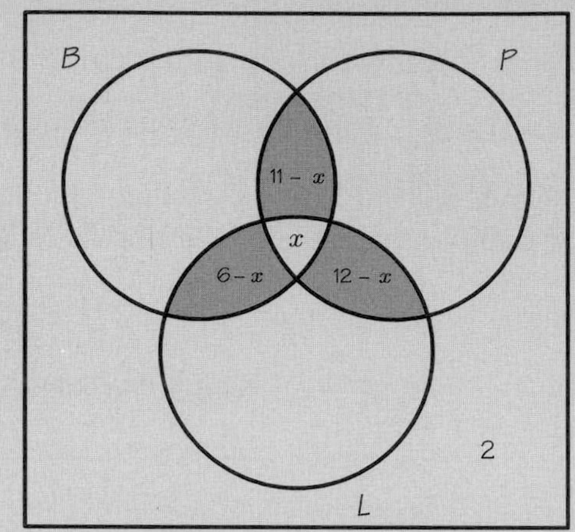

Continue working outwards; now consider the regions which belong to one group only. For example, a total of 19 people have a bicycle, so the number who have a bicycle but neither a phone nor a laptop should be $19-(11-x)-(6-x)-x=2+x$.

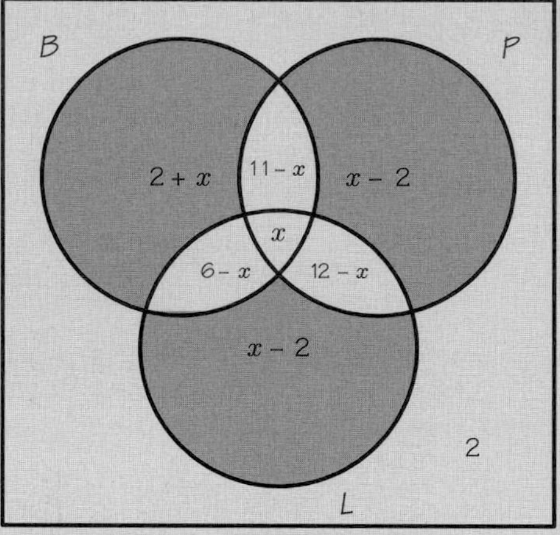

Use the fact that there are 32 people in the class to form an equation.

$$(2+x)+(11-x)+x+(6-x)$$
$$+(x-2)+(12-x)+(x-2)+2=32$$
$$\Leftrightarrow\ 29+x=32$$
$$\Leftrightarrow\quad x=3$$

Therefore three people have a bicycle, a phone and a laptop.

Venn diagrams are particularly useful when thinking about conditional probability. We can use the given information to exclude parts of the Venn diagram that are not relevant.

Worked example 17.15

Daniel has 18 toys: 12 are made of plastic and 13 are red; 2 are neither red nor plastic.

Daniel chooses a toy at random.

(a) Find the probability that it is a red plastic toy.

(b) If it is a red toy, find the probability that it is plastic.

We need to find the size of the intersection. We can do this by putting the given information into a Venn diagram.

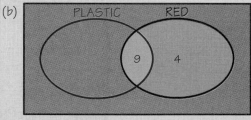

(a)

We know that there are 18 toys in total.

$$(12-x)+x+(13-x)+2=18$$
$$\Leftrightarrow 27-x=18$$
$$\Leftrightarrow x=9$$
$$\therefore \text{P(plastic and red)}=\frac{9}{18}=\frac{1}{2}$$

This is asking for a conditional probability. We can focus on the red toys.

(b)

9 out of 13 red toys are plastic

$$\therefore \text{P(plastic} \mid \text{red)}=\frac{9}{13}$$

When calculating conditional probabilities, it is often easier to use Venn diagrams rather than the formula in Key point 17.7. It is acceptable to do this in the examination.

In the previous two examples we used Venn diagrams to represent frequencies, but they can also represent probabilities, and the same methods work.

Some people find Venn diagrams to be a useful way of understanding the formula $P(A \mid B)=\frac{P(A \cap B)}{P(B)}$. Do visual arguments tend to be clearer than mathematical arguments? If so, why?

Worked example 17.16

Events A and B are such that $P(A)=0.6$, $P(B)=0.7$ and $P(A\cup B)=0.9$. Find $P(B'|A')$.

We can find $P(A\cap B)$ from the given information, using Key point 17.4.

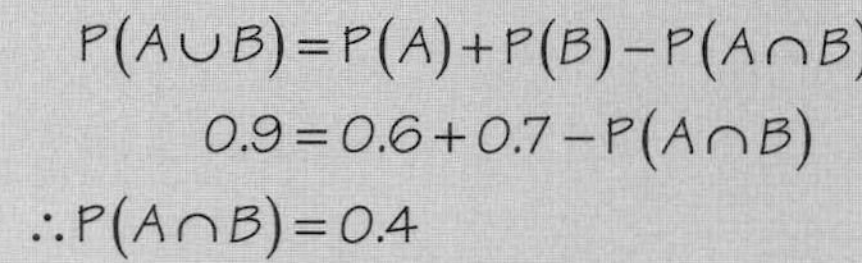

$$P(A\cup B)=P(A)+P(B)-P(A\cap B)$$
$$0.9=0.6+0.7-P(A\cap B)$$
$$\therefore P(A\cap B)=0.4$$

Draw a Venn diagram.
Label the central intersection first, and then work outwards.
For example, the region corresponding to A but not B has probability $0.6 - 0.4 = 0.2$.

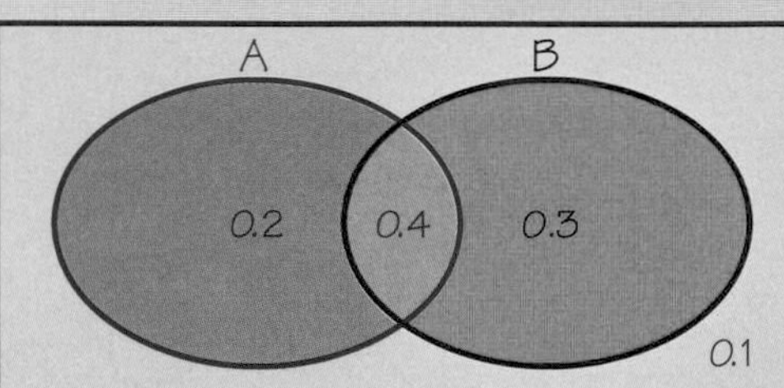

The probability of not being in A is $0.1 + 0.3 = 0.4$. Out of this, the probability of not being in B is 0.1. So

$$P(B'|A')=\frac{0.1}{0.4}=\frac{1}{4}$$

Exercise 17G

1. Out of 145 students in a college, 34 play football, 18 play badminton, and 5 play both sports.

(a) Draw a Venn diagram showing this information.

(b) How many students play neither sport?

(c) What is the probability that a randomly chosen student plays badminton?

(d) If we know that the chosen student plays football, what is the probability that they also play badminton? *[6 marks]*

2. Out of 145 students in a college, 58 study Mathematics, 47 study Economics and 72 study neither of the two subjects.

(a) Draw a Venn diagram to show this information.

(b) How many students study both subjects?

(c) A student tells you that she studies Mathematics. What is the probability that she studies both Mathematics and Economics? *[5 marks]*

3. Denise conducts a survey about food preferences in her college. She asks students which of the three meals – spaghetti bolognese, chilli con carne, and vegetable curry – they would eat. She finds that, out of the 145 students:

43 would eat spaghetti bolognese

80 would eat vegetable curry

20 would eat both the spaghetti and the curry

24 would eat both the curry and the chilli

35 would eat both the chilli and the spaghetti

12 would eat all three meals

10 would not eat any of the three meals

(a) Draw a Venn diagram showing this information.

(b) How many students would eat only spaghetti bolognese?

(c) How many students would eat chilli?

(d) What is the probability that a randomly selected student would eat only one of the three meals?

(e) Given that a student would eat only one of the three meals, what is the probability that they would eat curry?

(f) Find the probability that a randomly selected student would eat at least two of the three meals. *[12 marks]*

4. The probability that a person has dark hair is 0.7, the probability that they have blue eyes is 0.4, and the probability that they have both dark hair and blue eyes is 0.2.

(a) Draw a Venn diagram showing this information.

(b) Find the probability that a person has neither dark hair nor blue eyes.

(c) Given that a person has dark hair, find the probability that they also have blue eyes.

(d) Given that a person does not have dark hair, find the probability that they have blue eyes.

(e) Are the characteristics of having dark hair and having blue eyes independent? Explain your answer. *[11 marks]*

5. The probability that it rains on any given day is 0.45, and the probability that it is cold is 0.6. The probability that it is neither cold nor raining is 0.25.

(a) Find the probability that it is both cold and raining.

(b) Draw a Venn diagram showing this information.

(c) Given that it is raining, find the probability that it is not cold.

(d) Given that it is not cold, find the probability that it is raining.

(e) Are the events 'raining' and 'cold' independent? Explain your answer and show any supporting calculations. *[12 marks]*

17H Selections with and without replacement

In this section we look at a particular example which illustrates the difference between dependent and independent events.

Suppose you have a box containing 10 white and 10 dark chocolates, and you pick two chocolates without looking. We can think of this as two events happening one after the other (even if the two chocolates were taken out in one go) and draw a tree diagram to show the outcomes of each event and their probabilities. What is the probability that both chocolates are white? For the first chocolate, the probabilities of getting the white or dark types are the same: $\mathrm{P}(\text{first white}) = \mathrm{P}(\text{first dark}) = \frac{10}{20} = \frac{1}{2}$. However, the probabilities for the second chocolate depend on what the first one was. If the first chocolate was white, then there are 9 white and 10 dark chocolates remaining in the box. So the probability that the second chocolate is also white would be $\frac{9}{19}$. Note that this is *not* P(second white) but rather the conditional probability P(second white | first white). The probability that *both* chocolates are white is therefore

$$\mathrm{P}(\text{first white} \cap \text{second white}) = \mathrm{P}(\text{second white} \mid \text{first white})\,\mathrm{P}(\text{first white})$$
$$= \frac{9}{19} \times \frac{1}{2} = \frac{9}{38}$$

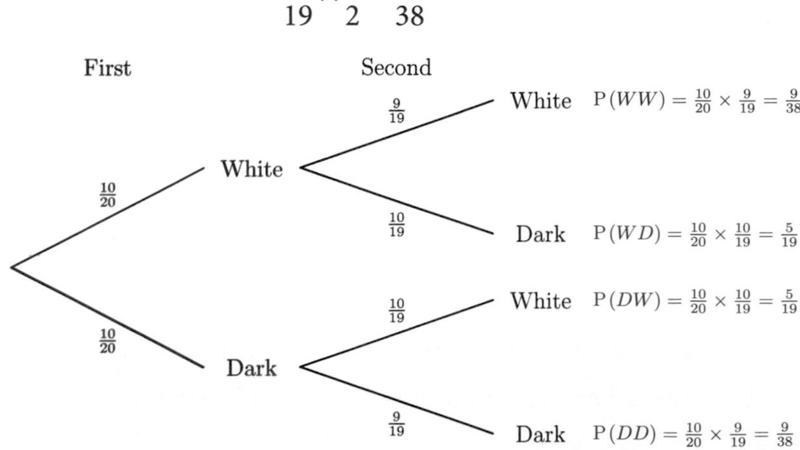

To find the probability of the second chocolate being white, we look at the tree diagram:

$$\begin{aligned}
&\text{P(second white)}\\
&= \text{P(second white} \cap \text{first white)} + \text{P(second white} \cap \text{first dark)}\\
&= \text{P(second white} \mid \text{first white) P(first white)}\\
&\quad + \text{P(second white} \mid \text{first dark) P(first dark)}\\
&= \frac{9}{19} \times \frac{1}{2} + \frac{10}{19} \times \frac{1}{2}\\
&= \frac{19}{38} = \frac{1}{2}
\end{aligned}$$

Notice that $\text{P}(\text{both white}) \neq \text{P}(\text{first white})\text{P}(\text{second white})$ because the types of the first and second chocolates are not independent.

Contrast this with the situation where you pick one chocolate, put it back in the box, and then select another one (called selection *with replacement*). This time, $\text{P}(\text{second white} \mid \text{first white}) = \frac{10}{20} = \frac{1}{2}$.

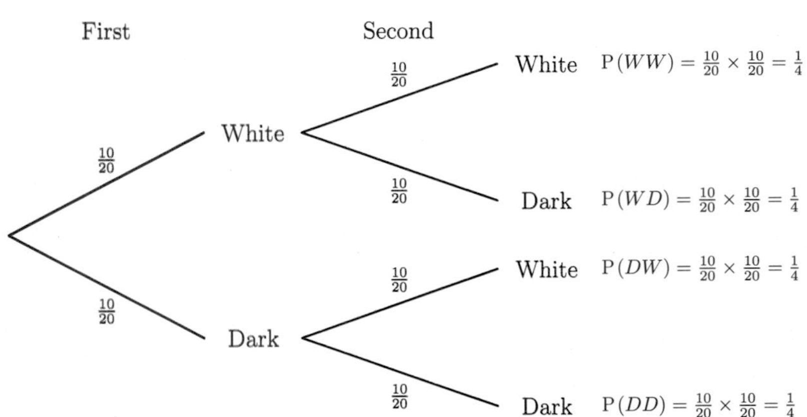

Using the new tree diagram, the probability that both chocolates are white is:

$$\begin{aligned}
\text{P(first white} \cap \text{second white)} &= \text{P(second white} \mid \text{first white) P(first white)}\\
&= \frac{1}{2} \times \frac{1}{2} = \frac{1}{4}
\end{aligned}$$

The probability that the second chocolate is white is

$$\begin{aligned}&\text{P(second white)}\\&= \text{P(second white} \mid \text{first white) P(first white)}\\&\quad + \text{P(second white} \mid \text{first dark) P(first dark)}\\&= \frac{1}{2}\times\frac{1}{2}+\frac{1}{2}\times\frac{1}{2}\\&= \frac{1}{2}\end{aligned}$$

Note that this probability is the same as when we did the selections without replacement. This time, however, P(both white) = P(first white)P(second white), so the types of the two chocolates are independent. This is to be expected, as replacing the first chocolate means that the choice of the second chocolate is not affected by the type of the first.

Worked example 17.17

A bag contains 7 green and 5 yellow balls. Two balls are selected at random, one at a time. Find the probability that the two balls are of different colours if the selection is made

(a) with replacement (b) without replacement.

Draw a tree diagram. The probabilities for the second ball are the same as for the first.

(a)

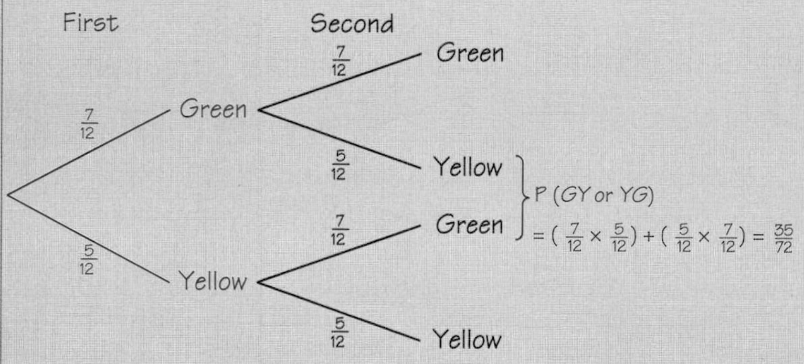

First		Second	
$\frac{7}{12}$	Green	$\frac{7}{12}$	Green
		$\frac{5}{12}$	Yellow
$\frac{5}{12}$	Yellow	$\frac{7}{12}$	Green
		$\frac{5}{12}$	Yellow

P (GY or YG) $= \left(\frac{7}{12}\times\frac{5}{12}\right)+\left(\frac{5}{12}\times\frac{7}{12}\right)=\frac{35}{72}$

There are two branches corresponding to the two balls being of different colours.

$$\text{P(different colours)} = \frac{7}{12}\times\frac{5}{12}+\frac{5}{12}\times\frac{7}{12} = 0.486 \text{ (3SF)}$$

→

continued . . .

Draw a new tree diagram. This time, since the first ball is not put back, the probabilities for the second ball are out of 11.

(b)

First — Second

Green ($\frac{7}{12}$): Green ($\frac{6}{11}$), Yellow ($\frac{5}{11}$)

Yellow ($\frac{5}{12}$): Green ($\frac{7}{11}$), Yellow ($\frac{4}{11}$)

P (GY or YG) $= (\frac{7}{12} \times \frac{5}{11}) + (\frac{5}{12} \times \frac{7}{11}) = \frac{35}{66}$

$$P(\text{different colours}) = \frac{7}{12} \times \frac{5}{11} + \frac{5}{12} \times \frac{7}{11}$$
$$= 0.530 \text{ (3SF)}$$

Exercise 17H

1. Sumaiya's pencil case contains five blue and three red pens. She selects two pens without looking. What is the probability that they are both blue? *[3 marks]*

2. A bag contains 100 sweets, 35 of which are strawberry flavoured. Ivo picks two sweets at random. Find the probability that at least one is strawberry flavoured. *[4 marks]*

3. Isabelle has three blue scarves and two purple scarves. Each day she picks a scarf at random. Find the probability that she wears a blue scarf on two consecutive days. *[4 marks]*

4. A bag contains 12 black and 15 red counters. A counter is picked from the bag and not replaced. A second counter is then picked from the bag. What is the probability that this second counter is red? *[4 marks]*

5. At the start of each turn in a game, you select two tokens out of a bag containing 13 blue and 13 orange tokens. You win an extra point if the two tokens are of different colours. Are you more likely to win the extra point if you select the tokens with or without replacement? *[7 marks]*

6. A bag contains the same number of red and yellow balls.

(a) One ball is selected and replaced. Another ball is then selected. Show that the probability that the two balls are of different colours is $\frac{1}{2}$.

(b) Two balls are selected without replacement. Find the smallest total number of balls so that the probability of selecting two balls of different colours is less than 0.53. *[9 marks]*

Summary

- Probability is a measure of how likely an event is, varying from 0 for impossible events up to 1 for events that are certain to happen.
- The probability of an event occurring can be estimated from the frequency of occurrence in prior data (empirical probability) or predicted by considering what proportion of the **sample space** – the list of all possible outcomes – corresponds to the event (theoretical probability).
- If the event we are interested in is a function of two outcomes (e.g. if it is the sum or product of two rolled dice), a convenient way of listing the sample space is in a probability grid diagram.
- **Venn diagrams** are a useful tool for understanding how different events can be combined and working out the associated probabilities. When calculating probabilities, label the intersection of all the groups with an unknown and work outwards.
- The probability of event A or event B or both occurring is the union of A and B: $\mathrm{P}(A \cup B) = \mathrm{P}(A) + \mathrm{P}(B) - \mathrm{P}(A \cap B)$

  If the events are mutually exclusive, then $\mathrm{P}(A \cap B) = 0$ and the formula becomes $\mathrm{P}(A \cup B) = \mathrm{P}(A) + \mathrm{P}(B)$.

  A particular case of mutually exclusive events is any event A and its **complement** A' (the event of A not happening), and we have $\mathrm{P}(A) + \mathrm{P}(A') = 1$.
- The probability of events A and B both occurring is the intersection of A and B: $\mathrm{P}(A \cap B)$.
- The outcomes of a sequence of events can be displayed in a **tree diagram**. The probability of following the path $A \to B$ in a tree diagram is $\mathrm{P}(A \cap B) = \mathrm{P}(A)\mathrm{P}(B|A)$ where $\mathrm{P}(B|A)$ is the probability of B occurring if we already know that A has occurred, a **conditional probability**.

- Conditional probabilities can be found from tree diagrams or Venn diagrams, using the formula

$$P(B|A) = \frac{P(A \cap B)}{P(A)}$$

- If A and B are **independent events**, $P(B|A) = P(B)$ and $P(A \cap B) = P(A)P(B)$.
- Selections with and without replacement are special cases of independent and non-independent events.

Introductory problem revisited

A woman gives birth to non-identical twins. One of them is a girl. What is the probability that the other one is a girl?

There are four equally likely possibilities for the twins' sexes:

First child	Second child
Boy	Boy
Boy	Girl
Girl	Boy
Girl	Girl

If we are told that one of the twins is a girl we can exclude the first case. This leaves three equally likely situations, of which only one consists of two girls; therefore the probability is $\frac{1}{3}$.

If you find this result intriguing, you may like to explore the famous 'Monty Hall problem'.

A word of warning before we finish: it is very tempting to argue that the probability should be $\frac{1}{2}$, as the probability of the second child being a girl is independent of the sex of the first child. This would indeed be the correct answer if the question had said that the *first child* is a girl, rather than that *one of the children* is a girl. Our intuition about probabilities is often flawed, which is why it is important to develop precise mathematical methods and use the language accurately.

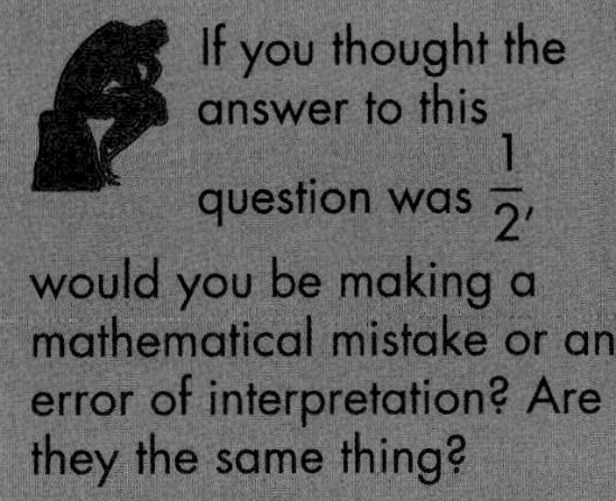

If you thought the answer to this question was $\frac{1}{2}$, would you be making a mathematical mistake or an error of interpretation? Are they the same thing?

Mixed examination practice 17

Short questions

1. A drawer contains 6 red socks, 4 black socks and 8 white socks. Two socks are picked at random. What is the probability that they are of the same colour? *[5 marks]*

2. In a bilingual school there is a class of 21 students. In this class, 15 of the students speak Spanish as their first language, and 12 of these 15 are Argentine. The other 6 students in the class speak English as their first language, and 3 of these 6 are Argentine.

A student is selected at random from the class and is found to be Argentine. Find the probability that the student speaks Spanish as his/her first language. *[4 marks]*

(*© IB Organization 1999*)

3. The probability that it rains on a summer's day in a certain town is 0.2. In this town, the probability that the daily maximum temperature exceeds 25°C is 0.3 when it rains and 0.6 when it does not rain. Given that the maximum daily temperature exceeded 25°C on a particular summer's day, find the probability that it rained on that day. *[6 marks]*

4. Given that $(A \cup B)' = \varnothing$, $\mathrm{P}(A' | B) = \frac{1}{5}$ and $\mathrm{P}(A) = \frac{14}{15}$, find $\mathrm{P}(B)$. *[5 marks]*

Long questions

1. **(a)** A large bag of sweets contains 8 red and 12 yellow sweets. Two sweets are chosen at random from the bag without replacement. Find the probability that two red sweets are chosen.

(b) A small bag contains 4 red and n yellow sweets. Two sweets are chosen without replacement from this bag. If the probability that two red sweets are chosen is $\frac{2}{15}$, show that $n = 6$.

Ayesha has one large bag and two small bags of sweets. She selects a bag at random and then picks two sweets from the bag without replacement.

(c) Calculate the probability that two red sweets are chosen.

(d) Given that two red sweets are chosen, find the probability that Ayesha had selected the large bag. *[15 marks]*

2. (a) If $\mathrm{P}(X)$ represents a probability, state the range of $\mathrm{P}(X)$.

(b) Express $\mathrm{P}(A)-\mathrm{P}(A\cap B)$ in terms of $\mathrm{P}(A)$ and $\mathrm{P}(B\mid A)$.

(c) (i) Show that $\mathrm{P}(A\cup B)-\mathrm{P}(A\cap B)=\mathrm{P}(A)\left(1-\mathrm{P}(B\mid A)\right)+\mathrm{P}(B)\left(1-\mathrm{P}(A\mid B)\right.$.

(ii) Hence explain why $\mathrm{P}(A\cup B)\geq \mathrm{P}(A\cap B)$. *[9 marks]*

3. The probability that a student plays badminton is 0.3. The probability that a student plays neither football nor badminton is 0.5, and the probability that a student plays both sports is x.

(a) Draw a Venn diagram showing this information.

(b) Find the probability that a student plays football but not badminton.

Given that a student plays football, the probability that they also play badminton is 0.5.

(c) Find the probability that a student plays both badminton and football.

(d) Hence complete your Venn diagram. What is the probability that a student plays only badminton?

(e) Given that a student plays only one sport, what is the probability that they play badminton? *[13 marks]*

4. Two women, Ann and Bridget, play a game in which they take it in turns to throw an unbiased six-sided die. The first woman to throw a '6' wins the game. Ann is the first to throw.

(a) Find the probability that

(i) Bridget wins on her first throw

(ii) Ann wins on her second throw

(iii) Ann wins on her nth throw.

(b) Let p be the probability that Ann wins the game. Show that $p=\frac{1}{6}+\frac{25}{36}p$.

(c) Find the probability that Bridget wins the game.

(d) Suppose that the game is played six times. Find the probability that Ann wins more games than Bridget. *[17 marks]*

(© IB Organization 2001)

18 Probability distributions

In this chapter you will learn:

- what a random variable is and how to list its possible values
- how to predict the average value of a random variable
- how to calculate the probability of getting a certain number of successes over a fixed number of trials – the binomial distribution
- about a distribution that models many naturally occurring random variables – the normal distribution.

Introductory problem

A casino offers a game in which a coin is tossed repeatedly. If the first head occurs on the first throw you get £2, if the first head occurs on the second throw you get £4, if the first head is on the third throw you get £8, and so on, with the prize doubling each time. How much should the casino charge for this game if they want to make a profit?

In statistics we find the mean, standard deviation and other measures of centre or spread from data we have already collected. In real life, however, it is often useful to be able to predict these quantities in advance. Even though, in a random situation, it is impossible to predict the outcome of a single event, such as one roll of a die, it turns out that if you look at enough events, the average can be predicted quite precisely.

The idea of being able to predict averages but not individual events is central to many areas of knowledge. For example, economists cannot predict what an individual will do when interest rates increase, but they can predict the average effect on the economy. A physicist knows that in a waterfall, any particular water molecule may actually be moving upwards, but on average the flow is definitely going to be downwards.

18A Random variables

A **random variable** is a quantity whose value depends on chance – for example, the outcome when a die is rolled. If the probabilities associated with each possible value are known, useful mathematical calculations can be made. A random variable is conventionally represented by a capital letter, and the values that the random variable can take are represented by the corresponding lower-case letter. For instance, if we let the random variable X be the outcome when a die is rolled, in one particular experiment you may find that $x = 2$.

Recall that the sample space of a random event is the list of all possible outcomes of the event. The sample space of a random variable, together with the probabilities associated with all the values in the list, is called the **probability distribution** of the variable; this information is best displayed in a table.

Worked example 18.1

Make a table to show the probability distribution of the outcome of rolling a fair six-sided die.

Make a list of all the values that the random variable can take. Then write down the probability of each value occurring.

Let X be the outcome of rolling the die.

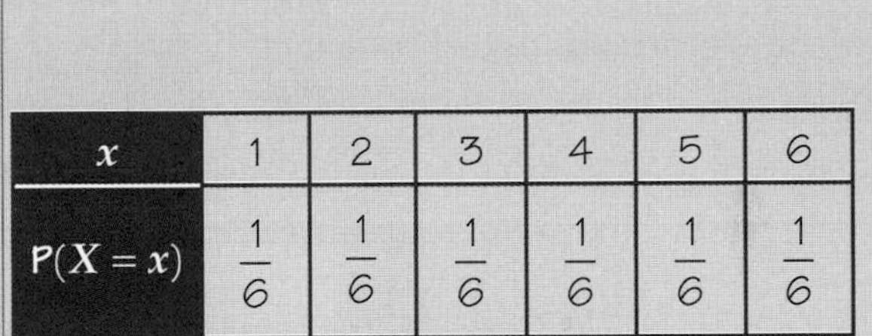

x	1	2	3	4	5	6
$P(X = x)$	$\frac{1}{6}$	$\frac{1}{6}$	$\frac{1}{6}$	$\frac{1}{6}$	$\frac{1}{6}$	$\frac{1}{6}$

The probabilities in a probability distribution cannot be just any numbers.

KEY POINT 18.1

The total of all the probabilities in a probability distribution must always equal 1.

This fact can be useful if we do not have complete information about the probabilities.

Worked example 18.2

In a game at a fair, a ball is thrown at a rectangular target. The dimensions of the target (in metres) are as shown. The probability of hitting each region is proportional to its area. The prize for hitting a region is a number of chocolates equal to the number shown in that region. Find the probability distribution of the number of chocolates won.

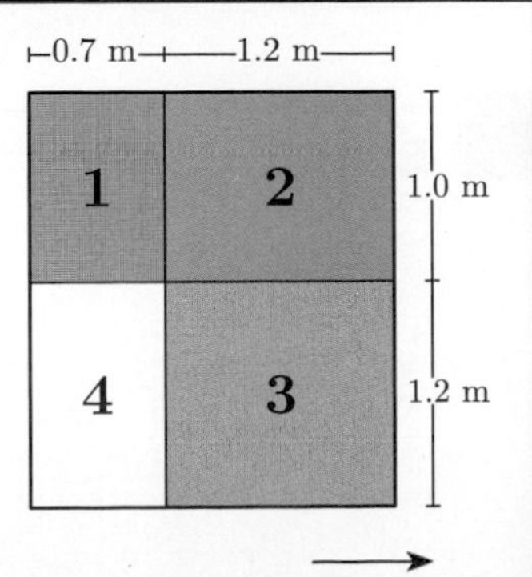

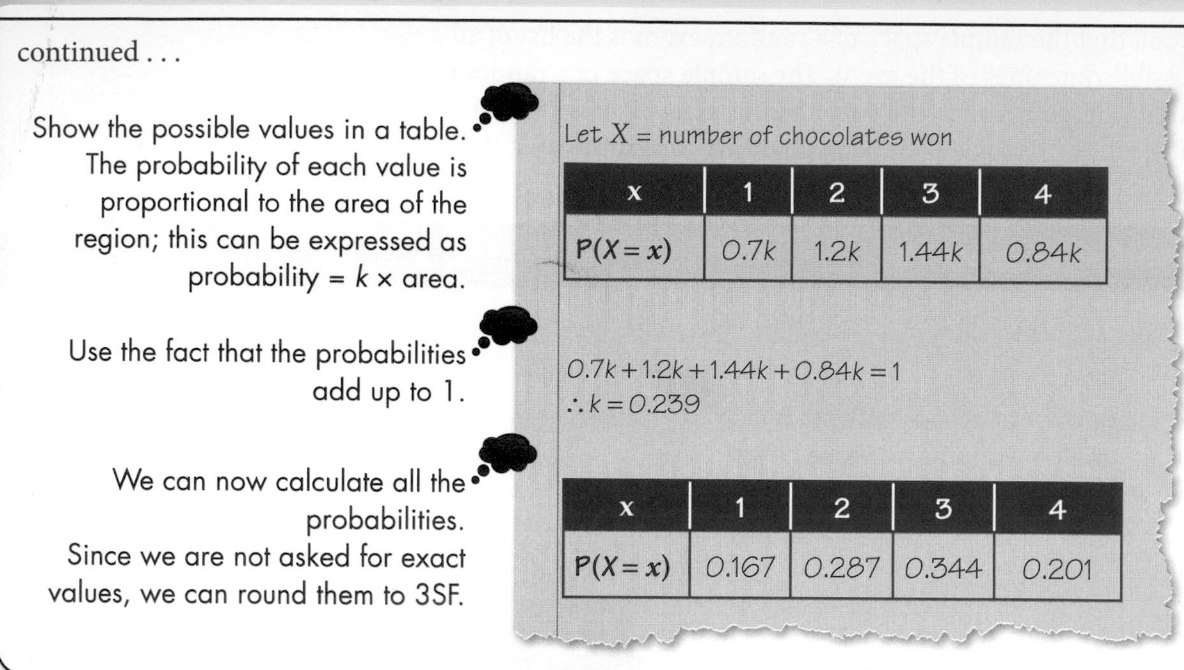

continued . . .

Show the possible values in a table. The probability of each value is proportional to the area of the region; this can be expressed as probability = $k \times$ area.

Let X = number of chocolates won

x	1	2	3	4
$P(X=x)$	$0.7k$	$1.2k$	$1.44k$	$0.84k$

Use the fact that the probabilities add up to 1.

$0.7k + 1.2k + 1.44k + 0.84k = 1$
$\therefore k = 0.239$

We can now calculate all the probabilities. Since we are not asked for exact values, we can round them to 3SF.

x	1	2	3	4
$P(X=x)$	0.167	0.287	0.344	0.201

An obvious question to ask about a random variable is what value is it *most likely* to have. This value, whose associated probability is the highest, is called the **mode**. In the above example, the random variable X has mode 3, which means that the most likely number of chocolates you will win is three. A random variable may not have a mode – for example, the outcomes of a fair die are all equally likely – or it may have more than one mode. In particular, if the largest probability corresponds to two of the outcomes, the random variable is said to be **bimodal**.

Another question we might ask is: if we were to play the above game many times, *on average* how many chocolates would we expect to win? The answer is not necessarily the same as the most likely outcome. We will see how to answer this question in the next section.

Exercise 18A

In this exercise you will need to use tools from chapter 17, in particular tree diagrams. For question 2(c) you may want to look back at chapter 6 on geometric sequences.

1. For each of the following, make a table to represent the probability distribution of the random variable described.

(a) A fair coin is thrown four times. The random variable W is the number of tails obtained.

(b) Two fair dice are thrown. The random variable D is the difference between the larger and the smaller score, or zero if they are the same.

(c) A fair die is thrown once. The random variable X is calculated as half the result if the die shows an even number, or one higher than the result if the die shows an odd number.

(d) A bag contains six red and three green counters. Two counters are drawn at random from the bag without replacement. The random variable G is the number of green counters remaining in the bag.

(e) Karl picks a card at random from a standard pack of 52 cards. If he draws a diamond, he stops; otherwise, he replaces the card and continues to draw cards at random, with replacement, until he has either drawn a diamond or drawn a total of four cards. The random variable C is the total number of cards drawn.

(f) Two fair four-sided spinners, each labelled 1, 2, 3 and 4, are spun. The random variable X is the product of the two values shown.

2. Find the missing value k for each probability distribution.

(a) (i)

x	3	7	9	11
$P(X=x)$	$\frac{1}{2}$	$\frac{1}{4}$	$\frac{1}{8}$	k

(ii)

x	5	6	7	10
$P(X=x)$	0.2	0.3	k	0.5

(b) (i) $P(Y=y)=ky$ for $x=1,2,3,4$

(ii) $P(X=x)=\frac{k}{x}$ for $x=1,2,3,4$

(c) (i) $P(X=x)=k(0.1)^x$ for $x\in\mathbb{N}$

(ii) $P(R=r)=k(0.9)^r$ for $r\in\mathbb{N}$

$\mathbb{N}$ is the set of natural numbers, $\{0,1,2,3,\ldots\}$.

See Prior Learning section G on the CD-ROM for a review of number sets.

3. In a game, a player rolls a biased four-sided die. The probability of each possible score is shown below.

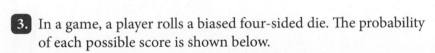

Score	1	2	3	4
Probability	$\frac{1}{3}$	$\frac{1}{4}$	k	$\frac{1}{5}$

Find the probability that the total score is 4 after two rolls. *[5 marks]*

18B Expectation of a discrete random variable

EXAM HINT

The expectation gives the *theoretical* expected mean. In any particular series of trials, the actual mean value may be different. Also, do not confuse the expected value with the most likely value (the mode).

If you roll a fair die many times, you would expect the average score to be around 3.5, the mean of the numbers 1 to 6. However, if the sides of the die were labelled 1, 2, 3, 4, 6 and 6, you would expect the average to be higher, because the probability of getting a 6 is higher than for each of the other possible outcomes. The **expectation** of a random variable is the average value you would get if you were to repeatedly measure the variable an infinite number of times.

KEY POINT 18.2

The **expectation** (or mean value) of a random variable X is written $\mathrm{E}(X)$ and calculated as

$$\mathrm{E}(X) = \mu = \sum_x x\,\mathrm{P}(X = x)$$

Worked example 18.3

The random variable X has probability distribution as shown in the table. Calculate $\mathrm{E}(X)$.

x	1	2	3	4	5	6
$\mathrm{P}(X=x)$	$\frac{1}{10}$	$\frac{1}{4}$	$\frac{1}{10}$	$\frac{1}{4}$	$\frac{1}{5}$	$\frac{1}{10}$

The formula tells us to calculate the product $x\mathrm{P}(X = x)$ for all possible values of x and add up the results.

$$\mathrm{E}(X) = 1\times\frac{1}{10} + 2\times\frac{1}{4} + 3\times\frac{1}{10} + 4\times\frac{1}{4} + 5\times\frac{1}{5} + 6\times\frac{1}{10}$$

$$= \frac{7}{2}$$

Just as the mean of a set of integers need not be an integer itself, so the expectation of a random variable need not be one of the values that the variable can take.

Exercise 18B

1. Calculate the expectation of each of the following random variables.

(a) (i)

x	1	2	3	4
$\text{P}(X = x)$	0.4	0.3	0.2	0.1

(ii)

w	8	9	10	11
$\text{P}(W = w)$	0.4	0.3	0.2	0.1

(b) (i) $\text{P}(X = x) = \frac{x^2}{14}$ for $x = 1,2,3$

(ii) $\text{P}(X = x) = \frac{1}{x}$ for $x = 2,3,6$

2. A random variable X has probability distribution $\text{P}(X = x) = k(x+1)$ for $x = 2,3,4,5,6$.

(a) Show that $k = 0.04$.

(b) Find $\text{E}(X)$. *[5 marks]*

3. The random variable V has probability distribution as shown in the table and $\text{E}(V) = 6.3$. Find the value of k.

v	1	2	5	8	k
$\text{P}(V = v)$	0.2	0.3	0.1	0.1	0.3

[4 marks]

4. A random variable X has its probability distribution given by $\text{P}(X = x) = k(x+3)$, where x is 0, 1, 2 or 3.

(a) Show that $k = \frac{1}{18}$.

(b) Find the exact value of $\text{E}(X)$. *[6 marks]*

5. The probability distribution of a random variable X is given by $\text{P}(X = x) = kx(4-x)$ for $x = 1,2,3$.

(a) Find the value of k.

(b) Find $\text{E}(X)$. *[6 marks]*

6. A fair six-sided die with sides numbered 1, 1, 2, 2, 2, 5 is thrown. Find the expected mean of the score. *[6 marks]*

7. The table below shows the probability distribution of a random variable X.

x	0	1	2	3
$P(X=x)$	0.1	p	q	0.2

Given that $E(X)=1.5$, find the values of p and q. *[6 marks]*

8. A biased die with four faces is used in a game. A player pays 5 counters to roll the die. The table below shows the possible scores on the die, the probability of each score, and the number of counters the player receives in return for each score.

Score	1	2	3	4
Probability	$\frac{1}{2}$	$\frac{1}{4}$	$\frac{1}{5}$	$\frac{1}{20}$
Number of counters player receives	4	5	15	n

Find the value of n so that the player gets an expected profit of 3.25 counters per roll. *[5 marks]*

9. In a game, a player pays an entrance fee of $\$n$. He then selects one number from 1, 2, 3 or 4 and rolls three 4-sided dice.

If his chosen number appears on all three dice, he wins four times his entrance fee.

If his number appears on exactly two of the dice, he wins three times the entrance fee.

If his number appears on exactly one die, he wins \$1.

If his number does not appear on any of the dice, he wins nothing.

(a) Copy and complete the following probability table.

Player's profit (\$)	$-n$		$2n$	$3n$
Probability		$\frac{27}{64}$		

(b) The game organiser wants to make a profit over many plays of the game. Given that he must charge a whole number of cents, what is the minimum entrance fee the organiser should charge? *[10 marks]*

18C The binomial distribution

Some probability distributions come up so often that they have been given names and formal notation. One of the most important of these is the **binomial distribution**.

A binomial distribution arises when an experiment (or 'trial') with two possible outcomes is repeated a set number of times. The word 'binomial' refers to the two possible outcomes; conventionally, one of them is called a 'success' and the other a 'failure'. If the probability of 'success' remains constant and the trials are conducted independently of each other, then the total number of successes can be modelled using the binomial distribution.

KEY POINT 18.3

The binomial distribution models the number of successful outcomes in a fixed number of trials, provided the following conditions are satisfied:

- Each trial has two possible outcomes.
- The trials are independent of each other.
- The probability of success is the same in every trial.

If n is the number of trials, p is the probability of a success, and the random variable X is the total number of successes, then X follows a binomial distribution with n trials and probability of success p, written $X \sim \mathrm{B}(n, p)$.

EXAM HINT

You need to know the conditions under which the binomial distribution can be used and be able to interpret them in context.

So what is this distribution? Let us consider a specific example: suppose a die is rolled four times; what is the probability of getting exactly two fives?

There are four trials, so $n = 4$. In this context, it makes sense to label getting a 5 as 'success', so we have $p = \frac{1}{6}$. The probability of a 'failure' (getting any number other than 5) is therefore $\frac{5}{6}$. One way of getting two fives is if on the first two rolls we get a five and on the next two rolls we get something else. The probability of this happening is $\frac{1}{6} \times \frac{1}{6} \times \frac{5}{6} \times \frac{5}{6} = \left(\frac{1}{6}\right)^2 \left(\frac{5}{6}\right)^2$. But this is not the only way in which two fives can occur. The two fives may be on the first and third or second and fourth rolls. In fact, we have to consider all the ways in which we can pick two trials out of the four for the 5 to turn up in. This can be done by drawing a tree diagram. We only need to include the branches along which exactly two fives occur.

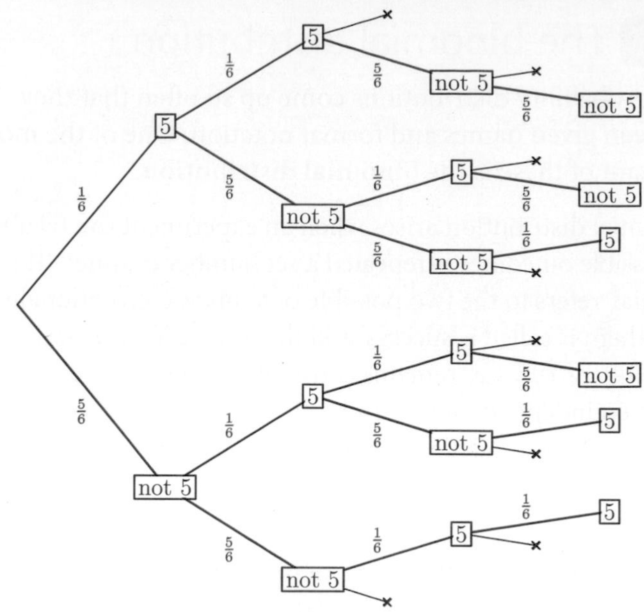

Each of the paths giving 'two fives' has the same probability, $\left(\frac{1}{6}\right)^2\left(\frac{5}{6}\right)^2$. The total number of paths giving the outcome 'two fives' is 6. So if X is the random variable 'number of fives thrown when four dice are rolled', then we can say that $\text{P}(X=2)=6\left(\frac{1}{6}\right)^2\left(\frac{5}{6}\right)^2$.

Generalising this reasoning, consider n trials in which the probability of a success is p, and suppose we are interested in the probability of obtaining r successes. If we imagine representing the n trials on a tree diagram, each relevant path (along which exactly r successes occur) will have probability $p^r(1-p)^{n-r}$, because r of the outcomes are successes (each occurring with probability p) and the remaining $n-r$ outcomes are failures (each occurring with probability $1-p$). It turns out that the number of paths that give r successes is given by the binomial coefficient $\binom{n}{r}$. This leads to the following general formula for the probabilities of the binomial distribution.

We met binomial coefficients in chapter 7 when studying the binomial expansion. You can find binomial coefficients with your calculator or by using the formula given in the Formula booklet.

KEY POINT 18.4

If $X \sim \text{B}(n,p)$, then

$$\text{P}(X=r)=\binom{n}{r}p^r(1-p)^{n-r} \text{ for } r=0,1,2\ldots,n$$

The useful thing about identifying a binomial distribution is that you can then apply standard results, such as the formula above, without having to go through the earlier argument with tree diagrams every time.

Worked example 18.4

Rohir has a 30% chance of correctly answering a multiple-choice question. He takes a test in which there are ten multiple-choice questions.

(a) What is the probability that Rohir gets exactly four of the questions correct? Give your answer to five significant figures.

(b) Suggest which requirements for a binomial distribution might not be satisfied in this situation.

Define the random variable (if not already given in the question).

(a) Let X be the number of correct answers out of the ten.

Identify the probability distribution.

$X \sim B(10, 0.3)$

Write down the formula for the probability required, and calculate the answer.

$n = 10, p = 0.3, r = 4$

$P(X = 4) = \binom{10}{4}(0.3)^4(0.7)^6$

$= 0.20012$ (5SF)

Consider the conditions for the distribution to apply.

(b) Binomial distribution requires:
two outcomes at each trial
trials independent of each other
constant probability of success in each trial.

Are there any requirements that are not met in this context? There are two outcomes, and trials are independent (answering one question does not make it easier or harder to answer another).

The questions may not all be of the same difficulty, so there may not be a constant probability of success.

Most calculators can find binomial probabilities if you specify the values of n, p and r. Sometimes you may want to find the probability of a *range* of numbers of successes (r values); you could in principle work out the probabilities for the different r values and then add them all up, but this can be very time-consuming. Fortunately, calculators usually have a function that gives the probability of getting up to (and including) a certain number of successes – this is called a **cumulative probability**.

EXAM HINT
See Calculator skills sheet 12 on the CD-ROM for how to find binomial probabilities and cumulative probabilities on your calculator.

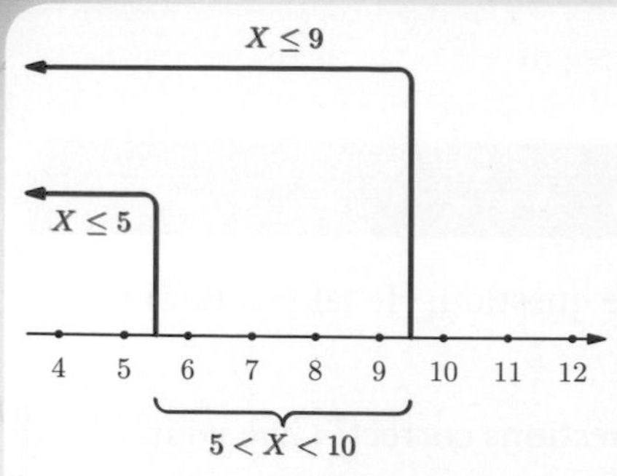

For example, if you are asked to find the probability that the number of successes is greater than 10, you can use your calculator to find the cumulative probability $P(X \le 10)$; then the probability you want, $P(X > 10)$, is just $1 - P(X \le 10)$. If you need the probability of getting more than 5 but fewer than 10 successes, this is $P(5 < X < 10) = P(X \le 9) - P(X \le 5)$, as shown on the number line.

Worked example 18.5

Anna shoots at a target 15 times. The probability that she hits the target on any shot is 0.6. Find the probability that she hits the target more than 5 but at most 10 times.

Define the random variable.

Let X be the number of times Anna hits the target.

State the probability distribution.

$X \sim B(15, 0.6)$

Write down the probability to be found, and express it in terms of probabilities that can be found on the GDC.

From GDC:

$$P(5 < X \le 10) = P(X \le 10) - P(X \le 5)$$
$$= 0.7827 - 0.0338$$
$$= 0.749 \quad (3\text{ SF})$$

EXAM HINT

Even when you are using a calculator to find probabilities, you should still write your solution in correct mathematical notation (not calculator notation). You must state what distribution you used and which probabilities you found using the GDC. Remember to give the answer to 3 significant figures.

Now that we can calculate probabilities for different numbers of successes in a binomial distribution, we can ask what is the expected mean number of successes. As we noted in section 18B, this is not the same as the most likely number of successes.

Suppose that all students in a large school take a multiple-choice test with 12 questions, each with 5 possible answers (only one of which is correct). If the students all decide to guess answers randomly, what is the expected average number of correct answers? The scores for each individual student will vary, but it seems plausible that the average will be around $12 \times \frac{1}{5} = 2.4$.

Using the formula for the expectation, it can be proved that this is indeed the case. It is also possible to show that the variance of the scores is $12 \times \frac{1}{5} \times \frac{4}{5} = 1.92$.

KEY POINT 18.5

> If $X \sim \mathrm{B}(n, p)$, then its expectation (mean) and variance are given by
>
> $$\mathrm{E}(X) = np$$
>
> $$\mathrm{Var}(X) = np(1-p)$$

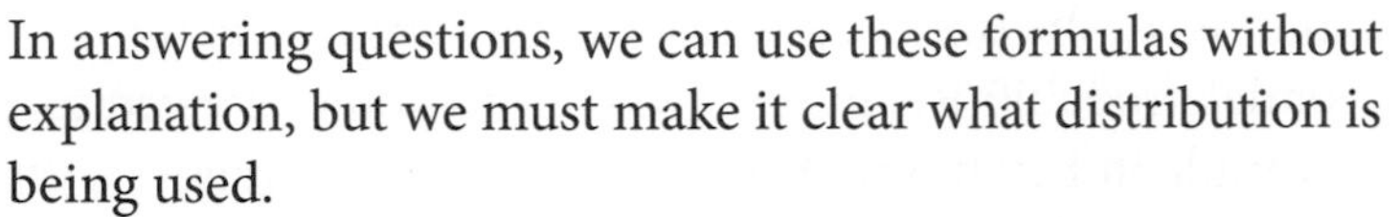

In answering questions, we can use these formulas without explanation, but we must make it clear what distribution is being used.

The variance was introduced in section 16B; it is the square of the standard deviation, a measure of the spread of values of a random variable.

Worked example 18.6

A bag contains a large number of balls, two-thirds of which are green. Ten balls are selected one by one, with each ball being replaced before the next one is selected. Find the mean and standard deviation of the number of green balls selected.

Define the random variable.

Let G be the number of green balls selected.

State the distribution. There are 10 trials, and in each trial the probability of selecting a green ball is always $\frac{2}{3}$, so G follows a binomial distribution.

$G \sim B\left(10, \frac{2}{3}\right)$

Use the formula for expectation.

$\mathrm{E}(X) = 10 \times \frac{2}{3} = \frac{20}{3}$

Use the formula for variance. Then take the square root to get the standard deviation.

$\mathrm{Var}(X) = 10 \times \frac{2}{3} \times \frac{1}{3} = \frac{20}{9}$

$\therefore \sigma = \sqrt{\frac{20}{9}} = \frac{2\sqrt{5}}{3}$

Although most of the time you will be using your calculator to find binomial probabilities, in some situations you may need to use the formula in Key point 18.4, as in the next example.

Worked example 18.7

A random variable X has distribution $\mathrm{B}(15, p)$. Given that $\mathrm{P}(X = 9) = 0.105$, find the possible values of p.

Use the formula in Key point 18.4 to write $\mathrm{P}(X = 9)$ in terms of P. Set this equal to 0.105 to get an equation for p.

$\mathrm{P}(X = 9) = \binom{15}{9} p^9 (1-p)^6 = 0.105$

→

continued . . .

Use the GDC to solve this equation. Remember that only values between 0 and 1 make sense for p.

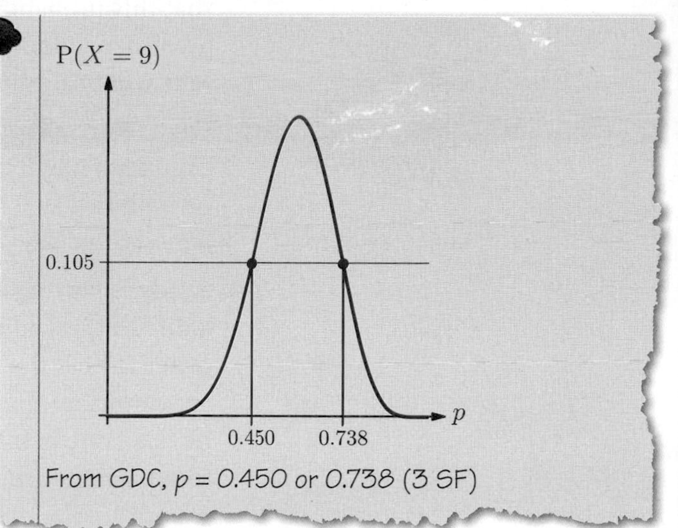

Exercise 18C

1. The random variable X has a binomial distribution with $n=8$ and $p=0.2$. Calculate the following probabilities.
   (a) (i) $P(X=3)$ (ii) $P(X=4)$
   (b) (i) $P(X\le 3)$ (ii) $P(X\le 2)$
   (c) (i) $P(X>3)$ (ii) $P(X>4)$
   (d) (i) $P(X<5)$ (ii) $P(X<3)$
   (e) (i) $P(X\ge 3)$ (ii) $P(X\ge 1)$
   (f) (i) $P(3<X\le 6)$ (ii) $P(1\le X<4)$

2. Given that $Y\sim B\left(5,\frac{1}{2}\right)$, find the exact value of
   (a) (i) $P(Y=1)$ (ii) $P(Y=0)$
   (b) (i) $P(Y\ge 1)$ (ii) $P(Y\le 1)$
   (c) (i) $P(Y>4)$ (ii) $P(Y\le 3)$

3. Find the mean and variance of the following random variables.
   (a) (i) $Y\sim B\left(100,\frac{1}{10}\right)$ (ii) $X\sim B\left(16,\frac{1}{2}\right)$
   (b) (i) $X\sim B(15,0.3)$ (ii) $Y\sim B(20,0.35)$
   (c) (i) $Z\sim B\left(n-1,\frac{1}{n}\right)$ (ii) $X\sim B\left(n,\frac{2}{n}\right)$

4. (a) Jake beats Marco at chess in 70% of their games. Assuming that this probability is constant and that the results of games are independent of each other, what is the probability that Jake will beat Marco in at least 16 of their next 20 games?

   (b) On a television channel, the news is shown at the same time each day. The probability that Salia watches the news on a given day is 0.35. Calculate the probability that on 5 consecutive days she watches the news on exactly 3 days.

   (c) Sandy is playing a computer game and needs to accomplish a difficult task at least three times in five attempts in order to pass the level. There is a 1 in 2 chance that he accomplishes the task each time he tries, unaffected by how he has done before. What is the probability that he will pass to the next level?

5. 15% of students at a large school travel by bus. A random sample of 20 students is taken.

   (a) Explain why the number of students in the sample who travel by bus follows only approximately a binomial distribution.

   (b) Use the binomial distribution to estimate the probability that exactly five of the students in the sample travel by bus.

[3 marks]

6. A coin is biased so that when it is tossed the probability of obtaining heads is $\frac{2}{3}$. The coin is tossed 4050 times. Let X be the number of heads obtained. Find the expected value of X.

[3 marks]

7. A biology test consists of eight multiple-choice questions. Each question has four answers, only one of which is correct. At least five correct answers are required to pass the test. Sheila has not studied for the test, so answers each question at random.

   (a) What is the probability that Sheila answers exactly five questions correctly?

   (b) What is the expected number of correct answers Sheila will give?

   (c) Find the variance of the number of correct answers Sheila gives.

   (d) What is the probability that Sheila manages to pass the test?

[7 marks]

8. Suppose that 0.8% of people in a country have a particular cold virus at any time. On a single day, a doctor sees 80 patients.

(a) What is the probability that exactly two of them have the virus?

(b) What is the probability that three or more of them have the virus?

(c) State an assumption you have made in these calculations. *[5 marks]*

9. Given that $Y \sim \text{B}(12, p)$ and that the mean of Y is 4.8, find the value of p. *[3 marks]*

Question 10 is the problem posed to Pierre de Fermat in 1654 by a professional gambler who could not understand why he was losing. It inspired Fermat (with the assistance of Pascal) to set up probability as a rigorous mathematical discipline.

10. With a fair die, which is more likely: rolling 3 sixes in 4 throws or rolling a five or a six in 5 out of 6 throws? *[6 marks]*

11. A drawer contains 5 red socks and 5 blue socks. Two socks are removed without replacement.

(a) Show that the probability of taking a red sock second depends on the outcome of the first sock taken, i.e. the events are dependent.

(b) Show that the probability of taking a red sock second equals the probability of taking a red sock first, i.e. the probability is constant.

12. Over a one-month period, Ava and Sven play a total of n games of tennis. The probability that Ava wins any game is 0.4. The result of each game played is independent of any other game played. Let X denote the number of games won by Ava over the one-month period.

(a) Find an expression for $\text{P}(X = 2)$ in terms of n.

(b) If the probability that Ava wins two games is 0.121 correct to three decimal places, find the value of n.

[5 marks]

13. A die is biased so that the probability of rolling a six is p. If the probability of rolling 2 sixes in 12 throws is 0.283 (to three significant figures), find the possible values of p correct to two decimal places. *[5 marks]*

14. X is a binomial random variable where the number of trials is 5 and the probability of success in each trial is p. Find the possible values of p if $\text{P}(X = 3) = 0.3087$. *[5 marks]*

18D The normal distribution

There are many situations where a random variable is most likely to be close to its average value, and values further away from the average become increasingly unlikely. The **normal distribution** is a model of such situations.

The normal distribution is a *continuous* distribution, used to model continuous data or a continuous random variable, where each value can be any real number within a certain interval – examples include measurements of height and time. For a continuous distribution, unlike for the *discrete* distributions we met in sections 18A–C, we cannot list all possible values of the variable in a table; we can only calculate the probability of the variable taking values in a specified range.

A continuous distribution is commonly represented by a curve, where the probability of the variable being between two specified values is equal to the *area* under the curve between those two values. The diagrams below show several examples of normal distributions. The values of the random variable X are plotted on the x-axis, and the shaded area represents the probability given beneath each graph.

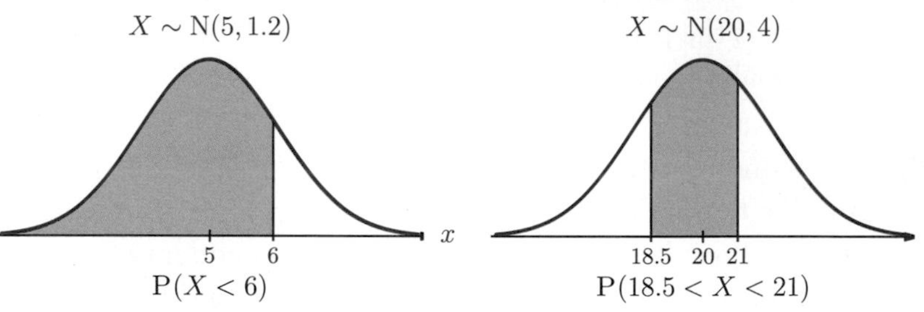

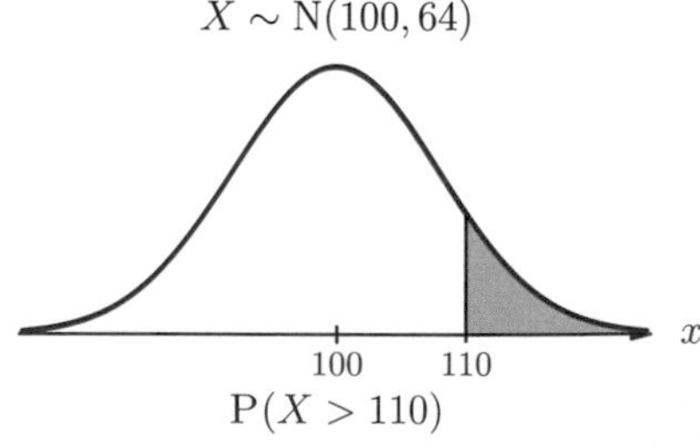

EXAM HINT

Be careful with the notation: σ^2 is the variance, so $X \sim N(10, 9)$ has standard deviation $\sigma = 3$.

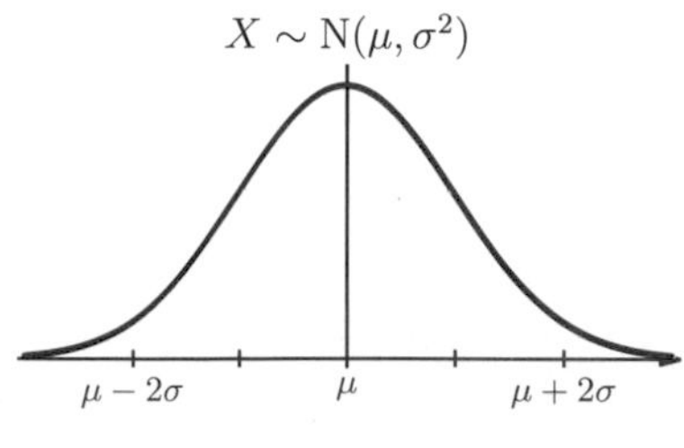

To describe a particular normal distribution, all that is needed is its mean and variance. If a random variable X follows a normal distribution with mean μ and variance σ^2, we write $X \sim N(\mu, \sigma^2)$. The peak of the normal distribution curve is at the mean. The standard deviation σ determines the width (i.e. spread) of the curve; values of x that lie further than two standard deviations from the mean are very unlikely.

Historically, cumulative probabilities for the normal distribution, i.e. probabilities of the form $P(X \le x)$, were recorded in tables. Many people still use such tables if they don't have access to a calculator. Since it is not feasible to make tables for every possible combination of μ and σ values, values of the random variable need to be converted into 'Z-scores', described below, before they can be looked up in a table.

You can find probabilities of normal distributions using your calculator. You need to enter the mean and standard deviation, and specify values x_1 and x_2 to obtain the probability $P(x_1 \le X \le x_2)$. You can also calculate probabilities of the form $P(X \ge x)$ or $P(X \le x)$.

EXAM HINT
See Calculator skills sheet 13 on the CD-ROM for details of how to calculate normal probabilities.

It is often helpful to sketch a graph to get a visual representation of the probability you are trying to find. Graphs can also provide a useful check of your answer, as they show you whether you should expect the probability to be smaller or greater than 0.5.

Worked example 18.8

The average height of people in a town is 170 cm, and the standard deviation of the heights is 10 cm. What is the probability that a randomly selected resident is

(a) shorter than 165 cm

(b) between 180 cm and 190 cm tall

(c) taller than 176 cm?

State the distribution.

Let X be the height of a town resident. Then

$X \sim N(170, 100)$

Identify the probability to be found and use a calculator to find it.

(a) $P(X < 165)$

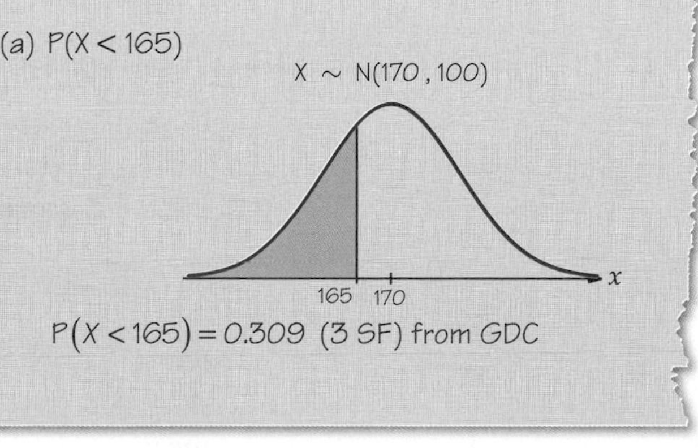

$P(X < 165) = 0.309$ (3 SF) from GDC

→

continued . . .

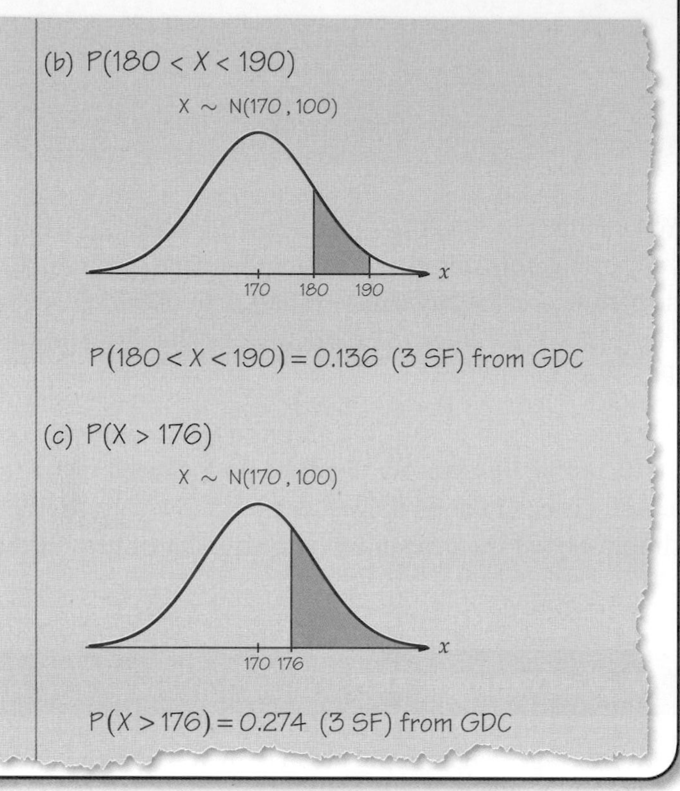

(b) P(180 < X < 190)
X ~ N(170, 100)
170
180
190
x
P(180 < X < 190) = 0.136 (3 SF) from GDC
(c) P(X > 176)
X ~ N(170, 100)
170 176
x
P(X > 176) = 0.274 (3 SF) from GDC

If a normally distributed random variable has mean 120, should a value of 150 be considered unusually large? The answer depends on how spread out the variable is, which is measured by its standard deviation. If the standard deviation of this variable is 30, then a value around 150 would be quite common; however, if the standard deviation were 5, then 150 would be very unusual.

The probability of a random variable being less than a given value is called **cumulative probability**. For a normally distributed variable, it turns out that this probability depends only on the number of standard deviations the value is from the mean. This distance in terms of number of standard deviations is called the **Z-score**.

KEY POINT 18.6

For $X \sim N(\mu, \sigma^2)$, the Z-score of the value x measures the number of standard deviations that x is away from the mean:

$$z = \frac{x - \mu}{\sigma}$$

Worked example 18.9

Suppose that $X \sim \mathrm{N}(15, 6.25)$.

(a) How many standard deviations is $x = 16.1$ away from the mean?

(b) Find the value of X which is 1.2 standard deviations below the mean.

The number of standard deviations away from the mean is measured by the Z-score.

(a) $z = \dfrac{x - \mu}{\sigma}$

6.25 is the variance! We need to take the square root to find the standard deviation.

$\sigma = \sqrt{6.25} = 2.5$

$\therefore z = \dfrac{16.1 - 15}{2.5} = 0.44$

So 16.1 is 0.44 standard deviations away from the mean.

Values below the mean have a negative Z-score.

(b) $z = -1.2$

means that

$-1.2 = \dfrac{x - 15}{2.5}$

$\Rightarrow x - 15 = -3$

$\Rightarrow x = 12$

If we have a random variable $X \sim N(\mu, \sigma^2)$, we can create a new random variable Z which takes values equal to the Z-scores of the values of X. In other words, for each x there is a corresponding $z = \dfrac{x - \mu}{\sigma}$; this is called the *standardised value.* It turns out that, whatever the original mean and standard deviation of X, this new random variable Z always has a normal distribution with mean 0 and variance 1, called the **standard normal distribution**: $Z \sim N(0,1)$. This is an extremely important property of normal distributions, and it is especially useful in situations when the mean and standard deviation of X are not known (see section 18E).

Think about the transformations of graphs that we studied in chapter 5: the normal distribution curves for X and Z are related via a horizontal translation by μ units and a horizontal stretch with scale factor σ.

Before graphical calculators became available (which is not so long ago!), people used tables showing cumulative probabilities of the standard normal distribution. Because of their importance, these probabilities were given special notation: $\Phi(z) = \text{P}(Z \le z)$. Although you don't have to use this notation, you should understand what it means as you may still encounter it in some books.

KEY POINT 18.7

The (cumulative) probabilities of X and Z are related by

$$\text{P}(X \le x) = \text{P}\left(Z \le \frac{x-\mu}{\sigma}\right)$$

Worked example 18.10

Let $X \sim N(6, 0.5^2)$. Write the following in terms of probabilities of Z.

(a) $\text{P}(X \le 6.1)$ (b) $\text{P}(5 < X < 7)$ (c) $\text{P}(X > 6.5)$

Here $x = 6.1$, so we calculate the corresponding $z = \frac{x-\mu}{\sigma}$.

(a) $\mu = 6, \sigma = 0.5$

$\text{P}(x \le 6.1) = \text{P}\left(Z \le \frac{6.1-6}{0.5}\right)$

$= \text{P}(Z \le 0.2)$

The relationship between probabilities of X and Z in Key point 18.7 is stated for cumulative probabilities, so convert to that form first.

(b) $\text{P}(5 < X < 7) = \text{P}(X < 7) - \text{P}(X < 5)$

$= \text{P}\left(Z < \frac{7-6}{0.5}\right) - \text{P}\left(Z < \frac{5-6}{0.5}\right)$

$= \text{P}(Z < 2) - \text{P}(Z < -2)$

$= \text{P}(-2 < Z < 2)$

(c) $\text{P}(X > 6.5) = 1 - \text{P}(X \le 6.5)$

$= 1 - \text{P}\left(Z \le \frac{6.5-6}{0.5}\right)$

$= 1 - \text{P}(Z \le 1)$

$= \text{P}(Z > 1)$

As you can see from parts (b) and (c) of the above example, you don't actually have to convert probabilities into the form $\text{P}(X \le k)$ every time; you can simply replace the x values by the corresponding z values (Z-scores).

Exercise 18D

1. Find the following probabilities.
   (a) $X \sim \text{N}(20,100)$
      (i) $\text{P}(X \le 32)$ (ii) $\text{P}(X < 12)$
   (b) $Y \sim \text{N}(4.8,1.44)$
      (i) $\text{P}(Y > 5.1)$ (ii) $\text{P}(Y \ge 3.4)$
   (c) $R \sim \text{N}(17,2)$
      (i) $\text{P}(16 < R < 20)$ (ii) $\text{P}(17.4 < R < 18.2)$
   (d) Q has a normal distribution with mean 12 and standard deviation 3.
      (i) $\text{P}(Q > 9.4)$ (ii) $\text{P}(Q < 14)$
   (e) F has a normal distribution with mean 100 and standard deviation 25.
      (i) $\text{P}(|F - 100| < 15)$ (ii) $\text{P}(|F - 100| > 10)$

2. Find the Z-score corresponding to the given value of X.
   (a) (i) $X \sim \text{N}(12,2^2)$, $x = 13$
      (ii) $X \sim \text{N}(38,7^2)$, $x = 45$
   (b) (i) $X \sim \text{N}(20,9)$, $x = 15$
      (ii) $X \sim \text{N}(162,25)$, $x = 160$

3. Given that $X \sim \text{N}(16,2.5^2)$, write the following in terms of probabilities of the standard normal variable.
   (a) (i) $\text{P}(X < 20)$ (ii) $\text{P}(X < 19.2)$
   (b) (i) $\text{P}(X \ge 14.3)$ (ii) $\text{P}(X \ge 8.6)$
   (c) (i) $\text{P}(12.5 < X < 16.5)$ (ii) $\text{P}(10.1 \le X \le 15.5)$

4. The battery life of a certain brand of laptop batteries follows a normal distribution with mean 16 hours and standard deviation 5 hours. A particular battery has a life of 10.2 hours.
   (a) How many standard deviations below the mean is this battery life?
   (b) What is the probability that a randomly chosen battery has a life shorter than this? *[6 marks]*

5. Weights of a certain breed of cat follow a normal distribution with mean 16 kg and variance 16 kg². In a sample of 2000 such cats, estimate the number that will have a weight above 13 kg. *[6 marks]*

6. When Ali participates in long-jump competitions, the lengths of his jumps are normally distributed with mean 5.2 m and standard deviation 0.7 m.

(a) What is the probability that Ali will record a jump between 5 m and 5.5 m?

(b) Ali needs to jump 6 m to qualify for the school team.

(i) What is the probability that he will qualify with a single jump?

(ii) If he is allowed three jumps, what is the probability that he will qualify for the school team? *[7 marks]*

7. If $D \sim \text{N}(250, 400)$, find

(a) $\text{P}(D > 265 \cap D < 280)$

(b) $\text{P}(D > 265 \mid D < 280)$

(c) $\text{P}(D < 242 \cup D > 256)$ *[6 marks]*

8. If $Q \sim \text{N}(4, 160)$, find

(a) $\text{P}(5 < |Q|)$

(b) $\text{P}(Q > 5 \mid 5 < |Q|)$ *[6 marks]*

9. The weights of apples in a certain shipment are normally distributed with mean weight 150 g and standard deviation 25 g. Supermarkets classify apples as 'medium' if their weights are between 120 g and 170 g.

(a) What proportion of apples in this shipment are 'medium'?

(b) In a bag of 10 apples, what is the probability that there are at least 8 medium apples? *[6 marks]*

10. The wingspan of a species of pigeon is normally distributed with mean 60 cm and standard deviation 6 cm. A pigeon of this species is chosen at random.

(a) Find the probability that its wingspan is greater than 50 cm.

(b) Given that this pigeon's wingspan is greater than 50 cm, find the probability that it is greater than 55 cm.

[6 marks]

11. Grains of sand are believed to have normally distributed widths with mean 2 mm and variance $0.25\ \text{mm}^2$.

(a) Find the probability that a randomly chosen grain of sand is wider than 1.5 mm.

(b) The sand is passed through a filter which blocks grains wider than 2.5 mm. The sand that has passed through the filter is examined. What is the probability that a randomly chosen grain of filtered sand is wider than 1.5 mm? *[6 marks]*

12. The amount of paracetamol per tablet of a pain-relieving medicine is normally distributed with mean 500 mg and standard deviation 160 mg. A dose containing less than 300 mg is ineffective in alleviating toothache. In a trial of this medicine on 20 people suffering from toothache, what is the probability that two or more people get less than the effective dose? *[6 marks]*

18E The inverse normal distribution

In section 18D we saw how to find probabilities when we were given information about a normally distributed random variable, such as values that it should lie between. In real life there are many situations where we need to work backwards from given probabilities to estimate corresponding values of the variable. Doing so requires the **inverse normal distribution**.

EXAM HINT
Remember that p must be a cumulative probability.

KEY POINT 18.8

For a given value of probability p, the inverse normal distribution gives the value of x such that $P(X \le x) = p$.

Many books also use the $\Phi(z)$ notation mentioned in section 18D to write inverse normal distributions: If $P(X \le x) = p$, then $\Phi^{-1}(p) = z = \frac{x - \mu}{\sigma}$.

You can use your calculator to find values of an inverse normal distribution: you need to enter the values of p, μ and σ, and then the calculator will return the value of x. If the probability you are given is $P(X > x)$, you may have to calculate $P(X \le x) = 1 - P(X > x)$ first.

EXAM HINT

Calculator skills sheet 13 on the CD-ROM explains how to work with inverse normal distributions. Some calculators are able to find the value of x such that $P(X > x) = p$ as well.

Worked example 18.11

The size of men's feet is thought to be normally distributed with mean 22 cm and variance 25 cm². A shoe manufacturer wants only 5% of men to be unable to find shoes large enough for them. How big should their largest shoe be?

Convert the question into mathematical terms.

Let X = length of a man's foot
Then $X \sim N(22,25)$
We need the value of x such that
$P(X > x) = 0.05$

Use the inverse normal distribution. Since the information we are given is $P(X > x)$, we first convert it into a cumulative probability of the form $P(X \leq x)$.

$P(X \leq x) = 1 - P(X > x) = 0.95$
$\Rightarrow x = 30.2$ (from GDC)
So their largest shoe must fit a foot 30.2 cm long.

EXAM HINT

Estimating parameters will involve solving equations – sometimes simultaneous equations. As the numbers are usually not 'nice', you may want to use your calculator.

One of the main applications of statistics is to estimate parameters of the distribution from information found in the data. For example, suppose we know that a certain random variable can be described as normally distributed, but we don't know the mean or standard deviation. How can we estimate the unknown parameter(s) using other information available from the data? This is where the standard normal distribution comes in useful: we can replace all the X values by their Z-scores, which follow a distribution $N(0,1)$ where all parameters are known.

Worked example 18.12

The masses of gerbils are thought to be normally distributed with standard deviation 8.3 g. It is found that 30% of gerbils have a mass of more than 65 g. Estimate the mean mass of a gerbil.

Convert the question into mathematical terms.

Let X = mass of a gerbil
Then $X \sim N(\mu, 8.3^2)$
and we know $P(X > 65) = 0.3$

Convert the probability into the form $P(X \le k)$.

$\therefore P(X \le 65) = 0.7$

Use the inverse normal distribution for Z and $z = \frac{x-\mu}{\sigma}$.

$P(Z \le z) = 0.7 \Rightarrow z = 0.524$ (from GDC)

where $z = \frac{x-\mu}{\sigma} = \frac{65-\mu}{8.3}$

Now we can solve for μ.

$\therefore \frac{65-\mu}{8.3} = 0.524$

$\Rightarrow \mu = 60.6\,g$

Exercise 18E

1. (a) If $X \sim N(14, 49)$, find the value of x for which
   (i) $P(X < x) = 0.8$ (ii) $P(X < x) = 0.46$
   (b) If $X \sim N(36.5, 10)$, find the value of x for which
   (i) $P(X > x) = 0.9$ (ii) $P(X > x) = 0.4$
   (c) If $X \sim N(0, 12)$, find the value of x for which
   (i) $P(|X| < x) = 0.5$ (ii) $P(|X| < x) = 0.8$

2. (a) If $X \sim N(\mu, 4)$, find μ given that
   (i) $P(X > 4) = 0.8$ (ii) $P(X > 9) = 0.2$
   (b) If $X \sim N(8, \sigma^2)$, find σ given that
   (i) $P(X \le 19) = 0.6$ (ii) $P(X \le 0) = 0.3$

3. If $X \sim N(\mu, \sigma^2)$, find μ and σ given that
   (a) (i) $P(X > 7) = 0.8$ and $P(X < 6) = 0.1$
   (ii) $P(X > 150) = 0.3$ and $P(X < 120) = 0.4$
   (b) (i) $P(X > 0.1) = 0.4$ and $P(X \ge 0.6) = 0.25$
   (ii) $P(X > 700) = 0.8$ and $P(X \ge 400) = 0.99$

4. IQ tests are designed to have a mean of 100 and a standard deviation of 20. What IQ score is needed to be in the top 2% of all scores? *[5 marks]*

5. Rabbits' masses are normally distributed with an average of 2.6 kg and a variance of 1.44 kg^2. A vet decides that the heaviest 20% of rabbits are 'obese'. What is the minimum mass of an obese rabbit? *[5 marks]*

6. A manufacturer knows that his machines produce bolts whose diameters follow a normal distribution with standard deviation 0.02 cm. He takes a random sample of bolts and finds that 6% of them have diameter greater than 2 cm. Find the mean diameter of the bolts. *[6 marks]*

7. The times taken for students to complete a test are normally distributed with a mean of 32 minutes and standard deviation of 6 minutes.

(a) Find the probability that a randomly chosen student completes the test in less than 35 minutes.

(b) 90% of students complete the test in less than t minutes. Find the value of t.

(c) A random sample of 8 students had the time they spent on the test recorded. Find the probability that exactly 2 of these students completed the test in less than 30 minutes.

[7 marks]

8. An old textbook says that the range of data can be estimated as 6 times the standard deviation. If the data is normally distributed, what percentage of the data is within this range? *[6 marks]*

9. (a) 30% of sand from Playa Gauss falls through a sieve with gaps of width 1 mm, but 90% passes through a sieve with 2 mm gaps. Assuming that the diameters of the grains are normally distributed, estimate the mean and standard deviation of the sand grain diameter.

(b) 80% of sand from Playa Fermat falls through a sieve with gaps of width 2 mm, and 40% of this filtered sand passes through a sieve with 1 mm gaps. Assuming that the diameters of the grains are normally distributed, estimate the mean and standard deviation of the sand grain diameter.

[7 marks]

Summary

- A **random variable** is a quantity whose value depends on chance. The **probability distribution** of the random variable is a list of all the possible outcomes together with their associated probabilities.
- Even though the outcome of any one observation of a random variable is impossible to determine, the **expectation** – i.e. the expected mean value – of observations can be predicted quite accurately by the formula

$$E(X)=\sum_{x} x\,P(X=x)$$

- Among a fixed number n of independent trials (each with two possible outcomes) with a constant probability p of success in each trial, the total number of successes X follows a **binomial distribution**: $X \sim B(n, p)$.
  - The probability of getting x successes is $P(X=r)=\binom{n}{r}p^r(1-p)^{n-r}$, $r = 0, 1, \ldots, n$, which can be found using your calculator.
  - The mean $(E(X))$ of the binomial distribution is np.
  - The variance $(\mathrm{Var}(X))$ is $np(1-p)$.
- The **normal distribution** is a continuous distribution which can be used to model many physical situations. A normal distribution is completely defined by its mean μ and variance σ^2. Given that $X \sim N(\mu,\sigma^2)$, you can use a calculator to find probabilities of the form $P(x_1 \le X \le x_2)$, $P(X \le x)$ or $P(X \ge x)$ if you enter the values of μ, σ and x_1, x_2 or x.
- If we know probabilities relating to a variable that follows a normal distribution, we can deduce information about the values of the variable by using the **inverse normal distribution**: $P(X \le x) = p$, where p is probability.
- For $X \sim N(\mu,\sigma^2)$, the **Z-score** of the value x measures the number of standard deviations that x is from the mean:

$$z=\frac{x-\mu}{\sigma}$$

The random variable Z whose values are these Z-scores follows a normal distribution with mean 0 and standard deviation 1, called the **standard normal distribution** $(Z \sim N(0,1))$. This can be useful when trying to calculate the μ and σ^2 of a given normal distribution.

If we put in a **cumulative probability** p, a calculator can tell us the value of z such that $P(Z \le z) = p$, from which we can then deduce information about the value of x, μ or σ using the Z-score relation above.

Introductory problem revisited

A casino offers a game in which a coin is tossed repeatedly. If the first head occurs on the first throw you get £2, if the first head occurs on the second throw you get £4, if the first head is on the third throw you get £8, and so on, with the prize doubling each time. How much should the casino charge for this game if they want to make a profit?

The probability of getting heads on the first throw is $\frac{1}{2}$, so $\text{P}(\text{win £2}) = \frac{1}{2}$. The probability of the first head being on the second throw is $\text{P}(\text{tails}) \times \text{P}(\text{heads}) = \frac{1}{4}$, so $\text{P}(\text{win £4}) = \frac{1}{4}$. The probability of the first head being on the third throw is $\text{P}(\text{tails}) \times \text{P}(\text{tails}) \times \text{P}(\text{heads}) = \frac{1}{8}$, so $\text{P}(\text{win £8}) = \frac{1}{8}$.

If the random variable X is the number of pounds won, then the probability distribution is as follows:

X	2	4	8	...	2^n	...
$\text{P}(X = x)$	$\frac{1}{2}$	$\frac{1}{4}$	$\frac{1}{8}$	...	$\frac{1}{2^n}$	...

Therefore the expected amount of winnings is

$$\text{E}(X) = 2 \times \frac{1}{2} + 4 \times \frac{1}{4} + 8 \times \frac{1}{8} + \cdots = 1 + 1 + 1 + \cdots$$

This sum continues for ever, so $\text{E}(X) = \infty$; that is, the expected payout over a long period of time is infinite – the casino cannot possibly charge enough to cover the expected payout.

Even though the expected payout is infinite, if you were offered the opportunity to play this game you should think twice. The calculation of E(X) assumes that you can play the game infinitely many times, and in reality this is of course not possible. This is an example of a famous fallacy known as 'Gambler's Ruin'.

Mixed examination practice 18

Short questions

1. A factory that makes bottles knows that, on average, 1.5% of its bottles are defective. Find the probability that in a randomly selected sample of 20 bottles, at least one bottle is defective. *[4 marks]*

2. A biased die with four faces is used in a game. A player pays 10 counters to roll the die and receives a number of counters equal to the value shown on the die. The table below shows the different values on the die and the probability of each occurring.

Value	1	5	10	N
Probability	$\frac{1}{2}$	$\frac{1}{5}$	$\frac{1}{5}$	$\frac{1}{10}$

Find the value represented by N, given that the player has an expected loss of one counter each time he plays the game. *[5 marks]*

3. The test scores of a group of students are normally distributed with mean 62 and variance 144.

(a) Find the percentage of students with scores above 80.

(b) What is the lowest score achieved by the top 5% of the students? *[6 marks]*

4. When a boy bats at baseball, the probability that he hits the ball is 0.4. In a practice session he gets pitched 12 balls; let X denote the total number of balls he hits. Assuming that his attempts are independent of each other, find

(a) $\mathrm{E}(X)$

(b) $\mathrm{P}(X \le \mathrm{Var}(X))$ *[5 marks]*

5. The adult of a certain breed of dog has average height 0.7 m with variance 0.05 m^2. If the heights follow a normal distribution, find the probability that of six independently selected dogs of this breed, exactly four are over 0.75 m tall. *[5 marks]*

6. When Robyn shoots an arrow at a target, the probability that she hits the target is 0.6. In a competition she has eight attempts to hit the target. If she gets at least seven hits on target, she will qualify for the next round.

(a) Find the probability that she hits the target exactly 4 times.

(b) Find the probability that she fails to qualify for the next round. *[6 marks]*

7. A company producing light bulbs knows that the probability of a new light bulb being defective is 0.5%.

(a) Find the probability that a pack of six light bulbs contains at least one defective bulb.

(b) Mario buys 20 packs of six light bulbs. Find the probability that more than four of the packs contain at least one defective light bulb. *[6 marks]*

8. 200 people are asked to estimate the size of an angle: 16 gave an estimate which was less than 25°, and 42 gave an estimate which was greater than 35°. Assuming that the data follows a normal distribution, estimate its mean and standard deviation. *[6 marks]*

9. When a fair die is rolled n times, the probability of getting at most two sixes is 0.532 correct to three significant figures.

(a) Find the value of n.

(b) Find the probability of getting exactly two sixes. *[7 marks]*

Long questions

1. A bag contains a very large number of ribbons. One-quarter of the ribbons are yellow and the rest are blue. Ten ribbons are selected at random from the bag.

(a) Find the expected number of yellow ribbons selected.

(b) Find the probability that exactly six of the selected ribbons are yellow.

(c) Find the probability that at least two of the selected ribbons are yellow.

(d) Find the most likely number of yellow ribbons selected.

(e) What assumption have you made about the probability of selecting a yellow ribbon? *[11 marks]*

2. The probability that each student forgets to do homework is 5%, independently of whether other students do homework or not. If at least one student forgets to do homework, the whole class has to do a test.

(a) If there are 12 students in a class, find the probability that the class will have to do a test.

(b) For a class with n students, write down an expression for the probability that the class will have to do a test.

(c) Hence find the smallest number of students in the class such that the probability of the class having to do a test is at least 80%. *[12 marks]*

3. Two children, Alan and Belle, each throw two fair cubical dice simultaneously. The score for each child is the sum of the two numbers shown on their respective dice.

(a) (i) Calculate the probability that Alan obtains a score of 9.

(ii) Calculate the probability that Alan and Belle both obtain a score of 9.

(b) (i) Calculate the probability that Alan and Belle obtain the same score.

(ii) Deduce the probability that Alan's score exceeds Belle's score.

(c) Let X denote the largest number shown on the four dice.

(i) Show that $\mathrm{P}(X \leq x) = \left(\frac{x}{6}\right)^4$ for $x = 1, 2, \ldots, 6$.

(ii) Copy and complete the following probability distribution table.

X	1	2	3	4	5	6
$\mathrm{P}(X = x)$	$\frac{1}{1296}$	$\frac{15}{1296}$				$\frac{671}{1296}$

(iii) Calculate $\mathrm{E}(X)$. *[13 marks]*

(*© IB Organization 2002*)

19 Questions crossing chapters

One of the hardest features of the International Baccalaureate is that examination questions can draw on different areas of the syllabus. This chapter brings together questions of this type, so you may find it very challenging. Indeed, some of the questions are at the highest difficulty level that could be expected to come up in the exam. Do not be disheartened if you cannot finish a question; try to extract as many marks from it as possible – that is how to get a top grade! Although some questions may look unfamiliar and daunting, if you can avoid being intimidated, we hope you will find that they are not impossible. In the long questions you will see that later parts are sometimes easier than earlier ones, particularly after 'show that' parts.

On your first pass through this chapter, you may find it a useful exercise to simply identify which topics each question links together – it is not always obvious! There is an index of what topics are covered in what questions available online (education.cambridge.org/standard).

Some of these questions are on the border of the International Baccalaureate syllabus, but then again, so are some recent examination questions!

Some exam tips

- Remember to use your reading time effectively:
  - Decide which order to do the questions in. In particular, several long questions can be easier than the last few short questions, and are worth more marks!
  - Think about which questions can be done on the calculator.
  - Practise using your reading time on your practice papers.
  - Try to classify which section of the course each question is about.

- Just because you cannot do part (a) of a question does not mean you cannot do later parts. As you have seen, sometimes later parts are easier than earlier parts.
- If you cannot do an early part of a question, you can show how you would have used the answer in later parts; you will still gain marks.
- Look for links between parts of multi-part questions. They often act as hints.
- Plan your time before you go into the exam. Decide whether you work better quickly with lots of time for checking, or working slowly but not having much checking time.
- Do not get distracted if you cannot do some questions; for whatever grade you want, you do not have to get 100%!
- Practise checking your answers; this is not as easy a skill as it seems. Particularly in the calculator paper; you should be able to use your calculator to check your work.
- Scavenge for marks. A blank response is guaranteed to score zero. If you have a sensible idea write it down as some marks may be awarded for what might seem to be a minor point. However, do not waste too much time on a question where you feel uncertain about your method. Leave these questions to the end.

Short questions

1. What is the probability of getting an average of 3 on two rolls of a fair die? *[6 marks]*

2. The sum of the first n terms of an arithmetic sequence is $S_n = 3n + 2n^2$. Find the common difference of the sequence. *[6 marks]*

3. If $f(x) = |x|$, sketch $f'(x)$ for $-2 \le x \le 2,\ x \ne 0$. *[5 marks]*

4. If $\boldsymbol{u} = \begin{pmatrix} x \\ x \\ 1 \end{pmatrix}$ and $\boldsymbol{v} = \begin{pmatrix} x \\ 1 \\ x \end{pmatrix}$, find $\int \boldsymbol{u}.\boldsymbol{v}\,\mathrm{d}x$. *[6 marks]*

5. What is the average value of the first n terms of a geometric progression with first term a and common ratio r? *[4 marks]*

6. Three data items are collected: 3, x^2 and x. Find the smallest possible value of the mean. *[6 marks]*

7. The discrete random variable X has the probability distribution $\mathrm{P}(X = x) = \ln kx$ for $x = 1,2,3,4$. Find the exact value of k. *[6 marks]*

8. If $f(x) = \sin(x)$, give the single transformation which maps $f(x)$ to $g(x) = 1 - \cos(x)$. *[4 marks]*

9. The graph of $y = \ln x$ can be transformed into the graph of $y = \ln kx$ by either a horizontal stretch or a vertical translation.

(a) State the stretch factor of the horizontal stretch.

(b) Find the vertical translation vector. *[4 marks]*

10. The sequence u_n is defined by $u_n = 0.5^n$.

(a) Find the exact value of $\sum_0^{10} u_r$

(b) Find the exact value of $\sum_0^{10} \ln(u_r)$ *[7 marks]*

11. The functions f and g are defined by $f(x) = 3x + 1$ and $g(x) = ax^2 - x + 5$. Find the value of a such that $f(g(x)) = 0$ has equal roots. *[7 marks]*

12. Find the positive solution of the equation $\int_0^y x^2 + 1\,\mathrm{d}x = 4$. *[5 marks]*

13. For what values of x is the series $x^2 - x + (x^2 - x)^2 + (x^2 - x)^3 + \cdots$ convergent? *[6 marks]*

14. $\boldsymbol{u}$ and $\boldsymbol{v}$ are vectors such that $\boldsymbol{u} \cdot \boldsymbol{v} = 0$. If $|\boldsymbol{u}| = 2$ and $|\boldsymbol{v}| = 3$, find $|\boldsymbol{u} - \boldsymbol{v}|$. *[4 marks]*

15. Theo repeatedly rolls a fair die until he gets a six.

(a) Show that the probability of him getting the six on the third roll is $\frac{25}{216}$.

(b) Let p_r be the probability of getting the first six on the rth roll. Find an expression for p_r in terms of r.

(c) Prove algebraically that $\sum_{r=1}^{r=\infty} p_r = 1$. *[9 marks]*

16. If $0 < x < 1$, evaluate exactly the quantity

$$\int_0^{1/2} \left(\sum_{i=0}^{i=\infty} x^i \right) \mathrm{d}x$$ *[6 marks]*

17. A rod of length l is inclined at an angle θ to the x-axis. A cone is formed by rotating this rod around the x-axis. Find the maximum possible volume of this cone as θ varies.

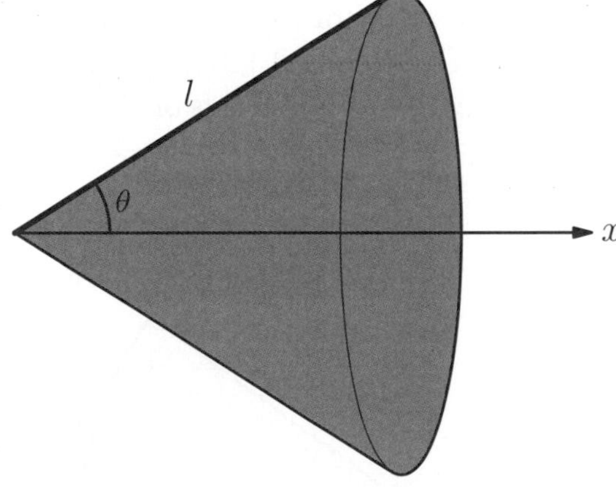

[8 marks]

18. The diagram shows two unit vectors, $\boldsymbol{a}$ and $\boldsymbol{b}$, with angle 2θ between them.

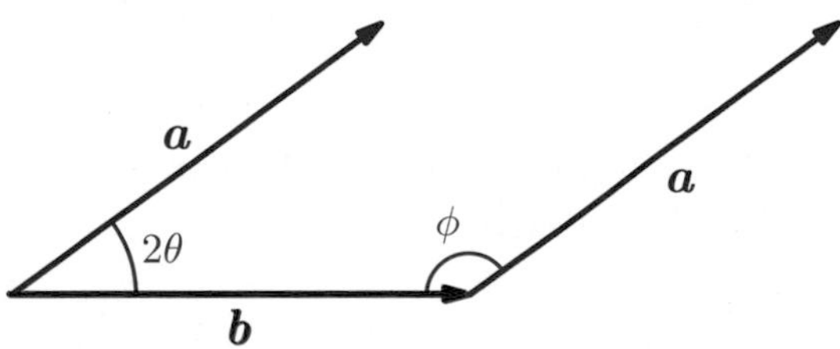

(a) Write down the size of the angle ϕ in terms of θ.

(b) Express $|\boldsymbol{a}+\boldsymbol{b}|^2$ in the form $k\cos^2\theta$. *[6 marks]*

19. The function f is defined for $x > 3$ by $f(x) = \ln(x^2 - 9) - \ln(x+3) - \ln x$.

(a) Express $f(x)$ in the form $\ln(g(x))$.

(b) Find an expression for $f^{-1}(x)$. *[6 marks]*

20. (a) What transformation is required to go from the graph of $y = \ln x$ to the graph of $y = \ln(x^2)$?

(b) What transformation is required to go from the graph of $y = \ln x$ to the graph of $y = \log_{10} x$? *[6 marks]*

21. The probability distribution of a discrete random variable X is given by

$$\mathrm{P}(X = x) = \frac{4(p)^x}{5} \quad \text{for } x \in \mathbb{N}$$

Find the value of p. *[6 marks]*

22. (a) By considering $(1+x)^n$ or otherwise, prove that

$$\sum_{r=0}^{r=n} \binom{n}{r} = 2^n$$

(b) Evaluate

$$\sum_{r=0}^{r=n} (-1)^n \binom{n}{r}$$

[8 marks]

23. The diagram shows a sector AOB of a circle of radius 1 and centre O, where $\mathrm{A\hat{O}B} = \theta$. The lines $[\mathrm{AB_1}]$, $[\mathrm{A_1B_2}]$, $[\mathrm{A_2B_3}]$ etc. are perpendicular to (OB), and $\mathrm{A_1B_1}$, $\mathrm{A_2B_2}$ etc. are all arcs of circles with centre O.

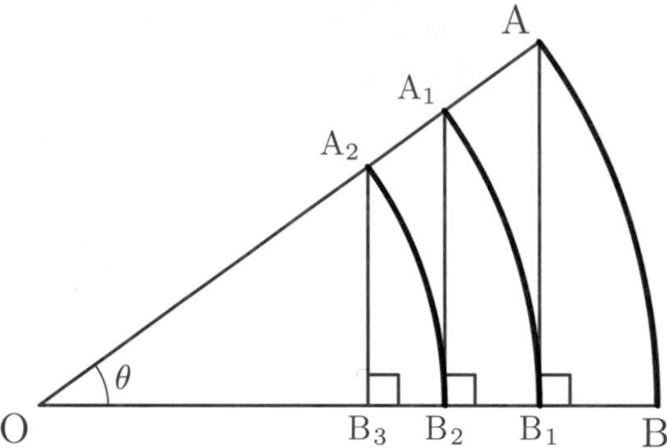

Calculate the sum to infinity of the arc lengths
$\mathrm{AB} + \mathrm{A_1B_1} + \mathrm{A_2B_2} + \mathrm{A_3B_3} + \cdots$.

[7 marks]

(© IB Organization 2004)

24. (a) If $y = \mathrm{e}^x + \mathrm{e}^{-x}$, express x in terms of y.

(b) Show that the sum of all possible values of x is zero. *[8 marks]*

25. Find the volume of revolution formed when the region enclosed by the graph of $y = \mathrm{e}^x$ and the lines $y = 1$ and $x = 1$ is rotated by 2π around the line $y = 1$. *[6 marks]*

26. The probability of an event occurring is found to be $\frac{1}{7}(x^2-14x+38)$ where x is known to be an integer parameter. Find all possible values of x. *[6 marks]*

27. Two vectors $\boldsymbol{a}$ and $\boldsymbol{b}$ have the same non-zero length, x. If $(\boldsymbol{a}+\boldsymbol{b})\cdot(\boldsymbol{a}+\boldsymbol{b})=6x$, find the smallest possible value of x. *[6 marks]*

Long questions

1. Daniel and Theo play a game with a biased coin. There is a probability of $\frac{1}{5}$ of the coin showing a head and a probability of $\frac{4}{5}$ of it showing a tail. The boys take it in turns to toss the coin. If the coin shows a head, the player who tossed the coin wins the game. If the coin shows a tail, the other player has the next toss. Daniel plays first and the game continues until there is a winner.

   (a) Write down the probability that Daniel wins on his first toss.

   (b) Calculate the probability that Theo wins on his first toss.

   (c) Calculate the probability that Daniel wins on his second toss.

   (d) Show that the probability of Daniel winning is $\frac{5}{9}$.

   (e) State the probability of Theo winning.

   (f) The boys play the game with a different coin and find that the probability of Daniel winning is twice the probability of Theo winning. Find the probability of this coin showing a head. *[14 marks]*

2. The table shows the values and gradient of $f(x)$ at various points.

x	0	1	2	3	4
$f(x)$	4	2	3	4	6
$f'(x)$	7	9	−3	4	2

   (a) Evaluate $f\circ f(3)$.

   (b) The graph $y=g(x)$ is formed by translating the graph of $y=f(x)$ by a vector $\begin{pmatrix}2\\3\end{pmatrix}$ and then reflecting it in the x-axis. Find $g'(2)$. *[6 marks]*

3. A function is defined by

$$f(x)=2x+\frac{1}{2}\sin 2x-\tan x \text{ for } x\in\left[-\frac{\pi}{2},\frac{\pi}{2}\right]$$

   (a) Find $f'(x)$.

   (b) Show that the stationary points of $f(x)$ satisfy the equation $2\cos^4 x+\cos^2 x-1=0$.

   (c) Hence show that the function has exactly two stationary points. *[11 marks]*

4. **(a)** The value of the infinite series $\sum_{r=0}^{\infty} a^r$ is 1.5. Find a.

(b) Prove that $\frac{1}{1+x} = 1 - x + x^2 - x^3 + \cdots$ for $|x| < k$, stating the value of k.

(c) Show that $\ln(1+x) = x - \frac{x^2}{2} + \frac{x^3}{3} \cdots$

(d) Evaluate $\ln 1.1$ to 3 decimal places. *[12 marks]*

5. At a building site, the probability P(A) that all materials arrive on time is 0.85; the probability P(B) that the building will be completed on time is 0.60. The probability that the materials arrive on time and the building is completed on time is 0.55.

(a) Show that events A and B are *not* independent.

(b) All the materials arrive on time. Find the probability that the building will not be completed on time.

(c) A team of ten people is working on the building, including two plumbers. The number of hours a week worked by the people in the team is normally distributed with a mean of 42 hours, and 10% of the team work 48 hours or more a week. Find the probability that *both* plumbers work more than 40 hours in a given week. *[15 marks]*

(© *IB Organization 2002*)

6. The function f is given by $f(x) = \frac{2x+1}{x-3}$, $x \in \mathbb{R}$, $x \neq 3$.

(a) (i) Show that $y = 2$ is an asymptote of the graph of $y = f(x)$.

(ii) Find the vertical asymptote of the graph.

(iii) Write down the coordinates of the point P at which the asymptotes intersect.

(b) Find the points of intersection of the graph and the axes.

(c) Hence sketch the graph of $y = f(x)$, showing the asymptotes by dotted lines.

(d) Show that $f'(x) = \frac{-7}{(x-3)^2}$, and hence find the equation of the tangent at the point S where $x = 4$.

(e) The tangent at the point T on the graph is parallel to the tangent at point S. Find the coordinates of T.

(f) Show that P is the midpoint of $[ST]$.

[24 marks]

(© *IB Organization 1999*)

7. **(a)** Find the equation of the tangent line to the curve $y = \ln x$ at the point (e, 1), and verify that the origin is on this line.

(b) Show that $\frac{\mathrm{d}}{\mathrm{d}x}(x\ln x - x) = \ln x$

(c) The diagram shows the region enclosed by the curve $y = \ln x$, the tangent line in part (a), and the line $y = 0$.

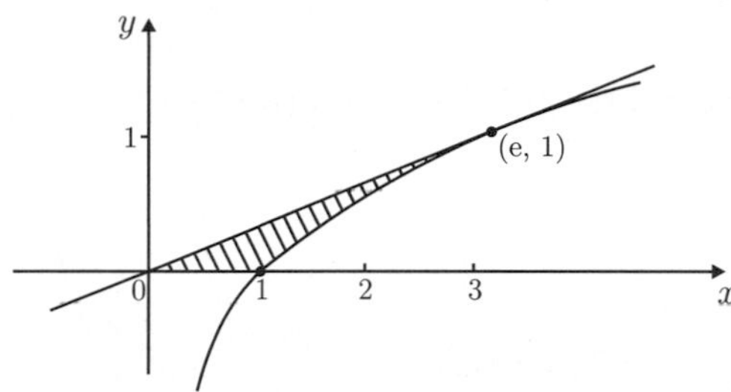

Use the result of part (b) to show that the area of this region is $\frac{1}{2}\mathrm{e} - 1$.

[11 marks]

(© *IB Organization 1999*)

8. The function f is given by $f(x) = (\sin x)^2 \cos x$. The following diagram shows part of the graph of $y = f(x)$.

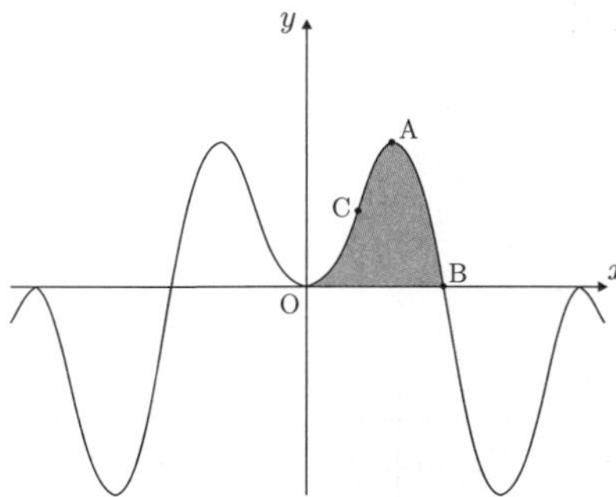

The point A is a maximum point, the point B lies on the x-axis, and the point C is a point of inflexion.

(a) Give the period of f.

(b) From consideration of the graph of $y = f(x)$, find to an accuracy of **one significant figure** the range of f.

(c) (i) Find $f'(x)$.

(ii) Hence show that at the point A, $\cos x = \sqrt{\frac{1}{3}}$.

(iii) Find the exact maximum value.

(d) Find the exact value of the x-coordinate at the point B.

(e) (i) Find $\int f(x)\,dx$.

(ii) Find the area of the shaded region in the diagram.

(f) Given that $f''(x) = 9(\cos x)^3 - 7\cos x$, find the x-coordinate at the point C.

[20 marks]

9. The diagram below shows the graphs of $f(x) = 1 + e^{2x}$, $g(x) = 10x + 2$, $0 \le x \le 1.5$.

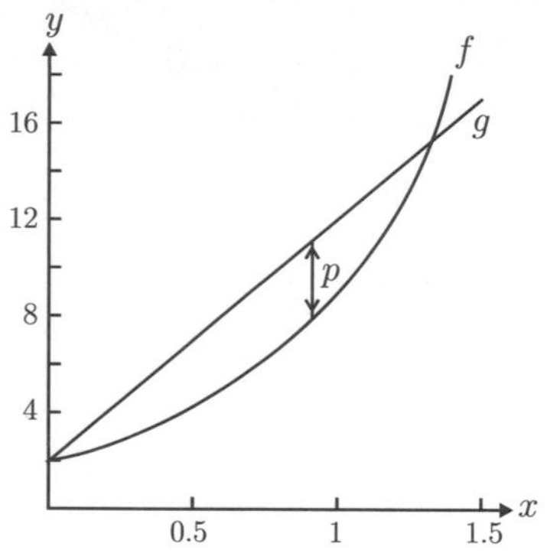

(a) (i) Write down an expression for the vertical distance p between the graphs of f and g.

(ii) Given that p has a maximum value for $0 \le x \le 1.5$, find the value of x at which this occurs.

The graph of $y = f(x)$ only is shown in the diagram below. When $x = a$, $y = 5$.

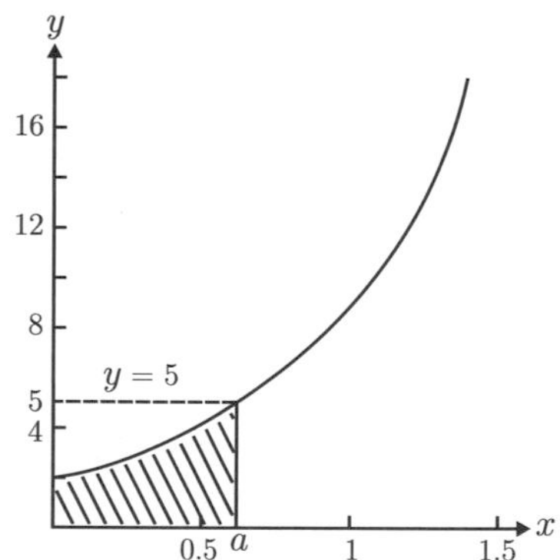

(b) (i) Find $f^{-1}(x)$.

(ii) *Hence* show that $a = \ln 2$.

(c) The region shaded in the diagram is rotated through 360° about the x-axis. Write down an expression for the volume obtained.

[11 marks]

(*© IB Organization 2005*)

10. Consider the functions f and g where $f(x) = 3x - 5$ and $g(x) = x - 2$.

(a) Find the inverse function, f^{-1}.

(b) Given that $g^{-1}(x) = x + 2$, find $(g^{-1} \circ f)(x)$.

(c) Given also that $(f^{-1} \circ g)(x) = \dfrac{x+3}{3}$, solve $(f^{-1} \circ g)(x) = (g^{-1} \circ f)(x)$.

Let $h(x) = \dfrac{f(x)}{g(x)}$, $x \neq 2$.

(d) (i) *Sketch* the graph of h for $-3 \le x \le 7$ and $-2 \le y \le 8$, including any asymptotes.

(ii) Write down the *equations* of the asymptotes.

(e) The expression $\dfrac{3x-5}{x-2}$ may also be written as $3 + \dfrac{1}{x-2}$. Use this to answer the following.

(i) Find $\int h(x)\,\mathrm{d}x$.

(ii) *Hence* calculate the *exact* value of $\int_3^5 h(x)\,\mathrm{d}x$.

(f) On your sketch, shade the region whose area is represented by $\int_3^5 h(x)\,\mathrm{d}x$.

[17 marks]

(*© IB Organization 2006*)

11. (a) If p and q are positive integers and $a < b$, find the x-coordinate of the stationary point on the curve $y = (x-a)^p(x-b)^q$ in the interval $a < x < b$.

(b) Sketch the graph in the case where $p = 2$ and $q = 3$.

(c) By considering the graph or otherwise, determine a condition involving p and/or q for this stationary point to be a local maximum.

[12 marks]

Answers

For answers that require a proof (normally indicated by: 'prove', 'show', 'verify' or 'explain') no answer has been provided.

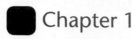

Chapter 1

Exercise 1A

1. (i) A1, B3, C2   (ii) A3, B1, C2

2. (a) (i) $2x^2+8x-10$ (ii) $5x^2-20x+15$
   (b) (i) $4x^2-8x-32$ (ii) $-x^2+3x-2$
   (c) (i) $3x^2-6x+6$ (ii) $4x^2+16x+11$
   (d) (i) $-4x^2+8x-5$ (ii) $-2x^2-8x-11$

3. (a) (i) $(0,-6)$ (ii) $(0,-3)$
   (b) (i) $(0,0)$ (ii) $(0,0)$
   (c) (i) $(0,2)$ (ii) $(0,6)$
   (d) (i) $(0,19)$ (ii) $(0,2)$

4. (a) (i) 5   (ii) 2
   (b) (i) −3   (ii) −1
   (c) (i) −2   (ii) 2

5. (a) (i) 3   (ii) 2
   (b) (i) 2   (ii) 5
   (c) (i) −3   (ii) −1

6. (a) (i) $a=2, b=-8, c=6$
   (ii) $a=5, b=5, c=-10$
   (b) (i) $a=-\frac{1}{4}, b=\frac{3}{4}, c=1$
   (ii) $a=-1, b=0, c=1$

7. (a) (i) $\left(\frac{2}{3},-\frac{1}{3}\right)$ (ii) $\left(-\frac{1}{4},-\frac{33}{8}\right)$
   (b) (i) $(0.2, 10.2)$ (ii) $(2,-1)$

8. (a) (i) −0.535, 1.87   (ii) −1,0.75
   (b) (i) −0.449, 4.45   (ii) −1.35, 1.85
   (c) (i) 3   (ii) 1.5

9. (a) (i) $x=2$ (ii) $x=-\frac{1}{4}$
   (b) (i) $x=\frac{3}{4}$ (ii) $x=\frac{1}{6}$

10. (a) (i) −3.46,2.12   (ii) −2.56,1.56
    (b) (i) −0.387, 1.72   (ii) −5.19,0.193

Exercise 1B

1. (a) (i) $(3,4)$ (ii) $(5,1)$
   (b) (i) $(2,-1)$ (ii) $(1,-5)$
   (c) (i) $(-1,3)$ (ii) $(-7,-3)$
   (d) (i) $(-2,-4)$ (ii) $(-1,5)$

2. (a) (i) $(x-3)^2-5$ (ii) $(x-5)^2-4$
   (b) (i) $(x+2)^2-3$ (ii) $(x+3)^2-12$
   (c) (i) $2(x-3)^2-13$ (ii) $3(x+1)^2+7$
   (d) (i) $-(x-1)^2-4$ (ii) $-(x+2)^2+5$
   (e) (i) $(x+1.5)^2-1.25$ (ii) $(x-2.5)^2+3.75$
   (f) (i) $2(x+1.5)^2+10.5$
   (ii) $2(x-1.25)^2-4.125$

3. (a) (i) $y=2(x-2)^2+4$ (ii) $y=3(x+1)^2-5$
   (b) (i) $y=-2(x+1)^2+3$ (ii) $y=-3(x-2)^2+1$

4. (a) $(x-3)^2+2$
   (b) 2

5. (a) $b=-3, c=6$
   (b) $a=2$

> **ANSWER HINT**
> (a) Did you notice that inside the bracket we had $x+b$?

6. (a) $2(x+1)^2-3$
   (b) $x=-1$
   (c) $x=-1\pm\sqrt{\frac{3}{2}}$

Exercise 1C

1 (a) (i) −2, 3   (ii) −1, 5
  (b) (i) −3, 0   (ii) 0, 2
  (c) (i) −2, 5   (ii) −1, 1
  (d) (i) $\frac{1}{2},-\frac{5}{3}$ (ii) $\frac{3}{4},-\frac{1}{3}$

2. (a) (i) −5, 1   (ii) 2, 4
   (b) (i) $\frac{3}{2},-2$ (ii) $2,-\frac{5}{3}$
   (c) (i) $\frac{3}{2},-\frac{1}{3}$ (ii) $\frac{5}{4},-\frac{1}{2}$
   (d) (i) −4, 3   (ii) −5, 2

3. (a) (i) $y=3x^2-15x+12$ (ii) $y=4x^2+4x-8$
   (b) (i) $y=-2x^2-2x+4$ (ii) $y=-x^2-6x-5$

4. (a) $(2x-3)(x+4)$
   (b) $(-4,0)$ and $\left(\frac{3}{2},0\right)$

5. $a=-\frac{3}{10}, b=-\frac{9}{10}, c=3$

Exercise 1D

1. (a) (i) 36 (ii) 68
   (b) (i) −47 (ii) −119
   (c) (i) 0 (ii) 0
   (d) (i) 49 (ii) 49

2. (a) (i) (ii) Two (b) (i) (ii) None
   (c) (i) (ii) One (d) (i) (ii) Two

3. (a) (i) $x=\frac{3\pm\sqrt{5}}{2}$ (ii) $x=\frac{1\pm\sqrt{5}}{2}$
   (b) (i) $x=-1,\frac{2}{3}$ (ii) $x=\frac{3\pm\sqrt{7}}{2}$
   (c) (i) $x=\frac{4}{3},-1$ (ii) $x=\frac{1}{2},-1$
   (d) (i) $x=2\pm\sqrt{7}$ (ii) $x=1,-\frac{3}{2}$

4. (a) (i) $k<\frac{1}{24}$ (ii) $k>-\frac{25}{12}$
   (b) (i) $k=\frac{3}{5}$ (ii) $k=-\frac{17}{24}$
   (c) (i) $k\ge-\frac{5}{4}$ (ii) $k\le\frac{1}{16}$
   (d) (i) $k>\frac{3}{8}$ (ii) $k<-\frac{25}{12}$
   (e) (i) $k=\frac{17}{4}$ (ii) $k=\frac{55}{32}$
   (f) (i) $k=1$ (ii) $k=\frac{1}{32}$
   (g) (i) $k<0$ (ii) $k<0$

5. $x=\frac{2\pm\sqrt{7}}{3}$

7. $m=\pm\sqrt{2}$

8. $k=\frac{11\pm2\sqrt{30}}{2}$

9. $k>\frac{9}{2}$

10. $c\ge\frac{17}{16}$

11. $m<-\frac{9}{16}$

12. $k=\pm9$

Exercise 1E

1. (a) (i) (−2, −3), (1, 0) (ii) (3, 0)
   (b) (i) (−3, −9), (4, 5) (ii) No intersection

2. (a) (i) $\left(-\frac{11}{5},-\frac{8}{5}\right)$, (3, 1) (ii) (−3, 3), (5, −1)
   (b) (i) (1, 3), (3,1) (ii) (−3, −5), (−5, −3)
   (c) (i) (−1, 6), (2, 3) (ii) (1, −3), (−1, −5)

3. (−4, 12), (3, 5)

4. $x=-0.25, y=2.88$ and $x=1, y=1$

6. $-1\pm2\sqrt{6}$

Exercise 1F

1. 1.5, 6.5

2. Area = $x(6-x)$; 9 cm^2

3. (a) $210x-2x^2$ (b) $x=52.5, y=105$

4. (a) 1.63 s (b) 3.27 m

5. (c) $x=24.2, y=7.38$

6. 25

Mixed examination practice 1

Short questions

1. (a) $(x+7)(x-2)$ (b) $x=-7, 2$

2. (a) Minimum (b) $a=3, b=7$

3. $a=-3, b=2, c=48$

4. $k+2$

5. (a) $p=-\frac{1}{2}, q=2$ (b) $\frac{3}{4}$

6.

Expression	Positive	Negative	zero
a		✓	
c		✓	
b^2-4ac			✓
b	✓		

7. (a) $(x-5)^2+10$ (b) $\frac{1}{1000}$

8. $3\pm2\sqrt{2}$

9. $k>4.5$

10. $k=-1\pm2\sqrt{3}$

11. (a) $\alpha=k-1, \beta=1$ (a) −3, 5

Long questions

1. (a) (i) $4x$ (ii) $2\pi y$

(b) $x = 2 - \frac{\pi}{2}y$

(d) 44.0%

2. (b) 6 km

3. (a) 9

(b) $y = -\frac{1}{5}x^2 - \frac{4}{5}x + \frac{21}{25}$

(c) $\left(\frac{4}{3}, \frac{25}{9}\right)$

Chapter 2

Exercise 2A

1. (a) (i) 6^7 (ii) 5^8
(b) (i) a^8 (ii) x^9
(c) (i) 7^{-3} (ii) 5^5
(d) (i) x^2 (ii) x^5
(e) (i) g^{-12} (ii) k^{-8}

2. (a) (i) 6^1 (ii) 5^{-2}
(b) (i) a^{-2} (ii) x^3
(c) (i) 5^9 (ii) 7^{15}
(d) (i) x^6 (ii) x^{11}
(e) (i) 2^2 (ii) 3^{-14}
(f) (i) g^6 (ii) k^{-8}

3. (a) (i) 2^{12} (ii) 3^{14}
(b) (i) 5^{-4} (ii) 7^{-6}
(c) (i) 11^2 (ii) 13^{15}
(d) (i) 2^{17} (ii) 3^3
(e) (i) 6^{12} (ii) 3^6

4. (a) (i) 2^{10} (ii) 3^{14}
(b) (i) 2^9 (ii) 2^{20}
(c) (i) 2^{13} (ii) 3^4
(d) (i) 2^9 (ii) 3^{11}
(e) (i) 2^{-6} (ii) 3^{-6}
(f) (i) 2^2 (ii) 3^{10}

5. (a) (i) $8x^6$ (ii) $9x^8$
(b) (i) $2x^6$ (ii) $3x^8$
(c) (i) $9a^{10}$ (ii) 2
(d) (i) $\frac{1}{2x}$ (ii) $\frac{y^2}{9}$
(e) (i) $\frac{2}{x}$ (ii) $3y^2$
(f) (i) $\frac{5x^2y^4}{9}$ (ii) $\frac{ab^5}{8}$
(g) (i) $\frac{p^3}{2q^2}$ (ii) $\frac{2^7 3^{10}}{x^7}$

6. (a) (i) $\frac{3}{4}$ (ii) $\frac{7}{81}$
(b) (i) $\frac{1}{36}$ (ii) $\frac{1}{1000}$
(c) (i) 40 (ii) $\frac{9}{64}$
(d) (i) $\frac{3}{4}$ (ii) $\frac{4}{27}$

7. (a) (i) 2 (ii) 2
(b) (i) 100 (ii) 3
(c) (i) $\frac{1}{5}$ (ii) $\frac{3}{4}$
(d) (i) 4 (ii) 125
(e) (i) 100 000 (ii) 27
(f) (i) $\frac{1}{32}$ (ii) $\frac{32}{243}$
(g) (i) $\frac{1}{2}$ (ii) $\frac{1}{7}$
(h) (i) $\frac{3}{4}$ (ii) $\frac{64}{27}$

8. (a) (i) x^3 (ii) x^{12}
(b) (i) $2x^5$ (ii) $\frac{1}{2x^4}$
(c) (i) $\frac{4}{3x^3}$ (ii) $\frac{y^{12}}{x^6}$

9. (a) (i) $\frac{5}{3}$ (ii) $-\frac{3}{2}$
(b) (i) $-\frac{1}{2}$ (ii) $-\frac{3}{4}$
(c) (i) 4 (ii) 2

10. 5×10^{-4}

11. 8 cm

12. (a) $\frac{1}{3}$ (b) 16 cm^2

13. 4

14. 0

15. 11

16. 4

17. 3

18. 3

Exercise 2B

1. (a) (i) $y = 0$

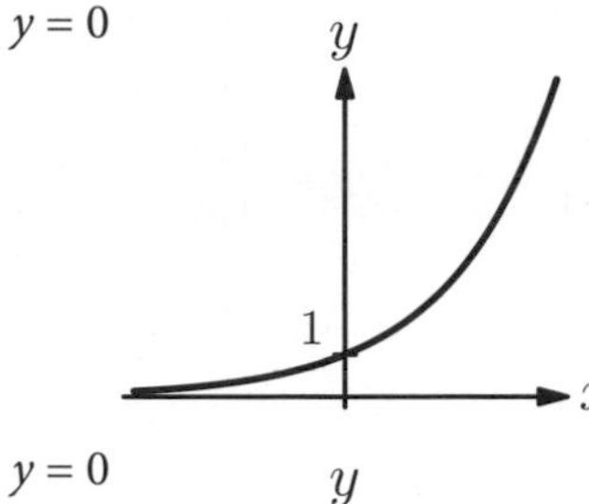

(ii) $y = 0$

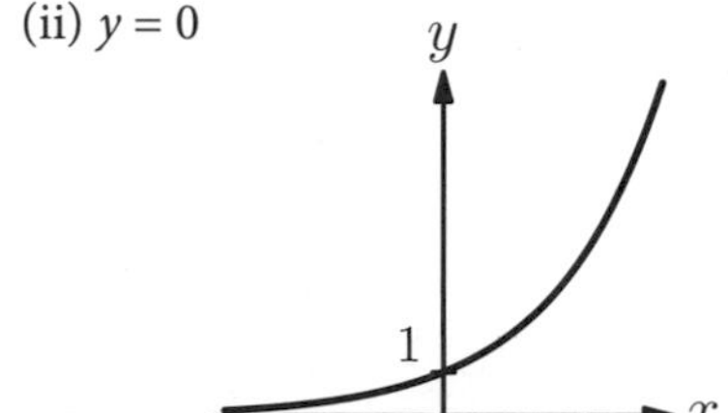

(b) (i) $y = 0$

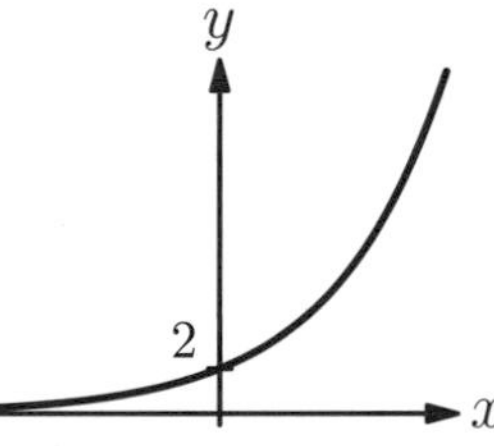

(ii) $y = 0$

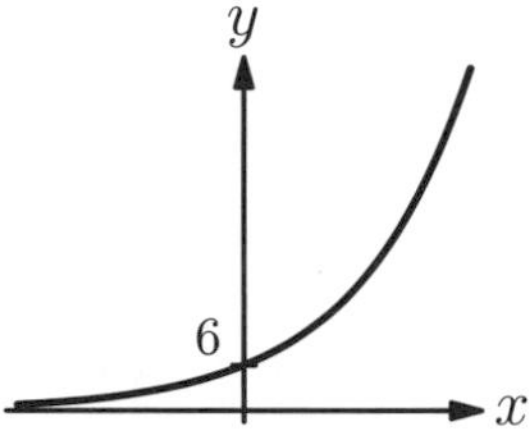

(c) (i) $y = 0$

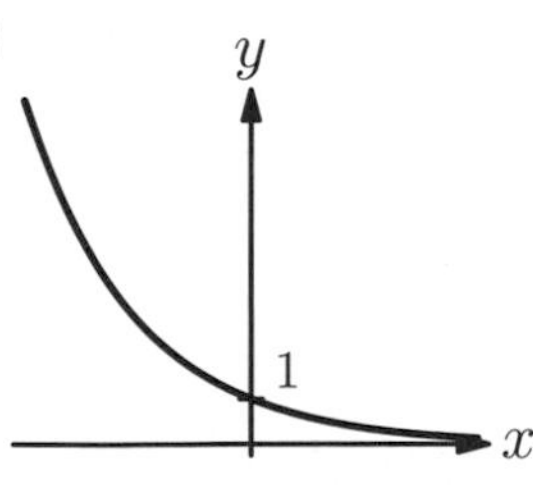

(ii) $y = 0$

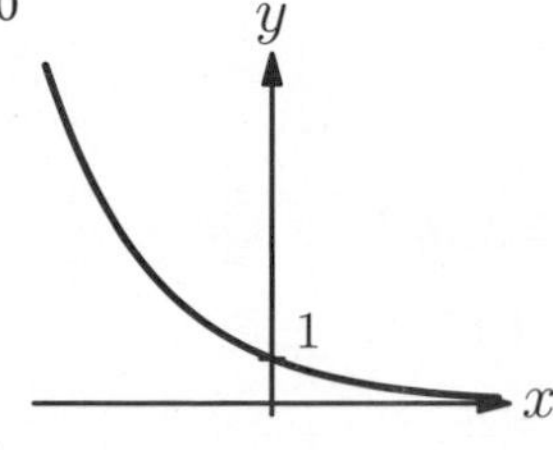

(d) (i)

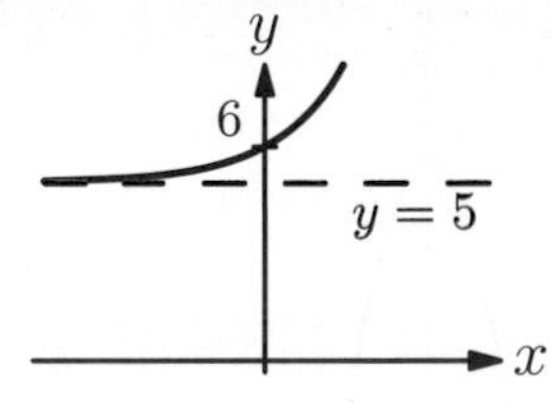

(ii)

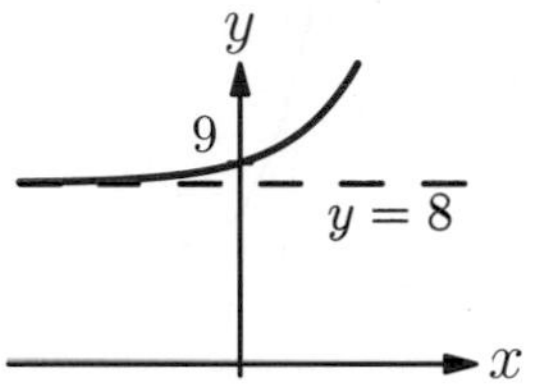

(e) (i)

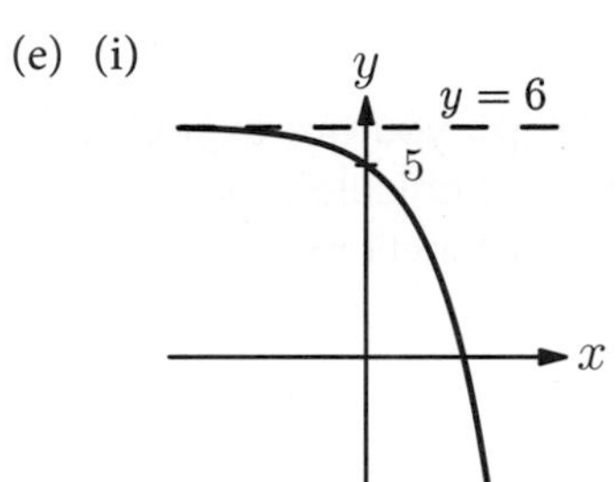

(ii)

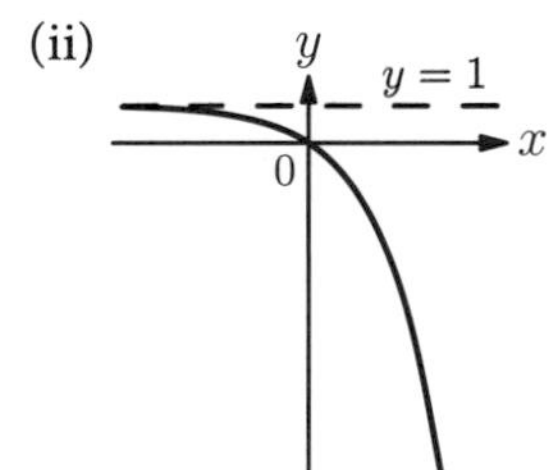

2. $13.31\,\text{m}^2$

3. (a)

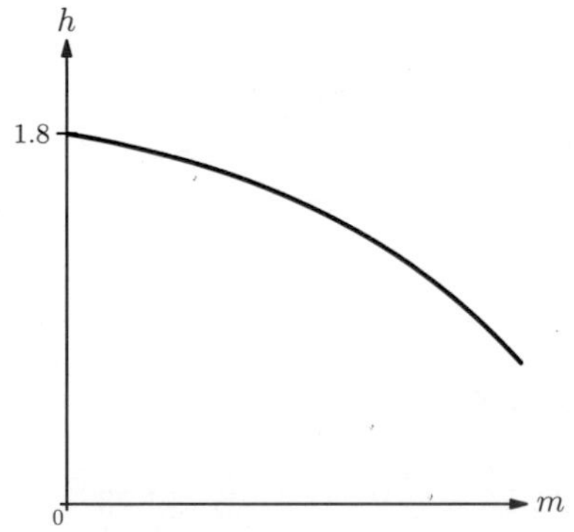

(b) 1.8 m
(c) 1.60 m
(d) The branch might break before reaching the ground.

4. (a)

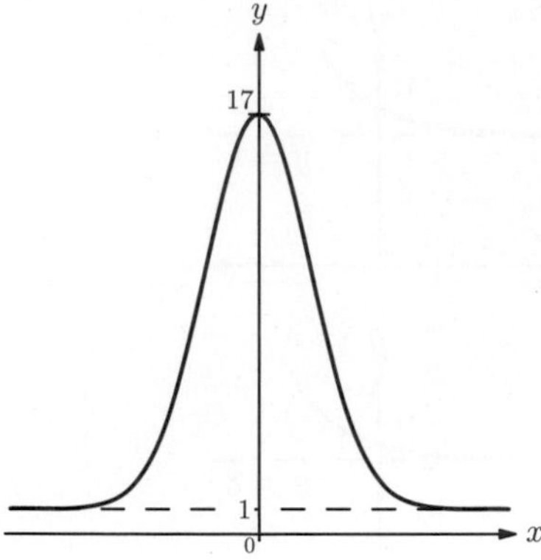

ANSWER HINT 4(a)
This is not a graph you are expected to know. Use your calculator to sketch unfamiliar functions.

(b) $x = \pm 0.866$

5. 41.2°C

6. (a) 0 m/s
(b) 40 m/s

7. (a) $A = 25, B = 100, k = 3$
(b) 26.0°C
(c)

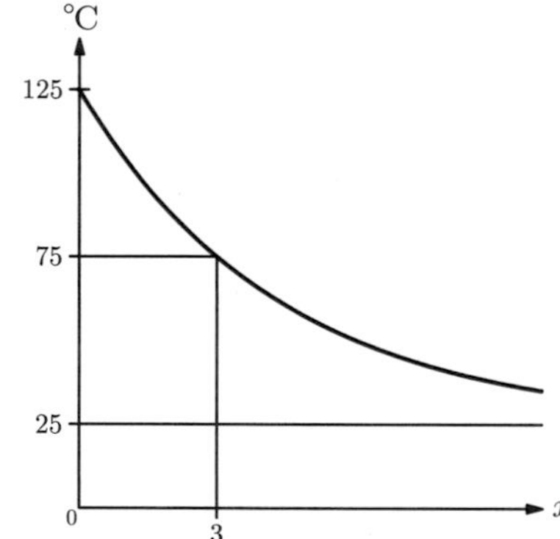

Exercise 2C

1. (a) (i) 3.72 (ii) −1.28
(b) (i) 8.15 (ii) 1.36
(c) (i) 7.39 (ii) 0.0498
(d) (i) 8.24 (ii) 0.00274

2. 2.718281809…

3. $e^4 + 4 + \frac{4}{e^4}$

Exercise 2D

1. (a) (i) 3 (ii) 2
(b) (i) 1 (ii) 1
(c) (i) 0 (ii) 0
(d) (i) −1 (ii) −3
(e) (i) $\frac{1}{2}$ (ii) $\frac{1}{3}$
(f) (i) $\frac{1}{2}$ (ii) $\frac{1}{2}$
(g) (i) $\frac{2}{3}$ (ii) $\frac{3}{4}$
(h) (i) $\frac{3}{2}$ (ii) $\frac{5}{4}$
(i) (i) $\frac{3}{4}$ (ii) $\frac{9}{4}$
(j) (i) $-\frac{1}{2}$ (ii) $-\frac{1}{2}$

2. (a) (i) 1.70 (ii) −0.602
(b) (i) −2.30 (ii) 2.30

3. (a) (i) $5\log x$ (ii) $5\log x$
(b) (i) $\log x \log y - \log y + 3\log x - 3$
(ii) $(\log x)^2 + 4\log x + 4$
(c) (i) $\frac{1}{\log b} + \frac{1}{\log a}$ (ii) $\log a + 1$

4. (a) (i) $x = 3^y$ (ii) $x = 16^y$
(b) (i) $x = a^{y+1}$ (ii) $x = a^{y^2}$
(c) (i) $x = \sqrt[3]{3y}$ (ii) $x = \sqrt{y}$

5. (a) (i) 32 (ii) 16
(b) (i) 0.4 (ii) 0.25
(c) (i) 6 (ii) 100

6. $x = 111$

7. $x = -3$

8. $x = \frac{e^2 + 1}{3}$

9. $9, \frac{1}{9}$

10. $x = 10^{1.5} = 31.6$

11. $x = \sqrt[9]{4} = 1.17$

12. $x = 81, y = 25$

13. 5.50

Exercise 2E

1. (a) (i) 4 (ii) $\frac{1}{2}$

(b) (i) 6 (ii) $\frac{3}{2}$

2. (a) (i) $y+z$ (ii) $z-x$

(b) (i) $3x$ (ii) $5y$

(c) (i) $z+7y$ (ii) $2x+y$

(d) (i) $x+2y-z$ (ii) $2x-y-3z$

(e) (i) $2-y-5z$ (ii) $1+y+2z$

3. (a) (i) $x=\frac{13}{7}$ (ii) $x=4$

(b) (i) $x=9$ (ii) $x=2$

(c) (i) $x=\frac{1}{4}$ (ii) $x=8$

(d) (i) $x=2^{\frac{12}{5}}=5.28$ (ii) $x=2^{10}=1024$

(e) (i) $x=8$ (ii) $x=4$

(f) (i) $x=\frac{1}{3}$ (ii) $x=8$

4. $x=\frac{1}{3}e^{\frac{3}{2}}$

5. (a) $a+2b$ (b) $2(a-b)$

6. $x=2,\frac{1}{2}$

7. (a) $x-4y$ (b) $2+2x+y+2z$

8. -1

9. (a) $2+\frac{y}{x}$ (b) $\frac{x+2z}{x+y}$

10. (a) $\frac{x-y-z}{y}=\frac{x-z}{y}-1$ (b) $\frac{y}{x}\times10^{x-y}$

Exercise 2F

1. (a) (i)

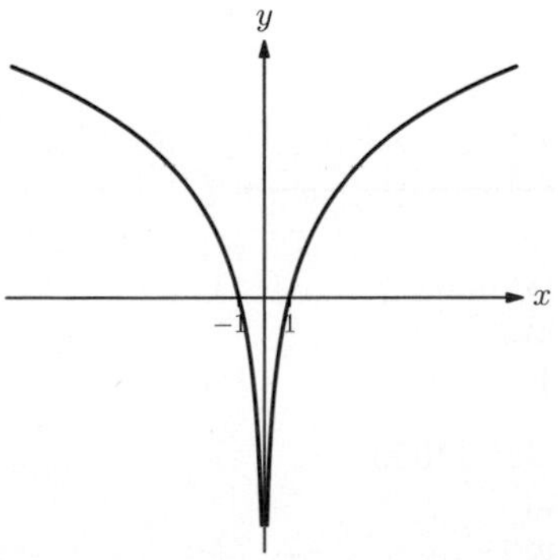

(ii)

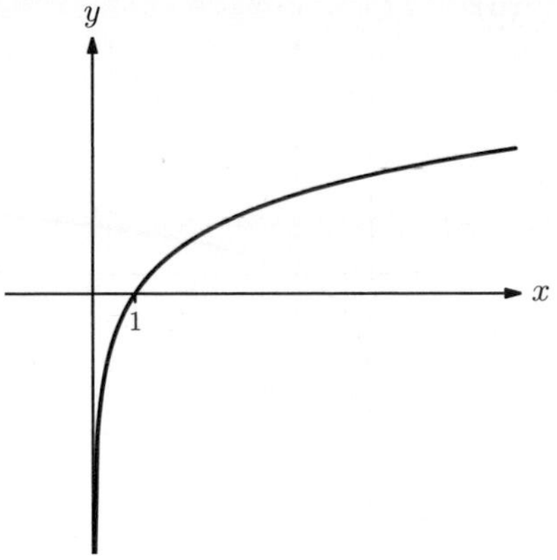

(b) (i)

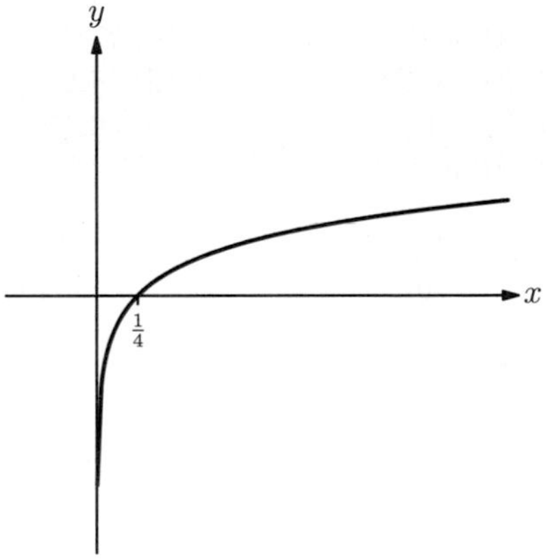

(ii)

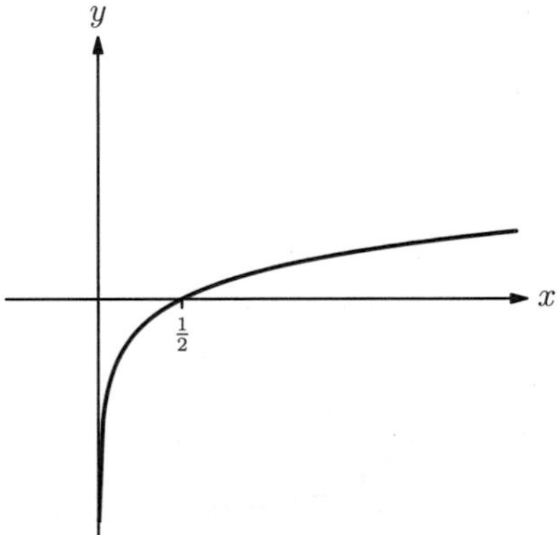

(c) (i)

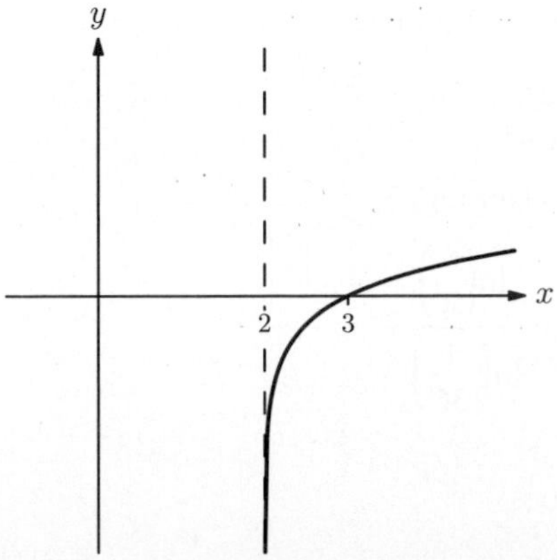

(ii)

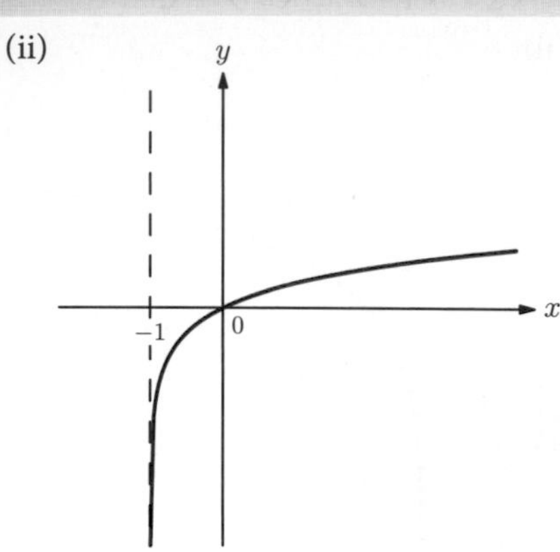

Exercise 2G

1. (a) (i) 2.45 (ii) 116
   (b) (i) −0.609 (ii) 4.62
   (c) (i) −1.71 (ii) 0.527
   (d) (i) 1.11 (ii) −2.98

2. (a) (i) $\dfrac{\ln 5}{2\ln 3}$ (ii) $\dfrac{\ln 7}{3\ln 10}$
   (b) (i) $\dfrac{\ln 2}{\ln 5-\ln 2}$ (ii) $\dfrac{2\ln 5}{\ln 5-\ln 3}$
   (c) (i) $\dfrac{\ln 3}{3\ln 2-1}$ (ii) $\dfrac{\ln 5}{2-\ln 2}$

3. (a) 100
   (b) 48 299
   (c) 2.24 hours

4. (a) 18
   (c) 64
   (d) 1:58 p.m.

5. (a) k
   (b)

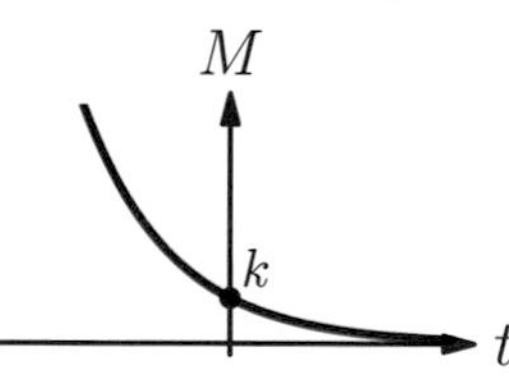

   (c) 2.31 minutes

6. $\dfrac{\log 15}{\log 45}$

7. $x = 10+\log_7 3$

8. $x = \dfrac{\ln\left(\dfrac{5}{4}\right)}{\ln\left(\dfrac{1}{36}\right)}$

ANSWER HINT

Sketch the graph.

9. (b) $x = 0.742$

Mixed examination practice 2

Short questions

1. $x = 24$

2. (a) $2a+\dfrac{b}{2}-c$
   (b) $\dfrac{a-1}{2}$
   (c) $\dfrac{b-c}{2}$

3. 1.68

4. $\dfrac{\ln 4}{\ln 5-2\ln 3}$

5. $x = e^{\frac{4}{3}} = 3.79, y = e^{\frac{10}{3}} = 28.0$

6. $x = 1\pm\sqrt{1-e^y}$

7. $x = \dfrac{\ln 8}{\ln 12}$

8. $a = b^{-2}$

9. $x = e^2$ or e^{-2}

Long questions

1. (a)

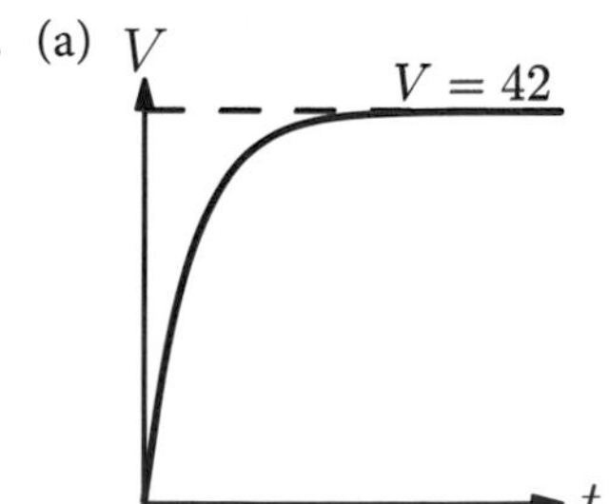

   (b) $0\ \text{m s}^{-1}$
   (c) $42\ \text{m s}^{-1}$
   (d) 3.71 s

2. (a) (i) $k = 37000$
   (b) 2750
   (c) 2039
   (d) $T = 7778\times 1.025^m$
   (e) 2.5%

3. (a) (i) \$2070 (ii) \$2375.37
(b) 20 years
(c)

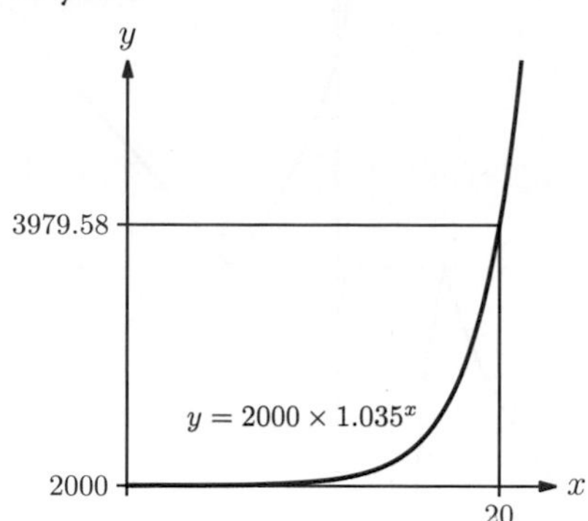

(d) 28
(e) \$2678.14

Chapter 3

Exercise 3A

1. (a) (i) $x = 3$ (ii) $x = -1$
(b) (i) $x = \frac{1}{2}, -\frac{3}{5}$ (ii) $x = 3, -3$
(c) (i) $x = 27, 1$ (ii) $x = 16, \frac{1}{81}$
(d) (i) $x = 7, \pm\sqrt{3}$ (ii) $x = \frac{6}{5}, -1, -4$

2. $x = 2$

3. $x = \dfrac{\log 2 - \log 7}{\log 2}$

4. $x = \frac{1}{3}, \pm 2$

Exercise 3B

1. (a) (i) $a = \pm\sqrt{3}, \pm\sqrt{7}$ (ii) $x = \pm 2, \pm\sqrt{3}$
(b) (i) $x = -\sqrt[3]{5}, \sqrt[3]{1.5}$ (ii) $a = 1, -2$
(c) (i) $x = \pm\sqrt{2 + \sqrt{6}}$ (ii) $x = \pm\sqrt{6}$
(d) (i) $x = 4, 16$ (ii) $x = 16, 36$

2. (a) $x = \ln 4$
(b) $x = 1, \dfrac{1}{\log 5}$
(c) $x = 1, \sqrt{2}$

3. (a) $x = \ln 4, \ln 5$
(b) $x = 2, \dfrac{\log 3}{\log 2}$
(c) $x = 3, 9$

4. $x = 0, 2$

5. $x = 0, \dfrac{\log 5}{\log a}$

6. $x = 2, 32$

Exercise 3C

1. (a) (i)

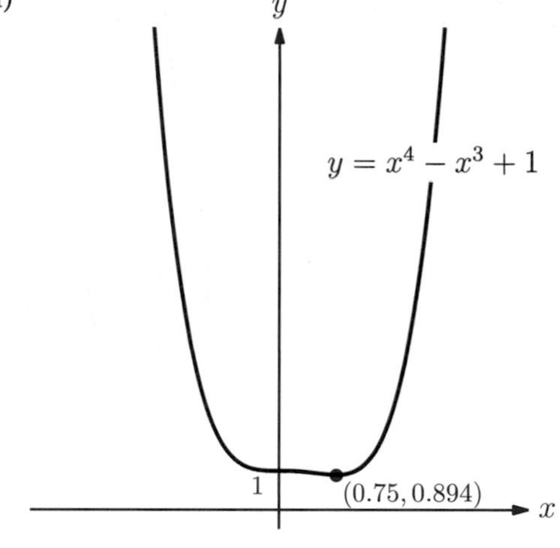

(ii)

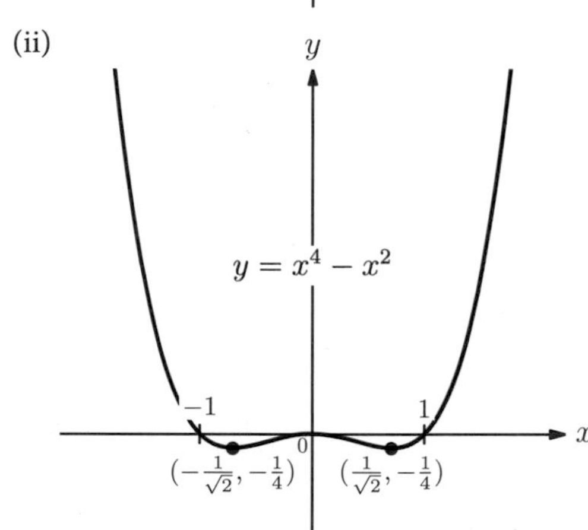

(b) (i)

y
$y = (x - 1)e^x$
x
1
(0, 1)

(ii)

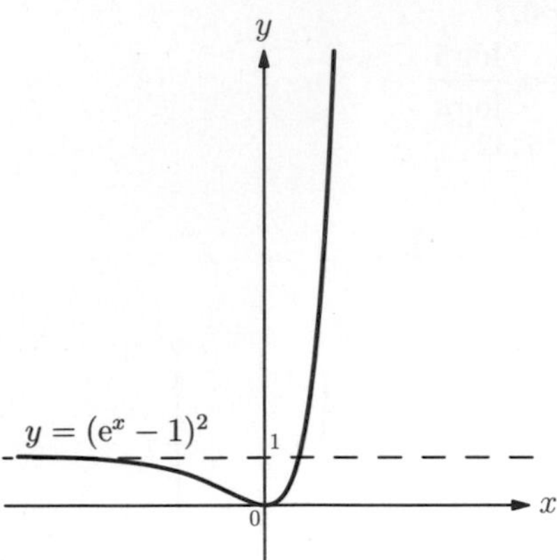

(c) (i)

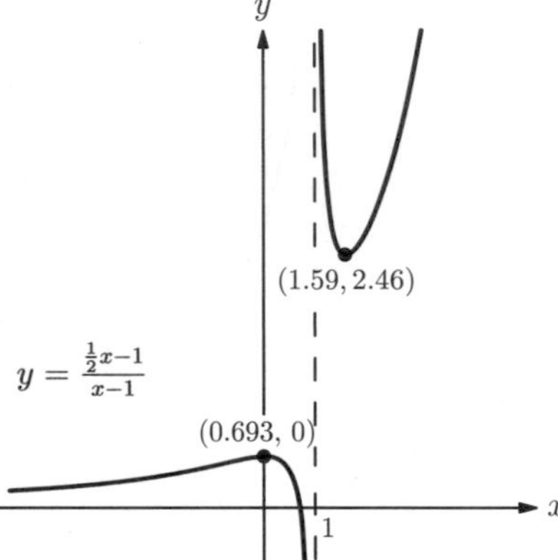

(ii)

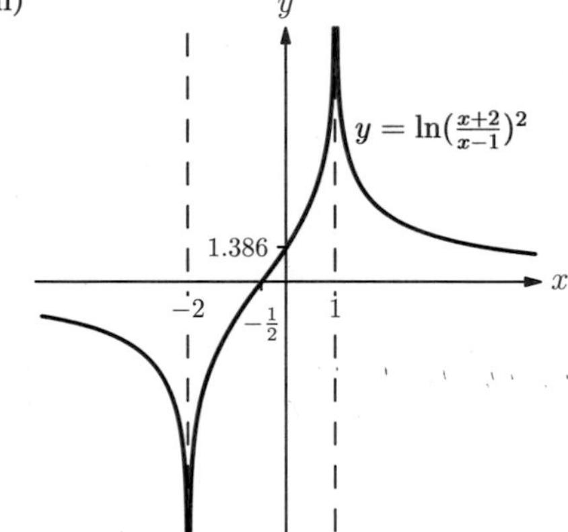

(d) (i)

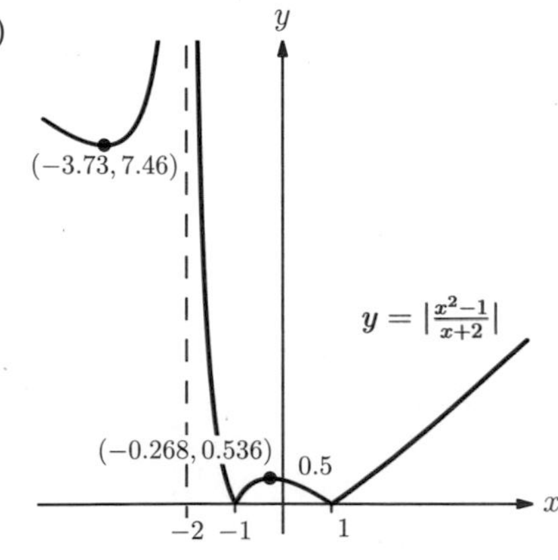

(ii)

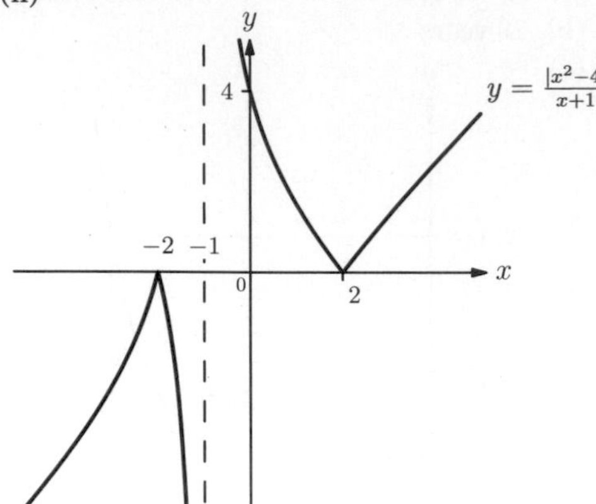

2.

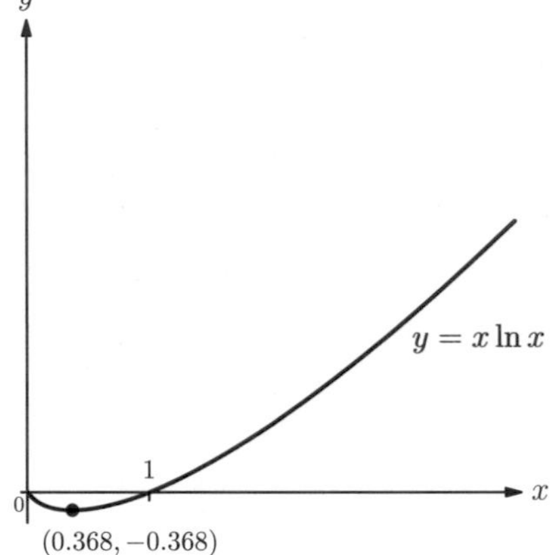

3.

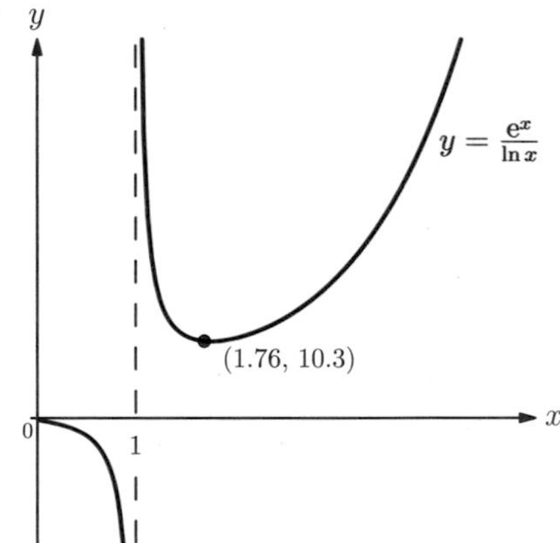

4.

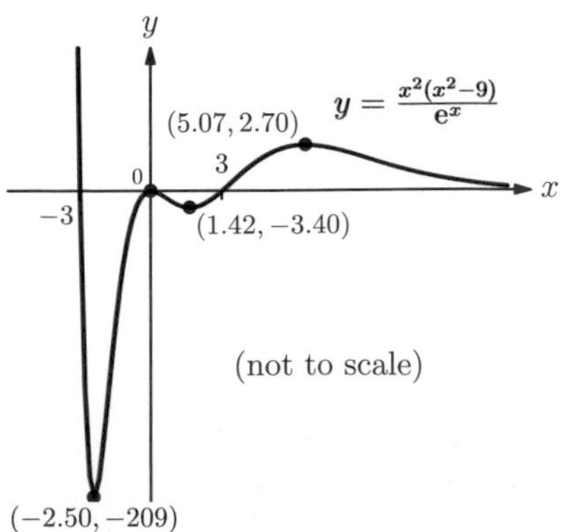

Exercise 3D

1. (a) (i) $x=-1.88, 0.347, 1.53$
   (ii) $x=-4.49$
   (b) (i) $x=0$ (ii) $x=-1.74$
   (c) (i) no solution (ii) $x=1, 1.43$
2. $x=1.53$
3. (a) 2 (b) 1 (c) 0
4. anything between 0.00125 and 0.00222

Mixed examination practice 3

1. (a)

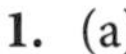

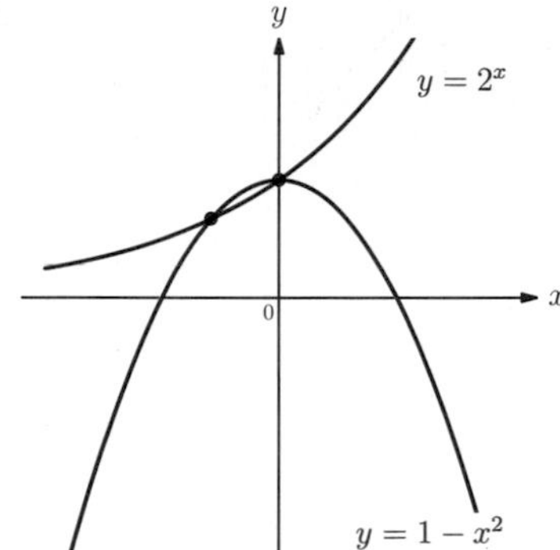

   (b) 2
2. 0.541
3. $x=e^3$
4. $x=-\frac{b}{a}$ and $x=c$
5. (a)

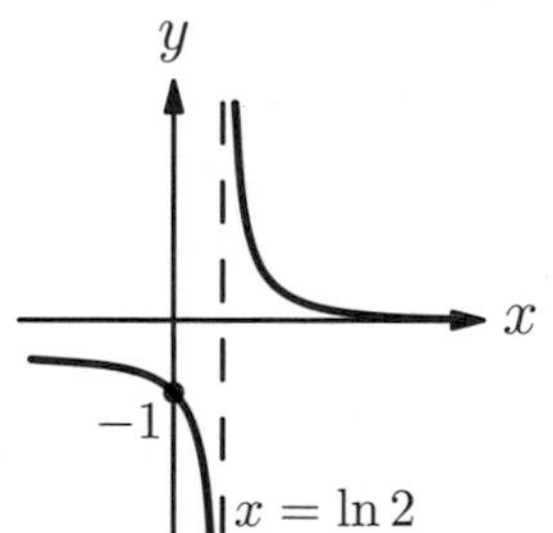

   (b) $x=\ln 2$
6. (a) $x=\pm 2, \pm 3$
7. $x=1$

Chapter 4

Exercise 4A

1. (a) (i) 24 (ii) 140
   (b) (i) 14 (ii) 4
   (c) (i) $3z^2-z$ (ii) $3a^2-a$
   (d) (i) $3x^2+5x+2$ (ii) $3x^2-13x+14$
   (e) (i) $-x$ (ii) $57x^2-11x$
   (f) (i) $\frac{3-x}{x^2}$ (ii) $3x-\sqrt{x}$
2. (a) (i) 3 (ii) 7
   (b) (i) 0 (ii) 1
   (c) (i) $1+\log_{10} y$ (ii) $1+\log_{10} z$
   (d) (i) $2+\log_{10} x$ (ii) $3+\log_{10} y$
   (e) (i) $2+3\log_{10} x$ (ii) 1
3. (a) (i) 4 (ii) -8
   (b) (i) $3x+1-\sqrt{y}$ (ii) $6x+4+2\sqrt{x}$
   (c) (i) $24x+2-6\sqrt{x}$ (ii) $6x^2+x-\sqrt{x^2+1}$

Exercise 4B

1. (a) Domain: $\mathbb{R}$; range: $]0,\infty[$
   (b) Domain: $\mathbb{R}$; range: $]0,\infty[$
   (c) Domain: $]0,\infty[$; range: $\mathbb{R}$
   (d) Domain: $]0,\infty[$; range: $\mathbb{R}$
2. (a) (i) $x\neq -2$ (ii) $x\neq 7$
   (b) (i) $x\neq 2$ or -4 (ii) $x\neq \pm 3$
   (c) (i) $y\geq 1$ (ii) $x\geq -3$
   (d) (i) $a>1$ (ii) $x<\frac{2}{5}$
   (e) (i) $x\neq 0$ or -1 (ii) $x\geq -1$
   (f) (i) $x\leq -\sqrt{5}$ or $x\geq \sqrt{5}$ (ii) $x\leq -3$ or $x\geq 1$
   (g) (i) $x\geq 0$ (ii) $x\geq -\frac{3}{2}$
3. (a) (i) $y\leq 7$ (ii) $y\geq 3$
   (b) (i) $y\geq 12$ (ii) $y\geq 5, y\in\mathbb{Z}$
   (c) (i) $y\geq 0$ (ii) $y\geq 0$
   (d) (i) $y\leq -1$ or $y>0$ (ii) $y>0$
4. $x\geq 5$
5. $x\geq 1, x\neq 2, x\neq 3$
6. $x<-2$ or $x>-1$
7. $x\leq \frac{1}{2}$ or $x>12$
8. (a) (i) $a\leq x<b$ (ii) $\varnothing$
   (b) $f(a)=\begin{cases}\ln(b-a) & \text{for } a<b\\ \text{undefined} & \text{for } a\geq b\end{cases}$

Exercise 4C

1. (a) (i) 5 (ii) 26
   (b) (i) $9x+8$
   (ii) $9x^2+12x+5$

(c) (i) $9\sqrt{a}+17$

(ii) $y^4-4y^3+8y^2-8y+5$

(d) (i) $9y^2+17$ (ii) $27z^2+36z+17$

2. (a) (i) x^2 (ii) x^3

(b) (i) $3x-5$ (ii) x^2+5x+6

(c) (i) $x+4$ (ii) $x^{\frac{2}{3}}$

(d) (i) $\ln(\ln x)$ (ii) $\ln\left(\frac{x+1}{3}\right)$

3. $x=0,-2$

4. $x=-\frac{1}{3}$

5. (a) $y\neq 2$

(b) $x=1.5$

(c) Domain: $x<-1$ or $x\geq 1.5$; range: $y>0$ and $y\neq\sqrt{2}$

6. (a) $\sqrt[3]{2x+3}$ (b) $2\sqrt[3]{x}+3$

7. (a) $a=-\frac{4}{3}, b=-\frac{2}{3}$

(b) $y\geq 0$

8. (a) x^2 is not always greater than 3

(b) $x\in\,]-\infty,-\sqrt{3}\,[\,\cup\,]\sqrt{3},\infty[$

9. $\frac{x}{6}-\frac{1}{3}$

Exercise 4D

1. (a) (i) $\frac{x-1}{3}$ (ii) $\frac{x+3}{7}$

(b) (i) $\frac{2x}{3x-2}$ (ii) $\frac{x}{1-2x}$

(c) (i) $\frac{bx-a}{x-1}$ (ii) $\frac{x-1}{bx-a}$,

(d) (i) $1-x$ (ii) $\frac{x-2}{3}$

(e) (i) $\frac{x^2+2}{3}$ (ii) $\frac{2-x^2}{5}$

(f) (i) $\frac{1-e^x}{5}$ (ii) $\frac{e^x-2}{2}$

(g) (i) $2\ln\left(\frac{x}{7}\right)$ (ii) $\frac{1}{10}\ln\left(\frac{x}{9}\right)$

(h) (i) $5-\sqrt{x+19}$ (ii) $-3+\sqrt{x+10}$

2. (a)

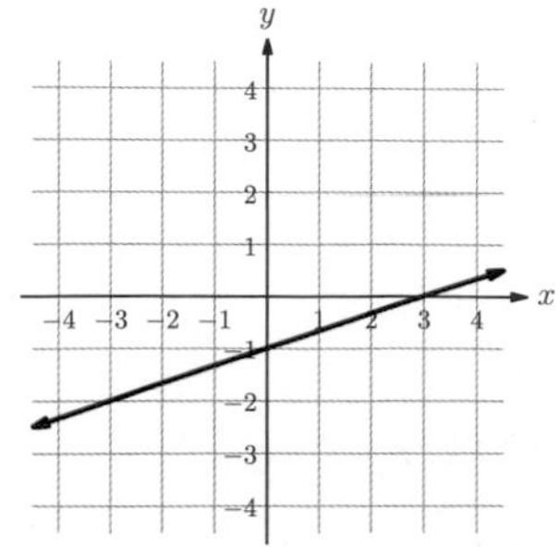

(b)

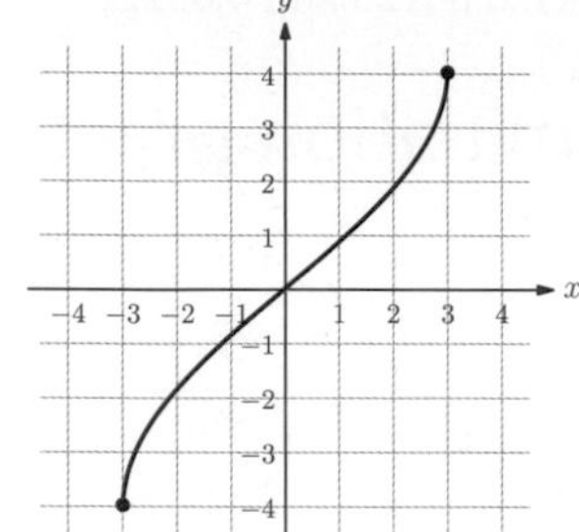

(c)

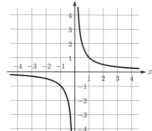

(d)

3. (a) -1 (b) 1

4. -23

5. $f^{-1}(x)=\frac{1}{2}\ln\left(\frac{x}{3}\right)$

6. $(f\circ g)^{-1}(x)=\sqrt[3]{\frac{x-3}{2}}$

7. (a) $\ln 3$

8. $x=-1$

9. $f^{-1}(x)=-\sqrt{\frac{9x+4}{1-x}}$, $x\neq 1$

10. (a) $f^{-1}(x)=\frac{e^x}{3}+1$

(b) $3x-3$

11. (b) $k=-3$

Exercise 4E

1. (a) (i) $\left(-\frac{1}{3},0\right),\left(0,\frac{1}{3}\right)$ (ii) $\left(-\frac{5}{2},0\right)$, $(0,5)$

(b) (i) $\left(\frac{3}{2},0\right),\left(0,-\frac{3}{7}\right)$ (ii) $\left(\frac{5}{3},0\right),\left(0,-\frac{5}{2}\right)$

2. (a) (i) $x = 1, y = 4$ (ii) $x = 7, y = 2$

(b) (i) $x = \frac{1}{2}, y = \frac{3}{2}$ (ii) $x = \frac{5}{3}, y = \frac{4}{3}$

(c) (i) $x = -\frac{5}{2}, y = -\frac{1}{2}$ (ii) $x = \frac{2}{3}, y = -\frac{2}{3}$

(d) (i) $x = 2, y = 0$ (ii) $x = -\frac{1}{2}, y = 0$

3. (a) (i)

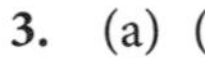

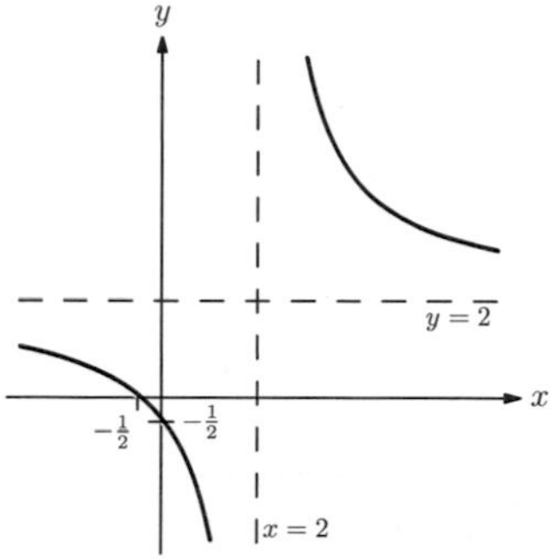

(ii)

(b) (i)

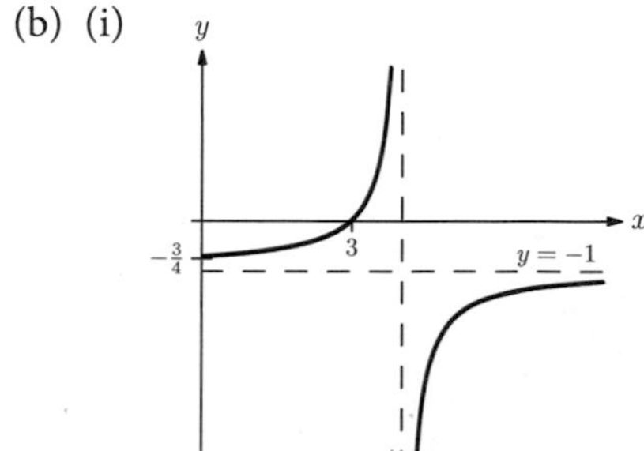

(ii)

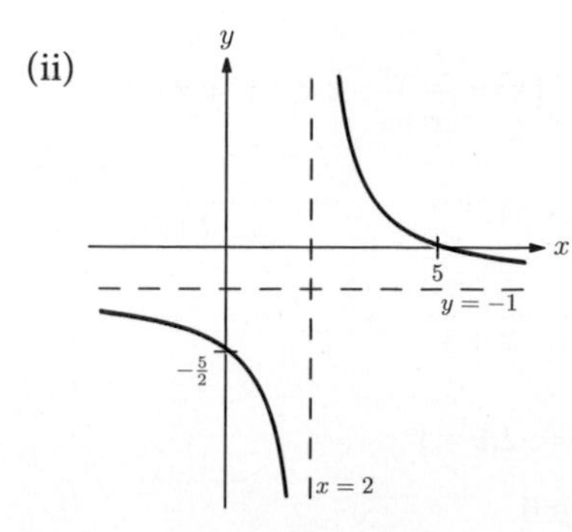

(c) (i)

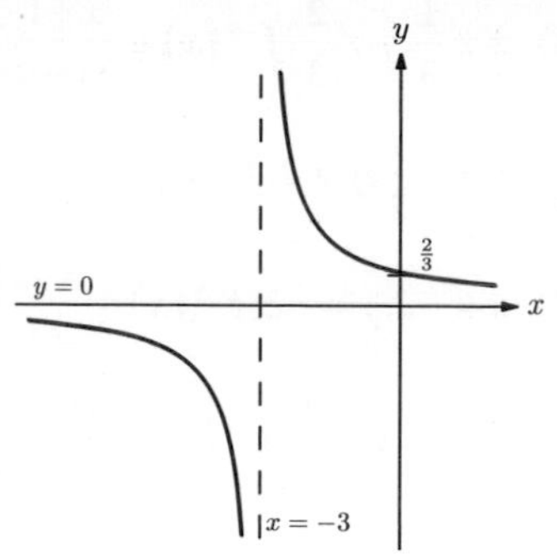

(ii)

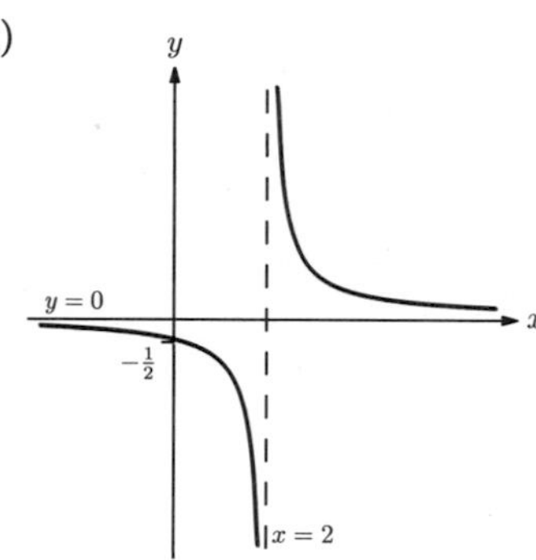

(d) (i)

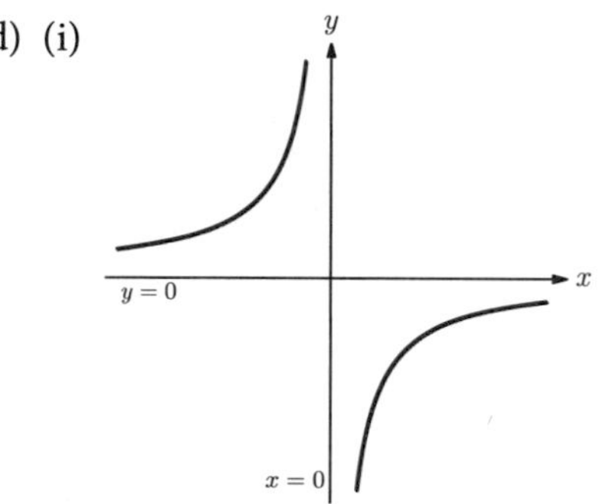

(ii)

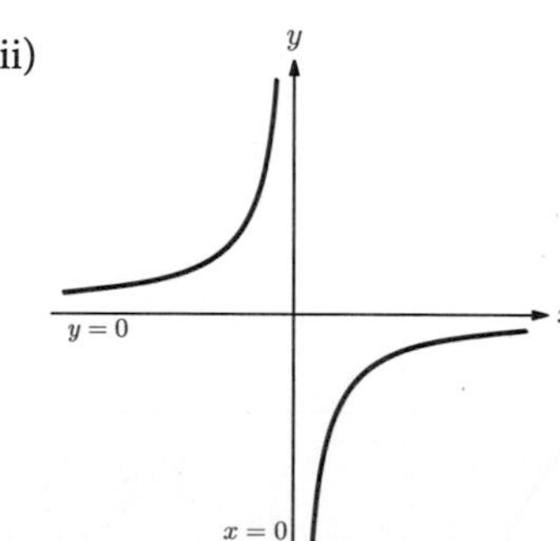

4. (a) (i) $x \neq 0, y \neq 0, f^{-1}(x) = \frac{3}{x}$

(ii) $x \neq 0, y \neq 0, f^{-1}(x) = \frac{7}{x}$

(b) (i) $x \neq 3, y \neq 0, f^{-1}(x) = \frac{3x+2}{x}$

(ii) $x \neq -1, y \neq 0, f^{-1}(x) = \frac{5-x}{x}$

(c) (i) $x \neq \frac{1}{3}, y \neq \frac{2}{3}, f^{-1}(x) = \frac{x+1}{3x-2}$

(ii) $x \neq -\frac{1}{2}, y \neq 2, f^{-1}(x) = \frac{-x-5}{2x-4}$

(d) (i) $x \neq -2, y \neq -2, f^{-1}(x) = \frac{5-2x}{x+2}$

(ii) $x \neq \frac{3}{4}, y \neq \frac{3}{4}, f^{-1}(x) = \frac{3x-1}{4x-3}$

5. $x = \frac{4}{5}$, $y = -\frac{3}{5}$

6. (a) $x \neq -3, y \neq 0$

(b) $f^{-1}(x) = \frac{1-3x}{x}$

7. (a)

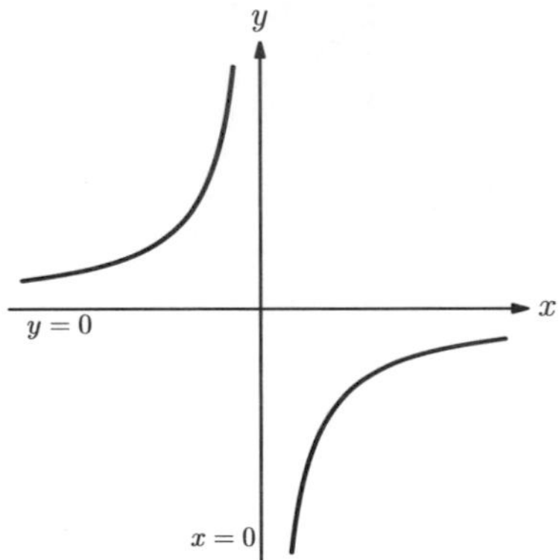

(b) $f^{-1}(x) = -\frac{3}{x}$

8.

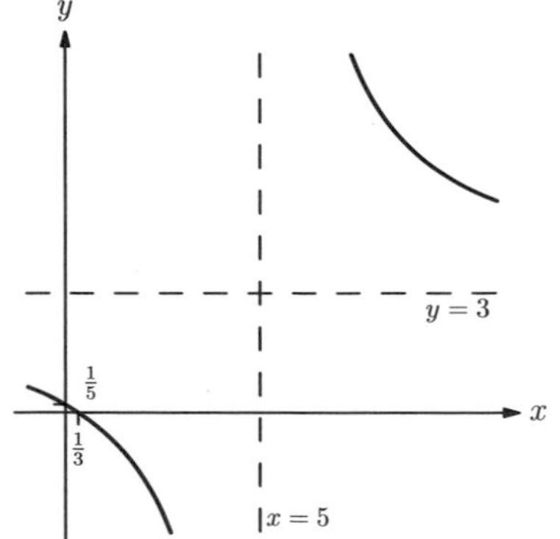

9. (a) $y \in \mathbb{R}, y \neq \frac{a}{2}$

(b) $f^{-1}(x) = \frac{8x+3}{2x-a}$

(c) 8

Mixed examination practice 4

Short questions

1. $4x^2 - 4x + 2$

2. $x = -\frac{1}{2}$

3. 0.549

4. (a) $x = 5, y = -4$

(b) $f^{-1}(x) = \frac{5x+3}{x+4}$

5. (a) $f^{-1}(x) = 3^x - 3$

(b) $f^{-1}(x) = \sqrt[3]{\ln\left(\frac{x}{3}\right) + 1}$

6. (a) $y = \log_2 x$ (b) $(1, 0)$

7. (a) $(x-3)^2 + 1$

(b) $\sqrt{x-1} + 3$

(c) $x \geq 1$

8. (a) $y \in \mathbb{R}, y \neq -1$

(b)

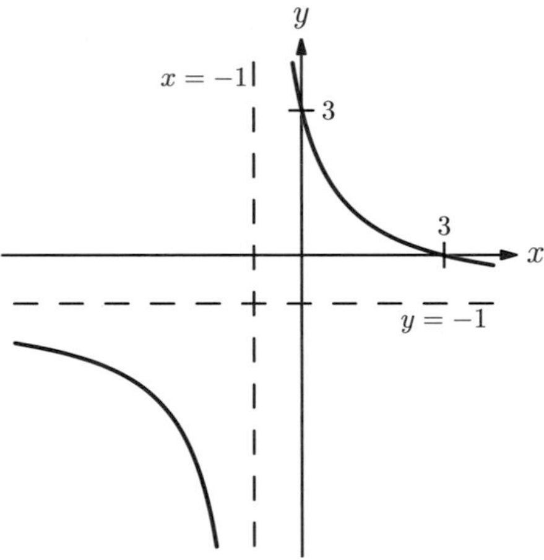

(c) $f^{-1}(x) = \frac{3-x}{x+1}$, $x \neq -1$, $y \neq -1$

9. (a) $(x-3)^2 - 7$

(b) $y > -7$

(c) $\sqrt{x+7} + 3$

10. (a) $a = -2, b = 1$

(b) $y \geq 0$

Long questions

1. (a) 10
(b) $4 - x^2$
(c) Reflections of each other in the line $y = x$
(d) (i) $\sqrt{x-1}$ (ii) $y \geq 3$ (iii) $x \geq 10$
(e) $x = -4, 1$

2. (a) (i) 15 (ii) $y \in \mathbb{R}$ (iii) $2z + 1$
(iv) $\dfrac{3x+5}{x-1}$ (v) $4x + 3$
(b) $f(x)$ can be 1, which is not in the domain of g
(c) (i) $\dfrac{x+3}{x-1}$
(ii) Reflections of each other in the line $y = x$
(iii) $x \neq 1$ (iv) $y \neq 1$

3. (a) $(x+2)^2 + 5$

(b)

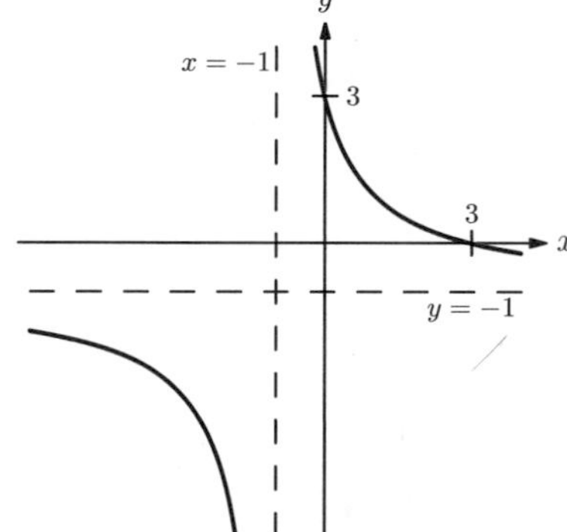

(c) Range of f is $y \geq 5$; range of g is $y > 0$
(d) $y > 9$

4. (a) $y = \dfrac{8x}{2x+3}$
(b)

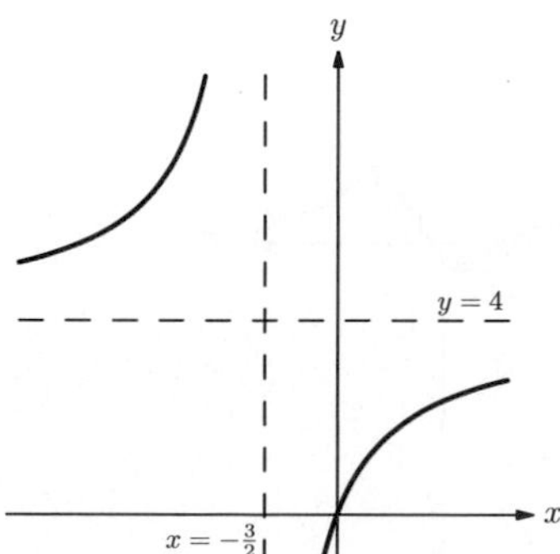

(c) $\dfrac{16x+8k}{4x+2k+3}$
(d) $x = -\dfrac{2k+3}{4}, y = 4$
(e) $(hg)(x) = (hg)^{-1}(x) = \dfrac{16x-76}{4x-16}$

Chapter 5

Exercise 5A

1. (a) (i)

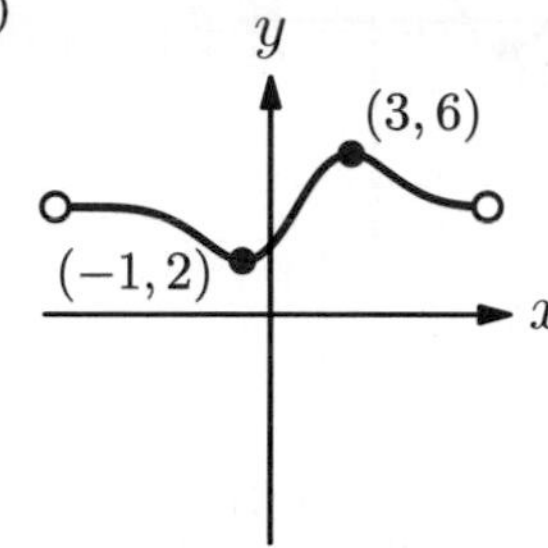

(ii)

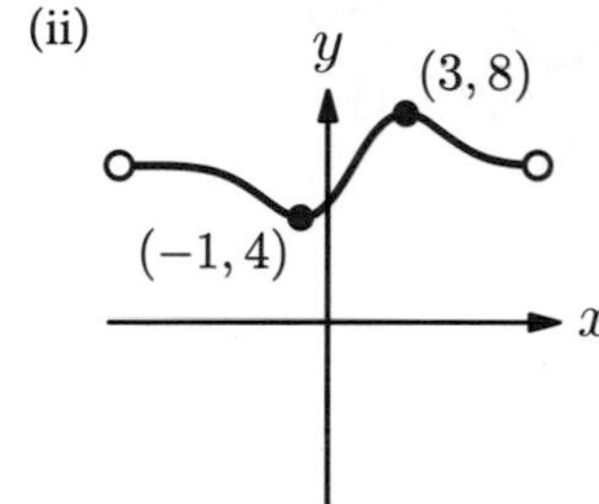

(b) (i)

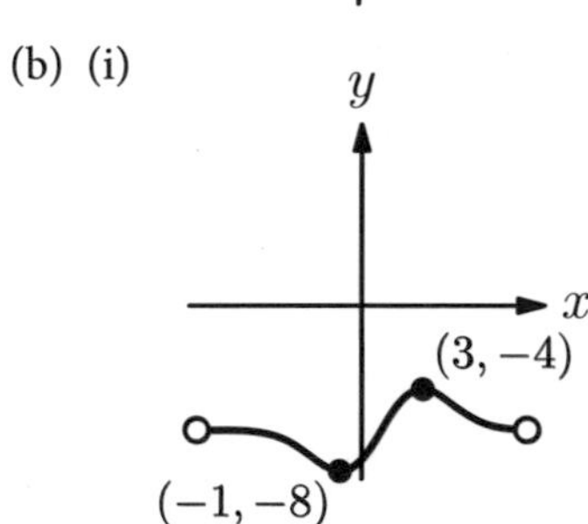

(ii)

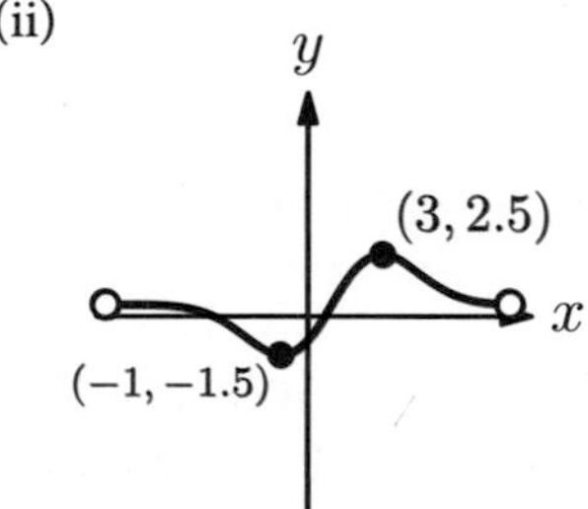

(c) (i)

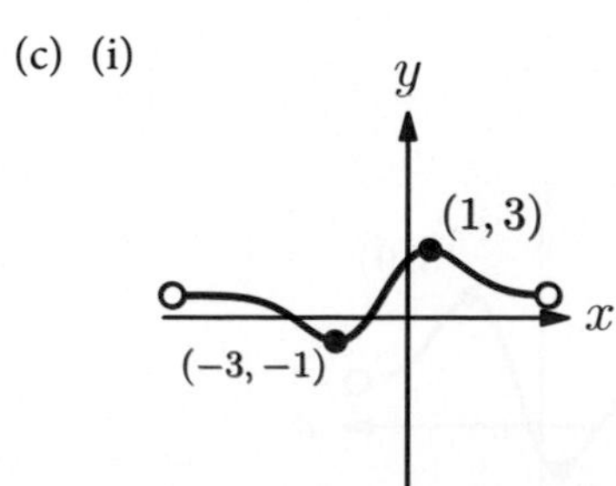

(ii)

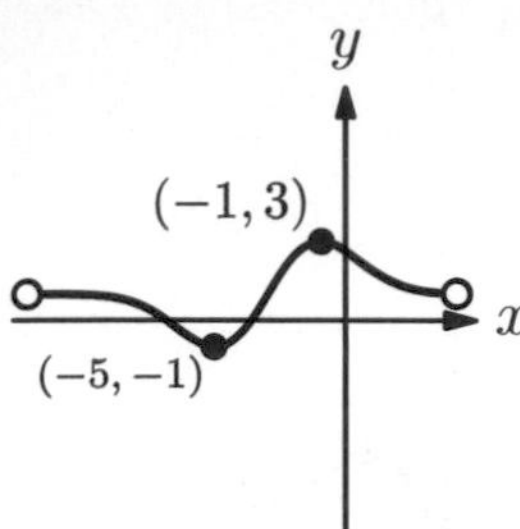

(d) (i)

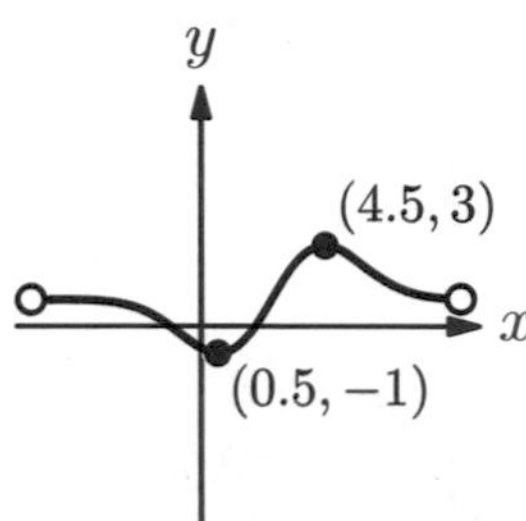

(ii)

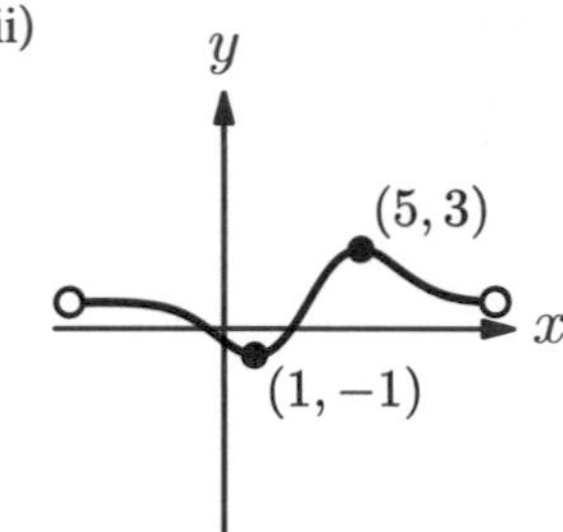

2. (a) (i) $y=3x^2+3$ (ii) $y=9x^3-7$
(b) (i) $y=7x^3-3x+4$ (ii) $y=8x^2-7x+6$
(c) (i) $y=4(x-5)^2$ (ii) $y=7(x+3)^2$
(d) (i) $y=3(x+4)^3-5(x+4)^2+4$
(ii) $y=(x-3)^3+6(x-3)+2$

3. (a) (i) Vertically down 5 units
(ii) Vertically down 4 units
(b) (i) Left 1 unit (ii) Left 5 units
(c) (i) Right 4 units (ii) Right 5 units
(d) (i) Left 3 units (ii) Right 2 units

Exercise 5B

1. (a) (i)

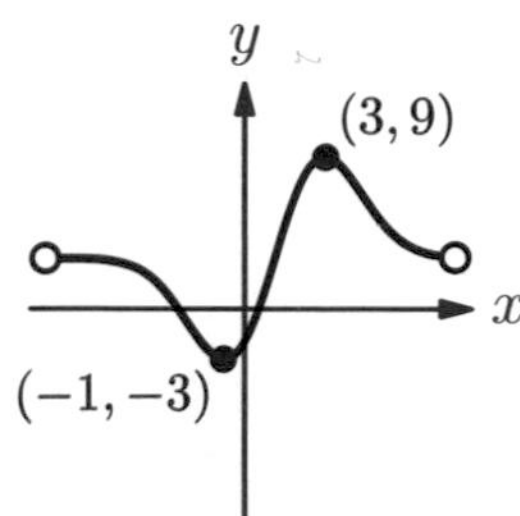

(ii)

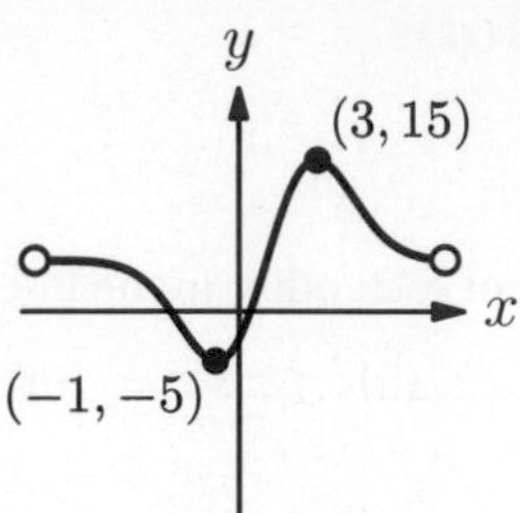

(b) (i)

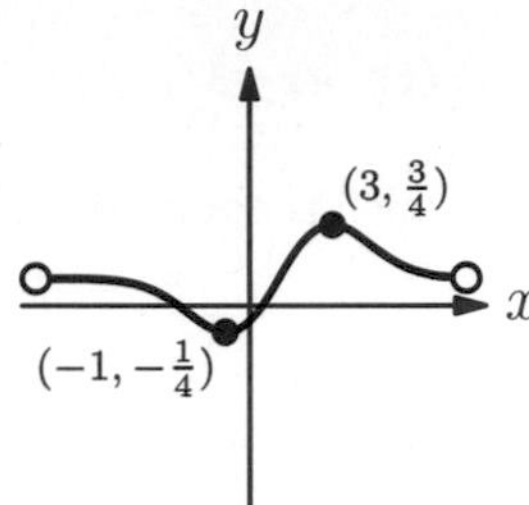

(ii)

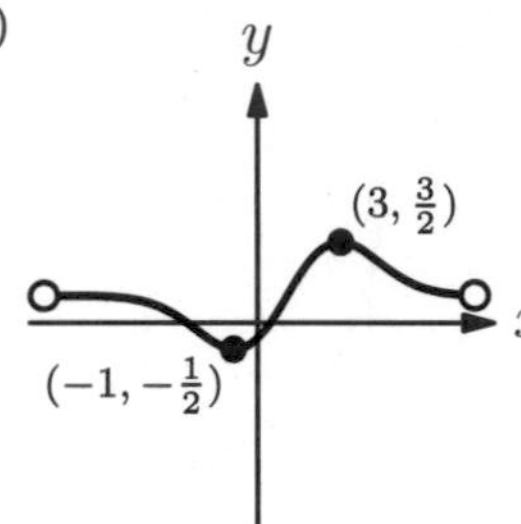

(c) (i)

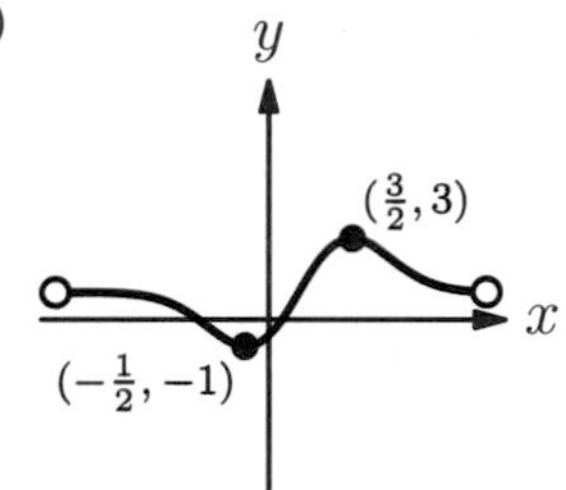

(ii)

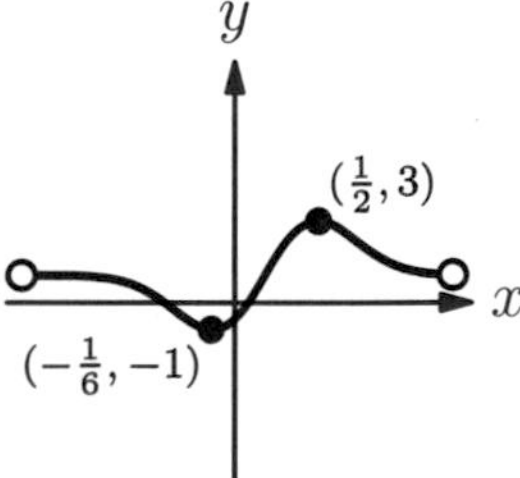

(d) (i)

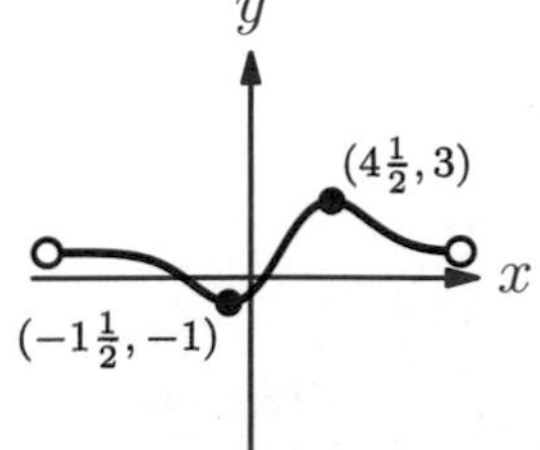

(ii)

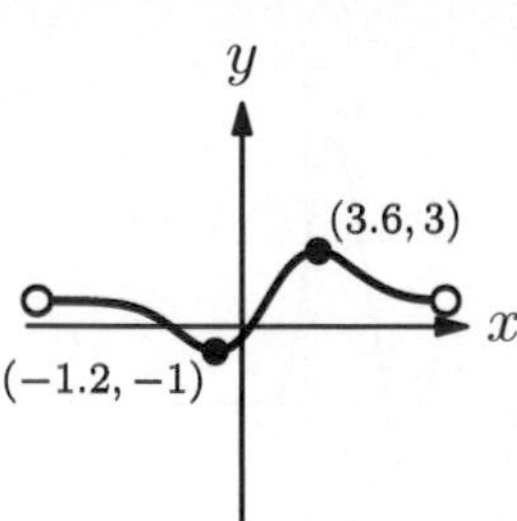

2. (a) (i) $y=21x^2$ (ii) $y=18x^3$

(b) (i) $y=\frac{1}{3}(7x^3-3x+6)$ (ii) $y=\frac{4}{5}(8x^2-7x+1)$

(c) (i) $y=4\left(\frac{x}{2}\right)^2$ (ii) $y=7\left(\frac{x}{5}\right)^2$

(d) (i) $y=3(2x)^3-5(2x)^2+4$

(ii) $y=\left(\frac{3x}{2}\right)^3+6\left(\frac{3x}{2}\right)+2$

3. (a) (i) Vertical stretch, scale factor 4
(ii) Vertical stretch, scale factor 6

(b) (i) Horizontal stretch, scale factor $\frac{1}{3}$

(ii) Horizontal stretch, scale factor $\frac{1}{4}$

(c) (i) Horizontal stretch, scale factor 2
(ii) Horizontal stretch, scale factor 5

(d) (i) Horizontal stretch, scale factor $\frac{1}{3}$

(ii) Horizontal stretch, scale factor 2

Exercise 5C

1. (a)

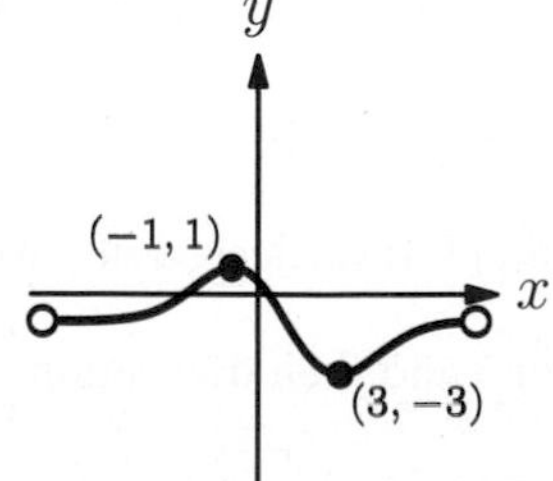

(b)

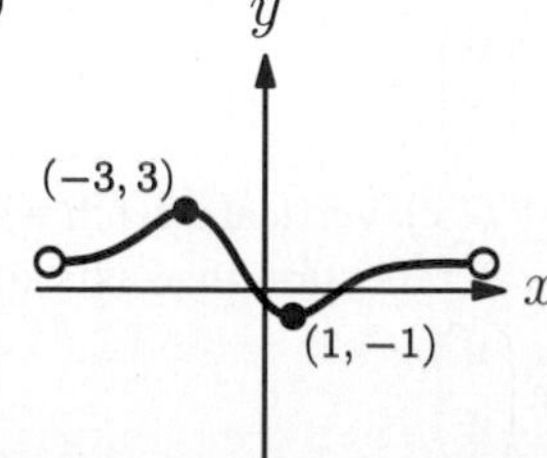

2. (a) (i) $y=-3x^2$ (ii) $y=-9x^3$
(b) (i) $y=-7x^3+3x-6$ (ii) $y=-8x^2+7x-1$
(c) (i) $y=4x^2$ (ii) $y=-7x^3$
(d) (i) $y=-3x^3-5x^2+4$ (ii) $y=-x^3-6x+2$

3. (a) (i) Reflection in the x-axis
(ii) Reflection in the x-axis
(b) (i) Reflection in the y-axis
(ii) Reflection in the y-axis
(c) (i) Reflection in the y-axis
(ii) Reflection in the x-axis
(d) (i) Reflection in the y-axis
(ii) Reflection in the y-axis

Exercise 5D

1. (a) $y=p(f(x)+c)$ (b) $y=f\left(\frac{x}{q}+d\right)$

2. (a) (i)

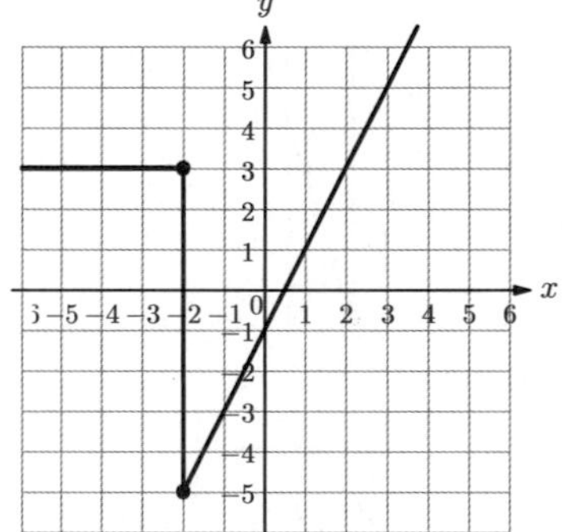

(ii)

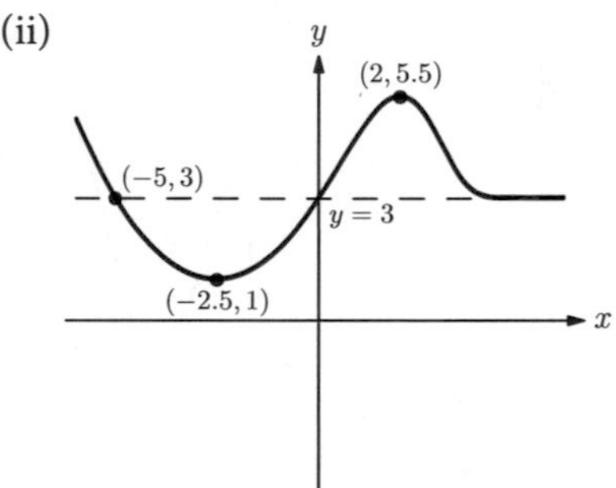

(b) (i)

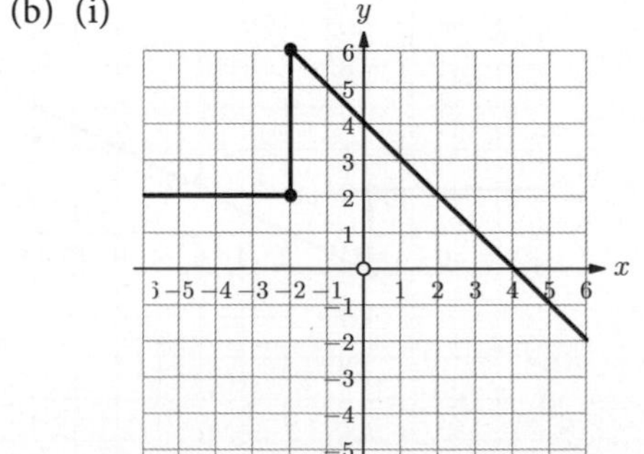

(ii)

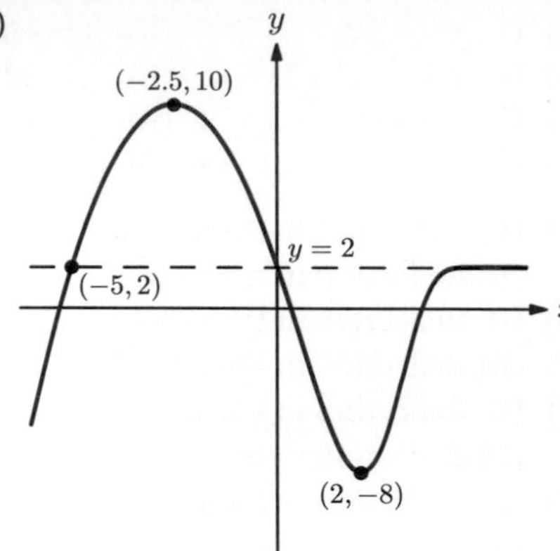

(c) (i)

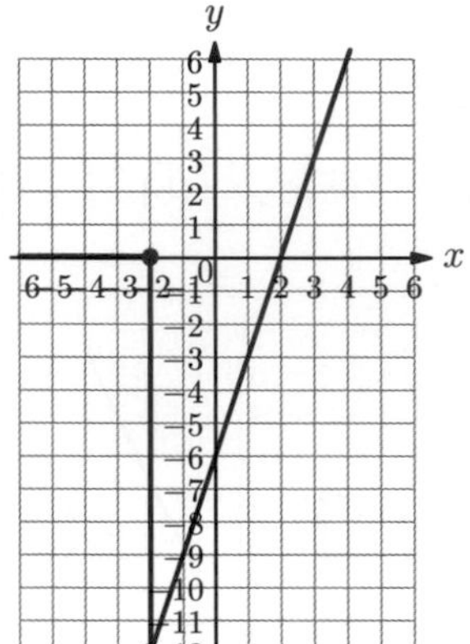

(ii)

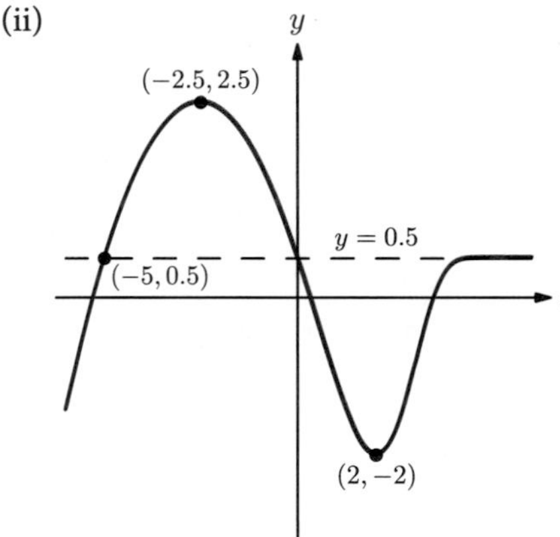

(d) (i)

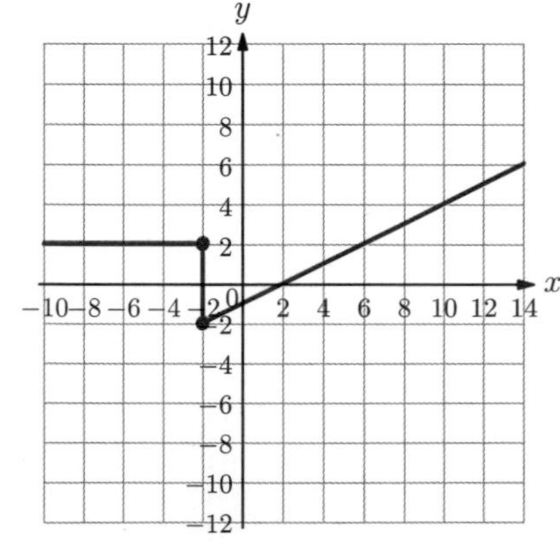

(ii)

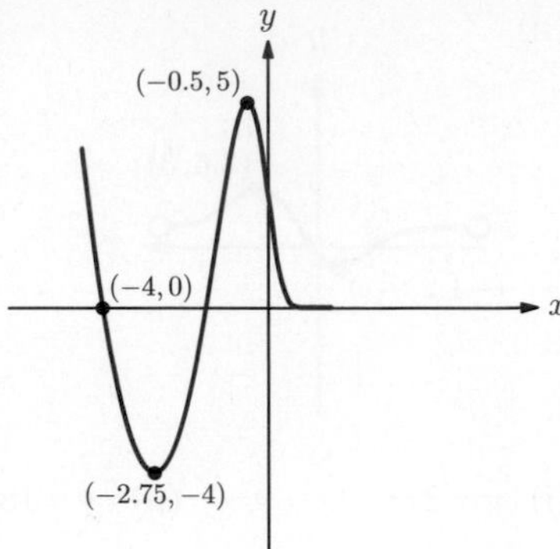

(e) (i)

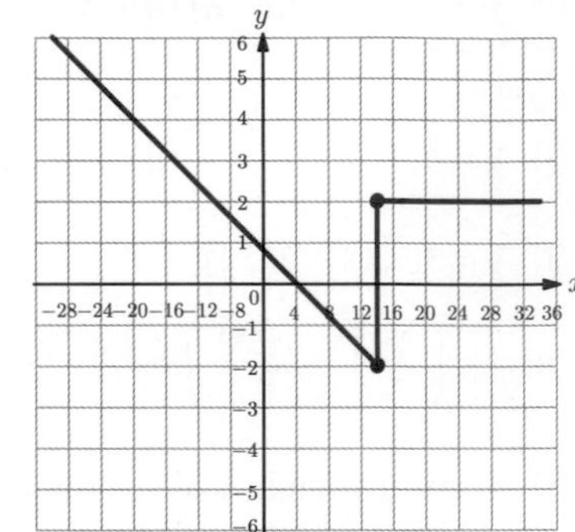

(ii)

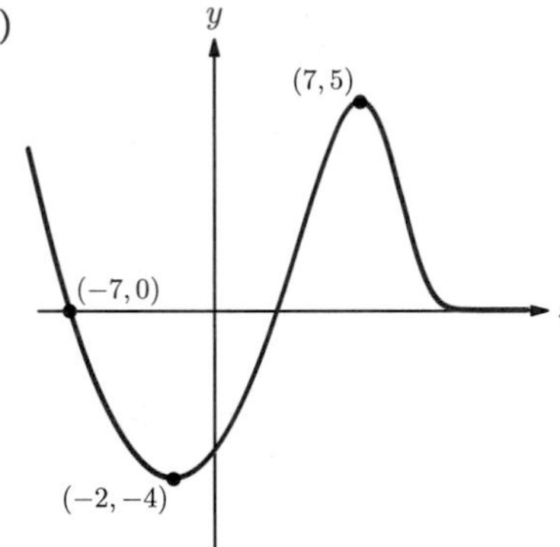

3. (a) (i) $k(x) = 2f(x) - 6$; vertical stretch with scale factor 2 and then translation $\begin{pmatrix} 0 \\ -6 \end{pmatrix}$

(ii) $k(x) = 5f(x) + 4$; vertical stretch with scale factor 5 and then translation $\begin{pmatrix} 0 \\ 4 \end{pmatrix}$

(b) (i) $h(x) = 5 - 3f(x)$; vertical stretch with scale factor 3, reflection in x-axis and translation $\begin{pmatrix} 0 \\ 5 \end{pmatrix}$

(ii) $h(x) = 4 - 8f(x)$; vertical stretch with scale factor 8, reflection in x-axis and translation $\begin{pmatrix} 0 \\ 4 \end{pmatrix}$

> **ANSWER HINT (3)**
> There are alternative answers; for example, (a)(i) could be translation $\begin{pmatrix}0\\-3\end{pmatrix}$ followed by vertical sketch with s.f.2.

4. (a) (i) $g(x)=6x^2-6$ (ii) $g(x)=x^2+1$
(b) (i) $g(x)=x^2+4$ (ii) $g(x)=7x^2-4$
(c) (i) $g(x)=4-2x^2$ (ii) $g(x)=6-2x^2$
(d) (i) $g(x)=5-x^2$ (ii) $g(x)=-3-3x^2$

5. (a) (i) $f(x+1)$; translation $\begin{pmatrix}-1\\0\end{pmatrix}$
(ii) $f(x-3)$; translation $\begin{pmatrix}3\\0\end{pmatrix}$
(b) (i) $f(2x)$; horizontal stretch with scale factor $\frac{1}{2}$; or $4f(x)$; vertical sketch with scale factor 4
(ii) $f\left(\frac{x}{3}\right)$; horizontal stretch with scale factor 3; or $\frac{1}{9}f(x)$; vertical sketch with scale factor $\frac{1}{9}$
(c) (i) $f(2x+2)$; translation $\begin{pmatrix}-2\\0\end{pmatrix}$ and then horizontal stretch with scale factor $\frac{1}{2}$ *or* horizontal stretch with scale factor $\frac{1}{2}$ and then translation $\begin{pmatrix}-1\\0\end{pmatrix}$
(ii) $f(3x-1)$; translation $\begin{pmatrix}1\\0\end{pmatrix}$ then horizontal stretch with scale factor $\frac{1}{3}$ *or* horizontal stretch with scale factor $\frac{1}{3}$ and then translation $\begin{pmatrix}1/3\\0\end{pmatrix}$

6. (a) (i) $g(x)=32x^2-16x-2$
(ii) $g(x)=8x^2+16x+4$
(b) (i) $g(x)=8x^2+64x+124$
(ii) $g(x)=\frac{9x^2}{2}-9x+\frac{1}{2}$
(c) (i) $g(x)=2x^2-12x+14$
(ii) $g(x)=2x^2+12x+14$

7. (a) (i) $g(x)=2f(x+1)-2$; translation by $\begin{pmatrix}-1\\-1\end{pmatrix}$, then vertical stretch with scale factor 2
(ii) $g(x)=3f(x-4)-40$; vertical stretch with scale factor 3, then translation by $\begin{pmatrix}4\\-40\end{pmatrix}$
(b) (i) $g(x)=f(x-3)-4$; translation by $\begin{pmatrix}3\\-4\end{pmatrix}$
(ii) $g(x)=-4f(x-1)+8$; vertical stretch with scale factor 4, then translation by $\begin{pmatrix}8\\1\end{pmatrix}$

8. $h(x)=4^{x+1}+16x-4$

9. (a)

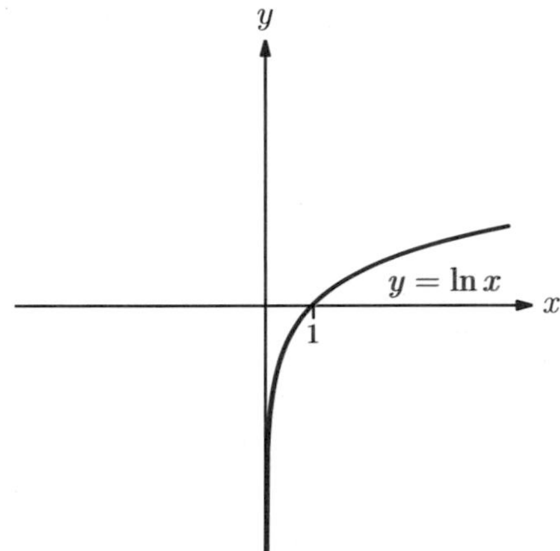

(b)

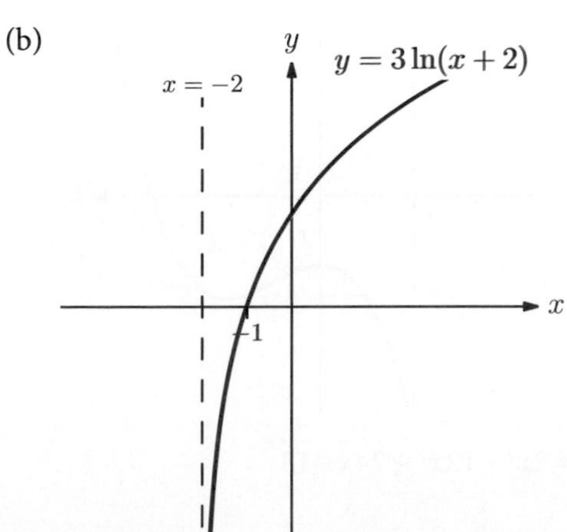

(c)

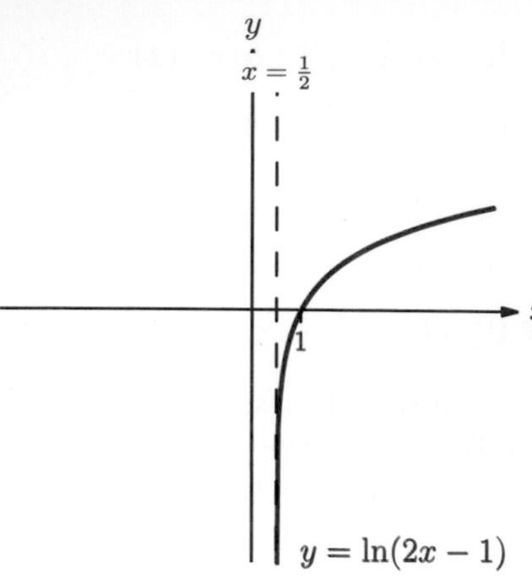

10. (i) $a = 5$, $b = -1$
(ii) $a = 16$, $b = 0$, $c = -25$

Mixed examination practice 5

Short questions

1. (a)

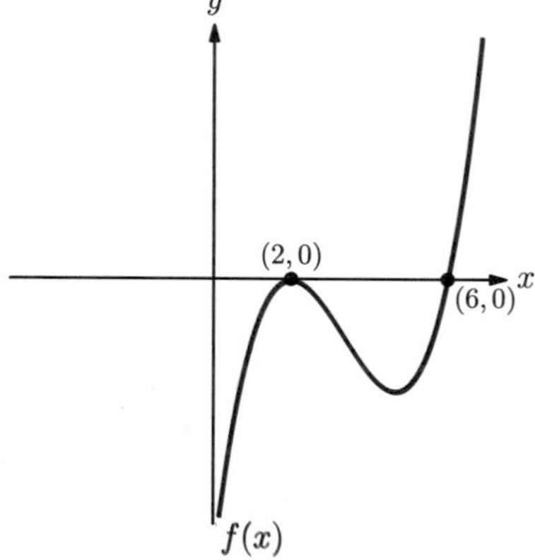

(b)

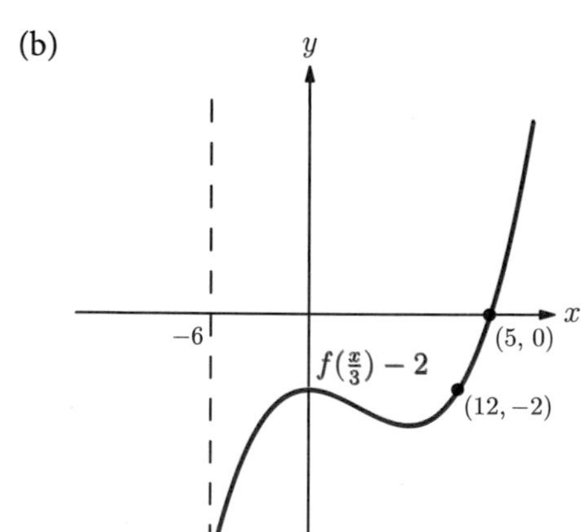

2. $y = 2x^2 - 12x^2 + 24x - 18$

3. (a)

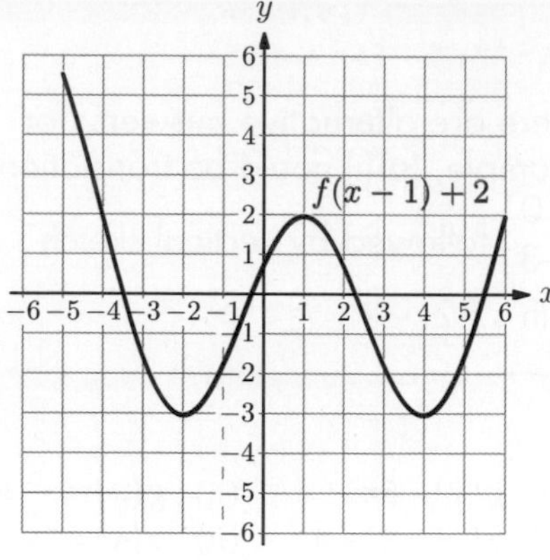

(b) $(-2, -3)$ and $(4, -3)$

4. Translation by $\begin{pmatrix} -3 \\ 0 \end{pmatrix}$ and vertical stretch with scale factor 3

5. (a) Vertical stretch with scale factor 3; horizontal stretch with scale factor 2

(b)

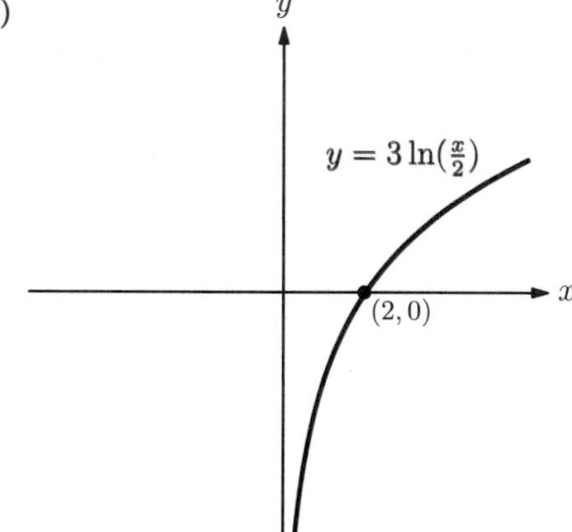

(c)

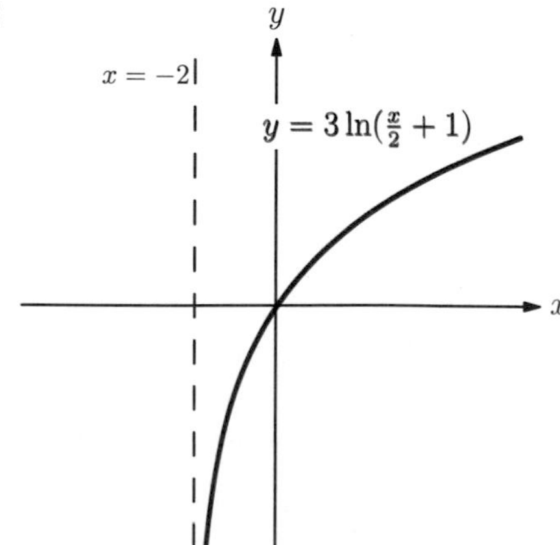

6.

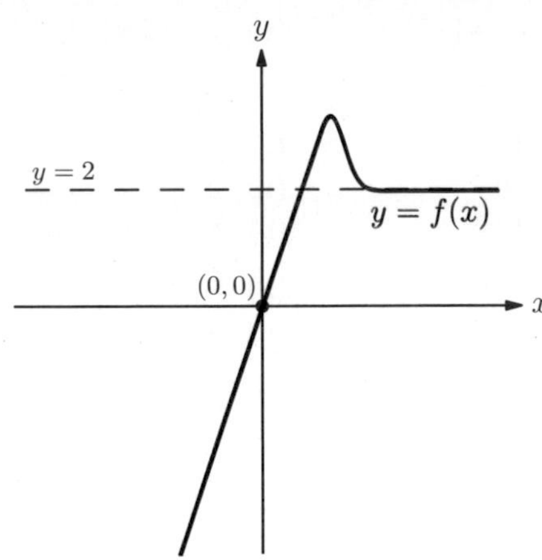

Long questions

1. (a) Translation by $\begin{pmatrix}2\\0\end{pmatrix}$ and vertical stretch with scale factor 3

(b) Translation by $\begin{pmatrix}3\\0\end{pmatrix}$ and translation by $\begin{pmatrix}0\\10\end{pmatrix}$

(c) Translation by $\begin{pmatrix}5\\10\end{pmatrix}$ and vertical stretch with scale factor 3

2. (a) Translation by $\begin{pmatrix}-2\\0\end{pmatrix}$

(b)

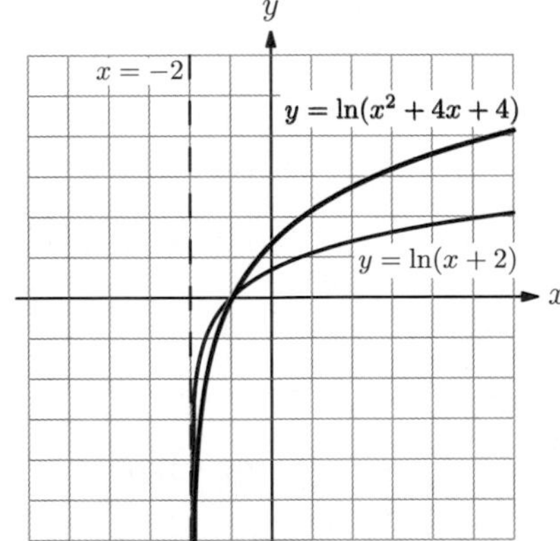

(c) (i) $\begin{pmatrix}2\\0\end{pmatrix}$ (ii) $a=-1, b=6, c=-10, d=-1$

3. (a) $y=3$
(b) $p=3, q=1$
(c) Translation with vector $\begin{pmatrix}2\\3\end{pmatrix}$
(d) $f^{-1}(x)=\dfrac{2x-5}{x-3}, x\neq 3$
(e) Reflection in the line $y=x$

Chapter 6

Exercise 6A

1. (a) (i) 3.1, 8.1, 13.1, 18.1, 23.1
(ii) 10, 6.2, 2.4, −1.4, −5.2
(b) (i) 0, 1, 4, 13, 40
(ii) 1, −1, −19, −181, −1639
(c) (i) 2, 3, 6, 18, 108 (ii) $2, 1, \frac{1}{2}, \frac{1}{2}, 1$
(d) (i) 3, 4, 8, 9, 13 (ii) −3, 3, −5, 7, −9
(e) (i) 0, 4, 8, 12, 16 (ii) 13, 11, 9, 7, 5

2. (a) (i) 5, 8, 11, 14, 17
(ii) −4.5, −3, −1.5, 0, 1.5
(b) (i) 0, 7, 26, 63, 124 (ii) 5, 20, 45, 80, 125
(c) (i) 3, 9, 27, 81, 243 (ii) $4, 2, 1, \frac{1}{2}, \frac{1}{4}$
(d) (i) 1, 4, 27, 256, 3125 (ii) 1, 0, −1, 0, 1

3. (a) (i) $u_{n+1}=u_n+3,\ u_1=7$
(ii) $u_{n+1}=u_n-0.8,\ u_1=1$
(b) (i) $u_{n+1}=2u_n,\ u_1=3$
(ii) $u_{n+1}=1.5u_n,\ u_1=12$
(c) (i) $u_{n+1}=u_n+n+1,\ u_1=1$
(ii) $u_{n+1}=(n+1)u_n, u_1=1$

4. (a) (i) $u_n=2n$ (ii) $u_n=2n-1$
(b) (i) $u_n=2^n$ (ii) $u_n=5^n$
(c) (i) $u_n=n^2$ (ii) $u_n=n^3$
(d) (i) $u_n=\dfrac{n}{n+1}$ (ii) $u_n=\dfrac{2n-1}{2^n}$

5. (a) 2 (b) $2\left(1+\dfrac{1}{n}\right)$

6. (a) 4, 8, 16 (b) (i) $u_n=2^n$

Exercise 6B

1. (a) (i) 27 (ii) 39
(b) (i) 116 (ii) $\dfrac{665}{48}$
(c) (i) $14b$ (ii) $19p$

2. (a) (i) $\sum_{2}^{43} r$ (ii) $\sum_{3}^{30} 2r$
(b) (i) $\sum_{1}^{6} \dfrac{1}{2^{r+1}}$ (ii) $\sum_{0}^{5} \dfrac{2}{3^r}$
(c) (i) $\sum_{r=2}^{10} 7ra$ (ii) $\sum_{r=1}^{19} r^b$

Exercise 6C

1. (a) (i) $u_n = 9+3(n-1)$ (ii) $u_n = 57+0.2(n-1)$
   (b) (i) $u_n = 12-(n-1)$ (ii) $u_n = 18-\frac{1}{2}(n-1)$
   (c) (i) $u_n = 1+3(n-1)$ (ii) $u_n = 9+10(n-1)$
   (d) (i) $u_n = 4-4(n-1)$ (ii) $u_n = 27-7(n-1)$
   (e) (i) $u_n = -17+11(n-1)$
   (ii) $u_n = -32+10(n-1)$
2. (a) (i) 33 (ii) 29
   (b) (i) 100 (ii) 226
3. (a) $a_n = 5+8(n-1)$ (b) 50
4. 121
5. 25th
6. 17
7. $a = 2, b = -3$
8. (b) 456

Exercise 6D

1. (a) (i) 3060 (ii) 1495
   (b) (i) 9009 (ii) 23798
   (c) (i) −204 (ii) 1470
   (d) (i) 667.5 (ii) 14.25
2. (a) (i) 13 (ii) 32 (iii) 53
   (b) $\frac{x}{2}$
3. $a = 15, d = -8$
4. (a) $S_n = \frac{n}{2}(3n+1)$ (b) 30
5. (a) 1, 5, 9 (b) $u_n = 4n-3$
6. 559
7. $a = 14, d = -8$
8. 55
9. $u_n = 6n-5$
10. 20°
11. 10300
12. 23926

Exercise 6E

1. (a) (i) $u_n = 6\times 2^{n-1}$ (ii) $u_n = 12\times(1.5)^{n-1}$
   (b) (i) $u_n = 20\times(0.25)^{n-1}$ (ii) $u_n = \left(\frac{1}{2}\right)^{n-1}$
   (c) (i) $u_n = (-2)^{n-1}$ (ii) $u_n = 5\times(-1)^{n-1}$
   (d) (i) $u_n = ax^{n-1}$ (ii) $u_n = 3\times(2x)^{n-1}$
2. (a) (i) 13 (ii) 7
   (b) (i) 10 (ii) 10
   (c) (i) 10 (ii) 8
3. (a) (i) 15 (ii) 31
   (b) (i) 33 (ii) 17
4. 39366
5. 10th
6. 16th
7. 2.5
8. ±384
9. 7 or −3.5
10. $a = -2, b = 4$
11. 7

Exercise 6F

1. (a) (i) 17089842
   (ii) $\frac{36855}{16} \approx 2300$
   (b) (i) 515 (ii) 9.49
   (c) (i) 39400 (ii) 9840
   (d) (i) 192 OR 64.0
   (ii) 2.44×10^7 or 1.63×10^7
2. (a) (i) 3 (ii) 0.2
   (b) (i) −6 (ii) −0.947
3. (a) 5 (b) $S_n = \frac{375(5^n - 1)}{4}$
4. $a = 5, r = 1.5$
5. 0.8 or −1.16
6. (a) 1.5 (b) 160

Exercise 6G

1. (a) (i) $\frac{27}{2}$ (ii) $\frac{196}{3}$
   (b) (i) $\frac{1}{3}$ (ii) $\frac{26}{33}$
   (c) (i) Divergent (ii) Divergent
   (d) (i) $\frac{25}{3}$ (ii) $\frac{18}{5}$
   (e) (i) Divergent (ii) $\frac{7}{3}$

2. (a) (i) $|x|<1$ (ii) $|x|<1$
(b) (i) $|x|<\frac{1}{3}$ (ii) $|x|<\frac{1}{10}$
(c) (i) $|x|<\frac{1}{5}$ (ii) $|x|<\frac{1}{3}$
(d) (i) $|x|<4$ (ii) $|x|<12$
(e) (i) $|x|<3$ (ii) $|x|<\frac{4}{5}$
(f) (i) $|x|>2$ (ii) $|x|>\frac{1}{2}$
(g) (i) $1<x<2$ (ii) $0<x<4$
(h) (i) $\frac{1}{2}<x<1$ (ii) $x<-0.5$
(i) (i) $|x|<1$ (ii) $|x|<\frac{1}{\sqrt[3]{4}}$

3. $-\frac{54}{5}$

4. (a) $S_n=\frac{18\left(1-\left(-\frac{1}{3}\right)^n\right)}{\frac{4}{3}}$ (b) $\frac{27}{2}$

5. (a) 3 (b) Divergent

6. (a) $\frac{2}{3}$ (b) 9

7. $\frac{1}{8}$

8. (a) $|x|<\frac{3}{2}$ (b) 5

9. 9

10. (a) $1<x<\frac{5}{3}$ (b) 7

11. (a) $x<0$ (b) $x=-3$

Exercise 6H

1. (a) £34.78 (b) £1194.05

2. (a) £60,500 (b) 22

3. (a) 5000×1.063^n
(b) $6786.35
(c) (i) $5000\times1.063^n>10000$
(ii) 12

4. (a) 10 (b) 23.7%

5. (a) $265.33 (b) 235

6. (a) 12 (b) Day 102

7. (a) 0.8192 m (b) 15.32 m

8. (b) $25000(1.04^n-1)$
(c) Year 29

Mixed examination practice 6

Short questions

1. 97.2

2. 13th

3. 2

4. 4.5

5. 19264

6. $0, -\frac{1}{4}$

7. $\ln\left(\frac{a^{69}}{b^{138}}\right)$

Long questions

1. (a) $10000+800n$
(b) 10000×1.05^n
(c) $n<19$ years

2. (a) $2n-1$
(b) 6
(c) 64

3. (a) n
(b) $\frac{n(n+1)}{2}$
(c) $\frac{n(n-1)}{2}+1$
(e) 32

4. (b) $150000\times1.06^n-\frac{500000\times(1.06^n-1)}{3}$
(c) 40

Chapter 7

Exercise 7A

1. (i) $792x^5y^7$ (ii) $11\,440a^7b^9$
(iii) $10c^3d^2$ (iv) $36a^2b^7$
(v) $15x^2y^4$

2. (a) 12
(b) 9375
(c) 3125

3. 0

Exercise 7B

1. (a) 1, 2, 1
(b) 1, 3, 3, 1
(c) 1, 5, 10, 10, 5, 1

2. (a) (i) 35 (ii) 36
(b) (i) 1 (ii) 1
(c) (i) 8 (ii) 45

3. (i) 4 (ii) 35
(iii) 7 (iv) 56

4. 240

5. (a) 5 (b) 80

6. (a) 10 (b) 180

Exercise 7C

1. (a) (i) 216 (ii) 20
(b) (i) $560x^3y^4$ (ii) $-280x^3y^4$
(c) (i) −5 (ii) 78030

2. (a) (i) $32-80x+80x^2-40x^3+10x^4-x^5$
(ii) $729+1458x+1215x^2+540x^3$
$+135x^4+18x^5+x^6$
(b) (i) $243x^5+405x^4y+270x^3y^2$
(ii) $16c^4-32c^3d+24c^2d^2$
(c) $8x^6-36x^5+54x^4-27x^3$

3. (a) $81-540x+1350x^2$ (b) 80.4614

4. $y^6+18y^7+135y^8+540y^9$

5. (a) $40x^3y^2$ (b) $-80x^2y^3$

6. −10500

7. $20412x^2$

8. 720

9. 56

10. (a) $128+1344x+6048x^2$
(b) (i) 322.88 (ii) 142.0448
(c) The answer in (ii) is more accurate; a smaller value of x means that higher-power terms are much smaller and therefore less important, so the error is less.

11. (a) $e^5+10e^3+40e+\frac{80}{e}+\frac{80}{e^3}+\frac{32}{e^5}$
(b) $2e^5+80e+\frac{160}{e^3}$

12. (a) 6 (b) 2

13. $16z^8+96z^5+216z^2+216z^{-1}+81z^{-4}$

14. (a) $(1-x^2)^n$ (b) $1-10x^2+45x^4$

15. (a) 3
(b) $27x^6y^3+135x^5y+225x^4y^{-1}+125x^3y^{-3}$

16. 80

17. −672

18. $-945x^5$

19. 79 200 000

20. 126

21. $a=2, n=5$

Mixed examination practice 7

Short questions

1. −101376

2. $8x^{-3}+60x^{-2}y+150x^{-1}y^2+125y^3$

3. $232-164\sqrt{2}$

4. −32

5. $x^8-8x^5+24x^2-32x^{-1}+16x^{-4}$

6. 5733

7. −5

Long questions

1. (a)

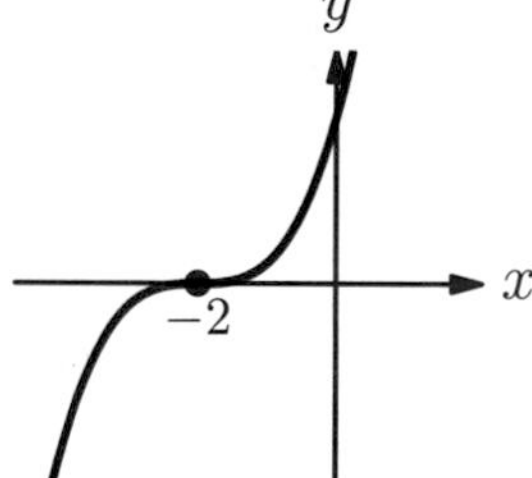

(b) $x^3+6x^2+12x+8$
(c) 8.012006001
(d) $x=-4$

2. (a) 5
(b) 0.5
(c) $32x^5+40x^4y+20x^3y^2+5x^2y^3$
(d) 3 240 200

Chapter 8

Exercise 8A

1. (a)

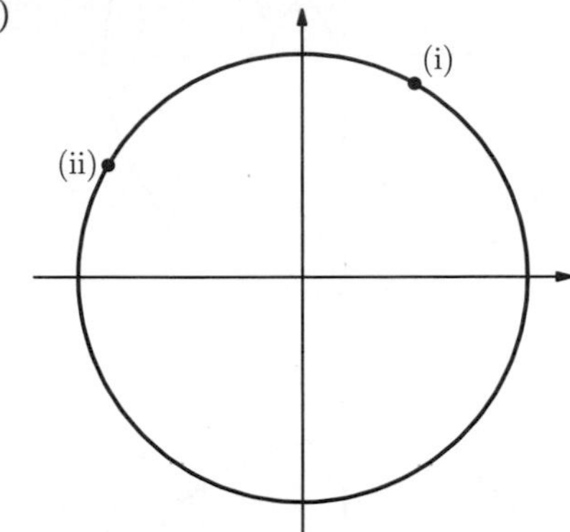

(b)

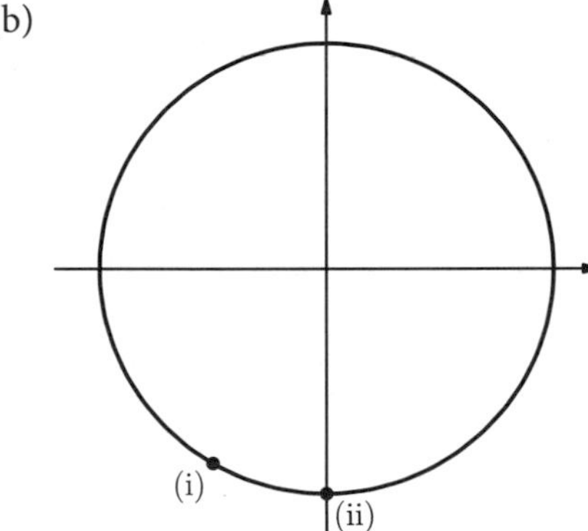

(c)

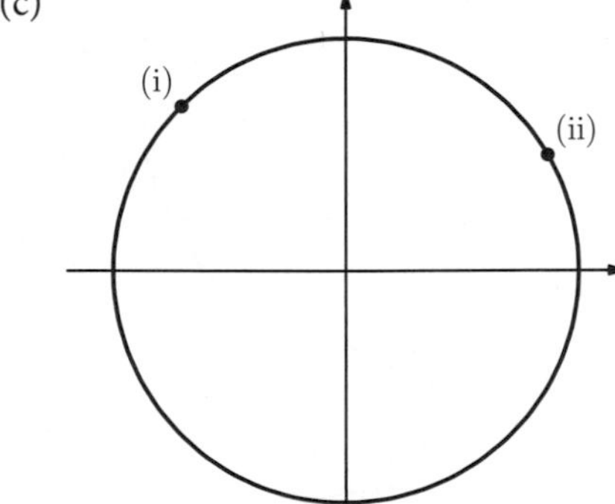

2. (a)

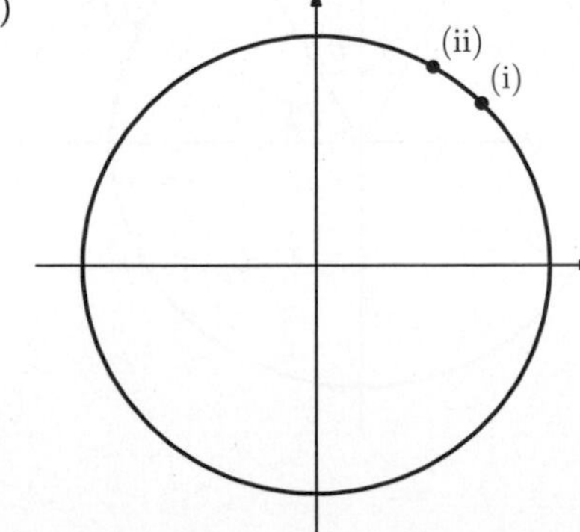

(b)

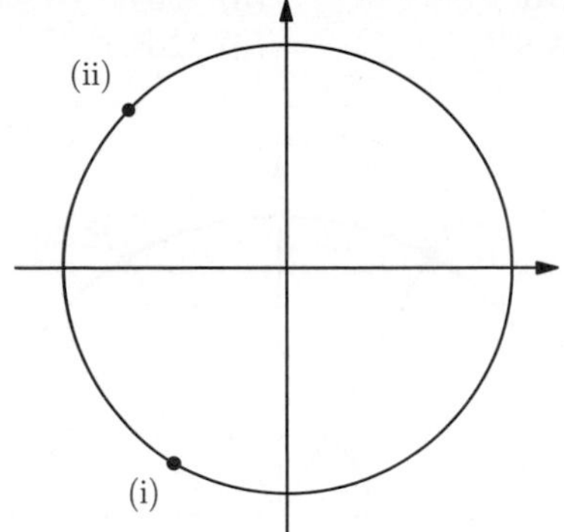

(c)

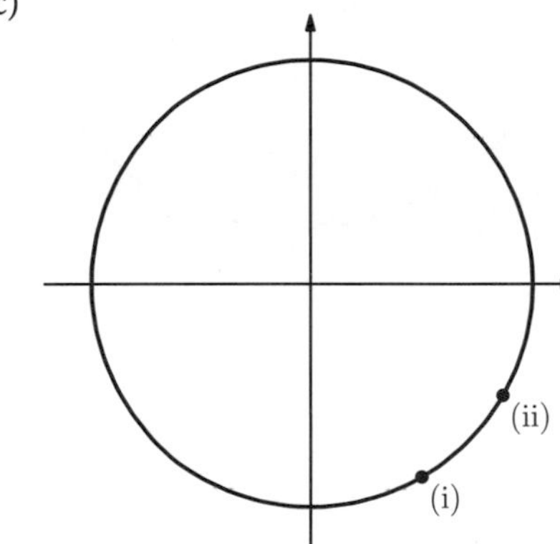

(d)

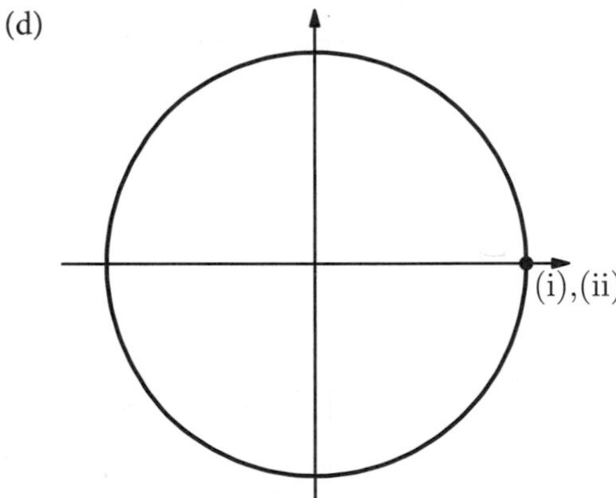

3. (a) (i) $\frac{3\pi}{4}$ (ii) $\frac{\pi}{4}$

(b) (i) $\frac{\pi}{2}$ (ii) $\frac{3\pi}{2}$

(c) (i) $\frac{2\pi}{3}$ (ii) $\frac{5\pi}{6}$

(d) (i) $\frac{5\pi}{18}$ (ii) $\frac{4\pi}{9}$

4. (a) (i) 5.585 (ii) 0.349

(b) (i) 4.712 (ii) 1.571

(c) (i) 1.134 (ii) 2.531

(d) (i) 1.745 (ii) 1.449

5. (a) (i) 60° (ii) 45°

(b) (i) 150° (ii) 120°

(c) (i) 270° (ii) 300°
(d) (i) 69.9° (ii) 265.3°

6. (a)

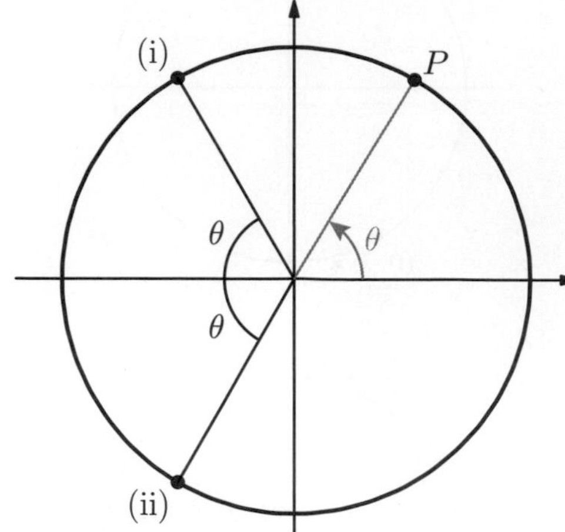

(b)

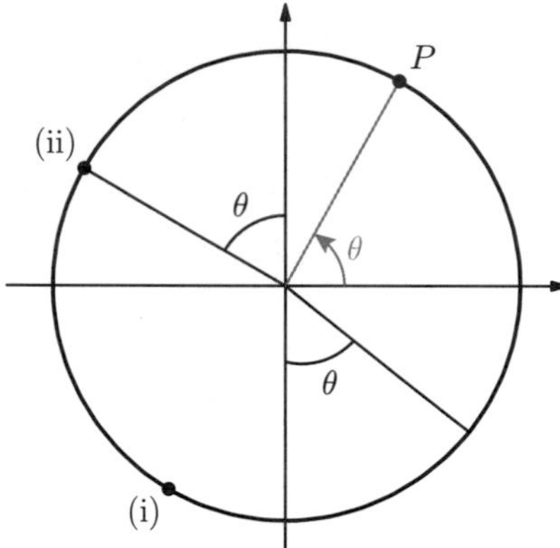

(c)

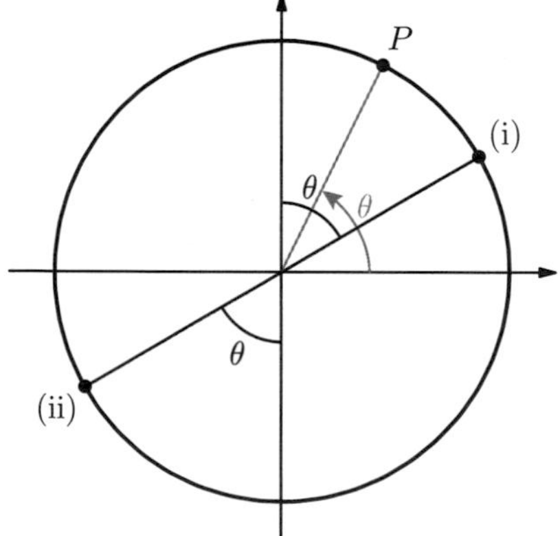

(d)

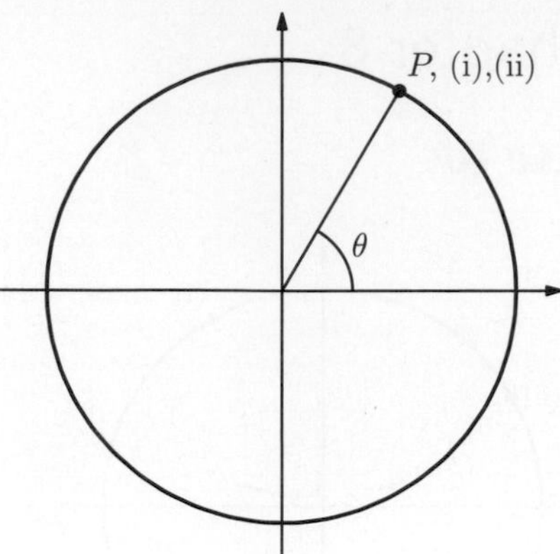

7. (a)

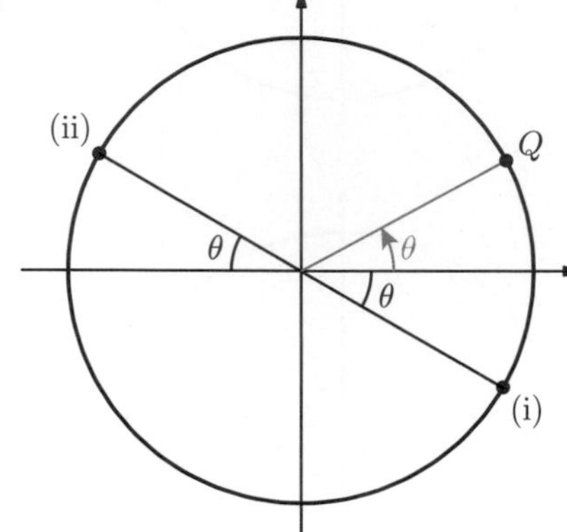

(b)

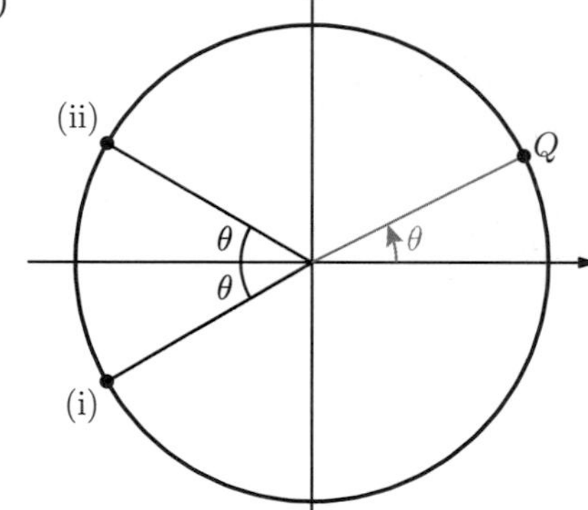

(c)

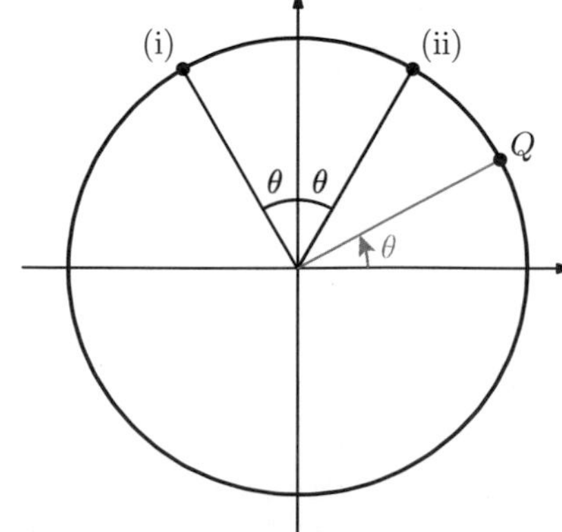

(d)

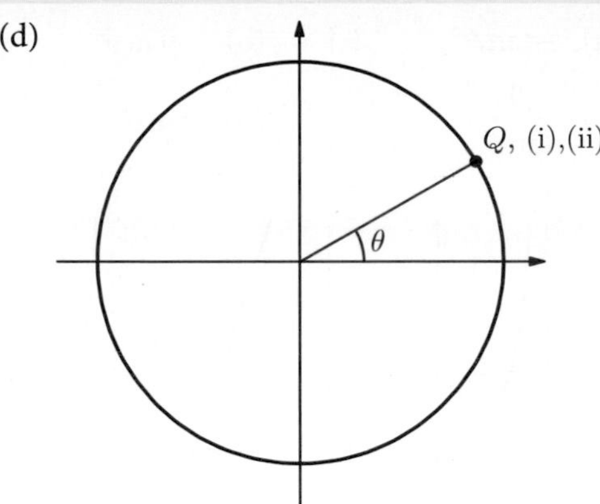

Exercise 8B

1. (a) $\sin x \approx 0.85$, $\cos x \approx 0.5$
   (b) $\sin x \approx -1$, $\cos x \approx 0$
   (c) $\sin x \approx 0.35$, $\cos x \approx -0.95$

2. (a) (i) 1 (ii) 0
   (b) (i) 1 (ii) −1
   (c) (i) −1 (ii) 0

3. (a) (i) 0 (ii) −1
   (b) (i) −1 (ii) 1
   (c) (i) 0 (ii) 0

4. (a) −0.809 (b) 0.809
   (c) 0.809 (d) −0.809

5. (a) −0.866 (b) −0.866
   (c) −0.866 (d) 0.866

6. (a) 0.766 (b) 0.766
   (c) −0.766 (d) −0.766

7. (a) 0.766 (b) 0.766
   (c) −0.766 (d) −0.766

8. (a) (i)

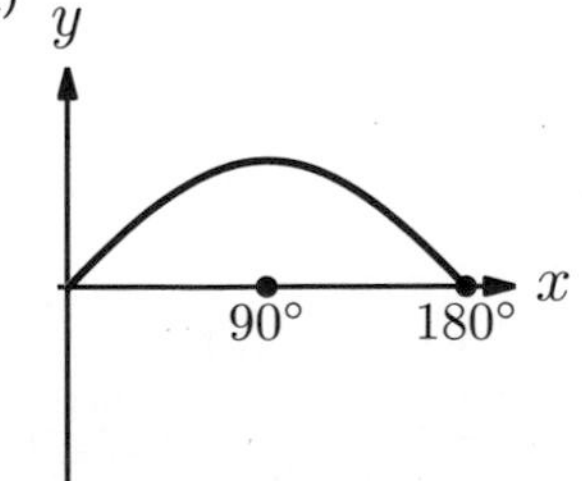

(ii)

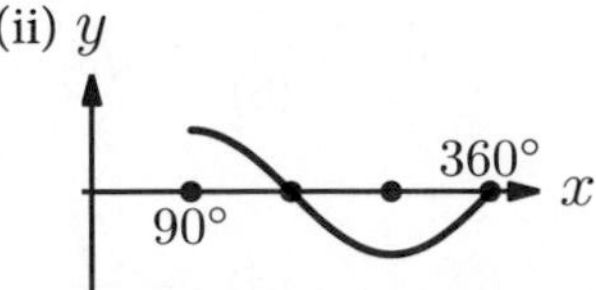

(b) (i)

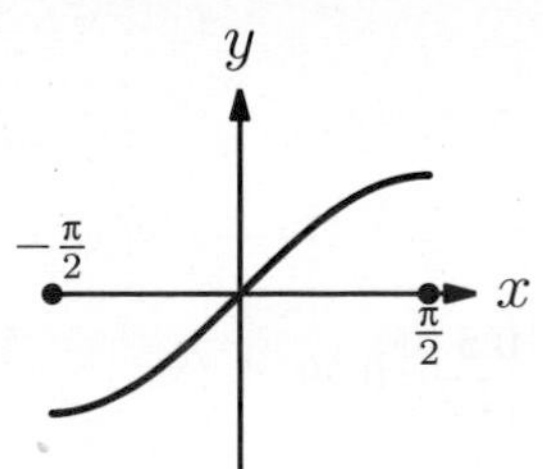

(ii)

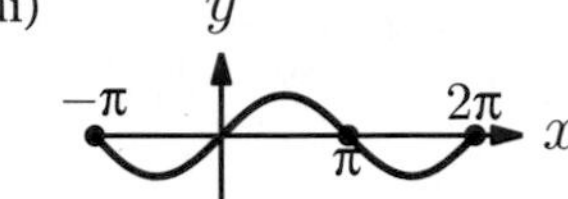

9. (a) (i)

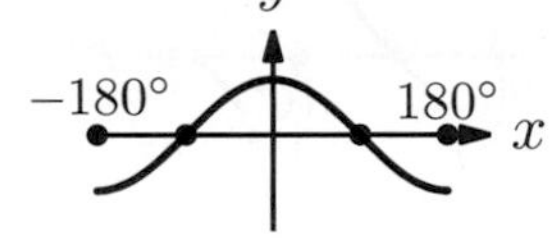

(ii)

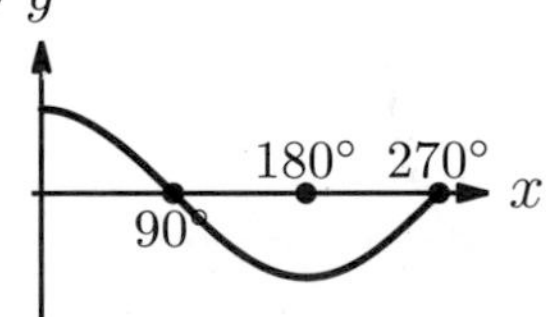

(b) (i)

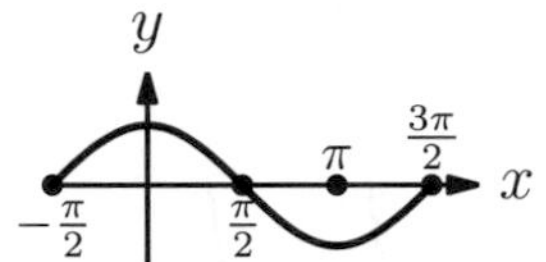

(ii)

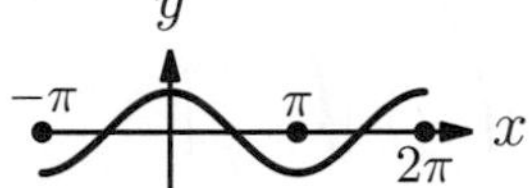

10. (a)

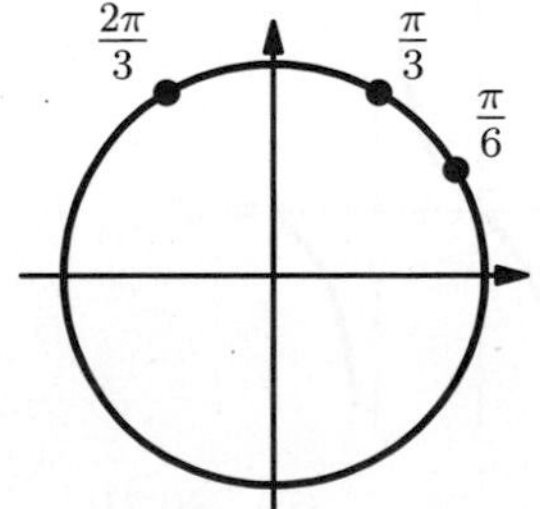

(b) (i) 0.5 (ii) −0.5

11. (a) (i) 0.315 (ii) 0.629
    (b) (i) 0.752 (ii) −0.711

12. (a) (i) 0.669 (ii) −0.978
    (b) (i) −0.766 (ii) −0.682

13. $-2\cos x$

14. $\sin x$

Exercise 8C

1. (a) $\tan x \approx \frac{0.5}{0.85} = 0.59$
   (b) $\tan x \approx \frac{-0.5}{-0.85} = 0.59$
   (c) $\tan x \approx \frac{-0.5}{0.85} = -0.59$

2. (a) (i)

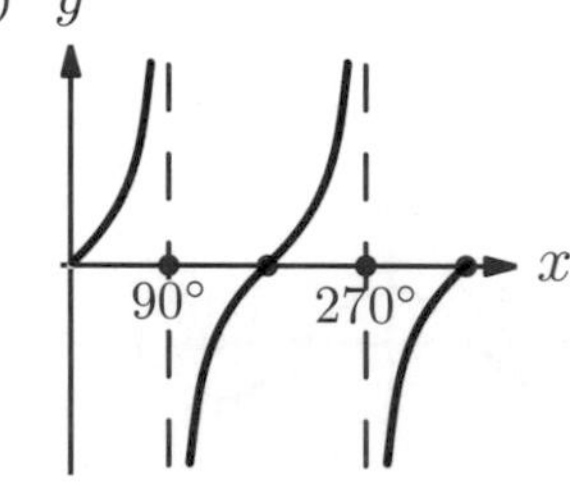

(ii)

y x −90° 90° 270°

(b) (i)

y x $\frac{\pi}{2}$ $\frac{3\pi}{2}$ $\frac{5\pi}{2}$

(ii)

y x $-\frac{\pi}{2}$ $\frac{\pi}{2}$

3. (a) (i) 2.57 (ii) 80.71
   (b) (i) −0.760 (ii) −1.62

4. (a) (i) 0.625 (ii) −0.213
   (b) (i) 0 (ii) 1.28

5. (a) $-\tan x$ (b) $-\frac{1}{\tan x}$
   (c) $\tan x$ (d) $\tan x$

6. (a) $-\tan\theta°$ (b) $-\tan\theta°$
   (c) $\frac{1}{\tan\theta°}$ (d) $\tan\theta°$

7. (i)

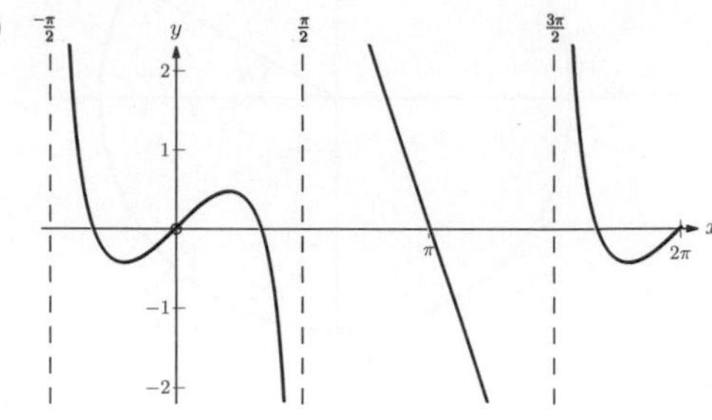

(ii)

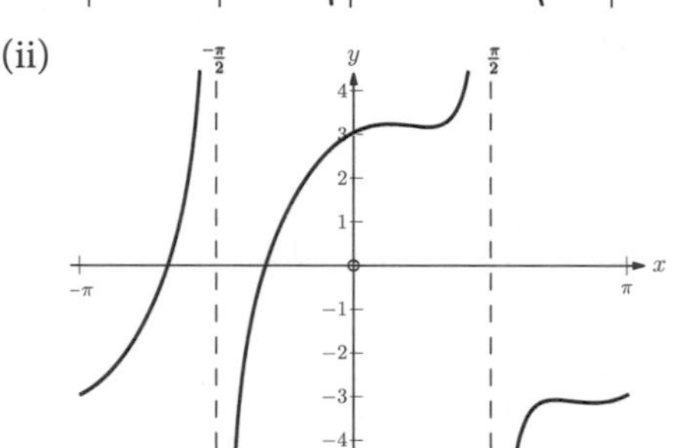

8. (i) 0, 180, 360 (ii) 57.9, 122

9. (i) max (0.805, 1.122); min (5.48, −1.122)
   (ii) max (−1.11, 2.24); min (2.03, −2.24)

10. (i) 1.87, 5.07 (ii) 0, 1.57, 3.14

Exercise 8D

1. (a) $-\frac{\sqrt{2}}{2}$ (b) 0
   (c) $-\frac{\sqrt{2}}{2}$ (d) −1

2. (a) $\frac{1}{2}$ (b) $-\frac{1}{2}$
   (c) $-\frac{1}{2}$ (d) $-\sqrt{3}$

3. (a) $\frac{\sqrt{2}}{2}$ (b) $\frac{\sqrt{2}}{2}$
   (c) $-\frac{\sqrt{2}}{2}$ (d) 1

4. (a) $-\frac{1}{2}$ (b) $-\frac{\sqrt{3}}{2}$
   (c) $\frac{\sqrt{3}}{3}$ (d) $-\frac{\sqrt{3}}{3}$

5. (a) $\frac{3}{4}$

(b) $\frac{\sqrt{2}+\sqrt{3}}{2}$

(c) $\frac{1-\sqrt{3}}{2}$

Exercise 8E

1. (a) (i)

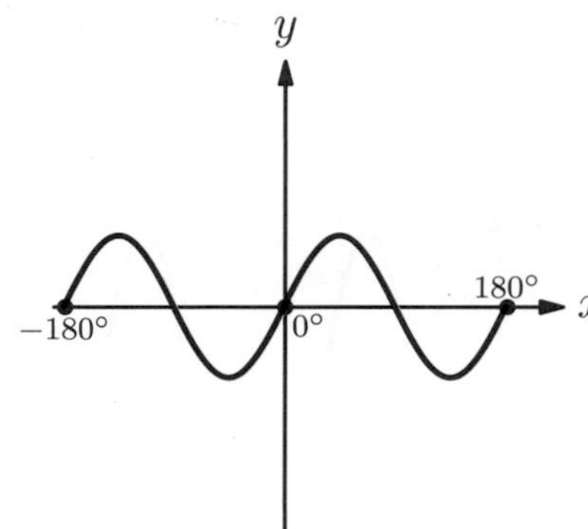

(ii)

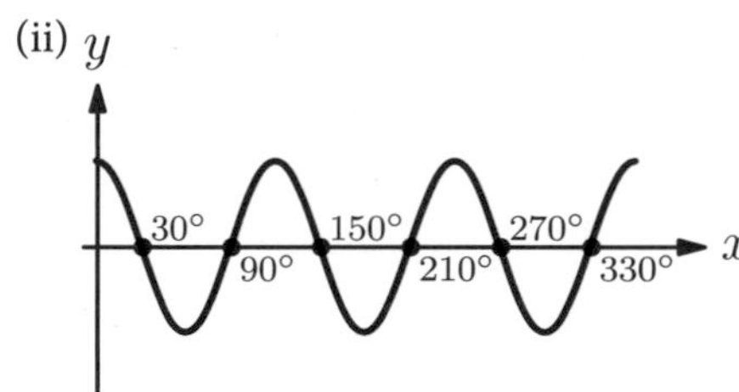

(b) (i)

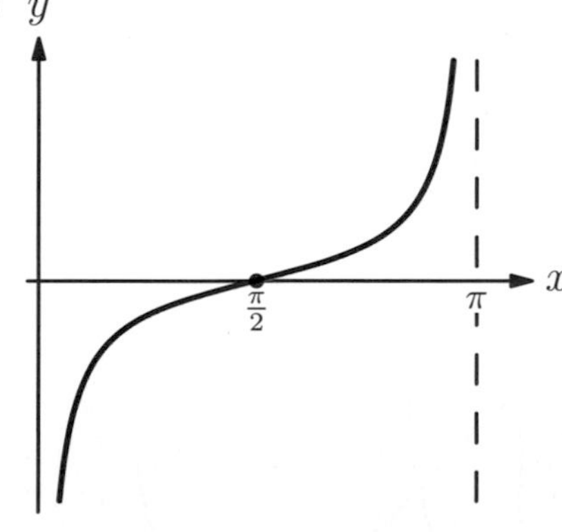

(ii)

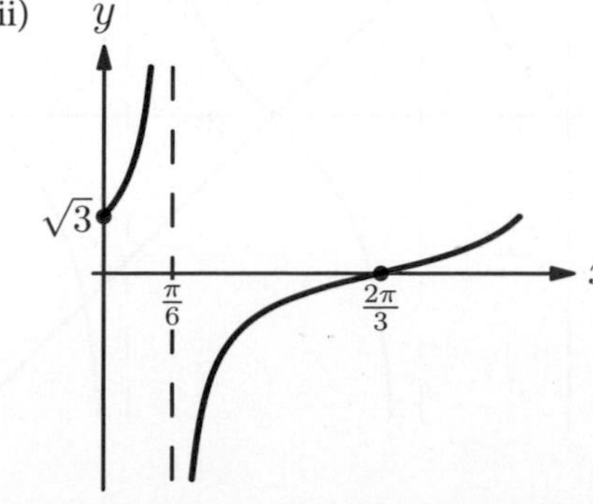

(c) (i)

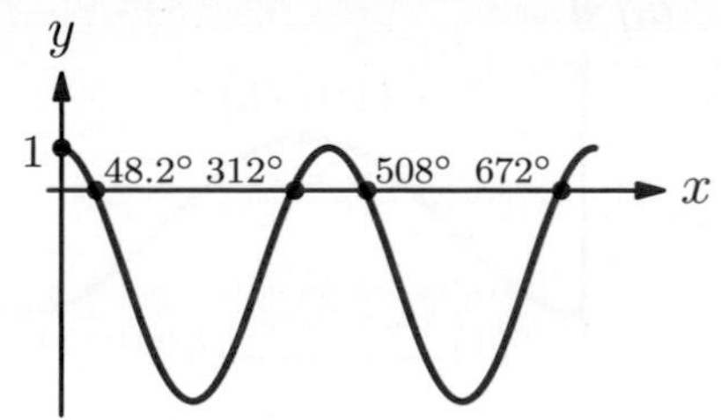

(ii)

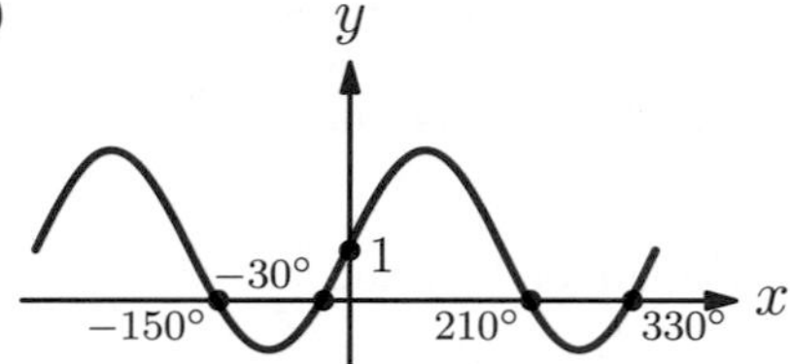

2. (a) (i)

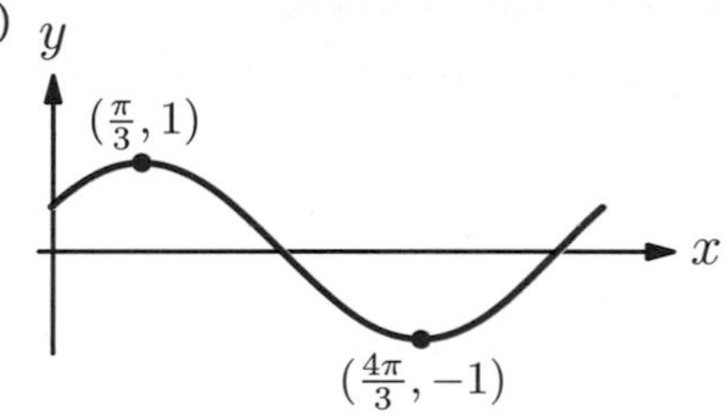

(ii)

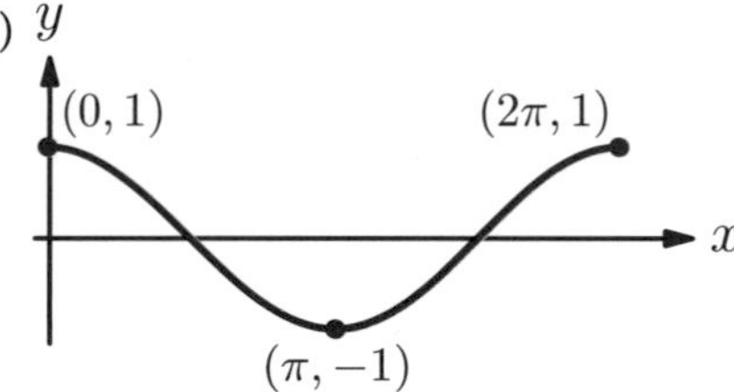

(b) (i)

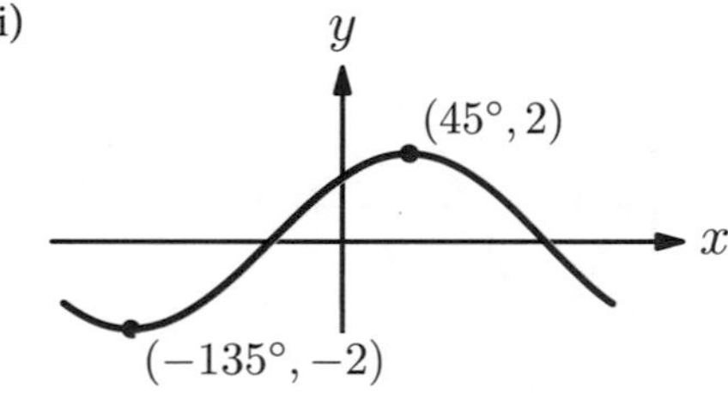

(ii)

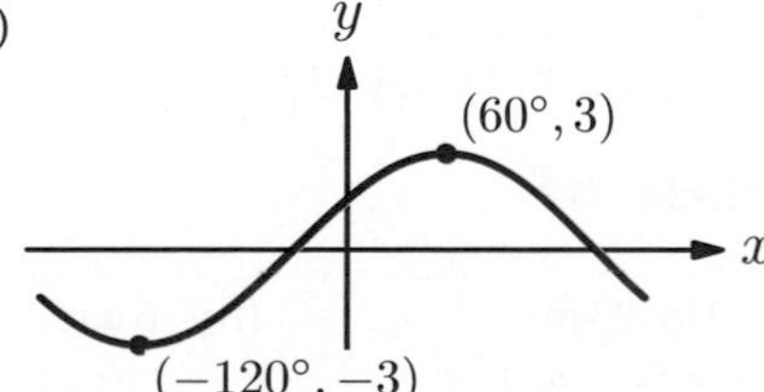

(c) (i)

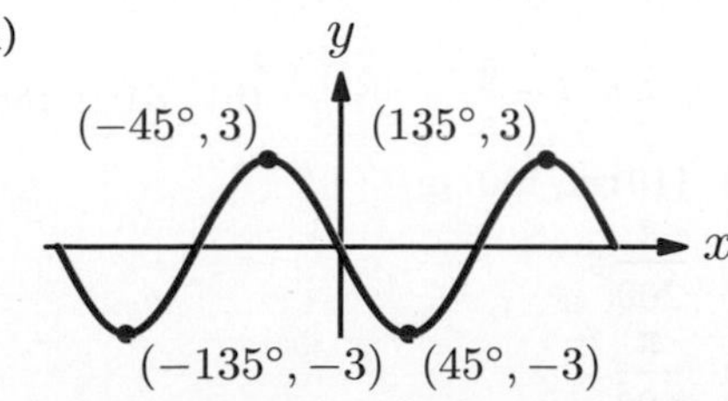

(ii)

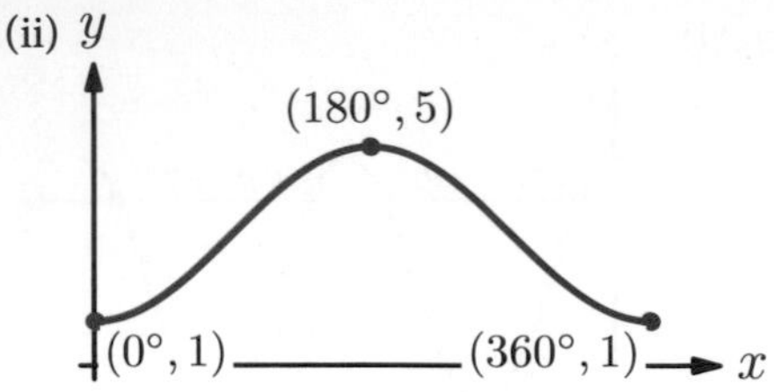

3. (a) Amplitude 3, period $\frac{\pi}{2}$

   (b) Amplitude ∞, period $\frac{\pi}{3}$

   (c) Amplitude 1, period $\frac{2\pi}{3}$

   (d) Amplitude 2, period 2

4. $p = 5, q = 2$

5. $a = 2, b = 20°$

6. (a)

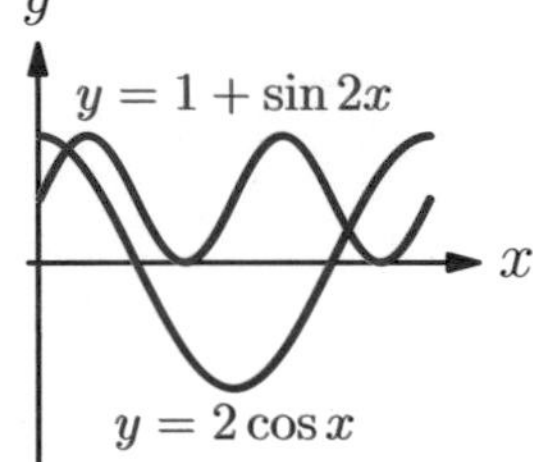

   (b) 2
   (c) 8

7. (a)

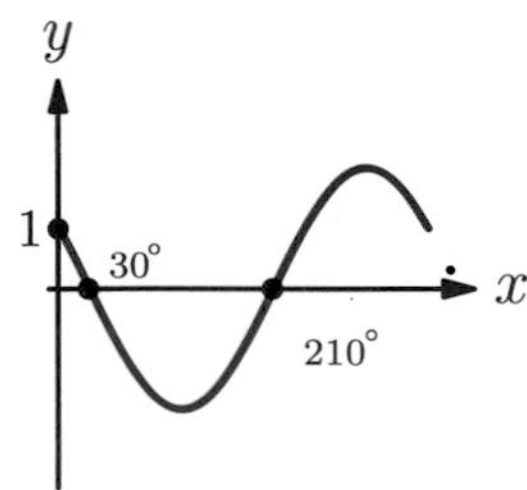

   (b) max (300°, 2); min (120°, −2)
   (c) max (300°, 1); min (120°, −3)

Exercise 8F

1. (a) 9 m, 23 m (b) 6 a.m.

2. $a = 1.5,\ b = \frac{\pi}{6},\ m = 4.5$

3. (a) $a = 5,\ k = \frac{\pi}{5}$ (b) 6.02 s and 8.98 s

4. (a) 110 cm, 130 cm
   (b) $\frac{\pi}{200}$ s
   (c) $\frac{\pi}{400}$ s

Mixed examination practice 8

Short questions

1. (a) 1.4 m (b) $\frac{2\pi}{3} = 2.09$ m

2. (a) 78.5 s
   (b) 377 m
   (c) 4.8 m/s

3. (a) π

   (b) $\left(\frac{\pi}{3}, 0\right), \left(\frac{5\pi}{6}, 0\right), \left(\frac{4\pi}{3}, 0\right), \left(\frac{11\pi}{6}, 0\right)$

   (c)

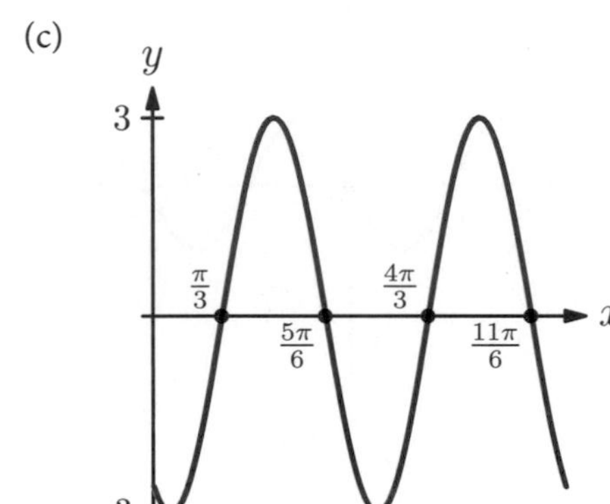

4. $a = 5,\ b = \frac{\pi}{4}$

Long questions

1. (a) (i) $\left(\frac{2\pi}{3}, \frac{3}{2}\right)$ (ii) $k = \frac{\pi}{6},\ c = \frac{1}{2}$

   (b) $-\frac{2\pi}{3},\ -2\pi,\ -\frac{8\pi}{3},\ -4\pi$

   (c) (i) 8 (ii) $\frac{10\pi}{3} - \alpha,\ 2\pi + \alpha$

2. (a)

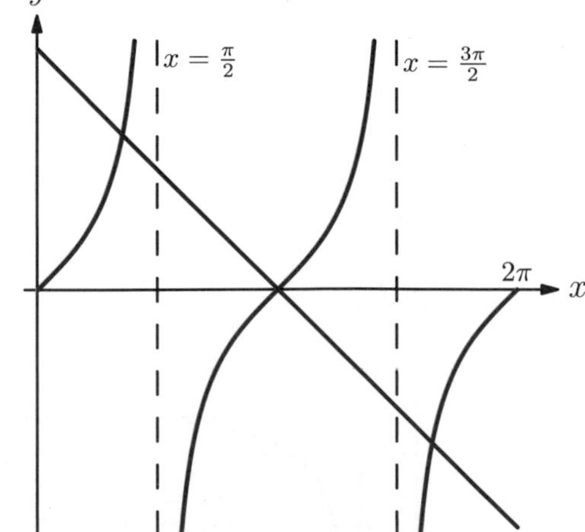

(b) (i) $\pi,\ 2\pi - x_0$ (ii) infinitely many

(c) (i) s, c (iii) $\sqrt{3},\ \frac{1}{\sqrt{3}}$ (iv) $\frac{\pi}{6},\ \frac{\pi}{3}$

3. (a) $-1;\ \pi$

(b) (i) translation $\begin{pmatrix} -\frac{\pi}{6} \\ 0 \end{pmatrix}$ and vertical stretch with scale factor 2.

(ii) $2;\ \frac{5\pi}{6}$

(c) (i) No; $\cos(A) \geq -1$ so $2\cos(A) + 3 \geq 1$, never 0.

(ii) $[1, 5]$

Chapter 9

Exercise 9A

1. (a) (i) 0.927 (ii) 0.201
(b) (i) −1.25 (ii) −0.927

2. (a) (i) $\frac{\pi}{6}$ (ii) $\frac{\pi}{6}$
(b) (i) $-\frac{\pi}{3}$ (ii) $\frac{3\pi}{4}$
(c) (i) $-\frac{\pi}{2}$ (ii) $\frac{\pi}{4}$

3. (a) (i) 44.4° (ii) 17.5°
(b) (i) 128.3° (ii) 138.6°
(c) (i) 81.1° (ii) −82.0°

4. (a) (i) 0.6 (ii) −0.3
(b) (i) −2 (ii) −1

5. (a) (i) 30°, 150° (ii) 45°, 135°
(b) (i) 60°, 300° (ii) 30°, 330°
(c) (i) 240°, 300° (ii) 210°, 330°
(d) (i) 45°, 225° (ii) 60°, 240°

6. (a) (i) $\frac{\pi}{6}, \frac{11\pi}{6}$ (ii) $\frac{\pi}{4}, \frac{7\pi}{4}$
(b) (i) $\frac{2\pi}{3}, \frac{4\pi}{3}$ (ii) $\frac{5\pi}{6}, \frac{7\pi}{6}$
(c) (i) $\frac{\pi}{4}, \frac{3\pi}{4}$ (ii) $\frac{\pi}{3}, \frac{2\pi}{3}$
(d) (i) $\frac{\pi}{6}, \frac{7\pi}{6}$ (ii) $\frac{3\pi}{4}, \frac{7\pi}{4}$

7. (a) (i) 26.7°, 153.3° (ii) 44.4°, 135.6°
(b) (i) ±138.6° (ii) ±101.5°
(c) (i) 18.4°, 198.4°, 378.4°, 558.4°
(ii) 53.1°, 233.1°, 413.1°, 593.1°
(d) (i) −138.2°, −41.8°, 221.8°, 318.2°
(ii) −165.5°, −14.5°, 194.5°, 345.5°

8. (a) (i) 0.644, 5.64, 6.93, 11.9
(ii) 0.841, 5.44, 7.12, 11.7
(b) (i) −2.21, −0.927, 4.07, 5.36
(ii) −2.78, −0.358, 3.50, 5.93
(c) (i) −0.588, 2.55 (ii) −1.25, 1.89
(d) (i) 0, 6.28, 12.6 (ii) 1.57, 4.71, 7.85, 11.0

9. (a) (i) 30°, 150°, −330°, −210°
(ii) 45°, 135°, −315°, −225°
(b) (i) ±180° (ii) −90°
(c) (i) −300°, −120° (ii) −315°, −135°
(d) (i) ±225°, ±135° (ii) ±210°, ±150°

10. (a) (i) $\pm\frac{5\pi}{3}, \pm\frac{\pi}{3}$ (ii) $\pm\frac{\pi}{6}, \pm\frac{11\pi}{6}$
(b) (i) $-\frac{2\pi}{3}, -\frac{\pi}{3}, \frac{4\pi}{3}, \frac{5\pi}{3}$
(ii) $-\frac{3\pi}{4}, -\frac{\pi}{4}, \frac{5\pi}{4}, \frac{7\pi}{4}$
(c) (i) $-\frac{\pi}{6}, \frac{5\pi}{6}$ (ii) $-\frac{\pi}{4}, \frac{3\pi}{4}$
(d) (i) $\frac{\pi}{2}, \frac{3\pi}{2}, \frac{5\pi}{2}$ (ii) $\pi, 2\pi$
(e) $-\frac{7\pi}{4}, -\frac{5\pi}{4}$

11. (a) (i) 5.74°, 174.3° (ii) −14.5°, 194.5°
(b) (i) 1.11, 5.17 (ii) 1.00, 5.28
(c) (i) 1.03, −2.11 (ii) 1.14, 4.29

12. $-\frac{\pi}{6}, -\frac{5\pi}{6}$

Exercise 9B

1. (a) (i) ±0.955, ±2.19
(ii) ±0.866, ±2.26
(b) (i) 48.2°, 132°, 228°, 312°
(ii) 52.2°, 128°, 232°, 308°

2. (a) (i) 0°, 180°, 360° (ii) 90°, 270°
(b) (i) $0, \pm\pi, 0.848, 2.29$ (ii) $\pm\frac{\pi}{2}, \pm 1.91$
(c) (i) 0.944, 1.30, 4.09, 4.44
(ii) $\frac{3\pi}{4}, \frac{7\pi}{4}$, 0.464, 3.61
(d) (i) $0, \pi, \frac{7\pi}{6}, \frac{11\pi}{6}, 2\pi$
(ii) $\frac{\pi}{2}, \frac{3\pi}{2}$, 0.983, 4.12
(e) (i) 60° (ii) No solutions

3. (a) (i) 35.3°, 145°, 215°, 325°
(ii) 22.1°, 97.9°, 142°, 218°, 262°, 338°
(b) (i) 0.266, 1.45, 2.36
(ii) 0.706, 3.01, 3.85, 6.15
(c) (i) −71.6°, 108° (ii) −132°, 48.4°

4. (a) (i) $\frac{\pi}{12}, \frac{5\pi}{12}, \frac{13\pi}{12}, \frac{17\pi}{12}$
(ii) $\frac{7\pi}{18}, \frac{11\pi}{18}, \frac{19\pi}{18}, \frac{23\pi}{18}, \frac{31\pi}{18}, \frac{35\pi}{18}$
(b) (i) 67.5°, 112.5°, 247.5°, 292.5°
(ii) ±20°, ±100°, ±140°
(c) (i) $\frac{\pi}{12}, \frac{\pi}{3}, \frac{7\pi}{12}, \frac{5\pi}{6}$ (ii) $\frac{\pi}{12}, \frac{7\pi}{12}$

5. (a) (i) 270°, 330° (ii) $0, \frac{2\pi}{3}$
(b) (i) $\frac{\pi}{6}, -\frac{\pi}{2}$ (ii) 75°, 345°
(c) (i) $\frac{3\pi}{4}, \frac{7\pi}{4}$ (ii) π

6. 1.01, 2.13

7. (a) $-\frac{1}{2}$ (b) 210°, 330°

8. $0, \pm\pi$

9. $\pm\sqrt{\frac{\pi}{6}}, \pm\sqrt{\frac{5\pi}{6}}, \pm\sqrt{\frac{13\pi}{6}}, \pm\sqrt{\frac{17\pi}{6}}$

Exercise 9C

1. (i) $\cos x = \frac{2\sqrt{2}}{3}, \tan x = \frac{\sqrt{2}}{4}$
(ii) $\cos x = \frac{3}{5}, \tan x = \frac{4}{3}$

2. (i) $\sin\theta = -\frac{2\sqrt{2}}{3}, \tan\theta = \sqrt{8}$
(ii) $\sin\theta = -\frac{\sqrt{7}}{4}, \tan\theta = \frac{\sqrt{7}}{3}$

3. (a) (i) $-\frac{2\sqrt{6}}{5}$ (ii) $\frac{\sqrt{3}}{2}$
(b) (i) $-\frac{4}{3}$ (ii) 0

4. (i) $\pm\frac{3}{\sqrt{13}}$ (ii) $\pm\frac{1}{\sqrt{5}}$

5. (a) 3 (b) 1
(c) −2 (d) −2
(e) 1 (f) $\frac{3}{2}$

6. (i) $4-\sin^2 x$ (ii) $2\cos^2 x - 1$

7. (a) $5-\frac{2}{\cos^2 x}$ (b) $\frac{1}{1-2\sin^2 x+\sin^4 x}$

8. (a) $\frac{1}{1+t^2}$ (b) $\frac{t^2}{1+t^2}$
(c) $\frac{1-t^2}{1+t^2}$ (d) $\frac{2+3t^2}{t^2}$

Exercise 9D

1. (a) (i) 33.7° (ii) 59.0°
(b) (i) 0.322 (ii) 1.89
(c) (i) 2.11, 5.25 (ii) 2.21, 5.36
(d) (i) −113°, 66.8° (ii) −101°, 78.7°

2. (a) (i) $\frac{\pi}{12}, \frac{5\pi}{12}$ (ii) $\frac{\pi}{6}, \frac{2\pi}{3}$
(b) (i) $\frac{\pi}{3}, \frac{5\pi}{6}, \frac{4\pi}{3}, \frac{11\pi}{6}$ (ii) $\frac{\pi}{4}$

3. (a) 0°, 135°, 180°, 315°, 360°
(b) $-\pi$, −2.55, 0, 0.588, π
(c) 26.6°
(d) $\frac{\pi}{2}, \frac{3\pi}{2}$, 2.50, 5.64

4. (a) (i) 45°, 135°, 225°, 315°
(ii) 54.7°, 125.3°, 234.7°, 305.3°
(b) (i) 45°, 135°, 225°, 315°
(ii) 0°, 180°, 360°

5. ±41.8°, ±138.2°

6. $\frac{\pi}{6}, \frac{5\pi}{6}, \frac{3\pi}{2}$

7. −0.253, −2.89, $-\frac{\pi}{2}$

8. $\frac{1}{3}$

9. (a) $-\frac{1}{2}, \frac{2}{3}$
(b) 48.2°, 120°, 240°, 311.8°

10. (b) $\frac{\pi}{4}, -\frac{3\pi}{4}$, 0.464, −2.68

Exercise 9E

1. (a) (i) $-\frac{7}{8}$ (ii) $\frac{1}{9}$
(b) (i) $\frac{2\sqrt{2}}{3}$ (ii) $\frac{4}{5}$
(c) (i) $\frac{4\sqrt{2}}{9}$ (ii) $\frac{24}{25}$

2. (a) $\frac{2-\sqrt{2}}{4}$

(b) $\dfrac{2-\sqrt{3}}{4}$

(c) $\dfrac{2+\sqrt{3}}{4}$

3. $\sqrt{2}-1$

4. (a) $\cos(6A)$ (b) $2\sin 10x$

(c) $3\cos b$ (d) $\dfrac{5}{2}\sin\left(\dfrac{2x}{3}\right)$

5. (a) $0, \pi, 2\pi$ (b) $90°$

(c) $\pm\dfrac{\pi}{2}$, 0.305, 2.84 (d) $0°, 180°, 360°$

6. $\pm0.955, \pm2.19$

> **ANSWER HINT**
> Did you use your GDC to solve this?

8. (a) $8\cos^4\theta - 8\cos^2\theta + 1$
(b) $8\sin^4\theta - 8\sin^2\theta + 1$

9. (b) $\dfrac{1-\cos x}{1+\cos x}$

10. $\dfrac{2a-b}{4a}$

Mixed examination practice 9

Short questions

1. −31.8, 148.2

2. (a) $\dfrac{\sqrt{5}}{3}$ (b) $\dfrac{1}{9}$

3. $\pm0.730, \pm2.41$

4.

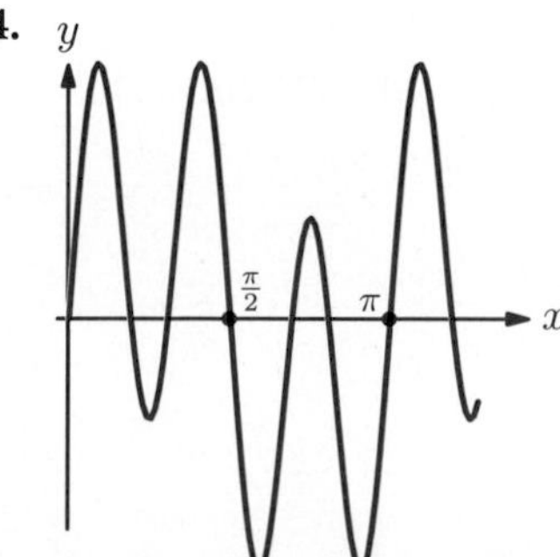

Period π

6. $\dfrac{\pi}{2}, \dfrac{3\pi}{2}, \dfrac{2\pi}{3}, \dfrac{4\pi}{3}$

7. 48.2°, 311.8°, 120°, 240°

8. $\dfrac{\pi}{6}, \dfrac{\pi}{2}, \dfrac{5\pi}{6}, \dfrac{3\pi}{2}$

Long questions

1. (a) 3π metres
(b) 5.05 m
(c) 1.50 m

2. (a)

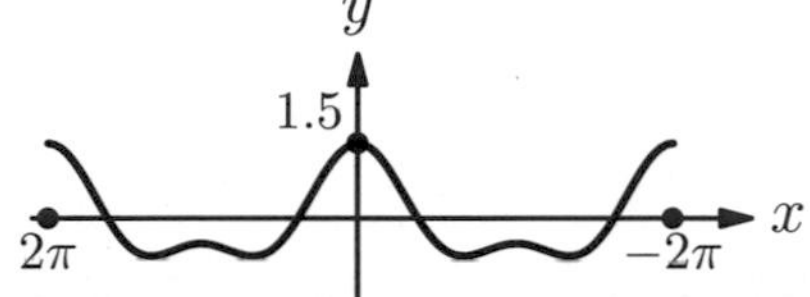

(b) 2π (c) $0, \pm\pi, \pm2\pi$
(d) 1.2 (e) (ii) $2\pi - x_0$

3. (a) ±4

(c) (i) 1 (ii) $\pm\dfrac{\pi}{3}, \pm\dfrac{5\pi}{3}$

(iii) 5 (iv) 7

Chapter 10

Exercise 10B

1. (a) (i) 6.04 (ii) 14.4
(b) (i) 10.6 cm (ii) 23.3 cm

2. (a) (i) 49.7 (ii) 59.2
(b) (i) 74.6 or 105 (ii) 62.0 or 118
(c) (i) 50.9 (ii) 54.4

3. 21.0°, 29.0°, 8.09 cm

4. $A = 49.9°$, $B = 95.1°$ and AC = 10.4 cm or
$A = 130.1°$, $B = 14.9°$ and AC = 2.69 cm

5. 9.94 cm

6. 23.3 m

Exercise 10C

1. (a) (i) 5.37 (ii) 3.44
(b) (i) 8.00 (ii) 20.5

2. (a) (i) 60.6° (ii) 120°
(b) (i) 81.5° (ii) 99.9°

3. (i) 106° (ii) 36.3°

4. 6.12 km

5. 7.95

6. 4.4

7. $2\sqrt{2}+\sqrt{41}$

Exercise 10D

1. (a) (i) 10.7 cm^2 (ii) 24.3 cm^2
   (b) (i) 27.6 cm^2 (ii) 26.2 cm^2

2. (i) 81.7°, 98.3° (ii) 60.9°, 119°

3. $LN = 17.7$ cm, area $= 29.7\text{ cm}^2$

4. $4\sqrt{3}$

Exercise 10E

1. (i) $\sqrt{134} = 11.6$ cm (ii) $\sqrt{96} = 9.80$ cm

2. Angles 47.6°, 59.7°, 72,7°; area 85.6 cm^2

3. 62.5°

4. $\sqrt{176} = 13.3$ cm

5. (a) $\sqrt{145} = 12.0$ cm (b) $\sqrt{290} = 17.0$ cm

6. (a) 18.8 m (b) 28.1 m

7. (a) $RA = \dfrac{h}{\tan\alpha}$ $RB = \dfrac{h}{\tan\beta}$
   (b) 13 m

Exercise 10F

1. (i) 7.8 cm (ii) 1.8 cm

2. (i) 82.2 cm (ii) 6.84 cm

3. 25 cm

4. (a) 0.938 (b) 53.7°

5. 2.53

6. 7.5 cm

7. 6.69 cm

8. 15.7 cm

9. 31.6 cm

10. $\left(\dfrac{25\pi}{6}+10\right)$ cm

11. 5 cm

12. $\dfrac{6\pi}{5}$

Exercise 10G

1. (i) 16.25 cm^2 (ii) 0.072 cm^2

2. (i) 463 cm^2 (ii) 4.79 cm^2

3. 0.8

4. 167°

5. $\sqrt{90} = 9.49$ cm

6. 11.3 cm

7. 5.14 cm^2

8. 48.4 cm^2

9. 2 cm or 1.5 cm

10. $\pi - 0.6 = 2.54$

Exercise 10H

1. (a) (i) 0.935 cm (ii) 3.39 cm
   (b) (i) 21.7 cm (ii) 15.8 cm

2. (a) (i) 1.89 cm (ii) 6.99 cm
   (b) (i) 52.5 cm (ii) 37.1 cm

3. (a) (i) 0.0595 cm^2 (ii) 1.21 cm^2
   (b) (i) 149 cm^2 (ii) 70.1 cm^2

4. (a) $\dfrac{25}{2}(\theta - \sin\theta)\text{ cm}^2$ (b) 2.08

5. (b) 70.1° (c) 3.67 cm^2

Mixed examination practice 10

Short questions

1. (a) $\dfrac{\pi}{3}$
   (b) 28.9 cm^2
   (c) 23.8 cm

2. 80 cm^2

3. 58.7°, 121.3°

4. (a) 8.09 m (b) 6.58 m

5. (a) 10.2 cm^2 (b) 18.8 cm

6. (b) 7

7. 12.3 cm^2

8. (a) 1.14 cm^2 (b) 2 cm^2

9. (a) $\dfrac{\pi}{2}-\theta$ (b) 47.7 cm^2

10. 4 cm or 13 cm

11. $2\sqrt{43}$

12. 7.23 cm^2

13. (a) $\dfrac{23}{32}$
    (b) $\dfrac{3\sqrt{55}}{32}$
    (c) $\dfrac{15\sqrt{55}}{4}\text{ cm}^2$

Long questions

1. (a) $25+\frac{x^2}{4}-5x\cos\theta$
   (c) 41.4°
2. (b) $r\sqrt{2}$
   (c) $\frac{\pi r^2}{4}$
   (d) $r^2\left(\frac{\pi}{2}-1\right)$
3. (b) $\pi r^2-\frac{1}{2}r^2\theta$
   (d) 2.50
4. (a) $\frac{4.42}{3x^2}$
   (b) $\frac{3x^2-2x-3}{2x^2}=\frac{3}{2}-\frac{1}{x}-\frac{3}{2x^2}$
   (d) (i) 1.24, 2.94 (ii) 1.86, 0.172
5. (b) $\frac{\sqrt{3}}{2}\le\cos\theta<1$ or $-1<\cos\theta\le-\frac{\sqrt{3}}{2}$
   (c) $0°<\theta\le 30°$ or $150°\le\theta<180°$
6. (a) (ii) $\sqrt{x^2+100}$
   (c) 38.7°
   (d) 5.63
   (e) (ii) $\frac{40}{3}$
7. (a) (i) 5 (ii) 144
   (b) (i) $z=10-x$
   (ii) $z^2=36+x^2-12x\cos Z$
   (e) (i) 12 (ii) isosceles
8. (a) $\frac{\pi}{2}$; a tangent to a circle makes a right angle with the radius
   (b) ABO_2P is a rectangle, because there are right angles at A and B, and AB is parallel to PO_2.
   (c) $\sqrt{600}=24.5$ cm
   (d) 1.369
   (e) 85.6 cm

Chapter 11

Exercise 11A

1. (a) (i) $\boldsymbol{b}$ (ii) $\boldsymbol{a}+\boldsymbol{b}$
   (b) (i) $-\boldsymbol{a}$ (ii) $-\frac{1}{2}\boldsymbol{a}$
   (c) (i) $\boldsymbol{a}+\frac{1}{2}\boldsymbol{b}$ (ii) $\frac{1}{2}\boldsymbol{b}-\frac{1}{2}\boldsymbol{a}$
2. (a) (i) $\boldsymbol{a}+\frac{4}{3}\boldsymbol{b}$ (ii) $\boldsymbol{a}+\frac{1}{2}\boldsymbol{b}$
   (b) (i) $-\frac{3}{2}\boldsymbol{a}+\boldsymbol{b}$ (ii) $-\frac{1}{2}\boldsymbol{b}+\frac{1}{2}\boldsymbol{a}$
   (c) (i) $\frac{3}{2}\boldsymbol{a}-\boldsymbol{b}$ (ii) $-\frac{4}{3}\boldsymbol{b}+\frac{1}{2}\boldsymbol{a}$
3. (a) (i) $\begin{pmatrix}4\\0\\0\end{pmatrix}$ (ii) $\begin{pmatrix}0\\-5\\0\end{pmatrix}$
   (b) (i) $\begin{pmatrix}3\\0\\1\end{pmatrix}$ (ii) $\begin{pmatrix}0\\2\\-1\end{pmatrix}$
4. (a) $\boldsymbol{b}-\boldsymbol{a}$
   (b) $\frac{1}{2}\boldsymbol{a}+\frac{1}{2}\boldsymbol{b}$
   (c) $4\boldsymbol{a}-3\boldsymbol{b}$
5. (a) $\overrightarrow{AB}=\begin{pmatrix}1\\2\end{pmatrix}$, $\overrightarrow{AC}=\begin{pmatrix}0.5\\1\end{pmatrix}$
   (b) (10, −2)
6. (a) $\begin{pmatrix}1\\-3\\7\end{pmatrix}$ (b) $\begin{pmatrix}3.5\\-0.5\\1.5\end{pmatrix}$
7. $\begin{pmatrix}3\\-4\end{pmatrix}$
8. $\begin{pmatrix}1.6\\0.8\\1.8\end{pmatrix}$
9. (a) $\frac{3}{2}\boldsymbol{i}+\frac{3}{2}\boldsymbol{j}-2\boldsymbol{k}$ (b) $\left(\frac{1}{2},\frac{13}{2},0\right)$
10. $\begin{pmatrix}0\\-1\\6\end{pmatrix}$

Exercise 11B

1. (a) (i) $\begin{pmatrix}21\\3\\36\end{pmatrix}$ (ii) $\begin{pmatrix}20\\-8\\12\end{pmatrix}$
   (b) (i) $\begin{pmatrix}2\\3\\9\end{pmatrix}$ (ii) $\begin{pmatrix}6\\-1\\5\end{pmatrix}$

(c) (i) $\begin{pmatrix} 11 \\ -3 \\ 8 \end{pmatrix}$ (ii) $\begin{pmatrix} -3 \\ 5 \\ 6 \end{pmatrix}$

(d) (i) $\begin{pmatrix} 10 \\ -3 \\ 11 \end{pmatrix}$ (ii) $\begin{pmatrix} 17 \\ 6 \\ 35 \end{pmatrix}$

2. (a) (i) $-5\boldsymbol{i} + 5\boldsymbol{k}$ (ii) $4\boldsymbol{i} + 8\boldsymbol{j}$
(b) (i) $\boldsymbol{i} - 3\boldsymbol{j} + 3\boldsymbol{k}$ (ii) $2\boldsymbol{j} + \boldsymbol{k}$
(c) (i) $4\boldsymbol{i} + 7\boldsymbol{k}$ (ii) $5\boldsymbol{i} - 4\boldsymbol{j} + 15\boldsymbol{k}$

3. (a) $-4\boldsymbol{i} + 2\boldsymbol{j} - \boldsymbol{k}$
(b) $-\frac{8}{3}\boldsymbol{i} + \frac{4}{3}\boldsymbol{j} - \frac{2}{3}\boldsymbol{k}$
(c) $4\boldsymbol{i} - 3\boldsymbol{j} + \boldsymbol{k}$
(d) $-\frac{1}{2}\boldsymbol{i} + \boldsymbol{j} - \frac{1}{2}\boldsymbol{k}$

4. $\begin{pmatrix} 2 \\ 0 \\ -3/4 \end{pmatrix}$

5. -2

6. $-\frac{4}{3}$

7. -2

8. $p = \frac{3}{8}, q = \frac{1}{8}$

Exercise 11C

1. $|\boldsymbol{a}| = 2\sqrt{5}, |\boldsymbol{b}| = \sqrt{26}, |\boldsymbol{c}| = 2\sqrt{5}, |\boldsymbol{d}| = \sqrt{2}$

2. $|\boldsymbol{a}| = \sqrt{21}, |\boldsymbol{b}| = \sqrt{2}, |\boldsymbol{c}| = \sqrt{21}, |\boldsymbol{d}| = \sqrt{2}$

3. (a) (i) $\sqrt{29}$ (ii) $\sqrt{2}$
(b) (i) $\sqrt{58}$ (ii) $\sqrt{5}$

4. (a) (i) $\sqrt{19}$ (ii) $\sqrt{38}$
(b) (i) $\sqrt{74}$ (ii) $\sqrt{13}$

5. (a) $\sqrt{53}$ (b) $\sqrt{94}$
(c) $\sqrt{53}$ (d) $\sqrt{2}$

6. (a) (i) $\frac{1}{3}\begin{pmatrix} 2 \\ 2 \\ 1 \end{pmatrix}$ (ii) $\frac{1}{3}\begin{pmatrix} 2 \\ 2 \\ -1 \end{pmatrix}$

(b) (i) $\frac{1}{\sqrt{3}}\begin{pmatrix} 1 \\ 1 \\ 1 \end{pmatrix}$ (ii) $\frac{1}{5}\begin{pmatrix} 4 \\ -1 \\ 2\sqrt{2} \end{pmatrix}$

7. $\pm 2\sqrt{6}$

8. $\frac{3}{2}$

9. $3, -\frac{5}{3}$

10. (a) $\begin{pmatrix} 4\sqrt{2} \\ -\sqrt{2} \\ \sqrt{2} \end{pmatrix}$ (b) $\begin{pmatrix} \sqrt{6} \\ -\sqrt{6}/2 \\ \sqrt{6}/2 \end{pmatrix}$

11. $-2, -\frac{23}{15}$

12. $t = \frac{1}{3}, d = \sqrt{\frac{14}{3}}$

Exercise 11D

1. (a) (i) 1.12 (ii) 1.17
(b) (i) 1.88 (ii) 1.13
(c) (i) 1.23 (ii) 1.77

2. (a) (i) $-\frac{5}{2\sqrt{21}}$ (ii) $-\frac{20}{\sqrt{570}}$

(b) (i) $-\frac{2}{\sqrt{102}}$ (ii) $\frac{1}{\sqrt{35}}$

(c) (i) 0 (ii) 0

3. (i) 61.0°, 74.5°, 44.5° (ii) 94.3°, 54.2°, 31.5°

4. (a) (i) No (ii) Yes
(b) (i) Yes (ii) No

5. 87.7°

6. 40.0°

7. (b) 73.2°, 106.8° (c) $\frac{5}{4}$

8. (b) 41.8°, 48.2° (c) $6\sqrt{5}$

Exercise 11E

1. (a) (i) 16 (ii) -56
(b) (i) 16 (ii) -16
(c) (i) 9 (ii) 9
(d) (i) -4 (ii) 0

2. (a) (i) $\frac{7}{3\sqrt{6}}$ (ii) $\frac{5}{\sqrt{39}}$

(b) (i) $\frac{2}{3}$ (ii) $\frac{1}{\sqrt{10}}$

3. (i) 48.2° (ii) 98.0°

4. (a) 19.2
(b) 3

6. (a) (i) $-\frac{1}{2}$ (ii) $\frac{2}{7}$

(b) (i) $\frac{4}{5}$ (ii) $0, \frac{3}{2}$

7. (a) 19
(b) 7
(c) 32

8. (a) 2
(b) 6

9. (a) $\frac{52}{9}$

10. (a) 1.6
(b) 21.3°, 68.7°, 90°
(c) 88.7

11. (a) $\overrightarrow{AC} = \boldsymbol{a}+\boldsymbol{b}$, $\overrightarrow{BD} = \boldsymbol{b}-\boldsymbol{a}$
(b) $|\boldsymbol{b}|^2 - |\boldsymbol{a}|^2$

12. (b) 2
(c) $4\sqrt{5}$

Exercise 11F

1. (a) (i) $r = \begin{pmatrix} 4 \\ -1 \end{pmatrix} + \lambda \begin{pmatrix} 1 \\ 4 \end{pmatrix}$ (ii) $r = \begin{pmatrix} 4 \\ 1 \end{pmatrix} + \lambda \begin{pmatrix} 2 \\ -3 \end{pmatrix}$

(b) (i) $r = \begin{pmatrix} 1 \\ 0 \\ 5 \end{pmatrix} + \lambda \begin{pmatrix} 1 \\ 3 \\ -3 \end{pmatrix}$ (ii) $\boldsymbol{r} = \begin{pmatrix} -1 \\ 1 \\ 5 \end{pmatrix} + \lambda \begin{pmatrix} 3 \\ -2 \\ 2 \end{pmatrix}$

(c) (i) $\boldsymbol{r} = \begin{pmatrix} 4 \\ 0 \end{pmatrix} + \lambda \begin{pmatrix} 2 \\ 3 \end{pmatrix}$ (ii) $\boldsymbol{r} = \begin{pmatrix} 0 \\ 2 \end{pmatrix} + \lambda \begin{pmatrix} 1 \\ -3 \end{pmatrix}$

(d) (i) $\boldsymbol{r} = \begin{pmatrix} 0 \\ 2 \\ 3 \end{pmatrix} + \lambda \begin{pmatrix} 1 \\ 0 \\ -3 \end{pmatrix}$ (ii) $r = \begin{pmatrix} 4 \\ -3 \\ 0 \end{pmatrix} + \lambda \begin{pmatrix} 2 \\ 3 \\ -1 \end{pmatrix}$

2. (a) (i) $r = \begin{pmatrix} 4 \\ 1 \end{pmatrix} + \lambda \begin{pmatrix} -3 \\ 1 \end{pmatrix}$ (ii) $r = \begin{pmatrix} 2 \\ 7 \end{pmatrix} + \lambda \begin{pmatrix} 2 \\ -9 \end{pmatrix}$

(b) (i) $r = \begin{pmatrix} -5 \\ -2 \\ 3 \end{pmatrix} + \lambda \begin{pmatrix} 9 \\ 0 \\ 0 \end{pmatrix}$ (ii) $r = \begin{pmatrix} 1 \\ 1 \\ 3 \end{pmatrix} + \lambda \begin{pmatrix} 9 \\ -6 \\ 3 \end{pmatrix}$

3. (a) (i) Yes (ii) Yes
(b) (i) No (ii) Yes

4. (b) (0, 3, 0)

5. (a) $\boldsymbol{r} = \begin{pmatrix} 7 \\ 1 \\ 2 \end{pmatrix} + \lambda \begin{pmatrix} -4 \\ -2 \\ 3 \end{pmatrix}$
(b) (−5, −5, 11) or (19, 7, −7)

6. (a) $\boldsymbol{r} = \begin{pmatrix} 2 \\ 1 \\ 4 \end{pmatrix} + \lambda \begin{pmatrix} 2 \\ -3 \\ 6 \end{pmatrix}$
(b) 7
(c) (−8, 16, −26) and (12, −14, 34)

Exercise 11G

1. (a) (i) 44.5° (ii) 56.5°
(b) (i) 26.6° (ii) 82.1°

2. (a) Perpendicular
(b) None (skew)
(c) Parallel
(d) Same line

3. (a) (i) (10, −7, −2) (ii) (4.5, 0, 0)
(b) (i) No intersection (ii) No intersection

4. $\left(\frac{64}{9}, \frac{4}{9}, \frac{19}{9}\right)$

5. $\frac{\sqrt{66}}{11}$

6. (a) (4, 1, −2)
(c) (1, 1, 2)
(d) $\frac{5\sqrt{26}}{2}$

7. 3

8. (a) $\left(\frac{5}{6}, \frac{19}{6}, \frac{9}{2}\right)$
(b) 48.5°
(d) $\frac{11\sqrt{11}}{6}(=6.08)$
(e) 4.55

9. (a) (9, −5, 8)
(c) (3, 4, −1)

10. (b) $\left(2+\sqrt{6}, -1-2\sqrt{6}, 2\sqrt{6}\right)$ or $\left(2-\sqrt{6}, 2\sqrt{6}-1, -2\sqrt{6}\right)$

Mixed examination practice 11

Short questions

1. $\boldsymbol{r} = \begin{pmatrix} 3 \\ -1 \\ 1 \end{pmatrix} + \lambda \begin{pmatrix} 3 \\ 1 \\ 0 \end{pmatrix}$

2. (a) $\frac{1}{2}\overrightarrow{AD} - \overrightarrow{AB}$

3. (11, 13, 8)

4. $\left(\frac{11}{3}, \frac{20}{3}, \frac{2}{3}\right)$ or $\left(-\frac{29}{3}, -\frac{20}{3}, \frac{22}{3}\right)$

5. (a) $r = \begin{pmatrix} 4 \\ 1 \\ 12 \end{pmatrix} + \lambda \begin{pmatrix} 1 \\ -3 \\ 2 \end{pmatrix}$

(b) $\left(\frac{31}{14}, \frac{89}{14}, \frac{59}{7}\right)$

6. 74.4°

7. $\frac{\pi}{2} - 2\theta$

8. 0

Long questions

1. (a) $\begin{pmatrix} 2 \\ 0 \\ k-7 \end{pmatrix}$

(c) (3, 6, 1)

(d) $-\frac{1}{\sqrt{10}}$

2. (b) $\sqrt{33}$

(c) 45.7°

(d) 4.11

3. (a) $\begin{pmatrix} -1+\frac{3}{k+1} \\ \frac{3}{k+1} \\ -4 \end{pmatrix}$

(b) 5

(c) $\left(\frac{3}{2}, \frac{3}{2}, 2\right)$

(d) $\sqrt{\frac{33}{2}}$

4. (a) (a, a^2)

(b) $\overrightarrow{PO} = \begin{pmatrix} -a \\ -a^2 \end{pmatrix}, \overrightarrow{PS} = \begin{pmatrix} -a \\ 4-a^2 \end{pmatrix}$

(c) $\sqrt{3}$

(d) $2\sqrt{3}$

5. (a) $\begin{pmatrix} 3t \\ 4t \end{pmatrix}$

(b) $\begin{pmatrix} 3t \\ 18-5t \end{pmatrix}$

(d) $t = 2$

(e) 2 hours

6. (a) $\begin{pmatrix} 3t \\ 5-4t \\ t \end{pmatrix}$

(d) 30 km

7. (b) (i) $\begin{pmatrix} \mu - 2\lambda + 8 \\ \mu + \lambda - 3 \\ -\mu + 8\lambda - 16 \end{pmatrix}$

(iii) $3\mu - 9\lambda + 21 = 0$

(iv) $P(1, 1, 2)$, $Q(4, -1, 3)$

(v) $\sqrt{14}$

8. (a) $r = \begin{pmatrix} -2 \\ 4 \\ 2 \end{pmatrix} + \lambda \begin{pmatrix} 1 \\ 1 \\ 0 \end{pmatrix}$

(b) $\frac{1}{2}$

(c) $3\sqrt{2}$

(d) $\frac{3\sqrt{2}}{2}$

Chapter 12

Exercise 12A

1. (a) (i)

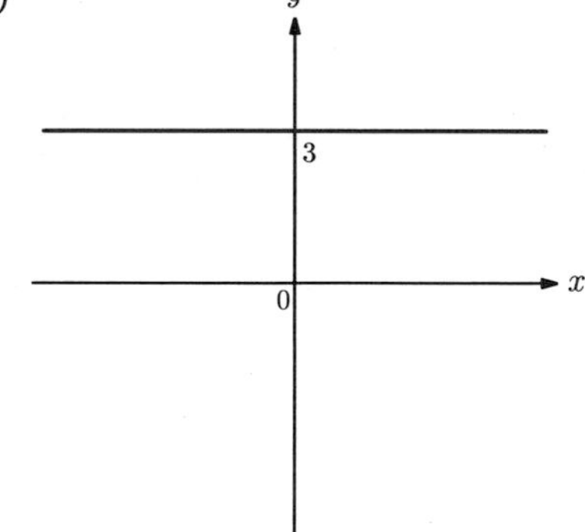

(ii)

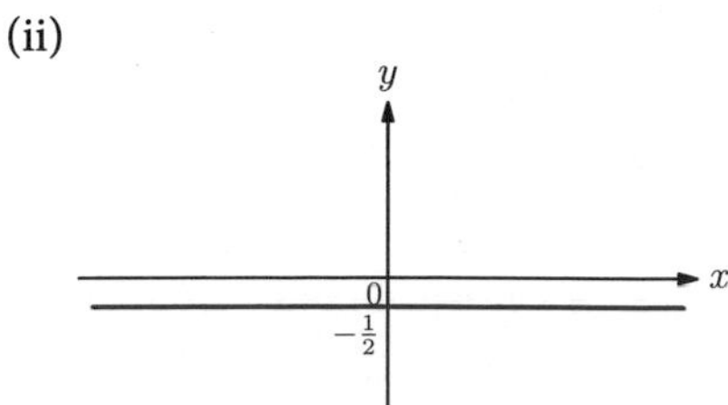

(b) (i)

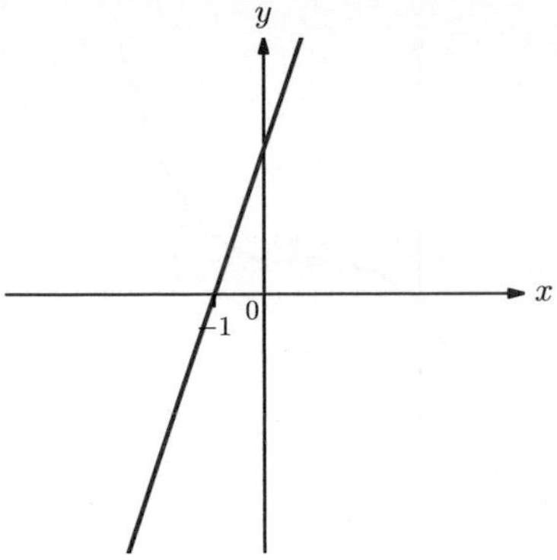

y, x, -1, 0

(ii)

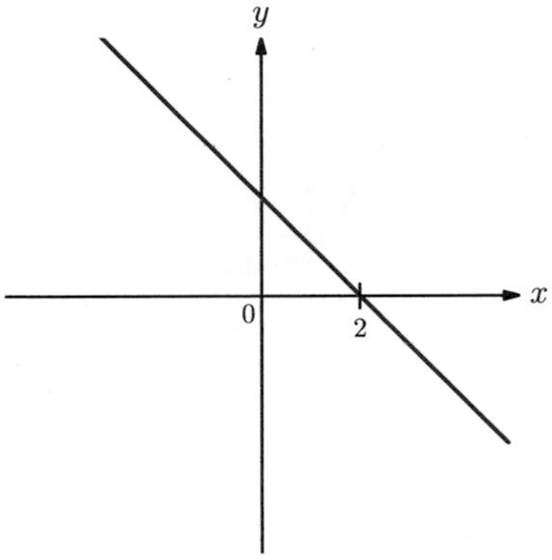

y, x, 0, 2

(c) (i)

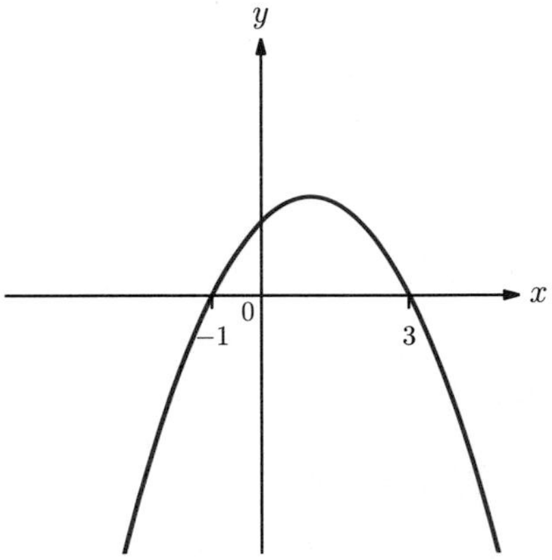

y, x, -1, 0, 3

(ii)

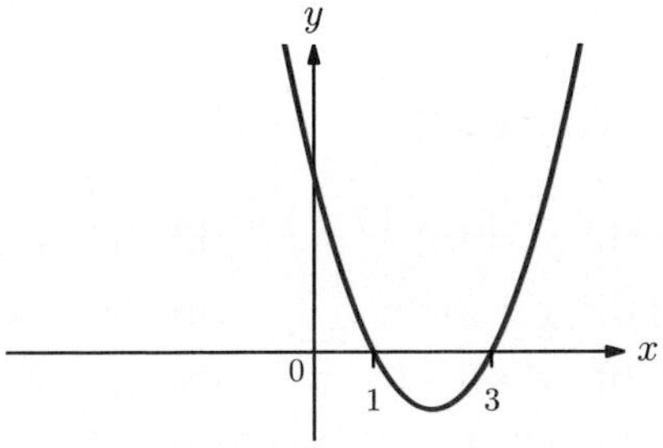

y, x, 0, 1, 3

(d) (i)

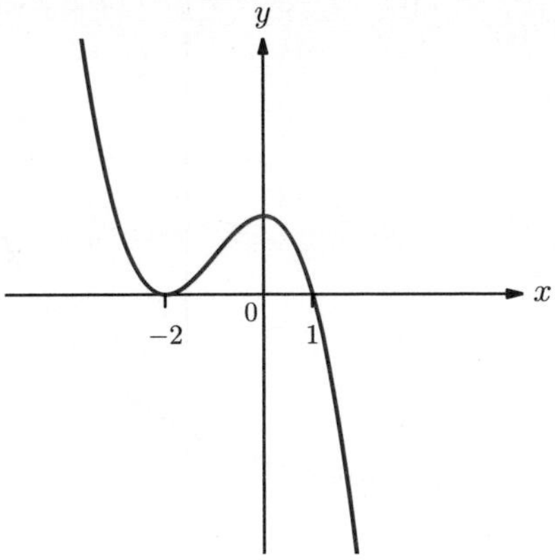

y, x, -2, 0, 1

(ii)

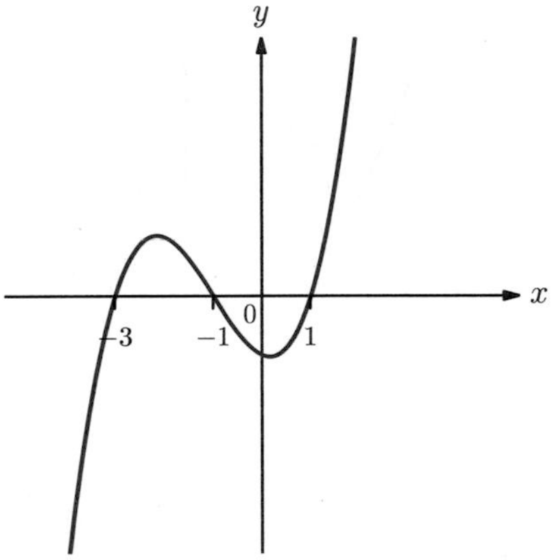

y, x, -3, -1, 0, 1

(e) (i)

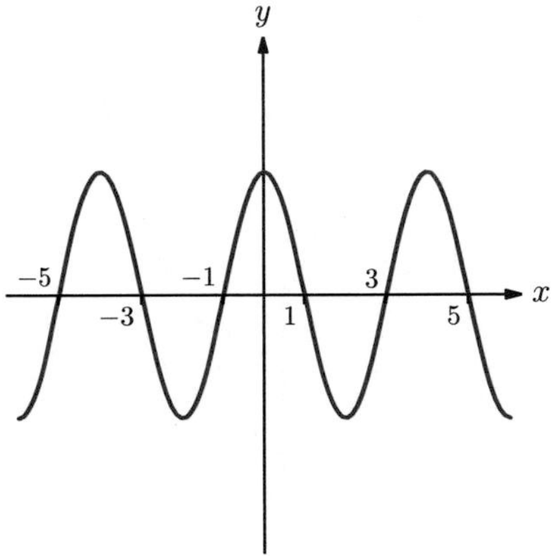

y, x, -5, -3, -1, 1, 3, 5

(ii)

y, x, -2, -1, 0, 1, 2

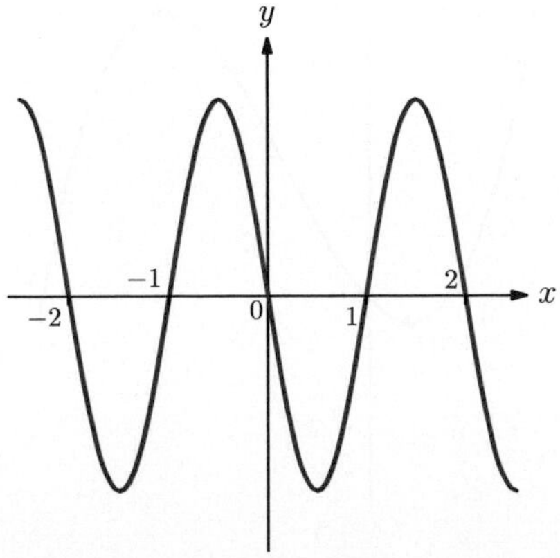

(f) (i)

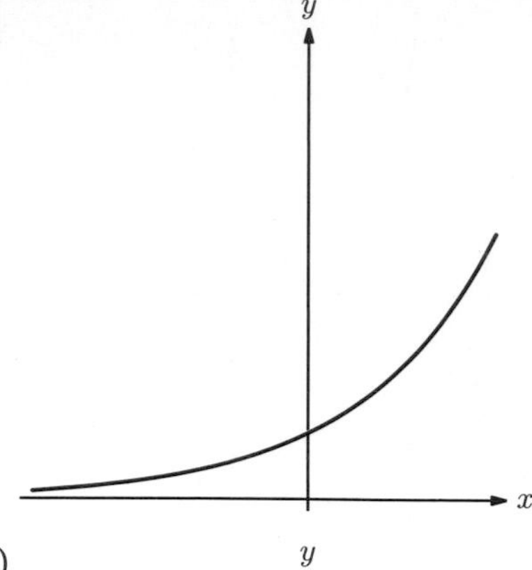

(ii)

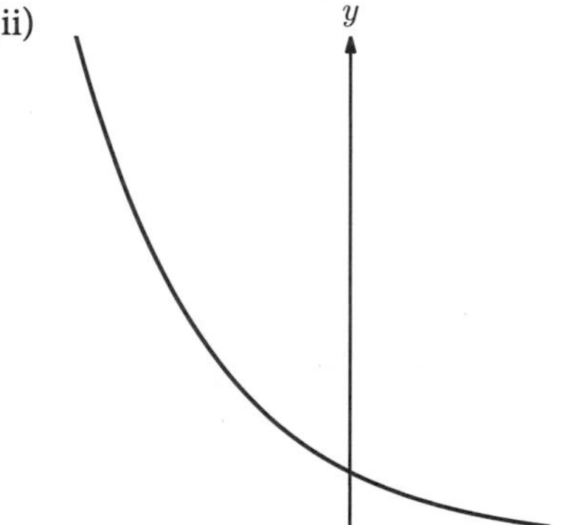

2. (a)

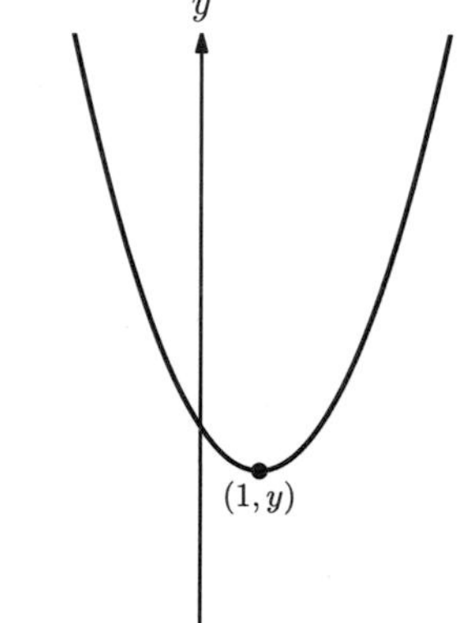

(b)

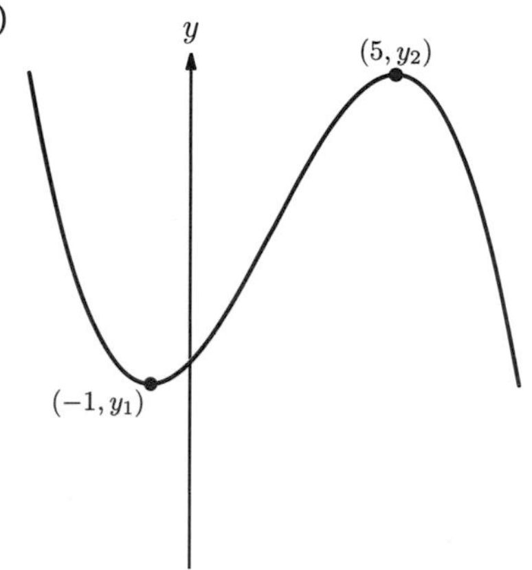

(c)

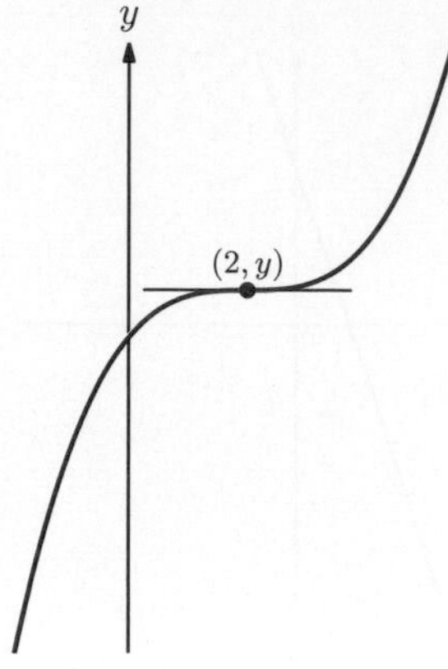

(d)

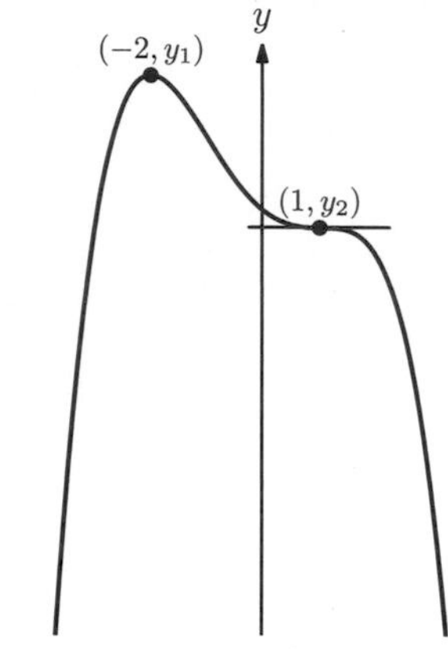

3. (a) Sometimes true
(b) Sometimes true
(c) Always true
(d) Sometimes true
(e) Sometimes true
(f) Sometimes true

Exercise 12B

1. (a) (i) $f'(x) = 3x^2$ (ii) $f'(x) = 4x^3$
(b) (i) $f'(x) = -4$ (ii) $f'(x) = 6x$
(c) (i) $f'(x) = 2x - 6$ (ii) $f'(x) = 2x - 3$

Exercise 12C

1. (a) (i) $y' = 4x^3$ (ii) $y' = 1$
(b) (i) $y' = 21x^6$ (ii) $y' = -20x^4$
(c) (i) $y' = 0$ (ii) $y' = 0$
(d) (i) $y' = 12x^2 - 10x + 2$ (ii) $y' = 8x^3 + 9x^2 - 1$
(e) (i) $y' = 2x^5$ (ii) $y' = -\frac{3}{2}x$

(f) (i) $y' = 7 - \frac{3}{2}x^2$ (ii) $y' = -20x^3 + x^4$

(g) (i) $y' = \frac{3}{2}x^{\frac{1}{2}}$ (ii) $y' = \frac{2}{3}x^{-\frac{1}{3}}$

(h) (i) $y' = 8x^{\frac{1}{3}}$ (ii) $y' = \frac{1}{2}x^{-\frac{1}{6}}$

(i) (i) $y' = 12x^3 - 2x + 6x^{-\frac{3}{5}}$

(ii) $y' = 3x^2 - x^{\frac{2}{3}} + \frac{2}{3}x^{-\frac{1}{2}}$

(j) (i) $y' = -x^{-2}$ (ii) $y' = 3x^{-4}$

(k) (i) $y' = -\frac{1}{2}x^{-\frac{3}{2}}$ (ii) $y' = 6x^{-\frac{7}{4}}$

(l) (i) $y' = 5 + \frac{4}{3}x^{-\frac{7}{2}}$ (ii) $y' = x^{-\frac{10}{7}} - 8x^{-7}$

2. (a) (i) $\frac{1}{3}x^{-\frac{2}{3}}$ (ii) $\frac{4}{5}x^{-\frac{1}{5}}$

(b) (i) $-6x^{-3}$ (ii) $4x^{-11}$

(c) (i) $-\frac{1}{2}x^{-\frac{3}{2}}$ (ii) $-2x^{-\frac{7}{4}}$

(d) (i) $9x^2 - 8x$ (ii) $\frac{7}{2}x^{\frac{5}{2}} - 3x^{\frac{1}{2}} + 4x^{-\frac{1}{2}}$

(e) (i) $\frac{4}{3}x^{\frac{1}{3}} + \frac{2}{3}x^{-\frac{2}{3}} - 1$ (ii) $2x - 8x^{-3}$

(f) (i) $9x^2 + 2x^{-2}$ (ii) $\frac{15}{2}x^{\frac{2}{3}} - \frac{1}{2}x^{-\frac{4}{3}}$

3. (a) (i) -1 (ii) $\frac{3}{2}$

(b) (i) $-2x - 1$ (ii) $4x^3 + 2$

Exercise 12D

1. (a) $\frac{dz}{dt}$

(b) $\frac{dQ}{dP}$

(c) $\frac{dR}{dm}$

(d) $\frac{dV}{dt}$

(e) $\frac{dy}{dx}$

(f) $\frac{d^2z}{dy^2}$

(g) $\frac{d^2H}{dm^2}$

2. (a) (i) $\frac{5}{3}x^{-\frac{2}{3}}$ (ii) $15q^4$

(b) (i) $3 - 7t^{-2}$ (ii) $1 - c^{-2}$

(c) (i) $18 + 6x$ (ii) $6t^{-3}$

3. (a) (i) 30 (ii) $\frac{227}{36}$

ANSWER HINT 3(a)

Did you think about doing this on the calculator?

(b) (i) 7 (ii) -29999.8

(c) (i) 12 (ii) -10

(d) (i) 24 (ii) 32

(e) (i) 6 (ii) $\frac{7}{2\sqrt{6}}$

4. (a) (i) $2ax + 1 - a$ (ii) $3x^2$

(b) (i) $\frac{1}{2}\sqrt{\frac{b}{a}}$ (ii) $6a^2v$

5. (a) (i) 54 (ii) 384

(b) (i) 8 (ii) $\frac{1}{108}$

(c) (i) 0 (ii) 42

6. (a) (i) 2 or -2 (ii) 1

(b) (i) 17 or -17 (ii) 6

7. (a) (i) $x > \frac{1}{2}$ (ii) $x < -1$

(b) (i) $x > 1$ (ii) $x < 0$

9. $(-0.199, 0.913)$, $(1.29, -0.181)$, $(3.91, 30.3)$

10. $x > -\frac{1}{3}$

11. $n!$

Exercise 12E

1. (a) (i) $y' = 3\cos x$ (ii) $y' = -2\sin x$

(b) (i) $y' = 2 + 5\sin x$ (ii) $y' = \frac{1}{\cos^2 x}$

(c) (i) $y' = \frac{\cos x - 2\sin x}{5}$

(ii) $y' = \frac{1}{2\cos^2 x} - \frac{1}{3}\cos x$

2. π

3. $\frac{22 - \pi^2}{12}$

4. $\frac{\pi}{4}, \frac{5\pi}{4}$

5. $x = \frac{\pi}{3}, \frac{2\pi}{3}, \frac{4\pi}{3}, \frac{5\pi}{3}$

Exercise 12F

1. (a) (i) $y' = 3e^x$ (ii) $y' = \frac{2e^x}{5}$

   (b) (i) $y' = \frac{-2}{x}$ (ii) $y' = \frac{1}{3x}$

   (c) (i) $y' = \frac{1}{5x} - 3 + 4e^x$ (ii) $y' = -\frac{e^x}{2} + \frac{3}{x}$

2. $2 - \frac{7}{\ln 4}$

3. $3 - \frac{1}{2\ln 3}$

4. $\ln 3$

5. $x > \ln 2$

6. 3

ANSWER HINT

Q6. Did you exclude the solution $x = -2$ because it cannot go into $g(x)$?

7. (a) (i) $y' = \frac{3}{x}$ (ii) $y' = \frac{1}{x}$

   (b) (i) $y' = e^3 e^x$ (ii) $y' = \frac{e^x}{e^3}$

   (c) (i) $y' = 2x$ (ii) $y' = 3e^2 x^2$

Exercise 12G

1. (a) Tangent: $11x - 4y - 4 = 0$;
   normal: $4x + 11y - 126 = 0$

   (b) Tangent: $4x - y + 1 - \pi = 0$;
   normal: $4x + 16y - \pi - 16 = 0$

2. $x - 5y - 10 - \ln 25 = 0$

3. $(-1, -4)$

4. 2.05, −0.0541

5. $y = 3x - \ln 4 + 2$

6. (0.410, 0.348)

Exercise 12H

1. (a) (i) (0, 0) local maximum;
   $\left(\frac{10}{3}, \frac{-500}{27}\right)$ local minimum

   (ii) (0, 0) local maximum; (2, −16) local minimum; (−2, −16) local minimum

   (b) (i) $\left(\frac{2\pi}{3}, \frac{3\sqrt{3}+2\pi}{6}\right)$ local maximum;
   $\left(-\frac{2\pi}{3}, -\frac{3\sqrt{3}+2\pi}{6}\right)$ local minimum

   (ii) (0, 3) local maximum; (π, −1) local minimum

   (c) (i) (4, ln 4 − 2) local maximum

   (ii) $\left(\ln\left(\frac{5}{2}\right), 5 - 5\ln\left(\frac{5}{2}\right)\right)$ local minimum

ANSWER HINT

In the exam you should give the value of $\frac{d^2y}{dx^2}$ for each stationary point to justify your classification

2. (−4, 92) local maximum; (2, −16) local minimum

3. $\left(\frac{1}{4}, -\frac{1}{4}\right)$ local minimum

4. (0.245, 4.12) local maximum;
   (3.39, −4.12) local minimum

6. $y \geq -21$

7. $y \geq 6 - 4\ln 4$

8. (0, 0) local minimum; $\left(-\frac{4}{k}, \frac{32}{k^2}\right)$ local maximum

Exercise 12I

1. $\left(\ln 2, 2 - (\ln 2)^2\right)$

2. (1, 4) and (−1, −10)

4. $\left(\frac{\pi}{2}, \frac{\pi}{2}\right)$ and $\left(\frac{3\pi}{2}, \frac{3\pi}{2}\right)$

ANSWER HINT

As the question doesn't state how many points of inflexion there are, you need to show that both of these are actually points of inflexion by checking the sign of $\frac{d^2y}{dx^2}$ on either side.

6.

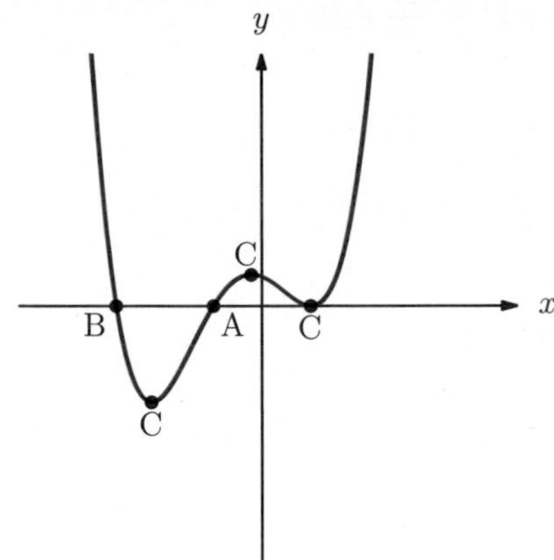

Exercise 12J

1. Minimum 1, maximum e
2. (a) $225\,\text{m}^2$
   (b) 60 m
3. Minimum $-6\sqrt{3}$, maximum 80
4. Minimum $3-3\ln 3$, maximum $e^2 - 6$
5. Minimum 0, maximum 4π
6. 2
7. 2.25
8. Minimum: 2 minutes; maximum: 4 minutes
9. (a) 40 million litres
   (b) After 1.6 and 3.8 days
10. (a) 2 units
    (b) 0 units
    (c) 1.94 units
11. (a) 4 litres
    (b) 41.5 litres
    (c) $t = 20$ seconds
12. (a) $(2x - \frac{x^2}{10})$ kJ
    (b) $10\,\text{m}^2$
    (c) $0 < x < 10$

Mixed examination practice 12

Short questions

1. $y = e^{\frac{\pi}{2}}x - \frac{\pi}{2}e^{\frac{\pi}{2}} + e^{\frac{\pi}{2}} + 2$
2. $x = 2$
3. $b = 8, c = -7$
4. $\left(\frac{1}{16}, \frac{7}{16}\right)$
5. $\left(2, -\frac{2}{3}\right)$
6. $x = \frac{\pi}{6} \pm k\pi$ local minima,
   $x = -\frac{\pi}{6} \pm k\pi$
   local maxima $(k \in \mathbb{Z})$
7.

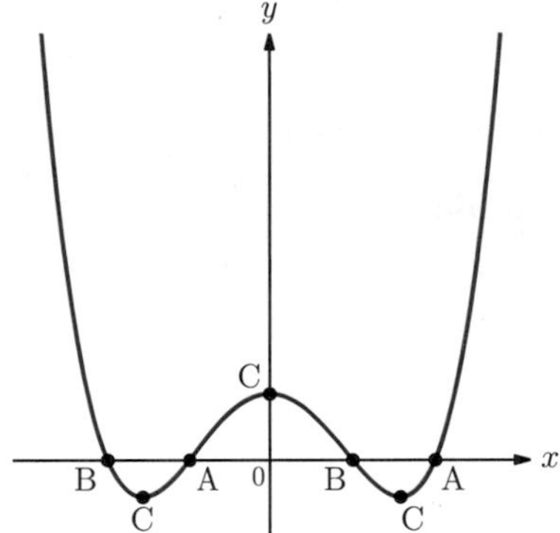

8. $3^{-1/4} = \frac{1}{\sqrt[4]{3}}$

Long questions

1. (b) $3a + b = 6$
   (c) $a = 1, b = 3$
   (d) $(-7, -192)$
2. (a) (i) $\left(-\frac{1}{3}, \frac{86}{27}\right)$
   (ii) $\left(\frac{1}{3}, \frac{70}{27}\right)$
   (b) (i) $y = -\frac{8}{9}x + \frac{78}{27}$
   (ii) $y = -\frac{8}{9}\left(x - \frac{3+2\sqrt{3}}{9}\right) + \frac{70}{27} - \frac{64\sqrt{3}}{243}$ or
   $y = -\frac{8}{9}\left(x - \frac{3-2\sqrt{3}}{9}\right) + \frac{70}{27} + \frac{64\sqrt{3}}{243}$
3. (a) (i) 11 000 (ii) 9.55 hours
   (b) (i) $\frac{dP}{dt} = e^t - 3$ (ii) 8.70 hours
   (c) (i) $\frac{d^2P}{dt^2} = e^t$ (ii) 9704

Chapter 13

Exercise 13A

1. (a) (i) $y = x^3$ (ii) $y = x^5$
   (b) (i) $y = \frac{1}{x}$ (ii) $y = \frac{1}{x^4}$
   (c) (i) $y = \sqrt{x}$ (ii) $y = \sqrt[3]{x}$
   (d) (i) $y = 2x^5$ (ii) $y = 4x^3$

Exercise 13B

1. (a) $\frac{3}{4}x^4$ + any three constants
   (b) Any three constants
2. (a) (i) $\frac{7}{5}x^5 + c$ (ii) $\frac{1}{9}x^3 + c$
   (b) (i) $-\frac{1}{2t} + c$ (ii) $-\frac{4}{y^2} + c$

Exercise 13C

1. (a) (i) $x^9 + c$ (ii) $x^{12} + c$
   (b) (i) $\frac{x^2}{2} + c$ (ii) $\frac{x^4}{4} + c$
   (c) (i) $9x + c$ (ii) $\frac{x}{2} + c$
   (d) (i) $\frac{x^6}{2} + c$ (ii) $\frac{9}{5}x^5 + c$
   (e) (i) $2x^{\frac{3}{2}} + c$ (ii) $\frac{9}{4}x^{\frac{4}{3}} + c$
   (f) (i) $-\frac{5}{x} + c$ (ii) $-\frac{1}{x^2} + c$
2. (a) (i) $3t + c$ (ii) $7z + c$
   (b) (i) $\frac{q^6}{6} + c$ (ii) $\frac{r^{11}}{11} + c$
   (c) (i) $\frac{15}{2}g^{\frac{8}{5}} + c$ (ii) $\frac{10}{9}y^{\frac{9}{2}} + c$
   (d) (i) $-\frac{4}{h} + c$ (ii) $-\frac{1}{3p^3} + c$
3. (a) (i) $\frac{x^3}{3} - \frac{x^4}{4} + 2x + c$ (ii) $\frac{x^5}{5} - x^2 + 5x + c$
   (b) (i) $-\frac{1}{6t^2} - \frac{1}{12t^3} + c$ (ii) $-\frac{5}{v} + \frac{1}{v^4} + c$
   (c) (i) $\frac{2}{5}x^{\frac{5}{2}} + c$ (ii) $\frac{18}{7}x^{\frac{7}{6}} + c$
   (d) (i) $\frac{x^4}{4} + x^3 + \frac{3x^2}{2} + x + c$
   (ii) $\frac{x^4}{4} + \frac{4x^3}{3} + 2x^2 + c$
4. $2\sqrt{x} + \frac{2}{3}x^{\frac{3}{2}} + c$

Exercise 13D

1. (a) (i) $2\ln x + c$ (ii) $3\ln x + c$
   (b) (i) $\frac{1}{2}\ln x + c$ (ii) $\frac{1}{3}\ln x + c$
   (c) (i) $\frac{x^2}{2} - \ln x + c$ (ii) $\frac{x^3}{3} + 5\ln x + c$
   (d) (i) $3\ln x - \frac{2}{x} + c$ (ii) $\ln x + \frac{2}{\sqrt{x}} + c$
2. (a) (i) $5e^x + c$ (ii) $9e^x + c$
   (b) (i) $\frac{2e^x}{5} + c$ (ii) $\frac{7e^x}{11} + c$
   (c) (i) $\frac{e^x}{2} + \frac{3x^2}{4} + c$ (ii) $\frac{e^x}{5} + \frac{x^4}{20} + c$

Exercise 13E

1. (a) (i) $-\cos x - \sin x + c$
   (ii) $3\sin x - 4\cos x + c$
   (b) (i) $\frac{x^2}{14} - \frac{\cos x}{7} + c$ (ii) $\frac{1}{9}x^{\frac{3}{2}} + \frac{\sin x}{6} + c$
   (c) (i) $x - \sin x + \cos x + c$
   (ii) $-2\cos x - \sin x + c$
2. $\pi\sin x - \pi x + c$
3. $\sin x - \cos x + c$

ANSWER HINT

Q3. Use a trigonometric identity to simplify first.

Exercise 13F

1. (a) (i) $y = \frac{x^2}{2} + 5$ (ii) $y = 2x^3 + 5$
   (b) (i) $y = 2\sqrt{x} + 4$ (ii) $y = -\frac{1}{x} + 4$
   (c) (i) $y = 2e^x + 2x - 1 - 2e$
   (ii) $y = e^x - 5$
   (d) (i) $y = x + \ln x - 1$ (ii) $y = \frac{1}{2}\ln x + 4$
   (e) (i) $y = \sin x - \cos x$ (ii) $y = 3\cos x + 1$

2. (a) $f(x)=\frac{1}{2}\ln x+c$

(b) $y=\frac{1}{2}\ln x-\frac{1}{2}\ln 2+7$

3. (a) -2

4. $y=\ln\frac{e^5}{x}$

Exercise 13G

1. (a) (i) 320 (ii) 28.5
(b) (i) 1 (ii) -2
(c) (i) $e-1$ (ii) $3e-\frac{3}{e}$

2. (a) (i) 0.995 (ii) 0.0997
(b) (i) 1.46 (ii) 1

3. $e^{\pi}+\pi+1$

5. 20

6. $a=16$

Exercise 13H

1. (a) (i) $\frac{7}{3}$ (ii) $\frac{1}{4}$
(b) (i) $\frac{2}{3}$ (ii) $\frac{22}{3}$
(c) (i) $\frac{11}{4}$ (ii) $\frac{79}{6}$

2. 9

3. (a) 6
(b) $\frac{22}{3}$

4. 2

ANSWER HINT

Q4. There is an easier way than splitting the integral into two parts.

5. $\frac{9}{2}$

Exercise 13I

1. (a) (i) $\frac{32}{3}$ (ii) $\frac{1}{6}$
(b) (i) 9 (ii) $\frac{1}{3}$
(c) (i) $\frac{9}{8}$ (ii) $\frac{1}{3}$

2. $\frac{32}{3}$

3. $e^2-\frac{11}{3}$

4. 0.462

6. $2-\sqrt{2}$

7. 8

8. 4

Mixed examination practice 13

Short questions

1. $f(x)=\frac{1}{2}-\cos x$

2. $\frac{4k^3}{3}$

3. $\ln x+\frac{2}{5}x^{\frac{5}{2}}+c$

4. (a) $a=\sqrt{2}$
(b) $\frac{1}{2}$

5. (a) (i) a^{n+1} (ii) $\frac{b^{n+1}}{n+1}-\frac{a^{n+1}}{n+1}$
(b) $n=3$

ANSWER HINT

Q5. You did not need to calculate an integral for the red area to answer this question.

6. $2\sqrt{3}-\frac{2}{3}\pi$

7. (a) Local minimum
(b) $x^3+3x^2-45x+100$

Long questions

1. (a) $3-e$
(b) 5
(c) $e^x+(3-e)x+2$
(d) $\frac{e+5}{2}$

2. (b) $(-a, 0)$ and $(3a, 8a^2)$

(c) $\frac{64}{3}a^3$

(d) $\frac{15}{16}$

Chapter 14

Exercise 14A

1. (a) (i) $15(3x+4)^4$ (ii) $35(5x+4)^6$
   (b) (i) $\frac{3}{2\sqrt{3x-2}}$ (ii) $\frac{1}{2\sqrt{x+1}}$
   (c) (i) $\frac{1}{(3-x)^2}$ (ii) $-\frac{4}{(2x+3)^3}$
   (d) (i) $10e^{10x+1}$ (ii) $-3e^{4-3x}$
   (e) (i) $4\cos 4x$ (ii) $-3\sin(3x+\pi)$
   (f) (i) $-\frac{1}{5-x}$ (ii) $-\frac{2}{3-2x}$
2. (a) (i) $7(2x-3)(x^2-3x+1)^6$
   (ii) $15x^2(x^3+1)^4$
   (b) (i) $(2x-2)e^{x^2-2x}$ (ii) $-3x^2e^{4-x^3}$
   (c) (i) $-6e^x(2e^x+1)^{-4}$ (ii) $20e^x(2-5e^x)^{-5}$
   (d) (i) $6x\cos(3x^2+1)$
   (ii) $-(2x+2)\sin(x^2+2x)$
   (e) (i) $-3\sin x\cos^2 x$ (ii) $4\cos x\sin^3 x$
   (f) (i) $\frac{2-15x^2}{(2x-5x)^3}$ (ii) $\frac{8x}{4x^2-1}$
   (g) (i) $\frac{16}{x}(4\ln x-1)^3$ (ii) $-\frac{5}{x}(\ln x+3)^{-6}$
3. (a) (i) $10(2x+3)^4$ (ii) $32(4x-1)^7$
   (b) (i) $4(5-x)^{-5}$ (ii) $7(1-x)^{-8}$
   (c) (i) $4\sin(1-4x)$ (ii) $\sin(2-x)$
   (d) (i) $\frac{5}{5x+2}$ (ii) $\frac{1}{x-4}$
4. (a) (i) $\frac{6\sin 3x}{\cos^3 3x}$ (ii) $4\tan(2x)\frac{1}{\cos^2 2x}$
   (b) (i) $6\sin(3x)\cos(3x)e^{\sin^2(3x)}$
   (ii) $\frac{2\ln(2x)}{x}e^{(\ln 2x)^2}$
   (c) (i) $-16\sin(2x)\cos(2x)(1-2\sin^2(2x))$
   (ii) $-24\sin 3x(4\cos 3x+1)$
   (d) (i) $\frac{6\sin 2x}{1-3\cos 2x}$ (ii) $\frac{5\sin 5x}{2-\cos 5x}$
5. $y=66x-11$
6. $y=\frac{27\sqrt{2}}{8}x-\frac{77}{12}$
7. $\left(\frac{\pi}{2}, e\right), \left(\frac{3\pi}{2}, e^{-1}\right)$
8. 7
9. (a) The left post, because $h(-1) > h(2)$
   (c) $\sqrt[3]{2}+\frac{1}{\sqrt[3]{4}}$

Exercise 14B

1. (a) (i) $(1+x)^3+3x(1+x)^2$
   (ii) $8x(x+3)^4+16x^2(x+3)^3$
   (b) (i) $2x\sin x+x^2\cos x$
   (ii) $5\tan x+\frac{5x}{\cos^2 x}$
   (c) (i) $e^x\ln x+\frac{e^x}{x}$ (ii) $e^x\sin x+e^x\cos x$
2. (a) (i) $2x\cos x-x^2\sin x$
   (ii) $-x^{-2}\sin x+x^{-1}\cos x$
   (b) (i) $-2x^{-3}\ln x+x^{-3}$ (ii) $3x^2\ln x+x^2$
   (c) (i) $3x^2\sqrt{2x+1}+x^3(2x+1)^{-\frac{1}{2}}$
   (ii) $-x^{-2}\sqrt{4x}+2x^{-1}(4x)^{-\frac{1}{2}}$
   (d) (i) $2e^{2x}\tan x+e^{2x}\frac{1}{\cos^2 x}$
   (ii) $e^{x+1}\sin 3x+3e^{x+1}\cos 3x$
3. (a) (i) $3(x+1)^3(x-2)^4(3x-1)$
   (ii) $(x-3)^6(x+5)^3(11x+23)$
   (b) (i) $(2x-1)^3(1-3x)^2(-42x+17)$
   (ii) $(1-x)^4(4x+1)(-28x+3)$
4. $(6x^2+4x+3)e^{2x}$
5. $y=2ex-e$
6. $(9x^2+12x+2)e^{3x}$

7. $x=-\frac{1}{2},2$

8. $\left(-\frac{2}{3},-\frac{2}{3\sqrt{3}}\right)$

9. $x=3,-\frac{1}{3},\frac{7}{4}$

10. (b) (0.538, 0.474), (1.82, −0.877), (3.29, 0.957), (4.81, −0.979)

11. $e^x(1+x)\cos(xe^x)$

12. (a) $\ln x+1$

(b) $x\ln x-x+C$

13. $\left(\frac{3\pi}{4},-\frac{\sqrt{2}}{2}e^{-\frac{3\pi}{4}}\right)$

14. $a=4,\ b=5$

15. (a) $y=e^{x\ln x}$

(b) $(\ln x+1)x^x$

(c) $(e^{-1},e^{-e^{-1}})$

Exercise 14C

1. (a) (i) $\frac{2}{(x+1)^2}$ (ii) $\frac{-5}{(x-3)^2}$

(b) (i) $\frac{x(2x+1)^{-\frac{1}{2}}-(2x+1)^{\frac{1}{2}}}{x^2}=\frac{-x-1}{x^2\sqrt{2x+1}}$

(ii) $\frac{2x(x-1)^{\frac{1}{2}}-\frac{1}{2}x^2(x-1)^{-\frac{1}{2}}}{x-1}=\frac{x(3x-4)}{2\sqrt{(x-1)^3}}$

(c) (i) $\frac{2(x^2-x-2)}{(x^2+2)^2}$ (ii) $-\frac{x^2+2x+4}{(1+x)^2}$

(d) (i) $\frac{1-\ln 3x}{x^2}$ (ii) $\frac{1-2\ln 2x}{x^3}$

2. (0, 0), (1, 1)

3. $y=\frac{\pi^2}{4}x+\frac{16-\pi^4}{8\pi}$

4. −1

5. $\left(e,\frac{1}{e}\right)$ local maximum

6. $0<x<2,\ x\neq 1$

7. $a=3,\ b=4,\ p=\frac{3}{2}$

Exercise 14D

1. (a) (i) 2 (ii) $\frac{49}{12}$

(b) (i) $2\sqrt{3}$ (ii) $4\sqrt{2}$

(c) (i) $4\sqrt{2}$ (ii) $\frac{8}{3}$

2. (a) $x(12-2x)^2$

(b) $x=2$

3. 48 cm^2

4. $\left(\frac{2\sqrt{3}}{3},\frac{8}{3}\right)$

5. (a) (i) $(\pi-x,\sin x)$ (ii) $(\pi-2x)\sin x$

(c) 1.12

6. 733 cm^3

7. 650 cm^3

8. (a) 3 and 3

(b) 0 and 6

9. (b) $r=5.56,\ h=7.86$

12. $\left(\sqrt{\frac{7}{2}},\frac{7}{2}\right)$

Mixed examination practice 14

Short questions

1. $\frac{16}{225}$

2. (a) $5e^{5x}$

(b) $\frac{3}{2\sqrt{3x+2}}$

(c) $5e^{5x}\sqrt{3x+2}+\frac{3e^{5x}}{2\sqrt{3x+2}}$

3. $\frac{5}{2}$

4. 15 m

5. (b) $\left(-\frac{\ln b}{c},\frac{a}{2b}\right)$

Long questions

1. (a) π

(b) (i) $e^x(\sin x+\cos x)$ (ii) 0

(d) (i) 0

(ii) $\left(\frac{\pi}{2},e^{\frac{\pi}{2}}\right)$

2. (a) $x=\frac{1}{2}$

(b) (0, 0) and (1, −1)

(c) (0, 0) local minimum; (1, −1) local maximum

(d)

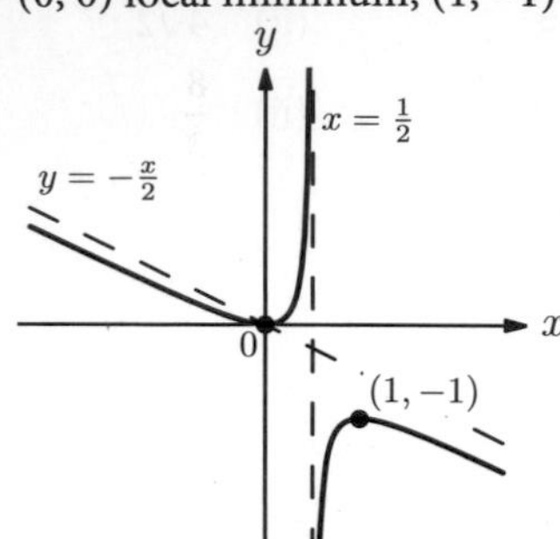

3. (b) (ii) $\frac{(\ln 2)^2 x^2 - 4x\ln 2 + 2}{2^x}$

(c) (i) $\frac{2}{\ln 2}$

Chapter 15

Exercise 15A

1. (a) (i) $(x+3)^5 + c$ (ii) $\frac{1}{6}(x-2)^6 + c$

(b) (i) $\frac{1}{32}(4x-5)^8 + c$ (ii) $2\left(\frac{1}{8}x+1\right)^4 + c$

(c) (i) $-\frac{1}{9}(4-x)^9 + c$ (ii) $-\frac{8}{7}\left(3-\frac{1}{2}x\right)^7 + c$

(d) (i) $\frac{1}{3}(2x-1)^{\frac{3}{2}} + c$ (ii) $-\frac{4}{5}(2-5x)^{\frac{7}{4}} + c$

(e) (i) $2(4-3x)^{-1} + c$ (ii) $4\left(2+\frac{x}{3}\right)^{\frac{3}{4}} + c$

2. (a) (i) $e^{3x} + c$ (ii) $\frac{1}{2}e^{2x+5} + c$

(b) (i) $2e^{\frac{1}{2}x} + c$ (ii) $6e^{\frac{2x-1}{3}} + c$

(c) (i) $2e^{-3x} + c$ (ii) $-\frac{1}{4}e^{-4x} + c$

(d) (i) $-\frac{3}{2}e^{-\frac{2}{3}x} + c$ (ii) $8e^{-\frac{x}{4}} + c$

3. (a) (i) $\ln(x+4) + c$ (ii) $\ln(5x-2) + c$

(b) (i) $\frac{2}{3}\ln(3x+4) + c$ (ii) $-4\ln(2x-5) + c$

(c) (i) $-\frac{1}{2}\ln(7-2x) + c$ (ii) $\frac{3}{4}\ln(1-4x) + c$

4. (a) $\frac{1}{3}\cos(2-3x) + c$

(b) $\frac{1}{2}\sin 4x + c$

5. (a) $\frac{1}{6}(2x-3)^3 + c$

(b) $\frac{1}{6}e^{6x} + c$

(c) $-\frac{1}{5}\ln(2-5x) + c$

6. Both are right:

$\frac{1}{3}\ln(3x) + c = \frac{1}{3}\ln x + \frac{1}{3}\ln 3 + c = \frac{1}{3}\ln x + c'$ where $c' = \frac{1}{3}\ln 3 + c$ is an unknown constant as well

7. 0.492

Exercise 15B

1. (a) (i) $\frac{1}{3}(x^2+2)^{\frac{3}{2}} + c$

(ii) $\frac{1}{3}(x^2+6x+4)^{\frac{3}{2}} + c$

(b) (i) $\frac{1}{3}\ln(x^3+1) + c$ (ii) $\frac{3}{2}\ln(x^2+5) + c$

(c) (i) $-\frac{1}{3}\cos^3 x + c$ (ii) $\frac{1}{2}(\ln x)^2 + c$

2. (a) (i) $\frac{1}{8}(x^2+3)^4 + c$ (ii) $\frac{1}{4}(x^2-1)^6 + c$

(b) (i) $\frac{1}{15}(3x^2-15x+4)^5 + c$

(ii) $\frac{1}{12}(x^3+3x^2-5)^4 + c$

(c) (i) $\ln(x^2+3) + c$

(ii) $2\ln(x^3-6x+1) + c$

(d) (i) $-\frac{2}{9}\cos^6 3x + c$ (ii) $\frac{1}{8}\sin^4 2x + c$

(e) (i) $\frac{1}{2}e^{3x^2-1} + c$ (ii) $\frac{3}{2}e^{x^2} + c$

(f) (i) $\ln\sqrt{e^{2x+3}+4} + c$ (ii) $\ln\sqrt[4]{3+4\sin x} + c$

3. e − 1

4. $\frac{2}{9}(x^3+5)^{\frac{3}{2}} + c$

5. $2\sqrt{e+1} - 2\sqrt{2}$

6. $e^5 - e^{-1}$

7. ln 8

8. (a) $\tan x = \frac{\sin x}{\cos x}$ (b) $-\ln(\cos x) + c$

9. $2\sqrt{3} - 2$

10. They are all right, with different constants of integration 'c', because

$\frac{1}{2}\sin^2 x = -\frac{1}{2}\cos^2 x + \frac{1}{2} = -\frac{1}{4}\cos 2x + \frac{1}{4}$ by trigonometric identities.

Exercise 15C

1. (a) (i) $v = -8e^{-2t}, a = 16e^{-2t}$

(ii) $v = -6e^{3t}, a = -18e^{3t}$

(b) (i) $v = \frac{5}{2}\cos\left(\frac{t}{2}\right), a = -\frac{5}{4}\sin\left(\frac{t}{2}\right)$

(ii) $v = 6\sin(2t), a = 12\cos(2t)$

2. (a) (i) $t^3 - t$ (ii) $\frac{1}{2}t - \frac{1}{8}t^4$

(b) (i) $2 - 2e^{-t}$ (ii) $t + \frac{1}{2}e^{2t} - \frac{1}{2}$

(c) (i) $3\ln\left(\frac{t+2}{2}\right)$ (ii) $3t - \ln(t+1)$

3. (a) (i) 1.73 (ii) 3.16
(b) (i) 2.22 (ii) 0.746
(c) (i) 3.23 (ii) 7.06

5. (a) 13.6 m
(b) 16.4 m

6. (a) 4.4 m
(b) 10.3 m

7. (a) $\frac{1-t^2}{(t^2+1)^2}$

(b) $\frac{1}{2}\ln(26) = 1.63$ (3SF)

8. $\frac{25}{4}$

9. (b) It reverses for 4 s and then moves forward.

(c) $5\frac{1}{3}$ m

(d) $26\frac{2}{3}$ m

(e) $21\frac{1}{3}$ m

(f) $t = 7$ s

(g) 16 m/s

Exercise 15D

1. (a) (i) $\frac{1524}{5}\pi$ (ii) $\frac{18}{7}\pi$

(b) (i) $\left(\frac{e^4}{4} + e^2 - \frac{1}{4}\right)\pi$

(ii) $\left(\frac{25}{2} - 4e^{-2} - \frac{e^{-4}}{2}\right)\pi$

(c) (i) 2π (ii) π

2. (a) (i) 101 (ii) 134
(b) (i) 12.6 (ii) 45.7
(c) (i) 3.59 (ii) 0.771

3. 19.0

4. π

5. $\sqrt[3]{\frac{4}{3}}$

6. (a) (0, 3) and (4, 19)

(b) $\frac{3008}{15}\pi = 630$ (3 SF)

Mixed examination practice 15

Short questions

1. (a) $-\frac{1}{3}\ln(1-3x) + c$

(b) $-\frac{1}{2}(2x+3)^{-1} + c$

2. $\ln(e^x + 1) + c$

3. 6.36

4. (a) $\ln x + 1$

(b) $x\ln x - x + c$

5. $\frac{\pi}{2}$

6. 1

7. $\ln 2$

8. (b) $\ln(x-2) - \frac{5}{x-2} + c$

9. $\ln(\ln x) + c$

Long questions

1. (a) $x + c$

(b) $\ln(\sin x + \cos x) + c$

(c) $\frac{1}{2}(x - \ln(\sin x + \cos x)) + c$

2. (b) $\frac{1}{2}x + \frac{1}{4}\sin 2x + c$

(c) $\frac{\pi}{2}$

3. (a) $-10\,\text{m/s}^2$
(b) $t = 0, 5$
(c) $\frac{25}{3} = 8.33\,\text{m}$
(d) 67 m
(e) 7.5 s

Chapter 16

Exercise 16A

1. (a) (i) Mean: 22.6; median 19; mode: none
(ii) Mean: 1.2; median 0.4; mode: none
(b) (i) Mean: $31\frac{1}{3}$; median 29; mode: 28
(ii) Mean: 58.5; median 51; mode: none

2. (i) Mean: $25\frac{5}{6}$; median 24.5; mode: 15
(ii) Mean: $4\frac{5}{6}$; median 4.5; mode: −8

4. (a) Sometimes
(b) Sometimes
(c) Sometimes
(d) Sometimes
(e) Always
(f) Sometimes
(g) Always
(h) Sometimes (e.g. not true for 1, 1, 2, 2, 2, 2, 5)

5. 18.3

6. (a) 84%
(b) 79%

7. 5 and 8

8. 8 or 9

Exercise 16B

1. (a) (i) $\sigma = 7.23$, IQR = 12.6
(ii) $\sigma = 6.57$, IQR = 13.5
(b) (i) $\sigma = 11.1$, IQR = 3
(ii) $\sigma = 35.3$, IQR = 72

2. (a) False
(b) Impossible to be sure; e.g. true for 20, 26, 26, 26, 26, 32
(c) True
(d) Impossible to be sure; e.g. true for 20, 20, 20, 20, 20, 32
(e) Impossible to be sure; e.g. true for 20, 21, 22, 23, 24, 32

3. 5

4. (a) 12
(b) 2.92

5. 21

Exercise 16C

1. (a) $\bar{x} = 12.1, \sigma = 1.90, Q^2 = 12$
(b) $\bar{x} = 0.263, \sigma = 0.137, Q^2 = 0.2$

2. (a) 17, 21
(b) 17, 20
(c) 16.5, 20.5
(d) 16, 20

3. (a) (i) $\bar{x} = 26.1, \sigma = 20.4$
(ii) $\bar{x} = 253, \sigma = 151$
(b) (i) $\bar{x} = 6.38, \sigma = 5.23$

ANSWER HINT
(b) The first group starts at 0, not −0.5!

(ii) $\bar{x} = 102, \sigma = 5.78$
(c) (i) $\bar{x} = 6.58, \sigma = 5.11$
(ii) $\bar{x} = 15.3, \sigma = 9.85$

4. (a) 1.5
(b) 1.84

5. $p = 14, q = 20$

6. $p = 13, q = 0$

Exercise 16D

1. (a) (i) Median ≈ 21 s; IQR ≈ 26 s

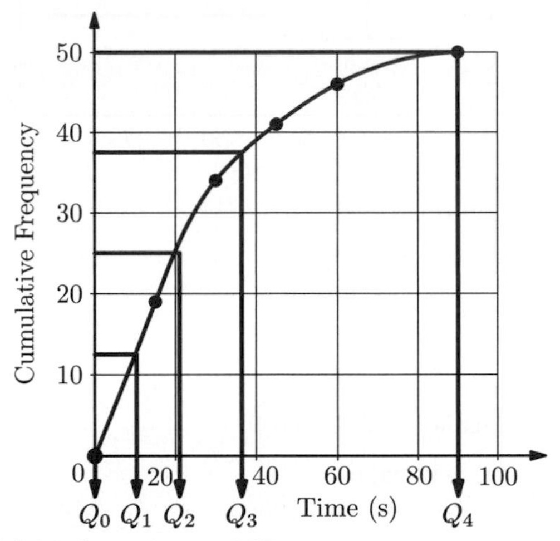

(ii) Median ≈ 233 g; IQR ≈ 154 g

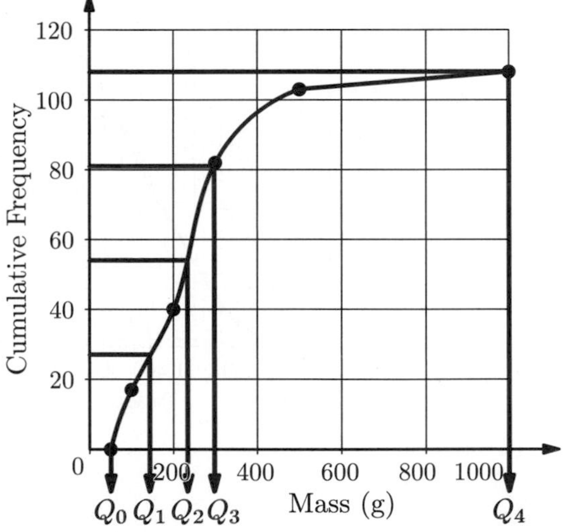

(b) (i) Median ≈ 4.5 cm; IQR ≈ 7 cm

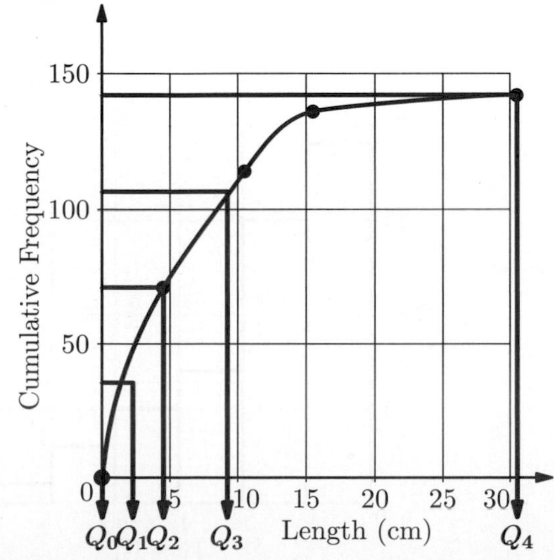

(ii) Median ≈ 102 W; IQR ≈ 8 W

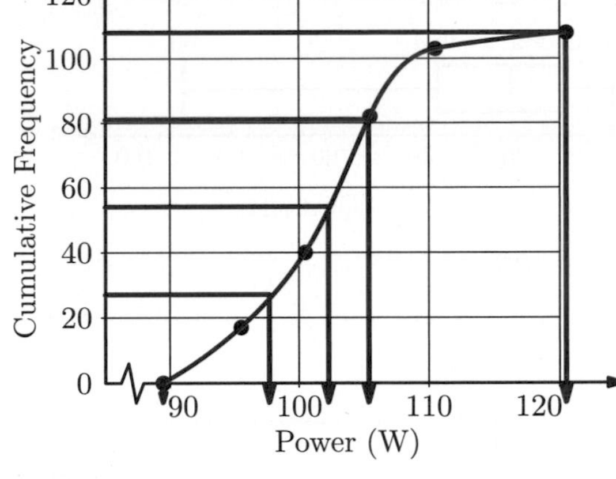

(c) (i) Median ≈ 4.3 years; IQR ≈ 6.7 years

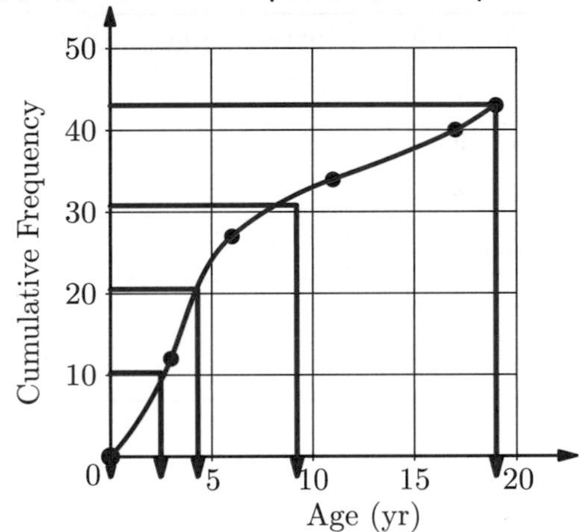

(ii) Median ≈ \$13.50; IQR ≈ \$14

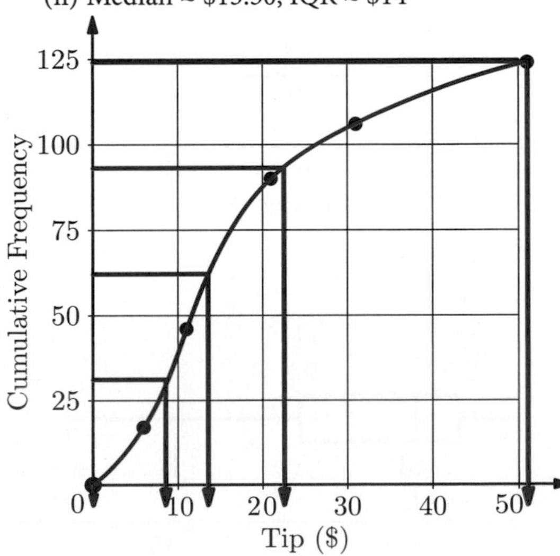

2. (a) (i)

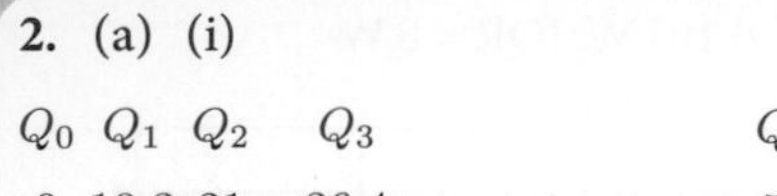

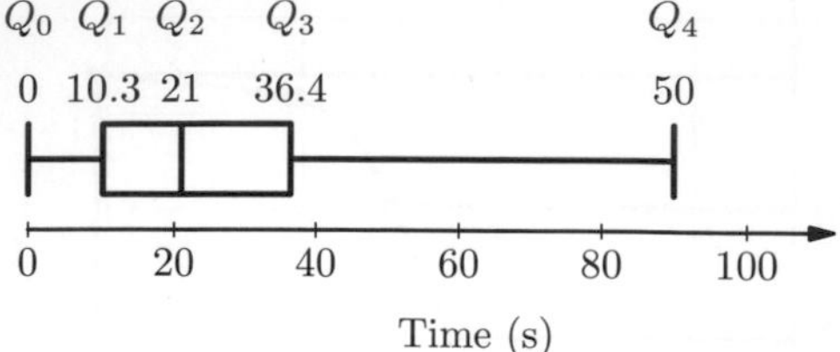

(ii)

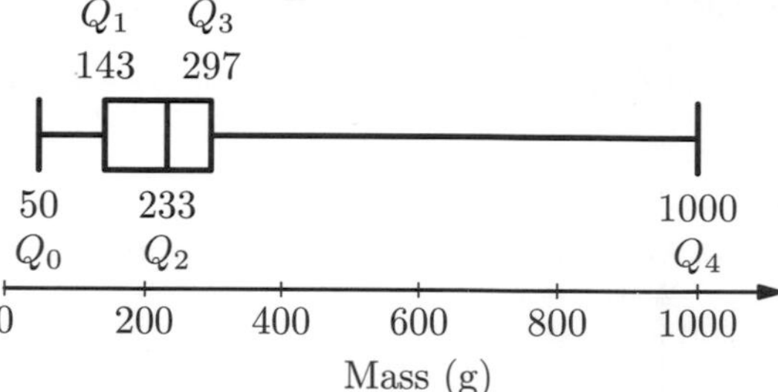

(b) (i)

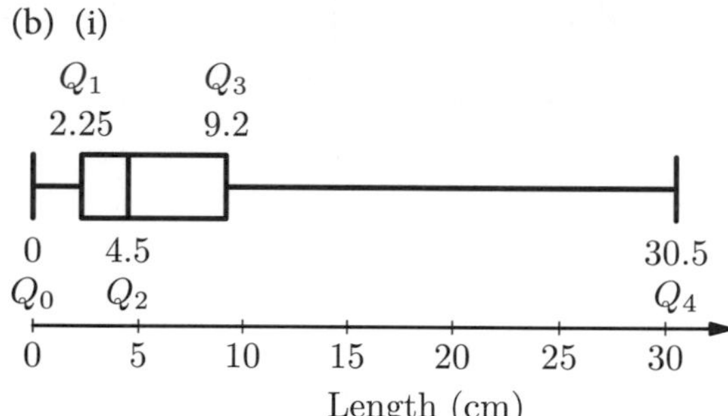

(ii)

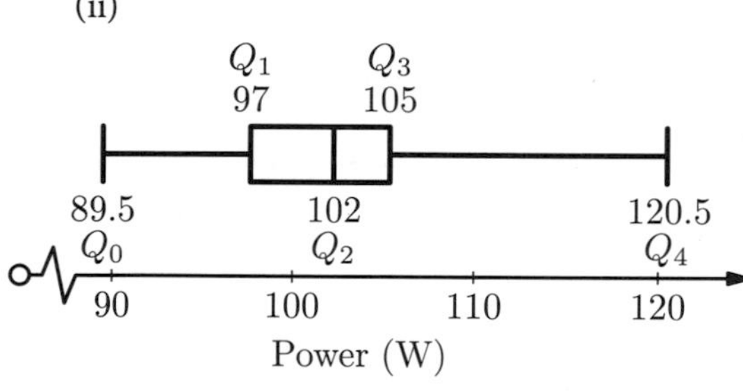

(c) (i)

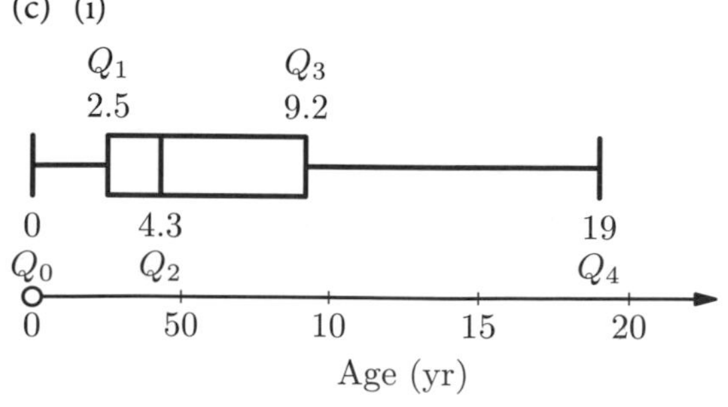

(ii)

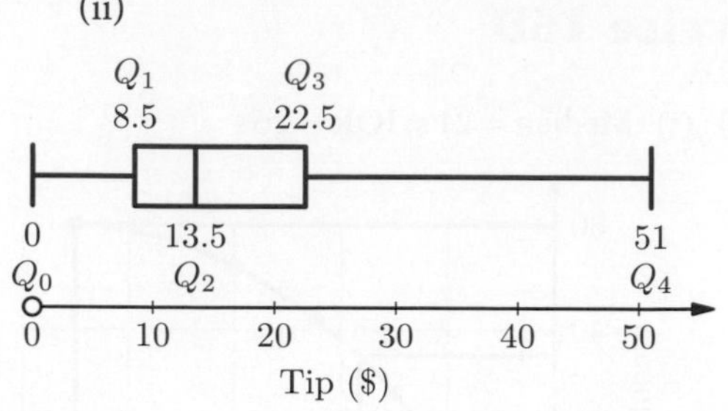

3. (a) 197 s
(b) 12 s
(c) $c \approx 191$, $d \approx 203$

4. (a) 53%
(b) 28

5. Median = 12, IQR = 9

6. (a) 417 pages
(b) 90, 143, 176, 196
(c)

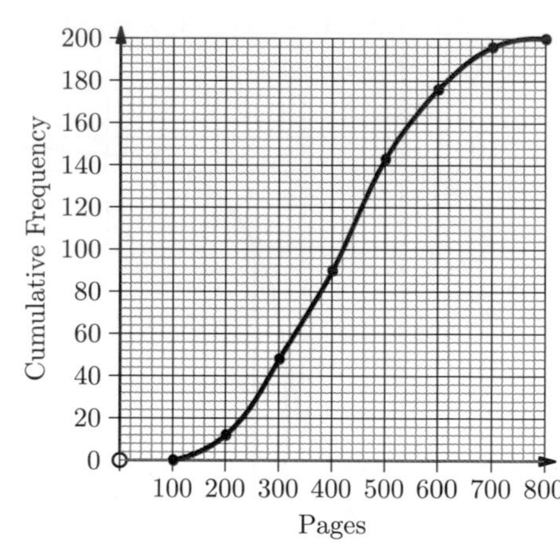

(d) 420 pages
(e) 210 pages
(f) 43%

Exercise 16E

1. (a) (i)

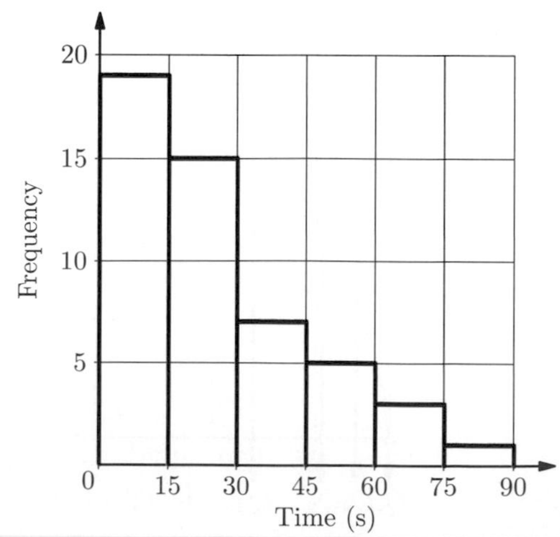

(ii)

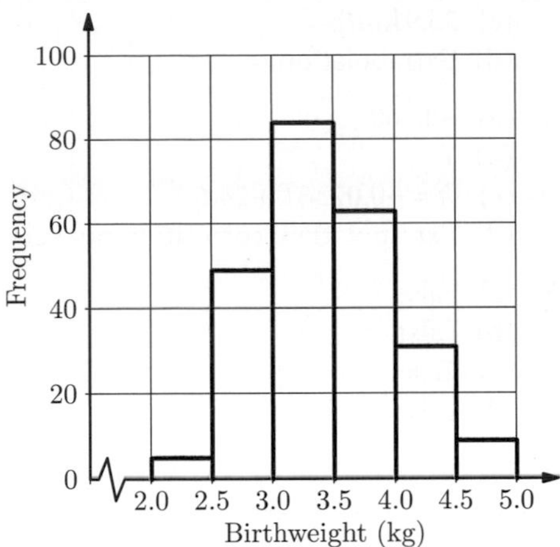

(b) (i)

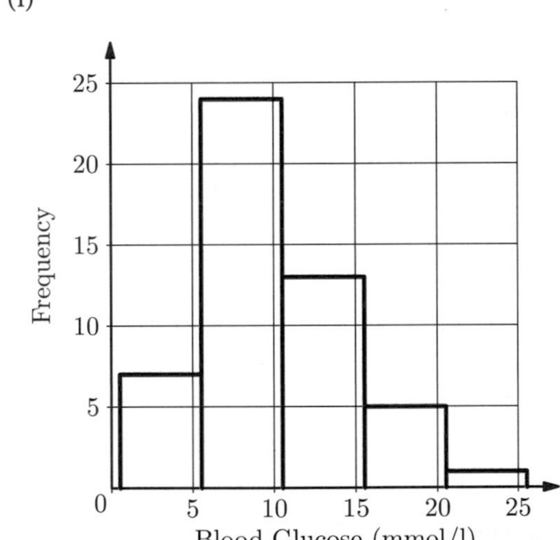

(ii)

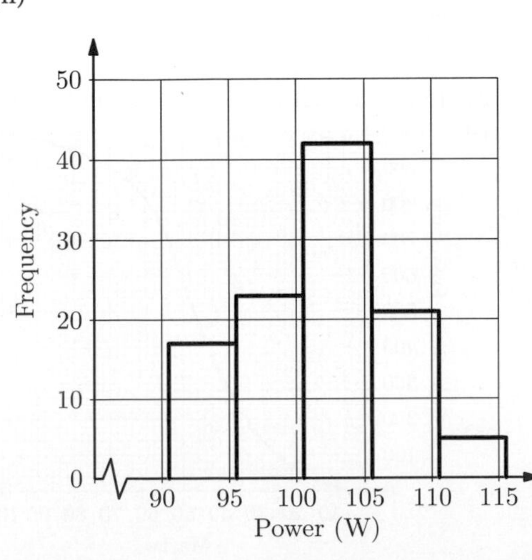

(c) (i)

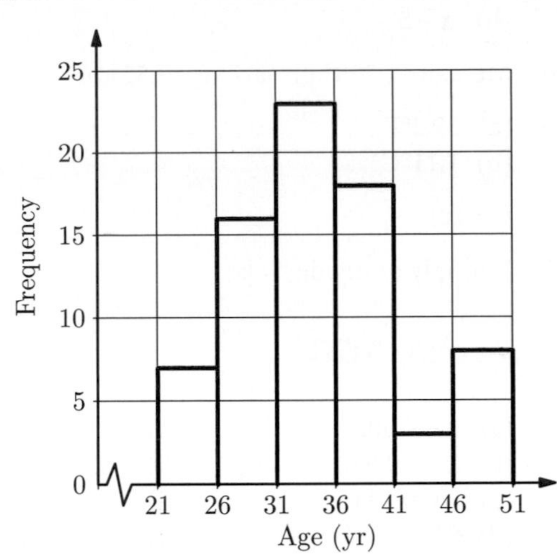

(ii)

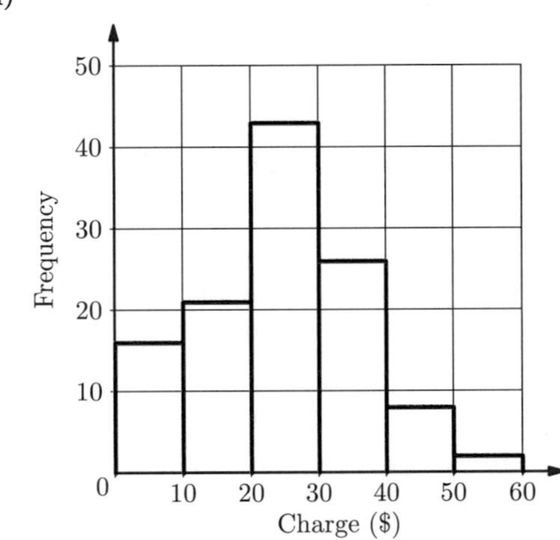

2. A3, B2, C1

3. $\bar{x} = 10, \sigma = 6.71$

Exercise 16F

1. (a) (i) $\bar{y} = 3, \sigma_y = 14$ (ii) $\bar{y} = 17, \sigma_y = 3$

(b) (i) $\bar{y} = 18.6, \sigma_y = 4.8$ (ii) $\bar{y} = 7, \sigma_y = 2$

(c) (i) $\bar{y} = -2, \sigma_y = 5$ (ii) $\bar{y} = 34, \sigma_y = 30$

(d) (i) $\bar{y} = 7, \sigma_y = 12$ (ii) $\bar{y} = 44, \sigma_y = 12$

2. (a) (i) Median 6.3, IQR 2.4
(ii) Median 4.1, IQR 2
(b) (i) Median 22.5, IQR 7.5
(ii) Median 9.6, IQR 7.2
(c) (i) Median 54.6, IQR 16.8
(ii) Median 86, IQR 72

3. (a) $x+1$
   (b) $x-5$

4. Median 11.328 kpl, variance 7.52 kpl^2

5. (a) 39.2°F
   (b) 1.11°C

6. $b = 10a$

7. Multiply or divide by $|x|$

Exercise 16G

1. (a) (i) 0.802 (ii) 0.770
   (b) (i) −0.942 (ii) −0.949
   (c) (i) 0.194 (ii) 0.441
   (d) (i) 1 (ii) −1

2. A: 1
   B: 4
   C: 2
   D: 3

3. (a) 0.990
   (b) There is a strong positive linear relationship.
   (c) No

4. (a) 0.876
   (b) There is a positive correlation.
   (c) Yes, since the claim does not relate to causation.

5. (a) 0.162
   (b) No, e.g. weak correlation, cannot talk about causation, small sample.

6. (a) −0.996
   (b) −0.996

Exercise 16H

1. (a) (i) $y=2.27x-0.489$
   (ii) $y=1.48x+0.296$
   (b) (i) $y=-0.258x+15.1$
   (ii) $y=-0.557x+57.7$
   (c) (i) $y=0.155x+1.98$
   (ii) $y=1.09x-5.37$
   (d) (i) $y=2x+1$
   (ii) $y=-x+10$

2. (a) 400
   (b) Cannot be found

3. (a) 0.962
   (b) d
   (c) 23.9 km/h
   (d) Extrapolation

4. (a) −0.700
   (b) T
   (c) $h=-0.0236T+24.6$
   (d) Extrapolation; correlation not very strong

5. (a) False
   (b) False
   (c) True
   (d) False

6. (a) (i) −0.328 (ii) 0.996
   (b) $y=1.11x^2-3.55$

Mixed examination practice 16

Short questions

1. (a) 24
   (b) 125
   (c) 124

2. (a) α: D, β: B, γ: C
   (b) (i) B (ii) A (iii) C

3. (a) 100
   (b) $a = 55$, $b = 75$

4. (a) $p=10f-100$
   (b) £730
   (c) 6000

5. 17

Long questions

1. (a) 11 cm
   (b) 8, 5, 4
   (c) 11.8 cm

2. (a) 165, 335, 595, 815, 950, 980, 1000
   (b)

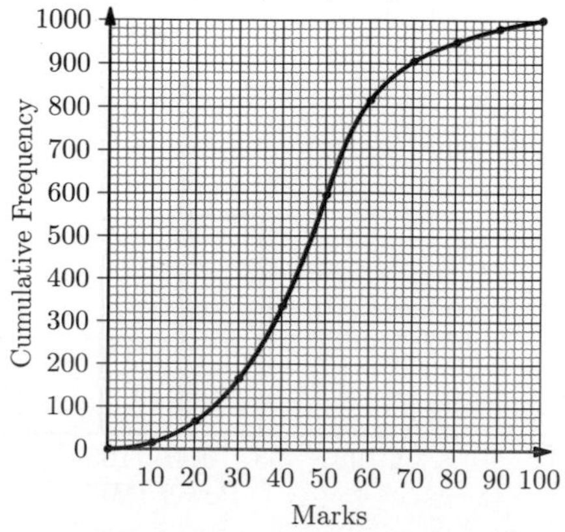

(c) (i) 46
(ii) 240
(iii) 63

3. (a) −0.660
(d) $y = -19.0x + 617$
(e) £617
(f) Extrapolation

4. (a) 0.945
(b) 37
(c) Extrapolation; dependent variable (ice creams sold) should not be used to predict the independent variable (temperature)

Chapter 17

Exercise 17A

1. (a) (i) 0.667 (ii) 0.150
(b) (i) 0.571 (ii) 0.400
(c) (i) 0.429 (ii) 0.100

2. (a) 5 (b) 75

3. 0.672

4. No; it is true only if the same number of bulbs were tested in each study.

Exercise 17B

1. (a) 1, 2, 3, 4, 5, 6
(b) RED, RDE, ERD, EDR, DRE, DER
(c) BBB, BBG, BGB, GBB, BGG, GBG, GGB, GGB (B = boy, G = girl)
(d) 1, 1, 1, 2, 3, 4

2. (a) (i) $\frac{1}{2}$ (ii) $\frac{1}{4}$
(b) (i) $\frac{1}{13}$ (ii) $\frac{4}{13}$
(c) (i) $\frac{18}{52}$ (ii) $\frac{4}{52}$
(d) (i) $\frac{3}{4}$ (ii) $\frac{9}{13}$
(e) (i) $\frac{25}{52}$ (ii) $\frac{44}{52}$
(f) (i) $\frac{10}{52}$ (ii) $\frac{12}{52}$

3. (a) (i) $\frac{6}{15}$ (ii) $\frac{5}{15}$
(b) (i) $\frac{11}{15}$ (ii) $\frac{9}{15}$
(c) (i) $\frac{9}{15}$ (ii) $\frac{10}{15}$
(d) (i) 0 (ii) 1
(e) (i) $\frac{4}{15}$ (ii) $\frac{6}{15}$
(f) (i) $\frac{6}{15}$ (ii) $\frac{11}{15}$
(g) (i) 0 (ii) 0

5. (a) $\frac{5}{36}$ (b) $\frac{22}{36}$
(c) $\frac{6}{36}$ (d) $\frac{7}{36}$
(e) $\frac{12}{36}$ (f) $\frac{14}{36}$

6. (a) $\frac{4}{32}$ (b) $\frac{19}{32}$
(c) $\frac{5}{32}$ (d) $\frac{7}{32}$
(e) $\frac{14}{32}$ (f) $\frac{16}{32}$

7. 115

8. $\frac{10}{216}$

Exercise 17C

1. (a) (i) 0.5 (ii) 1
(b) (i) $\frac{1}{6}$ (ii) 0.05
(c) (i) $\frac{4}{15}$ (ii) 0.2
(d) (i) 0.7 (ii) 0.11

2. (a) (i) $\frac{7}{20}$ (ii) 100%
(b) (i) 27.5% (ii) $\frac{7}{30}$
(c) (i) 55% (ii) 18.3%

3. (a) $P(x > 4)$
(b) $P(y \le 3)$
(c) 0
(d) 1
(e) P(fruit)
(f) P(apple)
(g) P(multiple of 4)
(h) P(rectangle)
(i) P(blue)
(j) $P(\text{blue} \cap \text{red})$

4. 5%
5. 0.4
6. 0.3
7. (a) 0.166
   (b) 0.041

Exercise 17D

1. (a) (i) 0.12 (ii) 0
   (b) (i) 0.24 (ii) 0.24
   (c) (i) $\frac{13}{20}$ (ii) $\frac{3}{4}$
2. $\frac{15}{91}$
3. $\frac{1}{6}$
4. (a) $\frac{19}{27}$
   (b) $\frac{25}{27}$
5. 0.048
6. $\frac{69}{110}$
7. 15 or 21

Exercise 17E

1. (a) (i) 0.21 (ii) $\frac{1}{15}$
   (b) (i) $\frac{15}{28}$ (ii) $\frac{5}{9}$
   (c) (i) 0.496 (ii) 0.4
   (d) (i) $\frac{1}{3}$ (ii) $\frac{4}{9}$
2. (a) (i) Yes (ii) No
   (b) (i) Yes (ii) No
3. (a) 0.3
   (b) 0.54
4. (a) 62.6%
   (b) 2.56%
   (c) 97.4%
5. (a) 0.410
   (b) 0.684

ANSWER HINT
(b) Did you consider the complement?

6. $\frac{14}{15}$

Exercise 17F

1. (a) $P(\text{prime} \cap \text{odd})$
   (b) $P(\text{Senegal} \cup \text{Taiwan})$
   (c) $P(\text{French}|\text{IB})$
   (d) $P(\text{heart}|\text{red})$
   (e) $P(\text{lives in Munich}|\text{German})$
   (f) $P(\text{not black} \cap \text{not white})$
   (g) $P(\text{potato}|\text{not cabbage})$
   (h) $P(\text{red}|\text{red} \cup \text{blue})$
2. (a) (i) $\frac{2}{3}$ (ii) $\frac{15}{28}$
   (b) (i) $\frac{5}{14}$ (ii) $\frac{5}{6}$
3. (a) (i) 0.1
   (b) $\frac{1}{6}$
4. (a) $\frac{1}{3}$
   (b) $\frac{7}{15}$
5. (a) $\frac{149}{240} = 0.621$
   (b) $\frac{125}{149} = 0.839$
6. (a) $\frac{64}{75} = 0.853$
   (b) $\frac{5}{32} = 0.156$
7. (a) $\frac{72}{160} = 0.45$
   (b) $\frac{9}{44} = 0.205$
8. (a) $\frac{2}{3}$
   (b) $\frac{4}{5}$
9. $\frac{4}{9}$
10. $\frac{1}{6}$

Exercise 17G

1. (a)

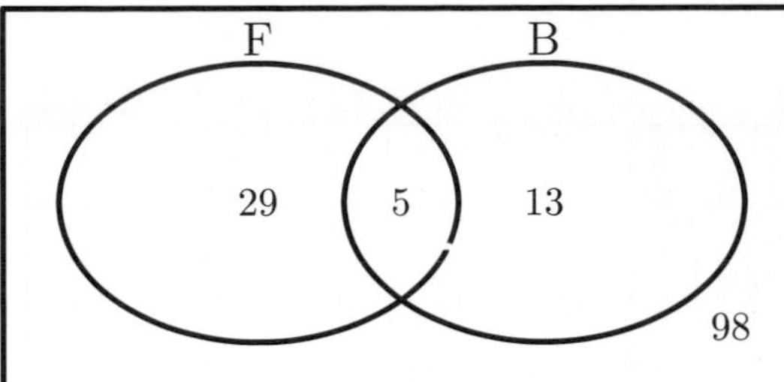

(b) 98

(c) $\frac{18}{145}$

(d) $\frac{5}{34}$

2. (a)

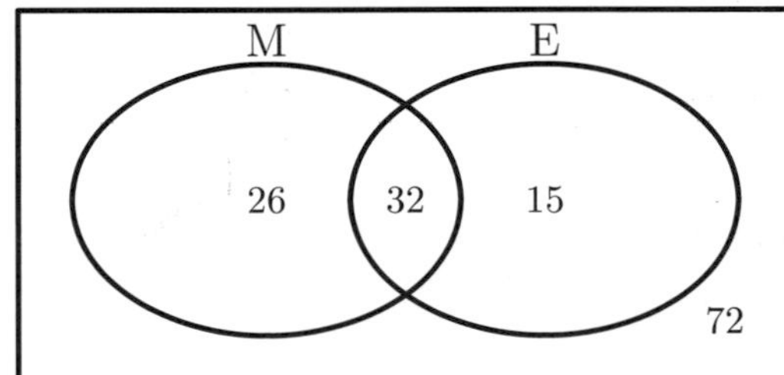

(b) 32

(c) $\frac{16}{29}$

3. (a) where C = chilli con carne, V = vegetable curry, B = spaghetti bolognese

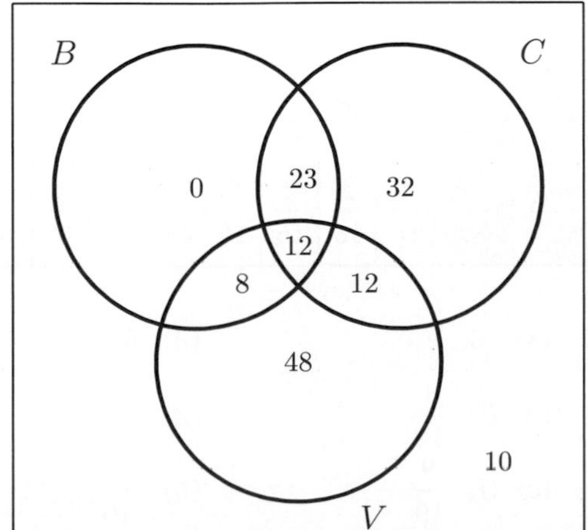

(b) 0
(c) 79

(d) $\frac{16}{29}$

(e) $\frac{3}{5}$

(f) $\frac{11}{29}$

4. (a)

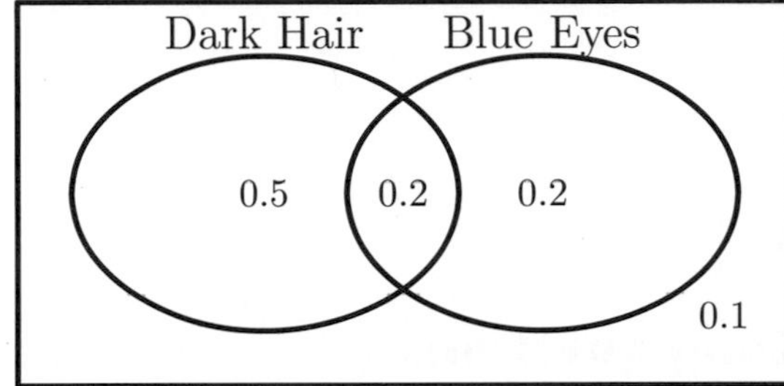

(b) 0.1

(c) $\frac{2}{7}$

(d) $\frac{2}{3}$

(e) No: $P(B \cap D) = 0.2, P(B)P(D) = 0.28$

5. (a) 0.3
(b)

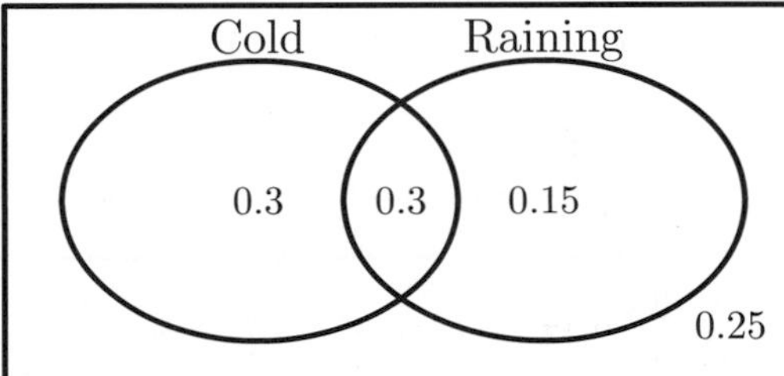

(c) $\frac{1}{3}$

(d) $\frac{3}{8}$

(e) No: $P(R \cap C) = 0.3$, $P(C)P(R) = 0.27$

Exercise 17H

1. $\frac{5}{14}$
2. 0.580
3. $\frac{9}{25}$
4. $\frac{5}{9}$

5. Without, because $\frac{13}{25} > \frac{1}{2}$

6. (b) 18

Mixed examination practice 17

Short questions

1. 0.320

2. 0.8

3. $\frac{1}{9} = 0.111$

4. $\frac{1}{3}$

Long questions

1. (a) $\frac{14}{95}$

   (c) 0.138

   (d) 0.356

2. (a) $0 \le P(X) \le 1$

   (b) $P(A) - P(B|A)P(A)$

3. (a)

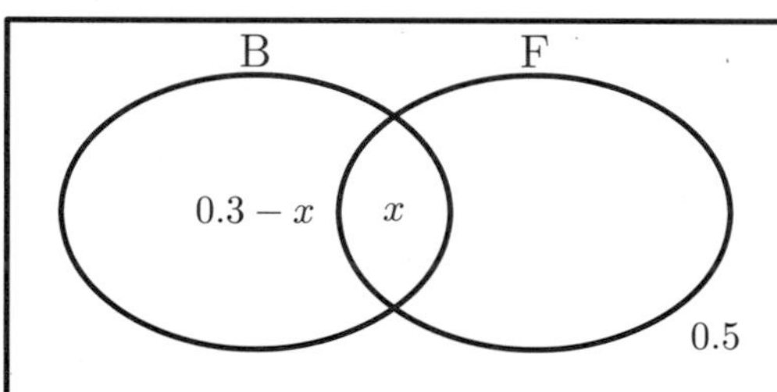

   (b) 0.2

   (c) 0.2

   (d) 0.1

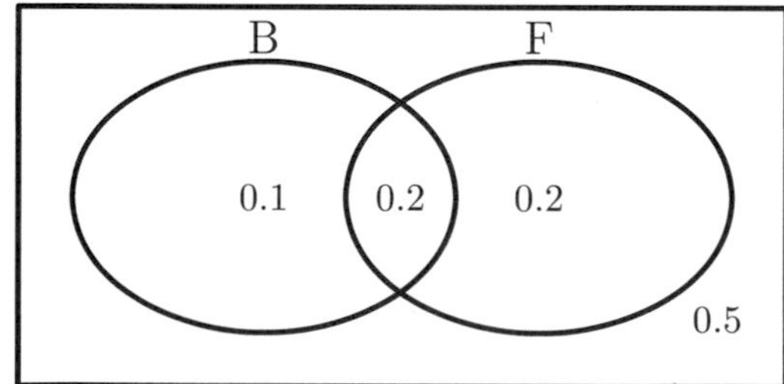

   (e) $\frac{1}{3}$

4. (a) (i) $\frac{5}{36}$ (ii) $\frac{25}{216}$ (iii) $\left(\frac{1}{6}\right)\left(\frac{5}{6}\right)^{2(n-1)}$

   (c) $\frac{5}{11}$

   (d) 0.432

Chapter 18

Exercise 18A

1. (a)

w	0	1	2	3	4
$P(W = w)$	$\frac{1}{16}$	$\frac{4}{16}$	$\frac{6}{16}$	$\frac{4}{16}$	$\frac{1}{16}$

   (b)

d	0	1	2	3	4	5
$P(D = d)$	$\frac{6}{36}$	$\frac{10}{36}$	$\frac{8}{36}$	$\frac{6}{36}$	$\frac{4}{36}$	$\frac{2}{36}$

   (c)

x	1	2	3	4	6
$P(X = x)$	$\frac{1}{6}$	$\frac{2}{6}$	$\frac{1}{6}$	$\frac{1}{6}$	$\frac{1}{6}$

   (d)

g	1	2	3
$P(G = g)$	$\frac{6}{72}$	$\frac{36}{72}$	$\frac{30}{72}$

   (e)

c	1	2	3	4
$P(C = c)$	$\frac{1}{4}$	$\frac{3}{16}$	$\frac{9}{64}$	$\frac{27}{64}$

   (f)

x	1	2	3	4	6	8	9	12	16
$P(X = x)$	$\frac{1}{16}$	$\frac{2}{16}$	$\frac{2}{16}$	$\frac{3}{16}$	$\frac{2}{16}$	$\frac{2}{16}$	$\frac{1}{16}$	$\frac{2}{16}$	$\frac{1}{16}$

2. (a) (i) $\frac{1}{8}$ (ii) 0

   (b) (i) $\frac{1}{10}$ (ii) $\frac{12}{25}$

   (c) (i) $\frac{9}{10}$ (ii) $\frac{1}{10}$

3. 0.207

Exercise 18B

1. (a) (i) 2 (ii) 9
   (b) (i) $\frac{36}{14} = 2.57$ (ii) 3

2. (b) 4.4

3. 14

4. (b) $\frac{32}{18}$

5. (a) $\frac{1}{10}$
   (b) 2

6. $\frac{13}{6}$

7. $p = 0.5, q = 0.2$

8. 40

9. (a)

Profit ($)	$-n$	$1-n$	$2n$	$3n$
Probability	$\frac{27}{64}$	$\frac{27}{64}$	$\frac{9}{64}$	$\frac{1}{64}$

   (b) $0.82

Exercise 18C

1. (a) (i) 0.147 (ii) 0.0459
   (b) (i) 0.944 (ii) 0.797
   (c) (i) 0.0563 (ii) 0.0104
   (d) (i) 0.990 (ii) 0.797
   (e) (i) 0.203 (ii) 0.832
   (f) (i) 0.0562 (ii) 0.776

2. (a) (i) $\frac{5}{32}$ (ii) $\frac{1}{32}$
   (b) (i) $\frac{31}{32}$ (ii) $\frac{6}{32}$
   (c) (i) $\frac{1}{32}$ (ii) $\frac{26}{32}$

3. (a) (i) $E(Y) = 10$, $Var(Y) = 9$
   (ii) $E(X) = 8$, $Var(X) = 4$
   (b) (i) $E(X) = 4.5$, $Var(X) = 3.15$
   (ii) $E(Y) = 7$, $Var(Y) = 4.55$
   (c) (i) $E(Z) = \frac{n-1}{n}, Var(Z) = \left(\frac{n-1}{n}\right)^2$
   (ii) $E(X) = 2, Var(X) = \frac{2(n-2)}{n}$

4. (a) 0.238
   (b) 0.181
   (c) 0.5

5. (a) The students in the sample may not be independent of each other (e.g. siblings) or sampling without replacement.
   (b) 0.103

6. 2700

7. (a) 0.0231
   (b) 2
   (c) 1.5
   (d) 0.0273

8. (a) 0.108
   (b) 0.0267
   (c) e.g. The probability that a person going to the doctor has the virus is the same as for the general population of the country.

9. 0.4

10. The second (because 0.0165 > 0.0154)

12. (a) $0.16\binom{n}{2}(0.6)^{n-2}$
    (b) 10

ANSWER HINT 12(b)
To solve this, you need to try some values of n or use tables on your calculator.

13. 0.14, 0.20

14. 0.494, 0.700

Exercise 18D

1. (a) (i) 0.885 (ii) 0.212
   (b) (i) 0.401 (ii) 0.878
   (c) (i) 0.743 (ii) 0.191
   (d) (i) 0.807 (ii) 0.748
   (e) (i) 0.451 (ii) 0.689

2. (a) (i) 0.5 (ii) 1
   (b) (i) −1.67 (ii) −0.4

3. (a) (i) $P(Z < 1.6)$ (ii) $P(Z < 1.28)$
   (b) (i) $P(Z \geq -0.68)$ (ii) $P(Z \geq -2.96)$

(c) (i) $P(-1.4 < Z < 0.2)$
(ii) $P(-2.36 \le Z \le -0.2)$

4. (a) 1.16
(b) 0.123

5. 1547

6. (a) 0.278
(b) (i) 0.127 (ii) 0.334

7. (a) 0.160 (b) 0.171 (c) 0.727

8. (a) 0.707 (b) 0.663

9. (a) 0.673 (b) 0.314

10. (a) 0.952 (b) 0.838

11. (a) 0.841 (b) 0.811

12. 0.640

Exercise 18E

1. (a) (i) 19.9 (ii) 13.3
(b) (i) 32.4 (ii) 37.3
(c) (i) 2.34 (ii) 4.44

2. (a) (i) 5.68 (ii) 7.32
(b) (i) 43.4 (ii) 15.3

3. (a) (i) $\mu = 8.91, \sigma = 2.27$
(ii) $\mu = 129.8, \sigma = 38.6$
(b) (i) $\mu = -0.201, \sigma = 1.19$
(ii) $\mu = 870, \sigma = 202$

4. 141

5. 3.61 kg

6. 1.97 cm

7. (a) 0.691
(b) 39.7
(c) 0.240

8. 99.7%

9. (a) $\mu = 1.29$ mm, $\sigma = 0.554$ cm
(b) $\mu = 1.36$ mm, $\sigma = 0.764$ cm

Mixed examination practice 18

Short questions

1. 0.261
2. 55
3. (a) 6.68%
(b) 82

4. (a) 4.8
(b) 0.0834

5. 0.149

6. (a) 0.232
(b) 0.894

7. (a) 0.0296
(b) 0.000244

8. $\mu = 31.4°, \sigma = 4.52°$

9. (a) 15
(b) 0.273

Long questions

1. (a) 2.5
(b) 0.0162
(c) 0.756
(d) 2
(e) It stays constant at 0.25

2. (a) 0.460
(b) $1 - (0.95)^n$
(c) 32

3. (a) (i) $\frac{1}{9}$ (ii) $\frac{1}{81}$

(b) (i) 0.113 (ii) 0.444
(c) (ii)

x	3	4	5
$P(X = x)$	$\frac{65}{1296}$	$\frac{175}{1296}$	$\frac{369}{1296}$

(iii) $\frac{6797}{1296} = 5.24$ *[13 marks]*

Chapter 19

Short questions

1. $\frac{5}{36}$

2. 4

3.

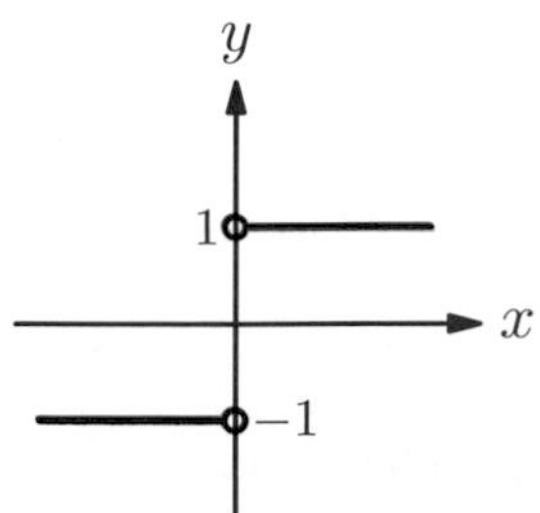

4. $\frac{1}{3}x^3+x^2+C$

5. $\frac{a(r^n-1)}{n(r-1)}$

6. $\frac{11}{12}$

7. $\frac{\sqrt[10]{e}}{2\sqrt[10]{27}}$

8. Translation by $\begin{pmatrix}\frac{\pi}{2}\\1\end{pmatrix}$

9. (a) $\frac{1}{k}$ (b) $\begin{pmatrix}0\\\ln k\end{pmatrix}$

10. (a) $\frac{2047}{1024}$ (b) $-55\ln 2$

11. $\frac{3}{64}$

12. $y=1.86$

13. $-0.618<x<1.62$

14. $\sqrt{13}$

15. (b) $\frac{1}{6}\left(\frac{5}{6}\right)^{r-1}$

16. $\ln 2$

17. $\frac{2\pi l^3}{9\sqrt{3}}$

18. (a) $\pi-2\theta$ (b) $4\cos^2\theta$

19. (a) $\ln\left(\frac{x-3}{x}\right)$ (b) $\frac{3}{1-e^x}$

20. (a) Vertical stretch with scale factor 2
(b) Vertical stretch with scale factor $\frac{1}{\ln 10}$ $(=\log_{10}e)$

21. $\frac{1}{5}$

22. (b) 0

23. $\frac{\theta}{1-\cos\theta}$

24. (a) $x=\ln\left(\frac{y\pm\sqrt{y^2-4}}{2}\right)$

25. $\left(\frac{1}{2}e^2-2e+\frac{5}{2}\right)\pi$

26. 3, 11

27. $\frac{3}{2}$

Long questions

1. (a) $\frac{1}{5}$ (b) $\frac{4}{25}$
(c) $\frac{16}{125}$ (e) $\frac{4}{9}$
(f) $\frac{1}{2}$

2. (a) 6 (b) -7

3. (a) $2+\cos 2x-\frac{1}{\cos^2 x}$

4. (a) $\frac{1}{3}$
(b) $k=1$
(d) 0.095

5. (b) $\frac{6}{17}$
(c) 0.443

6. (a) (ii) $x=3$
(iii) (3, 2)
(b) $\left(-\frac{1}{2},0\right),\left(0,-\frac{1}{3}\right)$
(c)

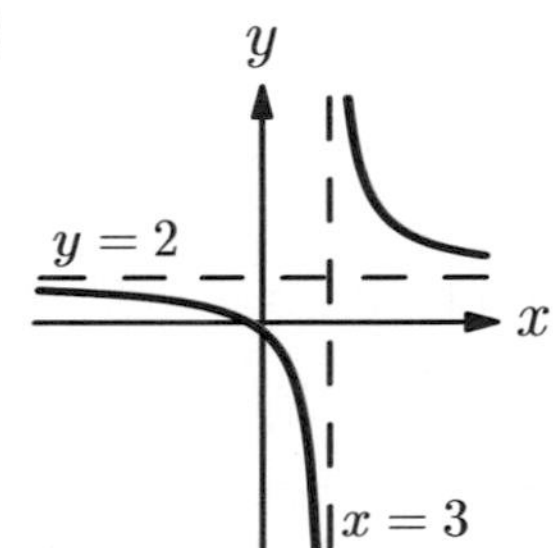

(d) $y=-7x+37$
(e) $(2,-5)$

7. (a) $y=\frac{1}{e}x$

8. (a) 2π
(b) $[-0.4, 0.4]$
(c) (i) $2\sin x\cos^2 x-\sin^3 x$
(iii) $\frac{2\sqrt{3}}{9}$
(d) $\frac{\pi}{2}$

(e) (i) $\frac{1}{3}\sin^3 x + c$

(ii) $\frac{1}{3}$

(f) 0.491

9. (a) (i) $10x + 1 - e^{2x}$

(ii) $\frac{\ln 5}{2} = 0.805$

(b) (i) $f^{-1}(x) = \frac{\ln(x-1)}{2}$

(c) $\int_0^{\ln 2} \pi(1 + e^{2x})^2 \, dx$

10. (a) $f^{-1}(x) = \frac{x+5}{3}$

(b) $3x - 3$

(c) $x = \frac{3}{2}$

(d) (i)

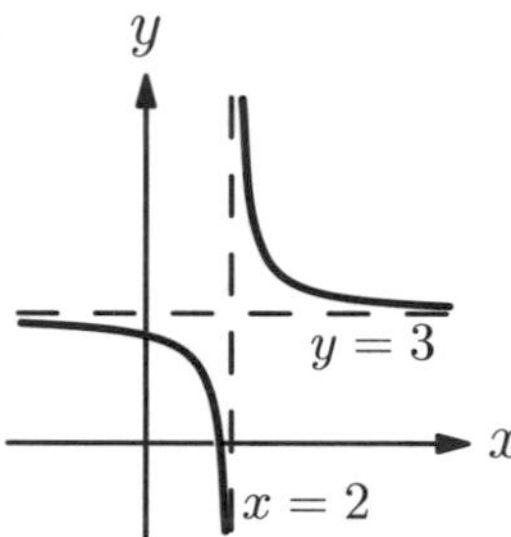

(ii) $x = 2, y = 3$

(e) (i) $3x + \ln(x-2) + c$

(ii) $6 + \ln 3$

(f)

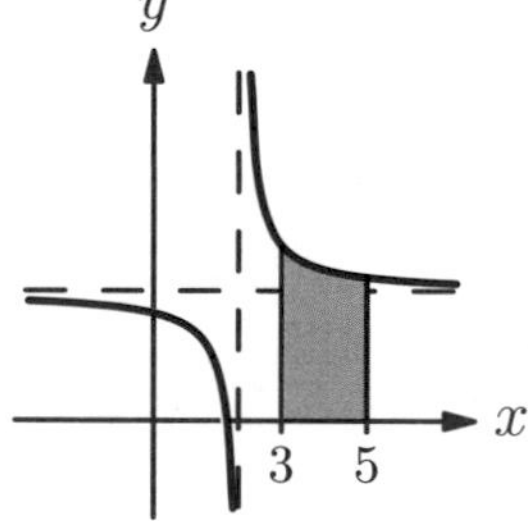

11. (a) $\frac{qa + pb}{p + q}$

(b)

(c) q should be even

Glossary

	Definition	Example
acceleration	The rate of change of velocity with respect to time.	An object falling under the influence of gravity has a constant acceleration: $a = \frac{\mathrm{d}v}{\mathrm{d}t}$
amplitude	The distance from the centre of an oscillation to an extreme point; often found by calculating half of the distance between the maximum and minimum values.	$y = 4\sin 3x$ has amplitude 4.
angle of depression	The angle below the horizontal.	A ship is observed at an angle of depression of $48°$ from a cliff top.
angle of elevation	The angle above the horizontal.	The top of a tower forms an angle of elevation of $16°$ from a point 30 m away.
arc	Part of the circumference of a circle between two points. For each pair of points on the circle there are two arcs: the larger is called the major arc; the smaller is called the minor arc.	The minor arc in the diagram has length $\frac{\pi}{3}$.
arcsin, arccos and arctan	The inverse functions of sine, cosine and tangent; they are useful for solving trigonometric equations.	$\arcsin\left(\frac{1}{2}\right) = \frac{\pi}{6}$
argument	An expression used as the input to a function.	The argument of $\cos(3x+1)$ is $3x+1$.
arithmetic sequence or **arithmetic progression**	A sequence in which the difference between consecutive terms is constant.	$3, 7, 11, 15, \ldots$ is an arithmetic sequence.
asymptote	An asymptote is a straight line which the graph approaches as either x or y gets very large.	The graph $y = \frac{1}{x-2}$ has asymptotes $x = 2$ and $y = 0$.
background level	The value that a function will approach after a sufficiently long time that the effect of any intervention has become negligible.	A model predicts that the temperature will drop to a background level of 25°C.
base	The number which is being multiplied with itself a certain number of times.	The base in $(xy)^5$ is xy.
base vectors	A set of vectors which can be used to describe other vectors.	In three dimensions we conventionally use the base vectors $\boldsymbol{i}, \boldsymbol{j}$ and $\boldsymbol{k}$.
bimodal	A probability distribution or data set which has two modes.	The data set 1, 1, 1, 3, 4, 4, 4 is bimodal.

binomial

Containing two terms.

$a+x$ is a binomial expression.

binomial coefficient $\binom{n}{r}$

A coefficient containing the term $a^{n-r}b^r$ in the expansion of $(a+b)^n$, usually denoted by $\binom{n}{r}$.

10 is a binomial coefficient in the expansion of $(1+x)^5$.

binomial distribution

A common distribution modelling the number of 'successes' occurring in a situation with a fixed number of independent trials and a constant probability of success.

The number of heads obtained when ten fair coins are tossed follows the binomial distribution $B(10, 0.5)$.

binomial theorem or **binomial expansion**

A formula for expanding $(a+b)^n$ into $n+1$ terms.

The first three terms in the binomial expansion of $(2x-3y)^5$ are $32x^5 - 240x^4y + 720x^3y^2$.

bivariate

Data consisting of paired measurements of two separate variables, both taken from the same source.

The following is a set of bivariate data collected from four students in a class:

Height (cm)	157	163	171	174
IB score	35	39	34	42

box and whisker plot

A diagram showing the median, lower and upper quartiles, and minimum and maximum values of a set of data.

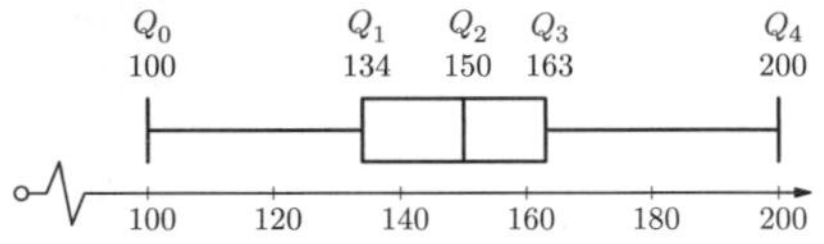

chain rule

A rule for differentiating composite functions:

$$\frac{dy}{dx} = \frac{dy}{du} \times \frac{du}{dx}$$

The derivative of $\sin x^2$ with respect to x can be found using the chain rule with a substitution $u = x^2$ to get $2x\cos x^2$.

change-of-base rule

A rule for converting logarithms to different bases.

$\log x$ can be converted into $\frac{\ln x}{\ln 10}$ using the change-of-base rule.

chord

A line connecting two points on a curve.

A chord connecting two points is always shorter than the minor arc between those two points.

coefficient

A number multiplying an algebraic expression.

The coefficient of x^2 in $5x^2+3$ is 5.

column vector

A vector described by its components written vertically.

$2\boldsymbol{i}+3\boldsymbol{j}$ can be written as the column vector $\begin{pmatrix} 2 \\ 3 \end{pmatrix}$.

complement

All relevant events other than the event in question.

The complement of rolling a 6 on a die is rolling a $1, 2, 3, 4$ or 5.

completed square form

A quadratic expression written in the form $a(x-h)^2+k$.

The completed square form is convenient for finding the vertex, which has coordinates (h, k).

component	The amount of displacement of a vector in the direction of a base vector.	The component of $\begin{pmatrix} 3 \\ 4 \\ -1 \end{pmatrix}$ in the $\boldsymbol{k}$ direction is -1.
composite function	A function applied to another function.	$fg(x) = \sin(x^2)$ is a composite function.
compound interest	Increasing an amount by a given ratio over a specific period of time, usually in a financial context.	If \$1000 was invested in a bank account at a rate of 5% interest compounded annually, the account balance will be \$1050 after one year.
concave-up or **concave-down**	A description of whether a graph is bending upwards or downwards, i.e. whether the gradient is increasing or decreasing. For example, a concave-up graph might look like 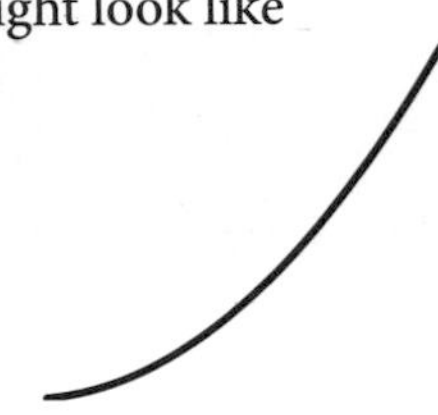 and a concave-down graph might look like 	The graph $y = x^3$ is concave-down when $x < 0$ and concave-up when $x > 0$.
conditional probability	The probability of an event occurring given that another event has occurred.	The conditional probability P (getting an ace on the second card | first card was an ace) is $\frac{3}{51}$.
constant of integration	A constant which reflects the fact that many different functions differentiate to give a particular function.	If you say that the integral of $\cos x$ is $\sin x$, then you are forgetting the constant of integration.
continuous	May take any value in a given interval.	Height is a continuous variable.
continuous random variable	A random variable which can take any value in a given interval.	The weight of a hamster is a continuous random variable.
convergent series	Where the sum of a sequence gets closer and closer to a particular number.	The sequence $\frac{1}{2}, -\frac{1}{3}, \frac{1}{4}, -\frac{1}{5}$ is convergent; it converges to zero.
correlation	A measure of association between two variables.	The height and weight of a person tend to be positively correlated.
cosine	A fundamental trigonometric function, often abbreviated to 'cos'; can be defined as the x-coordinate of a point on the unit circle.	$\cos\frac{\pi}{6} = \frac{\sqrt{3}}{2}$

cosine rule	A rule linking side lengths and angles in any triangle: $c^2 = a^2 + b^2 - 2ab\cos C$; $\cos C = \dfrac{a^2 + b^2 - c^2}{2ab}$	The cosine rule can be used to find the angles in a triangle when all of the side lengths are known.
cumulative frequency	The number of data items up to and including a certain value.	For the grouped data (see table below) the cumulative frequency corresponding to the data value '166.5' is 35.
cumulative probability	The probability of a random variable being less than or equal to a particular value.	If X is a binomially distributed random variable, the cumulative probability $\mathrm{P}(X \le 2)$ equals $\mathrm{P}(X=0)+\mathrm{P}(X=1)+\mathrm{P}(X=2)$.
deductive rule	A rule for generating terms of a sequence based on each term's position in the sequence.	$u_n = n^3 - 1$ is a deductive rule.
definite integration	Integration with limits; the result is a definite value.	$\int_0^1 e^x \,dx = e - 1$
degree	A unit for measuring angles: 1 degree or 1° is $\dfrac{1}{360}$ of a full rotation.	A right angle is 90°.
dependent variable	A variable that is not controlled directly in an experiment or survey.	In an experiment to determine whether petrol consumption is affected by the speed at which a car is driven, the dependent variable is the petrol consumption.
derivative	A function which gives the gradient of (the graph of) another function at every point of its domain.	The derivative of $3x^2 + 2$ is $6x$.
difference	The result of subtracting two numbers.	21 and 7 have a difference of 14.
differentiation	The process of finding the derivative of a function.	If we differentiate $\sin 2x$, we get $2\cos 2x$.
differentiation from first principles	Finding the derivative of a function by considering the limit of gradients of smaller and smaller chords.	The general formula for differentiation from first principles is $\lim\limits_{h\to 0}\dfrac{f(x+h)-f(x)}{h}$.
discrete	Restricted to fixed values in a given domain.	Shoe size is a discrete variable.

Height (cm)	Frequency
155–160	13
161–166	22
167–172	11

discriminant (Δ)	An expression which determines the number of solutions to a quadratic equation: $\Delta < 0 \rightarrow$ no solutions; $\Delta = 1 \rightarrow$ 1 solution; $\Delta > 0 \rightarrow$ two solutions	The discriminant of $x^2 + x + 12 = 0$ is negative, the equation has no solutions.
displacement	1. Displacement vector: A vector quantity representing the position of a point relative to another, i.e. the distance and direction from one point to another.	A ship has a displacement of $\begin{pmatrix} 3 \\ 6 \end{pmatrix}$ km relative to the lighthouse.
	2. In kinematics: How for something is away from the origin.	In a 400 metre race where the start and finish line are in the same place, an athlete's displacement upon finishing the race is 0 m.
displacement vector	A vector that represents how to get from one point to another; the displacement vector from point A to point B is written as $\overrightarrow{AB}$.	If A, B and C are three points, then $\overrightarrow{AC} = \overrightarrow{AB} + \overrightarrow{BC}$.
distance	In kinematics, the distance is how much ground is covered.	In a 400-metre race, an athlete runs a distance of 400 m.
divergent sequence	A sequence which does not get closer and closer to a particular number.	The sequence $1, 4, 9, 16, 25, \ldots$ is divergent.
domain	The set of all allowed input values of a function.	The domain of $f(x) = \sqrt{x+2}$ is $x \geq -2$.
doubleangle formula	An identity which expresses a trigonometric function involving 2θ in terms of trigonometric functions involving θ.	$\sin 2x = 2 \sin x \cos x$ is a double-angle formula.
equation	Two expressions which are equal for some values of the variable.	$x^2 = 9$ is an equation.
expectation	The expected mean of a probability distribution.	The following probability distribution has expectation $E(X) = 1.25$.

X	0	1	2
p	0.25	0.25	0.5

exponent form	A number or expression written in the form of a base raised to an exponent.	The exponent form of 32 is 2^5.
exponent or **power**	The number of times the base is multiplied together.	The exponent of x in x^7 is 7.
exponential decay	Something that can be modelled by a negative exponential function.	The mass of a radioactive isotope exhibits exponential decay.
exponential growth	Something that can be modelled by a positive exponential function.	A population of bacteria grows exponentially.
expression	A combination of numbers, variables and mathematical operations, containing no equals or inequality signs.	$\sin\left(\sqrt{x+3}\right)$ is an expression.

extrapolating or **extrapolation**	Estimating the value of the dependent variable corresponding to a value of the independent variable that lies outside the range of data.	For the data above, using the regression line to estimate the weight when the height is 181 is extrapolation.
factorised form	An expression written as a product of (usually) linear factors.	A quadratic function $y = a(x - p)(x - q)$ has zeros at $x = p$ and $x = q$.
function	A rule telling us how to calculate an output value given an input value.	$f: x \mapsto \sqrt{x+2}$ is a function.
geometric sequence or **geometric progression**	A sequence in which the ratio between consecutive terms is constant.	$3, 6, 12, 24, \ldots$ is a geometric progression.
gradient	The steepness of a line, measured as how far up it goes for each shift of one unit to the right.	The gradient of the line $y = 3x + 2$ is 3.
grouped data	A data set in which subsets of the original data values have been grouped together.	The following table shows a set of grouped data: (see table below)
growth factor	The factor that a function increases by (above the background level) when the independent variable increases by one unit.	The function $R = 12 \times 1.05^{2t}$ has a growth factor of 1.1025.
horizontal asymptote	A horizontal line of the form $y = a$ which a curve approaches.	$y = \frac{10x}{2x-3}$ has a horizontal asymptote $y = 5$.
hyperbola	A graph consisting of two curves which approach asymptotes and are mirror images of each other.	The graph $y = \frac{1}{x}$ is a hyperbola.
identity	Two expressions which are equal for every possible value of the variable.	$x^2 = x \times x$ is an identity.
identity function	The function which leaves its input unchanged, i.e. one whose output is exactly the same as its input.	The composite functions $f \circ f^{-1}$ and $f^{-1} \circ f$ are both equal to the identity function.
indefinite integration	Integration without limits; the result is a function plus a constant of integration.	$\int e^x \mathrm{d}x = e^x + c$
independent events	Two events whose probabilities are not affected by the outcome of each other.	A person's telephone number and the number of their house are independent events.

Grouped data example:

Weight of plants (g)	Frequency
[50,100[	17
[100,200[	23
[200,300[	42
[300,500[	21
[500,1000[	5

independent variable — A variable that we can control in an experiment or survey. — In an experiment to measure how the amount of sleep affects exam results, the independent variable is the number of hours of sleep.

initial value — The value of a function at time zero. — The speed of a car takes an initial value of $3\,\mathrm{m\,s^{-1}}$.

inner function — The function $g(x)$ in a composite function $f(x)=h(g(x))$, i.e. the function that is applied first. — The composite function $f(x)=\sin(x^2)$ has inner function $x \mapsto x^2$.

integration — The reverse process to differentiation. — The integral of x^{-1} with respect to x is $\ln x + c$.

integration by substitution — A method for turning one integral into another (easier) integral. — The integral of xe^{x^2} with respect to x can be found using the substitution $u=x^2$.

interpolating or **interpolation** — Estimating the value of the dependent variable corresponding to a value of the independent variable within the range of data already collected. — If we use the regression line $y=0.696x-57.4$ found from the data

Height (x)	151	153	158	161	161	172
Weight (y)	48	52	50	55	52	64

to estimate the weight when height is 157, we are interpolating.

interquartile range — A measure of how spread out the data is: the length of the interval covering the central 50% of values in the data set, calculated as the difference between the lower and the upper quartiles. — The interquartile range (IQR) of 1, 1, 4, 6, 8, 10, 12 is 9.

intersection — The combined event corresponding to two events both occurring. — The intersection of odd numbers less than 6 and prime numbers less than 6 is $\{3, 5\}$.

inverse function — A function which undoes the action of another function. — Finding the cube root is the inverse of cubing.

inverse normal distribution — A function which turns a cumulative probability into a Z-score; often denoted by $\Phi^{-1}(x)$. — In a normal distribution, the values in the top 20% are at least $\Phi^{-1}(0.8)=0.842$ standard deviations above the mean.

kinematics — The study of the movement of objects. — One important rule of kinematics is that the area under a graph of velocity against time gives the displacement.

limits of integration — The points between which a function is integrated in a definite integral. — The limits of the integral $\int_0^1 e^x \mathrm{d}x$ are 0 and 1.

line of best fit or **regression line**

A straight line modelling the relationship between two variables.

For the set of data

Height (x)	151	153	158	161	161	172
Weight (y)	48	52	50	55	52	64

the regression line has equation

$$y = 0.696x - 57.4$$

local maximum

A point around which the graph looks like

The graph $y = x^3 - 12x + 7$ has a local maximum at $(-2, 23)$.

local minimum

A point around which the graph looks like

The graph $y = x^3 - 12x + 7$ has a local minimum at $(2, 9)$.

logarithm to base *a* ($x = \log_a b$)

The answer to the question 'what power of the base a is this number?'

The logarithm to base 2 of 32 is 5.

lower interval boundary

Smallest possible value that data in a given group can take. This value is used in drawing histograms and cumulative frequency graphs.

In the group [100, 120[the lower interval boundary is 100. When heights have been rounded to the nearest cm, the group '155-160 has lower interval boundary of 154.5.

lower quartile

The value one quarter of the way up a list of data arranged in ascending order.

The lower quartile (LQ or Q_1) of 1, 1, 4, 6, 8, 10, 12 is 1.

magnitude

The size of a vector; the magnitude of a vector $\boldsymbol{v}$ is usually denoted by $|\boldsymbol{v}|$.

The magnitude of a velocity vector is the speed.

mean

An average found by dividing the sum of a set of data values by the number of data values in the set.

The mean of 6, 3 and 3 is 4.

median

An average found by identifying the central value of the data set when the data items are arranged in order.

The median of 6, 3 and 3 is 3.

mid-interval value

The mean of the upper and lower interval boundaries.

The mid-interval value of the group '155–160' is 157.5. Mid-interval values are used to estimate the mean of grouped data.

mode

An average found by identifying the most frequently occurring data item.

The mode of 6, 3 and 3 is 3.

modelling

Describing a real-world situation in terms of mathematical functions.

Tides can be modelled by a sine function.

negative exponential

A curve of the form $ka^x + c$ which is decreasing as x increases.

$y = \left(\frac{1}{2}\right)^x$ is a negative exponential curve.

normal — A line intersecting a graph such that it is perpendicular to the tangent at the point of intersection. — The normal to $y=x^2$ at $x=1$ is $y=\frac{1}{2}(3-x)$.

normal distribution — A common distribution modelling many naturally occurring continuous random variables. — The arm span of adults follows a normal distribution.

origin — A fixed reference point in space. — The origin is at the intersection of the x and y axes.

outer function — The function $h(x)$ in a composite function $f(x)=h(g(x))$. — The composite function $f(x)=\sin(x^2)$ has outer function $x \mapsto \sin x$.

outlier — An observation which is unusually large or small. — Usain Bolt's 100 m time record is an outlier.

parabola — The shape of the graph of a quadratic function. It has a single vertex (turning point) and a vertical line of symmetry. — The curve $y=x^2+4$ is a parabola.

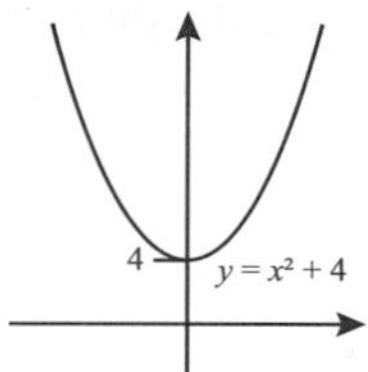

parallel — Lines or vectors which point in the same or opposite direction. — The vectors $\boldsymbol{i}-3\boldsymbol{j}$ and $6\boldsymbol{j}-2\boldsymbol{i}$ are parallel.

period — The interval between consecutive repeating units of a periodic function. — The period of $\cos 2x$ is π.

periodic function — A function whose graph repeats itself regularly. — $\sin(3x)+2$ is a periodic function.

point of inflexion — A place where a graph changes from concave-up to concave-down or vice versa. — The graph $y=x^3+3x^2-2x+1$ has a point of inflexion at $(-1,5)$.

position vector — A vector which represents displacement relative to the origin. — The point A(1, 2) has position vector $\begin{pmatrix}1\\2\end{pmatrix}$.

positive exponential — A curve of the form ka^x+c which is increasing as x increases. — $y=3^x$ is a positive exponential curve.

probability — A number between 0 and 1 (inclusive) which represents the likelihood of an event occurring. — When tossing a fair coin, the probability of getting a head is $\frac{1}{2}$.

probability distribution — A list of all possible outcomes of a random variable along with their probabilities. — The probability distribution for the number of heads obtained when two coins are tossed (H) is:

H	0	1	2
p	0.25	0.5	0.25

(Pearson's) product–moment correlation coefficient	A particular measure of correlation. It is usually denoted by r and can take values between -1 and 1.	The correlation coefficient for the data set Height: 151, 153, 158, 161, 161, 172 Weight: 48, 52, 50, 55, 52, 64 is $r=0.92$.
product rule	A rule for differentiating a product $y=u(x)v(x)$ of two functions: $\frac{dy}{dx}=u\frac{dv}{dx}+v\frac{du}{dx}$	The derivative of xe^x is xe^x+e^x by the product rule.
Pythagorean identity	An identity relating $\sin x$ and $\cos x$: $\sin^2 x+\cos^2 x=1$	The Pythagorean identity is useful in solving trigonometric equations.
quadrant	One of the four regions obtained when the plane is subdivided by a pair of coordinate axes. The first quadrant is the region with positive x and y coordinates; the quadrants are then numbered in an anticlockwise fashion.	The point $(3,-5)$ lies in the fourth quadrant.
quadratic function or **quadratic expression**	An expression involving only terms in x^2, x and numbers (constants).	The path of flight of a javelin can be modelled by a quadratic function.
quotient rule	A rule for differentiating a quotient (fraction) $y=\frac{u(x)}{v(x)}$ of two functions: $\frac{dy}{dx}=\frac{v\frac{du}{dx}-u\frac{dv}{dx}}{v^2}$	The derivative of $\tan x$ can be found by expressing $\tan x$ as $\frac{\sin x}{\cos x}$ and using the quotient rule.
radian	A unit for measuring angles: 1 radian is $\frac{1}{2\pi}$ of a full rotation.	A right angle is $\frac{\pi}{2}$ radians.
random variable	A quantity which can take a different value each time it is observed.	The outcome of rolling a die is a random variable.
range	1. The set of all possible outputs of a function defined on a specified domain. 2. A measure of spread of a data set, found by subtracting the smallest value from the largest value.	1. The range of $f(x)=x^2+3$ is $f(x)\geq 3$. 2. The range of $7,3,5,12,10$ is 9.
rate of change	How quickly a quantity changes as another quantity changes.	The rate of change of velocity with respect to time is acceleration.
rational function	A ratio of two polynomial functions.	$f(x)=\frac{2x-1}{x^2+3x-5}$ is a rational function.

reciprocal	The number 1 divided by another number or expression.	The reciprocal of 39 is $\frac{1}{39}$; the reciprocal of $\frac{2}{5}$ is $\frac{5}{2}$; the reciprocal of x^2 is $\frac{1}{x^2}$.
reciprocal function	A function of the form $f(x)=\frac{k}{x}$ where k is a constant.	$g(x)=\frac{-4}{x}$ is a reciprocal function.
recursive rule (also known as inductive)	A rule for generating terms of a sequence which depends upon previous results.	$u_{n+1}=5u_n$ is a recursive rule.
reverse chain rule	A method for integrating a product by recognising it as the result of a chain rule differentiation.	The integral of $x\cos x^2$ with respect to x can be seen to be $\frac{1}{2}\sin x^2+c$ by using the reverse chain rule.
root (or **solution**)	A value of a variable that makes an equation true.	3 is a root of $x^2+15=8x$.
sample space	A list of all possible equally likely outcomes.	The sample space when two coins are tossed can be represented by HH, HT, TH, TT.
scalar	A quantity which has size but no direction.	Energy is a scalar quantity.
scalar product or **dot product**	An operation which combines two vectors $\boldsymbol{a}$ and $\boldsymbol{b}$ to produce the scalar $\lvert\boldsymbol{a}\rvert\lvert\boldsymbol{b}\rvert\cos\theta$.	$\begin{pmatrix}3\\-2\end{pmatrix}\bullet\begin{pmatrix}3\\4\end{pmatrix}=1$
second derivative	The derivative of the derivative of a function.	The second derivative of x^3 is $6x$.
sector	A region in a circle enclosed by two radii and an arc. Each pair of radii defines two such regions: the larger is called the major sector; the smaller is called the minor sector.	The sector in the diagram has area $\frac{\pi}{6}$. 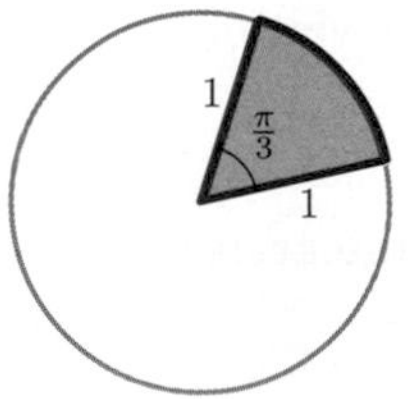
segment	A region in a circle enclosed by a chord and an arc. Each chord defines two such regions: the larger is called the major segment; the smaller is called the minor segment.	The segment below has area $\frac{\pi}{6}-\frac{\sqrt{3}}{4}$. 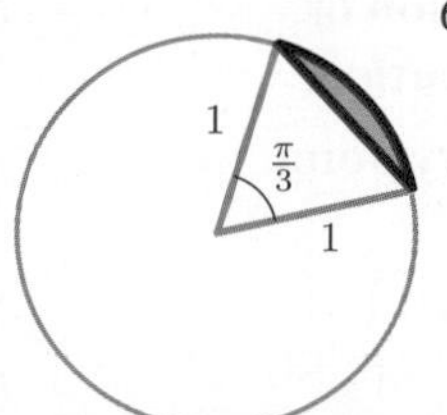
self-inverse function	A function whose inverse is the same as itself: $f^{-1}=f$.	$g(x)=\frac{-4}{x}$ is a self-inverse function.
sequence	A list of numbers in a specified order.	$1,4,9,16,\ldots$ is a sequence.

series	A sequence formed by summing terms from another sequence.	The harmonic series $1+\frac{1}{2}+\frac{1}{3}+\frac{1}{4}+\cdots$ is formed by summing the terms of the sequence $1,\frac{1}{2},\frac{1}{3},\frac{1}{4},\ldots$.
sigma notation (Σ)	A shorthand way of describing the sum of values with a common pattern or reference.	The nth square number can be expressed as $\sum_{k=1}^{n} 2k-1$.
simultaneous equations	A set of at least two equations involving more than one variable.	The intersection coordinates of two graphs can be found by solving a pair of simultaneous equations.
sine	A fundamental trigonometric function, often abbreviated to 'sin'; can be defined as the y-coordinate of a point on the unit circle.	$\sin\frac{\pi}{6}=\frac{1}{2}$
sine rule	A rule linking side lengths and angles in any triangle: $\frac{a}{\sin A}=\frac{b}{\sin B}=\frac{c}{\sin C}$	When using the sine rule to find an angle, there may be two possible answers.
skew lines	Two lines which are neither parallel nor intersecting.	The lines $x-2=\frac{y+4}{3}=\frac{z-1}{4}$ and $\boldsymbol{r}=\lambda\begin{pmatrix}1\\0\\1\end{pmatrix}$ are skew.
speed	A scalar quantity describing how fast an object is moving.	The magnitude of the velocity vector is the speed: $\lvert v\rvert$.
standard derivatives	Derivatives, given in the information booklet, which can be quoted without proof.	$\frac{\mathrm{d}}{\mathrm{d}x}(\tan x)=\frac{1}{\cos^2 x}$ is a standard derivative.
standard deviation	A measure of how spread out the data is, given by an average distance of data values from the mean.	The standard deviation of 1, 1, 4, 6, 8, 10, 12 is $\sqrt{\frac{110}{7}}$.
standard integrals	Integrals, given in the information booklet, which can be quoted without proof.	$\int\frac{1}{x}\,\mathrm{d}x=\ln x+c$ is a standard integral.
standard normal distribution or **Z-distribution**	A normal distribution with mean zero and standard deviation one, denoted by N(0,1).	If $X\sim \mathrm{N}(\mu,\sigma^2)$, then $\frac{X-\mu}{\sigma}$ follows a standard normal distribution.
stationary point	A point on a graph at which the gradient is zero.	The graph $y=x^3-12x+7$ has stationary points at $(2,-9)$ and $(-2,23)$.
subtends	When each end of a curve (or line) is joined by a straight line to a specified point, the angle enclosed by the two lines is said to be subtended by the curve at that point.	The diameter of a circle subtends an angle of 90° at any point on the circumference.

sum to infinity	The result of adding together all the terms of a never-ending sequence.	The sum to infinity of $1+\frac{1}{2}+\frac{1}{4}+\frac{1}{8}+\cdots$ is 2.
tangent	1. A trigonometric function, often abbreviated to 'tan'.	1. $\tan\frac{\pi}{3}=\sqrt{3}$
	2. A line which touches a curve without crossing it (except at points of inflexion).	2. A tangent to a circle meets any radius in a right angle.
term	1. A number in a sequence.	1. The third term of the sequence $2,5,10,17,\ldots$ is 10.
	2. A component of a sum.	2. The expression $3x^2y+2x$ consists of two terms.
tree diagram	A representation of events that shows the probability of each event occurring depending on previous outcomes.	When two cards are drawn without replacement from a standard deck of cards, the probabilities of drawing at least one heart can be represented in the following tree diagram: 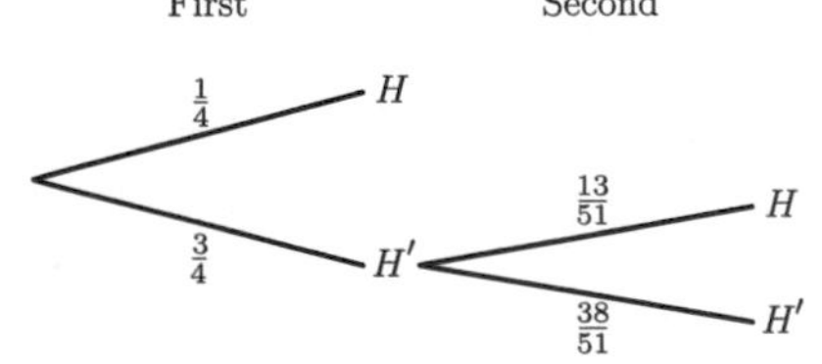
trigonometric function	One of the functions relating to ratios of lengths in a right-angled triangle or in the unit circle: sine, cosine, tangent, secant, cosecant or cotangent.	$\sin 4x$ is a trigonometric function.
turning point or **vertex**	A place where a graph changes from increasing to decreasing or vice versa.	The line of symmetry of a parabola passes through its vertex.
union	The combined event corresponding to either or both of two events occurring.	The union of odd numbers less than 6 and prime numbers less than 6 is $\{1,2,3,5\}$.
unit circle	A circle with radius one unit centred at the origin.	$\cos\theta$ is the x-coordinate of the point on the unit circle where the radius makes an angle θ with the positive x-axis.
unit vector	A vector with magnitude one.	$\frac{1}{\sqrt{3}}\begin{pmatrix}1\\-1\\-1\end{pmatrix}$ is a unit vector in the direction of $\begin{pmatrix}1\\-1\\-1\end{pmatrix}$.

upper interval boundary	The highest possible value that the data in a given group can take. This value is used in drawing histograms and cumulative frequency graphs.	When heights have been rounded to the nearest cm, the group '155–160' has upper interval boundary 160.5.
upper quartile	The value three quarters of the way up a list of data arranged in ascending order.	The upper quartile (UQ or Q_3) of 1, 1, 4, 6, 8, 10, 12 is 10.
variable	An unknown quantity, usually represented by an italic letter.	In the expression $3x^2$, the only variable is x.
variance	An indirect measure of how spread out the data is; it is the square of the standard deviation.	The variance of 1, 1, 4, 6, 8, 10, 12 is $\frac{110}{7}$.
vector	A quantity which has both size (magnitude) and direction.	Force is a vector quantity.
vector equation	An equation whose variables are vectors.	The vector equation of a line containing the points A and B is $\boldsymbol{r} = \boldsymbol{a} + \lambda(\boldsymbol{b} - \boldsymbol{a})$.
velocity	A vector quantity describing how fast an object is moving and in what direction.	Velocity is the rate of change of displacement with respect to time: $v = \frac{\mathrm{d}s}{\mathrm{d}t}$
Venn diagram	A representation of events as regions in a rectangular area (which represents the whole sample space).	If events A and B are mutually exclusive, their Venn diagram will look like
vertical asymptote	A vertical line of the form $x = a$ where a function is undefined.	$y = \ln(x-1)$ has a vertical asymptote $x = 1$.
volume of revolution	A solid shape formed by rotating a curve around an axis.	The volume of revolution of a straight line is a cone.
with respect to	A phrase for describing the controlled variable that is being changed in the process of differentiation or integration.	The derivative of ax^2 with respect to x is $2ax$.
zero of a function	A value of a variable that makes an expression equal to zero.	-2 is a zero of $x^2 + 5x + 6$.
Z-score	The number of standard deviations that a particular value lies above the mean.	In a normal distribution with mean 150 and standard deviation 10, the value 135 has a Z-score of -1.5.

Index

Acknowledgements

The authors and publishers are grateful for the permissions granted to reproduce materials in either the original or adapted form. While every effort has been made, it has not always been possible to identify the sources of all the materials used, or to trace all copyright holders. If any omissions are brought to our notice, we will be happy to include the appropriate acknowledgements on reprinting.

IB exam questions © International Baccalaureate Organization. We gratefully acknowledge permission to reproduce International Baccalaureate Organization intellectual property.

Cover image: David Robertson/Alamy

Diagrams in the coursebook and CD-ROM are created by Ben Woolley.

Photos on the CD-ROM: Supplementary sheet 3, page 3 John C. Hooten/Shutterstock; Fill-in proofs 3 Nicku/Shutterstock; Option 10, chapter 31, page 1 Edyta Pawlowska/Shutterstock

TI–83 fonts are reproduced on the calculator skills sheets on the CD-ROM with permission of Texas Instruments Incorporated.

Casio fonts are reproduced on the calculator skills sheets on the CD-ROM with permission of Casio Electronics Company Ltd (to access downloadable Casio resources go to www.casio.co.uk/education and http://edu.casio.com/dll).

Terms and conditions of use for the CD-ROM

This is a legal agreement between 'You' (which means the individual customer or the Educational Institution and its authorised users) and Cambridge University Press ('the Licensor') for *Mathematics Standard Level for the IB Diploma CD-ROM*. By placing this CD in the CD-ROM drive of your computer, You agree to the terms of this licence.

1 Limited licence

a You are purchasing only the right to use the CD-ROM and are acquiring no rights, express or implied, to it, other than those rights granted in this limited licence for not-for-profit educational use only.

b The Licensor grants You the licence to use one copy of this CD-ROM.

c You shall not: **(i)** copy or authorise copying of the CD-ROM, **(ii)** translate the CD-ROM, **(iii)** reverse-engineer, alter, adapt, disassemble or decompile the CD-ROM, **(iv)** transfer, sell, lease, lend, profit from, assign or otherwise convey all or any portion of the CD-ROM or **(v)** operate the CD-ROM from a mainframe system, except as provided in these terms and conditions.

d Permission is explicitly granted for use of the CD-ROM on a data projector, interactive whiteboard or other public display in the context of classroom teaching at a purchasing institution.

e If You are an Educational Institution, once a teacher ceases to be a member of the Educational Institution, all copies of the material on the CD-ROM stored on his/her personal computer must be destroyed and the CD-ROM returned to the Educational Institution.

f You are permitted to print reasonable copies of the printable resources on the CD-ROM. These must be used solely for use within the context of classroom teaching at a purchasing institution.

2 Copyright

a All original content is provided as part of the CD-ROM (including text, images and ancillary material) and is the copyright of the Licensor or has been licensed to the Licensor for use in the CD-ROM, protected by copyright and all other applicable intellectual-property laws and international treaties.

b You may not copy the CD-ROM except for making one copy of the CD-ROM solely for backup or archival purposes. You may not alter, remove or destroy any copyright notice or other material placed on or with this CD-ROM.

3 Liability and Indemnification

a The CD-ROM is supplied 'as is' with no express guarantee as to its suitability. To the extent permitted by applicable law, the Licensor is not liable for costs of procurement of substitute products, damages or losses of any kind whatsoever resulting from the use of this product, or errors or faults in the CD-ROM, and in every case the Licensor's liability shall be limited to the suggested list price or the amount actually paid by You for the product, whichever is lower.

b You accept that the Licensor is not responsible for the availability of any links within or outside the CD-ROM and that the Licensor is not responsible or liable for any content available from sources outside the CD-ROM to which such links are made.

c Where, through use of the original material, You infringe the copyright of the Licensor, You undertake to indemnify and keep indemnified the Licensor from and against any loss, cost, damage or expense (including without limitation damages paid to a third party and any reasonable legal costs) incurred by the Licensor as a result of such infringement.

4 Termination

Without prejudice to any other rights, the Licensor may terminate this licence if You fail to comply with the terms and conditions of the licence. In such an event, You must destroy all copies of the CD-ROM.

5 Governing law

This agreement is governed by the laws of England, without regard to its 'conflict of laws' provision, and each party irrevocably submits to the exclusive jurisdiction of the English courts. The parties disclaim the application of the United Nations Convention on the International Sale of Goods.